OVER 400 PAGES IN COLOR

by Paul Levitz

A DC PUBLICATION

The Golden Age of DC Comics

1935–1956

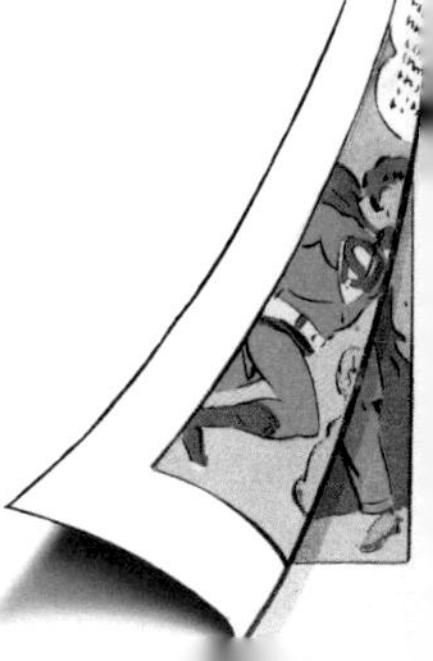

TASCHEN

Bibliotheca Universalis

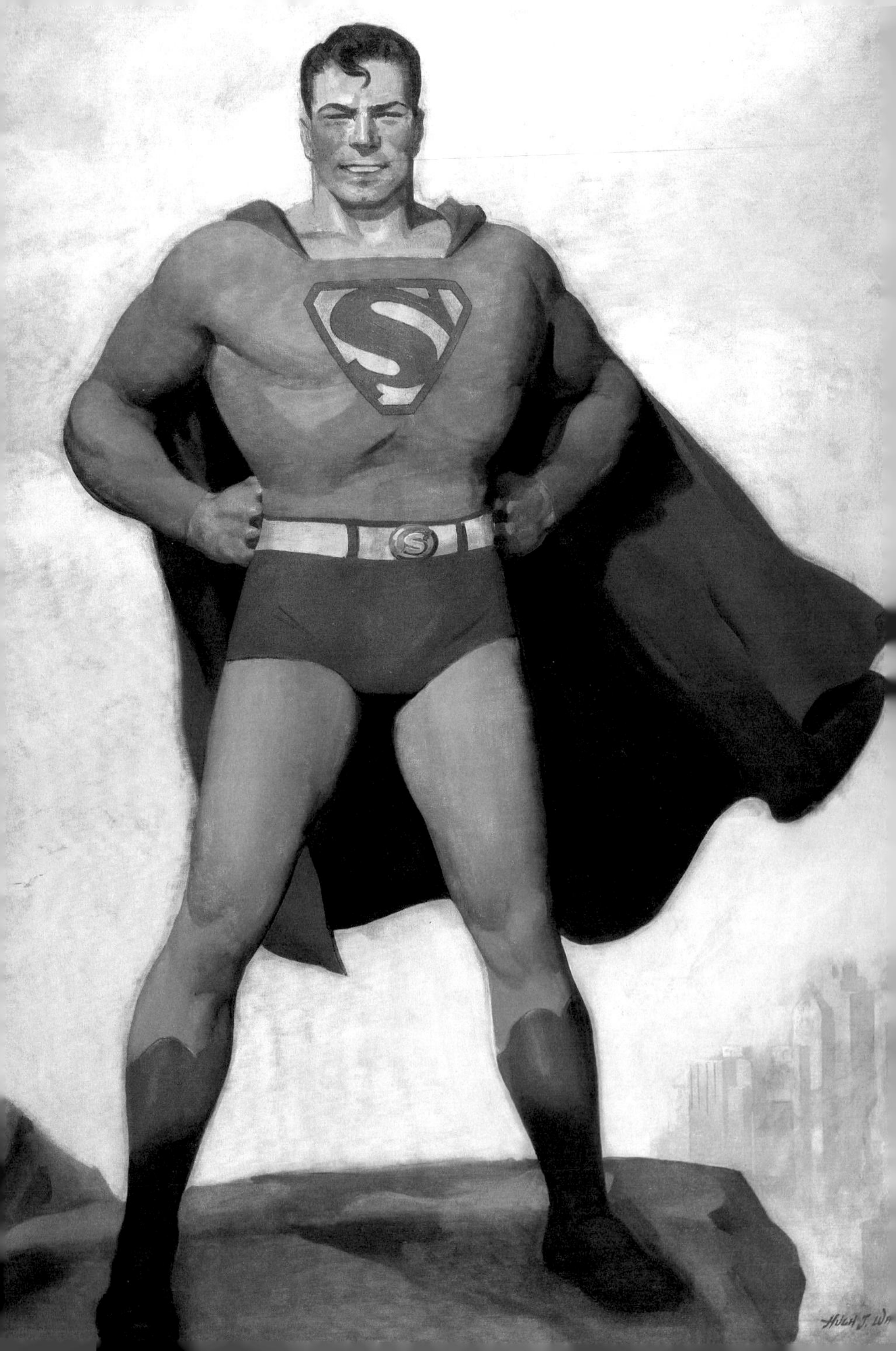

THERE ARE CHARACTERS AND THERE ARE CHARACTERS.

The characters portrayed in DC Comics are among the best-known fictional characters in the world, and their stories are best told by the wealth of visual imagery swirling through this book — and the three that will follow in this series — images that captured the popular imagination.

The real-life characters who created DC Comics are far less well known, and their stories, and the evolution of DC itself, are best told in narrative history, providing a context to the extraordinary events they presided over.

DC has published more than a million pages of comics and produced thousands of hours of television and animation, and dozens of films, serials, and cartoons made for the movie theaters…plus work in every other creative medium commercially viable in the past seven decades. For all the heft of what you're holding, it's only a small taste.

You could fill a shelf with books written about Superman alone, from Alvin Schwartz recalling sitting in a taxicab, meeting the living manifestation of the hero in *An Unlikely Prophet*, to Tom De Haven's scholarly *Our Hero: Superman on Earth*. Or consider that Les Klinger's four-volume annotation of *The Sandman* examines just that one Vertigo series. The depth of commentary and debate shows how these have become myths, tales told and retold, interpreted in search of their deepest meanings. The visuals selected here attempt to show some of the most amazing images, and to place DC's history in the larger context of the culture that shaped the company.

We have also tried to honor some of the thousands of talented, creative people who have contributed to DC and crafted modern myths in many different media to create larger-than-life reflections that help us understand our humanity and our world. Many of them led lives worthy of full biographies, and their work has been the subject of many monographs. They appear here too briefly, to introduce themselves and their most important moments in the pageant of DC's history.

No matter how familiar you are with DC, you will find pictures and moments that you don't know within these pages…and those of the next four volumes in this series. Culled from the supersized Eisner Award–winning tome *75 Years of DC Comics*, each volume focuses on a different era of DC's history: the Golden, Silver, and Bronze Ages of Comics, and then the periods we're denoting as Dark and Modern Ages. Each will include a new original interview with a legend of the era — Joe Kubert for the Golden Age, Neal Adams for the Silver Age, and so on — as well as significant new illustrations and updated essays by yours truly, particularly in the Modern Age volume for the exciting recent events in DC's history.

It's our hope that whether you first visited this world through a comic book's pages or a screen, or by putting on a Halloween costume, you'll find a connection to your own history here, and an invitation to explore.

Come, walk among the characters…and begin *before* the beginning…

— PAUL LEVITZ

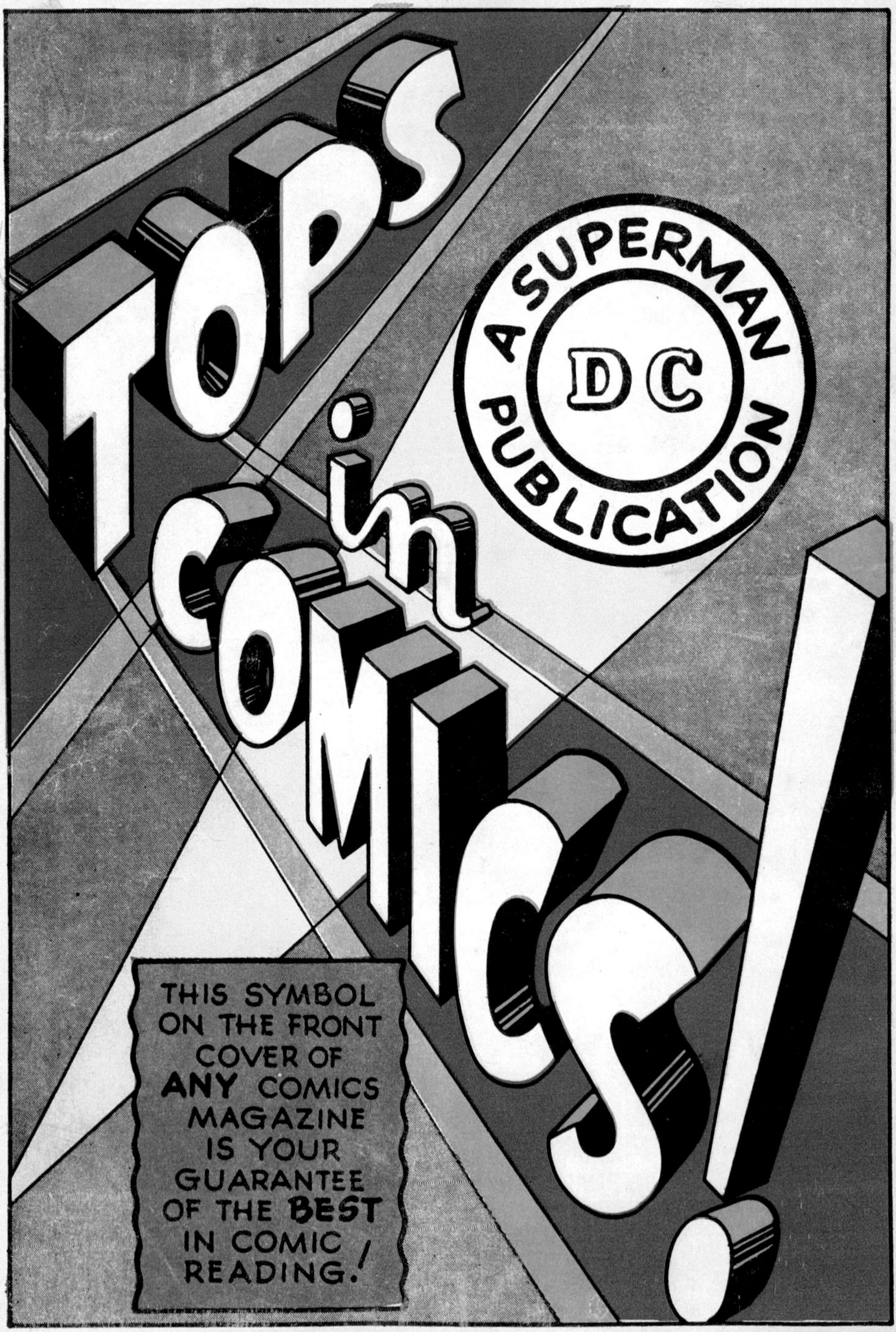
TOPS in COMICS!
A SUPERMAN DC PUBLICATION
THIS SYMBOL ON THE FRONT COVER OF ANY COMICS MAGAZINE IS YOUR GUARANTEE OF THE BEST IN COMIC READING!

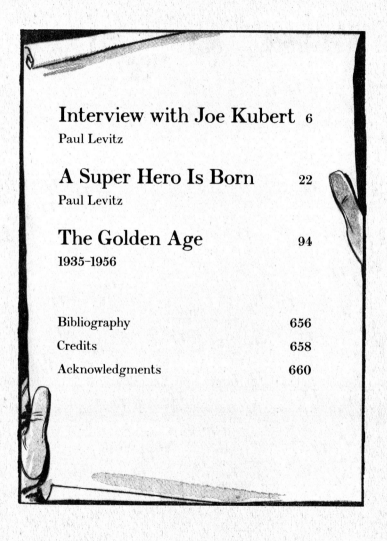

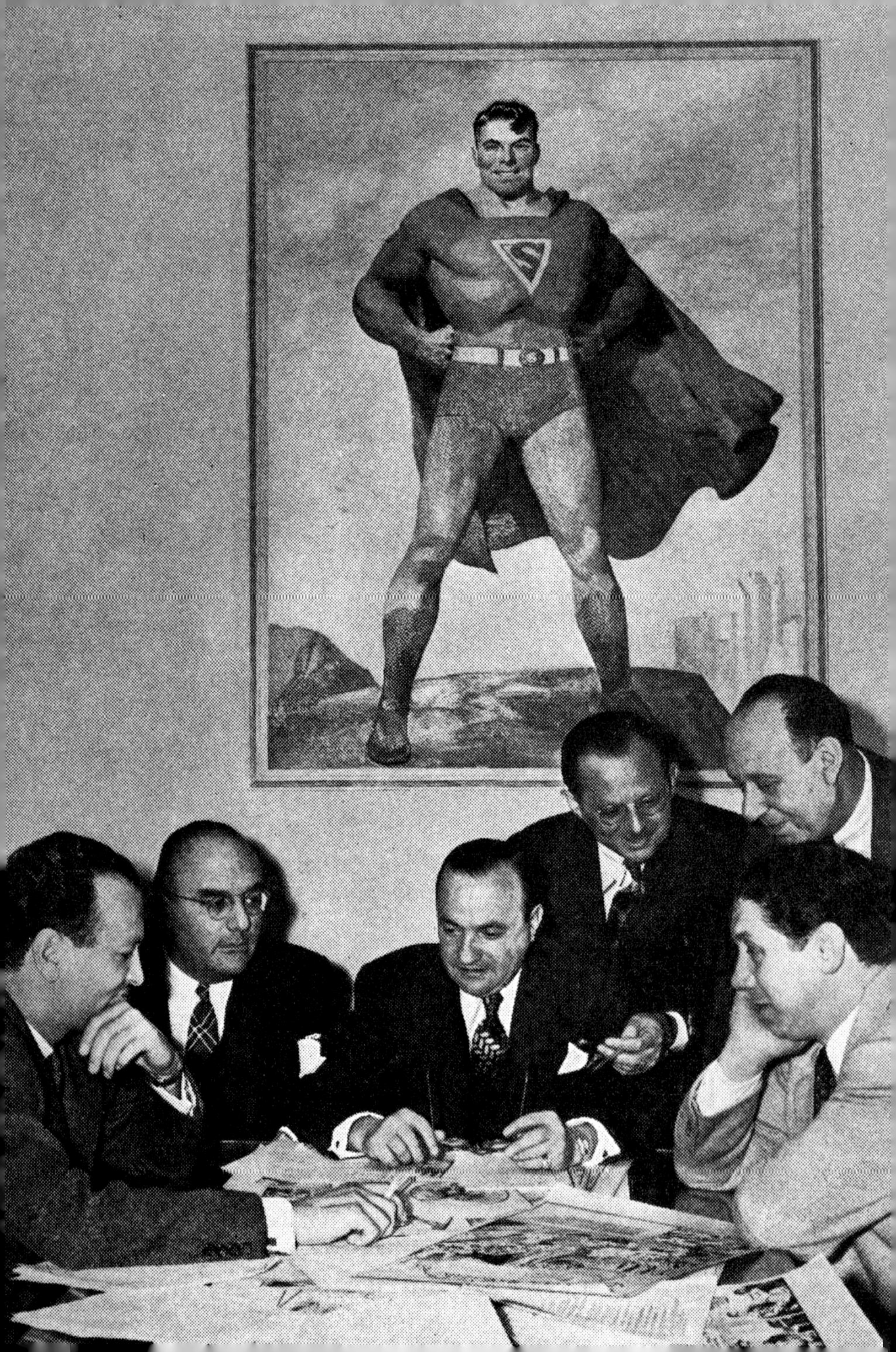

Interview with Joe Kubert

Paul Levitz

Born in Poland in 1926, Joe Kubert published his first solo work when he was 16. He started working for DC's All-American line and remained associated with the company, illustrating virtually every DC character and genre for over seven decades. In 1952, he cofounded a company to publish his legendary, oft-revived *Tor*, an early self-publishing effort. He returned to DC in 1955, teaming with Robert Kanigher to define the look of DC's war titles and illustrate Sgt. Rock, and in the early '60s drew an updated version of Hawkman. He served DC in an editorial capacity from 1967 to 1977, leaving after founding the Joe Kubert School of Cartoon and Graphic Art in Dover, New Jersey, a still-thriving institution.

The Kubert School has trained three generations of artists, many of whom have ended up in DC's pages after learning from one of the company's most prolific and versatile cover artists. Paul Levitz visited Kubert's office-cum-studio at the school on January 9, 2012, just months before his death on August 12 of the same year, to conduct this exclusive interview. "Walking into Joe's studio," Levitz reflected, "is a walk through history — artwork created at the Chesler Shop, one of the mythic sweatshops where the very first comics were crafted, lines the walls, predating even comics' Golden Age." Not to mention the original pages from Kubert himself reflecting his time as editor, writer, and artist on almost every DC genre.

You started at DC when you and comics were both young…
I was working for Shelly [Mayer at All-American, DC's sister company] while I was in high school. In fact, whenever I had a deadline that I couldn't meet, he was

DC COMICS EXECUTIVES
Photograph, (left to right) Robert Maxwell, Paul Sampliner, Harry Donenfeld, Jack Liebowitz, M. C. Gaines, Whitney Ellsworth, 1941. The role each of these men played was, by modern standards, fluid and ever changing. Liebowitz would say later, "We didn't bother much with titles in those days."

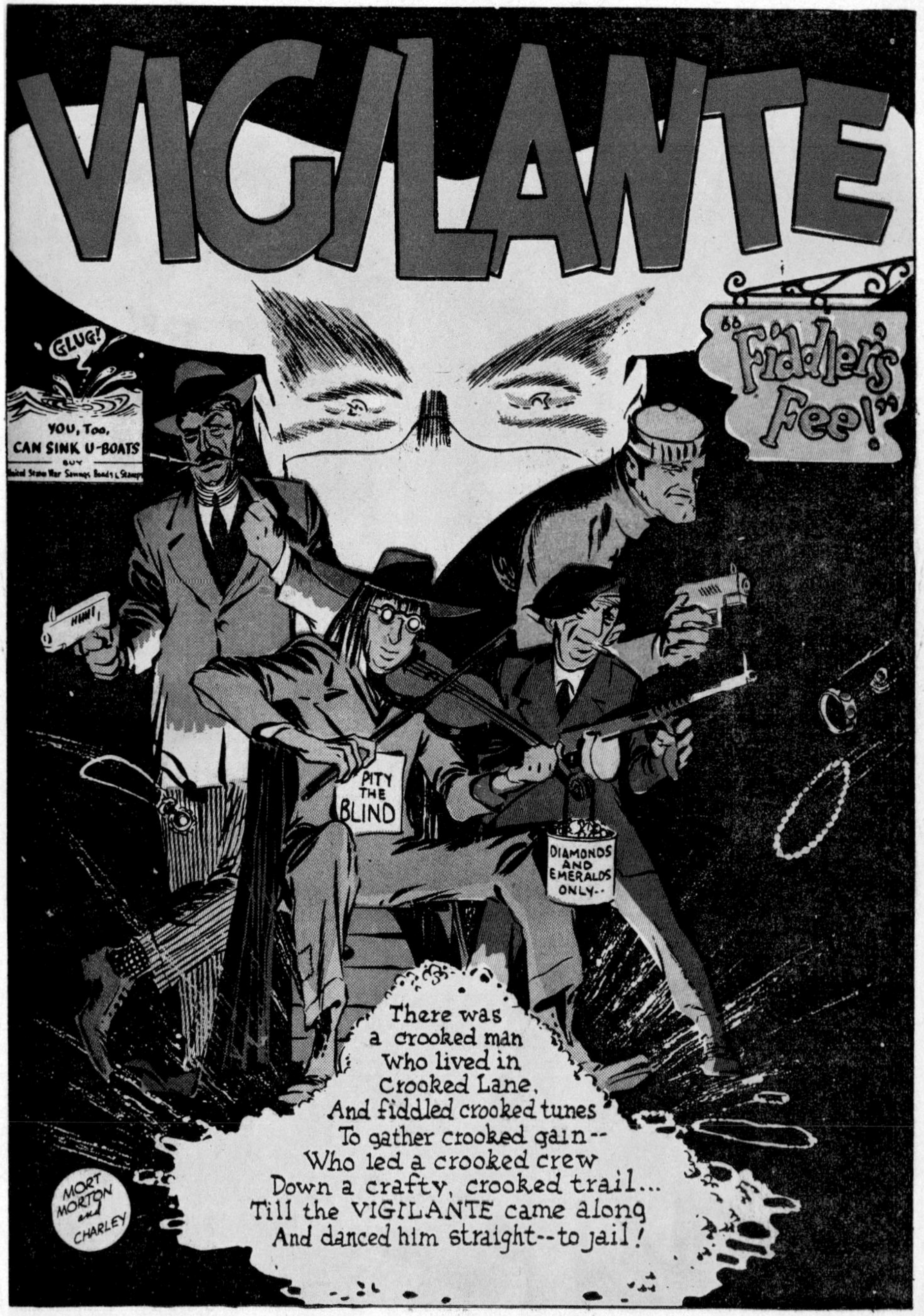

VIGILANTE
"Fiddler's Fee!"
GLUG!
YOU, Too, CAN SINK U-BOATS
BUY
PITY THE BLIND
DIAMONDS AND EMERALDS ONLY--
There was
a crooked man
Who lived in
Crooked Lane,
And fiddled crooked tunes
To gather crooked gain--
Who led a crooked crew
Down a crafty, crooked trail...
Till the VIGILANTE came along
And danced him straight--to jail!
MORT MORTON and CHARLEY

ACTION COMICS No. 59

Interior, "Fiddler's Fee"; script, unknown; pencils, Mort Meskin (as Mort Morton); inks, Charles Paris. April 1943. Longtime DC writer James Robinson also observed that Mort Meskin's art was "a kind of fusion between the energy of [Jack] Kirby and the cinematic structure of Jerry Robinson." There's also a bit of Will Eisner, as in this lyrical splash page that introduced the Vigilante's frequent opponent, the Fiddler.

STRAUSS PHOTO-ENGRAVING CO.

Jack Adler, a decade before joining DC's production department, color separating "Prince Valiant" Sunday page No. 36, 1937. Separators like Adler had to manually indicate the areas to be printed in each of four layers — cyan, magenta, yellow, and black — which, when printed in overlap, would produce a "full color" effect.

calling my home and my mother would tell him, "He's sick in bed, he can't get the stuff in on time." The first time I was working at DC [uptown] I was inking on [Mort] Meskin's stuff.

So uptown were the DC offices that were doing **Superman™** *and* **Batman™**, *while you were used to the printing district offices of All-American. Was there a different feeling uptown from downtown?*
Are you kidding? It was massive. It was ritzy. That was 480 Lex. First of all, you were so impressed by the painting of Superman that hung in the office there.

You're one of the first American comic book artists, and one of the youngest of that generation, starting even before your time at DC. Which artists were your most generous teachers?
They all were; every artist that I ever came across including Meskin, [Charlie] Biro, every guy helped me with what I was doing and what I wanted to do. They were a bunch of the kindest, nicest guys. Here I am — a kid, maybe 12, 13 years old — I knew nothing about anything.

  I think I recognized that there was some stuff that I really wanted to do. I guess most artists have an innate feeling that if they come across someone who has the same look or feel toward what they want to do that they did when they started, they'll do anything to help.

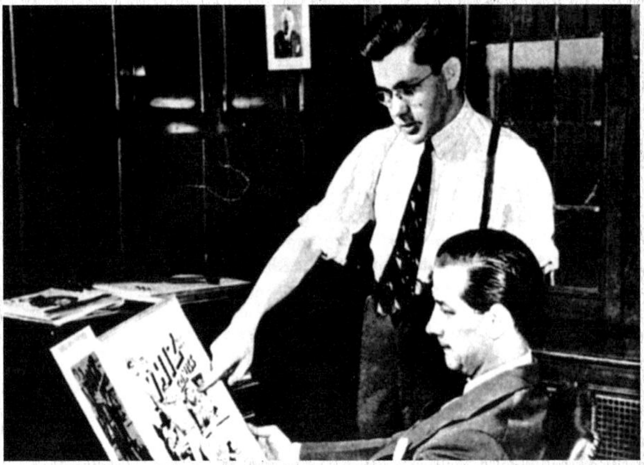

FAWCETT PUBLICATIONS
Charles Clarence Beck (standing), and Wilford Hamilton Fawcett Jr., 1942.

THE SPIRIT No. 60
Cover art detail, Will Eisner, July 20, 1941. The high point of the Eisner studio was *The Spirit*, with its spectacularly imaginative splash pages and integrated logos.

But also talent... something that makes you feel this kid is worth investing in.
I don't know if it's that at all. I don't think they're looking to get a return.

In legacy terms...
As far as recognizing talent, I can't judge my own work, but I never thought it was any good at all. In fact, when people show me the old stuff that I did, I can't even stand to look at it. It just looks terrible to me. So I doubt very much if it was a matter of showing talent at the time. They were just good guys who felt that this was a kid who really wants to learn.

In the early shops the conditions were awful. Which of the shop artists believed that people would still be looking at that work, 70-plus years later?
I don't think any of them were proud of what they were doing, or thought that what they were doing was worthwhile. It was a matter of making a buck. This was the Depression; every artist who was floating around was looking to make a buck someplace, and if it could possibly be while he was doing drawing...

What about Will Eisner?
I was just starting high school—Music & Art—and my buddy Norman [Maurer] and I used to go around looking

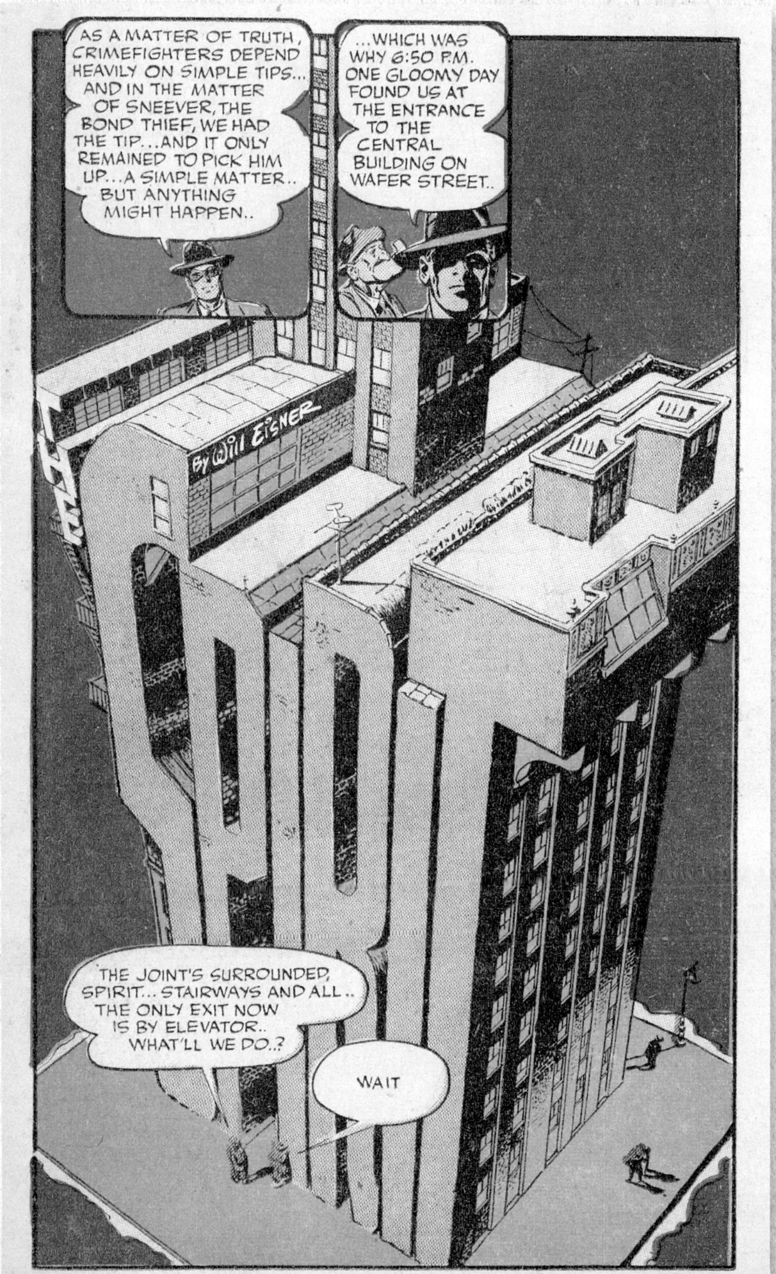
AS A MATTER OF TRUTH, CRIMEFIGHTERS DEPEND HEAVILY ON SIMPLE TIPS... AND IN THE MATTER OF SNEEVER, THE BOND THIEF, WE HAD THE TIP...AND IT ONLY REMAINED TO PICK HIM UP...A SIMPLE MATTER.. BUT ANYTHING MIGHT HAPPEN..
...WHICH WAS WHY 6:50 P.M. ONE GLOOMY DAY FOUND US AT THE ENTRANCE TO THE CENTRAL BUILDING ON WAFER STREET..
By Will Eisner
SPIRIT
THE JOINT'S SURROUNDED, SPIRIT... STAIRWAYS AND ALL.. THE ONLY EXIT NOW IS BY ELEVATOR.. WHAT'LL WE DO..?
WAIT

BATMAN No. 50

Interior, "Lights—Camera—Crime"; script, unknown; pencils, Bob Kane (Batman and Robin figures) and Lew Sayre Schwartz; inks, Charles Paris. December 1948–January 1949. "I began to accumulate material, a swipe file on locations and occupations. I would buy copies of *Popular Science* and *Popular Mechanics,* which covered every subject imaginable. I'd clip them and give these drawings to Bob Kane along with the story. I once found an article on a giant typewriter used for an exhibition at a trade show and used it as a prop in a script. It started the 'big prop' stories." —Bill Finger

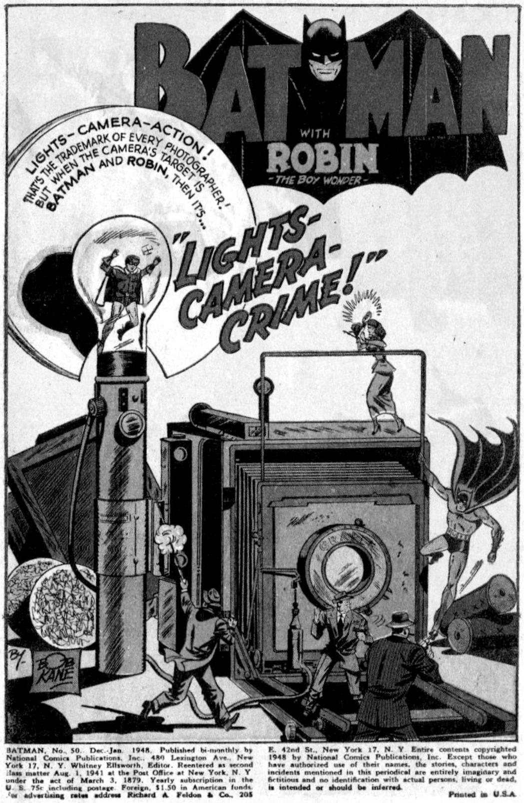
BATMAN
WITH
ROBIN
-THE BOY WONDER-
LIGHTS-CAMERA-ACTION! THAT'S THE TRADEMARK OF EVERY PHOTOGRAPHER! BUT WHEN THE CAMERA'S TARGET IS BATMAN AND ROBIN, THEN IT'S...
"LIGHTS-CAMERA-CRIME!"
BY-BOB KANE
BATMAN, No. 50. Dec.-Jan. 1948. Published bi-monthly by National Comics Publications, Inc., 480 Lexington Ave., New York 17, N. Y. Whitney Ellsworth, Editor. Reentered as second class matter Aug. 1, 1941 at the Post Office at New York, N. Y under the act of March 3, 1879. Yearly subscription in the U. S. 75c including postage. Foreign, $1.50 in American funds. For advertising rates address Richard A. Feldon & Co., 205 E. 42nd St., New York 17, N. Y. Entire contents copyrighted 1948 by National Comics Publications, Inc. Except those who have authorized use of their names, the stories, characters and incidents mentioned in this periodical are entirely imaginary and fictitious and no identification with actual persons, living or dead, is intended or should be inferred.
Printed in U.S.A.

for jobs. We were playing hooky and Will's was one of the first offices I went to. I got a job during the summer, not as an artist, and Will has often brought that to my attention; it was sweeping out the place. He wouldn't dare let me work on anybody else's stuff.

It was luck that I fell in. He was paying me $12.50 a week, coming in during the summer, which was great, a lot of money, almost as much as my father was making at the butcher store. But the fact that I got the job with Will was terrific.

Do you think that Will believed at that point that any of the work would survive and become art?

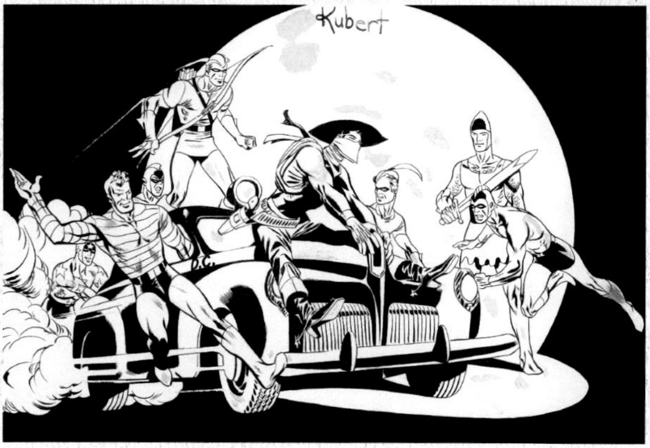
Kubert

SEVEN SOLDIERS OF VICTORY
Unpublished artwork, Joe Kubert, ca. 1944. One of Kubert's earliest samples, showing the Seven Soldiers of Victory, which may have led to his work on Vigilante.

He was always sure. I think that he was probably a hell of a lot more foresighted than most of the other people; he, even at that early time, saw a lot of stuff that was going to be going on in this particular medium that he wanted to catch hold of.

During the time when I worked for him, he worked in a separate room. Guys like me and Tex Blaisdell, and other

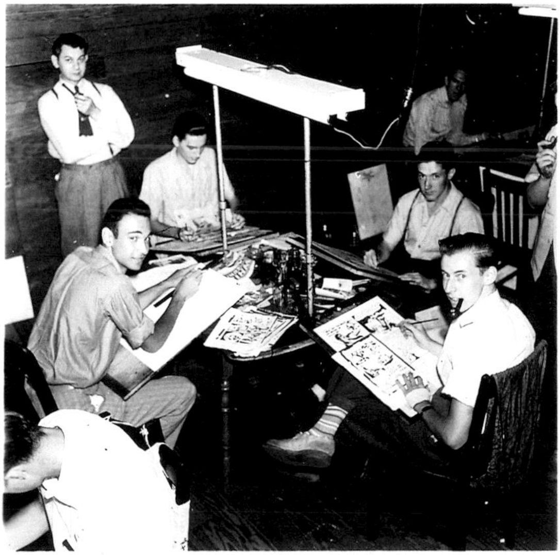

THE BINDER STUDIO
Photograph, clockwise from left, Jack Binder, Bob Boyajian, Victor Dowd, Ken Bald, and Ray Hartford. Early 1940s. Throughout the early 1940s, artist Jack Binder owned and oversaw an agency of artists and writers who packaged material for publishers including Fawcett, Lev Gleason, and Nedor. As young men, DC mainstays Carmine Infantino and Kurt Schaffenberger worked for Binder in his Fifth Avenue Manhattan office.

THE PRODUCTION ROOM

*Photograph, Sol Harrison
(standing to left, by cabinet)
with Jack Adler (center
of front row), 1940s.*
DC's separations were
produced in this room
at 487 Broadway.

THE BLUE BEETLE No. 1

*Cover art, Lou Fine, Winter
1939–1940.* One of Kubert's
heroes and inspirations, Lou
Fine was widely considered
to be one of the greatest
artists of the Golden Age
of Comics. He left his mark
on many characters still
published by DC today, such
as the Blue Beetle, the Ray,
and the Black Condor.

guys worked in the other room, so I never had a chance to talk to him...perhaps once...and I could sneak a peek in his room, see him working.

You're one of the good businessmen/artists from the Golden Age. Why were so few of the early comic artists interested in the business aspects of their work?
I always thought of doing other things, but never to the extent that I'd be willing to ever give up my drawing. I could never do that. Even when I started the [Kubert] school. If there was a question of my being able to do the work, my work, in addition to taking care of the school, I would have closed up the school years ago.

You collaborated with an enormous range of the writers in the business including DC's most prolific writers: Bob Kanigher, Gardner Fox, Bob Haney...
Bill Finger also. Bill was doing Hawkman scripts.

Can you contrast their styles?
Kanigher was a guy that I found easiest to work with. I think he understood better than I my strengths and weaknesses when he gave me a story. Once he gave me a 12-page story written on one sheet of paper, which he'd written on his lunch hour, which he did often.

He was so in tune with what I could do that he was able to describe in just two or three words a whole page of what

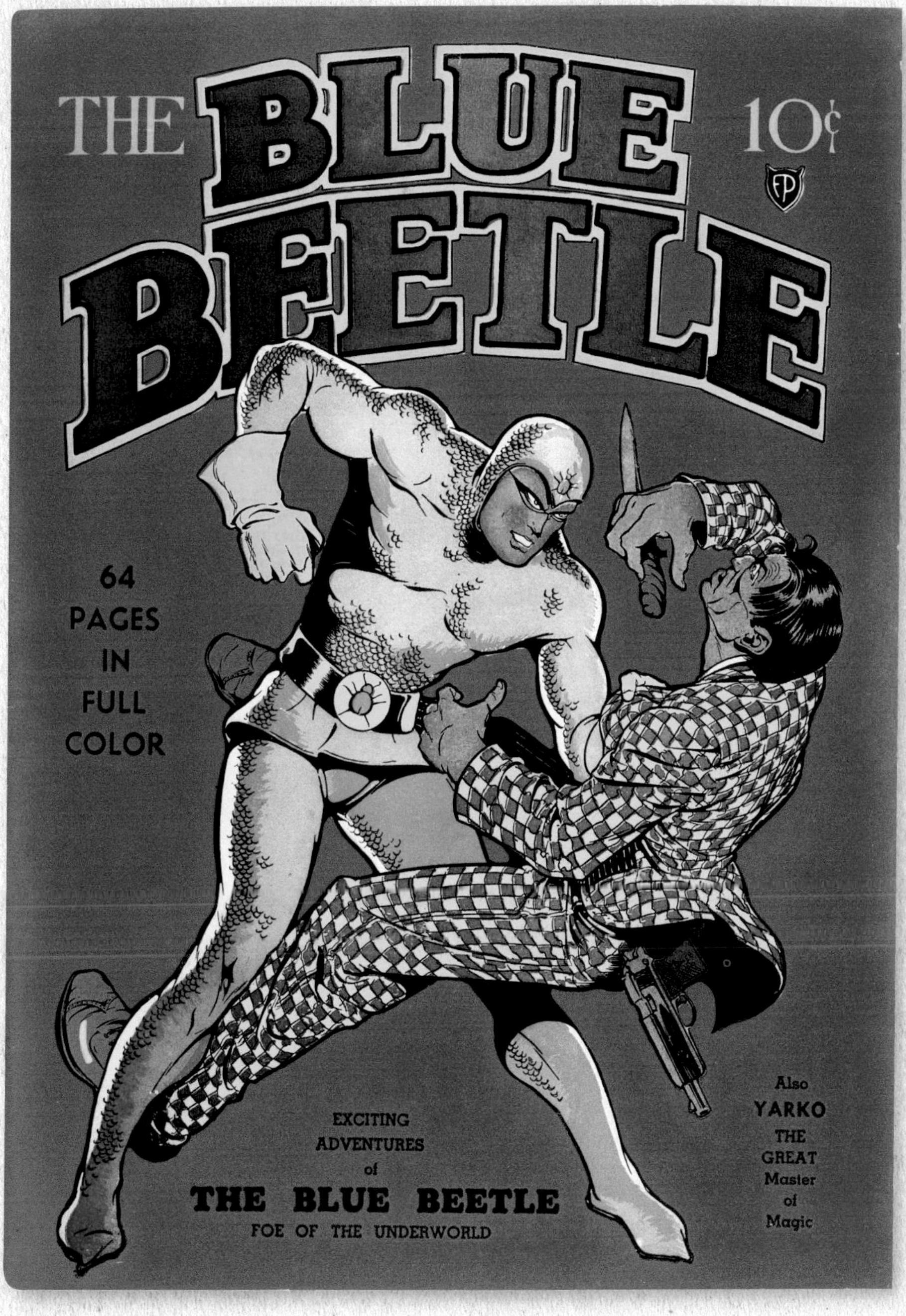
THE BLUE BEETLE 10¢
FP
64 PAGES IN FULL COLOR
EXCITING ADVENTURES of
THE BLUE BEETLE
FOE OF THE UNDERWORLD
Also YARKO THE GREAT Master of Magic

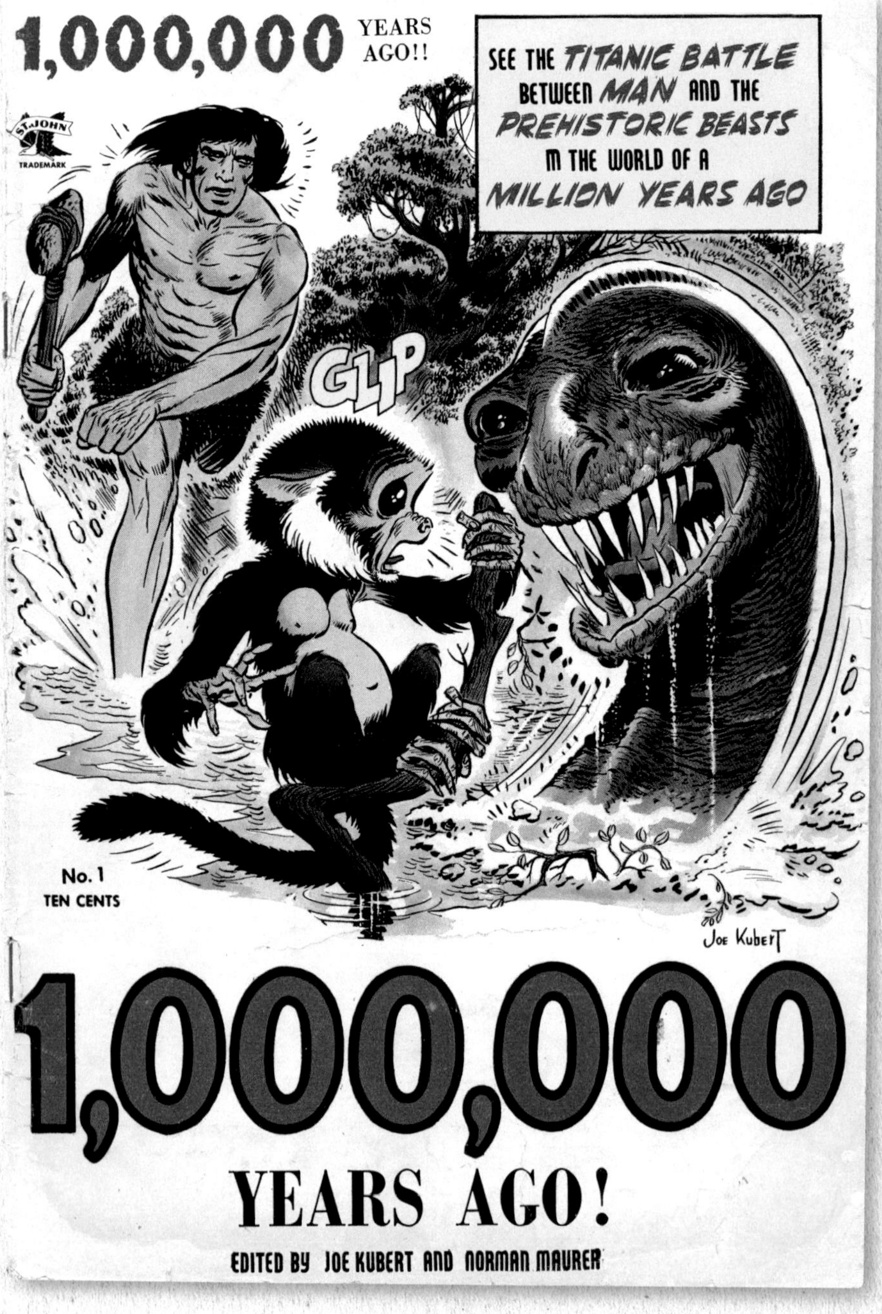
1,000,000 YEARS AGO!!
SEE THE TITANIC BATTLE BETWEEN MAN AND THE PREHISTORIC BEASTS IN THE WORLD OF A MILLION YEARS AGO
ST. JOHN TRADEMARK
GLIP
No. 1
TEN CENTS
JOE KUBERT
1,000,000
YEARS AGO!
EDITED BY JOE KUBERT AND NORMAN MAURER

I had to do. He allowed me to break down — which he never allowed any of the other artists to do — add panels, combine panels where I felt the flow would work better. That kind of freedom I appreciated very much, because it allowed me to change what I wanted. He was the easiest guy to work with.

With the other guys, it was much more specific when they described the panels and the action that was taking place, so I was locked in a lot more with the other scripts that I received. That's about the biggest difference.

Finger was famous, at least in his Batman scripts, for his giant objects. Did you find him a particularly visual writer to work with?

I remember one story — Hawkman was interred in the earth, in a kind of burial setup and a large rectangular stone is pushed in to cover it. The way he gets out, I thought was really clever. He comes by some pencils or rods and is able to slip them underneath and use them as rollers.

In the Golden Age, which of the artists tried to keep their originals?

I don't know that anybody thought it was worthwhile to keep their originals. It's one of the reasons that I think that all this hue and cry that people weren't given back their originals is a bunch of crap.

When did you begin keeping your art?

When I became conscious of the fact that others were doing it. Probably the mid-'60s... or I probably kept anything that came by me, simply because I hate to see artwork go whether it's mine or anyone else's. I've never been a collector, but if I see...if a kid sends me a drawing, I can't get rid of that either.

Did you ever work in DC's bullpen?

When I had corrections to make, but never on a regular basis. Those [boards] were only for the heavyweights. At the time, I was inking on Meskin's stuff, so I would come in and pick up the work or bring it back or show it to him.

1,000,000 YEARS AGO No. 1
Cover art, Joe Kubert, September 1953.
In 1953, Kubert and cartoonist Norman Maurer created Tor the caveman for St. John Publishing, but Kubert grew to so love the character that he purchased the rights and, under the DC banner, has revived the feature several times since.

GREEN LANTERN No. 35

Cover art, Joe Kubert, November–December 1948. Kubert's first cover for a DC comic other than Flash Comics. He would contribute covers to more than 50 titles, as DC's longest-running and most prolific cover artist.

Why hasn't his reputation survived?

My own theory on that is what happened to him happened to Lou Fine as well. When they got into doing advertising, you're suddenly playing with big money, not comic book stuff. You're not permitted to make mistakes; every job that comes through has to be decided on a committee basis. You can't please everybody, and least of all, you're not pleasing yourself. You're second-guessing all the time.

In comic books, you don't have the time to do that. So if you try different stuff, if you try new stuff, and it doesn't work, well, it's only one of 20 or 30 pages you've done. If during that testing period, something does work, the feeling of good stuff just stays with you, making you try again.

I was taught that the reader smells sincerity, and even if the craft is weak, would rather feel that than an insincere job told with craft. Looking back at the Golden Age, what was the magic that was pouring into the pages?

I think one of the reasons is the amount of work each of the artists had to turn out during that time. Because of that, they were willing to take chances on composition, storytelling…trying new and different approaches.

AT THE DRAWING BOARD

Photograph, Joe Kubert and Norman Maurer, published in 1,000,000 Years Ago!, September 1953.

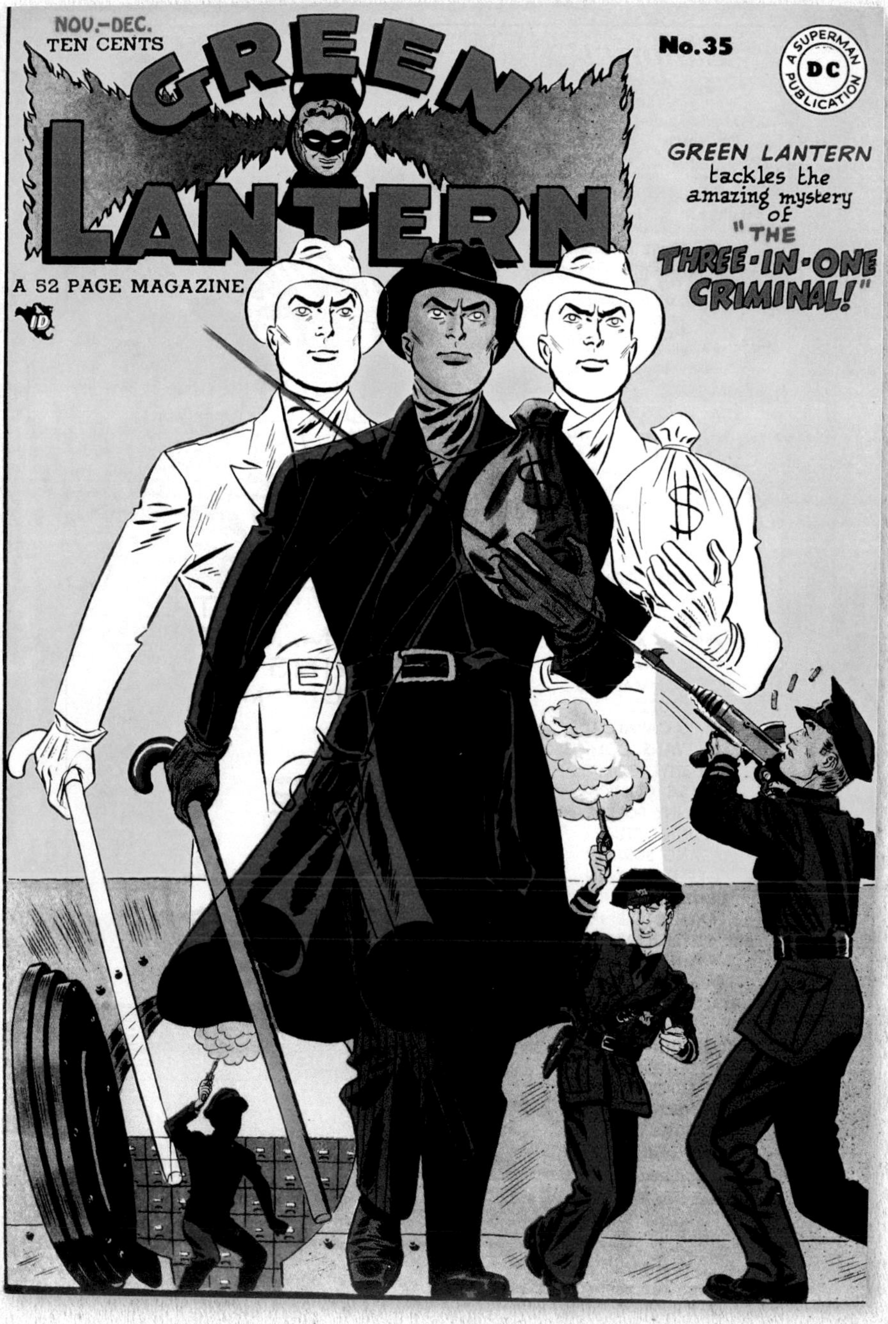
NOV.–DEC.
TEN CENTS
GREEN LANTERN
No.35
A SUPERMAN DC PUBLICATION
GREEN LANTERN tackles the amazing mystery of "THE THREE-IN-ONE CRIMINAL!"
A 52 PAGE MAGAZINE

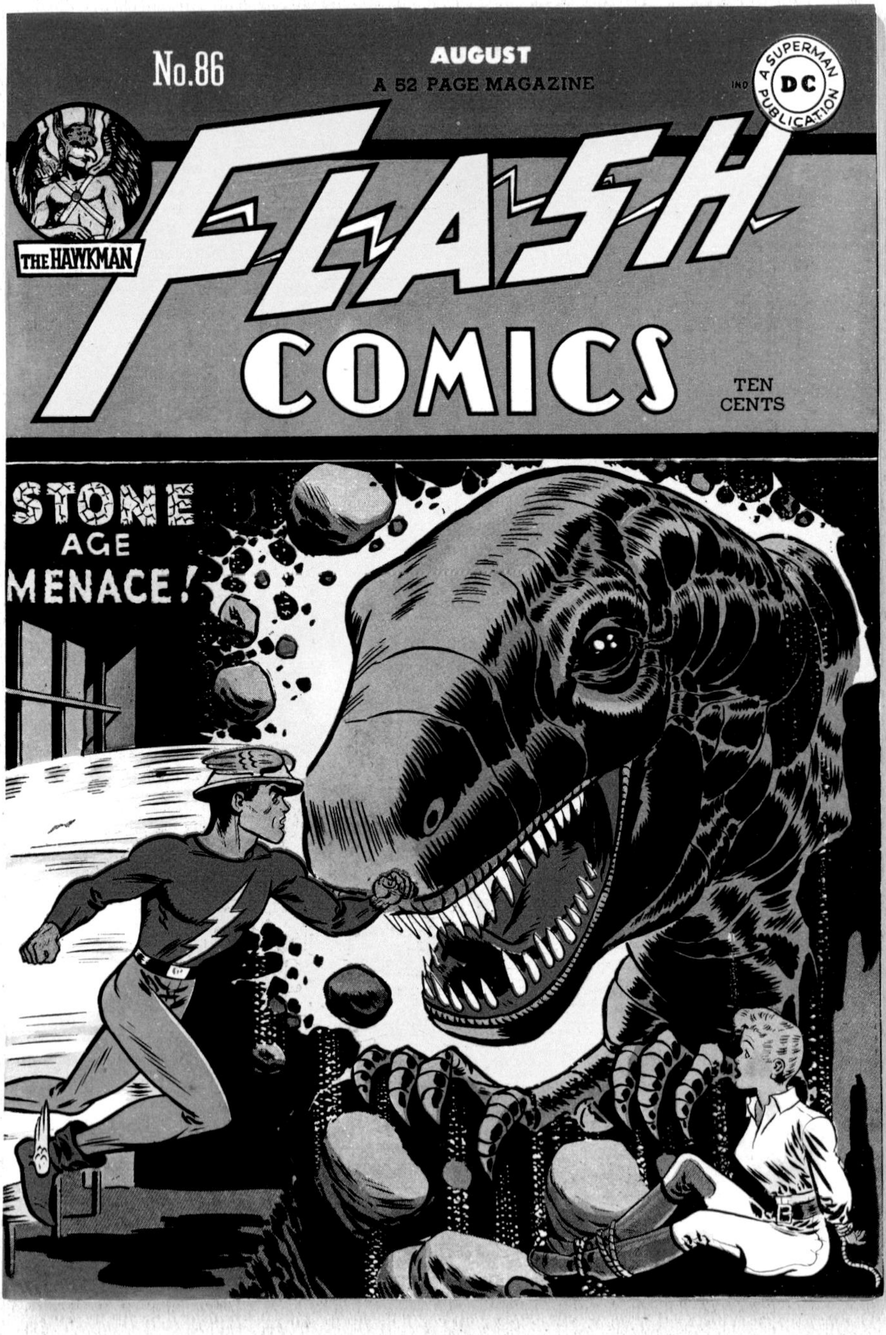
No.86
AUGUST
A 52 PAGE MAGAZINE
A SUPERMAN DC PUBLICATION
THE HAWKMAN
FLASH
COMICS
TEN CENTS
STONE AGE MENACE!

For a long time I would use anything — a pencil, a grease pencil, other materials, just to push it a little more. Because of the amount of work that had to be turned out, the fear of turning out something not so good never even entered my mind.

I still retain that feeling when I do the stuff I'm doing now. [Some artists are] afraid to really take chances. I think it's true of writers too; you're exposing yourself completely. Not only to ridicule, but jeopardizing how you make your livelihood, which is even more important.

I think it's even tougher on artists. It's easier for writers to feel like they can go back and fix the stuff, whereas with the artists there's a literal physical commitment — I have laid down my line. At least before the digital era.

People have said to me, the use of computers now is an assist to the artists because you can now alter it immediately on the computer. When you feel you can correct the mistakes that you've made, because of that sense that it's not irrevocable, you become less and less sure of the stroke that you're putting down. When you put down a brush or pen, a stroke is almost irrevocable.

If you give [the artist] a tool where he can take it back, you're losing an immediacy and the worst part of it is the artist himself suffers. If you start worrying about one stroke, you're done. And once you adopt the kind of feeling where you say to yourself, "I'm not afraid, and I'm going to do the best I can under the circumstances and it'll be the best work I can do at this time — my next job will be better and the next one will be a little better." You lose that if you have a piece of work that you feel you can work on forever, because that computer allows you to do that.

FLASH COMICS No. 86
Cover art, Joe Kubert, August 1947. Kubert's love for things prehistoric literally came crashing through the cover of the 1947 issue of *Flash Comics*, which introduced the Black Canary to the DC Universe.

SUPERMAN CONCEPT SKETCHES
FOLLOWING SPREAD: *Pencils, Joe Shuster, ca. 1936.* Joe Shuster's scratch paper shows less art than hand-lettered promotional text, including the use of the term "super hero" before there were any. The few graphics include early costume treatments and a prototype of Lois Lane.

A Super Hero Is Born

Paul Levitz

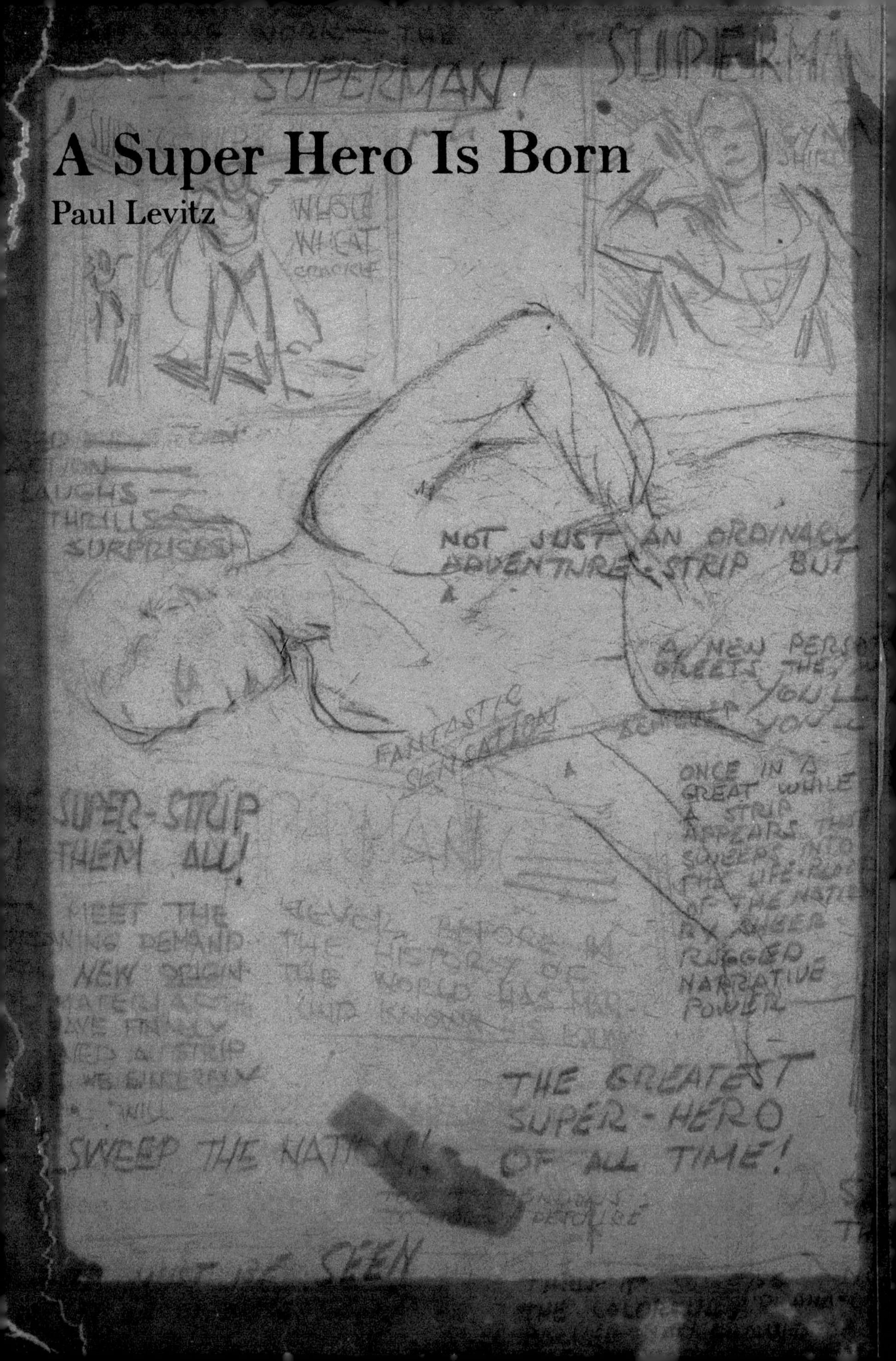

O BIG TO BE
DGED BY
RDINARY
ANDARDS

HE STRIP DESTINED
O SWEEP THE NATION!

THE MOST UNUSU
HUMOR - ADVENTU
STRIP EVER CREA

H HIT STRIP OF 1936
UPERMAN!

WRITE
UNDER TO
SUPERMAN

THE SINGU
EVENT SINCE THE
BIRTH OF COMIC-
STRIPS

IN

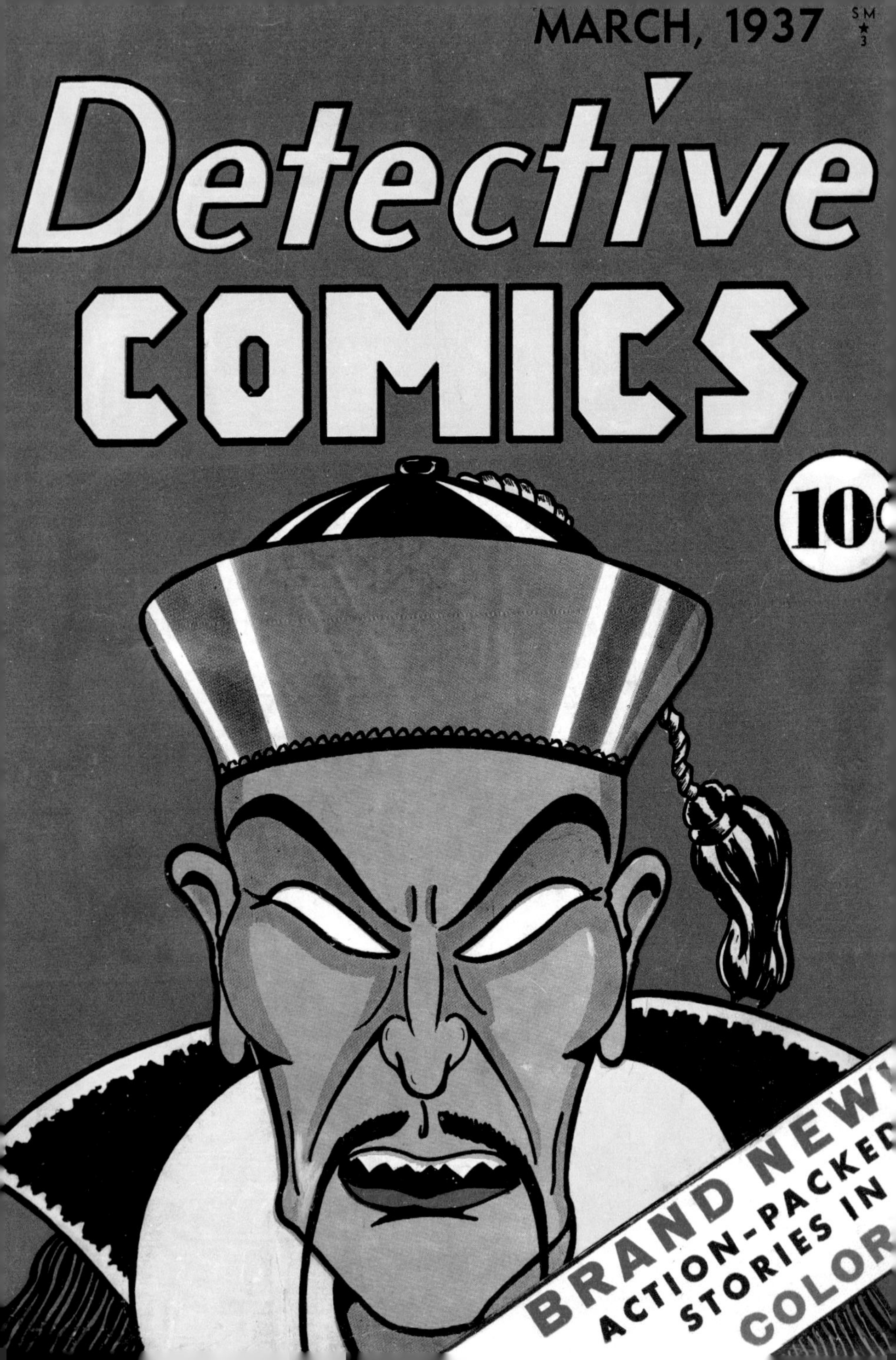
MARCH, 1937
SM
3
Detective
COMICS
10
BRAND NEW
ACTION-PACKED
STORIES IN
COLOR

THE STONE AGE

We have always gathered around as storytellers and crafted tales to bring the vastness of the universe down to a comfortable scale. To hold their audience, ancient storytellers used their tools: fire to make listeners comfortable, color to paint imagery on cave walls, even primitive drums for accompaniment. And they talked of gods and heroes, beings greater than humans, yet recognizable in their human emotions and needs. All that would change over the ages would be the storytellers' tools, as modern mythmaking evolved.

The newspaper comic strip, the clear creative forebear of early DC, emerged in New York by 1896, when R. F. Outcault's "Hogan's Alley" was using what are now very recognizable word balloons, and his principal character, the Yellow Kid, was on his way to being the first commercially important figure in this new art form. In 1897 the term *comic book* was first used for a magazine-format collection, filled with Outcault's "McFadden's Flats." By the 1930s, though, these formats began to be recognizable as the comic books of our lifetime.

STICK IT ON A NEWSSTAND AND SEE WHAT HAPPENS

In 1933, Max "M.C." Gaines was working as a salesman for Harry Wildenberg at Eastern Color Printing, where he helped develop the idea of folding a tabloid newspaper color comic section in half to make a publication slightly larger than the 21st-century comic book, which he then sold to marketers as premiums for products like milk of magnesia. Max was a man of entrepreneurial genius, founder of the only dynasty interwoven with DC's history for three generations, and cursed with luck and timing that prevented him from fully enjoying the fruits of his imagination.

According to the anecdotal history of the comics tribe, Gaines had the inspired idea to put 10¢ stickers on some copies of these giveaway reprint editions, and stuffed them into a newsstand on a Friday. They sold out by Monday morning. Bequeathing comics this tradition of inspiration over careful market research, Gaines gave

Cover art, Vin Sullivan, March 1937.
Detective Comics, the first successful comic book with a single theme, was perhaps inspired by publisher Harry Donenfeld's *Spicy Detective Stories* pulp. At a time when popular culture was rife with characters like Fu Manchu and Charlie Chan, the first issue of *Detective Comics* relied on a typical comic strip trope.

birth to the American comics industry, with a product whose format would endure with gradual changes but remain recognizably the same. By the summer of 1934, Eastern's *Famous Funnies* was a success others were imitating.

Surveying these developments was an even more colorful character, Major Malcolm Wheeler-Nicholson. Wheeler-Nicholson had an adventurous cavalry career, serving with Pershing and across Europe to the wastes of Siberia during the postrevolutionary wars in Russia. He took all these experiences and used them to fuel a writing career on his return to America, working in the pulp magazines (so named for the rough paper their interiors were printed on), and even creating his own syndicate to distribute his stories and comic strips to newspapers. One of his early efforts was a daily newspaper strip that adapted Robert Louis Stevenson's *Treasure Island* with artist Sven Elven in 1925, a feature Wheeler-Nicholson later reformatted for his comic books.

Combining his skill at developing new material with the nascent comic book market, Wheeler-Nicholson set up National Allied Publications on a card table at Manhattan's Hathaway Building on Fourth Avenue and launched the first American comic book sold on the basis of new content, *New Fun: The Big Comic Magazine*, and DC's history began in February 1935. An oversize tabloid with

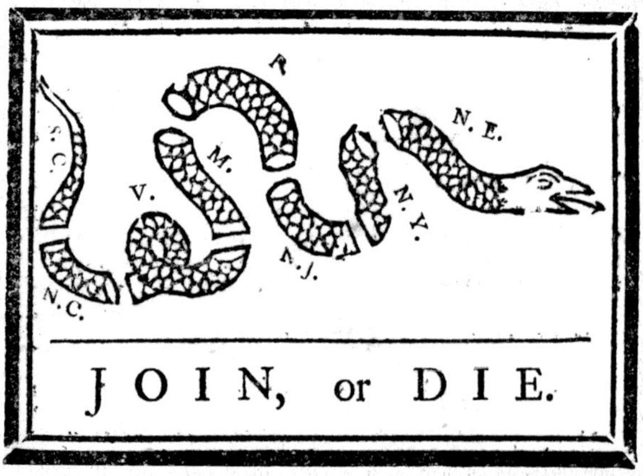
S.C.
N.C.
V.
M.
P.
N.J.
N.Y.
N.E.
JOIN, or DIE.

JOIN, OR DIE.
Pennsylvania Gazette *editorial cartoon, Benjamin Franklin, May 9, 1754.* The earliest comic strips grew out of the illustrative exaggeration and satire of political cartoons, which themselves evolved from the *caricatura* of the 16th century. Ben Franklin was an early proponent of the cartoon as propaganda, as his famously segmented snake, representing the "disunited state" ofthe colonies, shows.

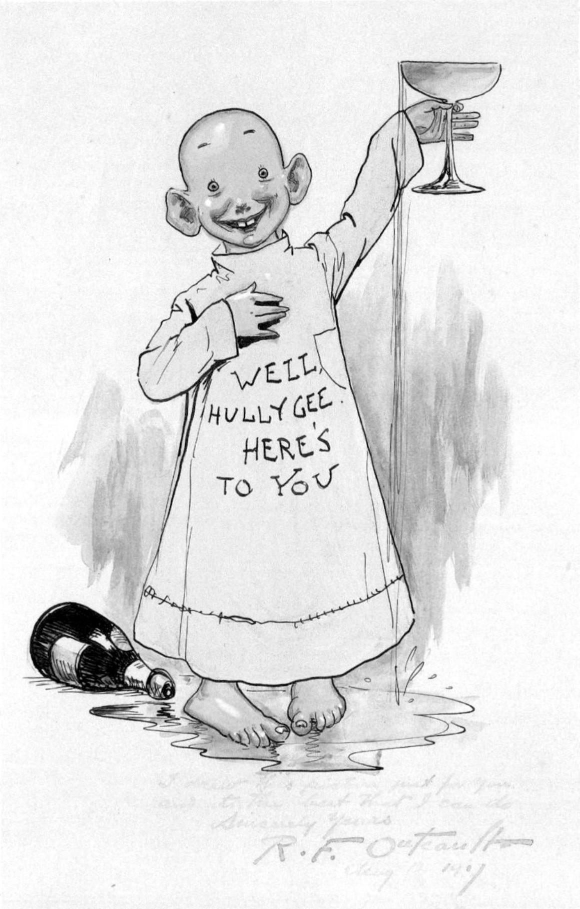
WELL,
HULLY GEE.
HERE'S
TO YOU

THE YELLOW KID

Pen and ink with watercolor wash, Richard F. Outcault, May 12, 1907. Commercial illustrator Richard Felton Outcault's Yellow Kid is generally considered the first comic strip protagonist popular enough to increase newspaper circulation. He is also thought to be the first to speak in dialogue balloons, although at first his dialogue "magically" appeared on his shirt, changing from one scene to the next.

black-and-white interiors (ignoring Gaines's use of color and smaller trim size), he ordered a run of 120,000 copies on the presses of the *Brooklyn Eagle* (Brooklyn had given up being an independent city less than 40 years earlier, but still enjoyed a hometown paper). *New Fun* didn't rely on the presold excitement of the strips it reprinted—if anything, it quietly ignored that some of the material was repurposed from Wheeler-Nicholson's syndicate.

Working with Wheeler-Nicholson on those early issues of *New Fun* were seminal figures in the birth of American comics and DC specifically. The man listed as

MAJOR WHEELER-NICHOLSON

Malcolm Wheeler-Nicholson, ca. 1917. Major Wheeler-Nicholson founded National Allied Publications, the precursor to DC Comics, and published the first comic books with all-new material. The World War I veteran preferred to be addressed as "Major," even as a civilian.

editor of the first four issues was Lloyd Jacquet. Jacquet went on to found one of the earliest "shops" that packaged original comics, Funnies Inc., including *Marvel Comics* No. 1 for Martin Goodman's new venture when Goodman added comics to his pulp publishing in 1939, thus making Jacquet essentially the founding editor of both DC *and* Marvel.

Also contributing to National's early issues were cartoonists Whitney Ellsworth, Vince Sullivan, and Sheldon Mayer (all three later editors with vital roles in DC's destiny), and Walt Kelly (whose "Pogo" would be regarded as one of the great American newspaper strips). And two young men from Cleveland began showing up in *New Fun* No. 6, as Jerome Siegel's and Joe Shuster's credit lines appeared on one-page strips named "Dr. Occult" and "Henri Duval."

FILLING THE RACKS, A COMIC AT A TIME

Despite the economic challenges of the late Depression, *New Fun* appears to have been successful. By the end of 1935, Wheeler-Nicholson collected some of the stories into *Big Book of Fun Comics*, the primal ancestor of DC's Annuals, and launched a companion title, *New Comics*. *New Fun Comics* became *More Fun Comics*, and by early 1936 both monthlies adopted the half-tabloid trim size that Gaines popularized, which enabled them to be easily displayed on the newsstands with the comic books reprinting famous strips...and the other original titles that would follow in their wake.

Adding these new titles meant new challenges as well. Wheeler-Nicholson started working with a better distributor to get his comics to those newsstands, a company called Independent News. Independent's principal owner, Harry Donenfeld, was very interested in this new field of comics, and was ready to help finance Wheeler-Nicholson's expansion.

Donenfeld came to the business through a long and colorful journey that would be paralleled by several other early figures in the comic book industry. Jewish immigrants who came to New York with entrepreneurial spirit and little else, they searched for opportunities in

NEW FUN No. 1

Cover art, "Jack Woods" one-page installment; script, unknown; pencils and inks, Lyman Anderson. February 1935.

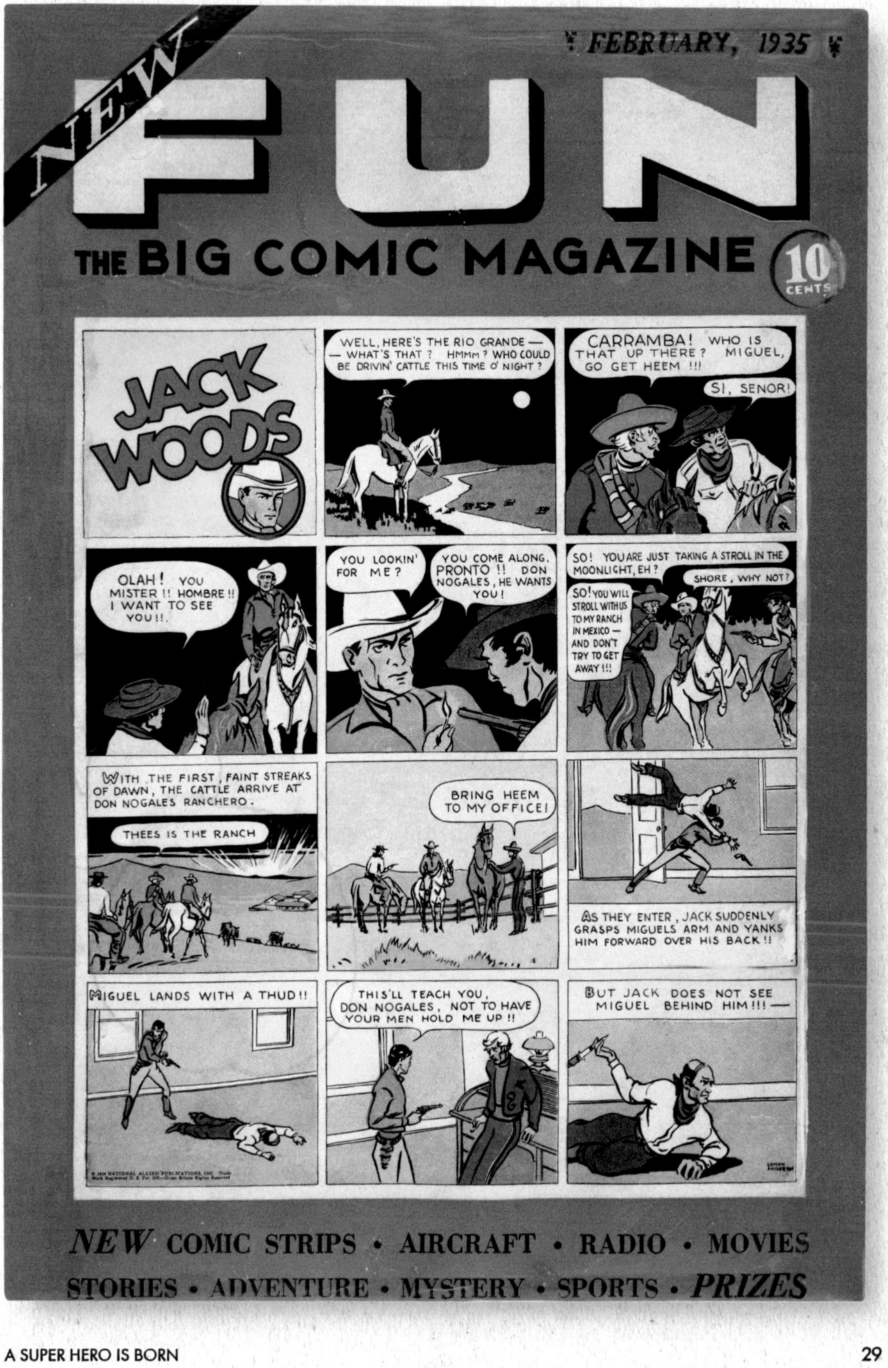
FEBRUARY, 1935
NEW
FUN
THE BIG COMIC MAGAZINE
10 CENTS
JACK WOODS
WELL, HERE'S THE RIO GRANDE — — WHAT'S THAT ? HMMM ? WHO COULD BE DRIVIN' CATTLE THIS TIME O' NIGHT ?
CARRAMBA! WHO IS THAT UP THERE? MIGUEL, GO GET HEEM !!!
SI, SENOR!
OLAH! YOU MISTER !! HOMBRE !! I WANT TO SEE YOU !!.
YOU LOOKIN' FOR ME?
YOU COME ALONG, PRONTO !! DON NOGALES, HE WANTS YOU!
SO! YOU ARE JUST TAKING A STROLL IN THE MOONLIGHT, EH?
SHORE, WHY NOT?
SO! YOU WILL STROLL WITH US TO MY RANCH IN MEXICO — AND DON'T TRY TO GET AWAY !!!
WITH THE FIRST, FAINT STREAKS OF DAWN, THE CATTLE ARRIVE AT DON NOGALES RANCHERO.
THEES IS THE RANCH
BRING HEEM TO MY OFFICE!
AS THEY ENTER, JACK SUDDENLY GRASPS MIGUELS ARM AND YANKS HIM FORWARD OVER HIS BACK !!
MIGUEL LANDS WITH A THUD !!
THIS'LL TEACH YOU, DON NOGALES, NOT TO HAVE YOUR MEN HOLD ME UP !!
BUT JACK DOES NOT SEE MIGUEL BEHIND HIM !!! —
NEW COMIC STRIPS • AIRCRAFT • RADIO • MOVIES
STORIES • ADVENTURE • MYSTERY • SPORTS • PRIZES

NEW ADVENTURE COMICS No. 12

Cover art, Whitney Ellsworth, January 1937. New Comics began its three-issue transformation into *Adventure* with this cover by Ellsworth, who had started out as "ghost" on the "Dumb Dora" and "Tillie the Toiler" newspaper strips before joining National's staff. Ellsworth would later become DC's editorial director and its first Hollywood-based producer.

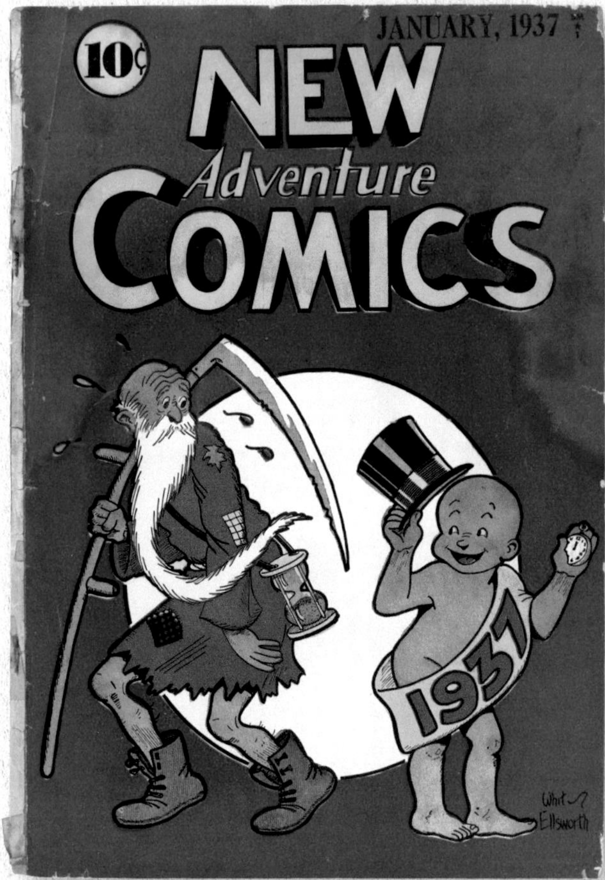
JANUARY, 1937
10¢
NEW
Adventure
COMICS
1937
Whit Ellsworth

many fields, and found entrance at the very bottom of the publishing industry. Among his business ventures, Donenfeld had been a partner with his older brothers in a small printing business in the 1920s, and then used that as leverage to become both printer and silent partner in a number of magazines. Frank Armer's pulp magazines were racy, and by the standards of the time often considered pornography; Donenfeld went from being Armer's partner to his competitor, with titles like *Hot Tales*, and then his successor when Armer went bankrupt. By then, Armer had a themed line of titles, including *Spicy Stories* and *Spicy Detective*, which in 1934, along with prose tales, lurid painted covers, and a few photographs of women in lingerie, included a simple comic strip called "Sally the Sleuth" by Adolphe Barreaux, who would later contribute to Wheeler-Nicholson's titles as well.

The risqué publishing line fit well with some of the connections the Damon Runyonesque Donenfeld made on the shadier sides of New York's streets, and it kept his printing presses rolling. The pulps also led to an opportunity to acquire a failing distribution company, Eastern News, which Donenfeld and his partners reshaped into Independent News.

Although it's likely that Donenfeld and his partners quietly retained interests in pulp magazines past the war years, by the mid-1930s Fiorello LaGuardia had become

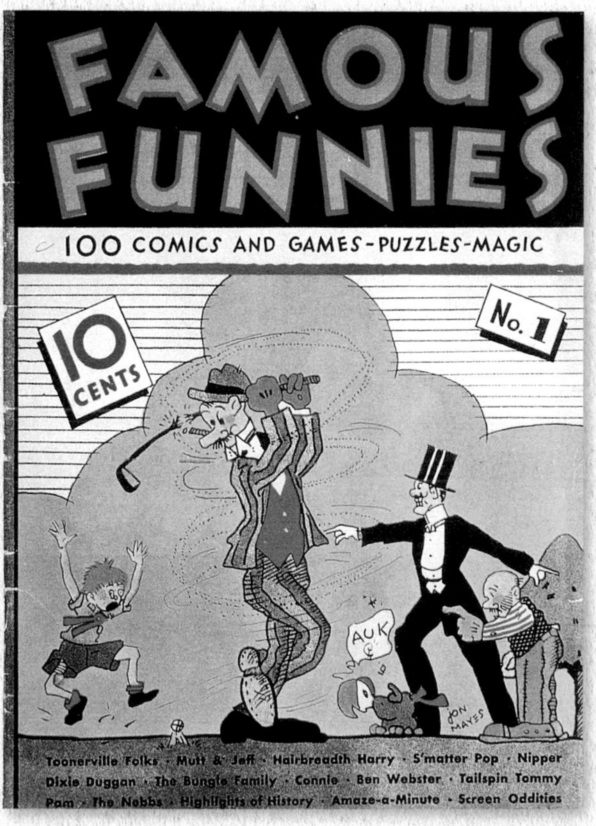

FAMOUS FUNNIES
100 COMICS AND GAMES - PUZZLES - MAGIC
10 CENTS
No. 1
AUK
JON MAYES
Toonerville Folks · Mutt & Jeff · Hairbreadth Harry · S'matter Pop · Nipper
Dixie Duggan · The Bungle Family · Connie · Ben Webster · Tailspin Tommy
Pam · The Nebbs · Highlights of History · Amaze-a-Minute · Screen Oddities

FAMOUS FUNNIES No. 1
Cover art, Jon Mayes (after "Mutt & Jeff" *creator Bud Fisher), July 1934.* Comics critic Ted White called M. C. Gaines "the Johnny Appleseed of comics" because Gaines worked for many publishers, "planting" new titles. His first employer in the field was Eastern Color, where his *Famous Funnies* introduced the standard comic book format.

THE BIG BOOK OF FUN COMICS No. 1

Cover art, various artists in panels excerpted from interior reprints, 1935. DC would introduce super hero reprint collections with its "Annuals" 24 years later, but originated the concept with this collection, reproducing the first four issues of *New Fun* in their entirety. Some 60 years later, DC revived the "Big Book" title for a series of black-and-white trade paperbacks from its Paradox Press imprint.

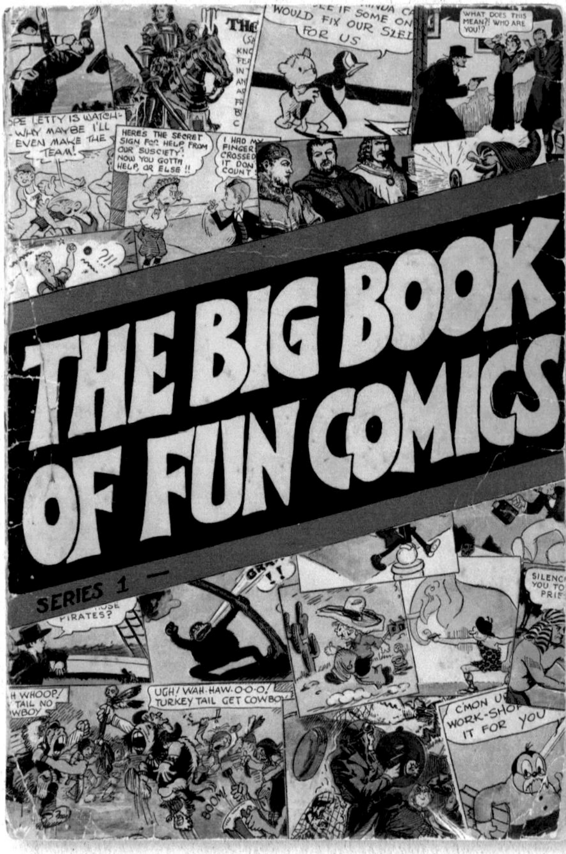

WOULD FIX OUR SLED
FOR US
WHAT DOES THIS MEAN?! WHO ARE YOU!?
EVEN MAKE THE TEAM!
HERES THE SECRET SIGN FOR HELP FROM OUR SUSCIETY! NOW YOU GOTTA HELP, OR ELSE !!
THE BIG BOOK OF FUN COMICS
SERIES 1 —
PIRATES?
UGH! WAH-HAW-O-O-O! TURKEY TAIL GET COWBO
WORK-SHO
IT FOR YOU

mayor of New York and was using legal leverage to push the racier magazines off newsstands. One of Donenfeld's employees took the rap (and a jail term) in a clash with the reform administration, and the magazines were toned down... slightly.

In a smaller but safer corner of the publishing world, Wheeler-Nicholson continued his expansion plans, with Vince Sullivan now on board as his editor. Sullivan cooked up *Detective Comics*, which for the first time focused content on a single theme, and developed longer stories, not mimicking the single-page approach of the Sunday newspaper section. One of these would be "Slam Bradley," a private-eye series from Siegel

MORE FUN COMICS No. 28

Cover art, Vin Sullivan, January 1938. Sullivan, who created this cover, also drew the first cover of *Detective* and urged DC management to launch Superman and Batman.

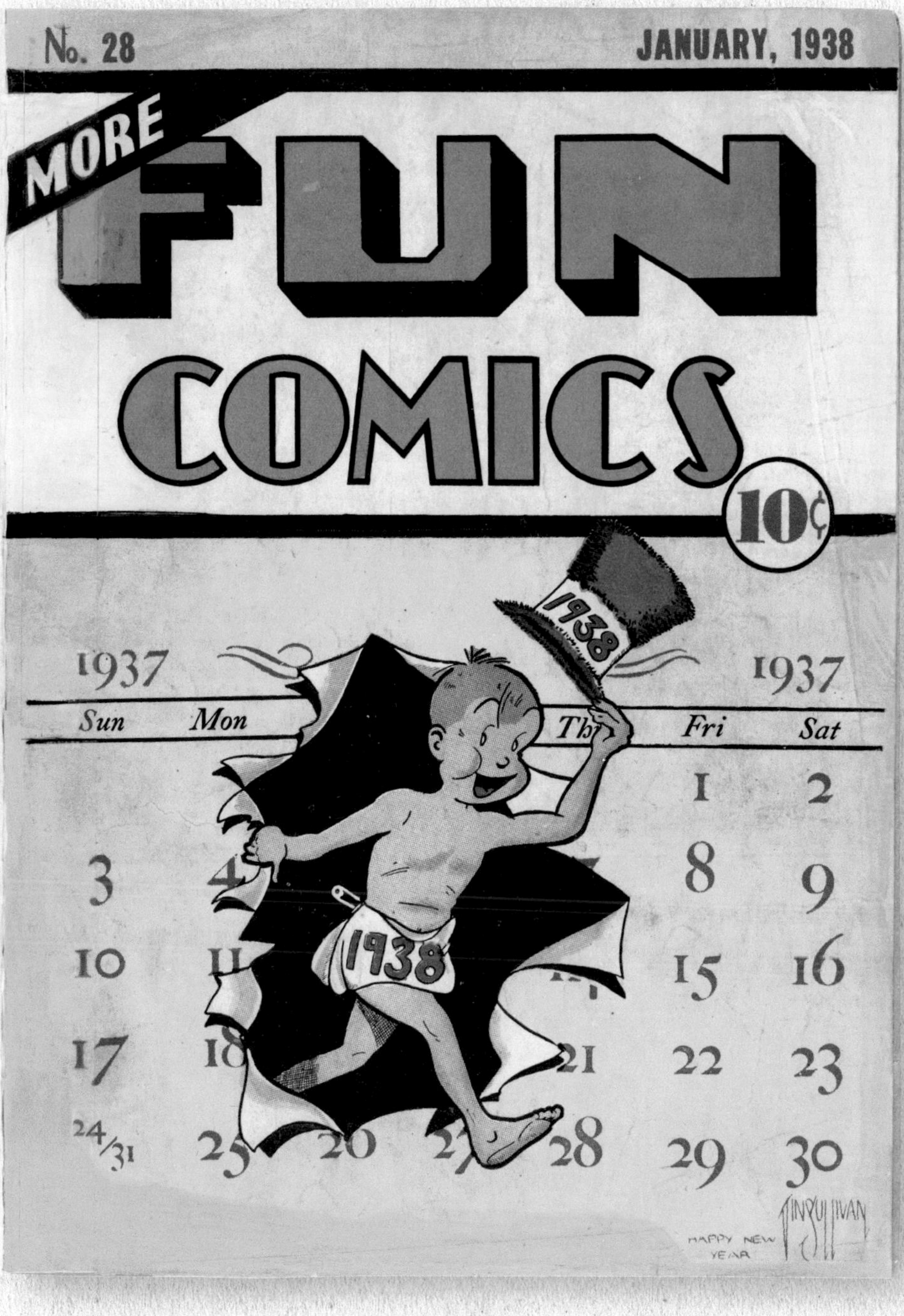
No. 28
JANUARY, 1938
MORE FUN COMICS
10¢
1938
1937
1937
Sun
Mon
Fri
Sat
1938
HAPPY NEW YEAR

SPICY DETECTIVE STORIES

Cover art, H. J. Ward, October 1938.
Harry Donenfeld, who would begin printing Wheeler-Nicholson's covers in 1935, was the publisher of such "racy" pulps as *Spicy Detective*, often with covers by Ward, of Superman portrait fame.

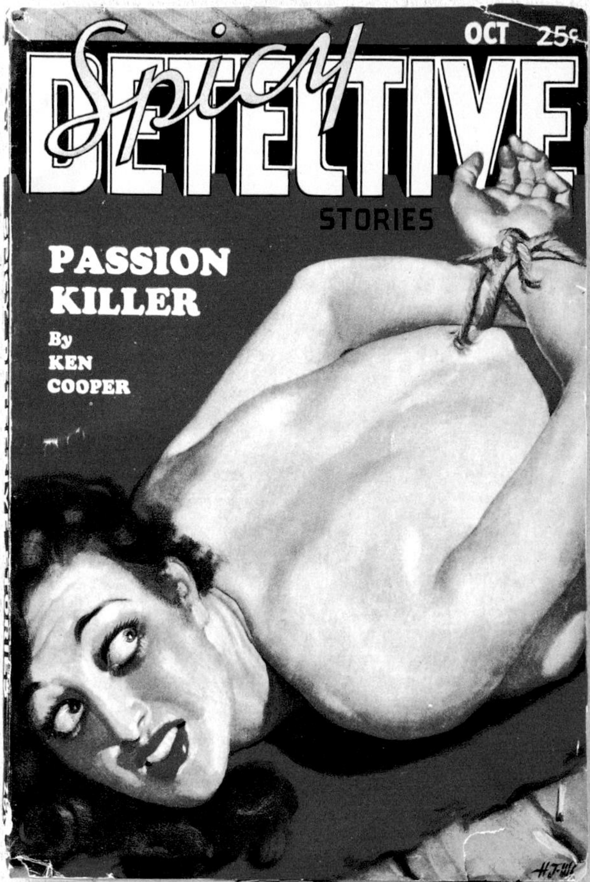

OCT 25¢
Spicy
DETECTIVE
STORIES
PASSION KILLER
By KEN COOPER

DETECTIVE COMICS No. 1

Interior, "Slam Bradley"; script, Jerry Siegel; pencils and inks, Joe Shuster. March 1937.
Before Superman, its creators presented one of comics' first private eyes, played more lightly than the hard-boiled types of Dashiell Hammett or Raymond Chandler.

and Shuster, who began to have a steady flow of work from National's three titles. But to produce *Detective* in 1937, Wheeler-Nicholson needed more capital, which Independent News arranged. Jack Liebowitz, Donenfeld's longtime accountant and business manager, became a partner in the newly formed Detective Comics Inc. as part of the arrangement.

Liebowitz was a precise man, given to measuring risk and reward possibilities carefully, and an early master of the uncertainties of newsstand distribution. Estimating suitable print runs in a fully returnable industry was always as much art as science (DC's extremes ranged

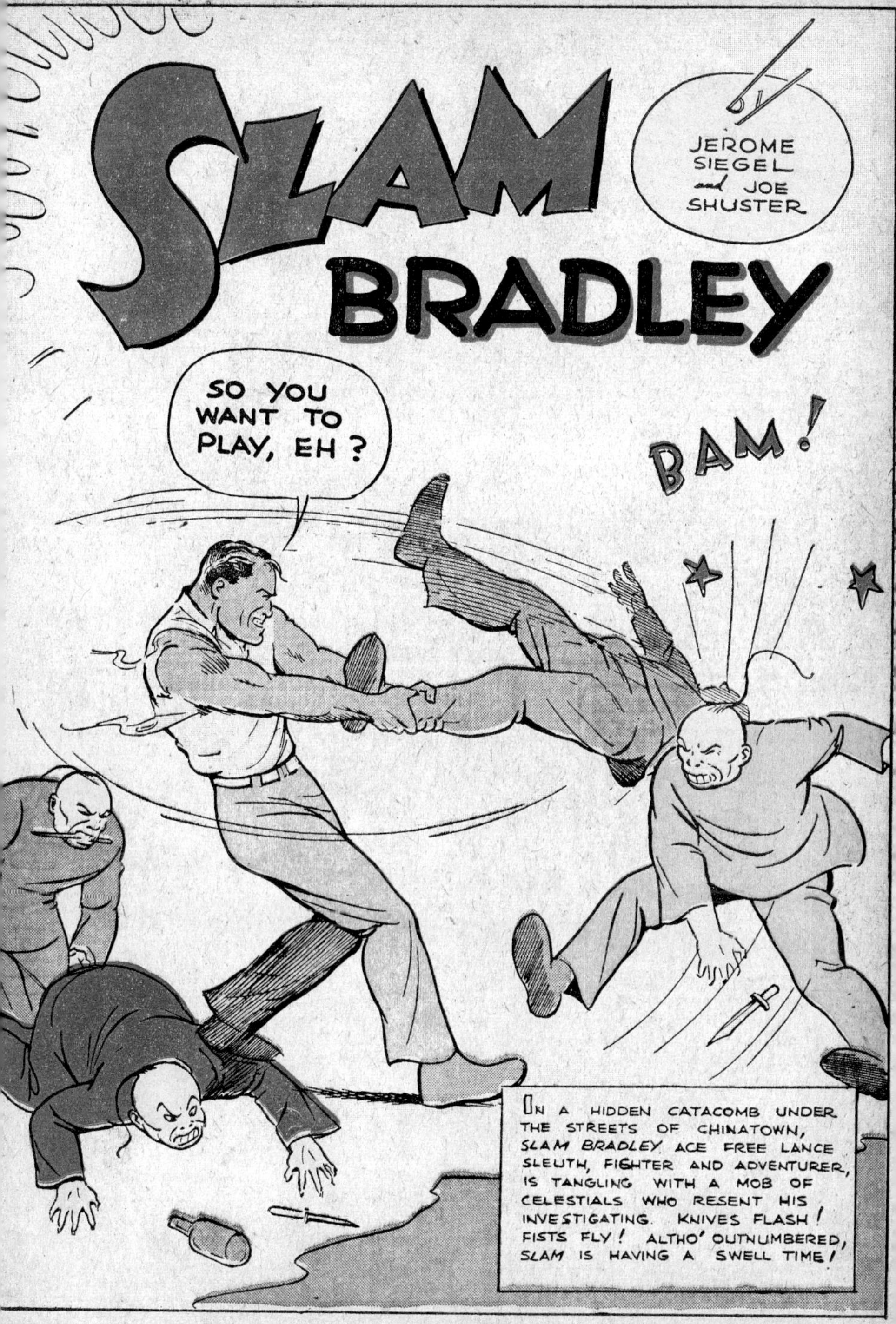
SLAM BRADLEY
BY JEROME SIEGEL and JOE SHUSTER
SO YOU WANT TO PLAY, EH?
BAM!
ON A HIDDEN CATACOMB UNDER THE STREETS OF CHINATOWN, SLAM BRADLEY ACE FREE LANCE SLEUTH, FIGHTER AND ADVENTURER, IS TANGLING WITH A MOB OF CELESTIALS WHO RESENT HIS INVESTIGATING. KNIVES FLASH! FISTS FLY! ALTHO' OUTNUMBERED, SLAM IS HAVING A SWELL TIME!

The REIGN of the SUPER-MAN
By
Herbert S. Fine
The breadline! Its row of downcast, disillusioned men; unlucky creatures who have found that life holds nothing but bitterness for them. The bread-line! Last resort of the starving vagrant.
With a contemptous sneer on his face, Professor Smalley watched the wretched unfortunates file past him. To him, who had come of rich parents and had never been forced to face the rigors of life, the miserableness of these men seemed deserved. It appeared to him that if they had the slightest ambition at all they could easily lift themselves from their terrible rut.
Another Thrilling Story By The Writer of ''Snaring The Master''
file past.
he inquired.
for you! Nothing crooked, I hope!''
Professor Smalley laughed. ''I assure you my intentions are purely humanitarian. But if you doubt ....''

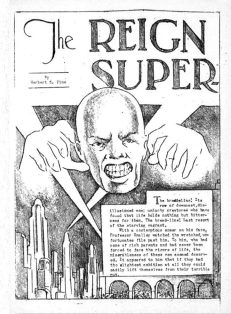

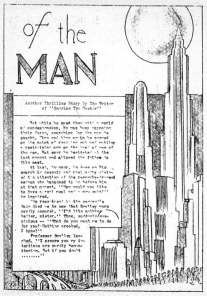

between 9% of a print run selling on an issue of *Jemm, Son of Saturn* and 90% on a television-fad-fueled issue of *Batman*). The balance was tipping rapidly from Wheeler-Nicholson's dreams to the harder-edged reality of his allies.

A series of further financial crises followed. Wheeler-Nicholson's ventures went under, and Donenfeld bought the assets out of bankruptcy court. Whether called National or Detective Comics, the company that would soon be known to the world as DC Comics was under new management.

Meanwhile, in Cleveland, two of the company's young contributors were engaged in their own frustrating quest. Jerry Siegel was a student at Glenville High, fascinated by science fiction and perhaps influenced by his own father's murder, when he dreamed up the idea of a Superman character with amazing powers. According to legend, he raced to his friend Joe Shuster's house and enlisted the artist in his dream.

The first incarnation of the idea was 1933's "The Reign of the Superman," a prose story by Siegel with illustrations by Shuster. Siegel published it in his own early fan magazine, *Science Fiction*, inspired by *The Time Traveller*, the prototypical fanzine from a group of New York fans including Julius Schwartz and Mort Weisinger. The tale explored the consequences of super-human power. The characters and concepts are unrecognizable, but it was part of a development process.

The next version was even more heavily connected to its science-fiction roots: Strongly influenced by Edgar Rice Burroughs's *John Carter of Mars* stories (in which an Earthman gains greater strength in the Red Planet's lesser gravity) and Philip Wylie's novel *Gladiator* (in which Hugo Danner is born with extraordinary powers), Siegel and Shuster's Superman became the epic prototype of the super hero. This was filled out by elements such as a colorful costume Shuster adapted from circus leotards, and the brilliant innovation of the Superman–Lois Lane–Clark Kent romantic triangle, which not only evoked the creators' own teenage challenges with Glenville's young women, but was an archetype that men and women would respond to for generations.

SCIENCE FICTION No. 3
Interior pages from mimeographed fanzine featuring "The Reign of the Superman"; script, Jerry Siegel; artist, Joe Shuster. January 1933.
Siegel and Shuster's fanzine, *Science Fiction*—which featured their first "Superman"—drew inspiration from *The Time Traveller*, published by Mort Weisinger and Julius Schwartz, who would later go on to edit "Superman" for DC. This prototype was not a hero, but a much darker personality who, as Siegel related under the pseudonym of Herbert S. Fine, could read minds, control others' thoughts, and ruled as "a veritable God."

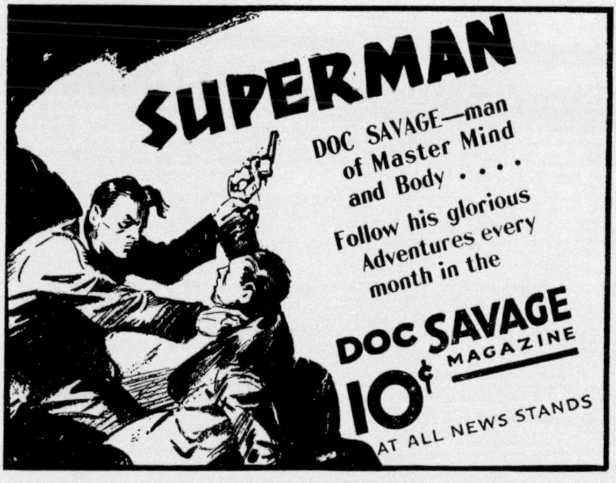

SUPERMAN
DOC SAVAGE—man of Master Mind and Body . . . .
Follow his glorious Adventures every month in the
DOC SAVAGE MAGAZINE
10¢
AT ALL NEWS STANDS

DOC SAVAGE MAGAZINE AD
Street & Smith house ad, artist unknown, 1934.

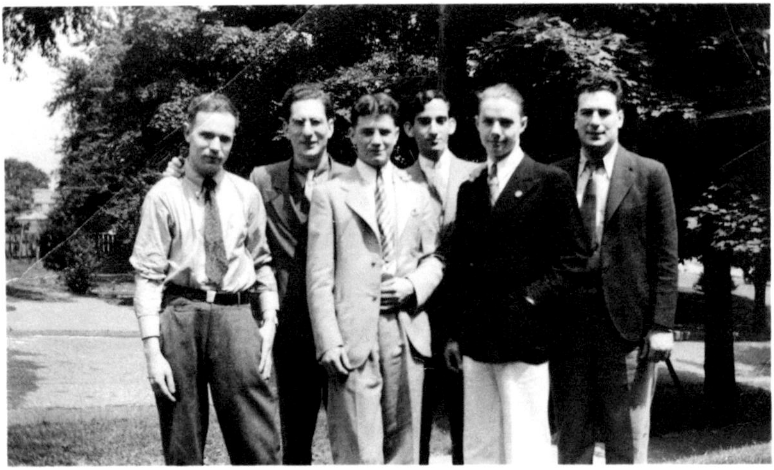

FANDOM'S FIRST
Julius Schwartz (second from left) and Mort Weisinger (right) with Fantasy Magazine *publisher Conrad H. Ruppert, writer Otto Binder,* Fantasy Fan *editor Charles D. Hornig, and "number-one fan" Jack Darrow, 1935.*

GLADIATOR
Book cover, author Philip Wylie, 1930.
Although the pair never acknowledged Hugo Danner as an influence, many have long conjectured that Siegel and Shuster found inspiration in Wylie's gladiator, who set out "to stamp crime off the face of the Earth" and become "a super-detective, following and summarily punishing every criminal until no one dared to commit a felony."

NO ONE WILL WANT TO READ THIS "SUPERMAN"

This new "Superman" was developed as a newspaper strip, and the boys worked up samples to send around. In all entertainment the most predictable successes are those closely modeled on previous hits, and the riskiest (though occasionally greatest) are those without a clear precedent. Although "Superman" had elements from other media, it felt like a completely new concept...and newspaper syndicate after syndicate rejected it.

Disappointed by the reaction, Siegel even contacted other artists, hoping a different visual look would enable his strip to succeed, but Siegel returned to Shuster and continued to pile up rejection slips.

THE GOLDEN AGE DAWNS

Overall, the 1930s were a dark decade in America, between the overwhelming weight of the Depression and the gathering clouds of war abroad. Only President Franklin D. Roosevelt's warm voice coming through the radio offered hope, and people were ready for a new kind of hero...they simply didn't know where he'd come from. Certainly no one expected much from the early comic books beyond a smile and a few minutes of entertainment, mostly from characters reminiscent of the newspaper strips. Editors or production managers would assemble an issue by going to their bulky metal flat files full of artwork and plucking out stories, perhaps trying to balance the themes, perhaps not. Envision Vince Sullivan at National's offices at 480 Lexington Avenue, just north of New York's Grand Central Terminal, pulling open drawers as he considered what would become *Action Comics* No.1, the launch of the company's fourth title. Regular contributors Homer Fleming and Bill Ely had offerings on hand, and new ones were ready, too: Fred Guardineer with Zatara, who spoke backward to work magic; Bernard Baily with Tex Thomson, the future Mister America; and Shelly Moldoff with a gag page for the inside back cover. But a sizeable hole remained.

History fails us here, for success has so many fathers. Many people have claimed a role godfathering Superman's

ABANDONED SUPERMAN PROTOTYPE

Lone surviving page of Jerry Siegel and Joe Shuster's rejected first Superman comic, 1933.

GLADIATOR
PHILIP WYLIE
BORZOI BOOKS

A SCIENCE FICTION STORY in CARTOONS
The SUPERMAN
THE MOST ASTOUNDING FICTION CHARACTER OF ALL TIME
10¢

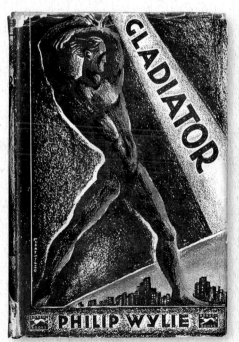

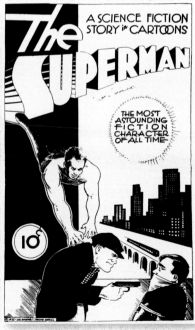

ACTION COMICS No. 1 HOUSE AD
Cover art, Joe Shuster, May 1938.
The historic first appearance of Superman in *Action Comics* No. 1 was proclaimed in this advertisement from *New Adventure Comics* No. 26. Many copies of *Action* No. 1 were mutilated thanks to a coloring contest that required kids to tear out the last page of the Superman tale.

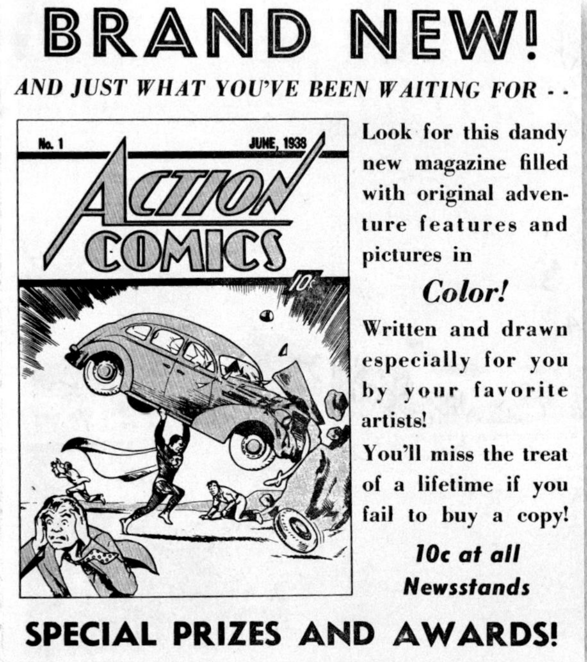
BRAND NEW!
AND JUST WHAT YOU'VE BEEN WAITING FOR - -
No. 1
JUNE, 1938
ACTION COMICS
10¢
Look for this dandy new magazine filled with original adventure features and pictures in
Color!
Written and drawn especially for you by your favorite artists!
You'll miss the treat of a lifetime if you fail to buy a copy!
10c at all Newsstands
SPECIAL PRIZES AND AWARDS!

EARLY SUPERMAN CONCEPT SKETCH
Pencils, Joe Shuster, ca. 1936.
Here, "The Superman" is still very much a work in progress, as yet without the distinctive costume, which was unlike anything seen before. Its originality did not extend to the name Superman, however. Credit for that term belongs, of course, to Friedrich Nietzsche, who in 1883 wrote, "Man is a rope, fastened between animal and Superman, a rope over an abyss. A dangerous going-across, a dangerous wayfaring, a dangerous looking-back, a dangerous shuddering and staying still."

birth in that first publication; from then-fading founder Malcolm Wheeler-Nicholson to Max Gaines (who was running the McClure Syndicate, where Superman had been submitted) and his perspicacious sidekick, Shelly Mayer (who had been contributing comic strips to DC since *New Comics* No. 1, when he was 17). But Sullivan was already commissioning Siegel and Shuster's stories for National. In any case, there's no dispute that the first story was bought to fill that hole in *Action* for a legendary $130 (the then-high page rate of $10 for the 13-page tale) contract signed by Jack Liebowitz, who himself claimed to have picked out the since-classic cover image, the now-iconic man lifting a car that became part of our visual language as a symbol of physical strength. Sadly, the business ramifications of that transaction include a long history of dispute, which would require a very different book to be told. But indisputably, the cultural ramifications were phenomenal: *Action Comics* No. 1 sold out and went through multiple printings, and an icon was born, leaping

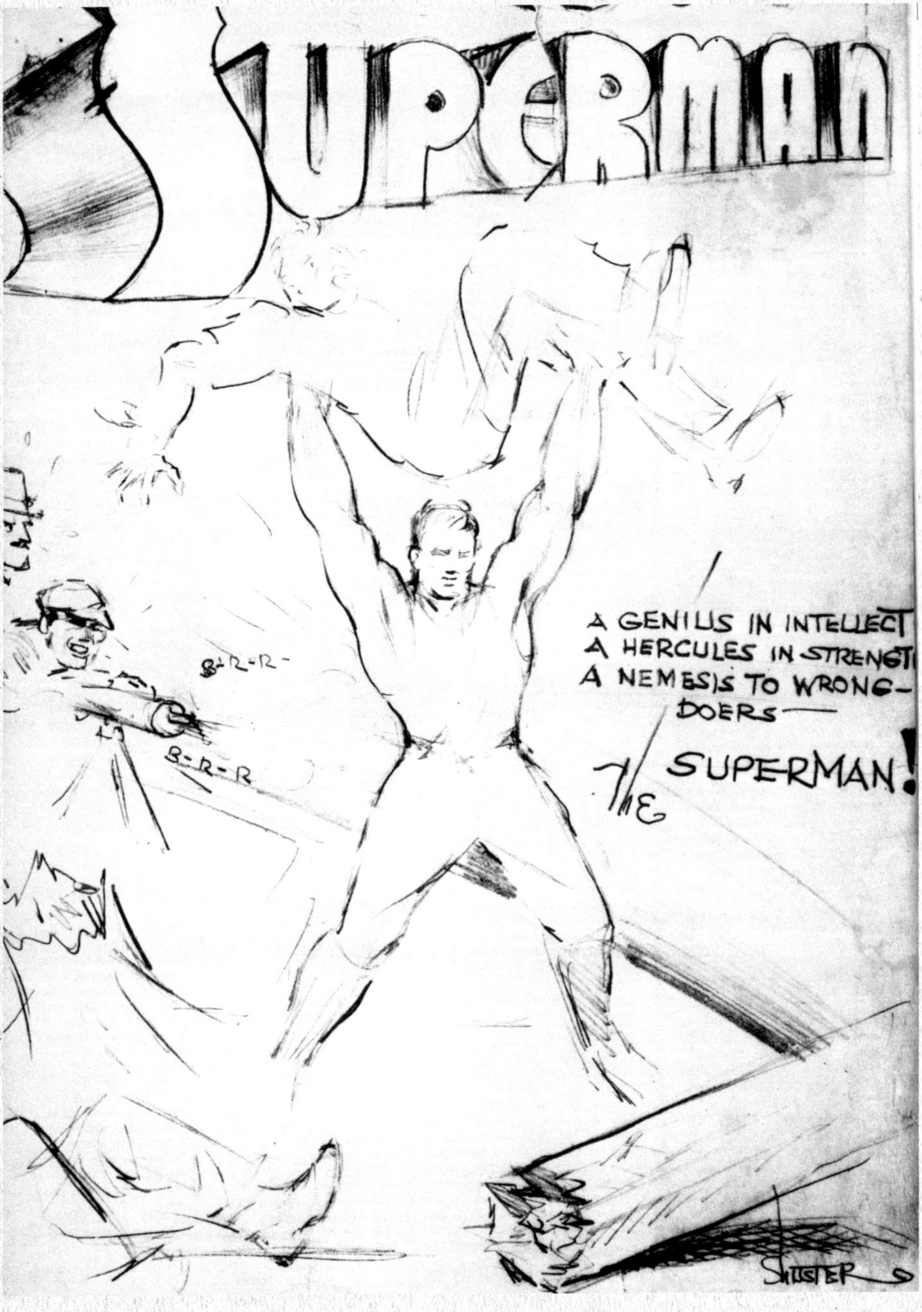
SUPERMAN
B-R-R-
B-R-R
A GENIUS IN INTELLECT
A HERCULES IN STRENGT
A NEMESIS TO WRONG-
DOERS
THE SUPERMAN!
SHUSTER

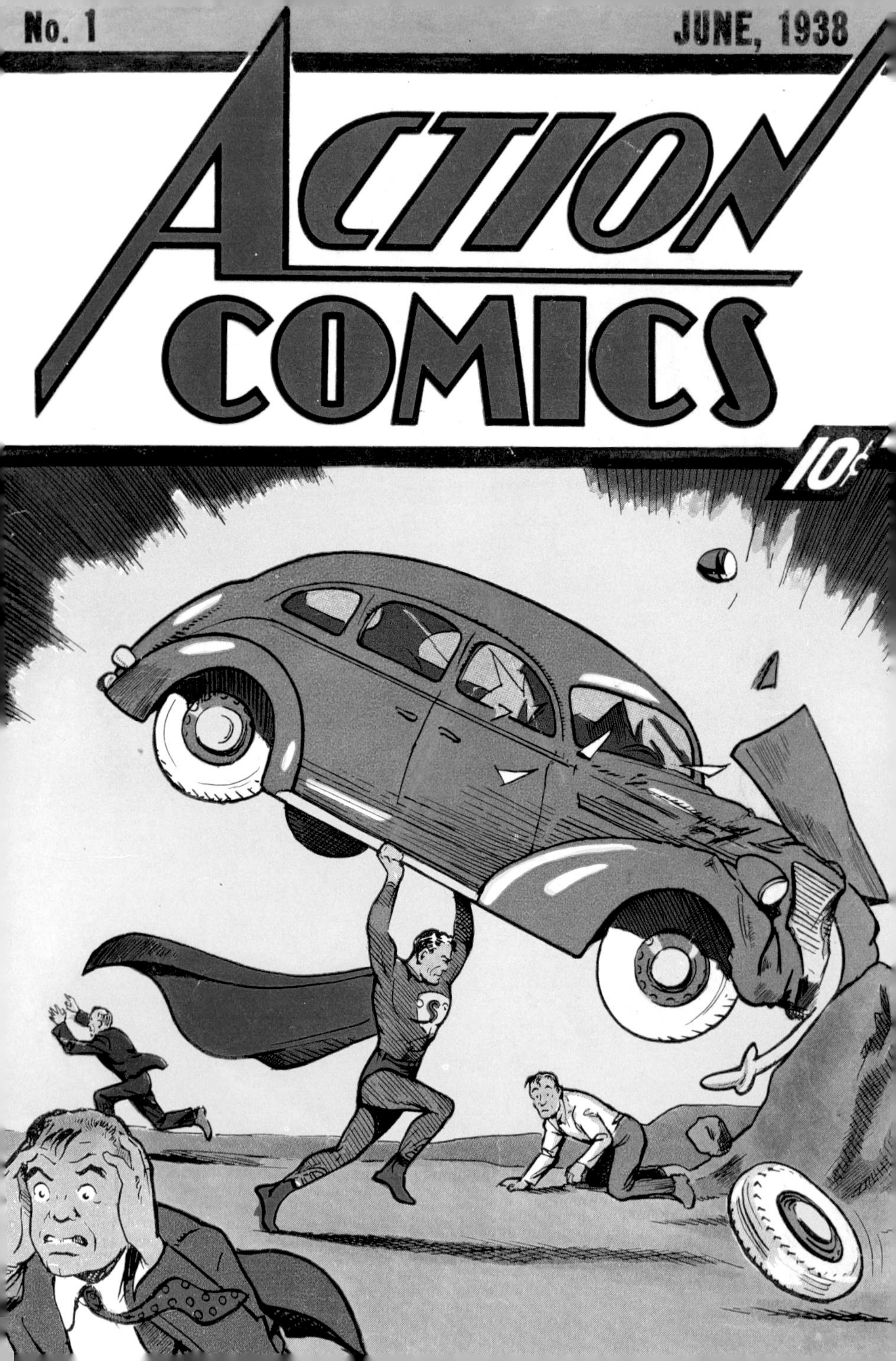
No. 1
JUNE, 1938
ACTION COMICS
10¢

over tall buildings and changing the face of American comics forever. In an era when the popular culture moved more slowly, as films rolled out town by town, television was in few homes, and only radio had the power to create "instant events" as Orson Welles would prove a few months later with his *War of the Worlds* broadcast, Superman was a phenomenon. The Golden Age had begun.

Superman mixed fundamental wish-fulfillment themes together in a new way: The aspiration that if only Lois would look beyond the glasses and see that Clark was really a Superman touched the inner milquetoast, and Superman's physical abilities to act out solutions ordinary mortals could only fantasize about was an enduring meme. Add in a touch of Moses in the

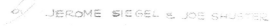

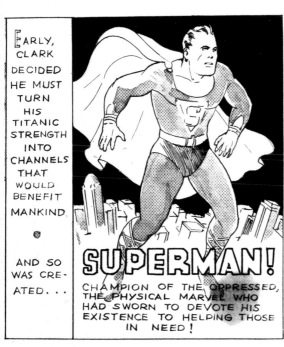

ACTION COMICS No. 1
Cover art, Joe Shuster, June 1938.
In his first appearance, Superman's back story is still vague — very much a work in progress. Later revisions establish how the orphanage never discovers the superbaby's powers, so as not to compromise his secret identity. Subsequent issues also state that Superman did not come from a race of superbeings, but rather he gains his powers on Earth due to geophysical differences between it and Krypton. In addition to the issue's historic content, its small print run helped make *Action Comics* No. 1 the "holy grail of comic collectors." An unrestored mint-condition copy sold for $1.5 million in early 2010.

JEROME SIEGEL & JOE SHUSTER
EARLY, CLARK DECIDED HE MUST TURN HIS TITANIC STRENGTH INTO CHANNELS THAT WOULD BENEFIT MANKIND.
AND SO WAS CRE-ATED . . .
SUPERMAN!
CHAMPION OF THE OPPRESSED, THE PHYSICAL MARVEL WHO HAD SWORN TO DEVOTE HIS EXISTENCE TO HELPING THOSE IN NEED!

"SUPERMAN" NEWSPAPER STRIP
Panel from rejected comic strip; script, Jerry Siegel; pencils and inks, Joe Shuster. Ca. 1936.
None of Siegel and Shuster's newspaper samples would go to waste. This art, too, would eventually be used, in slightly altered form.

AND SO BEGINS
OF THE MOST SEN
OF ALL TI

Their Perseverance Rewarded

JOE SCHUSTER AND JERRY SIEGEL

'Superman' Is Coming to
Plain Dealer Sunday

SIEGEL & SHUSTER
Newspaper clipping,
Cleveland Plain Dealer,
January 18, 1939.

ACTION COMICS No. 1
Interiors, "Superman"; script,
Jerry Siegel; pencils and inks,
Joe Shuster, June 1938.

bulrushes reset as a child rocketed from a doomed planet (named Krypton by Siegel in a nod to its fellow noble gas, helium, where Edgar Rice Burroughs's John Carter had discovered his greater-than-normal strength from the lesser gravity of Mars) and a bulletproof skin that would have saved Siegel's father, and the hero was born.

Superman's success was so great that Siegel and Shuster got one of their wishes almost immediately: On January 12, 1939, "Superman" debuted as a daily newspaper strip, with a Sunday strip added later that year. This more than doubled the amount of Superman material being created, and vastly extended the audience the character could reach. The phenomenon continued, with a special *World's Fair* one-shot comic issued in April starring Superman and other DC heroes, sold only at

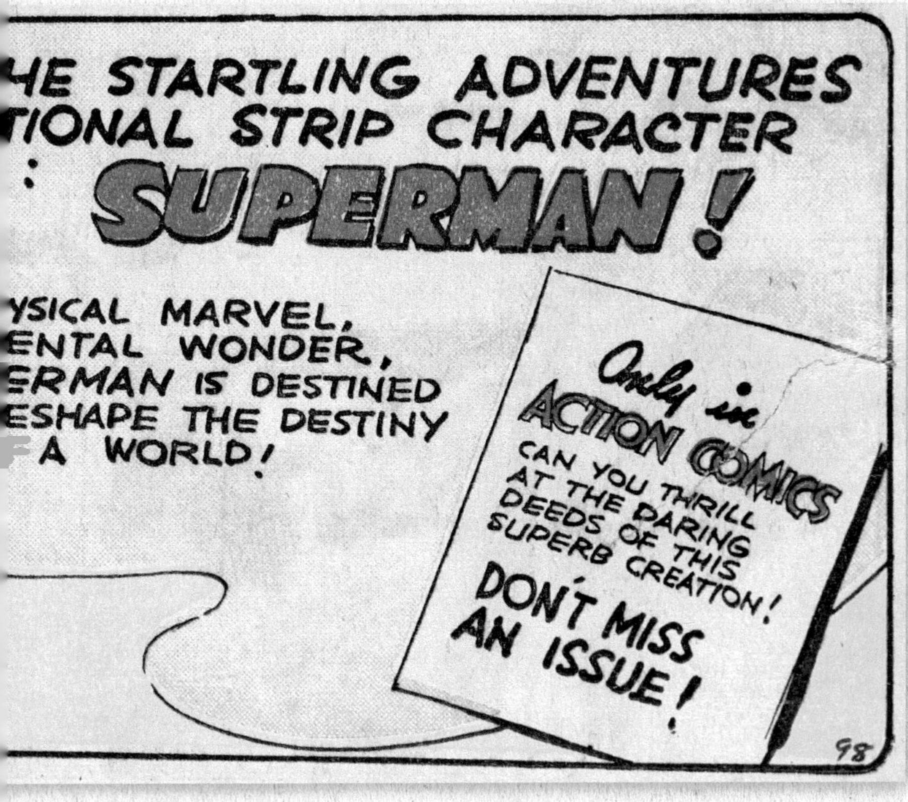
HE STARTLING ADVENTURES
TIONAL STRIP CHARACTER
: SUPERMAN!
YSICAL MARVEL,
ENTAL WONDER,
ERMAN IS DESTINED
ESHAPE THE DESTINY
A WORLD!
Only in
ACTION COMICS
CAN YOU THRILL AT THE DARING DEEDS OF THIS SUPERB CREATION!
DON'T MISS AN ISSUE!
98

the New York fairgrounds at the unprecedented price of 25 cents. And in May, the first four stories from *Action* were collected into *Superman* No. 1, the first solo title for a comic book character. When that comic started running new material with the second quarterly issue, the demand for art was so great that it was clear Shuster would need a substantial Superman art studio team.

A NEW DAY, AND A NEW KNIGHT IN COMICS . . .

Sullivan liked what happened with Superman, so he reached out to Bob Kane, who was contributing a number of short humor features to the National line, and asked him for a new hero. Kane sketched out a scallop-winged character called The Bat-Man, and at Sullivan's suggestion

"AND DAGWOOD BUMSTEAD, SUBSTITUTE"

Political cartoon, New York Journal-American*; art, Burris Jenkins Jr., 1940.* Less than two years after his debut, Superman was famous enough to join this lineup of comic stars — though historians might scratch their heads at the lumping together of heroes and humor figures.

"SUPERMAN" NEWSPAPER STRIP

Script, Jerry Siegel; pencils and inks, Joe Shuster and assistants. June 21, 1941. Possibly because it was his creators' preferred medium, Superman's newspaper strip was often the "leading edge" of his development in the '40s. The mature "Shuster style," mainly the creation of the many employees in the artist's studio, was in evidence here earlier than in the comics.

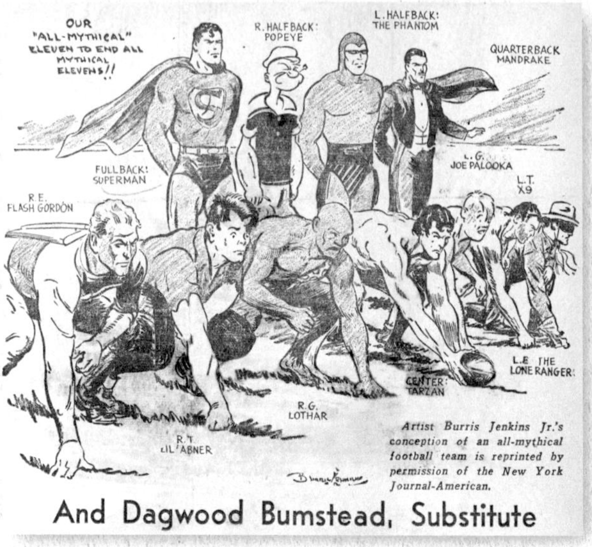
OUR "ALL-MYTHICAL" ELEVEN TO END ALL MYTHICAL ELEVENS!!
R. HALFBACK: POPEYE
L. HALFBACK: THE PHANTOM
QUARTERBACK MANDRAKE
FULLBACK: SUPERMAN
L.G. JOE PALOOKA
L.T. X9
R.E. FLASH GORDON
L.E THE LONE RANGER:
CENTER: TARZAN
R.G. LOTHAR
R.T LIL'ABNER
Artist Burris Jenkins Jr.'s conception of an all-mythical football team is reprinted by permission of the New York Journal-American.
And Dagwood Bumstead, Substitute

brought in writer Bill Finger to assist as his ghostwriter. They refined the character, which would forever be the dark icon of the DC Universe to Superman's bright image, and launched him in *Detective Comics* No. 27. Drawing inspiration from *The Shadow* and other pulps, and from films of the day, Batman would grow in distinctiveness from month to month, acquiring his tragic origin and becoming an enduring star. He was a more aspirational character than Superman — a hero you could theoretically choose to become if tragedy struck your family. Every reader could instantly pick whether Superman or Batman was his favorite character, so different were these two primal super heroes.

Kane and Finger were alumni of DeWitt Clinton High School in the Bronx, New York, a fertile breeding ground for early comics talent that also sent forth Will Eisner (already at work on a project that would earn National's ire, and later, so viewed as the ideal creator of comics that the industry's version of the Oscars would be named after him) and was about to graduate Stan Lee (who would co-create most of the Marvel Comics cast).

Comics were beginning to look like a winner to Harry Donenfeld. But rather than increase his risks with

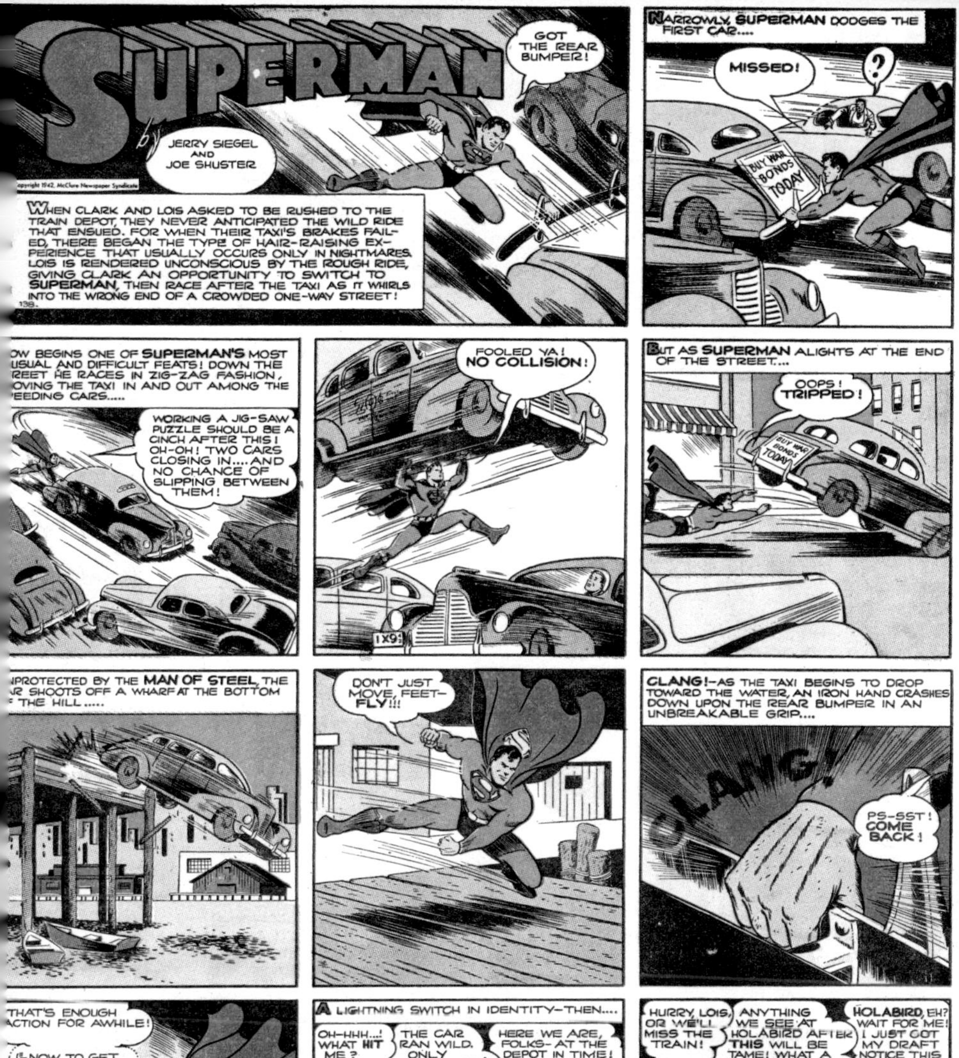
SUPERMAN
by JERRY SIEGEL AND JOE SHUSTER
opyright 1942, McClure Newspaper Syndicate
GOT THE REAR BUMPER!
WHEN CLARK AND LOIS ASKED TO BE RUSHED TO THE TRAIN DEPOT, THEY NEVER ANTICIPATED THE WILD RIDE THAT ENSUED. FOR WHEN THEIR TAXI'S BRAKES FAILED, THERE BEGAN THE TYPE OF HAIR-RAISING EXPERIENCE THAT USUALLY OCCURS ONLY IN NIGHTMARES. LOIS IS RENDERED UNCONSCIOUS BY THE ROUGH RIDE, GIVING CLARK AN OPPORTUNITY TO SWITCH TO SUPERMAN, THEN RACE AFTER THE TAXI AS IT WHIRLS INTO THE WRONG END OF A CROWDED ONE-WAY STREET!
138.
NARROWLY, SUPERMAN DODGES THE FIRST CAR....
MISSED!
?
BUY WAR BONDS TODAY
OW BEGINS ONE OF SUPERMAN'S MOST USUAL AND DIFFICULT FEATS! DOWN THE REET HE RACES IN ZIG-ZAG FASHION, OVING THE TAXI IN AND OUT AMONG THE PEEDING CARS.....
WORKING A JIG-SAW PUZZLE SHOULD BE A CINCH AFTER THIS! OH-OH! TWO CARS CLOSING IN....AND NO CHANCE OF SLIPPING BETWEEN THEM!
FOOLED YA! NO COLLISION!
1X9
BUT AS SUPERMAN ALIGHTS AT THE END OF THE STREET....
OOPS! TRIPPED!
BUY WAR BONDS TODAY
NPROTECTED BY THE MAN OF STEEL, THE AR SHOOTS OFF A WHARF AT THE BOTTOM F THE HILL.....
DON'T JUST MOVE, FEET- FLY!!!
CLANG!-AS THE TAXI BEGINS TO DROP TOWARD THE WATER, AN IRON HAND CRASHES DOWN UPON THE REAR BUMPER IN AN UNBREAKABLE GRIP....
CLANG!
PS-SST! COME BACK!
THAT'S ENOUGH ACTION FOR AWHILE!
(-NOW TO GET BACK INTO THE TAXI AS CLARK KENT BEFORE ANYONE NOTICES!-)
BONDS TODAY!
1X9
A LIGHTNING SWITCH IN IDENTITY—THEN....
OH-HHH...! WHAT HIT ME?
THE CAR RAN WILD. ONLY SUPERMAN'S INTERFERENCE SAVED US!
HERE WE ARE, FOLKS- AT THE DEPOT IN TIME! HOW ABOUT THAT FIVE SPOT YOU PROMISED ME?
HURRY, LOIS, OR WE'LL MISS THE TRAIN!
ANYTHING WE SEE AT HOLABIRD AFTER THIS WILL BE TAME! WHAT A PLEASURE TO THINK WE'VE SEEN THE LAST OF THAT INSANE TAXI DRIVER!
HOLABIRD, EH? WAIT FOR ME! I JUST GOT MY DRAFT NOTICE THIS MORNING, ASSIGNING ME THERE!

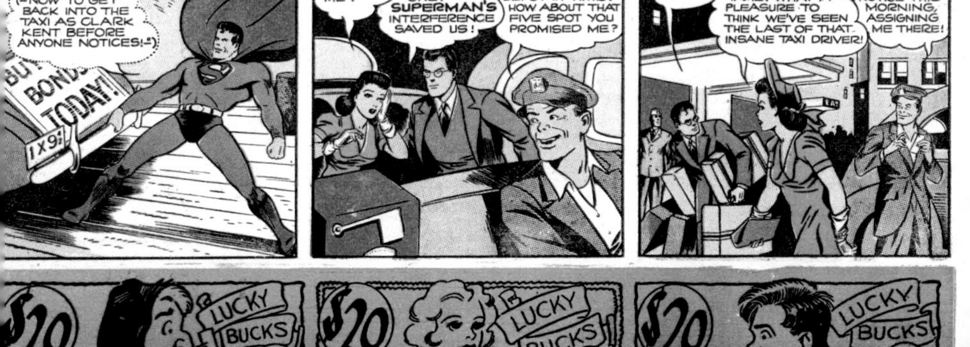
$20
LUCKY BUCKS
20
PLAY MONEY
$20
LUCKY BUCKS
20
PLAY MONEY
$20
LUCKY BUCKS
20
PLAY MONEY

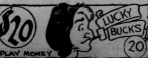

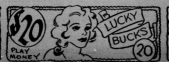

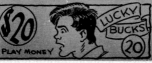

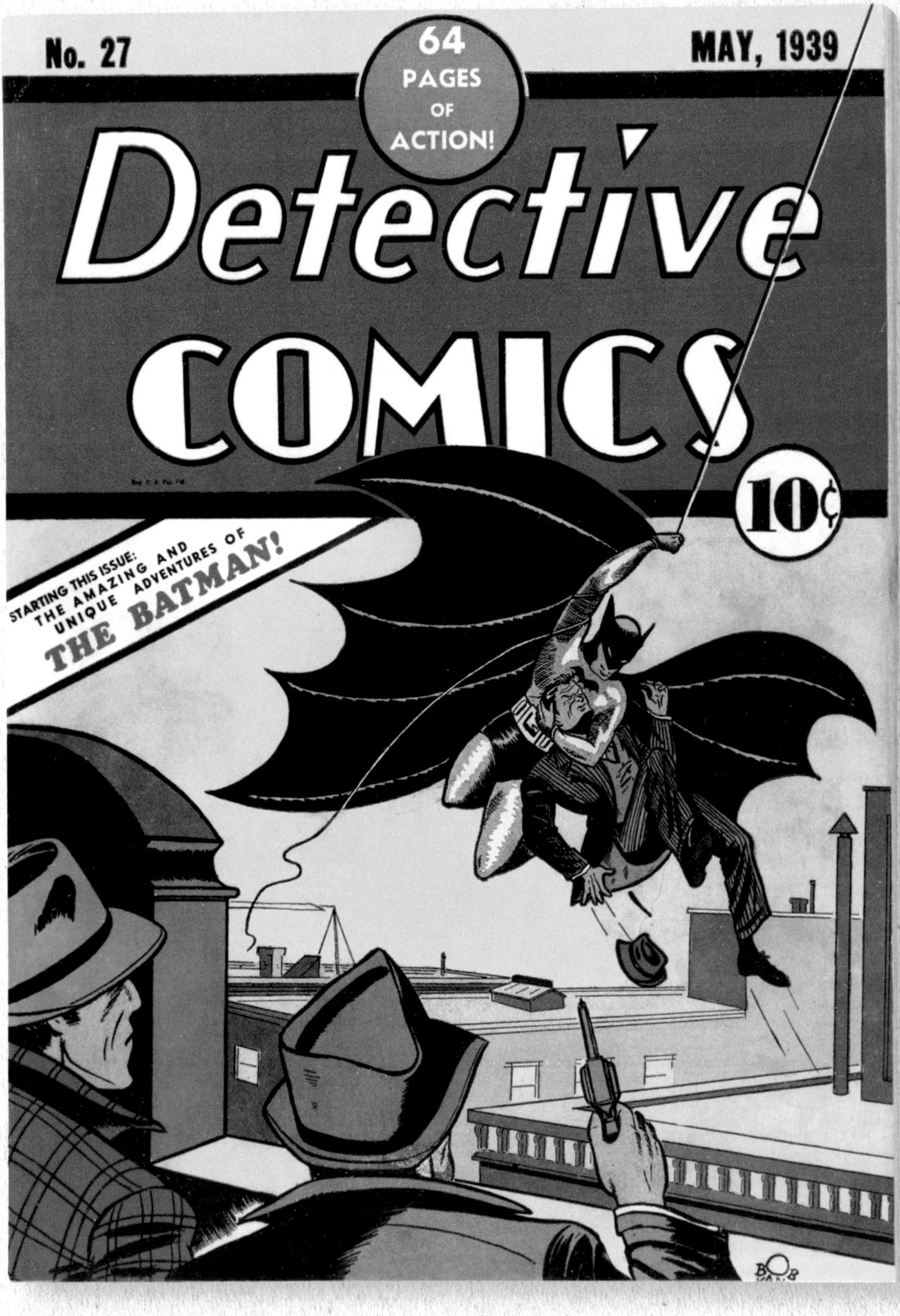
No. 27
64 PAGES OF ACTION!
MAY, 1939
Detective COMICS
10¢
STARTING THIS ISSUE: THE AMAZING AND UNIQUE ADVENTURES OF THE BATMAN!
BOB

unproven titles, he made a deal just to distribute a new line that Gaines and Mayer were launching from downtown offices at 225 Lafayette Street. He would market these with his titles, help with contracts and printing, and in return he convinced Gaines to take in Liebowitz as a partner. Liebowitz's eye for business detail would balance Gaines's entrepreneurial energy, and the still very young Mayer was there to provide a singular editorial viewpoint.

Gaines and Mayer started with two titles in March 1939: *All-American Comics* (also the name of the new company), whose stars included Hop Harrigan, a daring aerialist, and the ill-fated *Movie Comics*, originally intended to be published by Emil Strauss's Photochrome, the engraver who had been producing color separations for early comics. Rather than being written and drawn by cartoonists, the main features in *Movie Comics* were assembled out of colorized publicity stills for minor films (though *Gunga Din* surprised even its producers) by Photochrome staffers (and early comics' colorists) including Sol Harrison and Jack Adler. The rest of the issues were filled with comics about the movies. *Movie Comics* would disappear after six issues, the first casualty in the as-yet-unnamed comics line, and comics tied to films wouldn't become a major product for decades thereafter. Photochrome went back to engraving, and Gaines's third title repackaged the newspaper strip "Mutt & Jeff," like the reprints he had handled as a printing salesman, and this title became an enduring success that would last almost 20 years.

All-American's fourth title really added to the future DC Universe: *Flash Comics* No. 1 introduced the eponymous Fastest Man Alive, as Jay Garrick became a modern Mercury after a lab accident, and also Hawkman, in an origin in which his link to the ancient Egyptians was revealed. Gardner Fox was already a busy writer for National (and destined to become DC's second most prolific writer overall, with more than 1,500 stories) for whom he had developed the first Sandman (in *Adventure Comics* No. 40). Fox practiced law only briefly before shifting to writing, and would lock himself away to pound the keyboard all day long, writing for the pulps as well

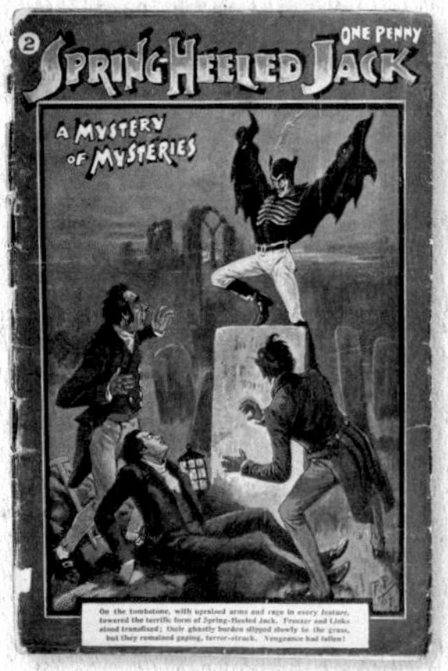
2
ONE PENNY
SPRING-HEELED JACK
A MYSTERY OF MYSTERIES

SPRING-HEELED JACK No. 2

Penny dreadful, ca. 1904. Bat imagery inspiring fear is an old idea, shown in this pulp precursor's recasting of Jack the Ripper as the nemesis of grave robbers.

DETECTIVE COMICS No. 27

Cover art, Bob Kane, May 1939. After seeing what Superman did for *Action*, editor Vin Sullivan invited many of his contributors to submit concepts for a super heroic investigator to boost *Detective*'s sales likewise. The "Crimson Avenger" on the cover of No. 22 hadn't done the trick, but Batman did, and got the regular cover spot from No. 35 (January 1940) onward.

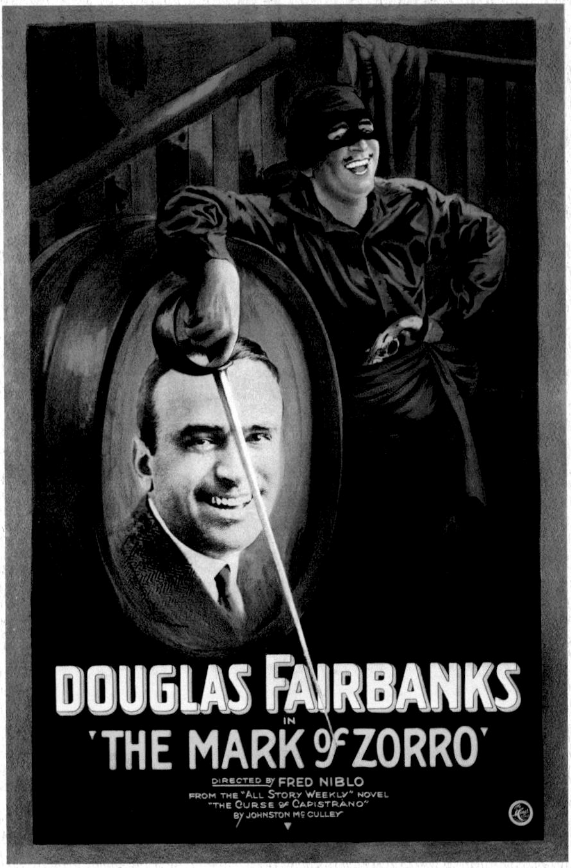
DOUGLAS FAIRBANKS
IN
'THE MARK OF ZORRO'
DIRECTED BY FRED NIBLO
FROM THE "ALL STORY WEEKLY" NOVEL
"THE CURSE OF CAPISTRANO"
BY JOHNSTON McCULLEY

THE MARK OF ZORRO
Movie poster; starring Douglas Fairbanks. 1920. The film starring the swashbuckling masked man had an enormous impact on Batman's Bob Kane, who formed a boyhood club called the Zorros.

THE SHADOW
Cover, George Rozen, December 15, 1937. The pulp and radio hero is believed by many to have had more than a passing influence on Batman's early stories. *Shadow* historians have documented thematic similarities between the first story in *Detective* and a 1936 *Shadow* story entitled "Partners in Peril." There was even a *Shadow* villain in that year called the Joker.

as the comics. Fox collaborated with Harry Lampert on *The Flash*. Lampert had probably met Mayer at the legendary Fleischer animation studio and followed him to All-American; Fox also teamed with Dennis Neville, who made his DC debut on *Hawkman*.

The trend toward costumed heroes continued, with the established writers adding series to their assignments: Fox did Doctor Fate with Howard Sherman for *More Fun* and Starman with Jack Burnley for *Adventure*, Siegel added the Spectre to *More Fun* with the ubiquitous Baily, Finger continued his collaborative pattern by signing on to script Martin Nodell's Green

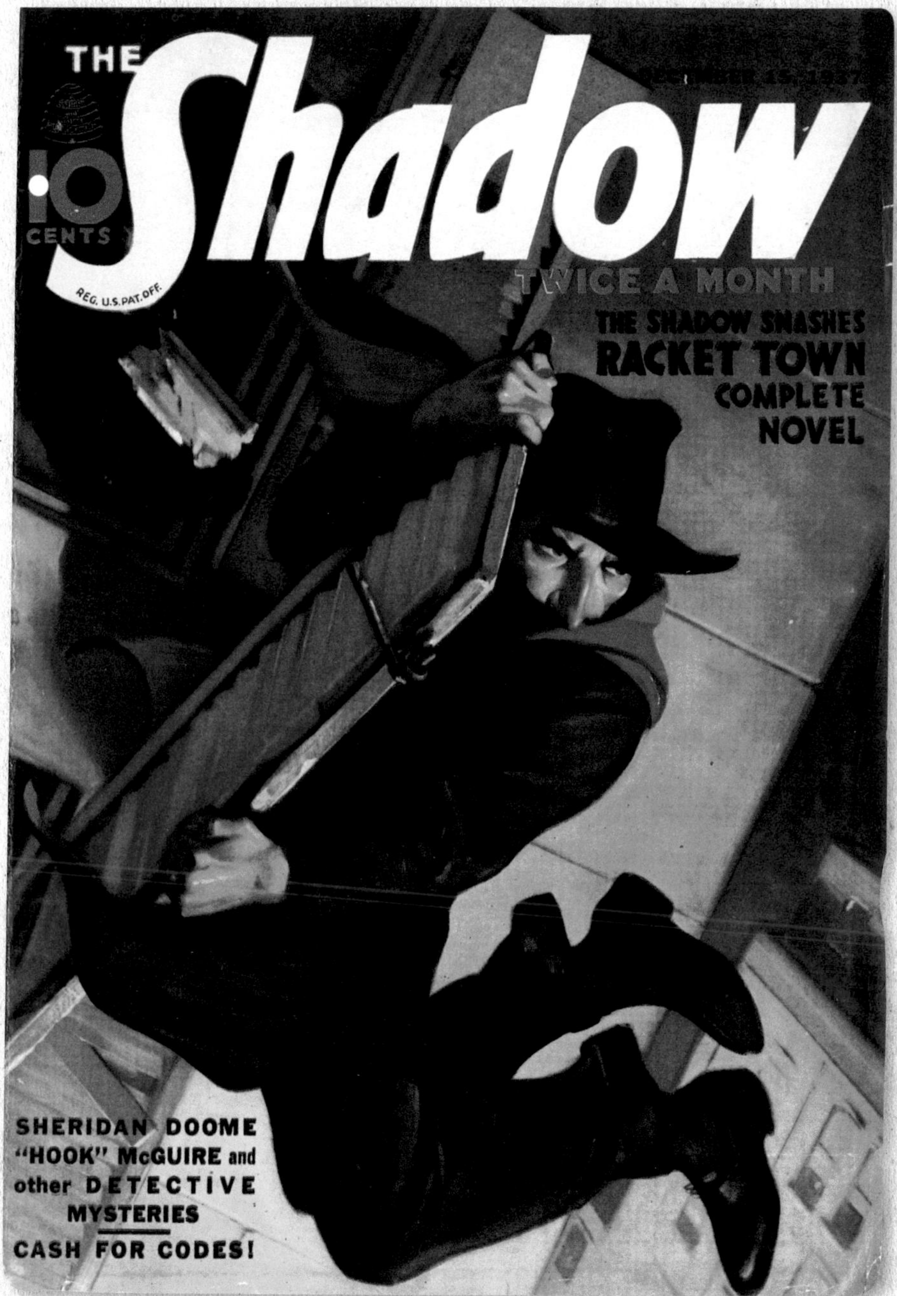
THE Shadow
10 CENTS
REG. U.S. PAT. OFF.
TWICE A MONTH
THE SHADOW SNASHES
RACKET TOWN
COMPLETE
NOVEL
SHERIDAN DOOME
"HOOK" McGUIRE and
other DETECTIVE
MYSTERIES
CASH FOR CODES!

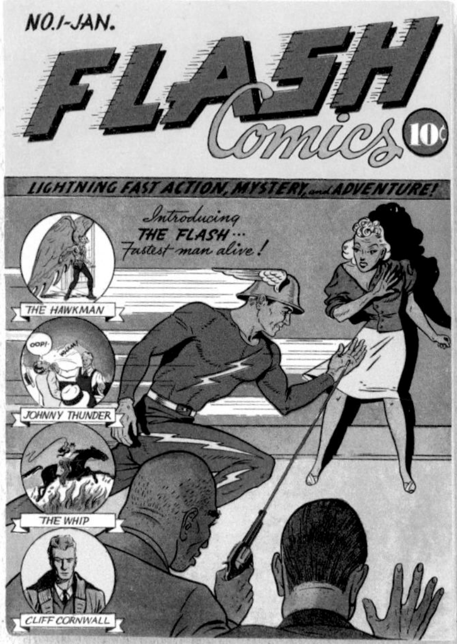

NO.1-JAN.
FLASH
Comics
10¢
LIGHTNING FAST ACTION, MYSTERY, and ADVENTURE!
Introducing
THE FLASH...
Fastest man alive!
THE HAWKMAN
OOP!
JOHNNY THUNDER
THE WHIP
CLIFF CORNWALL

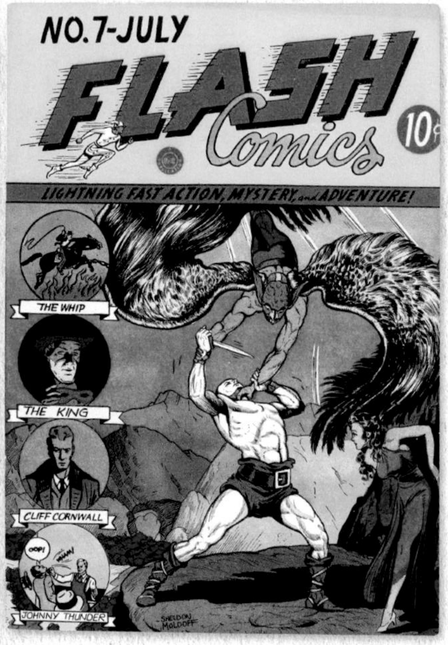

NO.7-JULY
FLASH
Comics
10¢
LIGHTNING FAST ACTION, MYSTERY, and ADVENTURE!
THE WHIP
THE KING
CLIFF CORNWALL
OOP!
JOHNNY THUNDER
SHELDON MOLDOFF

FLASH COMICS No. 1
Cover art, Sheldon Moldoff, January 1940.

FLASH COMICS No. 7
Cover art, Sheldon Moldoff, July 1940.

Lantern for *All-American Comics*, and Ken Fitch, whose contributions to DC dated from *New Fun* No. 1, worked on Hourman with Baily for *Adventure*. There was even a new anthology, *All-Star Comics*; probably put together by pulling extra stories from the flat files for the first time drawing on both the National and All-American characters, despite their slightly different ownership and the three miles between them.

AN EXPLOSION OF HEROES

What these new super heroes shared was clarity of concept and freshness, for the idea of heroism matched with this level of extraordinary ability hadn't been explored before. The pulp heroes, or their predecessors in the dime novels, were fundamentally human, perhaps "trained to near-super-human abilities" as was Doc Savage. The comic writers took this a step beyond, and gave their stars abilities unattainable in the real world. Because the creative territory was new, they had primal names: Starman possessed the power of the stars (harnessed

ADVENTURE COMICS No. 40
Cover art, Creig Flessel, July 1939.
In this issue *Adventure* got its first recurring — but not regular — cover star. But many would argue that the Sandman was not a super hero per se: He wore a suit and had no super powers.

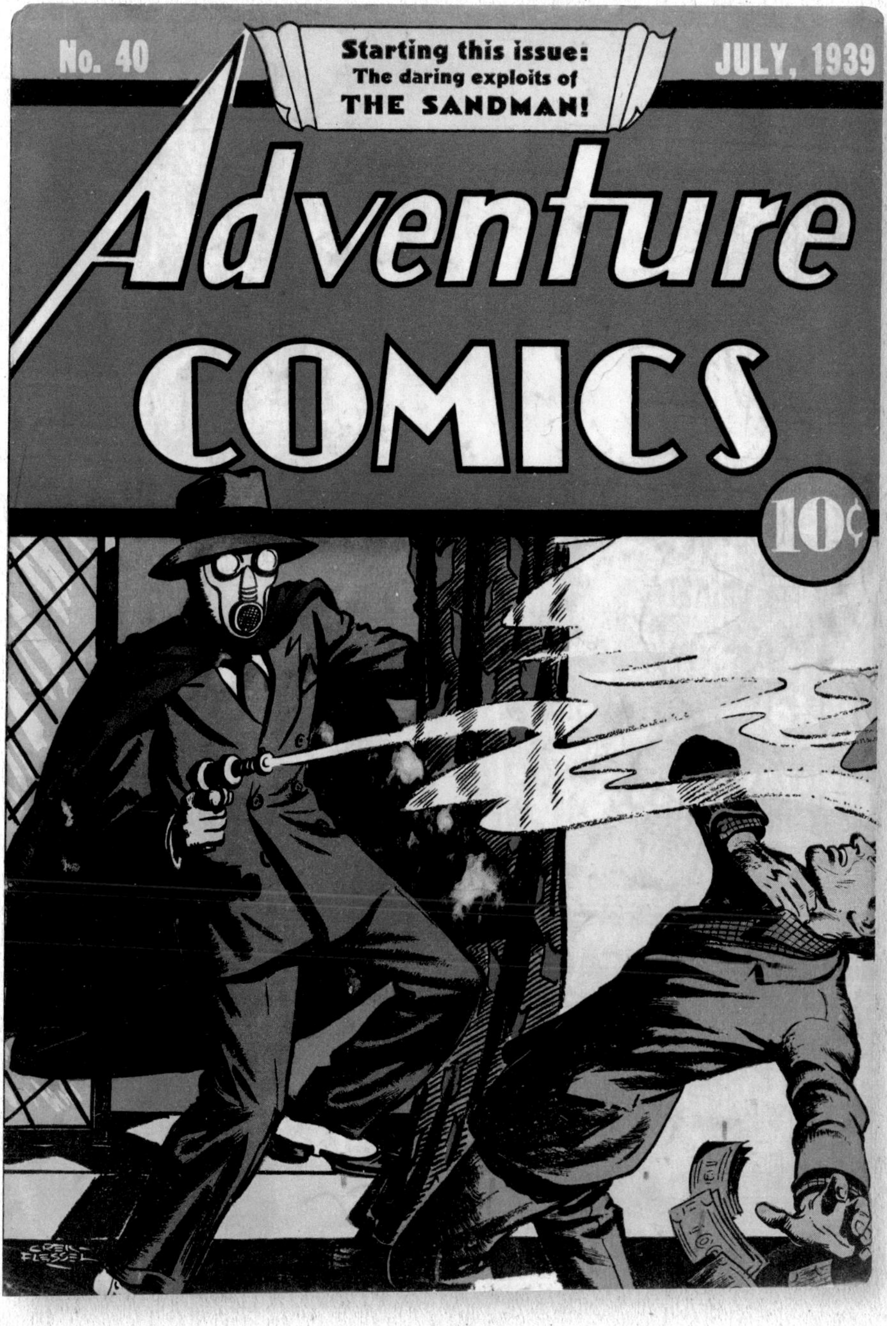
No. 40
Starting this issue:
The daring exploits of
THE SANDMAN!
JULY, 1939
Adventure
COMICS
10¢
CREIG-
FLESSEL

MUTT & JEFF No. 1
Cover art, Harry Lampert, Summer 1939.
Comic art critics might argue that Lampert was a better stylistic mimic in cartooning than a naturalistic illustrator as *The Flash*'s artist. Here he "specs" the style of "Mutt & Jeff" creator Harry Conway "Bud" Fisher perfectly. He and others did so for 103 covers.

MUTT & JEFF
10c
BY
BUD FISHER
ISN'T IT REMARKABLE HOW THOSE BACK WHEELS ARE HOLDING OUT? I THOUGHT THEY LOOKED KINDA WOBBLY THIS MORNING!!
HEY! HEY!
?
ENTIRE CONTENTS COPYRIGHTED - PUBLISHED BY ALL-AMERICAN COMICS INC....

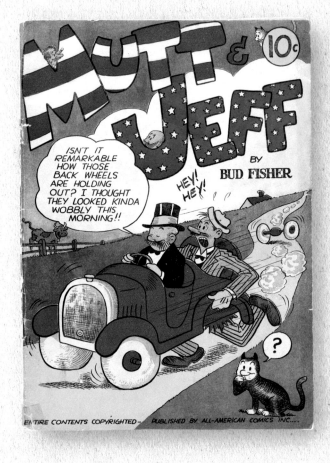

through his gravity rod), Hourman had his super powers for an hour (after taking a Miraclo pill), and so on. If nothing else, DC would have the heritage of the best names in the business and some of the best "high concepts."

What they lacked was distinctive ethnicity, cultural identity, or internal conflict. The immigrant publishers and talent wanted to pass as part of the American majority and to have their characters pass, too. Many of the creators changed their names (Bob Kahn to Bob Kane, Jacob Kurtzburg to Jack Kirby, and on and on), and all chose to label their heroes innocuously. The heroes took their powers for granted, their missions as the natural outcome of their gifts, and the idea that anything from injuries

MORE FUN COMICS No. 52
Cover art, Bernard Baily, February 1940.

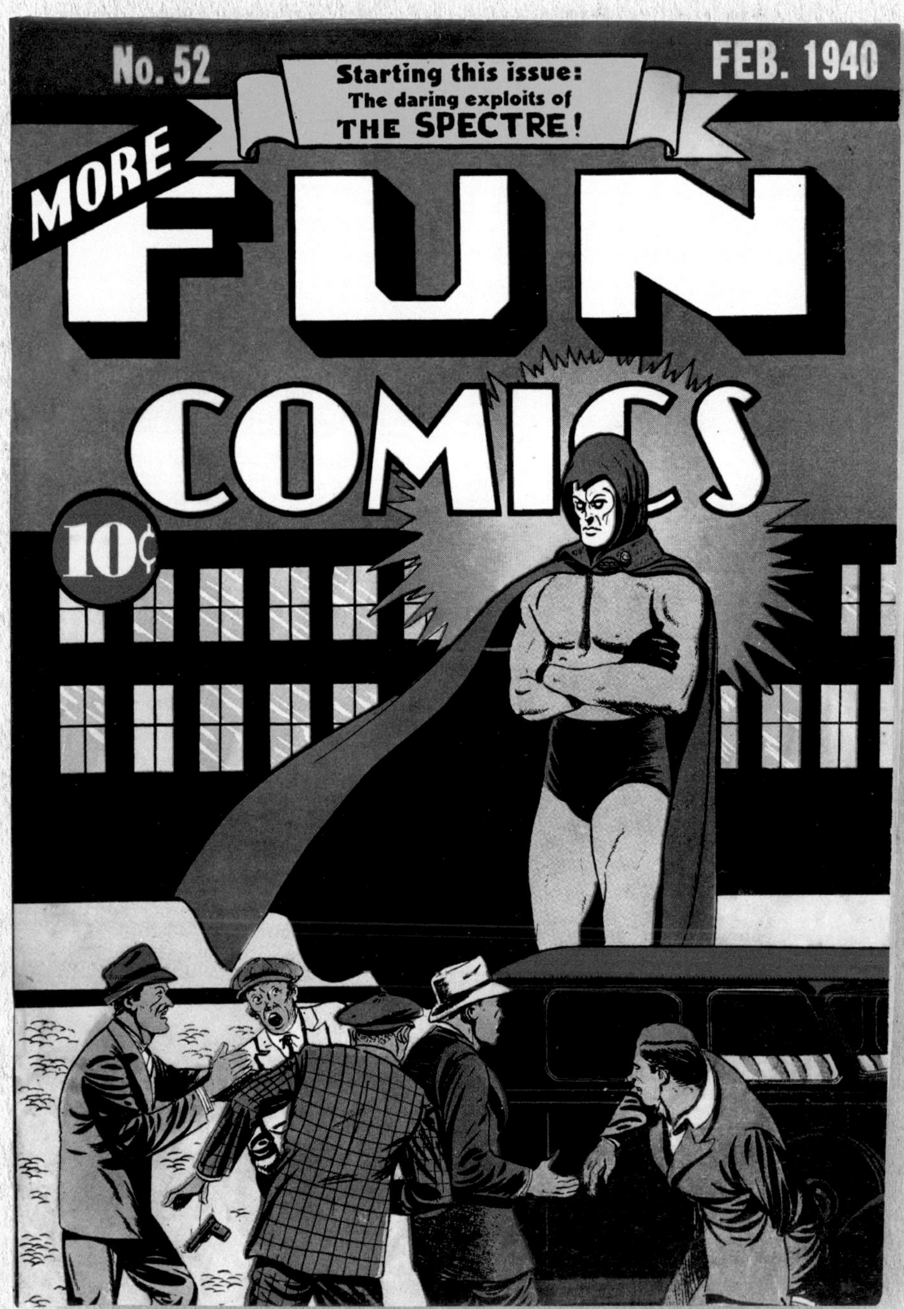
No. 52
Starting this issue:
The daring exploits of
THE SPECTRE!
FEB. 1940
MORE
FUN
COMICS
10¢

ADVENTURE COMICS
No. 81

Interior, "Starman": script, Gardner Fox; pencils, Mort Meskin (as Mort Morton Jr.); inks, George Roussos (as Inky Roussos). December 1942. Upon his debut in *Adventure* No. 61 (April 1941), no one could predict Starman would become a long-running—if oft-reconceived—character. As of 2010, there have been at least nine different heroes who have used the name, one them being a Star*girl.* Over the years, writers have delighted in finding ways to make the disparate versions fit into a unified mythology.

to post-traumatic stress would enter their lives was the furthest thing from their minds.

Other publishers were noticing the trend, too. Former Donenfeld accountant Victor Fox had bought his old boss's interest in a small publisher named Burns, and launched its comic line with a Superman knockoff named Wonder Man by Eisner, which debuted to instant (and successful) litigation from his old employers. The more solidly established Fawcett Publications asked for its own Superman, and staffers Bill Parker and C.C. Beck drew on the gods of classical mythology to create Captain Marvel for *Whiz Comics.* Parker and Beck gave birth to the one hero who would outsell Superman in the Golden Age (and lead to a long and complex litigation, which would end only when Fawcett was ready to exit the comics business).

As 1940 began the combined line was large enough to need an identity, and the first DC symbol showed up on the cover of *Action* No. 23 (with Lex Luthor making his first appearance inside). The official story was always that it meant Detective Comics, after the company's first themed title (and one of the uptown shop's official names, Detective Comics Inc.), but a quiet alternative was that it meant Donenfeld's Comics, at least to the principal owner (who had once operated DM Publishing for Donenfeld's magazines, and Donny Press). People in the industry continued to call the company National, but to readers, it was DC forever after…even though it took 36 more years to become the company's name. The simple symbol created as a trademark would change over the decades, but remained an identifiable anchor that settled permanently in the upper-left-hand corner of the covers.

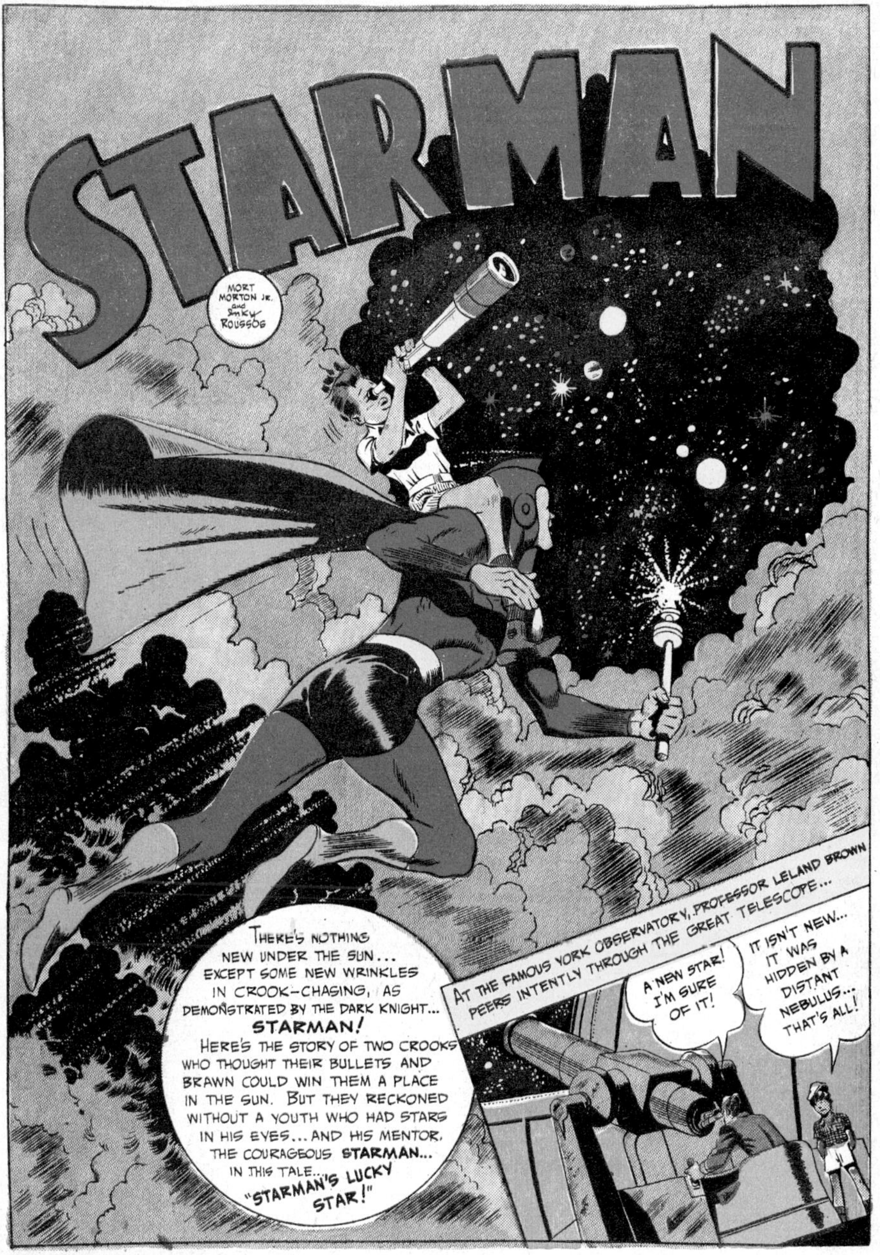
STARMAN
MORT MORTON JR. and INKY ROUSSOS
THERE'S NOTHING NEW UNDER THE SUN... EXCEPT SOME NEW WRINKLES IN CROOK-CHASING, AS DEMONSTRATED BY THE DARK KNIGHT... STARMAN! HERE'S THE STORY OF TWO CROOKS WHO THOUGHT THEIR BULLETS AND BRAWN COULD WIN THEM A PLACE IN THE SUN. BUT THEY RECKONED WITHOUT A YOUTH WHO HAD STARS IN HIS EYES... AND HIS MENTOR, THE COURAGEOUS STARMAN... IN THIS TALE... "STARMAN'S LUCKY STAR!"
AT THE FAMOUS YORK OBSERVATORY, PROFESSOR LELAND BROWN PEERS INTENTLY THROUGH THE GREAT TELESCOPE...
A NEW STAR! I'M SURE OF IT!
IT ISN'T NEW... IT WAS HIDDEN BY A DISTANT NEBULUS... THAT'S ALL!

WONDER COMICS No. 1
Cover art, Will Eisner, May 1939.

OFF THE PAGE AND INTO THE WIDER WORLD . . .

By whatever name, the DC office uptown was growing faster, even if All-American was adding more titles. Besides the comics themselves, publicist Allen Ducovny and pulp writer Bob Maxwell teamed up to produce *The Adventures of Superman*, a syndicated radio series starting in 1940, featuring Bud Collyer as the Man of Steel. To celebrate its success, Ducovny arranged for "Superman Day" to be declared at the New York World's Fair, ushering in for the first time a live Man of Tomorrow,

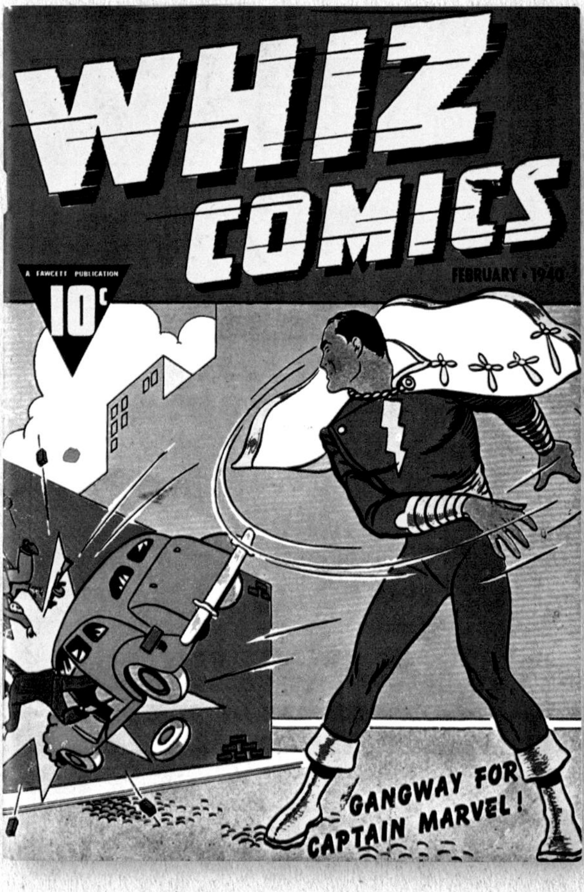
WHIZ COMICS
A FAWCETT PUBLICATION
10¢
FEBRUARY · 1940
GANGWAY FOR CAPTAIN MARVEL!

WHIZ COMICS No. 2
Cover art, C. C. Beck, February 1940. DC pressed its 1941 suit over Captain Marvel more aggressively than those against other Superman imitators, especially when "The Big Red Cheese" began outselling the Man of Steel and became the first to reach the movie screen that same year. The action wended its way through the courts for a full decade, with Fawcett winning the first judgment. But DC prevailed on appeal in 1951 and, by 1953, the Captain, like Fawcett Comics itself, would be gone.

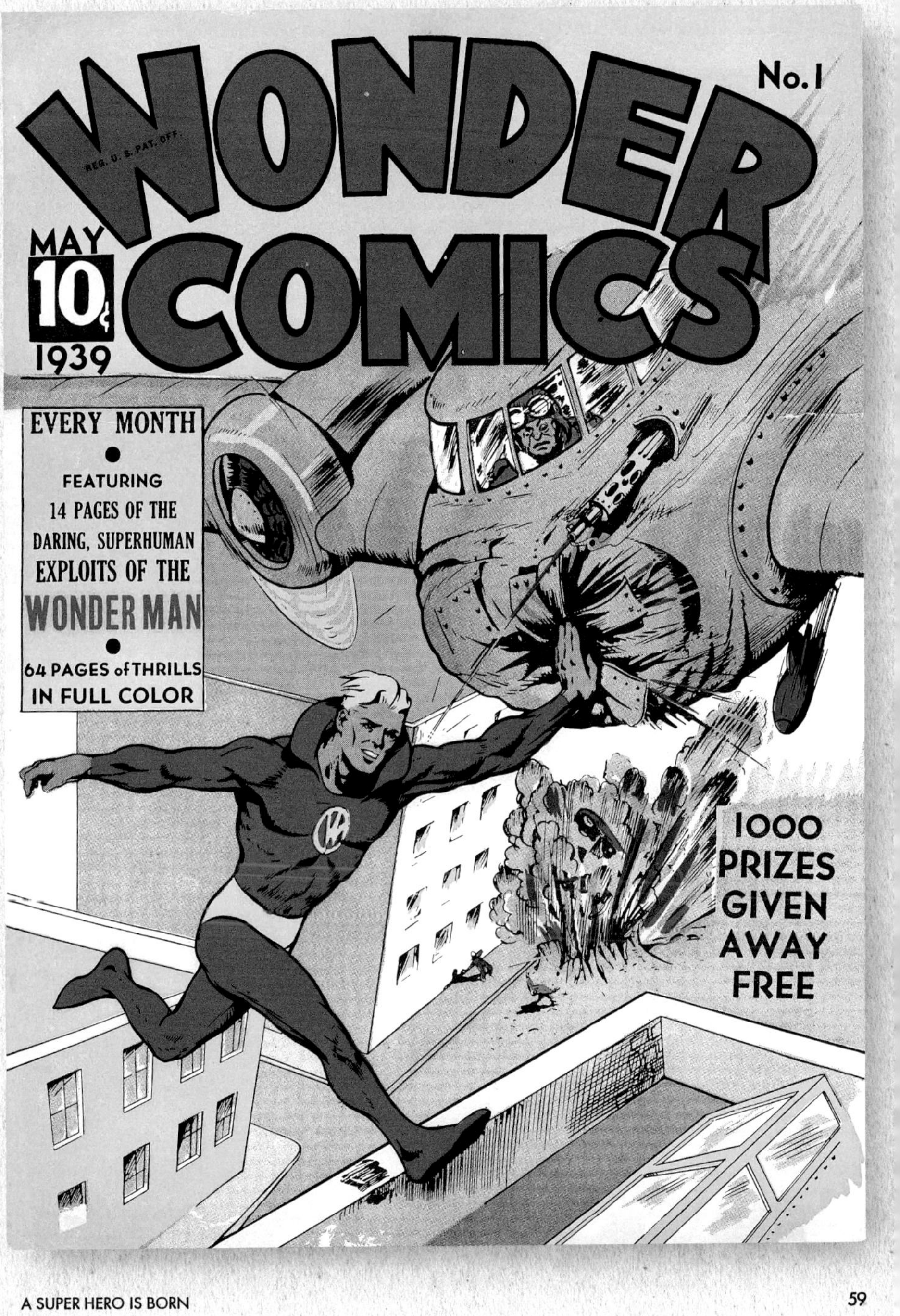
WONDER COMICS
REG. U. S. PAT. OFF.
No. 1
MAY
10¢
1939
EVERY MONTH
FEATURING
14 PAGES OF THE
DARING, SUPERHUMAN
EXPLOITS OF THE
WONDER MAN
64 PAGES of THRILLS
IN FULL COLOR
1000
PRIZES
GIVEN
AWAY
FREE

onto a mobile stage, astounding attendees across the fairgrounds. Siegel and Shuster and DC executives were feted in the shade of the Trylon and Perisphere, as audiences basked in the fair's theme of "For Peace and Freedom" while the early phases of World War II began to storm across Europe.

Many opportunities for Superman were opening up... and a 1940 deal with Fleischer Studios for a series of 17 big-budget *Superman* theatrical cartoon shorts that would be released by Paramount Pictures over the next three years meant that the explosion was just beginning. The animators had long connections to comics (Mayer, Lampert, and Kirby had worked there as kids), and

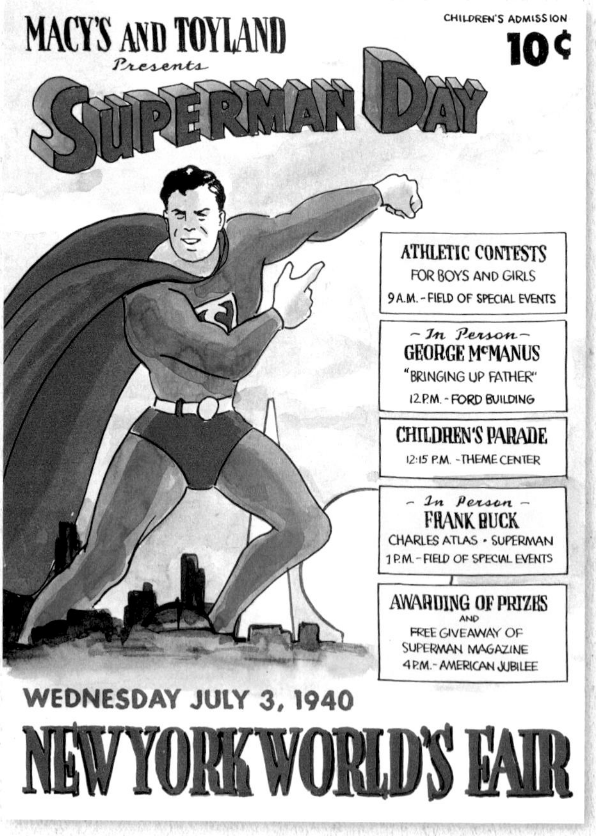

MACY'S AND TOYLAND
Presents
SUPERMAN DAY
CHILDREN'S ADMISSION
10¢
ATHLETIC CONTESTS
FOR BOYS AND GIRLS
9 A.M. - FIELD OF SPECIAL EVENTS
- In Person -
GEORGE McMANUS
"BRINGING UP FATHER"
12 P.M. - FORD BUILDING
CHILDREN'S PARADE
12:15 P.M. - THEME CENTER
- In Person -
FRANK BUCK
CHARLES ATLAS • SUPERMAN
1 P.M. - FIELD OF SPECIAL EVENTS
AWARDING OF PRIZES
AND
FREE GIVEAWAY OF
SUPERMAN MAGAZINE
4 P.M. - AMERICAN JUBILEE
WEDNESDAY JULY 3, 1940
NEW YORK WORLD'S FAIR

SUPERMAN DAY, NEW YORK WORLD'S FAIR
Poster, artist unknown, July 3, 1940.

SUPERMAN RADIO SHOW
Promotional flag, ca. 1940.

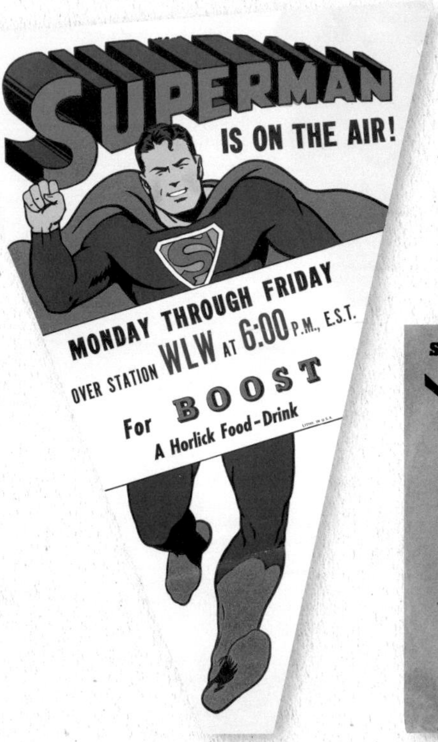
SUPERMAN
IS ON THE AIR!
MONDAY THROUGH FRIDAY
OVER STATION WLW AT 6:00 P.M., E.S.T.
For BOOST
A Horlick Food-Drink

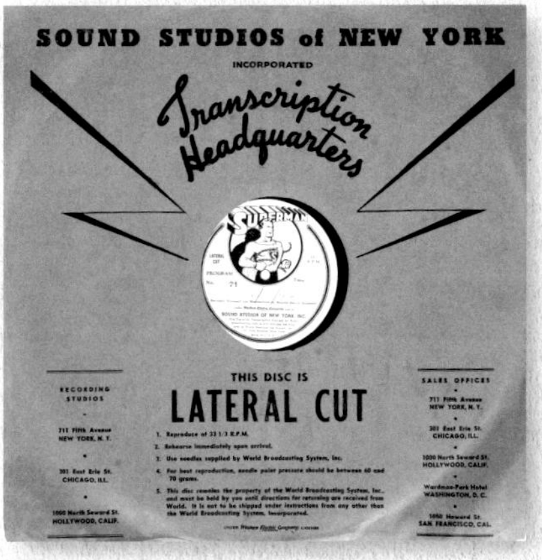
SOUND STUDIOS of NEW YORK
INCORPORATED
Transcription Headquarters
THIS DISC IS
LATERAL CUT

depicted a Superman who truly could fly... and garnered an Academy Award nomination for DC's first big-screen project. With simple, archetypical plots (and in some cases, unfortunately, stereotypically racist portrayals of African tribesmen or Axis opponents), the scripts for the cartoons have receded into history, but the art deco–influenced art style created for them lived on to be reborn in the Warner Bros. Animation cartoons starring DC heroes two generations later.

The Superman art studio near Cleveland's Playhouse Square was pouring out work, and Bob Kane started to emulate them by bringing on a talented young assistant—or perhaps sidekick is a better term? Jerry Robinson joined Kane just in time to contribute to the origin stories of Robin in *Detective* No. 38 and the Joker and Catwoman in *Batman* No. 1, as a second DC star

SUPERMAN RADIO BROADCAST ACETATE
33⅓ rpm record, "Lighthouse Point" (programs 71–72, episodes 2 and 3), broadcast February–March 1944.
A syndicated *Superman* radio show, produced by DC, began in 1940, later moving to the Mutual network and then to ABC for its final season in 1950. The hit series introduced many elements that would appear in the comics only later, such as Perry White, Jimmy Olsen, and kryptonite.

earned his solo quarterly title. Before long, Robinson was working out of a growing bullpen in the DC offices, and, with the unabashed enthusiasm of the young, managed to collect and preserve some of the very few pages of original art to survive from those days.

On the editorial side, Vince Sullivan had left for greener pastures, eventually founding the competing Magazine Enterprises comics company, which had a 15-year run, though never re-creating the success he'd had at DC. Whit Ellsworth, Sullivan's fellow assistant editor and cartoonist in the Wheeler-Nicholson days, returned, and would lead the uptown editorial team through the rest of the Golden Age.

Downtown at All-American, Mayer and Fox cooked up one of the biggest ideas in super hero history: What if the varied stars of *All-Star Comics* actually met and worked together? In popular culture today, the idea of a crossover permeates television, film, and novels, and is

one of the great engines of comics...but in 1941, the idea of
mixing separate properties together was radical...and an
enduring-enough hit that *Justice Society of America* (*JSA*)
ran to the end of the Golden Age (even, by some scholars'
logic, defining the end of the Golden Age when it stopped).
It was radical as well, in that it took advantage of the DC
and All-American talent pools' tendency to do more than
one series, so that writers and artists could relatively easily
work in the different styles of the different features. And
as the *JSA* series evolved, the look of the feature would
become as close as DC got to a "house style" for its super
heroes—a single visual approach that could capture the
charm of the characters, even if it inherently compromised
the more singular approaches of the original cartoonists
or their successors. The heroes' personalities would be
synchronized a bit, too, leaving no room for a vengeful
ghost like the Spectre to be in conflict with Superman's
sworn goal of preserving life.

**FLEISCHER STUDIOS
SUPERMAN STILLS**
*Animation stills, director,
Seymour Kneitel,
September 26, 1941.*
The opening frames of the
1940s Superman theatrical
shorts distilled the essence
of the Man of Steel into
a few lines and images
that included a shot of
the caped hero dissolving
into mild-mannered
reporter Clark Kent.

MARSTON'S LIE DETECTOR

The invention in operation, 1930s. William Moulton Marston was an indefatigable promoter of the lie detector and staged many demonstrations of it in use. In the comics, he had Wonder Woman's magic lasso force anyone bound by it to obey her and tell the truth.

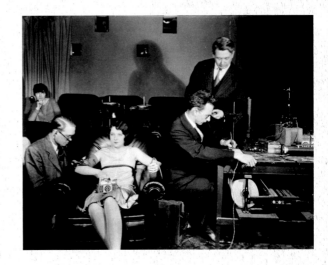

FROM AN EXPERIMENT TO AN INSTITUTION

With the first great growth spurt over, both companies continued to expand to meet the demand for their heroes: More titles like *World's Best Comics* (soon rechristened *World's Finest*) with Superman and Batman headlining a massive 96-page collection (as opposed to the 64-page format of the regular 10-cent titles), *All-Flash* and *Green Lantern* solo quarterlies, and one new anthology, the first from DC since *Action: Star-Spangled Comics*, with Siegel and Hal Sherman collaborating on the Star-Spangled Kid, the first young hero with an adult sidekick, reversing the now year-old stereotype. The second issue of *Star-Spangled* introduced a new DC logo, which would last into the 1960s.

More editors were coming on board, too. Murray Boltinoff, a former screenwriter and journalist, became Ellsworth's assistant, starting a record 45-year career in DC editorial. From the pulp magazines, Jack Schiff, Mort Weisinger, and Bernie Breslauer came to DC. Like the pulps, comics followed the practice of having their editors write stories to supplement their duties (and pay). Weisinger rapidly contributed three new heroes for *More Fun* — Green Arrow, Aquaman, and Johnny Quick — and Vigilante for *Action*, then led a gang of

ALL-STAR COMICS No. 3

Cover art, E. E. Hibbard, winter 1940–1941. Back-issue pricing expert Robert Overstreet called the first super hero team-up "a breakthrough concept, second in importance only to [their] creation [itself]." It endures today, 70 years later, more popular than ever.

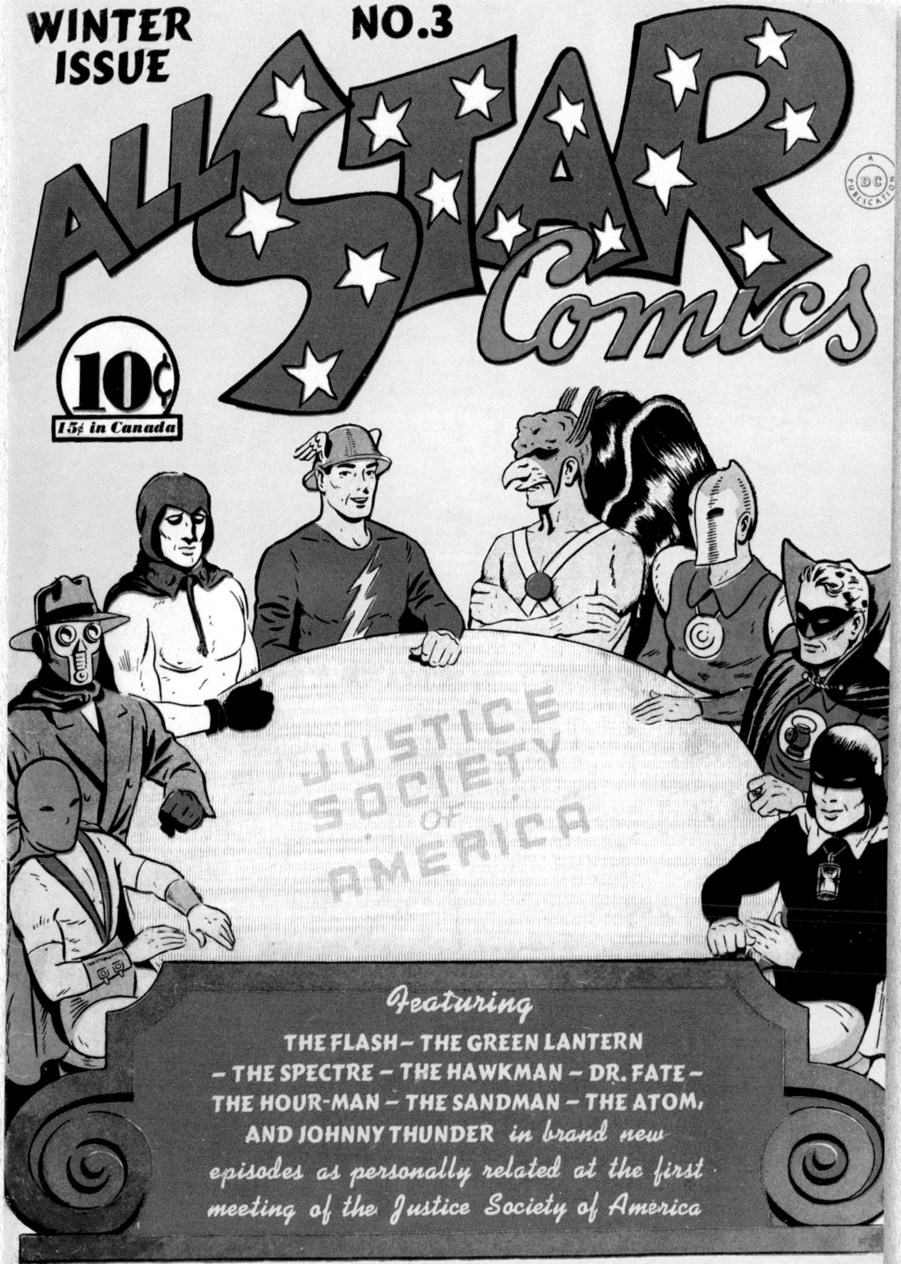
WINTER ISSUE
NO.3
ALL STAR Comics
A DC PUBLICATION
10¢
15¢ in Canada
JUSTICE SOCIETY OF AMERICA
Featuring
THE FLASH – THE GREEN LANTERN – THE SPECTRE – THE HAWKMAN – DR. FATE – THE HOUR-MAN – THE SANDMAN – THE ATOM, AND JOHNNY THUNDER in brand new episodes as personally related at the first meeting of the Justice Society of America

**H. G. PETER
ILLUSTRATION**
*Interior, "Dame Fashion's
Merry-Go-Round,"* Judge
Magazine, *ca. 1908.*

LEADING COMICS No. 1
*Cover art, Mort Meskin,
Winter 1941–1942.*

writers in launching DC's answer to *All-Star, Leading
Comics,* with the Seven Soldiers of Victory as a short-
lived group of heroes who didn't make it into the JSA.
Weisinger's fondness for two characters he helped develop,
Green Arrow and Aquaman, allowed them to be the only
DC heroes to survive continuously in the back features
through the rest of the Golden Age and deep into the
Silver. Weisinger would soon forsake comics writing to
focus on nonfiction, but would guide other writers' tales
for decades. Schiff was courtlier, methodical, and became
the company's grammarian and living stylebook.

While virtually every aspect of the DC Universe was
being constructed by young talent, a very different chain
of circumstances led to Wonder Woman's birth. William
Moulton Marston was a polymath, educated both as
a lawyer and a psychologist, and his journey included
becoming a novelist, self-help author, and magazine

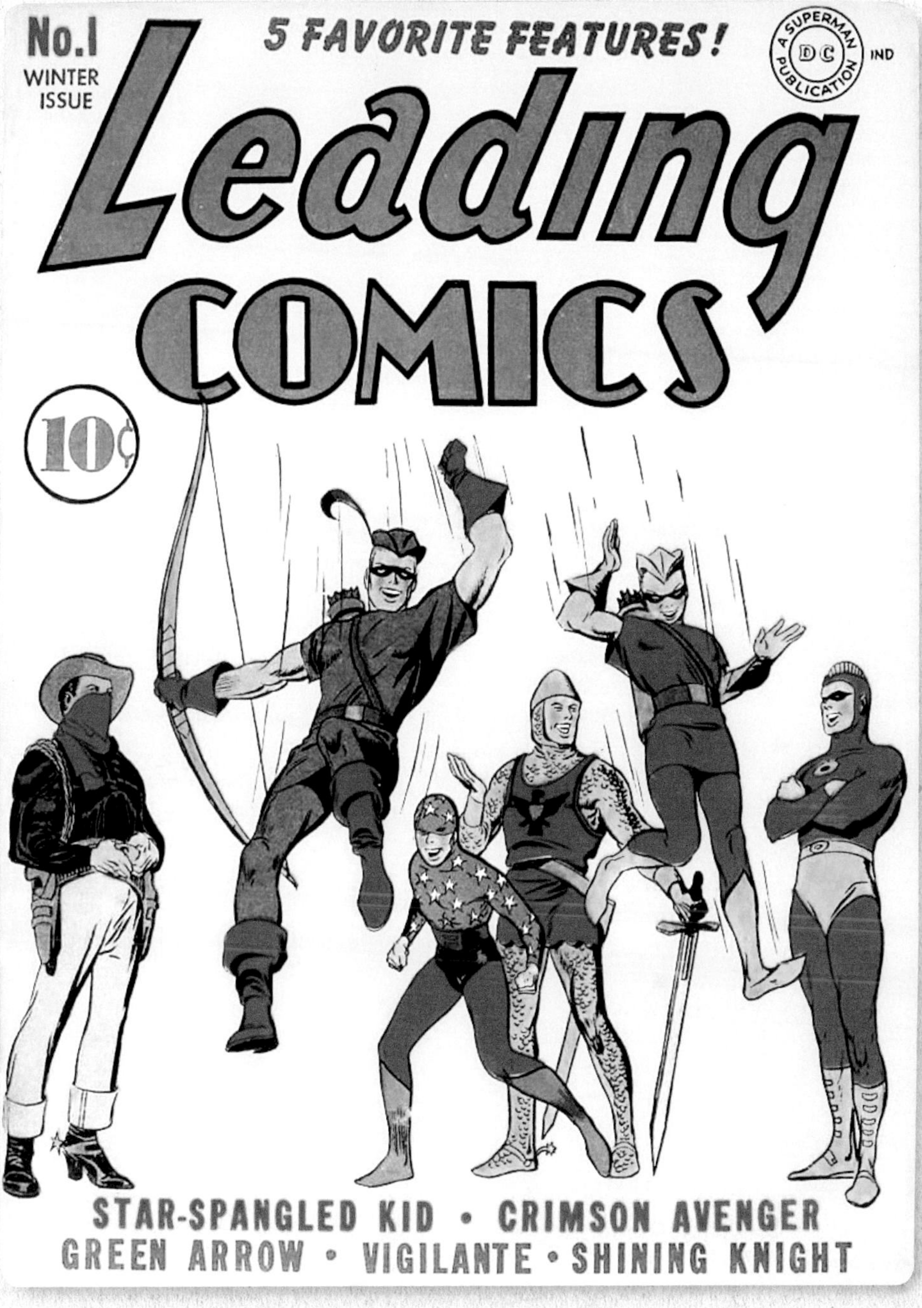
No.1
WINTER ISSUE
5 FAVORITE FEATURES!
A SUPERMAN DC PUBLICATION
IND
Leading COMICS
10¢
STAR-SPANGLED KID • CRIMSON AVENGER
GREEN ARROW • VIGILANTE • SHINING KNIGHT

WESTERN COMICS No. 4
Interior, "The Four Notches of Hate"; script, unknown; pencils, Mort Meskin; inks, George Roussos. July–August 1948. "Just take a moment to think about the Vigilante," *Starman* writer James Robinson once suggested. "How at the time a cowboy mystery man was just not done… no skin-tight mask or costume. Add to that that he rode a motor bike and operated in the city. Meskin was a brave talent to be sure."

writer. Marston's article on the emerging importance of comics caught Gaines's eye, and led to invitations to serve on DC's Advisory Board (a group of luminaries designed to ward off criticism that comics were bad for children) as well as to write for the company. Marston combined his interests in mythology, social behavior, and women and began writing a series of adventures that played off his theories of dominance and submission as social roles. H. G. Peter, a 61-year-old cartoonist with roots going back to *Judge*, a classic late-19th/early-20th-century magazine full of powerful political cartoons, brought a unique sensibility to the artwork as well.

Wonder Woman premiered in *All-Star* No. 8, then immediately went on to star in a new All-American anthology, *Sensation Comics*, and would add her own quarterly shortly thereafter. She was an instantly iconic figure, and equally controversial, with fierce debate among the Advisory Board members, psychologists, Gaines, Mayer, and their new editorial associate, Dorothy Roubicek (the first woman on DC's editorial staff) about Wonder Woman's effect on children… the presumed audience of all comics at the time.

The young women among Wonder Woman's readers were oblivious to the subtexts of Marston's stories, but were captivated by the heroine who had been divinely enlivened from clay, on a Paradise Island inhabited only by women straight out of Greek myth. Her lasso of truth (echoing Marston's scientific interests as an early popularizer of the lie detector), her invisible plane, mental radio, and bracelets flashing bullets away inspired young Gloria Steinem, who would be her most famous fan… and help make her a feminist icon decades later.

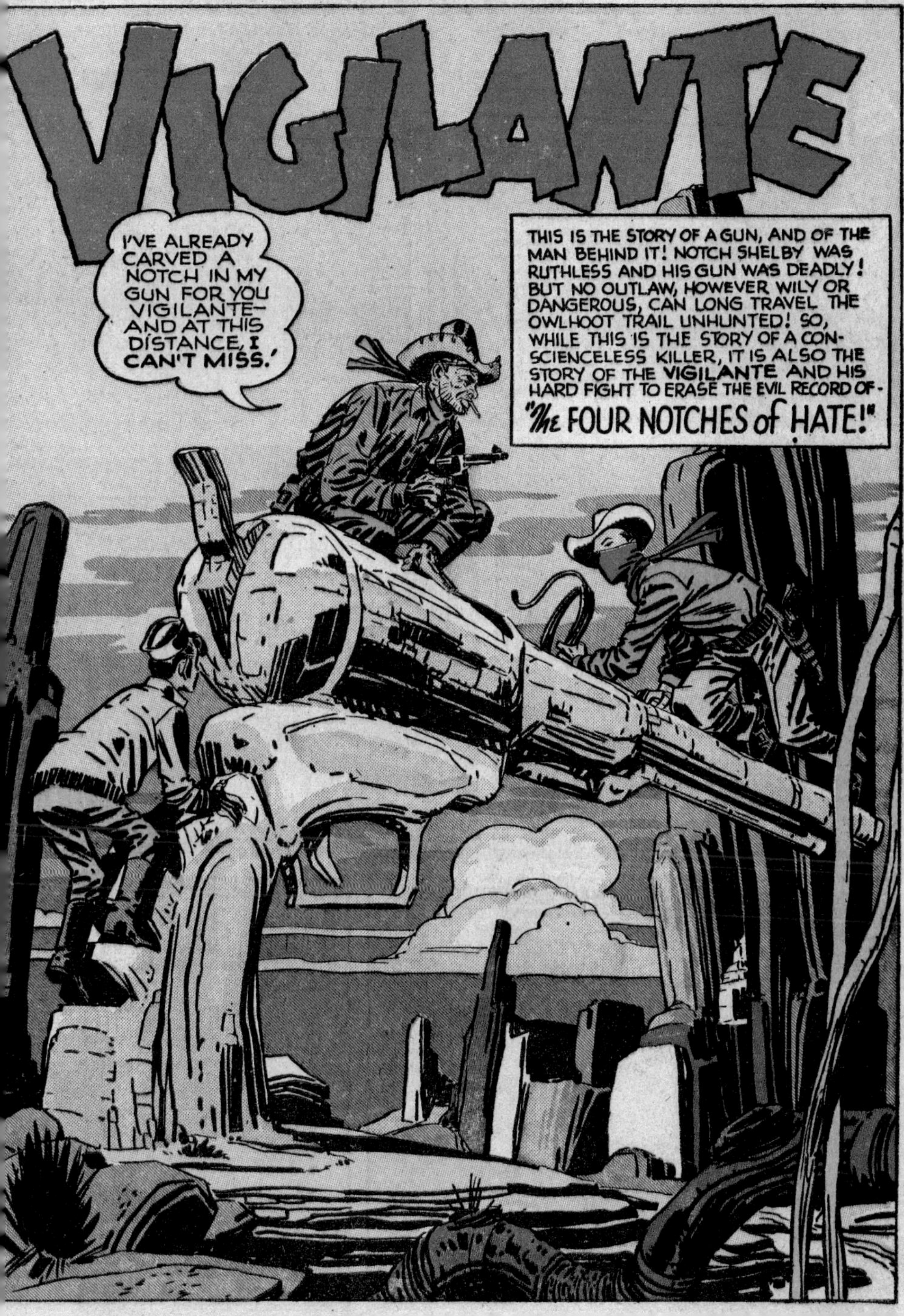
VIGILANTE
I'VE ALREADY CARVED A NOTCH IN MY GUN FOR YOU VIGILANTE— AND AT THIS DISTANCE, I CAN'T MISS.'
THIS IS THE STORY OF A GUN, AND OF THE MAN BEHIND IT! NOTCH SHELBY WAS RUTHLESS AND HIS GUN WAS DEADLY! BUT NO OUTLAW, HOWEVER WILY OR DANGEROUS, CAN LONG TRAVEL THE OWLHOOT TRAIL UNHUNTED! SO, WHILE THIS IS THE STORY OF A CONSCIENCELESS KILLER, IT IS ALSO THE STORY OF THE VIGILANTE AND HIS HARD FIGHT TO ERASE THE EVIL RECORD OF-
"The FOUR NOTCHES of HATE!"

OFF TO WAR

While a small war over Wonder Woman's costume waged at 225 Lafayette, the real war began outside, with ramifications for every aspect of comics. Servicemen became a new audience in growing numbers, as well as evangelists who would carry American comics across the globe, and their number would eventually include many of DC's editors, writers, and artists as the draft began to pull more and more men into the military. War and home-front themes quickly showed up on covers and in the stories themselves, and people needed the escape of imagination more than ever.

Comics pioneers Joe Simon and Jack Kirby had created Captain America for the competing Timely Comics linc

THE NEW SENSATION

A LIVELY, ROMANTIC PAPER FOR THE PERIOD

Vol. I. NEW YORK, JULY 7, 1873. No. 4.

The Intruder, the Fastest Girl, with Flashing Eyes, Stood with two Revolvers Pointing at the two Principals of the Festive Board.

THE FASTEST GIRL IN NEW YORK.

BY COLONEL CABOT.

CHAPTER VI.—Continued.

"Well, Mac," she said, after the passage-at-arms had concluded, and she had thrown herself upon one of the lounges, "every cock, they say, fights best on his native heath, or words to that effect, and I suppose the rule will apply to every hen as well, and every pullet, eh? I don't know as I shall ever wrestle with you on your own vantage ground, but who can tell what time may bring to pass?—time works wonders, it is said."

Stepping to the floor, she said, as Mac picked up his hat from the piano, "Don't be in a hurry, it's only three o'clock now, and there is no hour at which people are locked in here. This is 'Liberty Hall,' you bet—come when you please, stay as long as you please, and—well, go when you get ready, of course, else, I suppose, it wouldn't be 'Liberty Hall.' Don't go, now, though, before we have another bottle. No more? Oh, but you will, though—a parting drink, you know. You can't refuse—and I'll drink Heidsick with you."

Stepping to the buffet, she took a bottle of "Piper Heidsick," passed her by Bacchus, with a knife to cut the strings. The whitest cambric handkerchief could have been rubbed over the bottle without soiling its whiteness in the least, so clean it was.

"Pop goes the weasel!" exclaimed the gay beauty, as the cork flew ceilingward from the bottle. Filling the glasses, she called out to Prince to "come to the front," which he did at once.

Looking archly at him, as she raised her glass, and then at Mac, she said:

"When shall we three meet again?" and then tossed off the amber liquid, sparkling with a thousand gems.

"One more, Mac! What! can't take any more? But you must, my dear fellow—one more!"

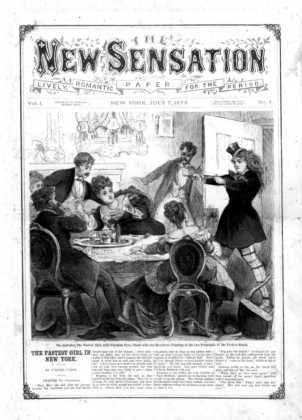

THE NEW SENSATION
Vol. 1 No. 4

Story paper, cover, "The Fastest Girl in New York"; script, Colonel Cabot; art, unknown. 1872.

The role of women in American society was changing rapidly as Wonder Woman was born, but it was a process with roots in previous decades… even back to this earlier "Sensation."

The Newest of the 'DC' magazines
NO.1 JANUARY
SENSATION COMICS
A SUPERMAN DC PUBLICATION
10¢
Featuring
THE SENSATIONAL
NEW ADVENTURE
STRIP CHARACTER-
Wonder Woman!

Fantastic Novels
SEPT.
20¢
PEOPLE OF THE GOLDEN ATOM
By Ray Cummings
A.Merritt
COMPLETE IN THIS ISSUE

SENSATION COMICS No. 1
Cover art, H. G. Peter and Jon L. Blummer, January 1942. Flashing her iconic bullet-deflecting bracelets, Wonder Woman leaped into her own series, headlining All-American's latest monthly.

FANTASTIC NOVELS
Cover art, "People of the Golden Atom," art, F. R. Paul, September 1940.
The argument over whether powerful women should also be illustrated to emphasize their sexuality goes on even today in comics, but had deep roots in pulp fiction.

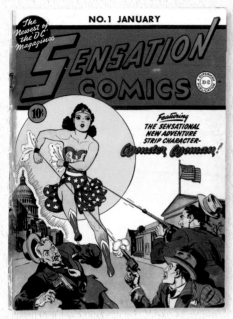

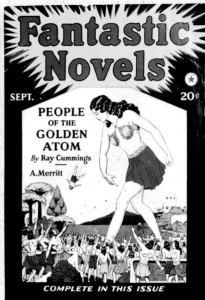

early in 1941, but the tide rushing toward the United States' entry into World War II made their images of Cap punching Hitler a hit. Dissatisfied with their share of the proceeds, Simon and Kirby left Timely and struck a lucrative deal at DC, becoming the first comics talent to secure royalties on sales of their work from DC (Marston had such a deal on Wonder Woman, but his prior success as a writer and public figure clearly put him in a very different class). Simon and Kirby took over existing DC features Manhunter and Sandman in *Adventure*, giving both characters more heroic new looks, and developed two new features, with kid protagonists: the Newsboy Legion for *Star-Spangled* and Boy Commandos for *Detective*. *Boy Commandos* became its own title as well, and the royalty checks from it were instrumental in keeping their studio going through their war service. They became the first star talent in comics, with their names blazoned on the covers to help sell copies.

Another comics star also was rushing to war, as Will Eisner and his studio developed Blackhawk as the lead

ALL-STAR COMICS No. 8
Cover art, E. E. Hibbard, December 1941–January 1942.

feature for *Military Comics* from Everett "Busy" Arnold's Quality Comics. Modeled on the Lafayette Squadron of World War I, the Blackhawk team became a sort of Foreign Legion of pilots facing all variety of dangers, and so would be able to continue beyond the war itself (and even beyond the Golden Age).

While wartime was beginning to make manpower and paper scarce, All-American managed to add a new production manager, taking on early comics colorist and engraver Sol Harrison, and launched *Picture Stories from the Bible* and one more anthology, *Comic Cavalcade*, a

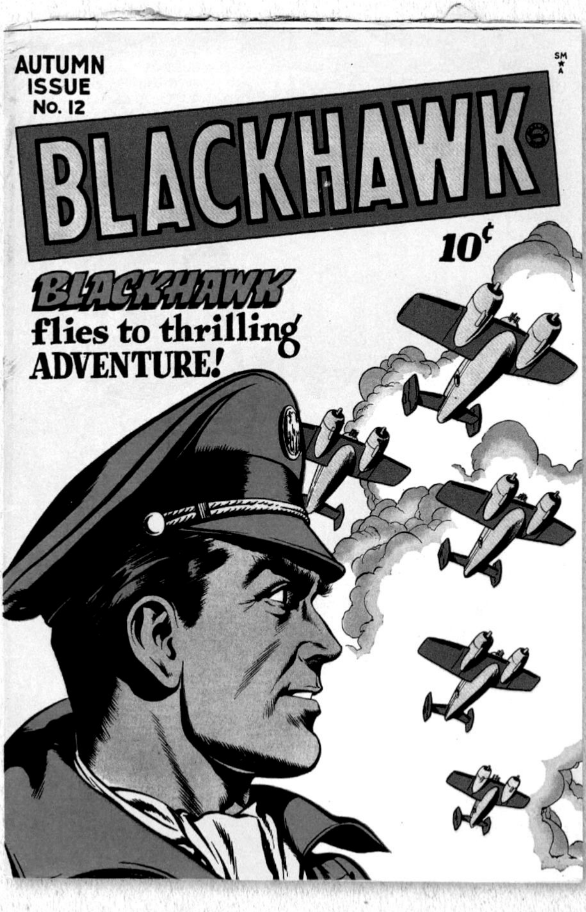
AUTUMN ISSUE No. 12
BLACKHAWK
10¢
BLACKHAWK flies to thrilling ADVENTURE!

BLACKHAWK No. 12
Cover art, Al Bryant, autumn 1946.
A prewar feature about a Polish aviator resisting the Nazis, Blackhawk was acquired by DC in 1957, but it was first published by Quality Comics.

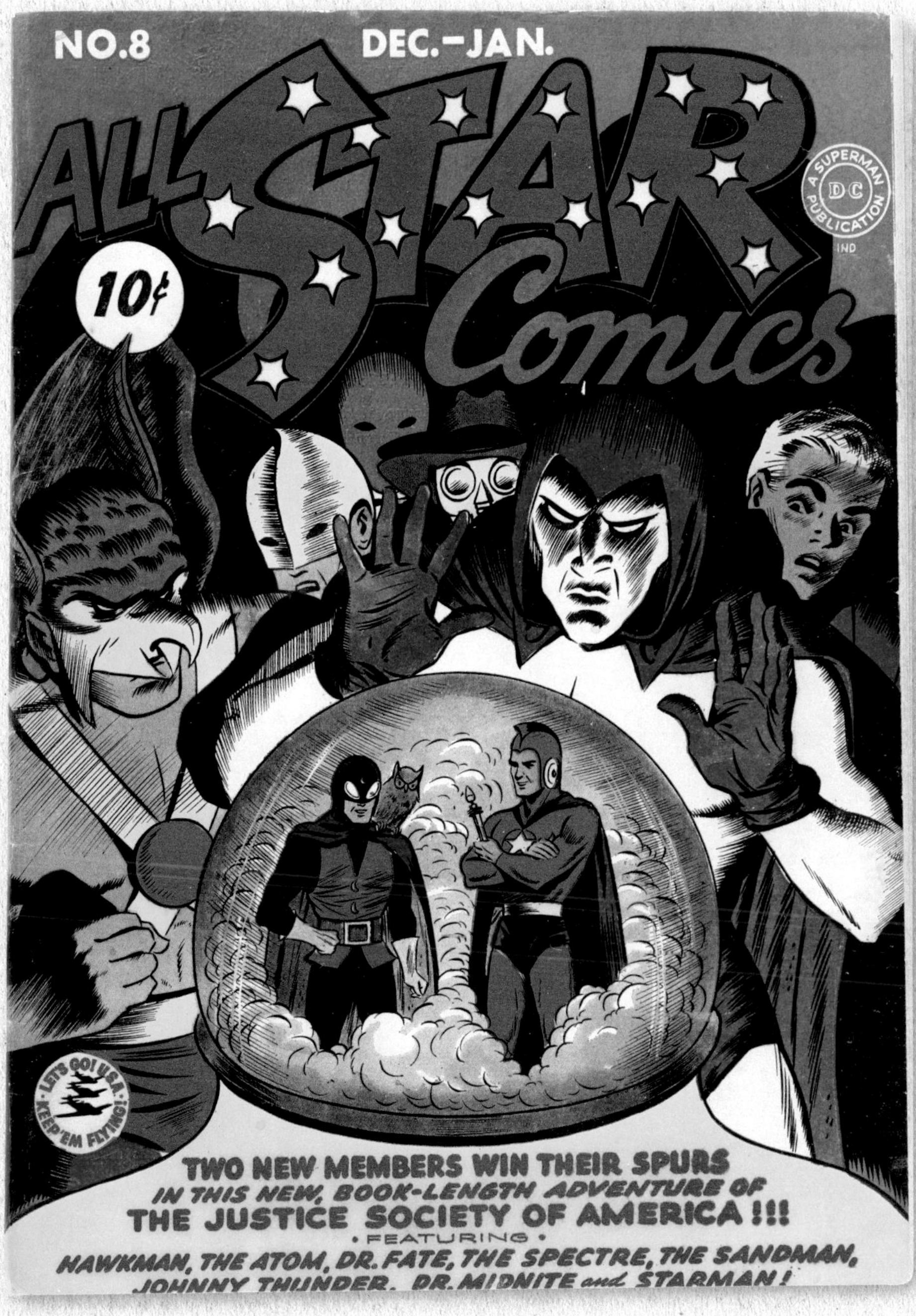
NO.8
DEC.-JAN.
ALL STAR Comics
10¢
A SUPERMAN DC PUBLICATION
IND
LET'S GO! U.S.A. KEEP 'EM FLYING!
TWO NEW MEMBERS WIN THEIR SPURS
IN THIS NEW, BOOK-LENGTH ADVENTURE OF
THE JUSTICE SOCIETY OF AMERICA !!!
• FEATURING •
HAWKMAN, THE ATOM, DR. FATE, THE SPECTRE, THE SANDMAN,
JOHNNY THUNDER, DR. MIDNITE and STARMAN!

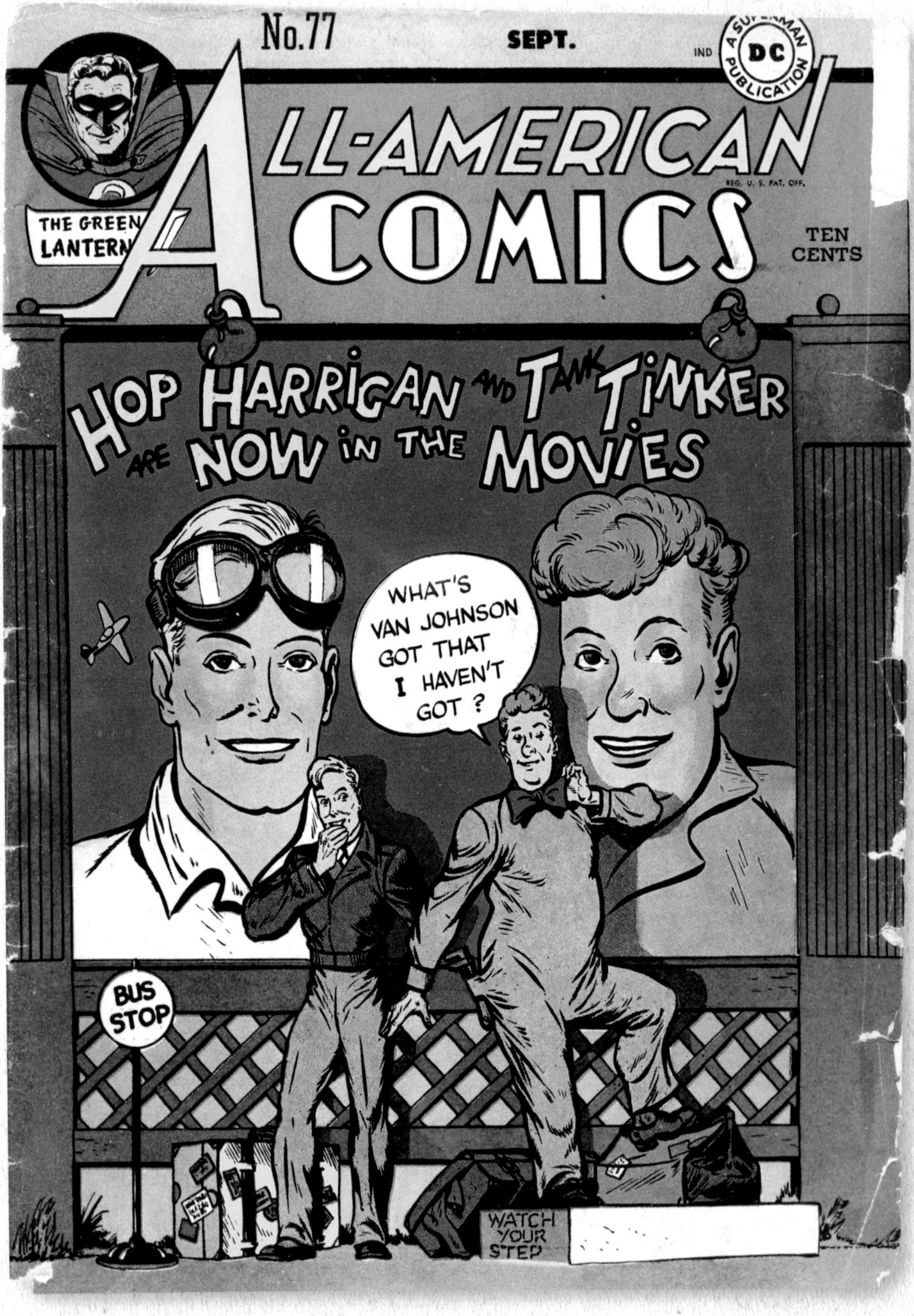
No.77
SEPT.
IND
A SUPERMAN DC PUBLICATION
ALL-AMERICAN COMICS
REG. U. S. PAT. OFF.
THE GREEN LANTERN
TEN CENTS
HOP HARRIGAN AND TANK TINKER ARE NOW IN THE MOVIES
WHAT'S VAN JOHNSON GOT THAT I HAVEN'T GOT ?
BUS STOP
WATCH YOUR STEP

15-cent title that featured its big three (the Flash, Green Lantern, and Wonder Woman) and was modeled on the uptown *World's Finest*...With that, as 1942 ended, so did the expansion of DC's super hero line, which would not add a non–Superman Family title for the next 16 years.

In 1943, the tide began to turn. Wartime paper rationing cut the number of issues published each year for many titles, and page counts throughout the line shrank from 64 to 48 pages (making many features disappear faster than Zatara could say "raeppasid"). Outside the comics, the DC mythology continued to grow, as George Lowther wrote the first Superman novel and introduced the hypothesis that his powers may have slowly appeared during puberty — a concept the comics wouldn't adopt for decades. A *Batman* movie serial from Columbia Pictures brought DC to life on the screen for the first time, with Lewis Wilson in the title role, and Batman received his own newspaper strip thanks to the added exposure. But the only new title uptown was *All-Funny*, starting a trend that would snowball over the next few years. Alvin Schwartz and DC vet George Storm contributed *Buzzy*, a teen series trying to cash in on *Archie's* momentum, and the following year it graduated to its own title.

All-American took a different direction, launching *Funny Stuff*, filled with amusing animals, including Mayer's own J. Rufus Lion. Mayer assembled DC's first "annual" of original stories, with the *Big All-American Comic Book* including all of their stars...and a story by the bespectacled assistant editor Mayer brought on at the recommendation of science-fiction pulp writer Alfred Bester, who was moonlighting doing comics and crafting Green Lantern's oath. The new kid was Julie Schwartz, who with Mort Weisinger had created one of the earliest science-fiction fanzines and gone on to be a prestigious science-fiction literary agent — a career that no longer paid the rent in the tough times of the war. Schwartz read his first comic on the train going in for his interview with Mayer, and stayed for the rest of his life. The All-American team would be rounded out by the arrival of Robert Kanigher, an experienced writer of comics and many other media, who would become DC's most prolific writer,

ALL-AMERICAN COMICS No. 77
Cover art, Jon L. Blummer, September 1946.
The cover copy refers to the 15-chapter *Hop Harrigan* Saturday-morning serial released by Columbia Pictures that year. It starred William Bakewell as Hop and Sumner Getchell as Tank Tinker. Like most of the movie serials based on DC comics, it wasn't particularly faithful to the source material.

far outpacing Fox. With Schwartz and Kanigher on the bench, all of the key editors who would drive DC for the next two decades were in place at one of the two offices.

As the war was ending in 1945, All-American declared its own war, with DC uptown—banishing the DC logo from its covers as Gaines tried to secede. The civil war was brief, and the AA symbol flew across only a few months of covers while issues of *All-Star* were hurriedly redrawn to replace DC heroes with the Lafayette Street crew. Often in war, the side with the most resources wins...and Gaines ended up being bought out by Donenfeld and Liebowitz, going off with *Picture Stories from the Bible* to start his own EC ("Educational Comics") line, before tragically dying in a boating accident in 1947.

The tide of change continued to accelerate away from the heroes: Dell Comics had achieved great success with its Disney comics titles (the flagship of which, *Walt Disney Comics & Stories,* would peak at more than 3 million circulation) and Warner Bros.' *Looney Tunes,* so to compete, DC introduced *Real Screen Funnies,* bringing the Fox and the Crow and other cartoon characters from the movies; *Leading Comics* abandoned its heroes for funny animals; and after briefly starring Superboy, *More Fun* sent him and all the rest of its surviving heroes over to *Adventure Comics* and once again lived up to its name with

THE BIG ALL-AMERICAN COMIC BOOK No. 1

Cover art, various artists, 1944. All-American's first attempt at an omnibus, at 132 pages of original content, featured most of its heroes, as well as some humor features. It is considered among the rarest of AA publications, priced on the collector's market at more than $15,000.

THE ADVENTURES OF SUPERMAN

Novel, interior; script, George Lowther; art, Joe Shuster. 1942.

"You say if Krypton is destroyed we can escape to the Planet Earth. How could we live there, Jor-el?... It takes a hundred Earth People together to do what one man on Krypton can do alone! They have not the power to fly, but must walk at snail's pace on the Earth's surface! They cannot breathe beneath the sea!"
—Rozan, from George Lowther's *Adventures of Superman*

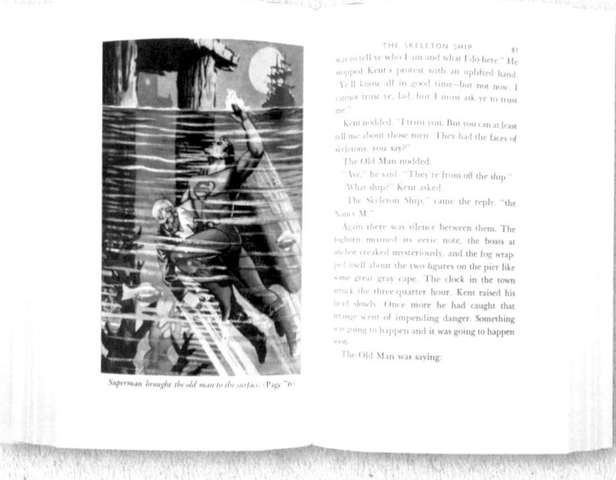
Superman brought the old man to the surface. (Page 76)
THE SKELETON SHIP 81
was to tell ye who I am and what I do here." He stopped Kent's protest with an uplifted hand. "Ye'll know all in good time—but not now. I cannot trust ye, lad, but I must ask ye to trust me."
Kent nodded. "I trust you. But you can at least tell me about those men. They had the faces of skeletons, you say?"
The Old Man nodded.
"Aye," he said. "They're from off the ship."
"What ship?" Kent asked.
"The Skeleton Ship," came the reply, "the Nancy M."
Again there was silence between them. The foghorn moaned its eerie note, the boats at anchor creaked mysteriously, and the fog wrapped itself about the two figures on the pier like some great gray cape. The clock in the town struck the three-quarter hour. Kent raised his head slowly. Once more he had caught that strange scent of impending danger. Something was going to happen and it was going to happen soon.
The Old Man was saying:

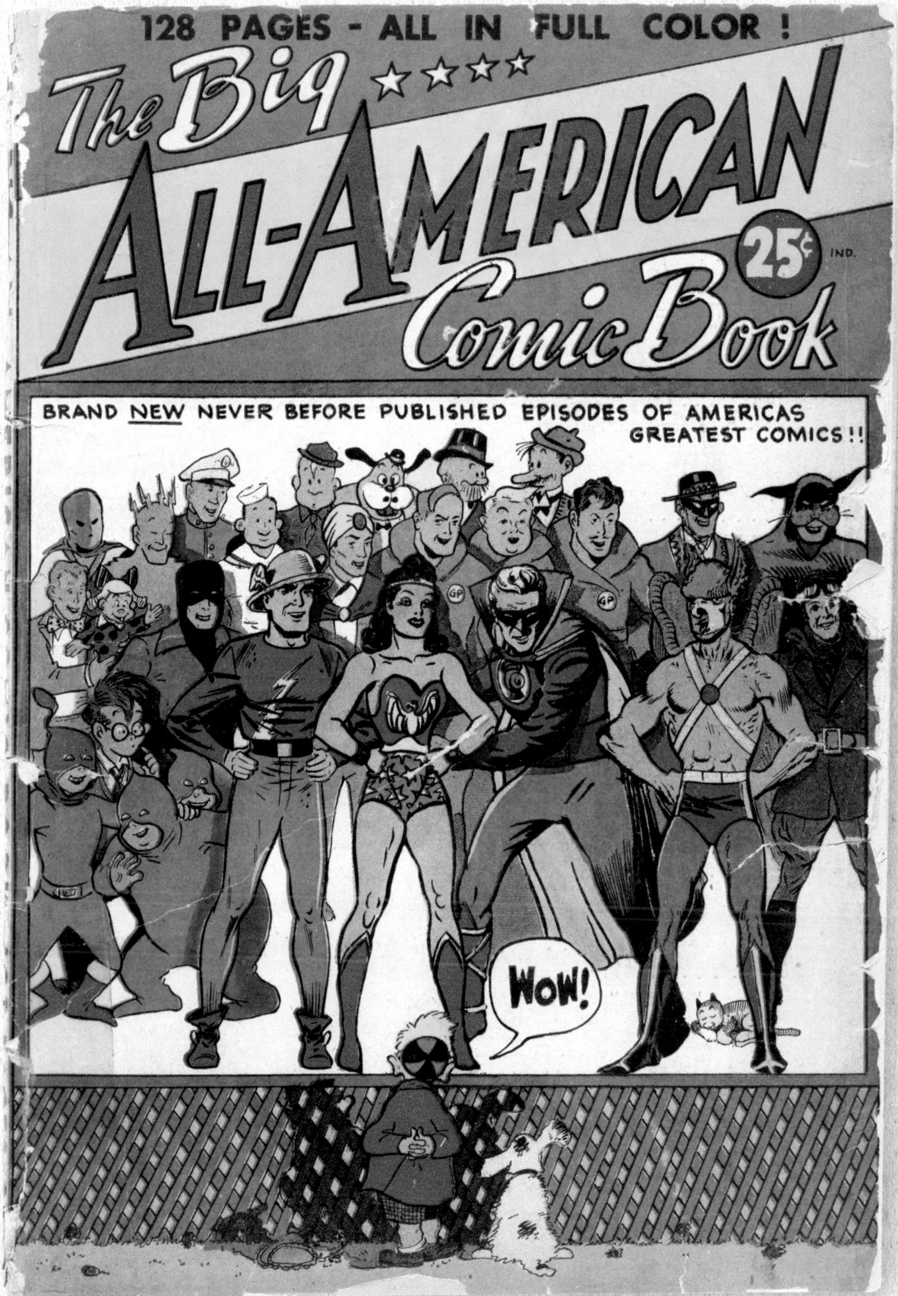
128 PAGES - ALL IN FULL COLOR !
The Big All-American Comic Book
25¢
IND.
BRAND NEW NEVER BEFORE PUBLISHED EPISODES OF AMERICAS GREATEST COMICS!!
GP
GP
WOW!

stars like dopey twins Dover and Clover. *Star-Spangled Comics* made Robin its centerpiece with a new solo series (even if Batman did show up as a constant chaperone). Half of the DC titles starring super heroes other than the enduring Superman, Batman, and Wonder Woman were gone.

The media connections continued to grow while publishing faced its problems. All-American finally got its big screen moment with a *Hop Harrigan* movie serial, bringing Jon Blummer's character to life in 1946. The same Columbia relationship resulted in a *Vigilante* serial in 1947, but by then, the tide had definitively shifted. Perhaps with the war won and the Depression over, the newly confident nation was prepared to fight its own battles…or perhaps people were simply ready to return to ordinary human-scale challenges that could be handled with our natural abilities instead of ones beyond mortal attainment: buying homes in the fast-sprouting suburbs and new cars, and looking forward to an age of prosperity.

THE GILT BEGINS TO FADE . . .

Date the postwar fading chapter of the Golden Age from the events in 1947: Seeking a new engine to drive its success, DC reached out to license three successful radio shows, *A Date with Judy*, *Gangbusters*, and *Mr. District Attorney*; canceled *More Fun Comics*, where the company's history began; and launched only two new titles, *Western Comics* (marking the beginning of another trend) and the first DC title to ever debut without an anthology appearance, *Leave It to Binky*. Binky, another follower in Archie's footsteps, was Mayer's last editorial creation, executed by Hal Seegar (another Fleischer alumnus) and Bob Oksner, both making their DC debuts. Though only 30, Mayer's health was suffering, his longtime boss Gaines was gone, and his drawing hand was itching.

It's hard to overstate Shelly Mayer's impact on DC and comics' Golden Age — set aside his considerable role in the beginnings of five of DC's six most important heroes, he was a powerful (if not always kindly) father figure to the only slightly younger artists who filled the halls, many of whom qualified as his personal discoveries (including

FOR THE FIRST TIME IN COLORED CONTINUITY
A DC PUBLICATION
PICTURE STORIES from the BIBLE
10¢
NOAH
RUTH
JOSEPH
JONAH
MOSES
SAUL
ESTHER
OLD TESTAMENT EDITION NUMBER ONE

YOU CAN'T BEAT THE LAW!
A SUPERMAN PUBLICATION DC
No. 1 DEC. JAN.
A 52 PAGE MAGAZINE
TEN CENTS
GANG BUSTERS
IN THIS ISSUE! A CRIME CONFESSION... "MURDER WAS MY BUSINESS!"
ABC
BASED ON THE SMASH RADIO HIT!

PICTURE STORIES FROM THE BIBLE No. 1
Cover art, Don Cameron, 1942.

GANG BUSTERS No. 1
Cover art, Howard Sherman, December 1947–January 1948.

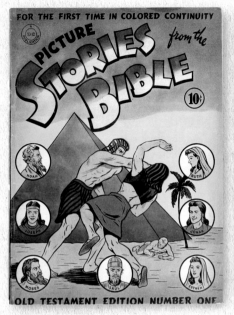

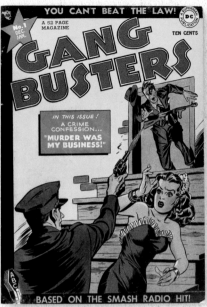

Joe Kubert, future DC President Carmine Infantino and artists' artist Alex Toth). The anecdotes are endless: Mayer ripping up pages, calling home to an artist's mother to get him to meet his deadlines, encouraging another to finish school before being given assignments, and on and on. Decades later, the formidable Kanigher was still nervous about being in the same room with his old boss. Mayer's own feature, *Scribbly*, which he debuted at other publishers and brought to All-American, is recognized as a primal ancestor of the graphic novel memoir for telling the tale of an aspiring young cartoonist, as the 19-year-old Mayer was when it began. *Scribbly* had run in *All-American Comics*, and when Mayer gave up his desk, it became its own title for the next few years. In many ways, when Mayer left the building, the Golden Age of Comics went with him.

If there is a quintessence to the Golden Age, then, it was the sense of possibility — both in the characters, who were exploring the potential for humans to reach abilities that previously had not been deeply explored

THE ADVENTURES OF REX THE WONDER DOG No. 24
Cover art, Gil Kane. November–December 1955.
Streak the Wonder Dog usually had to share covers with Green Lantern, but Rex got his own title. Woof!

ALL-AMERICAN COMICS No. 99
Cover art, Alex Toth, July 1948.
As the popularity of super heroes waned, Green Lantern took a back seat to Streak the Wonder Dog. The canine hero went into limbo with his guardian, but his spirit lived on in the 1950s *Rex the Wonder Dog* comic book.

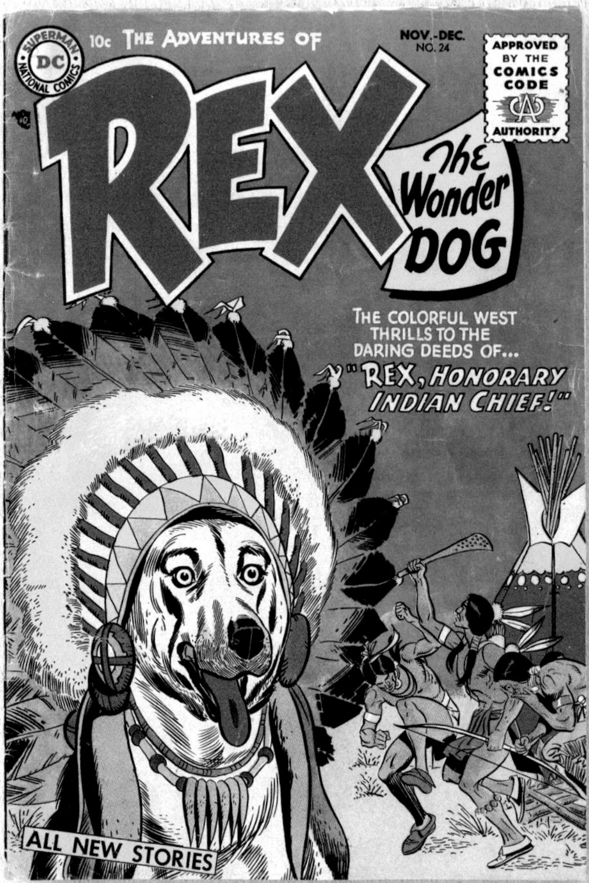
10¢ THE ADVENTURES OF
NOV.-DEC. NO. 24
APPROVED BY THE COMICS CODE AUTHORITY
SUPERMAN DC NATIONAL COMICS
REX
The Wonder DOG
THE COLORFUL WEST THRILLS TO THE DARING DEEDS OF...
"REX, HONORARY INDIAN CHIEF!"
ALL NEW STORIES

in fiction, and in the creators, who were almost all young people in that first flush of discovery of their talents. Both did amazing and unprecedented things, for a while.

. . . BUT THE GOLDEN AGE OF DC CONTINUES

Yet there's a divergence between the Golden Age of Comics and the Golden Age of DC at this point. Follow the comics publishing side of the company, and the postwar years into the early 1950s tell a consistent if difficult tale. DC and All-American consolidated at 480 Lexington Avenue under the editorial leadership of Whit

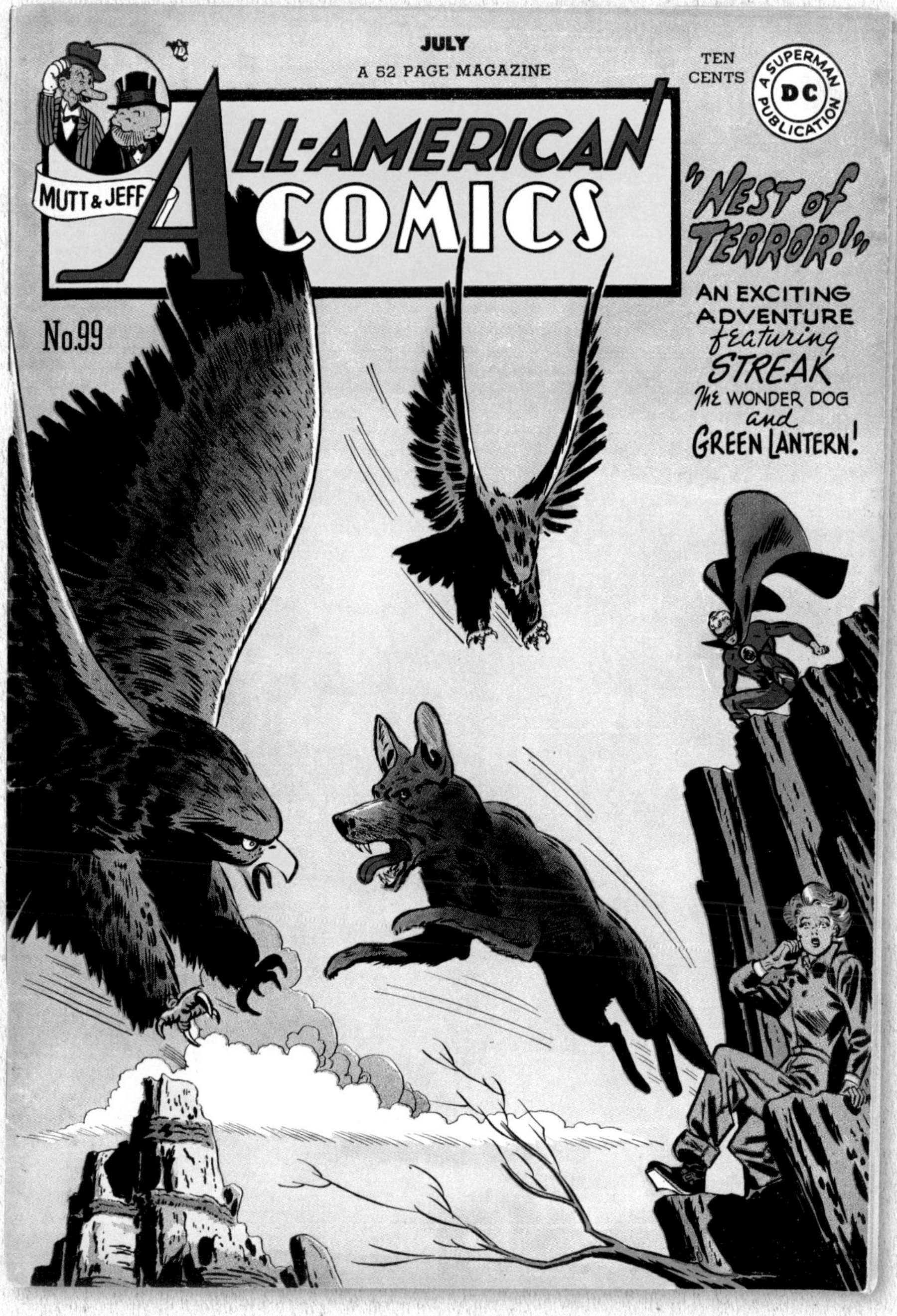
JULY
A 52 PAGE MAGAZINE
TEN CENTS
A SUPERMAN DC PUBLICATION
MUTT & JEFF
ALL-AMERICAN COMICS
No.99
"NEST OF TERROR!"
AN EXCITING ADVENTURE featuring STREAK THE WONDER DOG and GREEN LANTERN!

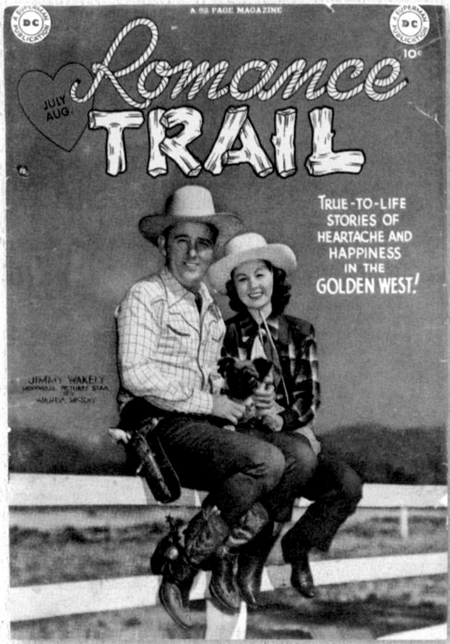
Romance
TRAIL
JULY AUG.
10¢
TRUE-TO-LIFE STORIES OF HEARTACHE AND HAPPINESS IN THE GOLDEN WEST!
JIMMY WAKELY

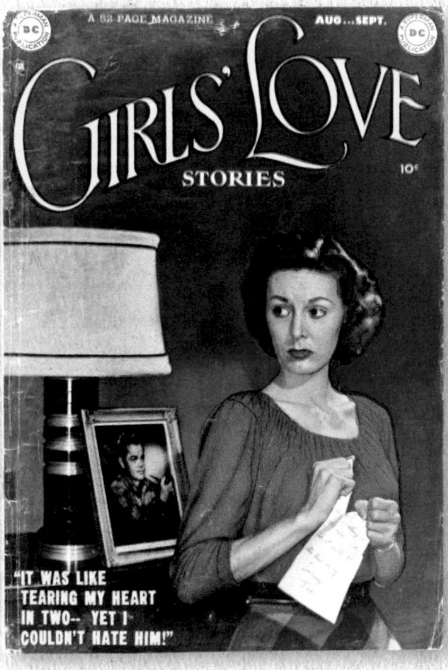
AUG...SEPT.
GIRLS' LOVE
STORIES
10¢
"IT WAS LIKE TEARING MY HEART IN TWO-- YET I COULDN'T HATE HIM!"

ROMANCE TRAIL No. 1
Cover art, July–August 1949. "On newsstands all over the U.S. last week, new-style comic books with such come-on titles as *Sweethearts, Romantic Secrets, Teen-Age Romances* and *Young Love* were outselling all others, even the blood and thunder variety." —*Time* magazine, 1949

GIRLS' LOVE STORIES No. 1
Cover art, August–September 1949. The DC romance comics line that began with this issue would last almost three decades and inspire the pop art movement to reconceptualize the comic book images into museum pieces.

Ellsworth. The number of issues published each year rose steadily, from just over 200 in 1947 to over 350 by 1955, but with each issue contributing fairly modestly to the company's success, other than the Superman titles. There was an almost endless appetite for new genres to replace the disappearing super heroes (by 1950, only the big three would be able to carry titles). *All-American* became *All-American Western,* and *All-Star, All-Star Western,* were joined by *Dale Evans, Hopalong Cassidy,* and even *Jimmy Wakely* (of whom, his newly assigned editor Schwartz commented, "Who the fuck is Jimmy Wakely?"). *Girls' Love Stories* and *Girls' Romances* were launched as the building blocks of a line that would endure for more than 25 years, answering the success Prize Comics had with Simon and Kirby's invention of romance comics, after misfires like *Miss Beverly Hills of Hollywood* and *Romance Trail.* Kanigher created—and mostly wrote—war comics as soon as the dust of WWII had settled, launching *Our Army at War* and converting titles to create *Star-Spangled War Stories* and *All-American Men of War*. Schwartz returned to his science-fiction roots, with *Strange Adventures* and *Mystery in Space*. Even the coonskin-cap craze of the '50s was answered with adventure titles from *Tomahawk*, through *Daniel Boone*, *Frontier Fighters*, and *The Brave and the Bold*. There was a continuing flow of more of the same in all these genres, ending with the debut of Mayer's most charming and enduring creation, *Sugar and Spike*, as 1956 began.

And the presence of the heroes continued to shrink, with the last blow being the disappearance of the Justice Society after *All-Star Comics* No. 57, in 1950. Even the comics themselves shrank, with page counts

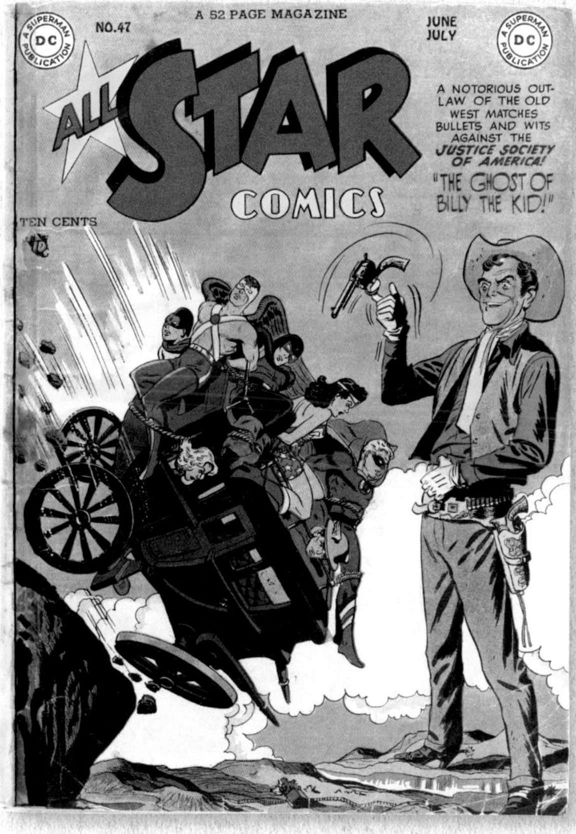
A 52 PAGE MAGAZINE
NO. 47
JUNE
JULY
SUPERMAN DC PUBLICATION
SUPERMAN DC PUBLICATION
ALL STAR
COMICS
TEN CENTS
A NOTORIOUS OUT-LAW OF THE OLD WEST MATCHES BULLETS AND WITS AGAINST THE JUSTICE SOCIETY OF AMERICA!
"THE GHOST OF BILLY THE KID!"

ALL-STAR COMICS No. 47
Cover art, Irwin Hasen and Bob Oksner, June–July 1949. The prominence of the Western figure here didn't seem to have ominous implications for the Justice Society of America at the time, but it *was* a harbinger of things to come: In just two short years, the super heroes would be banished and retired from duty as the title became *All-Star Western* with No. 58 (April–May 1951).

SUPERMAN AND THE MOLE MEN

Set photograph, Harry Donenfeld (front left) with crew members and actors portraying Mole Men, 1951.

SUPERMAN IN EXILE

Movie poster, 20th Century Fox, 1954. This one-sheet promotes one of five "features" that were actually compilations of episodes from the TV series' second season. The episode titles are shown in the blue boxes with white text.

slipping from 48 pages to 40 in the early 1950s before stabilizing at the 32-page format in 1954, which would be the predominant size for periodical comics into the next century. *World's Finest* shrank, too, despite its two big-name stars, going from a fat 15-cent title to an ordinary 10-center, and teaming up Superman and Batman so they could both fit in each issue.

The only newcomer to the heroic ranks could be found if you looked very carefully, in a story hidden in the back pages of *Detective Comics* in 1955. Written by Joe Samachson and drawn by Joe Certa, it featured a plainclothes cop with mysterious powers because he was really the Manhunter from Mars. The only other additions to the heroic ranks were the two young members of the Superman family: Superboy getting a book of his own, and *Superman's Pal, Jimmy Olsen*, a creation of the radio series. But while radio had been Jimmy's birthplace, he became a star on television, the rising power in American culture.

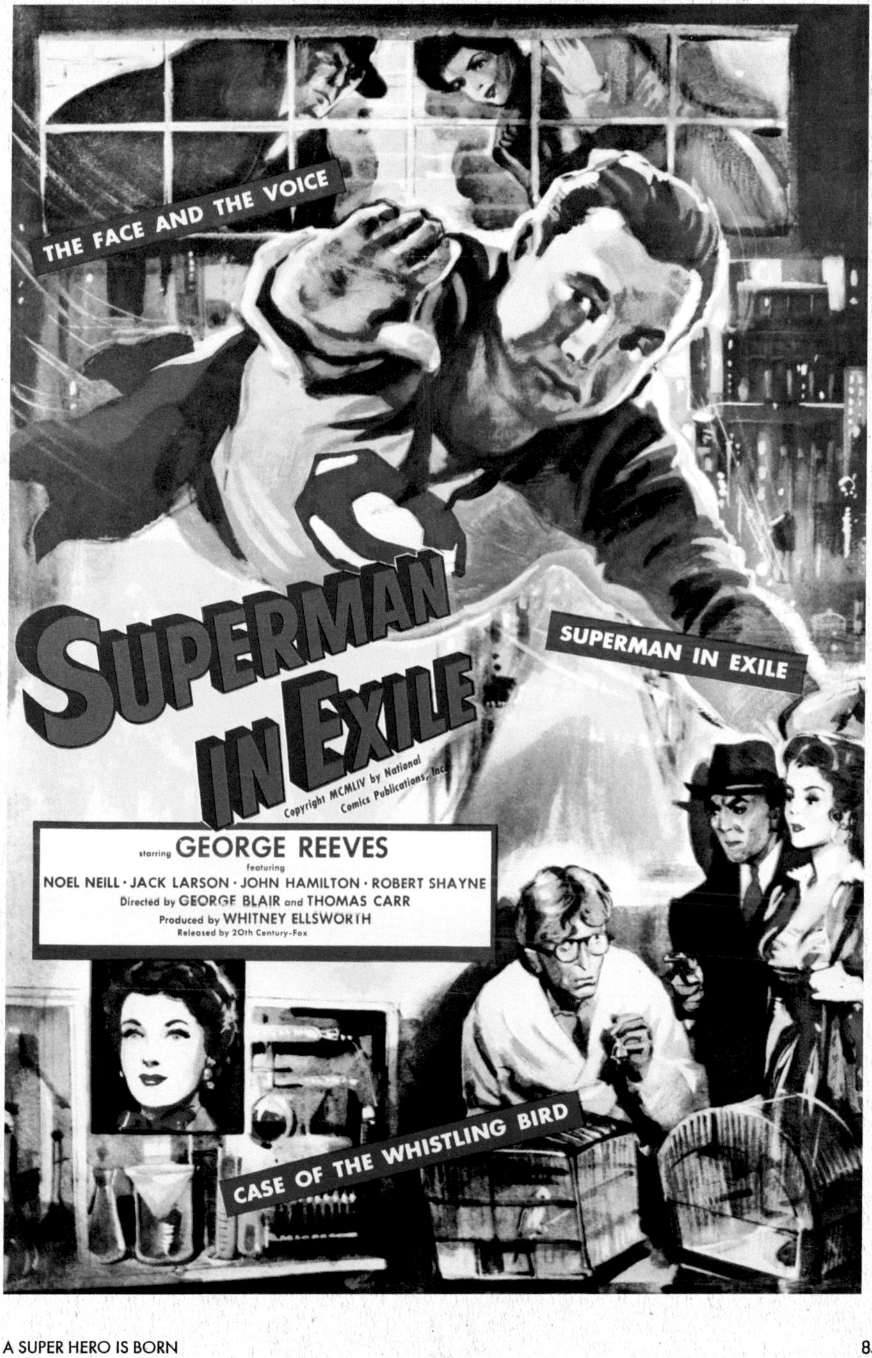
THE FACE AND THE VOICE
SUPERMAN IN EXILE
SUPERMAN IN EXILE
Copyright MCMLIV by National Comics Publications, Inc.
starring GEORGE REEVES
featuring
NOEL NEILL · JACK LARSON · JOHN HAMILTON · ROBERT SHAYNE
Directed by GEORGE BLAIR and THOMAS CARR
Produced by WHITNEY ELLSWORTH
Released by 20th Century-Fox
CASE OF THE WHISTLING BIRD

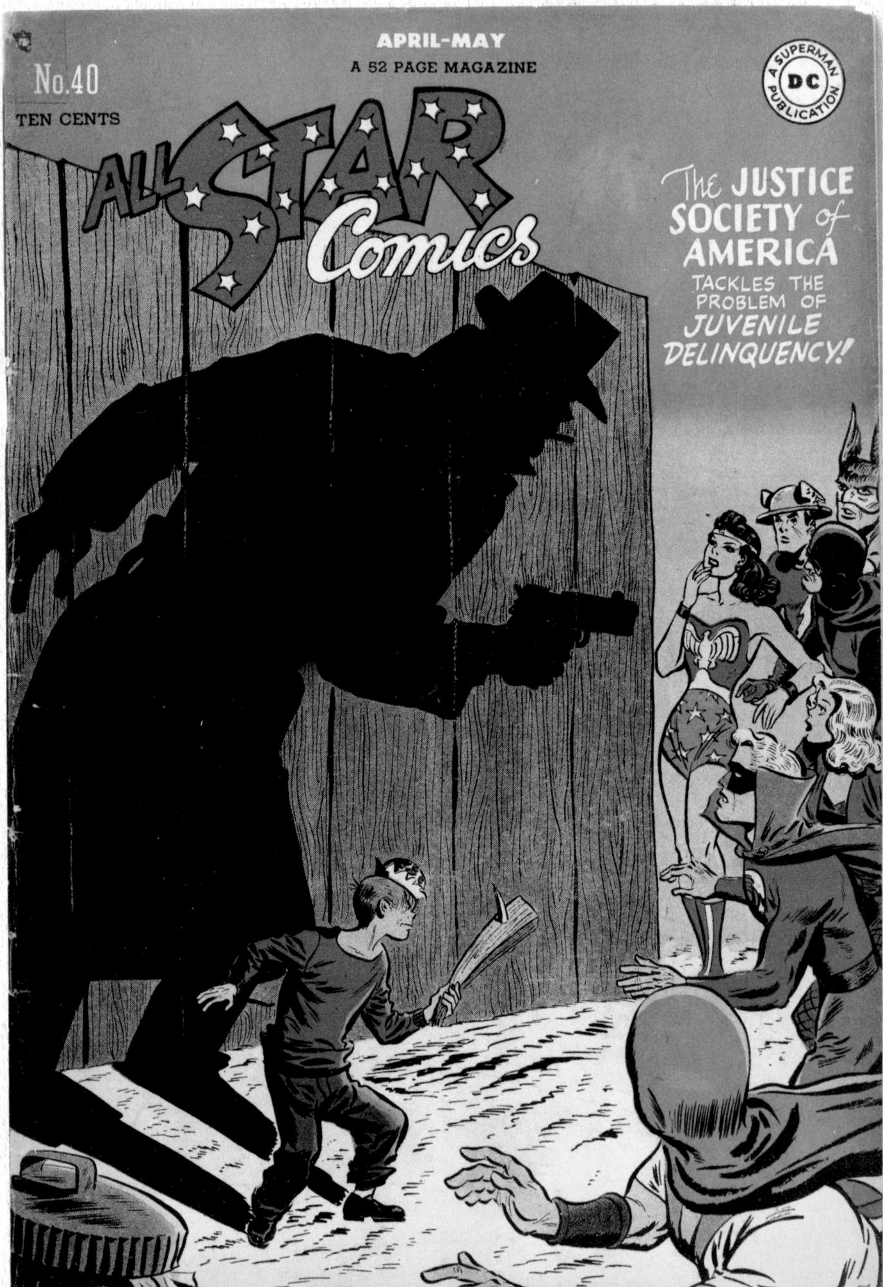
APRIL-MAY
A 52 PAGE MAGAZINE
No.40
TEN CENTS
A SUPERMAN DC PUBLICATION
ALL STAR Comics
The JUSTICE SOCIETY of AMERICA TACKLES THE PROBLEM OF JUVENILE DELINQUENCY!

It was television that would ultimately stretch out the Golden Age for DC. The movie serials had continued to build on the heroes' visibility, *Superman* starring Kirk Alyn as the Man of Steel and Noel Neill as Lois in 1948 and 1950, *Congo Bill* (1948), and *Batman and Robin* (1949). But the serials were fading and radio drama was as well, spelling an end to *Superman* in 1951.

Robert Maxwell was dispatched from the radio series to Hollywood so DC could make its own television series of *The Adventures of Superman*. The pilot episodes were constructed as a short movie, permitting theatrical release of *Superman and the Mole Men* in 1951 by Lippert Pictures, with George Reeves taking over as Superman and Phyllis Coates as Lois. With the success of the pilot, a series was quickly (and inexpensively) produced and syndicated, hitting the air in 1952, with a cast that included Jack Larson as Jimmy Olsen and John Hamilton as Perry White. Noel Neill stepped back in to reprise her role as Lois after the first season of production.

ALL STAR COMICS No. 40
Cover art, Carmine Infantino and Frank Giacoia, April–May 1948.

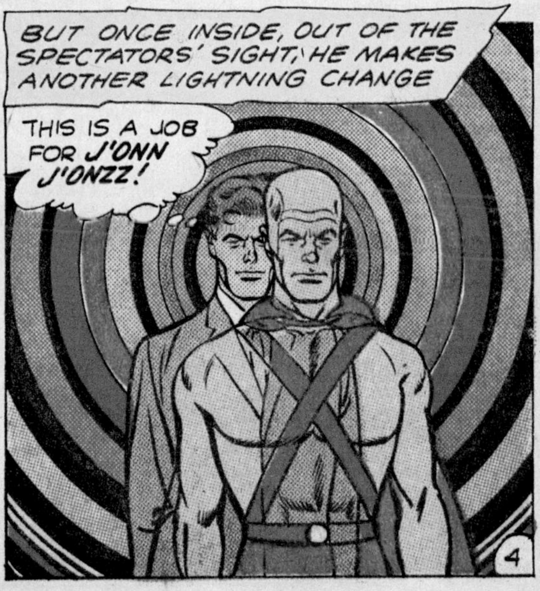
BUT ONCE INSIDE, OUT OF THE SPECTATORS' SIGHT, HE MAKES ANOTHER LIGHTNING CHANGE
THIS IS A JOB FOR J'ONN J'ONZZ!
4

DETECTIVE COMICS No. 287
Interior, "J'onn J'onzz's Kid Brother"; script, Jack Miller; art, Joe Certa. January 1961. The last super hero of the last moments of the Golden Age.

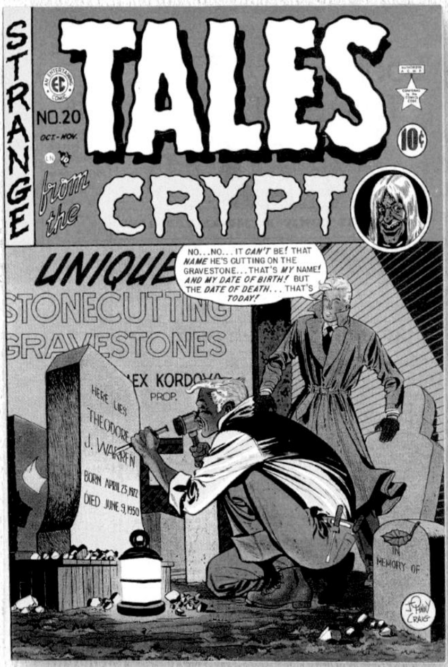
STRANGE
TALES from the CRYPT
NO.20
OCT-NOV.
10¢
NO...NO... IT CAN'T BE! THAT NAME HE'S CUTTING ON THE GRAVESTONE... THAT'S MY NAME! AND MY DATE OF BIRTH! BUT THE DATE OF DEATH... THAT'S TODAY!
UNIQUE
STONECUTTING
GRAVESTONES
EX KORDOVA
PROP.
HERE LIES
THEODORE
J. WARREN
BORN APRIL 23, 1912
DIED JUNE 9, 1950
IN MEMORY OF

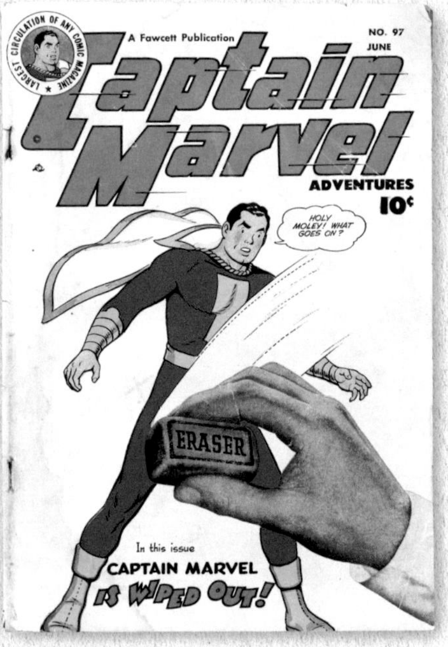
LARGEST CIRCULATION OF ANY COMIC MAGAZINE
A Fawcett Publication
NO. 97
JUNE
Captain Marvel
ADVENTURES
10¢
HOLY MOLEY! WHAT GOES ON?
ERASER
In this issue
CAPTAIN MARVEL
IS WIPED OUT!

TALES FROM THE CRYPT No. 20
Cover art, Johnny Craig, October–November 1950. Arguably the best-known title of EC Comics' horror line, *Tales from the Crypt* evolved from the comparatively tame *Crime Patrol* title.

CAPTAIN MARVEL ADVENTURES No. 97
Cover art, C. C. Beck, June 1949.

The series' success promoted sales of dress-up costumes and a wide variety of merchandise, with Kellogg's sponsoring the show. Commercials even showed Reeves and Larson sharing a breakfast table laden with Kellogg's best... but not allowing Neill to join them, in the curious Puritanism of the time. More importantly, the affection viewers (particularly young viewers) had for the portrayals of Superman and his television family reforged his bonds with the public.

Superman comics were outselling any other adventure titles and enabled DC to outlast a long list of competitors, while Fawcett (and Captain Marvel) and many others vanished. Comics came under a multipronged assault in the 1950s, with a proliferation of weak titles crowding newsstands, just as families were starting to move out to the suburbs, taking their kids away from easy access to newsstands entirely. And two successful genres, crime and horror, went a bit further than society was comfortable with: *Crime Does Not Pay* (from Lev Gleason, a small

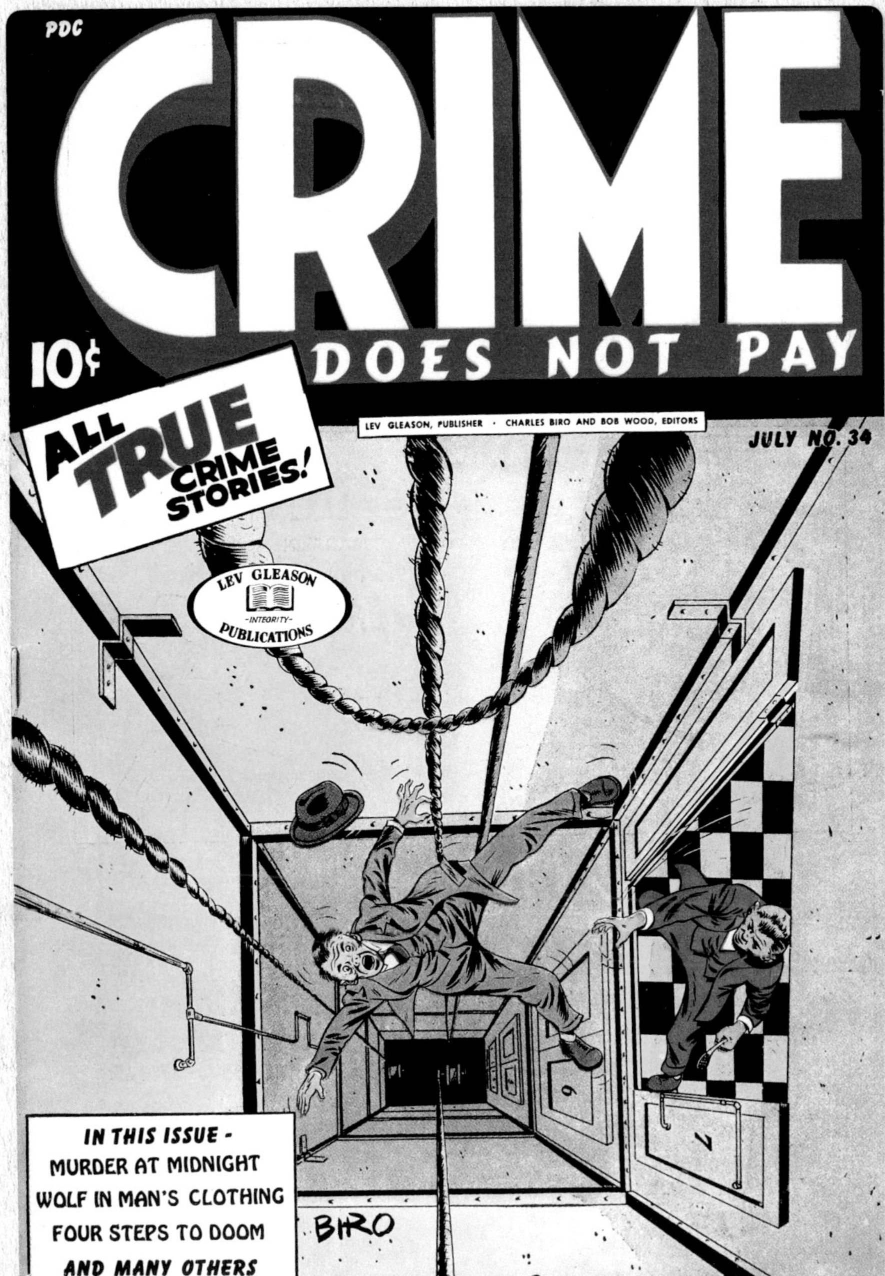
PDC
CRIME
10¢
DOES NOT PAY
ALL TRUE CRIME STORIES!
LEV GLEASON, PUBLISHER · CHARLES BIRO AND BOB WOOD, EDITORS
JULY NO. 34
LEV GLEASON
-INTEGRITY-
PUBLICATIONS
IN THIS ISSUE -
MURDER AT MIDNIGHT
WOLF IN MAN'S CLOTHING
FOUR STEPS TO DOOM
AND MANY OTHERS
BIRO

CRIME DOES NOT PAY No. 34

PREVIOUS PAGE: *Cover art, Charles Biro, July 1944.* Lev Gleason's *Crime Does Not Pay* specialized in stories torn from real life. The sensationalized, adult nature of its content eventually attracted more than 1 million readers per issue along with critics who charged that true crime comics like it were corrupting youth.

BEFORE
AFTER

COMICS CODE PRESS CONFERENCE

Photograph, Comics Magazine Association of America representative Charles F. Murphy takes questions against a backdrop of original and sanitized EC Comics panels, New York City, 1954.

BURNING COMIC BOOKS

Photograph, fifth-graders at the Jenkins School, Scituate, Massachusetts, one of many communities that participated in bonfires of comic books deemed dangerous for children in the pre–Comics Code era. December 22, 1948.

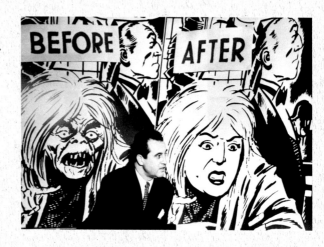

comics publisher) started in the early '40s but peaked in the early '50s and attracted many imitators, and All-American founder Max Gaines's son Bill Gaines's EC built a line of horror comics such as *Tales from the Crypt*, setting new standards for quality art and storytelling, but also for graphic gore.

Social crusaders blamed comics as the cause of juvenile delinquency and other social ills (on evidence as spurious as polling delinquents and finding that they had all read comics—as had virtually every other American child at the time), and Gaines ended up defending his line before a Senate subcommittee hearing. In the witch-hunt and scapegoat-driven political culture of 1950s America, comics were an easy target, with publishers who were disproportionately Jewish and leaned toward the left wing, even if there was no trace of either characteristic in the comics themselves. With sales battered by the rise of newsstandless suburbia, alternative forms of entertainment on television, and publicity-seeking rabble-rousers going to lengths like staging comic book burnings, it was clear something would have to give.

DC and other publishers banded together to form a self-regulating Comics Code, sanitizing any publications that came anywhere near the challenged genres (DC's *House of Mystery*, *House of Secrets*, and *Tales of the Unexpected* were already harmless by comparison, and got even

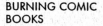

C. C. BECK CARTOON

Beck on the Superman–Captain Marvel trial, 1981. Acerbic *Captain Marvel* co-creator C. C. Beck had little sympathy for DC in its lawsuit against Fawcett Comics.

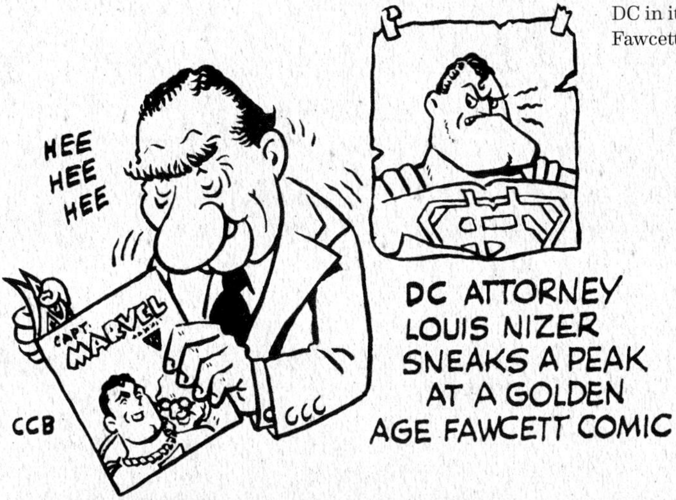

HEE
HEE
HEE
CAPT. MARVEL
CCB
CCC
DC ATTORNEY
LOUIS NIZER
SNEAKS A PEAK
AT A GOLDEN
AGE FAWCETT COMIC

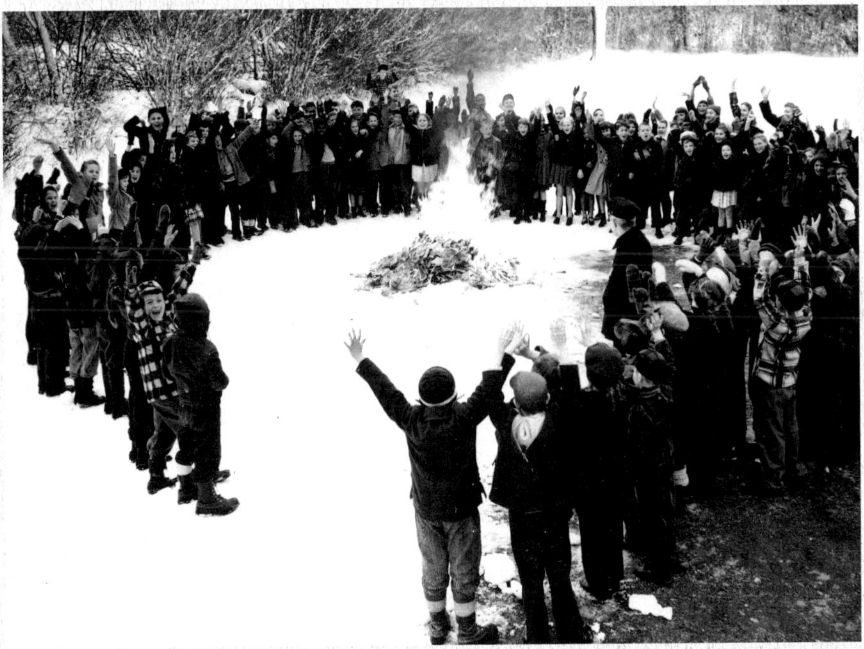

less threatening under the Code's review). Words were banned, ranging from "terror" to "flick" (which, when hand lettered, could close up and take on a whole other meaning). Society was safe, but publishers began to fold, or radically reduce their lines even under the Code. Only Dell, thriving with its Disney and Looney Tunes licenses, didn't feel the need for the Code…and DC sailed onward, now under the dual protection of Superman and the Code seal on its covers.

LOOKING BACK AT THE GOLD

Just as there's a certain magic to recalling all the firsts in our lives, fans and scholars alike have continued to mark the years between the birth of *Superman* and the arrival of the claustrophobia of the Comics Code as an unequalled Golden Age for comics. Often awkward, amateurish, and filled with many features quickly forgotten (by readers and their creators alike), the energy that pervaded the Golden Age took what had been a marketing format and made it a true American art form. Distinct in style, tone, and attitude, American comics would evolve massively over the next few decades, but never completely lose touch with their origins in these times. And for DC, the iconic heroes birthed in the Golden Age would forever define the company's public identity, serve as its trademarks, and provide the superstrength that would support hundreds of experiments, imitators, and innovations alike. With the lasting gifts of the Golden Age's modern myth-makers, DC would possess both economic invulnerability and cultural immortality well into the next century.

FLASH COMICS No. 104
Cover art, Joe Kubert, February 1949.
The last issue of *Flash Comics* brought an end to the solo adventures of the Flash, Hawkman, and Black Canary, although they survived a few years longer as members of the Justice Society in *All-Star Comics*.

PAUL LEVITZ

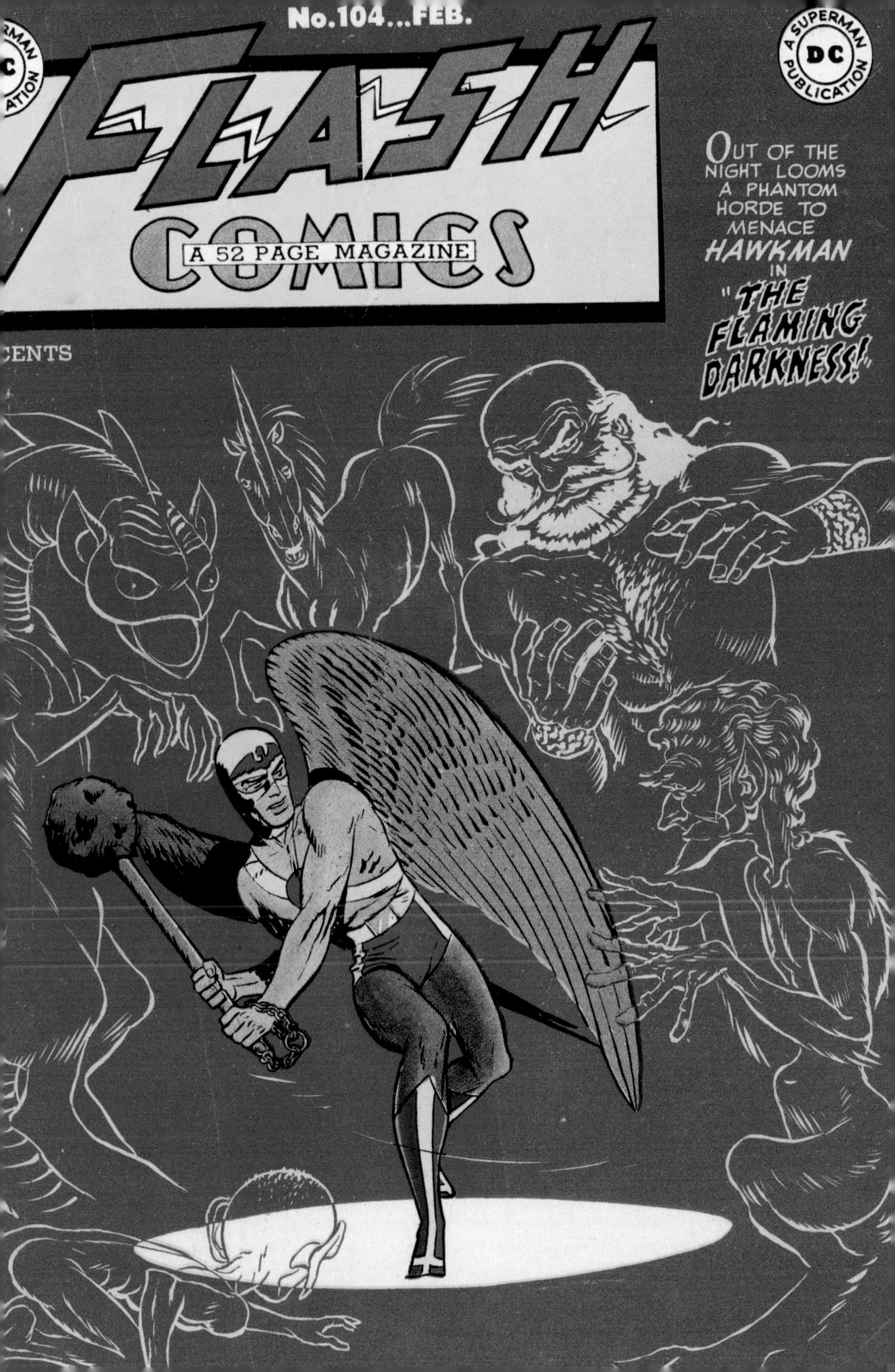

No.104...FEB.
FLASH COMICS
A 52 PAGE MAGAZINE
A SUPERMAN DC PUBLICATION
CENTS
OUT OF THE NIGHT LOOMS A PHANTOM HORDE TO MENACE HAWKMAN IN "THE FLAMING DARKNESS!"

The Golden Age

1935–1956

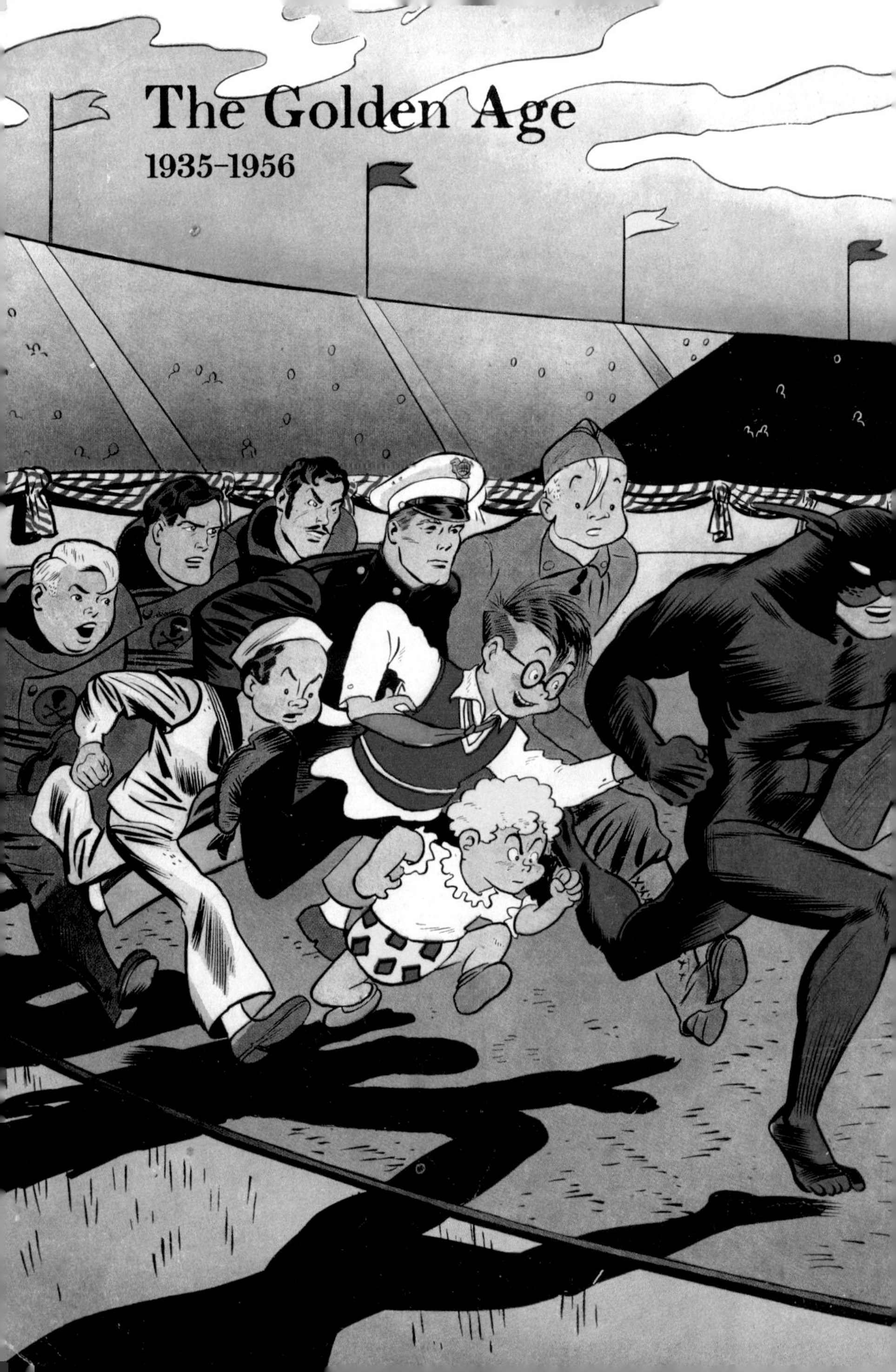

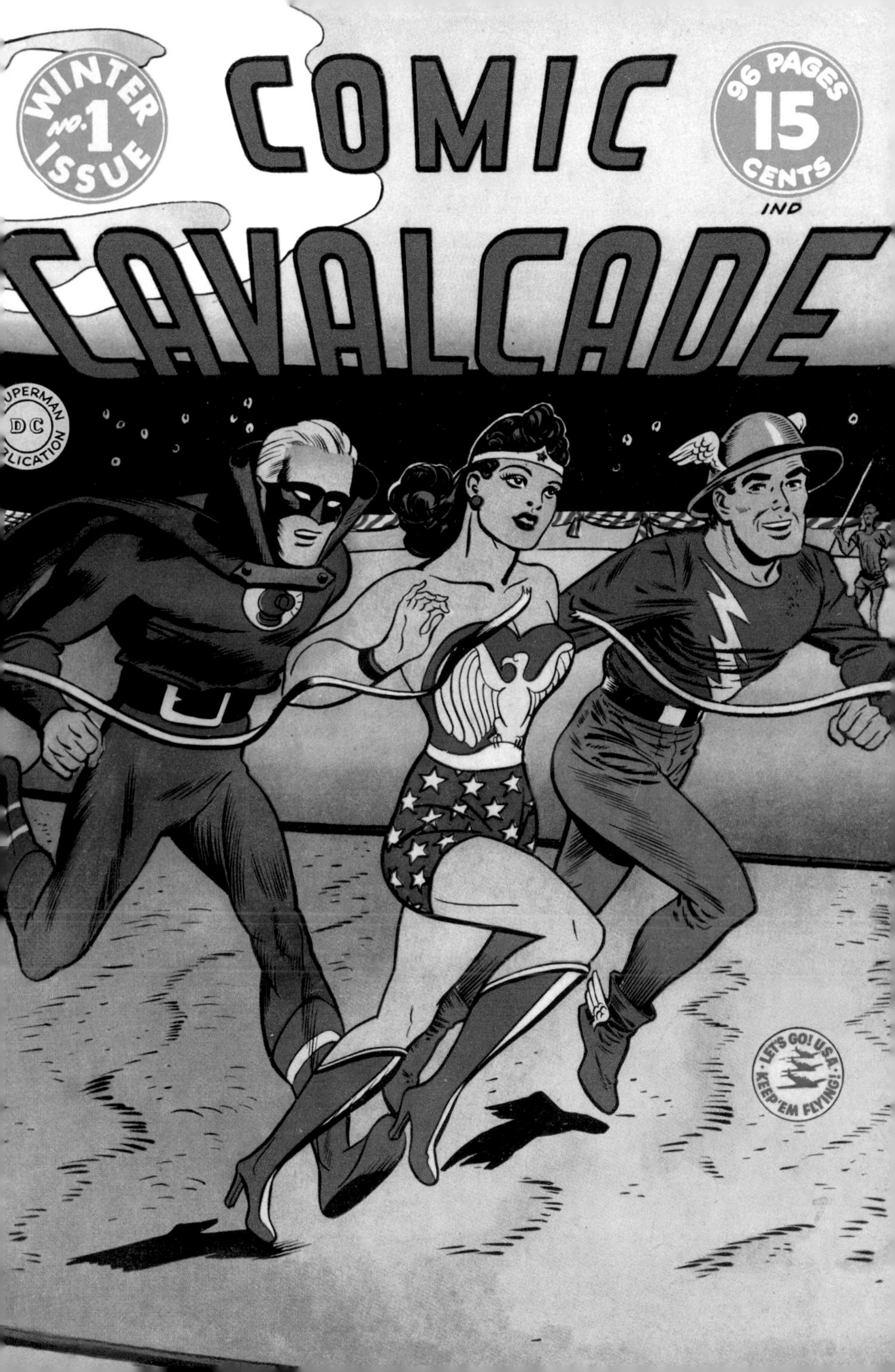

WINTER ISSUE No. 1
COMIC
96 PAGES 15 CENTS
IND
CAVALCADE
SUPERMAN DC PUBLICATION
LET'S GO! U.S.A. KEEP 'EM FLYING!

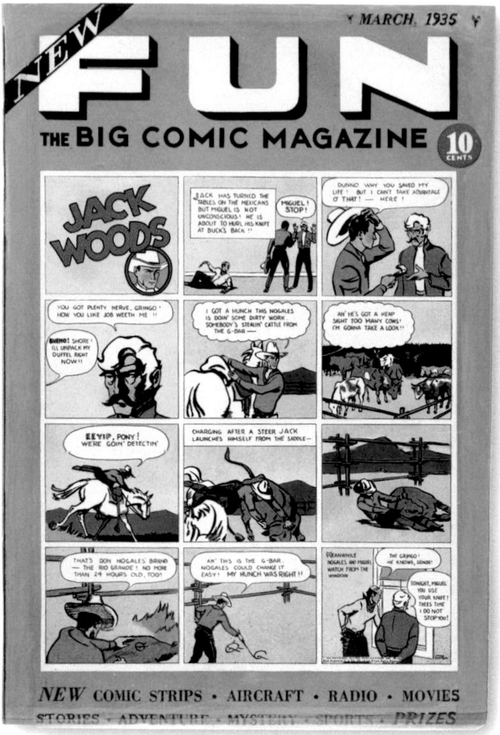
NEW
MARCH, 1935
FUN
THE BIG COMIC MAGAZINE
10 CENTS
JACK WOODS
JACK HAS TURNED THE TABLES ON THE MEXICANS BUT MIGUEL IS NOT UNCONSCIOUS! HE IS ABOUT TO HURL HIS KNIFE AT BUCK'S BACK!!
MIGUEL! STOP!
DUNNO WHY YOU SAVED MY LIFE! BUT I CAN'T TAKE ADVANTAGE O' THAT! — HERE!
YOU GOT PLENTY NERVE, GRINGO! HOW YOU LIKE JOB WEETH ME !!
BUENO! SHORE! I'LL UNPACK MY DUFFEL RIGHT NOW!!
I GOT A HUNCH THIS NOGALES IS DOIN' SOME DIRTY WORK. SOMEBODY'S STEALIN' CATTLE FROM THE G-BAR —
AN' HE'S GOT A HEAP SIGHT TOO MANY COWS! I'M GONNA TAKE A LOOK!!
EEYIP, PONY! WE'RE GOIN' DETECTIN'
CHARGING AFTER A STEER JACK LAUNCHES HIMSELF FROM THE SADDLE—
THAT'S DON NOGALES' BRAND — THE RIO GRANDE! NO MORE THAN 24 HOURS OLD, TOO!
AN' THIS IS THE G-BAR. NOGALES COULD CHANGE IT EASY! MY HUNCH WAS RIGHT!!
MEANWHILE NOGALES AND MIGUEL WATCH FROM THE WINDOW
THE GRINGO! HE KNOWS, SENOR!
TONIGHT, MIGUEL YOU USE YOUR KNIFE! THEES TIME I DO NOT STOP YOU!
NEW COMIC STRIPS • AIRCRAFT • RADIO • MOVIES
STORIES • ADVENTURE • MYSTERY • SPORTS • PRIZES

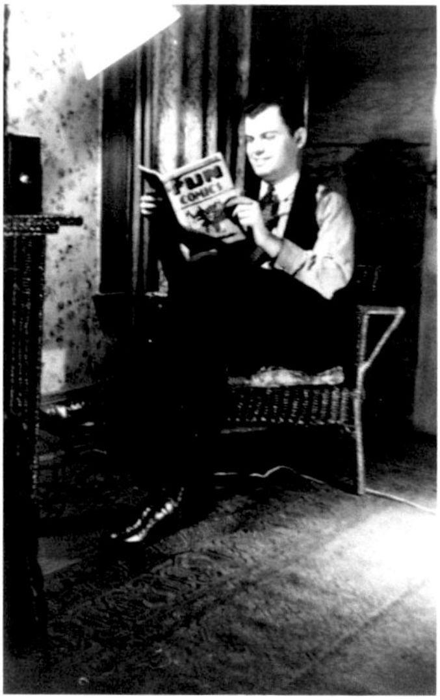
FUN COMICS

COMIC CAVALCADE No. 1

PREVIOUS SPREAD: *Cover art, Frank Harry, winter 1942–1943.*

NEW FUN No. 2

Cover art, "Jack Woods" one-page installment; script, unknown; pencils and inks, Lyman Anderson. March 1935. Two decades before letter columns, readers had their say. The winner of the popularity poll in *New Fun* No. 1 was published in this issue, and "Don Drake" replaced "Jack Woods" on the cover of *New Fun* No. 3.

MORE FUN

Unidentified man reads an early issue of More Fun, *1937.*

NEW FUN No. 3

Cover art, "Don Drake on the Planet Saro" one-page installment; script, Ken Fitch; pencils and inks, Clem Gretter. April 1935.

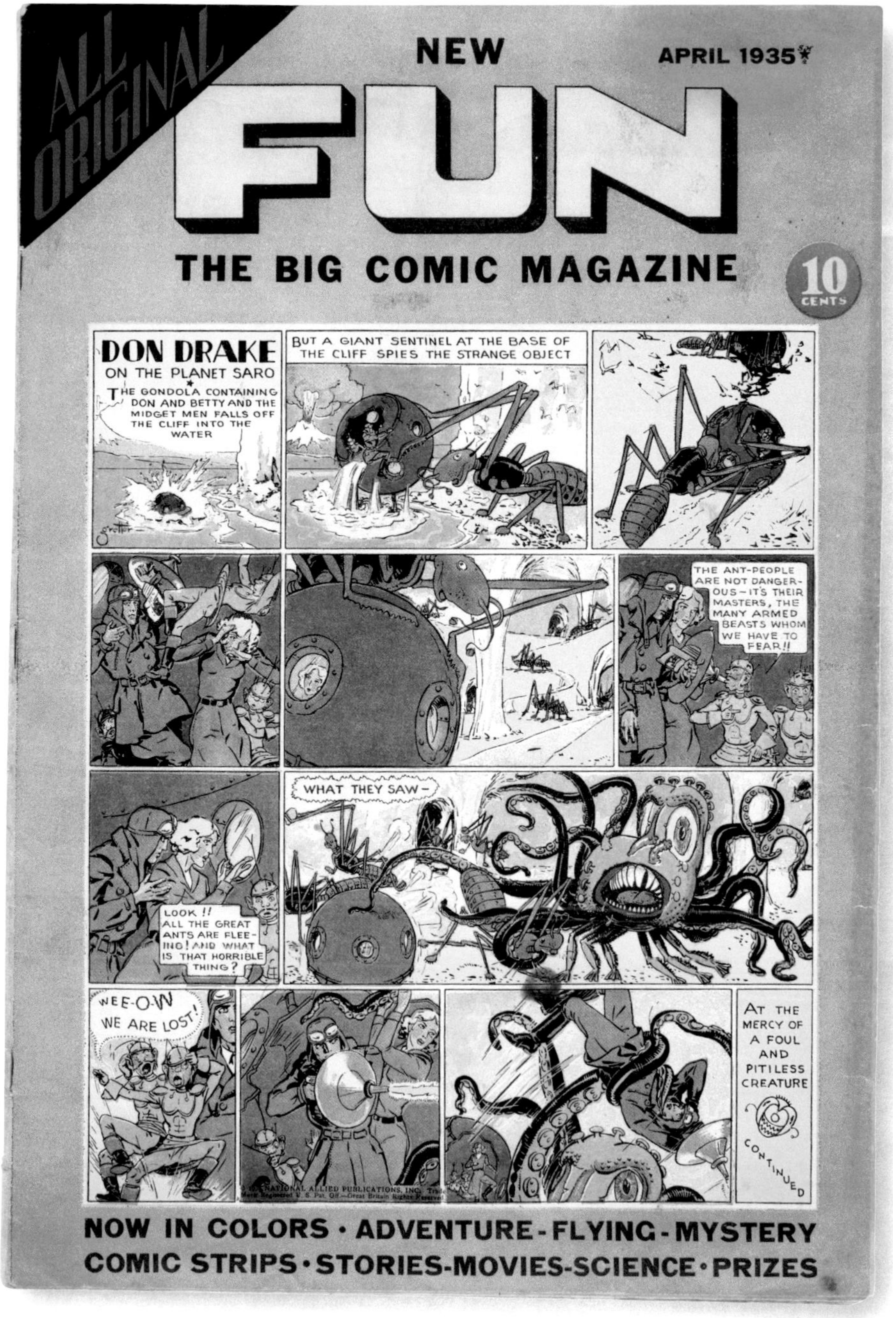

ALL ORIGINAL
NEW
APRIL 1935
FUN
THE BIG COMIC MAGAZINE
10 CENTS
DON DRAKE
ON THE PLANET SARO
THE GONDOLA CONTAINING DON AND BETTY AND THE MIDGET MEN FALLS OFF THE CLIFF INTO THE WATER
BUT A GIANT SENTINEL AT THE BASE OF THE CLIFF SPIES THE STRANGE OBJECT
THE ANT-PEOPLE ARE NOT DANGEROUS – IT'S THEIR MASTERS, THE MANY ARMED BEASTS WHOM WE HAVE TO FEAR!!
WHAT THEY SAW –
LOOK !! ALL THE GREAT ANTS ARE FLEEING! AND WHAT IS THAT HORRIBLE THING?
WEE-O-W WE ARE LOST!
AT THE MERCY OF A FOUL AND PITILESS CREATURE
CONTINUED
NOW IN COLORS · ADVENTURE - FLYING - MYSTERY
COMIC STRIPS · STORIES - MOVIES - SCIENCE · PRIZES

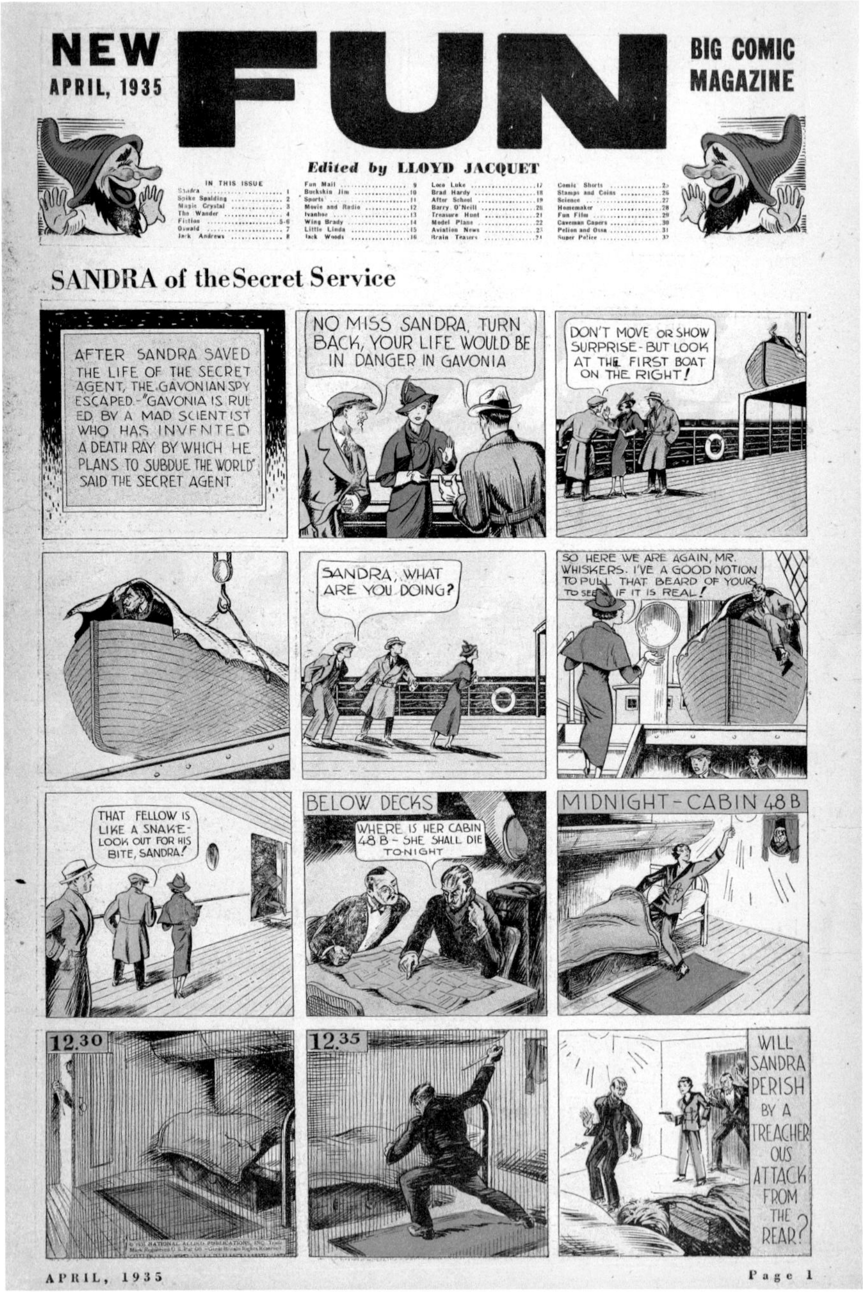

NEW FUN

APRIL, 1935

BIG COMIC MAGAZINE

***Edited by* LLOYD JACQUET**

IN THIS ISSUE

SANDRA of the Secret Service

AFTER SANDRA SAVED THE LIFE OF THE SECRET AGENT, THE GAVONIAN SPY ESCAPED.-"GAVONIA IS RULED BY A MAD SCIENTIST WHO HAS INVENTED A DEATH RAY BY WHICH HE PLANS TO SUBDUE THE WORLD" SAID THE SECRET AGENT.
NO MISS SANDRA, TURN BACK, YOUR LIFE WOULD BE IN DANGER IN GAVONIA
DON'T MOVE OR SHOW SURPRISE - BUT LOOK AT THE FIRST BOAT ON THE RIGHT!
SANDRA, WHAT ARE YOU DOING?
SO HERE WE ARE AGAIN, MR. WHISKERS. I'VE A GOOD NOTION TO PULL THAT BEARD OF YOURS TO SEE IF IT IS REAL!
THAT FELLOW IS LIKE A SNAKE - LOOK OUT FOR HIS BITE, SANDRA!
BELOW DECKS
WHERE IS HER CABIN 48 B - SHE SHALL DIE TO-NIGHT
MIDNIGHT - CABIN 48 B
12.30
12.35
WILL SANDRA PERISH BY A TREACHEROUS ATTACK FROM THE REAR?

APRIL, 1935 Page 1

NEW FUN No. 3

Interior, "Sandra of the Secret Service" one-page installment; script and art, Charles Flanders. April 1935.
Feisty females were a staple of the early National titles. Sandra, one name only, joined such other adventurers as "Dale Daring" and "Hope Hazard, G-Woman" in tales of a poor man's — or woman's — "Jane Arden," a popular newspaper strip of the day.

MORE FUN Nos. 7 & 8

BELOW LEFT: *Cover art, "Little Linda" one-page installment; script and art, Whitney Ellsworth. January 1936.*
BELOW RIGHT: *Cover art, "Spike" one-page installment; script and art, Vin Sullivan. February 1936.* A work in progress: *New Fun* was renamed *More Fun* with issue No. 7. Of the first six *New Funs*, four cover-featured adventure strips. Now, a decidedly humorous and younger-skewing feature took the cover spot, as if to test who was reading.

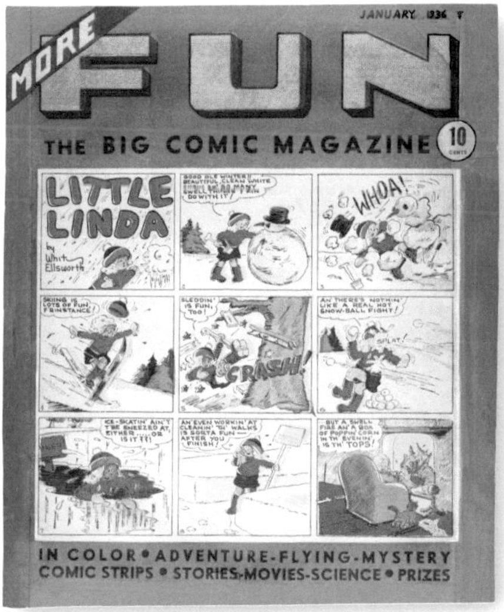
JANUARY 1936
MORE
FUN
THE BIG COMIC MAGAZINE
10 CENTS
LITTLE LINDA
by Whit Ellsworth
WHOA!
SKIING IS LOTS OF FUN, F'RINSTANCE!
SLEDDIN' IS FUN, TOO!
CRASH!
AN' THERE'S NOTHIN' LIKE A REAL HOT SNOW-BALL FIGHT!
SPLAT!
ICE-SKATIN' AIN'T T'BE SNEEZED AT, EITHER .....OR IS IT ??!
AN' EVEN WORKIN' AT CLEANIN' TH' WALKS IS SORTA FUN — AFTER YOU FINISH!
BUT A SWELL FIRE AN' A BOX OF POPPIN' CORN IN TH' EVENIN' IS TH' TOPS!
IN COLOR • ADVENTURE-FLYING-MYSTERY
COMIC STRIPS • STORIES-MOVIES-SCIENCE • PRIZES

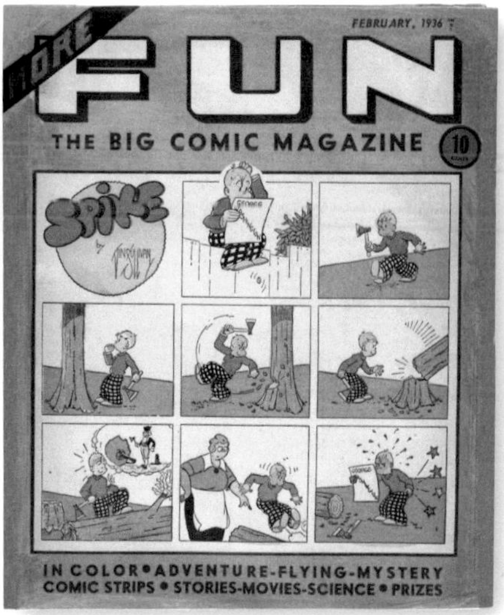
FEBRUARY, 1936
MORE
FUN
THE BIG COMIC MAGAZINE
10
SPIKE
IN COLOR • ADVENTURE-FLYING-MYSTERY
COMIC STRIPS • STORIES-MOVIES-SCIENCE • PRIZES

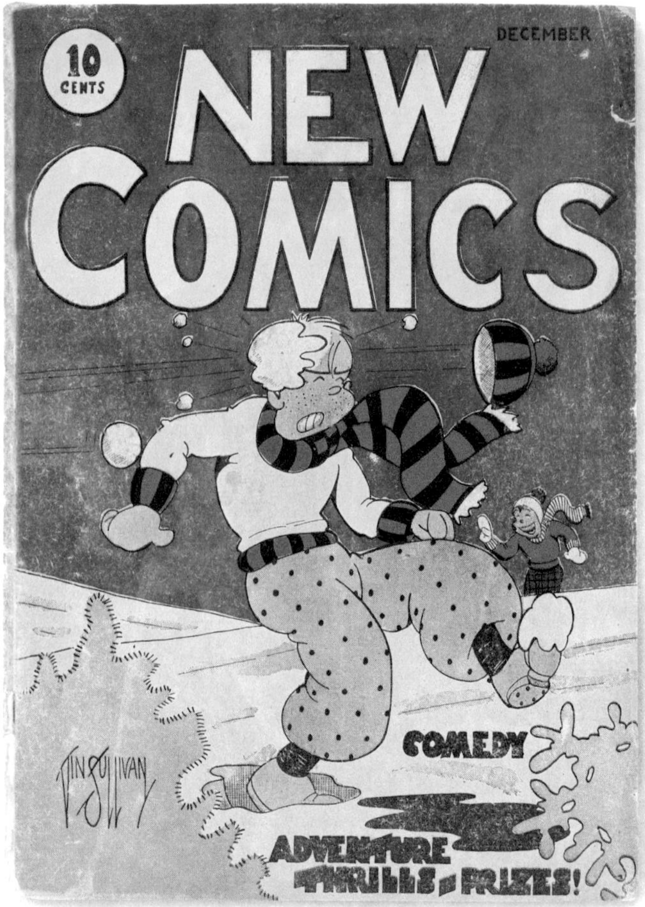
10 CENTS
DECEMBER
NEW COMICS
VIN SULLIVAN
COMEDY
ADVENTURE
THRILLS & PRIZES!

NEW COMICS No. 1

Cover art, Vin Sullivan. December 1935. With the publication of its second title in 1935, DC continued to grow, adding some 40,000 more issues in the next 75 years.

NEW ADVENTURE COMICS No. 26

Interior, "The Adventures of Rusty and His Pals"; script and art, Bob Kane. May 1938. "This five-page strip didn't advance humor cartoonist Bob (Batman) Kane's career until it became high adventure, complete with a logo that imitated 'Terry and the Pirates,' and a better writer." —Bill Finger

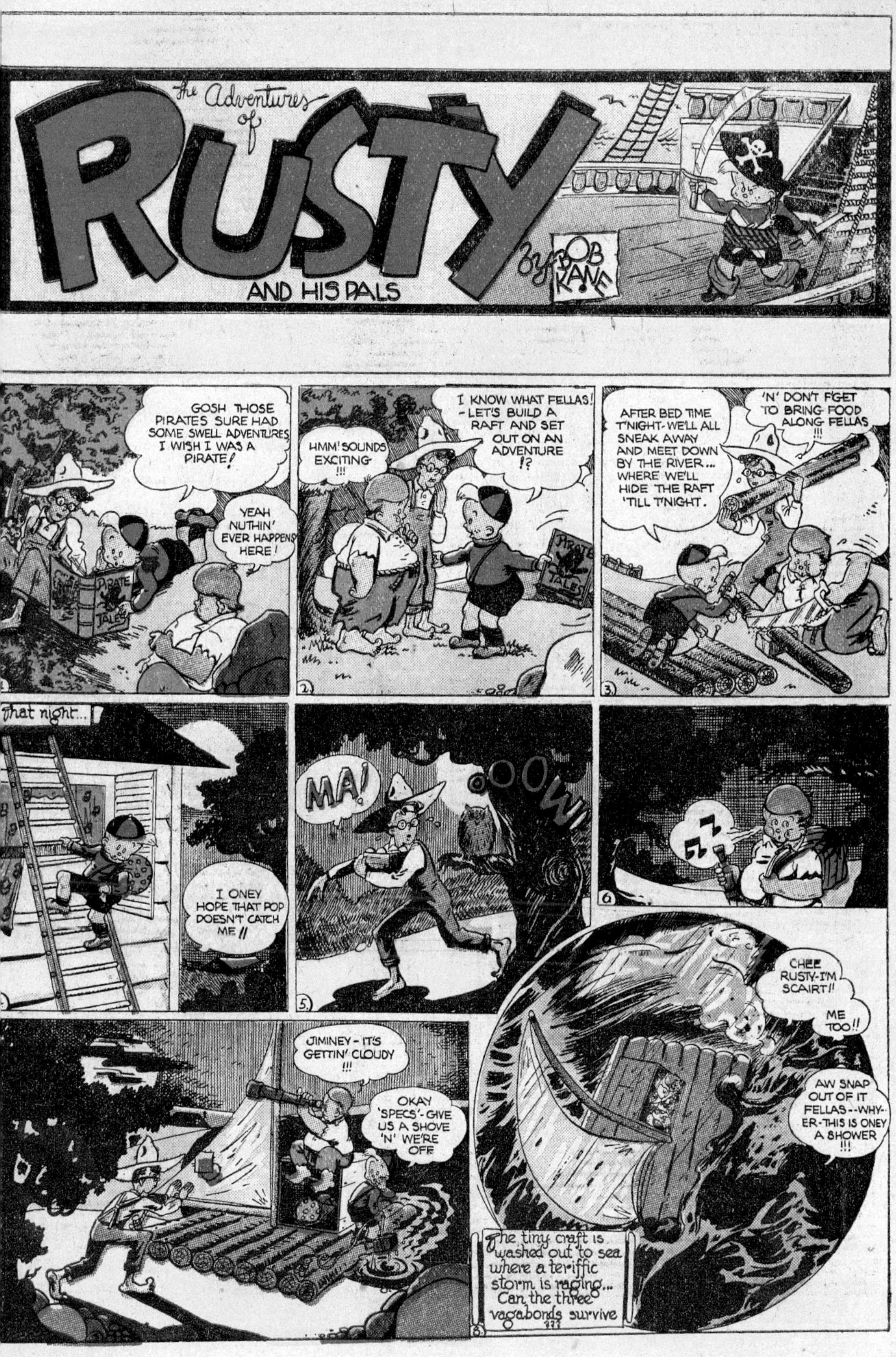
the Adventures of
RUSTY
AND HIS PALS
by BOB KANE
GOSH THOSE PIRATES SURE HAD SOME SWELL ADVENTURES I WISH I WAS A PIRATE!
YEAH NUTHIN' EVER HAPPENS HERE!
PIRATE TALES
HMM! SOUNDS EXCITING !!!
I KNOW WHAT FELLAS! - LET'S BUILD A RAFT AND SET OUT ON AN ADVENTURE !?
PIRATE TALES
AFTER BED TIME T'NIGHT - WE'LL ALL SNEAK AWAY AND MEET DOWN BY THE RIVER... WHERE WE'LL HIDE THE RAFT 'TILL T'NIGHT.
'N' DON'T F'GET TO BRING FOOD ALONG FELLAS !!!
That night...
I ONEY HOPE THAT POP DOESN'T CATCH ME!!
MA!
OOOW!
Z Z
JIMINEY - IT'S GETTIN' CLOUDY !!!
OKAY 'SPECS'- GIVE US A SHOVE 'N' WE'RE OFF
CHEE RUSTY-I'M SCAIRT!!
ME TOO!!
AW SNAP OUT OF IT FELLAS--WHY-ER-THIS IS ONEY A SHOWER !!!
The tiny craft is washed out to sea where a teriffic storm is raging... Can the three vagabonds survive ???

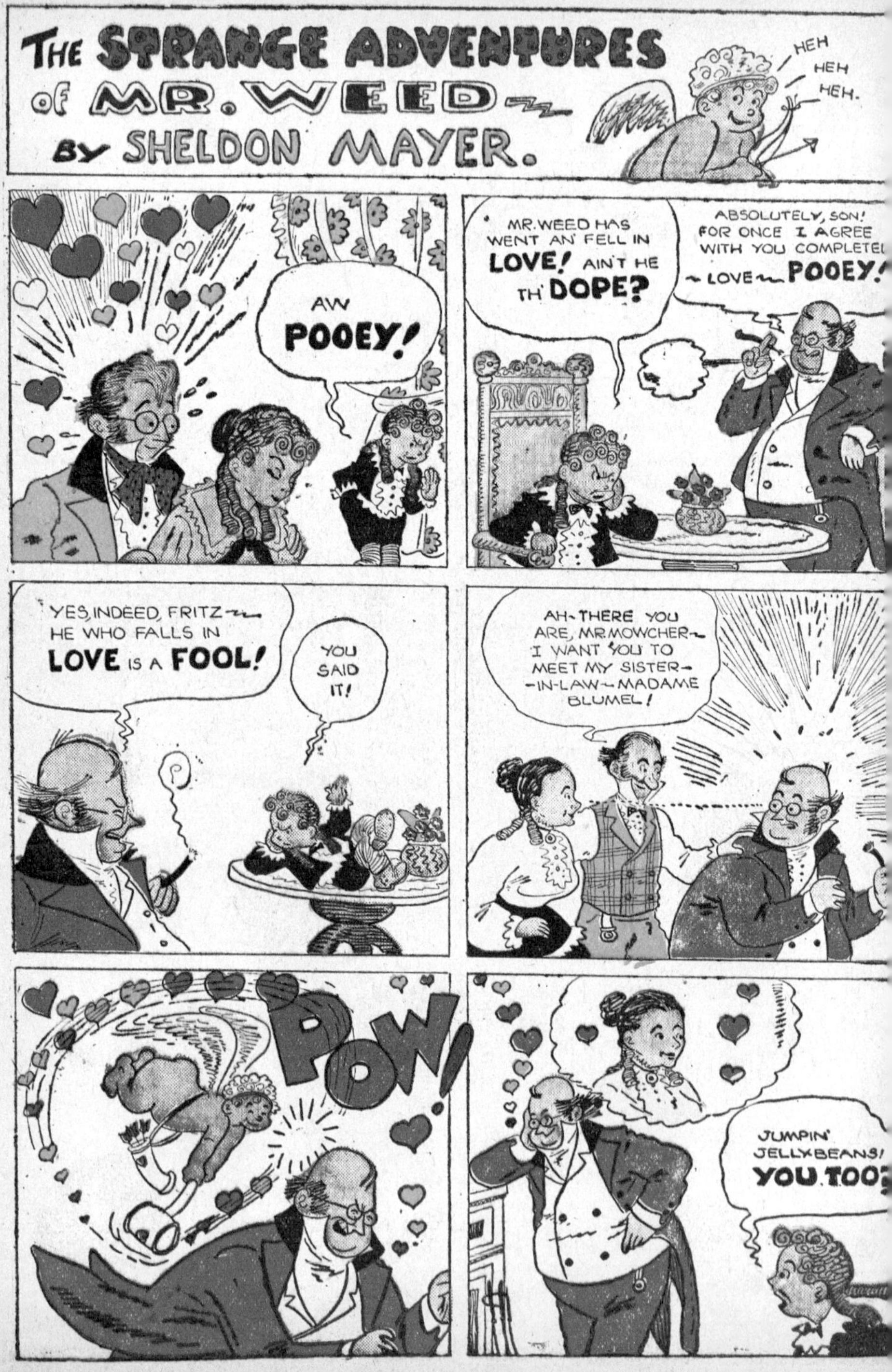
THE STRANGE ADVENTURES of MR. WEED
BY SHELDON MAYER.
HEH HEH HEH.
AW POOEY!
MR. WEED HAS WENT AN' FELL IN LOVE! AIN'T HE TH' DOPE?
ABSOLUTELY, SON! FOR ONCE I AGREE WITH YOU COMPLETEL- LOVE POOEY!
YES, INDEED, FRITZ HE WHO FALLS IN LOVE IS A FOOL!
YOU SAID IT!
AH-THERE YOU ARE, MR. MOWCHER- I WANT YOU TO MEET MY SISTER-IN-LAW- MADAME BLUMEL!
POW!
JUMPIN' JELLYBEANS! YOU TOO

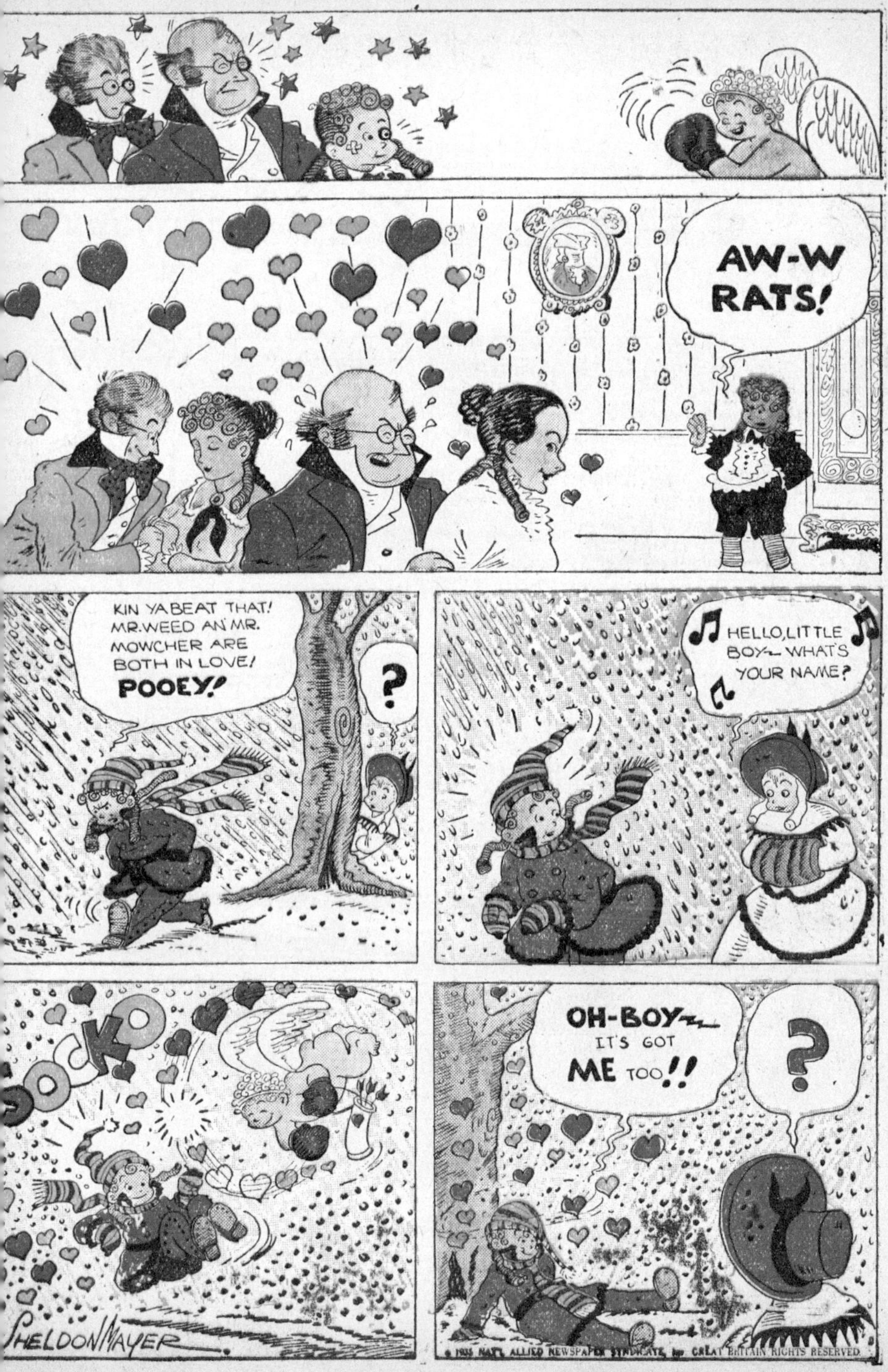
AW-W RATS!
KIN YA BEAT THAT! MR. WEED AN' MR. MOWCHER ARE BOTH IN LOVE! POOEY!
?
HELLO, LITTLE BOY— WHAT'S YOUR NAME?
SOCKO
OH-BOY— IT'S GOT ME TOO!!
?
SHELDON MAYER
© 1935 NAT'L ALLIED NEWSPAPER SYNDICATE, Inc GREAT BRITAIN RIGHTS RESERVED

NEW COMICS No. 3

PREVIOUS SPREAD: *Interiors, "The Strange Adventures of Mr. Weed" serial: script and art, Sheldon Mayer. February 1936.* Paradoxically, Mayer's lifelong relationship with DC began because Wheeler-Nicholson could not pay him. As an alternative to freelancing, Mayer began working for M. C. Gaines, who later hired Mayer as editor-in-chief of the All-American line. Neither *Scribbly* nor *Sugar and Spike*, the humor titles for which Mayer is best remembered, displayed the surrealism of the curiously named "Mr. Weed," however.

NEW BOOK OF COMICS No. 1

Cover art, various artists in panels excerpted from interior reprints, 1937. If 1935's *Big Book of Fun Comics* sold, why not a *New Book of Comics*? The decision to issue another reprint collection must have been sound, as a second volume followed, cover-dated spring 1938.

NEW ADVENTURE COMICS No. 18

Cover art, Creig Flessel, August 1937. The dynamic composition of this early action scene demonstrates why Flessel adapted easily to super heroes, pencilling "The Sandman" in the '40s and contributing regularly to *Superboy* until 1959.

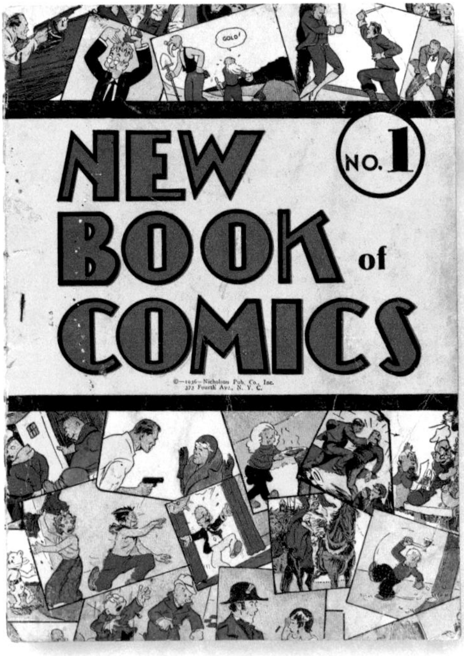
GOLD!
NEW BOOK of COMICS
NO. 1
©—1936—Nicholson Pub. Co., Inc.
373 Fourth Ave., N. Y. C.

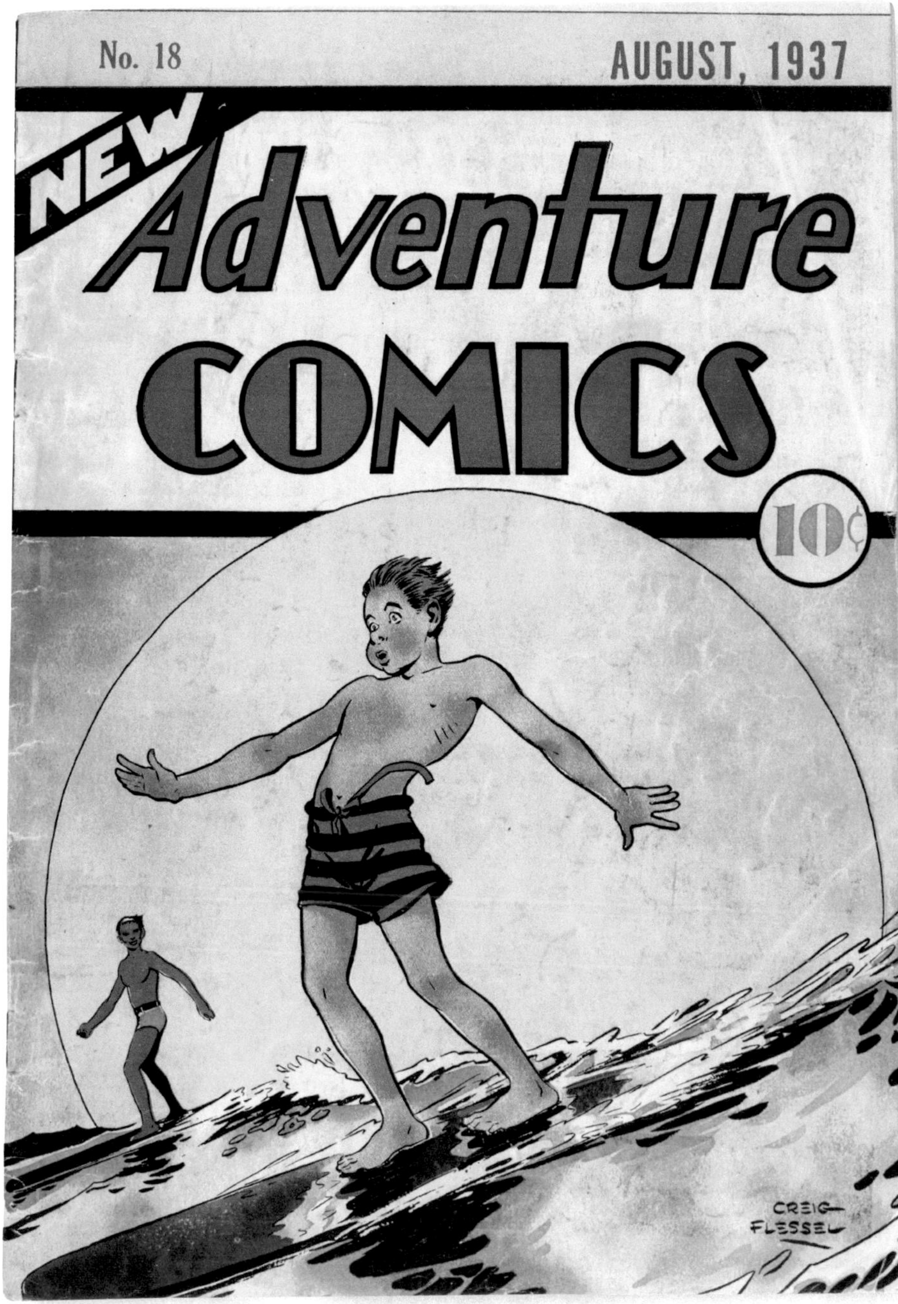
No. 18
AUGUST, 1937
NEW
Adventure
COMICS
10¢
CREIG
FLESSEL

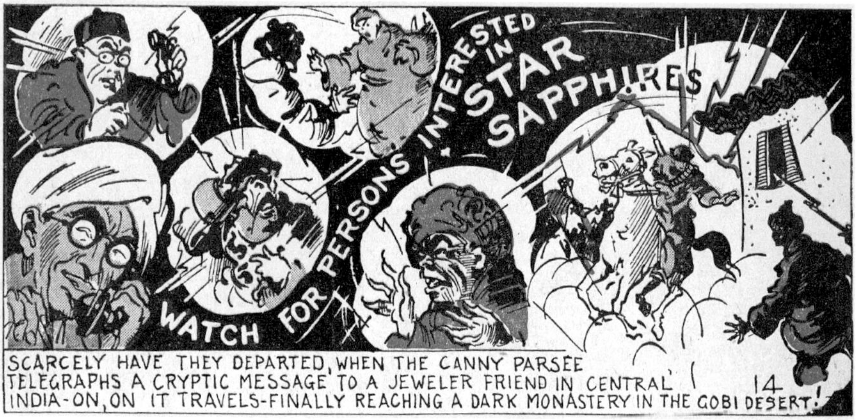
WATCH FOR PERSONS INTERESTED IN STAR SAPPHIRES
SCARCELY HAVE THEY DEPARTED, WHEN THE CANNY PARSEE TELEGRAPHS A CRYPTIC MESSAGE TO A JEWELER FRIEND IN CENTRAL INDIA-ON, ON IT TRAVELS-FINALLY REACHING A DARK MONASTERY IN THE GOBI DESERT!
14

"The smoke was thicker than you'd see in the comics.... It was a crashing place for everybody: transients, cartoonists, Nicholson's friends, people waiting at a job or killing time, salesmen."

—CREIG FLESSEL

NEW ADVENTURE COMICS No. 17

Interior, "The Monastery of the Blue God" serial; script, Malcolm Wheeler-Nicholson; pencils and inks, Munson Paddock. July 1937. The Major's titles were a curious hodgepodge of state-of-the-art graphic storytelling and antiquated techniques, cobbled together as they were from sample strips by new talent trying to break into newspaper syndication and veterans in the twilight of their careers. Paddock, then 51, was one of the latter. Since 1907 he had been rendering in a style influenced by Charles Dana Gibson, and his approach to formal elements such as balloons and captions was more reminiscent of Richard F. Outcault than Chester Gould.

NEW ADVENTURE COMICS No. 22

Interior, "G-Woman"; script and art, unknown. December 1937. Not to be confused with Hope Hazard, just plain "G-Woman" was June Justis, a federal investigator whose adventures were even more moribund than Hazard's. By now it was becoming clear that the two- and three-page serialized format, inspired by newspaper strips, was vitiating the stories' suspense, especially when months elapsed between installments.

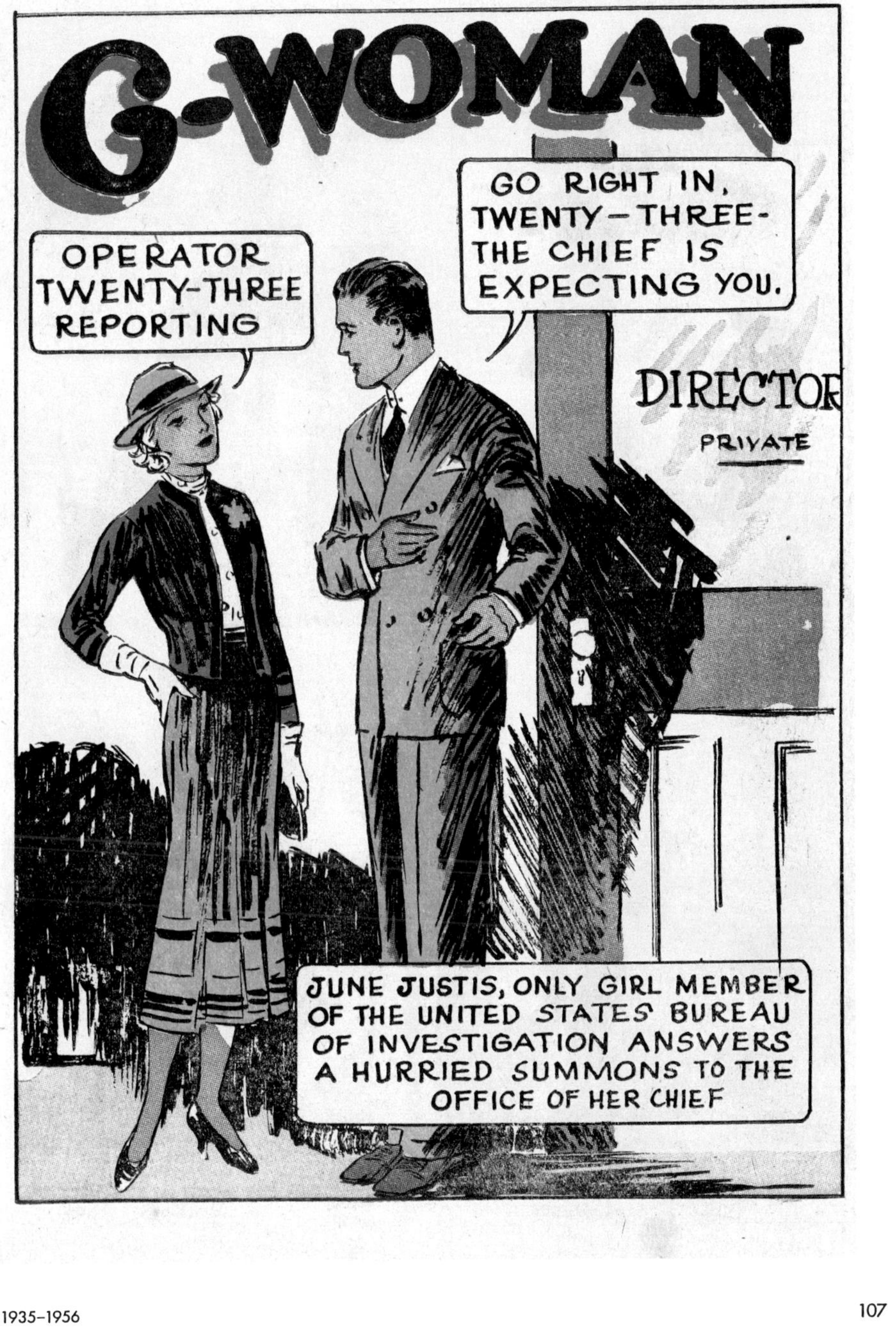
G-WOMAN
OPERATOR TWENTY-THREE REPORTING
GO RIGHT IN, TWENTY-THREE- THE CHIEF IS EXPECTING YOU.
DIRECTOR
PRIVATE
JUNE JUSTIS, ONLY GIRL MEMBER OF THE UNITED STATES BUREAU OF INVESTIGATION ANSWERS A HURRIED SUMMONS TO THE OFFICE OF HER CHIEF

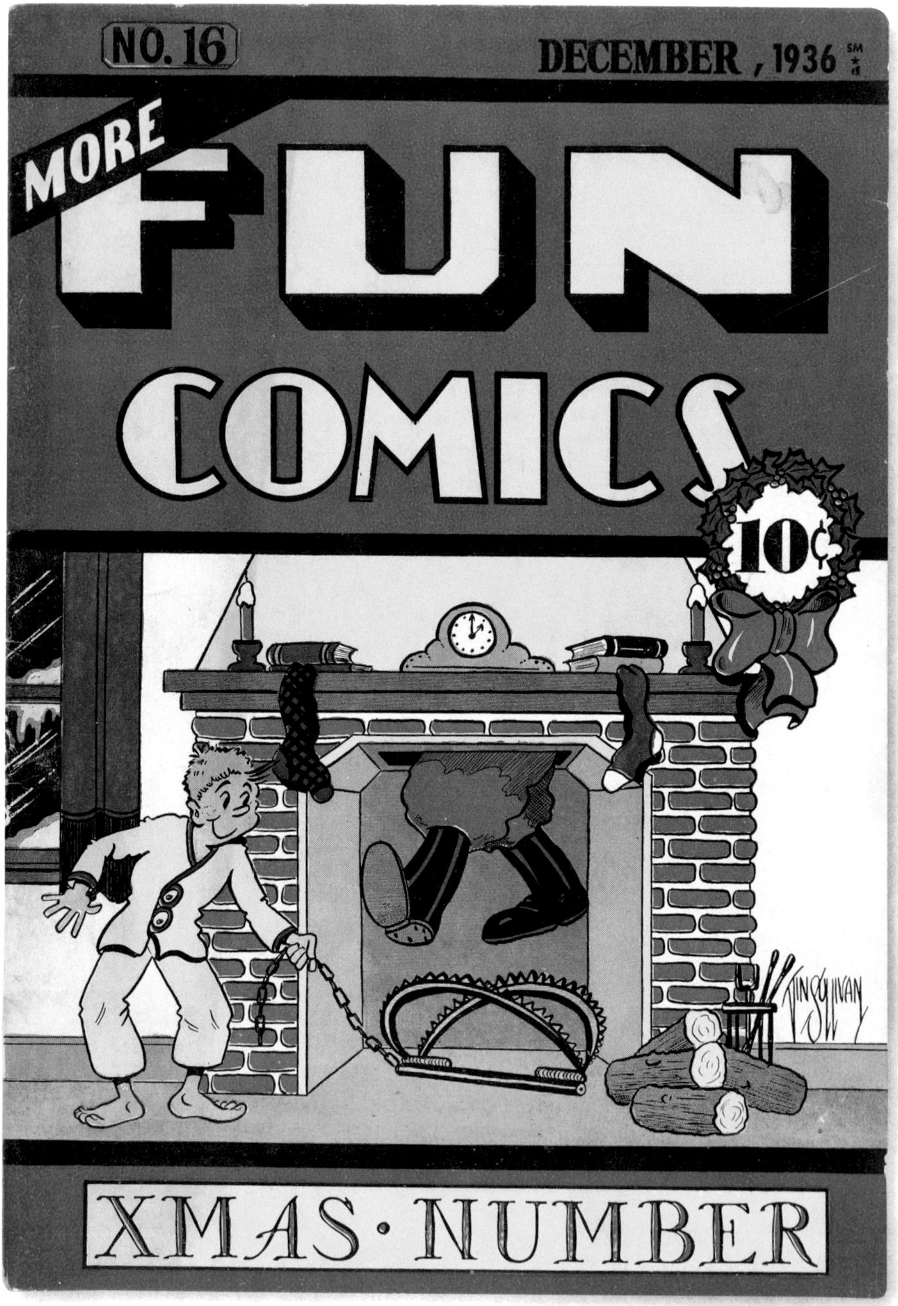
NO. 16
DECEMBER, 1936
MORE
FUN
COMICS
10¢
XMAS · NUMBER

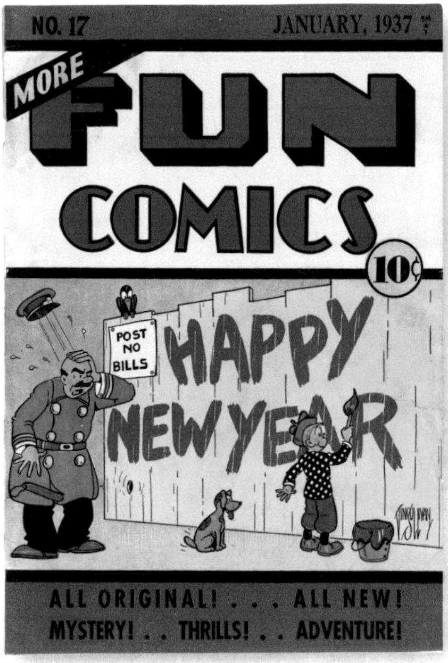
NO. 17
JANUARY, 1937
MORE
FUN
COMICS
10¢
POST
NO
BILLS
HAPPY
NEW YEAR
ALL ORIGINAL! . . . ALL NEW!
MYSTERY! . . THRILLS! . . ADVENTURE!

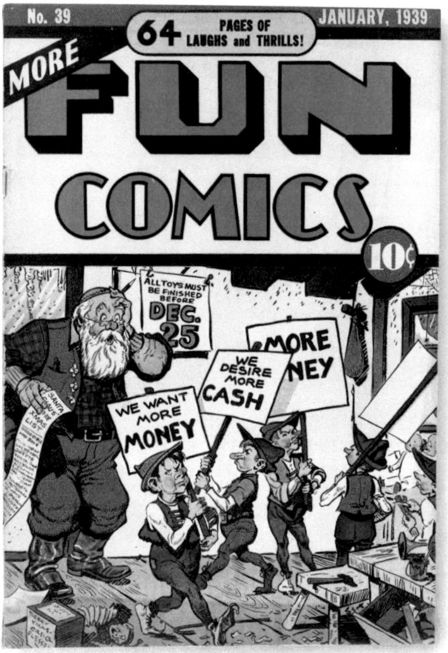
No. 39
64 PAGES OF LAUGHS and THRILLS!
JANUARY, 1939
MORE
FUN
COMICS
10¢
ALL TOYS MUST BE FINISHED BEFORE DEC. 25
WE WANT MORE MONEY
WE DESIRE MORE CASH

MORE FUN COMICS No. 16

Cover art, Vin Sullivan, December 1936. The last issue of the final year of Wheeler-Nicholson's vision. By the end of 1937 the Major would be gone, forced out and handed a consolation prize of a percentage of this title's profits for 10 years. Almost exactly to the date — specifically, November 1947 (the 127th issue) — *More Fun* would follow its creator into comic book oblivion.

MORE FUN COMICS No. 17

Cover art, Vin Sullivan, January 1937. As Jack Liebowitz steered *More Fun* toward an emphasis on adventure over humor, relying more heavily on the greater sophistication of talent like Flessel and Fred Guardineer, cartoonists such as Sullivan faced a dwindling demand for the light touch exhibited in his seasonal scenes. Sullivan would leave DC in 1940, and eventually found his own comics company, Magazine Enterprises.

MORE FUN COMICS No. 39

Cover art, Creig Flessel, January 1939. Stone Age readers delighted in the masterful rendering Flessel brought to other genres as well. Flessel's last work for the company appeared in *Prez* No. 4 (March 1974).

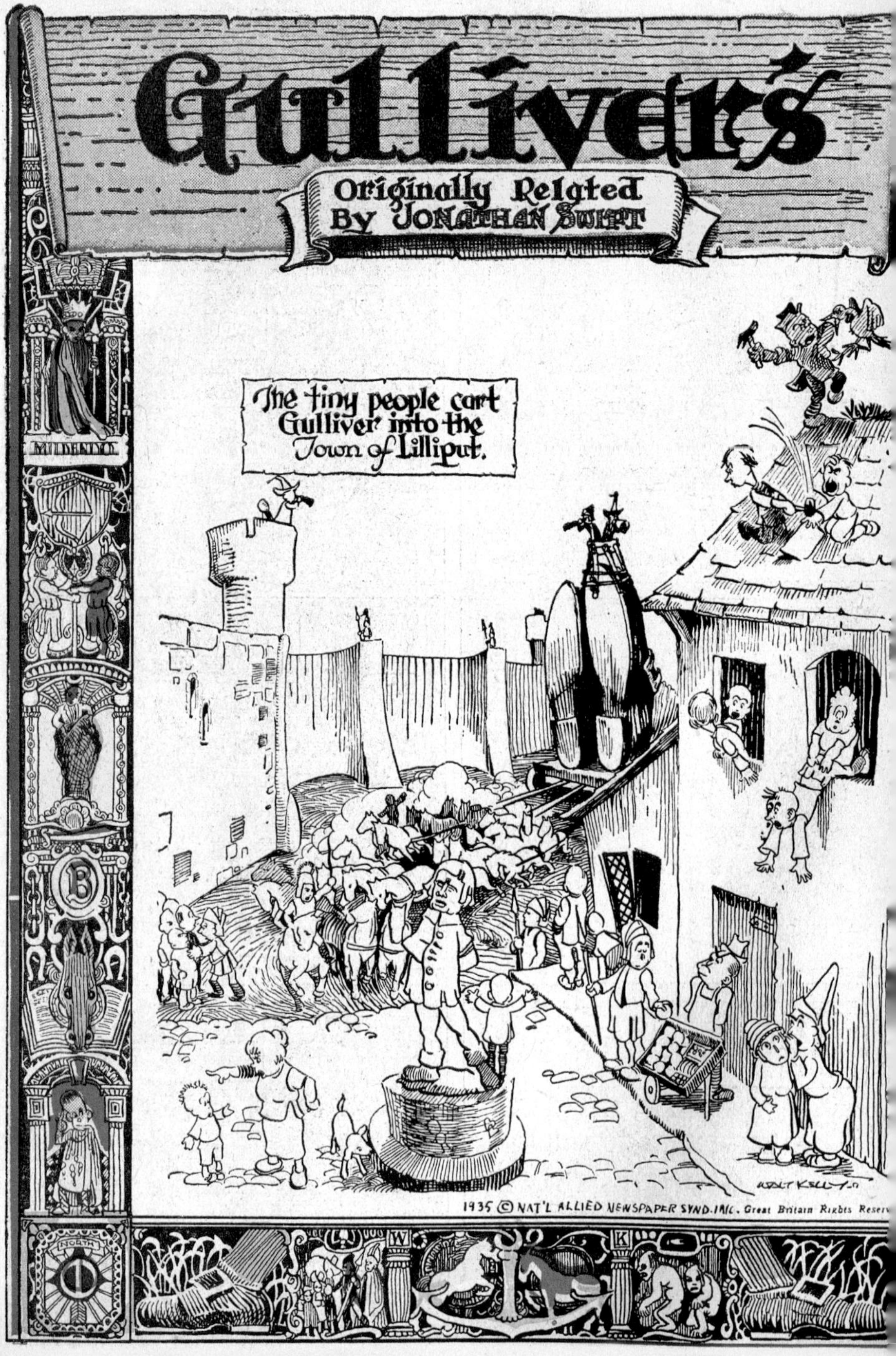
Gulliver's
Originally Related By Jonathan Swift
The tiny people cart Gulliver into the Town of Lilliput.
WALT KELLY
1935 © NAT'L ALLIED NEWSPAPER SYND. INC. Great Britain Rights Reserv

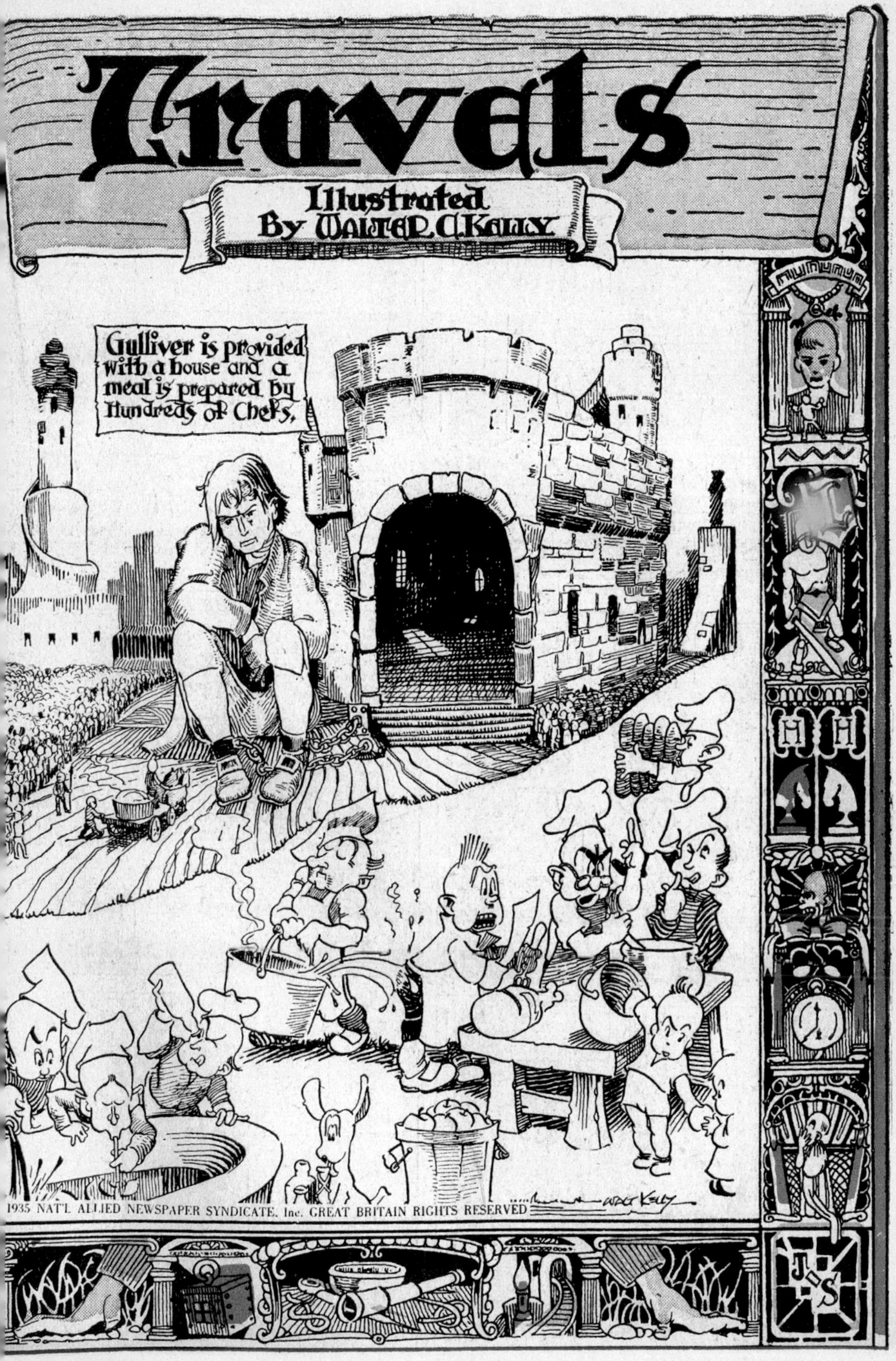
Travels
Illustrated By Walter C. Kelly
Gulliver is provided with a house and a meal is prepared by hundreds of Chefs.
1935 NAT'L ALLIED NEWSPAPER SYNDICATE, Inc. GREAT BRITAIN RIGHTS RESERVED
WALT KELLY

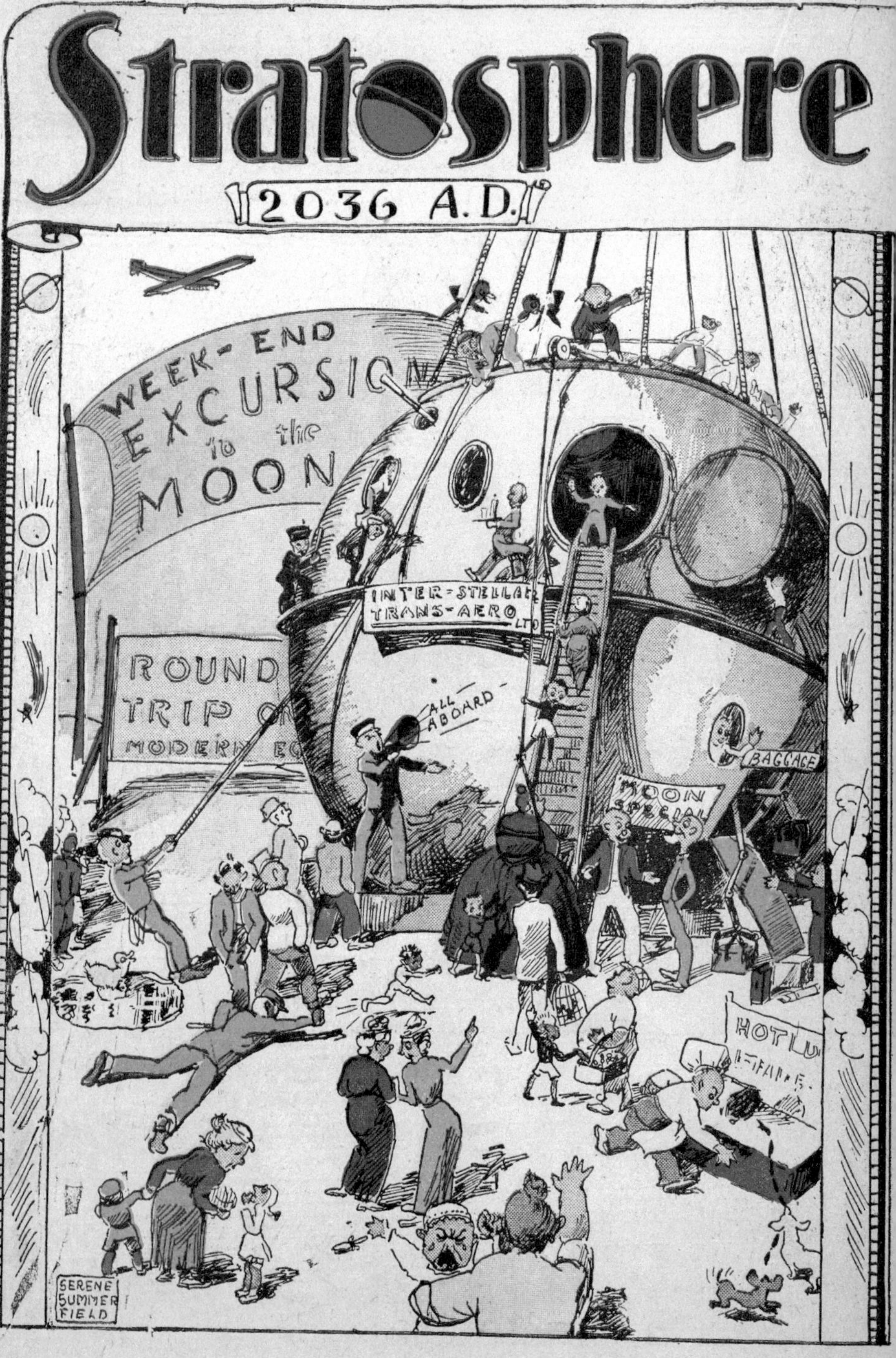
Stratosphere
2036 A.D.
WEEK-END EXCURSIO to the MOON
INTER-STELLAR TRANS-AERO LTD
ROUND TRIP
ALL ABOARD
BAGGAGE
MOON SPECIAL
SERENE SUMMERFIELD

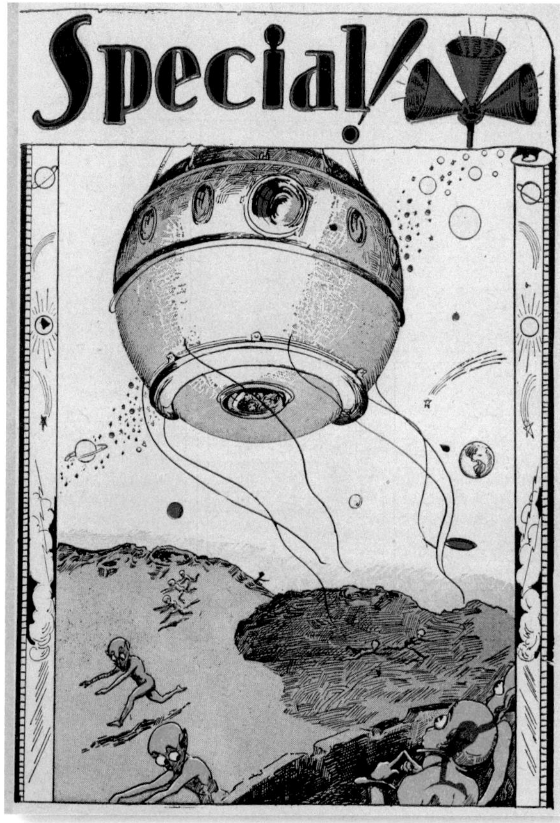
Special!

NEW COMICS No. 2

PREVIOUS SPREAD: *Interiors, "Gulliver's Travels"; script and art, Walt Kelly (adapted from Jonathan Swift). January 1936.* Sholly Mayer claimed to have bonded, on the basis of being "stiffed" by Wheeler-Nicholson, with the soon-to-be Disney animator Kelly. This story was one of the few that he did for DC, some 13 years before the debut of his hugely successful newspaper strip, "Pogo."

NEW COMICS Nos. 4 & 5

THIS SPREAD AND FOLLOWING SPREAD: *Interiors, "Stratosphere Special 2036 A.D."; script and art, Serene Summerfield. March–April and June 1936.* No one today remembers Serene Summerfield, but there must have been a certain lack of serenity among those discovering his—her?—vision of the future, antiquated even by 1930s standards: It owed much more to Jules Verne than *Thrilling Wonder Stories.*

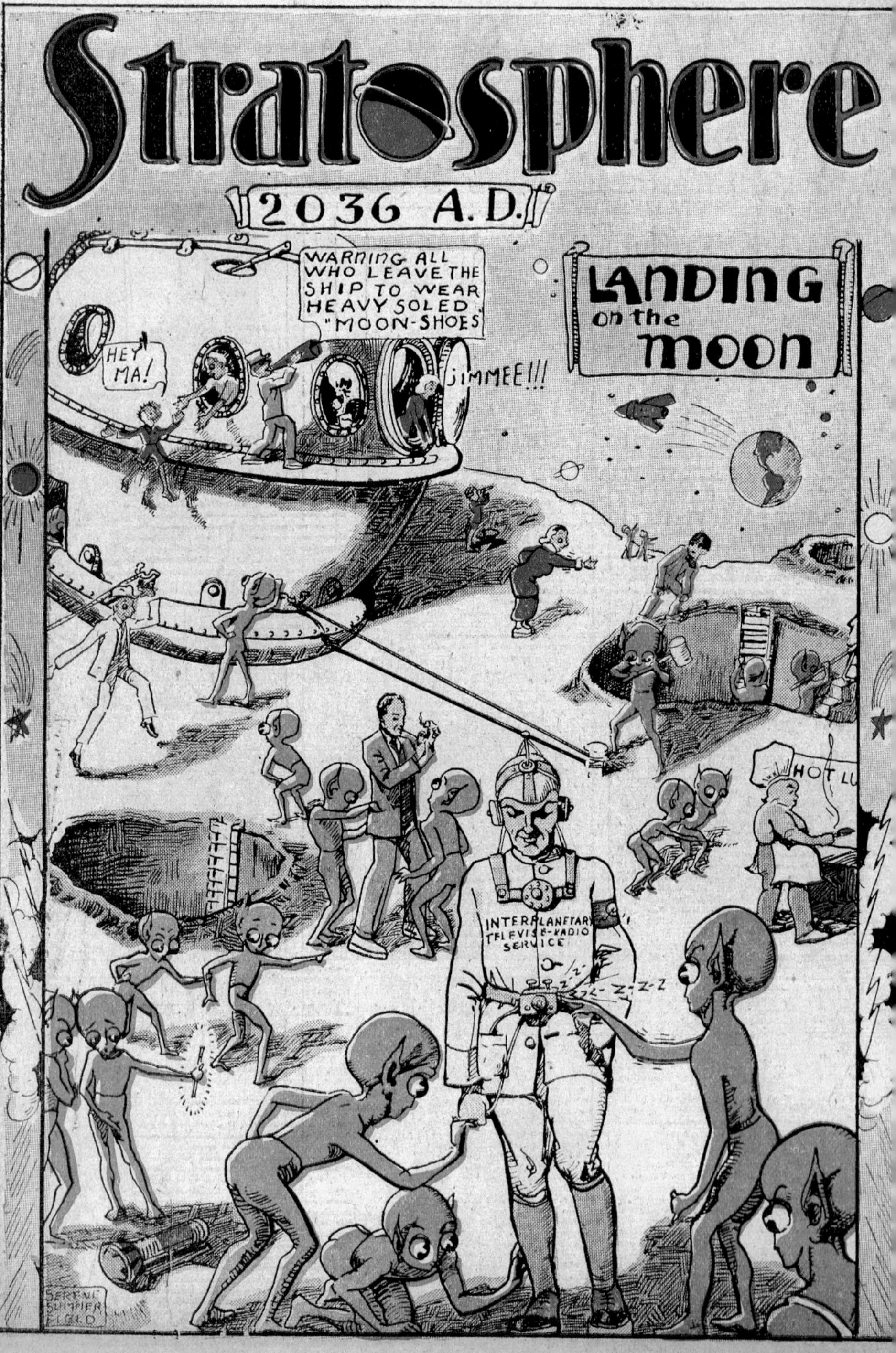
Stratosphere
2036 A.D.
LANDING on the MOON
WARNING ALL WHO LEAVE THE SHIP TO WEAR HEAVY SOLED "MOON-SHOES
HEY MA!
JIMMEE!!!
INTERPLANETARY TELEVISE-RADIO SERVICE
Z-Z-Z
HOT LU

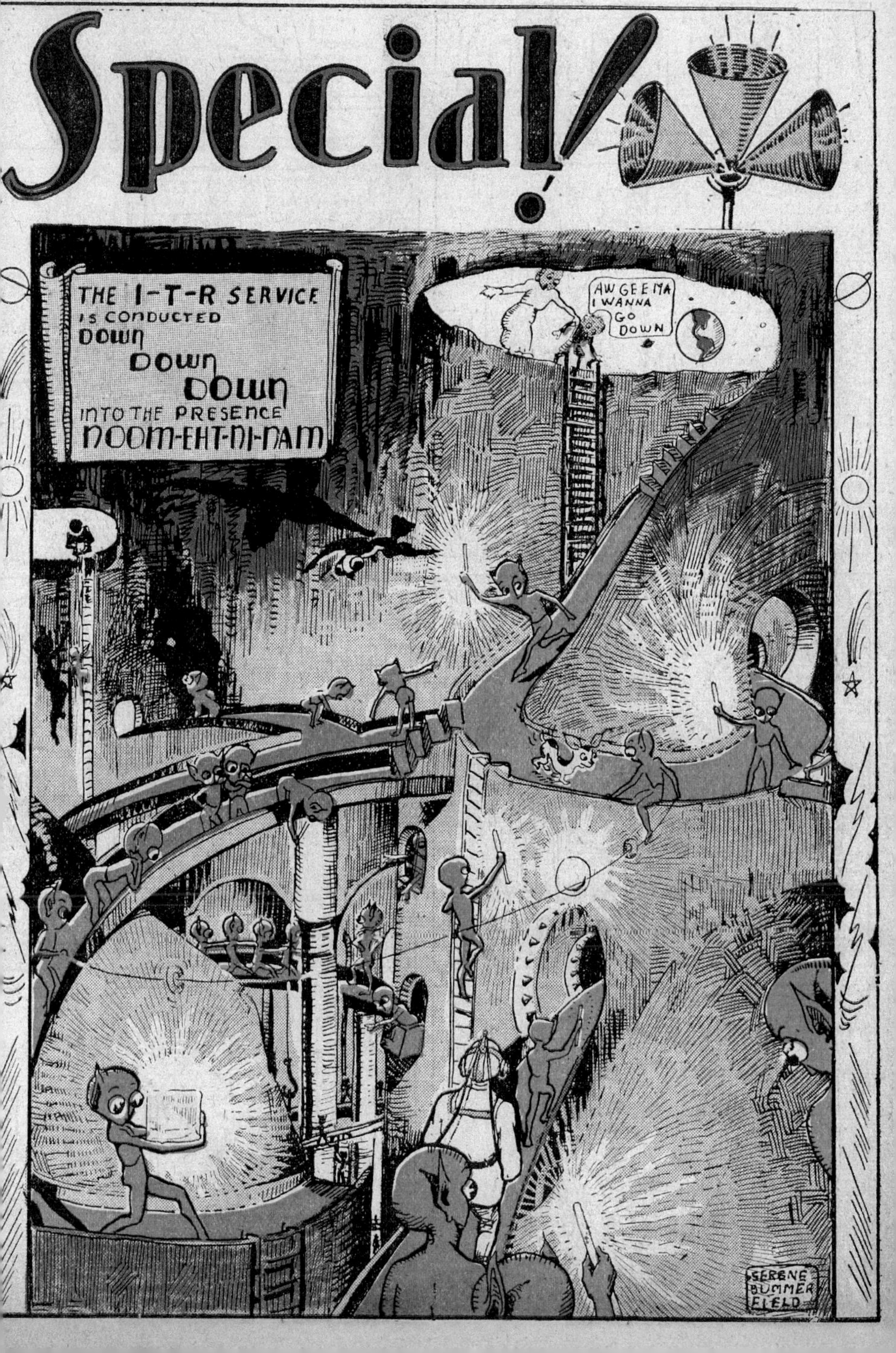
Special!
THE I-T-R SERVICE IS CONDUCTED
DOWN
DOWN
DOWN
INTO THE PRESENCE
NOOM-EHT-NI-NAM
AW GEE MA I WANNA GO DOWN
SERENE SUMMER FIELD

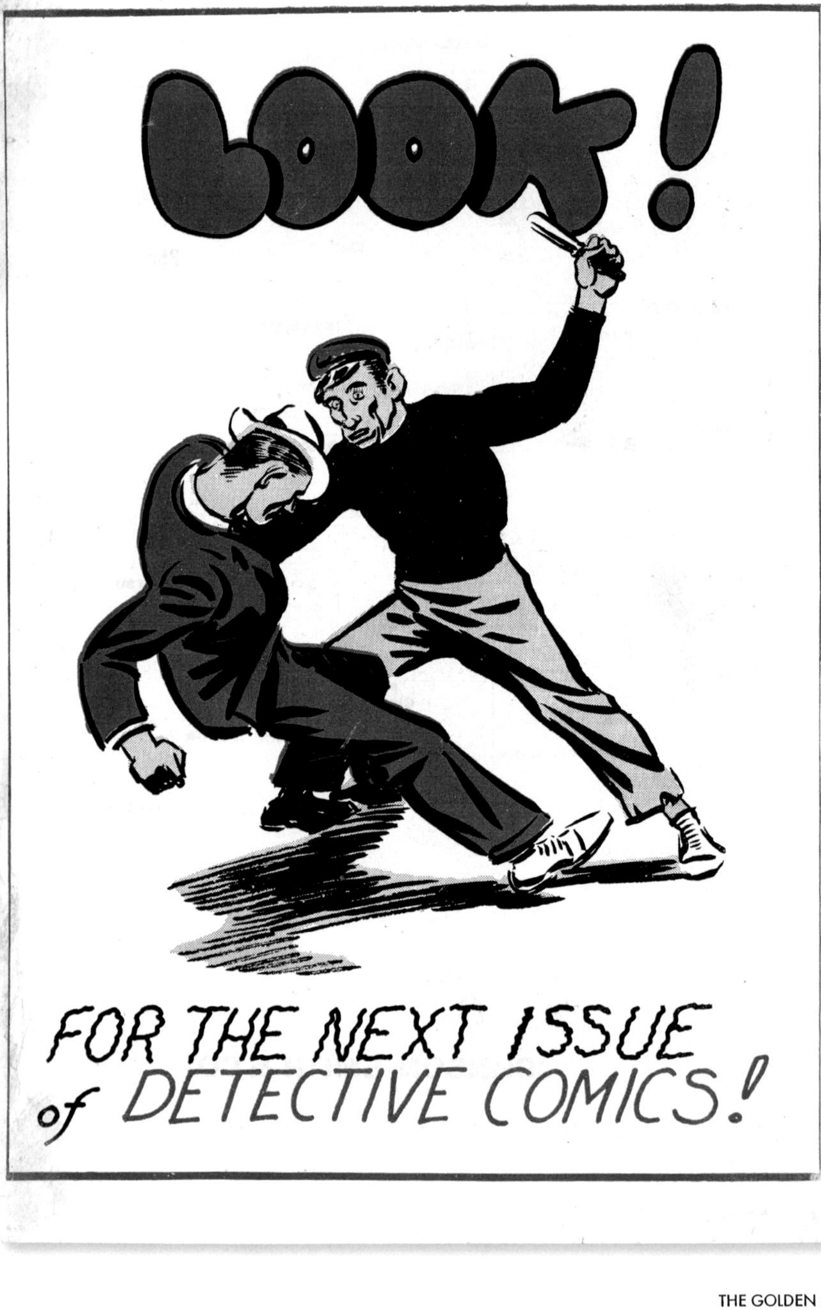
LOOK!
FOR THE NEXT ISSUE
of DETECTIVE COMICS!

DETECTIVE COMICS HOUSE AD

Interior, Detective Comics *No. 3, artist unknown, May 1937.* Using pages in one comic to promote the next issue or even another title from the same company as a "house ad" was a concept that developed slowly in comics, probably because the early editors were uncertain what would be in the next issue, unlike today, when issues are planned out well in advance.

NEW ADVENTURE COMICS No. 16

Cover art, attributed Creig Flessel, June 1937. The third Siegel and Shuster contribution was an obvious appeal to "Dick Tracy" fans, right down to the yellow fedora of its star, Steve Carson. It also facilitated DC's canny adoption of a promotional device that was a staple of children's radio at the time: the fan club, replete with "official" mail-order gear. Siegel and Shuster would repeat this gimmick later with the *Supermen of America,* but without "breaking the fourth wall" quite so blatantly to do it.

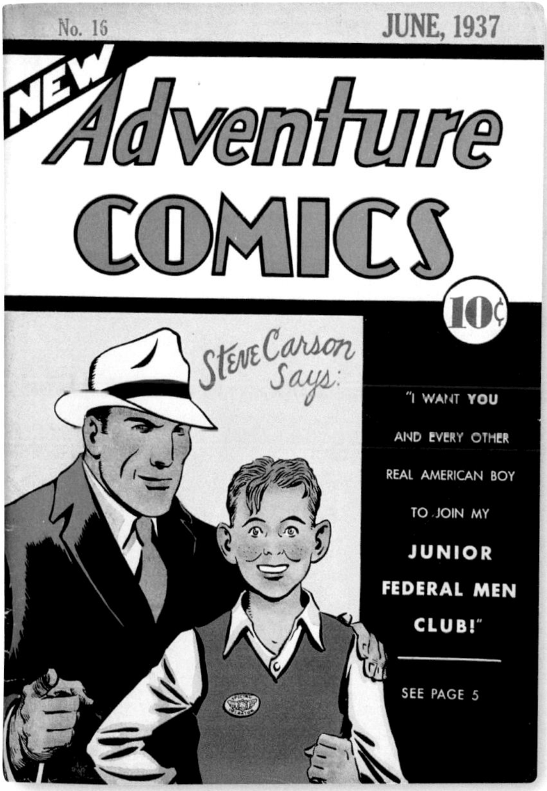
No. 16
JUNE, 1937
NEW
Adventure
COMICS
10¢
Steve Carson Says:
"I WANT YOU AND EVERY OTHER REAL AMERICAN BOY TO JOIN MY JUNIOR FEDERAL MEN CLUB!"
SEE PAGE 5

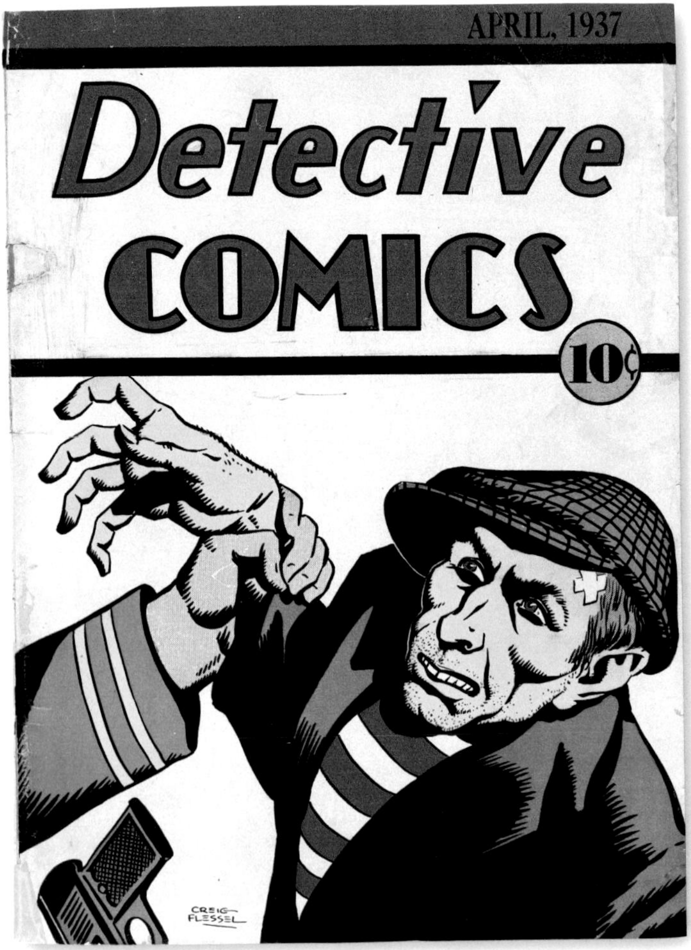
APRIL, 1937
Detective
COMICS
10¢
CREIG FLESSEL

DETECTIVE COMICS No. 2

Cover art, Creig Flessel, April 1937.

DETECTIVE COMICS No. 4

Cover art, Creig Flessel, June 1937. Still in search of the cover star it would not find until its 27th issue, *Detective* continued to give its regular cover artist Flessel a workout in search of provocative imagery suitable to the theme. Stalled for several issues, Flessel and DC's art directors chose to go with a series of trench-coated Dick Tracy imitations.

No. 4 JUNE, 1937

Detective COMICS

10¢

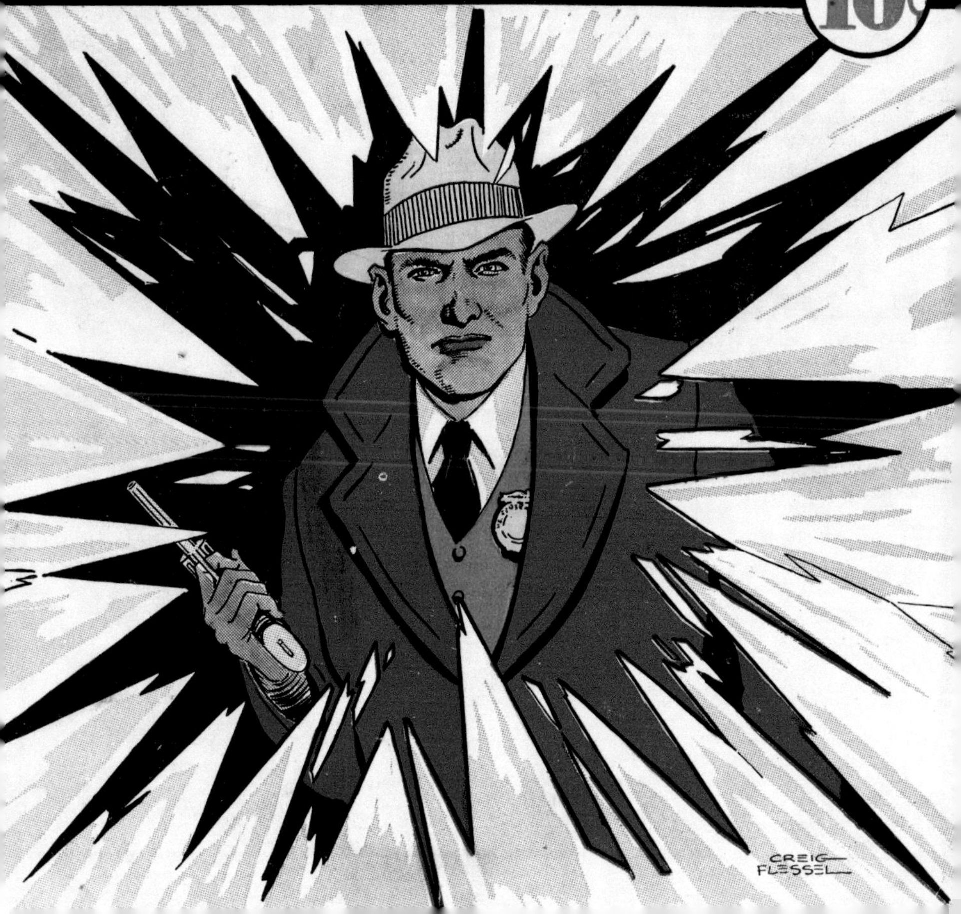
CREIG
FLESSEL

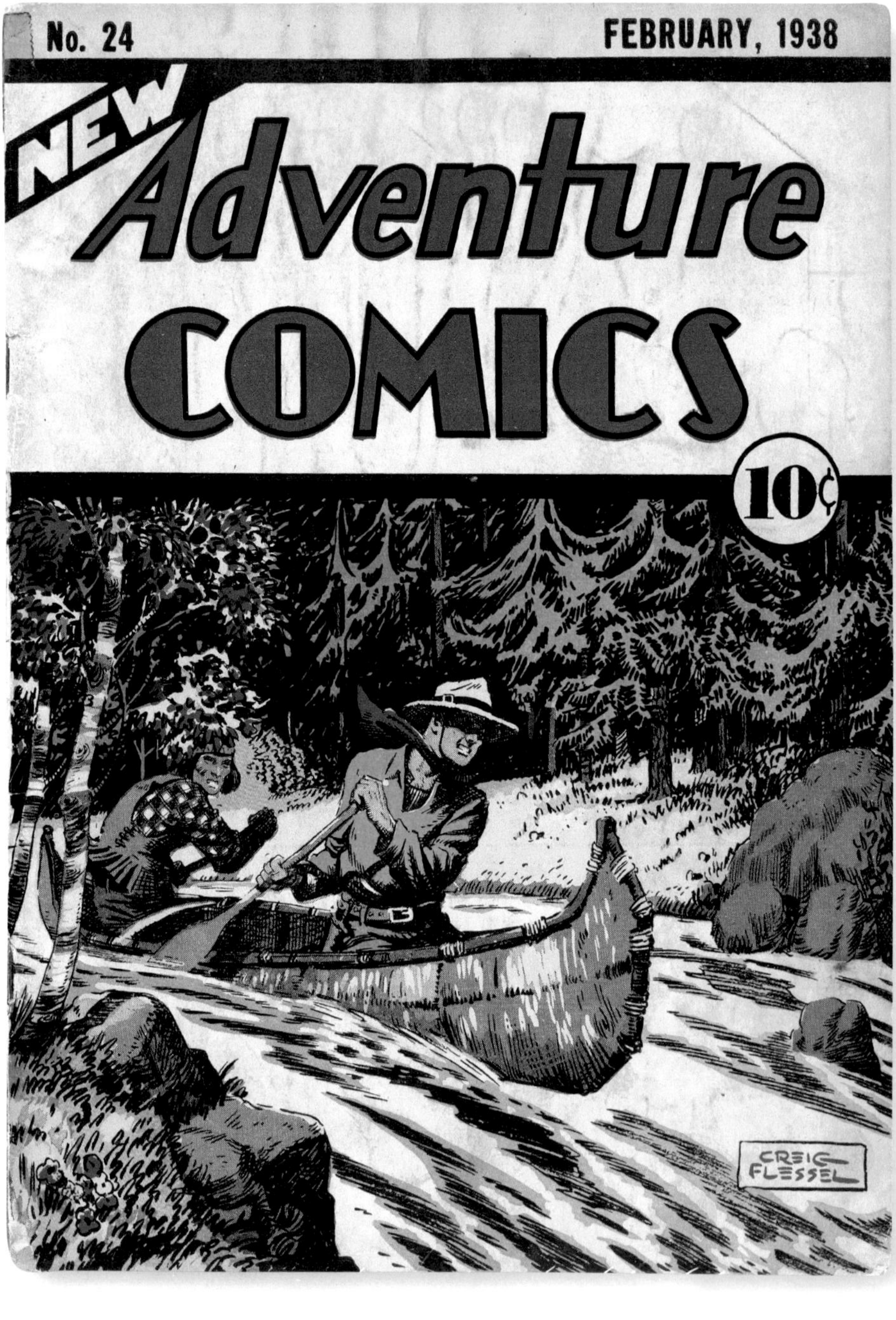
No. 24
FEBRUARY, 1938
NEW
Adventure
COMICS
10¢
CREIG
FLESSEL

NEW ADVENTURE COMICS No. 24

Cover art, Creig Flessel, February 1938. By 1938, *Adventure Comics'* cover images consistently reflected its eponymous theme. Gone was the occasional note of whimsy, as would be the banner containing the word "New" within a year. Letterer Ira Schnapp had long ago redesigned the "Comics" in *More Fun Comics'* logo in the same distinctive type style used here and on *Detective Comics*. It would recur on DC's first new title, *Action Comics*. The first visually identifiable comic book branding had been born.

ADVENTURE COMICS No. 61

Interior, "Steve Conrad, Adventurer"; script and art, Jack Lehti. April 1941.

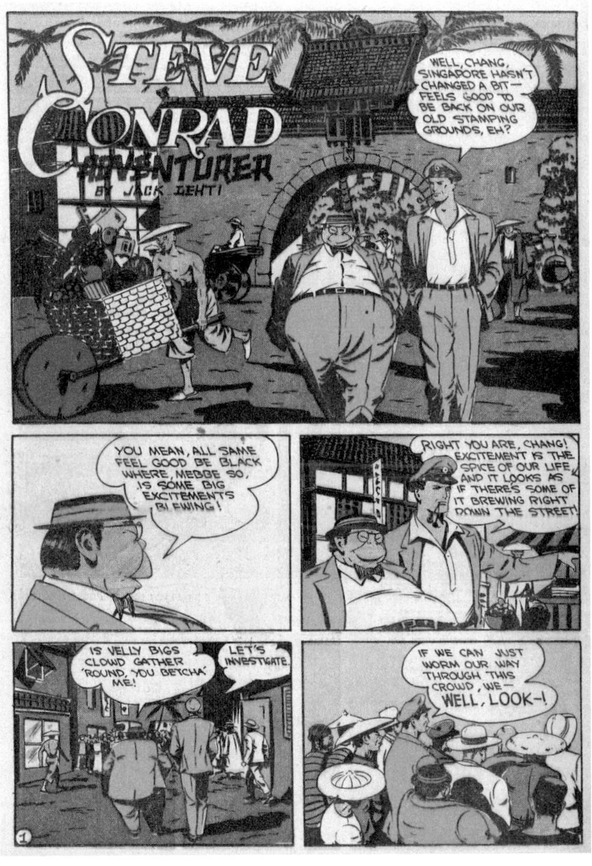

STEVE CONRAD ADVENTURER
BY JACK LEHTI
WELL, CHANG, SINGAPORE HASN'T CHANGED A BIT— FEELS GOOD TO BE BACK ON OUR OLD STAMPING GROUNDS, EH?
YOU MEAN, ALL SAME FEEL GOOD BE BLACK WHERE, MEBBE SO, IS SOME BIG EXCITEMENTS BLEWING!
RIGHT YOU ARE, CHANG! EXCITEMENT IS THE SPICE OF OUR LIFE, AND IT LOOKS AS IF THERE'S SOME OF IT BREWING RIGHT DOWN THE STREET!
IS VELLY BIGS CLOWD GATHER 'ROUND, YOU BETCHA' ME!
LET'S INVESTIGATE.
IF WE CAN JUST WORM OUR WAY THROUGH THIS CROWD, WE— WELL, LOOK—!
1

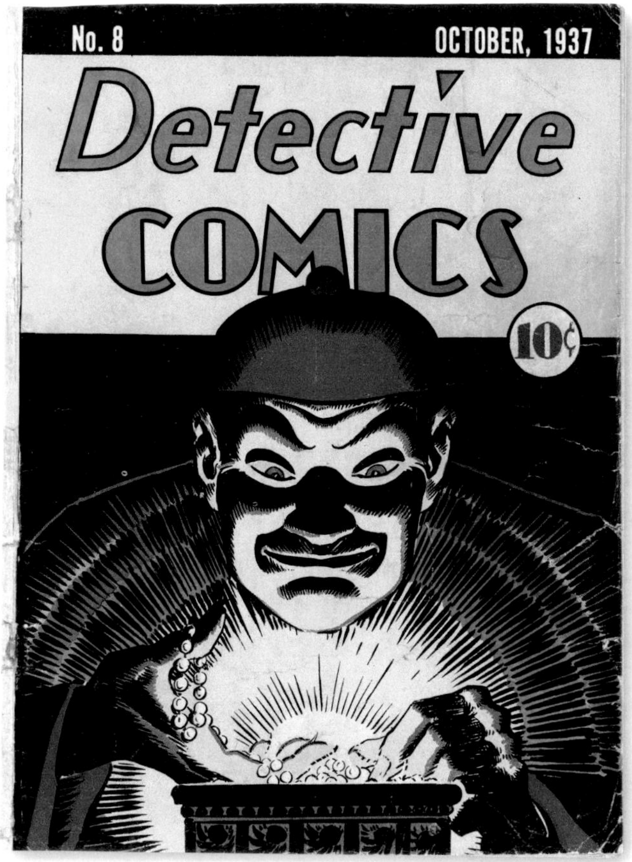
No. 8
OCTOBER, 1937
Detective
COMICS
10¢

DETECTIVE COMICS No. 8

Cover art, Creig Flessel, October 1937.

MORE FUN COMICS No. 20

Interior, "Bob Merritt and His Flying Pals" serial; script, Malcolm Wheeler-Nicholson; pencils and inks, Leo O'Mealia. May 1937. The straight side of "Andy Handy": Veteran newspaper cartoonist O'Mealia, who had begun working out of Harry "A" Chesler's shop, was repeatedly called upon to lend his lush rendering to simple adventure strips like this one. All were knockoffs of *Tom Swift*ian boys' dime novels, already woefully old-fashioned, with titles like "Barry O'Neill" and "Inspector Donald and Bobby." Leo the Lion, as O'Mealia was called, gave them better than they deserved, along with his trademark lion-cartoon signature.

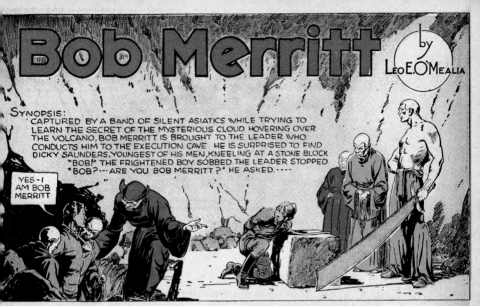

Bob Merritt

by Leo E. O'Mealia

SYNOPSIS:
CAPTURED BY A BAND OF SILENT ASIATICS WHILE TRYING TO LEARN THE SECRET OF THE MYSTERIOUS CLOUD HOVERING OVER THE VOLCANO, BOB MERRITT IS BROUGHT TO THE LEADER WHO CONDUCTS HIM TO THE EXECUTION CAVE. HE IS SURPRISED TO FIND DICKY SAUNDERS, YOUNGEST OF HIS MEN, KNEELING AT A STONE BLOCK "BOB!" THE FRIGHTENED BOY SOBBED THE LEADER STOPPED "BOB?---ARE YOU BOB MERRITT?" HE ASKED.----

YES - I AM BOB MERRITT

ALL THE FREE GOLD IN THE CRATER IS LOADED ON OUR TRANSPORTS. TO INSURE OUR SAFE DEPARTURE WITH IT WE HAD DECIDED TO BOMB YOUR CAMP THEN FINISH THE SURVIVORS WITH BULLET AND BAYONET. YOU CAN PREVENT THIS, BOB MERRITT, AND NEITHER SIDE WILL LOSE A MAN.

THIS GOLD IS NOT YOURS - IT RIGHTFULLY BELONGS TO MY MEN. WE CAME TO ALASKA TO MINE IT AND WE WILL NOT SURREND---

YOU WILL WRITE RATHER THAN SEE THIS BOY TORTURED. HISS FIRST CUT OFF THE LEFT ARM.

3. IT ISS MY SUGGESTION THAT YOU WRITE A NOTE TO YOUR MEN CALLING UP-ON THEM TO SURRENDER YOUR CAMP AND PLANES TO US AND TO DEPART PEACEABLY.

HUH - I WILL DO NOTHING OF THE KIND

5. WAIT !! I'LL WRITE BUT YOU MUST GIVE MY MEN TWO HOURS TO FIND SHELTER

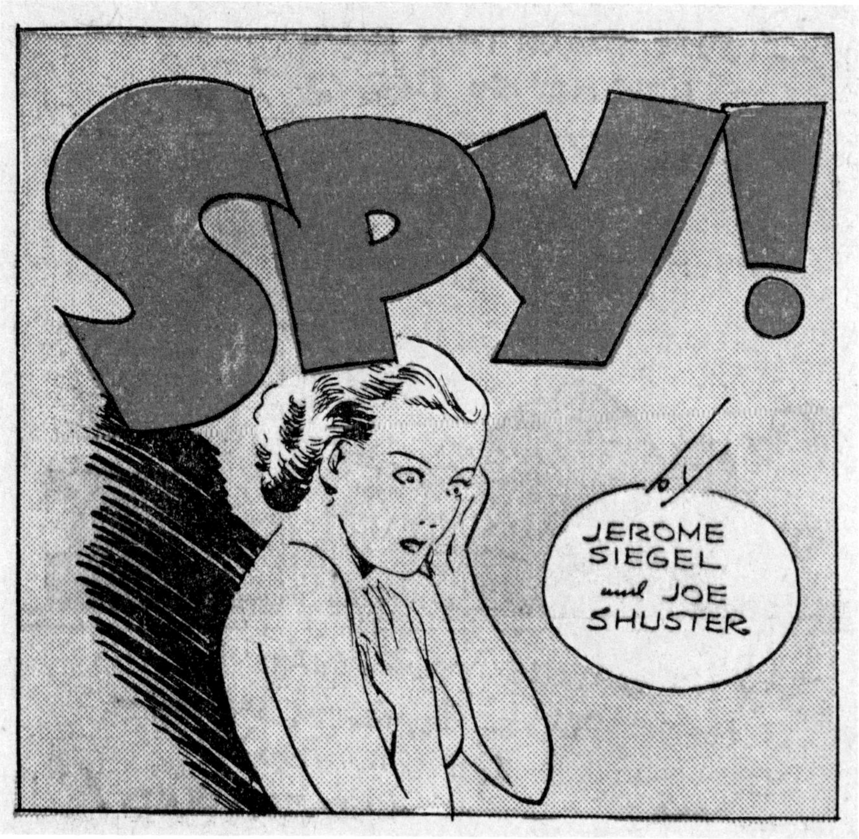
SPY!
by
JEROME SIEGEL
and JOE SHUSTER

"It was also a time of fads, follies, and fancies; the wacky, witless, and inane.... The comics reflected society's contradictions and its need for escape with the development of two disparate forms—adventure strips and comedy strips."

—JERRY ROBINSON

DETECTIVE COMICS No. 3

Interior, "Spy" serial; script, Jerry Siegel; pencils and inks, Joe Shuster. May 1937. Even before their greatest creation debuted, Siegel and Shuster were among DC's most prolific contributors. Between 1935 and 1938, the pair wrote and drew six different features, many appearing monthly. "Spy" was the last of these, beginning life, for one issue, as "Bart Regan, Spy." It debuted in *Detective* and ran until 1944, with Mart Bailey, followed by many others, taking over the art chores in No. 29 (July 1939). Siegel continued as writer till mid-1941.

DETECTIVE COMICS No. 1

Interior, "Slam Bradley"; script, Jerry Siegel; pencils and inks, Joe Shuster. March 1937. The fifth of Siegel and Shuster's more reality-based, pre-Superman features demonstrated that the pair's work was often at its best when aiming for laughs—here supplied by comical sidekick Shorty Morgan. "Bradley" enjoyed a long run, ending in 1949 and by far outlasting not only Siegel and Shuster's tenure as suppliers, but their entire working relationship with DC.

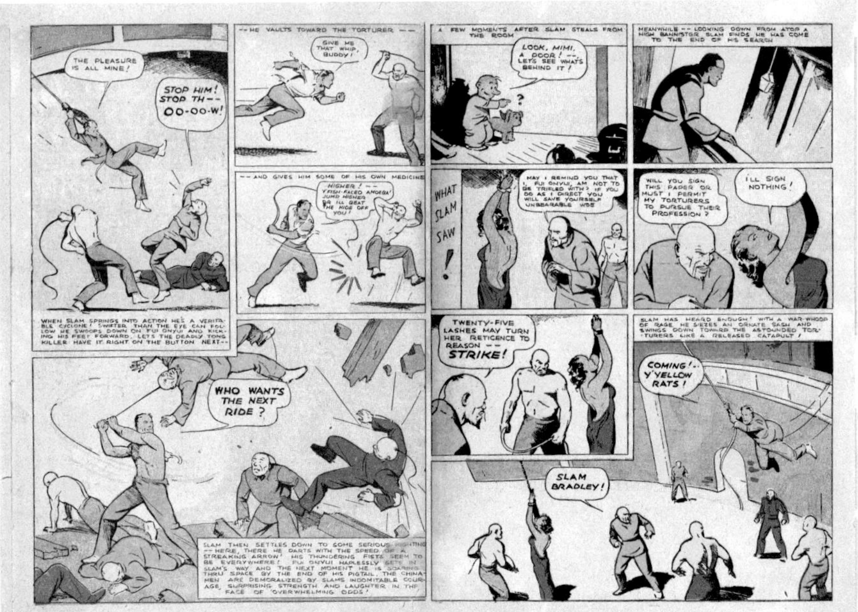

THE PLEASURE IS ALL MINE!
STOP HIM! STOP TH-- OO-OO-W!
WHEN SLAM SPRINGS INTO ACTION HE'S A VERITABLE CYCLONE! SWIFTER THAN THE EYE CAN FOLLOW HE SWOOPS DOWN ON FUI ONYUI AND KICKING HIS FEET FORWARD, LETS THE DEADLY TONG KILLER HAVE IT RIGHT ON THE BUTTON NEXT--
--HE VAULTS TOWARD THE TORTURER --
GIVE ME THAT WHIP, BUDDY!
--AND GIVES HIM SOME OF HIS OWN MEDICINE
HIGHER! -- Y'FISH-FACED AMOEBA! JUMP HIGHER OR I'LL BEAT THE HIDE OFF YOU!
WHO WANTS THE NEXT RIDE?
SLAM THEN SETTLES DOWN TO SOME SERIOUS --HERE, THERE HE DARTS WITH THE SPEED STREAKING ARROW! HIS THUNDERING FISTS TO BE EVERYWHERE! FUI ONYUI HAPLESSLY IN SLAM'S WAY AND THE NEXT MOMENT HE IS THRU SPACE BY THE END OF HIS PIGTAIL. THE CHINAMEN ARE DEMORALIZED BY SLAMS INDOMITABLE COURAGE, SURPRISING STRENGTH AND LAUGHTER IN THE FACE OF OVERWHELMING ODDS!
A FEW MOMENTS AFTER SLAM STEALS FROM THE ROOM
LOOK, MIMI, A DOOR! --, LET'S SEE WHAT'S BEHIND IT!
?
MEANWHILE -- LOOKING DOWN FROM ATOP A HIGH BANNISTER SLAM FINDS HE HAS COME TO THE END OF HIS SEARCH
WHAT SLAM SAW!
MAY I REMIND YOU THAT I, FUI ONYUI, AM NOT TO BE TRIFLED WITH? IF YOU DO AS I DIRECT YOU WILL SAVE YOURSELF UNBEARABLE WOE
WILL YOU SIGN THIS PAPER OR MUST I PERMIT MY TORTURERS TO PURSUE THEIR PROFESSION?
I'LL SIGN NOTHING!
TWENTY-FIVE LASHES MAY TURN HER RETICENCE TO REASON -- STRIKE!
SLAM HAS HEARD ENOUGH! WITH A WAR-WHOOP OF RAGE HE SIEZES AN ORNATE SASH AND SWINGS DOWN TOWARD THE ASTOUNDED TORTURERS LIKE A RELEASED CATAPULT!
COMING!.. Y'YELLOW RATS!
SLAM BRADLEY!

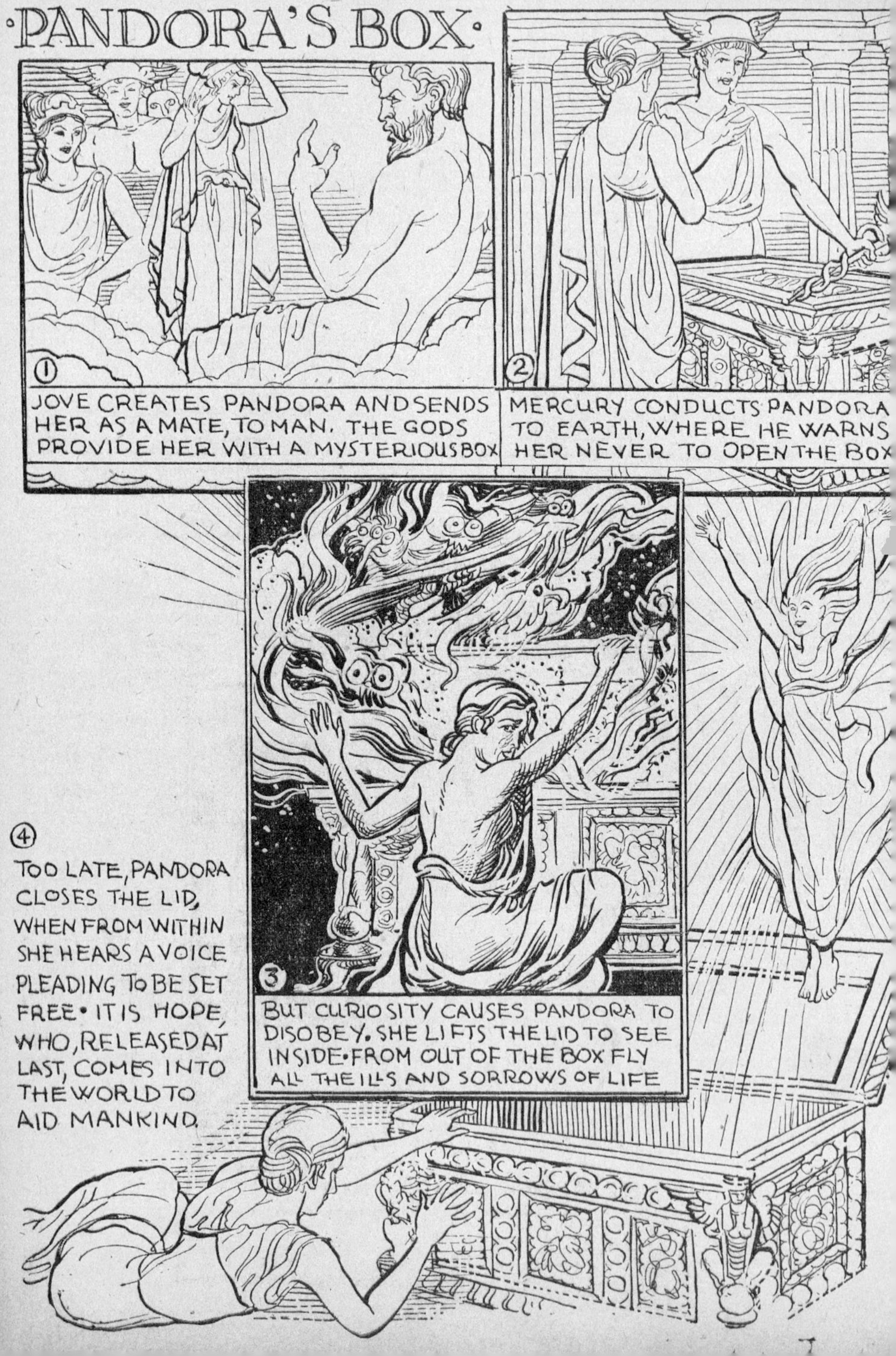
PANDORA'S BOX
1
JOVE CREATES PANDORA AND SENDS HER AS A MATE, TO MAN. THE GODS PROVIDE HER WITH A MYSTERIOUS BOX
2
MERCURY CONDUCTS PANDORA TO EARTH, WHERE HE WARNS HER NEVER TO OPEN THE BOX
3
BUT CURIOSITY CAUSES PANDORA TO DISOBEY. SHE LIFTS THE LID TO SEE INSIDE. FROM OUT OF THE BOX FLY ALL THE ILLS AND SORROWS OF LIFE
4
TOO LATE, PANDORA CLOSES THE LID, WHEN FROM WITHIN SHE HEARS A VOICE PLEADING TO BE SET FREE. IT IS HOPE, WHO, RELEASED AT LAST, COMES INTO THE WORLD TO AID MANKIND.

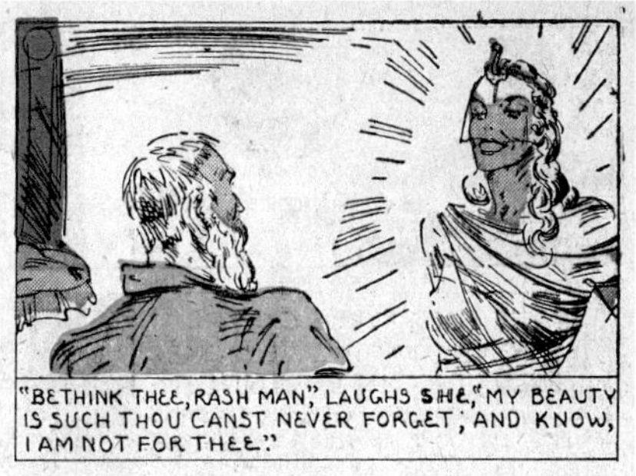
"BETHINK THEE, RASH MAN," LAUGHS SHE,"MY BEAUTY IS SUCH THOU CANST NEVER FORGET; AND KNOW, I AM NOT FOR THEE."

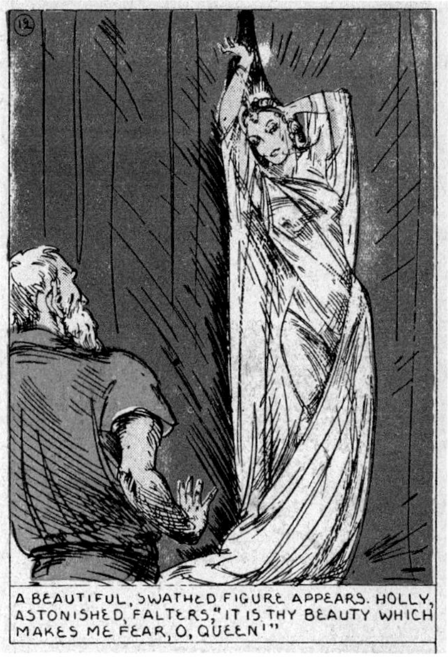
A BEAUTIFUL, SWATHED FIGURE APPEARS. HOLLY, ASTONISHED, FALTERS,"IT IS THY BEAUTY WHICH MAKES ME FEAR, O, QUEEN!"

NEW COMICS No. 5

Interior, "Pandora's Box"; script and art, attributed H.C. Kiefer. June 1936. Wheeler-Nicholson's fondness for Greco-Roman mythology surfaced frequently in his comics. In its bowdlerizing of Bulfinch, inadvertent or otherwise — accompanied by illustrations drawing on influences unfamiliar to readers of the time — "Pandora's Box" anticipated the *Wonder Woman* that was to follow, which the Major had nothing to do with. It even employed the same Cecil B. DeMille–like use of classicism to justify sexy images. All that's missing is the spandex.

NEW ADVENTURE COMICS Nos. 14 & 20

Interiors, "She" serial; script, Malcolm Wheeler-Nicholson (adapted from H. Rider Haggard); pencils and inks, Sven Elven. March and October 1937. Wheeler-Nicholson's claims to have been a soldier of fortune suggest he identified with H. Rider Haggard. In the tale of Horace Holly's encounter with the mystic queen Ayesha, the writer who gave the world Allan Quatermain also gave Elven subject matter suited to his outdated style. By 1937, Alex Raymond and Milton Caniff were setting the standards for adventure strip art, and Elven — better known for the bizarre "Cosmo, Phantom of Disguise" in *Detective* — was sorely outclassed.

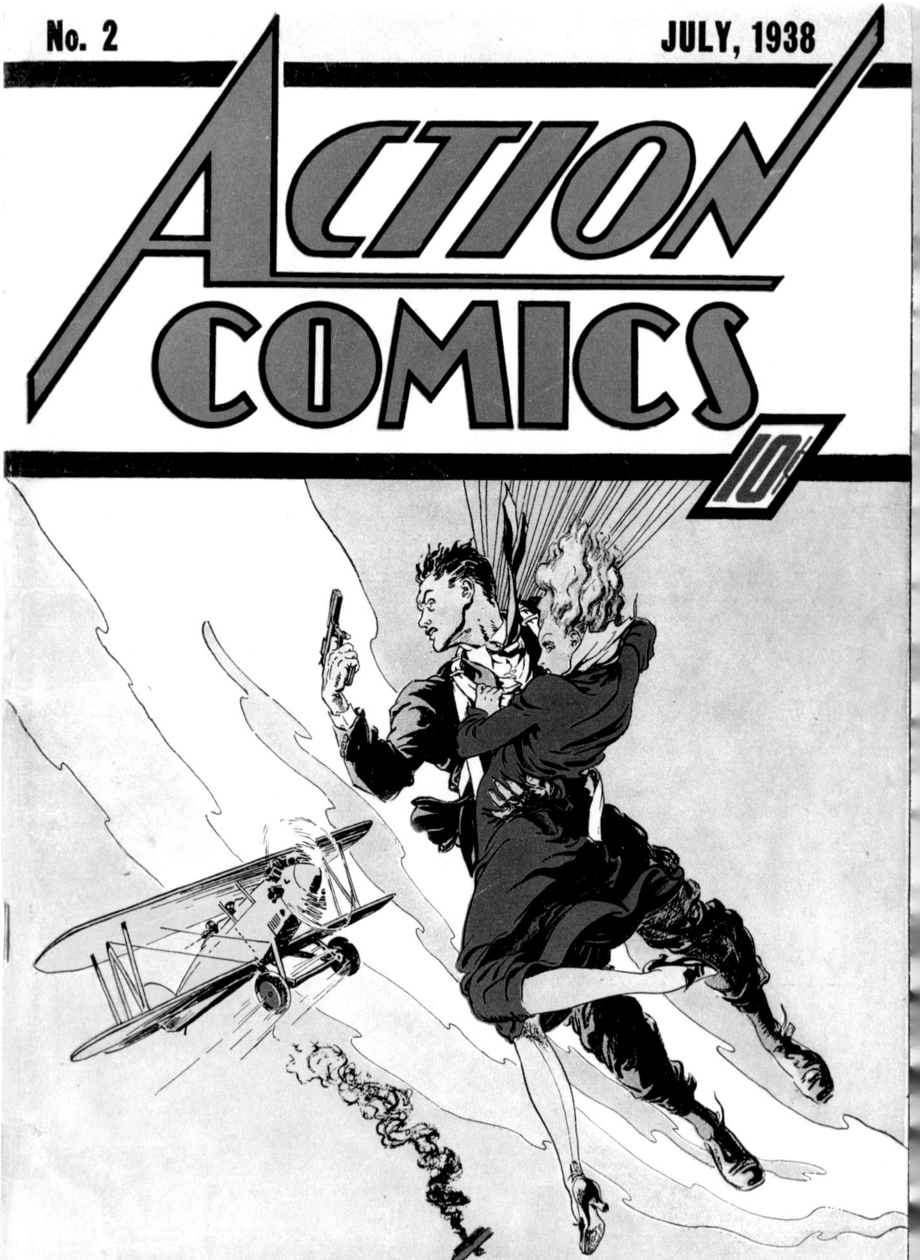
No. 2
JULY, 1938
ACTION COMICS
10¢
LEO E. O'MEALIA

ACTION COMICS No.2

Cover art, Leo O'Mealia, July 1938. One of the major contributors to the infant DC Comics was Leo O'Mealia, whose intricate, realistic art stood out among inexperienced illustrators trying to break into the business. Born in 1884, O'Mealia had a long career as a political cartoonist and newspaper illustrator before being tapped to illustrate some of Major Malcolm Wheeler-Nicholson's serialized features such as "Barry O'Neill" and "Bob Merritt and His Flying Pals".

ACTION COMICS No. 3

Cover art, Leo O'Mealia, August 1938.

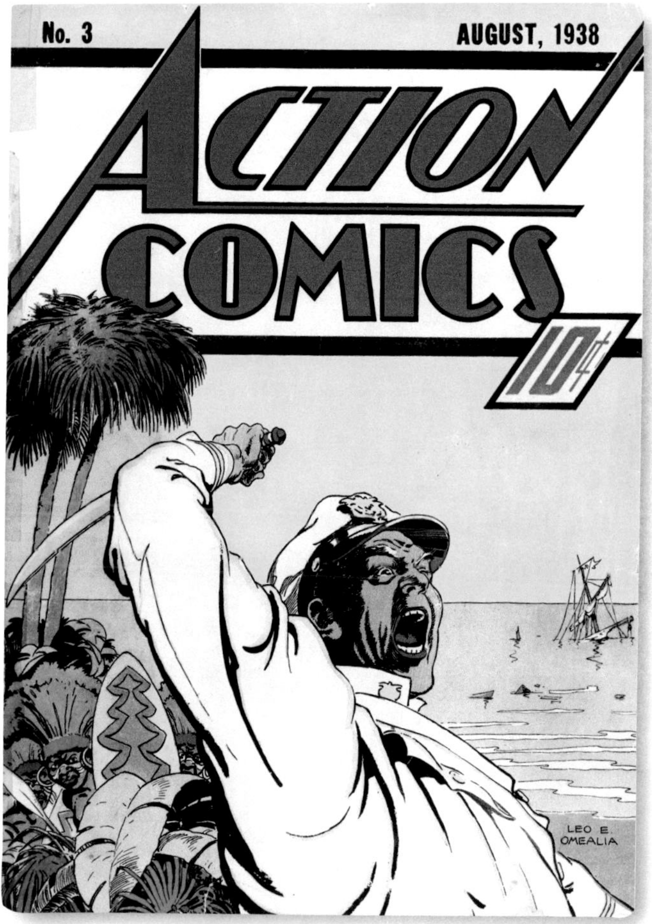
No. 3
AUGUST, 1938
ACTION COMICS
10¢
LEO E. OMEALIA

ACTION COMICS No. 4

Cover art, Leo O'Mealia, September 1938.

ACTION COMICS No. 6

Cover art, Leo O'Mealia, November 1938.

NEW ADVENTURE COMICS No. 24

FOLLOWING SPREAD: *Interior, "Boomerang Jones"; script and art, Fred Guardineer (as Stan Babcock). February 1938.* Boomerang Jones was just one of several plainclothes heroes whose exploits filled this title's pages without producing a breakout hit. It would not be until Superman's influence was felt throughout comics, and the costumed Hourman burst on the scene in *Adventure* No. 48 (March 1940), that its cover star would be found.

No. 4
SEPTEMBER, 1938
ACTION COMICS
10¢

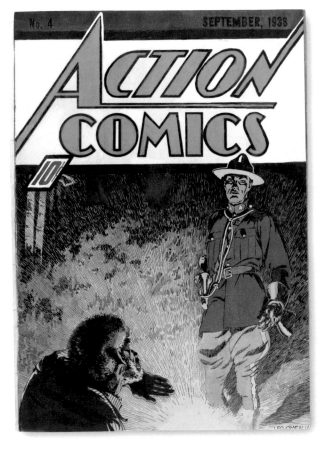

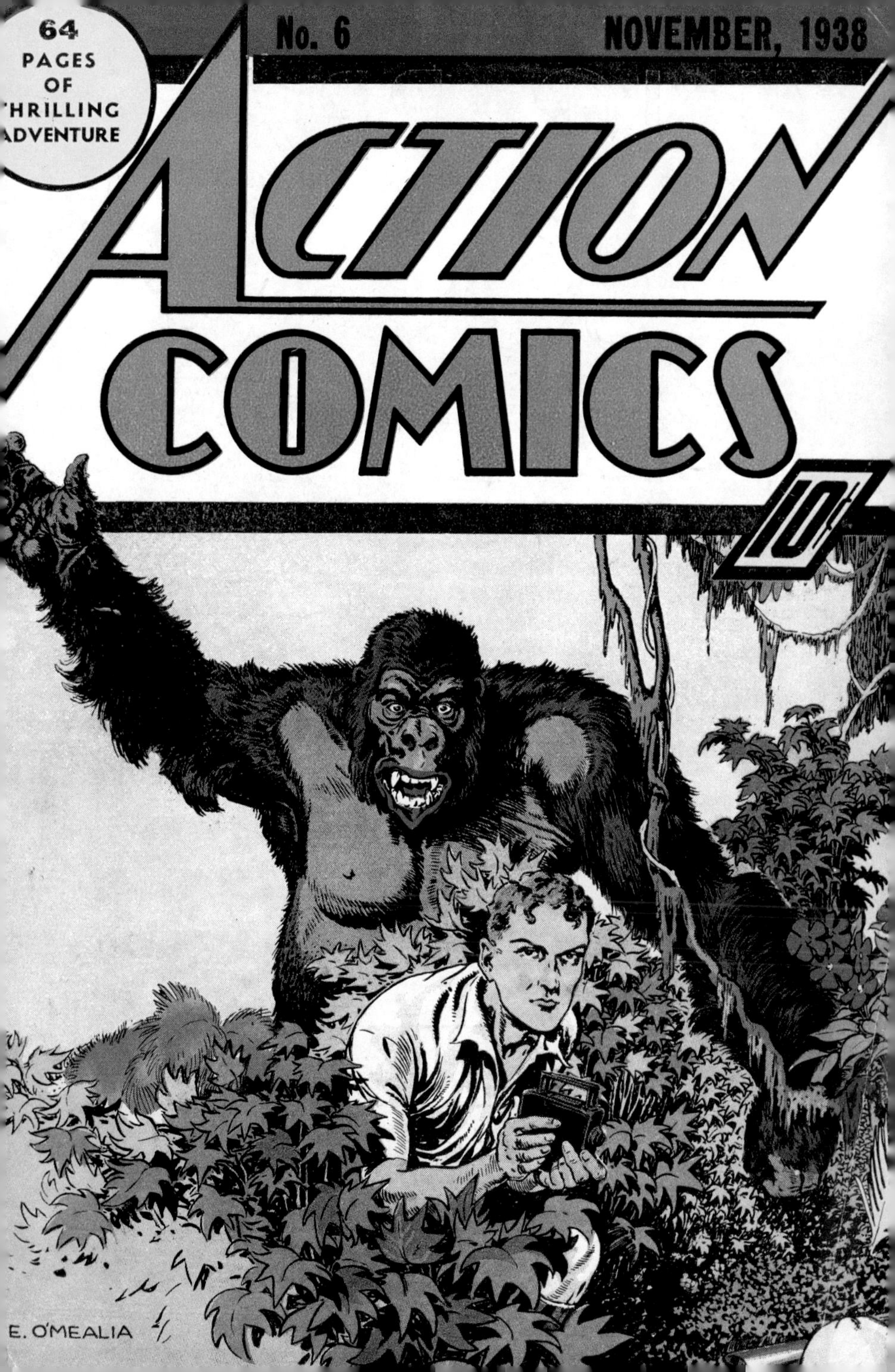
64 PAGES OF THRILLING ADVENTURE
No. 6
NOVEMBER, 1938
ACTION COMICS
10¢
E. O'MEALIA

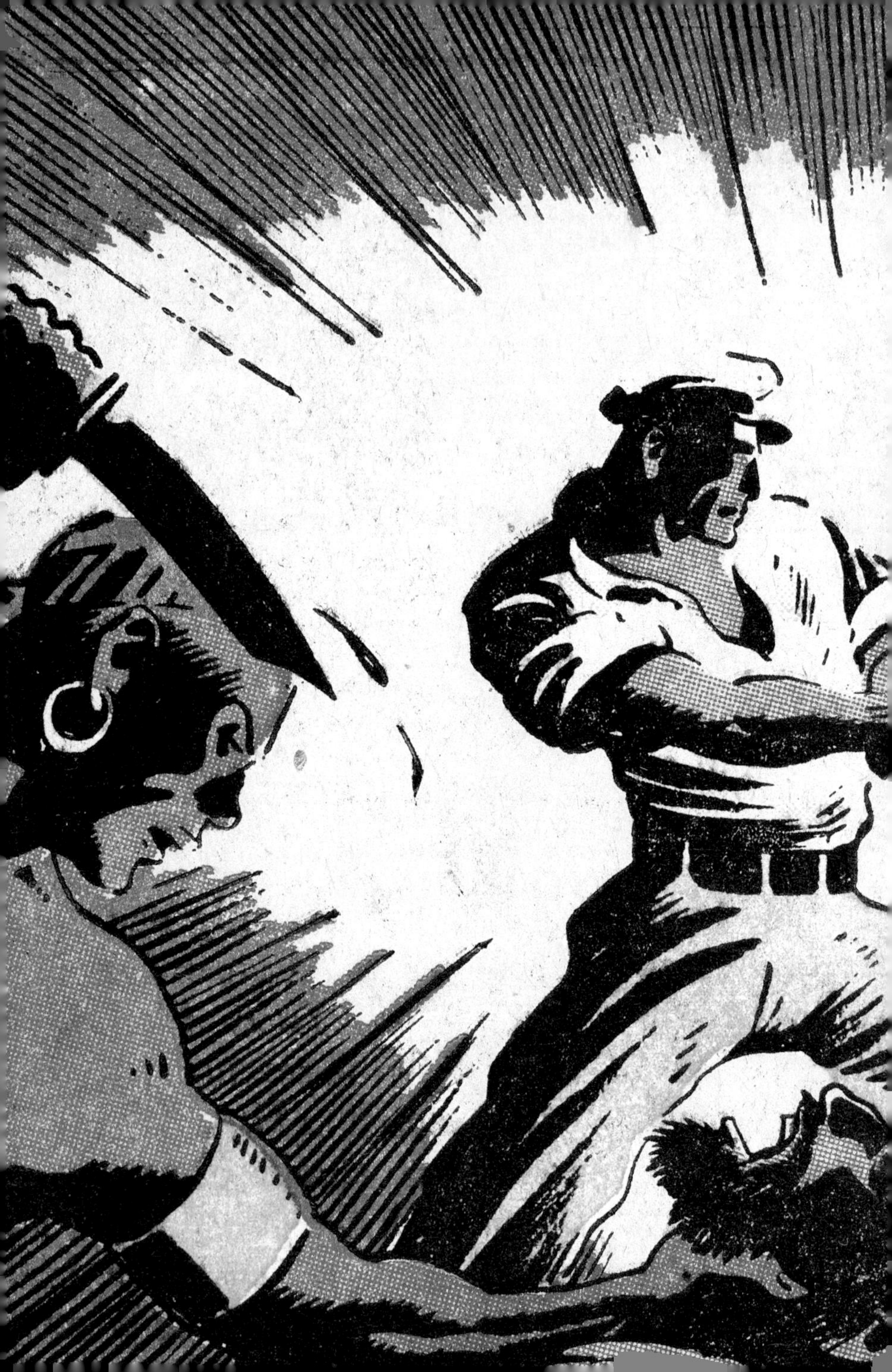

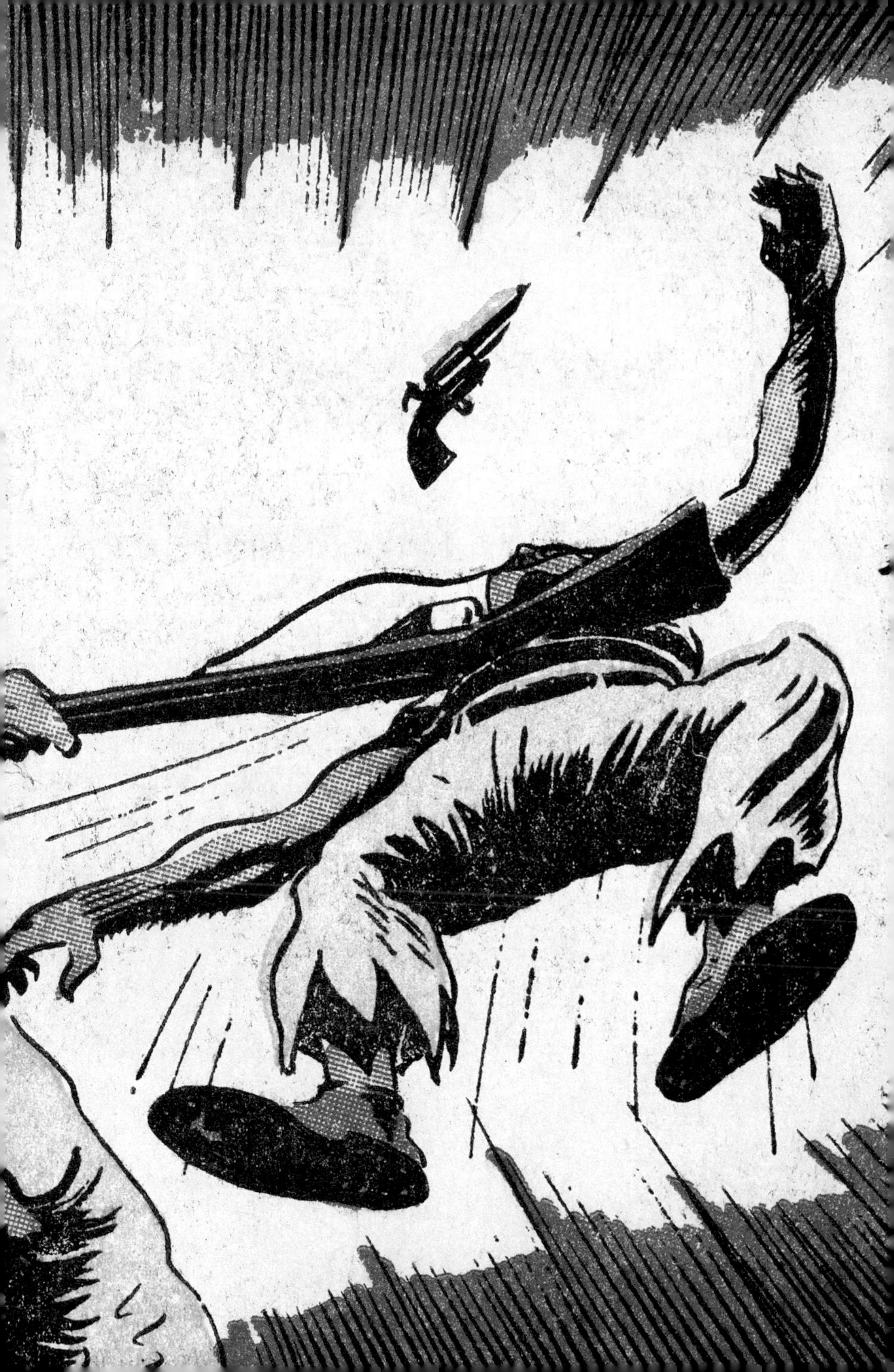

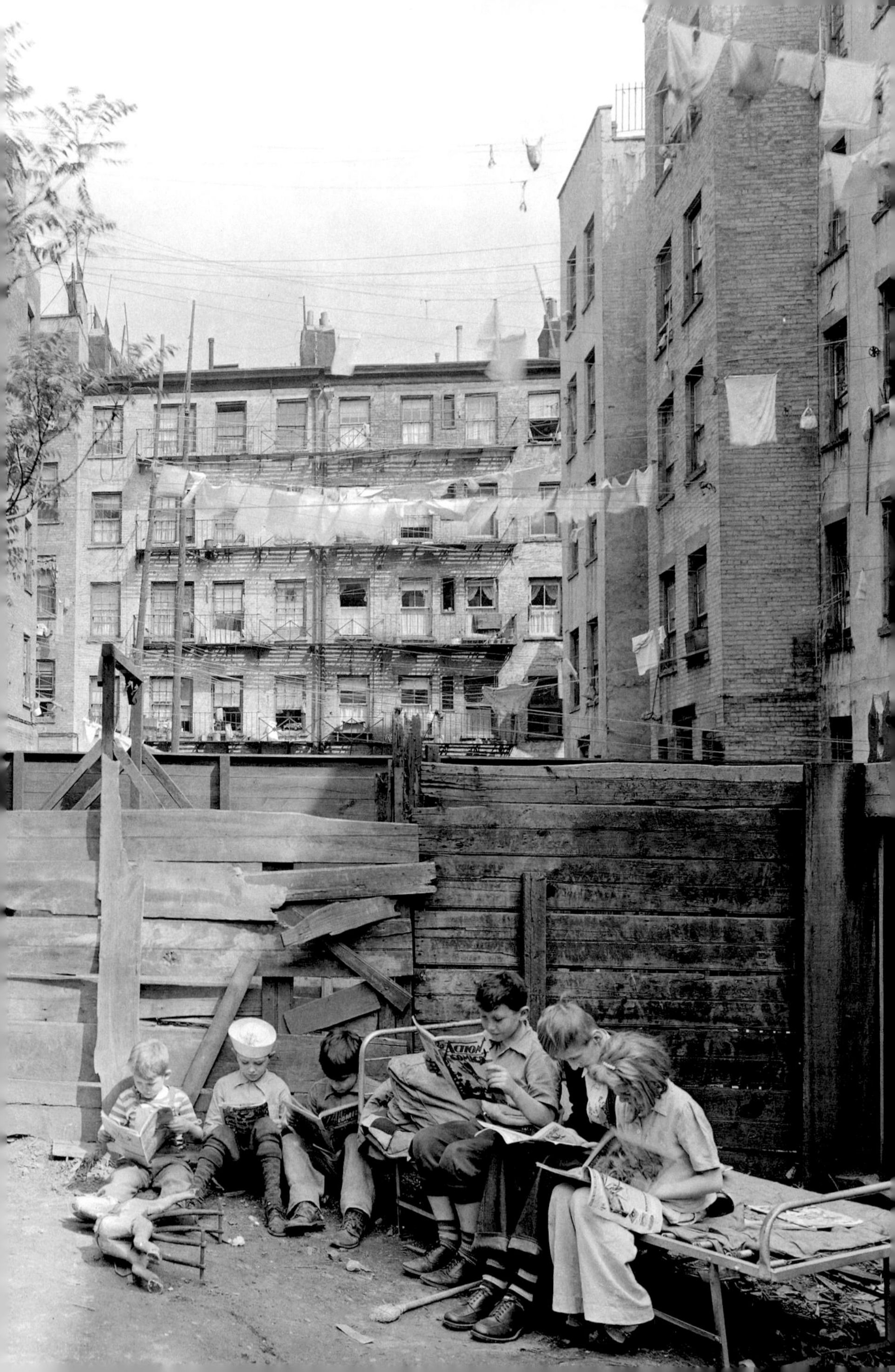
ACTION
COMICS

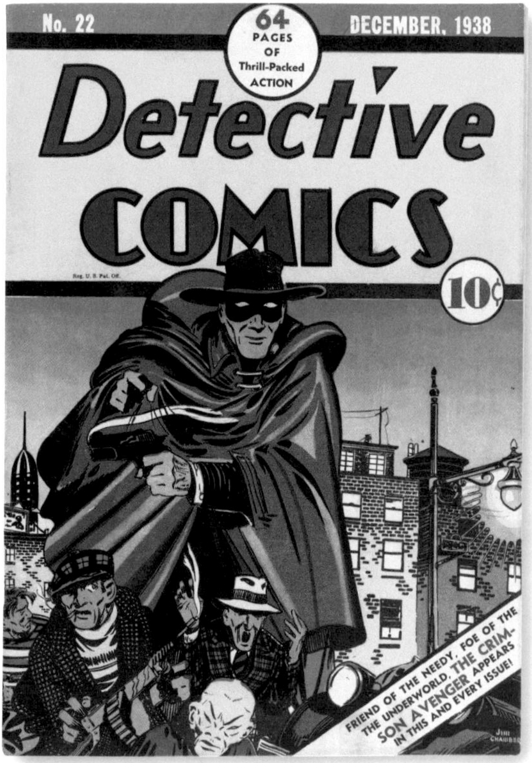
No. 22
64 PAGES OF Thrill-Packed ACTION
DECEMBER, 1938
Detective
COMICS
10¢
FRIEND OF THE NEEDY, FOE OF THE UNDERWORLD, THE CRIMSON AVENGER APPEARS IN THIS AND EVERY ISSUE!

CHILDREN READING COMICS

Tenement courtyard, New York, 1943.

Early DC comics, like the copy of *Action Comics* No. 62 being read here, provided low-cost escapism from the worst of times, whether the waning days of the Great Depression or the height of World War II. Immigrants living in urban tenements like these begat not only the first readers of DC comics, but also some of the first young people to *create* them.

DETECTIVE COMICS No. 22

Cover art, Jim Chambers, December 1938.

DC's first masked mystery man owed much to the pulps in general and to the Green Hornet specifically. Like that famous fictional hero, the Crimson Avenger was a crusading newspaper publisher with an Asian chauffeur and later partner. Once Batman took over as *Detective Comics'* star and a new breed of hero emerged, the Crimson Avenger and sidekick Wing received a makeover with colorful skintight red and yellow costumes.

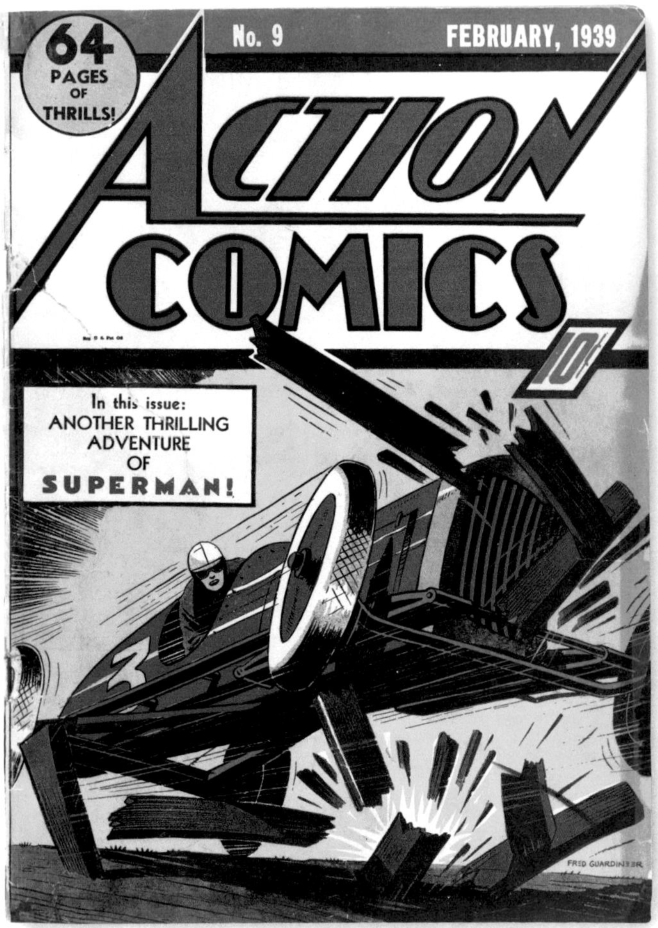
64 PAGES OF THRILLS!
No. 9
FEBRUARY, 1939
ACTION COMICS
10¢
In this issue: ANOTHER THRILLING ADVENTURE OF SUPERMAN!
FRED GUARDINEER

ACTION COMICS No. 9

Cover art, Fred Guardineer, February 1939. Cover artist Fred Guardineer was represented inside *Action Comics* with features starring all-around athlete Pep Morgan and Zatara the magician.

NEW ADVENTURE COMICS No. 26

Cover art, Creig Flessel, May 1938. The month before Superman's debut, DC's diverse anthology featured 17 series in its 64 pages, including two humor series by Bob Kane and Siegel and Shuster's *Federal Men*, as well as the unfortunately named *Nadir*.

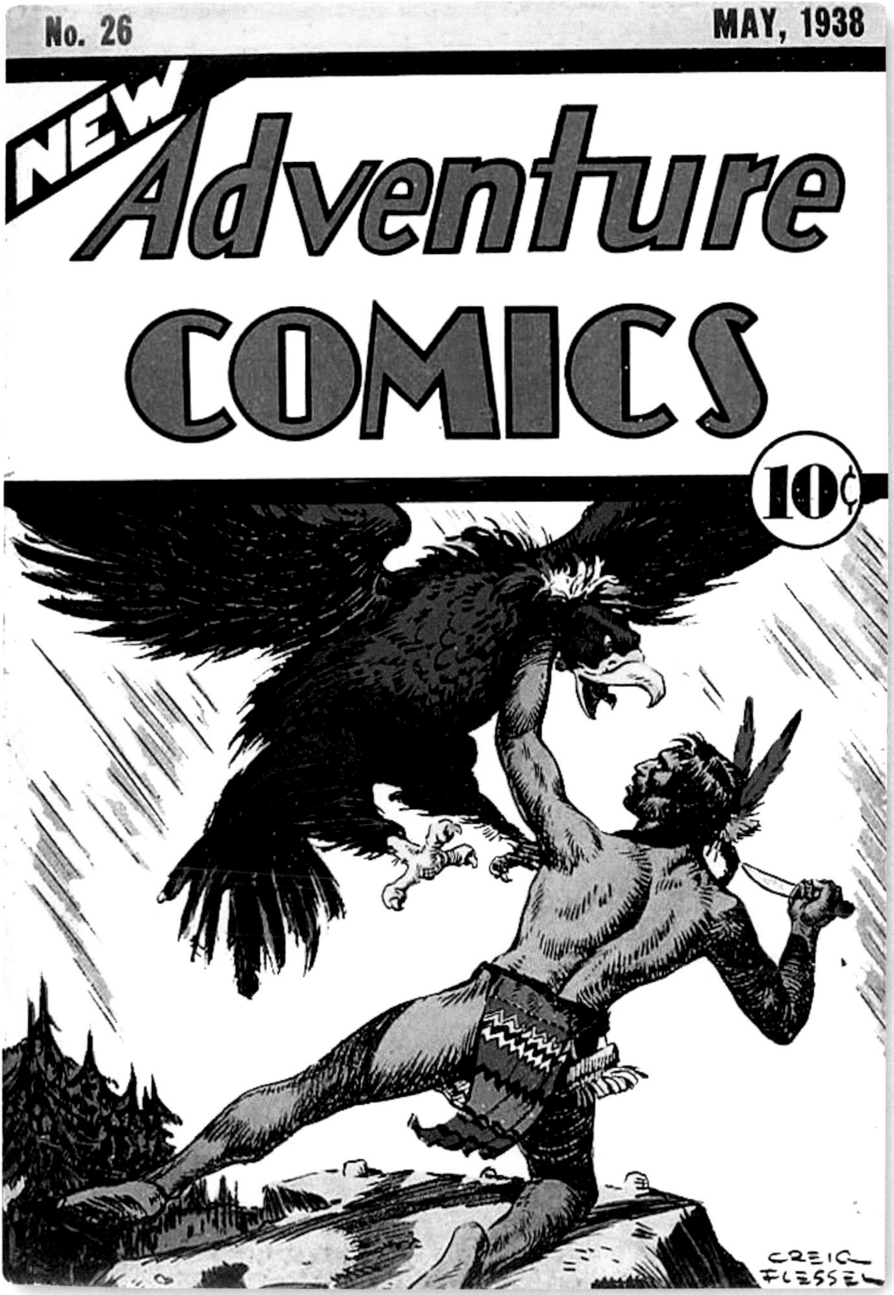
No. 26
MAY, 1938
NEW
Adventure
COMICS
10¢
CREIG FLESSEL

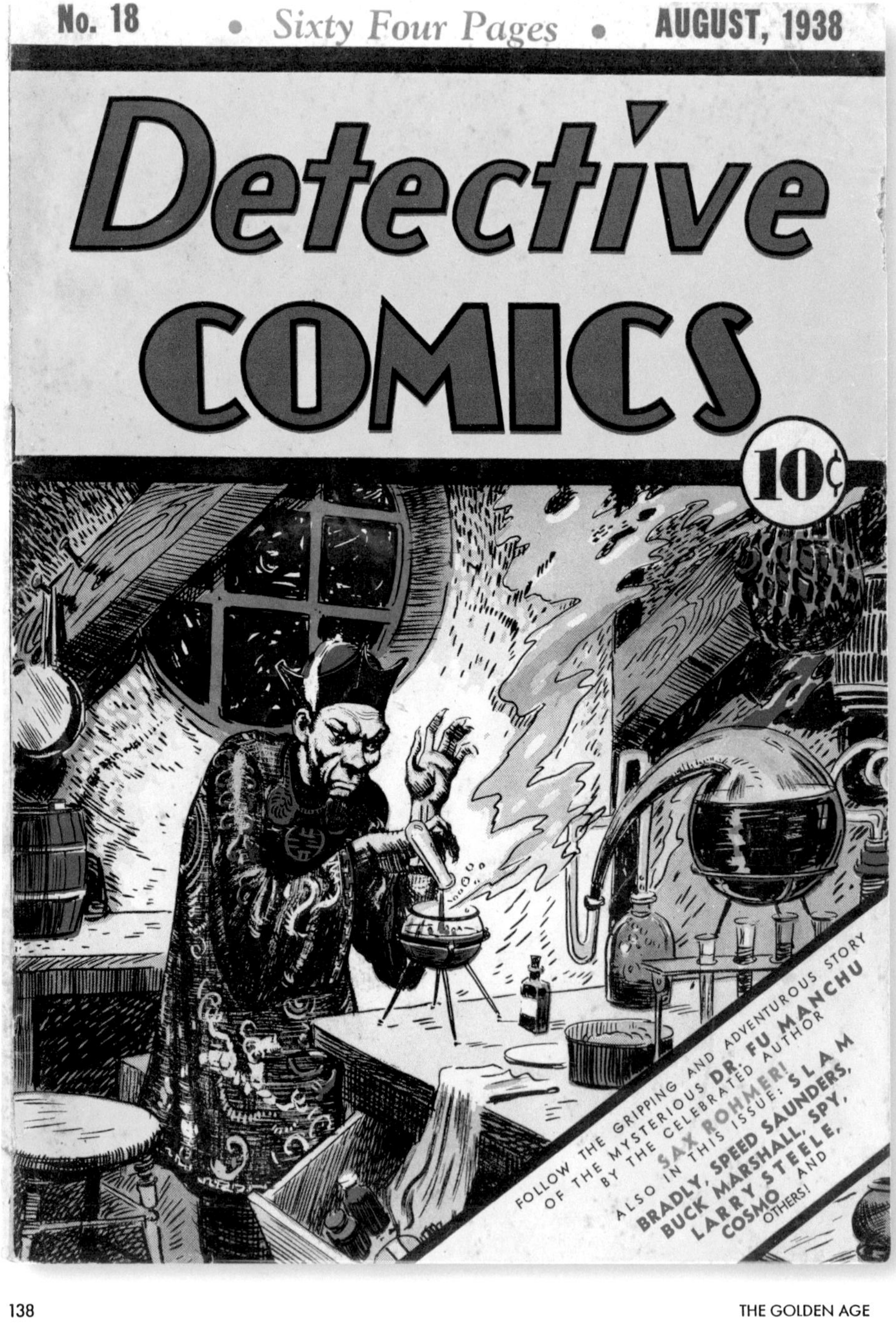
No. 18 • Sixty Four Pages • AUGUST, 1938
Detective COMICS
10¢
FOLLOW THE GRIPPING AND ADVENTUROUS STORY OF THE MYSTERIOUS DR. FU MANCHU BY THE CELEBRATED AUTHOR SAX ROHMER!
ALSO IN THIS ISSUE: SLAM BRADLY, SPEED SAUNDERS, BUCK MARSHALL, SPY, LARRY STEELE, COSMO AND OTHERS!

DETECTIVE COMICS Nos. 18,19 & 20

OPPOSITE AND FOLLOWING SPREAD: *Cover art, Creig Flessel (Nos. 18 and 19) and Leo O'Mealia (No. 20), August–October 1938.* *Detective Comics* made history as the first comic book devoted to a single theme. Characters such as Bruce Nelson, Speed Saunders, and Cosmo, the Phantom of Disguise, brought criminals to justice in every issue, although the star features were arguably the rough-and-tumble Slam Bradley and government agent Spy, produced by future Superman creators Jerry Siegel and Joe Shuster. Covers generally featured generic adventure scenes, although No. 18's rendition of Fu Manchu was an exception.

DETECTIVE COMICS No. 6

Cover art, Creig Flessel, August 1937.

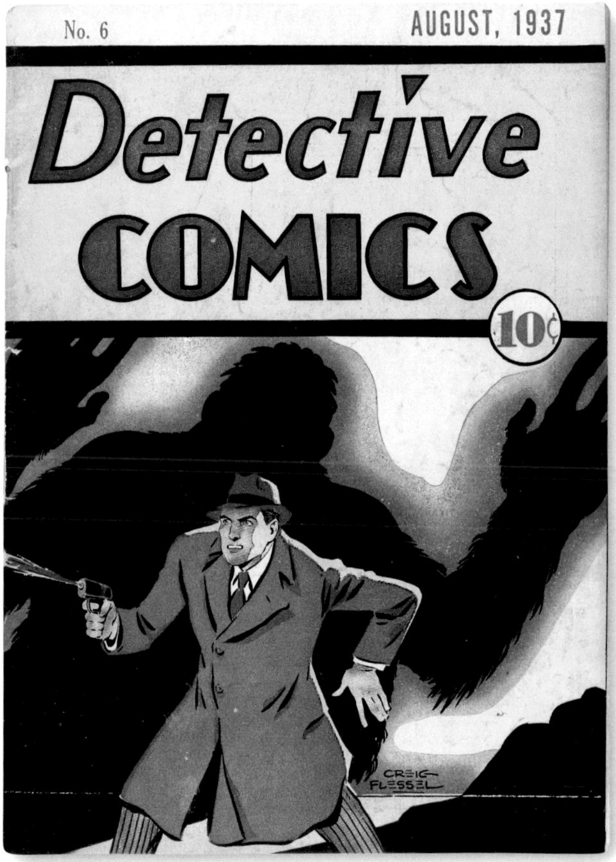
No. 6
AUGUST, 1937
Detective
COMICS
10¢
CREIG FLESSEL

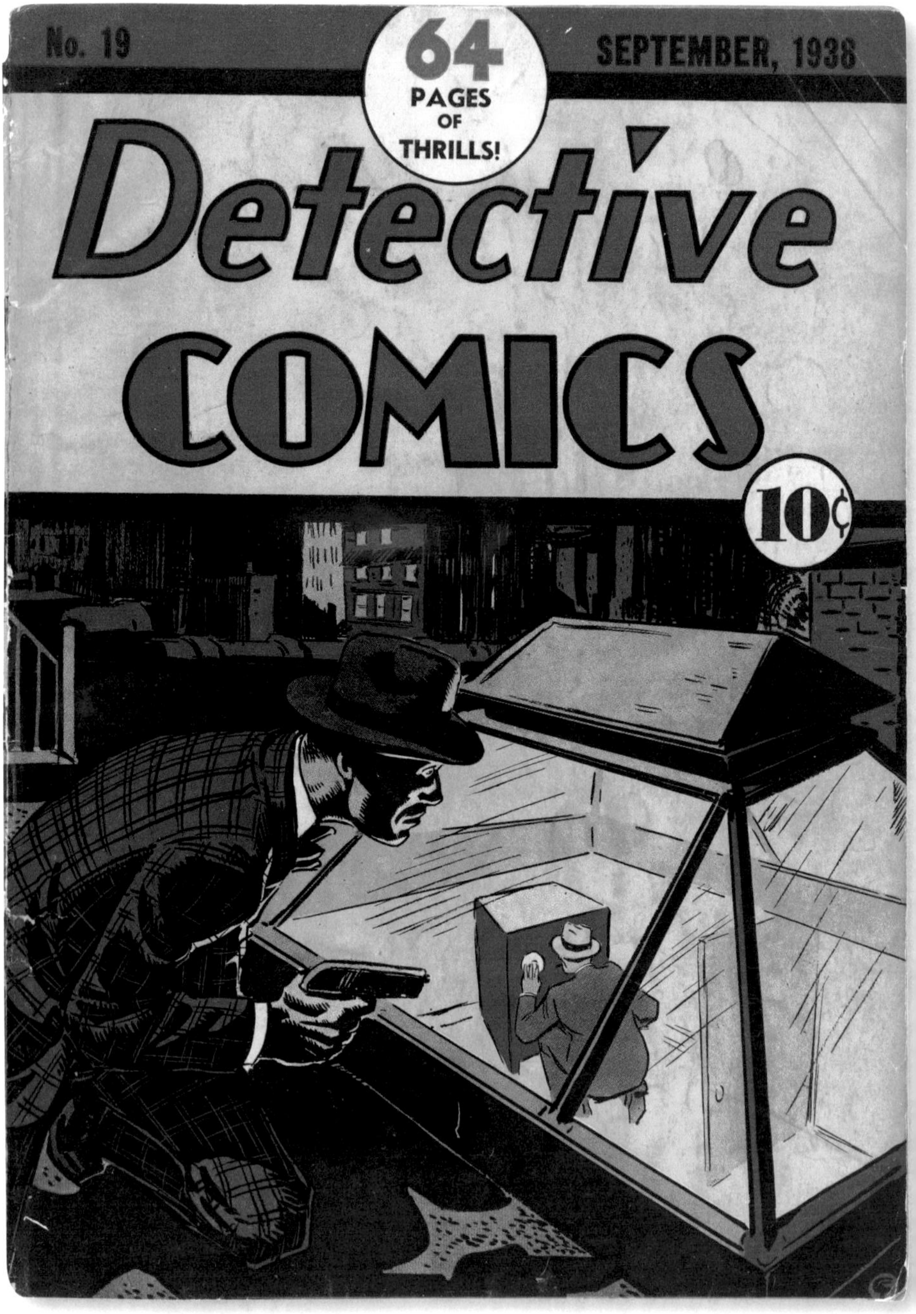
No. 19
64
PAGES
OF
THRILLS!
SEPTEMBER, 1938
Detective
COMICS
10¢

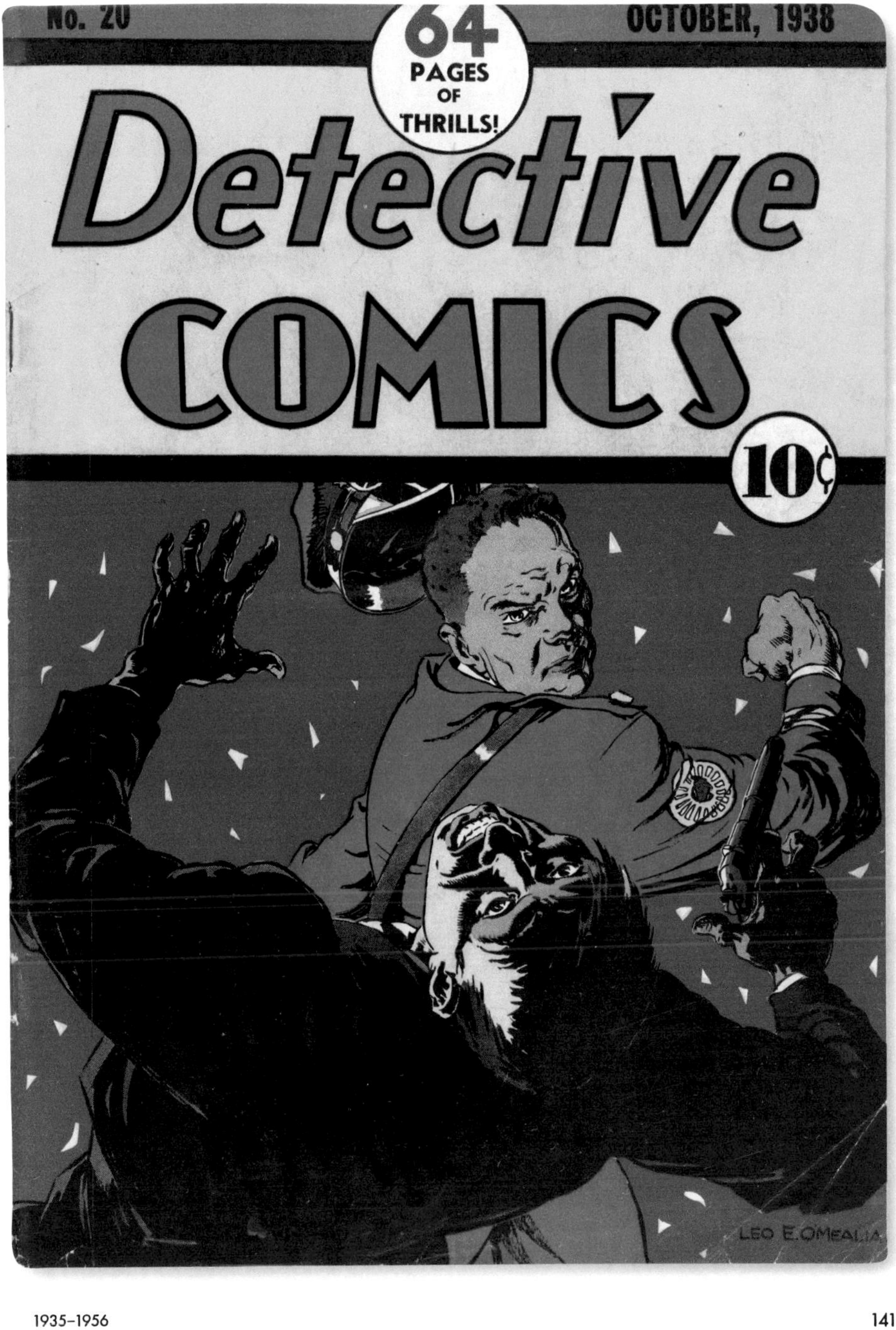
No. 20
64 PAGES OF THRILLS!
OCTOBER, 1938
Detective COMICS
10¢
LEO E. O'MEALIA

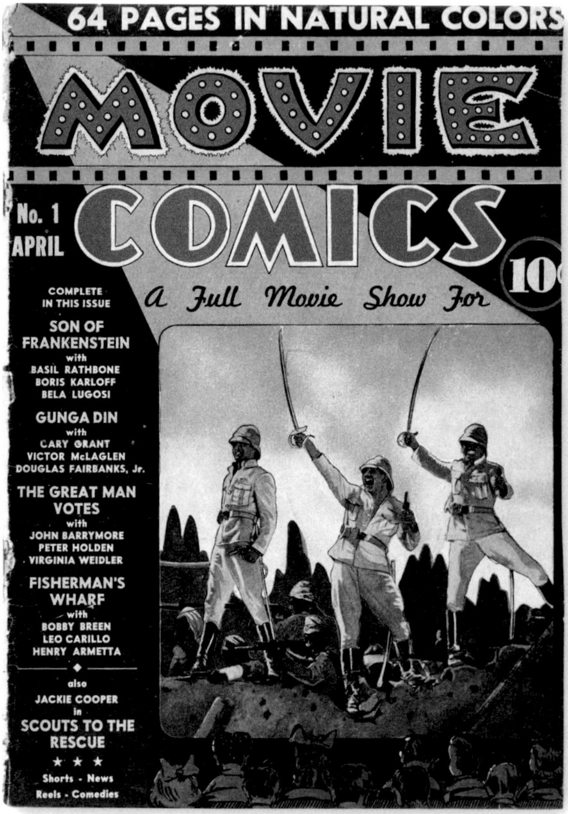
64 PAGES IN NATURAL COLORS
MOVIE
No. 1
APRIL
COMICS
10¢
A Full Movie Show For
COMPLETE IN THIS ISSUE
SON OF FRANKENSTEIN
with
BASIL RATHBONE
BORIS KARLOFF
BELA LUGOSI
GUNGA DIN
with
CARY GRANT
VICTOR McLAGLEN
DOUGLAS FAIRBANKS, Jr.
THE GREAT MAN VOTES
with
JOHN BARRYMORE
PETER HOLDEN
VIRGINIA WEIDLER
FISHERMAN'S WHARF
with
BOBBY BREEN
LEO CARILLO
HENRY ARMETTA
also
JACKIE COOPER
in
SCOUTS TO THE RESCUE
Shorts - News
Reels - Comedies

MOVIE COMICS No. 1

Cover art, airbrushing, and photo coloring, Jack Adler and Emery Gondor, April 1939. The second All-American title had no "box office" to speak of, and disappeared after six issues.

MOVIE COMICS No. 1

Interior, "The Adventures of Phoozy"; script, unknown; airbrushed photo art, Jack Adler. April 1939. Few elements of *Movie Comics* were as bizarre as Phoozy, a one-page featurette that tapped into the popularity of kid film shorts like Hal Roach's *Our Gang* series. Sol Harrison said that all the images in *Movie Comics* were produced at "actual printed size, as opposed to the large size other comic art was drawn. This was because we could not reproduce the halftones. We also had to prepare it for color, and if you look at it in the terms of what we did, using halftones, it was darn good reproduction."

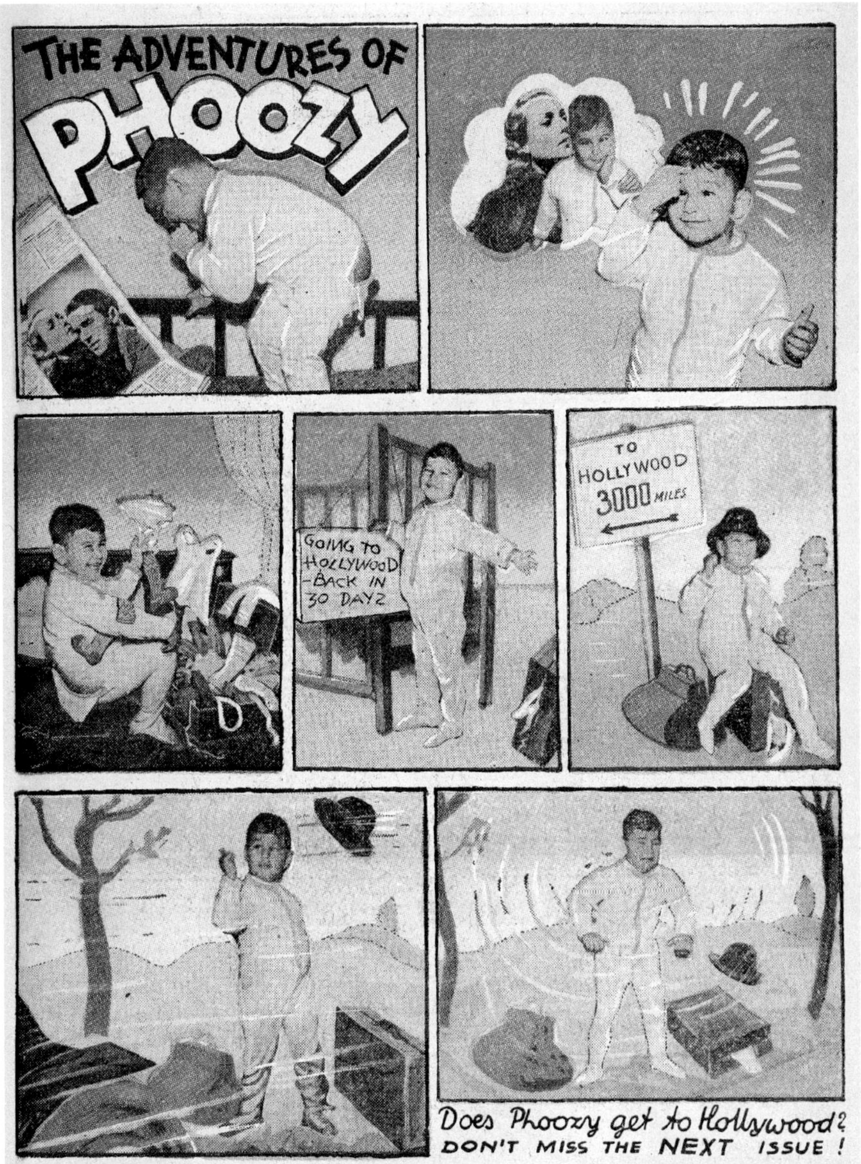
THE ADVENTURES OF
PHOOZY
GOING TO HOLLYWOOD -BACK IN 30 DAYZ
TO HOLLYWOOD 3000 MILES
Does Phoozy get to Hollywood?
DON'T MISS THE NEXT ISSUE!

MOVIE COMICS No. 3

Interior, "East Side of Heaven"; script, unknown (adapting William Conselman screenplay); airbrushed photo art, Jack Adler and Emery Gondor. June 1939. "In most cases, we did not have the photographs that fit the story. We had to piece heads, hats, uniforms together, flop faces and fit the various pieces together." —Sol Harrison

MOVIE COMICS No. 6

Cover art, artist unknown, September–October 1939. Movie Comics never caught on with readers, a consequence of lack of access to many of 1939's most popular films and a general inability to compete with glossy movie magazines.

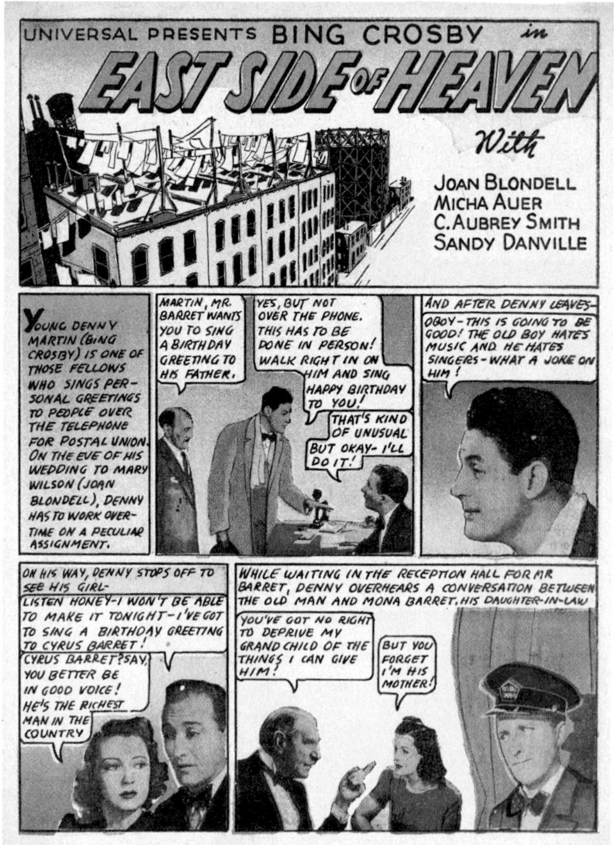

UNIVERSAL PRESENTS BING CROSBY in
EAST SIDE of HEAVEN
With
JOAN BLONDELL
MICHA AUER
C. AUBREY SMITH
SANDY DANVILLE
YOUNG DENNY MARTIN (BING CROSBY) IS ONE OF THOSE FELLOWS WHO SINGS PERSONAL GREETINGS TO PEOPLE OVER THE TELEPHONE FOR POSTAL UNION. ON THE EVE OF HIS WEDDING TO MARY WILSON (JOAN BLONDELL), DENNY HAS TO WORK OVERTIME ON A PECULIAR ASSIGNMENT.
MARTIN, MR. BARRET WANTS YOU TO SING A BIRTHDAY GREETING TO HIS FATHER.
YES, BUT NOT OVER THE PHONE. THIS HAS TO BE DONE IN PERSON! WALK RIGHT IN ON HIM AND SING HAPPY BIRTHDAY TO YOU!
THAT'S KIND OF UNUSUAL BUT OKAY- I'LL DO IT!
AND AFTER DENNY LEAVES-
OBOY- THIS IS GOING TO BE GOOD! THE OLD BOY HATES MUSIC AND HE HATES SINGERS- WHAT A JOKE ON HIM!
ON HIS WAY, DENNY STOPS OFF TO SEE HIS GIRL-
LISTEN HONEY- I WON'T BE ABLE TO MAKE IT TONIGHT- I'VE GOT TO SING A BIRTHDAY GREETING TO CYRUS BARRET!
CYRUS BARRET? SAY, YOU BETTER BE IN GOOD VOICE! HE'S THE RICHEST MAN IN THE COUNTRY
WHILE WAITING IN THE RECEPTION HALL FOR MR BARRET, DENNY OVERHEARS A CONVERSATION BETWEEN THE OLD MAN AND MONA BARRET, HIS DAUGHTER-IN-LAW
YOU'VE GOT NO RIGHT TO DEPRIVE MY GRAND CHILD OF THE THINGS I CAN GIVE HIM!
BUT YOU FORGET I'M HIS MOTHER!

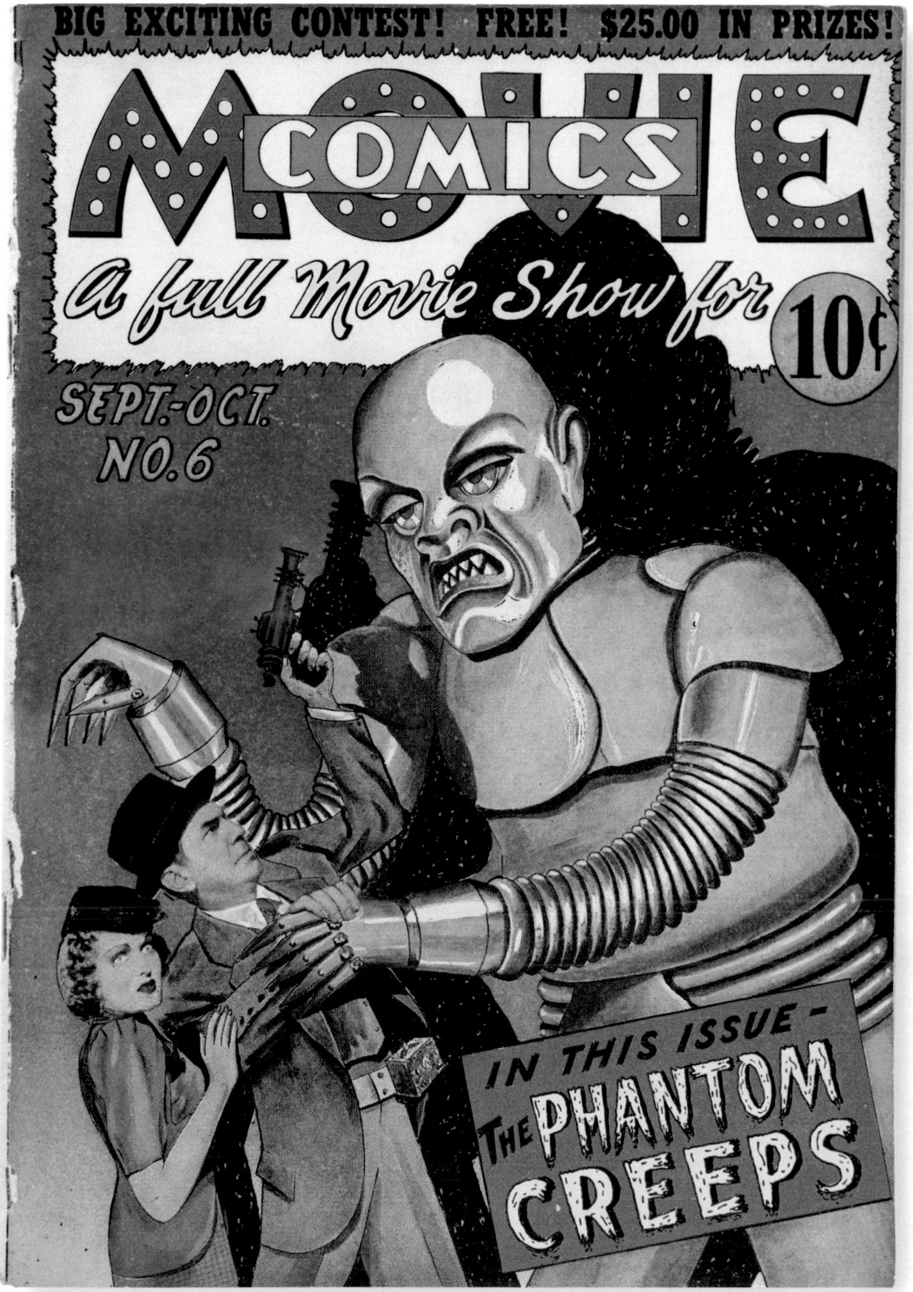
BIG EXCITING CONTEST! FREE! $25.00 IN PRIZES!
MOVIE COMICS
a full Movie Show for
10¢
SEPT.-OCT.
NO.6
IN THIS ISSUE -
THE PHANTOM CREEPS

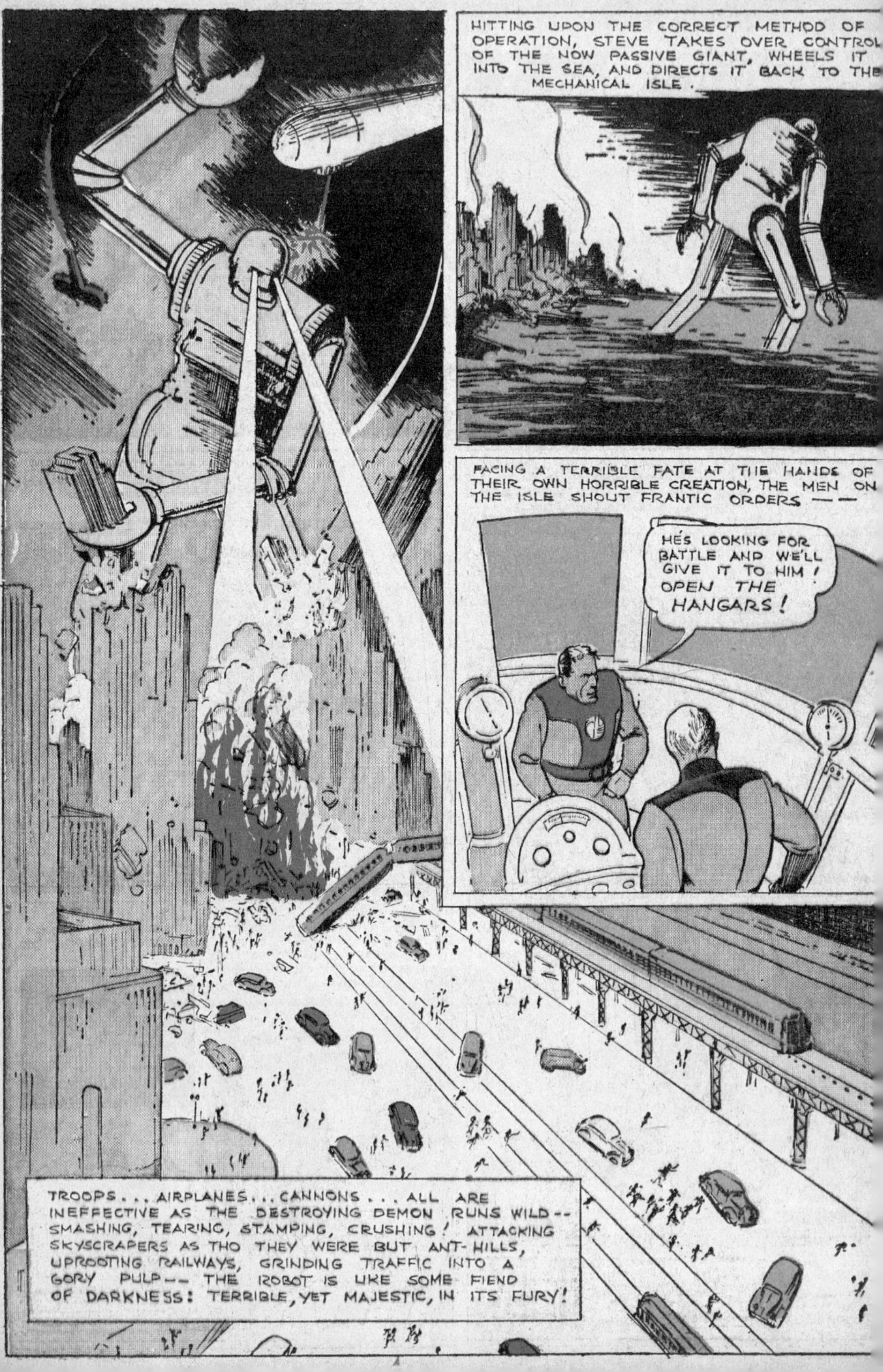
HITTING UPON THE CORRECT METHOD OF OPERATION, STEVE TAKES OVER CONTROL OF THE NOW PASSIVE GIANT, WHEELS IT INTO THE SEA, AND DIRECTS IT BACK TO THE MECHANICAL ISLE.
FACING A TERRIBLE FATE AT THE HANDS OF THEIR OWN HORRIBLE CREATION, THE MEN ON THE ISLE SHOUT FRANTIC ORDERS ——
HE'S LOOKING FOR BATTLE AND WE'LL GIVE IT TO HIM! OPEN THE HANGARS!
TROOPS... AIRPLANES... CANNONS... ALL ARE INEFFECTIVE AS THE DESTROYING DEMON RUNS WILD-- SMASHING, TEARING, STAMPING, CRUSHING! ATTACKING SKYSCRAPERS AS THO THEY WERE BUT ANT-HILLS, UPROOTING RAILWAYS, GRINDING TRAFFIC INTO A GORY PULP-- THE ROBOT IS LIKE SOME FIEND OF DARKNESS: TERRIBLE, YET MAJESTIC, IN ITS FURY!

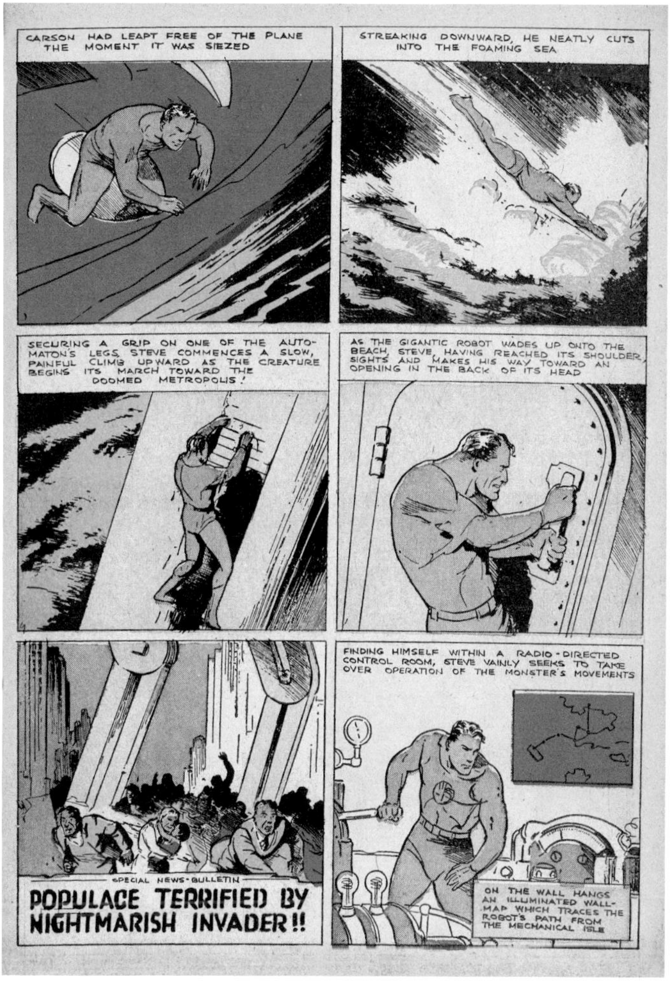
CARSON HAD LEAPT FREE OF THE PLANE THE MOMENT IT WAS SIEZED
STREAKING DOWNWARD, HE NEATLY CUTS INTO THE FOAMING SEA
SECURING A GRIP ON ONE OF THE AUTOMATON'S LEGS, STEVE COMMENCES A SLOW, PAINFUL CLIMB UPWARD AS THE CREATURE BEGINS ITS MARCH TOWARD THE DOOMED METROPOLIS!
AS THE GIGANTIC ROBOT WADES UP ONTO THE BEACH, STEVE, HAVING REACHED ITS SHOULDER, SIGHTS AND MAKES HIS WAY TOWARD AN OPENING IN THE BACK OF ITS HEAD
SPECIAL NEWS-BULLETIN
POPULACE TERRIFIED BY NIGHTMARISH INVADER!!
FINDING HIMSELF WITHIN A RADIO-DIRECTED CONTROL ROOM, STEVE VAINLY SEEKS TO TAKE OVER OPERATION OF THE MONSTER'S MOVEMENTS
ON THE WALL HANGS AN ILLUMINATED WALL-MAP WHICH TRACES THE ROBOT'S PATH FROM THE MECHANICAL ISLE

NEW COMICS No. 10

THIS SPREAD AND FOLLOWING SPREAD: *Interior, "Federal Men"; script, Jerry Siegel; art, Joe Shuster. November 1936.* This was the first of Siegel and Shuster's features to abandon a realistic format in favor of embracing their love of pulp science fiction. A seven-part serial found Steve Carson and his government forces opposing a super-scientific combine called the Invisible Empire that ultimately unleashed a giant robot on the United States' east coast.

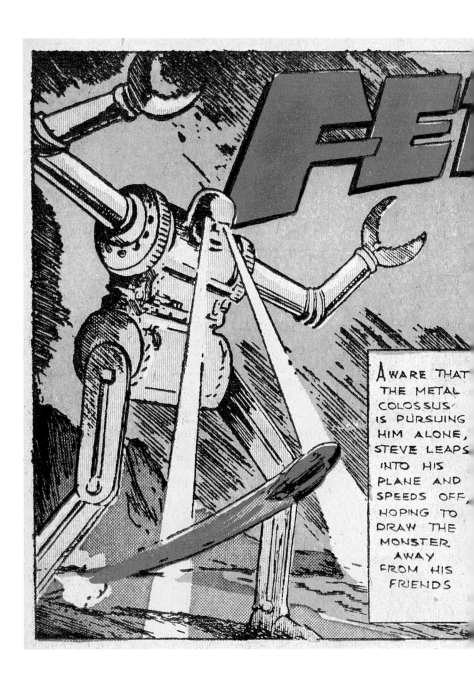

AWARE THAT THE METAL COLOSSUS IS PURSUING HIM ALONE, STEVE LEAPS INTO HIS PLANE AND SPEEDS OFF, HOPING TO DRAW THE MONSTER AWAY FROM HIS FRIENDS

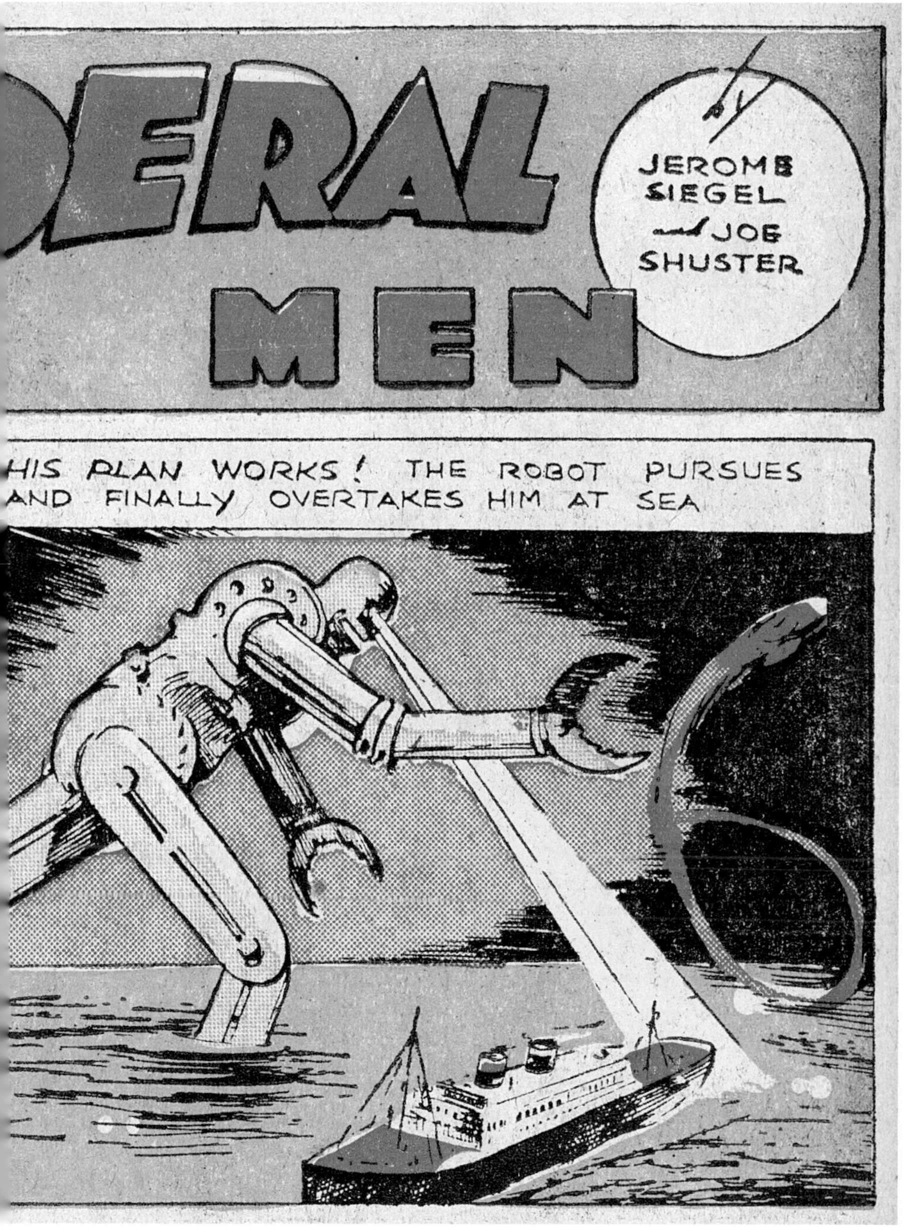

ERAL
MEN
by
JEROME SIEGEL
and JOE SHUSTER
HIS PLAN WORKS! THE ROBOT PURSUES
AND FINALLY OVERTAKES HIM AT SEA

KING KONG

Film still; gorilla model, Marcel Delgado; Empire State Building model, Willis O'Brien. 1933. With significant implications for the 1930s' newest medium, comics, the Depression accelerated the popularity of science fiction among mass audiences, beginning with Hugo Gernsbach's pulps of the late '20s and the surprise smash hit of 1933, *King Kong*.

DETECTIVE COMICS No. 2

Interior, "Slam Bradley"; script, Jerry Siegel; pencils and inks, Joe Shuster. April 1937. Anyone wondering what might have been in Jerry Siegel's mind when he said that "Slam Bradley was a dry run for Superman" need only compare this image to the splash page of "The Mysterious Mr. Mxyztplk" (*Superman* No. 30, September–October 1944). The compositions are similar, and the design of Shorty Morgan was clearly "cannibalized" for the other-dimensional imp.

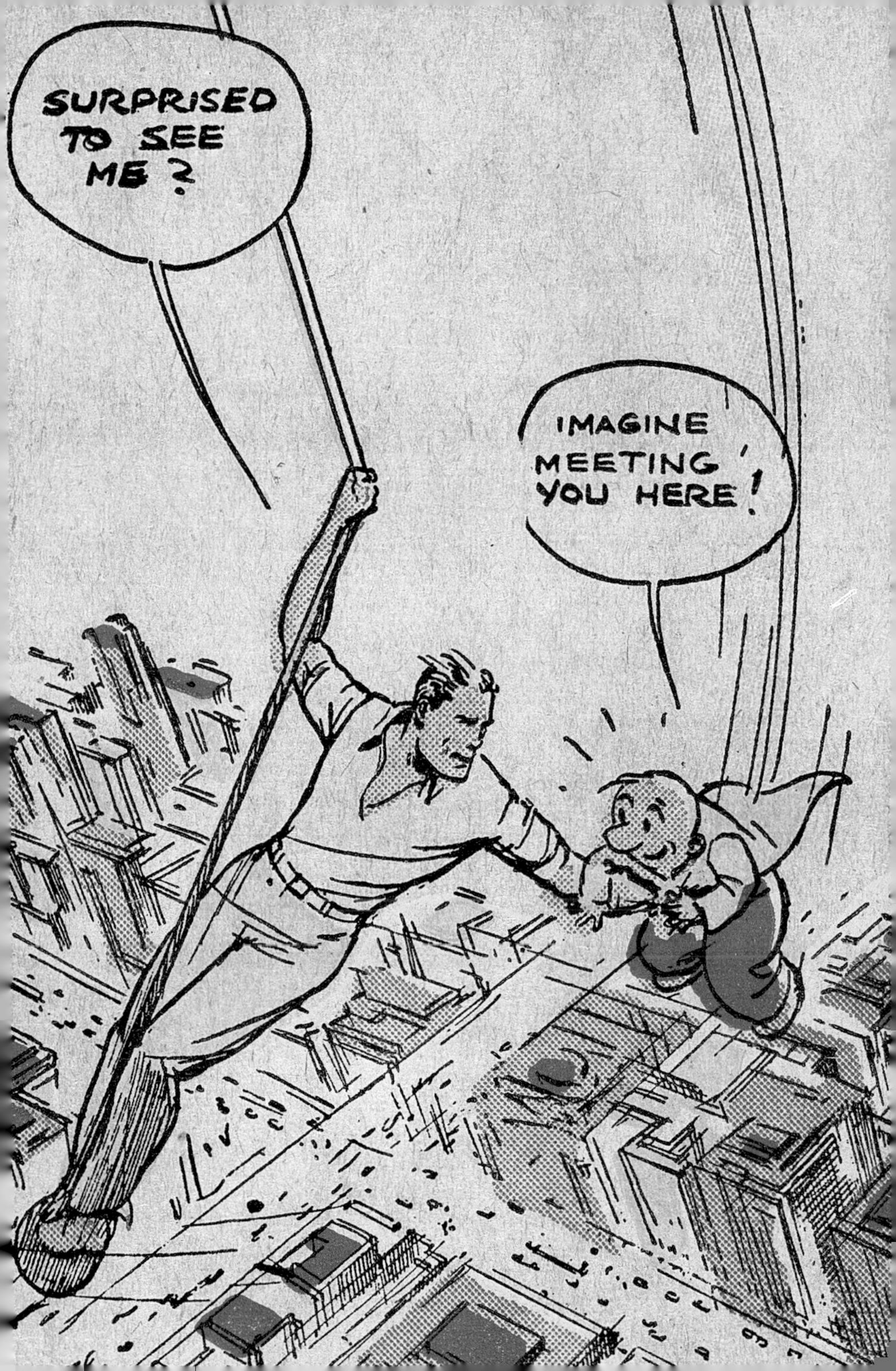
SURPRISED TO SEE ME?
IMAGINE MEETING YOU HERE!

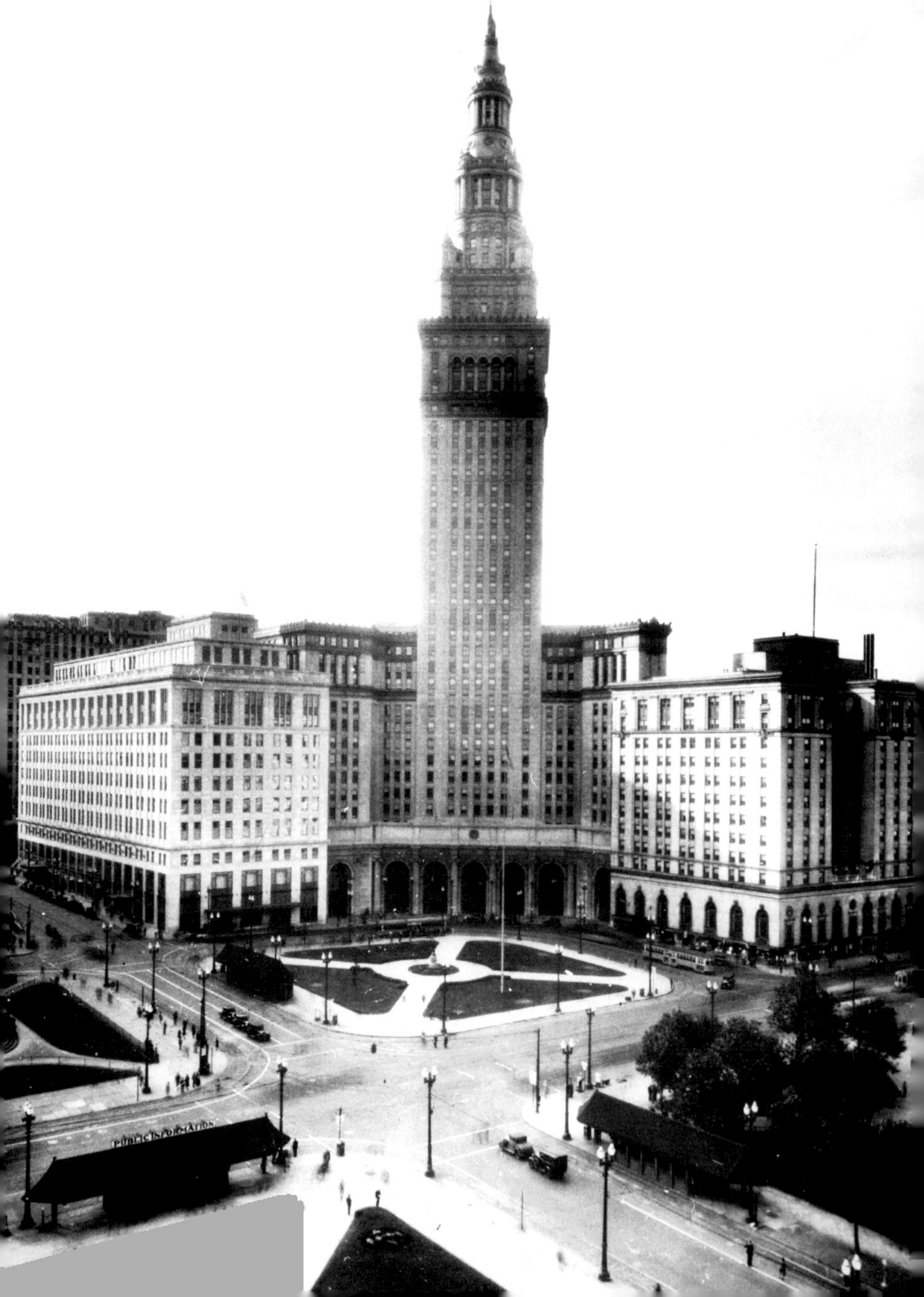
PUBLIC INFORMATION

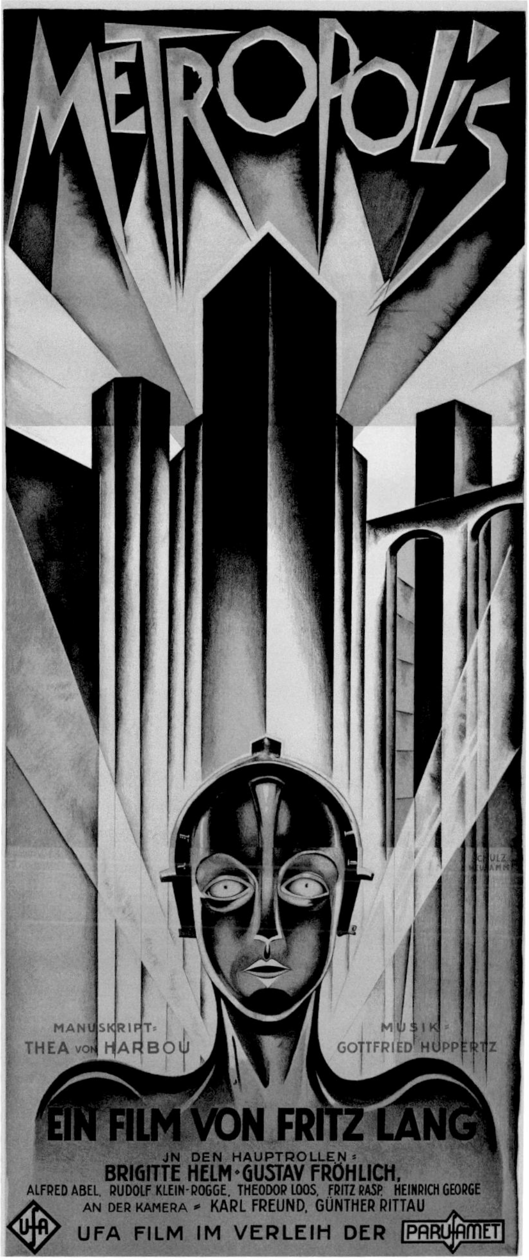
METROPOLIS
MANUSKRIPT:
THEA VON HARBOU
MUSIK:
GOTTFRIED HUPPERTZ
EIN FILM VON FRITZ LANG
JN DEN HAUPTROLLEN:
BRIGITTE HELM · GUSTAV FRÖHLICH,
ALFRED ABEL, RUDOLF KLEIN-ROGGE, THEODOR LOOS, FRITZ RASP, HEINRICH GEORGE
AN DER KAMERA: KARL FREUND, GÜNTHER RITTAU
UFA
UFA FILM IM VERLEIH DER PARUFAMET

TERMINAL TOWER

Photograph, Cleveland, Ohio, landmark frequented by teenagers Jerry Siegel and Joe Shuster, ca. 1935. The interpretation of the steel and concrete canyons over which Siegel and Shuster's heroes soared — before *and* after Superman — was inspired as much by real life as popular culture. In Cleveland rose the 1930s' second-tallest skyscraper. King Kong climbed the first.

METROPOLIS MOVIE POSTER

Poster art, Heinz Schulz-Neudamm, 1927. Science fiction also influenced Shuster's creative vision by arriving, at an impressionable age, in the form of Fritz Lang's German expressionist film. Not only did *Metropolis*'s art deco architectural design elements start to make their way into his cityscapes, the film's name ended up being used by Siegel for Superman's home on Earth.

Occult dons the uniform which is handed to him.

Guard this sword well and it shall never fail you. It is no ordinary weapon as you will learn soon enough. And now you must go, for there is little time.

MORE FUN COMICS No. 15

Interior, "Dr. Occult, Ghost Detective" serial: script, Jerry Siegel (as Leger); pencils and inks, Joe Shuster (as Reuths), November 1936. This panel is contemporaneous with Shuster's 1936 sketches of a prototype Superman costume. All show him considering the trapeze artist's trunks, as well as the cape and chest emblem seen here—as if Shuster wanted to test the character in print.

MORE FUN COMICS No. 16

Interior, "Dr. Occult, Ghost Detective" serial: script, Jerry Siegel (as Leger); pencils and inks, Joe Shuster (as Reuths). December 1936. This and "Henri Duval"—the first two Siegel and Shuster comic book features—supposedly ran under the pseudonym "Leger and Reuths" *only* because there was already so much other material by the pair in print. The Major didn't want to reveal the small size of his talent pool. Not surprisingly, even the spelling of "Leger" sometimes varied.

THE COMICS MAGAZINE No. 1

FOLLOWING SPREAD: *Interior, "Dr. Mystic the Occult Detective"; script, Jerry Siegel; pencils and inks, Joe Shuster. July 1936.*

DR. OCCULT
GHOST DETECTIVE

by LEGAR-REUTHS

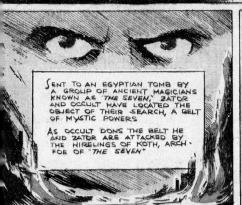

SENT TO AN EGYPTIAN TOMB BY A GROUP OF ANCIENT MAGICIANS KNOWN AS *THE SEVEN*, ZATOR AND OCCULT HAVE LOCATED THE OBJECT OF THEIR SEARCH, A BELT OF MYSTIC POWERS

AS OCCULT DONS THE BELT HE AND ZATOR ARE ATTACKED BY THE HIRELINGS OF KOTH, ARCH-FOE OF *THE SEVEN*

A SLIGHT TOUCH UPON ONE OF THE BELT'S BUTTONS SENDS THE ASTOUNDED DR OCCULT WHIRLING HELPLESSLY UP INTO THE AIR — —

— —WHILE ZATOR TRIPS BEFORE THE SWORD OF A MERCILESS OPPONENT!

OCCULT! TO ME!

HEARING ZATOR'S SHOUT, OCCULT PLUNGES RECKLESSLY DOWN TOWARD HIM, KNOWING HOWEVER THAT HE CANNOT ARRIVE IN TIME. HIS FINGER HAPPENS TO STRIKE ONE OF THE BUTTONS ON THE BELT . . .

HE STIFFENED IN MID-AIR, THEN STRUCK THE GROUND AND SMASHED TO BITS!

THE BELT! IT — —TURNED HIM TO STONE!

FRIGHTENED AT THEIR COMRADE'S FATE, THE REMAINING ATTACKERS FLEE IN TERROR!

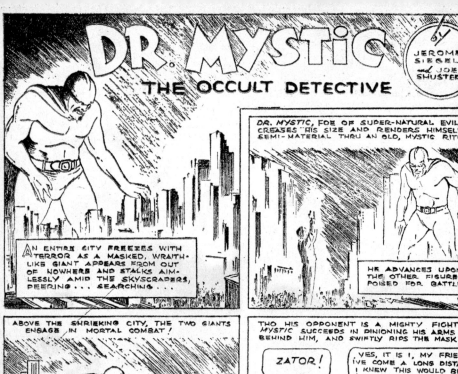

DR. MYSTIC
THE OCCULT DETECTIVE

JEROME SIEGEL and JOE SHUSTER

AN ENTIRE CITY FREEZES WITH TERROR AS A MASKED, WRAITH-LIKE GIANT APPEARS FROM OUT OF NOWHERE AND STALKS AIMLESSLY AMID THE SKYSCRAPERS, PEERING.... SEARCHING...

DR. MYSTIC, FOE OF SUPER-NATURAL EVIL, CREASES HIS SIZE AND RENDERS HIMSELF SEMI-MATERIAL THRU AN OLD, MYSTIC RITU...

HE ADVANCES UPON THE OTHER FIGURE, POISED FOR BATTLE.

ABOVE THE SHRIEKING CITY, THE TWO GIANTS ENGAGE IN MORTAL COMBAT!

THO HIS OPPONENT IS A MIGHTY FIGHTER MYSTIC SUCCEEDS IN PINIONING HIS ARMS BEHIND HIM, AND SWIFTLY RIPS THE MASK

ZATOR!

YES, IT IS I, MY FRIEN. I'VE COME A LONG DISTA. I KNEW THIS WOULD BE THE EASIEST WAY TO LOCATE YOU, THAT YO WOULD WAGE BATTLE W. ME IF I APPEARED AS A MENACE.

IT'S GOOD TO SEE YOU, ZATOR! HOW ARE "THE SEVEN"?

IT IS BECAUSE OF THEM I SEEK YOU. -- THEY WISH YOU TO COME IMMEDIATELY. LET US HURRY!

BEFORE THE SHOCKED EYES OF THE CITY, THE TWO GIANT FIGURES LOCK ARMS COMRADE-LY -- AND VANISH !

THRU THE SPIRIT WORLD, FLASHING ALO. AT A SPEED GREATER THAN THAT OF LIGHT ITSELF, HURTLE THE DE-MATERIAL. BODIES OF MYSTIC AND ZATOR BOUND FOR INDIA AND "THE SEVEN"

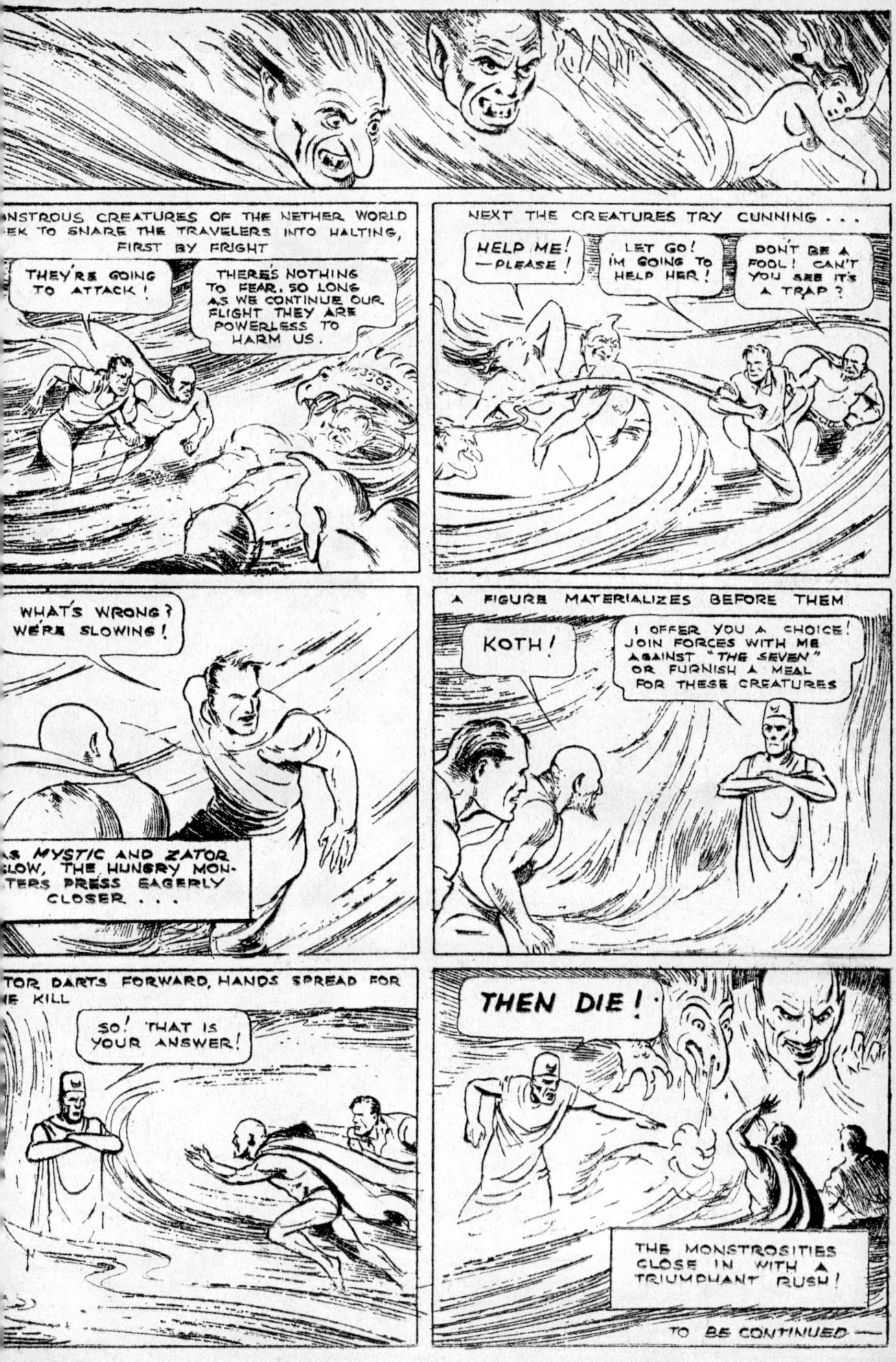

NSTROUS CREATURES OF THE NETHER WORLD
EK TO SNARE THE TRAVELERS INTO HALTING,
FIRST BY FRIGHT
THEY'RE GOING TO ATTACK!
THERE'S NOTHING TO FEAR. SO LONG AS WE CONTINUE OUR FLIGHT THEY ARE POWERLESS TO HARM US.
NEXT THE CREATURES TRY CUNNING . . .
HELP ME! —PLEASE!
LET GO! I'M GOING TO HELP HER!
DON'T BE A FOOL! CAN'T YOU SEE IT'S A TRAP?
WHAT'S WRONG? WE'RE SLOWING!
AS MYSTIC AND ZATOR SLOW, THE HUNGRY MONSTERS PRESS EAGERLY CLOSER . . .
A FIGURE MATERIALIZES BEFORE THEM
KOTH!
I OFFER YOU A CHOICE! JOIN FORCES WITH ME AGAINST "THE SEVEN" OR FURNISH A MEAL FOR THESE CREATURES
TOR DARTS FORWARD, HANDS SPREAD FOR
E KILL
SO! THAT IS YOUR ANSWER!
THEN DIE!
THE MONSTROSITIES CLOSE IN WITH A TRIUMPHANT RUSH!
TO BE CONTINUED—

SUPERMAN

JEROME SIEGEL & JOE SHUSTER

AS A DISTANT PLANET WAS DESTROYED BY OLD AGE, A SCIENTIST PLACED HIS INFANT SON WITHIN A HASTILY DEVISED SPACE-SHIP, LAUNCHING IT TOWARD EARTH!

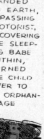

WHEN THE VEHICLE LANDED ON EARTH, A PASSING MOTORIST, DISCOVERING THE SLEEPING BABE WITHIN, TURNED THE CHILD OVER TO AN ORPHAN-AGE

ATTENDANTS, UNAWARE THE CHILD'S PHYSICAL STRUCTURE WAS MILLIONS OF YEARS ADVANCED OF THEIR OWN, WERE ASTOUNDED AT HIS FEATS OF STRENGTH

WHEN MATURITY WAS REACHED, HE DISCOVERED HE COULD EASILY :

LEAP 1/8TH OF A MILE; HURDLE A TWENTY-STORY BUILDING...

RAISE TREMENDOUS WEIGHTS...

...RUN FASTER THAN AN EXPRESS TRAIN...

...AND THAT NOTHING LESS THAN A BURSTING SHELL COULD PENETRATE HIS SKIN!

EARLY, CLARK DECIDED HE MUST TURN HIS TITANIC STRENGTH INTO CHANNELS THAT WOULD BENEFIT MANKIND . AND SO WAS CREATED...

SUPERMAN!

CHAMPION OF THE OPPRESSED, THE PHYSICAL MARVEL WHO HAD SWORN TO DEVOTE HIS EXISTENCE TO HELPING THOSE IN NEED!

A SCIENTIFIC EXPLANATION OF CLARK KENT'S AMAZING STRENGTH

KENT HAD COME FROM A PLANET WHOSE INHABITANTS' PHYSICAL STRUCTURE WAS MILLIONS OF YEARS ADVANCED OF OUR OWN. UPON REACHING MATURITY, THE PEOPLE OF HIS RACE BECAME GIFTED WITH TITANIC STRENGTH!

--INCREDIBLE? NO! FOR EVEN TODAY ON OUR WORLD EXIST CREATURES WITH SUPER-STRENGTH

THE LOWLY ANT CAN SUPPORT WEIGHTS HUNDREDS OF TIMES ITS OWN.

THE GRASSHOPPER LEAPS WHAT TO MAN WOULD BE THE SPACE OF SEVERAL CITY BLOCKS.

Jerry Siegel & Joe Shuster

"It was 1933 and we were in the depths of the Great Depression. The world was full of cruel injustices, and in Europe war seemed imminent. I wondered what I would do if I could make things better. What would I do if I weren't so meek and mild, and if I were stronger than anyone else on Earth?"

—JERRY SIEGEL

ACTION COMICS No. 1
Interior, "Superman"; script, Jerry Siegel; art, Joe Shuster. June 1938. Superman's origin came out bit by bit. Readers wouldn't see the planet Krypton and meet the hero's parents Jor-L and Lora until the newspaper strip premiered in early 1939. Later in 1939, a two-page recap of Superman's birth explained how the infant Kal-L was adopted on Earth by John and Mary Kent.

JERRY SIEGEL & JOE SHUSTER
Photograph, at the drawing table, published in The Saturday Evening Post, *June 21, 1941.*

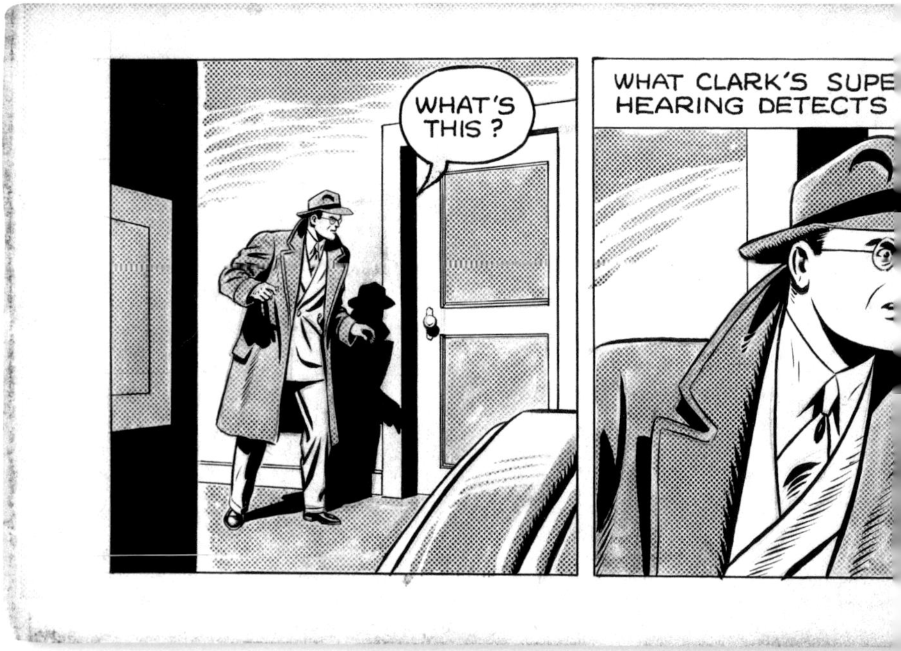
WHAT'S THIS ?
WHAT CLARK'S SUPE
HEARING DETECTS

"SUPERMAN" DAILY COMIC STRIP

Original art, first draft for newspaper comic strip: script, Jerry Siegel; pencils and inks, Joe Shuster Studio. Final strip published April 11, 1947. With newspaper circulations in the millions, popular comic strips like "Little Orphan Annie" and "Dick Tracy" became household names and made their creators extremely wealthy. Jerry Siegel and Joe Shuster aspired to that sort of prestigious role when they first conceived Superman as a comic book and were elated when the character finally acquired his own comic strip only months after the publication of *Action Comics* No. 1.

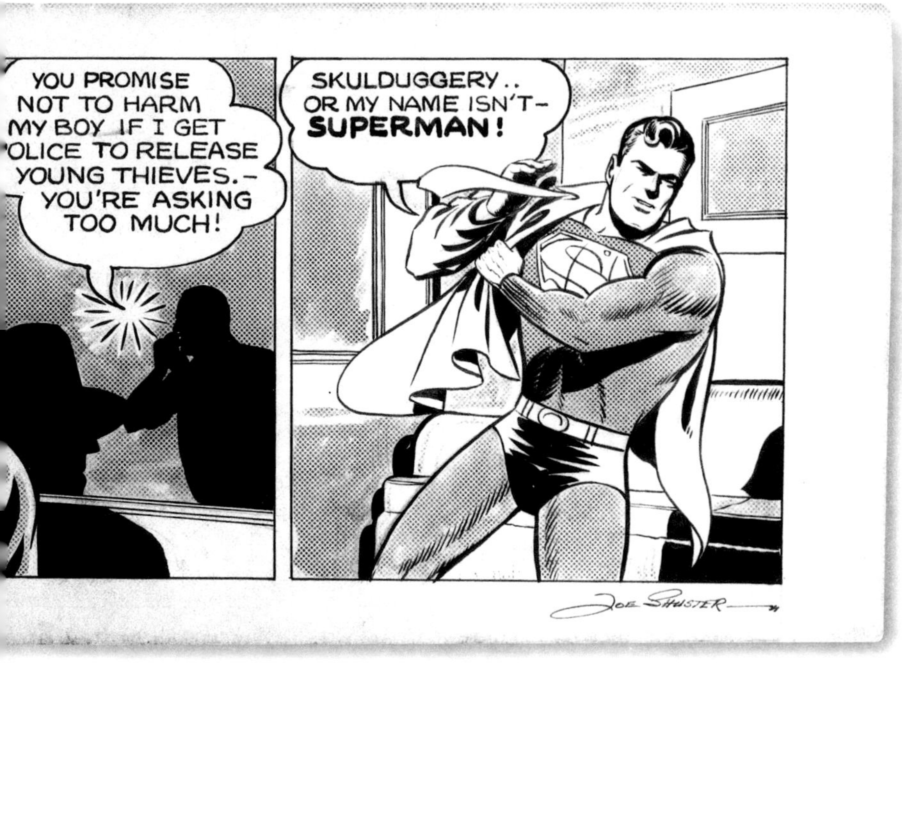
YOU PROMISE NOT TO HARM MY BOY IF I GET 'OLICE TO RELEASE YOUNG THIEVES.- YOU'RE ASKING TOO MUCH!
SKULDUGGERY.. OR MY NAME ISN'T- **SUPERMAN!**
JOE SHUSTER

CLARK KENT
MEEK, DAILY
PLANET REPORTER

SUPERMAN
CHAMPION OF THE
HELPLESS *and* OPPRESSED

ONE AND SAME!

"SUPERMAN" NEWSPAPER STRIP

Script, Jerry Siegel; pencils and inks, Joe Shuster.
November 12, 1939. Superman's double identity is so
universally familiar today that it's hard to imagine a
time when it needed to be explained to readers.

SUPERMAN No. 1

Cover art, Joe Shuster, summer 1939. "Though to all outward
appearances he is now a normal young man of twenty-five,
these gifts include such attributes as a skin impervious to
knife or bullet, the ability to leap over skyscrapers, to run
faster than an express train, to soar through the air, crush
steel or rock in his bare hands, scale buildings like a fly, catch
cannon balls in mid-flight and lift and smash tremendous
weights. He can also on occasion render beautiful young
ladies unconscious by pressing a nerve situated at the back
of the neck." —Slater Brown, *The New Republic*, 1940

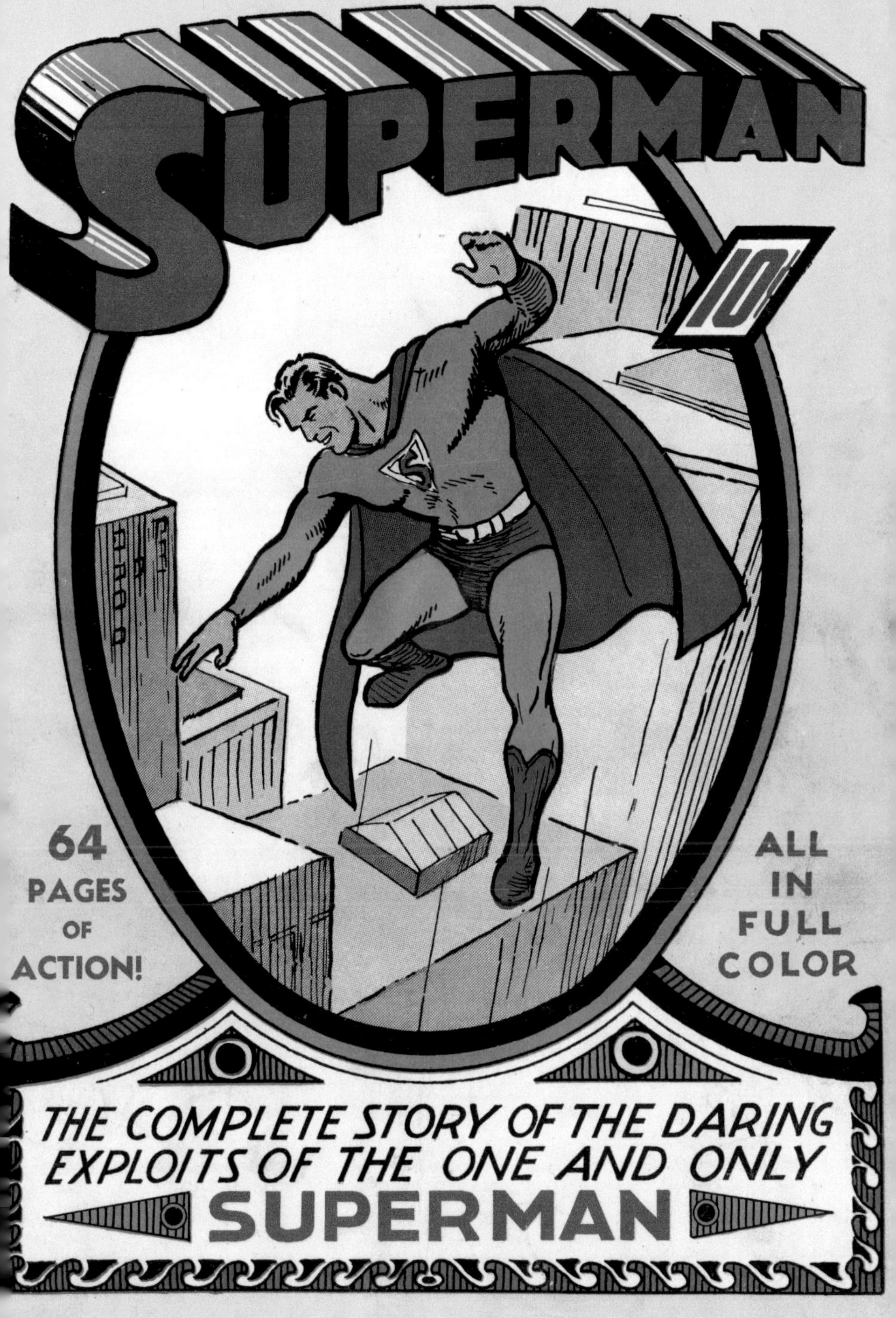
SUPERMAN
10¢
64 PAGES OF ACTION!
ALL IN FULL COLOR
THE COMPLETE STORY OF THE DARING EXPLOITS OF THE ONE AND ONLY
SUPERMAN

THE "FUNNIES," LONG SERIOUS, ARE READ BY EVERY CHILD, MOST GROWNUPS, AND ARE A TREMENDOUS INFLUENCE. IS IT GOOD OR BAD?

BY OLIVE RICHARD

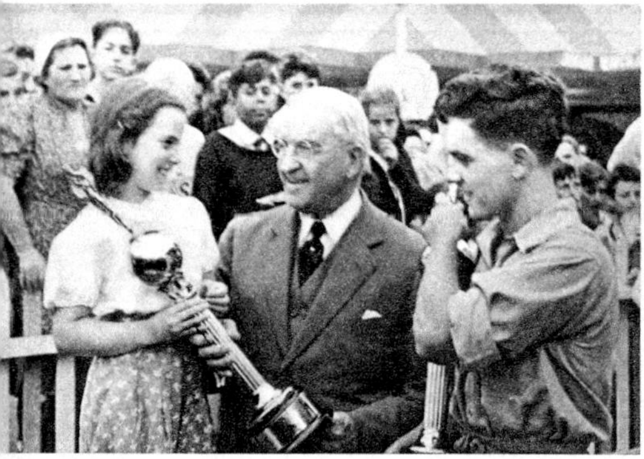

Thousands of youngsters belong to Supermen of America clubs. At the New York World's Fair in July, Maureen Reynolds and William Aronis (shown here with Harvey Gibson, Fair head) were judged Supergirl and Superboy in a contest on Superman Day

riousness, the death knell of comedy appeal in the comics was sounded.

"FOR the better part of two decades," Dr. Marston continued, "about 200 story strips marched steadily along in the Sunday and daily newspapers, then—*presto!*—'Superman' appeared. Comics evolution took another huge jump ahead. Superman—the supernatural, the stupendous, the great and ultimate embodiment of all childhood dreams of strength and power! Until the advent of Superman nearly all story-strip characters had retained some human characteristics and limitations. Their adventures were real in the sense that they exposed themselves to danger as ordinary humans do and suffered various defeats, hard knocks, and painful injuries in the course of winning their inevitable victories. But Superman can't be hurt. His skin sheds bullets like raindrops; he can't be crushed, drowned, burned, poisoned, or otherwise injured. His strength is colossal; he leaps over skyscrapers, runs faster than a bullet, and pushes ocean liners ahead of him while swimming underwater."

Here I broke in. "Oh, I know about Superman!" I exclaimed. "I'm always hearing tales of his greatness, but I don't think children will go on liking that sort of character."

"That," said Dr. Marston, "is precisely what the editors and publishers thought when Superman was first offered to them four or five years ago. Superman was created by Jerry Siegel, a young comics continuity writer from Cleveland. Like most comics originators, Jerry was intensely serious. He believed that the real superman of the future would be somebody with vast power who would use his invincible strength to right human wrongs. Superman is created in the image of that ideal; a man who changes from weak-kneed, ordinary Clark Kent, newspaper reporter, to fabulously powerful Superman at the call of wrong to be righted. Siegel offered Superman to practically every syndicate in the country for five years, only to meet consistent rejection. But he persisted. Finally, three years ago, Siegel sent his brain child to advertising executive M. C. Gaines, a former school principal and the originator of the comics monthly magazine. Mr. Gaines, now publisher of a number of leading publications of this type, had the insight into fundamental emotional appeals which other publishers had lacked. He placed the 'Superman' story strip in *Action Comics* and also induced the McClure Newspaper Syndicate to distribute it. From that

(*Please turn to page* 22)

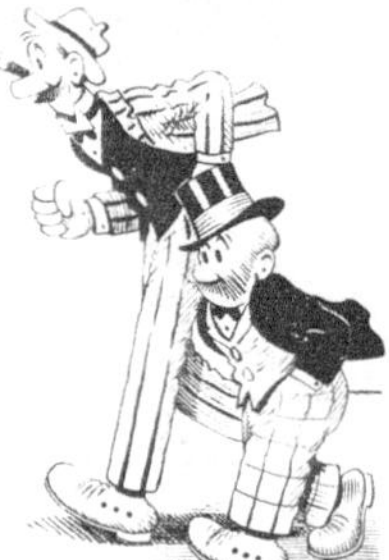

"Mutt and Jeff," now the oldest strip published, is one of the few that still try to keep a large following solely on the basis of humor

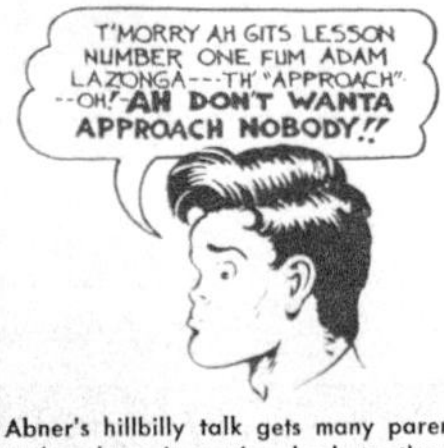
T'MORRY AH GITS LESSON NUMBER ONE FUM ADAM LAZONGA---TH' "APPROACH" --OH!-AH DON'T WANTA APPROACH NOBODY!!

Li'l Abner's hillbilly talk gets many parents down when they hear it coming back to them out of the mouths of their babes. But Dr. Marston thinks that it need not be viewed entirely with alarm

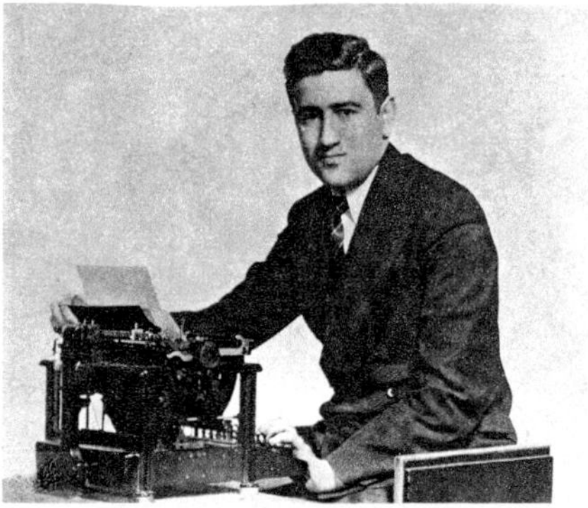

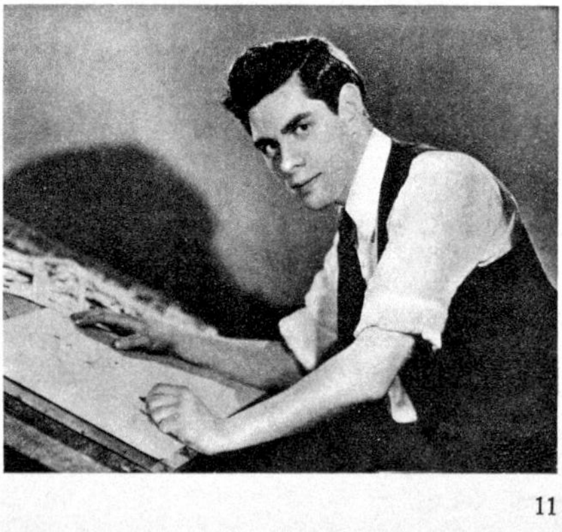

Jerry Siegel (above, right), a comics continuity writer from Cleveland, created "Superman" and then found (as usually happens) that no one wanted it—until he met M. C. Gaines, originator of the comics monthly magazine, who had more insight into fundamental emotional appeals. Joe Shuster (at the right) draws the "Superman" strip

COMIC BOOK FEATURE

Article, "Don't Laugh at the Comics," Family Circle *Magazine; writer, Olive Richard. October 25, 1940.* As Superman's popularity grew, Siegel and Shuster became stars in their own right.

SUPERMAN No. 19

Interior, "Case of the Funny Paper Crimes," featuring Jerry Siegel; script, Jerry Siegel; pencils, Ed Dobrotka; inks, John Sikela. November–December 1942. Jerry Siegel was one of the rare comic book creators who was so well known that he could give Dick Grayson an autograph in a Batman story or be parodied as the alter ego of cartoonist-turned-villain Funny Face in this Superman adventure.

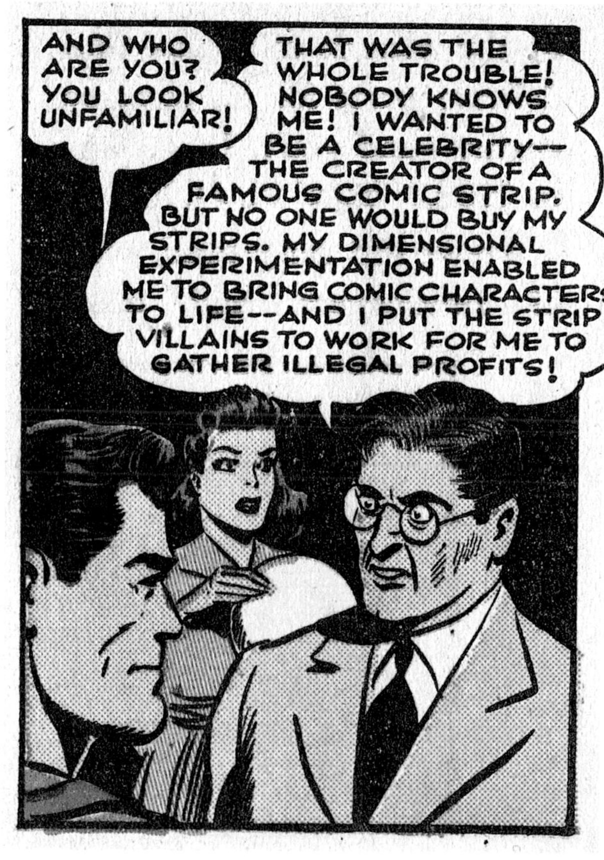
AND WHO ARE YOU? YOU LOOK UNFAMILIAR!
THAT WAS THE WHOLE TROUBLE! NOBODY KNOWS ME! I WANTED TO BE A CELEBRITY-- THE CREATOR OF A FAMOUS COMIC STRIP. BUT NO ONE WOULD BUY MY STRIPS. MY DIMENSIONAL EXPERIMENTATION ENABLED ME TO BRING COMIC CHARACTERS TO LIFE--AND I PUT THE STRIP VILLAINS TO WORK FOR ME TO GATHER ILLEGAL PROFITS!

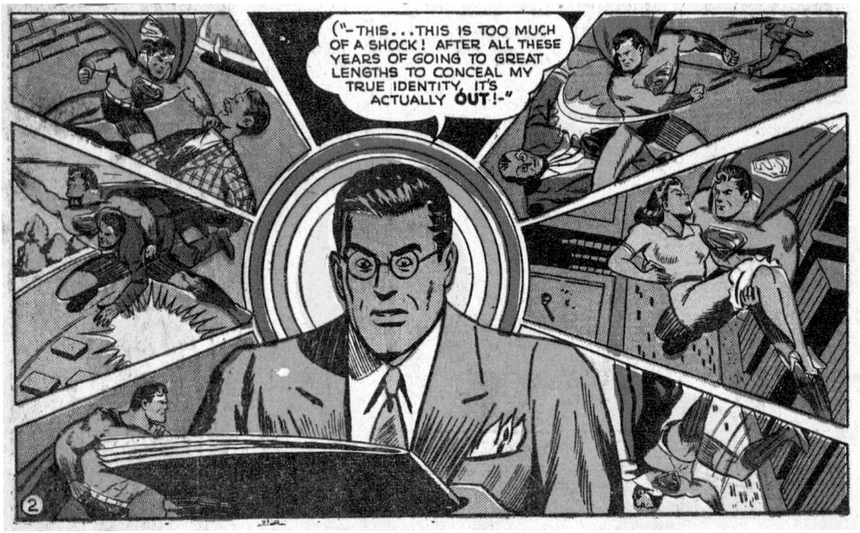
("-THIS...THIS IS TOO MUCH OF A SHOCK! AFTER ALL THESE YEARS OF GOING TO GREAT LENGTHS TO CONCEAL MY TRUE IDENTITY, IT'S ACTUALLY OUT!-"
2

SUPERMAN No. 20

Interior, "Superman's Secret Revealed"; script, Jerry Siegel; pencils, Ed Dobrotka; inks, John Sikela. January–February 1943. "In the silent films, my hero was Douglas Fairbanks Sr., who was very agile and athletic.... He had a stance which I often used in drawing Superman. You'll see in many of his roles—including Robin Hood—that he always stood with his hands on his hips and his feet spread apart, laughing—taking nothing seriously. Clark Kent, I suppose, had a little bit of [bespectacled comic actor] Harold Lloyd in him." —Joe Shuster

SUPERMAN No. 20

Interior, "Superman's Secret Revealed"; script, Jerry Siegel; pencils, Ed Dobrotka; inks, John Sikela. January–February 1943. "Superman was the ultimate assimilationist fantasy. The mild manners and glasses that signified a class of nerdy Clark Kents was, in no way, our real truth. Underneath the schmucky facade there lived Men of Steel! Jerry Siegel's accomplishment was to chronicle the smart Jewish boy's American dream.... It wasn't Krypton that Superman really came from; it was the planet Minsk or Lodz or Vilna or Warsaw." —Jules Feiffer

SUPERMAN No. 13

FOLLOWING SPREAD: *Interiors, "The Archer"; script, Jerry Siegel; pencils and inks, Leo Nowak. November–December 1941.*

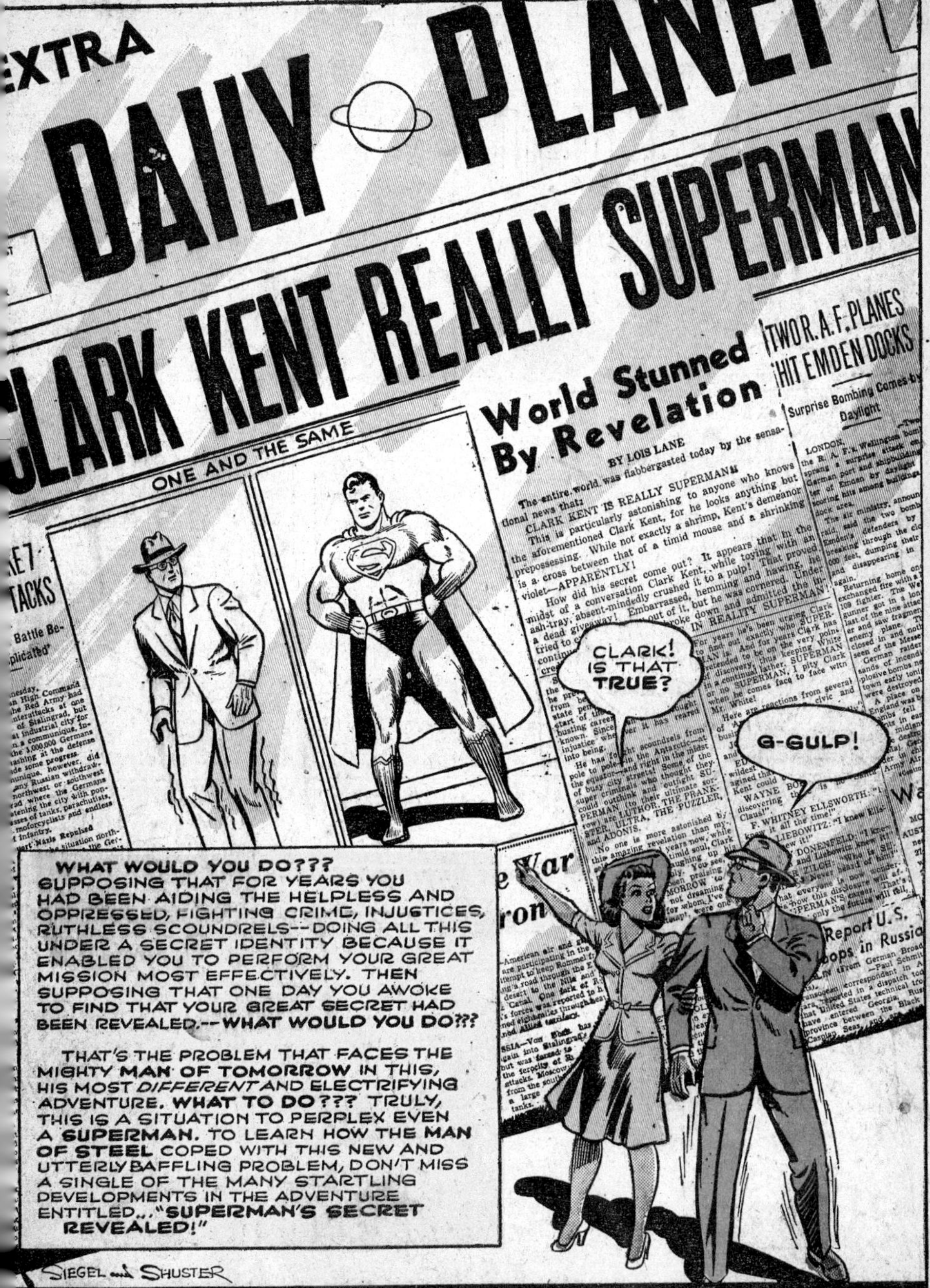

EXTRA
DAILY PLANET
CLARK KENT REALLY SUPERMAN
TWO R.A.F. PLANES HIT EMDEN DOCKS
Surprise Bombing Comes by Daylight
World Stunned By Revelation
BY LOIS LANE
The entire world was flabbergasted today by the sensational news that:
CLARK KENT IS REALLY SUPERMAN!!
ONE AND THE SAME
CLARK! IS THAT TRUE?
G-GULP!
WHAT WOULD YOU DO??? SUPPOSING THAT FOR YEARS YOU HAD BEEN AIDING THE HELPLESS AND OPPRESSED, FIGHTING CRIME, INJUSTICES, RUTHLESS SCOUNDRELS--DOING ALL THIS UNDER A SECRET IDENTITY BECAUSE IT ENABLED YOU TO PERFORM YOUR GREAT MISSION MOST EFFECTIVELY. THEN SUPPOSING THAT ONE DAY YOU AWOKE TO FIND THAT YOUR GREAT SECRET HAD BEEN REVEALED.--WHAT WOULD YOU DO???
THAT'S THE PROBLEM THAT FACES THE MIGHTY MAN OF TOMORROW IN THIS, HIS MOST DIFFERENT AND ELECTRIFYING ADVENTURE. WHAT TO DO??? TRULY, THIS IS A SITUATION TO PERPLEX EVEN A SUPERMAN. TO LEARN HOW THE MAN OF STEEL COPED WITH THIS NEW AND UTTERLY BAFFLING PROBLEM, DON'T MISS A SINGLE OF THE MANY STARTLING DEVELOPMENTS IN THE ADVENTURE ENTITLED..."SUPERMAN'S SECRET REVEALED!"
SIEGEL and SHUSTER
THE GREATEST SCOOP OF ALL TIME!

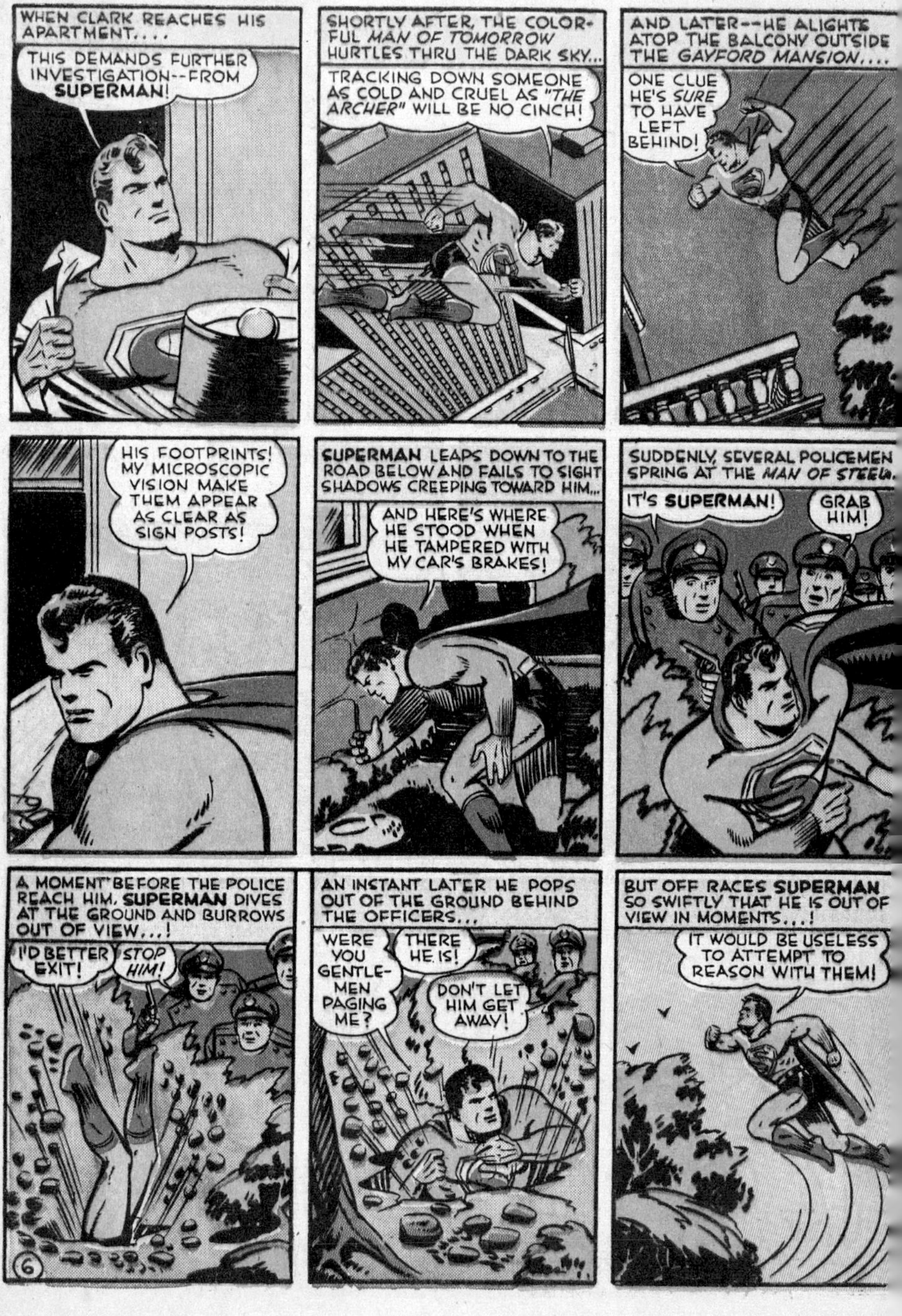

WHEN CLARK REACHES HIS APARTMENT....
THIS DEMANDS FURTHER INVESTIGATION--FROM SUPERMAN!
SHORTLY AFTER, THE COLORFUL MAN OF TOMORROW HURTLES THRU THE DARK SKY...
TRACKING DOWN SOMEONE AS COLD AND CRUEL AS "THE ARCHER" WILL BE NO CINCH!
AND LATER--HE ALIGHTS ATOP THE BALCONY OUTSIDE THE GAYFORD MANSION....
ONE CLUE HE'S SURE TO HAVE LEFT BEHIND!
HIS FOOTPRINTS! MY MICROSCOPIC VISION MAKE THEM APPEAR AS CLEAR AS SIGN POSTS!
SUPERMAN LEAPS DOWN TO THE ROAD BELOW AND FAILS TO SIGHT SHADOWS CREEPING TOWARD HIM...
AND HERE'S WHERE HE STOOD WHEN HE TAMPERED WITH MY CAR'S BRAKES!
SUDDENLY, SEVERAL POLICEMEN SPRING AT THE MAN OF STEEL.
IT'S SUPERMAN!
GRAB HIM!
A MOMENT BEFORE THE POLICE REACH HIM, SUPERMAN DIVES AT THE GROUND AND BURROWS OUT OF VIEW...!
I'D BETTER EXIT!
STOP HIM!
AN INSTANT LATER HE POPS OUT OF THE GROUND BEHIND THE OFFICERS...
WERE YOU GENTLEMEN PAGING ME?
THERE HE IS!
DON'T LET HIM GET AWAY!
BUT OFF RACES SUPERMAN SO SWIFTLY THAT HE IS OUT OF VIEW IN MOMENTS...!
IT WOULD BE USELESS TO ATTEMPT TO REASON WITH THEM!
6

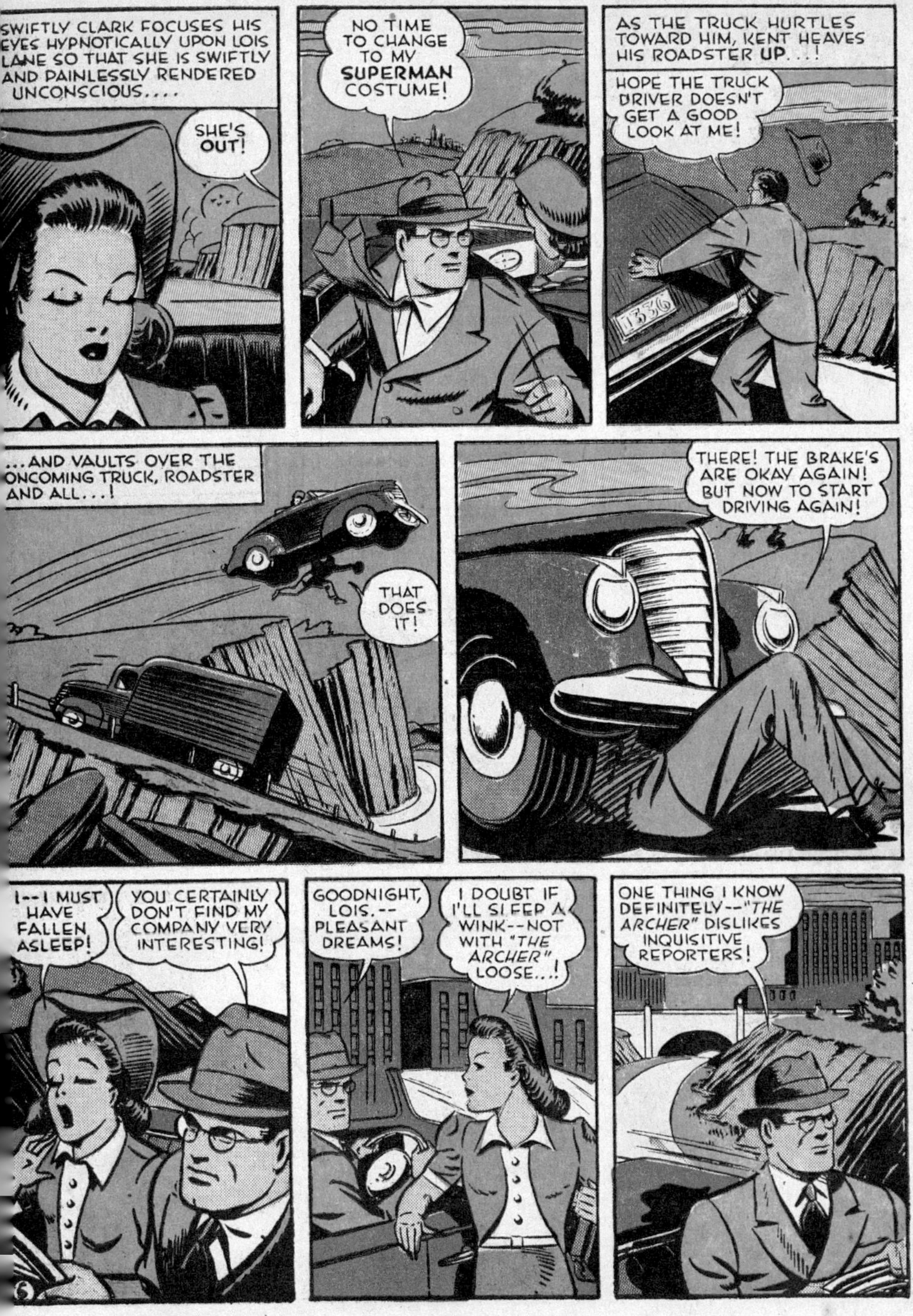
SWIFTLY CLARK FOCUSES HIS EYES HYPNOTICALLY UPON LOIS LANE SO THAT SHE IS SWIFTLY AND PAINLESSLY RENDERED UNCONSCIOUS....
SHE'S OUT!
NO TIME TO CHANGE TO MY SUPERMAN COSTUME!
AS THE TRUCK HURTLES TOWARD HIM, KENT HEAVES HIS ROADSTER UP...!
HOPE THE TRUCK DRIVER DOESN'T GET A GOOD LOOK AT ME!
1336
...AND VAULTS OVER THE ONCOMING TRUCK, ROADSTER AND ALL...!
THAT DOES IT!
THERE! THE BRAKE'S ARE OKAY AGAIN! BUT NOW TO START DRIVING AGAIN!
I--I MUST HAVE FALLEN ASLEEP!
YOU CERTAINLY DON'T FIND MY COMPANY VERY INTERESTING!
GOODNIGHT, LOIS.-- PLEASANT DREAMS!
I DOUBT IF I'LL SLEEP A WINK--NOT WITH "THE ARCHER" LOOSE...!
ONE THING I KNOW DEFINITELY--"THE ARCHER" DISLIKES INQUISITIVE REPORTERS!

John Sunlight hit
again, again . . .

strength to fetch them.

John Sunlight took the heaviest sledge.

"Stay here." His eyes smoldered in the almost-black cups which his eye sockets had become. "Stay here."

He stood and gave each of them hypnotic attention in turn.

"None of you must ever go near that blue dome," he said with stark intensity.

He did not say what would happen if they disobeyed; did not voice a single threat. It was not his way to give physical threats; no one had ever heard him do so. Because it is easy to threaten a man's body, but difficult to explain how a terrible thing can happen to a mind. That kind of a threat would not sound convincing, or even anything but silly.

But they knew when they heard him. And he knew, too, that not one of them would go near the Strange Blue Dome. He had not exerted his hideous sway over them for months for nothing.

It took a longer time for John Sunlight to make his way back to the vast blue thing. He planted his feet wide, and raised the sledge hammer, and gathered all his great strength—his strength was more incredible than anyone could have imagined, even starved as he was—and hit the blue dome.

There was a single clear ringing note, as if a great bell had been tapped once, and the sound doubtless carried for miles, although it did not seem loud.

John Sunlight lowered the sledge hammer, examined the place where he had struck. He made his growling. It was a low and beastly growl, almost the only emotional sound he ever made. Too, the bestial growl was almost the only meaty, physical thing he ever did. Otherwise he seemed to be composed entirely of a frightful mind.

DOC SAVAGE'S FORTRESS OF SOLITUDE

Interior. Doc Savage *No. 68. "The Fortress of Solitude";
script, Lester Dent; artist, Paul Orban. October 1938.*
Pulp adventurer Clark "Doc" Savage had a great influence
not only on Superman creator Jerry Siegel but also future
editor Mort Weisinger. It was the latter who relocated the
Man of Steel's secret hideaway to the Arctic and dubbed it
the Fortress of Solitude after Savage's 1930s sanctuary.

SUPERMAN No. 17

*Interior, "Muscles for Sale"; script, Jerry Siegel; pencils and inks,
John Sikela. July–August 1942.* Superman originally found time
to unwind in a secret mountain retreat north of Metropolis
whose ornate entrance ought to have caught someone's
attention. The citadel included a state-of-the-art gym,
trophies, and a laboratory. In *Superman* No. 58 (1949),
the retreat was moved to "the polar wastes" and referred
to as the Fortress of Solitude for the first time.

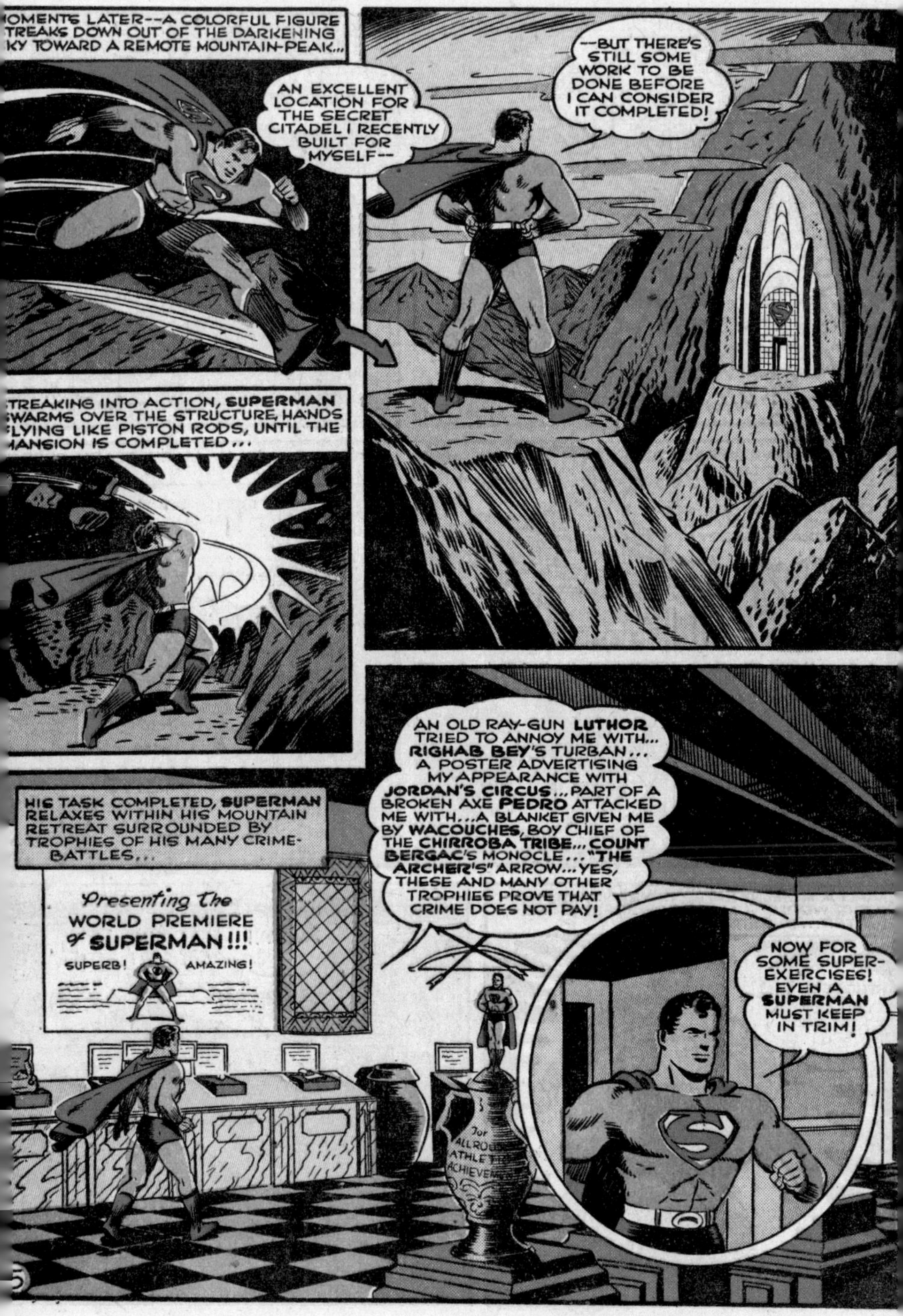

MOMENTS LATER--A COLORFUL FIGURE STREAKS DOWN OUT OF THE DARKENING SKY TOWARD A REMOTE MOUNTAIN-PEAK...
AN EXCELLENT LOCATION FOR THE SECRET CITADEL I RECENTLY BUILT FOR MYSELF--
--BUT THERE'S STILL SOME WORK TO BE DONE BEFORE I CAN CONSIDER IT COMPLETED!
STREAKING INTO ACTION, SUPERMAN SWARMS OVER THE STRUCTURE, HANDS FLYING LIKE PISTON RODS, UNTIL THE MANSION IS COMPLETED...
HIS TASK COMPLETED, SUPERMAN RELAXES WITHIN HIS MOUNTAIN RETREAT SURROUNDED BY TROPHIES OF HIS MANY CRIME-BATTLES...
Presenting the WORLD PREMIERE of SUPERMAN!!!
SUPERB! AMAZING!
AN OLD RAY-GUN LUTHOR TRIED TO ANNOY ME WITH... RIGHAB BEY'S TURBAN... A POSTER ADVERTISING MY APPEARANCE WITH JORDAN'S CIRCUS... PART OF A BROKEN AXE PEDRO ATTACKED ME WITH... A BLANKET GIVEN ME BY WACOUCHES, BOY CHIEF OF THE CHIRROBA TRIBE... COUNT BERGAC'S MONOCLE... "THE ARCHER'S" ARROW... YES, THESE AND MANY OTHER TROPHIES PROVE THAT CRIME DOES NOT PAY!
NOW FOR SOME SUPER-EXERCISES! EVEN A SUPERMAN MUST KEEP IN TRIM!

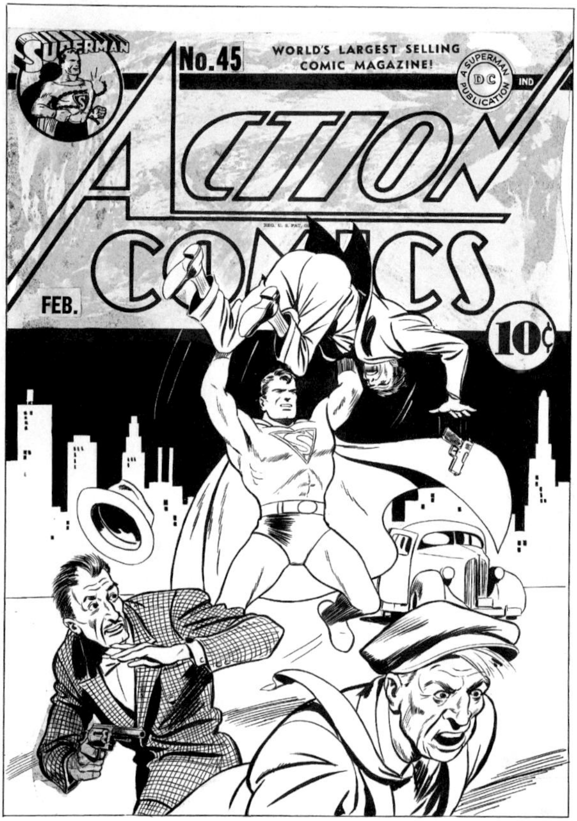
SUPERMAN
No. 45
WORLD'S LARGEST SELLING
COMIC MAGAZINE!
A SUPERMAN DC PUBLICATION
IND
ACTION
COMICS
FEB.
10¢

ACTION COMICS No. 45

Original cover art, Fred Ray, February 1942.
The early Superman could be a fearsome presence, even killing a handful of early opponents.

SUPERMAN No. 17

Interior, "Man or Superman?"; script, Jerry Siegel; pencils, Joe Shuster; inks, John Sikela. July–August 1942. Three years into their working relationship, Lois Lane finally notices that there is something a little suspicious about her mild-mannered fellow reporter, Clark Kent, and begins the first in a seemingly endless series of efforts to prove that he is really Superman.

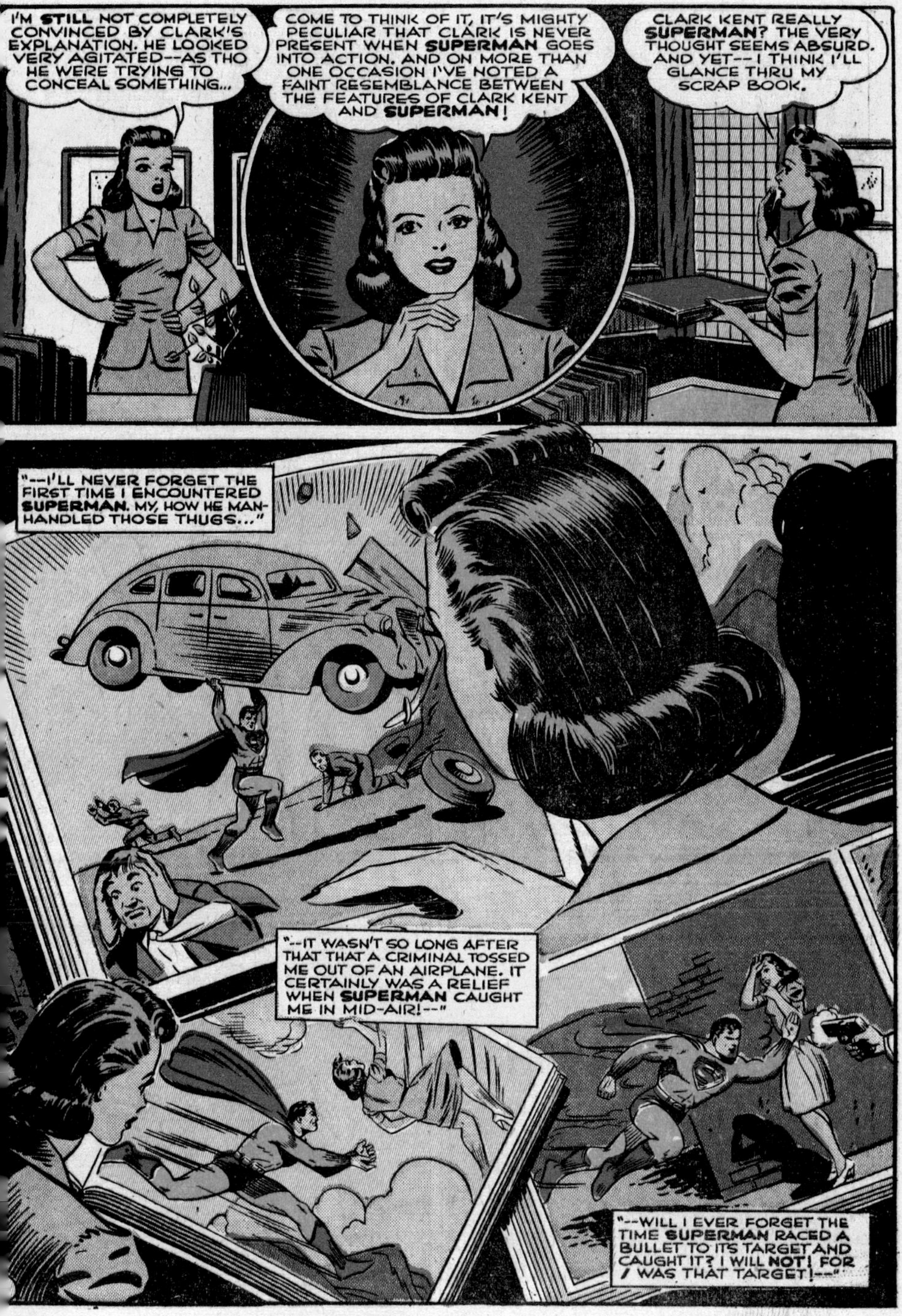

I'M STILL NOT COMPLETELY CONVINCED BY CLARK'S EXPLANATION. HE LOOKED VERY AGITATED--AS THO HE WERE TRYING TO CONCEAL SOMETHING...
COME TO THINK OF IT, IT'S MIGHTY PECULIAR THAT CLARK IS NEVER PRESENT WHEN SUPERMAN GOES INTO ACTION. AND ON MORE THAN ONE OCCASION I'VE NOTED A FAINT RESEMBLANCE BETWEEN THE FEATURES OF CLARK KENT AND SUPERMAN!
CLARK KENT REALLY SUPERMAN? THE VERY THOUGHT SEEMS ABSURD. AND YET-- I THINK I'LL GLANCE THRU MY SCRAP BOOK.
"--I'LL NEVER FORGET THE FIRST TIME I ENCOUNTERED SUPERMAN. MY, HOW HE MAN-HANDLED THOSE THUGS..."
"--IT WASN'T SO LONG AFTER THAT THAT A CRIMINAL TOSSED ME OUT OF AN AIRPLANE. IT CERTAINLY WAS A RELIEF WHEN SUPERMAN CAUGHT ME IN MID-AIR!--"
"--WILL I EVER FORGET THE TIME SUPERMAN RACED A BULLET TO ITS TARGET AND CAUGHT IT? I WILL NOT! FOR I WAS THAT TARGET!--"

SUPERMAN No. 5

Cover art, Wayne Boring and Paul Lauretta, summer 1940. "Back then, comic books were the stepchild of the publishing industry. Mostly, they were looked down on, except by their millions of ardent readers." —Jerry Siegel

ACTION COMICS No. 29

Interior, "Superman"; script, Jerry Siegel; pencils and inks, Jack Burnley. October 1940. The early Superman was very much a populist crusader, as in this story, in which he intervenes on behalf of elderly citizens victimized by an insurance scam linked to a pharmacy. "Jerry was one of the first I can remember—at least in the comic books—who really used the style of a screenwriter. He would describe each scene, and the shot used—long shot, medium, close-up, overhead shot. It was marvelous.... He would study the techniques of the movie serials, but he never saw a written screenplay." —Joe Shuster

No.5
SUMMER ISSUE
SUPERMAN
10¢

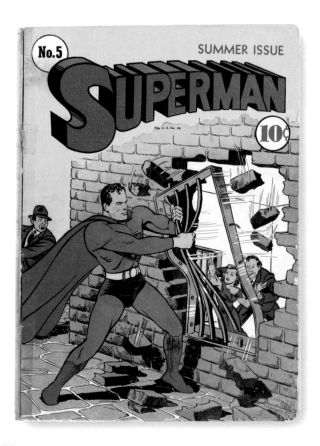

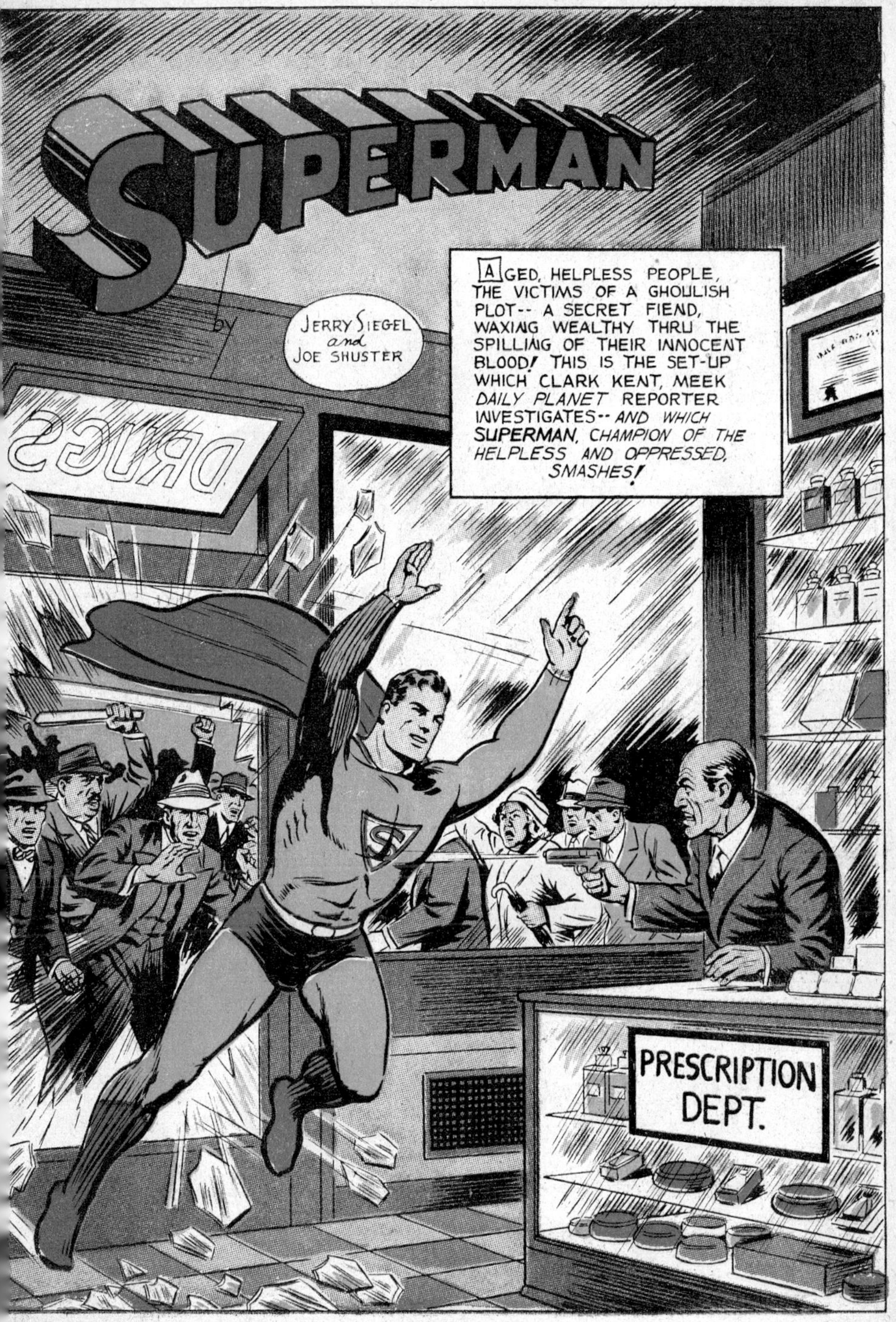
SUPERMAN
by JERRY SIEGEL and JOE SHUSTER
AGED, HELPLESS PEOPLE, THE VICTIMS OF A GHOULISH PLOT-- A SECRET FIEND, WAXING WEALTHY THRU THE SPILLING OF THEIR INNOCENT BLOOD! THIS IS THE SET-UP WHICH CLARK KENT, MEEK DAILY PLANET REPORTER INVESTIGATES-- AND WHICH SUPERMAN, CHAMPION OF THE HELPLESS AND OPPRESSED, SMASHES!
DRUGS
PRESCRIPTION DEPT.

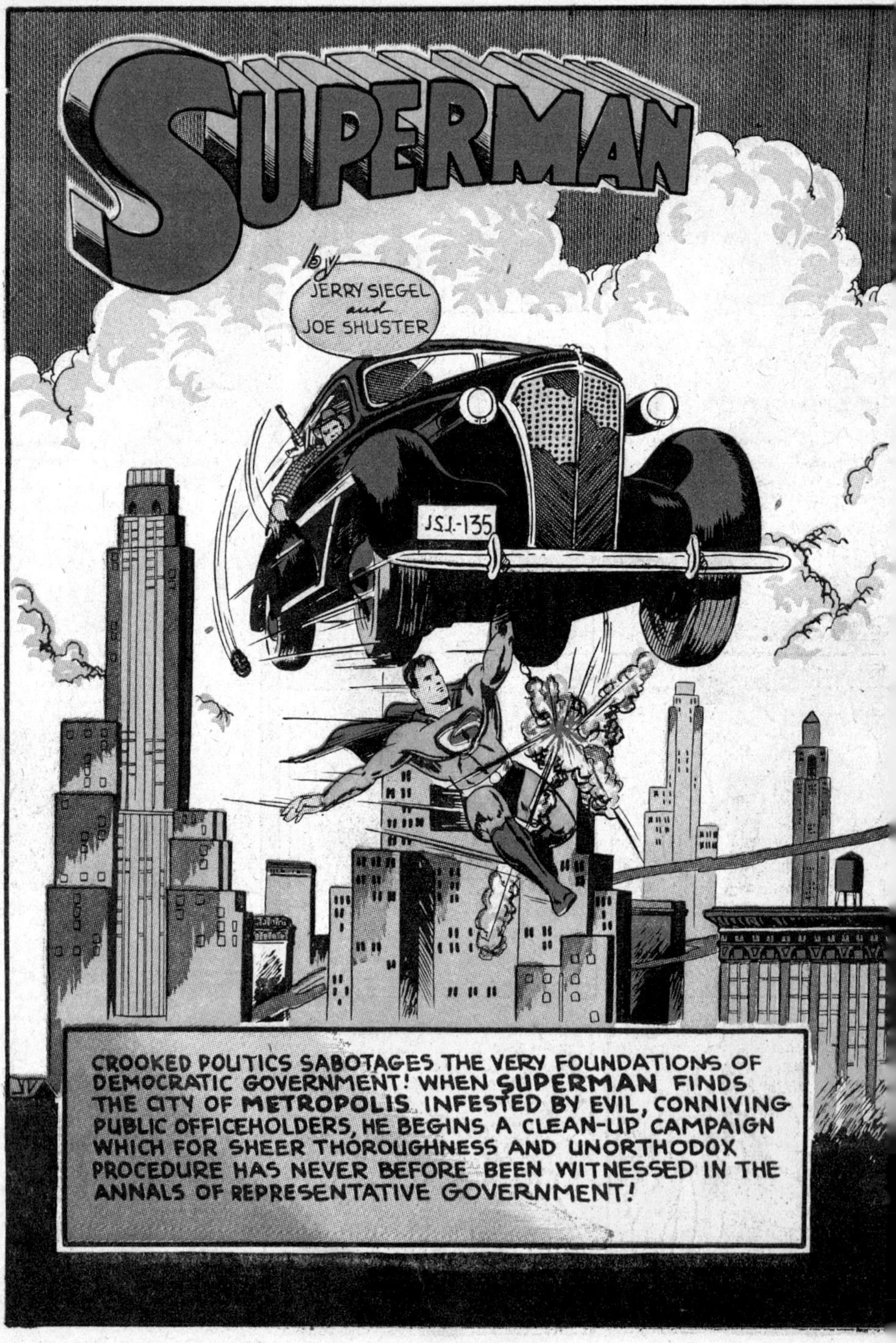
SUPERMAN
by JERRY SIEGEL and JOE SHUSTER
JSI.-135
CROOKED POLITICS SABOTAGES THE VERY FOUNDATIONS OF DEMOCRATIC GOVERNMENT! WHEN SUPERMAN FINDS THE CITY OF METROPOLIS INFESTED BY EVIL, CONNIVING PUBLIC OFFICEHOLDERS, HE BEGINS A CLEAN-UP CAMPAIGN WHICH FOR SHEER THOROUGHNESS AND UNORTHODOX PROCEDURE HAS NEVER BEFORE BEEN WITNESSED IN THE ANNALS OF REPRESENTATIVE GOVERNMENT!

"The passage of time…has only confirmed Superman's position as the Odin-figure amidst a munificent mythology of comic titans. He has witnessed a genesis of super-copies born, grow, change, struggle, die and be welcomed into the sanctum sanctorum of super hero Valhalla. He has endured. And as long as he continues, his patriarchal presence will be felt."

—JIM STERANKO

SUPERMAN No. /

Interior, "Superman"; script, Jerry Siegel; pencils and inks, Wayne Boring. November–December 1940. "I liked Joe Shuster's Superman. It was an awkward style, it wasn't a great style, but he told a story very well. When you saw his Superman pick up an automobile, it looked great. I mean, look at this little man picking up an automobile—you know, fantastic. But today, when Superman picks up an automobile, you say, 'Well, that's no big trick. Look at the muscles on this guy. I mean, he could probably pick up two automobiles.'" —Sheldon Moldoff

ACTION COMICS No. 50

PAGE 178: *Cover art, Fred Ray, July 1942.*

ACTION COMICS No. 13

PAGE 179: *Cover art, Joe Shuster, June 1939.*

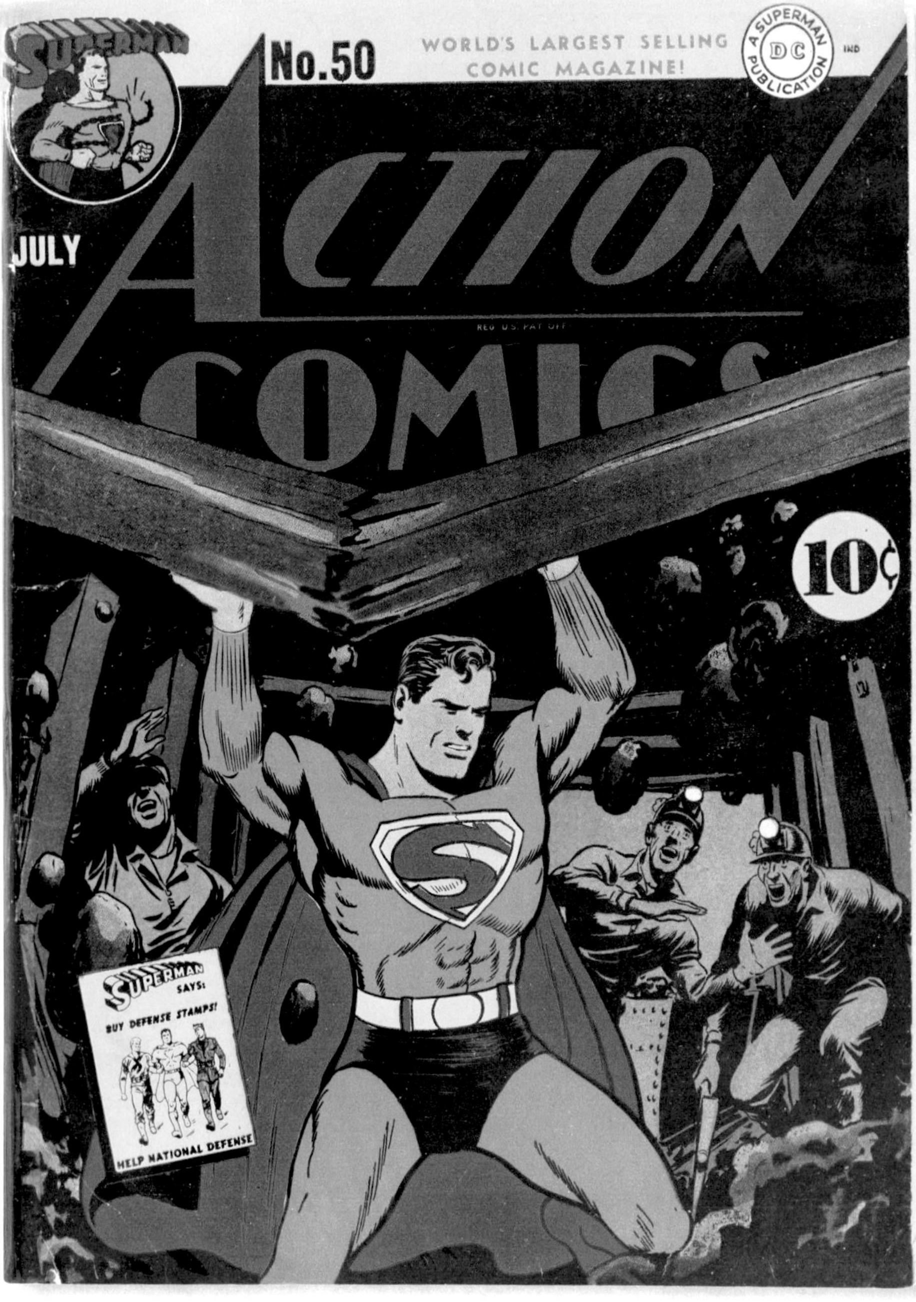

SUPERMAN
No.50
WORLD'S LARGEST SELLING
COMIC MAGAZINE!
A SUPERMAN
DC
PUBLICATION
JULY
ACTION
REG. U.S. PAT. OFF.
COMICS
10¢
SUPERMAN
SAYS:
BUY DEFENSE STAMPS!
HELP NATIONAL DEFENSE

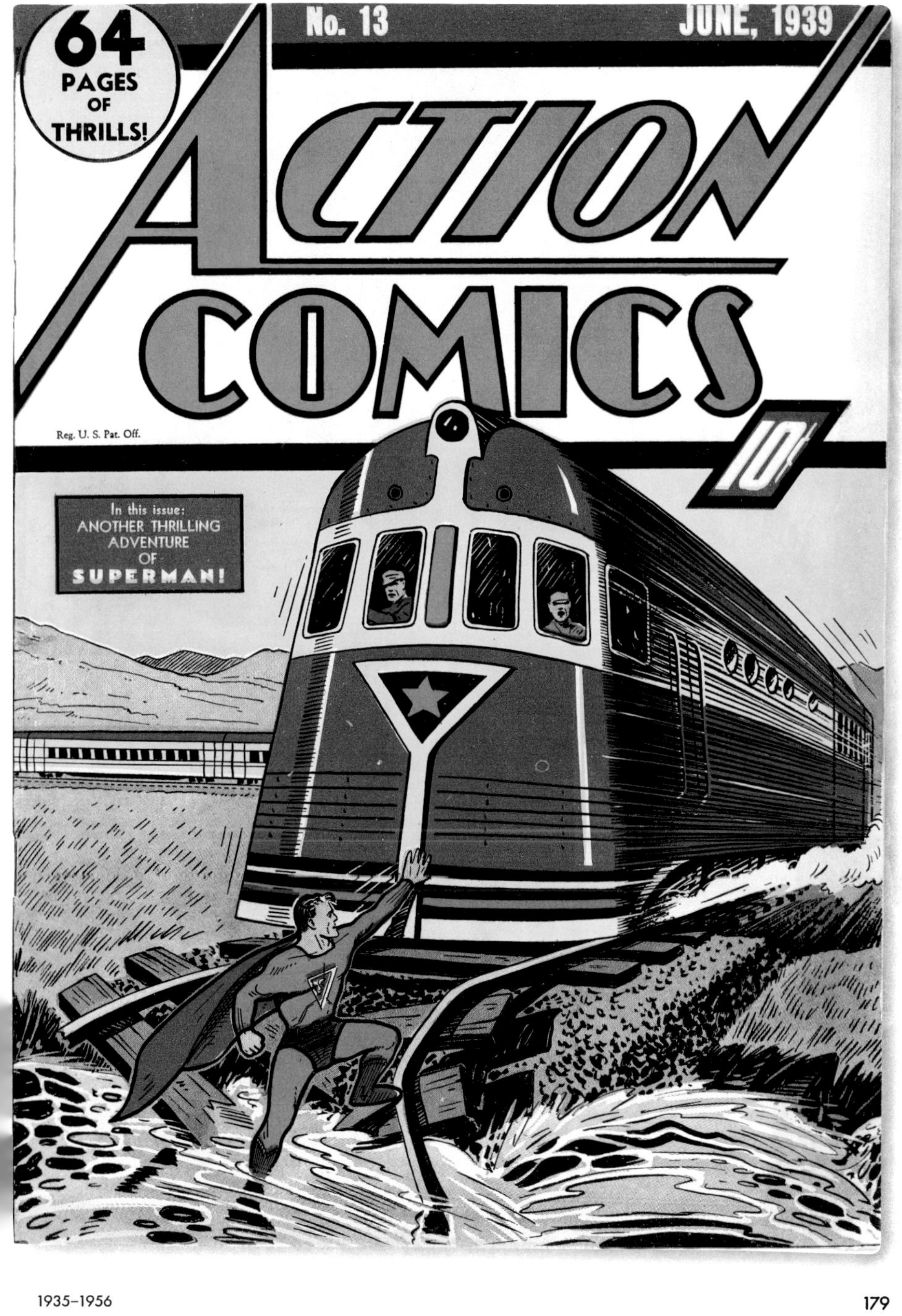
64 PAGES OF THRILLS!
No. 13
JUNE, 1939
ACTION COMICS
Reg. U. S. Pat. Off.
10¢
In this issue:
ANOTHER THRILLING ADVENTURE OF
SUPERMAN!

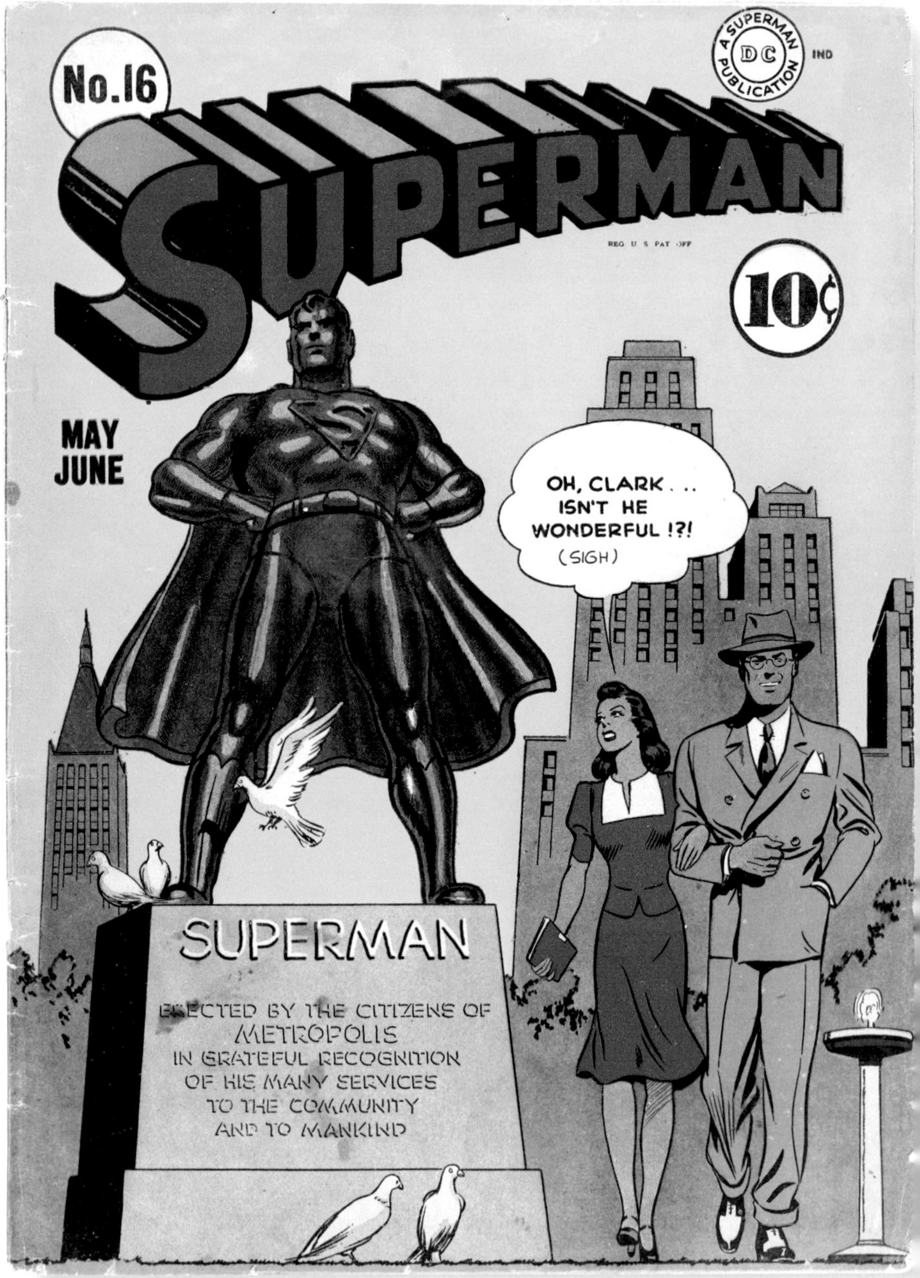
No.16
A SUPERMAN PUBLICATION
DC
IND
SUPERMAN
REG U S PAT OFF
10¢
MAY
JUNE
OH, CLARK . . . ISN'T HE WONDERFUL !?!
(SIGH)
SUPERMAN
ERECTED BY THE CITIZENS OF
METROPOLIS
IN GRATEFUL RECOGNITION
OF HIS MANY SERVICES
TO THE COMMUNITY
AND TO MANKIND

SUPERMAN
No.41
JULY...AUG...TEN CENTS
SUPERMAN
6
DUE DATE!
SUPERMAN

No.9
SUPERMAN
10¢
MARCH
APRIL
WORLD'S
GREATEST
ADVENTURE-STRIP
CHARACTER

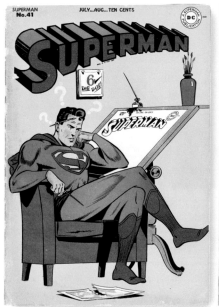

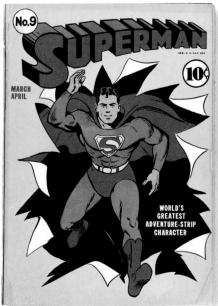

SUPERMAN No. 16

Cover art, Fred Ray, May–June 1942. The real Metropolis, in Illinois, has its own Superman statue with the simple invocation "Truth—Justice—The American Way." The town hosts an annual Superman celebration.

SUPERMAN No. 41

Cover art, Wayne Boring and George Roussos, July–August 1946. Even Superman could be stumped when it came to creating a vivid image to put on his covers. Wayne Boring made the process look easy. Originally hired to help ghost Joe Shuster's art on the "Superman" comic strip, Boring was subsequently brought over to comic books by editor Mort Weisinger. Like Shuster's iconic original, Wayne Boring's barrel-chested, larger-than-life Superman became the template that other artists on the character sought to imitate through the late 1940s and 1950s.

SUPERMAN No. 9

Cover art, Fred Ray, March–April 1941. Renowned for his Golden Age super hero covers, Fred Ray was also a respected Revolutionary War historian. He spent more than two decades drawing DC's Tomahawk feature, which was set in that era, and produced a number of historical comics pamphlets.

SUPERMAN TOY

Painted doll, 1939. Produced by the Novelty and Ideal Toy Company, this first Superman figure was jointed and made of wood.

SUPERMAN BREAD ADVERTISEMENT

Schouten's Sunrise Bread, 1940s. The logical topping for Superman Bread would have been Superman Peanut Butter. Unfortunately, that particular licensing deal didn't come to pass until the early 1980s.

COMIC BOOK WINDOW DISPLAY

Photograph, location unknown, with Detective Comics *No. 138,* Captain Marvel *No. 88,* Captain Marvel Jr. *No. 64,* Master Comics *No. 95, and* Dick Tracy Monthly *No. 8, 1948.*

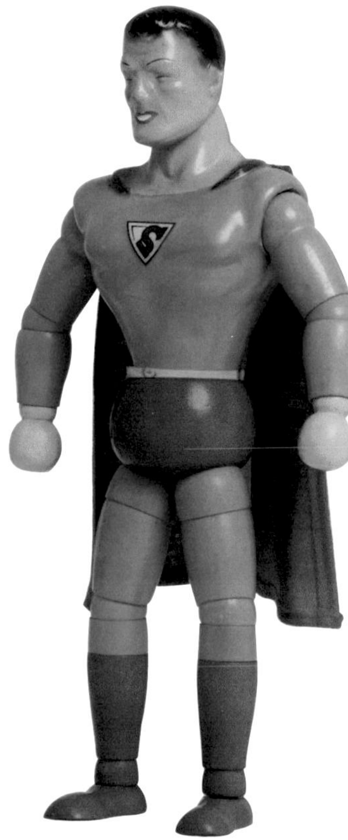

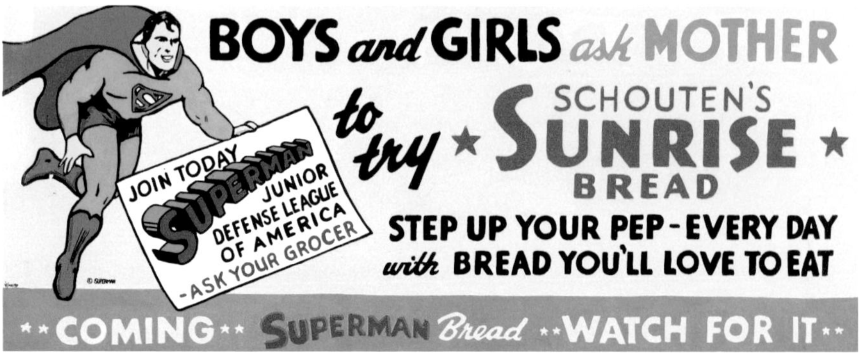

BOYS and GIRLS ask MOTHER
to try
SCHOUTEN'S
SUNRISE
BREAD
JOIN TODAY
SUPERMAN
JUNIOR
DEFENSE LEAGUE
OF AMERICA
-ASK YOUR GROCER
STEP UP YOUR PEP - EVERY DAY
with BREAD YOU'LL LOVE TO EAT
COMING
SUPERMAN Bread
WATCH FOR IT

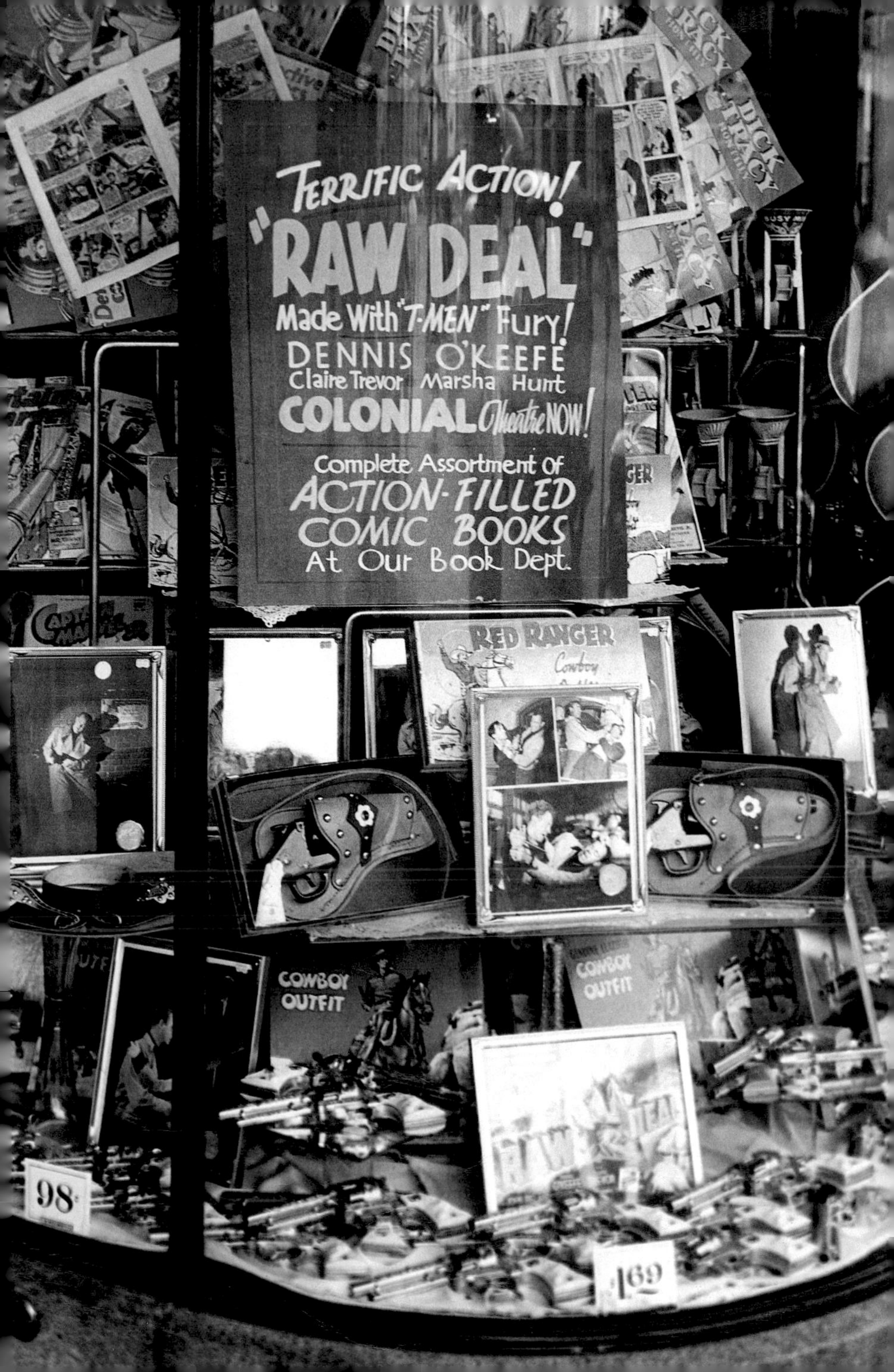
TERRIFIC ACTION!
"RAW DEAL"
Made With "T-MEN" Fury!
DENNIS O'KEEFE
Claire Trevor Marsha Hunt
COLONIAL Theatre NOW!
Complete Assortment Of
ACTION-FILLED
COMIC BOOKS
At Our Book Dept.
RED RANGER
Cowboy
COWBOY OUTFIT
COWBOY OUTFIT
98¢
1.69

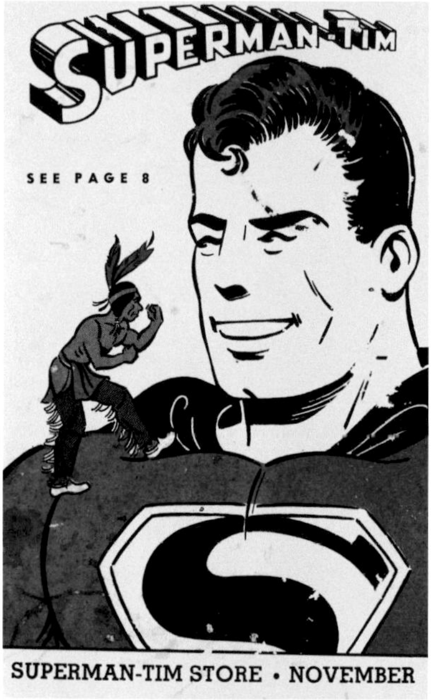
SUPERMAN-TIM
SEE PAGE 8
SUPERMAN-TIM STORE • NOVEMBER

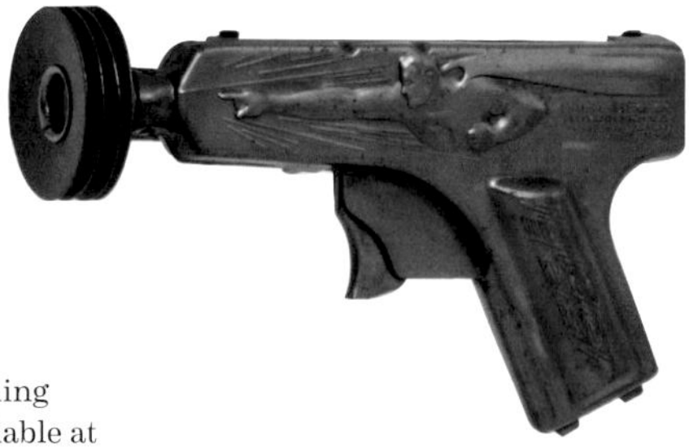

SUPERMAN-TIM

Booklet, November 1942. The Superman-Tim clothing line promoted its wares through a magazine available at participating department stores. Superman's involvement was mostly restricted to spot illustrations, although he did meet Tim in some actual comics episodes later, including one featuring the Norse god Thor.

KRYPTO-RAYGUN

Superman toy, 1940. In order to justify the existence of a licensed toy, a story in *Action Comics* No. 32 showed Superman devising a Krypto-Raygun that was a combination camera and projector.

SUPERMAN No. 21

Cover art, Jack Burnley, March–April 1943. Originally a two-man operation, Superman soon welcomed a satellite team of creators who were charged with chronicling his adventures. Although Jerry Siegel scripted all the Superman stories in this issue, artists Ed Dobrotka, Leo Nowak, Pete Riss, George Roussos, and John Sikela joined Joe Shuster in drawing it.

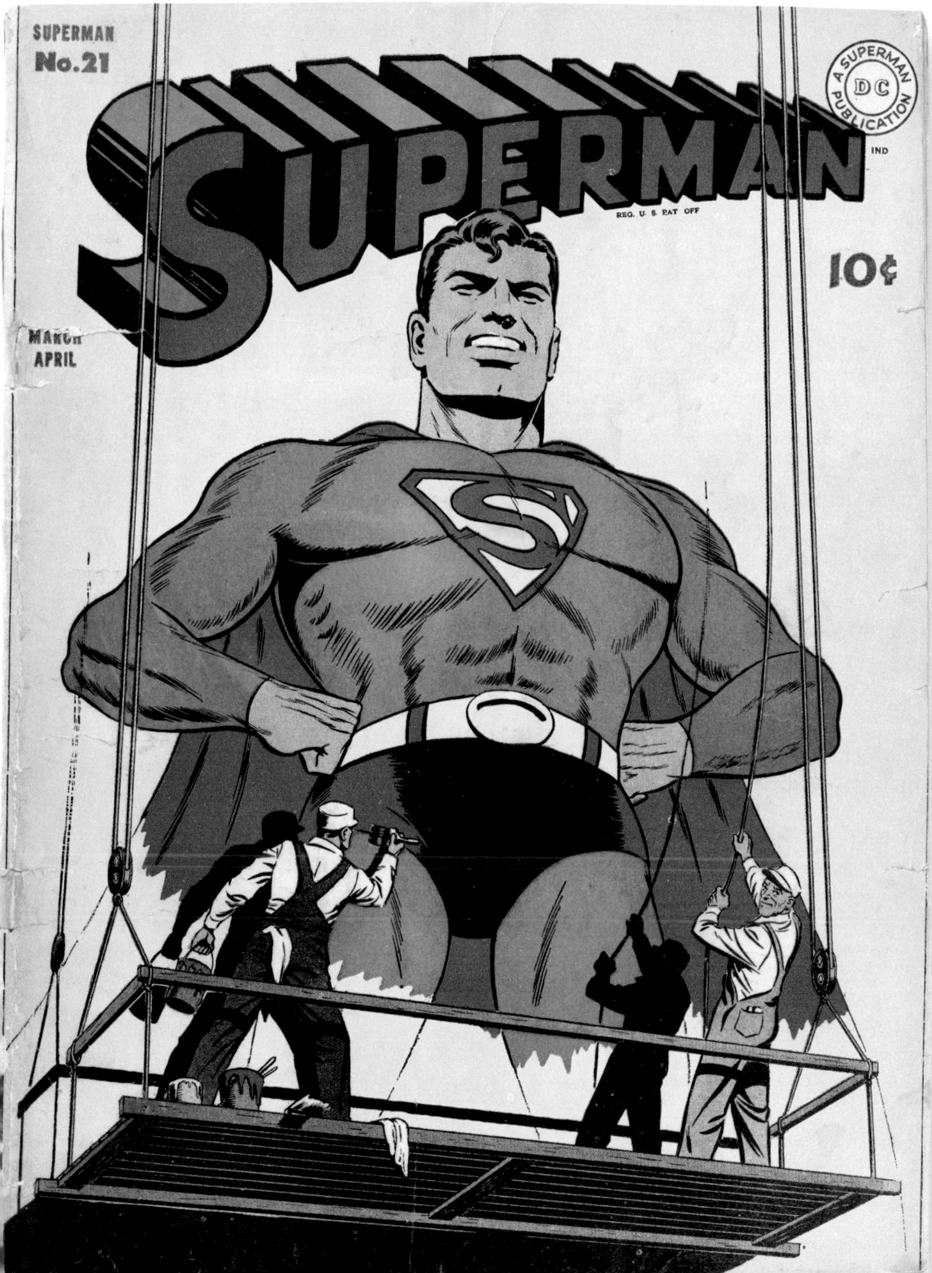
SUPERMAN
No.21
SUPERMAN
A SUPERMAN DC PUBLICATION
IND
REG. U. S. PAT OFF
10¢
MARCH
APRIL

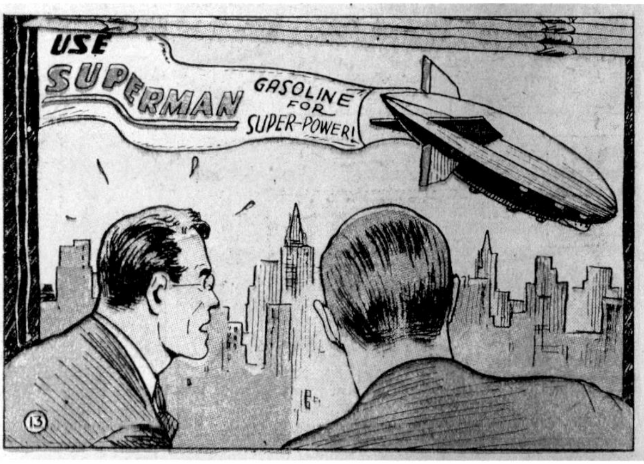
USE SUPERMAN GASOLINE FOR SUPER-POWER!

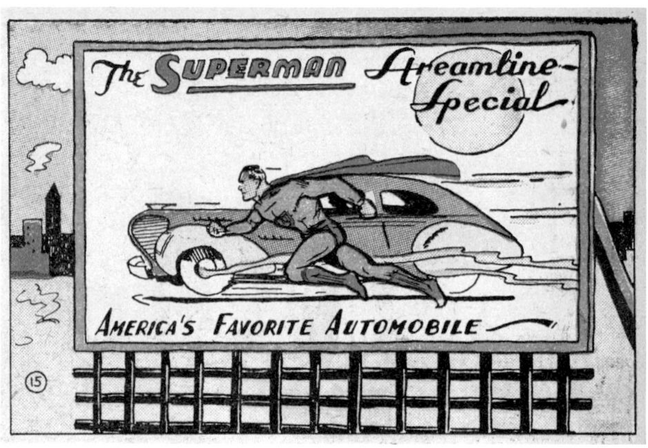
The SUPERMAN Streamline-Special
AMERICA'S FAVORITE AUTOMOBILE

ACTION COMICS No. 6

Interiors, "Superman"; script, Jerry Siegel; pencils and inks, Joe Shuster. November 1938. Superman's licensing potential was apparent to Jerry Siegel almost from the start, as seen in these examples cooked up by a crook claiming to be the Man of Steel's agent. DC quickly launched Superman Inc. as a licensing arm — later to grow into Licensing Corporation of America.

ACTION COMICS No. 33

Interior, "Superman"; script, Jerry Siegel; pencils and inks, Jack Burnley. February 1941. Superman's rescue of a drowning Lois Lane is one of the most vivid story pages of the Golden Age, a tribute to Jack Burnley's design skill and the realistic character work he honed while working as a sports cartoonist.

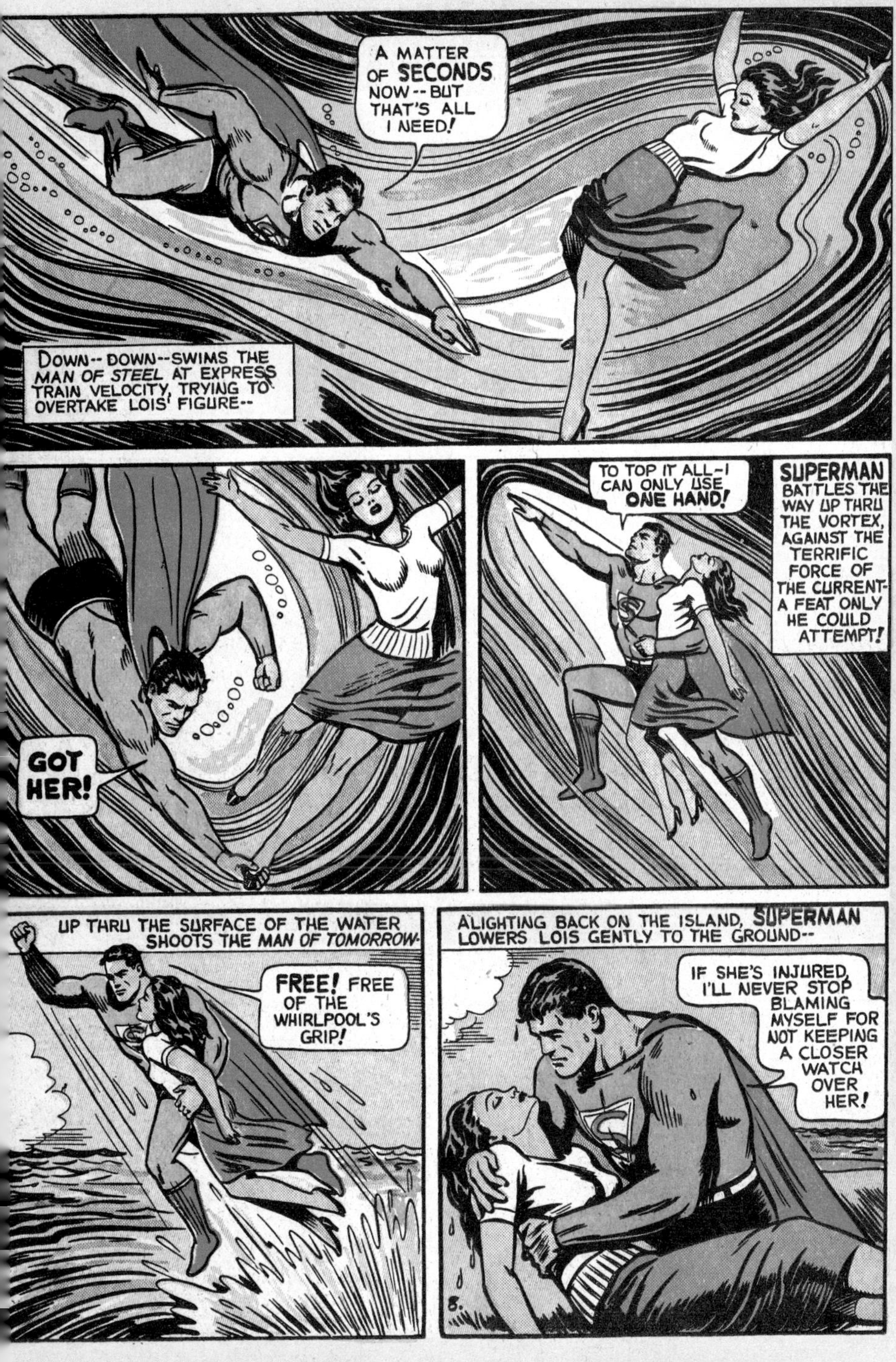
A MATTER OF SECONDS NOW -- BUT THAT'S ALL I NEED!
DOWN -- DOWN -- SWIMS THE MAN OF STEEL AT EXPRESS TRAIN VELOCITY, TRYING TO OVERTAKE LOIS' FIGURE --
GOT HER!
TO TOP IT ALL - I CAN ONLY USE ONE HAND!
SUPERMAN BATTLES THE WAY UP THRU THE VORTEX, AGAINST THE TERRIFIC FORCE OF THE CURRENT - A FEAT ONLY HE COULD ATTEMPT!
UP THRU THE SURFACE OF THE WATER SHOOTS THE MAN OF TOMORROW -
FREE! FREE OF THE WHIRLPOOL'S GRIP!
ALIGHTING BACK ON THE ISLAND, SUPERMAN LOWERS LOIS GENTLY TO THE GROUND --
IF SHE'S INJURED, I'LL NEVER STOP BLAMING MYSELF FOR NOT KEEPING A CLOSER WATCH OVER HER!
8.

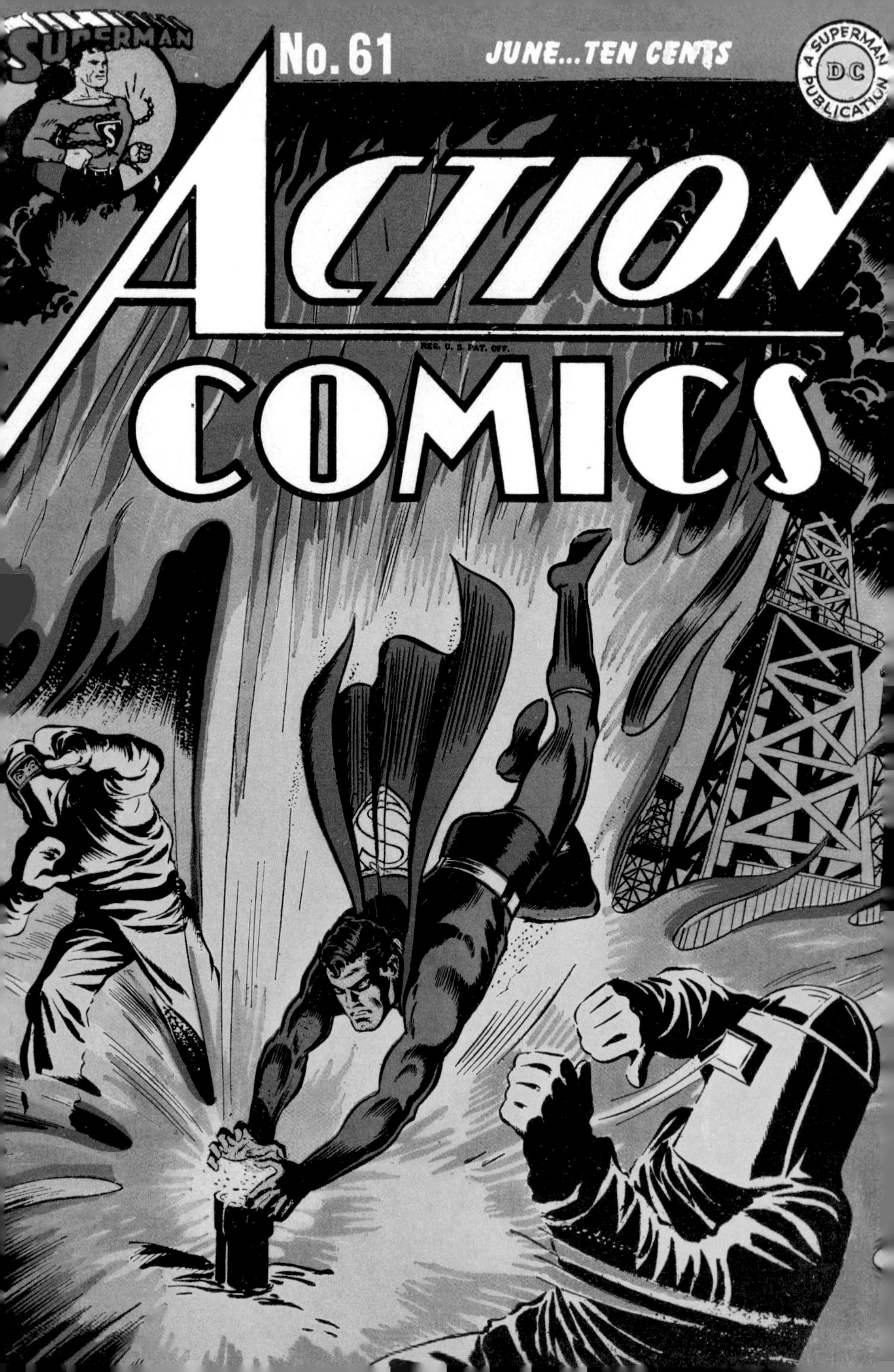
SUPERMAN
No. 61
JUNE...TEN CENTS
A SUPERMAN DC PUBLICATION
ACTION
REG. U. S. PAT. OFF.
COMICS

Superman
No.108
Ten Cents
Action Comics
May 1947
A Superman DC Publication

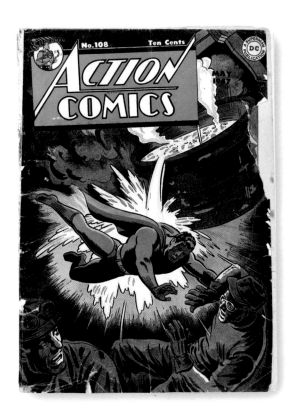

"Fire can't burn him, knives can't cut him, bullets can't hurt him.... In fact, there's nothing known to man that can harm even a hair on Superman's head!"

—SUPERMAN NO. 107, AUGUST 1956

ACTION COMICS No. 61
Cover art, Jack Burnley, June 1943.

ACTION COMICS No. 108
Cover art, Jack Burnley and Stan Kaye, May 1947.
Most of Jack Burnley's covers derived from rough sketches drawn by editor Whitney Ellsworth. "I wasn't interested in thinking up ideas for covers," the artist explained.

ACTION COMICS No. 14

Interior, "Superman": script, Jerry Siegel; pencils and inks, Paul Cassidy. July 1939. Superman's first recurring nemesis was the Ultra-Humanite, a bald scientist who eventually transplanted his brain into the body of a beautiful actress before vanishing from view.

SUPERMAN No. 4

Interior, "Superman": script, Jerry Siegel; pencils and inks, Paul Cassidy Spring 1940. In his earliest appearances, the evil Luthor had a shock of red hair. His trademark bald image came about when an artist looked at an earlier story for reference and mistakenly assumed the hairless henchman in the tale was Luthor himself.

ACTION COMICS No. 23

Interior, "Superman": script, Jerry Siegel; pencils, Joe Shuster; inks, Paul Cassidy. April 1940.

ONLY ONE OBSTACLE CONFRONTS ME— SUPERMAN! HE MUST BE WIPED OUT! IT'S A TERRIFIC TASK.... BUT MY TREMENDOUS BRAIN CAN DEVISE SOME WAY TO TRICK HIM!
- MEANWHILE -
THE END

QUIBBLING ASIDE--YOU AGREED TO MATCH ME AT ANY FEAT. WELL, IMPETUOUS ONE, ARE YOU PREPARED TO RACE MY SKY-VESSELS AROUND THE WORLD?
LET'S GO!
40

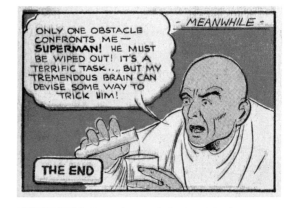

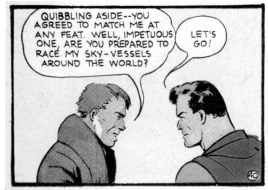

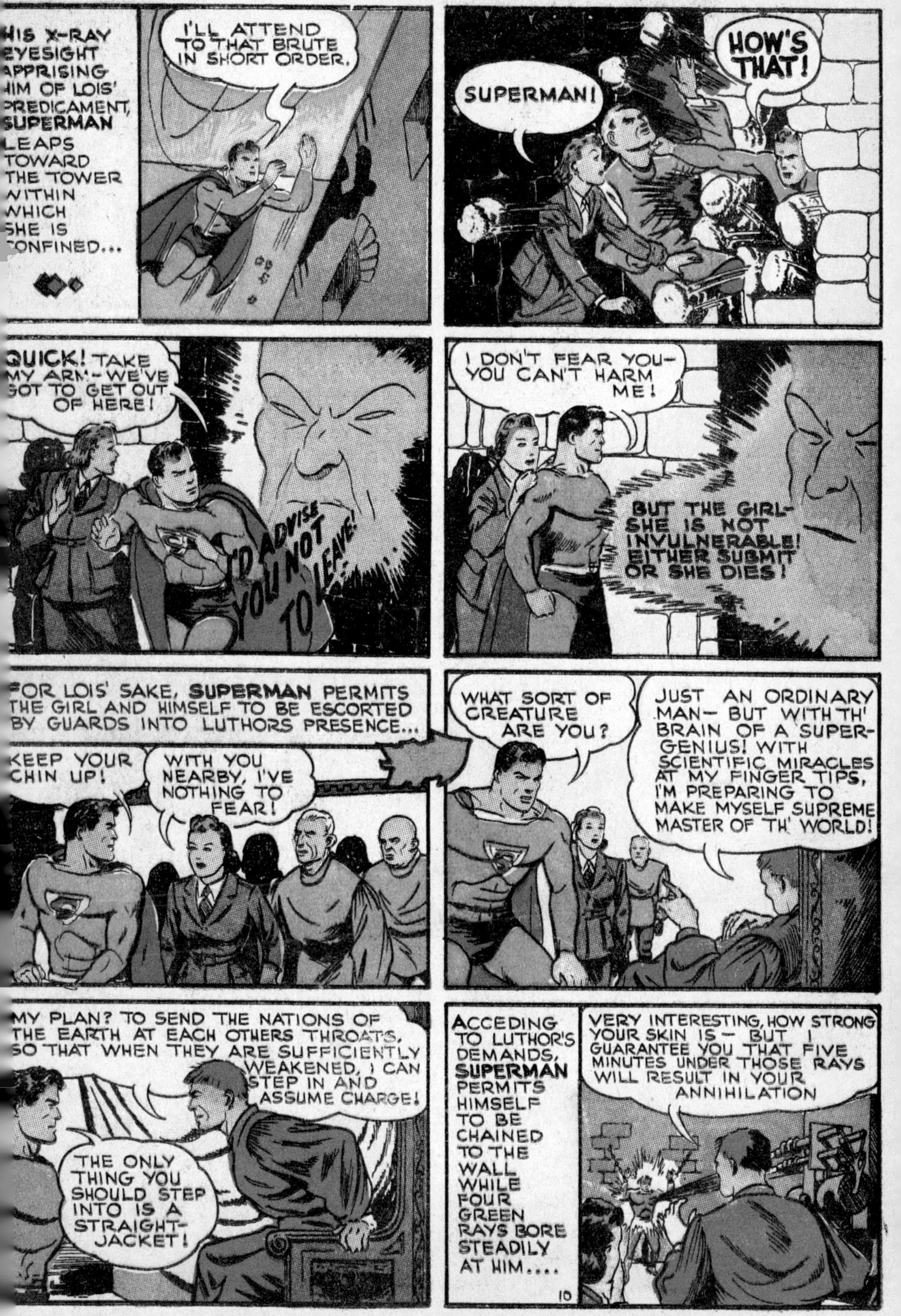
HIS X-RAY EYESIGHT APPRISING HIM OF LOIS' PREDICAMENT, SUPERMAN LEAPS TOWARD THE TOWER WITHIN WHICH SHE IS CONFINED...
I'LL ATTEND TO THAT BRUTE IN SHORT ORDER.
SUPERMAN!
HOW'S THAT!
QUICK! TAKE MY ARM- WE'VE GOT TO GET OUT OF HERE!
I'D ADVISE YOU NOT TO LEAVE!
I DON'T FEAR YOU- YOU CAN'T HARM ME!
BUT THE GIRL- SHE IS NOT INVULNERABLE! EITHER SUBMIT OR SHE DIES!
FOR LOIS' SAKE, SUPERMAN PERMITS THE GIRL AND HIMSELF TO BE ESCORTED BY GUARDS INTO LUTHORS PRESENCE...
KEEP YOUR CHIN UP!
WITH YOU NEARBY, I'VE NOTHING TO FEAR!
WHAT SORT OF CREATURE ARE YOU?
JUST AN ORDINARY MAN- BUT WITH TH' BRAIN OF A SUPER-GENIUS! WITH SCIENTIFIC MIRACLES AT MY FINGER TIPS, I'M PREPARING TO MAKE MYSELF SUPREME MASTER OF TH' WORLD!
MY PLAN? TO SEND THE NATIONS OF THE EARTH AT EACH OTHERS THROATS, SO THAT WHEN THEY ARE SUFFICIENTLY WEAKENED, I CAN STEP IN AND ASSUME CHARGE!
THE ONLY THING YOU SHOULD STEP INTO IS A STRAIGHT-JACKET!
ACCEDING TO LUTHOR'S DEMANDS, SUPERMAN PERMITS HIMSELF TO BE CHAINED TO THE WALL WHILE FOUR GREEN RAYS BORE STEADILY AT HIM....
VERY INTERESTING, HOW STRONG YOUR SKIN IS — BUT I GUARANTEE YOU THAT FIVE MINUTES UNDER THOSE RAYS WILL RESULT IN YOUR ANNIHILATION
10

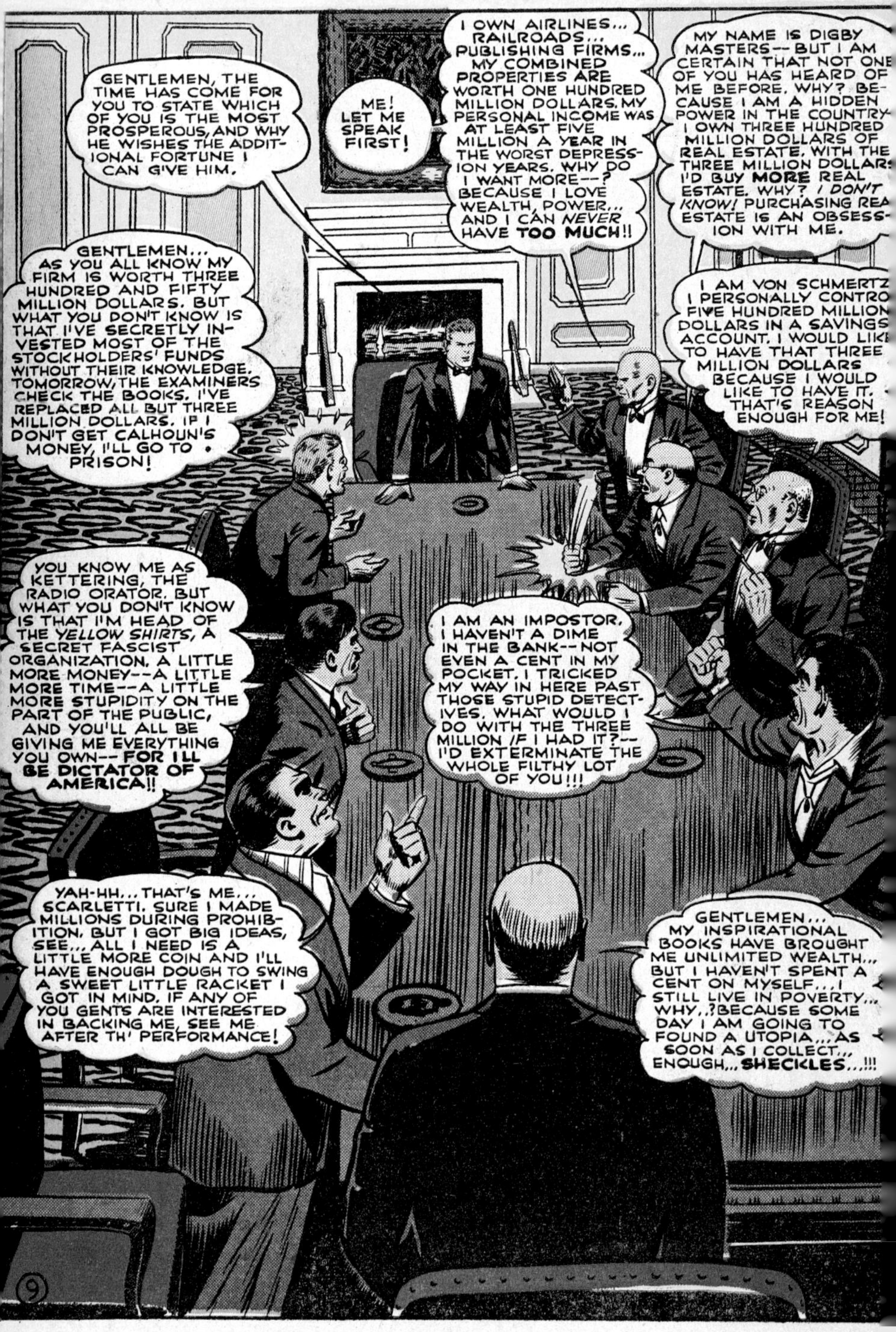
GENTLEMEN, THE TIME HAS COME FOR YOU TO STATE WHICH OF YOU IS THE MOST PROSPEROUS, AND WHY HE WISHES THE ADDITIONAL FORTUNE I CAN GIVE HIM.
ME! LET ME SPEAK FIRST!
I OWN AIRLINES... RAILROADS... PUBLISHING FIRMS... MY COMBINED PROPERTIES ARE WORTH ONE HUNDRED MILLION DOLLARS. MY PERSONAL INCOME WAS AT LEAST FIVE MILLION A YEAR IN THE WORST DEPRESSION YEARS. WHY DO I WANT MORE--? BECAUSE I LOVE WEALTH, POWER... AND I CAN NEVER HAVE TOO MUCH!!
MY NAME IS DIGBY MASTERS-- BUT I AM CERTAIN THAT NOT ONE OF YOU HAS HEARD OF ME BEFORE. WHY? BECAUSE I AM A HIDDEN POWER IN THE COUNTRY- I OWN THREE HUNDRED MILLION DOLLARS OF REAL ESTATE. WITH THE THREE MILLION DOLLARS I'D BUY MORE REAL ESTATE. WHY? I DON'T KNOW! PURCHASING REAL ESTATE IS AN OBSESSION WITH ME.
GENTLEMEN... AS YOU ALL KNOW MY FIRM IS WORTH THREE HUNDRED AND FIFTY MILLION DOLLARS. BUT WHAT YOU DON'T KNOW IS THAT I'VE SECRETLY INVESTED MOST OF THE STOCKHOLDERS' FUNDS WITHOUT THEIR KNOWLEDGE. TOMORROW, THE EXAMINERS CHECK THE BOOKS. I'VE REPLACED ALL BUT THREE MILLION DOLLARS. IF I DON'T GET CALHOUN'S MONEY, I'LL GO TO PRISON!
I AM VON SCHMERTZ. I PERSONALLY CONTROL FIVE HUNDRED MILLION DOLLARS IN A SAVINGS ACCOUNT. I WOULD LIKE TO HAVE THAT THREE MILLION DOLLARS BECAUSE I WOULD LIKE TO HAVE IT. THAT'S REASON ENOUGH FOR ME!
YOU KNOW ME AS KETTERING, THE RADIO ORATOR. BUT WHAT YOU DON'T KNOW IS THAT I'M HEAD OF THE YELLOW SHIRTS, A SECRET FASCIST ORGANIZATION. A LITTLE MORE MONEY--A LITTLE MORE TIME--A LITTLE MORE STUPIDITY ON THE PART OF THE PUBLIC, AND YOU'LL ALL BE GIVING ME EVERYTHING YOU OWN-- FOR I'LL BE DICTATOR OF AMERICA!!
I AM AN IMPOSTOR. I HAVEN'T A DIME IN THE BANK--NOT EVEN A CENT IN MY POCKET. I TRICKED MY WAY IN HERE PAST THOSE STUPID DETECTIVES. WHAT WOULD I DO WITH THE THREE MILLION IF I HAD IT?-- I'D EXTERMINATE THE WHOLE FILTHY LOT OF YOU!!!
YAH-HH... THAT'S ME... SCARLETTI. SURE I MADE MILLIONS DURING PROHIBITION, BUT I GOT BIG IDEAS, SEE... ALL I NEED IS A LITTLE MORE COIN AND I'LL HAVE ENOUGH DOUGH TO SWING A SWEET LITTLE RACKET I GOT IN MIND. IF ANY OF YOU GENTS ARE INTERESTED IN BACKING ME, SEE ME AFTER TH' PERFORMANCE!
GENTLEMEN... MY INSPIRATIONAL BOOKS HAVE BROUGHT ME UNLIMITED WEALTH... BUT I HAVEN'T SPENT A CENT ON MYSELF... I STILL LIVE IN POVERTY... WHY..? BECAUSE SOME DAY I AM GOING TO FOUND A UTOPIA... AS SOON AS I COLLECT... ENOUGH... SHECKLES...!!!
9

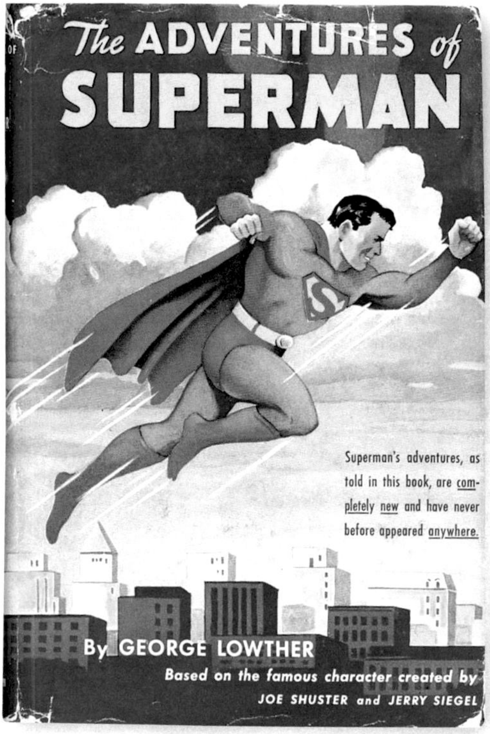
The ADVENTURES of
SUPERMAN
Superman's adventures, as told in this book, are completely new and have never before appeared anywhere.
By GEORGE LOWTHER
Based on the famous character created by
JOE SHUSTER and JERRY SIEGEL

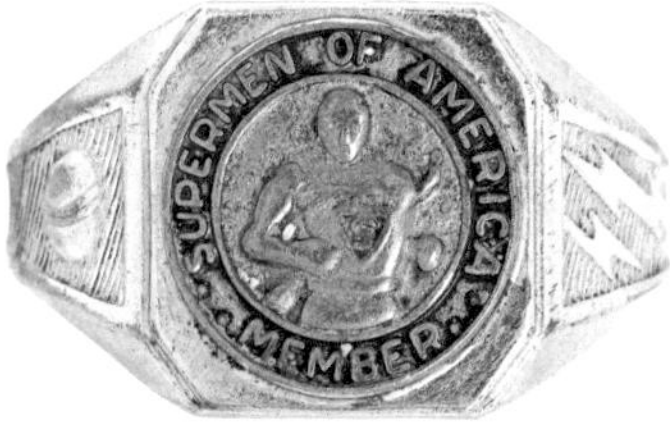
SUPERMEN OF AMERICA
MEMBER

SUPERMAN No. 47

Interior, "Powerstone"; script, Jerry Siegel; art, John Sikela. April 1942.

THE ADVENTURES OF SUPERMAN

Cover art, Joe Shuster, 1942. The Adventures of Superman radio writer George Lowther penned the first prose novelization of Superman, with illustrations by the Shuster studio. Lowther used the space to explore themes other media wouldn't get to for years — from life on Krypton and in Smallville, to what it's like to discover you have superpowers as a young man.

SUPERMEN OF AMERICA RING

Fan club premium, 1940. Of the 1,600 rings originally produced, only around a dozen are known to still exist. They command premium prices from collectors.

HARRY DONENFELD AND SUPER-CAKE

Photograph, Donenfeld (second from right) and party guests, ca. 1945.

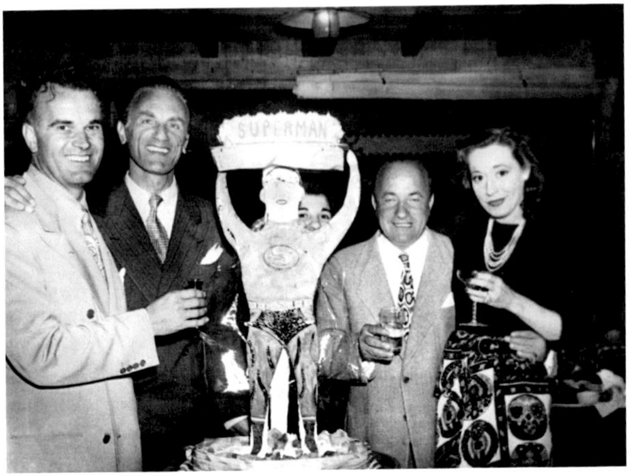
SUPERMAN

SUPERMAN No. 28

Interior, "Lois Lane, Girl Reporter"; script, Don Cameron; pencils and inks, Ed Dobrotka. May–June 1944. Wartime paper shortages necessitated fewer pages in most comic books. In the place of a traditional 12-page Superman story, a four-page Lois Lane feature began appearing in the comic book from No. 28 to No. 42 in 1946.

SUPERMAN RADIO SCRIPT

"Superman, Episode I"; script, Allen Ducovny and Robert Maxwell. Ca. February 1940. The signature introduction to Superman appeared in this seminal radio script and was soon revised to the familiar, "Look! Up in the sky! It's a bird! It's a plane! It's Superman!"

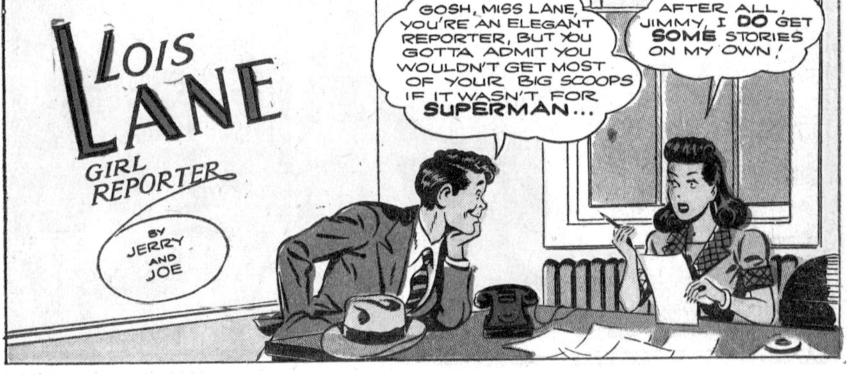
LOIS LANE
GIRL REPORTER
BY JERRY AND JOE
GOSH, MISS LANE, YOU'RE AN ELEGANT REPORTER, BUT YOU GOTTA ADMIT YOU WOULDN'T GET MOST OF YOUR BIG SCOOPS IF IT WASN'T FOR SUPERMAN...
AFTER ALL, JIMMY, I DO GET SOME STORIES ON MY OWN!

VOICES:	One, Two, and Three, in opening, CAN BE DOUBLED.
NARRATOR:	Bright, attention-catching voice, able to adapt itself to fantastic theme.
JOREL:	Super scientist of the planet Krypton. Early 30's...energetic forceful, loving husband and father. Finest type of man.
ROZAN:	Head of Krypton Council. Middle-aged man. Calm, Baldwin-type, refusing to recognise danger when it stares him in the face.
LARA:	Jorel's wife and Superman's mother. Average good wife and mother, ready to sacrifice herself for her baby. Late 20's. Should, however- give some indication of belonging to a Super race.
SUPERMAN:	As known.
NOTE:	The character of Jorel Rozan, and Lara should all convey an impression of "gods-among-men."

- - - - - - - - - - - - -

C.O.	OPENING THEME...HOLD... OUT ABRUPTLY FOR:
NARR:	A new, exciting radio programme, featuring the thrilling adventures of an amazing and INCREDIBLE personality...Fast than an aeroplane..more powerful than a locomotive..
C.O.	"WHOOSH" OF WIND.
NARR:	Impervious to bullets..
C.O.	THE 'SUPERMAN' WIND EFFECT.
VOICE ONE:	Up in the sky...look!
VOICE TWO:	It's a giant bird!
SUPERMAN:	No it's not -- it's -- SUPERMAN!
C.O.	THE SUPERMAN WIND EFFECT AGAIN...SEGUE INTO THEME, AND OUT FOR...

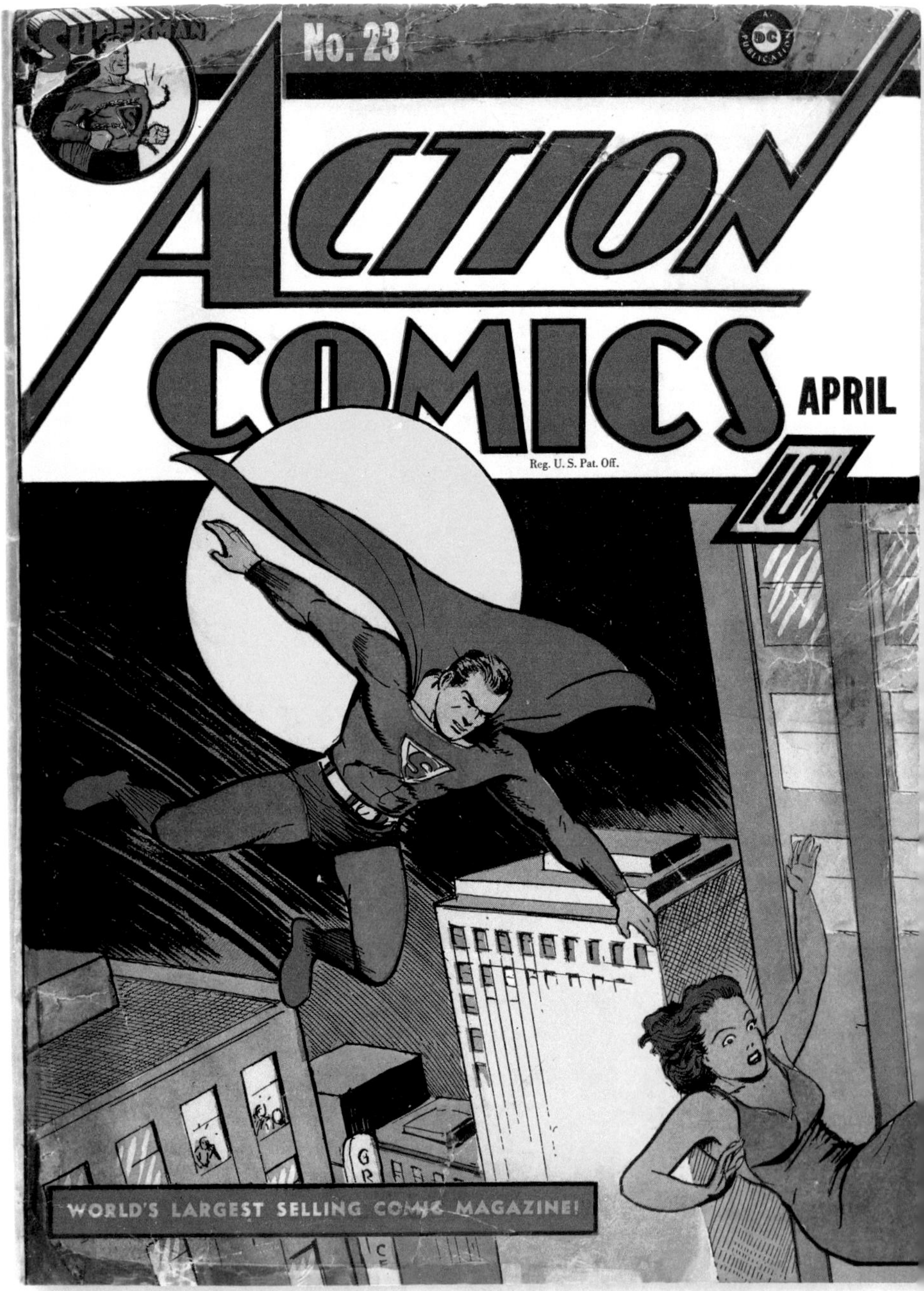
SUPERMAN
No. 23
A DC PUBLICATION
ACTION
COMICS
APRIL
Reg. U. S. Pat. Off.
10¢
WORLD'S LARGEST SELLING COMIC MAGAZINE!

ACTION COMICS No. 23

Cover art, Joe Shuster and Paul Cassidy, April 1940.
The generic rescue scene of this issue's cover gave no hint that a decades-old rivalry was about to begin. Intervening in the war between the countries of Toran and Galonia, Superman fought the scientific weaponry of a red-haired scientist named Luthor.

SUPERMAN No. 57

Cover art, Wayne Boring and Stan Kaye, March–April 1949.
Lois Lane's legacy was said to extend far into 2949 A.D., where Superman once met her supposed descendant Lois 4XR. By that point, everyone on Earth possessed the same set of powers that were once unique to the Man of Steel.

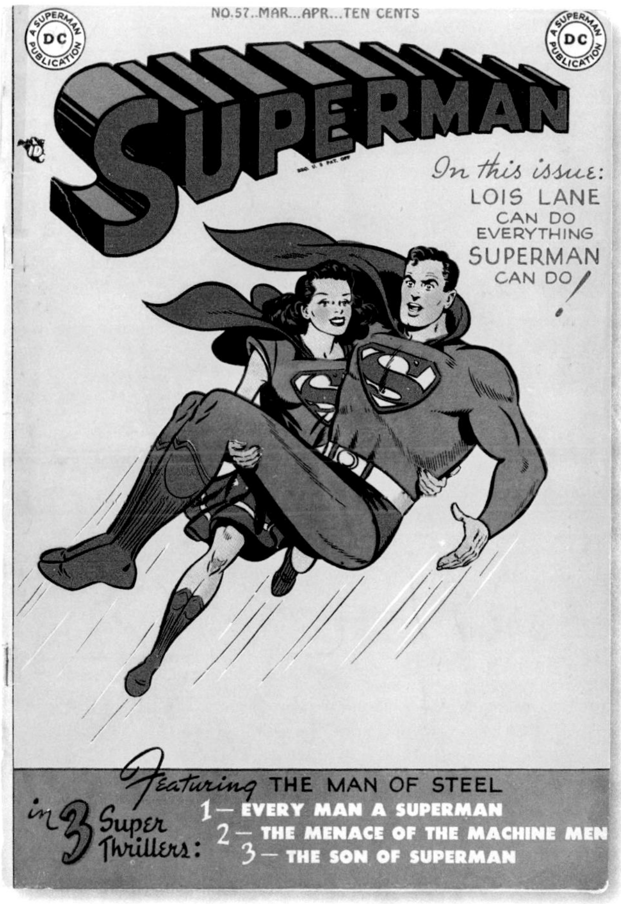
NO.57..MAR...APR...TEN CENTS
A SUPERMAN DC PUBLICATION
SUPERMAN
In this issue:
LOIS LANE CAN DO EVERYTHING SUPERMAN CAN DO!
Featuring THE MAN OF STEEL
in 3 Super Thrillers:
1—EVERY MAN A SUPERMAN
2—THE MENACE OF THE MACHINE MEN
3—THE SON OF SUPERMAN

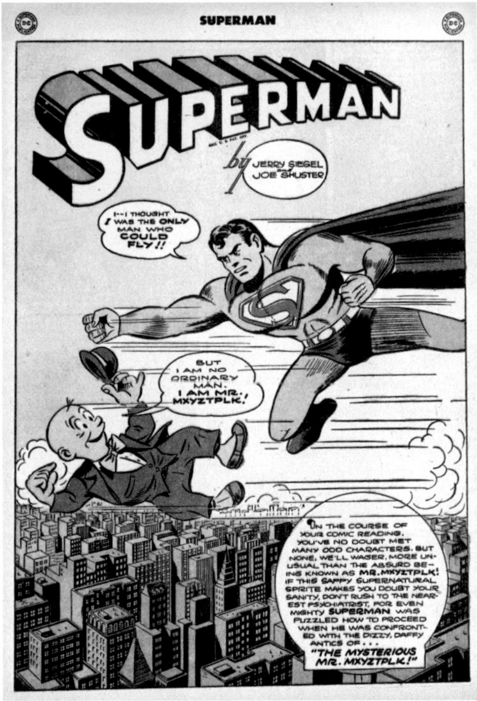
SUPERMAN
SUPERMAN
by JERRY SIEGEL and JOE SHUSTER
I--I THOUGHT I WAS THE ONLY MAN WHO COULD FLY!!
BUT I AM NO ORDINARY MAN. I AM MR. MXYZTPLK!
IN THE COURSE OF YOUR COMIC READING, YOU'VE NO DOUBT MET MANY ODD CHARACTERS. BUT NONE, WE'LL WAGER, MORE UNUSUAL THAN THE ABSURD BEING KNOWN AS MR. MXYZTPLK! IF THIS SAPPY SUPERNATURAL SPRITE MAKES YOU DOUBT YOUR SANITY, DON'T RUSH TO THE NEAREST PSYCHIATRIST, FOR EVEN MIGHTY SUPERMAN WAS PUZZLED HOW TO PROCEED WHEN HE WAS CONFRONTED WITH THE DIZZY, DAFFY ANTICS OF . . . "THE MYSTERIOUS MR. MXYZTPLK!"

SUPERMAN No. 30

Interior, "The Mysterious Mr. Mxyztplk"; script, Jerry Siegel; pencils, Joe Shuster and Ira Yarbrough; inks, Joe Shuster. September–October 1944. As war continued, the world grew darker, and Superman's adventures became lighter, particularly with the addition of Mr. Mxyztplk, wa prankster from the Fifth Dimension who enjoyed nothing more than creating magical pranks in the more humdrum earthly plane. The imp's name was inspired by Joe Btfsplk, a comedic jinx who appeared in Al Capp's popular "Li'l Abner" comic strip.

SUPERMAN No. 48

Interior, "The Man Who Stole the Sun"; script, Jerry Siegel; pencils, John Sikela; inks, attributed George Roussos. September–October 1947. "Villains, whatever fate befell them in the obligatory last panel, were infinitely better equipped than those silly, hapless heroes. Not only comics, but life taught us that. Those of us raised in ghetto neighborhoods were being asked to believe that crime didn't pay? Tell that to the butcher! Nice guys finished last; landlords, first.... It was not to be believed that any ordinary human could combat them. More was required. Someone with a call." —Jules Feiffer

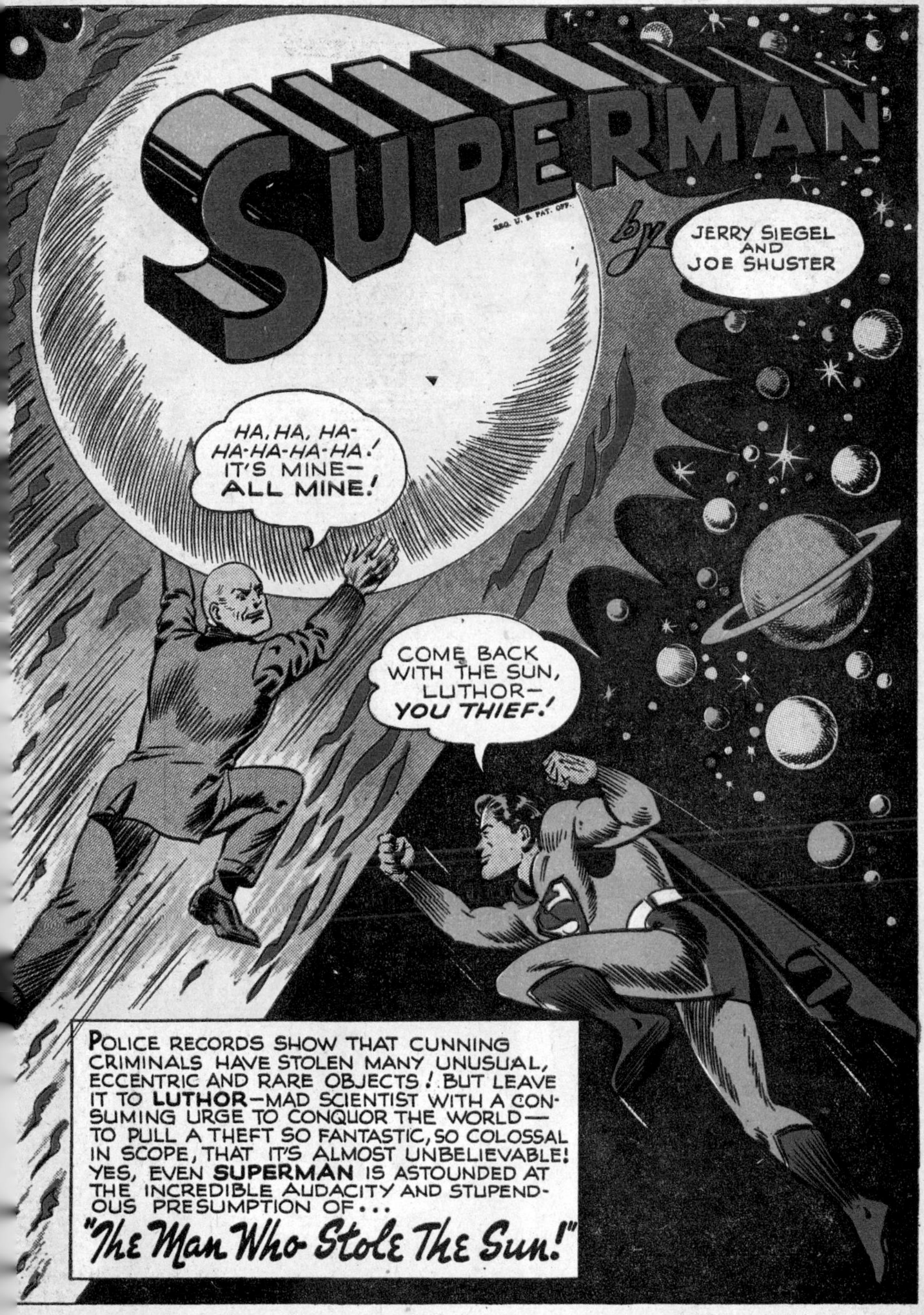
SUPERMAN
REG. U. S. PAT. OFF.
by JERRY SIEGEL AND JOE SHUSTER
HA, HA, HA-HA-HA-HA-HA-HA! IT'S MINE—ALL MINE!
COME BACK WITH THE SUN, LUTHOR—YOU THIEF!
POLICE RECORDS SHOW THAT CUNNING CRIMINALS HAVE STOLEN MANY UNUSUAL, ECCENTRIC AND RARE OBJECTS! BUT LEAVE IT TO LUTHOR—MAD SCIENTIST WITH A CONSUMING URGE TO CONQUOR THE WORLD—TO PULL A THEFT SO FANTASTIC, SO COLOSSAL IN SCOPE, THAT IT'S ALMOST UNBELIEVABLE! YES, EVEN SUPERMAN IS ASTOUNDED AT THE INCREDIBLE AUDACITY AND STUPENDOUS PRESUMPTION OF...
"The Man Who Stole The Sun!"

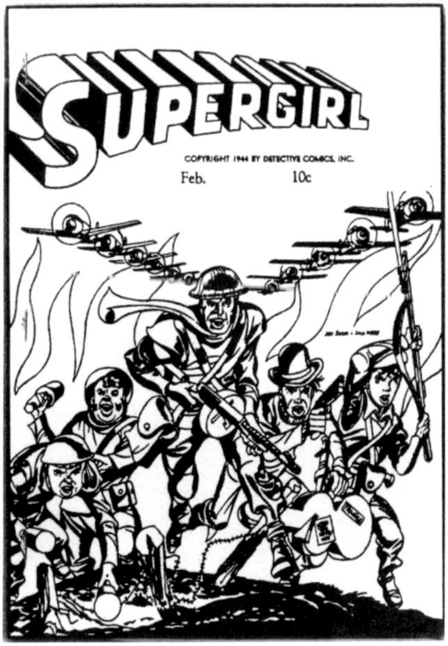
SUPERGIRL
COPYRIGHT 1944 BY DETECTIVE COMICS, INC.
Feb.
10c

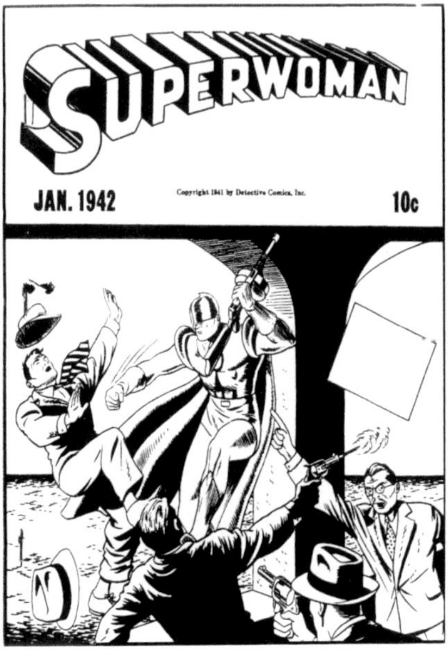
SUPERWOMAN
JAN. 1942
Copyright 1941 by Detective Comics, Inc.
10c

SUPERGIRL AND SUPERWOMAN ASHCANS

ABOVE LEFT: *Cover art, Jack Kirby and Joe Simon, February 1944.* ABOVE RIGHT: *Cover art, Howard Sherman, January 1942.* Fearful of rival publishers capitalizing on Superman, National trademarked female variations of his name on unsolicited comic books created strictly to protect their hero.

SUPERMAN No. 74

Cover art, Win Mortimer, January–February 1952.

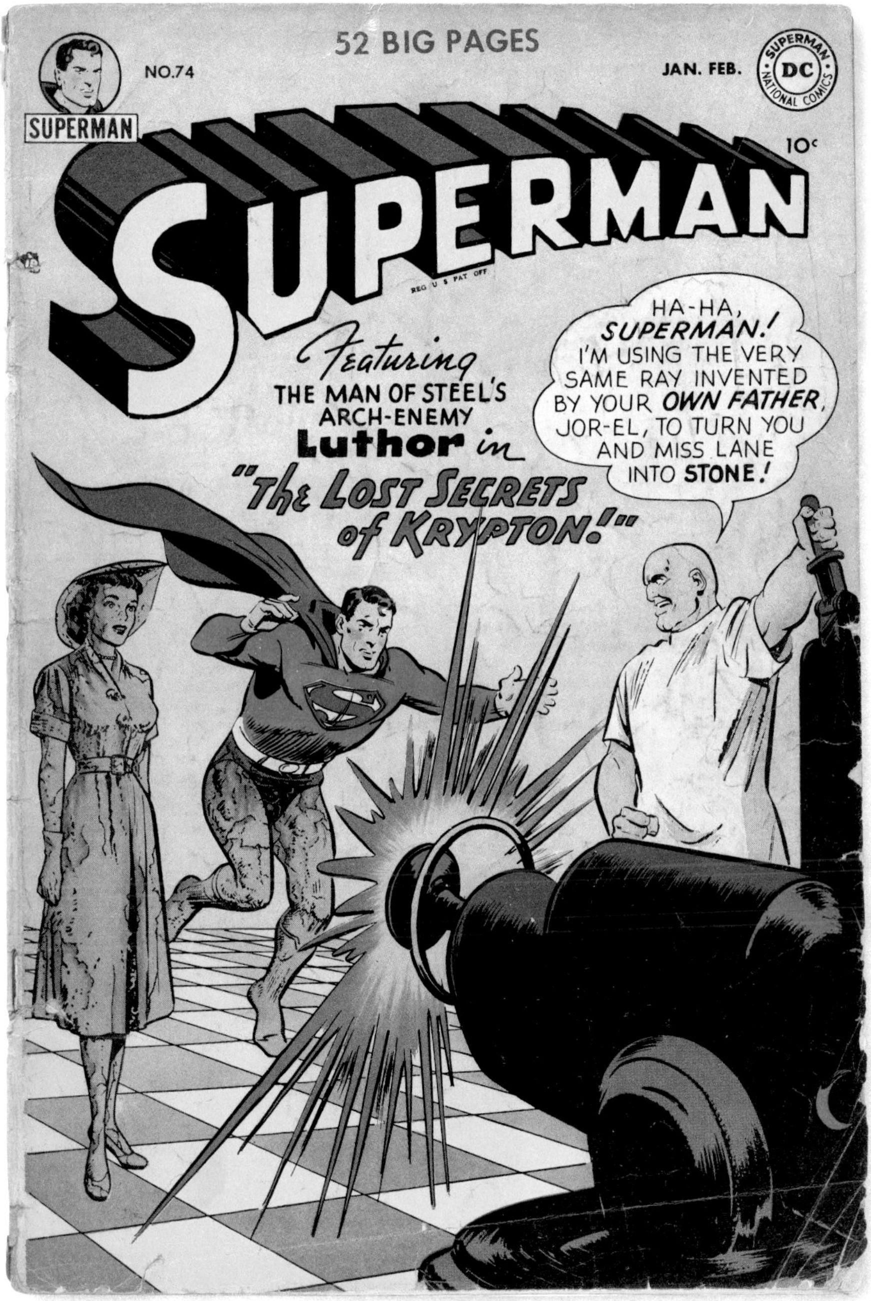

52 BIG PAGES
NO.74
JAN. FEB.
SUPERMAN
SUPERMAN DC NATIONAL COMICS
10¢
SUPERMAN
REG. U. S. PAT. OFF.
Featuring THE MAN OF STEEL'S ARCH-ENEMY Luthor in "The Lost Secrets of Krypton!"
HA-HA, SUPERMAN! I'M USING THE VERY SAME RAY INVENTED BY YOUR OWN FATHER, JOR-EL, TO TURN YOU AND MISS LANE INTO STONE!

ACTION COMICS No. 156

Cover art, Al Plastino, May 1951. Although Lois Lane continued to adopt the Superwoman name in dreams and reality, two other women later shared the name with her. The first was an evil member of the Crime Syndicate who first fought the Justice League and Justice Society in 1964, while the second was a time traveler named Kristin Wells who assumed the persona in 1983.

ACTION COMICS No. 60

Interior, "Lois Lane—Superwoman"; script, Jerry Siegel; pencils and inks, George Roussos. May 1943. Superwoman Lois Lane acquired her superpowers via a blood tranfusion, but in the end it was revealed as just a dream. In 1951 Lois became Superwoman for real, but this time she couldn't control her abilities and, even worse, learned that she was a pawn of evil Lex Luthor.

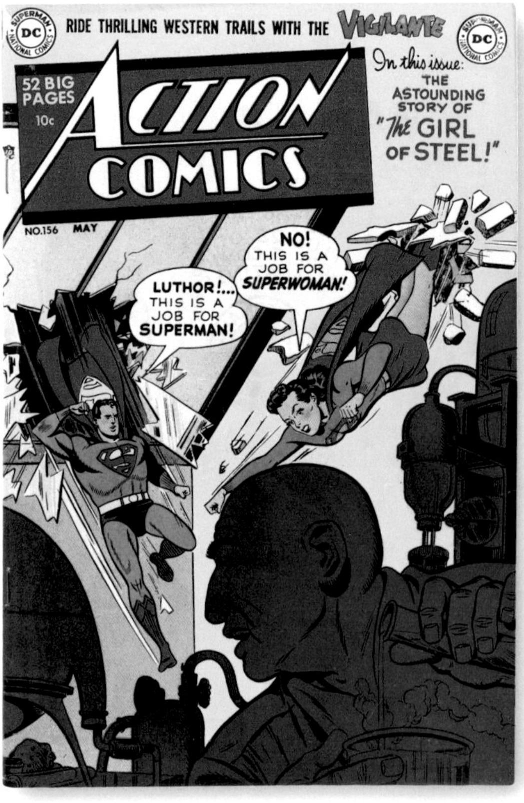
RIDE THRILLING WESTERN TRAILS WITH THE VIGILANTE
52 BIG PAGES 10c
ACTION COMICS
NO.156 MAY
In this issue: THE ASTOUNDING STORY OF "The GIRL OF STEEL!"
LUTHOR!... THIS IS A JOB FOR SUPERMAN!
NO! THIS IS A JOB FOR SUPERWOMAN!

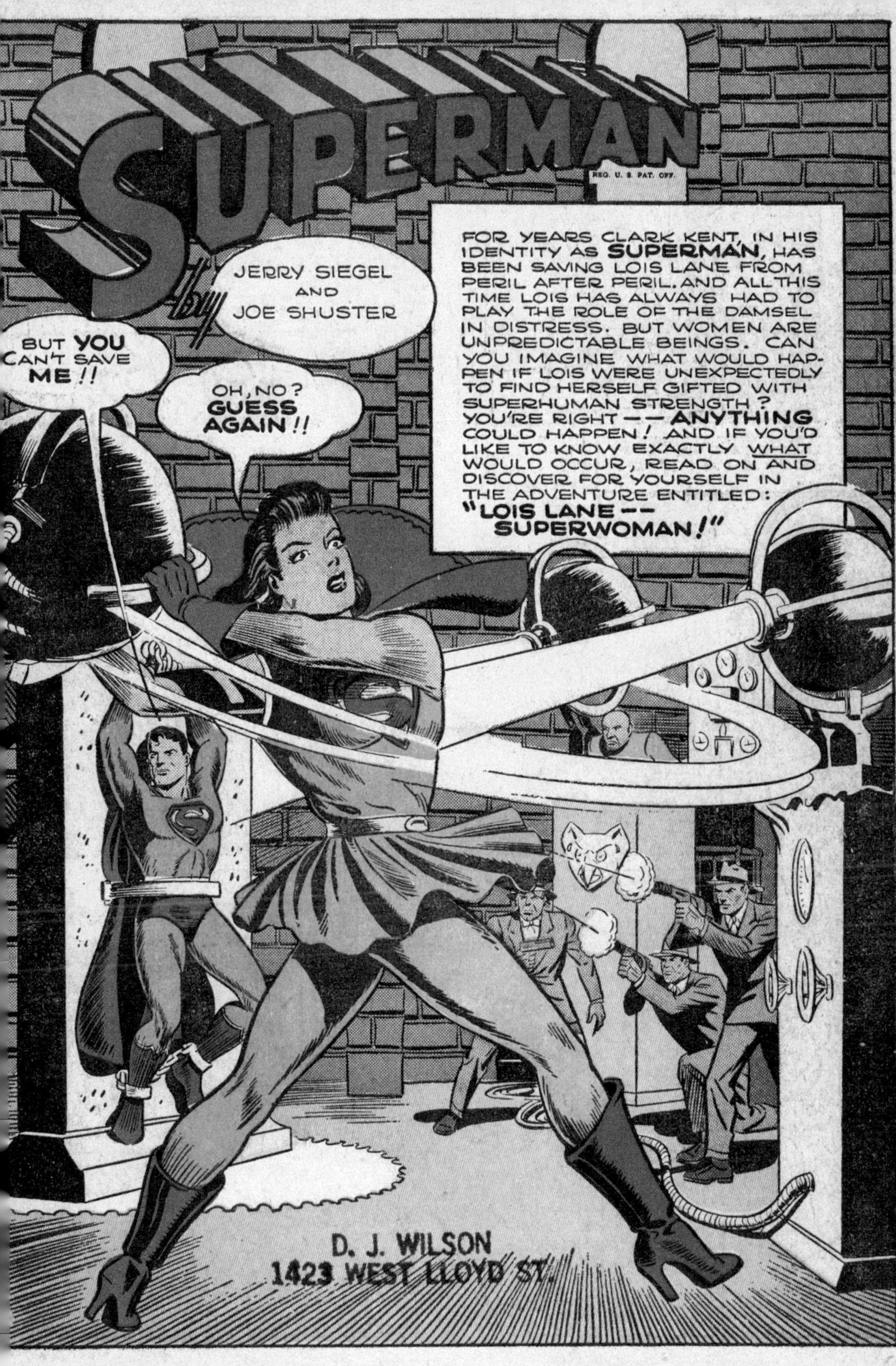
SUPERMAN
REG. U. S. PAT. OFF.
by
JERRY SIEGEL AND JOE SHUSTER
FOR YEARS CLARK KENT, IN HIS IDENTITY AS SUPERMAN, HAS BEEN SAVING LOIS LANE FROM PERIL AFTER PERIL. AND ALL THIS TIME LOIS HAS ALWAYS HAD TO PLAY THE ROLE OF THE DAMSEL IN DISTRESS. BUT WOMEN ARE UNPREDICTABLE BEINGS. CAN YOU IMAGINE WHAT WOULD HAPPEN IF LOIS WERE UNEXPECTEDLY TO FIND HERSELF GIFTED WITH SUPERHUMAN STRENGTH? YOU'RE RIGHT -- ANYTHING COULD HAPPEN! AND IF YOU'D LIKE TO KNOW EXACTLY WHAT WOULD OCCUR, READ ON AND DISCOVER FOR YOURSELF IN THE ADVENTURE ENTITLED: "LOIS LANE -- SUPERWOMAN!"
BUT YOU CAN'T SAVE ME!!
OH, NO? GUESS AGAIN!!
D. J. WILSON
1423 WEST LLOYD ST.

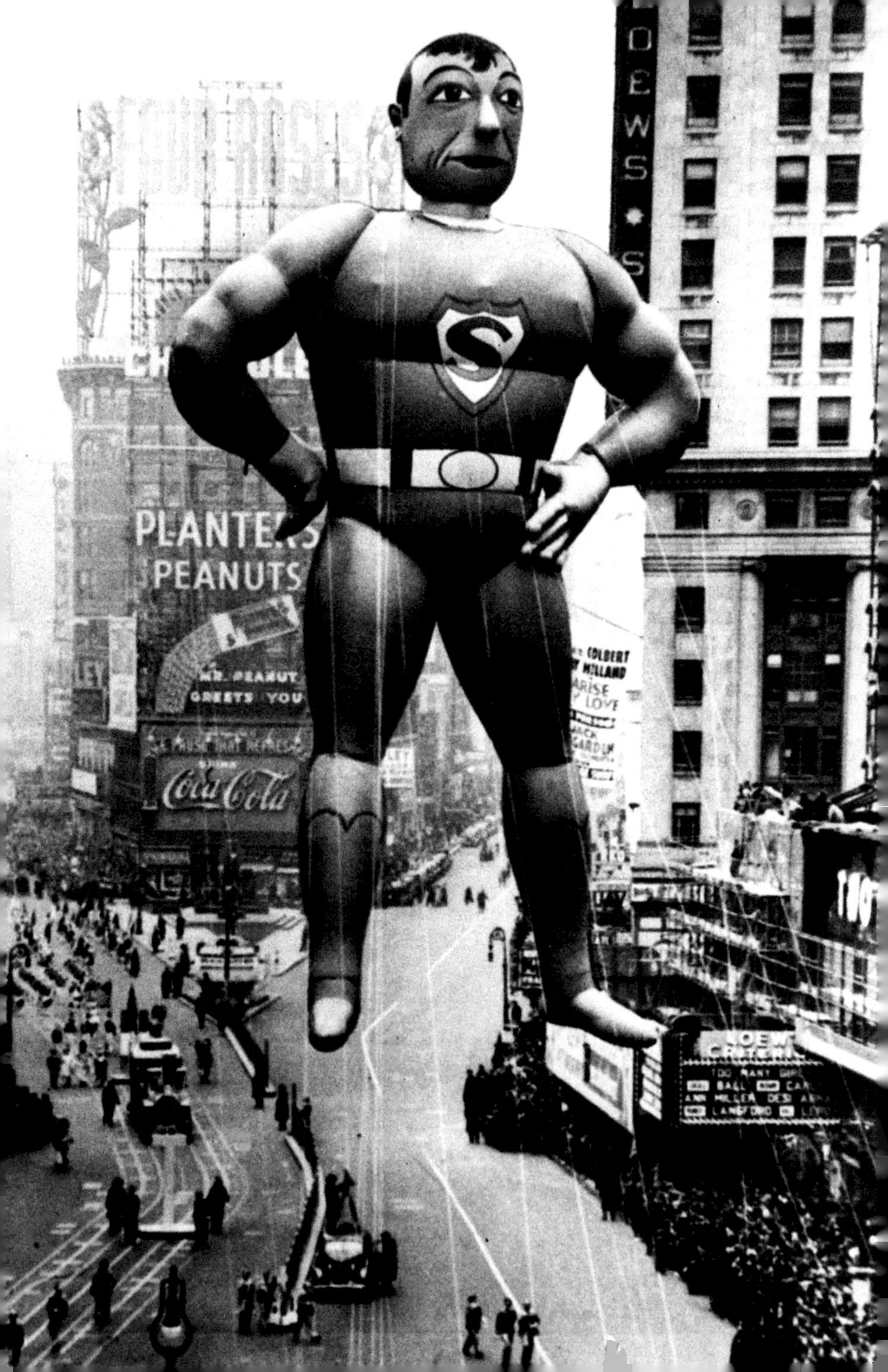
PLANTERS
PEANUTS
MR. PEANUT
GREETS YOU
Coca-Cola
COLBERT
MILLAND

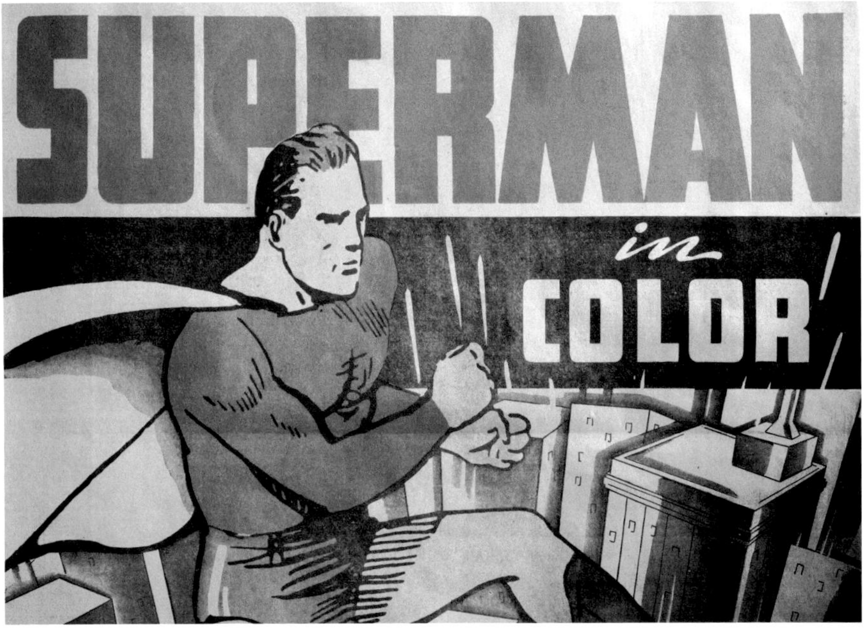
SUPERMAN
in
COLOR

MACY'S THANKSGIVING DAY PARADE

Superman balloon, Times Square, New York, November 21, 1940. The Macy's Thanksgiving Day Parade in New York began featuring balloon characters in 1927 with Felix the Cat, but Superman's debut in 1940 took him to new heights. Broadcast on radio at that time, the parade later became a television staple of the American family holiday as the turkey slowly roasted.

SUPERMAN IN COLOR AD

Advertising art, Joe Shuster, 1939.

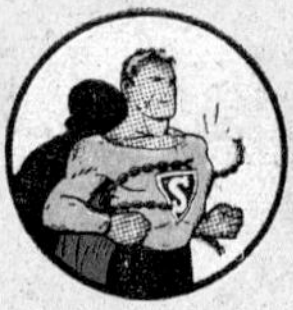

SUPER STRENGTH

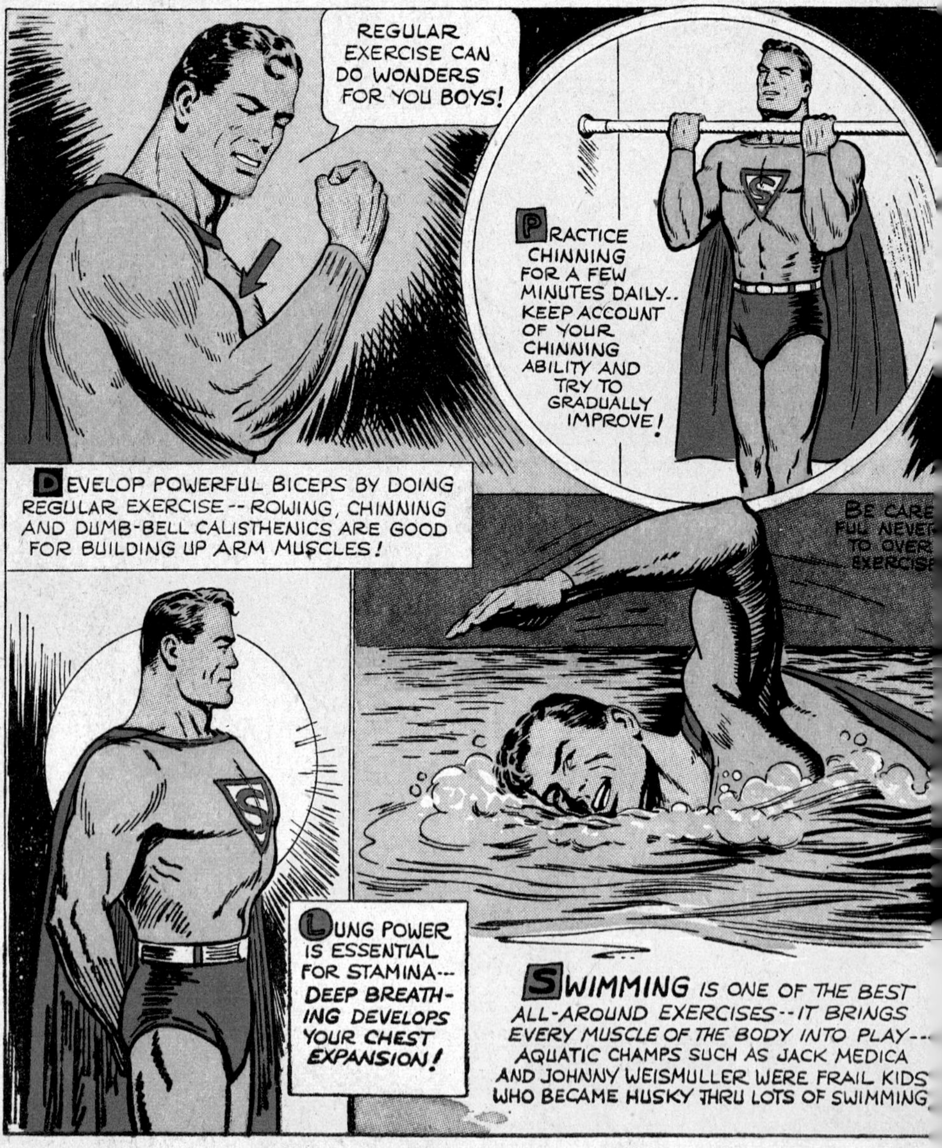
REGULAR EXERCISE CAN DO WONDERS FOR YOU BOYS!
PRACTICE CHINNING FOR A FEW MINUTES DAILY.. KEEP ACCOUNT OF YOUR CHINNING ABILITY AND TRY TO GRADUALLY IMPROVE!
DEVELOP POWERFUL BICEPS BY DOING REGULAR EXERCISE -- ROWING, CHINNING AND DUMB-BELL CALISTHENICS ARE GOOD FOR BUILDING UP ARM MUSCLES!
BE CARE
FUL NEVE
TO OVER
EXERCIS
LUNG POWER IS ESSENTIAL FOR STAMINA--- DEEP BREATHING DEVELOPS YOUR CHEST EXPANSION!
SWIMMING IS ONE OF THE BEST ALL-AROUND EXERCISES--IT BRINGS EVERY MUSCLE OF THE BODY INTO PLAY--- AQUATIC CHAMPS SUCH AS JACK MEDICA AND JOHNNY WEISMULLER WERE FRAIL KIDS WHO BECAME HUSKY THRU LOTS OF SWIMMING.

SUPERMAN No. 6

Interior, "Super Strength"; script, Jerry Siegel; pencils and inks, Jack Burnley. September–October 1940. No kid could really become Superman through these exercises any more than they could gain the strength of Popeye through devouring spinach. Still, the intentions of pages like these (a variation of which appeared in *Batman*) were good.

O LOBINHO No. 10

Cover art, artist unknown, 1941. Journalist Adolfo Aizen spearheaded the publication of translated U.S. comics in Brazil in the 1930s and 1940s in inexpensive magazines like this.

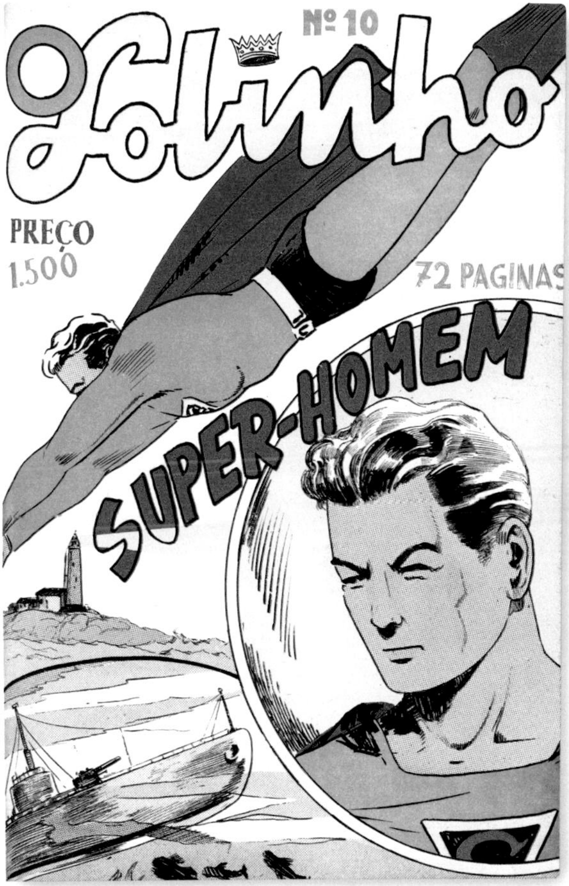

Nº 10
O Lobinho
PREÇO
1.500
72 PAGINAS
SUPER-HOMEM

CARTOON PARODIES

TOP LEFT: *Animation still, "A Hatful of Dreams." Paramount Pictures: director, George Pal. 1945.* TOP RIGHT: *Animation still, "Super Lulu," Famous Studios: director, Bill Tytla. November 21, 1947.* ABOVE: *Animation still, "Super-Rabbit," Merrie Melodies, Warner Bros.: director, Chuck Jones. April 3, 1943.* Superman's place as a cultural icon was readily apparent by the mid-1940s, when several animation studios were eager to build shorts around the now-familiar tropes surrounding the hero.

SUPER-BABE

Doll, 1947. As a precursor to the release of the 1948 *Superman* movie serial, Macy's offered this exclusive rubber doll for the 1947 Christmas season at a then-expensive $5.59 retail.

BOY COMMANDOS No. 24

Cover art, Jack Kirby and unknown inker, November–December 1947. Although the costume is strictly from the comics, the dialogue on this cover shows the clear influence of the popular *Adventures of Superman* radio show with riffs on its trademark lines like "Up, up, and away" and "It's a bird, it's a plane…"

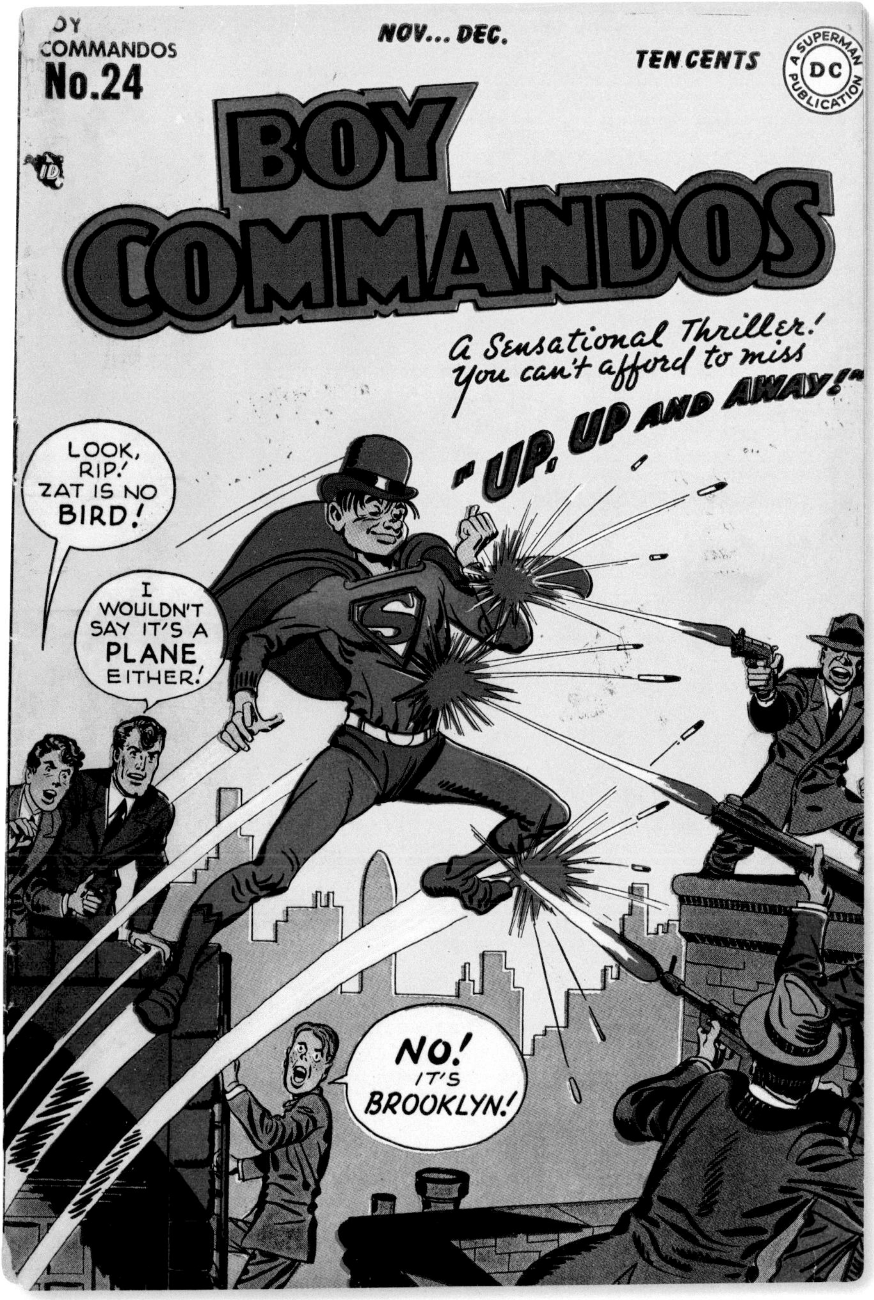
BOY COMMANDOS
No.24
NOV... DEC.
TEN CENTS
A SUPERMAN PUBLICATION DC
BOY COMMANDOS
A Sensational Thriller! You can't afford to miss
"UP, UP AND AWAY!"
LOOK, RIP! ZAT IS NO BIRD!
I WOULDN'T SAY IT'S A PLANE EITHER!
NO! IT'S BROOKLYN!

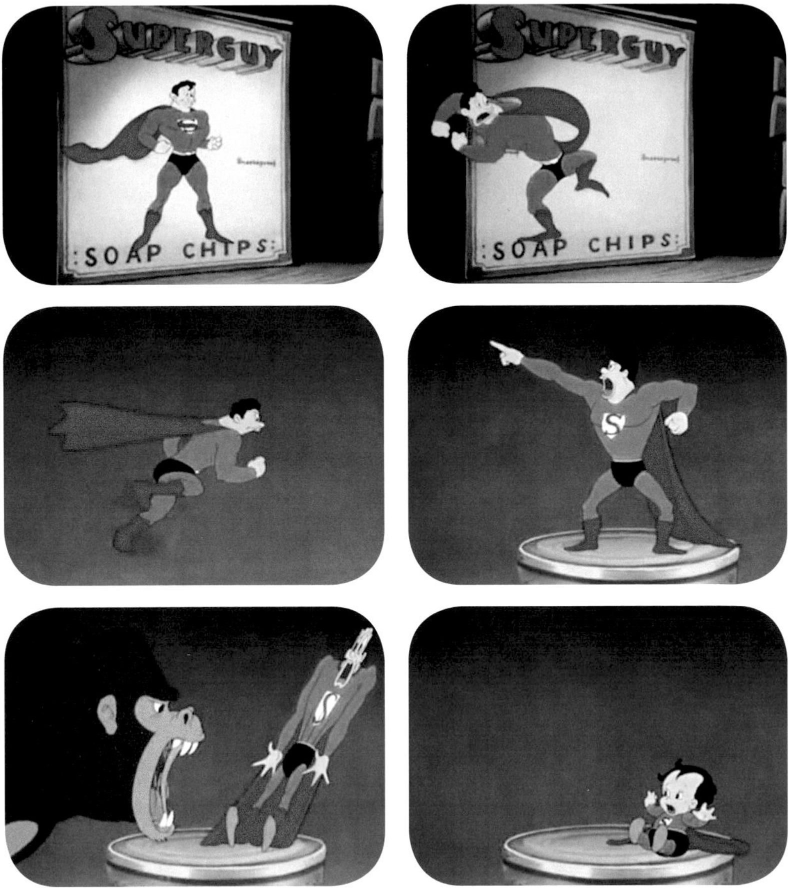
SUPERGUY
SOAP CHIPS
SUPERGUY
SOAP CHIPS

MERRIE MELODIES SUPERMAN SPOOF

Animation stills, "Goofy Groceries"; director, Robert Clampett; March 29, 1941. Superman quickly became a popular target for parody, beginning with this animated sequence from Warner Bros. Other cartoon jabs came in Terrytoons' 1942 *The Mouse of Tomorrow* and a 1943 Bugs Bunny episode entitled *Super-Rabbit.*

COMIC CAVALCADE No. 23

Cover art, Alex Toth (adult figures) and Harry Lampert (children and fence), October–November 1947. The wish fulfillment inherent in super heroes is clearly on display here. The girl playing Wonder Woman is Cotton-Top Katie, the star of a kids humor feature seen in *Comic Cavalcade, All-American Comics,* and other titles.

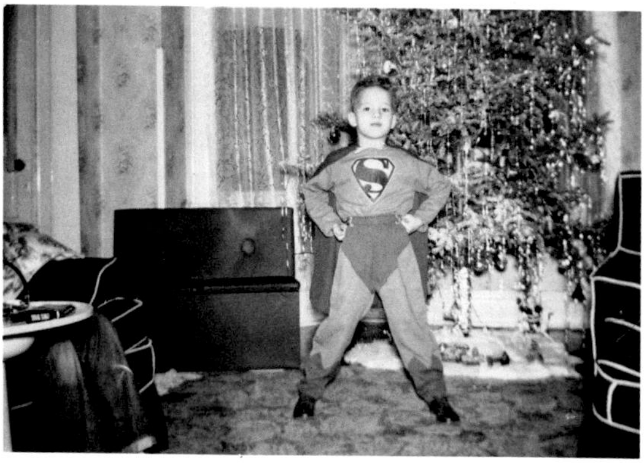

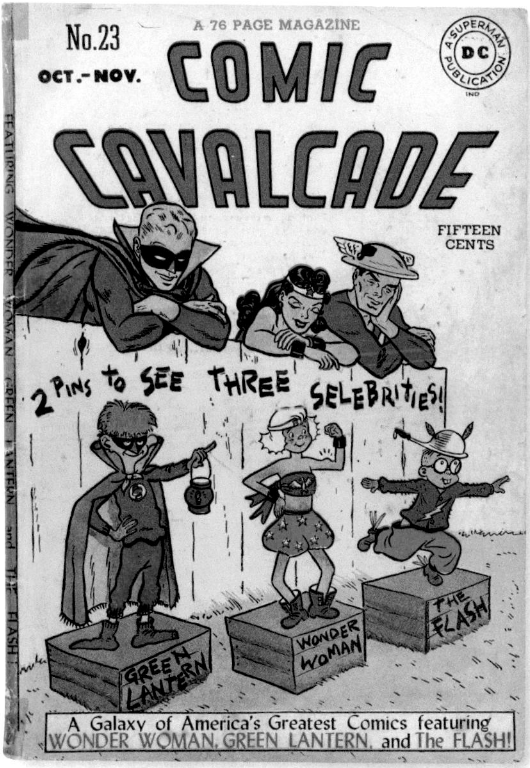
No.23
A 76 PAGE MAGAZINE
OCT.-NOV.
COMIC CAVALCADE
A SUPERMAN DC PUBLICATION
FIFTEEN CENTS
FEATURING WONDER WOMAN GREEN LANTERN and THE FLASH!
2 PINS TO SEE THREE SELEBRITIES!
GREEN LANTERN
WONDER WOMAN
THE FLASH
A Galaxy of America's Greatest Comics featuring
WONDER WOMAN, GREEN LANTERN, and The FLASH!

A SUPERMAN CHRISTMAS
Photograph, anonymous, ca. 1940. "Superman's appeal was one of intrinsic simplicity. Kids understood it better than anyone. His costume was more colorful, more flamboyant than the Phantom's. His method of operation more direct than Dick Tracy. And he was stronger than Tarzan, Buck Rogers, and everyone else put together. He lacked the adult, sophisticated veneer of Flash Gordon, the talkativeness of Terry. In short, he was the graphic representation of the ultimate childhood dream-self."
—Jim Steranko

DOUBLE ACTION COMICS No. 2 ASHCAN

OPPOSITE: *Cover art, John Richard Flanagan.* BELOW: *Interior, "Crime Never Pays" reprint; script and art, unknown. January 1940.* There are only three copies of *Double Action Comics* No. 2 known to exist, and no verified copies have ever surfaced of a No. 1. That's because ashcans weren't for sale; they existed purely for trademark and copyright registration and were generally produced in single-digit quantities and filed away. Those rare copies that have survived the decades have become such collector's items that they can sell at auctions for tens of thousands of dollars.

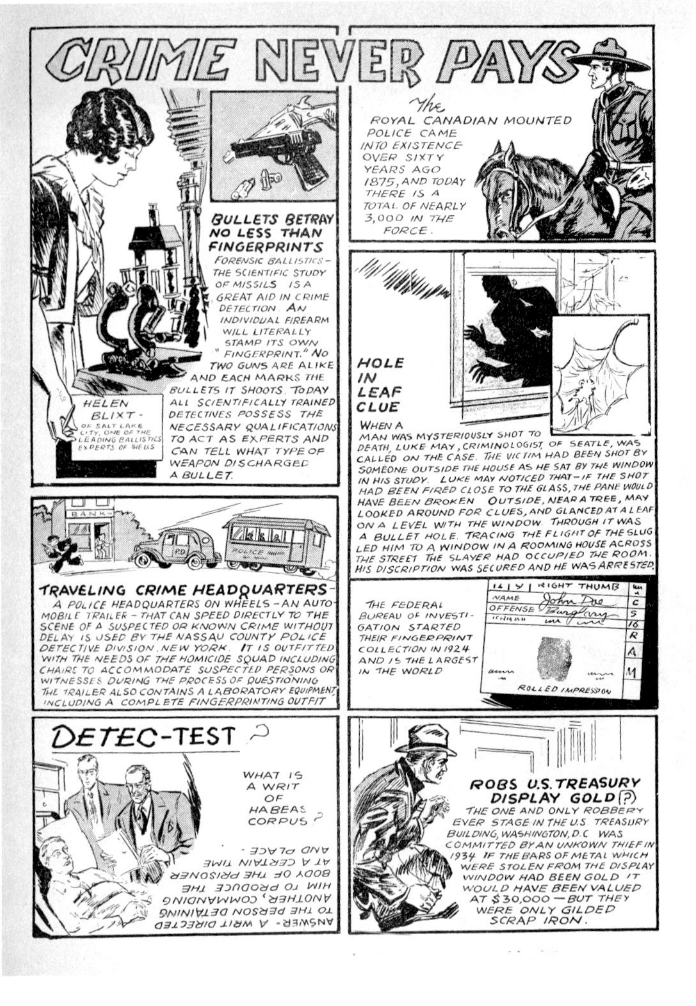

CRIME NEVER PAYS
BULLETS BETRAY NO LESS THAN FINGERPRINTS
FORENSIC BALLISTICS – THE SCIENTIFIC STUDY OF MISSILS IS A GREAT AID IN CRIME DETECTION. AN INDIVIDUAL FIREARM WILL LITERALLY STAMP ITS OWN "FINGERPRINT." NO TWO GUNS ARE ALIKE AND EACH MARKS THE BULLETS IT SHOOTS. TODAY ALL SCIENTIFICALLY TRAINED DETECTIVES POSSESS THE NECESSARY QUALIFICATIONS TO ACT AS EXPERTS AND CAN TELL WHAT TYPE OF WEAPON DISCHARGED A BULLET.
HELEN BLIXT - OF SALT LAKE CITY, ONE OF THE LEADING BALLISTICS EXPERTS OF THE U.S
The ROYAL CANADIAN MOUNTED POLICE CAME INTO EXISTENCE OVER SIXTY YEARS AGO 1875, AND TODAY THERE IS A TOTAL OF NEARLY 3,000 IN THE FORCE.
HOLE IN LEAF CLUE
WHEN A MAN WAS MYSTERIOUSLY SHOT TO DEATH, LUKE MAY, CRIMINOLOGIST, OF SEATLE, WAS CALLED ON THE CASE. THE VICTIM HAD BEEN SHOT BY SOMEONE OUTSIDE THE HOUSE AS HE SAT BY THE WINDOW IN HIS STUDY. LUKE MAY NOTICED THAT – IF THE SHOT HAD BEEN FIRED CLOSE TO THE GLASS, THE PANE WOULD HAVE BEEN BROKEN. OUTSIDE, NEAR A TREE, MAY LOOKED AROUND FOR CLUES, AND GLANCED AT A LEAF ON A LEVEL WITH THE WINDOW. THROUGH IT WAS A BULLET HOLE. TRACING THE FLIGHT OF THE SLUG LED HIM TO A WINDOW IN A ROOMING HOUSE ACROSS THE STREET. THE SLAYER HAD OCCUPIED THE ROOM. HIS DISCRIPTION WAS SECURED AND HE WAS ARRESTED.
BANK
P.D
POLICE
TRAVELING CRIME HEADQUARTERS -
A POLICE HEADQUARTERS ON WHEELS – AN AUTOMOBILE TRAILER – THAT CAN SPEED DIRECTLY TO THE SCENE OF A SUSPECTED OR KNOWN CRIME WITHOUT DELAY IS USED BY THE NASSAU COUNTY POLICE DETECTIVE DIVISION, NEW YORK. IT IS OUTFITTED WITH THE NEEDS OF THE HOMICIDE SQUAD INCLUDING CHAIRS TO ACCOMMODATE SUSPECTED PERSONS OR WITNESSES DURING THE PROCESS OF QUESTIONING. THE TRAILER ALSO CONTAINS A LABORATORY EQUIPMENT, INCLUDING A COMPLETE FINGERPRINTING OUTFIT
THE FEDERAL BUREAU OF INVESTIGATION STARTED THEIR FINGERPRINT COLLECTION IN 1924 AND IS THE LARGEST IN THE WORLD
RIGHT THUMB
NAME John Doe
OFFENSE Burglary
C
5
16
R
A
M
ROLLED IMPRESSION
DETEC-TEST
WHAT IS A WRIT OF HABEAS CORPUS?
ANSWER - A WRIT DIRECTED TO THE PERSON DETAINING ANOTHER, COMMANDING HIM TO PRODUCE THE BODY OF THE PRISONER AT A CERTAIN TIME AND PLACE.
ROBS U.S. TREASURY DISPLAY GOLD (?)
THE ONE AND ONLY ROBBERY EVER STAGE IN THE U.S. TREASURY BUILDING, WASHINGTON, D.C. WAS COMMITTED BY AN UNKOWN THIEF IN 1934. IF THE BARS OF METAL WHICH WERE STOLEN FROM THE DISPLAY WINDOW HAD BEEN GOLD IT WOULD HAVE BEEN VALUED AT $30,000 — BUT THEY WERE ONLY GILDED SCRAP IRON.

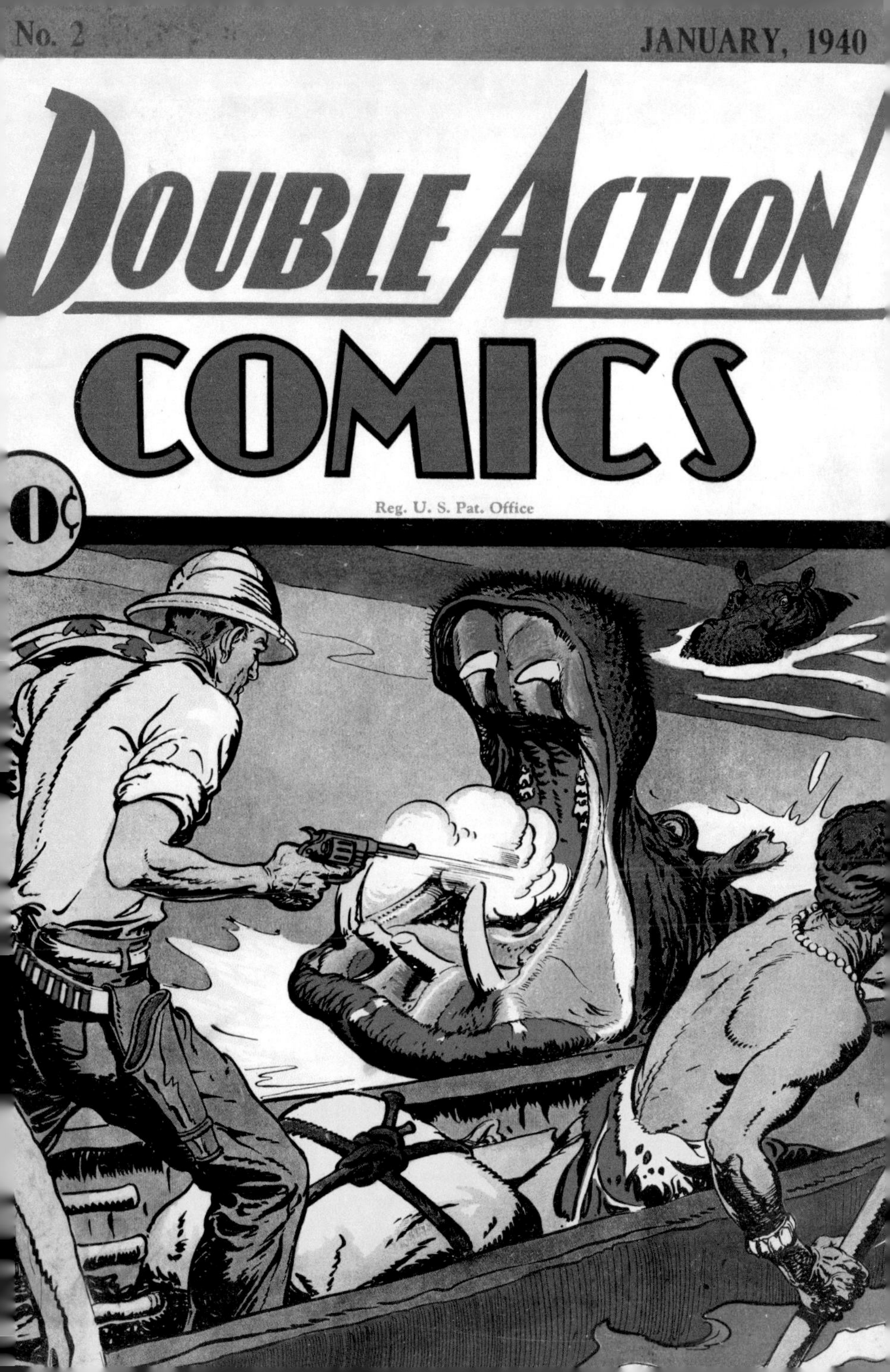
No. 2
JANUARY, 1940
DOUBLE ACTION
COMICS
10¢
Reg. U. S. Pat. Office

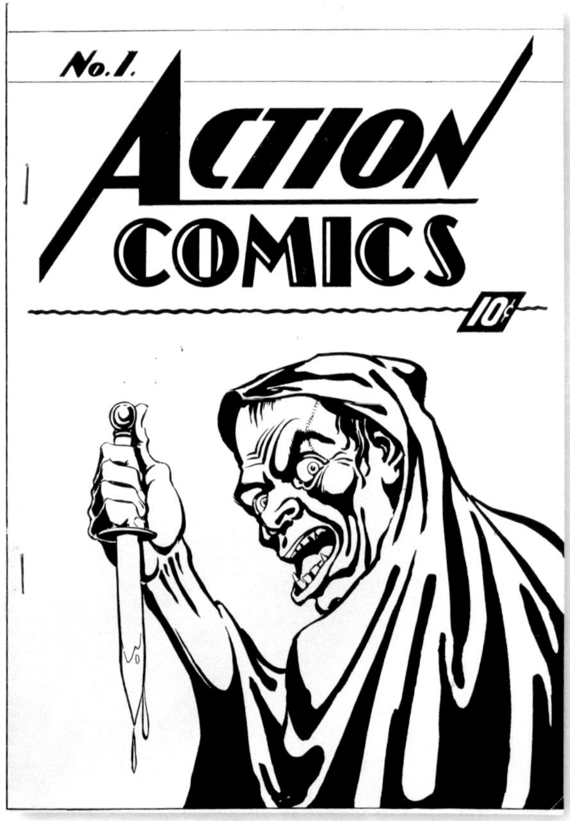
No. 1.
ACTION
COMICS
10¢

ACTION COMICS, SUPERBOY, & FLASH COMICS ASHCANS

ABOVE: *Cover art, Creig Flessel, 1938.*

OPPOSITE: *Cover art, Leo E. O'Mealia, December 1939.*

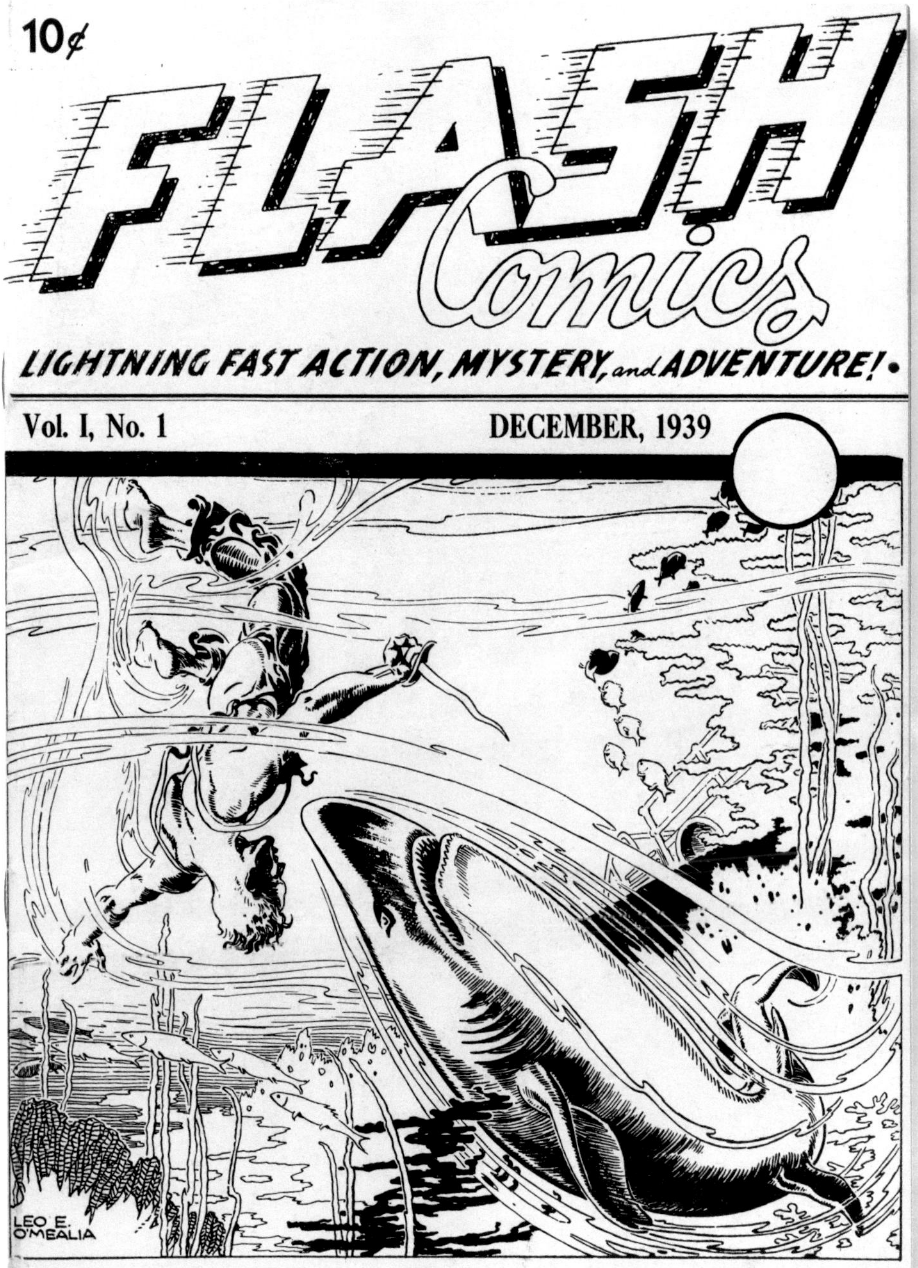
10¢
FLASH
Comics
LIGHTNING FAST ACTION, MYSTERY, and ADVENTURE!
Vol. I, No. 1
DECEMBER, 1939
LEO E. O'MEALIA

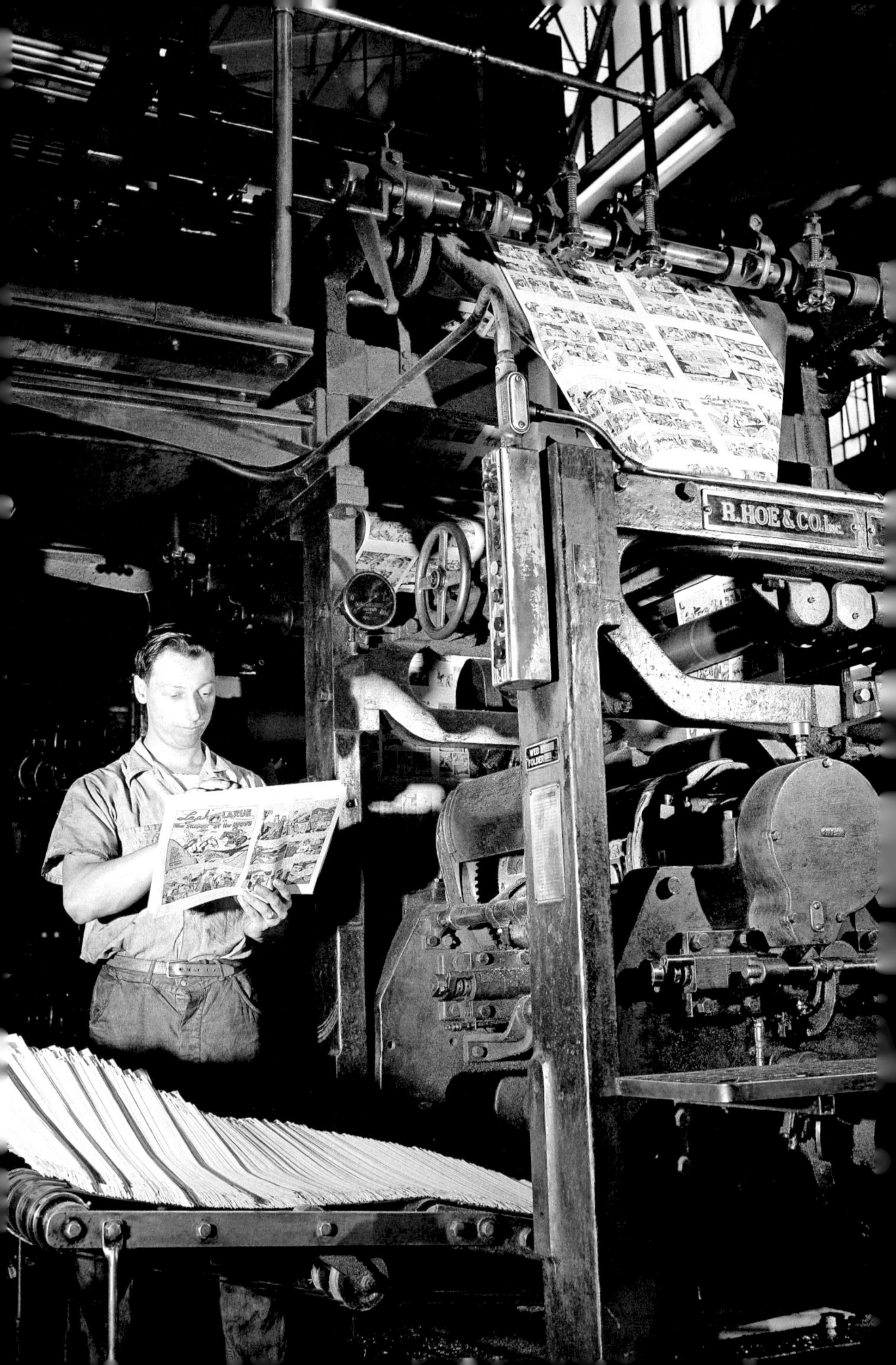
R.HOE & CO.Inc.

THE PRINTING PROCESS

Photo, C. T. Dearing company pressroom, Louisville, Kentucky, 1950. Giant rolls of cheap newsprint came off rail-road cars directly into the plant, to be fed seamlessly through a long press, with each color being applied in turn, then dried, cut, and folded into 16- or 32-page sections. Thousands were produced every hour. Covers printed separately. Then interiors and covers were placed on a bindery line, which would collate, staple, and trim the books into their final form.

FOUR-COLOR SEPARATIONS

FOLLOWING SPREAD: *Separating process, cover art for* All-American Western *No. 125, Alex Toth and Sy Barry, April–May 1952.* The four-color plates used for the lithography of comics were black, magenta, yellow, and cyan. Comic covers would use a wider range of tones than interiors, which permitted no shades of black in the mix until the 1980s. Editors and production staff could review this "progressive proof" of a cover, which enabled them to see and ask for subtle adjustments. Interiors weren't proofed in color.

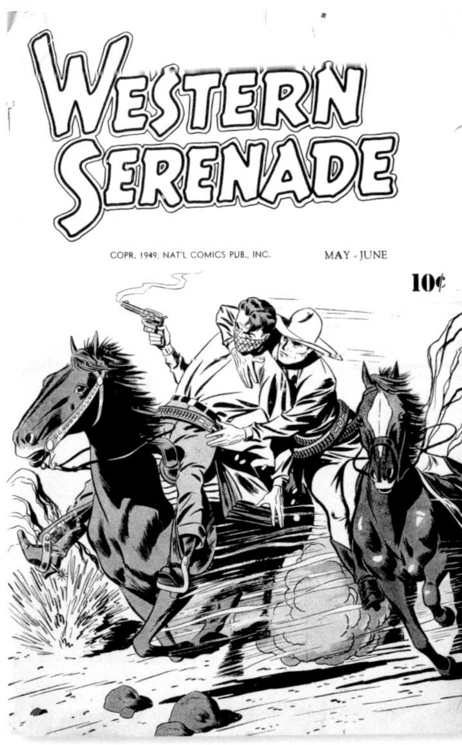
WESTERN SERENADE
COPR. 1949, NAT'L COMICS PUB., INC.
MAY - JUNE
10¢

WESTERN SERENADE ASHCAN

Cover art, Howard Sherman, May–June 1949.

A THRILLING "FOLEY of the FIGHTING FIFTH" ADVENTURE
ALL AMERICAN
Western
10¢
SIZZLING BULLETS PURSUE
DEATH!

Western

SUPERMAN DC NATIONAL COMICS
APR. MAY NO.12
Western
WE'VE BEEN WAITIN' FOR THIS, THUNDER! YOU'RE A PERFECT TARGET! HAW HAW!
Johnny Thunder IN A GRIM GAME OF

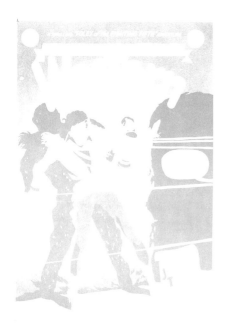

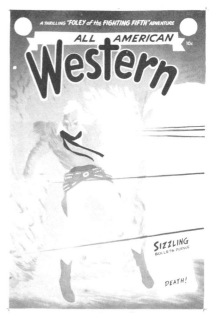

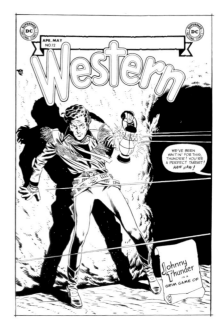

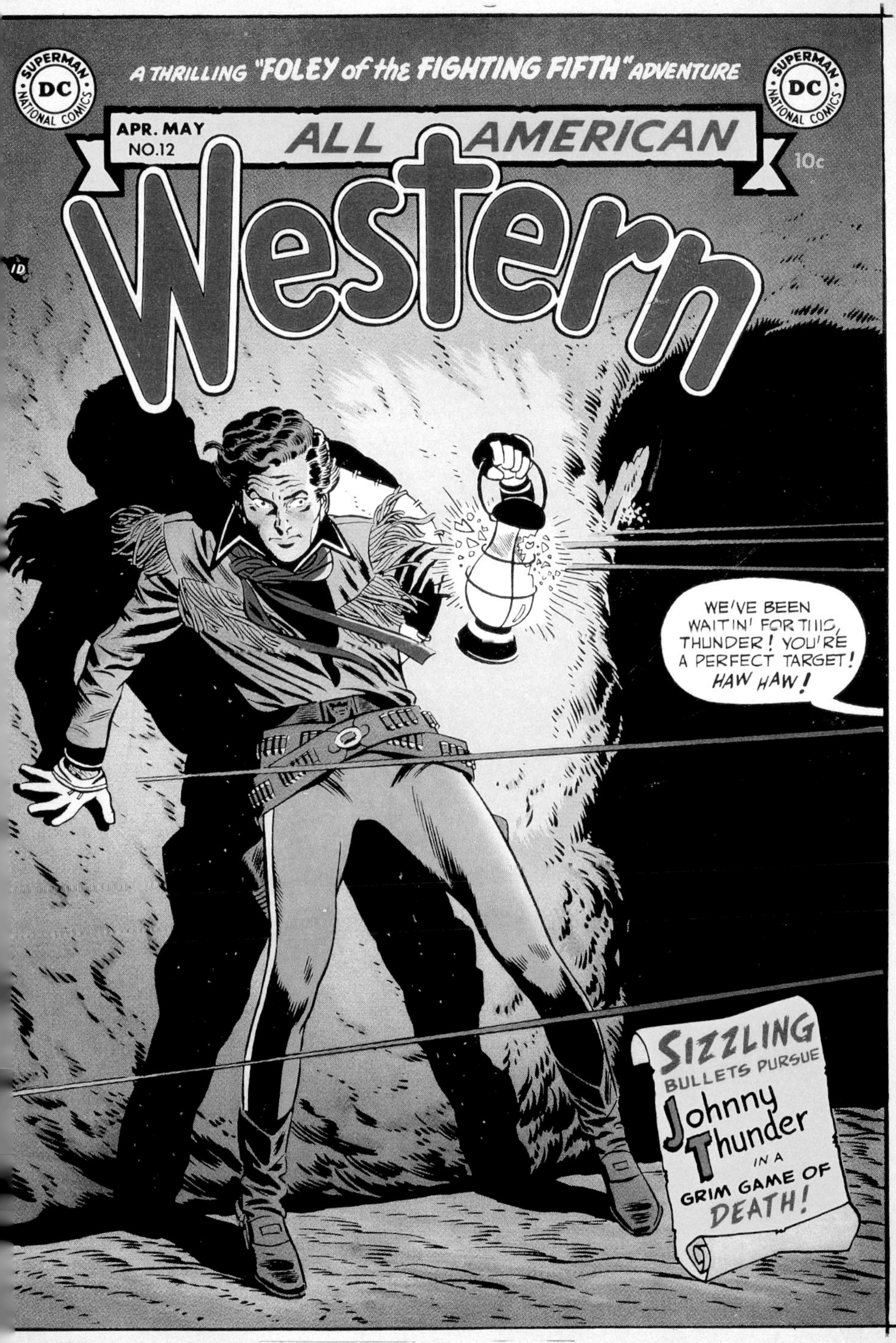

SUPERMAN DC NATIONAL COMICS
A THRILLING "FOLEY of the FIGHTING FIFTH" ADVENTURE
SUPERMAN DC NATIONAL COMICS
APR. MAY
NO.12
ALL AMERICAN
Western
10c
WE'VE BEEN WAITIN' FOR THIS, THUNDER! YOU'RE A PERFECT TARGET! HAW HAW!
SIZZLING BULLETS PURSUE Johnny Thunder IN A GRIM GAME OF DEATH!

THE STEPS OF PRODUCTION

World Color Press *magazine, 1977, featuring photos of every stage of the production process, 1930s–1950s. World Color Press* created complete Sunday comic sections for newspapers well before the Golden Age, but the process it used remained similar decades later: editorial would move to the publishers, but any text material would still require typesetting in a composing room, the engraved metal plates produced by color separation would still need adjustment by routing, and preparing the books for shipment took advantage of the central location of their plants around St. Louis.

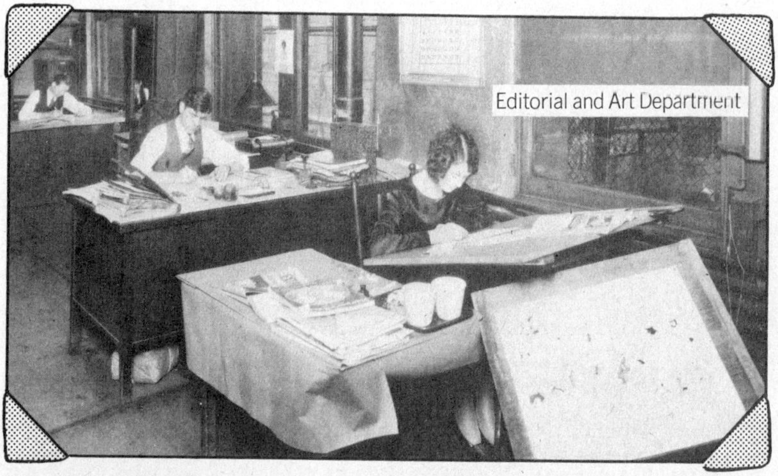

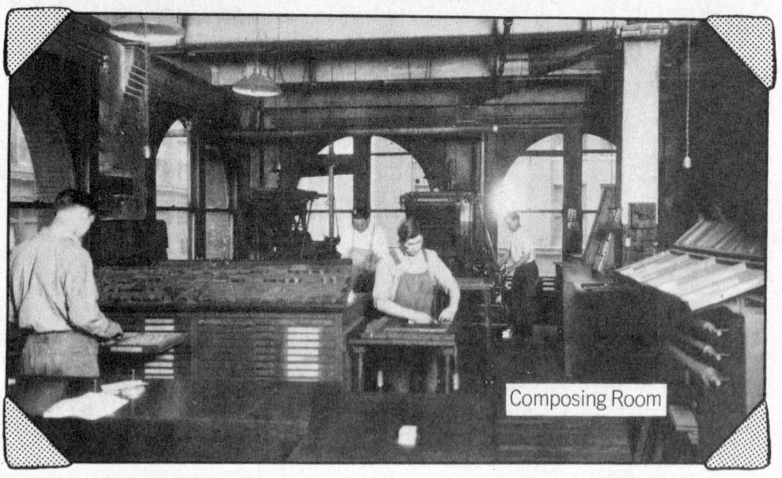

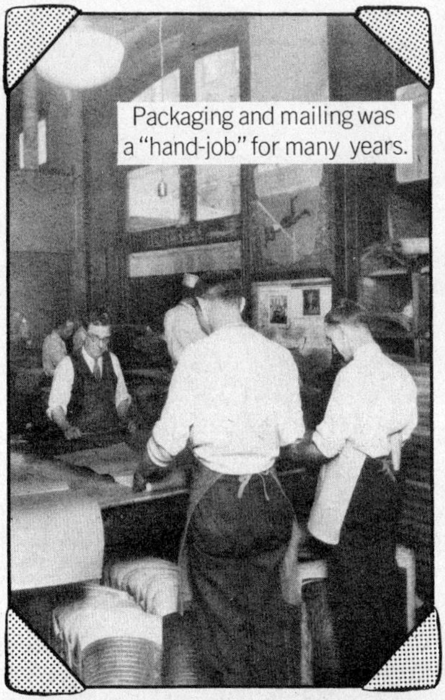

Packaging and mailing was a "hand-job" for many years.

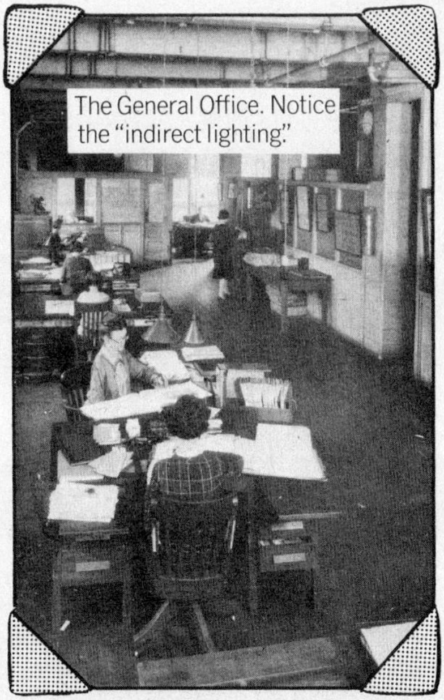

The General Office. Notice the "indirect lighting."

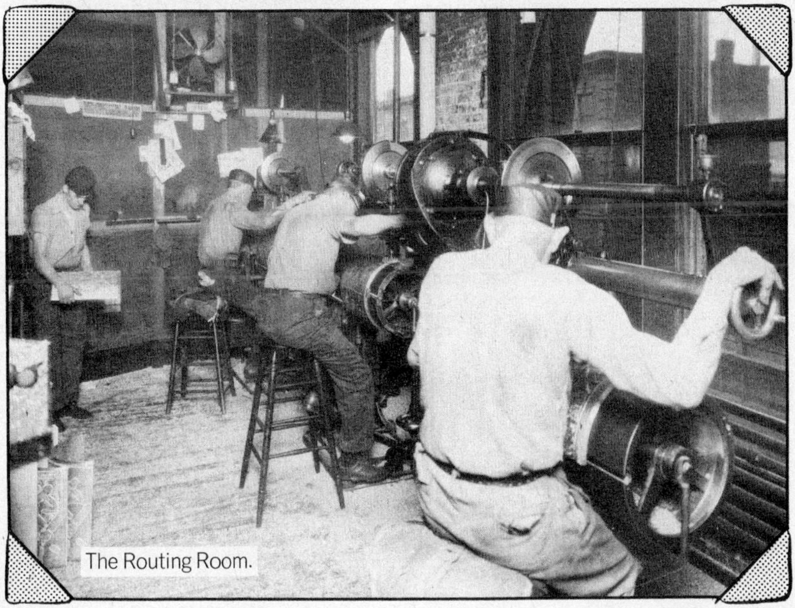

The Routing Room.

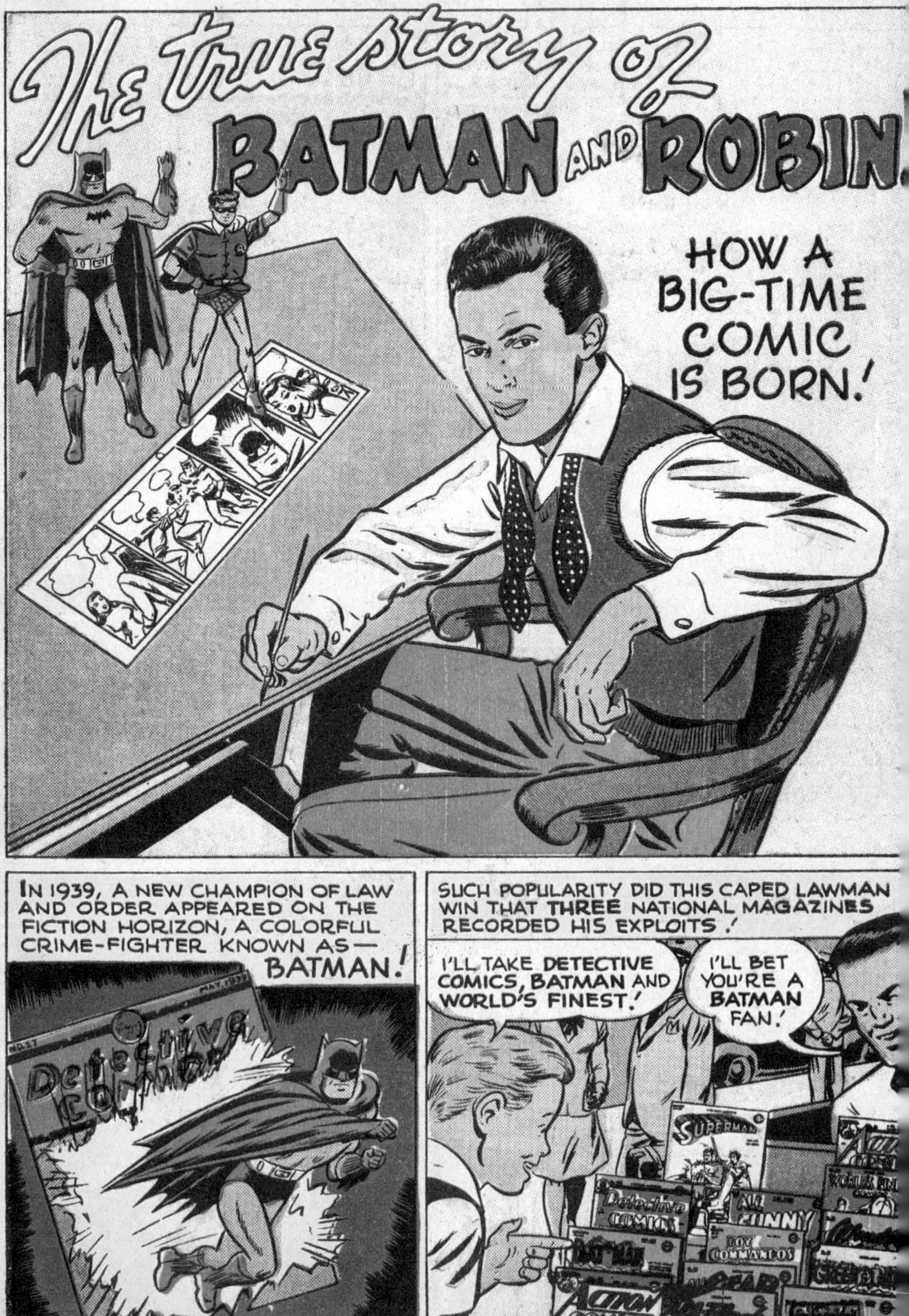
The true story of
BATMAN AND ROBIN
HOW A BIG-TIME COMIC IS BORN!
IN 1939, A NEW CHAMPION OF LAW AND ORDER APPEARED ON THE FICTION HORIZON, A COLORFUL CRIME-FIGHTER KNOWN AS— BATMAN!
MAY, 1939
Detective Comics
SUCH POPULARITY DID THIS CAPED LAWMAN WIN THAT THREE NATIONAL MAGAZINES RECORDED HIS EXPLOITS!
I'LL TAKE DETECTIVE COMICS, BATMAN AND WORLD'S FINEST!
I'LL BET YOU'RE A BATMAN FAN!
SUPERMAN
Detective COMICS
BOY COMMANDOS

Bob Kane

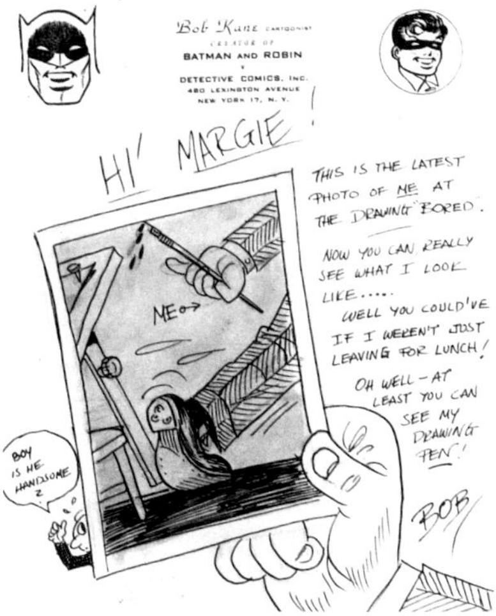

Bob Kane CARTOONIST
CREATOR OF
BATMAN AND ROBIN
DETECTIVE COMICS, INC.
480 LEXINGTON AVENUE
NEW YORK 17, N. Y.
HI' MARGIE!
THIS IS THE LATEST PHOTO OF ME AT THE DRAWING BORED.
NOW YOU CAN REALLY SEE WHAT I LOOK LIKE.....
WELL YOU COULD'VE IF I WEREN'T JUST LEAVING FOR LUNCH!
OH WELL - AT LEAST YOU CAN SEE MY DRAWING PEN!
BOB
ME
BOY IS HE HANDSOME ?

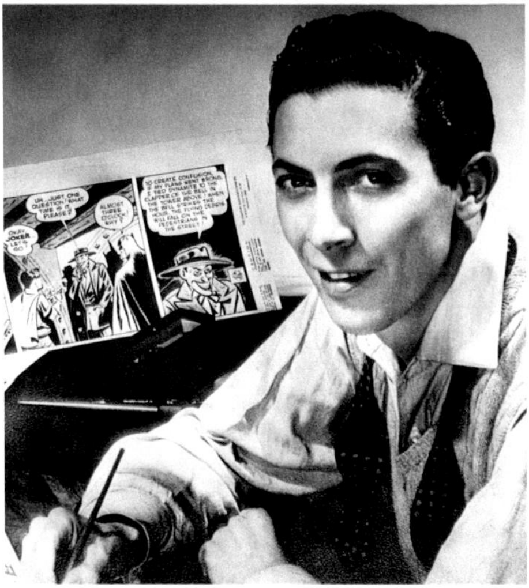

REAL FACT COMICS No. 5

Interior, "The True Story of Batman and Robin"; script, Jack Schiff, Mort Weisinger, and Bernie Breslauer; pencils and inks, Win Mortimer. November–December 1946. This five-page story presented a fanciful answer to the question, "How did Batman come to be?" Among the revelations: Bob Kane's mother sewed a Batman costume for a friend to model so Kane could draw him; the idea for the Joker came from another friend squirting Kane with a gag lapel flower in a novelty store; and Robin was inspired by a letter from a young reader who wrote, "I would like to see Batman have a partner…someone who can share the secret of his identity."

BOB KANE, SELF-PORTRAIT CARTOON

Letter to a fan, 1940s.

BOB KANE

Photograph, at the drawing board, "Batman" comic strip in background, 1944. Like many young men, Bob Kane aspired to create his own newspaper strip. One of his first DC features — Rusty and His Pals — was inspired by Milton Caniff's comic strip "Terry and the Pirates."

"Kane's strength…lay not in his draftsmanship (which was never quite believable), but in his total involvement in what he was doing (which made everything believable)….because Kane's was an authentic fantasy, a genuine vision, so that however one might nitpick the components, the end product remained an impregnable whole: gripping and original."

—JULES FEIFFER

DETECTIVE COMICS No. 33
Interiors, "The Batman Wars Against the Dirigible of Doom"; writer, Gardner Fox; pencils, Bob Kane (primary figures) and Sheldon Moldoff (backgroun ds). November 1939. "We can all understand Bruce [Wayne]'s grief, we can all understand his frustration at having to watch helplessly as the lives of the most important people in his young life are taken uselessly, and we can all understand his need to do something to avenge the deaths of his parents. The origin of the Batman is grounded, therefore, in emotion. An emotion that is primal and timeless and dark." —Dick Giordano

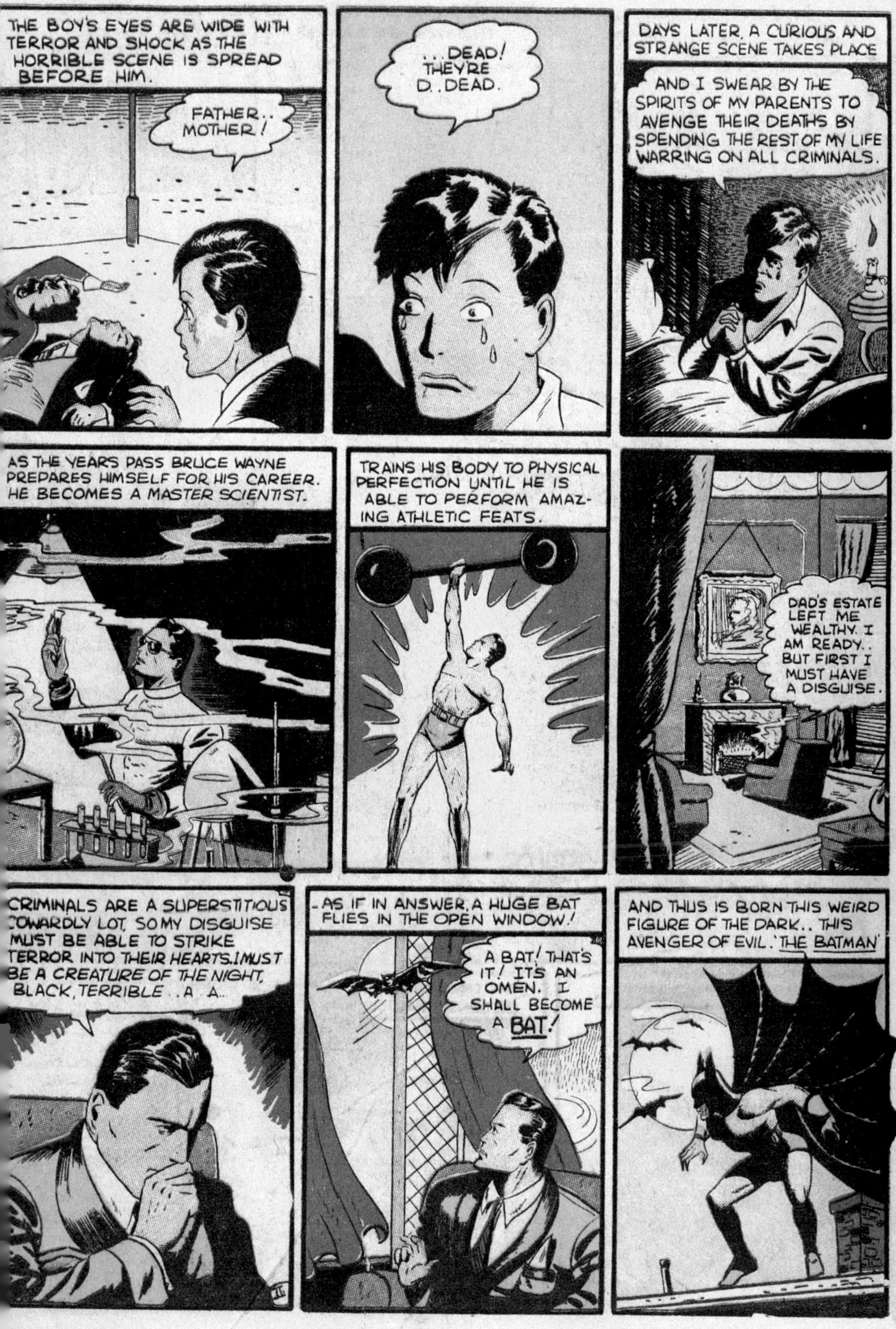
THE BOY'S EYES ARE WIDE WITH TERROR AND SHOCK AS THE HORRIBLE SCENE IS SPREAD BEFORE HIM.
FATHER.. MOTHER!
...DEAD! THEY'RE D..DEAD.
DAYS LATER, A CURIOUS AND STRANGE SCENE TAKES PLACE
AND I SWEAR BY THE SPIRITS OF MY PARENTS TO AVENGE THEIR DEATHS BY SPENDING THE REST OF MY LIFE WARRING ON ALL CRIMINALS.
AS THE YEARS PASS BRUCE WAYNE PREPARES HIMSELF FOR HIS CAREER. HE BECOMES A MASTER SCIENTIST.
TRAINS HIS BODY TO PHYSICAL PERFECTION UNTIL HE IS ABLE TO PERFORM AMAZING ATHLETIC FEATS.
DAD'S ESTATE LEFT ME WEALTHY. I AM READY.. BUT FIRST I MUST HAVE A DISGUISE.
CRIMINALS ARE A SUPERSTITIOUS COWARDLY LOT, SO MY DISGUISE MUST BE ABLE TO STRIKE TERROR INTO THEIR HEARTS. I MUST BE A CREATURE OF THE NIGHT, BLACK, TERRIBLE..A A..
-AS IF IN ANSWER, A HUGE BAT FLIES IN THE OPEN WINDOW!
A BAT! THAT'S IT! IT'S AN OMEN. I SHALL BECOME A BAT!
AND THUS IS BORN THIS WEIRD FIGURE OF THE DARK.. THIS AVENGER OF EVIL. 'THE BATMAN'

THE BAT

Film still, actress Louise Fazenda, 1926. "I recalled seeing a movie around 1926 called *The Bat,* in which the villain wore a batlike costume which was quite awesome. The main difference being that I changed my character into a hero. I felt that this awesome costume on my hero would throw fear and respect into all the villains that he would encounter in his many exciting adventures." —Bob Kane

BLACK BOOK DETECTIVE

Cover art, Rudolph Belarski, Winter 1951.

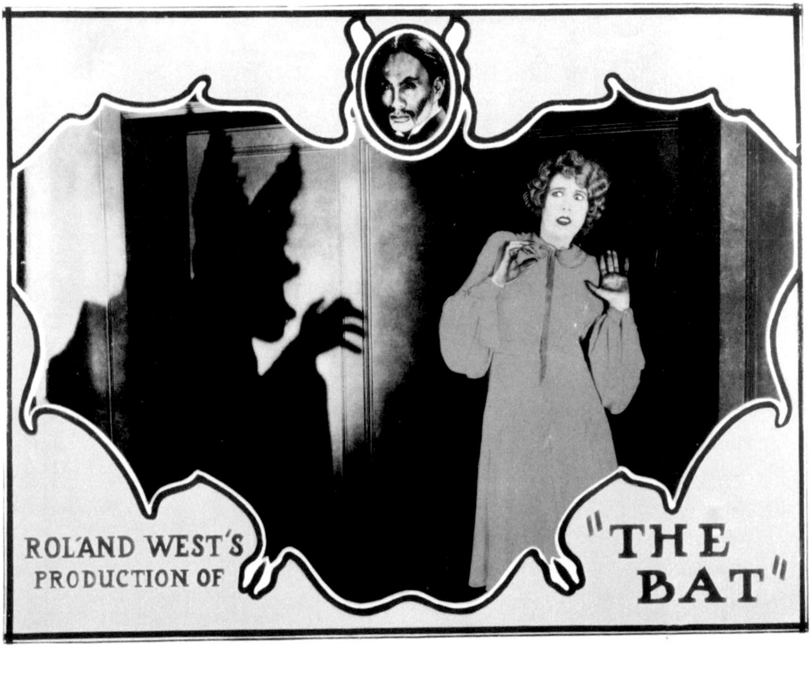
ROLAND WEST'S
PRODUCTION OF
"THE BAT"

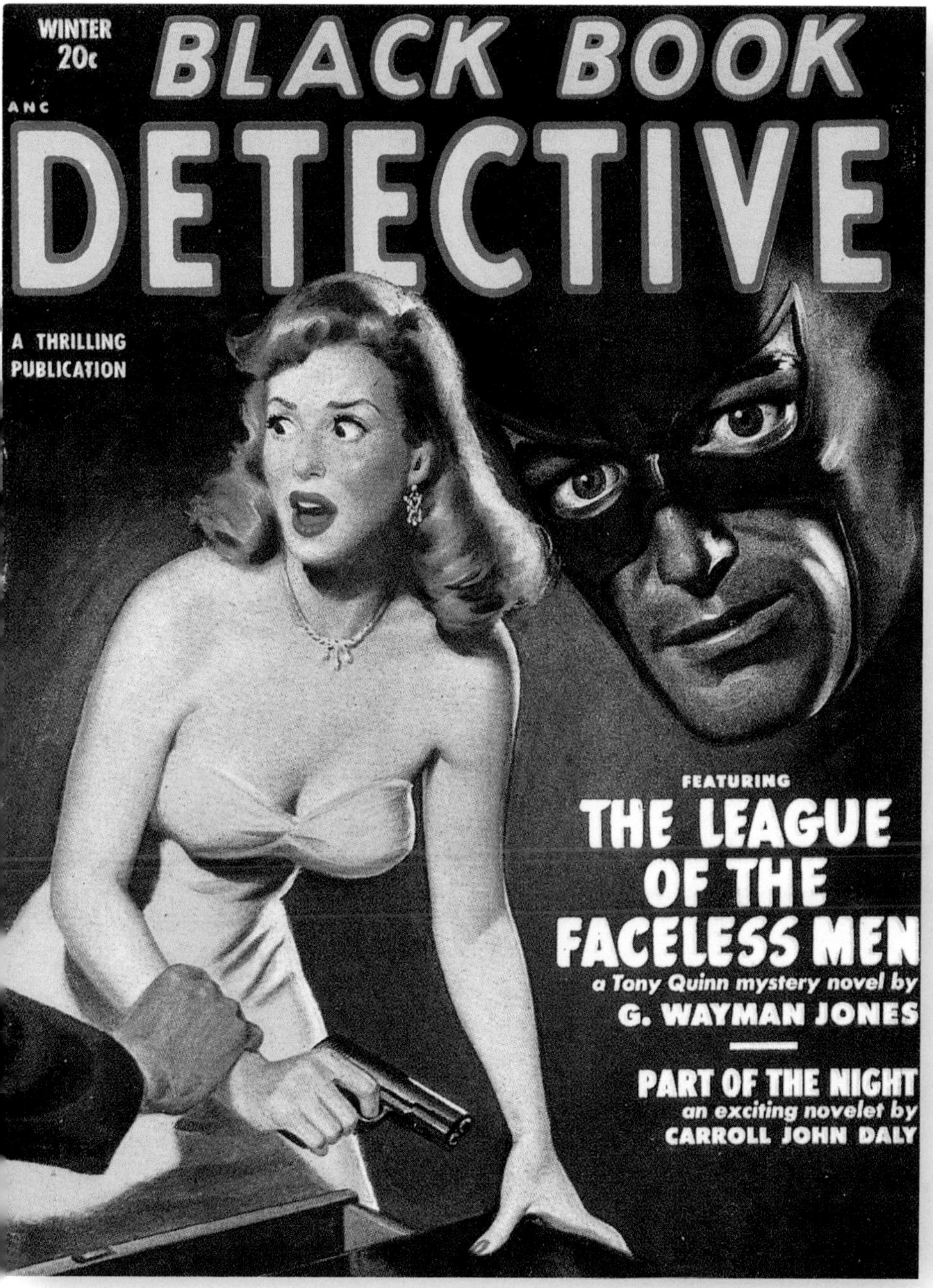
WINTER
20¢
BLACK BOOK
ANC
DETECTIVE
A THRILLING PUBLICATION
FEATURING
THE LEAGUE OF THE FACELESS MEN
a Tony Quinn mystery novel by
G. WAYMAN JONES
PART OF THE NIGHT
an exciting novelet by
CARROLL JOHN DALY

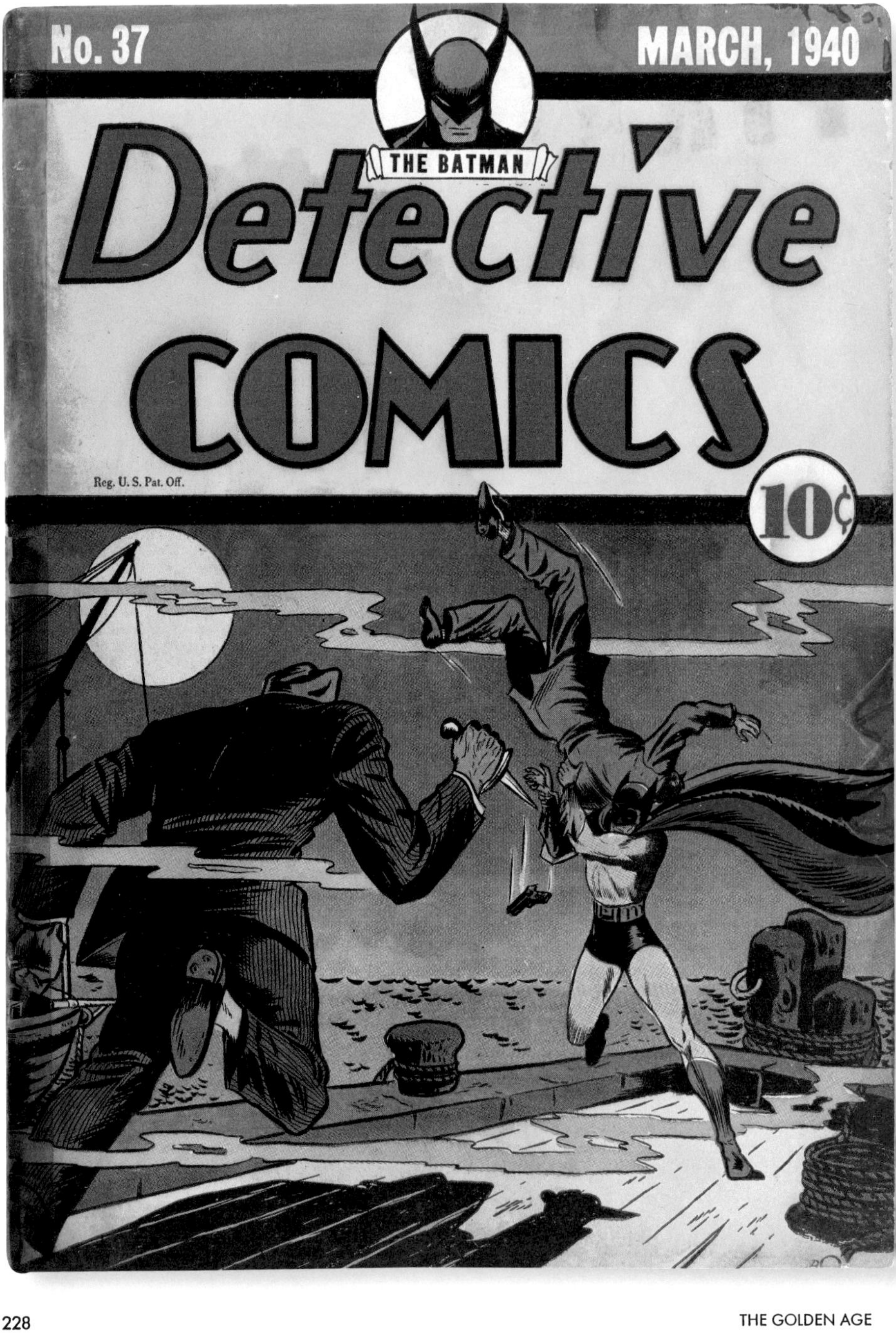
No. 37
MARCH, 1940
THE BATMAN
Detective
COMICS
Reg. U. S. Pat. Off.
10¢

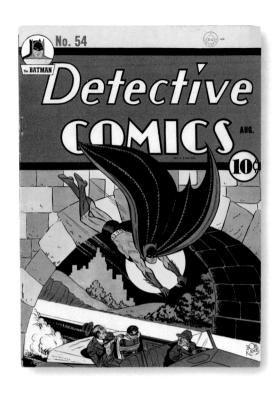

No. 54
The BATMAN
Detective
COMICS
AUG.
10¢
BOB KANE

DETECTIVE COMICS No. 37

Cover art, Bob Kane, March 1940. During his first year in existence, Batman fought a darker breed of villain than the more colorful characters he would later be known for, notably mad scientists Doctor Death and Hugo Strange. That darkness was reflected back by Batman, who killed both of Doctor Death's brutish henchmen and shot the Monk and his lovely sidekick Dala—both vampires—in their hearts with silver bullets.

DETECTIVE COMICS No. 54

Cover art, Bob Kane, Jerry Robinson, and George Roussos. August 1941. Following a brutal assault on Robin in 1941, a caption cautioned, "Woe to all criminals, for now, the Batman has become a terrible figure of vengeance."

DETECTIVE COMICS No. 27

Interior, "The Case of the Chemical Syndicate"; script, Bill Finger; pencils and inks, Bob Kane. May 1939.

The "Batman" who appears in *Detective* No. 27 is not yet fully formed but many of the hallmarks are already there, notably the hero's grim demeanor, his other identity of Bruce Wayne, and his police connection in Commissioner Gordon.

ORIGINAL BATMAN ART

Art, Bob Kane, 1940s.

THE BATMAN SURVEYS HIS GROUND CAUTIOUSLY...

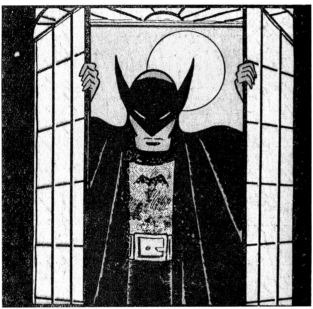

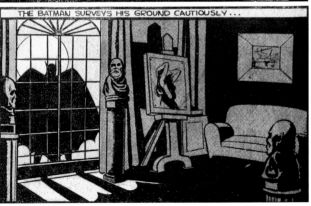

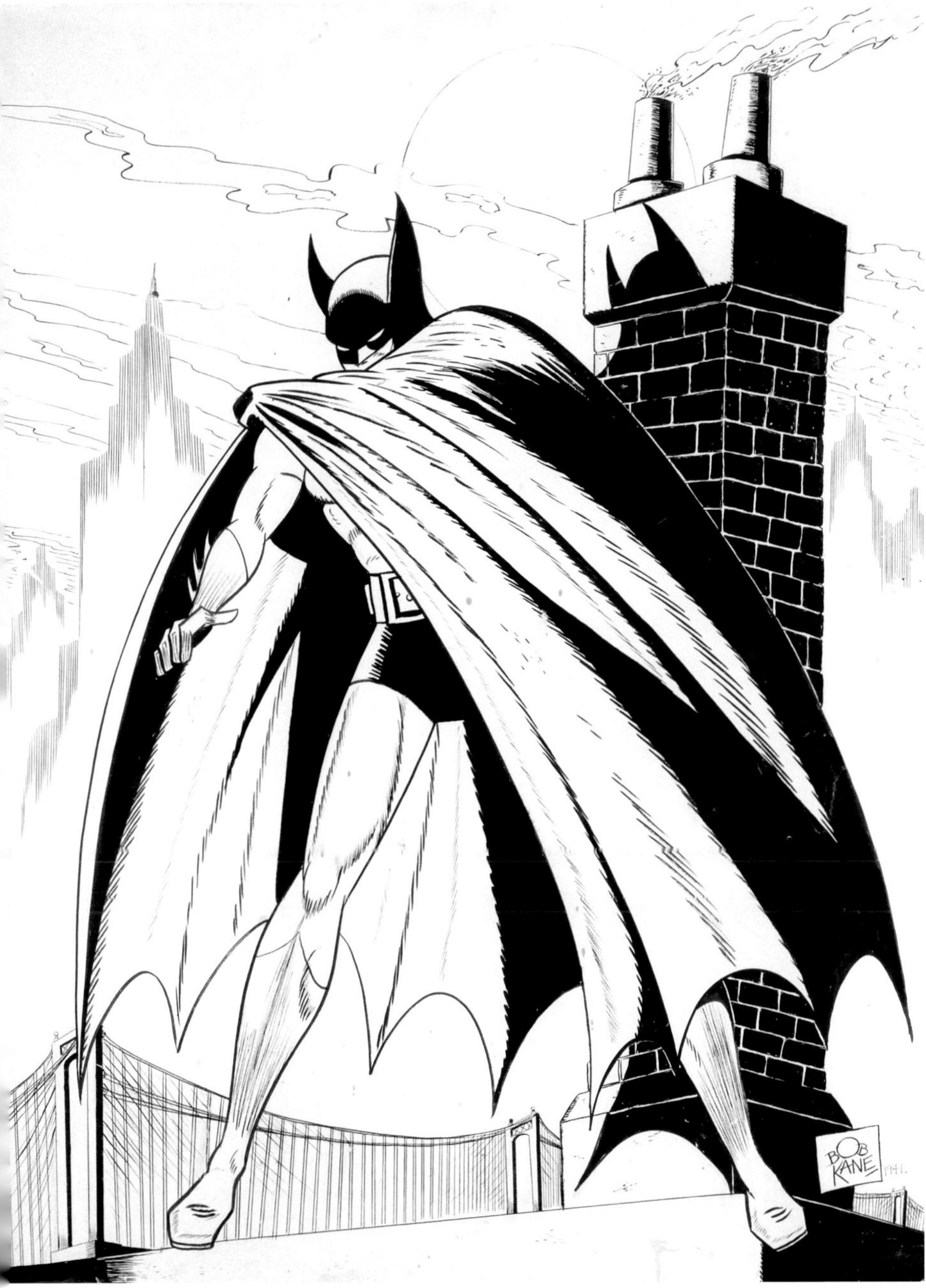
BOB KANE
1941.

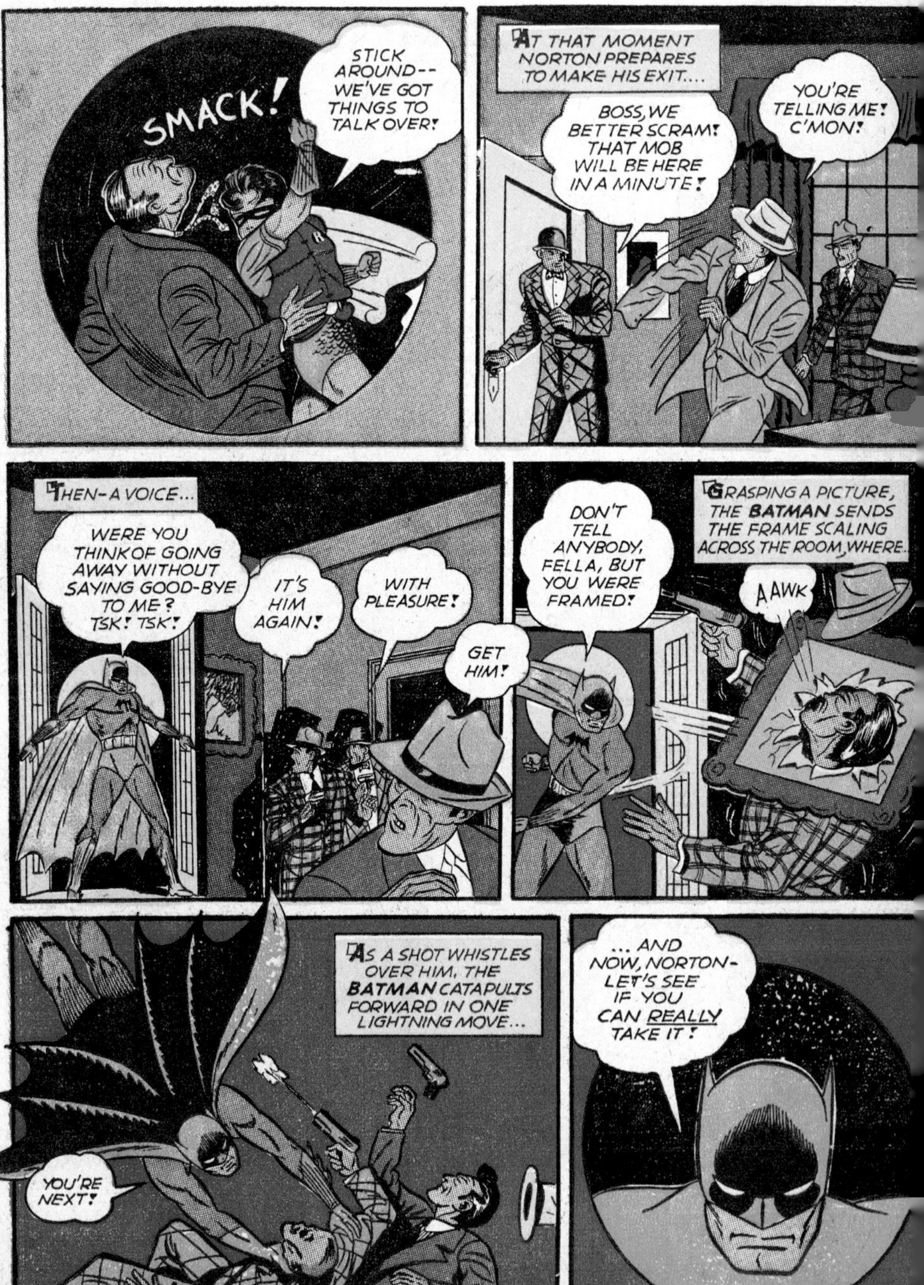
SMACK!
STICK AROUND-- WE'VE GOT THINGS TO TALK OVER!
AT THAT MOMENT NORTON PREPARES TO MAKE HIS EXIT....
BOSS, WE BETTER SCRAM! THAT MOB WILL BE HERE IN A MINUTE!
YOU'RE TELLING ME! C'MON!
THEN-A VOICE...
WERE YOU THINKOF GOING AWAY WITHOUT SAYING GOOD-BYE TO ME? TSK! TSK!
IT'S HIM AGAIN!
WITH PLEASURE!
GET HIM!
GRASPING A PICTURE, THE BATMAN SENDS THE FRAME SCALING ACROSS THE ROOM, WHERE...
DON'T TELL ANYBODY, FELLA, BUT YOU WERE FRAMED!
AAWK
AS A SHOT WHISTLES OVER HIM, THE BATMAN CATAPULTS FORWARD IN ONE LIGHTNING MOVE...
YOU'RE NEXT!
... AND NOW, NORTON- LET'S SEE IF YOU CAN REALLY TAKE IT!

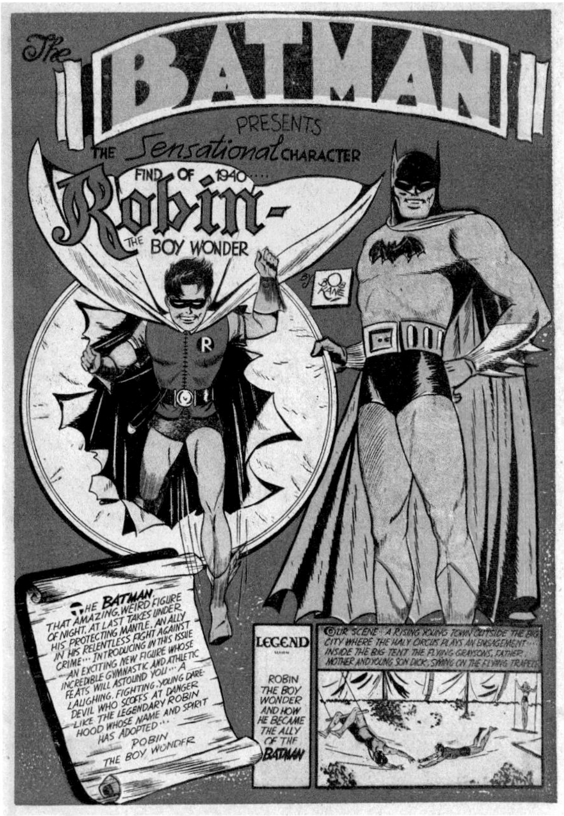

The BATMAN
PRESENTS
THE Sensational CHARACTER FIND OF 1940...
Robin-
THE BOY WONDER
by BOB KANE
THE BATMAN, THAT AMAZING, WEIRD FIGURE OF NIGHT, AT LAST TAKES UNDER HIS PROTECTING MANTLE AN ALLY IN HIS RELENTLESS FIGHT AGAINST CRIME... INTRODUCING IN THIS ISSUE —AN EXCITING NEW FIGURE WHOSE INCREDIBLE GYMNASTIC AND ATHLETIC FEATS WILL ASTOUND YOU... A LAUGHING, FIGHTING, YOUNG DARE-DEVIL WHO SCOFFS AT DANGER LIKE THE LEGENDARY ROBIN HOOD WHOSE NAME AND SPIRIT HAS ADOPTED... ROBIN THE BOY WONDER
LEGEND
ROBIN THE BOY WONDER AND HOW HE BECAME THE ALLY OF THE BATMAN
OUR SCENE: A RISING YOUNG TOWN OUTSIDE THE BIG CITY WHERE THE HALY CIRCUS PLAYS AN ENGAGEMENT... INSIDE THE BIG TENT THE FLYING GRAYSONS, FATHER, MOTHER AND YOUNG SON DICK, SWING ON THE FLYING TRAPEZE

DETECTIVE COMICS No. 43

Interior, "The Case of the City of Terror"; script, Bill Finger; pencils, Bob Kane; inks, Jerry Robinson and George Roussos. September 1940. Following the introduction of Robin, the nature of Batman evolved quickly from simply a fearsome creature of the night to a symbol of empowerment to the helpless. In this story, the newly formed Dynamic Duo visited a small town and helped its populace rise up against the racketeers who were terrorizing them.

DETECTIVE COMICS No. 38

Interior, "Robin the Boy Wonder"; script, Bill Finger; pencils, Bob Kane; inks, Jerry Robinson. April 1940. It was Bob Kane's teenage assistant Jerry Robinson who observed that Batman's new partner was like a young Robin Hood and suggested calling him Robin. "I recall adding the final touch on Bob's sketch of Robin," the artist said. "A small 'R' monogram on his vest."

WORLD'S FINEST COMICS No. 7

Interior, "The North Pole Crimes"; script, Bill Finger; pencils, Bob Kane; inks, Jerry Robinson. Autumn 1942. The banter between Batman and Robin brought a lighter tone to the series that was also reflected in many of the comic books it influenced. It was another crucial step in distinguishing super heroes from the serious, even grim, vigilantes of the pulps.

BATMAN No. 1

Cover art, Bob Kane (Batman and Robin) and Jerry Robinson (background), spring 1940. The introduction of Robin had a transformative effect on Batman, humanizing the character and adding depth to the series' straightforward gothic adventure stories. The notion of a reader-identification character proved a remarkably canny business move, as well, that doubled sales and moved Batman into the same orbit as Superman.

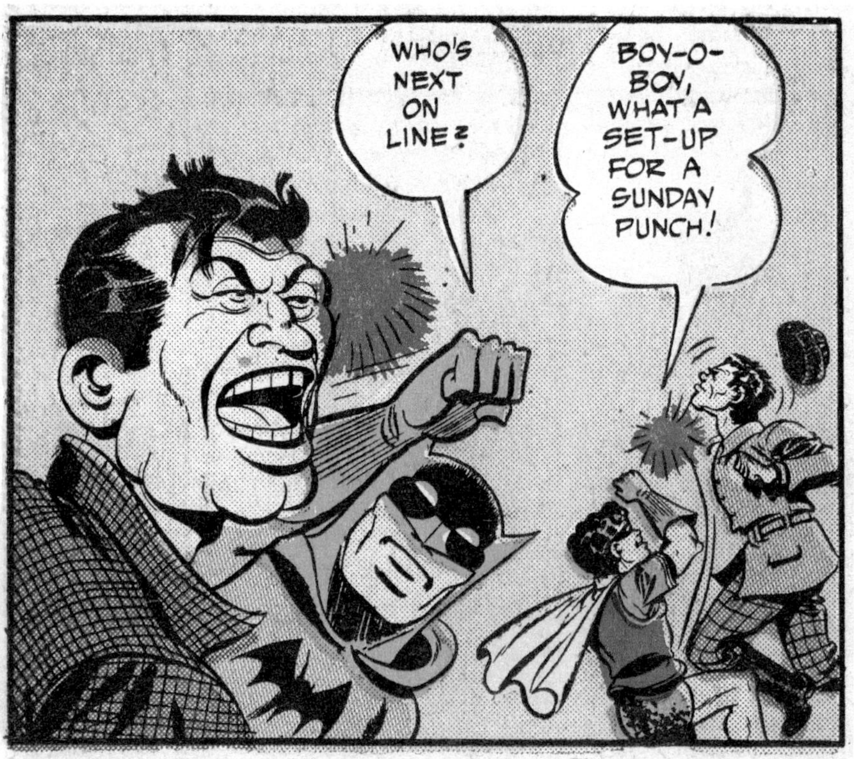
WHO'S NEXT ON LINE?
BOY-O-BOY, WHAT A SET-UP FOR A SUNDAY PUNCH!

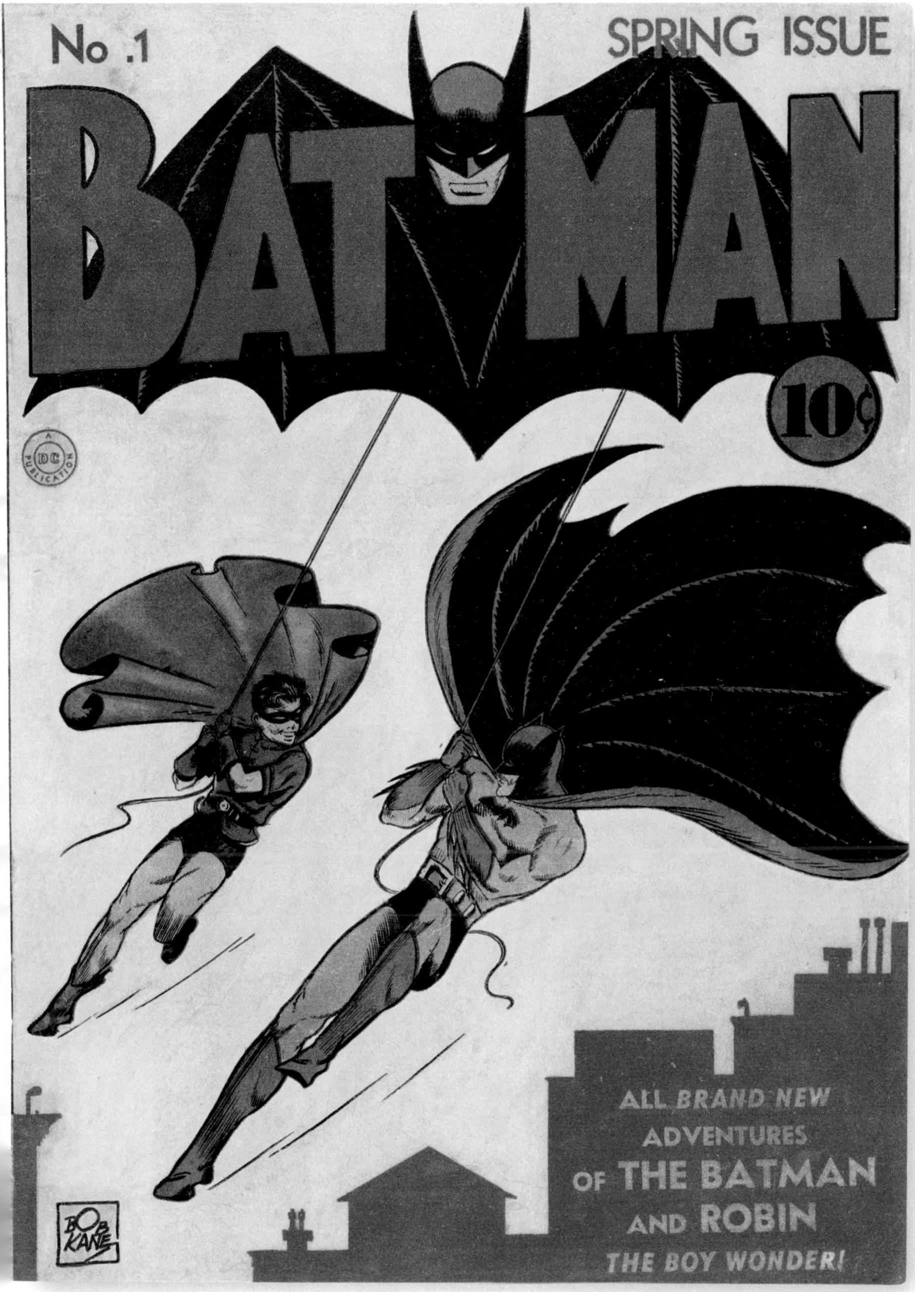
No. 1
SPRING ISSUE
BATMAN
10¢
A DC PUBLICATION
BOB KANE
ALL BRAND NEW
ADVENTURES
OF THE BATMAN
AND ROBIN
THE BOY WONDER!

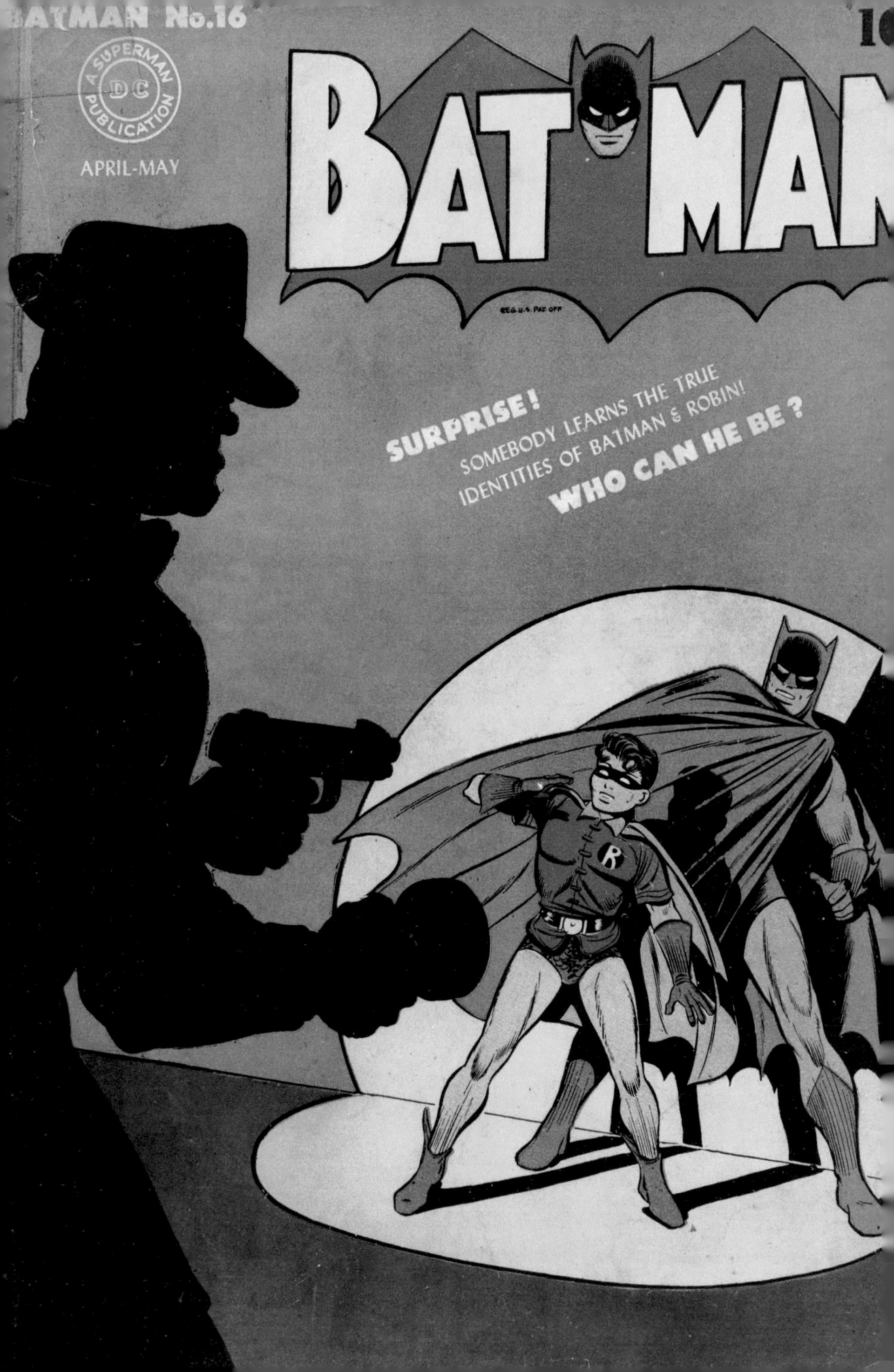
BATMAN No.16
A SUPERMAN DC PUBLICATION
APRIL-MAY
10
BATMAN
REG. U.S. PAT. OFF.
SURPRISE!
SOMEBODY LEARNS THE TRUE IDENTITIES OF BATMAN & ROBIN!
WHO CAN HE BE?
R

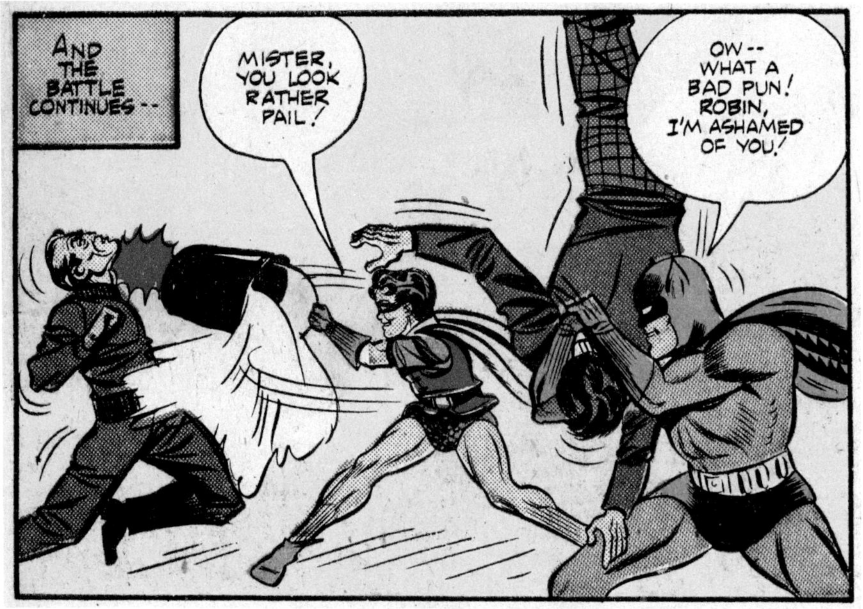
AND THE BATTLE CONTINUES --
MISTER, YOU LOOK RATHER PAIL!
OW -- WHAT A BAD PUN! ROBIN, I'M ASHAMED OF YOU!

BATMAN No. 16
Cover art, Jerry Robinson, April–May 1943. Atypical of its era was this cover "teasing" the reader with its third story's major plot twist. It is most notable for its iconic Jerry Robinson image of Batman and Robin, which was reprinted countless times over the years on book jackets and merchandise. Ironically for a cover based on interior content, this one is coy regarding the most memorable thing about the story in question: the introduction of Alfred the butler!

BATMAN No. 9
Interior, "The White Whale"; script, Bill Finger; pencils, Bob Kane; inks, Jerry Robinson and George Roussos. February–March 1942. Batman and Robin's spectacular success made sidekicks imperative in nearly every major super hero launch of the early 1940s. Timely had Captain America and Bucky and the Human Torch and Toro, Fawcett had Mr. Scarlet and Pinky, MLJ had the Shield and Rusty, and DC itself introduced Green Arrow and Speedy, among others. The concept was so entrenched by 1941 that Jerry Siegel could reverse the stereotypes with the teenage Star-Spangled Kid and his adult partner, Stripesy.

DETECTIVE COMICS No. 42

Cover art, Bob Kane and Jerry Robinson, August 1940.

DETECTIVE COMICS No. 150

Cover art, Jim Mooney, August 1949. The Bat-Signal was a vivid symbol of the sea change in Batman's series since the introduction of Robin. Once sought by the authorities for taking the law into his own hands, the Caped Crusader was made an honorary member of the police department by Commissioner Gordon in 1941. By the end of the year in *Detective Comics* No. 60, a spotlight with a bat on its lens was mounted on police headquarters and aimed toward the sky whenever the Dynamic Duo was needed.

No. 42
The BATMAN
Detective
COMICS
AUG.
10¢
BOB KANE

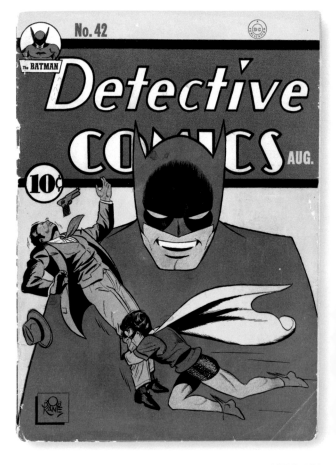

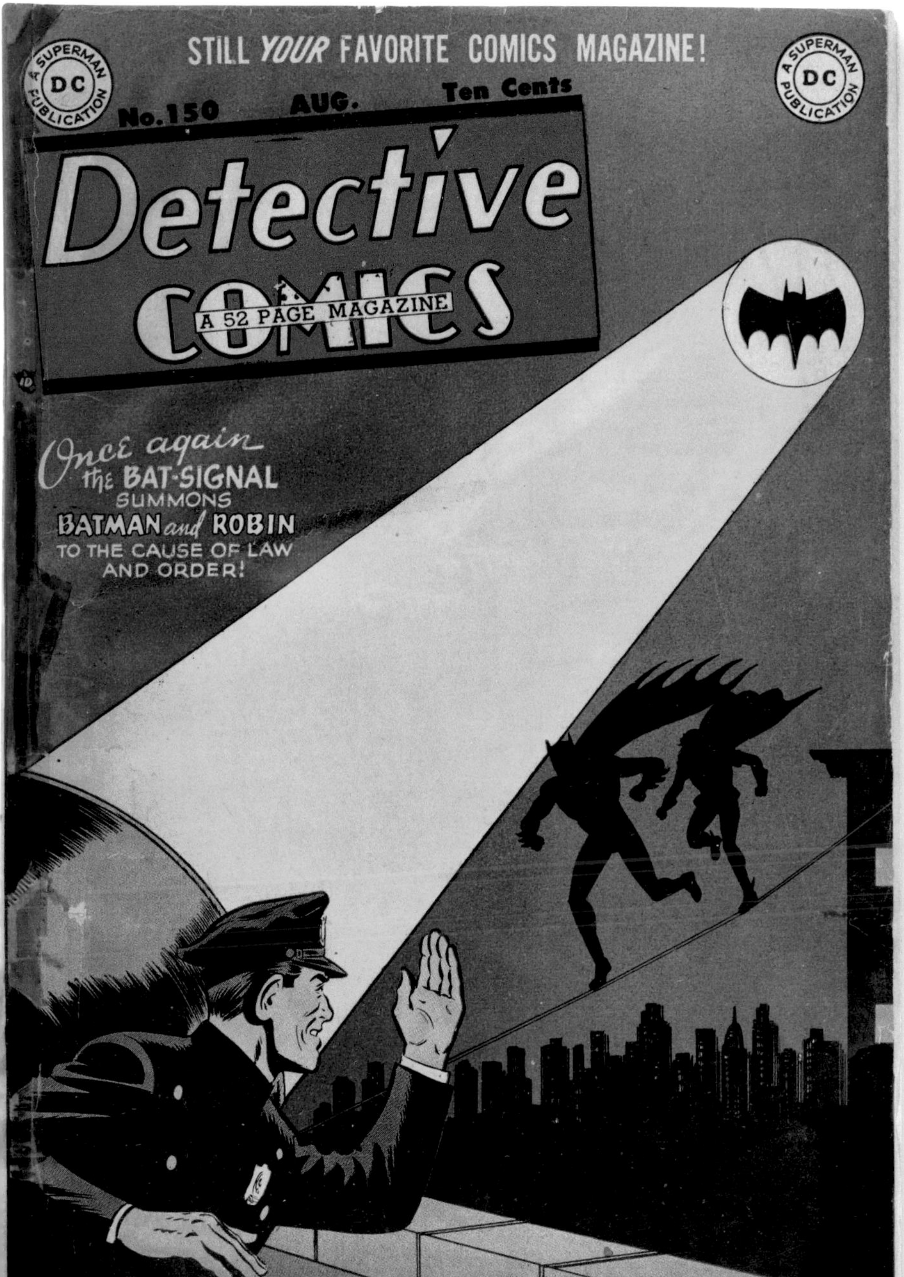
STILL YOUR FAVORITE COMICS MAGAZINE!
A SUPERMAN DC PUBLICATION
No. 150
AUG.
Ten Cents
Detective COMICS
A 52 PAGE MAGAZINE
A SUPERMAN DC PUBLICATION
Once again the BAT-SIGNAL SUMMONS BATMAN and ROBIN TO THE CAUSE OF LAW AND ORDER!

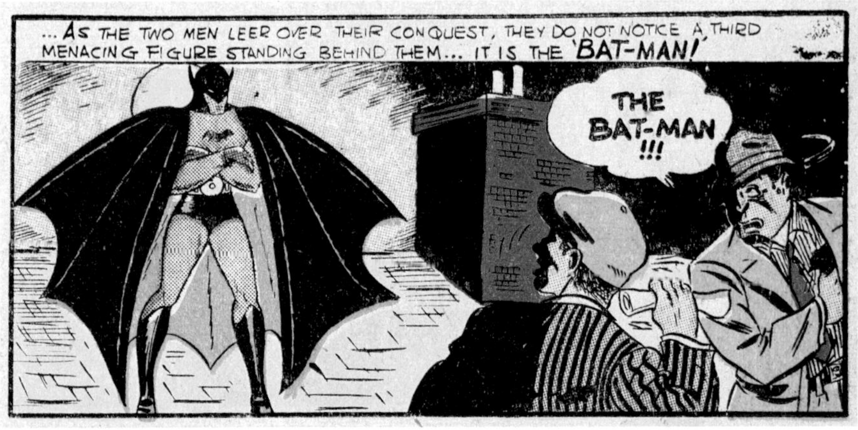
...AS THE TWO MEN LEER OVER THEIR CONQUEST, THEY DO NOT NOTICE A THIRD MENACING FIGURE STANDING BEHIND THEM... IT IS THE 'BAT-MAN!'
THE BAT-MAN !!!

DETECTIVE COMICS No. 27

Interior, "The Case of the Chemical Syndicate"; script, Bill Finger; pencils and inks, Bob Kane. May 1939.

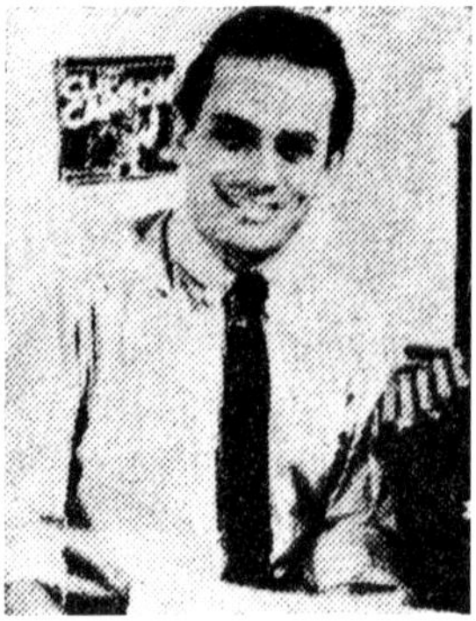

BILL FINGER

Photograph, published in Green Lantern *No. 1, Fall 1941.* From the start of his collaboration with Bob Kane, Bill Finger contributed crucial details to the development of Batman. Noting that Kane's initial drawings were too similar to Superman, Finger suggested a bat-eared cowl, gloves, and a scalloped cape rather than wings.

BATMAN No. 31

Interior, "Punch and Judy"; script, Bill Finger; pencils, Jerry Robinson; inks, George Roussos. October–November 1945. Bill Finger wrote full scripts with complete captions, dialogue, and art direction before any artwork was assigned to an illustrator.

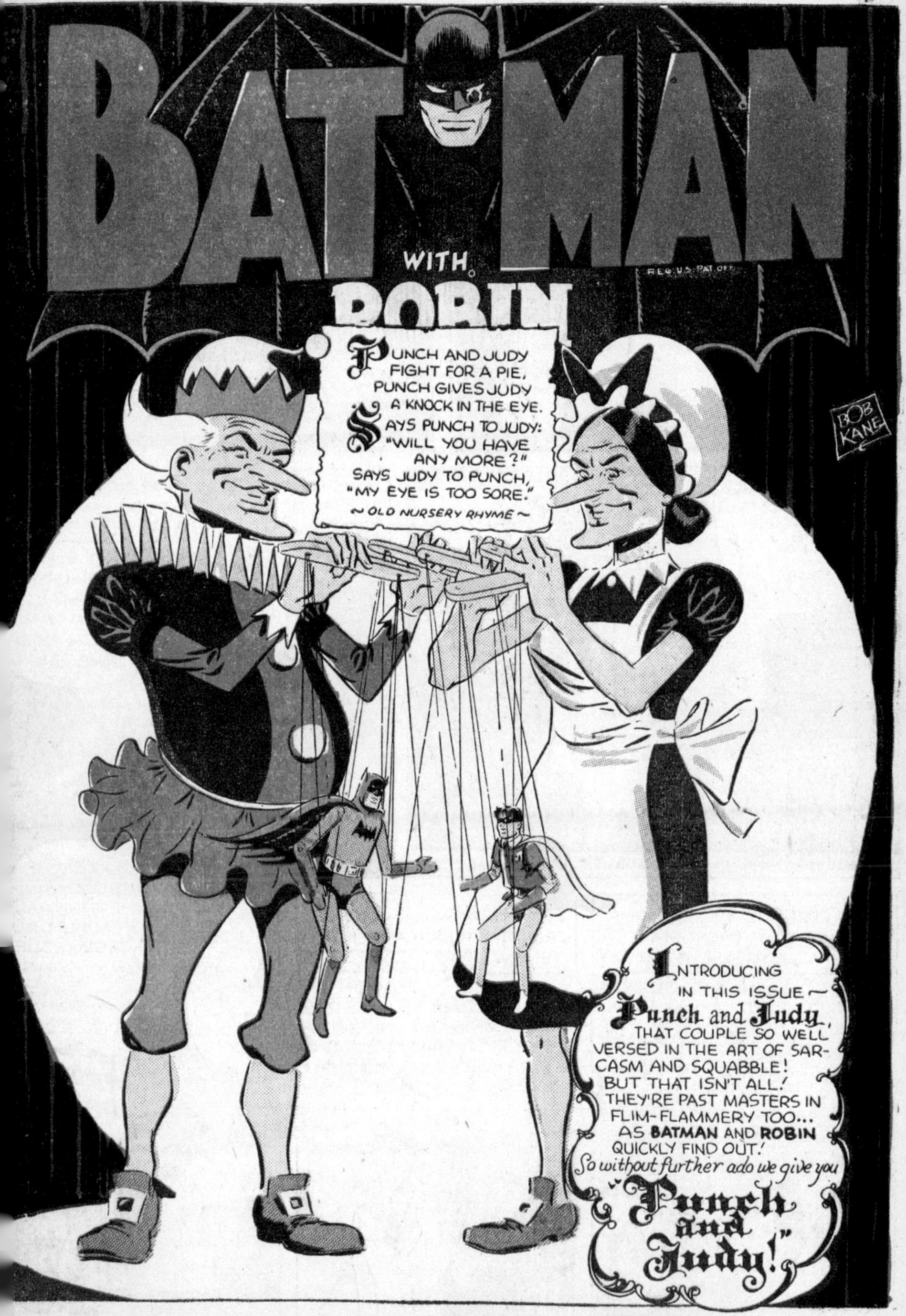
BATMAN
WITH ROBIN
REG. U.S. PAT. OFF.
PUNCH AND JUDY
FIGHT FOR A PIE,
PUNCH GIVES JUDY
A KNOCK IN THE EYE.
SAYS PUNCH TO JUDY:
"WILL YOU HAVE
ANY MORE?"
SAYS JUDY TO PUNCH,
"MY EYE IS TOO SORE."
~OLD NURSERY RHYME~
BOB KANE
INTRODUCING
IN THIS ISSUE—
Punch and Judy,
THAT COUPLE SO WELL
VERSED IN THE ART OF SAR-
CASM AND SQUABBLE!
BUT THAT ISN'T ALL!
THEY'RE PAST MASTERS IN
FLIM-FLAMMERY TOO...
AS BATMAN AND ROBIN
QUICKLY FIND OUT!
So without further ado we give you
"Punch and Judy!"

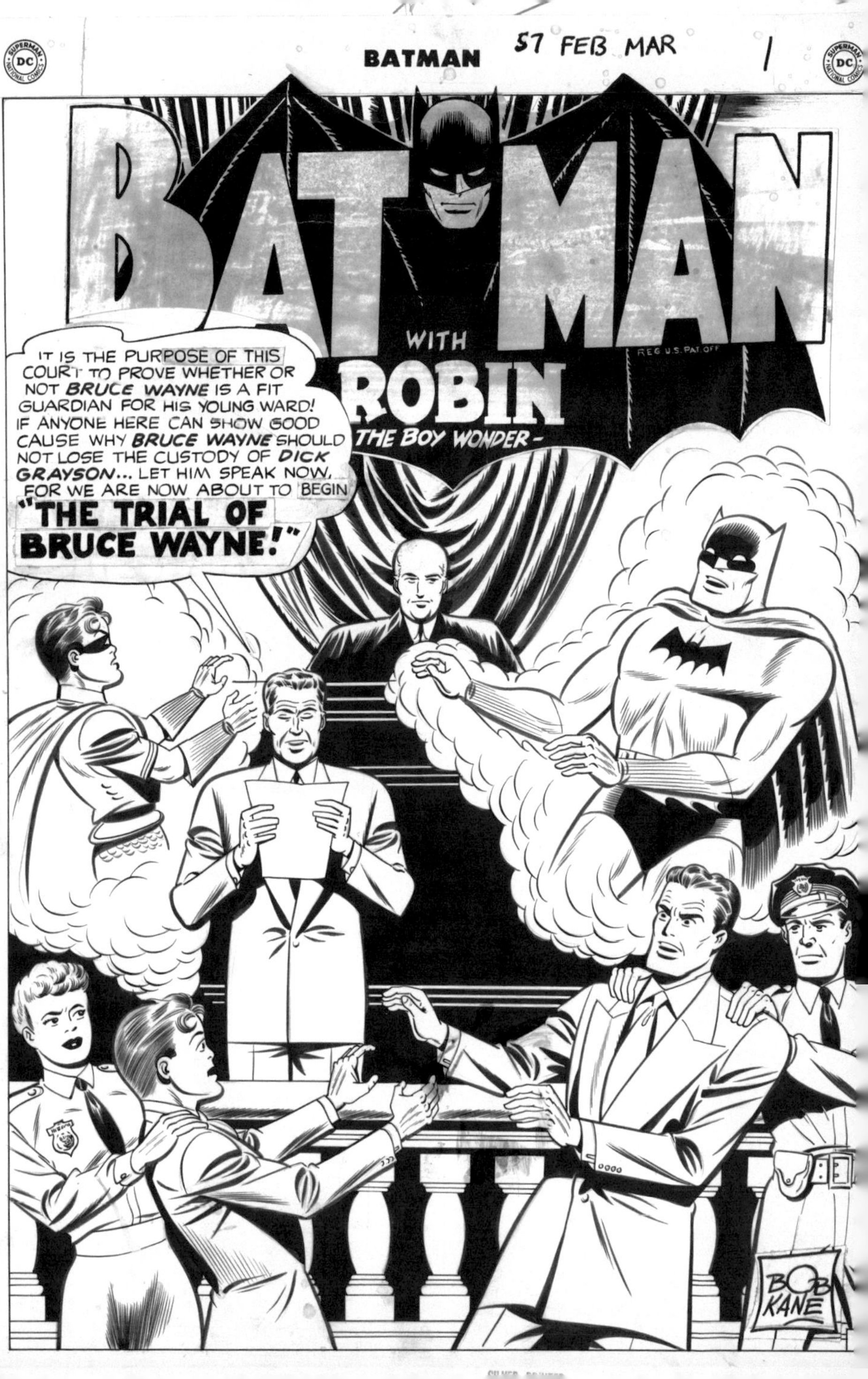
BATMAN
57 FEB MAR
1
BATMAN
WITH
ROBIN
THE BOY WONDER -
REG. U.S. PAT. OFF
IT IS THE PURPOSE OF THIS COURT TO PROVE WHETHER OR NOT BRUCE WAYNE IS A FIT GUARDIAN FOR HIS YOUNG WARD! IF ANYONE HERE CAN SHOW GOOD CAUSE WHY BRUCE WAYNE SHOULD NOT LOSE THE CUSTODY OF DICK GRAYSON... LET HIM SPEAK NOW, FOR WE ARE NOW ABOUT TO BEGIN "THE TRIAL OF BRUCE WAYNE!"
BOB KANE

ENROUTE TO STATE PRISON FOR THE CRIMINAL INSANE, THE JOKER, FAMED FOE OF THE BATMAN AND ROBIN, EXTRACTS FROM WITHIN HIS JACKET, FOUR UNRELATED OBJECTS...
A STRAIGHT NAIL...A CIGARETTE BUTT...A WOODEN MATCH...A PAPER BAG...AND ESCAPE!
FIRST, THE NAIL! USELESS FOR OPENING HANDCUFFS-UNLESS YOU KNOW HOW!
AND I KNOW HOW! NEXT, THE MATCH AND THE CIGARETTE STUB!
AND FINALLY...THE PAPER BAG! THE MOMENT HAS COME!
127
Copyright 1944 by Detective Comics, Inc. Dist. by McClure Newspaper Syndicate
Copyright 1944 by Detective Comics, Inc. Dist. by McClure Newspaper Syndicate

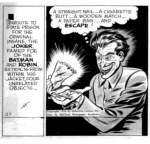

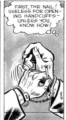

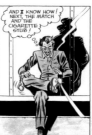

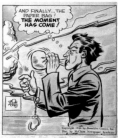

BATMAN No. 57

Original interior art, "The Trial of Bruce Wayne!"; script, Bill Finger; pencils, Dick Sprang; inks, Charles Paris. February–March 1950. Separation anxiety was a frequent way for Bill Finger and other writers to wring strong emotion out of Bruce Wayne's paternal bond with Dick Grayson. Early stories in *Batman* No. 5 and *Detective Comics* No. 60 saw Batman succumb to bleak rage when he believed Robin was mortally wounded. A story in *Batman* No. 20 even saw Dick's relatives successfully win custody of the boy in a scheme to claim part of the Wayne fortune.

MUCH AS I HATE TO TAKE HUMAN LIFE, I'M AFRAID THIS TIME IT'S NECESSARY!
RAT-TAT-TAT-TAT-TAT

"BATMAN" DAILY COMIC STRIP

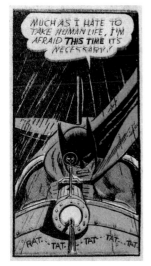

Newspaper comic strip; script, Bill Finger; pencils, Bob Kane; inks, Charles Paris. March 27, 1944. "Almost every famous character ever created had a kind of simplistic, definitive design that was easily recognizable, and that's what I was striving for with Batman." —Bob Kane

BATMAN No. 1

Interior, "Batman"; script, Bill Finger; pencils, Bob Kane; inks, Bob Kane and Jerry Robinson. Spring 1940. Published amid three Batman and Robin adventures in *Batman* No. 1 was a leftover story prepared before the Boy Wonder was introduced. A key sequence involved the Dark Knight mounting a machine gun in his plane and using it kill several marauding giants terrorizing the city. Bill Finger recalled editor Whitney Ellsworth emphatically instructing him to never have the hero take a human life again. With Robin's presence attracting a younger audience, Ellsworth believed a stronger code of honor was called for.

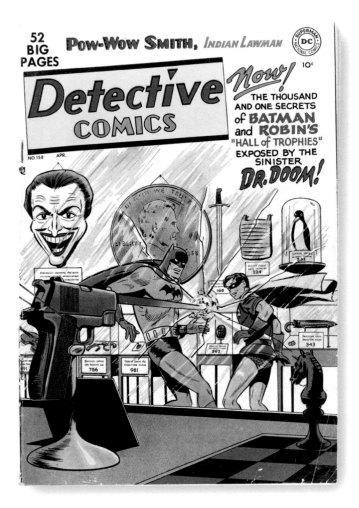

52 BIG PAGES
POW-WOW SMITH, INDIAN LAWMAN
SUPERMAN DC NATIONAL COMICS
10¢
Detective COMICS
NO.158 APR.
Now! THE THOUSAND AND ONE SECRETS of BATMAN and ROBIN'S "HALL of TROPHIES" EXPOSED BY THE SINISTER DR. DOOM!
224
165
343
562
756
981

DETECTIVE COMICS No. 158

Cover art, Win Mortimer, April 1950. Few details of the Batcave are as memorable as its trophy room. Amid the generic items shown here are genuine pieces from early stories, such as the giant penny from *World's Finest Comics* No. 30.

DETECTIVE COMICS No. 31

Cover art, Bob Kane, September 1939. With the interior lead story in *Detective* No. 31, Gardner Fox became the first writer other than Bill Finger to script the series. Most significantly, this issue introduced an early form of the Batplane (the Batgyro) and Bruce Wayne's fiancée Julie Madison.

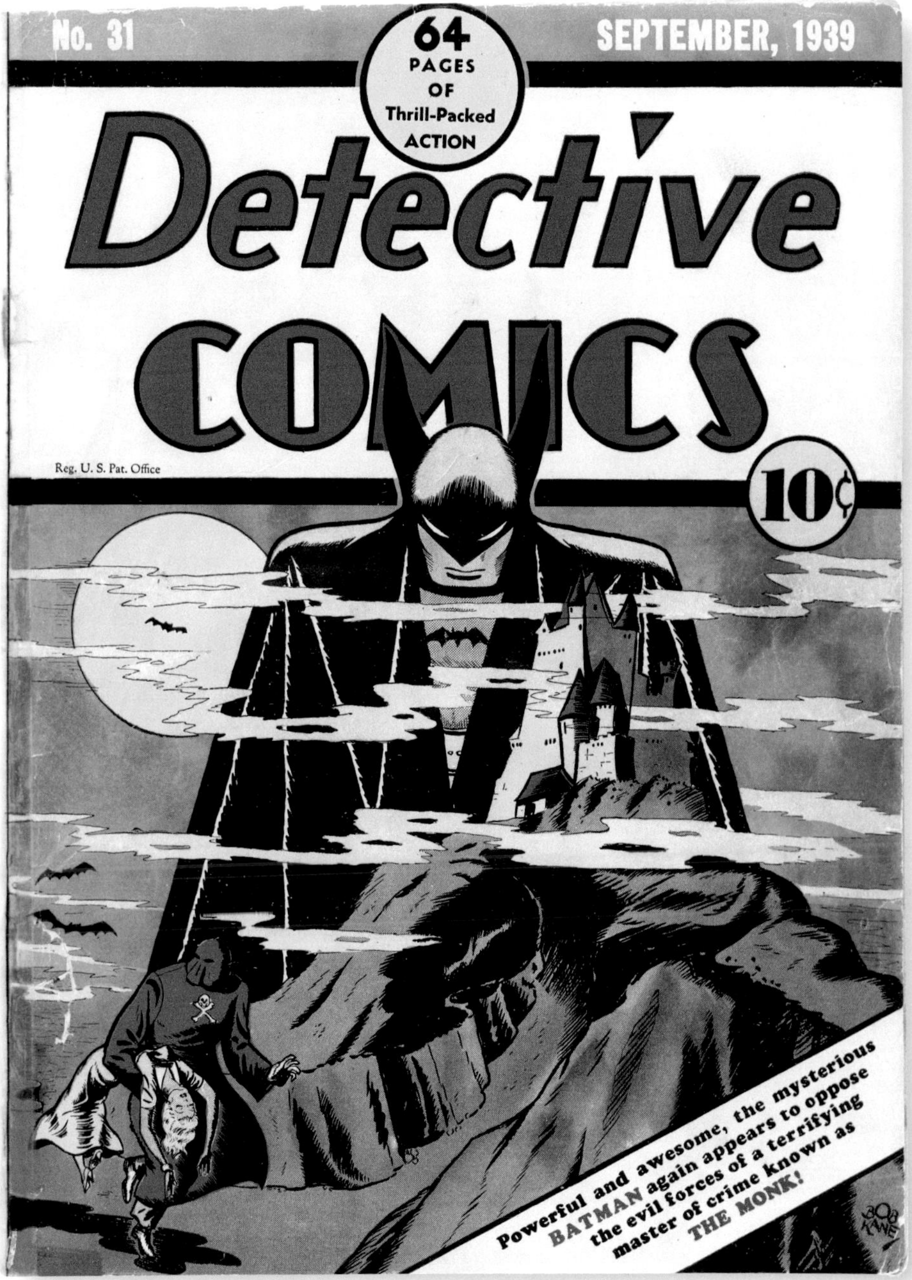
No. 31
64 PAGES OF Thrill-Packed ACTION
SEPTEMBER, 1939
Detective COMICS
Reg. U. S. Pat. Office
10¢
Powerful and awesome, the mysterious BATMAN again appears to oppose the evil forces of a terrifying master of crime known as THE MONK!
BOB KANE

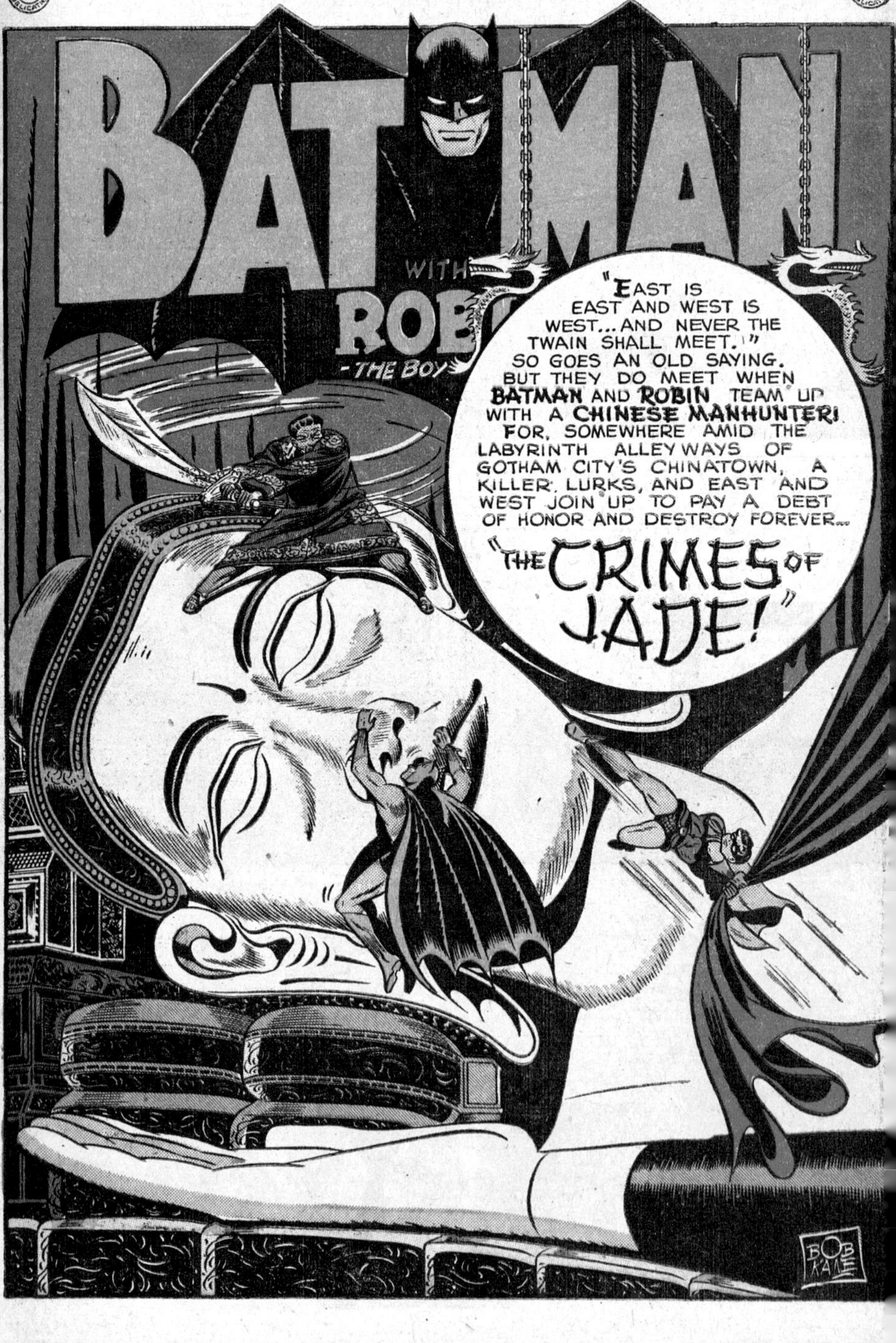
BATMAN
WITH ROB
-THE BOY
"EAST IS EAST AND WEST IS WEST... AND NEVER THE TWAIN SHALL MEET." SO GOES AN OLD SAYING. BUT THEY DO MEET WHEN BATMAN AND ROBIN TEAM UP WITH A CHINESE MANHUNTER! FOR, SOMEWHERE AMID THE LABYRINTH ALLEYWAYS OF GOTHAM CITY'S CHINATOWN, A KILLER LURKS, AND EAST AND WEST JOIN UP TO PAY A DEBT OF HONOR AND DESTROY FOREVER...
"THE CRIMES OF JADE!"
BOB KANE

DETECTIVE COMICS No. 139

Interior, "The Crimes of Jade"; script, Bill Finger; pencils, Dick Sprang; inks, Charles Paris. September 1948. Larger-than-life heroes required backgrounds to match. From giant pennies and huge statues to enormous working models of everyday objects, oversize set pieces were a hallmark of Bill Finger's stories. Countless younger writers have incorporated giant objects into their own Batman adventures as a way of paying homage.

BATMAN No. 81

Cover art, Win Mortimer, December 1954. Although the flip of a giant coin was the central menace in Two-Face's return to crime, Batman and Robin first had to escape onrushing billiard balls on a gargantuan pool table.

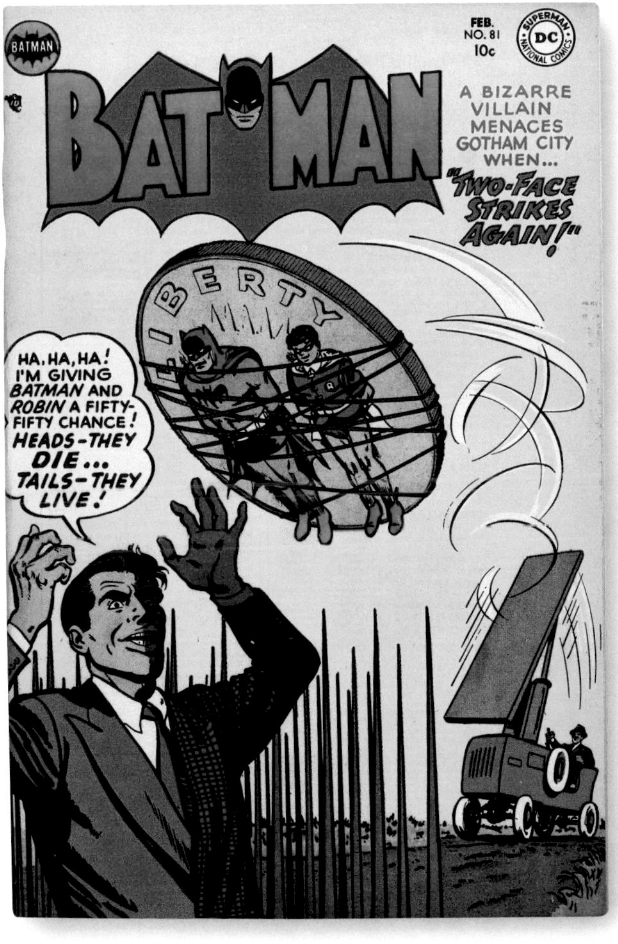

BATMAN
FEB. NO. 81 10c
SUPERMAN DC NATIONAL COMICS
BATMAN
A BIZARRE VILLAIN MENACES GOTHAM CITY WHEN...
"TWO-FACE STRIKES AGAIN!"
LIBERTY
HA, HA, HA! I'M GIVING BATMAN AND ROBIN A FIFTY-FIFTY CHANCE! HEADS-THEY DIE... TAILS-THEY LIVE!

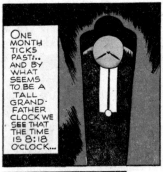

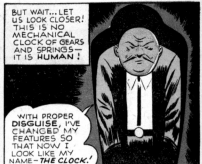

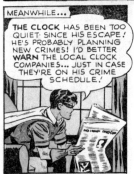

ONE MONTH TICKS PAST!.. AND BY WHAT SEEMS TO BE A TALL GRAND-FATHER CLOCK WE SEE THAT THE TIME IS 8:18 O'CLOCK...
BUT WAIT... LET US LOOK CLOSER! THIS IS NO MECHANICAL CLOCK OF GEARS AND SPRINGS— IT IS HUMAN!
WITH PROPER DISGUISE, I'VE CHANGED MY FEATURES SO THAT NOW I LOOK LIKE MY NAME—THE CLOCK.!
MEANWHILE...
THE CLOCK HAS BEEN TOO QUIET SINCE HIS ESCAPE! HE'S PROBABLY PLANNING NEW CRIMES! I'D BETTER WARN THE LOCAL CLOCK COMPANIES... JUST IN CASE THEY'RE ON HIS CRIME SCHEDULE.!

STAR SPANGLED COMICS No. 74

ABOVE: *Interior, "The Clock Strikes"; script, Bill Finger; art, Jim Mooney. November 1947.* Robin shared many recurring enemies with Batman but had only one nemesis who was all his own. The Clock appeared in four episodes of the Boy Wonder's series in *Star Spangled Comics* between 1947 and 1949. Bill Finger crafted a new version of the time-themed villain in a 1959 *Batman* story and later wrote a Clock King episode for the 1966 *Batman* TV show. OPPOSITE: *Cover art, Jim Mooney, November 1947.*

STAR SPANGLED COMICS No. 79

FOLLOWING SPREAD: *Interiors, "Zero Hour"; script, Bill Finger; pencils, Jim Mooney; inks, John Giunta. April 1948.* Bill Finger maintained a massive collection of files that he could reference for his comic book scripts. Along with clippings from magazines like *Popular Science*, he also devoted folders to subjects like birds and related trivia. A file on topics related to time undoubtedly informed Finger's Clock stories.

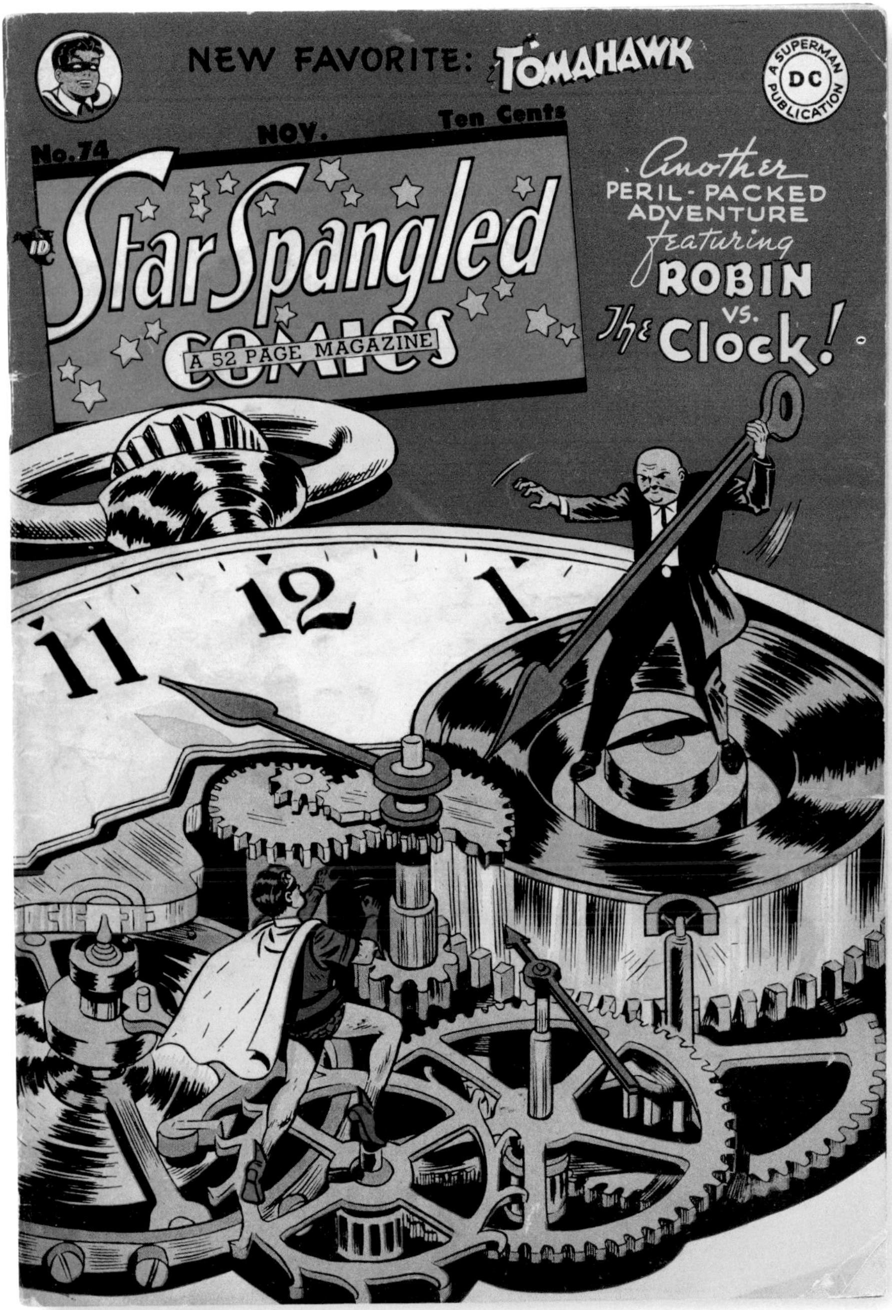
NEW FAVORITE: TOMAHAWK
A SUPERMAN DC PUBLICATION
No.74
NOV.
Ten Cents
Star Spangled COMICS
A 52 PAGE MAGAZINE
Another PERIL-PACKED ADVENTURE featuring ROBIN VS. The Clock!
12
1
11

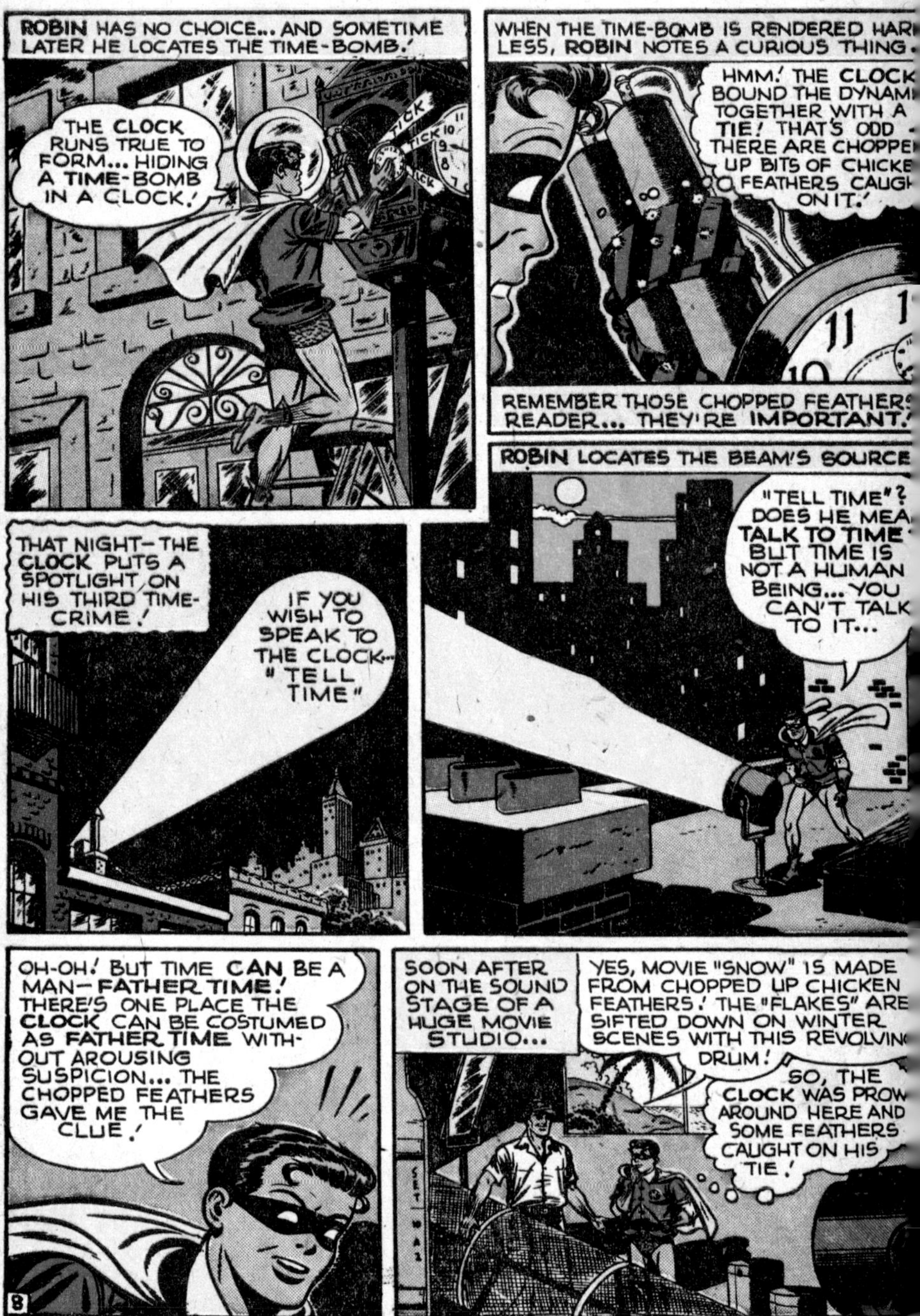
ROBIN HAS NO CHOICE... AND SOMETIME LATER HE LOCATES THE TIME-BOMB!
THE CLOCK RUNS TRUE TO FORM... HIDING A TIME-BOMB IN A CLOCK!
TICK
TICK
WHEN THE TIME-BOMB IS RENDERED HAR LESS, ROBIN NOTES A CURIOUS THING.
HMM! THE CLOCK BOUND THE DYNAM TOGETHER WITH A TIE! THAT'S ODD - THERE ARE CHOPPE UP BITS OF CHICKE FEATHERS CAUG ON IT!
REMEMBER THOSE CHOPPED FEATHER READER... THEY'RE IMPORTANT!
THAT NIGHT—THE CLOCK PUTS A SPOTLIGHT ON HIS THIRD TIME-CRIME!
IF YOU WISH TO SPEAK TO THE CLOCK... "TELL TIME"
ROBIN LOCATES THE BEAM'S SOURCE
"TELL TIME"? DOES HE MEA TALK TO TIME BUT TIME IS NOT A HUMAN BEING... YOU CAN'T TALK TO IT...
OH-OH! BUT TIME CAN BE A MAN—FATHER TIME! THERE'S ONE PLACE THE CLOCK CAN BE COSTUMED AS FATHER TIME WITHOUT AROUSING SUSPICION... THE CHOPPED FEATHERS GAVE ME THE CLUE!
8
SOON AFTER ON THE SOUND STAGE OF A HUGE MOVIE STUDIO...
YES, MOVIE "SNOW" IS MADE FROM CHOPPED UP CHICKEN FEATHERS! THE "FLAKES" ARE SIFTED DOWN ON WINTER SCENES WITH THIS REVOLVIN DRUM!
SO, THE CLOCK WAS PROW AROUND HERE AND SOME FEATHERS CAUGHT ON HIS TIE!

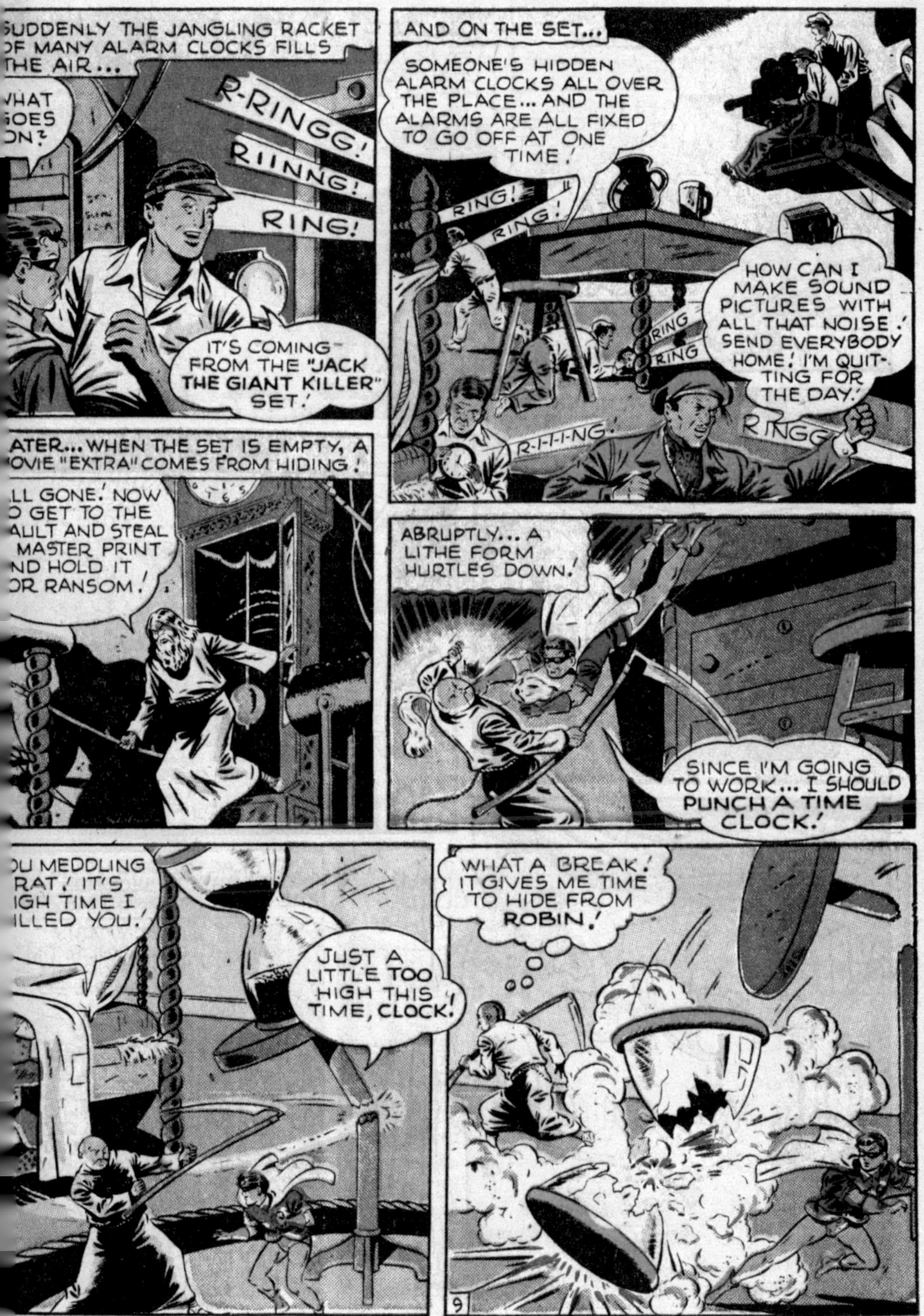
SUDDENLY THE JANGLING RACKET OF MANY ALARM CLOCKS FILLS THE AIR...
WHAT GOES ON?
R-RINGG!
RIINNG!
RING!
IT'S COMING FROM THE "JACK THE GIANT KILLER" SET!
AND ON THE SET...
SOMEONE'S HIDDEN ALARM CLOCKS ALL OVER THE PLACE... AND THE ALARMS ARE ALL FIXED TO GO OFF AT ONE TIME!
RING!
RING!
RING
RING
HOW CAN I MAKE SOUND PICTURES WITH ALL THAT NOISE! SEND EVERYBODY HOME! I'M QUITTING FOR THE DAY!
R-I-I-I-NG!
RINGG
LATER... WHEN THE SET IS EMPTY, A MOVIE "EXTRA" COMES FROM HIDING!
ALL GONE! NOW TO GET TO THE VAULT AND STEAL MASTER PRINT AND HOLD IT FOR RANSOM!
ABRUPTLY... A LITHE FORM HURTLES DOWN!
SINCE I'M GOING TO WORK... I SHOULD PUNCH A TIME CLOCK!
YOU MEDDLING RAT! IT'S HIGH TIME I KILLED YOU!
JUST A LITTLE TOO HIGH THIS TIME, CLOCK!
WHAT A BREAK! IT GIVES ME TIME TO HIDE FROM ROBIN!
9

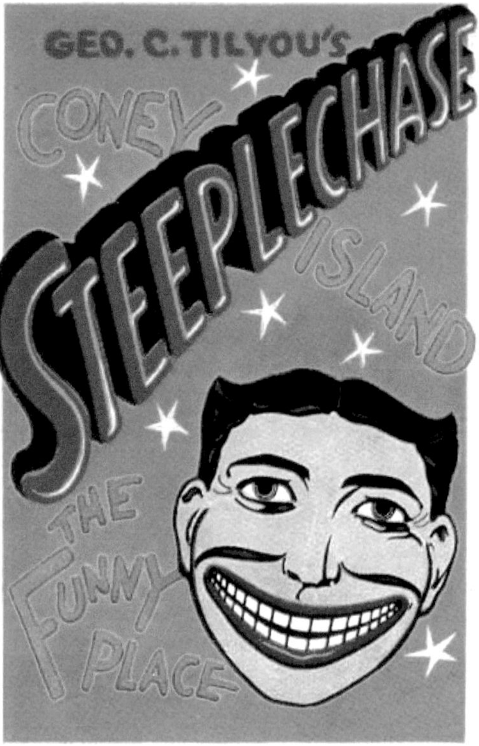
GEO. C. TILYOU'S
CONEY
STEEPLECHASE
ISLAND
THE
FUNNY
PLACE

THE FUNNY PLACE

Poster, Steeplechase Park, Coney Island, New York, ca. 1920. Twenty years before the Joker, this eerie wide-mouthed grin could be seen advertising for a New York amusement park.

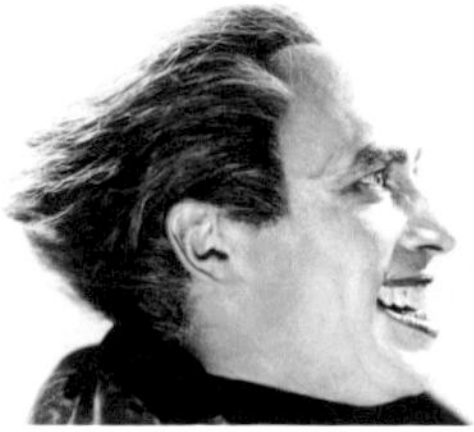

THE MAN WHO LAUGHS

Publicity still, Conrad Veidt, Universal Pictures, 1928. "The Conrad Veidt aspect was how the Joker physically looked: The *long* arms, the *long* hands, the very *long* face…the sadness of the character…the Joker, when you come down to it, is a very sad character." —Fred Finger

BATMAN No. 8

Interior, "The Cross-Country Crimes"; script, Bill Finger; pencils, Bob Kane; inks, Jerry Robinson and George Roussos. December 1941–January 1942. A nationwide manhunt was declared for the Joker after he shot FBI chief G. Henry Mover (a take on J. Edgar Hoover).

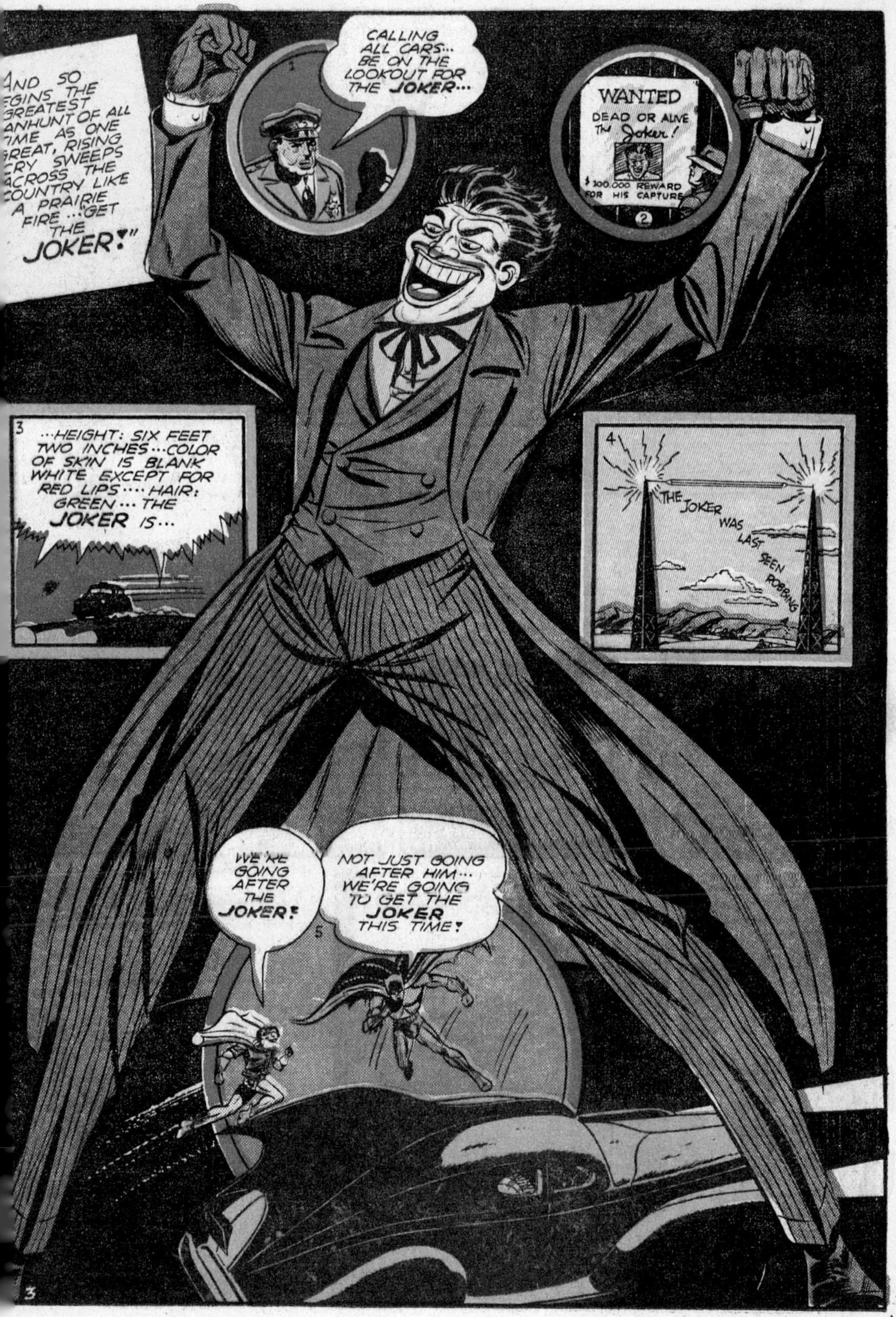
AND SO EGINS THE GREATEST ANHUNT OF ALL TIME AS ONE GREAT, RISING CRY SWEEPS ACROSS THE COUNTRY LIKE A PRAIRIE FIRE ..."GET THE JOKER!"
CALLING ALL CARS... BE ON THE LOOKOUT FOR THE JOKER...
WANTED
DEAD OR ALIVE
The Joker!
$100,000 REWARD FOR HIS CAPTURE
...HEIGHT: SIX FEET TWO INCHES...COLOR OF SKIN IS BLANK WHITE EXCEPT FOR RED LIPS.... HAIR: GREEN... THE JOKER IS...
THE JOKER WAS LAST SEEN ROBBING
WE'RE GOING AFTER THE JOKER!
NOT JUST GOING AFTER HIM... WE'RE GOING TO GET THE JOKER THIS TIME!

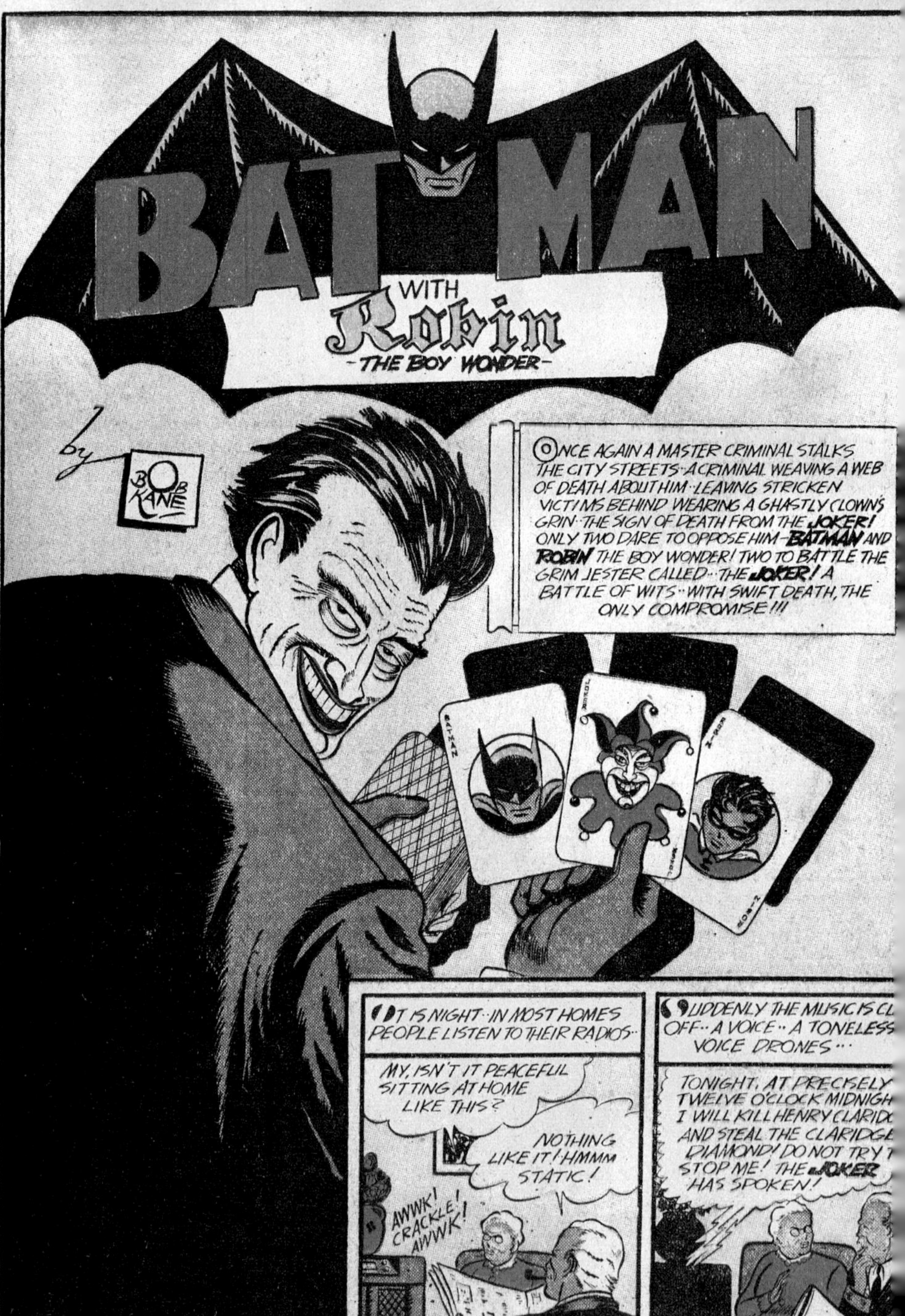
BATMAN
WITH
Robin
-THE BOY WONDER-
by BOB KANE
ONCE AGAIN A MASTER CRIMINAL STALKS THE CITY STREETS--A CRIMINAL WEAVING A WEB OF DEATH ABOUT HIM--LEAVING STRICKEN VICTIMS BEHIND WEARING A GHASTLY CLOWN'S GRIN--THE SIGN OF DEATH FROM THE JOKER! ONLY TWO DARE TO OPPOSE HIM--BATMAN AND ROBIN THE BOY WONDER! TWO TO BATTLE THE GRIM JESTER CALLED--THE JOKER! A BATTLE OF WITS--WITH SWIFT DEATH, THE ONLY COMPROMISE!!!
BATMAN
JOKER
ROBIN
IT IS NIGHT--IN MOST HOMES PEOPLE LISTEN TO THEIR RADIOS--
MY, ISN'T IT PEACEFUL SITTING AT HOME LIKE THIS?
NOTHING LIKE IT! HMMM STATIC!
AWWK! CRACKLE! AWWK!
SUDDENLY THE MUSIC IS CL
OFF--A VOICE--A TONELESS VOICE DRONES--
TONIGHT, AT PRECISELY TWELVE O'CLOCK MIDNIGH I WILL KILL HENRY CLARIDG AND STEAL THE CLARIDGE DIAMOND! DO NOT TRY T STOP ME! THE JOKER HAS SPOKEN!

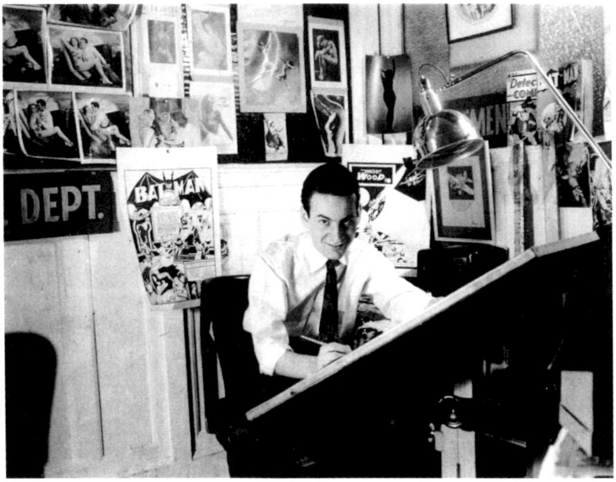
DEPT.
BATMAN

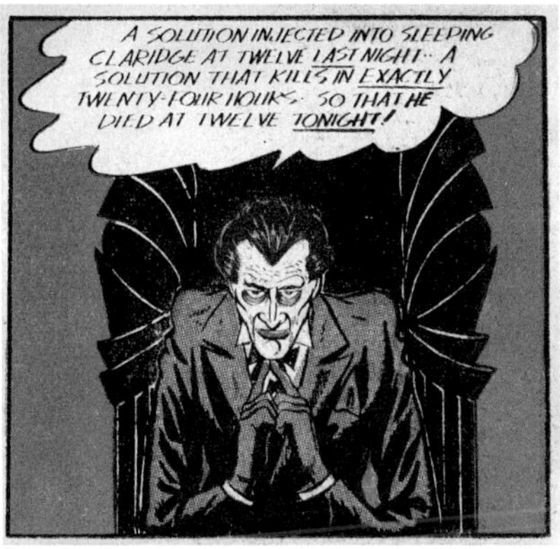
A SOLUTION INJECTED INTO SLEEPING CLARIDGE AT TWELVE LAST NIGHT-- A SOLUTION THAT KILLS IN EXACTLY TWENTY-FOUR HOURS-- SO THAT HE DIED AT TWELVE TONIGHT!

BATMAN No. 1

OPPOSITE AND ABOVE: *Interior, "Batman"; script, Bill Finger; pencils, Bob Kane; inks, Jerry Robinson. Spring 1940.*

JERRY ROBINSON

Photograph, Robinson at his drawing board, 1941.
"People in the [comics] field immediately noticed the resemblance of the name, 'Robin,' to my own name, Robinson," recalled Bob Kane's young art assistant, Jerry Robinson. "I remember receiving a lot of teasing about it and it bothered me at the time. When you're 17 or 18 and desperately trying to appear older, you don't want to be known as 'the Boy Wonder.'"

DETECTIVE COMICS No. 69

Original cover art, Jerry Robinson, November 1942.
College student/artist Jerry Robinson took great pride in helping give birth to the Joker and was one of the few Golden Age artists to preserve original art like this piece.

DETECTIVE COMICS No. 62

Original cover art, Jerry Robinson. April 1942. The Joker helped DC laugh all the way to the bank. Between 1940 and 1954, the garish villain appeared in a jaw-dropping 65 stories as well as separate continuities in the "Batman" daily and Sunday newspaper comic strips. During his lengthy period of bouts with the Caped Crusader, the Joker shifted from a twisted murderer to a comparatively benign prankster.

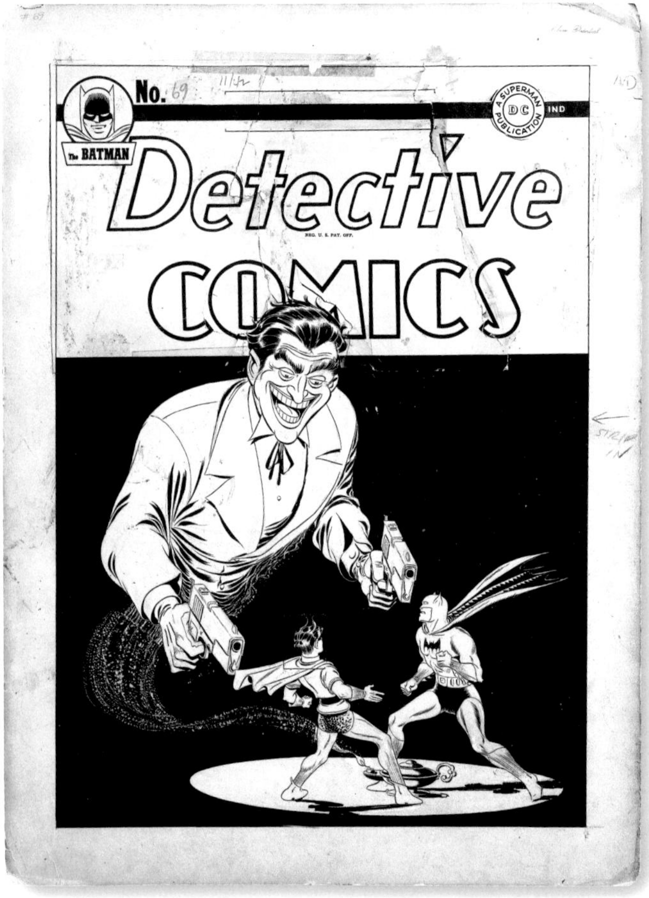

No.
The BATMAN
A SUPERMAN DC PUBLICATION
IND
Detective
REG. U. S. PAT. OFF.
COMICS

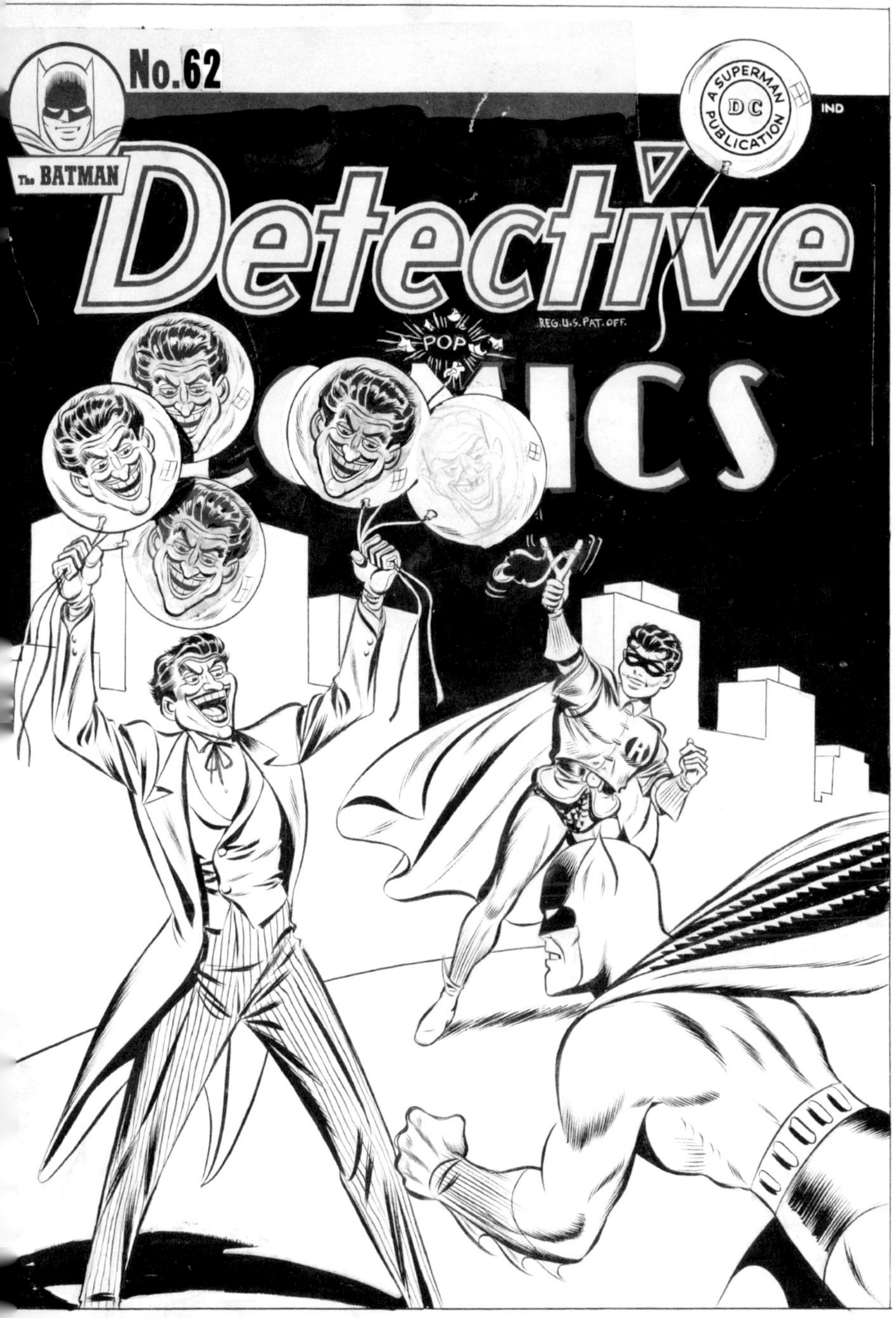

No. 62
The BATMAN
A SUPERMAN DC PUBLICATION
IND
Detective
REG. U.S. PAT. OFF.
POP
COMICS

from the collection of jerry robinson

STRANGE FIGURE INDEED...STRANGE FIGURE WITH WOMAN'S BODY AND CAT'S HEAD.....

BATMAN No. 3

Interior, "The Batman vs. the Cat-Woman"; script, Bill Finger; pencils, Bob Kane; inks, Jerry Robinson and George Roussos. Fall 1940. "Lovely girl! What eyes! Maybe I'll bump into her again sometime." Batman was quite taken with the lovely thief called the Cat, so much so that he "accidentally" let her escape more than once. By their third encounter, the mystery woman had hidden her features behind a cat's head and renamed herself the Catwoman.

BATMAN No. 62

Interior, "The Secret Life of the Catwoman"; script, Bill Finger; pencils, Bob Kane (Batman and Robin figures) and Lew Sayre Schwartz; inks, Charles Paris. December 1950–January 1951. Much as he'd done with Two-Face, Bill Finger attempted to reform Catwoman in 1950 by revealing that she was actually an amnesia victim named Selina Kyle. She pulled out her costume twice to fight other criminals—one of them her own brother—but Catwoman held more story potential as a bad girl who Batman couldn't tame, and she returned to crime in 1953.

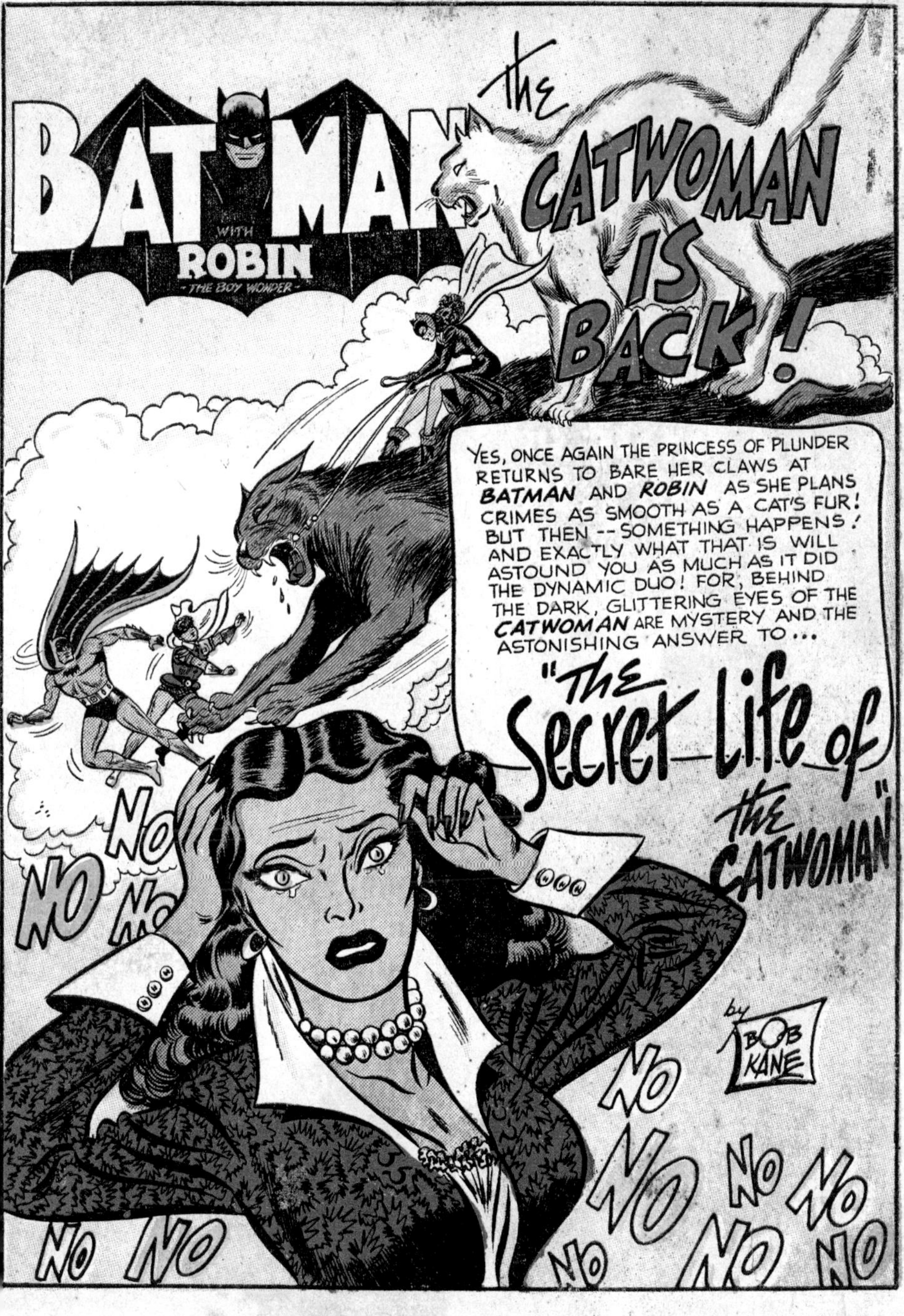
BATMAN WITH ROBIN -THE BOY WONDER-
THE CATWOMAN IS BACK!
YES, ONCE AGAIN THE PRINCESS OF PLUNDER RETURNS TO BARE HER CLAWS AT BATMAN AND ROBIN AS SHE PLANS CRIMES AS SMOOTH AS A CAT'S FUR! BUT THEN -- SOMETHING HAPPENS! AND EXACTLY WHAT THAT IS WILL ASTOUND YOU AS MUCH AS IT DID THE DYNAMIC DUO! FOR, BEHIND THE DARK, GLITTERING EYES OF THE CATWOMAN ARE MYSTERY AND THE ASTONISHING ANSWER TO...
"THE SECRET LIFE OF THE CATWOMAN"
NO NO NO
by BOB KANE
NO NO NO NO NO NO NO NO NO NO

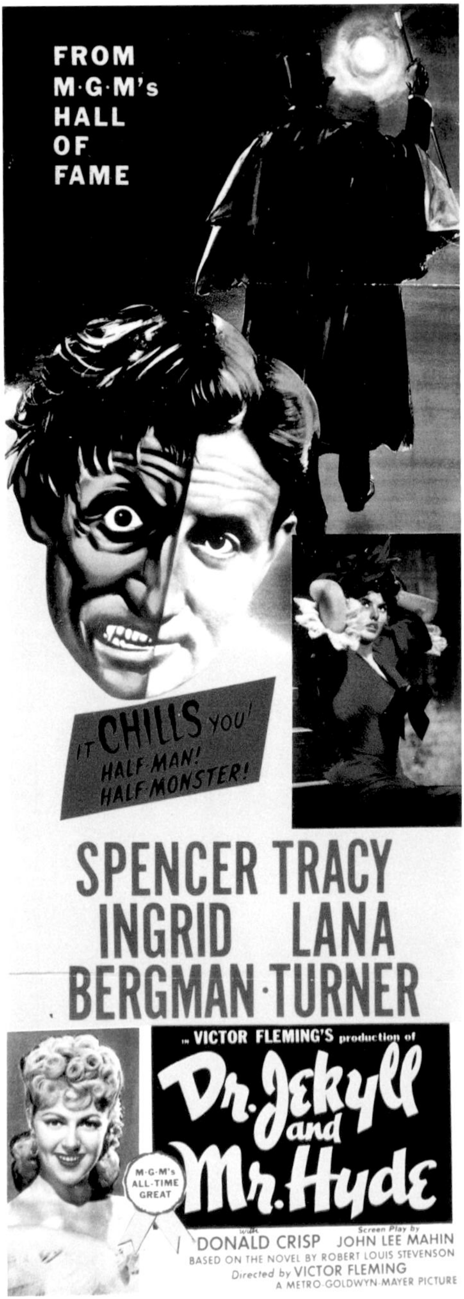
FROM
M·G·M's
HALL
OF
FAME
IT CHILLS YOU!
HALF-MAN!
HALF-MONSTER!
SPENCER TRACY
INGRID BERGMAN · LANA TURNER
IN VICTOR FLEMING'S production of
Dr. Jekyll and Mr. Hyde
M·G·M's ALL-TIME GREAT
with DONALD CRISP
Screen Play by JOHN LEE MAHIN
BASED ON THE NOVEL BY ROBERT LOUIS STEVENSON
Directed by VICTOR FLEMING
A METRO-GOLDWYN-MAYER PICTURE

DR. JEKYLL AND MR. HYDE

Movie poster, director, Victor Fleming, MGM, 1941. Two-Face's shifts between good and evil recalled Robert Louis Stevenson's 1886 novella *Strange Case of Dr. Jekyll and Mr. Hyde*. Among its many film adaptations was a 1941 version starring Spencer Tracy that debuted less than a year before the first Two-Face story in *Detective Comics* No. 66.

BATMAN No. 81

Interior, "Two-Face Strikes Again"; script, David Vern Reed; pencils, Dick Sprang; inks, Charles Paris. February 1954. Two-Face was one of Batman's great enemies, a handsome district attorney whose features were partially destroyed by a vengeful mobster. With each flip of a two-headed coin that was defaced on one side, he determined whether his next actions would be in the cause of good or evil. Three issues' worth of give and take between Batman and Two-Face end with the character surrendering, undergoing plastic surgery, and marrying his girlfriend. Despite the character's popularity, writer Bill Finger refused to undo his happy ending. David V. Reed was less sentimental and had the character's plastic surgery undone in this 1954 story.

BAT MAN

With

ROBIN
THE BOY WONDER

A HIDEOUS FACE, SPLIT DOWN THE MIDDLE! A HEART TWISTED AND WARPED WITH HATE! A BRAIN PACKED WITH DECEIT AND CUNNING! THESE ARE THE TRADE-MARKS OF ONE OF THE MOST AMAZING CRIMINALS EVER TO STALK THE GOTHAM CITY UNDERWORLD--- THE MAN CALLED **TWO-FACE!** NOW HE'S BACK---MORE DANGEROUS THAN EVER! BACK WITH A LUST FOR STRANGE REVENGE THAT CHALLENGES EVERY NERVE AND FIBER OF THE GALLANT CRIMEFIGHTERS, **BATMAN** AND **ROBIN THE BOY WONDER** IN THE STORY CALLED...

TWO-FACE
STRIKES
AGAIN!

BOB KANE

1

ATMAN, No. 81, February, 1954. Published 8 times yearly— monthly, except Jan., May, July, and Nov., by National Comics ublications, Inc., 480 Lexington Ave., New York 17, N. Y. hitney Ellsworth, Editor. Reentered as second class matter ug. 1, 1941 at the Post Office at New York, N. Y. under e act of March 3, 1879. Yearly subscription in the U. S. .00 including postage. Foreign, $2.00 in American funds.

For advertising rates address Richard A. Feldon & Co., 205 E. 42nd St., New York 17, N. Y. Entire contents copyrighted 1953 by National Comics Publications, Inc. Except for those who have authorized use of their names, the stories, characters and incidents mentioned in this periodical are entirely imaginary and fictitious and no identification with actual persons, living or dead, is intended or should be inferred.   Printed in U.S.A.

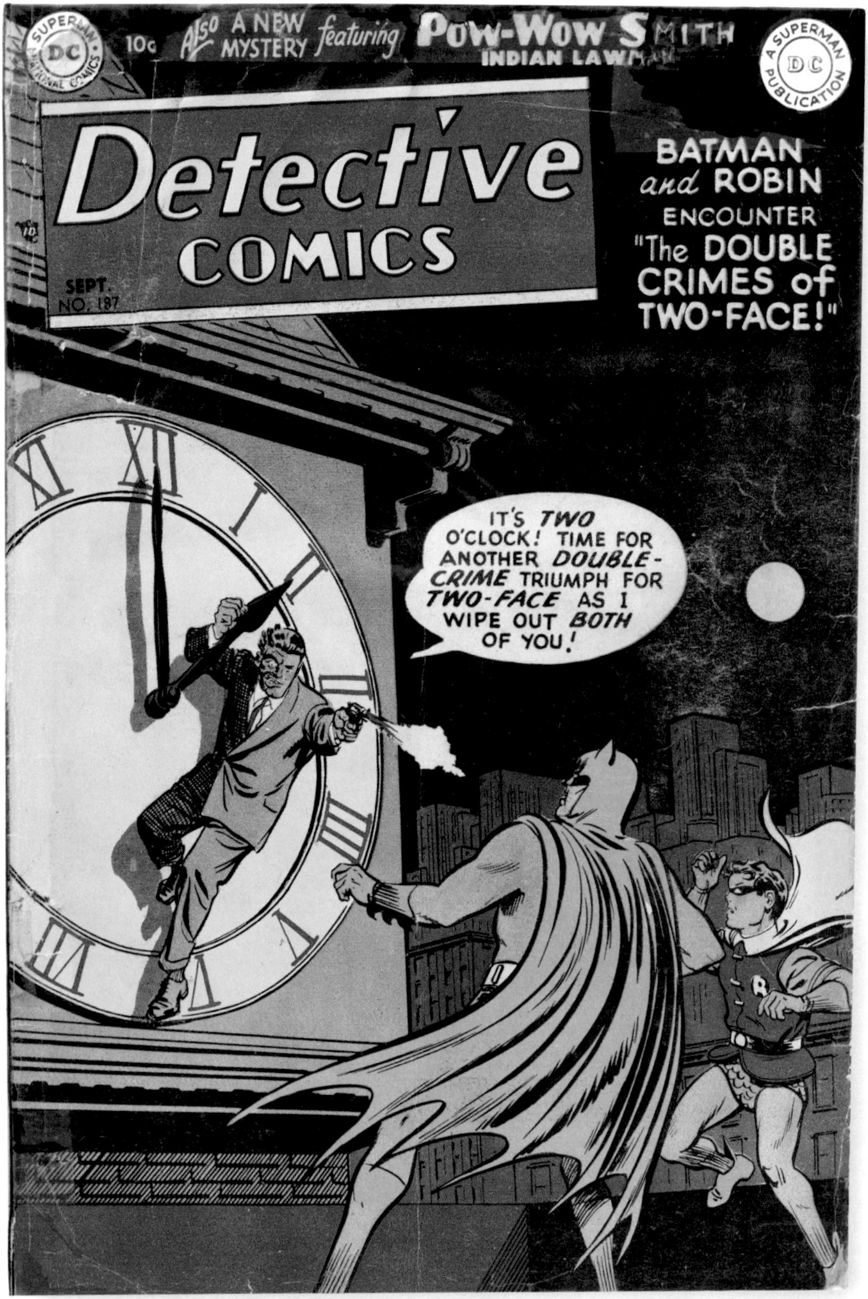

SUPERMAN DC NATIONAL COMICS
10¢
ALSO A NEW MYSTERY featuring POW-WOW SMITH
INDIAN LAWMAN
A SUPERMAN DC PUBLICATION
Detective COMICS
SEPT. NO. 187
BATMAN and ROBIN ENCOUNTER "The DOUBLE CRIMES of TWO-FACE!"
IT'S TWO O'CLOCK! TIME FOR ANOTHER DOUBLE-CRIME TRIUMPH FOR TWO-FACE AS I WIPE OUT BOTH OF YOU!

BATMAN
No.42
AUG...SEPT.
TEN CENTS
A SUPERMAN PUBLICATION
DC
BATMAN
A 52 PAGE
MAGAZINE
The PARTNERS IN PERIL
face the steel-clawed
fury of
The CATWOMAN

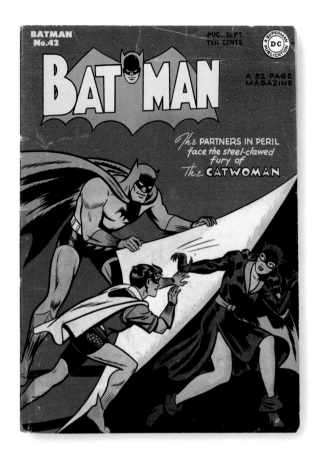

DETECTIVE COMICS No. 187

Cover art, Win Mortimer, September 1952. In the absence of the original Two-Face, Bill Finger brought back variations of the character three times. After a dark variation on the original story in the "Batman" Sunday comic strip, a pair of imposters took on the role in *Batman* Nos. 50 and 68.

BATMAN No. 42

Cover art, Jack Burnley and Charles Paris, August–September 1947. The Catwoman finally settled on a costume in 1947, adopting a purple dress slit up the side with a green cape and steel-clawed gloves. The visuals served her well through the remainder of her Golden Age appearances and remained popular enough in the 1970s that a more modern costume was abandoned in favor of the classic old one.

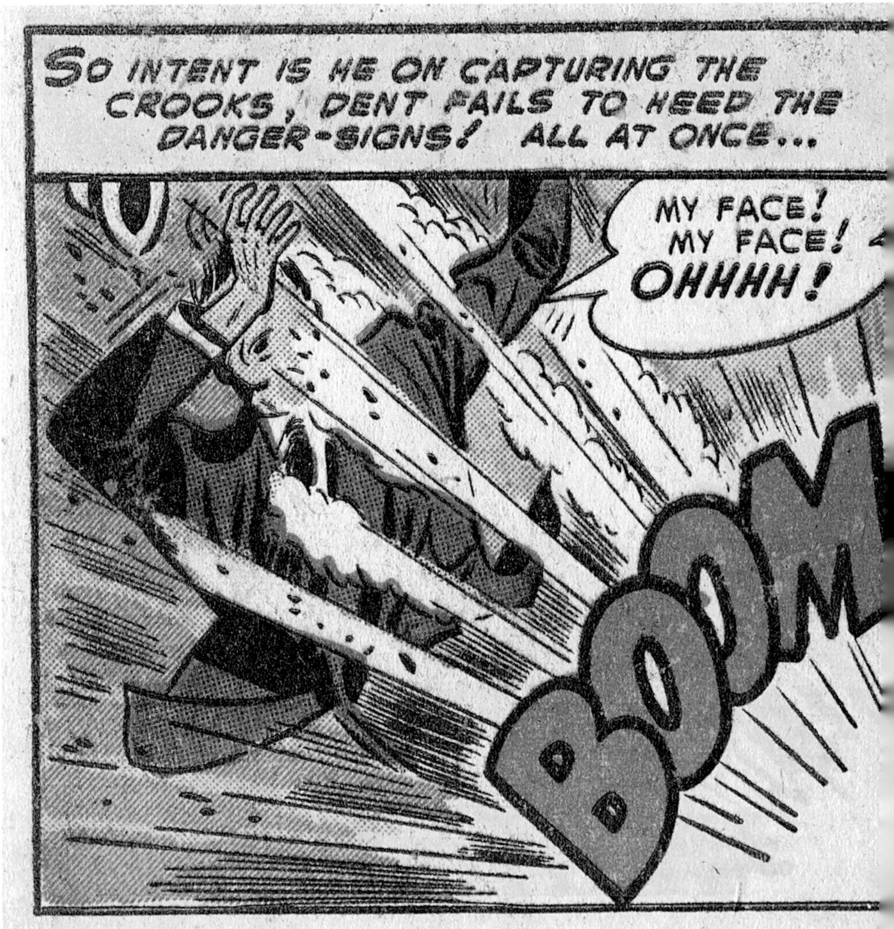
SO INTENT IS HE ON CAPTURING THE CROOKS, DENT FAILS TO HEED THE DANGER-SIGNS! ALL AT ONCE...
MY FACE! MY FACE! OHHHH!
BOOM

BATMAN No. 81

Interior, "Two-Face Strikes Again"; script, David Vern; pencils, Dick Sprang; inks, Charles Paris. February 1954.

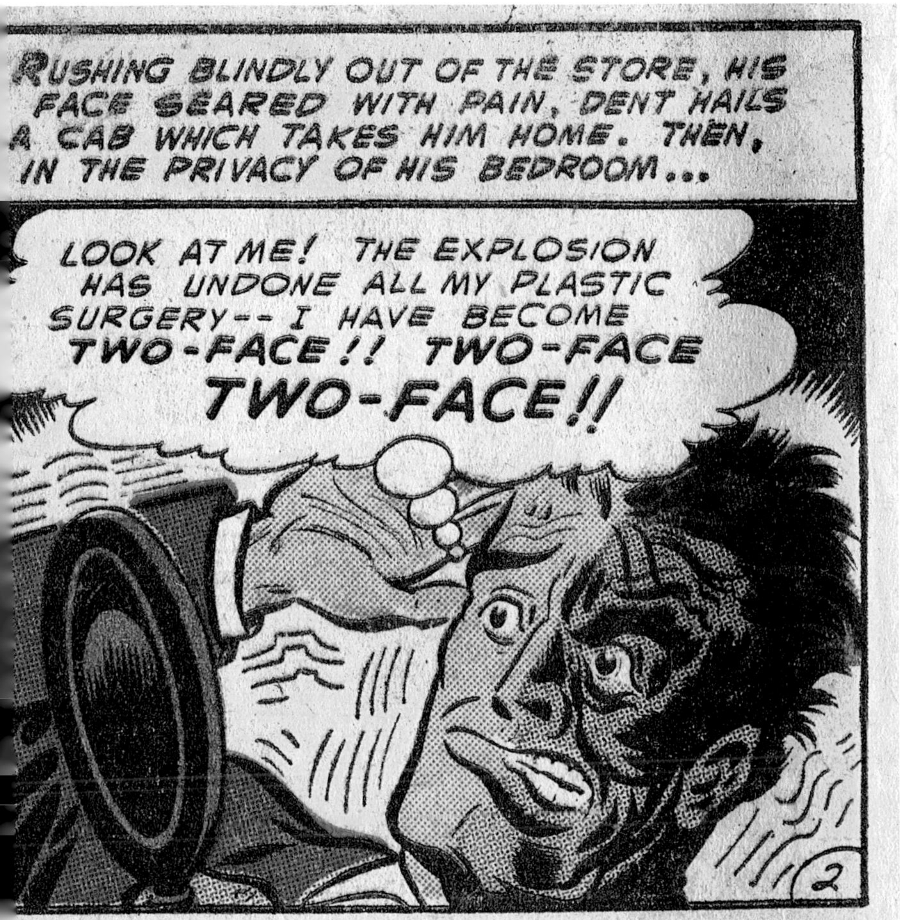
RUSHING BLINDLY OUT OF THE STORE, HIS FACE SEARED WITH PAIN, DENT HAILS A CAB WHICH TAKES HIM HOME. THEN, IN THE PRIVACY OF HIS BEDROOM...
LOOK AT ME! THE EXPLOSION HAS UNDONE ALL MY PLASTIC SURGERY-- I HAVE BECOME TWO-FACE!! TWO-FACE TWO-FACE!!
2

BY THE TIME THE DENSE SMOKE CLEARS...

THE RIDDLER WILL GET AWAY— AND I CAN'T FOLLOW HIM, KNOWING EAGLE WILL SUFFOCATE INSIDE THAT PUZZLE!

NOW *BATMAN* MATCHES HIS WITS AGAINST A HIGHLY COMPLEX PUZZLE, WITH A LIFE AT STAKE IF HE FAILS!

I'LL NEVER FIND THE SECRET OF THIS PUZZLE IN TIME TO SAVE HIM!

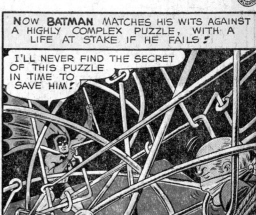

WAIT! THE LITTLE NICKS ON SOME OF THESE STEEL RODS WERE OBVIOUSLY MADE WHEN THE RODS SCRAPED AGAINST EACH OTHER!

BY CAREFULLY FOLLOWING THE TINY NICKS SHOWING HOW THE RODS WERE FITTED TOGETHER, *BATMAN* UNDOES THE PUZZLE!

JUST IN TIME, TOO!

UHHH!

AFTERWARDS... IT IS A GRIM *BATMAN* WHO REJOINS *ROBIN!*

THE RIDDLER'S STAGING A CRIME-CHARADE IN THIS TOWN THAT WE'VE GOT TO STOP! THAT MAN'S DANGEROUS!

MEANWHILE...

THAT WILL DO NICELY FOR MY FINAL CHALLENGE TO *BATMAN* AND *ROBIN*— A RIDDLE TO RID ME OF THEM— FOR GOOD!

HIGGINS CANNED CORN

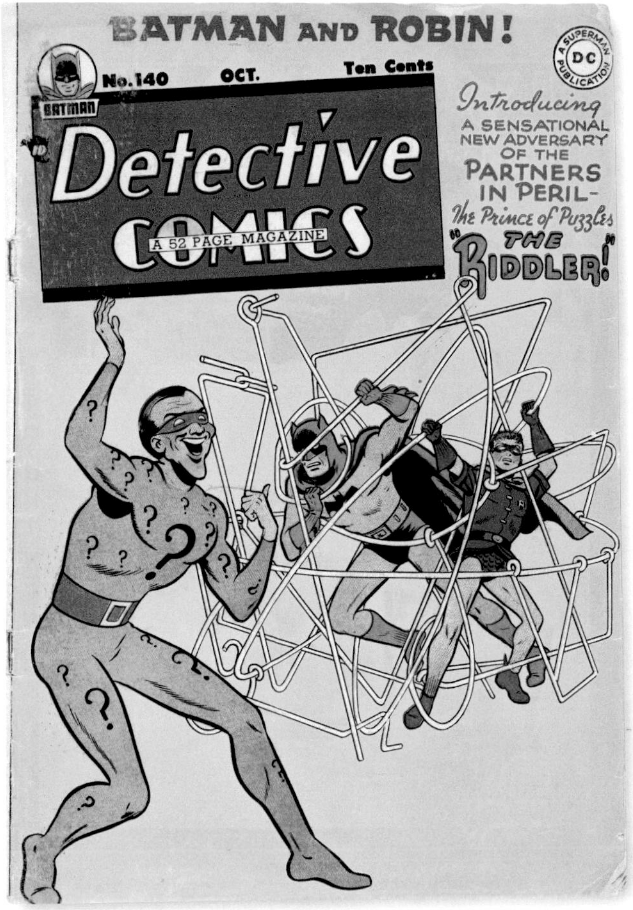
BATMAN AND ROBIN!
No. 140
OCT.
Ten Cents
BATMAN
Detective
COMICS
A 52 PAGE MAGAZINE
A SUPERMAN PUBLICATION
DC
Introducing
A SENSATIONAL
NEW ADVERSARY
OF THE
PARTNERS
IN PERIL-
The Prince of Puzzles
"THE
RIDDLER!"

DETECTIVE COMICS No. 140

OPPOSITE: *Interior, "The Riddler"; script, Bill Finger; pencils, Dick Sprang; inks, Charles Paris. October 1948.* ABOVE: *Cover art, Win Mortimer.* "What I tried to pull off was making movies in frozen frame, drawn images that produced a recognition and feeling of dramatic movement, lighting, and setting, cutting from close-up to long shot, bird's eye to ground-level view, and perspective untamed. All comic art pages are a collection of images. But how do you arrange them to establish danger, serenity, suspense, fear, and humor; how do you interpret a script with gusto, liveliness, vigor, and authentic substance?" —Dick Sprang

DETECTIVE COMICS No. 73

Cover art, Bob Kane, Jerry Robinson, and George Roussos, March 1943.

DETECTIVE COMICS No. 126

Cover art, Jack Burnley and Charles Paris, August 1947.
"While doing his best to emulate Bob Kane's style, Jack [Burnley] couldn't help but bring a more naturalistic approach to the work. His Batman lived in a world more recognizably our own — less *The Cabinet of Dr. Caligari* and more *Casablanca.*"
— Bill Schelly

No.73
BOY COMMANDOS
ALL THIS AND BATMAN TOO!
A SUPERMAN DC PUBLICATION
IND
The BATMAN
Detective
REG. U. S. PAT. OFF.
MARCH
10¢
COMICS
BY POPULAR DEMAND
"RETURN OF THE SCARECROW"
In A Brand-New Story

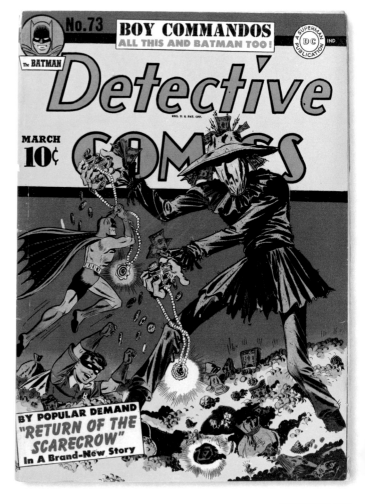

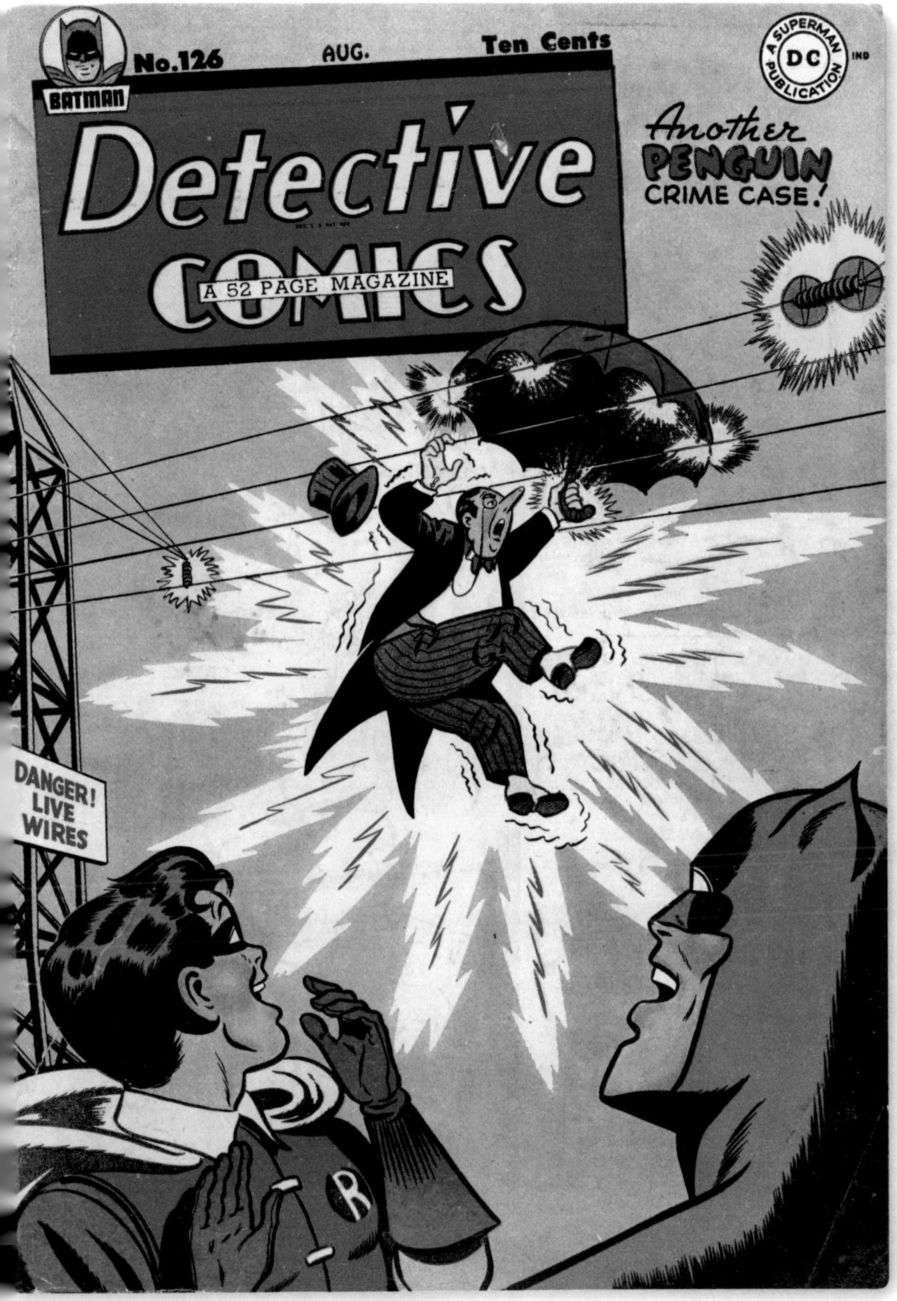
BATMAN
No.126
AUG.
Ten Cents
A SUPERMAN DC PUBLICATION
IND
Detective
COMICS
A 52 PAGE MAGAZINE
Another
PENGUIN
CRIME CASE!
DANGER!
LIVE
WIRES
R

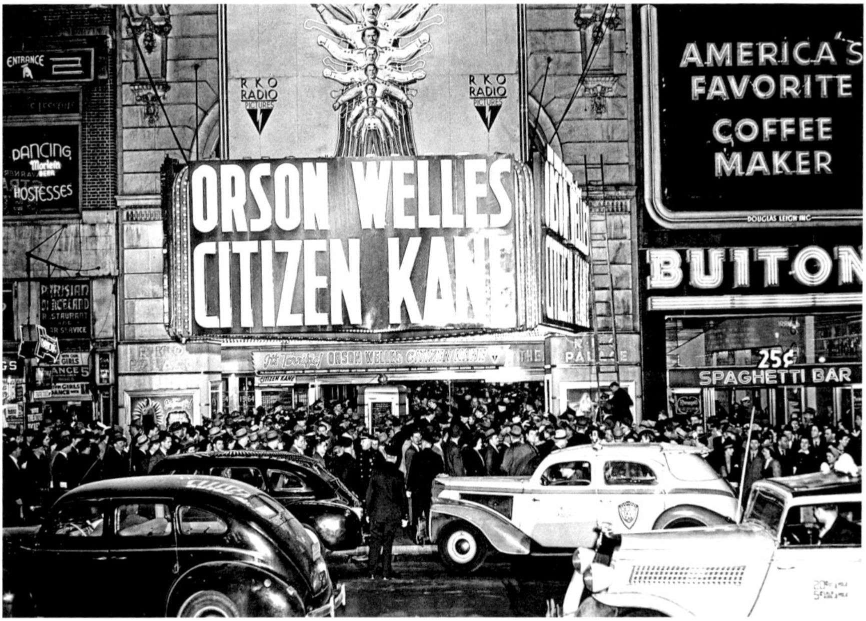
ENTRANCE
RKO RADIO PICTURES
AMERICA'S FAVORITE COFFEE MAKER
DANCING
HOSTESSES
ORSON WELLES
CITIZEN KANE
25¢
SPAGHETTI BAR

WORLD PREMIERE OF CITIZEN KANE

Photograph, RKO Palace in New York City, May 1, 1941. "We were a generation. We thought of ourselves the way the men who began movies must have. We were out to be splendid — somehow.... Experiments in the use of angle shots were carried on. Arguments raged: Should angle shots be used for their own sake or for the sake of furthering the story? Everyone went back to study *Citizen Kane*. Rumors spread that Welles, himself, had read and learned from comic books! What a great business!" — Jules Feiffer

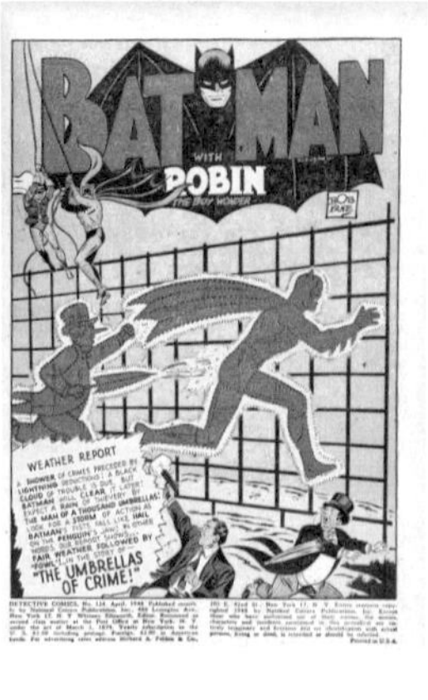
BATMAN
WITH ROBIN
WEATHER REPORT
"THE UMBRELLAS OF CRIME!"

DETECTIVE COMICS No. 134

Interior, "The Umbrellas of Crime"; script, Bill Finger; pencils, Jim Mooney; inks, Charles Paris. April 1948. Inspired by a smartly dressed bird in ads for Kool Cigarettes, the Penguin began life as a ruthless murderer, but his plump comical image showed greater potential as a lighter character forever involved in crimes involving birds and umbrellas that had been reconfigured as weapons. The rogue made 32 appearances between 1941 and 1956 — plus a memorable turn in the "Batman" Sunday comic strip — before being retired for several years.

DETECTIVE COMICS No. 114

Interior, "Acrostic of Crime"; script, Don Cameron; pencils and inks, Win Mortimer. August 1946.

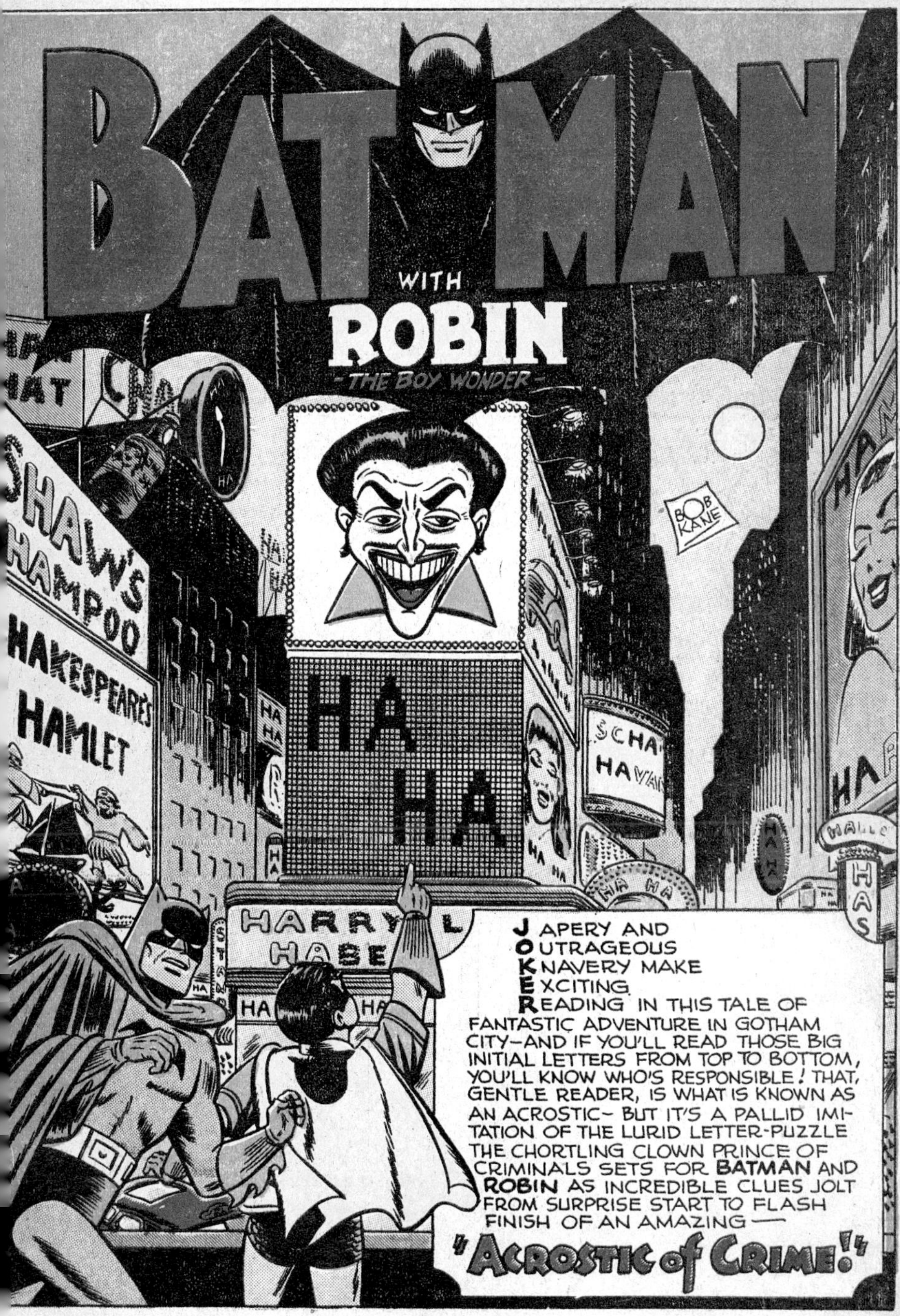
BATMAN
WITH
ROBIN
-THE BOY WONDER-
BOB KANE
SHAW'S SHAMPOO
SHAKESPEARE'S HAMLET
HA HA
HARRY L HABE
JAPERY AND
OUTRAGEOUS
KNAVERY MAKE
EXCITING
READING IN THIS TALE OF FANTASTIC ADVENTURE IN GOTHAM CITY—AND IF YOU'LL READ THOSE BIG INITIAL LETTERS FROM TOP TO BOTTOM, YOU'LL KNOW WHO'S RESPONSIBLE! THAT, GENTLE READER, IS WHAT IS KNOWN AS AN ACROSTIC— BUT IT'S A PALLID IMITATION OF THE LURID LETTER-PUZZLE THE CHORTLING CLOWN PRINCE OF CRIMINALS SETS FOR BATMAN AND ROBIN AS INCREDIBLE CLUES JOLT FROM SURPRISE START TO FLASH FINISH OF AN AMAZING —
"ACROSTIC of CRIME!"

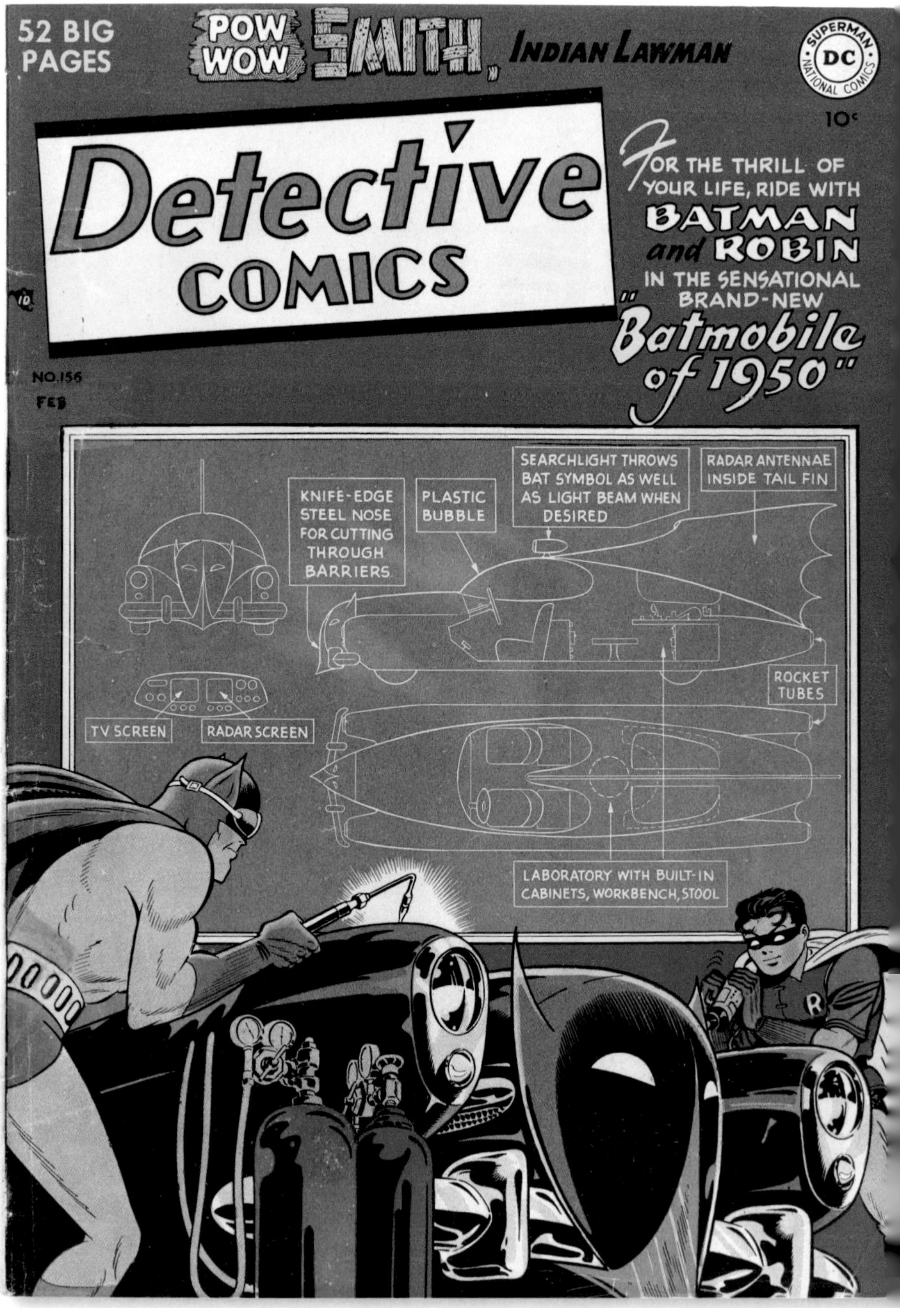
52 BIG PAGES
POW WOW SMITH, INDIAN LAWMAN
SUPERMAN DC NATIONAL COMICS
10¢
Detective COMICS
NO.156
FEB
FOR THE THRILL OF YOUR LIFE, RIDE WITH BATMAN and ROBIN IN THE SENSATIONAL BRAND-NEW "Batmobile of 1950"
KNIFE-EDGE STEEL NOSE FOR CUTTING THROUGH BARRIERS
PLASTIC BUBBLE
SEARCHLIGHT THROWS BAT SYMBOL AS WELL AS LIGHT BEAM WHEN DESIRED
RADAR ANTENNAE INSIDE TAIL FIN
ROCKET TUBES
TV SCREEN
RADAR SCREEN
LABORATORY WITH BUILT-IN CABINETS, WORKBENCH, STOOL
R

BATMAN No. 5 & DETECTIVE COMICS No. 156

OPPOSITE: *Cover art, Dick Sprang, February 1950.* BELOW LEFT: *Interior, "Crime Does Not Pay"; script, Bill Finger; pencils, Bob Kane; inks, Jerry Robinson and George Roussos. Spring 1941.*
Les Daniels notes that "the first Batmobile really worthy of the name, a midnight-blue 'super-charged car' with a scalloped tail fin and a bat-shaped battering ram, appeared in *Batman* No. 5." When the vehicle finally crashed, the time was ripe for a bigger, better "Batmobile of 1950," complete with cutaway diagrams. In his autobiography, Bob Kane ruefully recalled being on the set of the 1943 *Batman* serial and asking where the Batmobile was. Pointing to an ordinary car, the director snapped that Kane "was standing right in front of it."

DETECTIVE COMICS No. 48

BELOW RIGHT: *Interior, "The Secret Cavern"; script, Bill Finger; pencils, Bob Kane; inks, Jerry Robinson and George Roussos. February 1941.* Comics historian Les Daniels writes, "Batman has been driving around in a fast car since his first appearance, but in the beginning it was just a scarlet sedan. Later he had a blue convertible, which at least matched his color scheme. In 1941 a modest hood ornament in the shape of a bat was added, allowing captions to at last call the car 'the Batmobile'—but it was red again."

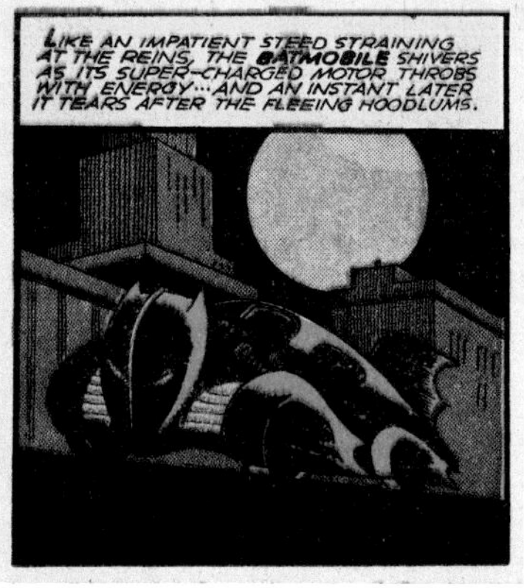
LIKE AN IMPATIENT STEED STRAINING AT THE REINS, THE BATMOBILE SHIVERS AS ITS SUPER-CHARGED MOTOR THROBS WITH ENERGY... AND AN INSTANT LATER IT TEARS AFTER THE FLEEING HOODLUMS.

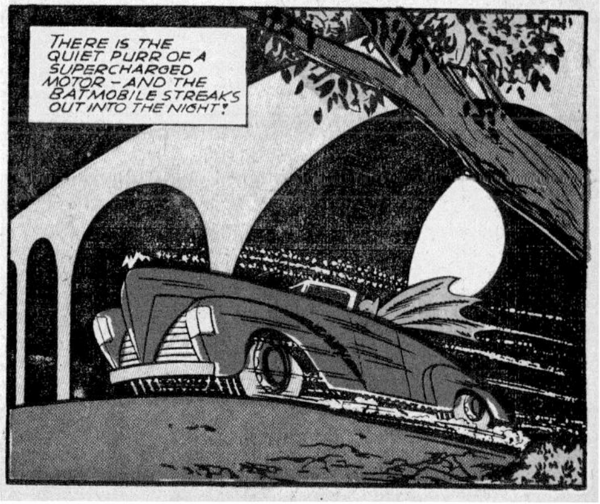
THERE IS THE QUIET PURR OF A SUPERCHARGED MOTOR - AND THE BATMOBILE STREAKS OUT INTO THE NIGHT!

GRAHAM
for 1939
Beauty Graham "Spirit of Motion" styling wins first awards at four important Continental salons; influences 1939 design of many American manufacturers.
Economy Graham proves its economy under A.A.A. supervision by defeating all other contestants in three successive Gilmore Yosemite Economy runs. (Average in 1938 event, 25.77 miles per gallon.)
Comfort Graham's wide seats, deep luxurious cushions, scientifically balanced weight and equalized spring rates combine to produce a ride that's restful and relaxing.
Performance Graham invites critical comparisons in all departments of motor car performance: speed, pickup in high, get-away, driving ease, riding qualities, economy.
IT LOOKS LIKE A MILLION... IT'S PRICED FOR THE MILLIONS

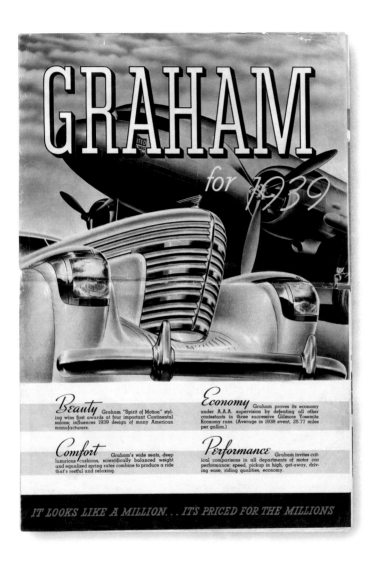

GRAHAM FOR 1939
Automobile brochure, 1939.

BATMAN No. 20
Cover art, Dick Sprang, December 1943–January 1944.

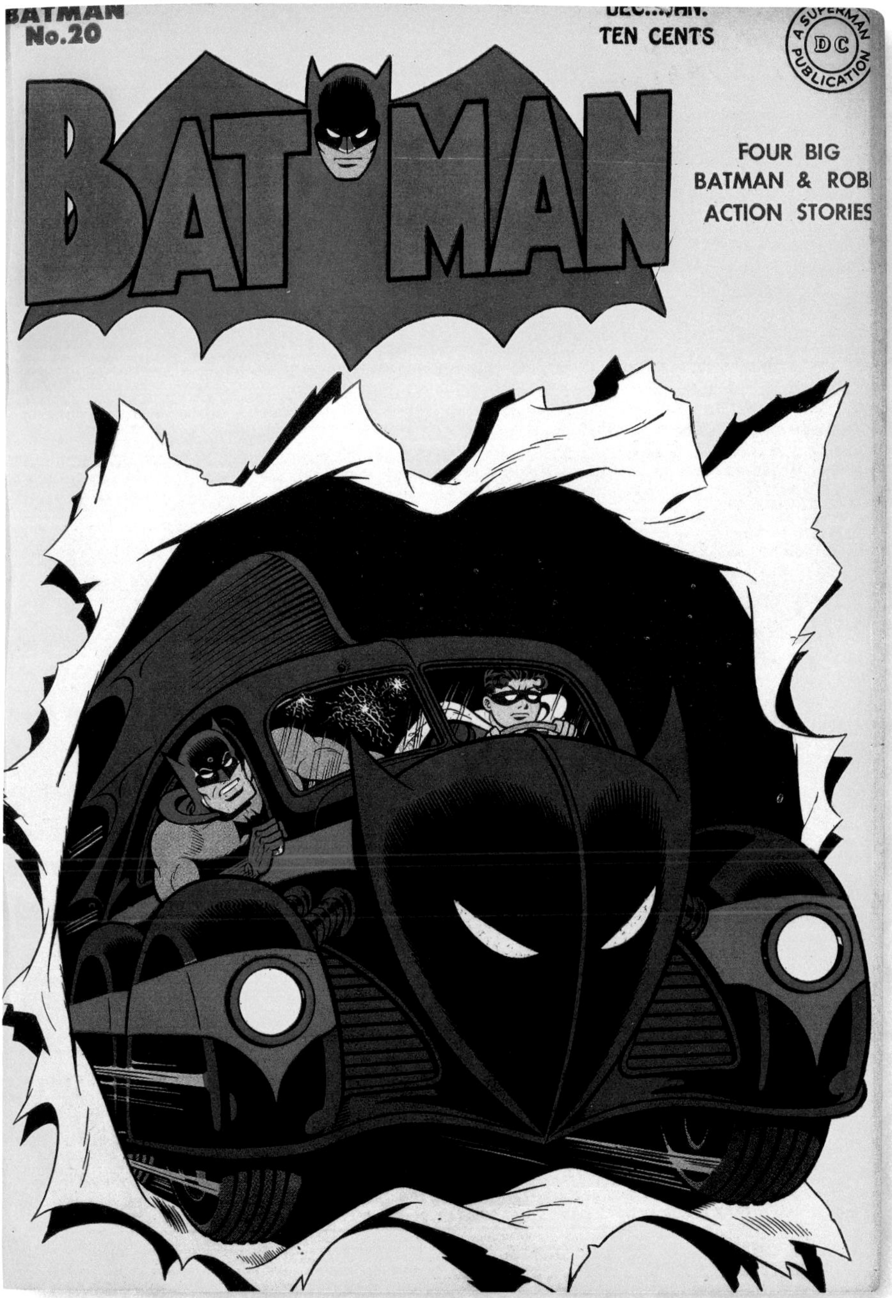
BATMAN
No.20
DEC.-JAN.
TEN CENTS
A SUPERMAN DC PUBLICATION
BATMAN
FOUR BIG
BATMAN & ROBI
ACTION STORIES

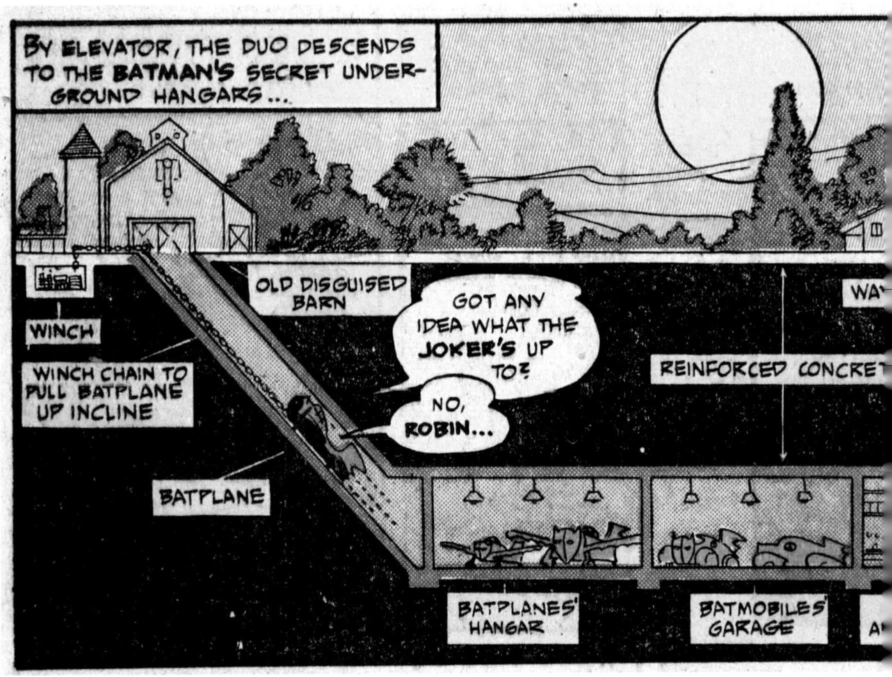
BY ELEVATOR, THE DUO DESCENDS TO THE BATMAN'S SECRET UNDER-GROUND HANGARS...
OLD DISGUISED BARN
WINCH
WINCH CHAIN TO PULL BATPLANE UP INCLINE
GOT ANY IDEA WHAT THE JOKER'S UP TO?
NO, ROBIN...
BATPLANE
REINFORCED CONCRET
BATPLANES' HANGAR
BATMOBILES' GARAGE

BATMAN No. 12

Interior, "The Wizard of Words"; script, Bill Finger; pencils, Bob Kane; inks, Jerry Robinson. August–September 1942. Intricate diagrams such as this first detailed glimpse of Batman's secret headquarters—not yet called the Batcave—helped reinforce the mythology that Bill Finger was constructing around the character. Updated and expanded versions of this panel would be inserted into other Batman stories at intervals through the 1940s, 1950s, and beyond.

DETECTIVE COMICS No. 165

Interior, "The Strange Costumes of Batman"; script, Edmond Hamilton; pencils, Dick Sprang; inks, Charles Paris. November 1950. In addition to wetsuits, Batman and Robin had to create a full-fledged Batmarine in 1954 when they were submerged in Gotham Harbor over a two-day period.

SECRET
LABORATORY

SECRET
ELEVATOR

BATMAN'S "FROG MAN" DIVING SUIT—FIRST USED BY BRITISH NAVY MEN TO SWIM UNOBSERVED TO DISCONNECT GERMAN UNDERWATER MINES AND PREPARE THE WAY FOR INVASION ON D-DAY!

FACE MASK GLASS WINDOW
EXHALING PIPE
EXHALING BREATHING BAG
OXYGEN VALVE
FRONT WEIGHT

HELMET
INHALING PIPE
COLLAR
INHALING BREATHING BAG
OXYGEN BOTTLE
RUBBERIZED STOCKINET SUIT

FRONT
FINS

REGENERATING CHAMBER ALLOWS AIR TO BE BREATHED OVER AGAIN

BACK WEIGHT

BACK

7

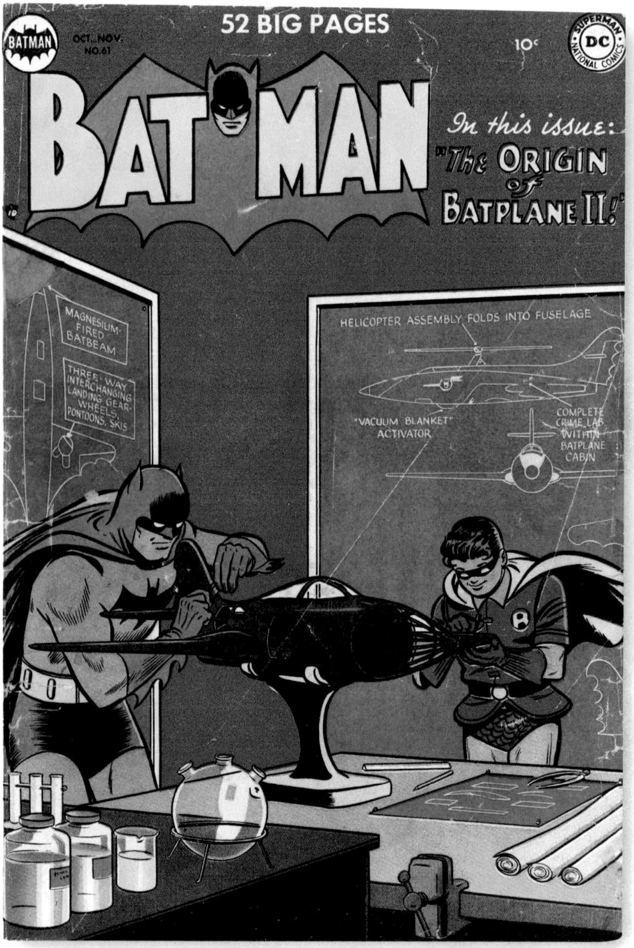
BATMAN
OCT.-NOV.
NO.61
52 BIG PAGES
10¢
SUPERMAN
DC
NATIONAL COMICS
BATMAN
In this issue:
"The ORIGIN of BATPLANE II!"
MAGNESIUM-FIRED BATBEAM
THREE-WAY INTERCHANGING LANDING GEAR-WHEELS, PONTOONS, SKIS
HELICOPTER ASSEMBLY FOLDS INTO FUSELAGE
"VACUUM BLANKET" ACTIVATOR
COMPLETE CRIME LAB WITHIN BATPLANE CABIN

BATMAN No. 61

ABOVE: *Cover art, Win Mortimer, October–November 1950.*
OPPOSITE: *Interior, "The Birth of Batplane II"; script, David Vern Reed; pencils, Dick Sprang; inks, Charles Paris. October–November 1950.* Technology was improving at a rapid pace, and Batman needed to stay on the cutting edge. Bill Finger was canny enough to realize that such upgrades ought to be an event for readers and concocted elaborate stories that required new models of the Batplane and Batmobile. One of the amazing features of the new, improved Batplane was its ability to retract its wings and function underwater as the Batmarine.

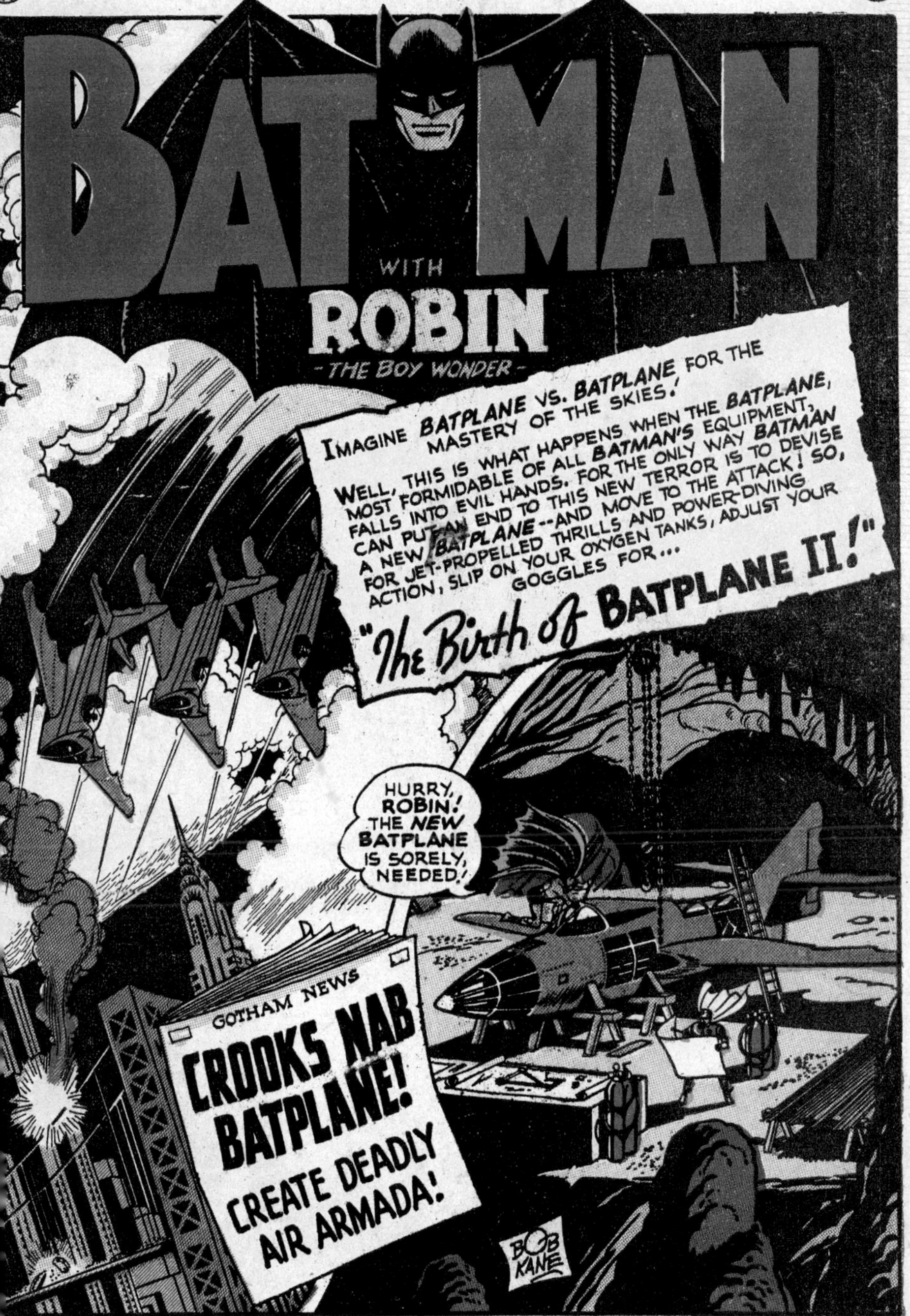
BATMAN
WITH
ROBIN
-THE BOY WONDER-
IMAGINE BATPLANE VS. BATPLANE FOR THE MASTERY OF THE SKIES!
WELL, THIS IS WHAT HAPPENS WHEN THE BATPLANE, MOST FORMIDABLE OF ALL BATMAN'S EQUIPMENT, FALLS INTO EVIL HANDS. FOR THE ONLY WAY BATMAN CAN PUT AN END TO THIS NEW TERROR IS TO DEVISE A NEW BATPLANE--AND MOVE TO THE ATTACK! SO, FOR JET-PROPELLED THRILLS AND POWER-DIVING ACTION, SLIP ON YOUR OXYGEN TANKS, ADJUST YOUR GOGGLES FOR...
"The Birth of BATPLANE II!"
HURRY, ROBIN! THE NEW BATPLANE IS SORELY NEEDED!
GOTHAM NEWS
CROOKS NAB BATPLANE!
CREATE DEADLY AIR ARMADA!
BOB KANE

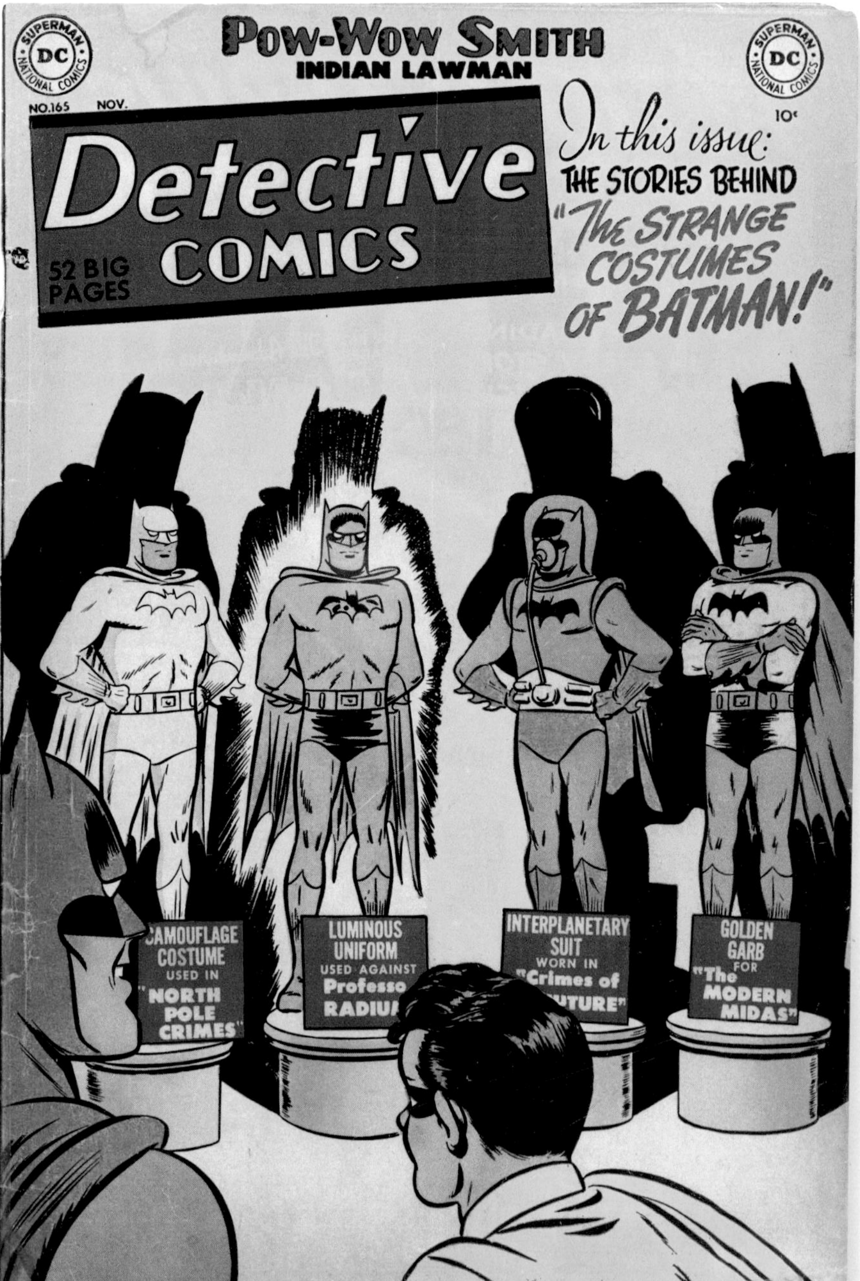
SUPERMAN DC NATIONAL COMICS
POW-WOW SMITH
INDIAN LAWMAN
SUPERMAN DC NATIONAL COMICS
NO.165 NOV.
10¢
Detective COMICS
52 BIG PAGES
In this issue:
THE STORIES BEHIND
"The STRANGE COSTUMES OF BATMAN!"
CAMOUFLAGE COSTUME USED IN "NORTH POLE CRIMES"
LUMINOUS UNIFORM USED AGAINST Professo RADIU
INTERPLANETARY SUIT WORN IN "Crimes of UTURE"
GOLDEN GARB FOR "The MODERN MIDAS"

DETECTIVE COMICS No. 165

Cover art, Win Mortimer, November 1950. Decades before action figure manufacturers created specialty costumes for its toy line, Bill Finger incorporated such outfits into his stories, culminating with the semiretrospective "Strange Costumes of Batman" that included a surprising new addition for Robin's wardrobe in the episode's climax.

BATMAN No. 11

Cover art, Fred Ray and Jerry Robinson, June–July 1942.

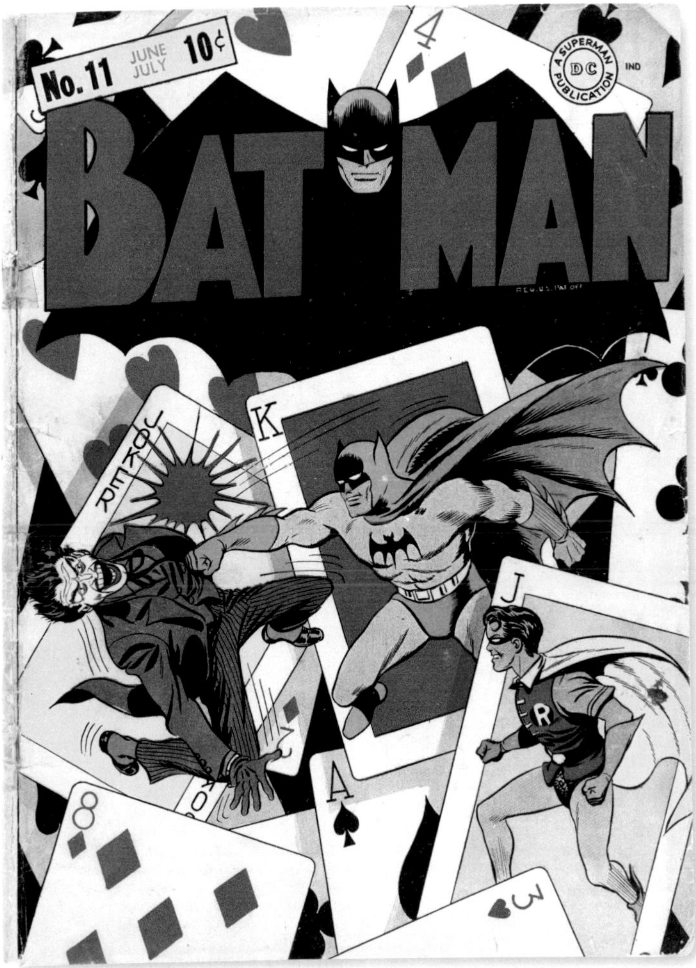
No. 11
JUNE JULY
10¢
A SUPERMAN DC PUBLICATION
IND
BATMAN
JOKER

O Lobinho
Nº 7
BATMAN
O Homem-Morcego

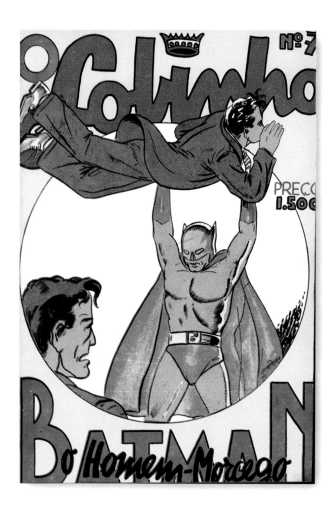

O LOBINHO No. 7

Cover art, artist unknown, 1940. When Batman's adventures were first reprinted in Brazil, the details of his costume were clearly not yet familiar. In a crude re-creation of a panel from *Batman* No. 2, an unknown artist for *O Lobinho* left off the Caped Crusader's chest icon, not to mention his shirt and tights.

ITALIAN BATMAN COMICS

Cover art, "I Due Parker" and "La Candela della Morte," artists unknown, Le Edizioni Mondiali, *1948.*

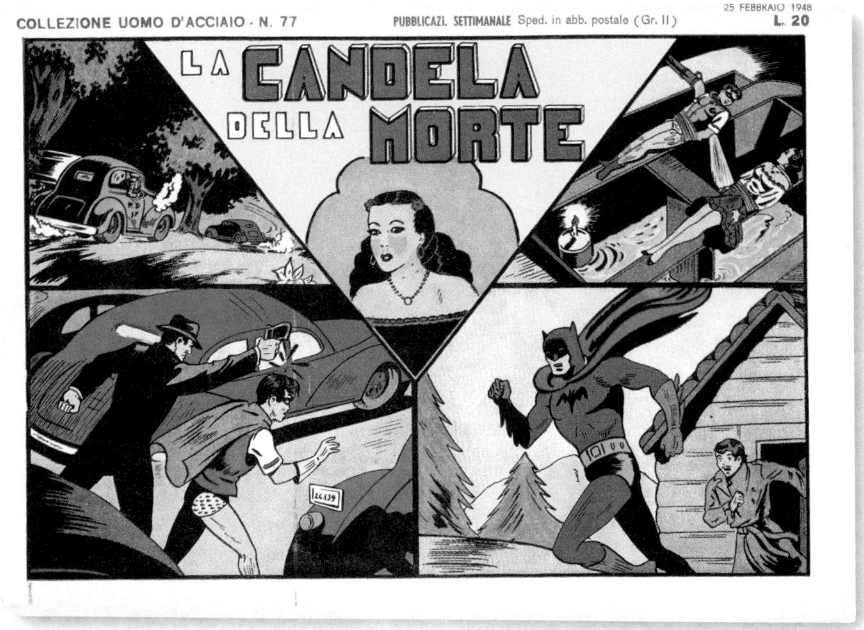
COLLEZIONE UOMO D'ACCIAIO - N. 77
PUBBLICAZI. SETTIMANALE Sped. in abb. postale (Gr. II)
25 FEBBRAIO 1948
L. 20
LA CANDELA DELLA MORTE

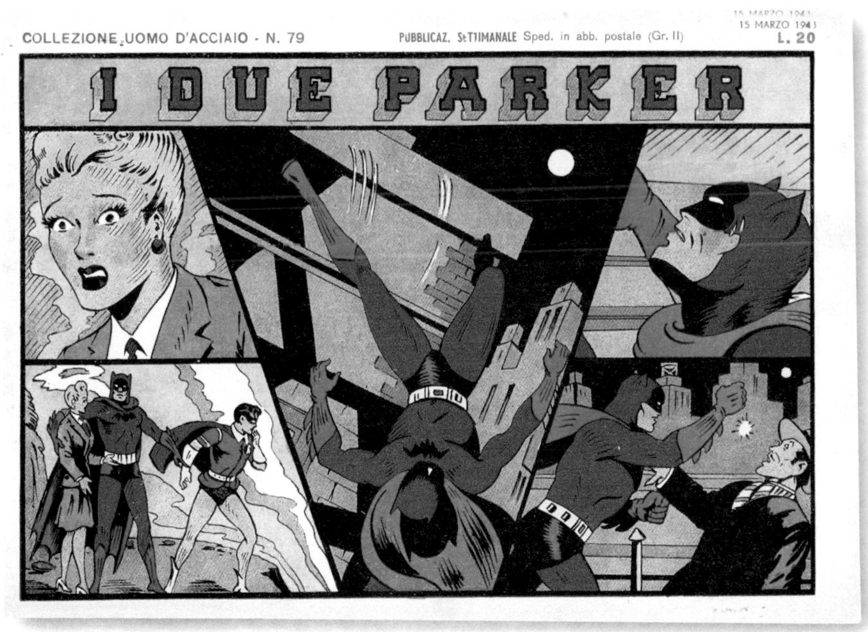
COLLEZIONE UOMO D'ACCIAIO - N. 79
PUBBLICAZ. SETTIMANALE Sped. in abb. postale (Gr. II)
15 MARZO 1943
L. 20
I DUE PARKER

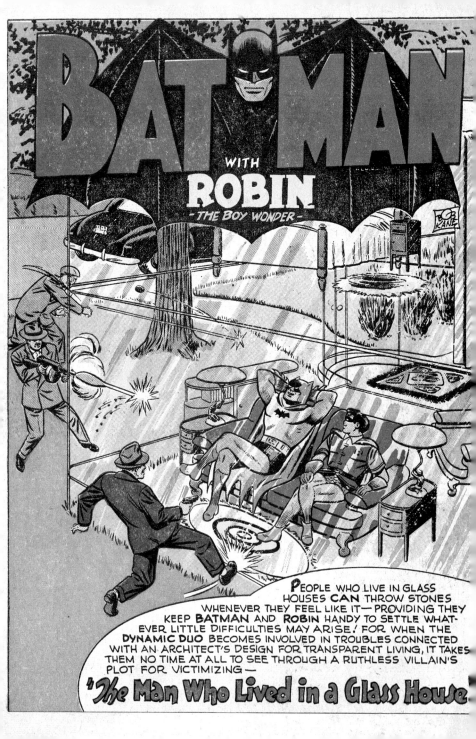

BAT MAN

WITH ROBIN
- THE BOY WONDER -

BOB KANE

PEOPLE WHO LIVE IN GLASS HOUSES **CAN** THROW STONES WHENEVER THEY FEEL LIKE IT— PROVIDING THEY KEEP **BATMAN** AND **ROBIN** HANDY TO SETTLE WHATEVER LITTLE DIFFICULTIES MAY ARISE! FOR WHEN THE **DYNAMIC DUO** BECOMES INVOLVED IN TROUBLES CONNECTED WITH AN ARCHITECT'S DESIGN FOR TRANSPARENT LIVING, IT TAKES THEM NO TIME AT ALL TO SEE THROUGH A RUTHLESS VILLAIN'S PLOT FOR VICTIMIZING—

"The Man Who Lived in a Glass House!"

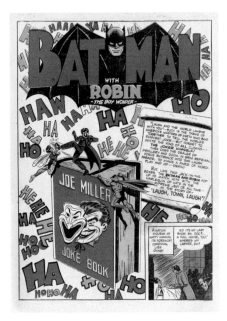

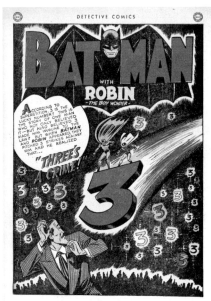

BATMAN
WITH
ROBIN
-THE BOY WONDER-
"LAUGH AND THE WORLD LAUGHS WITH YOU"--SUCH IS THE THEME OF AMERICA'S MASTERS OF MIRTH WHO BAND TOGETHER TO TELL THE WORLD'S FUNNIEST JOKE---BUT FORGET TO INVITE THE KING OF ALL CLOWNS--- THE JOKER HIMSELF! THEN DOES THE DEALER OF DROLLERY AND DOOM, IN GRIM REPRISAL, FORCE ENTRANCE INTO THIS LAUGH PARADE, TO MAKE A FARCE OF WORD-PLAY AND OF---DEATH!
BUT, LIKE TWO JACK-IN-THE-BOXES, THE BATMAN AND ROBIN POP UP TO MATCH WITS WITH THE HARLEQUIN OF HATE IN THE SUPREME JEST OF ALL TIME... IN THE STORY OF-
"LAUGH, TOWN, LAUGH"!
JOE MILLER
JOKE BOOK
A NATION MOURNS AS HAPPY HANSON, ITS FOREMOST COMEDIAN, LIES DYING!
SO IT'S MY LAST SHOW, EH, DOC?... A FULL HOUSE, TOO! WHERE'S MY LAWYER, EH?

DETECTIVE COMICS
BATMAN
WITH
ROBIN
-THE BOY WONDER-
ACCORDING TO SUPERSTITION, 3 IS THE LUCKY NUMBER! THIS IS THE STORY OF ONE MAN WHO NOT ONLY BELIEVED IT—BUT ALSO BELIEVED 3 MADE HIM IMMUNE TO THE LAW! BUT WHEN BATMAN AND ROBIN APPEARED, THEY PITCHED 3 STRIKES AGAINST HIM AND HE REALIZED THAT...
"THREE'S A CRIME!"

DETECTIVE COMICS No. 115

Interior, "The Man Who Lived in a Glass House!"; script, Don Cameron; pencils and inks, Win Mortimer. September 1946. A prolific DC contributor from 1940 until his death in 1954, Don Cameron wrote dozens of Batman stories that introduced villains such as Tweedledum and Tweedledee, and the Cavalier. His crowning achievement was *Batman* No. 16's "Here Comes Alfred," which featured the first appearance of Bruce Wayne's beloved butler.

DETECTIVE COMICS No. 146

Interiors, "Three's a Crime"; script, Bill Finger; pencils and inks, Dick Sprang. April 1949. As other Batman artists moved on, Sprang became one of the principal illustrators of the feature. He distilled the Bob Kane look into its boldest, most cartoony form with eye-catching splash pages and layouts. Sprang's name was unknown when he retired in 1963, but his style was so distinctive and recognizable that fans of a later generation were able to properly celebrate his work.

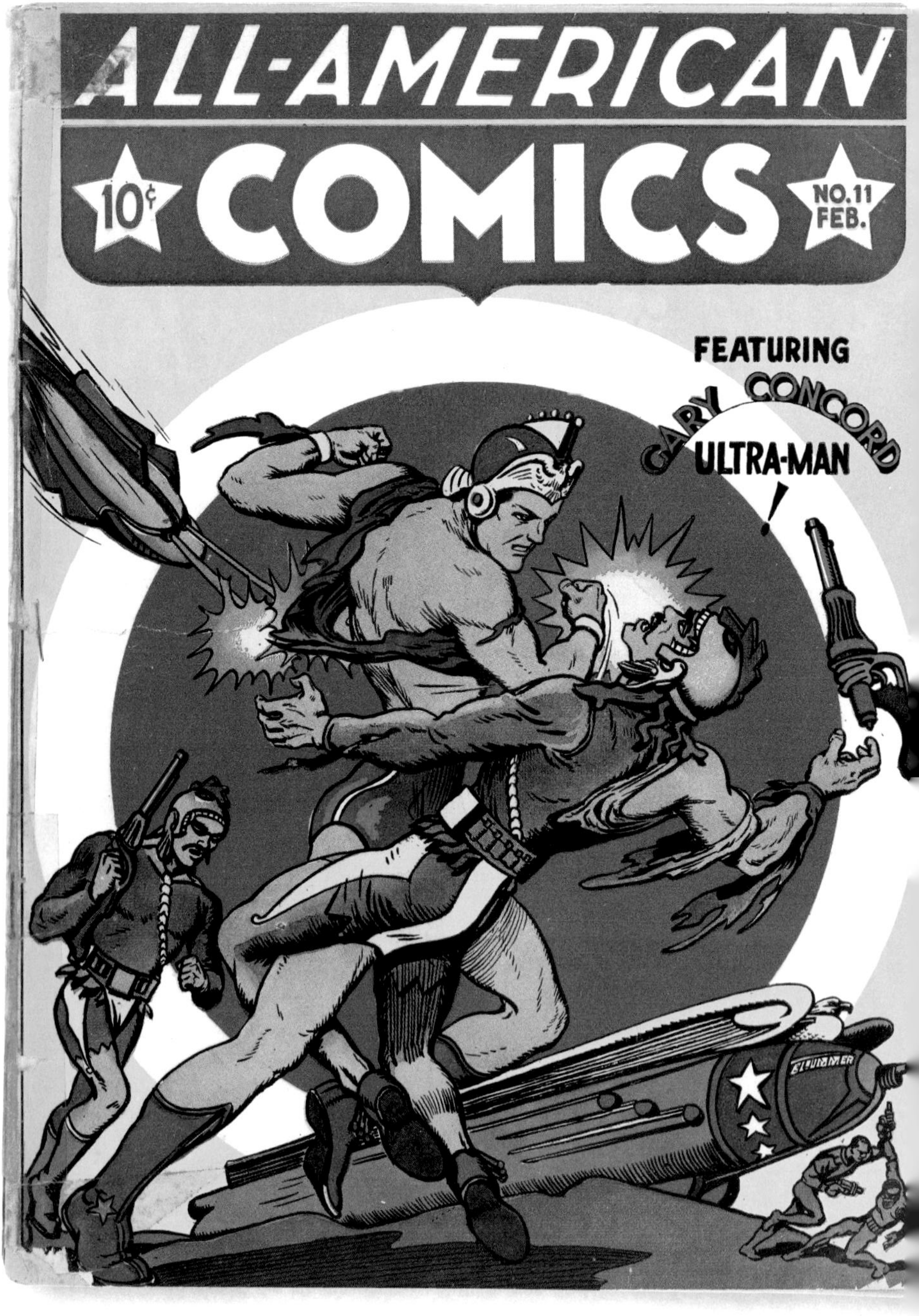
ALL-AMERICAN
COMICS
10¢
NO. 11
FEB.
FEATURING
GARY CONCORD
ULTRA-MAN
!

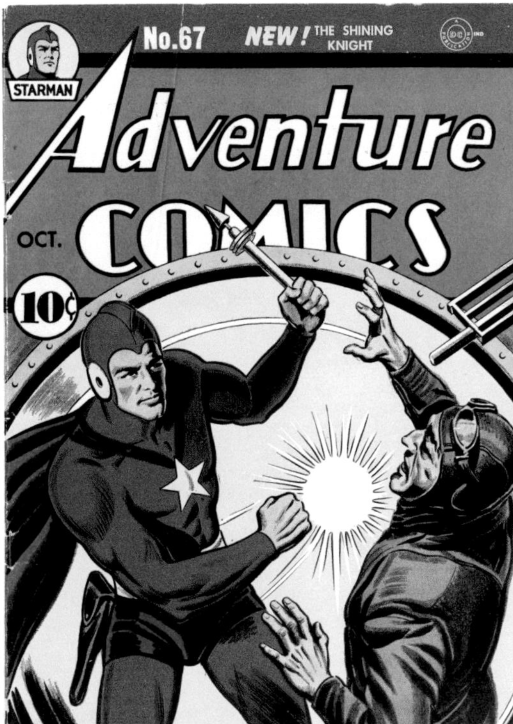
STARMAN
No.67
NEW! THE SHINING KNIGHT
Adventure
COMICS
OCT.
10¢

ALL-AMERICAN COMICS No. 11

Cover art, Jon L. Blummer, February 1940. Ultra-Man was All-American's first science-fiction feature and was probably influenced by elements from the "Buck Rogers" comic strip. Rogers was a 20th-century man who awoke 500 years in the future. Ultra-Man's Gary Concord had a similar experience, but his heroic adventures were quickly bypassed and he died of old age by the end of the second installment. At that point, his son Gary II became Ultra-Man for the duration of its short run.

ADVENTURE COMICS No. 67

Cover art, Jack Burnley, April 1941. Socialite Ted Knight used a gravity rod powered by "infra-rays from the distant stars" to take flight as Starman, a hero that illustrator Jack Burnley recalled was created by committee. In an editorial meeting, Jack Liebowitz, Whitney Ellsworth, Jack Schiff, Bernie Breslauer, and Murray Boltinoff met with the artist to devise a character that they envisioned as the next Superman, but he never caught fire as they had hoped.

ALL-AMERICAN COMICS No. 16

Cover art, Sheldon Moldoff, July 1940. The sole survivor of a train wreck, Alan Scott recovered a magical lantern from the wreckage, fashioned an emerald ring to channel its powers, and adopted the heroic persona of Green Lantern. Created by Martin Nodell, the hero was further developed by writer Bill Finger.

ALL-AMERICAN COMICS No. 21

Cover art, Sheldon Moldoff, December 1940. Influenced by popular Flash Gordon cartoonist Alex Raymond, Sheldon Moldoff brought a dynamic realism to the early *Green Lantern* covers.

GREEN LANTERN No. 1

Cover art, Howard Purcell, fall 1941. "The subway platform was crowded. There was some kind of delay; the train was not coming into the station. On the tracks, I could see a trainman holding a red lantern as he checked the rails. Then he hid behind a pole, waving a *green lantern*, indicating that all was now safe. At last, the train pulled in, and I had a title: Green Lantern. It still sounded good by the time I reached home—and to me, that meant it was safe to go ahead." —Martin Nodell

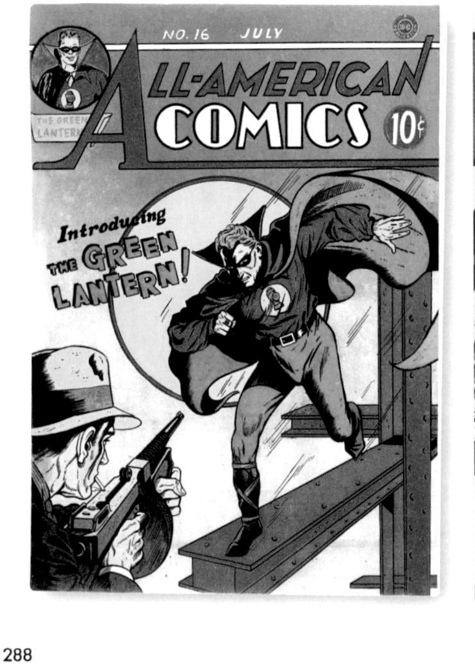
NO. 16 JULY
ALL-AMERICAN COMICS
10¢
THE GREEN LANTERN
Introducing THE GREEN LANTERN!

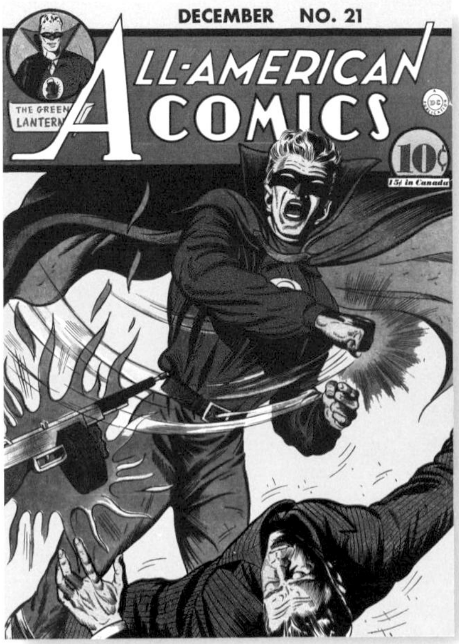
DECEMBER NO. 21
ALL-AMERICAN COMICS
THE GREEN LANTERN
10¢
15¢ in Canada

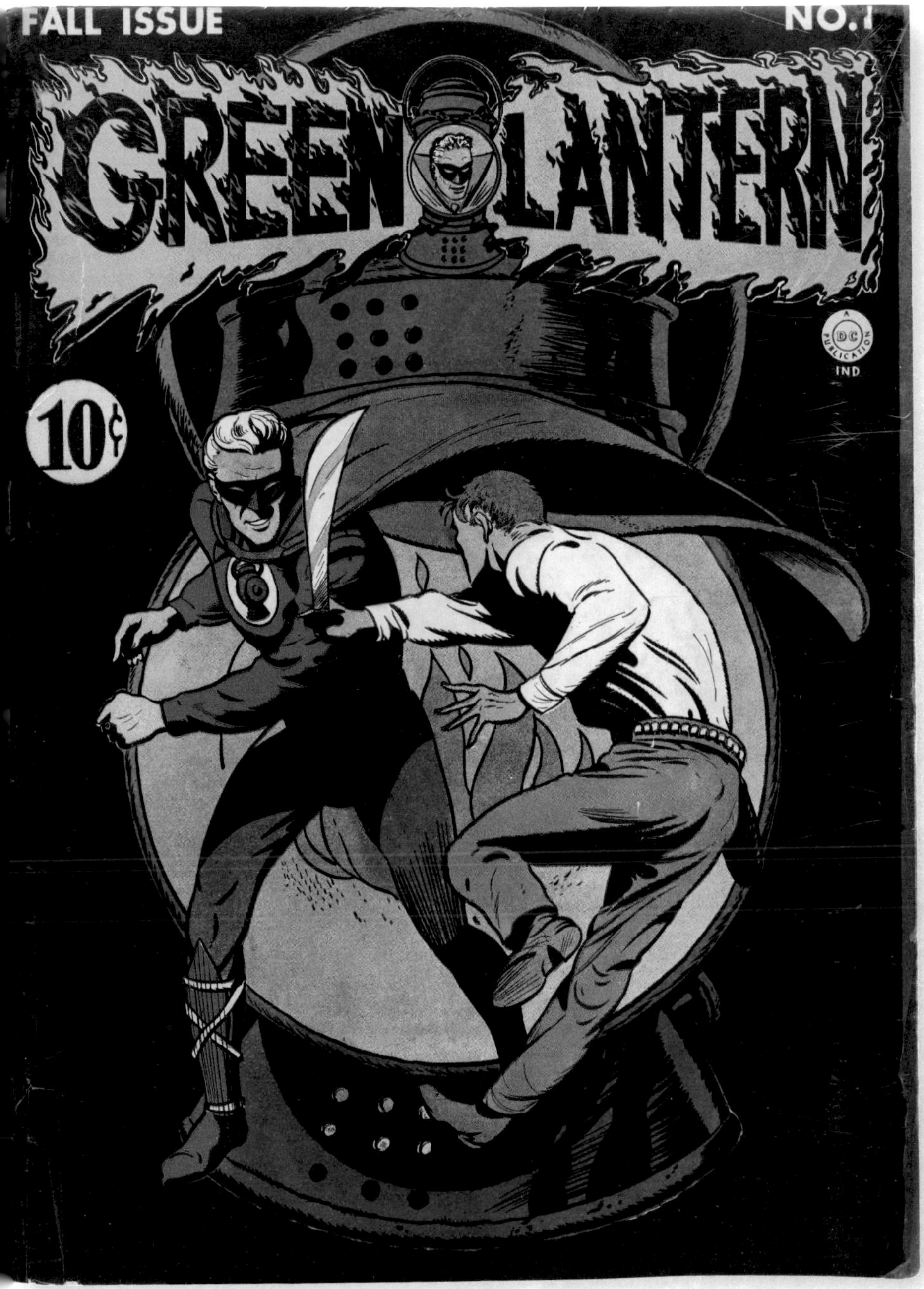
FALL ISSUE
NO.1
GREEN LANTERN
A DC PUBLICATION
IND
10¢

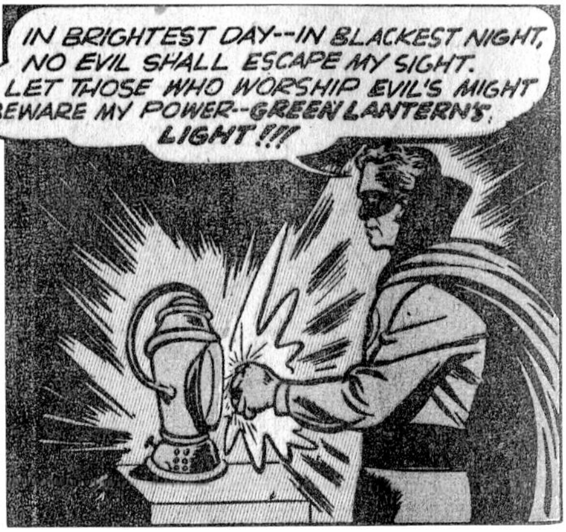
IN BRIGHTEST DAY--IN BLACKEST NIGHT, NO EVIL SHALL ESCAPE MY SIGHT. LET THOSE WHO WORSHIP EVIL'S MIGHT BEWARE MY POWER--GREEN LANTERN'S LIGHT!!!

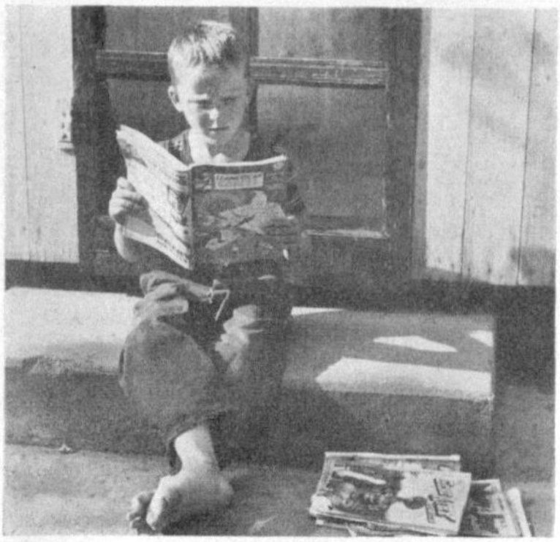

COMICS DO NOT COUNT but Leo likes them best and sandwiches a lot of them into his reading program. Two of his favorites: Superman and Batman.

GREEN LANTERN No. 10

Interior, "The Man Who Wanted the World"; script, Alfred Bester; pencils and inks, Martin Nodell. Winter 1943–1944. Science-fiction author Alfred Bester, noted for his classic 1950s novels *The Demolished Man* and *The Stars My Destination*, spent a fertile period writing *Green Lantern* during the mid-1940s. Beyond his scripts featuring the debuts of enduring villains like Solomon Grundy and Vandal Savage, the author also wrote the rhyming oath that the hero used when recharging his power ring, which he did every 24 hours, by touching it to his magic green lantern.

COMICS DO NOT COUNT

Article, "Feathers for Reading", Life, September 29, 1947. Most educators and librarians held comic books in disdain, absolutely convinced that children's minds could only be nourished by proper books. They surely must have despaired upon seeing a *Life* magazine article declaring that, despite winning a library contest by reading 157 "real" books, Iowa boy Leo Farrell still considered his favorite printed material to be comics.

GREEN LANTERN No. 13

Cover art, Irwin Hasen, Fall 1944. Many cartoonists of the 1940s longed for the prestige of drawing a newspaper comic strip. Irwin Hasen was one of the few who achieved that dream, producing the Dondi feature from 1955 to 1986.

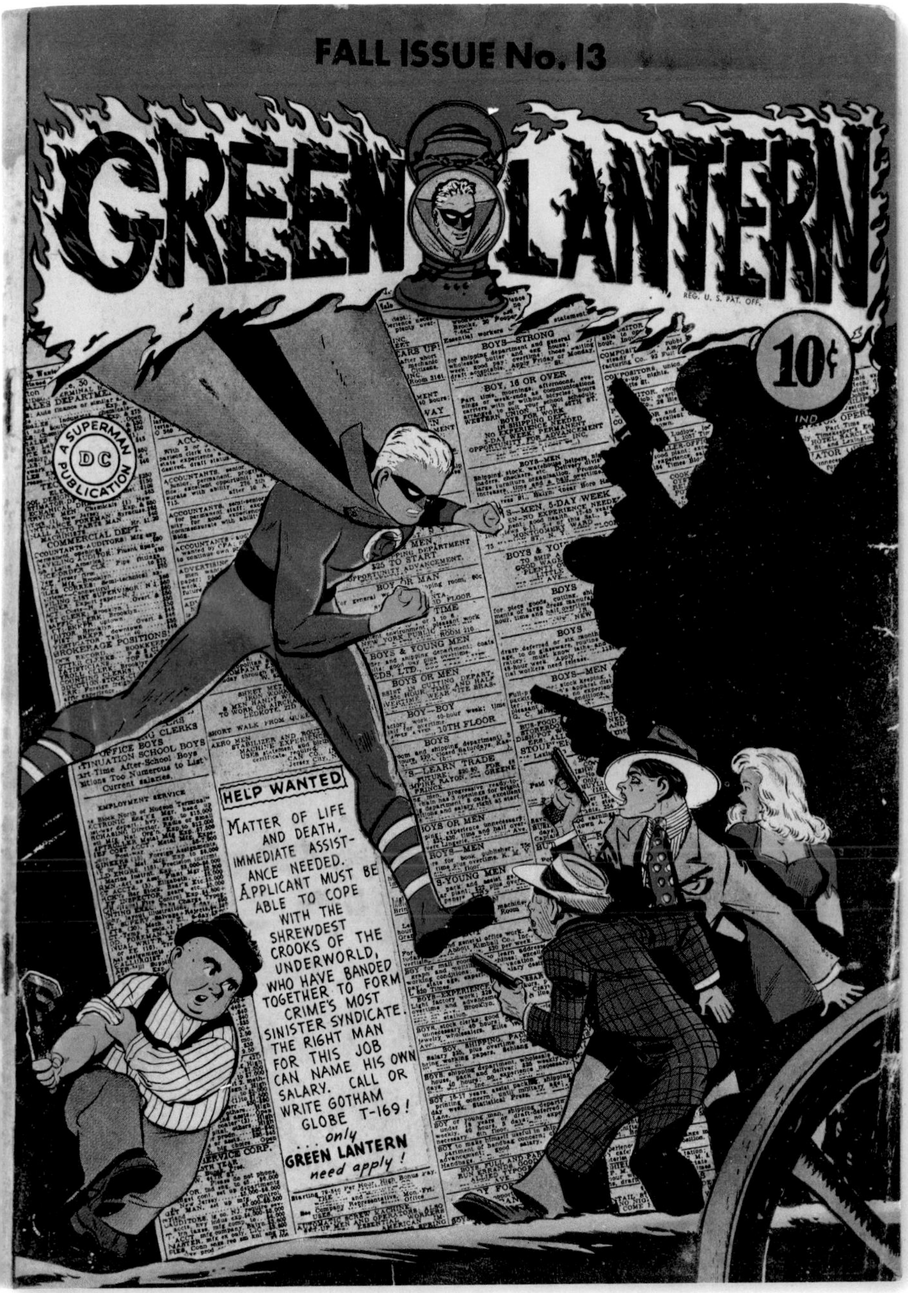
FALL ISSUE No. 13
GREEN LANTERN
REG. U. S. PAT. OFF.
10¢
A SUPERMAN DC PUBLICATION
HELP WANTED
MATTER OF LIFE AND DEATH, IMMEDIATE ASSISTANCE NEEDED. APPLICANT MUST BE ABLE TO COPE WITH THE SHREWDEST CROOKS OF THE UNDERWORLD, WHO HAVE BANDED TOGETHER TO FORM CRIME'S MOST SINISTER SYNDICATE. THE RIGHT MAN FOR THIS JOB CAN NAME HIS OWN SALARY. CALL OR WRITE GOTHAM GLOBE T-169!
...only GREEN LANTERN need apply!

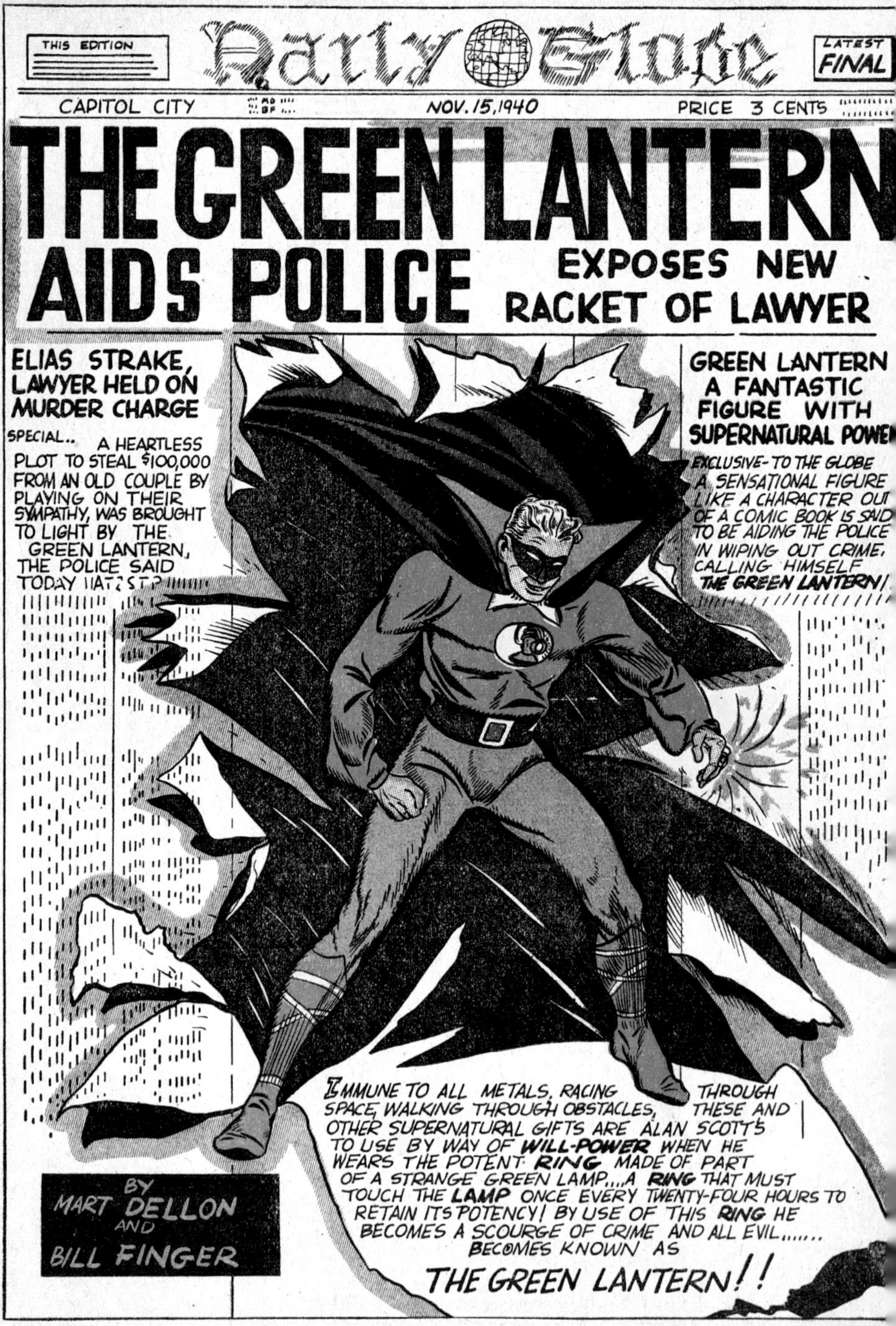
THIS EDITION
Daily Globe
LATEST FINAL
CAPITOL CITY
NOV. 15, 1940
PRICE 3 CENTS
THE GREEN LANTERN AIDS POLICE
EXPOSES NEW RACKET OF LAWYER
ELIAS STRAKE, LAWYER HELD ON MURDER CHARGE
SPECIAL.. A HEARTLESS PLOT TO STEAL $100,000 FROM AN OLD COUPLE BY PLAYING ON THEIR SYMPATHY, WAS BROUGHT TO LIGHT BY THE GREEN LANTERN, THE POLICE SAID TODAY
GREEN LANTERN A FANTASTIC FIGURE WITH SUPERNATURAL POWE
EXCLUSIVE-TO THE GLOBE A SENSATIONAL FIGURE LIKE A CHARACTER OUT OF A COMIC BOOK IS SAID TO BE AIDING THE POLICE IN WIPING OUT CRIME, CALLING HIMSELF THE GREEN LANTERN!
IMMUNE TO ALL METALS, RACING THROUGH SPACE, WALKING THROUGH OBSTACLES, THESE AND OTHER SUPERNATURAL GIFTS ARE ALAN SCOTT'S TO USE BY WAY OF WILL-POWER WHEN HE WEARS THE POTENT RING MADE OF PART OF A STRANGE GREEN LAMP,...A RING THAT MUST TOUCH THE LAMP ONCE EVERY TWENTY-FOUR HOURS TO RETAIN ITS POTENCY! BY USE OF THIS RING HE BECOMES A SCOURGE OF CRIME AND ALL EVIL...... BECOMES KNOWN AS
THE GREEN LANTERN!!
BY MART DELLON AND BILL FINGER

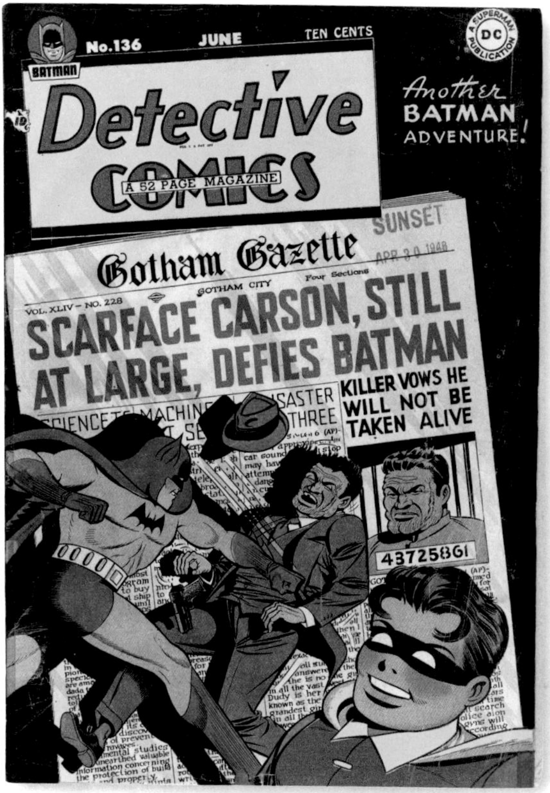
No.136
JUNE
TEN CENTS
BATMAN
A SUPERMAN PUBLICATION
DC
Detective
COMICS
A 52 PAGE MAGAZINE
Another
BATMAN
ADVENTURE!
SUNSET
Gotham Gazette
APR 30 1948
GOTHAM CITY
Four Sections
VOL. XLIV – NO. 228
SCARFACE CARSON, STILL AT LARGE, DEFIES BATMAN
KILLER VOWS HE WILL NOT BE TAKEN ALIVE
43725861

ALL-AMERICAN COMICS No. 22

Interior, "The Green Lantern Aids Police"; script, Bill Finger; pencils and inks, Martin Nodell (as Mart Dellon). January 1941. An interesting detail of the *Green Lantern* series was the fact that he lived in Gotham City just as Batman did (and yet somehow they never ran into each other). Gotham was a real-life nickname for New York City, but the real reason that the two heroes had the same address was because they shared a common writer, Bill Finger.

DETECTIVE COMICS No. 136

Cover art, Dick Sprang, June 1948. Batman's hometown has had many newspapers, but none have been mentioned as frequently as the *Gotham Gazette*, dating back to *Batman* No. 17. One episode in *World's Finest Comics* No. 80 discloses that Bruce Wayne was on the paper's board of directors and that *Daily Planet* editor Perry White worked there as a cub reporter.

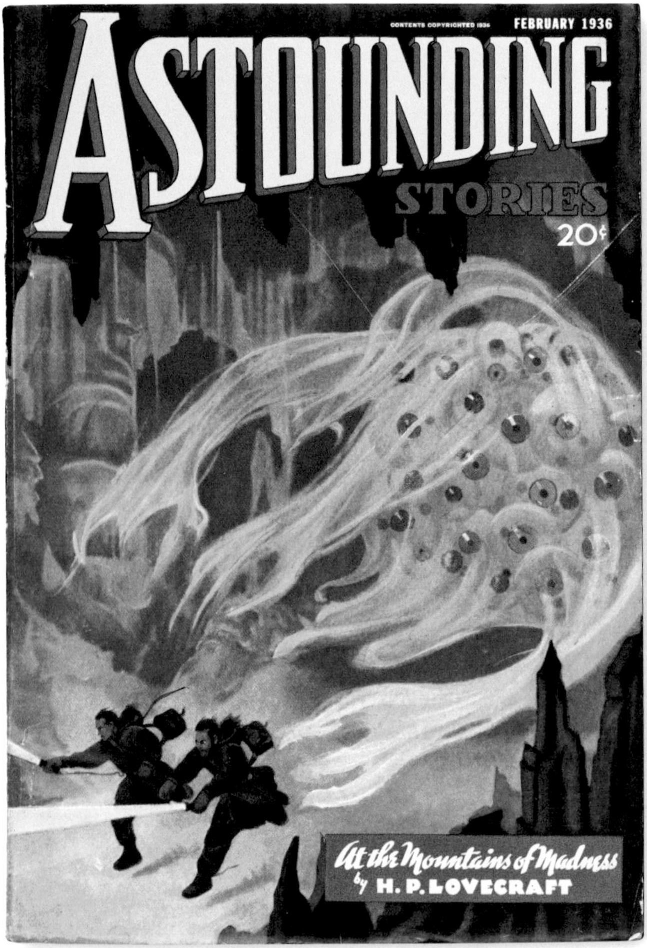
CONTENTS COPYRIGHTED 1936
FEBRUARY 1936
ASTOUNDING
STORIES
20¢
At the Mountains of Madness
by H. P. LOVECRAFT

ASTOUNDING STORIES

Cover art, Howard V. Brown; script, H. P. Lovecraft. February 1936.

ACTION COMICS No. 12

Cover art, Fred Guardineer, May 1939. Zatara was modeled after newspaper strip hero Mandrake the Magician. What made Zatara memorable was the fact that the magical commands that he spoke were real words spelled backward. At Quality Comics, Guardineer later worked on Tor the Magic Master and Merlin, both of whom also used backward magic.

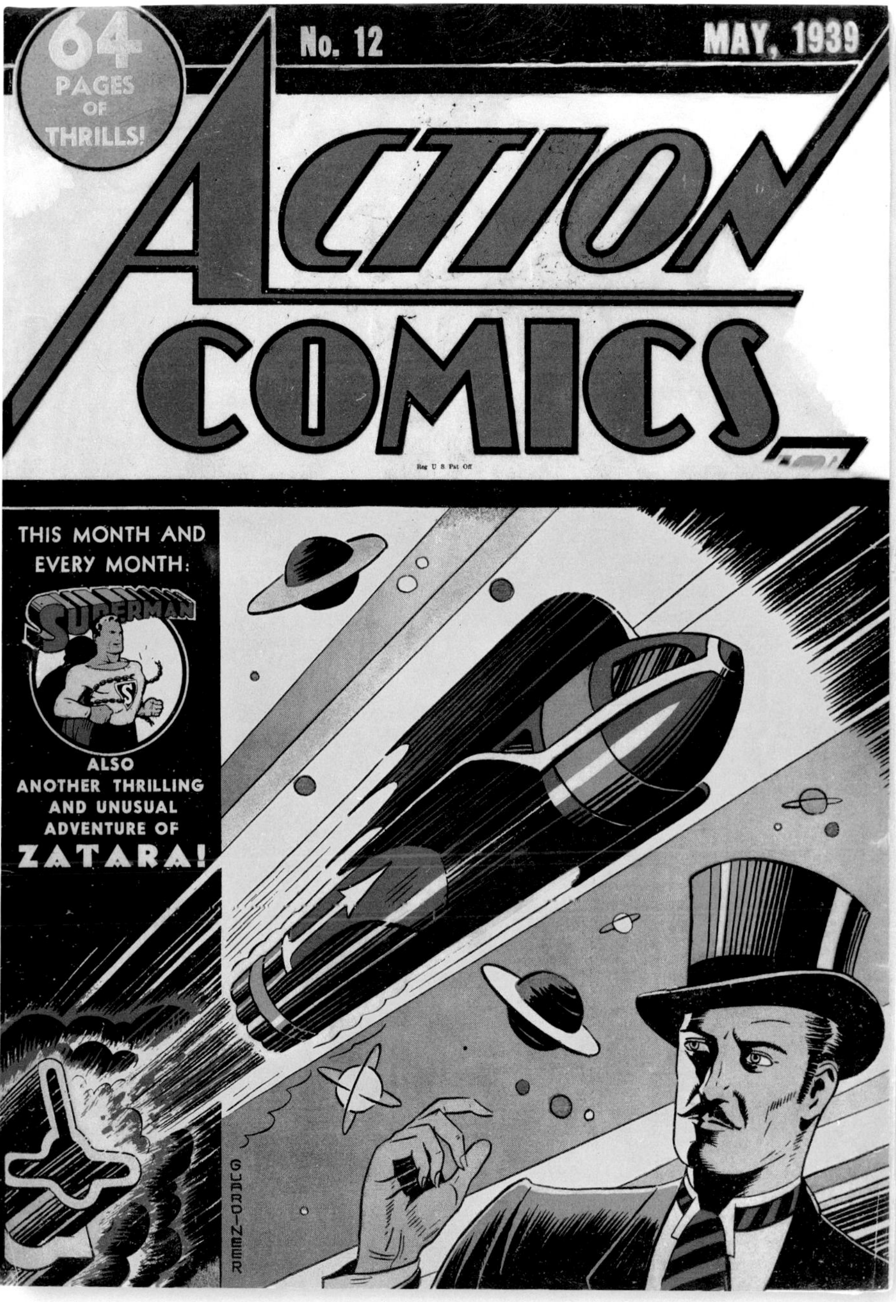
64 PAGES OF THRILLS!
No. 12
MAY, 1939
ACTION COMICS
Reg U S Pat Off
THIS MONTH AND EVERY MONTH:
SUPERMAN
ALSO ANOTHER THRILLING AND UNUSUAL ADVENTURE OF
ZATARA!
GUARDINEER

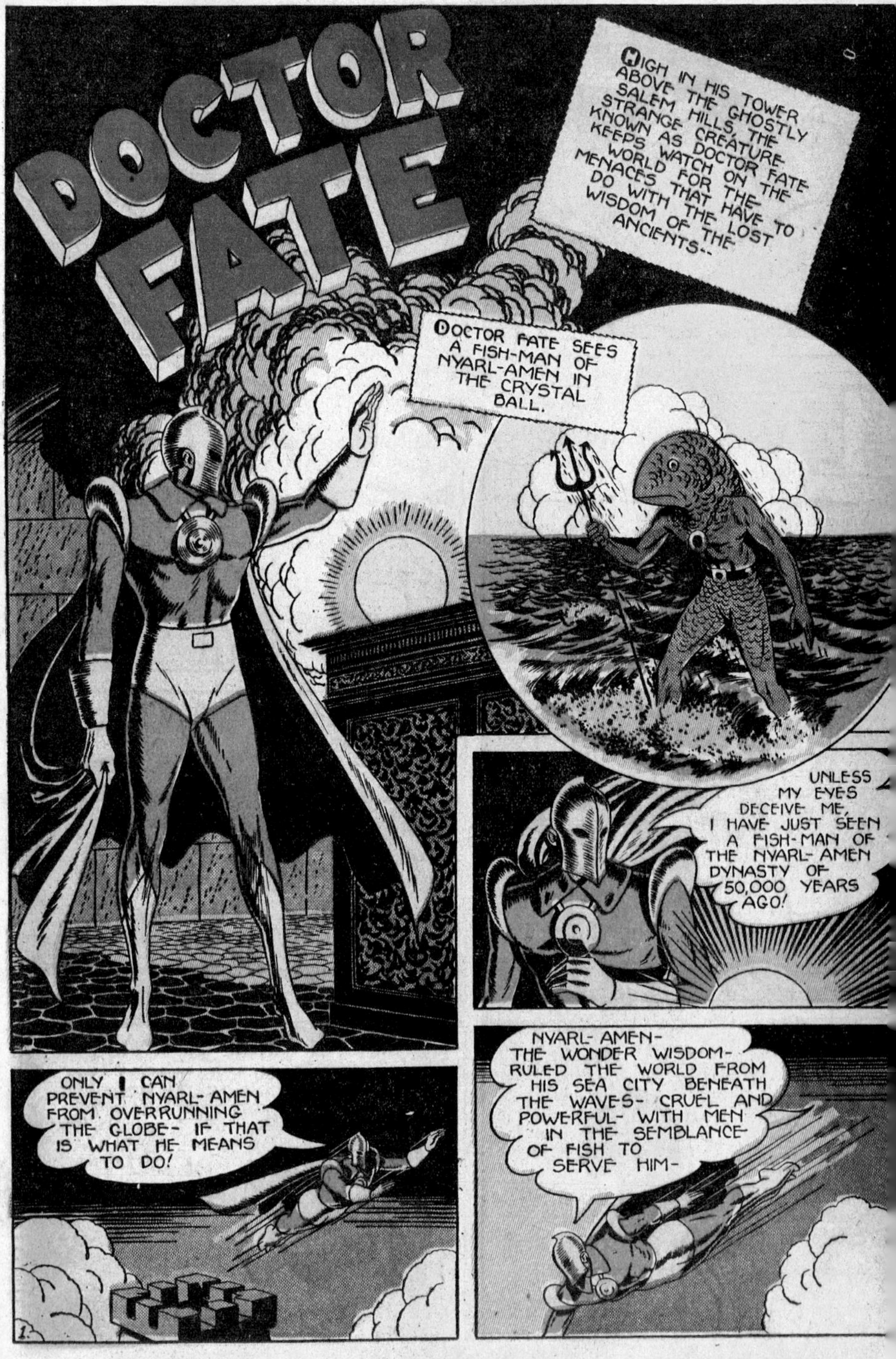
DOCTOR FATE
HIGH IN HIS TOWER ABOVE THE GHOSTLY SALEM HILLS, THE STRANGE CREATURE KNOWN AS DOCTOR FATE KEEPS WATCH ON THE WORLD FOR THE MENACES THAT HAVE TO DO WITH THE LOST WISDOM OF THE ANCIENTS--
DOCTOR FATE SEES A FISH-MAN OF NYARL-AMEN IN THE CRYSTAL BALL.
UNLESS MY EYES DECEIVE ME, I HAVE JUST SEEN A FISH-MAN OF THE NYARL-AMEN DYNASTY OF 50,000 YEARS AGO!
ONLY I CAN PREVENT NYARL-AMEN FROM OVERRUNNING THE GLOBE- IF THAT IS WHAT HE MEANS TO DO!
NYARL-AMEN- THE WONDER WISDOM- RULED THE WORLD FROM HIS SEA CITY BENEATH THE WAVES- CRUEL AND POWERFUL- WITH MEN IN THE SEMBLANCE OF FISH TO SERVE HIM-
1.

MORE FUN COMICS No. 65

Interior, "Doctor Fate"; script, Gardner Fox; pencils and inks, Howard Sherman. March 1941. The influence of fantasy writer H. P. Lovecraft was clear in this adventure, in which Doctor Fate fights the Fish-Men of Nyarl-Amen, evocative of Nyarlathotep in one of Lovecraft's stories.

MORE FUN COMICS No. 61

Cover art, Howard Sherman, November 1940. When not fighting supernatural menaces, Doctor Fate sequestered himself in a doorless tower that only he and his beloved Inza could magically pass through.

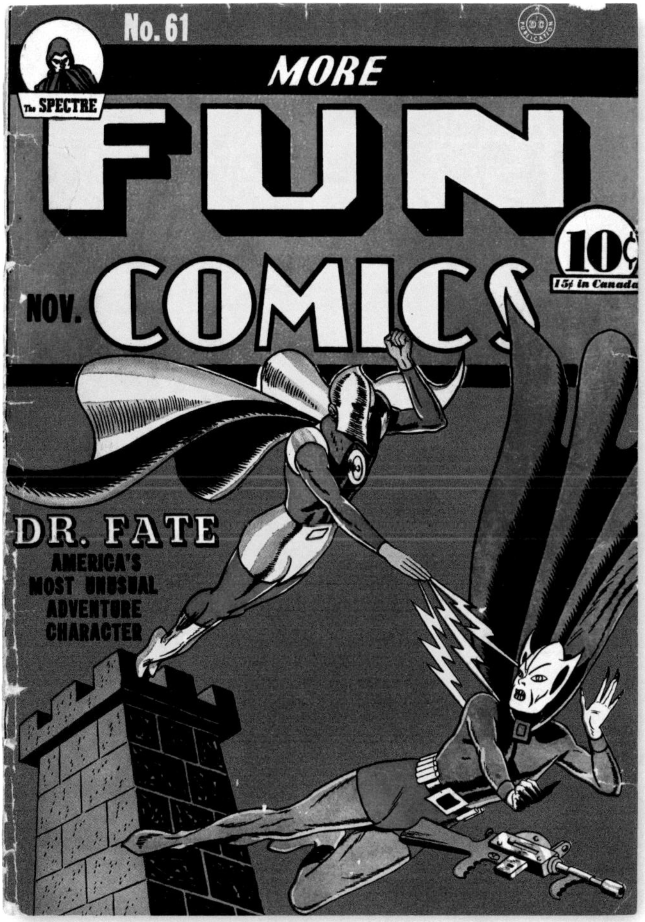
No. 61
The SPECTRE
MORE
FUN
COMICS
NOV.
10¢
15¢ in Canada
DR. FATE
AMERICA'S
MOST UNUSUAL
ADVENTURE
CHARACTER

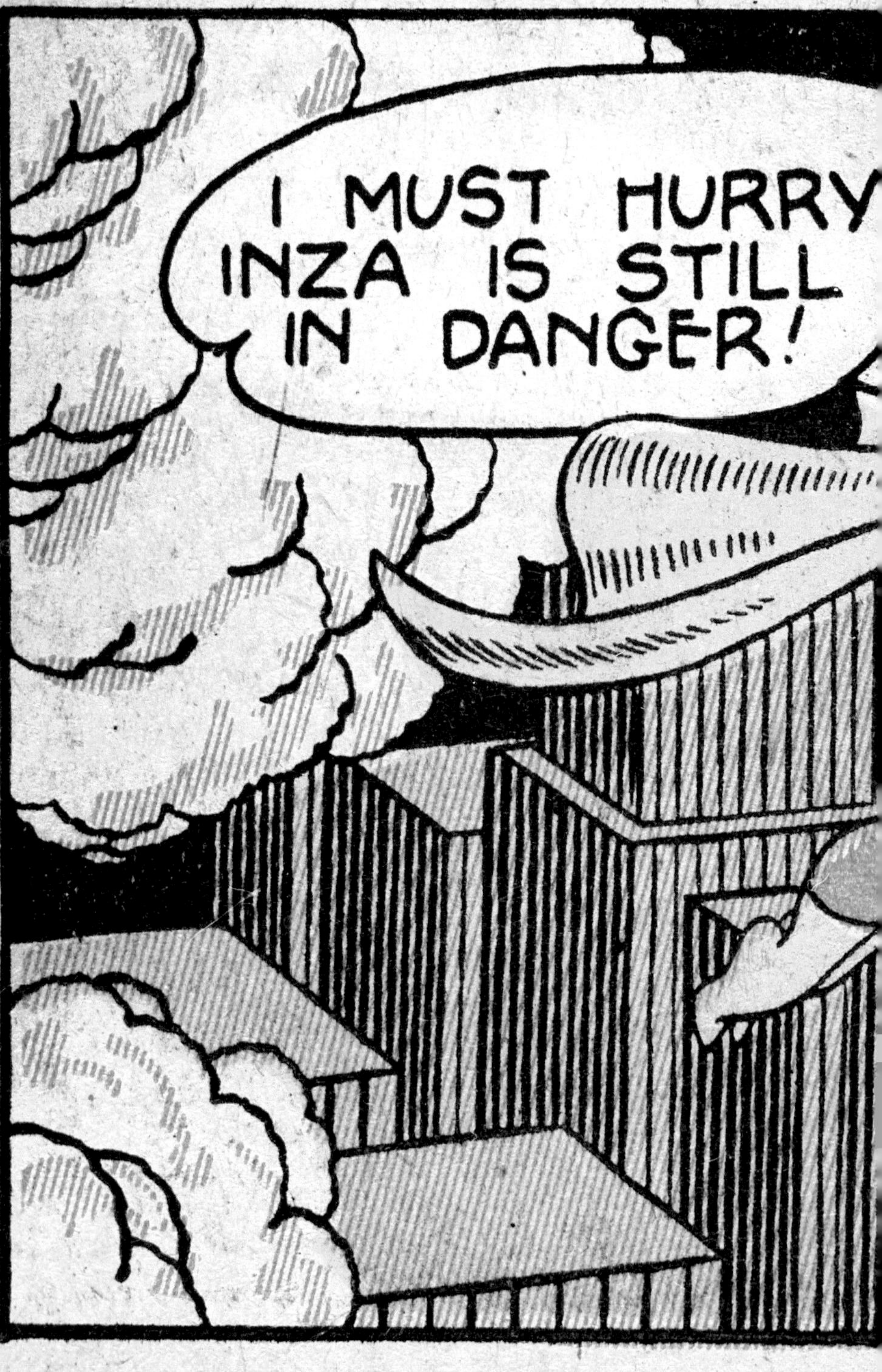
I MUST HURRY INZA IS STILL IN DANGER!

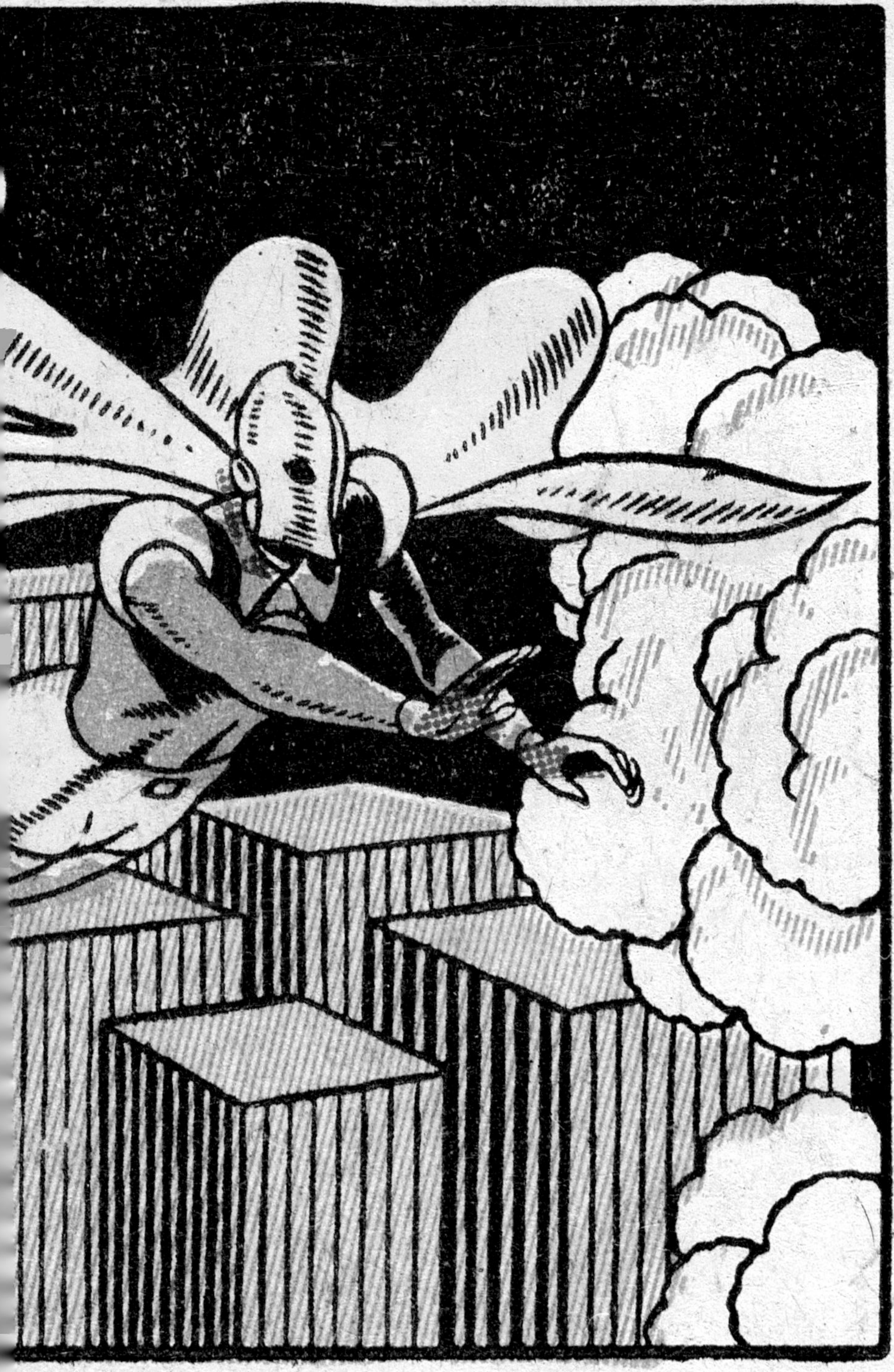

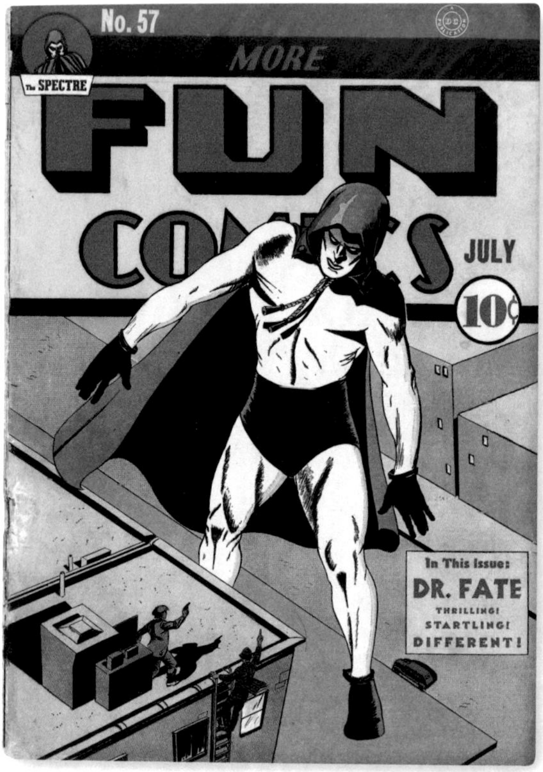
No. 57
MORE
FUN
COMICS
JULY
10¢
The SPECTRE
In This Issue:
DR. FATE
THRILLING!
STARTLING!
DIFFERENT!

ALL-STAR COMICS No. 3

PREVIOUS SPREAD: *Interior, "Doctor Fate"; script, Gardner Fox; pencils and inks, Howard Sherman. Winter 1940–1941.* Where other super heroes of the day tended to mostly confront relatively ordinary criminals, Doctor Fate clashed with menaces worthy of his supernatural power from the start. He fought a magical opposite number named Wotan and the ancient Mayan god Mayoor among others and literally went to Hell and back in his first year of existence. Howard Sherman's art gave the series a distinctive look, right down to the scalloped edges of each caption.

MORE FUN COMICS No. 57

Cover art, Bernard Baily, July 1940.

MORE FUN COMICS No. 69

Cover art, Howard Sherman, July 1941.

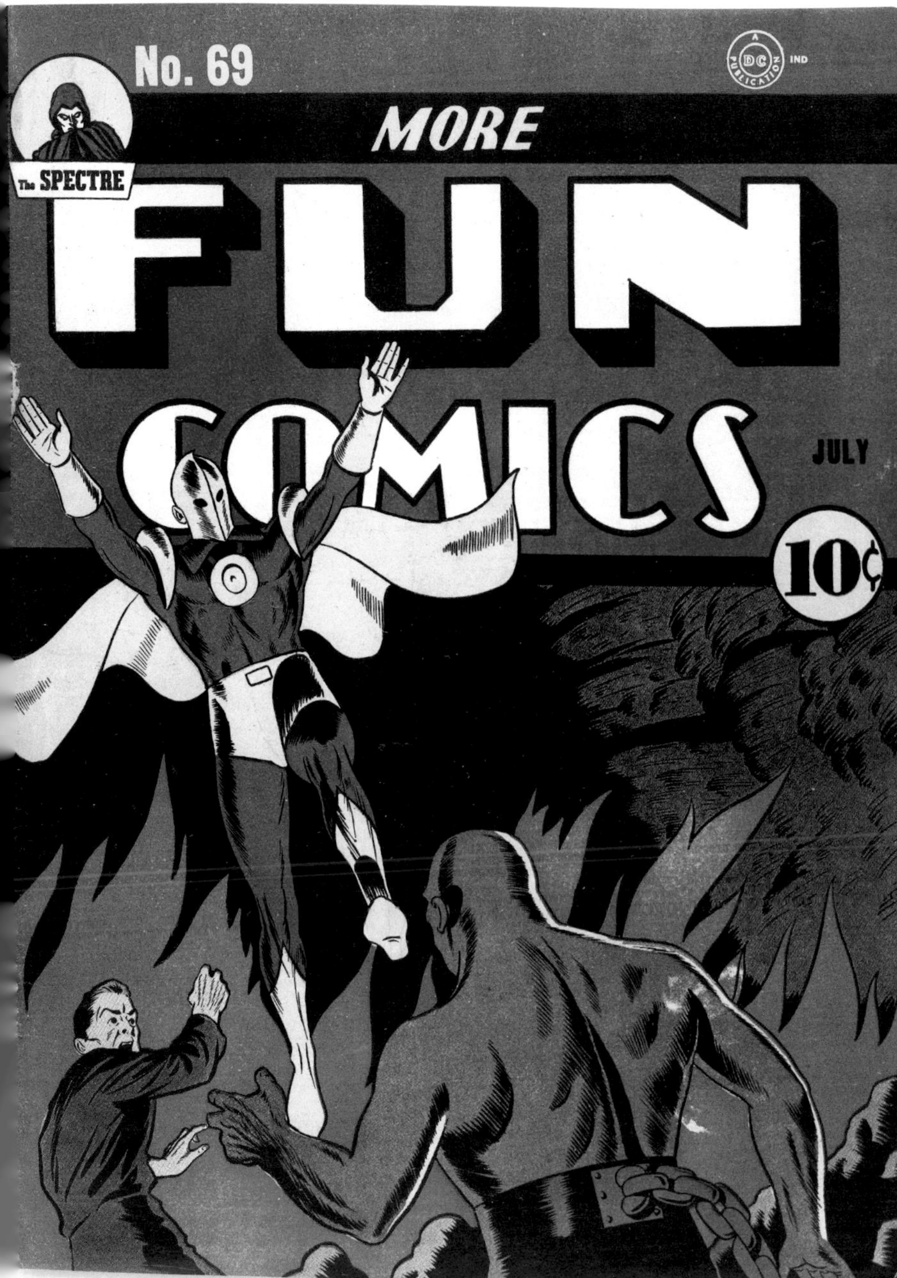
No. 69
A DC PUBLICATION
IND
MORE
FUN
COMICS
JULY
10¢
The SPECTRE

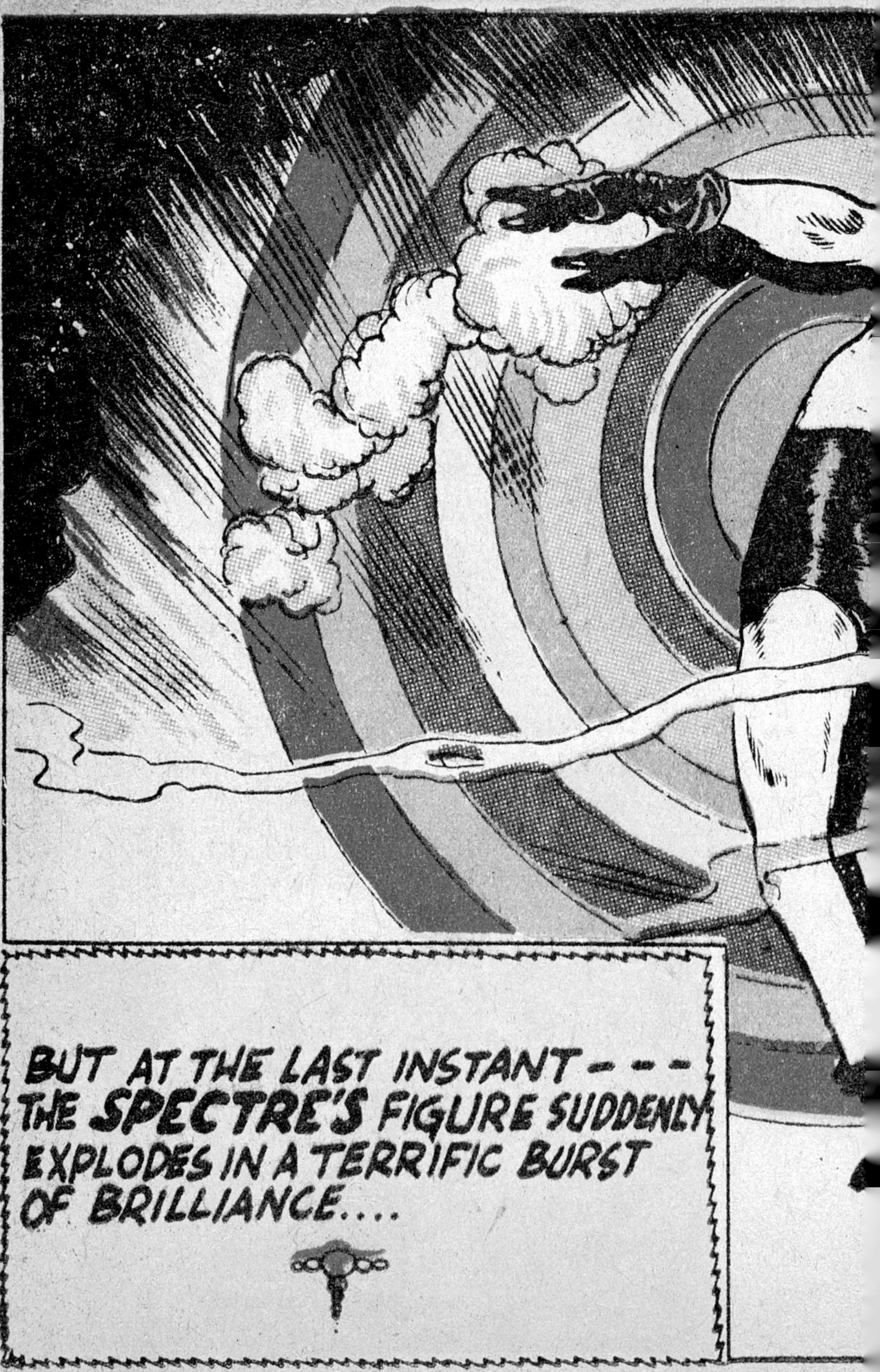
BUT AT THE LAST INSTANT---
THE SPECTRE'S FIGURE SUDDENLY EXPLODES IN A TERRIFIC BURST OF BRILLIANCE....

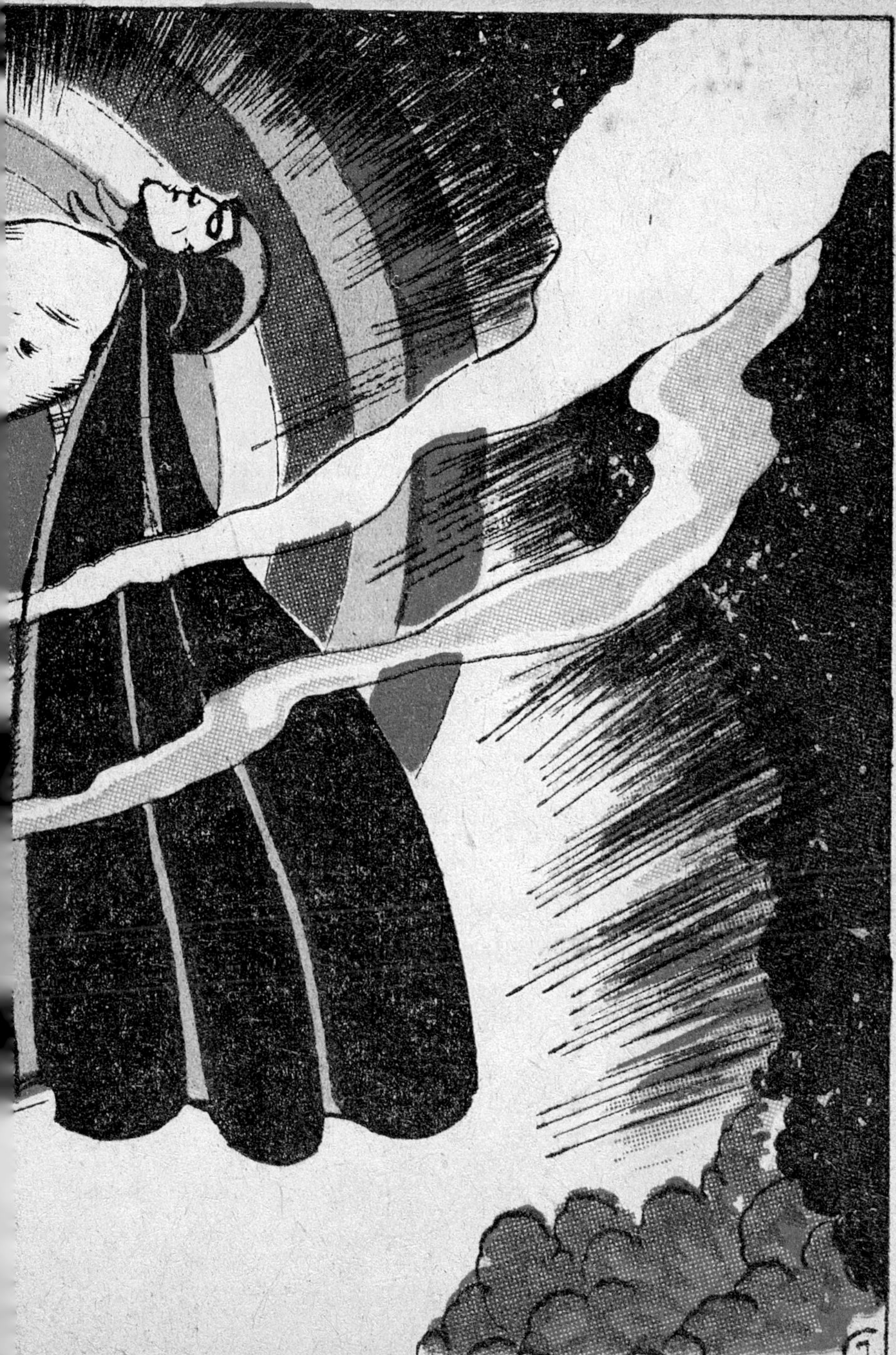
7

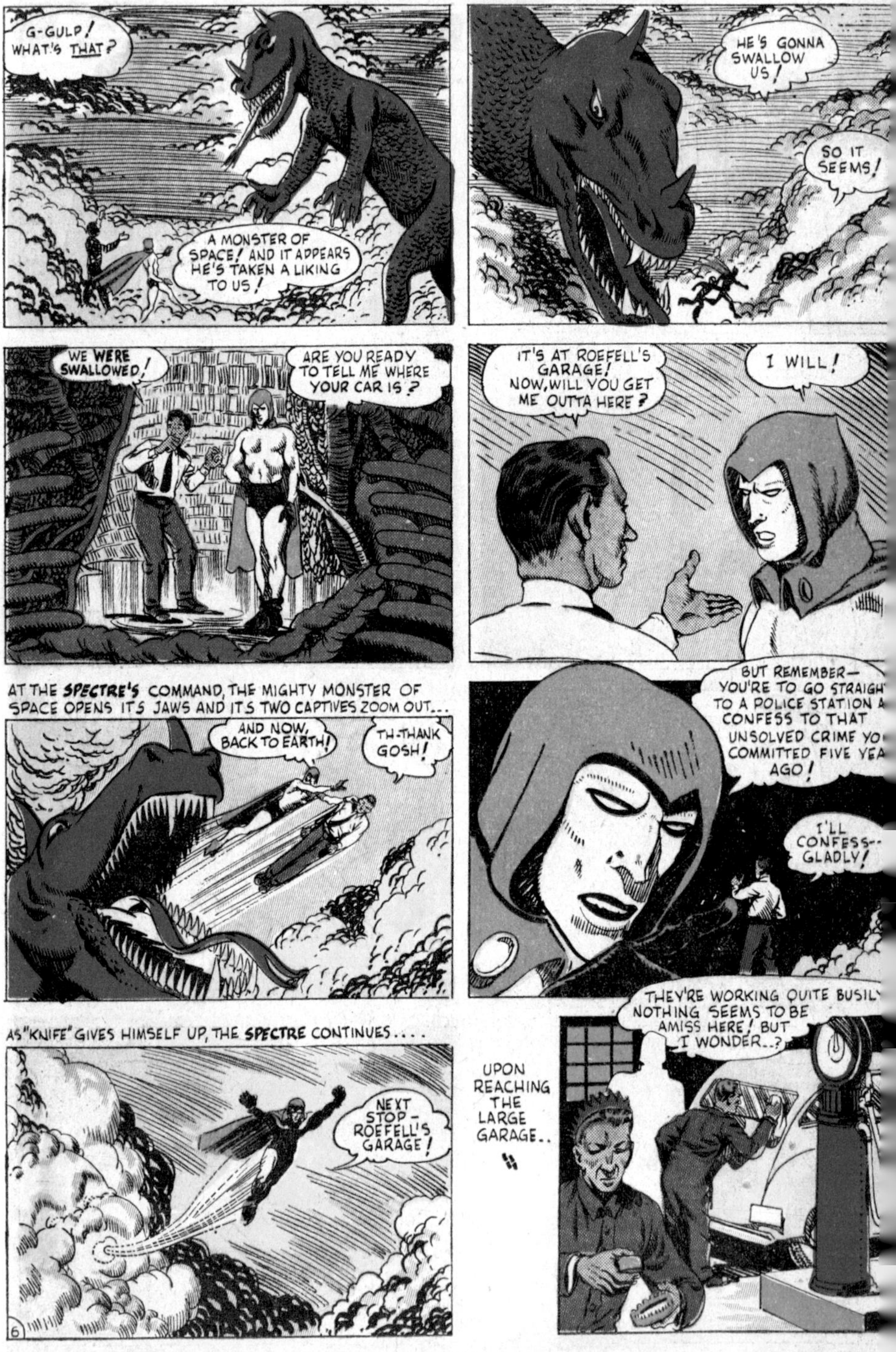
G-GULP! WHAT'S THAT?
A MONSTER OF SPACE! AND IT APPEARS HE'S TAKEN A LIKING TO US!
HE'S GONNA SWALLOW US!
SO IT SEEMS!
WE WERE SWALLOWED!
ARE YOU READY TO TELL ME WHERE YOUR CAR IS?
IT'S AT ROEFELL'S GARAGE! NOW, WILL YOU GET ME OUTTA HERE?
I WILL!
AT THE SPECTRE'S COMMAND, THE MIGHTY MONSTER OF SPACE OPENS ITS JAWS AND ITS TWO CAPTIVES ZOOM OUT...
AND NOW, BACK TO EARTH!
TH-THANK GOSH!
BUT REMEMBER— YOU'RE TO GO STRAIGH TO A POLICE STATION A CONFESS TO THAT UNSOLVED CRIME YO COMMITTED FIVE YEA AGO!
I'LL CONFESS-- GLADLY!
AS "KNIFE" GIVES HIMSELF UP, THE SPECTRE CONTINUES....
NEXT STOP - ROEFELL'S GARAGE!
UPON REACHING THE LARGE GARAGE..
THEY'RE WORKING QUITE BUSIL NOTHING SEEMS TO BE AMISS HERE! BUT I WONDER..?
6

"Badly drawn, badly written, and badly printed — a strain on young eyes and young nervous systems — the effect of these pulp-paper nightmares is that of a violent stimulant.... Unless we want a coming generation even more ferocious than the present one, parents and teachers throughout America must band together to break the 'comic' magazine."

— *CHICAGO DAILY NEWS*, MAY 8, 1940

MORE FUN COMICS No. 60

PREVIOUS SPREAD: *Interior, "The Spectre"; script, Jerry Siegel; pencils and inks, Bernard Baily. October 1940.* When the Spectre was compelled by a villain to use his awesome power against humanity, the ghostly avenger's celestial guardian stepped into break the spell.

MORE FUN COMICS No. 65

Interior, "The Spectre"; script, Jerry Siegel; pencils and inks, Bernard Baily. March 1941.

No. 64
MORE
FUN
COMICS
FEB.
10¢
The SPECTRE
BERNARD BAILY

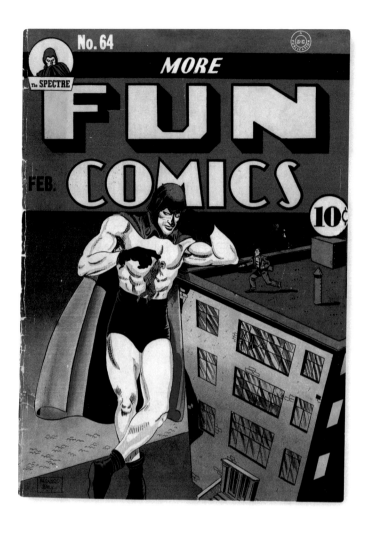

MORE FUN COMICS No. 64

Cover art, Bernard Baily, February 1941.

MORE FUN COMICS No. 54

Cover art, Bernard Baily, April 1940. The Spectre was Jerry Siegel's answer to how he was going to top Superman. When police detective Jim Corrigan was murdered, his ghost was empowered by a celestial voice to rain down vengeance on criminals. The Spectre could assume the proportions of a giant, travel in space, and inflict all manner of terrible fates to anyone who acted on the wickedness in his or her heart.

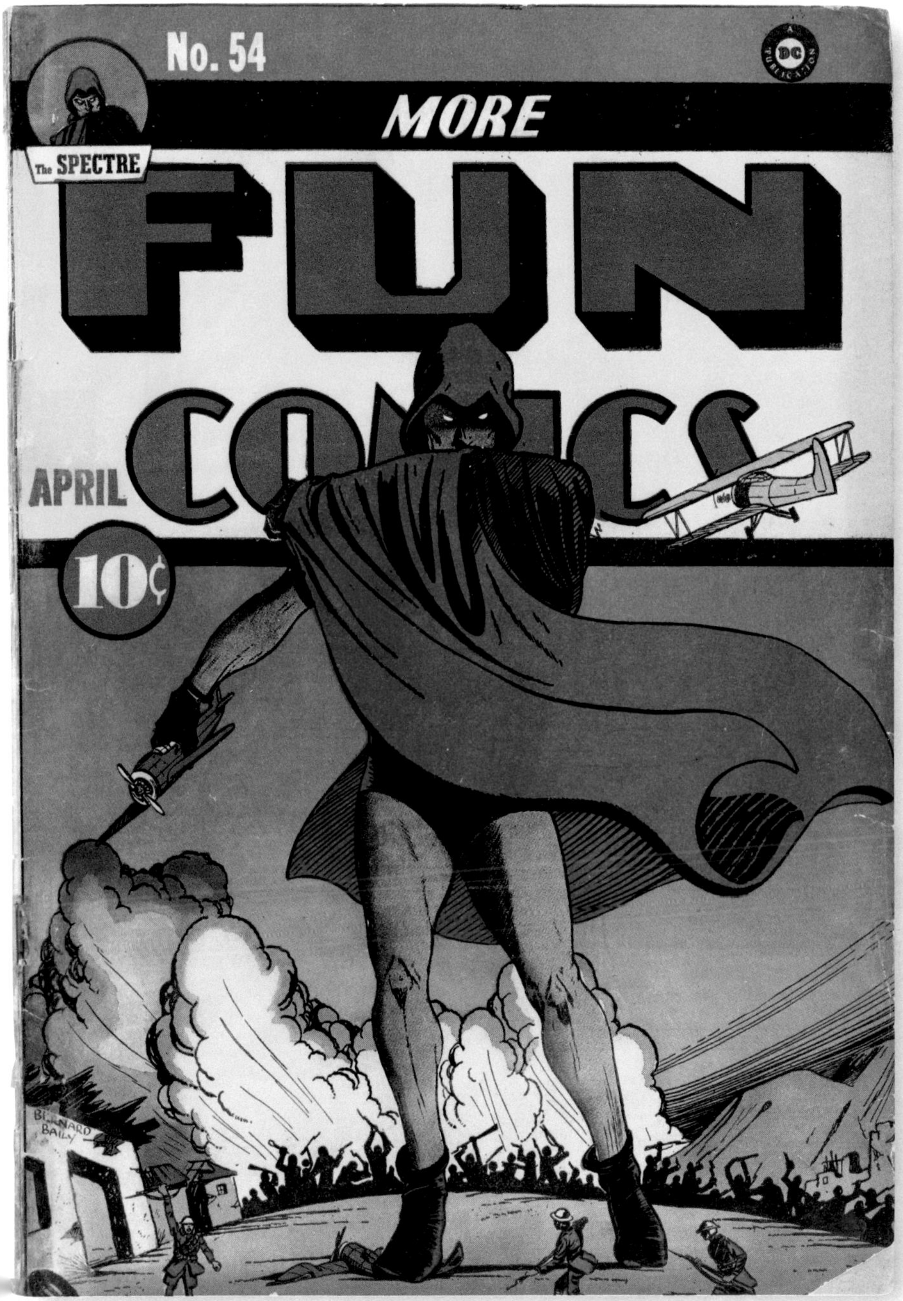
No. 54
The SPECTRE
MORE
FUN
COMICS
APRIL
10¢
BERNARD BAILY

The Flash
— FASTEST MAN ALIVE!
BY GARDNER FOX AND E·E·HIBBARD

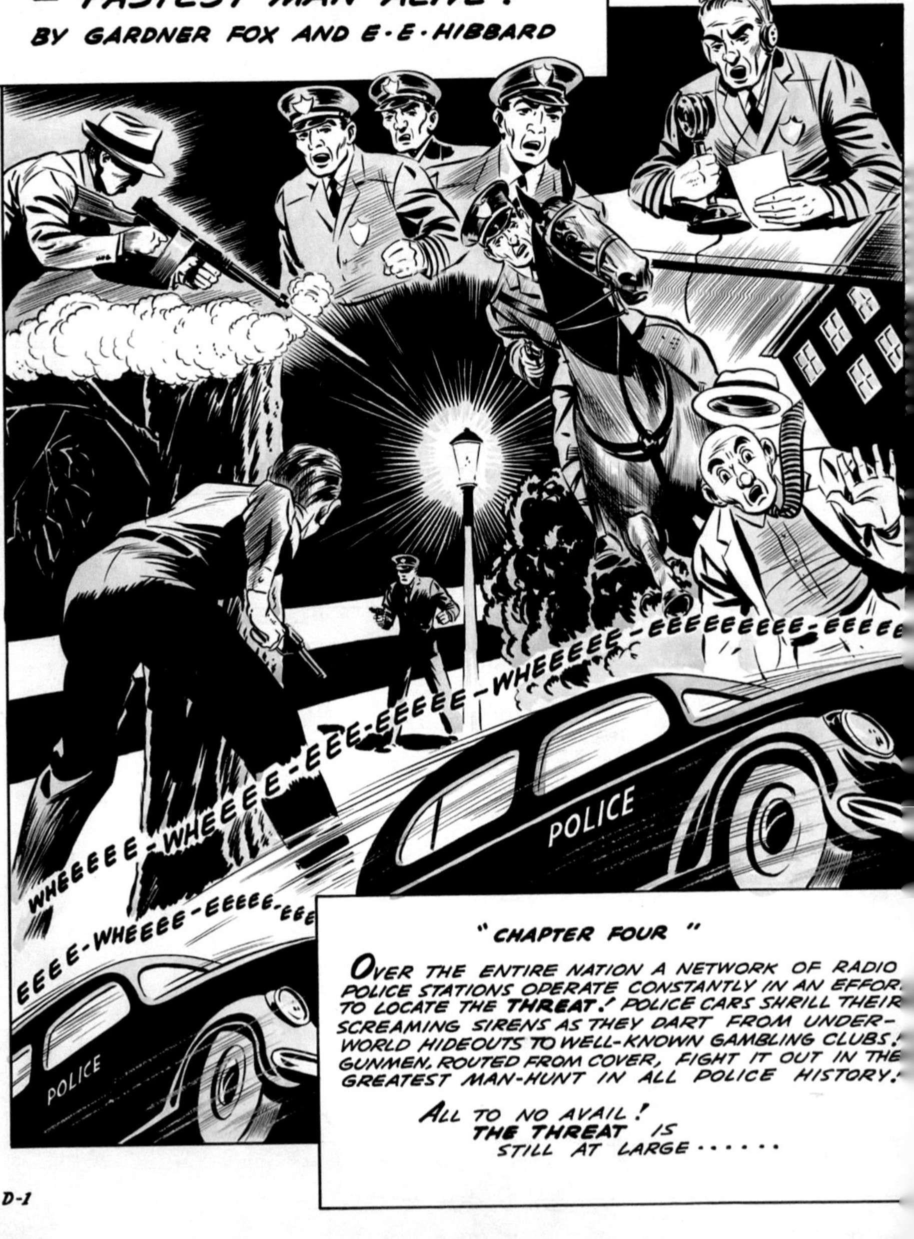

WHEEEEE-WHEEEEE-EEE-EEEEE-EEEEE-WHEEEEE-EEEEEEEEE-EEEEE
EEEE-WHEEEE-EEEEE-EEE
POLICE
POLICE
"CHAPTER FOUR"
OVER THE ENTIRE NATION A NETWORK OF RADIO POLICE STATIONS OPERATE CONSTANTLY IN AN EFFORT TO LOCATE THE THREAT! POLICE CARS SHRILL THEIR SCREAMING SIRENS AS THEY DART FROM UNDER-WORLD HIDEOUTS TO WELL-KNOWN GAMBLING CLUBS! GUNMEN, ROUTED FROM COVER, FIGHT IT OUT IN THE GREATEST MAN-HUNT IN ALL POLICE HISTORY!
ALL TO NO AVAIL! THE THREAT IS STILL AT LARGE......

ALL-FLASH COMICS No. 2

Original interior art, "Chapter Four"; script, Gardner Fox; pencils and inks, E. E. Hibbard. Fall 1941. This striking montage was a splash page from the story that introduced the villain the Threat. The actual page was printed in full color, but note the use of blue non-reproducing pencil to delineate shapes to facilitate inking.

FLASH PROMOTIONAL COMIC

Cover art, pencils and inks, Irwin Hasen, 1946. The Sultan of Speed starred in one of the earliest All-American "custom comics" (magazines produced as promotional giveaways rather than for sale at retail). This mini-version of *Flash Comics* measured 6.5 by 8.25 inches and was taped to twin packs of Wheaties cereal. In it, the Flash battled Dmane, a cosmic villain never seen in the regular comics, in a story by Gardner Fox. Johnny Thunder, the Ghost Patrol, and Hawkman were also squeezed into the tiny booklet.

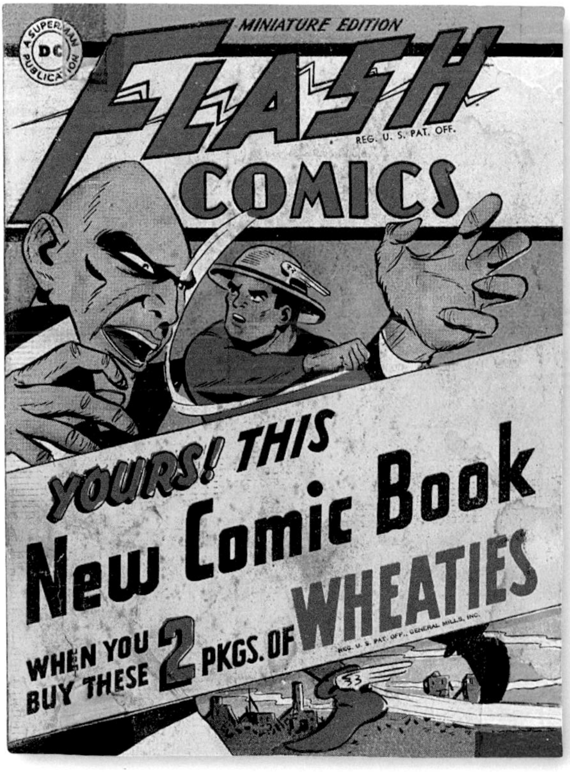
A SUPERMAN DC PUBLICATION
MINIATURE EDITION
FLASH
REG. U. S. PAT. OFF.
COMICS
YOURS! THIS
New Comic Book
WHEN YOU BUY THESE 2 PKGS. OF WHEATIES
REG. U. S. PAT. OFF., GENERAL MILLS, INC.

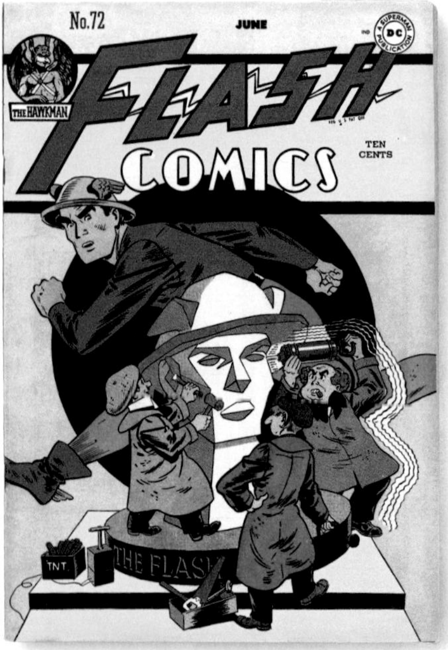
No.72
JUNE
FLASH
COMICS
TEN CENTS
THE HAWKMAN
TNT.
THE FLASH

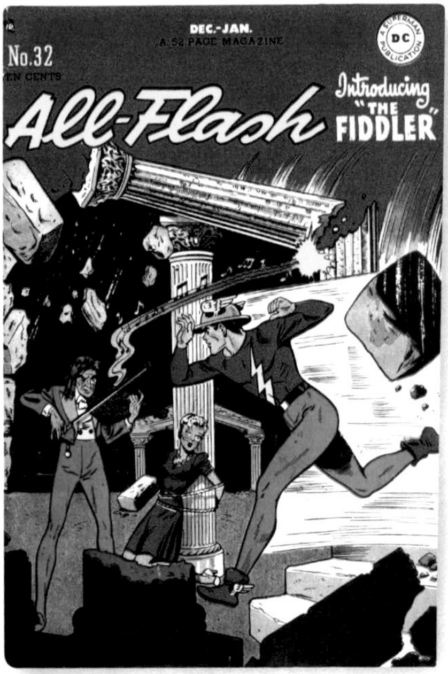
DEC.-JAN.
A 52 PAGE MAGAZINE
No.32
All-Flash
Introducing "THE FIDDLER"

FLASH COMICS No. 72

Cover art, pencils and inks, E. E. Hibbard, June 1947. A staple of 1940s comics starring long-suffering super heroes was the well-meaning but comically bumbling sidekick. Plastic Man was stuck with Woozy Winks, and the first Green Lantern had to put up with Doiby Dickles. But the poor Flash had three such stooges to contend with — Winky, Blinky, and Noddy — here bedeviling their hero on a cover.

ALL-FLASH No. 32

Cover art, Lee Elias and Moe Worthman, December 1947–January 1948.

ALL-FLASH No. 6

Cover art, E. E. Hibbard, September–October 1942.

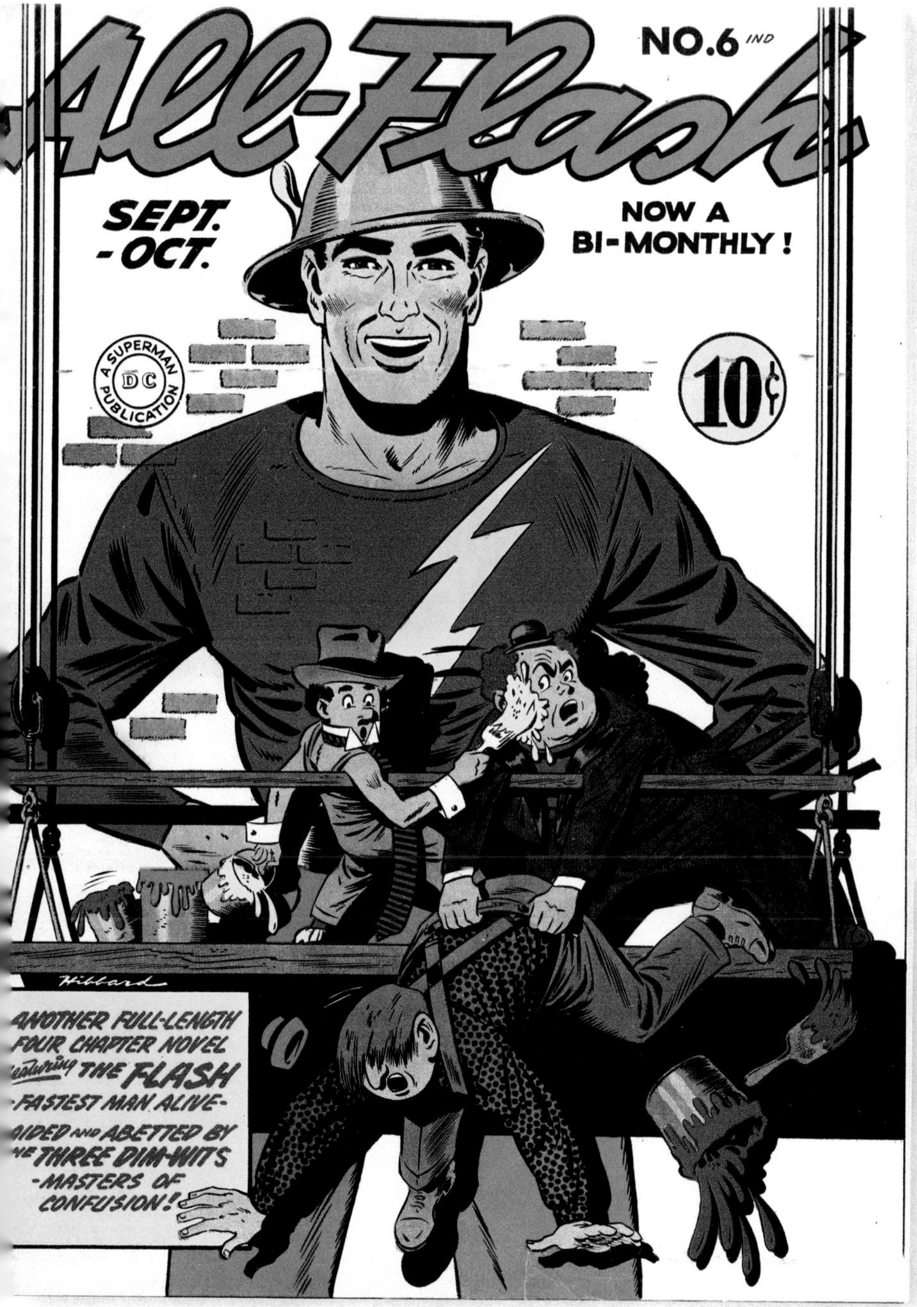
All-Flash
NO.6 IND
SEPT.
-OCT.
NOW A
BI-MONTHLY!
A SUPERMAN DC PUBLICATION
10¢
Hibbard
ANOTHER FULL-LENGTH
FOUR CHAPTER NOVEL
THE FLASH
-FASTEST MAN ALIVE-
AND ABETTED BY
THREE DIM-WITS
-MASTERS OF
CONFUSION!

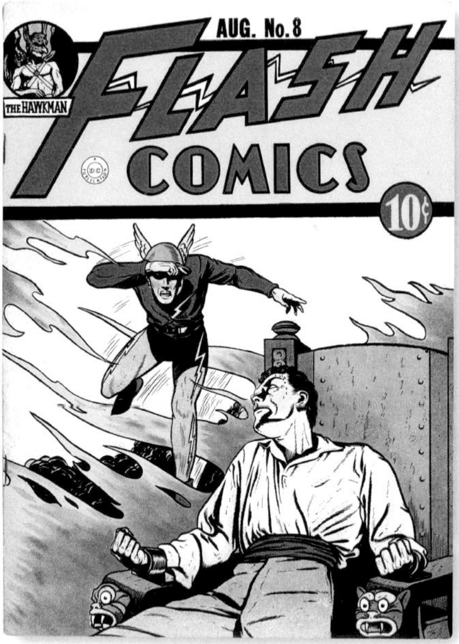
AUG. No. 8
THE HAWKMAN
FLASH
COMICS
10¢

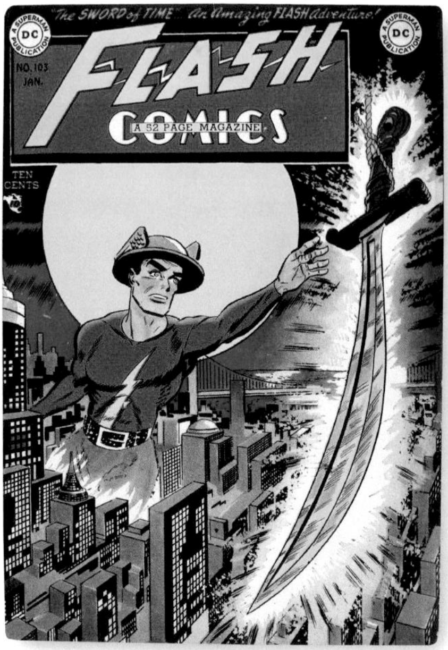
"The SWORD of TIME" An Amazing FLASH Adventure!
A SUPERMAN DC PUBLICATION
NO. 103
JAN.
FLASH
COMICS
A 52 PAGE MAGAZINE
TEN CENTS

FLASH COMICS No. 8

Cover art, Sheldon Moldoff, August 1940.

FLASH COMICS No. 103

Cover art, Carmine Infantino. January 1949. Although the comic book bore his name, the Flash graciously alternated covers with his co-star Hawkman. This was the final issue to feature the Scarlet Speedster on the cover.

FLASH COMICS No. 97

Cover art, Irwin Hasen, July 1948. A story with a sequence depicting a nightmare plaguing the Flash's girlfriend gave the feature's artists a rare opportunity to experiment with surrealism.

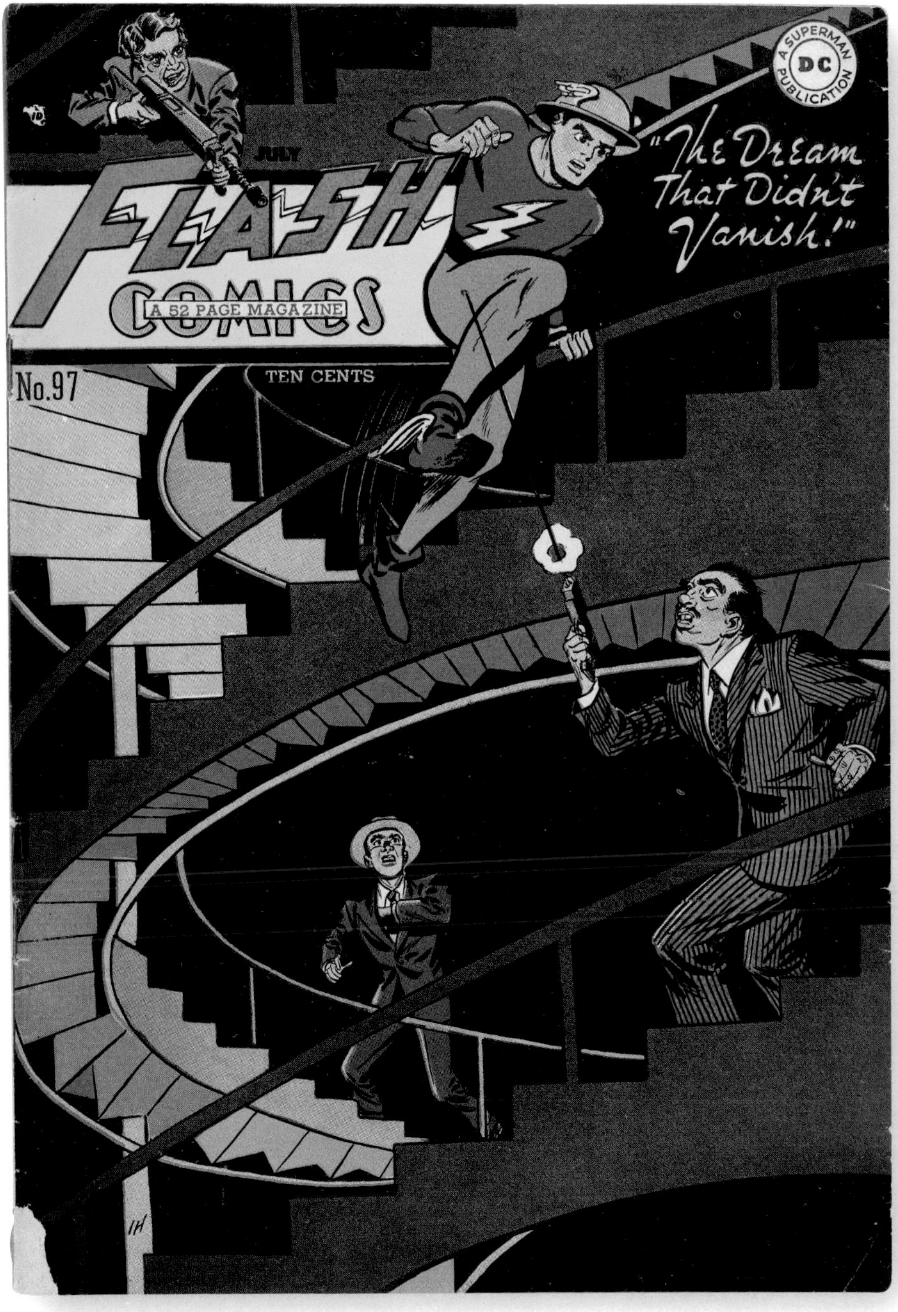

A SUPERMAN DC PUBLICATION
JULY
FLASH COMICS
A 52 PAGE MAGAZINE
No.97
TEN CENTS
"The Dream That Didn't Vanish!"

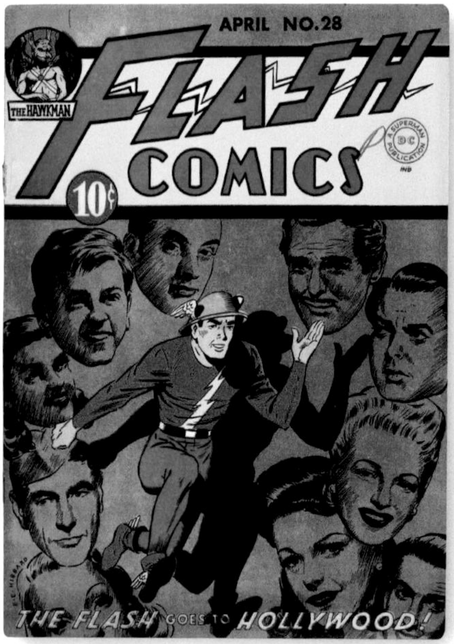
APRIL NO. 28
THE HAWKMAN
FLASH
COMICS
10¢
A SUPERMAN DC PUBLICATION
THE FLASH GOES TO HOLLYWOOD!

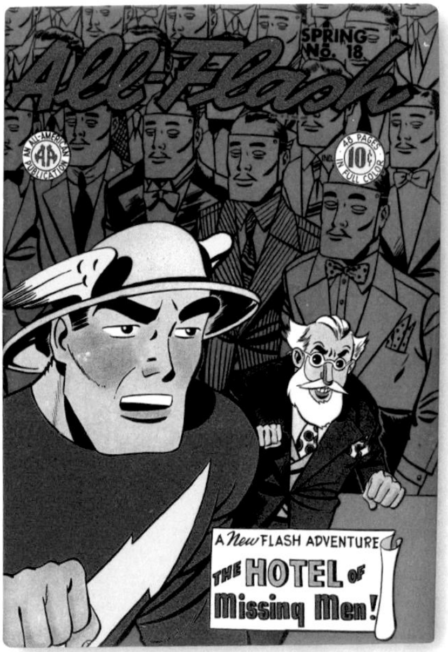
SPRING No. 18
All-Flash
AN ALL-AMERICAN PUBLICATION
AA
48 PAGES IN FULL COLOR
10¢
A New FLASH ADVENTURE
THE HOTEL of Missing Men!

FLASH COMICS No. 28

Cover art, E.E. Hibbard, April 1942.

ALL-FLASH No. 18

Cover art, Martin Naydel, Spring 1945.

FLASH COMICS No. 104

Interior, "The Rival Flash"; script, John Broome; pencils, Carmine Infantino; inks, Bernard Sachs. February 1949. Coming full circle in the final issue of his comic book, the Flash faced a rival speedster with ties to the accident that gave him his superpowers.

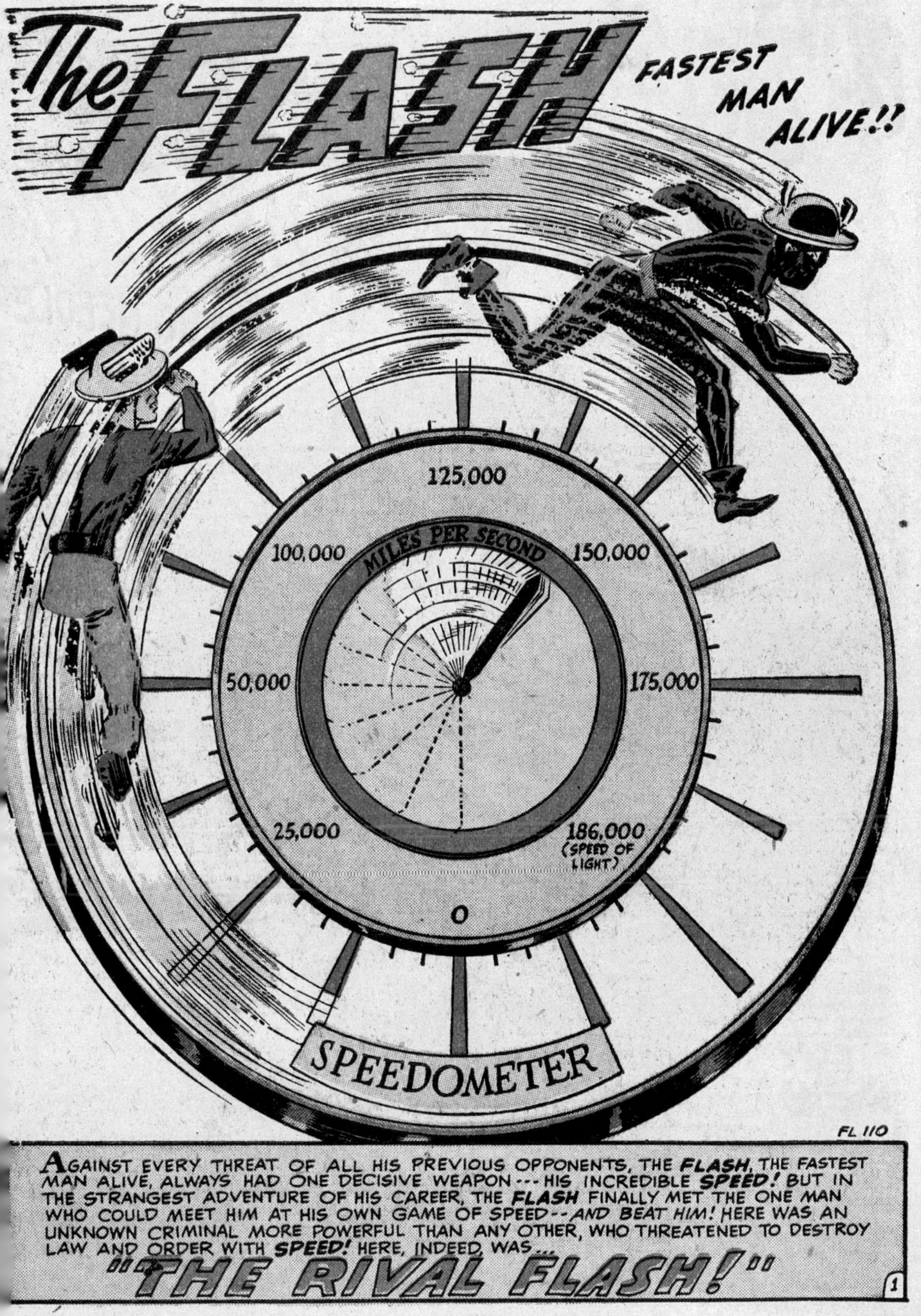
A SUPERMAN DC PUBLICATION
A SUPERMAN DC PUBLICATION
The FLASH
FASTEST MAN ALIVE!!
125,000
100,000
MILES PER SECOND
150,000
50,000
175,000
25,000
186,000 (SPEED OF LIGHT)
0
SPEEDOMETER
FL 110
AGAINST EVERY THREAT OF ALL HIS PREVIOUS OPPONENTS, THE FLASH, THE FASTEST MAN ALIVE, ALWAYS HAD ONE DECISIVE WEAPON --- HIS INCREDIBLE SPEED! BUT IN THE STRANGEST ADVENTURE OF HIS CAREER, THE FLASH FINALLY MET THE ONE MAN WHO COULD MEET HIM AT HIS OWN GAME OF SPEED -- AND BEAT HIM! HERE WAS AN UNKNOWN CRIMINAL MORE POWERFUL THAN ANY OTHER, WHO THREATENED TO DESTROY LAW AND ORDER WITH SPEED! HERE, INDEED, WAS...
"THE RIVAL FLASH!"
1

O LOBINHO No. 10

Interior, "The Flash"; script, Gardner Fox; art, E.E. Hibbard. Ca. 1941. The Flash became Joel Ciclone in this Brazilian reprint from *Flash Comics* No. 8.

FLASH COMICS No. 37

Cover art, Sheldon Moldoff, January 1943. Hawkman and Hawkgirl were inspired by the visuals of the hawk-men in Alex Raymond's "Flash Gordon" comic strip, but they became unique characters in their own right.

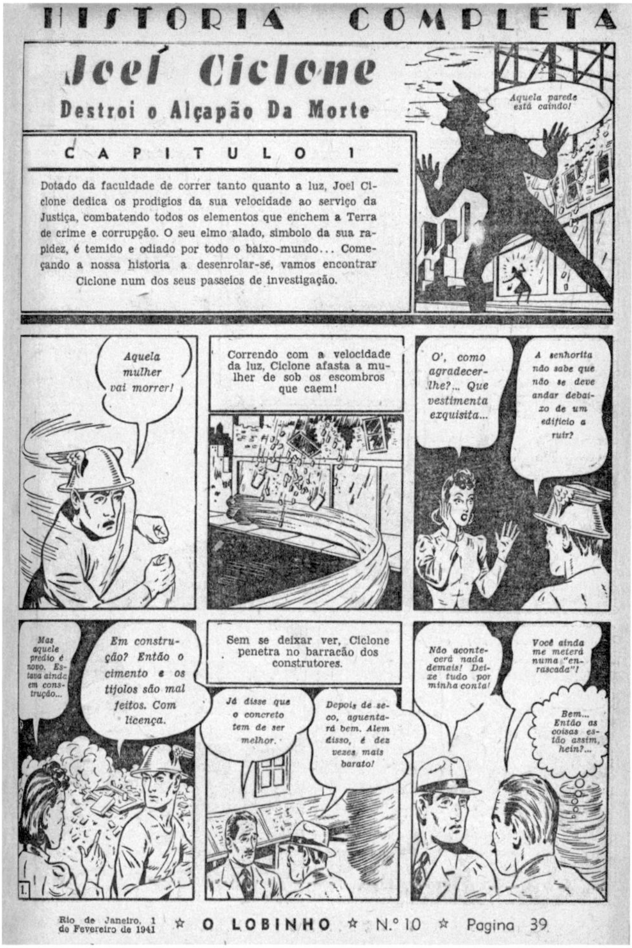
HISTORIA COMPLETA
Joel Ciclone
Destroi o Alçapão Da Morte
Aquela parede está caindo!
CAPITULO 1
Dotado da faculdade de correr tanto quanto a luz, Joel Ciclone dedica os prodigios da sua velocidade ao serviço da Justiça, combatendo todos os elementos que enchem a Terra de crime e corrupção. O seu elmo alado, simbolo da sua rapidez, é temido e odiado por todo o baixo-mundo... Começando a nossa historia a desenrolar-se, vamos encontrar Ciclone num dos seus passeios de investigação.
Aquela mulher vai morrer!
Correndo com a velocidade da luz, Ciclone afasta a mulher de sob os escombros que caem!
O', como agradecer-lhe?... Que vestimenta exquisita...
A senhorita não sabe que não se deve andar debaixo de um edificio a ruir?
Mas aquele predio é novo. Estava ainda em construção...
Em construção? Então o cimento e os tijolos são mal feitos. Com licença.
Sem se deixar ver, Ciclone penetra no barracão dos construtores.
Já disse que o concreto tem de ser melhor.
Depois de seco, aguentará bem. Alem disso, é dez vezes mais barato!
Não acontecerá nada demais! Deixe tudo por minha conta!
Você ainda me meterá numa "enrascada"!
Bem... Então as coisas estão assim, hein?...
Rio de Janeiro, 1 de Fevereiro de 1941 ☆ O LOBINHO ☆ N.º 10 ☆ Pagina 39

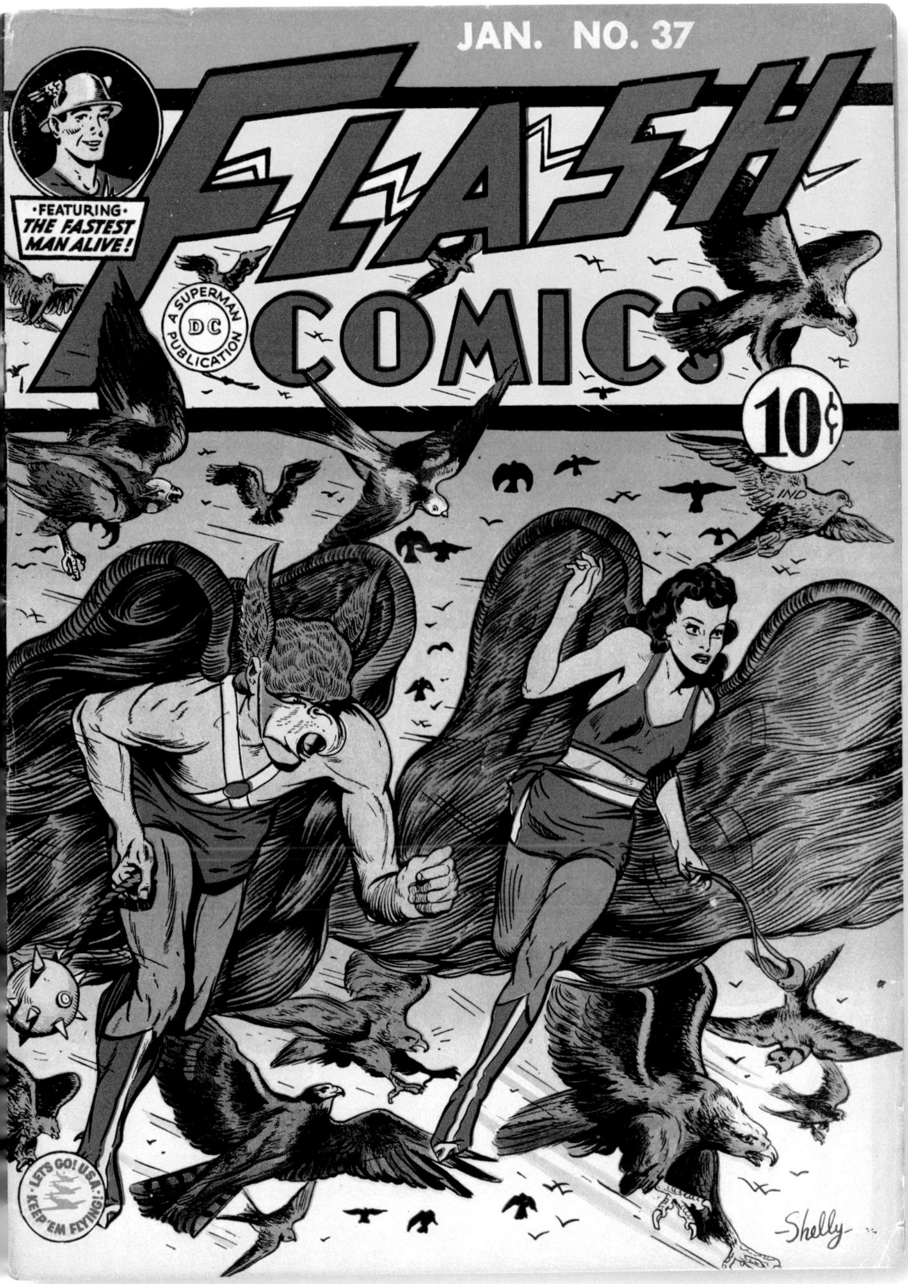

JAN. NO. 37
FLASH
COMICS
·FEATURING·
THE FASTEST
MAN ALIVE!
A SUPERMAN
DC
PUBLICATION
10¢
LET'S GO! U.S.A.
KEEP 'EM FLYING!
-Shelly-

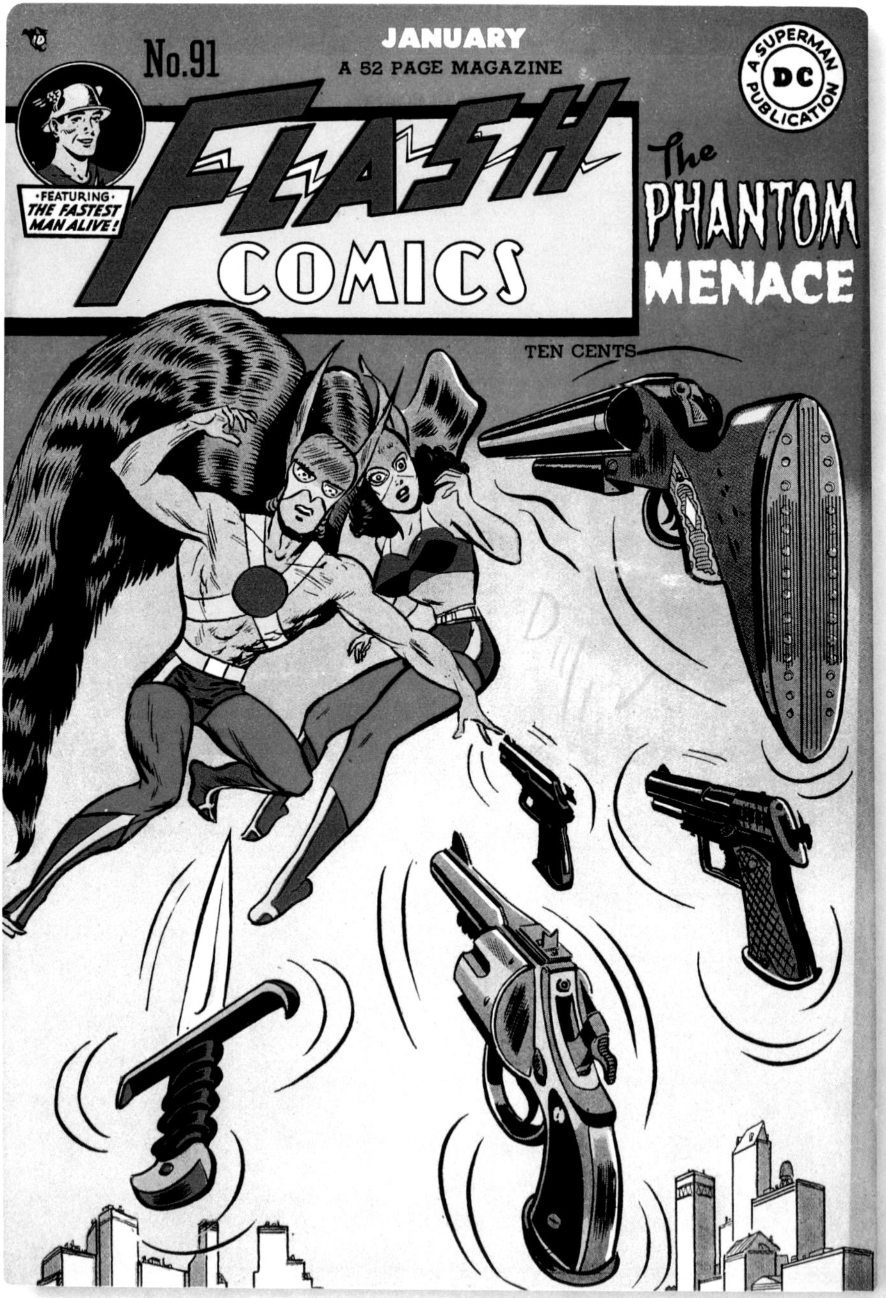
No. 91
JANUARY
A 52 PAGE MAGAZINE
A SUPERMAN PUBLICATION
DC
FLASH
COMICS
·FEATURING·
THE FASTEST MAN ALIVE!
The PHANTOM MENACE
TEN CENTS

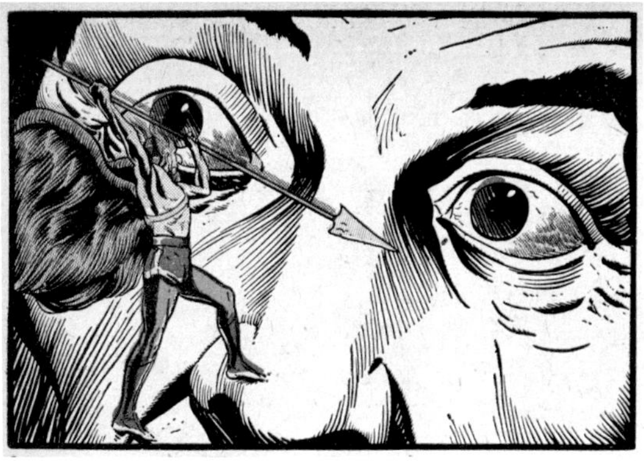

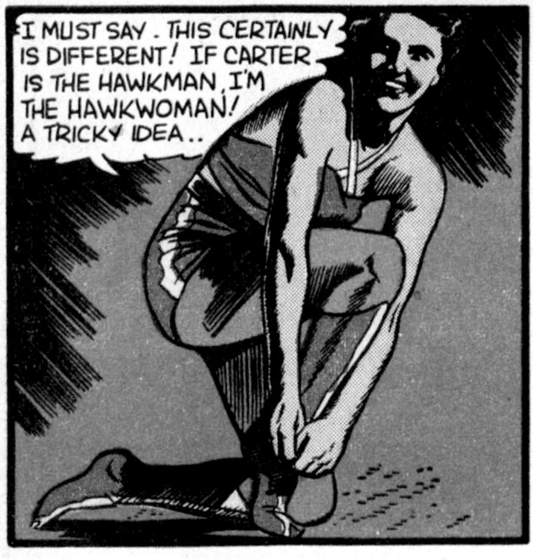
I MUST SAY . THIS CERTAINLY IS DIFFERENT! IF CARTER IS THE HAWKMAN, I'M THE HAWKWOMAN! A TRICKY IDEA..

FLASH COMICS No. 91
Cover art, Joe Kubert, January 1948. Joe Kubert was the last artist to draw the Hawkman feature in the 1940s and the first to illustrate its revival in the 1960s.

FLASH COMICS No. 91
Interior, "Hawkman"; script, Gardner Fox; art, Sheldon Moldoff. September 1941. A fan of pulp horror, writer Gardner Fox conceived a variety of monstrosities to threaten Hawkman, including a mad albino giant from Neptune.

FLASH COMICS No. 24
Interior, "Hawkman"; script, Gardner Fox; art, Sheldon Moldoff. December 1941. Although she initially called herself the Hawkwoman, Shiera Sanders soon succumbed to the conventions of the 1940s and became known as Hawkgirl.

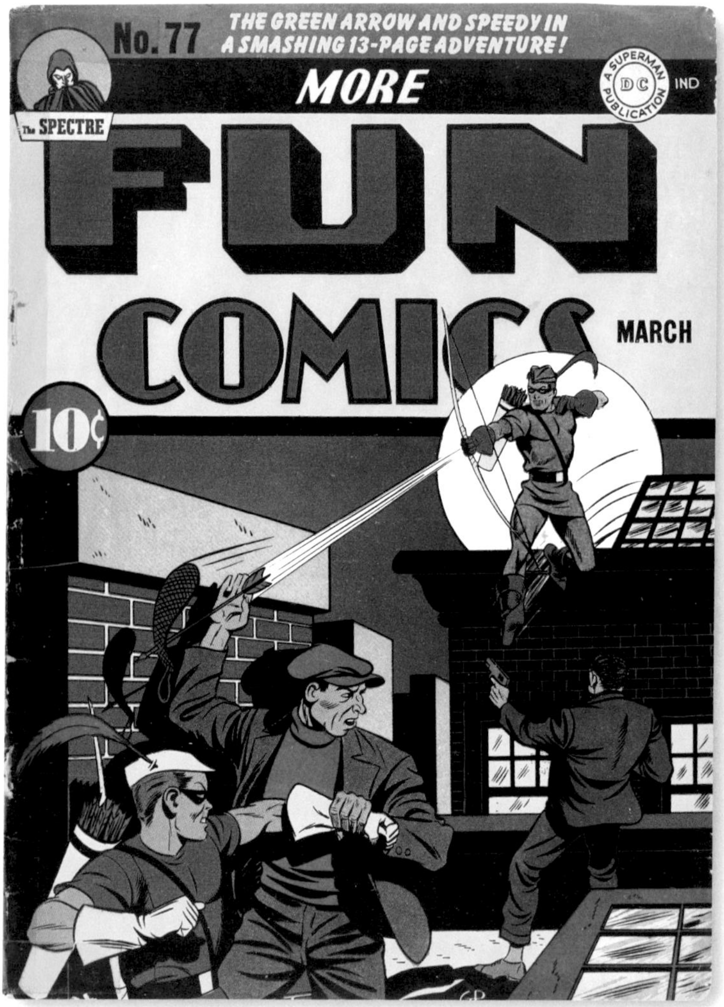
No. 77
THE GREEN ARROW AND SPEEDY IN
A SMASHING 13-PAGE ADVENTURE!
MORE
FUN
COMICS
The SPECTRE
A SUPERMAN DC PUBLICATION
IND
MARCH
10¢

MORE FUN COMICS No. 77
Cover art, George Papp, March 1942.

COMIC BOOK ROW
Photograph, July, ca. 1955. Scenes like this one, shot in the comics aisle of a New Orleans, Louisiana, drugstore, inspired many a retailer to snap, "Hey, kid, this ain't a library!"

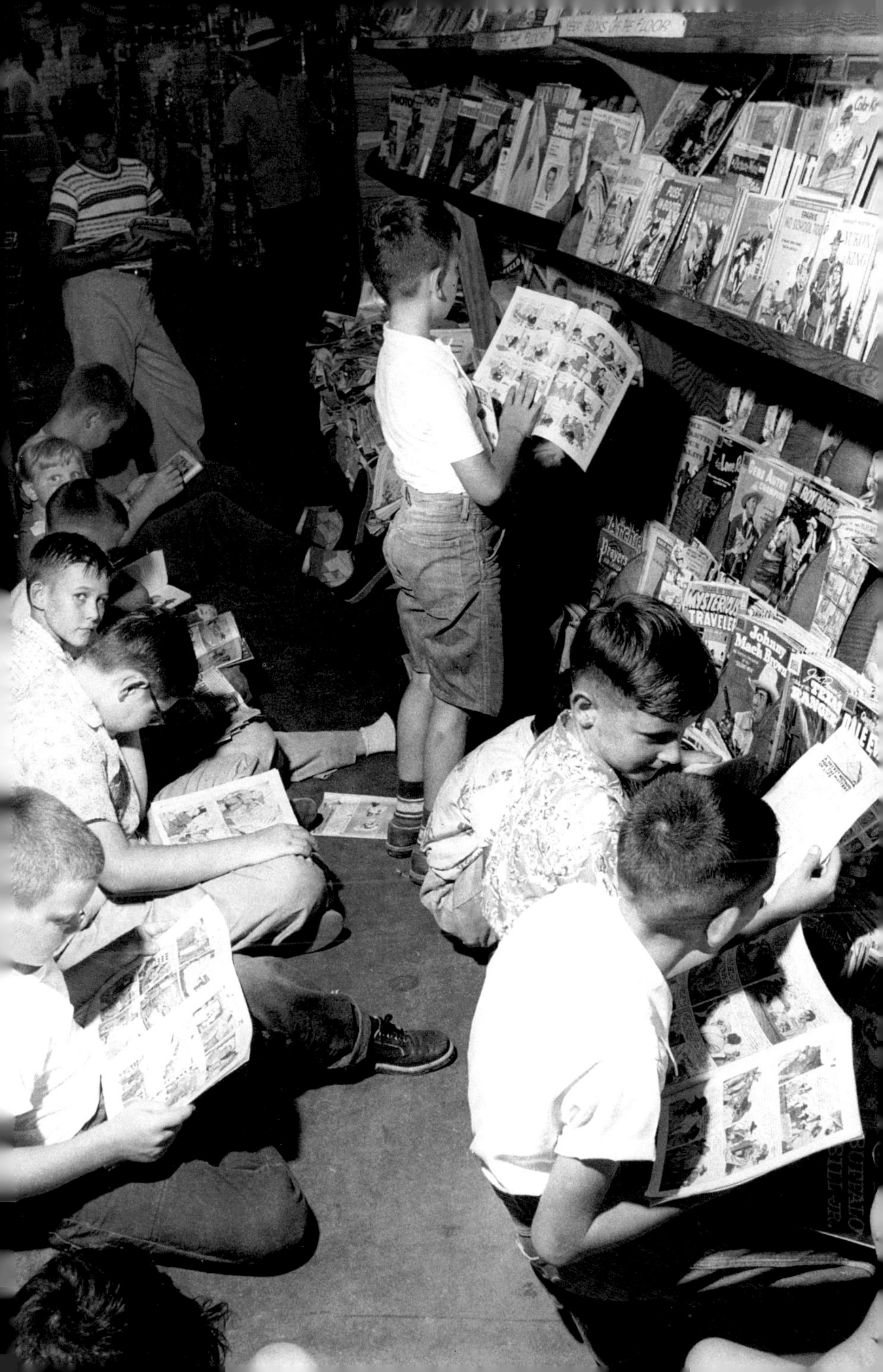
PHOTO
Johnny Mack Brown
Gene Autry
Archie
BUFFALO BILL JR.

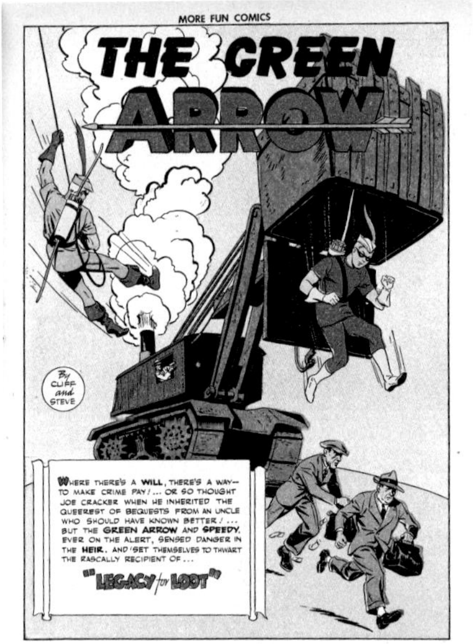
MORE FUN COMICS
THE GREEN ARROW
By CLIFF and STEVE
WHERE THERE'S A WILL, THERE'S A WAY— TO MAKE CRIME PAY! ... OR SO THOUGHT JOE CRACKER WHEN HE INHERITED THE QUEEREST OF BEQUESTS FROM AN UNCLE WHO SHOULD HAVE KNOWN BETTER! ... BUT THE GREEN ARROW AND SPEEDY, EVER ON THE ALERT, SENSED DANGER IN THE HEIR, AND SET THEMSELVES TO THWART THE RASCALLY RECIPIENT OF ...
"LEGACY for LOOT"

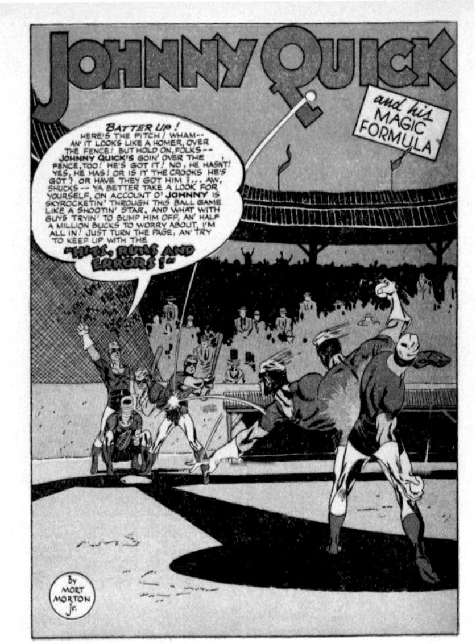
JOHNNY QUICK
and his MAGIC FORMULA
BATTER UP! HERE'S THE PITCH! WHAM-- AN' IT LOOKS LIKE A HOMER, OVER THE FENCE! BUT HOLD ON, FOLKS-- JOHNNY QUICK'S GOIN' OVER THE FENCE, TOO! HE'S GOT IT! NO, HE HASN'T! YES, HE HAS! OR IS IT THE CROOKS HE'S GOT? OR HAVE THEY GOT HIM ?... AW, SHUCKS-- YA BETTER TAKE A LOOK FOR YOURSELF, ON ACCOUNT O' JOHNNY IS SKYROCKETIN' THROUGH THIS BALL GAME LIKE A SHOOTIN' STAR, AND WHAT WITH GUYS TRYIN' TO BUMP HIM OFF, AN' HALF A MILLION BUCKS TO WORRY ABOUT, I'M ALL IN! JUST TURN THE PAGE, AN' TRY TO KEEP UP WITH THE "HITS, RUNS AND ERRORS!"
By MORT MORTON Jr.

MORE FUN COMICS No. 92

Interior, "Legacy for Loot"; script, unknown; pencils, Cliff Young; inks, Steve Brodie. July–August 1943.

MORE FUN COMICS No. 92

Interior, "Hits, Runs, and Errors"; script, unknown; pencils and inks, Mort Meskin (as Mort Morton Jr.). July–August 1943.

All-American's Flash was the preeminent speedster in comic books, but Mort Weisinger reasoned that DC needed one, too. Johnny Quick was the end result, enlivened considerably by Mort Meskin's energetic depiction of the superfast hero in action. Weisinger kept Johnny's feature running through 1954, six years after *Flash Comics* was canceled.

MORE FUN COMICS No. 85

Cover art, George Papp, November 1942.

ADVENTURE COMICS No. 48

*Cover art, Bernard Baily, March 1940.*Using a drug called Miraclo to alter his meek personality and enhance his strength, the Hour-Man briefly held the role of *Adventure Comics*' cover star.

ALL-AMERICAN COMICS No. 25

Interior, "Dr. Mid-Nite"; script, Charles Reizenstein; pencils and inks, Stan Aschmeier. April 1941.

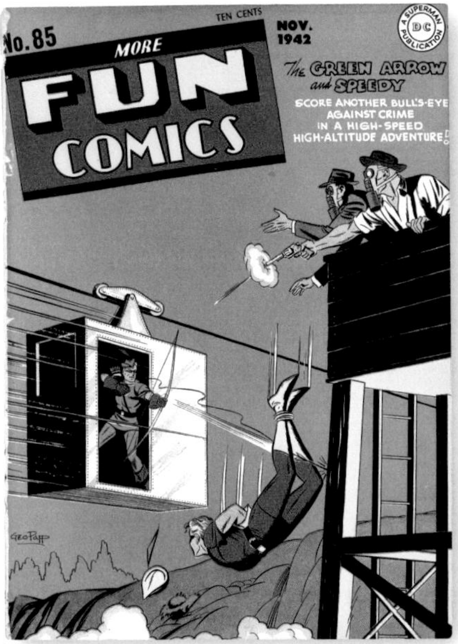
TEN CENTS
No.85
MORE FUN COMICS
NOV. 1942
The GREEN ARROW and SPEEDY
SCORE ANOTHER BULL'S-EYE AGAINST CRIME IN A HIGH-SPEED HIGH-ALTITUDE ADVENTURE!

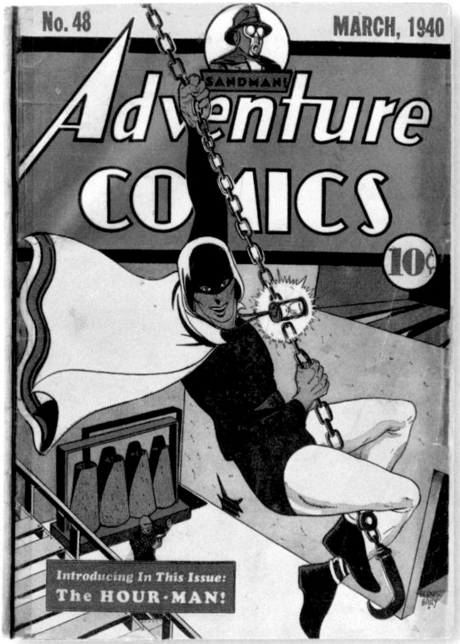
No. 48
MARCH, 1940
SANDMAN!
Adventure COMICS
10¢
Introducing In This Issue:
The HOUR-MAN!

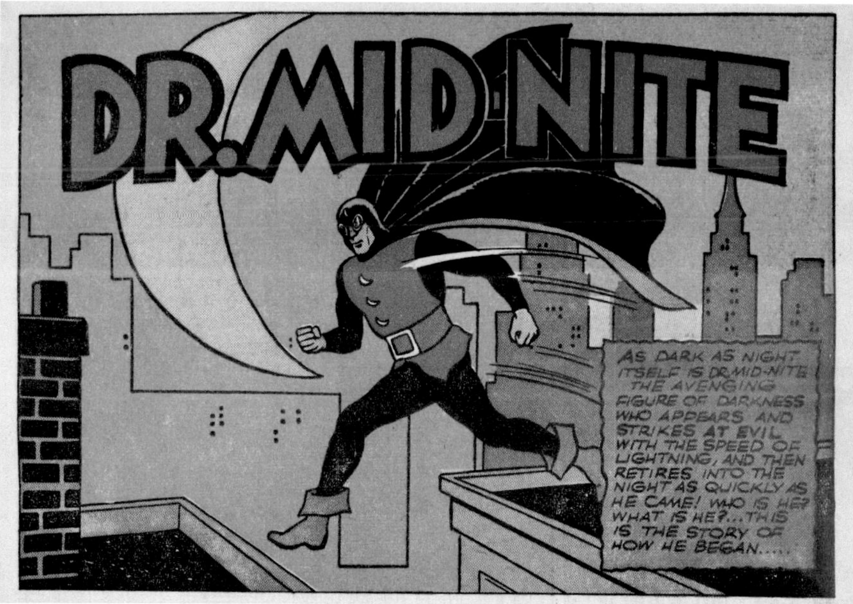
DR. MID-NITE
AS DARK AS NIGHT ITSELF IS DR. MID-NITE THE AVENGING FIGURE OF DARKNESS WHO APPEARS AND STRIKES AT EVIL WITH THE SPEED OF LIGHTNING, AND THEN RETIRES INTO THE NIGHT AS QUICKLY AS HE CAME! WHO IS HE? WHAT IS HE?... THIS IS THE STORY OF HOW HE BEGAN.....

AQUAMAN

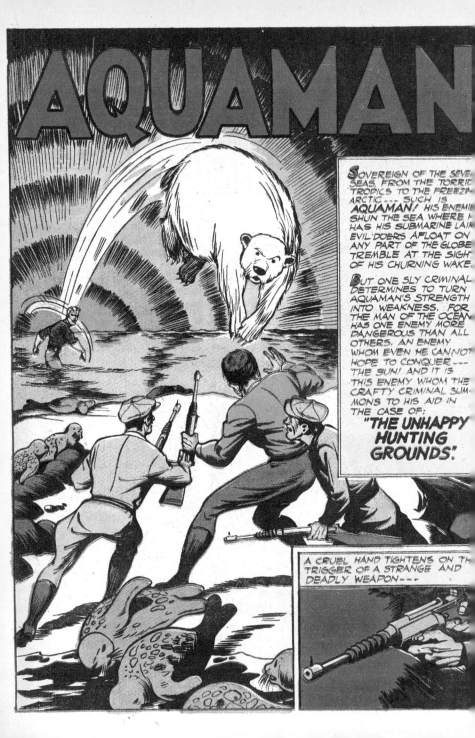

SOVEREIGN OF THE SEVEN SEAS, FROM THE TORRID TROPICS TO THE FREEZING ARCTIC... SUCH IS AQUAMAN! HIS ENEMIES SHUN THE SEA WHERE HE HAS HIS SUBMARINE LAIR. EVIL-DOERS AFLOAT ON ANY PART OF THE GLOBE TREMBLE AT THE SIGHT OF HIS CHURNING WAKE.

BUT ONE SLY CRIMINAL DETERMINES TO TURN AQUAMAN'S STRENGTH INTO WEAKNESS. FOR THE MAN OF THE OCEAN HAS ONE ENEMY MORE DANGEROUS THAN ALL OTHERS, AN ENEMY WHOM EVEN HE CANNOT HOPE TO CONQUER--- THE SUN! AND IT IS THIS ENEMY WHOM THE CRAFTY CRIMINAL SUMMONS TO HIS AID IN THE CASE OF:

"THE UNHAPPY HUNTING GROUNDS."

A CRUEL HAND TIGHTENS ON THE TRIGGER OF A STRANGE AND DEADLY WEAPON---

MORE FUN COMICS No. 85

Interior, "The Unhappy Hunting Grounds"; script, unknown; pencils and inks, Louis Cazeneuve. November 1942. Created as DC's answer to Timely's *Marvel Comics* star the Sub-Mariner, Aquaman could breathe underwater, had considerable strength and endurance, and, within a year of his debut, could mentally command sea life. Compared to the volatile Sub-Mariner, DC's aquatic hero was cool under pressure, even when fighting modern-day pirate Black Jack in 20 stories between 1941 and 1950.

STAR SPANGLED COMICS No. 3

Interior, "Dr. Weerd"; script, Jerry Siegel; art, Hal Sherman. December 1941. DC had high hopes for Jerry Siegel's Star-Spangled Kid and Stripesy concept, which twisted the hero/sidekick formula by making a wealthy teenager the leading man and his adult chauffeur the subordinate.

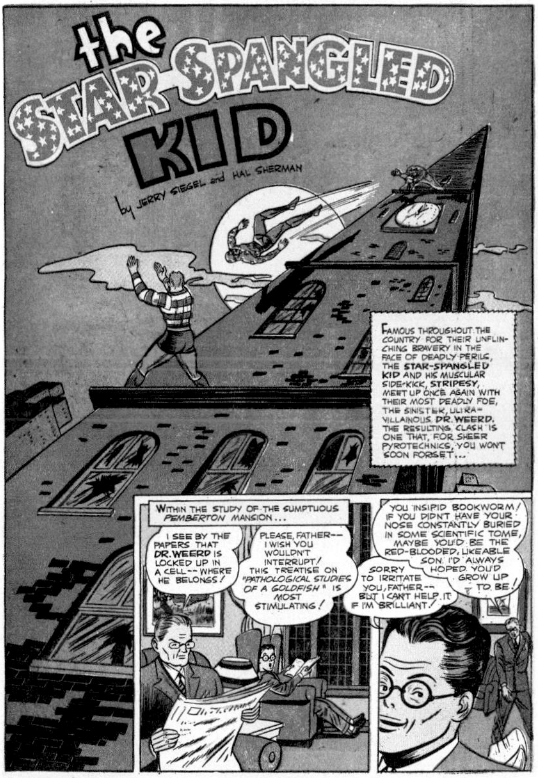
the STAR-SPANGLED KID
by JERRY SIEGEL and HAL SHERMAN
FAMOUS THROUGHOUT THE COUNTRY FOR THEIR UNFLINCHING BRAVERY IN THE FACE OF DEADLY PERILS, THE STAR-SPANGLED KID AND HIS MUSCULAR SIDE-KICK, STRIPESY, MEET UP ONCE AGAIN WITH THEIR MOST DEADLY FOE, THE SINISTER, ULTRA-VILLAINOUS DR. WEERD. THE RESULTING CLASH IS ONE THAT, FOR SHEER PYROTECHNICS, YOU WON'T SOON FORGET...
WITHIN THE STUDY OF THE SUMPTUOUS PEMBERTON MANSION...
I SEE BY THE PAPERS THAT DR. WEERD IS LOCKED UP IN A CELL--WHERE HE BELONGS!
PLEASE, FATHER--I WISH YOU WOULDN'T INTERRUPT! THIS TREATISE ON "PATHOLOGICAL STUDIES OF A GOLDFISH" IS MOST STIMULATING!
YOU INSIPID BOOKWORM! IF YOU DIDN'T HAVE YOUR NOSE CONSTANTLY BURIED IN SOME SCIENTIFIC TOME, MAYBE YOU'D BE THE RED-BLOODED, LIKEABLE SON I'D ALWAYS HOPED YOU'D GROW UP TO BE!
SORRY TO IRRITATE YOU, FATHER--BUT I CAN'T HELP IT IF I'M BRILLIANT!

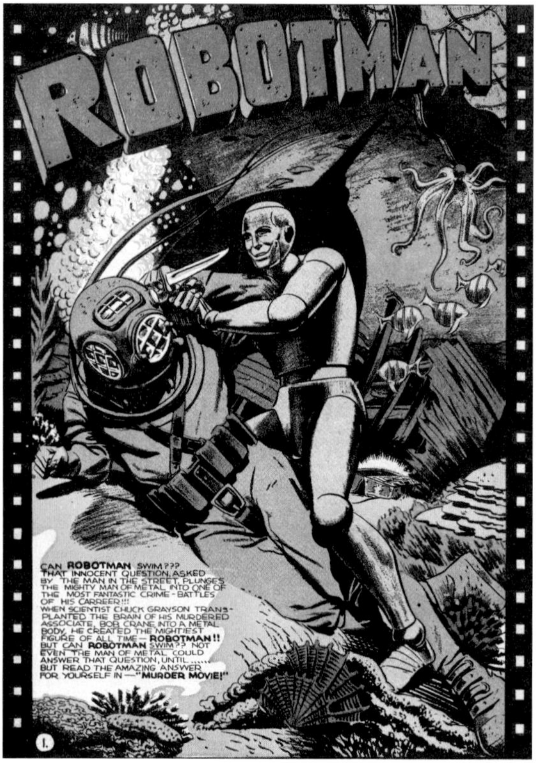
ROBOTMAN
CAN ROBOTMAN SWIM??? THAT INNOCENT QUESTION, ASKED BY THE MAN IN THE STREET, PLUNGES THE MIGHTY MAN OF METAL INTO ONE OF THE MOST FANTASTIC CRIME-BATTLES OF HIS CARREER!!! WHEN SCIENTIST CHUCK GRAYSON TRANS-PLANTED THE BRAIN OF HIS MURDERED ASSOCIATE, BOB CRANE, INTO A METAL BODY, HE CREATED THE MIGHTIEST FIGURE OF ALL TIME—ROBOTMAN!! BUT CAN ROBOTMAN SWIM?? NOT EVEN THE MAN OF METAL COULD ANSWER THAT QUESTION, UNTIL...... BUT READ THE AMAZING ANSWER FOR YOURSELF IN—"MURDER MOVIE!"
1.

STAR SPANGLED COMICS No. 14

Interior, "Murder Movie"; script, Jerry Siegel; art, Leo Nowak and the Shuster Shop. November 1942. In his somber early days, Robotman pined for the woman he'd loved as a human. Jerry Siegel named her Joan Carter, in honor of the former Lois Lane model (and his future wife).

STAR SPANGLED COMICS No. 36

Interior, "The Battle with the Beasts"; script, unknown; pencils and inks, Jimmy Thompson. September 1944. Making his debut in 1942, Jerry Siegel's Robotman was originally a scientist who—after being fatally shot by gangsters—survived by having his brain transplanted into a metal body. In other hands, that premise could have been the stuff of tragedy, but the arrival of artist Jimmy Thompson in 1943 brought comedic flair to the series, along with a slick style and vibrant splash pages and layouts. Robotman's series ended in 1953, but he lived happily ever after, regaining a human body in 1980.

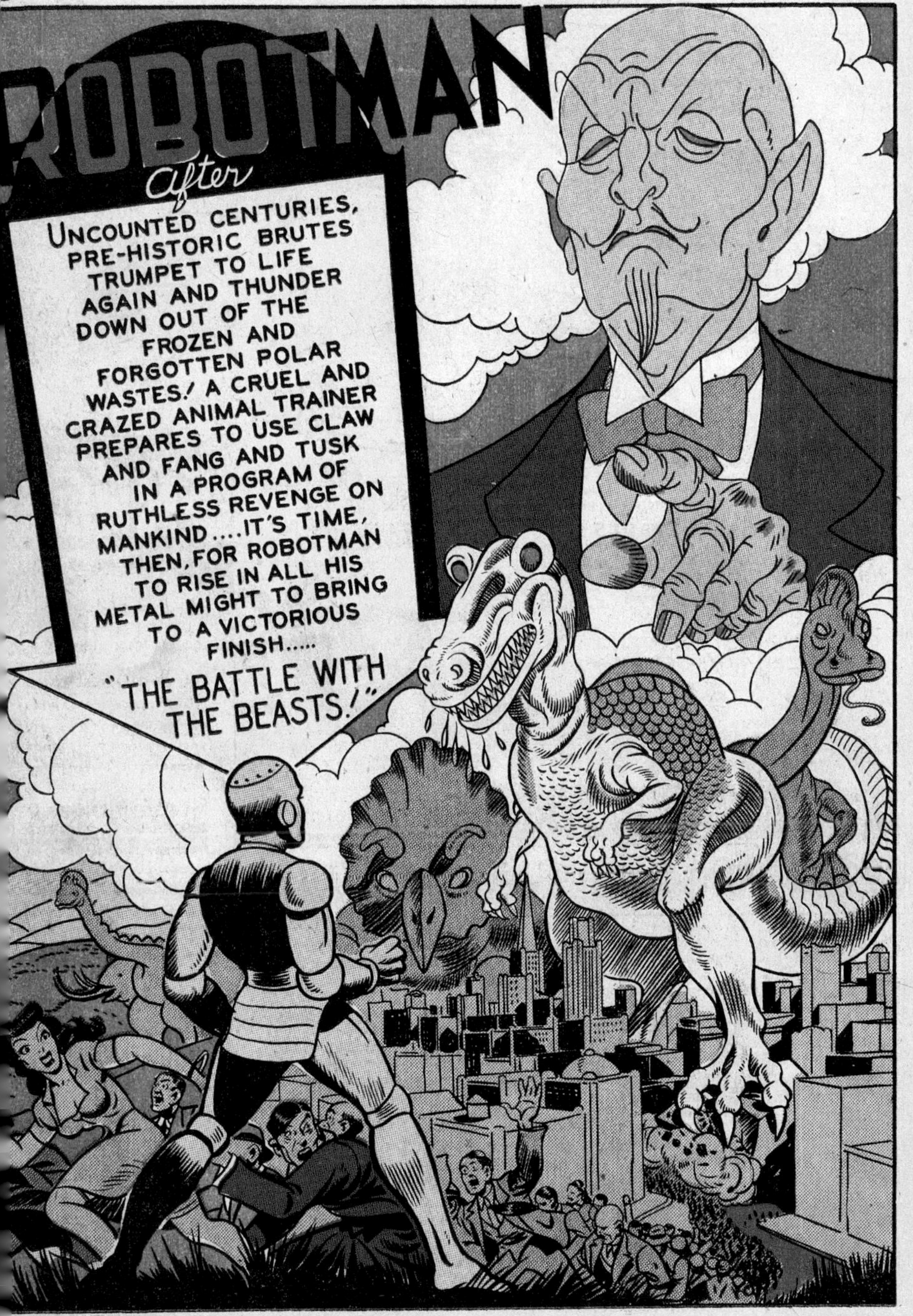
ROBOTMAN
after
UNCOUNTED CENTURIES, PRE-HISTORIC BRUTES TRUMPET TO LIFE AGAIN AND THUNDER DOWN OUT OF THE FROZEN AND FORGOTTEN POLAR WASTES! A CRUEL AND CRAZED ANIMAL TRAINER PREPARES TO USE CLAW AND FANG AND TUSK IN A PROGRAM OF RUTHLESS REVENGE ON MANKIND....IT'S TIME, THEN, FOR ROBOTMAN TO RISE IN ALL HIS METAL MIGHT TO BRING TO A VICTORIOUS FINISH.....
"THE BATTLE WITH THE BEASTS!"

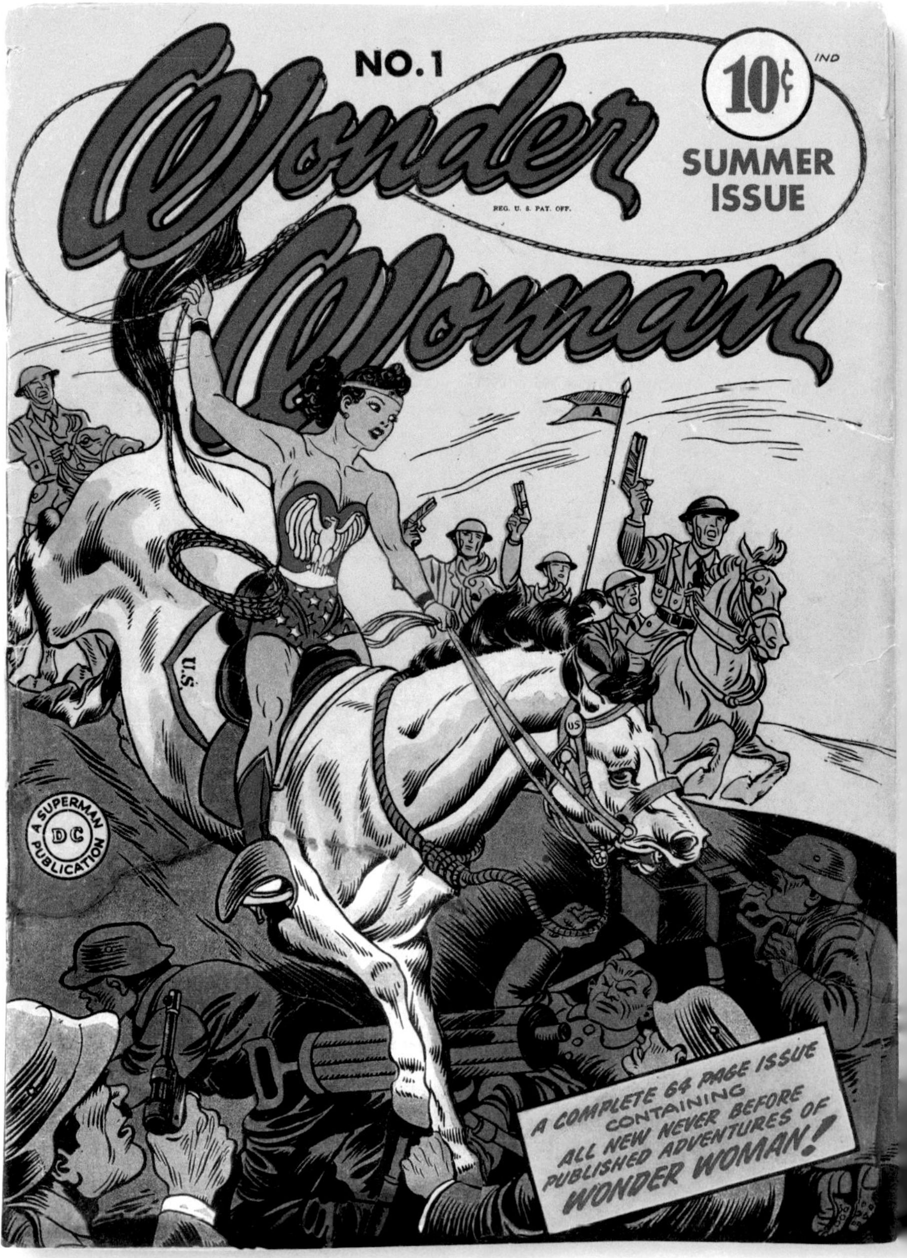
NO. 1
Wonder Woman
REG. U. S. PAT. OFF.
10¢
IND
SUMMER ISSUE
A SUPERMAN DC PUBLICATION
U.S.
A COMPLETE 64 PAGE ISSUE CONTAINING ALL NEW NEVER BEFORE PUBLISHED ADVENTURES OF WONDER WOMAN!

William Moulton Marston

"Marston was an early feminist, no question about it. He felt that a woman would and should be president someday. He was writing a feminist book, but he was dealing with a male audience...."

—SHELDON MAYER

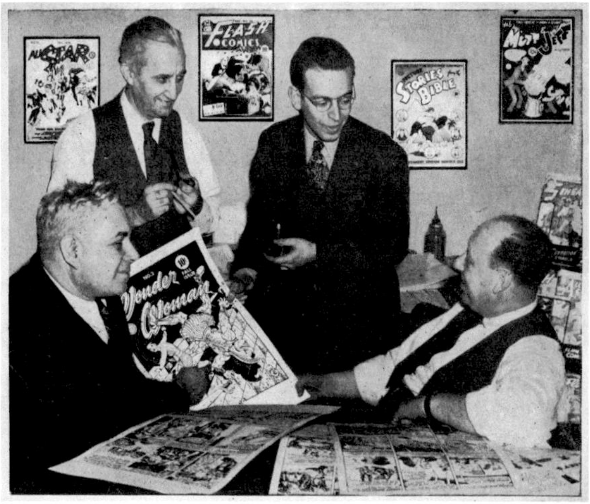
FLASH COMICS
Wonder Woman

WONDER WOMAN No. 1

Cover art, H. G. Peter, summer 1942. Superman and Batman each had to wait a year before being promoted to their own books, but Wonder Woman received the honor within 10 months. Notable among the first issue's contents was an expansion of the heroine's origin, first detailed in late 1941's *All-Star Comics* No. 8.

WONDER WOMAN CREATIVE TEAM

Photograph, left to right, William Moulton Marston, H. G. Peter, Sheldon Mayer, M. C. Gaines, 1942. "Here they are in Mr. Gaines's office discussing this second issue of *Wonder Woman* on a warm day in August. But I almost had to get Wonder Woman and her magic lasso to get them to pose..."
—Alice Marble

FIRST WONDER WOMAN SKETCHES

Concept art by H. G. Peter with notes from William Moulton Marston, ca. 1941. H. G. Peter's preliminary drawings of Wonder Woman were carefully scrutinized by Marston in his notes, but the costume appeared in comic books largely as it appeared here. The two notable differences were the covering of her bare midriff with a girdle and her footwear, which became red boots in the published account. Shortly after Marston's death in 1948, Wonder Woman began wearing sandals with straps running up her calf. Intermittent at first, the change was consistent by 1950.

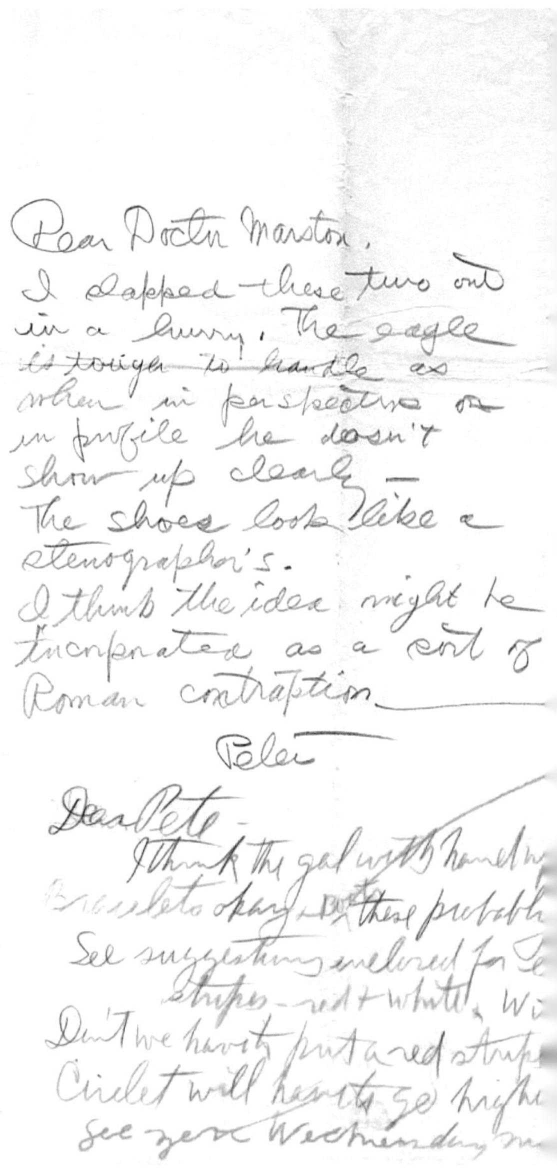

Dear Doctor Marston,
I slapped these two out in a hurry. The eagle is tougher to handle as when in perspective or in profile he doesn't show up clearly —
The shoes look like a stenographer's.
I think the idea might be incorporated as a sort of Roman contraption —
Peter

Dear Pete —
I think the gal with hair and
bracelets okay — but these probabl
See suggestions enclosed for
stripes — red + white, Wi
Don't we have to put a red stripe
Circlet will have to go highe
See you Wednesday m

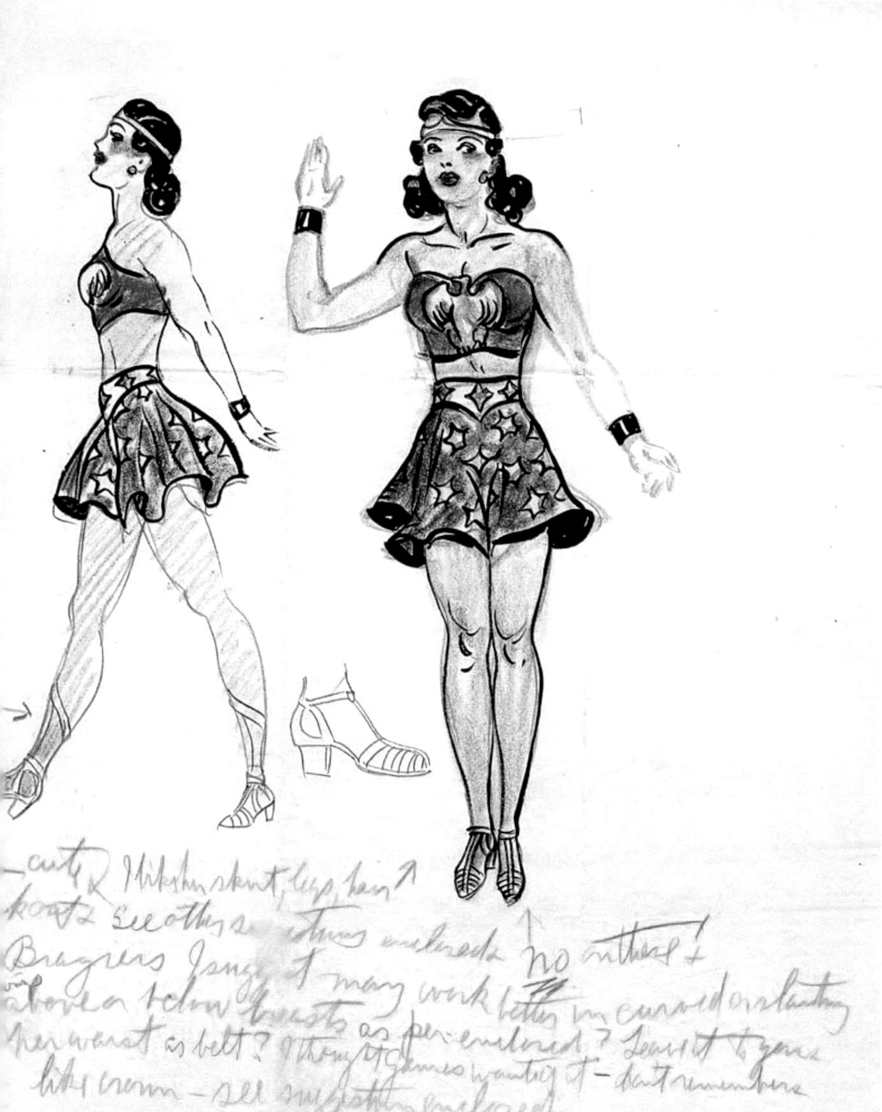
no others!

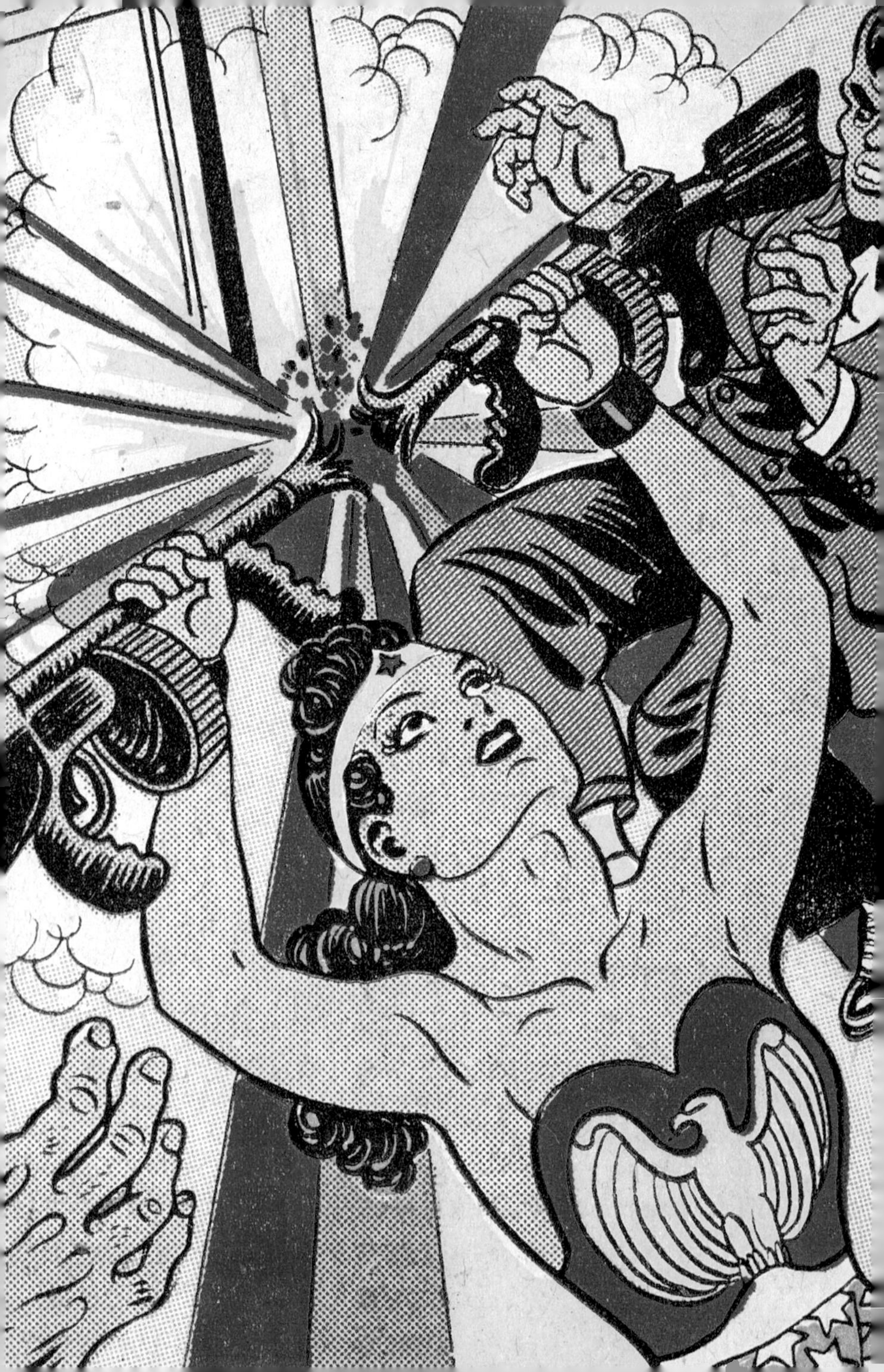

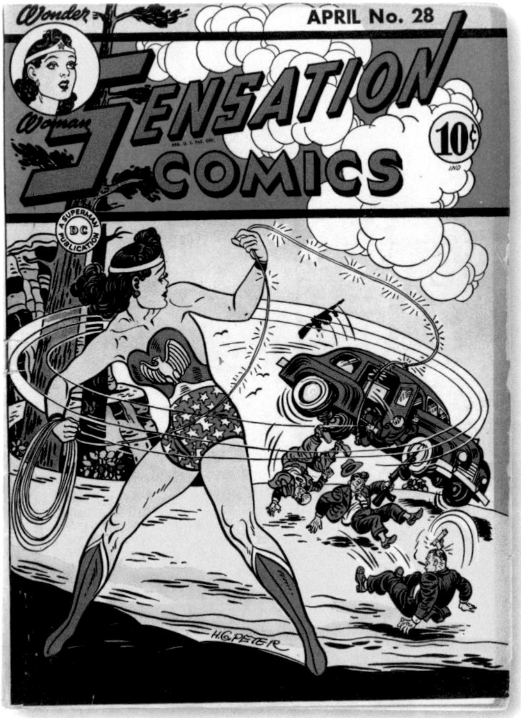
Wonder Woman
APRIL No. 28
SENSATION COMICS
10¢
A SUPERMAN DC PUBLICATION
H.G. PETER

WONDER WOMAN No. 12

Interior, "The Conquest of Venus"; script, Joye Murchison; pencils and inks, H. G. Peter. Spring 1945. Triumphing by turning two "masculine" weapons against each other is a quintessential example of Wonder Woman's paradoxical mission to "Man's World": to rid it of the violence spawned by males, but often using that very same violence in the process.

SENSATION COMICS No. 28

Cover art, H. G. Peter, April 1944. "What woman lacks is the dominance or self-assertive power to put over and enforce her love desires. I have given Wonder Woman this dominant force but have kept her loving, tender, maternal, and feminine in every other way. Her bracelets, with which she repels bullets and other murderous weapons, represent the Amazon Princess's submission to Aphrodite, Goddess of Love and Beauty. Her magic lasso, which compels anyone bound by it to obey Wonder Woman and which was given her by Aphrodite herself, represents woman's love charm and allure, with which she compels men and women to do her bidding." —William Moulton Marston, in a letter to Coulton Waugh

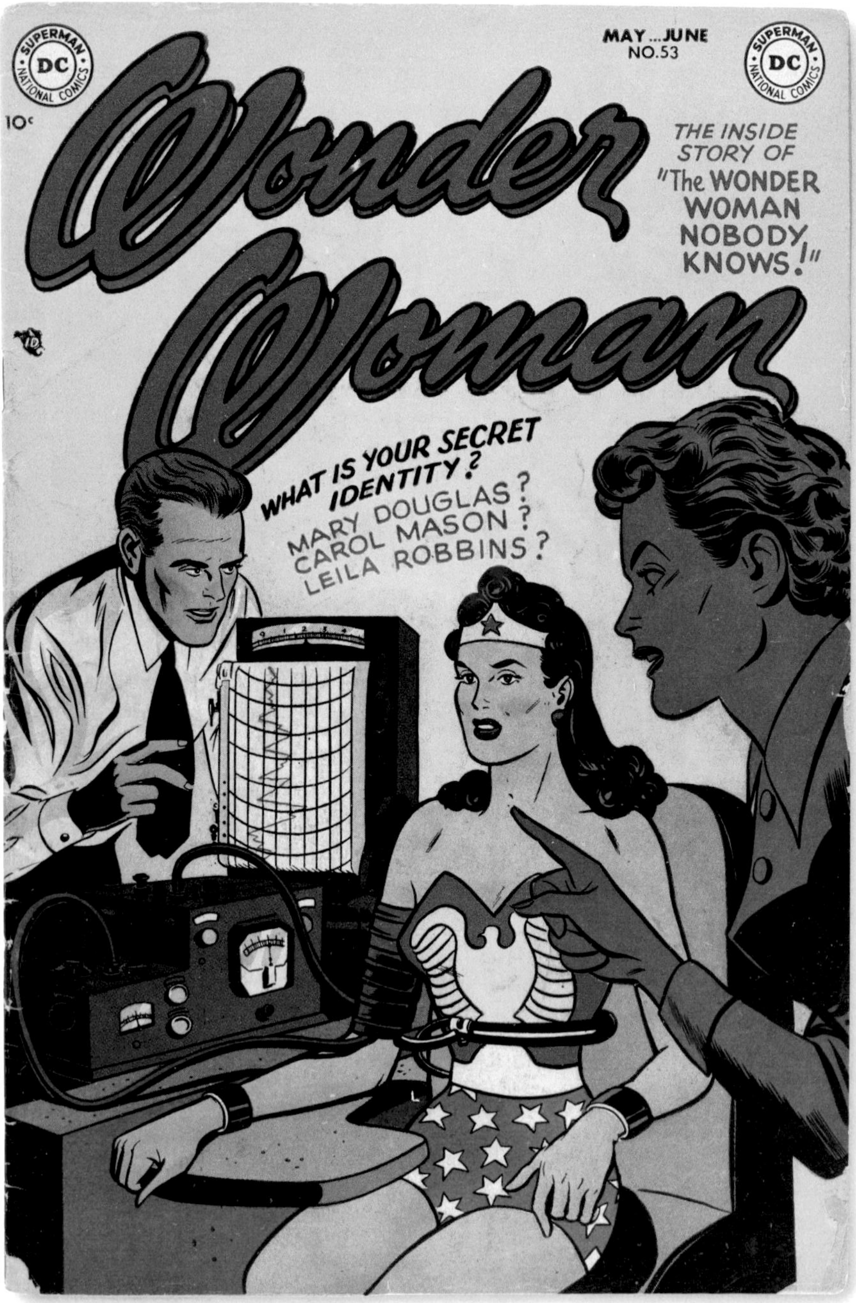
SUPERMAN DC NATIONAL COMICS
10¢
Wonder Woman
MAY...JUNE
NO.53
THE INSIDE STORY OF "The WONDER WOMAN NOBODY KNOWS!"
WHAT IS YOUR SECRET IDENTITY?
MARY DOUGLAS?
CAROL MASON?
LEILA ROBBINS?

WONDER WOMAN No. 53

Cover art, Irv Novick, May–June 1952. Here Wonder Woman is questioned while attached to the device that her creator, William Moulton Marston, was instrumental in inventing. Indeed, Marston provided his heroine with her own portable lie detector —a magic golden lasso—in 1942's *Sensation Comics* No. 6.

WONDER WOMAN UNPUBLISHED COVER

Original art, H.G. Peter, ca. 1945. Wonder Woman's ability to speed past cars was established from the moment she arrived in the United States. After outracing a theatrical promoter, she agreed to go on tour with her "Bullets and Bracelets" act to earn money before acquiring her Diana Prince alter ego.

SENSATION COMICS No. 1

Interior, "Wonder Woman"; script, William Moulton Marston; art, H.G. Peter. January 1942.

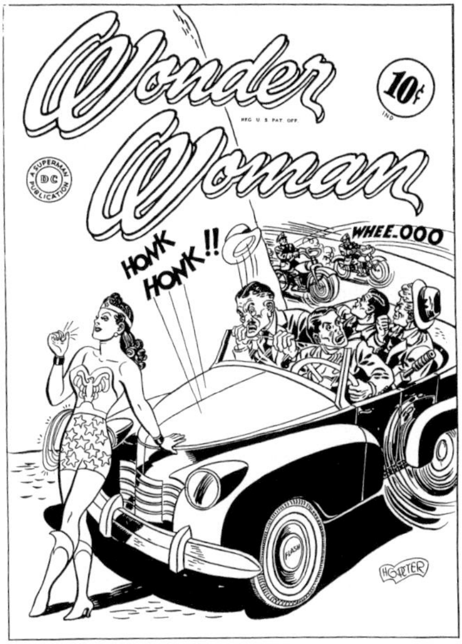
Wonder Woman
10¢
REG. U.S. PAT. OFF.
A SUPERMAN DC PUBLICATION
HONK HONK!!
WHEE.OOO
FLASH
HGPETER

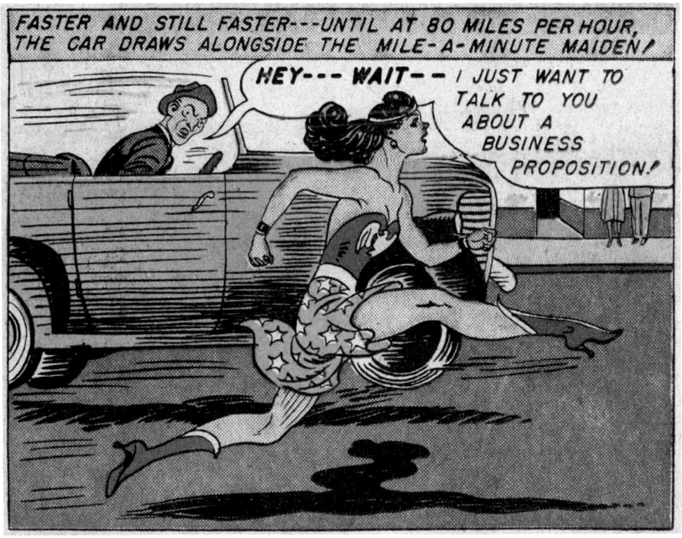
FASTER AND STILL FASTER---UNTIL AT 80 MILES PER HOUR, THE CAR DRAWS ALONGSIDE THE MILE-A-MINUTE MAIDEN!
HEY--- WAIT-- I JUST WANT TO TALK TO YOU ABOUT A BUSINESS PROPOSITION!

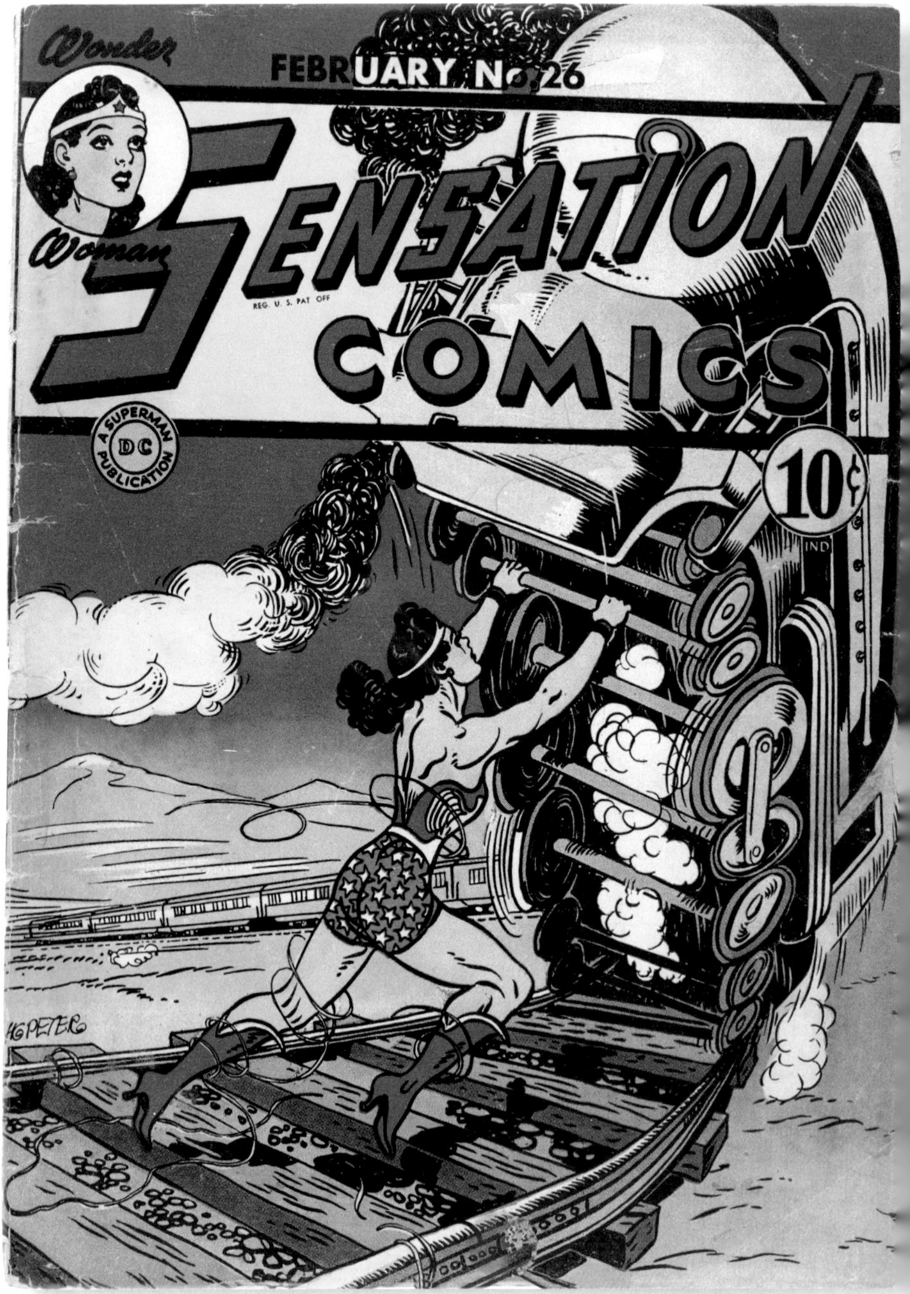
Wonder Woman
FEBRUARY No. 26
SENSATION COMICS
REG. U. S. PAT. OFF
A SUPERMAN DC PUBLICATION
10¢
IND
HG PETER

"Give them an alluring woman stronger than themselves to submit to, and they'll be proud to become her willing slaves!"
—WILLIAM MOULTON MARSTON

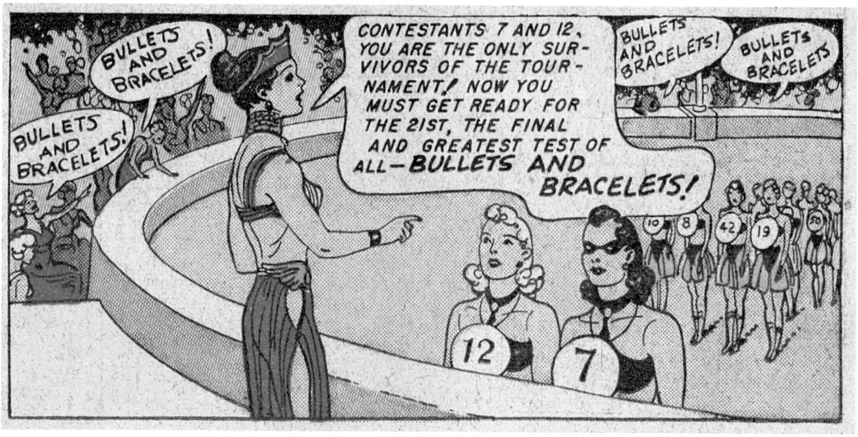
BULLETS AND BRACELETS!
BULLETS AND BRACELETS!
CONTESTANTS 7 AND 12, YOU ARE THE ONLY SURVIVORS OF THE TOURNAMENT! NOW YOU MUST GET READY FOR THE 21ST, THE FINAL AND GREATEST TEST OF ALL—BULLETS AND BRACELETS!
BULLETS AND BRACELETS!
BULLETS AND BRACELETS
12
7
10
8
42
19

SENSATION COMICS No. 26

Cover art, H. G. Peter, February 1944. Wonder Woman borrows a page from Superman's book and stops a locomotive in its tracks. But is it really her or her mother, Queen Hippolyte, who poses as her daughter in the issue's lead story, "The Masquerader"? Either way, the emulation of Man of Steel–style action was fitting for this title, which followed *Action Comics'* format of a dynamic super hero "fronting" a diverse array of backup features. Included in this issue were tales of the Black Pirate, Little Boy Blue, the Gay Ghost, Mr. Terrific, and Wildcat.

ALL-STAR COMICS No. 8

Interior, "Introducing Wonder Woman"; script, William Moulton Marston (as Charles Moulton); pencils and inks, H. G. Peter. December 1941–January 1942. The extraordinary competition of Bullets and Bracelets requires contestants to move fast enough to deflect shells fired from a gun with their metal wristbands. The Amazons are obviously made of sterner stuff than mere mortals, and Wonder Woman uses the stunt to earn money when she first arrives in the United States.

Wonder Woman
NOV. No. 35
SENSATION COMICS
10¢
A SUPERMAN DC PUBLICATION
HG PETER

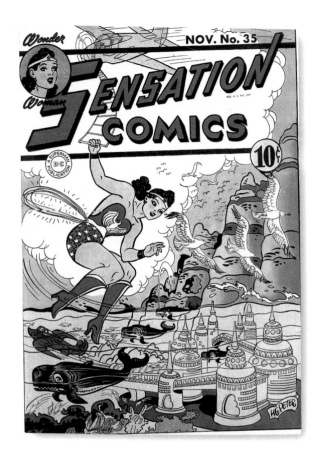

SENSATION COMICS No. 35

Cover art, H.G. Peter, November 1944. Wonder Woman had several adventures in two rival kingdoms of Atlantis, one ruled by the benevolent Queen Eeras and the other by wicked Queen Clea.

WONDER WOMAN No. 3

Cover art, H.G. Peter, February–March 1943. Wonder Woman differed from her male counterparts in the steadfast belief that villains were not beyond redemption. Such was the case with the Baroness Paula von Gunther, whom the Amazing Amazon eventually discovered was being coerced by Nazis. After rescuing the Baroness's daughter from a concentration camp, Wonder Woman successfully rehabilitated Paula and gained a trusted friend in the years that followed.

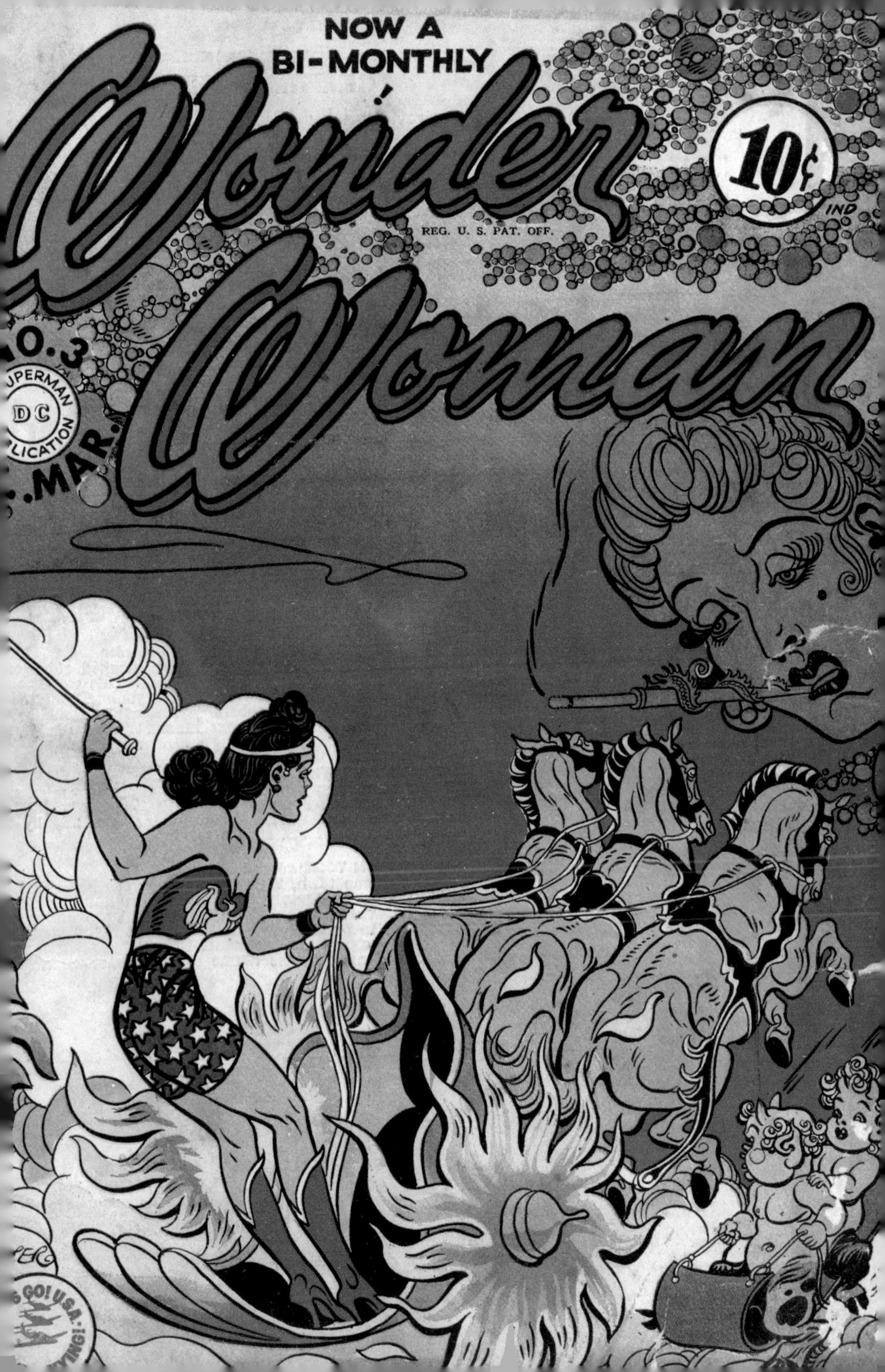
NOW A
BI-MONTHLY
Wonder Woman
REG. U. S. PAT. OFF.
10¢
IND
O. 3
UPERMAN
DC
LICATION
.MAR.

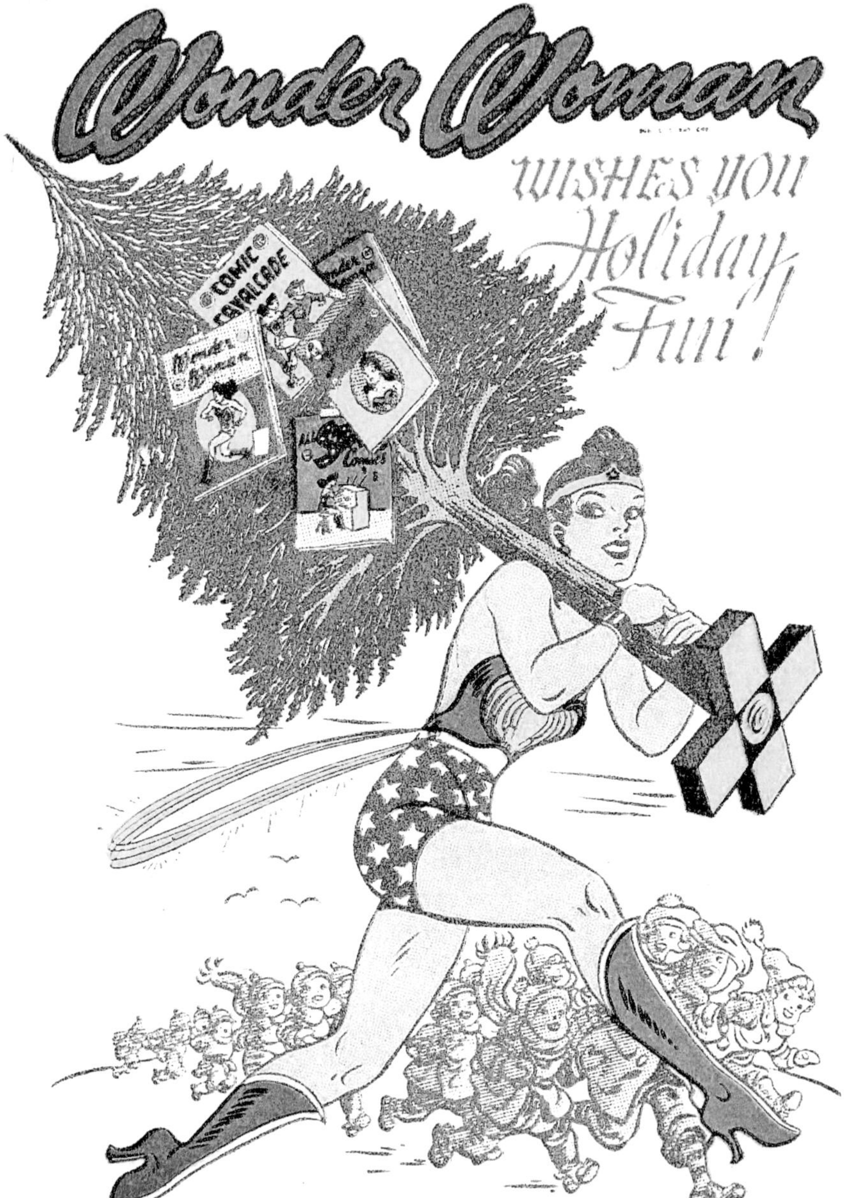

To

1943

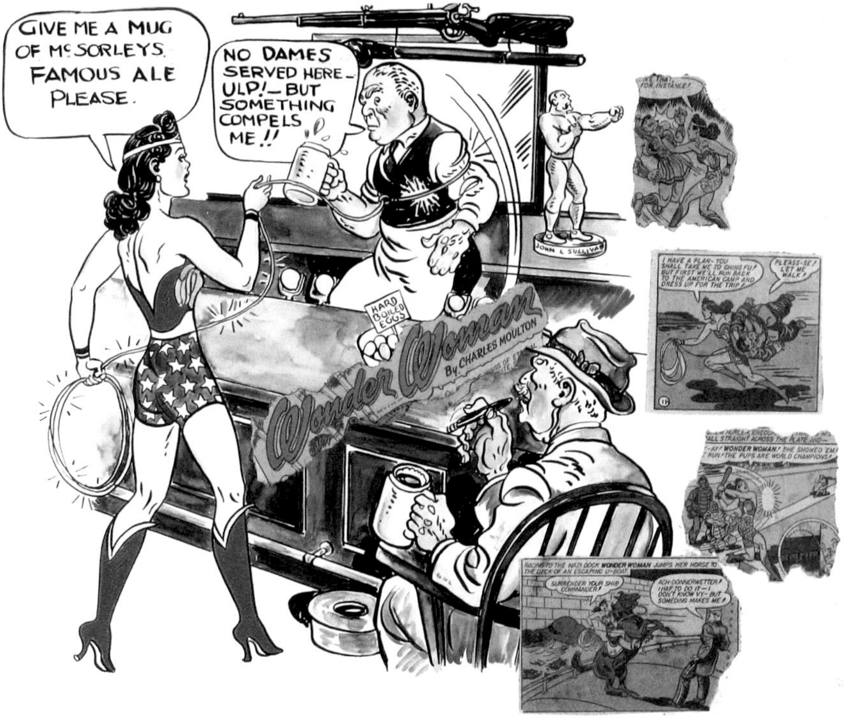
GIVE ME A MUG OF McSORLEYS FAMOUS ALE PLEASE.
NO DAMES SERVED HERE – ULP! – BUT SOMETHING COMPELS ME!!
HARD BOILED EGGS
Wonder Woman
By CHARLES MOULTON
JOHN L SULLIVAN
I HAVE A PLAN- YOU SHALL TAKE ME TO CHING FU! BUT FIRST WE'LL RUN BACK TO THE AMERICAN CAMP AND DRESS UP FOR THE TRIP!
PLEASS-SE! LET ME WALK!
SURRENDER YOUR SHIP COMMANDER!
ACH-DONNERWETTER! I HAF TO DO IT—I DON'T KNOW VY- BUT SOMEDING MAKES ME!

WONDER WOMAN CHRISTMAS CARD

Christmas card art, H.G. Peter, 1943.

McSORLEY'S FAMOUS ALE

Personalized art, H.G. Peter, ca. 1940s. H.G. Peter occasionally drew personalized pieces like this one, set at McSorley's Old Ale House, New York City's oldest Irish tavern.

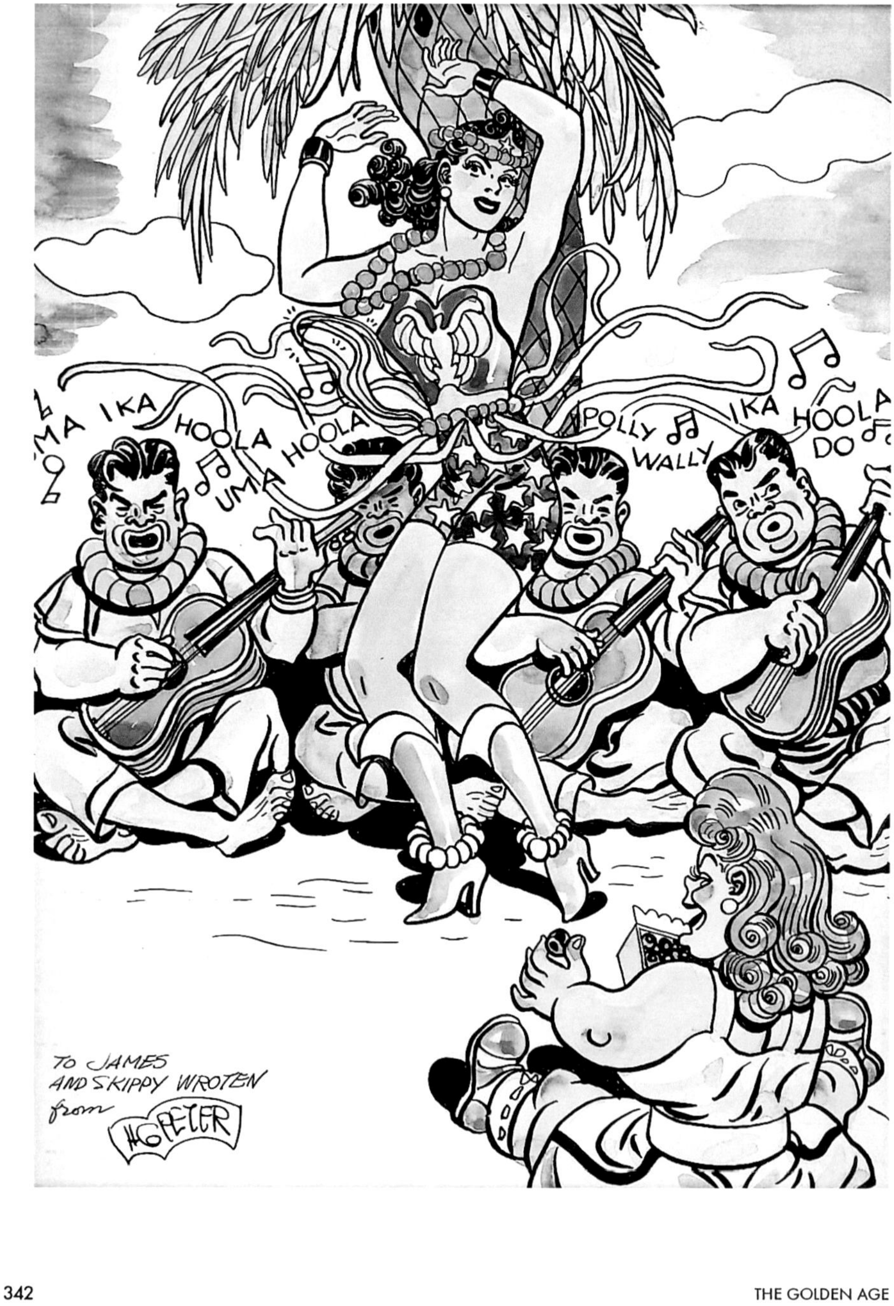
MA IKA
HOOLA
UMA HOOLA
POLLY
WALLY
IKA
HOOLA
DO
TO JAMES
AND SKIPPY WROTEN
from
HG PETER

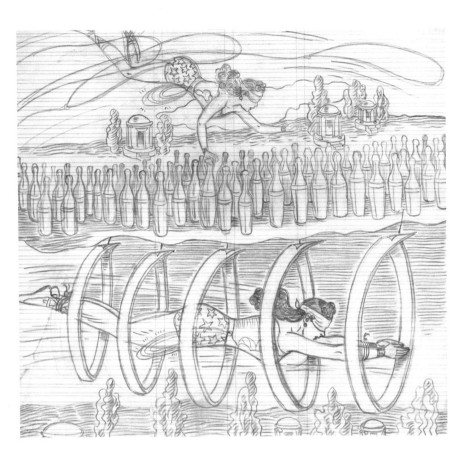

WONDER WOMAN HULA

Unpublished illustration, H. G. Peter, 1940s. Enjoying Wonder
Woman's hula dance is her comic sidekick, Etta Candy.
A mainstay of the series almost from the beginning, the
redheaded college student never backed down from a
challenge or rejected a box of chocolates. Within a few
years of Marston's death, sorority sisters Etta and the
Holliday Girls were quietly dropped.

WONDER WOMAN No. 75

Preliminary sketches, H. G. Peter, 1955. By the mid-1950s, Wonder
Woman was in the hands of writer-editor Robert Kanigher,
who began running an occasional series about the background
on the heroine's costume. These warm-up sketches by Peter
were part of a story that detailed the competition that earned
the Amazing Amazon her tiara.

ETTA CANDY VS "THE CHEETAH"
10 ROUNDS

ETTA LANDS A
ROUND-HOUSE
RIGHT TO THE JAW.

"THE CHEETAH"
LANDS A STINGING
LEFT TO THE
CANDY BELT.

ETTA CANDY VS. THE CHEETAH

Unpublished illustration, H.G. Peter, ca. 1940s. The schizophrenic
Cheetah, who struggled with her more benign persona
of Priscilla Rich, was a favored villainess of the Wonder
Woman creators.

"WONDER WOMAN" NEWSPAPER COMIC
STRIP BROCHURE

Cover art, artist unknown, 1944. A "Wonder Woman" newspaper
strip was introduced with great fanfare in 1944 but failed to
build much of a subscriber list and was canceled within a year.

INTERVIEW WITH DR. MARSTON

PAGE 346: *Article, "Don't Laugh at the Comics,"* Family Circle
Magazine; writer, Olive Richard; October 25, 1940. Marston
promoted himself as an authority on the young comic book
medium in a magazine article that attracted the attention of
All-American Publisher M.C. Gaines. Out of the conversations
between the two men, Wonder Woman was eventually born.

ALICE MARBLE FEATURE

PAGE 347: *Article, "Our Women Are Our Future,"*
Family Circle *Magazine; script, Olive Richard; August 14, 1942.*
Tennis champion Alice Marble enjoyed a position on
All-American's advisory board during the 1940s and
was *Wonder Woman*'s associate editor.

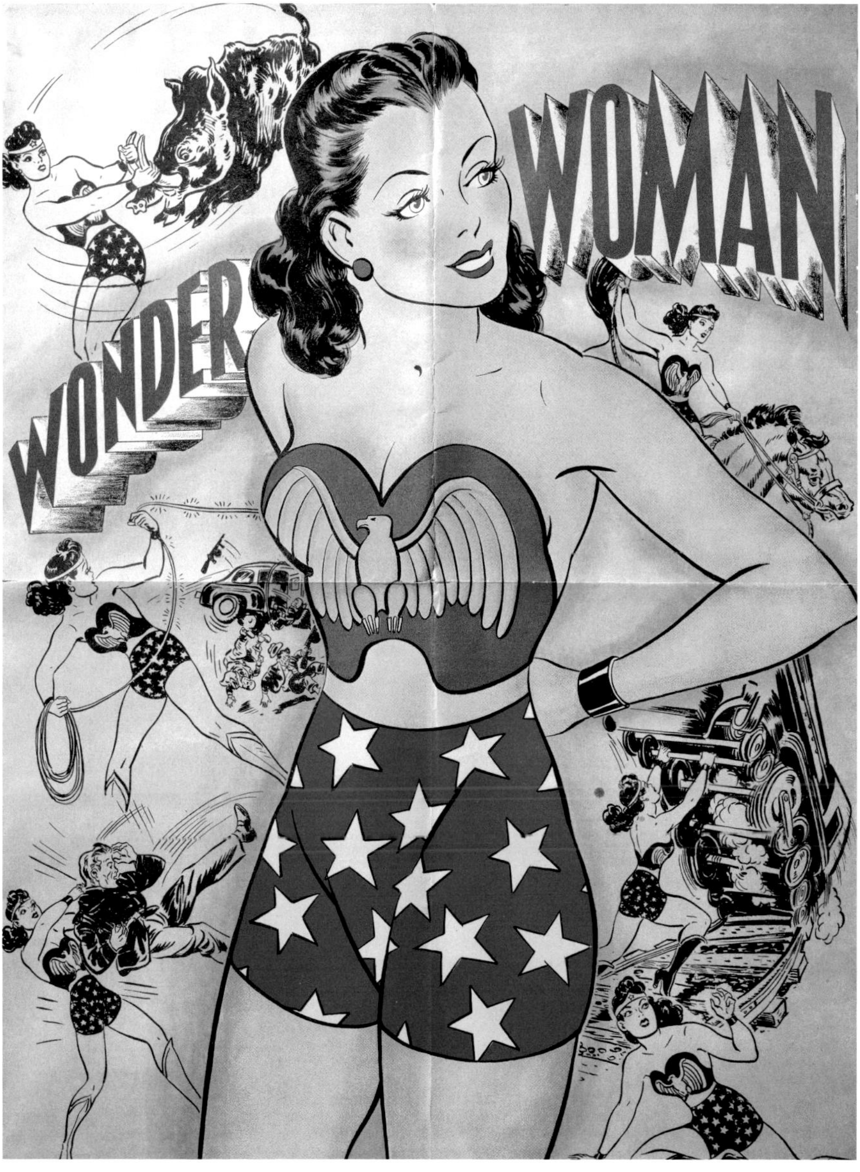
WONDER
WOMAN

DON'T LAUGH AT THE COMICS

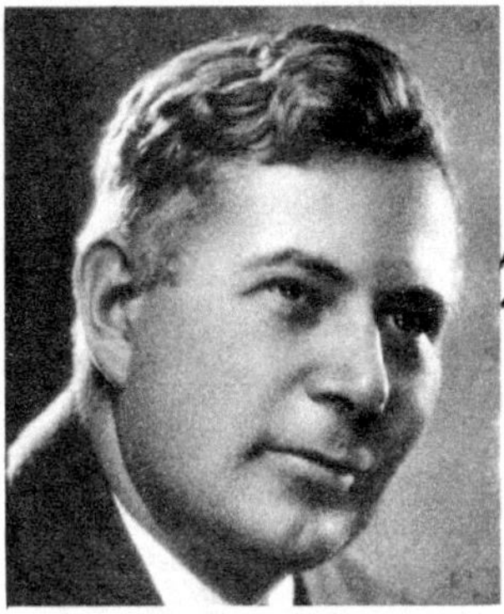

Everybody has always said it is story value—the primitive thrill of danger and adventure — that makes such strips as "Superman" so popular. But that's not the real reason, says Dr. Marston, Family Circle psychologist, who tells what he thinks it is

WHEN Orson Welles announced in the course of a radio melodrama that octopus men from Mars were invading New Jersey, and people by the thousands believed him, I thought the world had gone mad. It seemed incredible that rational human beings could accept such a fantastic "news announcement" as truth, that they could dash about ringing fire alarms, telephoning hospitals and police, and calling out the National Guard to repel the Martians.

But this is how Dr. William Moulton Marston, THE FAMILY CIRCLE psychologist, explained it. "This episode in American spoofology is attributable almost entirely to the comics," he told me. "Comic-strip stories like 'Buck Rogers,' appearing in daily newspapers and Sunday comics sections, and recently in monthly comics magazines, have created a world of fantasy that is almost as real to adults as it is to children. And that means that sane grownups sometimes cannot tell the difference between fact and fancy. There are millions of normal men and women today who have no mental resistance at all to tales of the weirdly impossible. No supernatural being is too illogical to believe in. Orson Welles' fascinating radio experiment proved that Americans today are living an imaginary mental life in a comics-created world!"

I know from observation in my own household that children read the so-called funnies morning, noon, and — unfortunately — night, and that while they're doing it there are no childish quarrels. Naturally, I had come to enjoy those peaceful interludes that followed the purchase of the magazines, but then Dr. Marston's statement made me begin to wonder if comics magazines were poisonous mental pacifiers, and I counted how many I personally had been buying. I found that the number was constantly increasing. Other parents made the same check, and among us we counted 84 different comics magazines. And the more enterprising youngsters traded them among themselves so that they might read all of them.

Parent-teacher groups, women's clubs, and other parents' organizations were starting to be a little worried over the possible harm such assiduous comics reading might do our future generations, when Stirling North, in *The Chicago Daily News,* added to the foment with his scathing indictment of the comics magazines. North pulled no punches when he said, "The lurid publications depend for their appeal upon mayhem, murder, torture, abduction, superman heroics, voluptuous females, blazing machine guns, and hooded justice." He added that parents and teachers throughout America would be forced to band together to break the hold of the comics.

With terrible visions of Hitlerian justice in mind, I went to Dr. Marston, whose common-

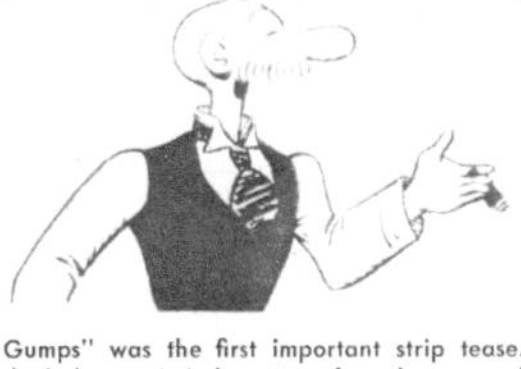

"The Gumps" was the first important strip tease. It marked the comics' departure from humor and piqued curiosity by never revealing quite all

sense and farseeing views usually quiet the tempest in the teapot.

"Do you know anything about comics magazines?" I asked. "Do you know how many are sold each month?"

If I thought the question might stick the Doctor, I was wrong — as usual. He said, "There are about 108 comics magazines on the newsstands. Sales figures show that between 10,000,000 and 12,000,000 magazines are sold every month. That means $1,000,000 or more are spent every month by comics fans. There are, besides, another 3,000,000 or 4,000,000 comics magazines sold quarterly. Surveys show that on the average four children read every book sold. That makes a total of somewhere between 40,000,000 and 50,000,000 juvenile readers per month. And another 12,000,000 to 16,000,000 readers every three months. The magazines sell for 10c apiece, which brings the yearly retail sales to between $14,000,000 and $15,000,000."

When I professed amazement at the Doctor's detailed knowledge of the subject, he told me that he had been doing research in this field for more than a year—and tha *had read almost every comics magazine lished during that time!* I told him that figures were pretty big for me, but th gathered that just about every child in A ica is reading these magazines.

"That's correct," Dr. Marston said. " surveys show that 86% of the parents e reading them also. Which is still more a ing. Nothing like the comics-magazine n ment has ever been known before. The co sections of Sunday newspapers long ago came the Sabbath-day bible of more 10,000,000 children. But now the comics azines have become their weekday textb and believe me, no youngsters ever stu their schoolbooks as they do these comics!"

"How do you explain their appeal?" I as "I always assumed that the appeal of cc to children was humor. But you never see laugh at the funnies. The one thing they most seriously in life is their comics-m zine reading. Why is that?"

"The comics long ago ceased to be hu ous," Dr. Marston said. "More than 30 ago Bud Fisher (Harry Conway) origi the comic strip that is now the oldest one lished—'Mutt and Jeff.' That was intend be funny and thousands of readers laughed Bud. A few years later, in 1917, along R. Sidney Smith with a serious story co ity and grotesque characters — 'The Gu You may think Andy Gump is a charact be laughed at, but Sidney Smith though an important human document. Even th morous hangover which persisted in the la able aspects of the chinless Andy was wiped out by such cartoon strips as 'O

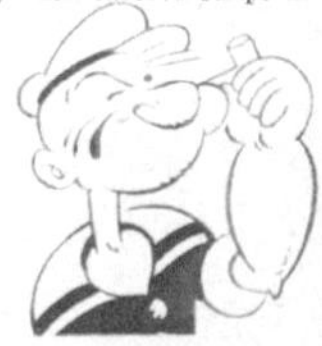

Popeye might be considered the forerunner perman in that he was one of the earliest cha to perform feats of strength that, althoug posterous, captured the imagination of you

Annie' and the avalanche of newspape ture-stories which flourished during t years following Andy Gump's debut. Les half a dozen of the whole lot were ev tended to be funny. And one of those—f ing Popeye—gained national popularit made its creator Segar rich; not b readers laugh at it, but because Popey spinach and from that previously de vegetable draws colossal strength to form feats that provoke admiration. As of newspaper story-strip characters d themselves to adventure with increasi

HE war news had me down. I had just ɔeen to see a friend whose husband, a l officer, was killed at Pearl Harbor. Com- ıome I bought a newspaper with a "Wake America!" editorial spread all over the t page. The general drift of it seemed to at the country is on the brink of ruin and we'd better wake up or else. Well, I was ke to the danger, all right, but I couldn't of anything more to do about it. I'd paid income taxes, bought war stamps and s, volunteered up to my neck for every nse project, cut out sugar and all pleasure with the car, and made the decision that ould look awful but patriotic in my old es.

ɪen to cap it all I turned on the radio and blared the voice of an expert war-news commentator telling us in 15 minutes of dismal prediction that we should prepare ourselves for much worse disasters than anything we had yet suffered. Women must do this and women must do that and women must be charming through it all. Usually some everyday incident comes up to stop one going through thought mazes of this kind, and it happened here. On the table where I was about to throw my hat with a Katharine Cornell gesture was a comics book with a brilliant-hued cover bearing the picture of a pretty girl in a scanty costume leaping aboard a racing motorboat.

A memory stirred; this must be the "daughter or the brain of Dr. William Moulton Marston, FAMILY CIRCLE psychologist" that I had seen recently in THE FAMILY CIRCLE.

"Well," I thought. "If Marston is whipping up comics stories while Rome burns, there must be a reason." So I clamped the hat on again and made tracks for Rye, New York.

The Doctor hadn't changed a bit. He was reading a comics magazine, which sport he relinquished with a chuckle and rose gallantly to his feet, a maneuver of major magnitude for this psychologic Nero Wolfe. "Hello, hello, my Wonder Woman!" cried the mammoth heartily. "I was just reading about you in this magazine. You're prettier than your prototype in the story strip and far more intellectual. Sit down and tell me all."

"I came to be told, and what's the idea of calling *me* Wonder Woman, and I don't feel like listening to any male sarcasm on account of I've heard too much already."

"Your bracelets," said the Doctor, taking

UR WOMEN ARE OUR FUTURE

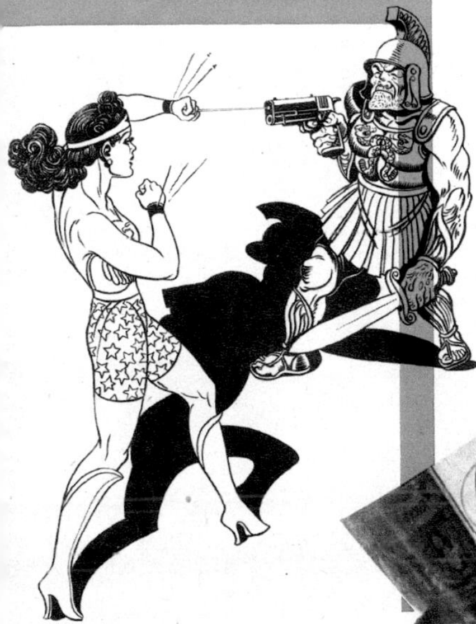

Women's feminine force can avail even against the brute force of war, says Dr. William Moulton Marston, whose fictional character Wonder Woman here symbolically repels the bullets of Mars with her magic bracelets. (Below) Alice Marble, who is associate editor of *Wonder Woman* magazine, exemplifies the influence of women in today's scheme of things

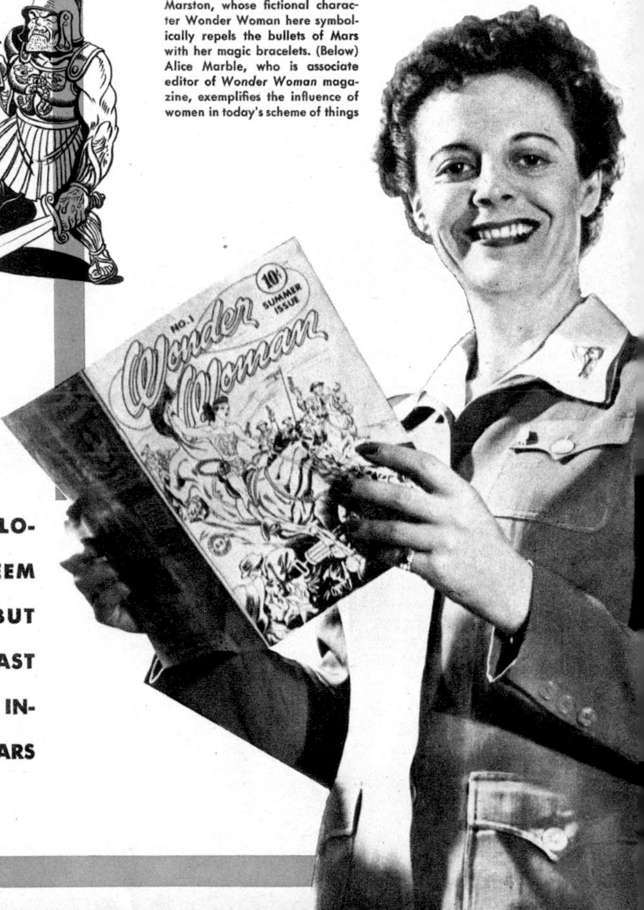
10¢
No. 1
SUMMER ISSUE
Wonder Woman

THIS EMINENT PSYCHOLOGIST'S THESIS MAY SEEM ILLUSORY AT FIRST, BUT JUST CONSIDER THE VAST INCREASE IN WOMEN'S INFLUENCE IN RECENT YEARS

BY OLIVE RICHARD

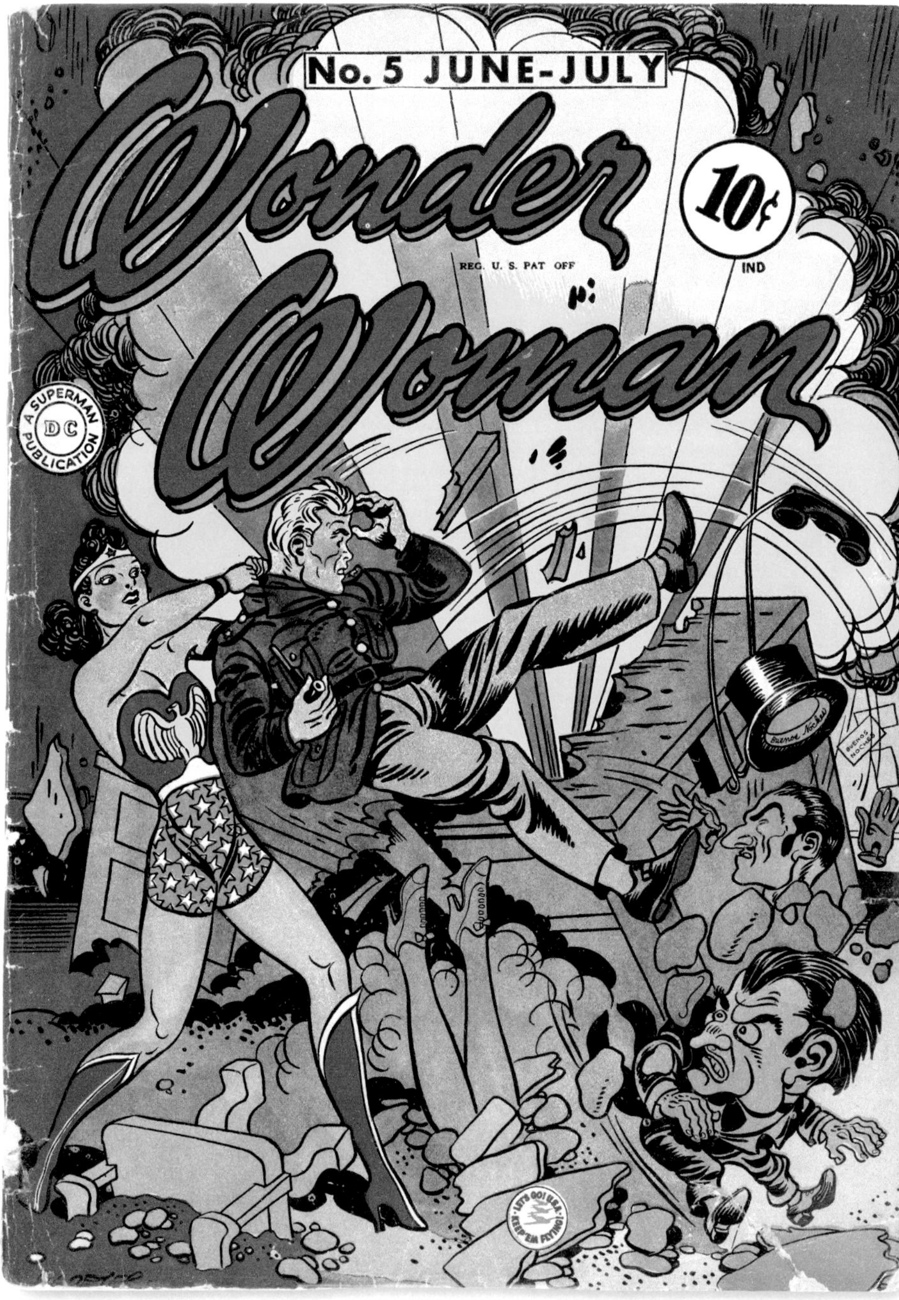
No. 5 JUNE-JULY
Wonder Woman
10¢
REG. U. S. PAT OFF
IND
A SUPERMAN DC PUBLICATION

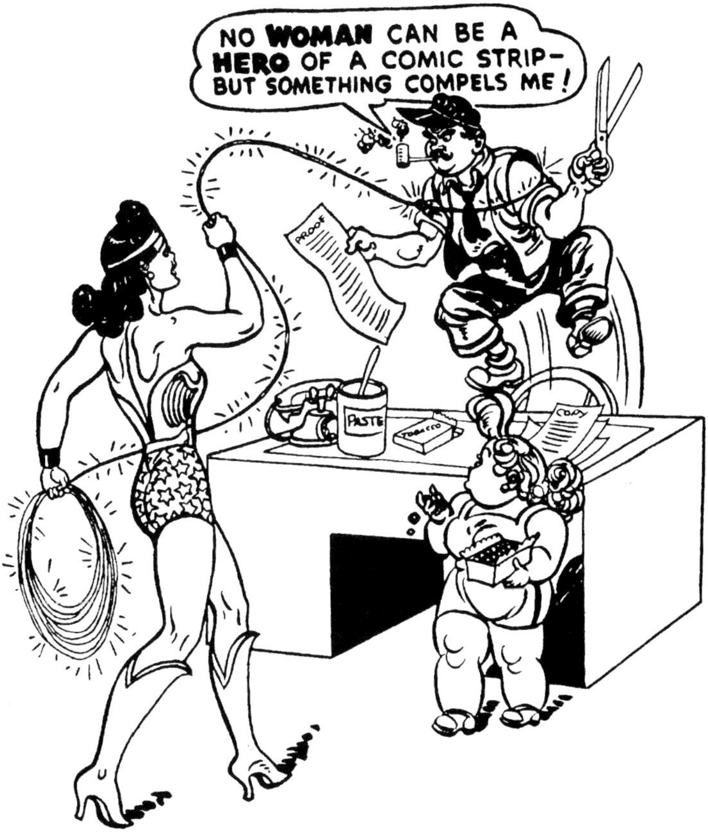
NO WOMAN CAN BE A HERO OF A COMIC STRIP– BUT SOMETHING COMPELS ME!
PROOF
PASTE
COPY

WONDER WOMAN No. 5

Cover art, H. G. Peter, June–July 1943. Colonel Steve Trevor was characterized by later generations as a "male Lois Lane" whose only functions seemed to be chasing after and being rescued by Wonder Woman. Under series creator William Moulton Marston, the soldier was far more of an equal partner. After Marston's death, Trevor became more of a frustrated lover, engaging in a futile campaign to convince Wonder Woman to marry him.

"WONDER WOMAN" COMIC STRIP TEASER

Promotional art, H.G. Peter, 1944.

WONDER WOMAN No. 2

Interior, "Wonder Woman"; script, William Moulton Marston; pencils and inks, H. G. Peter. Fall 1942. Part of Wonder Woman's appeal was the pure physicality of the character. Whether fighting the eight-foot-tall Mammotha or Mars, God of War, the Amazing Amazon struck down every obstacle in her path and empowered girls with the message that no challenge was insurmountable.

SENSATION COMICS No. 34

Cover art, H. G. Peter, October 1944. Grand adventures with invading armies and strange villains were balanced by more intimate stories in which Wonder Woman improved the lives of ordinary citizens. In "Edgar's New World," the kind-hearted Amazon provides a vision-impaired youngster with new glasses and discovers that his mother has been falsely imprisoned for his father's murder. Moved by the heroine's efforts to exonerate his mom, Edgar must break his glasses to save Wonder Woman's life later in the story.

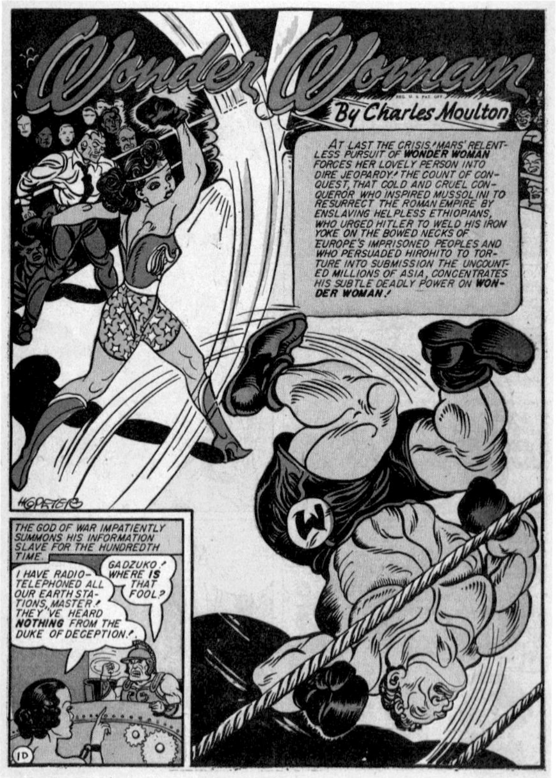
Wonder Woman
By Charles Moulton
AT LAST THE CRISIS! MARS' RELENTLESS PURSUIT OF WONDER WOMAN FORCES HER LOVELY PERSON INTO DIRE JEOPARDY! THE COUNT OF CONQUEST, THAT COLD AND CRUEL CONQUEROR WHO INSPIRED MUSSOLINI TO RESURRECT THE ROMAN EMPIRE BY ENSLAVING HELPLESS ETHIOPIANS, WHO URGED HITLER TO WELD HIS IRON YOKE ON THE BOWED NECKS OF EUROPE'S IMPRISONED PEOPLES AND WHO PERSUADED HIROHITO TO TORTURE INTO SUBMISSION THE UNCOUNTED MILLIONS OF ASIA, CONCENTRATES HIS SUBTLE DEADLY POWER ON WONDER WOMAN!
H.G. PETER
THE GOD OF WAR IMPATIENTLY SUMMONS HIS INFORMATION SLAVE FOR THE HUNDREDTH TIME.
GADZUKO! WHERE IS THAT FOOL?
I HAVE RADIO-TELEPHONED ALL OUR EARTH STATIONS, MASTER! THEY'VE HEARD NOTHING FROM THE DUKE OF DECEPTION!
1D

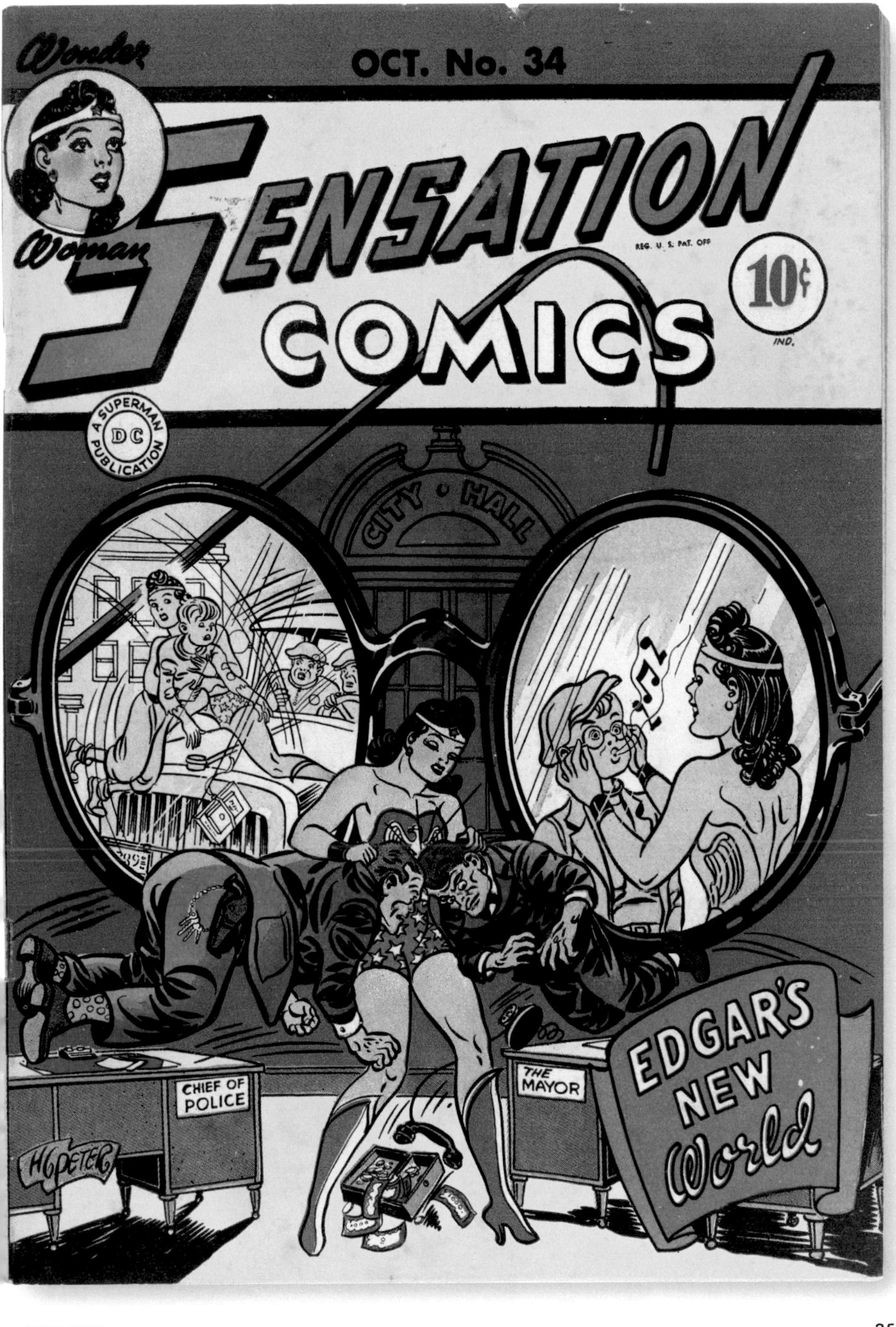
Wonder Woman
OCT. No. 34
SENSATION COMICS
REG. U. S. PAT. OFF
10¢
IND.
A SUPERMAN DC PUBLICATION
CITY • HALL
CHIEF OF POLICE
THE MAYOR
EDGAR'S NEW World
H.G.PETER

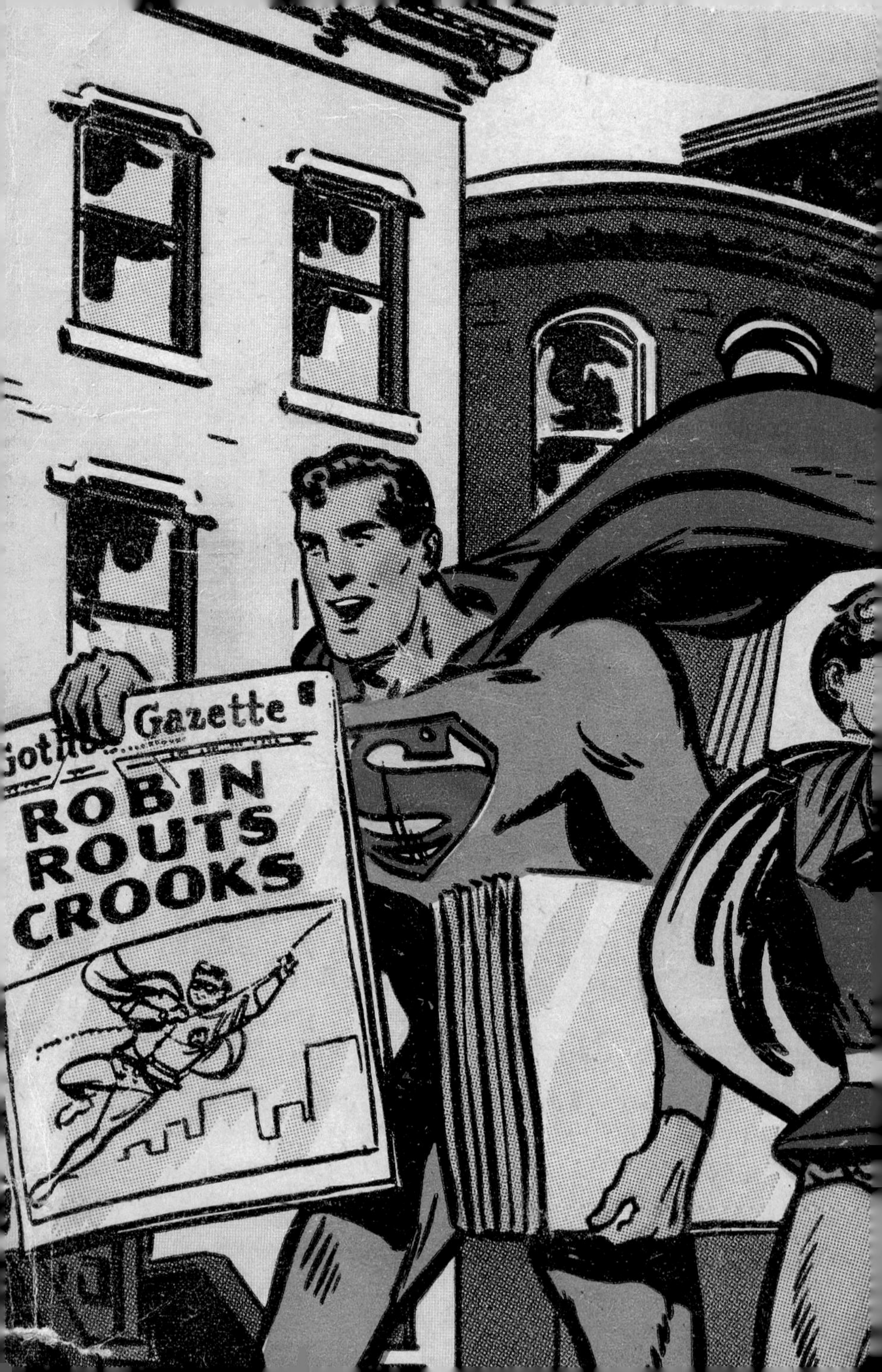
Gazette
ROBIN
ROUTS
CROOKS

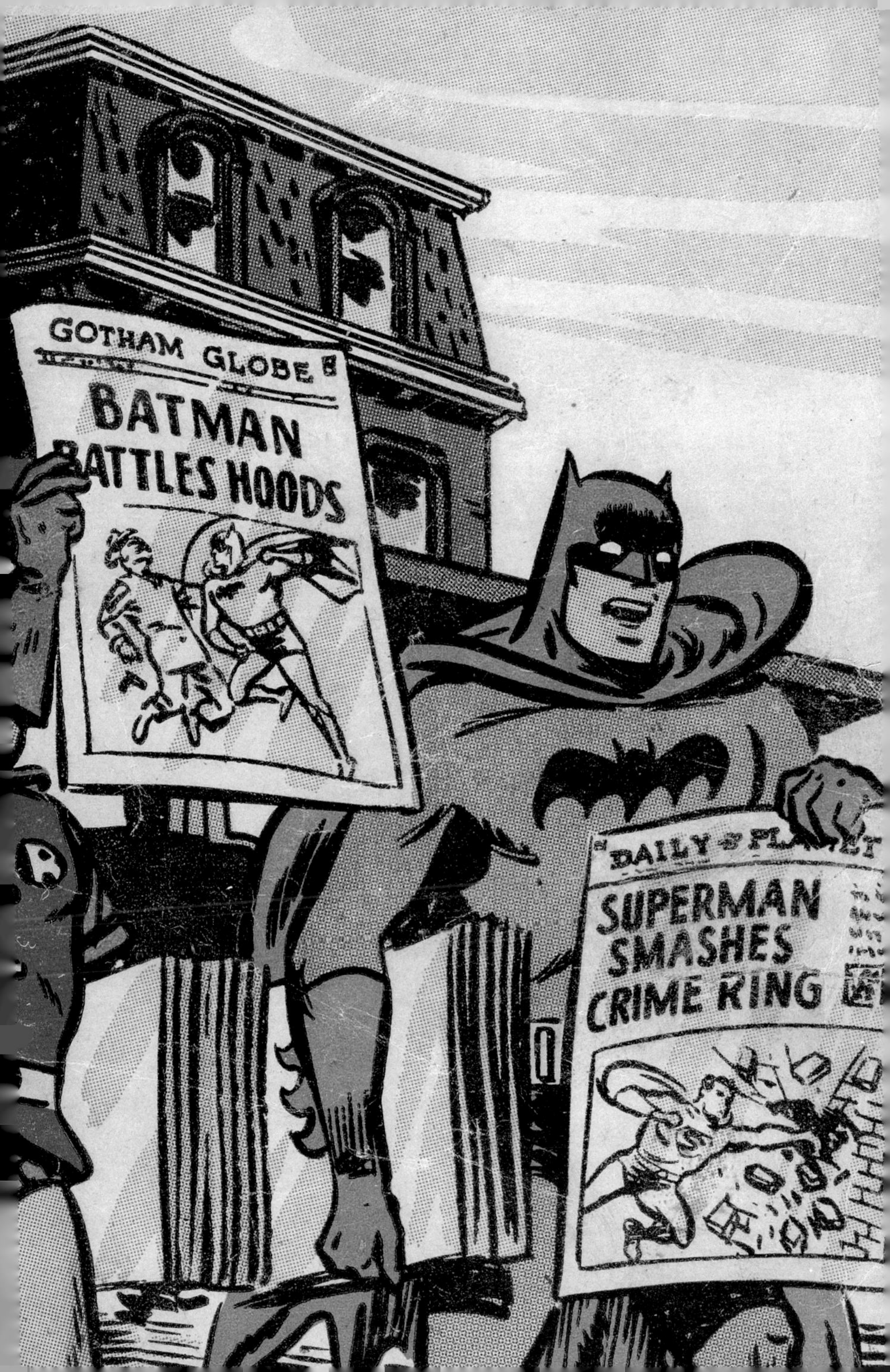
GOTHAM GLOBE
BATMAN
ATTLES HOODS
DAILY
SUPERMAN
SMASHES
CRIME RING

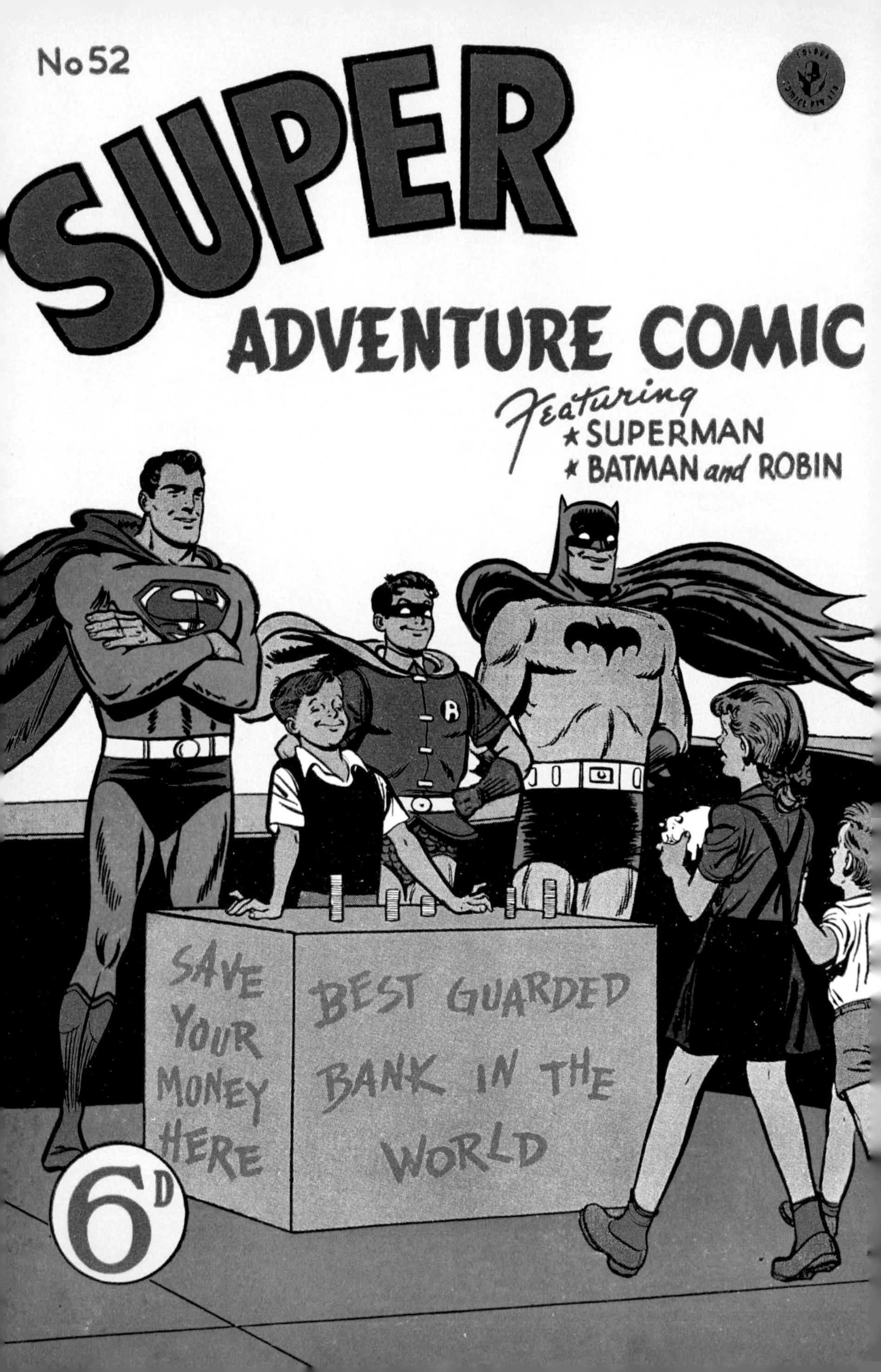
No 52
SUPER
ADVENTURE COMIC
Featuring
★ SUPERMAN
★ BATMAN and ROBIN
SAVE YOUR MONEY HERE
BEST GUARDED BANK IN THE WORLD
6D

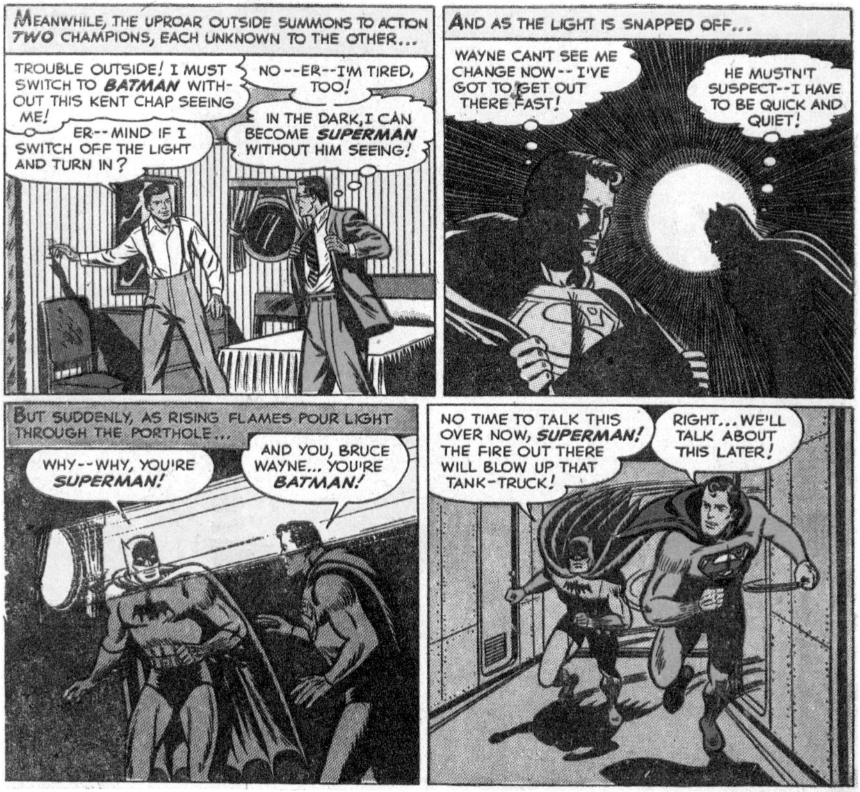
MEANWHILE, THE UPROAR OUTSIDE SUMMONS TO ACTION TWO CHAMPIONS, EACH UNKNOWN TO THE OTHER...
TROUBLE OUTSIDE! I MUST SWITCH TO BATMAN WITHOUT THIS KENT CHAP SEEING ME!
NO--ER--I'M TIRED, TOO!
ER--MIND IF I SWITCH OFF THE LIGHT AND TURN IN?
IN THE DARK, I CAN BECOME SUPERMAN WITHOUT HIM SEEING!
AND AS THE LIGHT IS SNAPPED OFF...
WAYNE CAN'T SEE ME CHANGE NOW--I'VE GOT TO GET OUT THERE FAST!
HE MUSTN'T SUSPECT--I HAVE TO BE QUICK AND QUIET!
BUT SUDDENLY, AS RISING FLAMES POUR LIGHT THROUGH THE PORTHOLE...
WHY--WHY, YOU'RE SUPERMAN!
AND YOU, BRUCE WAYNE... YOU'RE BATMAN!
NO TIME TO TALK THIS OVER NOW, SUPERMAN! THE FIRE OUT THERE WILL BLOW UP THAT TANK-TRUCK!
RIGHT... WE'LL TALK ABOUT THIS LATER!

WORLD'S FINEST COMICS No. 63

PREVIOUS SPREAD: *Cover art, Win Mortimer, March–April 1953.*

SUPER ADVENTURE COMIC No. 52

Cover art, Win Mortimer, October 1954. On DC's behalf, Carroll Rheinstrom spent decades traveling the world and sold the rights to translated comics stories in dozens of countries. Such was the case with this Australian title, which was filled with black and white reprints starring Superman, Batman, and others.

SUPERMAN No. 76

Interior, "The Mightiest Team in the World"; script, Edmond Hamilton; pencils, Curt Swan; inks, Stan Kaye and John Fischetti. May–June 1952. Superman and Batman met on radio in 1945, but in comics they met only on covers and briefly twice in *All-Star Comics*. A fateful shipboard encounter in *Superman* No. 76 was the beginning of their long comic book partnership.

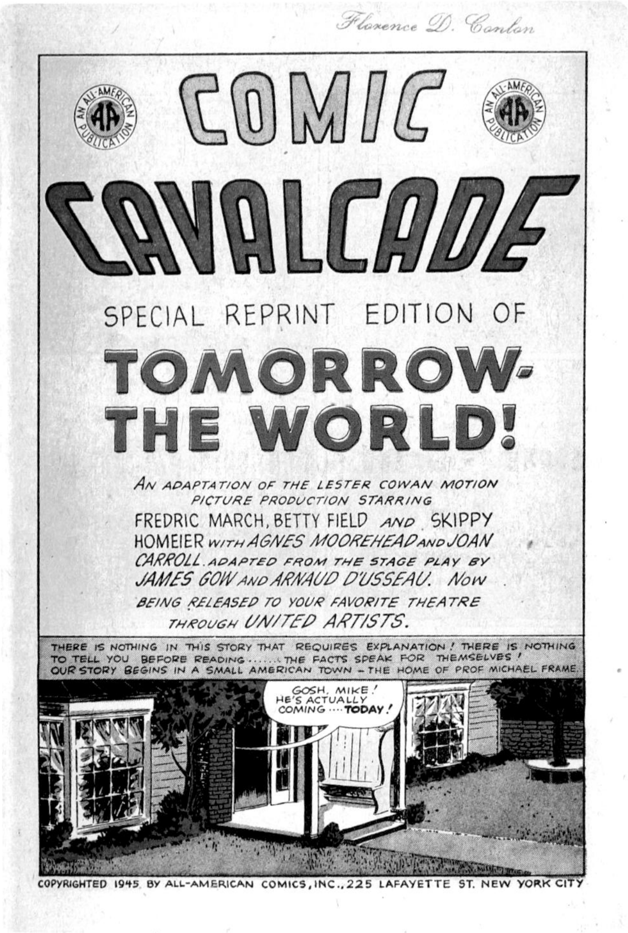
Florence D. Conlon
COMIC CAVALCADE
AN ALL-AMERICAN PUBLICATION
SPECIAL REPRINT EDITION OF
TOMORROW- THE WORLD!
AN ADAPTATION OF THE LESTER COWAN MOTION PICTURE PRODUCTION STARRING FREDRIC MARCH, BETTY FIELD AND SKIPPY HOMEIER WITH AGNES MOOREHEAD AND JOAN CARROLL. ADAPTED FROM THE STAGE PLAY BY JAMES GOW AND ARNAUD D'USSEAU. NOW BEING RELEASED TO YOUR FAVORITE THEATRE THROUGH UNITED ARTISTS.
THERE IS NOTHING IN THIS STORY THAT REQUIRES EXPLANATION! THERE IS NOTHING TO TELL YOU BEFORE READING...... THE FACTS SPEAK FOR THEMSELVES! OUR STORY BEGINS IN A SMALL AMERICAN TOWN - THE HOME OF PROF MICHAEL FRAME.
GOSH, MIKE! HE'S ACTUALLY COMING.... TODAY!
COPYRIGHTED 1945 BY ALL-AMERICAN COMICS, INC., 225 LAFAYETTE ST. NEW YORK CITY

COMIC CAVALCADE

Cover art, E.E. Hibbard. 1945. All-American reprinted several stories like this one (first published in *Comic Cavalcade* No. 10) as standalone giveaway pamphlets. An adaptation of a 1944 movie, "Tomorrow the World" dealt with Americans trying to free a German boy indoctrinated by Nazi propaganda.

COMIC CAVALCADE No. 3

Cover art, Frank Harry, Summer 1943.

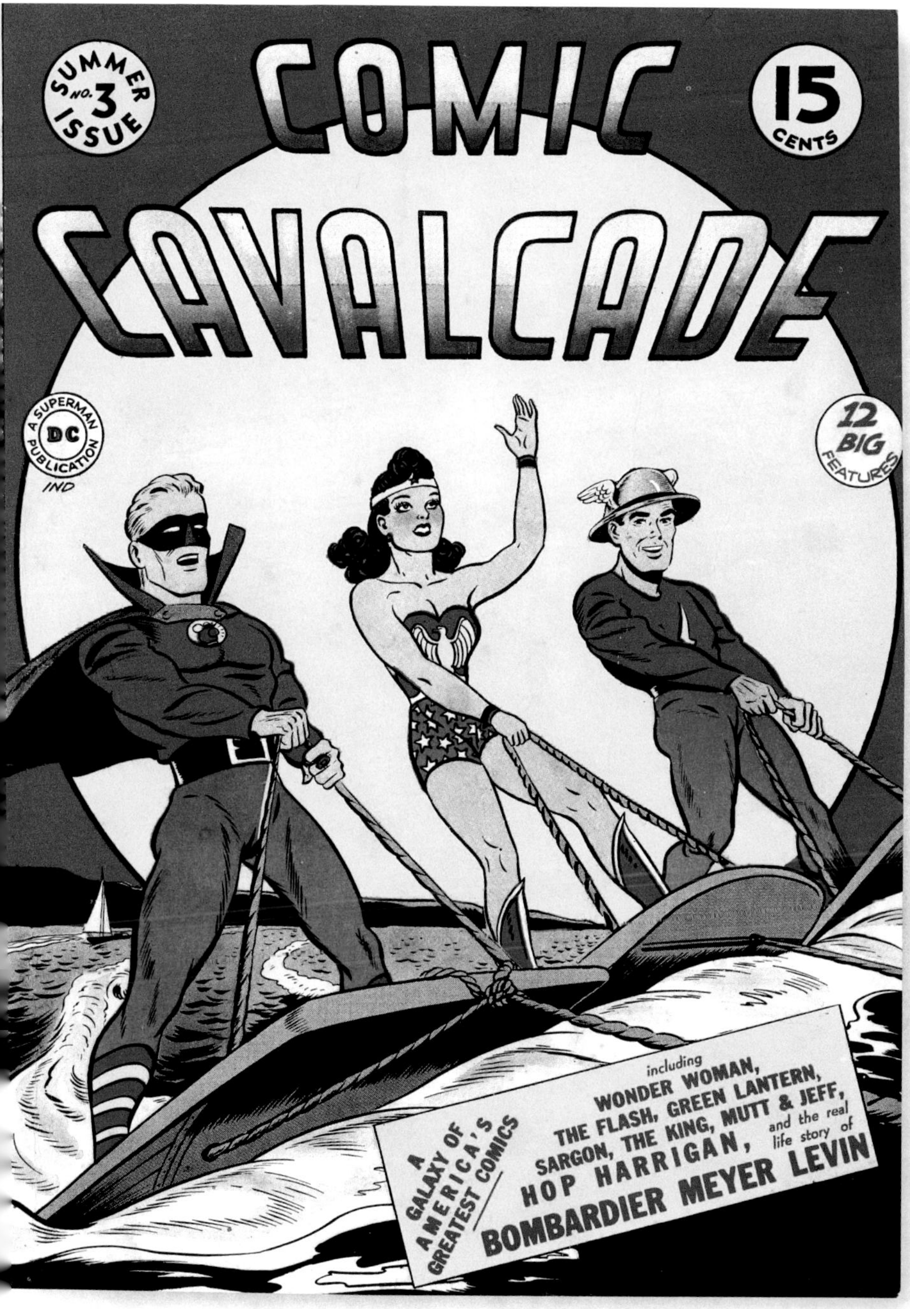
SUMMER NO. 3 ISSUE
COMIC CAVALCADE
15 CENTS
A SUPERMAN DC PUBLICATION
IND
12 BIG FEATURES
including
WONDER WOMAN,
THE FLASH, GREEN LANTERN,
SARGON, THE KING, MUTT & JEFF,
HOP HARRIGAN, and the real life story of
BOMBARDIER MEYER LEVIN
A GALAXY OF AMERICA'S GREATEST COMICS

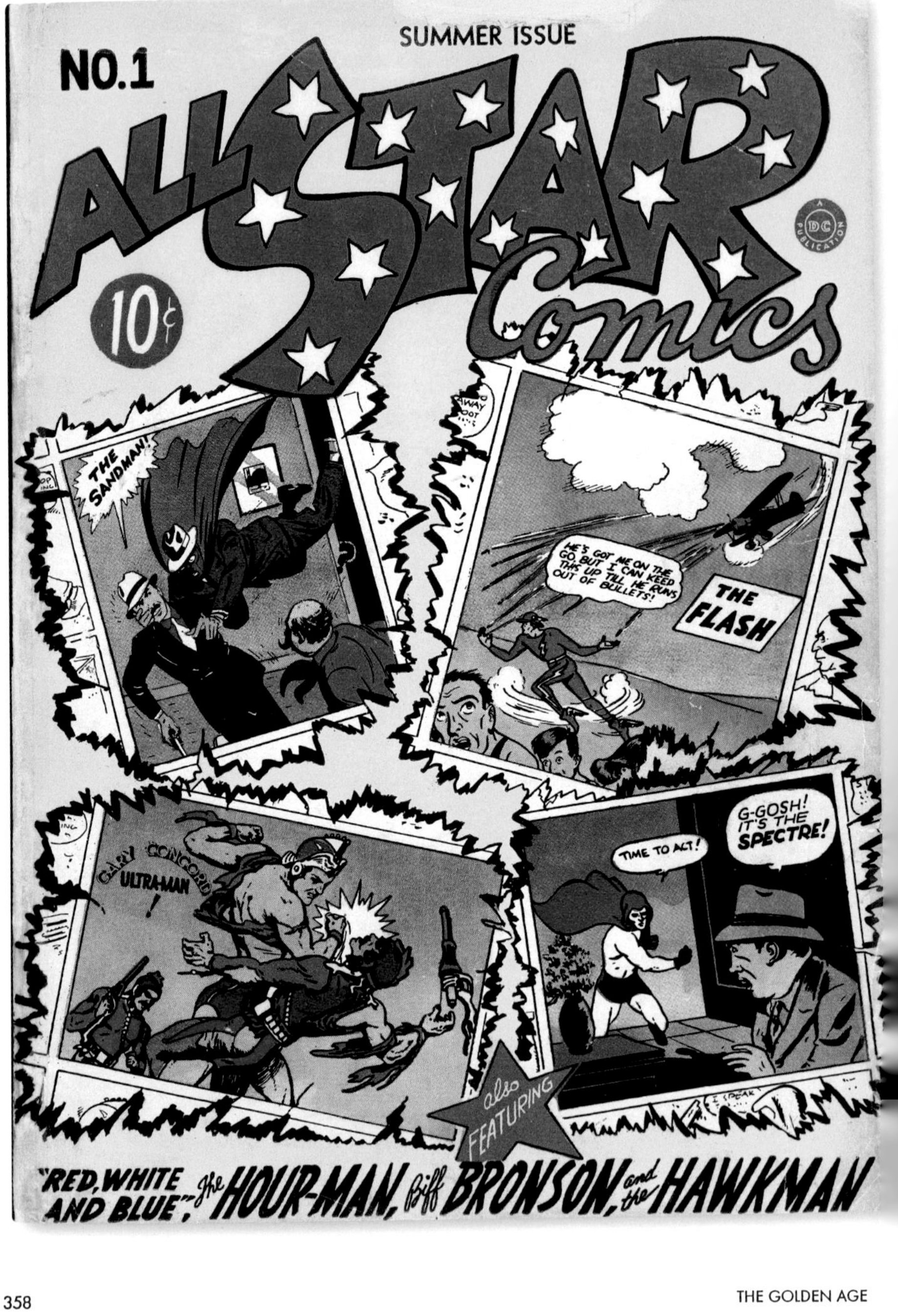
SUMMER ISSUE
NO.1
ALL STAR Comics
10¢
A DC PUBLICATION
THE SANDMAN!
HE'S GOT ME ON THE GO, BUT I CAN KEEP THIS UP TILL HE RUNS OUT OF BULLETS!
THE FLASH
GARY CONCORD ULTRA-MAN!
TIME TO ACT!
G-GOSH! IT'S THE SPECTRE!
also FEATURING
"RED, WHITE AND BLUE", the HOUR-MAN, Biff BRONSON, and the HAWKMAN

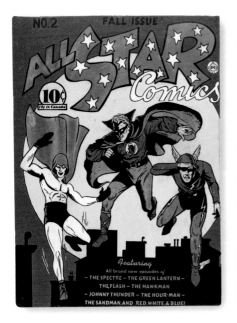

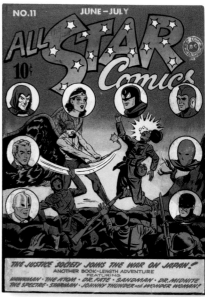

NO.2
FALL ISSUE
ALL STAR Comics
10¢
15¢ in Canada
Featuring
All brand new episodes of
- THE SPECTRE - THE GREEN LANTERN -
THE FLASH - THE HAWKMAN
- JOHNNY THUNDER - THE HOUR-MAN -
THE SANDMAN, AND RED, WHITE, & BLUE!

NO.11
JUNE-JULY
ALL STAR Comics
10¢
THE JUSTICE SOCIETY JOINS THE WAR ON JAPAN!
ANOTHER BOOK-LENGTH ADVENTURE
FEATURING
HAWKMAN · THE ATOM · DR. FATE · SANDMAN · DR. MIDNITE
THE SPECTRE · STARMAN · JOHNNY THUNDER and WONDER WOMAN!

ALL-STAR COMICS No. 1

Cover art, Creig Flessel, Harry Lampert, Jon L. Blummer, and Bernard Baily, Summer 1940. The first two issues of *All-Star Comics* functioned as a sampler of the All-American line with individual stories featuring the Sandman, the Spectre, Ultra-Man, the Flash, and others.

ALL-STAR COMICS No. 2

Cover art, Howard Purcell, Fall 1940. The cover stars of *More Fun Comics* (the Spectre), *All-American Comics* (Green Lantern), and *Flash Comics* (the Flash) were first united on the front of this comic book, an anthology that foreshadowed the formation of the Justice Society one issue later.

ALL-STAR COMICS No. 11

Cover art, Sheldon Moldoff, June–July 1942. Recognizing the All-Star heroes as the resource they were, the United States War Department rechristened them as The Justice Battalion of America for the duration of World War II.

ALL-STAR COMICS No. 16

Interior, "The Justice Society Fights for a United America": script, Gardner Fox; pencils and inks, Joe Gallagher. April–May 1943. With the advent of the U.S.'s entrance into World War II, the Junior Justice Society of America was formed as a fan club for readers of *All-Star Comics*. A 15-cent admission fee paid for a membership package that included a certificate, a metal badge, and an all-important secret decoder key that could be used to translate secret messages in future comics in the All-American line. Members of the Junior JSA even participated in occasional comic book stories as early as *All-Star Comics* No. 16 and as late as No. 40 in 1948.

ALL-STAR COMICS No. 16

Cover art, Frank Harry, April–May 1943. The Justice Society may have received the spotlight, but the point of the cover and its accompanying story was that everyone in the United States was on the same team when it came to defeating the global threat of the Axis powers.

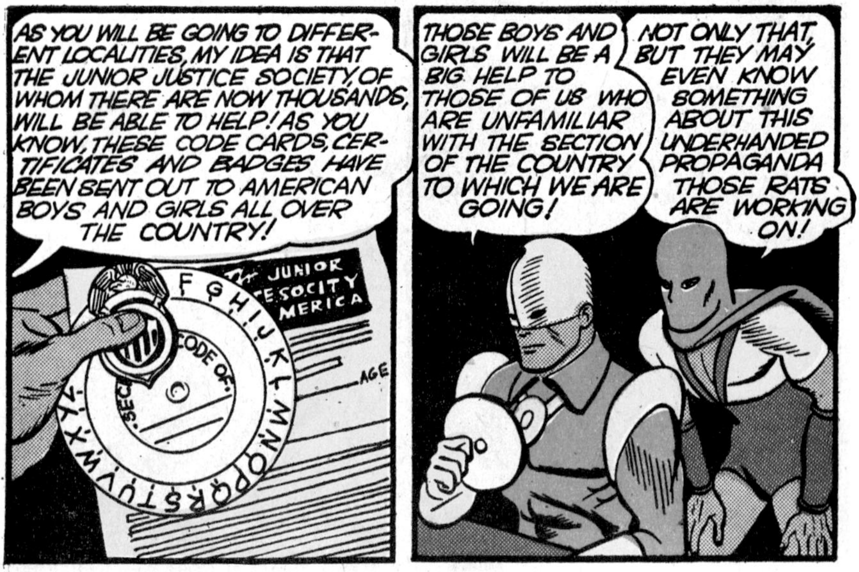
AS YOU WILL BE GOING TO DIFFERENT LOCALITIES, MY IDEA IS THAT THE JUNIOR JUSTICE SOCIETY, OF WHOM THERE ARE NOW THOUSANDS, WILL BE ABLE TO HELP! AS YOU KNOW, THESE CODE CARDS, CERTIFICATES AND BADGES HAVE BEEN SENT OUT TO AMERICAN BOYS AND GIRLS ALL OVER THE COUNTRY!
THOSE BOYS AND GIRLS WILL BE A BIG HELP TO THOSE OF US WHO ARE UNFAMILIAR WITH THE SECTION OF THE COUNTRY TO WHICH WE ARE GOING!
NOT ONLY THAT, BUT THEY MAY EVEN KNOW SOMETHING ABOUT THIS UNDERHANDED PROPAGANDA THOSE RATS ARE WORKING ON!

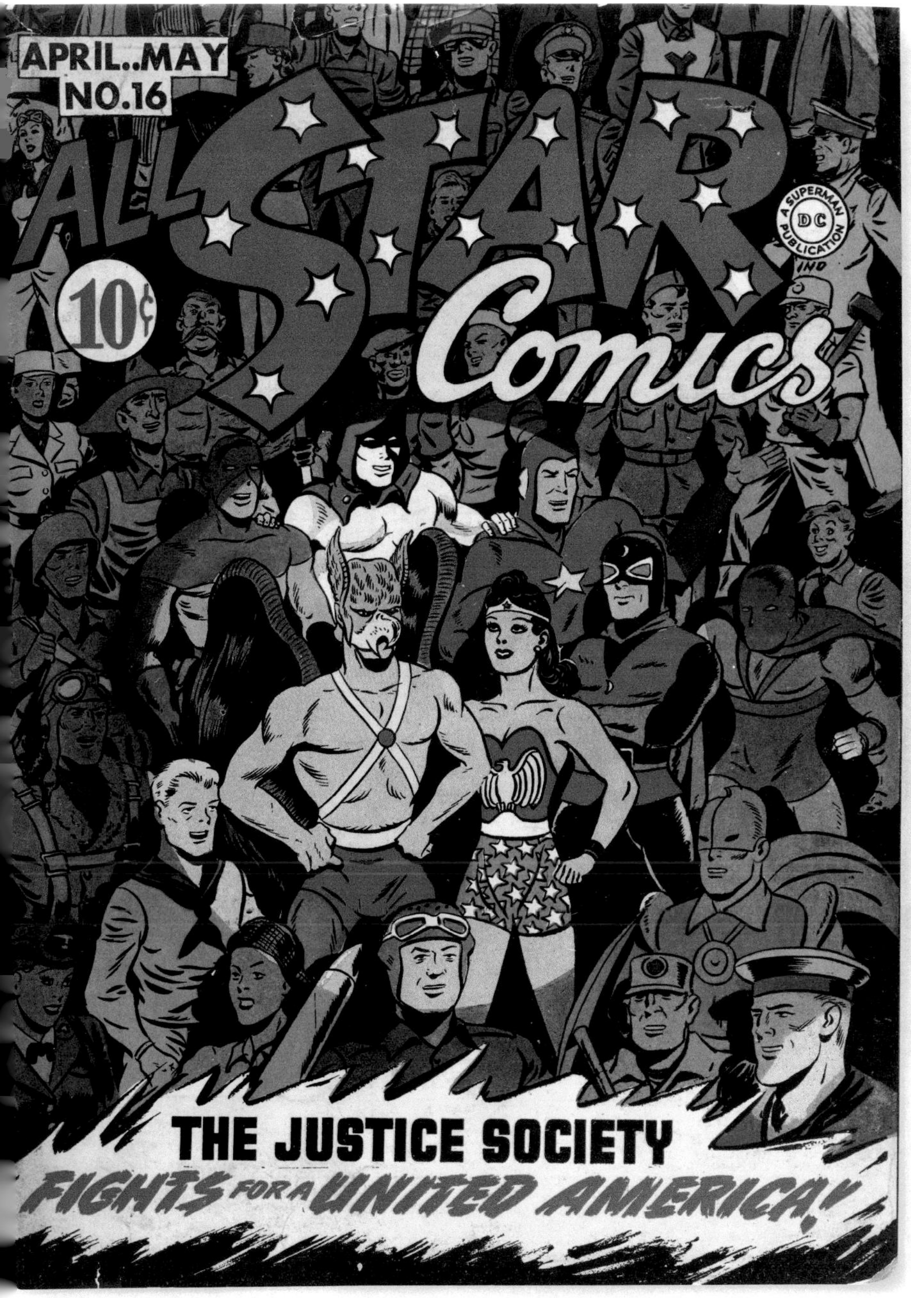
APRIL..MAY
NO.16
ALL STAR Comics
10¢
A SUPERMAN DC PUBLICATION
THE JUSTICE SOCIETY
FIGHTS FOR A UNITED AMERICA!

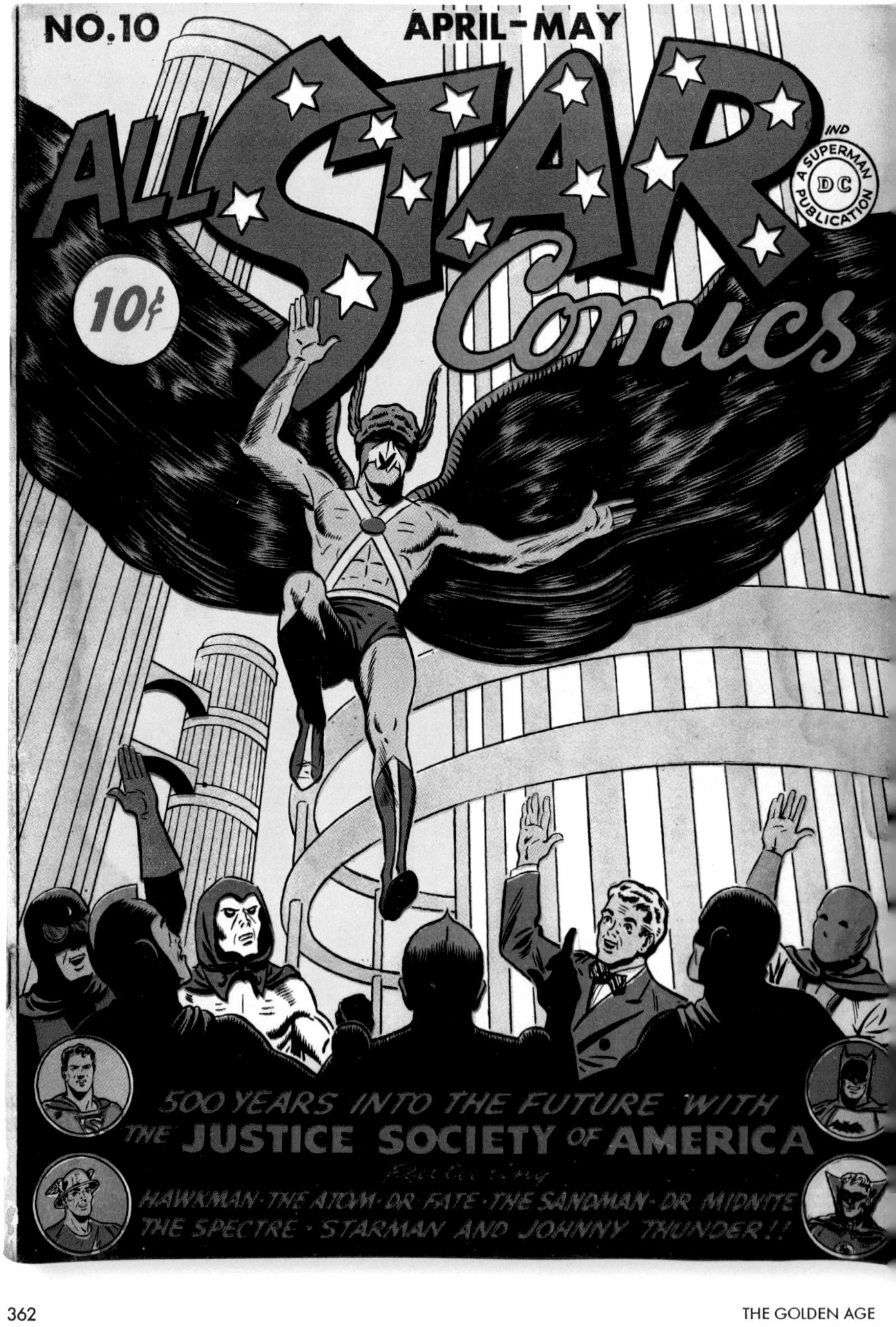
NO.10
APRIL-MAY
ALL STAR Comics
A SUPERMAN DC PUBLICATION
10¢
500 YEARS INTO THE FUTURE WITH
THE JUSTICE SOCIETY OF AMERICA
HAWKMAN · THE ATOM · DR FATE · THE SANDMAN · DR MIDNITE
THE SPECTRE · STARMAN AND JOHNNY THUNDER!!

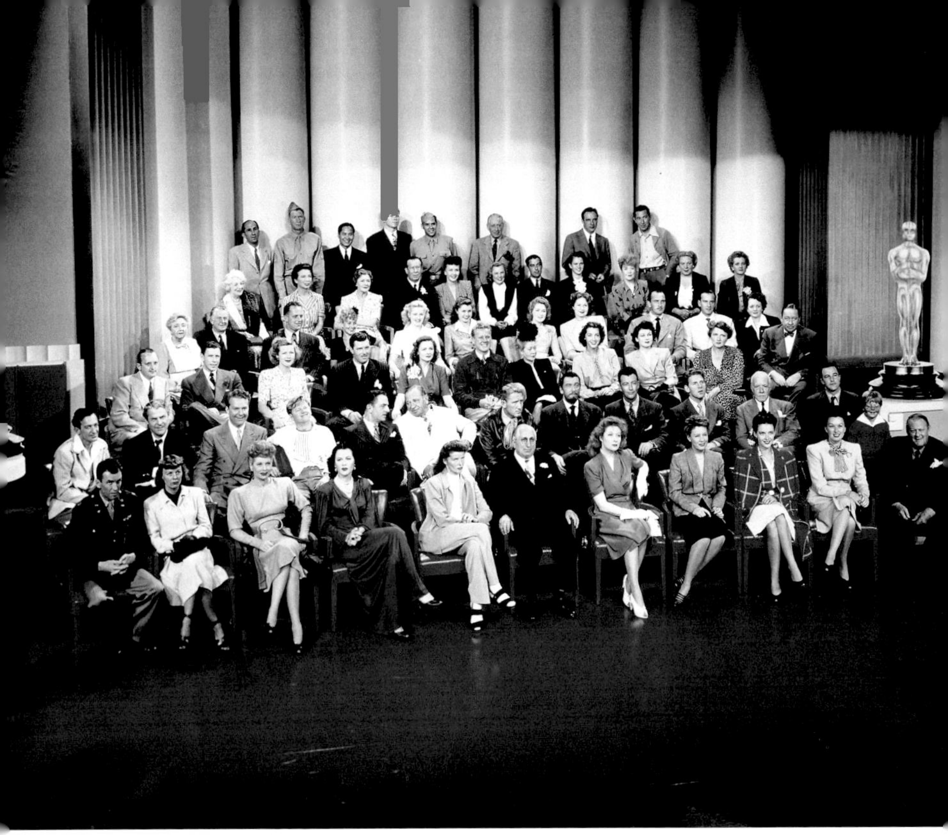

ALL-STAR COMICS No. 10

Cover art, E.E. Hibbard, April–May 1942. In a story produced prior to the 1941 Pearl Harbor attack (but published in early 1942), The Justice Society traveled to 2442 A.D. to assemble the components of a bomb defense formula that would protect the United States from attacks in the present.

MGM STUDIOS PORTRAIT

Photograph, Louis B. Mayer and 65 stars gathered for MGM's 20th anniversary, 1943. "Just as the movie studios had their individual trademarks, their way of lighting, their special approach to subject matter by which they could be identified even if one came in at the middle, so did comic books. National, who produced the DC line, was the MGM of the field. It had the great stars, the crisp-brittle lighting, the elder statesman touch — smoothly exciting, eschewing the more boisterous effects of its less wealthy competitors." — Jules Feiffer

ALL-STAR COMICS No. 33

OPPOSITE: *Cover art, Irwin Hasen.* BELOW: *Interior, "The Revenge of Solomon Grundy"; script, Gardner Fox; art, Irwin Hasen. February–March 1947.* The undead Solomon Grundy — typically an opponent of Green Lantern alone — represented perhaps the most physically powerful threat faced by The Justice Society to that point and ushered in a creative peak for the series that would encompass subsequent menaces like the Wizard, Degaton, and an entire Injustice Society.

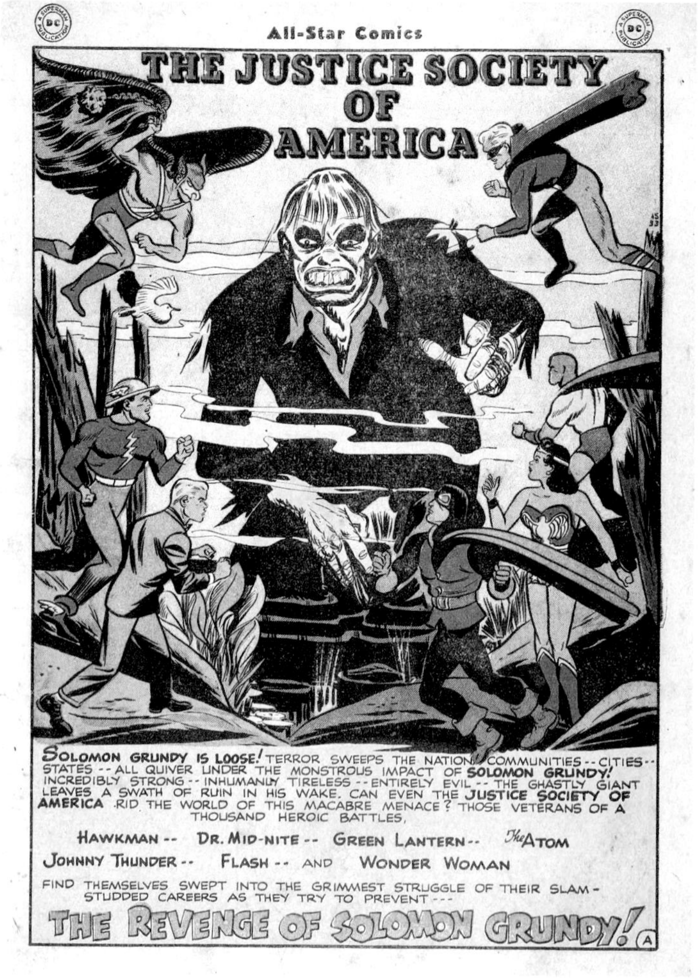
All-Star Comics
THE JUSTICE SOCIETY OF AMERICA
SOLOMON GRUNDY IS LOOSE! TERROR SWEEPS THE NATION! COMMUNITIES -- CITIES -- STATES -- ALL QUIVER UNDER THE MONSTROUS IMPACT OF SOLOMON GRUNDY! INCREDIBLY STRONG -- INHUMANLY TIRELESS -- ENTIRELY EVIL -- THE GHASTLY GIANT LEAVES A SWATH OF RUIN IN HIS WAKE. CAN EVEN THE JUSTICE SOCIETY OF AMERICA RID THE WORLD OF THIS MACABRE MENACE? THOSE VETERANS OF A THOUSAND HEROIC BATTLES,
HAWKMAN -- DR. MID-NITE -- GREEN LANTERN -- THE ATOM
JOHNNY THUNDER -- FLASH -- AND WONDER WOMAN
FIND THEMSELVES SWEPT INTO THE GRIMMEST STRUGGLE OF THEIR SLAM-STUDDED CAREERS AS THEY TRY TO PREVENT ---
THE REVENGE OF SOLOMON GRUNDY!
A

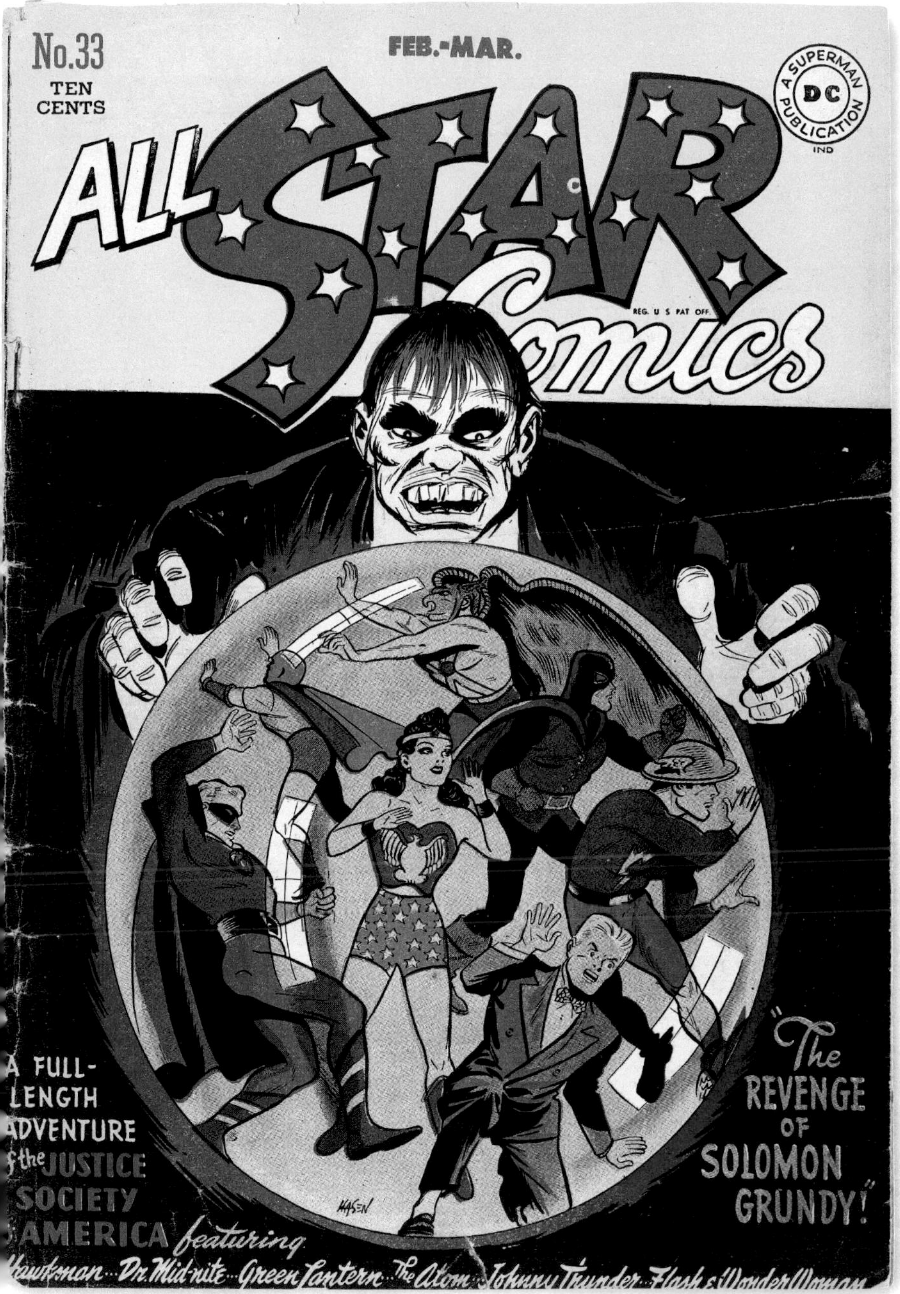
No.33
TEN CENTS
FEB.-MAR.
A SUPERMAN PUBLICATION
DC
IND
ALL STAR Comics
REG. U S PAT OFF.
A FULL-
LENGTH
ADVENTURE
the JUSTICE
SOCIETY
AMERICA featuring
Dr. Mid-nite...Green Lantern...The Atom...Johnny Thunder...
"The
REVENGE
OF
SOLOMON
GRUNDY!"
HASEN

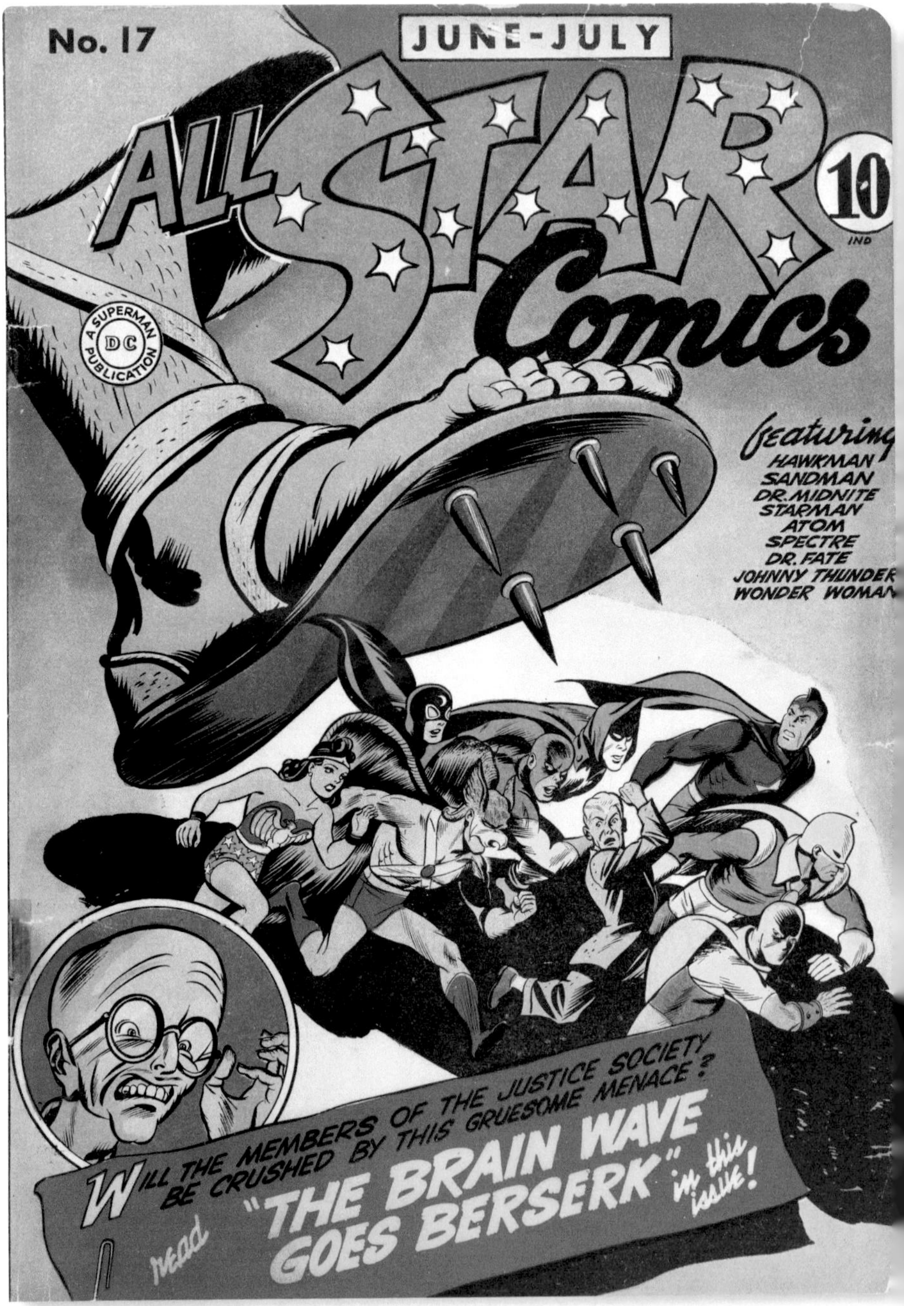
No. 17
JUNE-JULY
ALL STAR Comics
10¢
IND
A SUPERMAN DC PUBLICATION
featuring
HAWKMAN
SANDMAN
DR. MIDNITE
STARMAN
ATOM
SPECTRE
DR. FATE
JOHNNY THUNDER
WONDER WOMAN
WILL THE MEMBERS OF THE JUSTICE SOCIETY BE CRUSHED BY THIS GRUESOME MENACE?
read "THE BRAIN WAVE GOES BERSERK" in this issue!

The JUNIOR JUSTICE SOCIETY OF AMERICA

Headquarters: c/o All Star Comics
480 Lexington Ave., New York, N. Y.

This Certifies that:

Name Andrew James Todd Jr. Age 11

Address Grimes, Virginia

has been duly elected a charter member of this organization upon his or her pledge to help keep our country united in the face of enemy attempts to make us think we Americans are all different, because we are rich or poor; employer or worker; native or foreign-born; Gentile or Jew; Protestant or Catholic. And makes the further pledge to defeat this Axis propaganda, seeking to get us to fight among ourselves, so we cannot successfully fight our enemies--knowing full well that we are all AMERICANS believing in DEMOCRACY and are resolved to do everything possible to help win the war!

This membership is accepted by the above Charter Member upon his or her oath to keep secret the J. J. S. A. code and to follow the announcements of the JUNIOR JUSTICE SOCIETY OF AMERICA in every issue of "ALL-STAR COMICS".

In Witness of which I have this day set my seal and signature as follows:

Diana Prince
(WONDER WOMAN) . . . Secretary

Wonder Woman
REG. U. S. PAT. OFF.

No.

COPYRIGHTED 1942 BY ALL-AMERICAN COMICS INC.

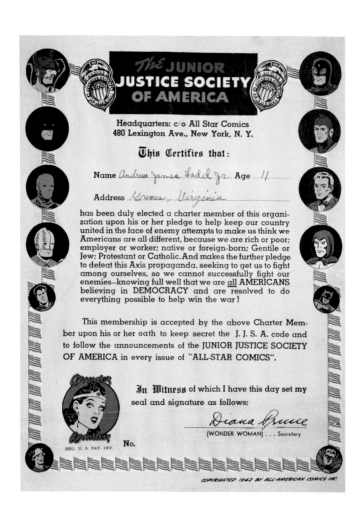

ALL-STAR COMICS No. 17
Cover art, Joe Gallagher, June–July 1943.

JUNIOR JUSTICE
SOCIETY OF AMERICA
Membership certificate, 1942.

No.34
TEN CENTS
APRIL-MAY
ALL STAR Comics
ANOTHER FULL-LENGTH ADVENTURE OF THE JUSTICE SOCIETY OF AMERICA
"THE WILES OF THE WIZARD" FEATURING
THE FLASH, DR.MID-NITE, ATOM, HAWKMAN, JOHNNY THUNDER AND WONDER WOMAN

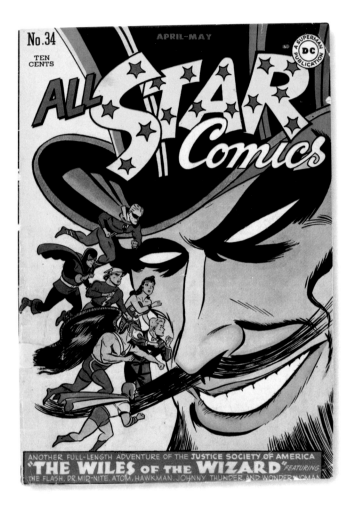

ALL-STAR COMICS No. 34

Cover art, Irwin Hasen, April-May 1947. The blank-eyed Wizard was one of The Justice Society's greatest foes, returning only three issues after his debut to attack them as part of the Injustice Society.

ALL-STAR COMICS No. 50

Cover art, Arthur Peddy and Bob Oksner, December 1949–January 1950. Near the end of its run, Green Lantern, Hawkman, Wonder Woman, and the Flash dominated the covers of *All-Star Comics* at the expense of lesser-known members of The Justice Society.

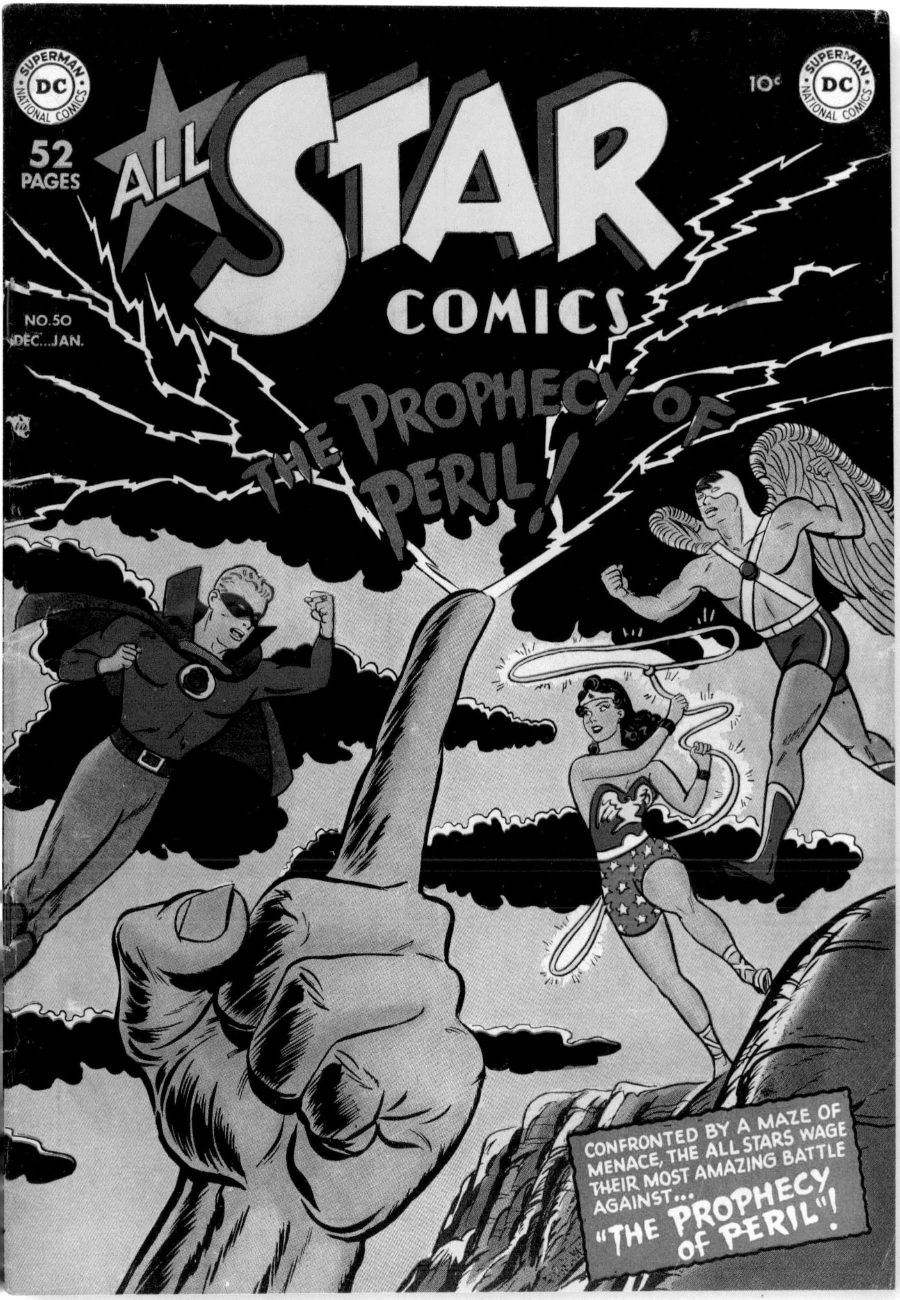
SUPERMAN DC NATIONAL COMICS
52 PAGES
ALL STAR COMICS
10¢
NO.50
DEC...JAN.
THE PROPHECY OF PERIL!
CONFRONTED BY A MAZE OF MENACE, THE ALL STARS WAGE THEIR MOST AMAZING BATTLE AGAINST... "THE PROPHECY OF PERIL"!

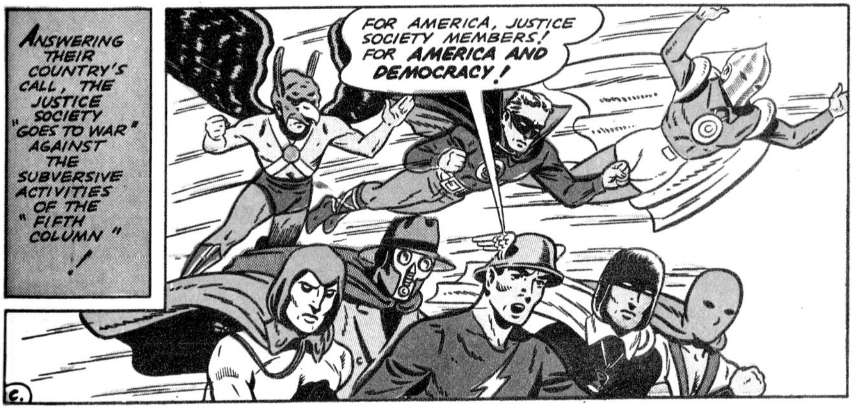
ANSWERING THEIR COUNTRY'S CALL, THE JUSTICE SOCIETY "GOES TO WAR" AGAINST THE SUBVERSIVE ACTIVITIES OF THE "FIFTH COLUMN"!
FOR AMERICA, JUSTICE SOCIETY MEMBERS! FOR AMERICA AND DEMOCRACY!

ALL-STAR COMICS No. 4

Interior, "For America and Democracy"; script, Gardner Fox; art, E.E. Hibbard. March–April 1941. After sitting around a table swapping stories in their first meeting, the nascent Justice Society was summoned to the office of FBI director J. Edgar Hoover and ordered to root out spies and saboteurs across the United States.

LEADING COMICS No. 7

Interior, "Wizard of Wisstark"; script, Joe Samachson; pencils, attributed Pierce Rice; inks, unknown. Summer 1943. "Before the *Magnificent Seven,* there was the Seven Soldiers of Victory; even more than The Justice Society (which I adored), I *loved* this bunch. Particularly, the Vigilante." —Harlan Ellison

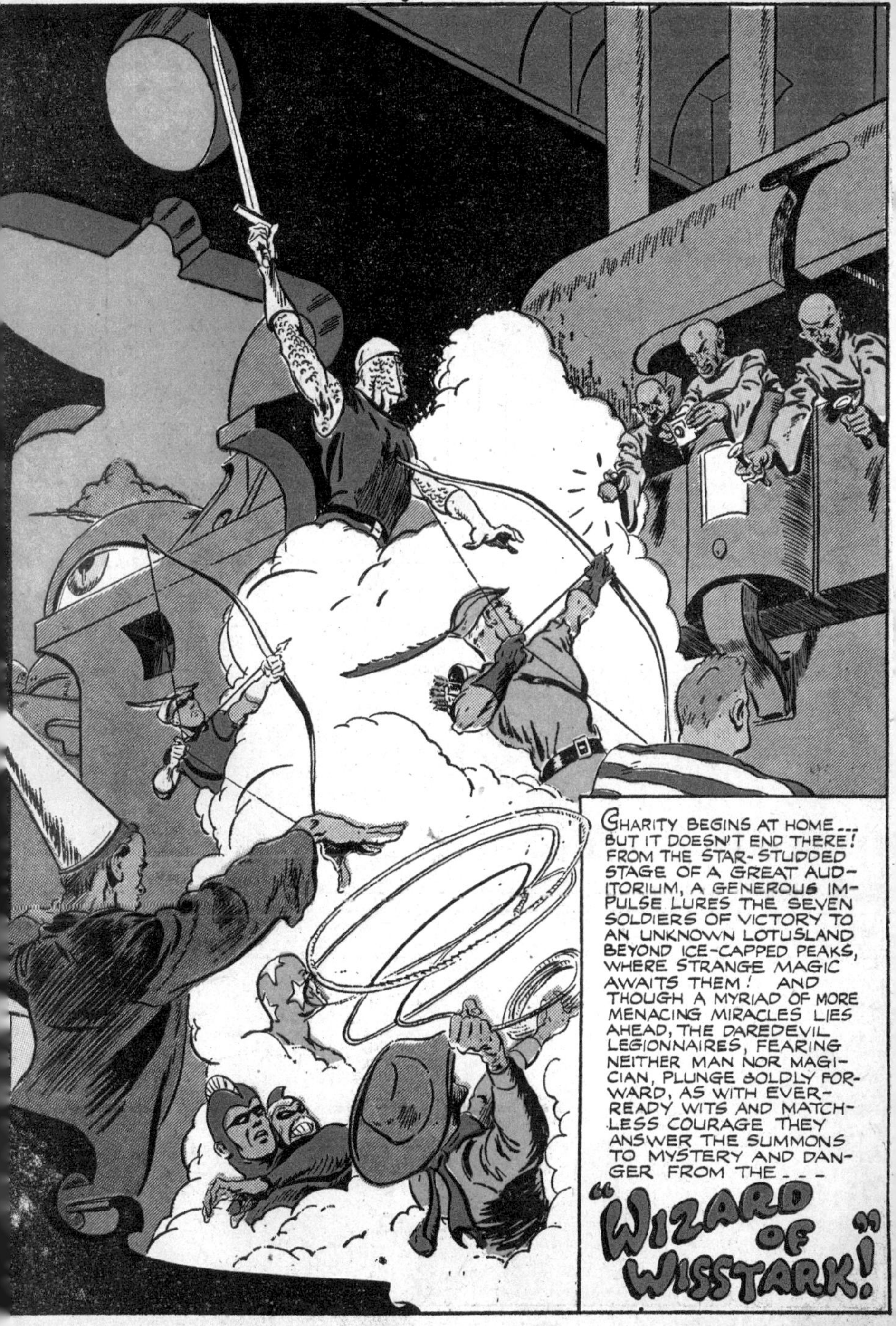
CHARITY BEGINS AT HOME... BUT IT DOESN'T END THERE! FROM THE STAR-STUDDED STAGE OF A GREAT AUDITORIUM, A GENEROUS IMPULSE LURES THE SEVEN SOLDIERS OF VICTORY TO AN UNKNOWN LOTUSLAND BEYOND ICE-CAPPED PEAKS, WHERE STRANGE MAGIC AWAITS THEM! AND THOUGH A MYRIAD OF MORE MENACING MIRACLES LIES AHEAD, THE DAREDEVIL LEGIONNAIRES, FEARING NEITHER MAN NOR MAGICIAN, PLUNGE BOLDLY FORWARD, AS WITH EVER-READY WITS AND MATCHLESS COURAGE THEY ANSWER THE SUMMONS TO MYSTERY AND DANGER FROM THE---
"WIZARD OF WISSTARK!"

96 Pages in FULL COLOR!
25¢
NEW YORK WORLD'S FAIR
COMICS
SUPERMAN
ZATARA
BUTCH The Pup
THE SANDMAN
GINGERSNAP
ALSO
Interesting and Unusual
Features, Stories and Pictures of the Fair
MYSTERY · THRILLS · ADVENTURE
THE ABOVE FAVORITES AND MANY OTHERS!

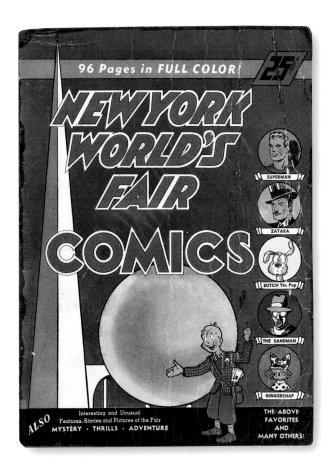

SUPERMAN DAY AT THE NEW YORK WORLD'S FAIR

16mm film stills, including M.C. Gaines (in hat) and Harry Donenfeld (on elephant). July 3, 1940. Only two years old, Superman already was a star to the American public, as evidenced by this promotion, attended by Jerry Siegel, Joe Shuster, and DC executives. *The Saturday Evening Post* later reported, "Superman Day at the World's Fair cracked all attendance records for any single children's event, drawing 36,000 of them at ten cents a head."

NEW YORK WORLD'S FAIR COMICS 1939

Cover art, Vin Sullivan and Fred Guardineer, 1939. The Sandman made his first published appearance in this comic book, released more than a month before his ongoing series began in *Adventure Comics* No. 40.

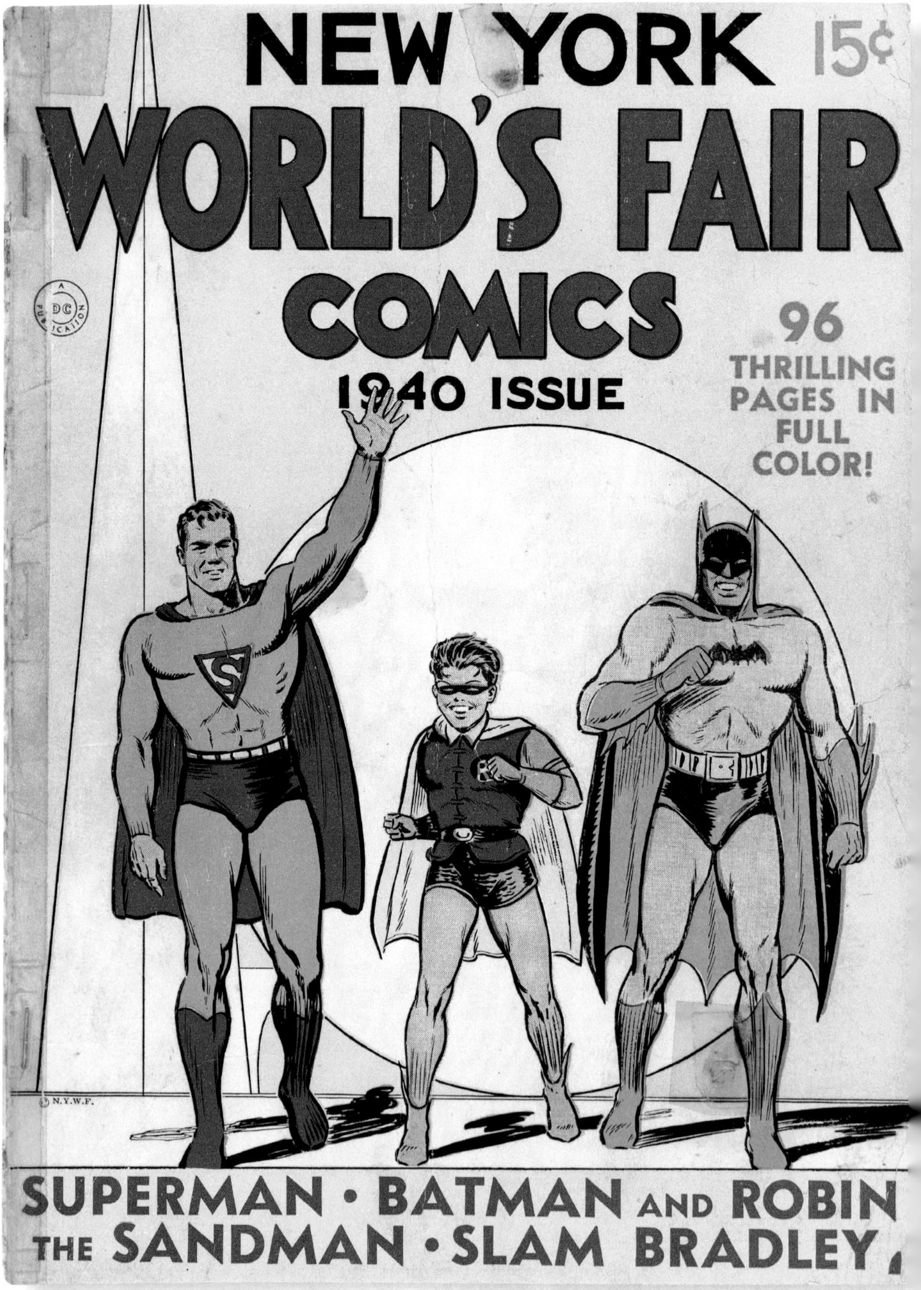
NEW YORK
15¢
WORLD'S FAIR
COMICS
1940 ISSUE
96 THRILLING PAGES IN FULL COLOR!
A DC PUBLICATION
© N.Y.W.F.
SUPERMAN · BATMAN AND ROBIN
THE SANDMAN · SLAM BRADLEY

NEW YORK WORLD'S FAIR No. 2

Cover art, Jack Burnley, 1940. Beyond representing artist Jack Burnley's first illustrations of Superman, the second issue of *New York World's Fair* was also the first time that the Man of Steel stood side by side with Batman and Robin, if only on the cover. Noting that the 15-cent price on the comic book (which was 100 pages rather than 68) didn't deter sales, DC decided to launch an ongoing series in that format that was initially titled *World's Best Comics*.

SUPERMAN AT WORLD'S FAIR

Photograph of actor Ray Middleton as Superman. July 3, 1940. Thirty-three-year-old Ray Middleton earned a place in history at the World's Fair as the first man to portray Superman in the flesh. The actor/singer went on to introduce the role of Frank Butler opposite Ethel Merman in 1946's *Annie Get Your Gun.*

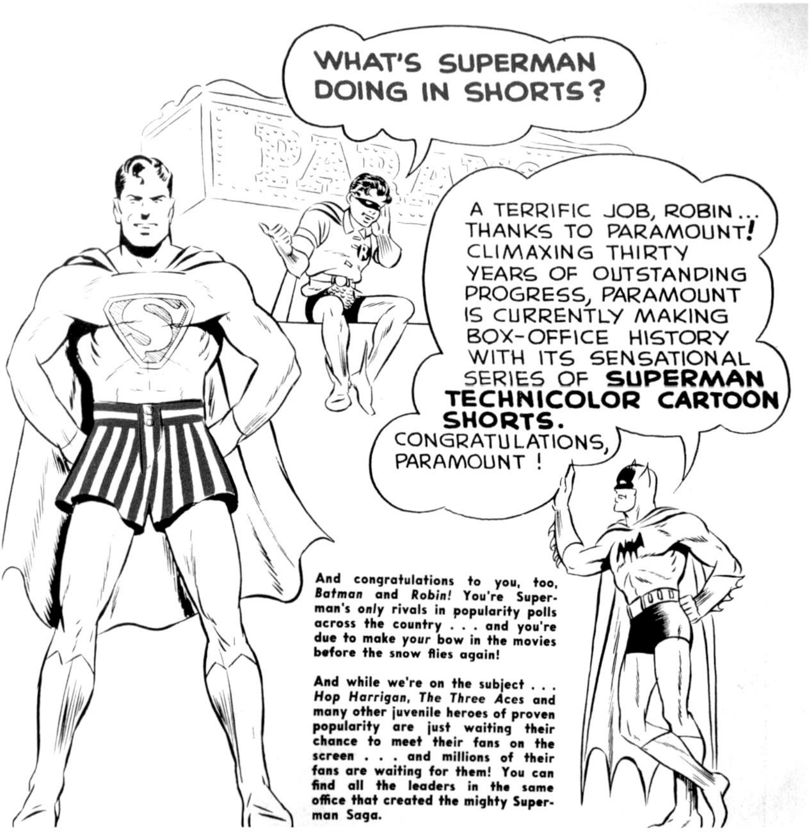
WHAT'S SUPERMAN DOING IN SHORTS?
A TERRIFIC JOB, ROBIN... THANKS TO PARAMOUNT! CLIMAXING THIRTY YEARS OF OUTSTANDING PROGRESS, PARAMOUNT IS CURRENTLY MAKING BOX-OFFICE HISTORY WITH ITS SENSATIONAL SERIES OF SUPERMAN TECHNICOLOR CARTOON SHORTS. CONGRATULATIONS, PARAMOUNT!
And congratulations to you, too, Batman and Robin! You're Superman's only rivals in popularity polls across the country . . . and you're due to make your bow in the movies before the snow flies again!
And while we're on the subject . . . Hop Harrigan, The Three Aces and many other juvenile heroes of proven popularity are just waiting their chance to meet their fans on the screen . . . and millions of their fans are waiting for them! You can find all the leaders in the same office that created the mighty Superman Saga.

SUPERMAN ANIMATED SHORTS

Advertisment, Fleischer Studios and Paramount Pictures, 1941. Batman and Superman also met in ads such as this one for the cartoons that Paramount Pictures began releasing in 1941. The animated short subjects—"shorts"—afforded Robin another opportunity to indulge his fondness for "groaner" plays on words, but the cartoon's success was no laughing matter. The series sustained 17 films over three years and earned an Academy Award nomination in its first year, under the producer-director team of Max and Dave Fleischer.

ALL-AMERICAN COMICS No. 18

Cover art, Sheldon Moldoff, September 1940. Clearly displayed in the background of this cover are the Perisphere and the towering Trylon, a pair of modernistic structures that were the centerpiece of the New York World's Fair.

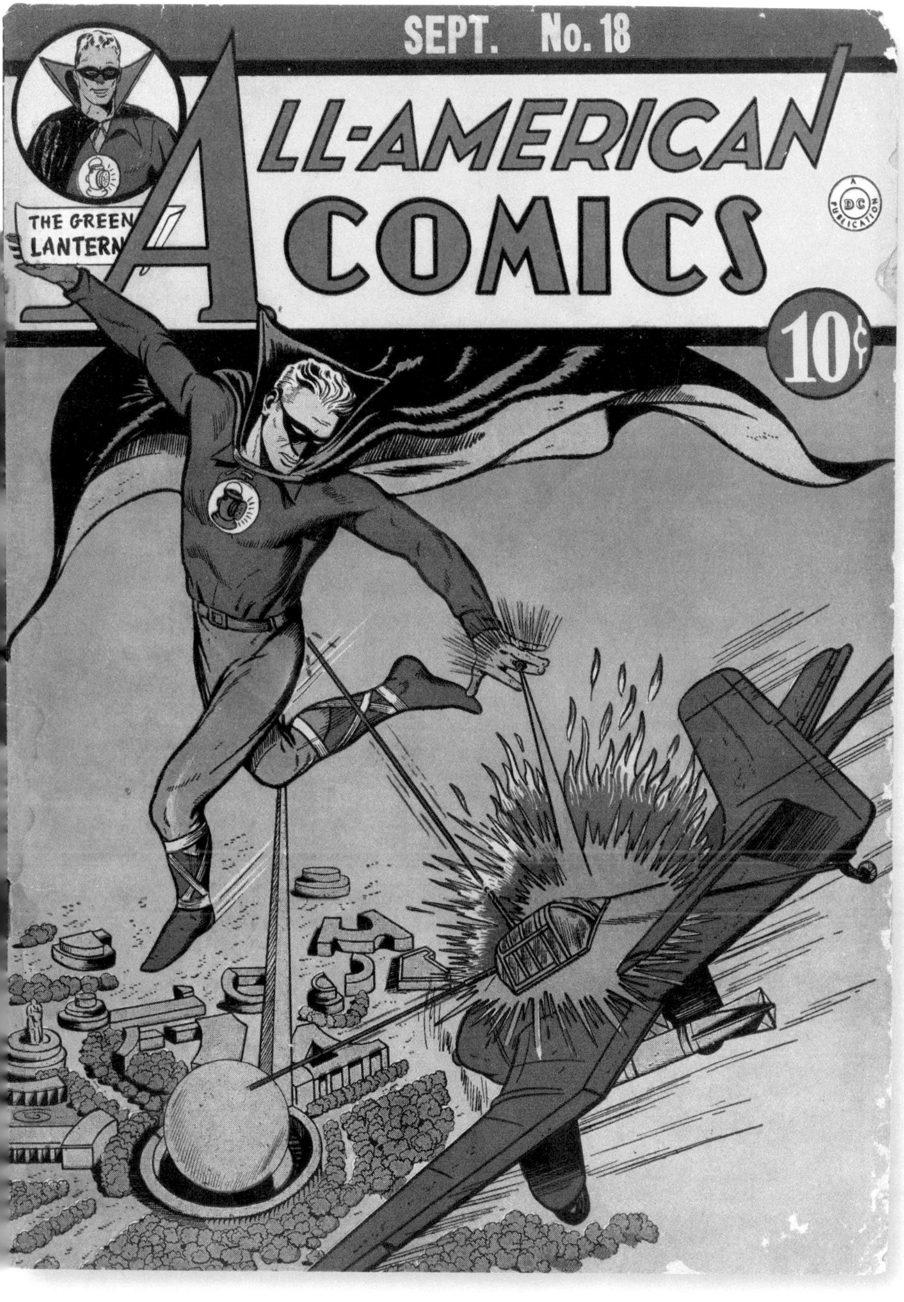
SEPT. No. 18
ALL-AMERICAN COMICS
THE GREEN LANTERN
A DC PUBLICATION
10¢

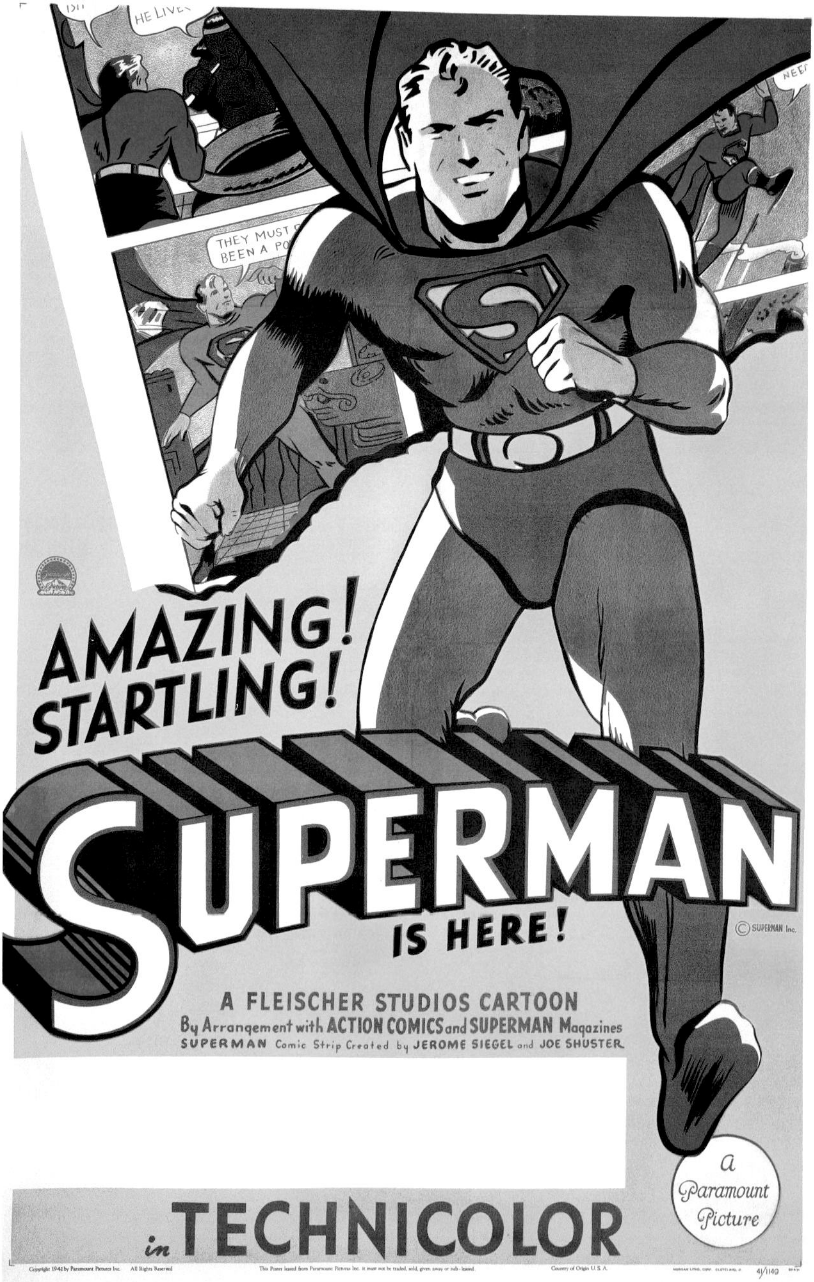
HE LIVE
THEY MUST
BEEN A PO
AMAZING!
STARTLING!
SUPERMAN
IS HERE!
© SUPERMAN Inc.
A FLEISCHER STUDIOS CARTOON
By Arrangement with ACTION COMICS and SUPERMAN Magazines
SUPERMAN Comic Strip Created by JEROME SIEGEL and JOE SHUSTER
a Paramount Picture
in TECHNICOLOR
Copyright 1941 by Paramount Pictures Inc. All Rights Reserved
This Poster leased from Paramount Pictures Inc. it must not be traded, sold, given away or sub-leased.
Country of Origin U.S.A.
41/1149

SUPERMAN IS HERE!

Poster, Max Fleischer's Superman *animated shorts, Fleischer Studios and Paramount Pictures, 1941.* "The Fleischer Superman cartoons were the first Hollywood cartoons not based on fairy tales or revolving around slapstick sight gags. They were the first to tell serious science-fiction stories in a strong visual style combining the art of Joe Shuster's comics with graphics straight off a pulp magazine cover. They are fast paced and exciting, and as far as I'm concerned, all the super hero movies of today — live action or animated — owe a tip of the hat to these remarkable cartoons." — Jerry Beck

STÅLMANNEN

Poster, Swedish release, 1941.

I DETTA PROGRAM INGÅR
MAX FLEISCHERS TECKNADE KORTFILM I FÄRG
STÅLMANNEN
[SUPER MAN]

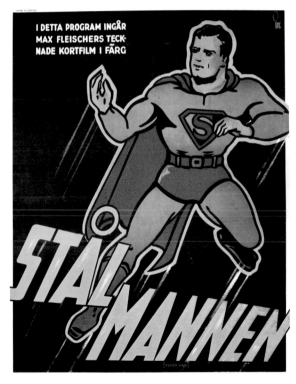

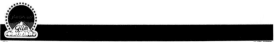

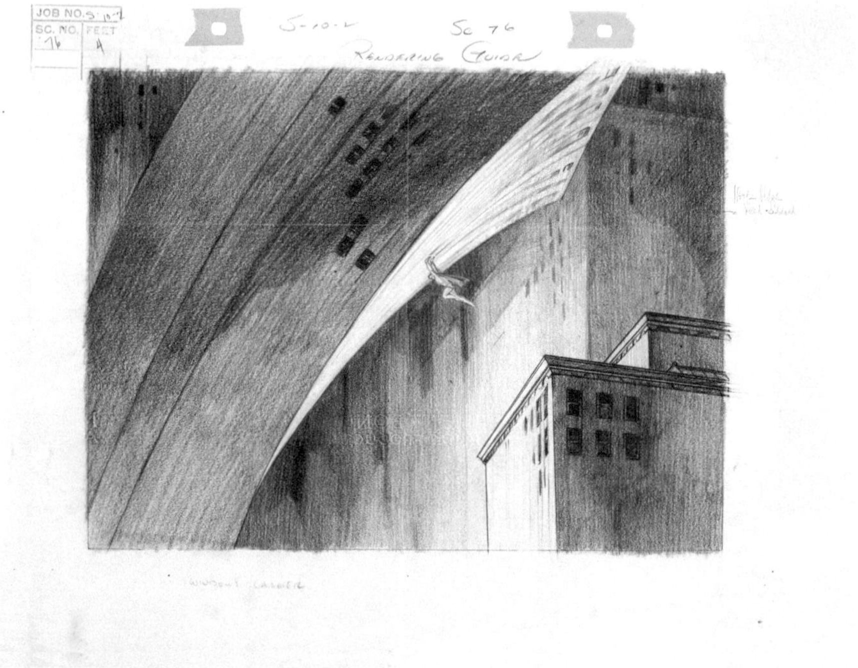
JOB NO. S-10-2
SC. NO. FEET
76 4
S-10-2
Sc 76
RENDERING GUIDE

FLEISCHER STUDIOS SUPERMAN

Layout drawing and animation cel detail. Superman *(first episode):*
producer, Max Fleischer: director, Dave Fleischer: animation, Steve
Muffati and Frank Endres. 1941. As a precursor to their official
Superman cartoon. Fleischer Studios first created a test reel.
"I couldn't figure how to make Superman look right without
spending a lot of money." director Dave Fleischer recalled.
"I told [Paramount] they'd have to spend $90,000 on each one."
That amount was about triple the traditional budget for similar
cartoons at the time. To his amazement, the studio agreed!

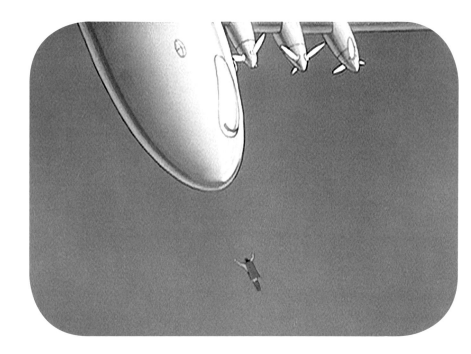

SUPERMAN, MATINEE IDOL

ABOVE AND OPPOSITE ABOVE: *Animation cels, animation, Myron Waldman and Nicholas Tafuri. September 18, 1942. "Billion Dollar Limited": animation, Frank Endres and Myron Waldman. January 9, 1942. "The Bulleteers": animation, Orestes Calpini and Graham Place. March 27, 1942. "Showdown": animation, Steve Muffati and Graham Place. October 16, 1942.*

The popularity of the Superman shorts extended to DC's comic books, where the Newsboy Legion could be found enjoying one of the films in 1942's *Star Spangled Comics* No. 11. Far more unusual, however, was the story in *Superman* No. 19, wherein Lois Lane and Clark Kent watched a cartoon that was a sequel to Fleischer's first installment in the series. At one point, noting that his secret identity was about to be revealed on screen, Clark created a distraction to keep Lois from noticing.

SUPERMAN TEST REEL IMAGE

OPPOSITE BELOW: *Animation cel; producer, Max Fleischer; director, Dave Fleischer. 1940.*

The actors providing the voices of Superman, Lois Lane, and Perry White were Bud Collyer, Joan Alexander, and Jackson Beck, the same trio performing those duties on the popular radio broadcast.

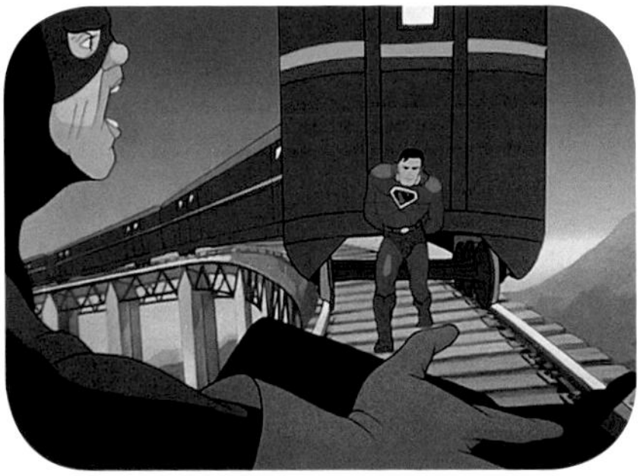
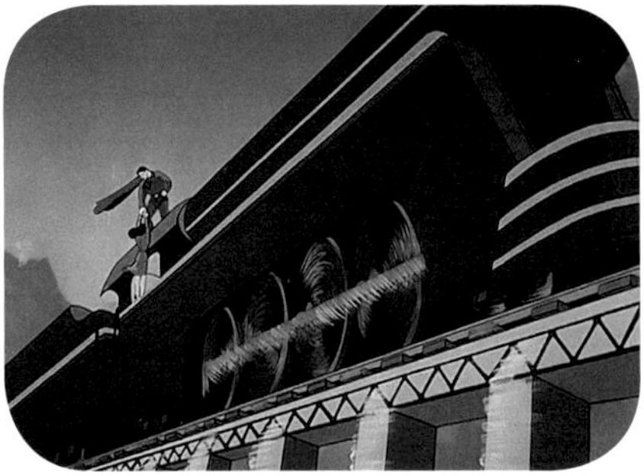
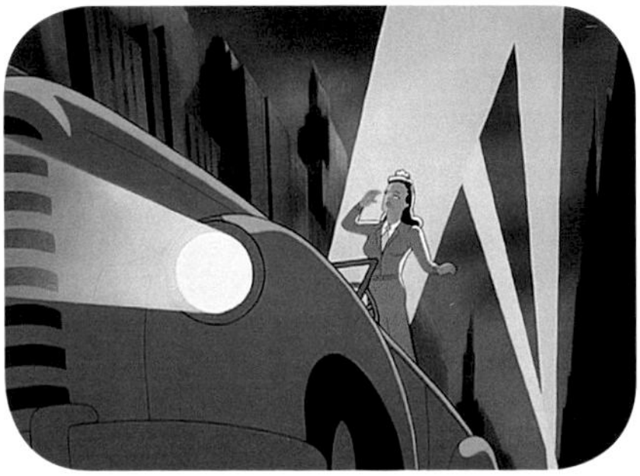
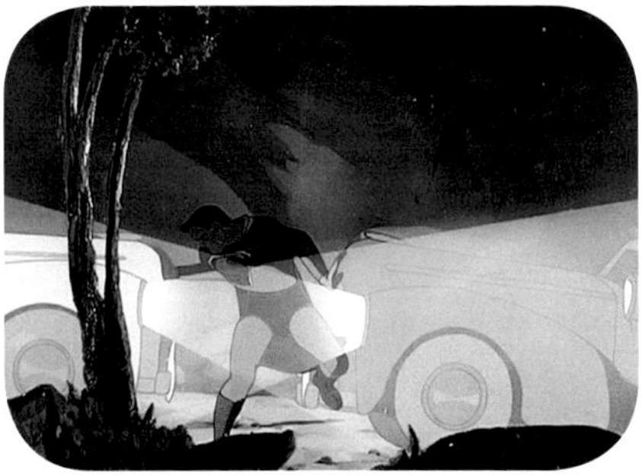
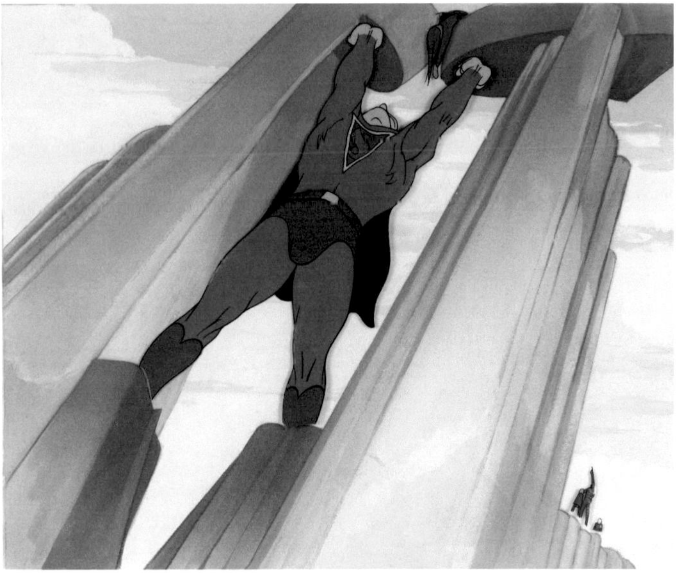

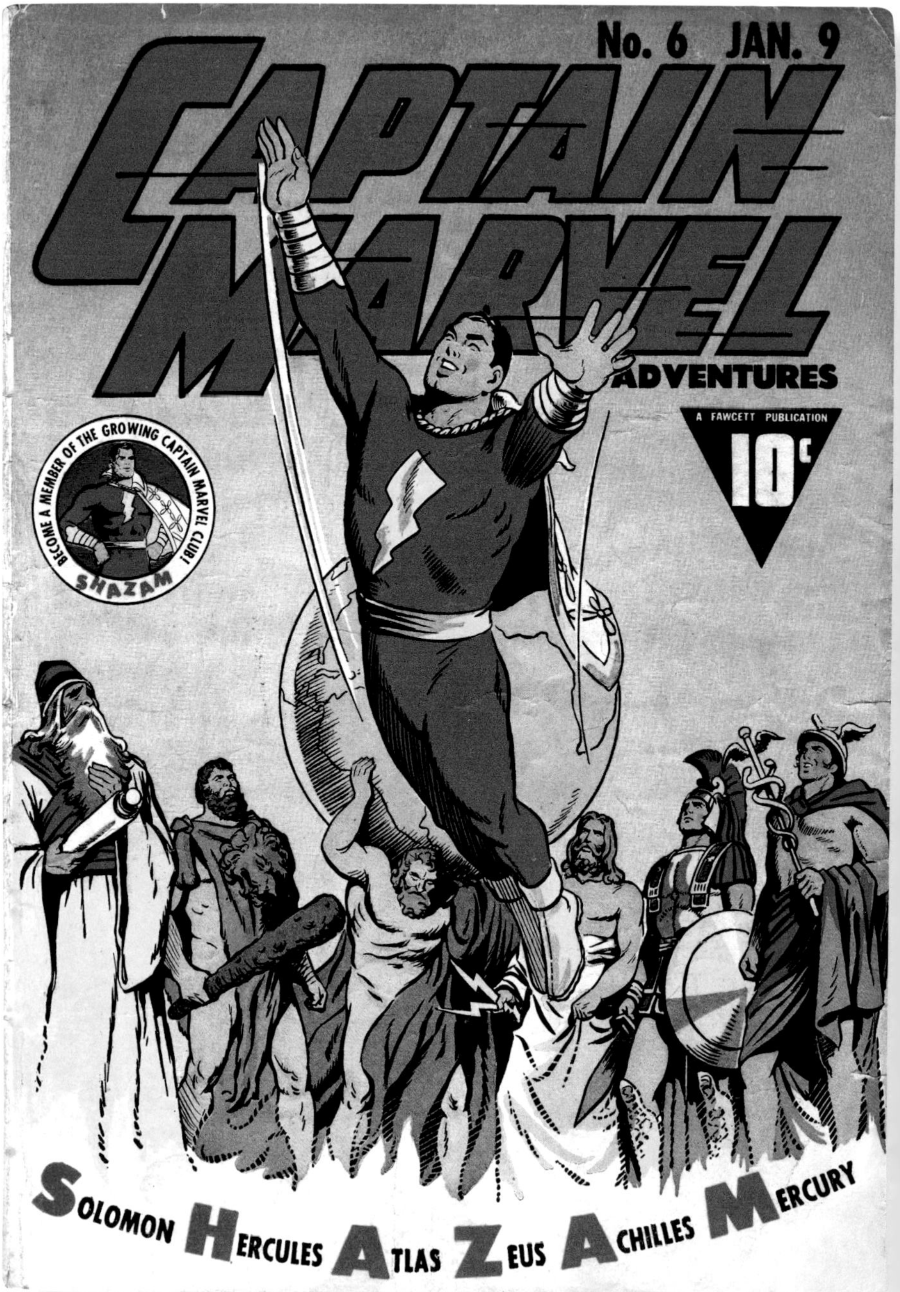
No. 6 JAN. 9
CAPTAIN MARVEL ADVENTURES
A FAWCETT PUBLICATION
10¢
BECOME A MEMBER OF THE GROWING CAPTAIN MARVEL CLUB!
SHAZAM
SOLOMON HERCULES ATLAS ZEUS ACHILLES MERCURY

C. C. Beck

CAPTAIN MARVEL ADVENTURES No. 6
Cover art, C.C. Beck and Pete Costanza, January 9, 1942.

C. C. BECK & THE FAWCETT ART STAFF
Photograph, Beck (standing). Seated, left to right, Marc Swayze, Richard Deane Taylor (aka Meyer Tuck Schneider), and Jack Keats: Fawcett Publications, Paramount Building, New York City. 1942. Under the art direction of Al Allard, Fawcett's talented crew of illustrators produced many of its Captain Marvel stories, adhering to the style established by C.C. Beck. A gifted mimic, Swayze was able to replicate Beck's look with ease and rivaled him in the number of pages produced during World War II. Other Fawcett comics were created by the Jack Binder shop in New Jersey.

CAPTAIN MARVEL ADVENTURES No. 80

Interior, "Captain Marvel in the Land of Surrealism"; writer, Otto Binder; art, C.C. Beck and Pete Costanza. January 1948. Artist C.C. Beck had strong opinions about what did and did not mak good comic book artwork. Similarly, painter Leonardo da Vinc took offense that his painting was interpreted as modern art and escorted Captain Marvel to a surreal dimension where he proved that he simply drew from life.

WHIZ COMICS No. 22

Cover art, C.C. Beck and Pete Costanza, October 3, 1941.

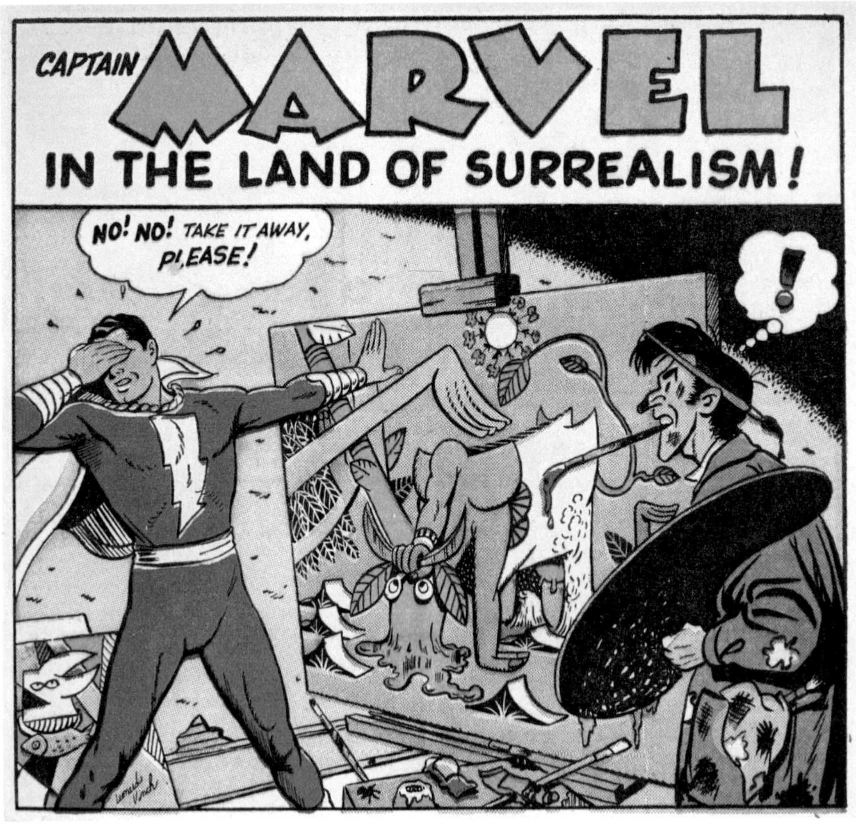
CAPTAIN MARVEL
IN THE LAND OF SURREALISM!
NO! NO! TAKE IT AWAY, PLEASE!
!

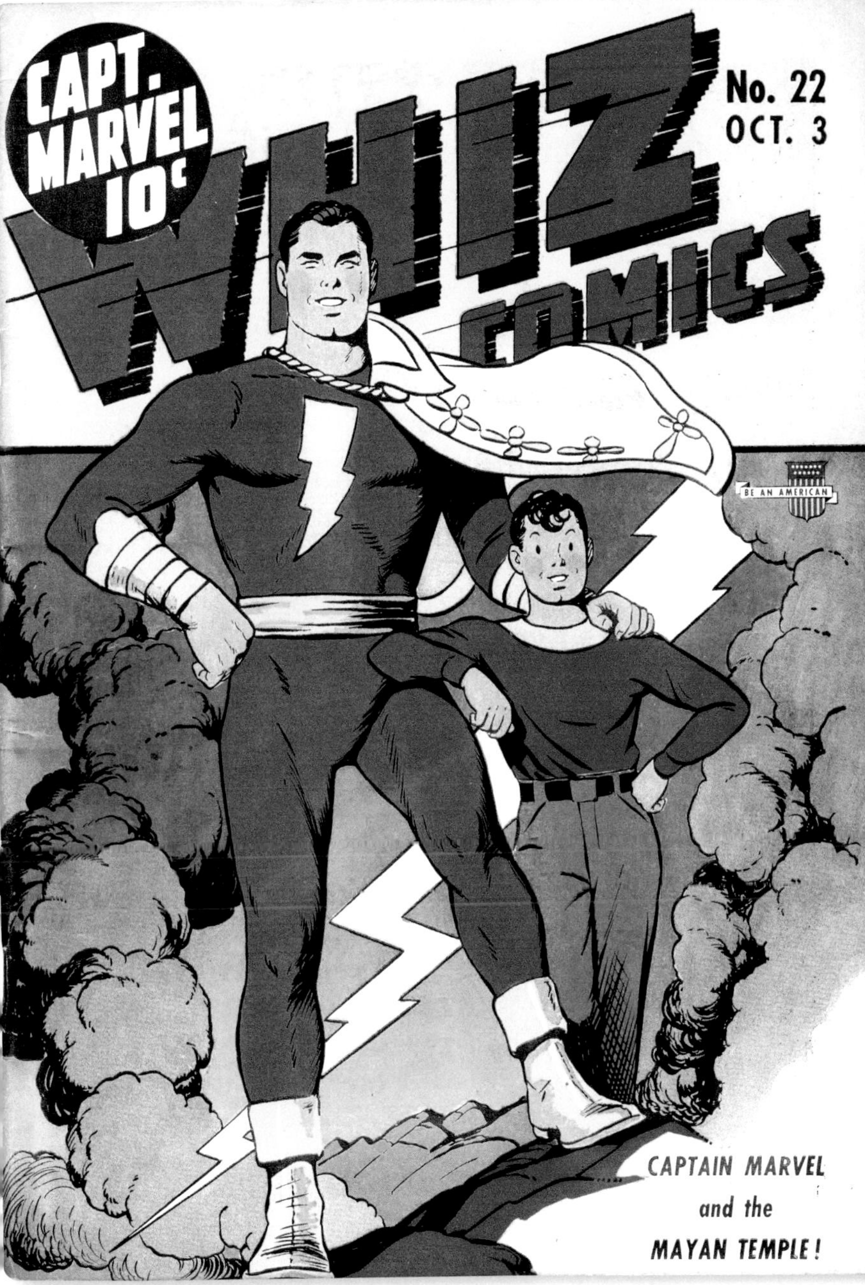
CAPT. MARVEL 10¢
WHIZ COMICS
No. 22
OCT. 3
BE AN AMERICAN
CAPTAIN MARVEL
and the
MAYAN TEMPLE!

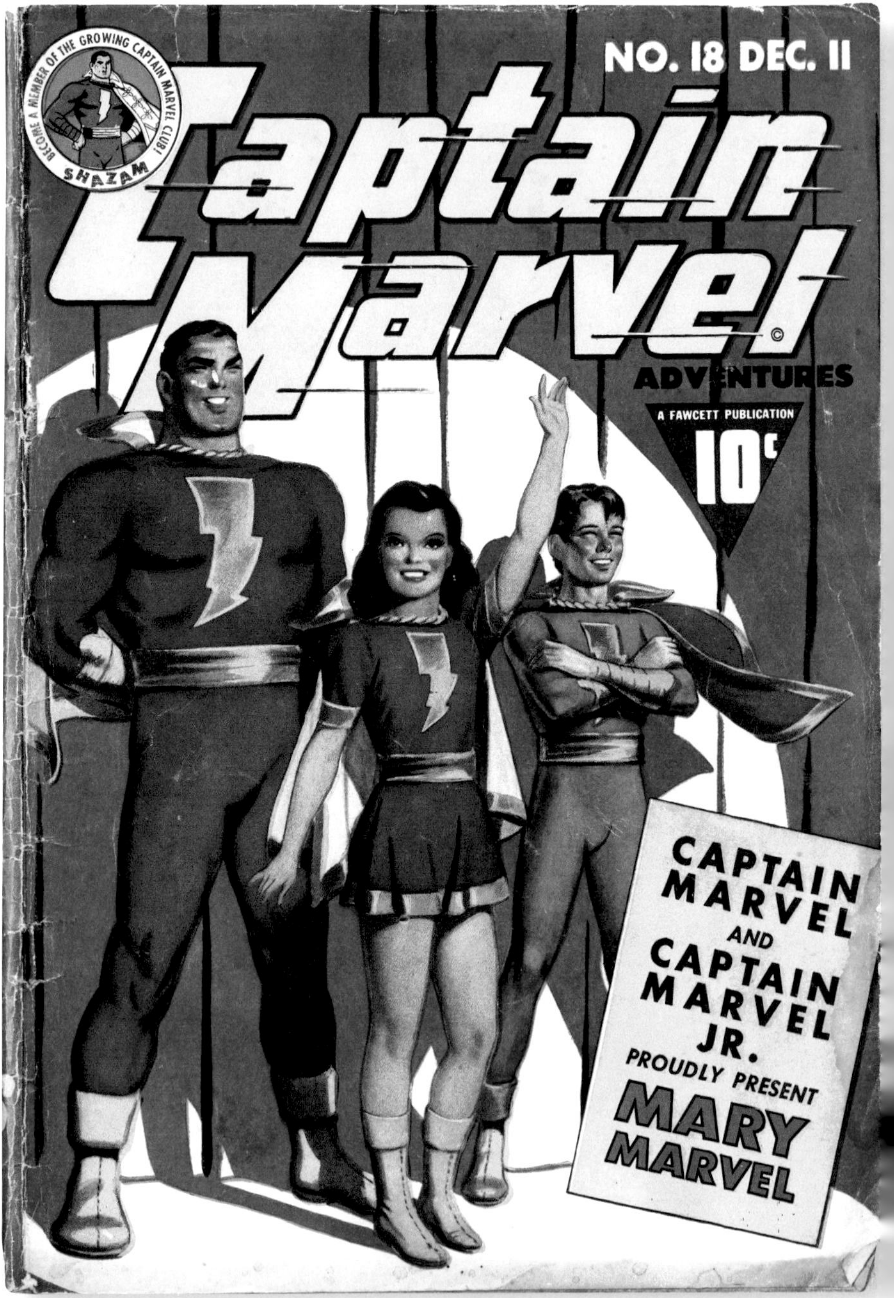
BECOME A MEMBER OF THE GROWING CAPTAIN MARVEL CLUB!
SHAZAM
NO. 18 DEC. 11
Captain Marvel ©
ADVENTURES
A FAWCETT PUBLICATION
10¢
CAPTAIN MARVEL AND CAPTAIN MARVEL JR. PROUDLY PRESENT
MARY MARVEL

"C.C. Beck's Captain Marvel, with its emphasis on magic and cartoony humor, was not only the most popular, by far, of the first-generation super hero comics, it was the one most clearly directed at the youngest readers."

— ART SPIEGELMAN
& FRANÇOISE MOULY

CAPTAIN MARVEL ADVENTURES No. 18
Cover art, C. C. Beck, December 11, 1942. The introduction of Mary Marvel created a Captain Marvel spinoff with special appeal to girls and completed the trinity known as the Marvel Family. The issue's painted cover was one of the first in comics and added a heretofore unrealized level of realism to the fanciful concept of super heroes.

MARVEL FAMILY HALLOWEEN
Photograph, anonymous, ca. 1945.

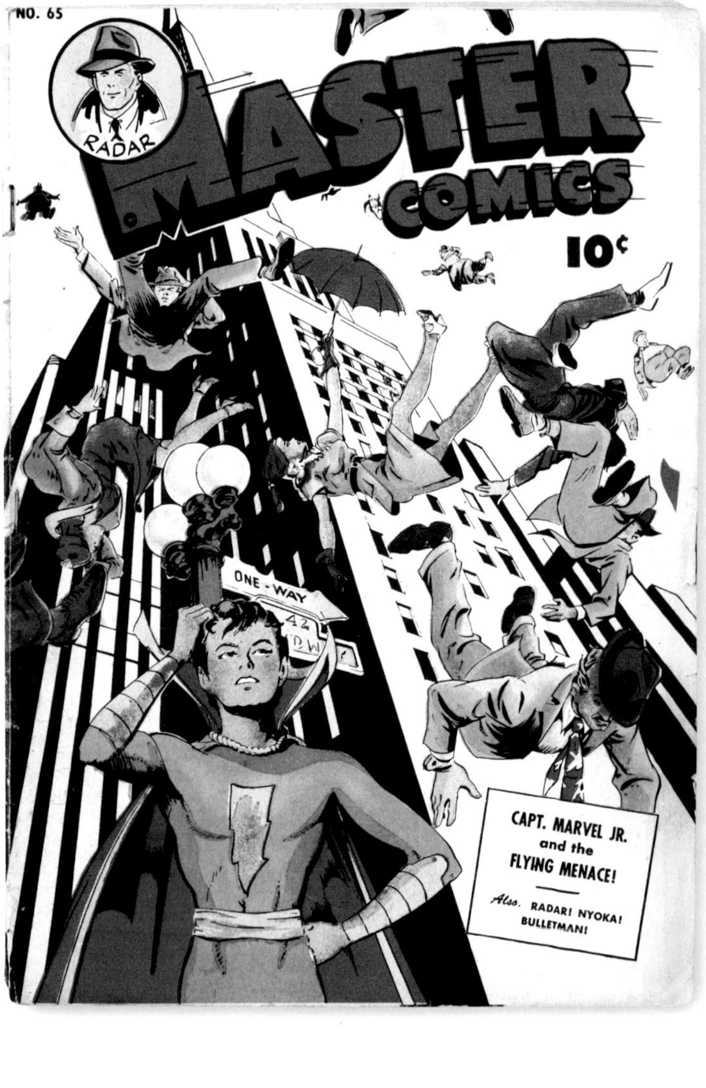
NO. 65
RADAR
MASTER COMICS
10¢
ONE-WAY
CAPT. MARVEL JR. and the FLYING MENACE!
Also. RADAR! NYOKA! BULLETMAN!

MASTER COMICS No. 65

Cover art, Bud Thompson, January 1946.

MARY MARVEL No. 9

Cover art, Jack Binder, February 1947. Captain Marvel Jr. successfully maintained his own comic book and a series in *Master Comics* through 1953. Mary Marvel was less fortunate, losing her namesake comic book in 1948.

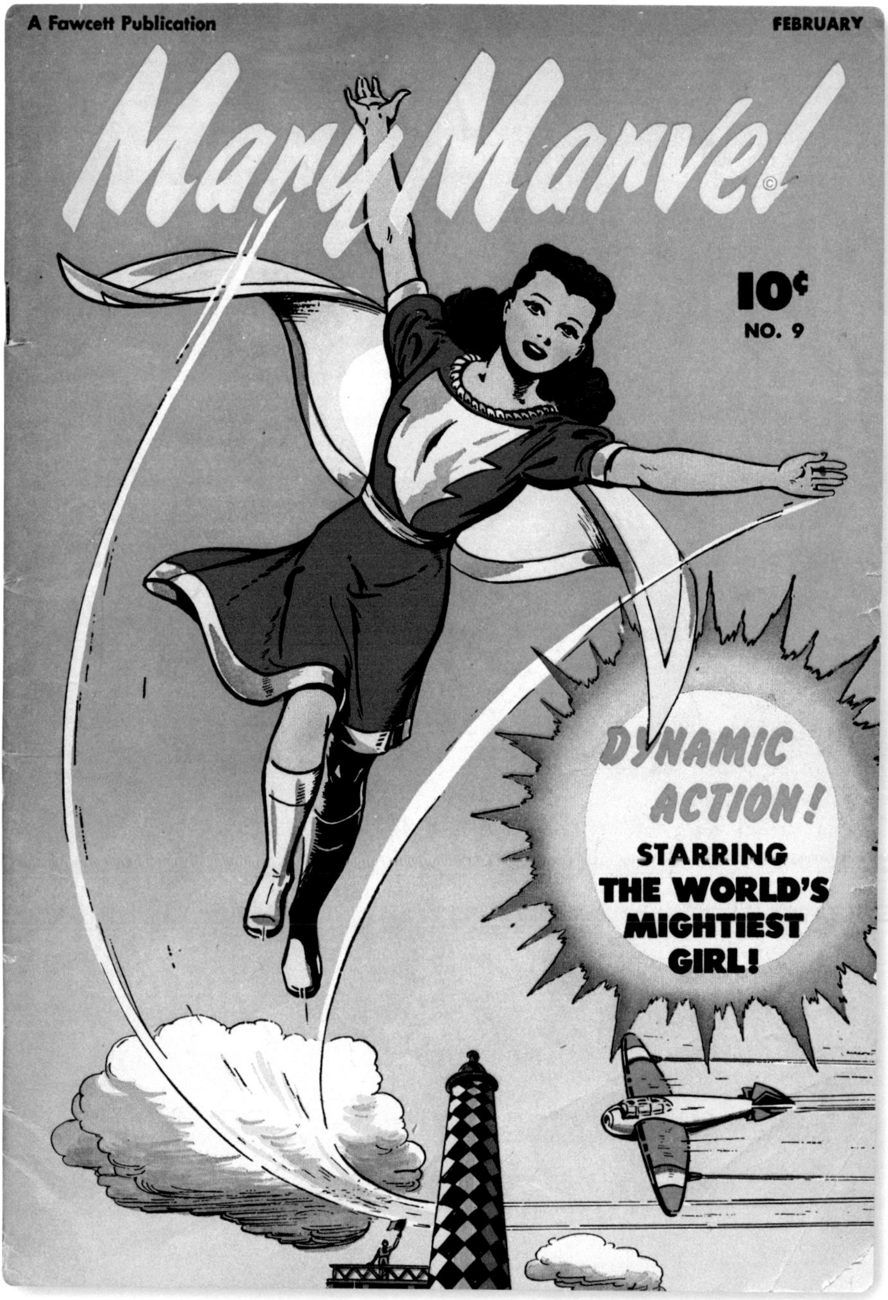
A Fawcett Publication
FEBRUARY
Mary Marvel ©
10¢
NO. 9
DYNAMIC ACTION!
STARRING THE WORLD'S MIGHTIEST GIRL!

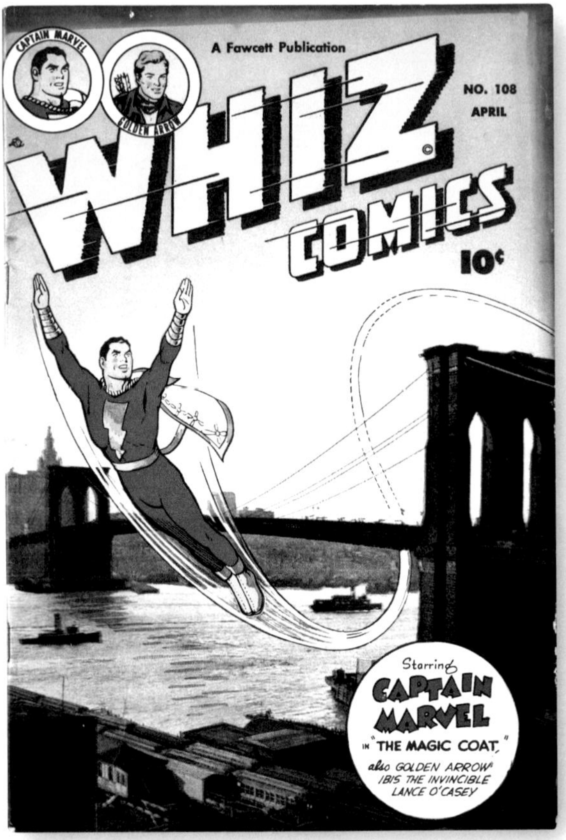
A Fawcett Publication
CAPTAIN MARVEL
GOLDEN ARROW
WHIZ COMICS
NO. 108
APRIL
10¢
Starring
CAPTAIN MARVEL
IN "THE MAGIC COAT"
also GOLDEN ARROW
IBIS THE INVINCIBLE
LANCE O'CASEY

WHIZ COMICS No. 108
Cover art, C. C. Beck and Pete Costanza, April 1949.

AFTER-SCHOOL SPECIAL
Photograph, January 1947.

"What I remember about comics is that they were the first things I could read on my own, and the first things I wanted to read on my own. They were the first heroes I read that belonged to the world outside the school doors.... but what I remember most of all is that they were mine."

—STEPHEN KING

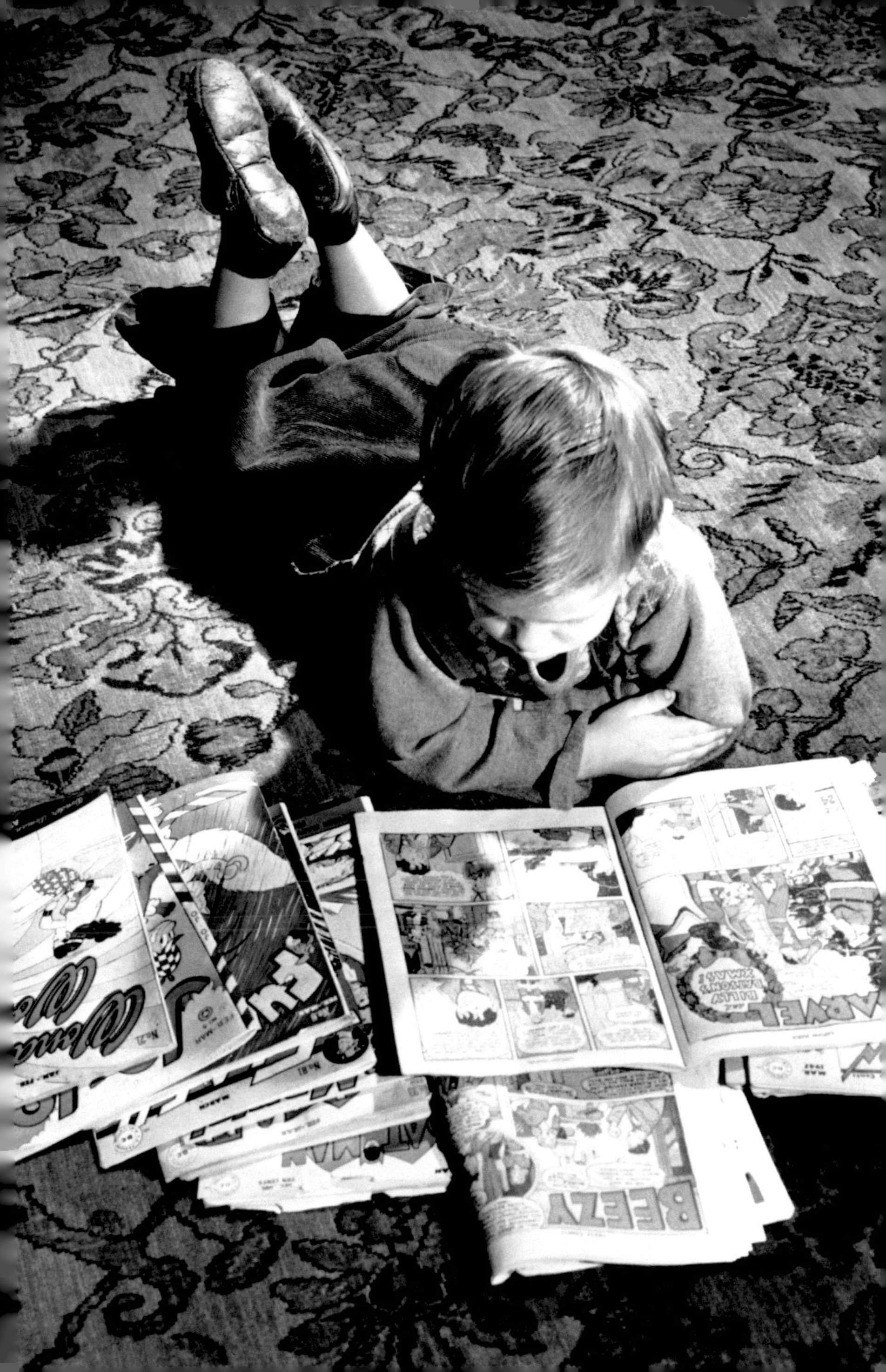
BEEZY

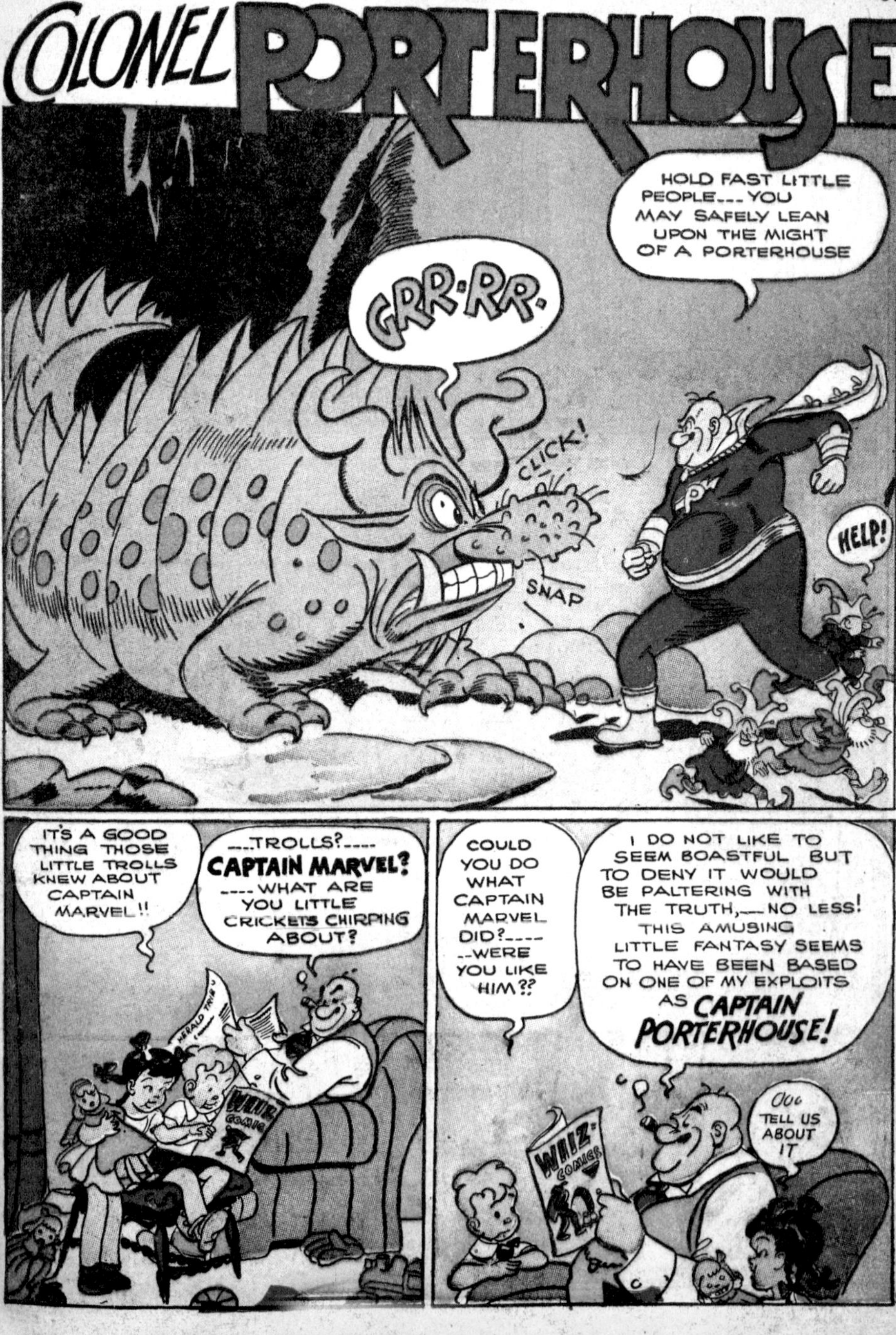
COLONEL PORTERHOUSE
HOLD FAST LITTLE PEOPLE--- YOU MAY SAFELY LEAN UPON THE MIGHT OF A PORTERHOUSE
GRR-RR.
CLICK!
SNAP
HELP!
IT'S A GOOD THING THOSE LITTLE TROLLS KNEW ABOUT CAPTAIN MARVEL!!
---TROLLS?---- CAPTAIN MARVEL? ----WHAT ARE YOU LITTLE CRICKETS CHIRPING ABOUT?
COULD YOU DO WHAT CAPTAIN MARVEL DID?---- --WERE YOU LIKE HIM??
I DO NOT LIKE TO SEEM BOASTFUL BUT TO DENY IT WOULD BE PALTERING WITH THE TRUTH,--NO LESS! THIS AMUSING LITTLE FANTASY SEEMS TO HAVE BEEN BASED ON ONE OF MY EXPLOITS AS CAPTAIN PORTERHOUSE!
Ooo TELL US ABOUT IT
WHIZ COMICS

WHIZ COMICS No. 37

Interior, "The Wee Folk"; script, unknown; pencils and inks, George Storm. November 1942. The Colonel Porterhouse humor feature devoted five successive issues to parodies of each hero in *Whiz Comics* before the series was renamed Skipper McGee and adopted a more generic premise involving tall tales.

WHIZ COMICS No. 20

Interior, "Crusher of Crime"; script, unknown; pencils, C.C. Beck; inks, Pete Costanza. August 8, 1941. Captain Marvel's creative team distinguished the feature by giving it a progressively lighter touch. Even at this early point, they were clearly having fun by situating the wicked Dr. Sivana in a laboratory stamped "Nefarious Research Inc."

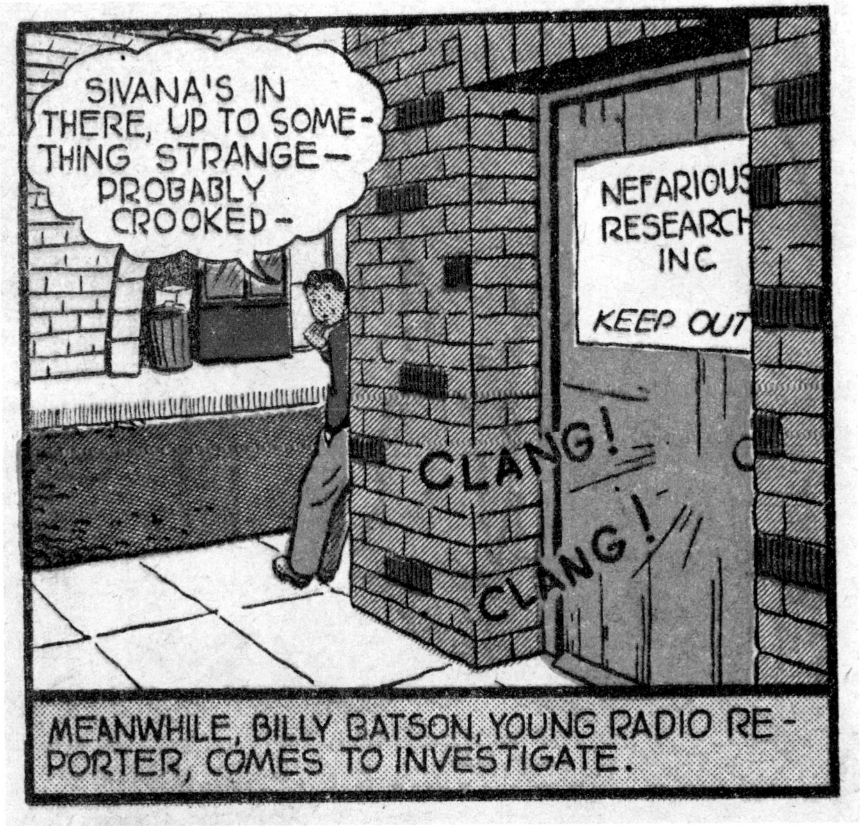
SIVANA'S IN THERE, UP TO SOME-THING STRANGE— PROBABLY CROOKED—
NEFARIOUS RESEARCH INC
KEEP OUT
CLANG!
CLANG!
MEANWHILE, BILLY BATSON, YOUNG RADIO RE-PORTER, COMES TO INVESTIGATE.

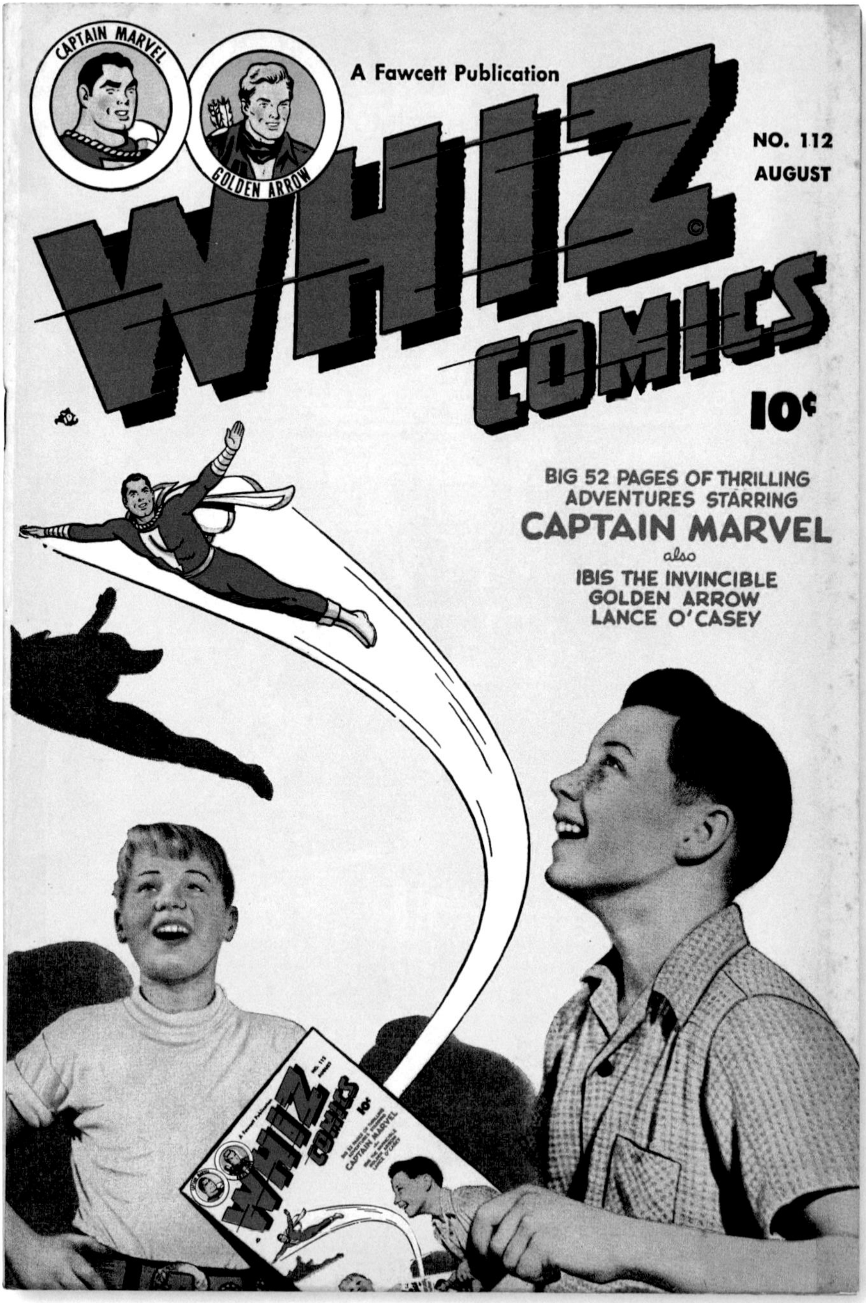
CAPTAIN MARVEL
GOLDEN ARROW
A Fawcett Publication
WHIZ COMICS
NO. 112
AUGUST
10¢
BIG 52 PAGES OF THRILLING ADVENTURES STARRING
CAPTAIN MARVEL
also
IBIS THE INVINCIBLE
GOLDEN ARROW
LANCE O'CASEY

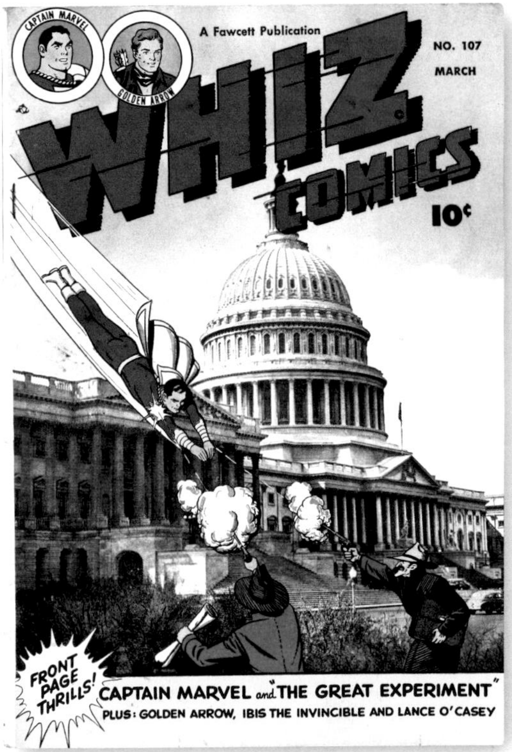
A Fawcett Publication
CAPTAIN MARVEL
GOLDEN ARROW
WHIZ COMICS
NO. 107
MARCH
10¢
FRONT PAGE THRILLS!
CAPTAIN MARVEL and THE GREAT EXPERIMENT"
PLUS: GOLDEN ARROW, IBIS THE INVINCIBLE AND LANCE O'CASEY

WHIZ COMICS No. 112

Cover art, C.C. Beck, August 1949. "Captain Marvel started out not as a copy of Superman, as so many have claimed, but as an answer to him. Cap's stories were highly imaginative, fanciful, and were as likely to take him to other worlds or into the past or future, involving talking animals and gnomes. Captain Marvel himself was humanly vulnerable; he smiled, laughed, gritted his teeth, and even broke a sweat sometimes."
—P.C. Hammerlinck

WHIZ COMICS No. 107

Cover art, C.C. Beck and Pete Costanza, March 1949.
One enormously popular series of stories involved Captain Marvel visiting different American cities, sometimes with a photograph of a famous landmark used as the background on the issue's cover. DC Comics writer and historian E. Nelson Bridwell added that "local magazine distributors and media people were often used in the tales—a fine way to get better distribution and publicity."

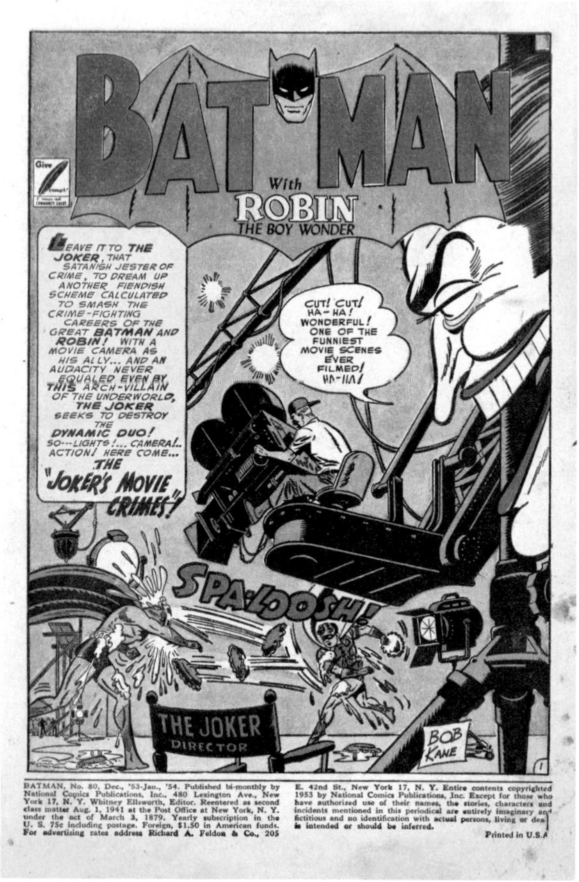
BATMAN
With
ROBIN
THE BOY WONDER
LEAVE IT TO THE JOKER, THAT SATANISH JESTER OF CRIME, TO DREAM UP ANOTHER FIENDISH SCHEME CALCULATED TO SMASH THE CRIME-FIGHTING CAREERS OF THE GREAT BATMAN AND ROBIN! WITH A MOVIE CAMERA AS HIS ALLY... AND AN AUDACITY NEVER EQUALED EVEN BY THIS ARCH-VILLAIN OF THE UNDERWORLD, THE JOKER SEEKS TO DESTROY THE DYNAMIC DUO! SO---LIGHTS!... CAMERA!.. ACTION! HERE COME... THE "JOKER'S MOVIE CRIMES"!
CUT! CUT! HA-HA! WONDERFUL! ONE OF THE FUNNIEST MOVIE SCENES EVER FILMED! HA-HA!
SPA-LOOSH!
THE JOKER
DIRECTOR
BOB KANE
1
BATMAN, No. 80, Dec., '53-Jan., '54. Published bi-monthly by National Comics Publications, Inc., 480 Lexington Ave., New York 17, N. Y. Whitney Ellsworth, Editor. Reentered as second class matter Aug. 1, 1941 at the Post Office at New York, N. Y. under the act of March 3, 1879. Yearly subscription in the U. S. 75c including postage. Foreign, $1.50 in American funds. For advertising rates address Richard A. Feldon & Co., 205 E. 42nd St., New York 17, N. Y. Entire contents copyrighted 1953 by National Comics Publications, Inc. Except for those who have authorized use of their names, the stories, characters and incidents mentioned in this periodical are entirely imaginary and fictitious and no identification with actual persons, living or dead is intended or should be inferred.
Printed in U.S.A

BATMAN No. 80

Interior, "The Joker's Movie Crimes"; script, attributed Bill Finger; pencils, Dick Sprang; inks, Charles Paris. December 1953–January 1954. Returning to life after execution in the electric chair in *Detective Comics* No. 64, the Joker was a changed man. Mark Waid observed that "his felonies became less macabre and more zany, his crimes revolving around gimmicks such as committing bizarre thefts in mysterious patterns or around weird themes.... It was a pretty fair trade: Joker stories became less moody but, on the whole, more memorable."

CAPTAIN MARVEL No. 72

Cover art, C. C. Beck, May 1947.

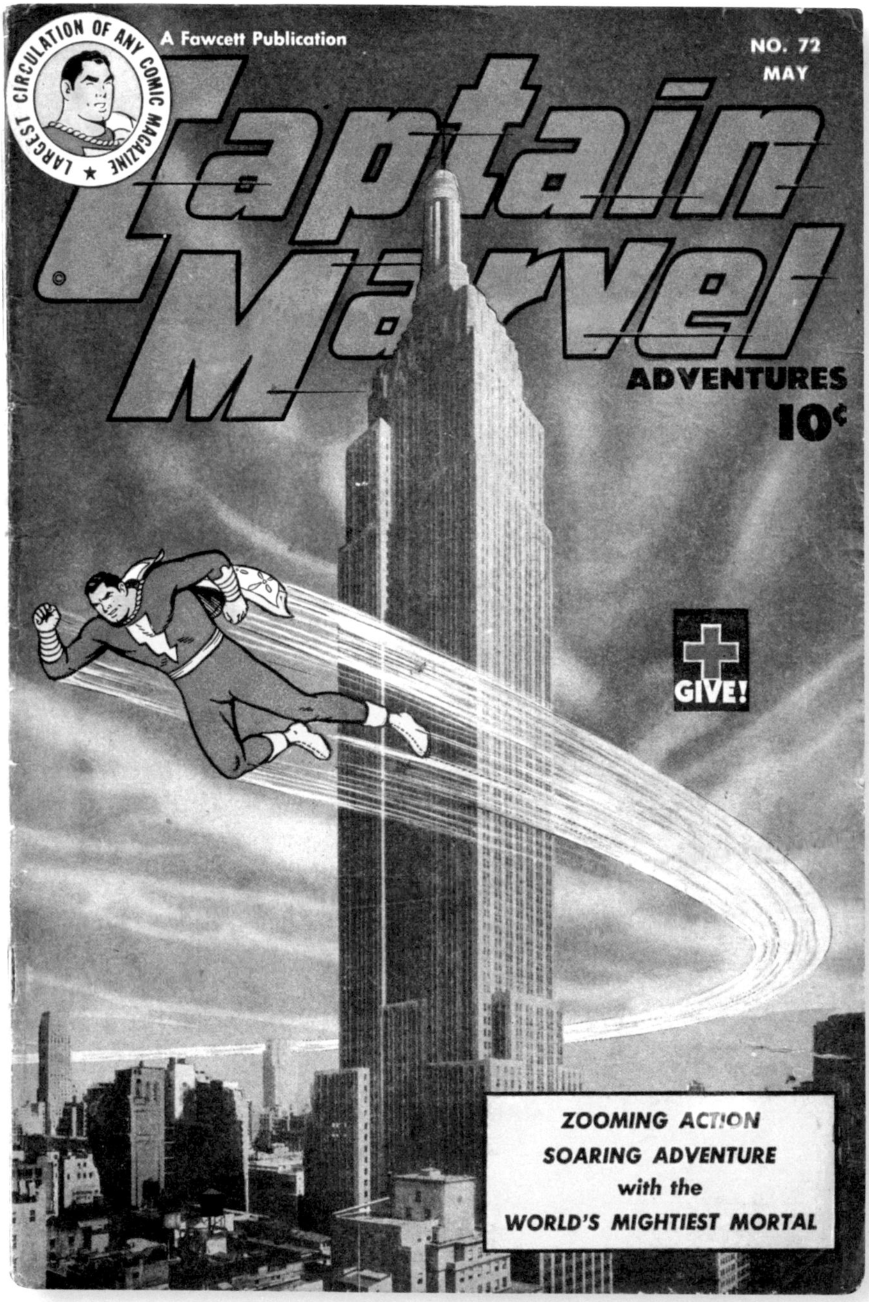
LARGEST CIRCULATION OF ANY COMIC MAGAZINE
A Fawcett Publication
NO. 72
MAY
Captain Marvel
ADVENTURES
10¢
GIVE!
ZOOMING ACTION
SOARING ADVENTURE
with the
WORLD'S MIGHTIEST MORTAL

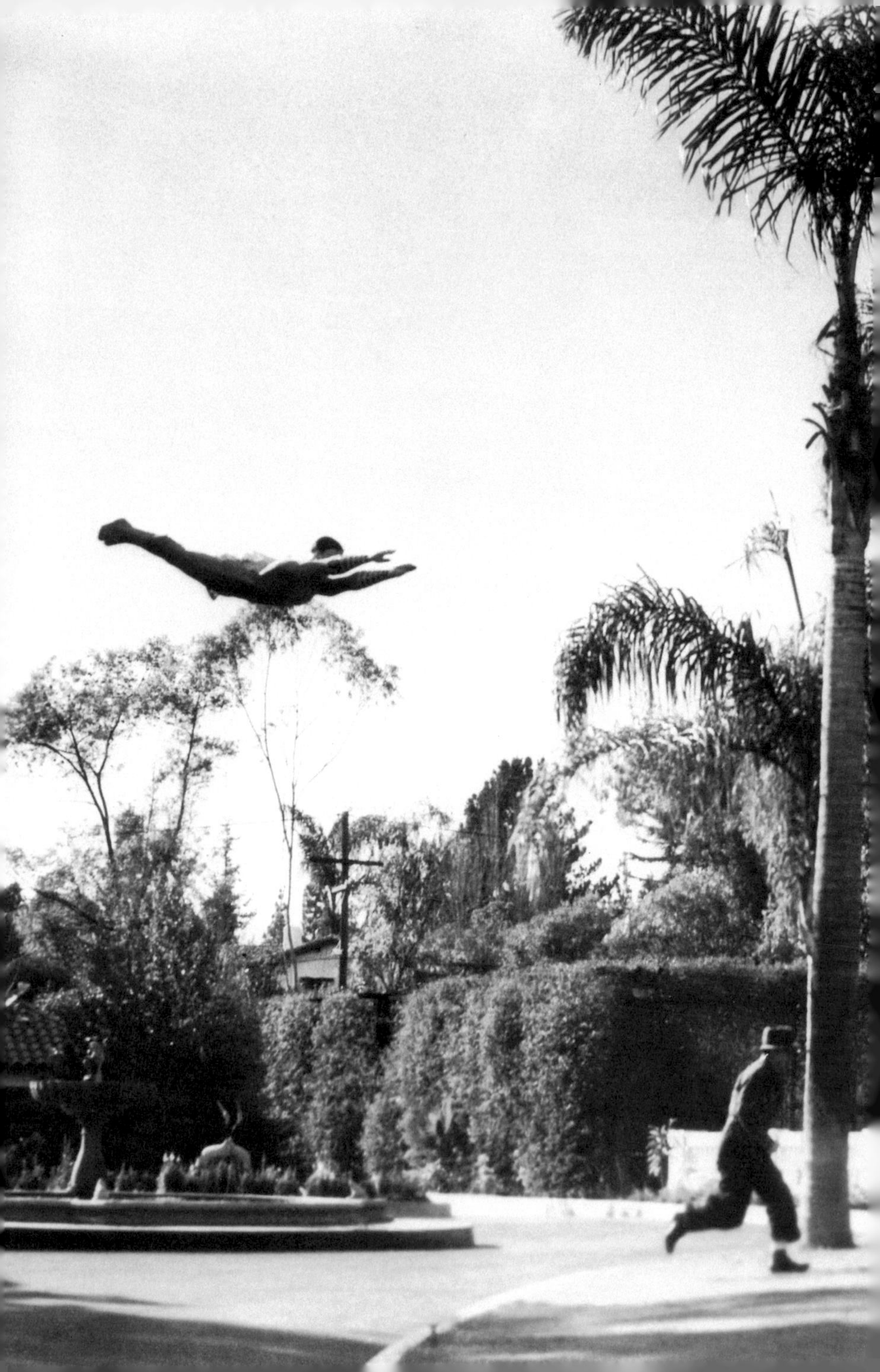

ADVENTURES OF CAPTAIN MARVEL MOVIE SERIAL

OPPOSITE: *Film still, 1941.* BELOW: *Poster, Republic Pictures, 1941. The Adventures of Captain Marvel* was regarded by many fans as not simply the best super hero entry of the era but one of the finest movie serials, period. The film's storyline was subsequently referred to in a Captain Marvel story in *Whiz Comics* No. 22, which introduced a character from the serial named Whitey Murphy into the comics.

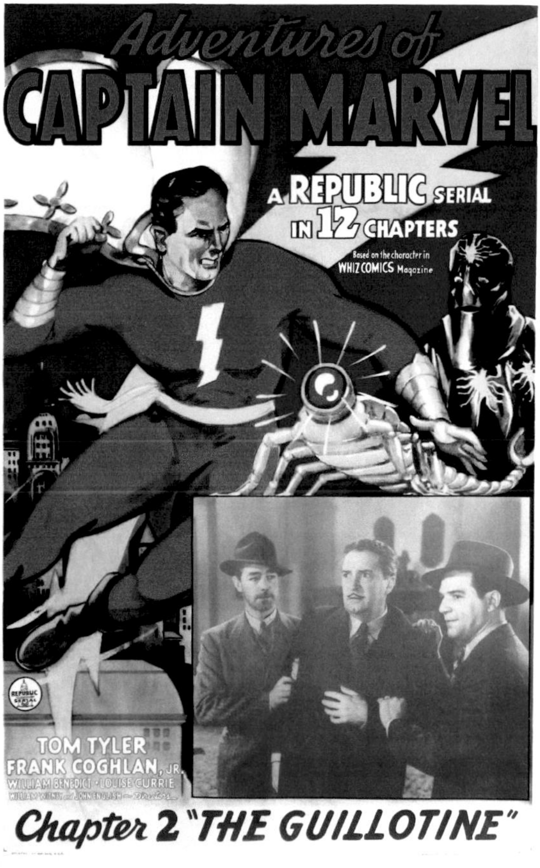

Adventures of
CAPTAIN MARVEL
A REPUBLIC SERIAL
IN 12 CHAPTERS
Based on the character in
WHIZ COMICS Magazine
TOM TYLER
FRANK COGHLAN, JR.
WILLIAM BENEDICT · LOUISE CURRIE
Chapter 2 "THE GUILLOTINE"

No.23
A 52 PAGE MAGAZINE
A SUPERMAN DC PUBLICATION
IND
Wonder Woman
TEN CENTS
MAY, JUNE
In this issue:
A Story From
Wonder Woman's
CHILDHOOD

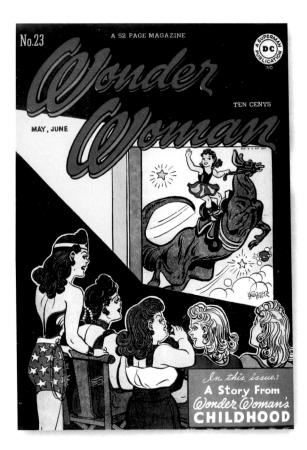

WONDER WOMAN No. 23

Cover art, H.G. Peter. May–June 1947. The notion of Amazon home movies featuring Wonder Woman as a child was revisited with a vengeance in the 1960s when the films were spliced together to depict the heroine interacting with her younger selves and mother as the Wonder Family.

AMERICA'S GREATEST COMICS No. 6

Cover art, C.C. Beck and Pete Costanza, February 17, 1943. *America's Greatest Comics* was Fawcett's version of All-American's *Comic Cavalcade* and DC's *World's Finest*. The 100-page, 15-cent comic book featured every major Fawcett hero, including movie serial stars Captain Marvel and Spy Smasher. Probably as a consequence of wartime paper rationing, the comic book lasted only eight issues before being discontinued in 1943.

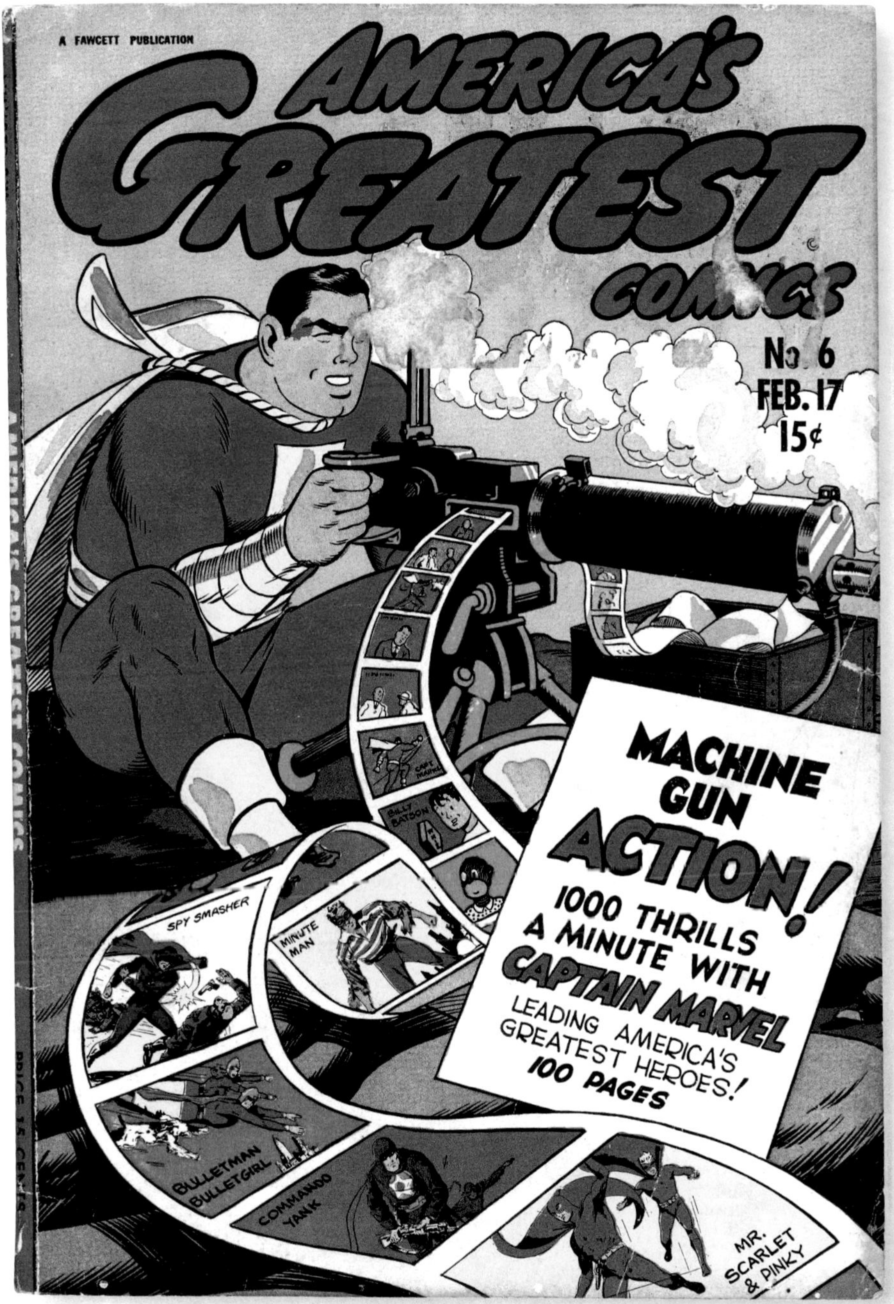
A FAWCETT PUBLICATION
AMERICA'S GREATEST COMICS
No. 6
FEB. 17
15¢
MACHINE GUN ACTION!
1000 THRILLS A MINUTE WITH CAPTAIN MARVEL
LEADING AMERICA'S GREATEST HEROES!
100 PAGES
BILLY BATSON
SPY SMASHER
MINUTE MAN
BULLETMAN BULLETGIRL
COMMANDO YANK
MR. SCARLET & PINKY

THE VIGILANTE SCRIPT

Script page, director, Wallace Fox; producer, Sam Katzman. 1947.

ACTION COMICS SOUVENIR EDITION

Cover art, Mort Meskin and George Roussos, 1947. The Vigilante movie serial was cause for two promotional issues, most notably the *Action Comics Souvenir Edition*. The 36-page digest-size comic book was entirely devoted to the Western hero. Published during the same period was a feature in *Real Fact Comics* No. 10 on the making of the serial.

MORE FUN COMICS No. 80

Cover art, George Papp, June 1942. Green Arrow and Speedy were modeled on the Batman and Robin template from the beginning, but a number of specific parallels sprang up between them as the 1940s wore on. The Wizard Archers drove an Arrowcar, were summoned to police headquarters by an Arrowsignal, and occasionally fought a mad clown called the Bull's-Eye.

COLUMBIA PROD. NO. 882-12
ESSKAY PRODUCTIONS PRESENT
"THE VIGILANTE"
PRODUCER:
SAM KATZMAN
DIRECTOR:
WALLACE FOX
RELEASED THROUGH
COLUMBIA PICTURES CORP.

FREE SOUVENIR EDITION
ACTION COMICS
IN HONOR OF
Columbia's
THRILLING NEW
MOVIE
SERIAL
"The VIGILANTE"

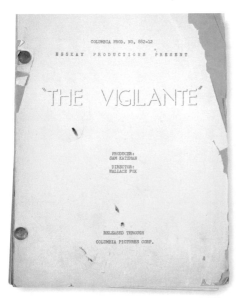

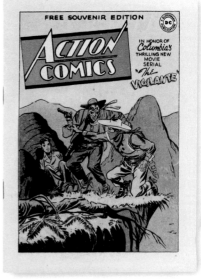

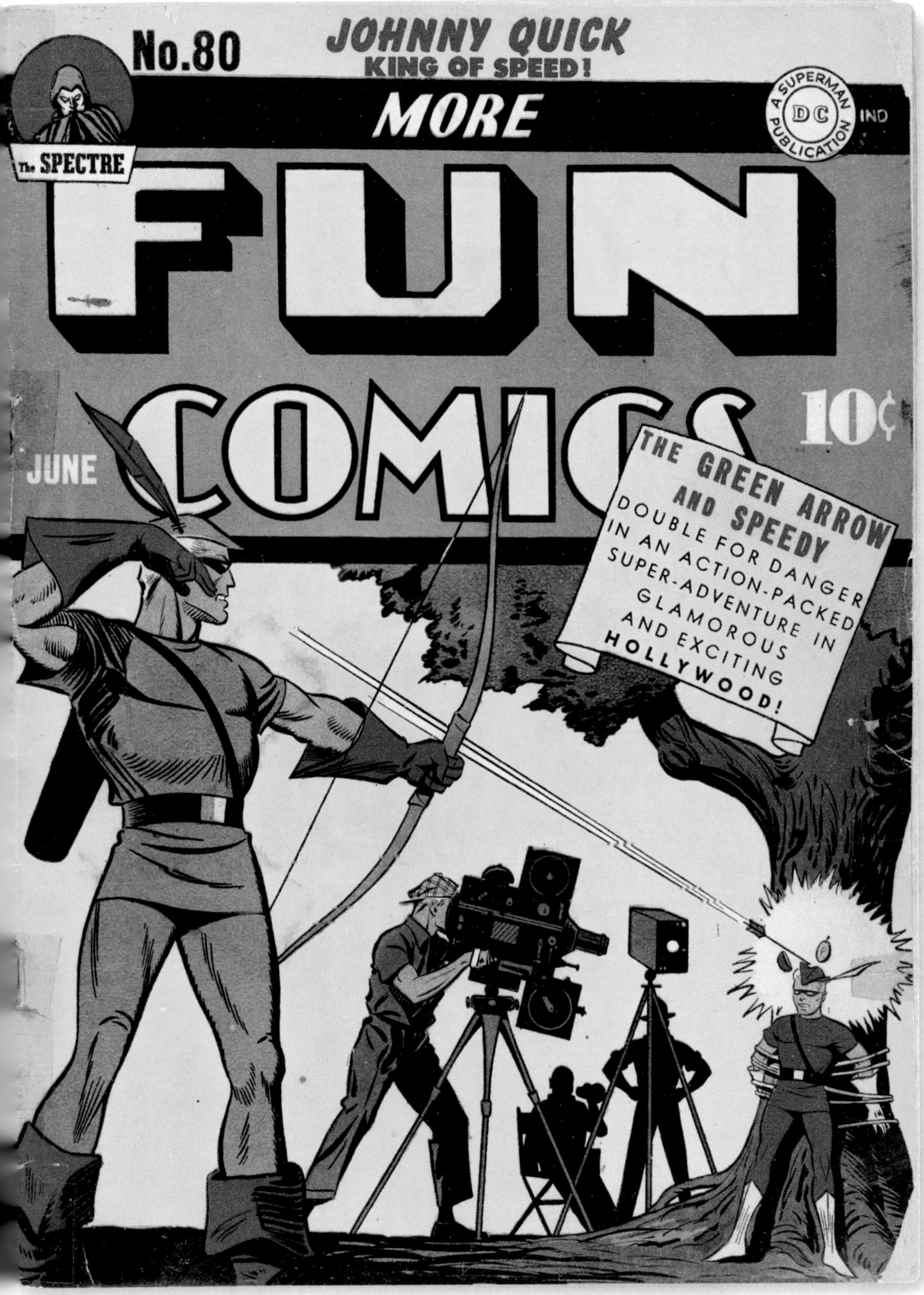
No.80
JOHNNY QUICK
KING OF SPEED!
MORE
A SUPERMAN DC PUBLICATION
IND
The SPECTRE
FUN
COMICS
10¢
JUNE
THE GREEN ARROW AND SPEEDY
DOUBLE FOR DANGER IN AN ACTION-PACKED SUPER-ADVENTURE IN GLAMOROUS AND EXCITING HOLLYWOOD!

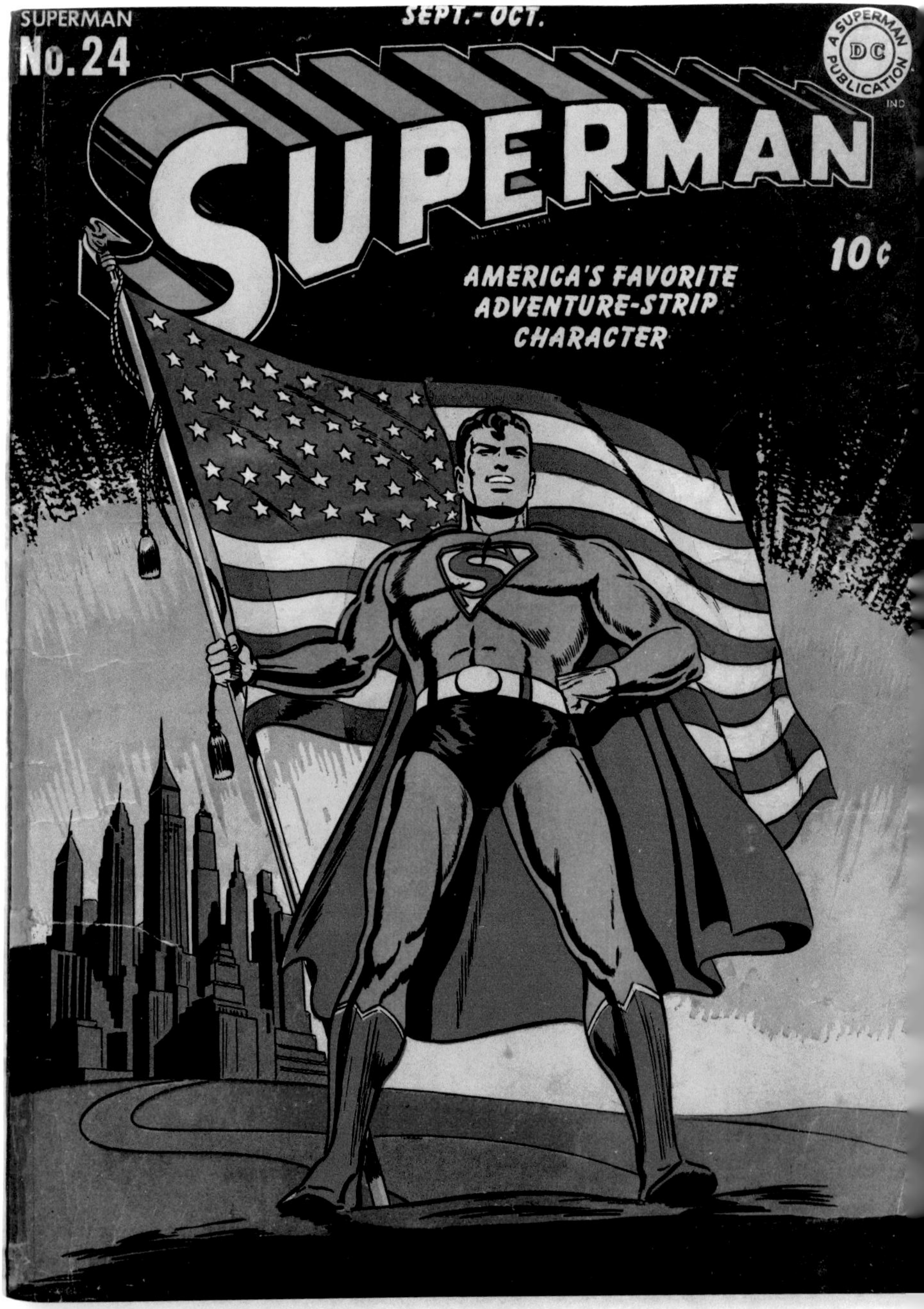
SUPERMAN
No. 24
SEPT.-OCT.
A SUPERMAN DC PUBLICATION INC
SUPERMAN
10¢
AMERICA'S FAVORITE
ADVENTURE-STRIP
CHARACTER

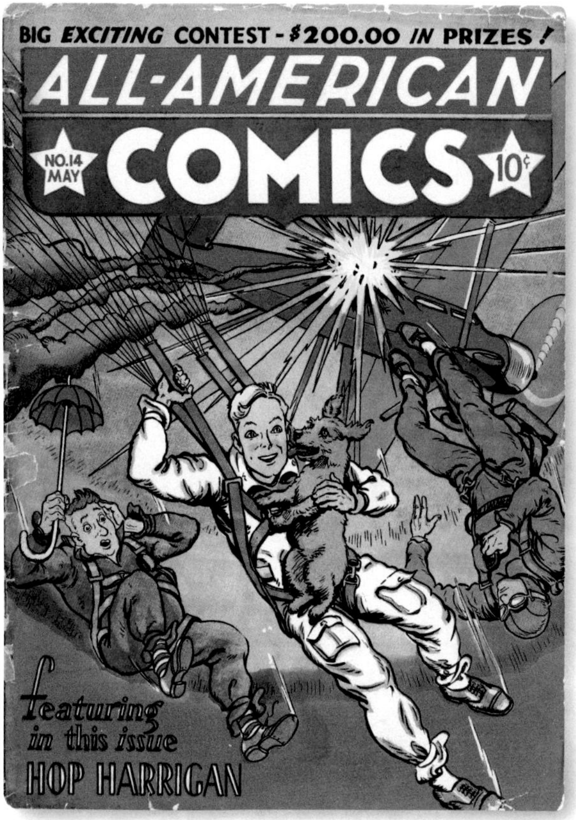
BIG EXCITING CONTEST - $200.00 IN PRIZES!
ALL-AMERICAN
COMICS
NO.14 MAY
10¢
featuring in this issue
HOP HARRIGAN

SUPERMAN No. 24

Cover art, Jack Burnley, September–October 1943.

ALL-AMERICAN COMICS No. 14

Cover art, Jon L. Blummer, May 1940.

LOOK MAGAZINE

FOLLOWING SPREAD: *Interiors, "How Superman Would End the War"; script, Jerry Siegel; pencils and inks, Joe Shuster. February 27, 1940.* This extraordinary two-page story, published nearly two years before the United States entered World War II, is also notable for the strange bedfellows that the conflict made. After Nazi Germany violated a nonaggression pact with Russia in 1941, Joseph Stalin threw his country's support behind the Allied forces.

★ ★ ★ HOW SUPERMAN WOULD END TH

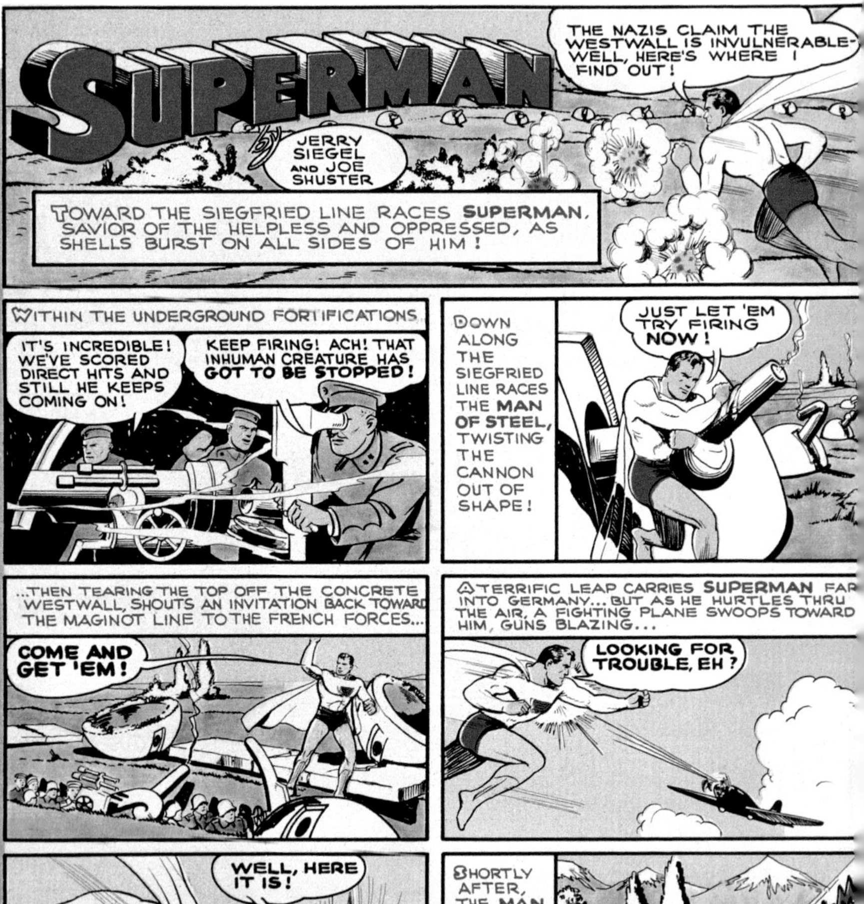
SUPERMAN
BY JERRY SIEGEL AND JOE SHUSTER
THE NAZIS CLAIM THE WESTWALL IS INVULNERABLE- WELL, HERE'S WHERE I FIND OUT!
TOWARD THE SIEGFRIED LINE RACES SUPERMAN, SAVIOR OF THE HELPLESS AND OPPRESSED, AS SHELLS BURST ON ALL SIDES OF HIM!
WITHIN THE UNDERGROUND FORTIFICATIONS...
IT'S INCREDIBLE! WE'VE SCORED DIRECT HITS AND STILL HE KEEPS COMING ON!
KEEP FIRING! ACH! THAT INHUMAN CREATURE HAS GOT TO BE STOPPED!
DOWN ALONG THE SIEGFRIED LINE RACES THE MAN OF STEEL, TWISTING THE CANNON OUT OF SHAPE!
JUST LET 'EM TRY FIRING NOW!
...THEN TEARING THE TOP OFF THE CONCRETE WESTWALL, SHOUTS AN INVITATION BACK TOWARD THE MAGINOT LINE TO THE FRENCH FORCES...
COME AND GET 'EM!
A TERRIFIC LEAP CARRIES SUPERMAN FAR INTO GERMANY... BUT AS HE HURTLES THRU THE AIR, A FIGHTING PLANE SWOOPS TOWARD HIM, GUNS BLAZING...
LOOKING FOR TROUBLE, EH?
WELL, HERE IT IS!
HIMMEL! VOS IS DISS?
SHORTLY AFTER, THE MAN OF TOMORROW STREAKS DOWN THROUGH THE CEILING OF HITLER'S RETREAT...
ZOOM-M

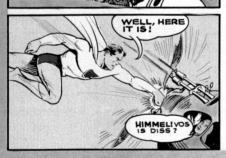

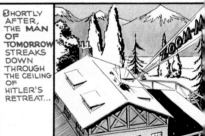

SIEGEL AND SHUSTER GAVE SUPERMAN A BIG JOB in this episode, when they assign him to solve the international situation just for LOOK, but such tasks are nothing n for him. He once stopped a war "somewhere in South America" by dumping a mu

WAR *drawn especially for* LOOK ★ ★ ★

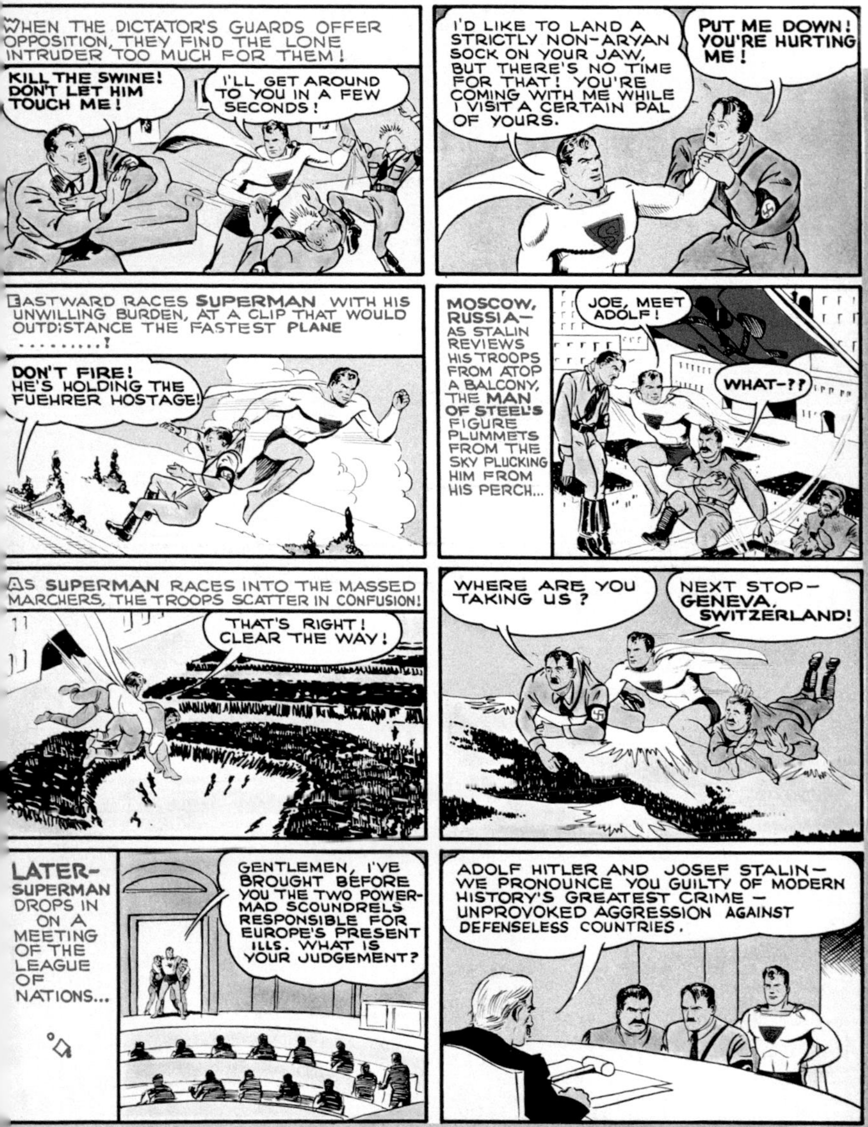

WHEN THE DICTATOR'S GUARDS OFFER OPPOSITION, THEY FIND THE LONE INTRUDER TOO MUCH FOR THEM!
KILL THE SWINE! DON'T LET HIM TOUCH ME!
I'LL GET AROUND TO YOU IN A FEW SECONDS!
I'D LIKE TO LAND A STRICTLY NON-ARYAN SOCK ON YOUR JAW, BUT THERE'S NO TIME FOR THAT! YOU'RE COMING WITH ME WHILE I VISIT A CERTAIN PAL OF YOURS.
PUT ME DOWN! YOU'RE HURTING ME!
EASTWARD RACES SUPERMAN WITH HIS UNWILLING BURDEN, AT A CLIP THAT WOULD OUTDISTANCE THE FASTEST PLANE ....!
DON'T FIRE! HE'S HOLDING THE FUEHRER HOSTAGE!
MOSCOW, RUSSIA— AS STALIN REVIEWS HIS TROOPS FROM ATOP A BALCONY, THE MAN OF STEEL'S FIGURE PLUMMETS FROM THE SKY PLUCKING HIM FROM HIS PERCH...
JOE, MEET ADOLF!
WHAT-??
AS SUPERMAN RACES INTO THE MASSED MARCHERS, THE TROOPS SCATTER IN CONFUSION!
THAT'S RIGHT! CLEAR THE WAY!
WHERE ARE YOU TAKING US?
NEXT STOP— GENEVA, SWITZERLAND!
LATER— SUPERMAN DROPS IN ON A MEETING OF THE LEAGUE OF NATIONS...
GENTLEMEN, I'VE BROUGHT BEFORE YOU THE TWO POWER-MAD SCOUNDRELS RESPONSIBLE FOR EUROPE'S PRESENT ILLS. WHAT IS YOUR JUDGEMENT?
ADOLF HITLER AND JOSEF STALIN— WE PRONOUNCE YOU GUILTY OF MODERN HISTORY'S GREATEST CRIME — UNPROVOKED AGGRESSION AGAINST DEFENSELESS COUNTRIES.

ıs profiteer into the trenches for a dose of his own medicine. On another occasion plucked two opposing generals from their tents and told them to settle their 'erences with bare fists. They knew no "differences," shook hands and made peace.

MAKING HEADLINES

Newspaper clipping, "Superman Claims Hitler 'Capture;' Reward Late," Cleveland Plain Dealer, *February 1940.*

SUPERMAN-TIM

Cover art, artist unknown, July 1943. For all his power, Superman couldn't truly end World War II in the pages of his own comic books without insulting the heroic sacrifices of the real-life men and women who were fighting overseas. That didn't mean that fantasy scenarios like this one from the Superman-Tim clothing line's brochures couldn't be acted out on the covers.

Superman Claims Hitler 'Capture;' Reward Late

It was announced on the front page of yesterday's Plain Dealer that a group of Pittsburgh residents had offered a reward of $1,000,000 in cash for the delivery of Adolf Hitler "alive, unwounded and unhurt" into the custody of the League of Nations.

Herr Hitler was captured on Feb. 27, 1940, by two Cleveland boys, Jerry Siegel and Joe Shuster. They were not content with capturing Hitler. They tossed in Josef Stalin for good measure.

And here's how:

Siegel writes the script and Shuster does the cartooning for a comic strip called Superman which appears daily in the Plain Dealer. Superman is a reporter at times for a daily paper. At other times he changes to a winged man of steel who defies time, space, fire, bullets, or what have you.

In the Feb. 27 issue of Look Magazine, Superman appeared in a two-page color layout in which he demonstrated how simple it was to capture the two bad boys. He first raced along the Siegfried Line, twisting the cannons out of shape as he ran. Then he tipped over the line's "pill boxes" and scattered them all over the landscape. It was then but the work of a few seconds and two or three pictures to grab Hitler by the neck, fly with him to Stalin's hangout in Moscow, then deliver both miscreants to the League of Nations in Geneva. There they were pronounced guilty of "modern history's greatest crime—unprovoked aggression against defenseless countries."

"These Pittsburghers are a little late with the idea," said Siegel in an interview last night. "Too, they only offer a million bucks. Joe and I will accept that, but we think we should receive more. After all, we got Stalin, too."

The syndicated Superman feature now reaches 10,000,000 readers daily, Siegel said. The man of steel is on a sponsored radio program, and bids have started to come in for his services in a movie.

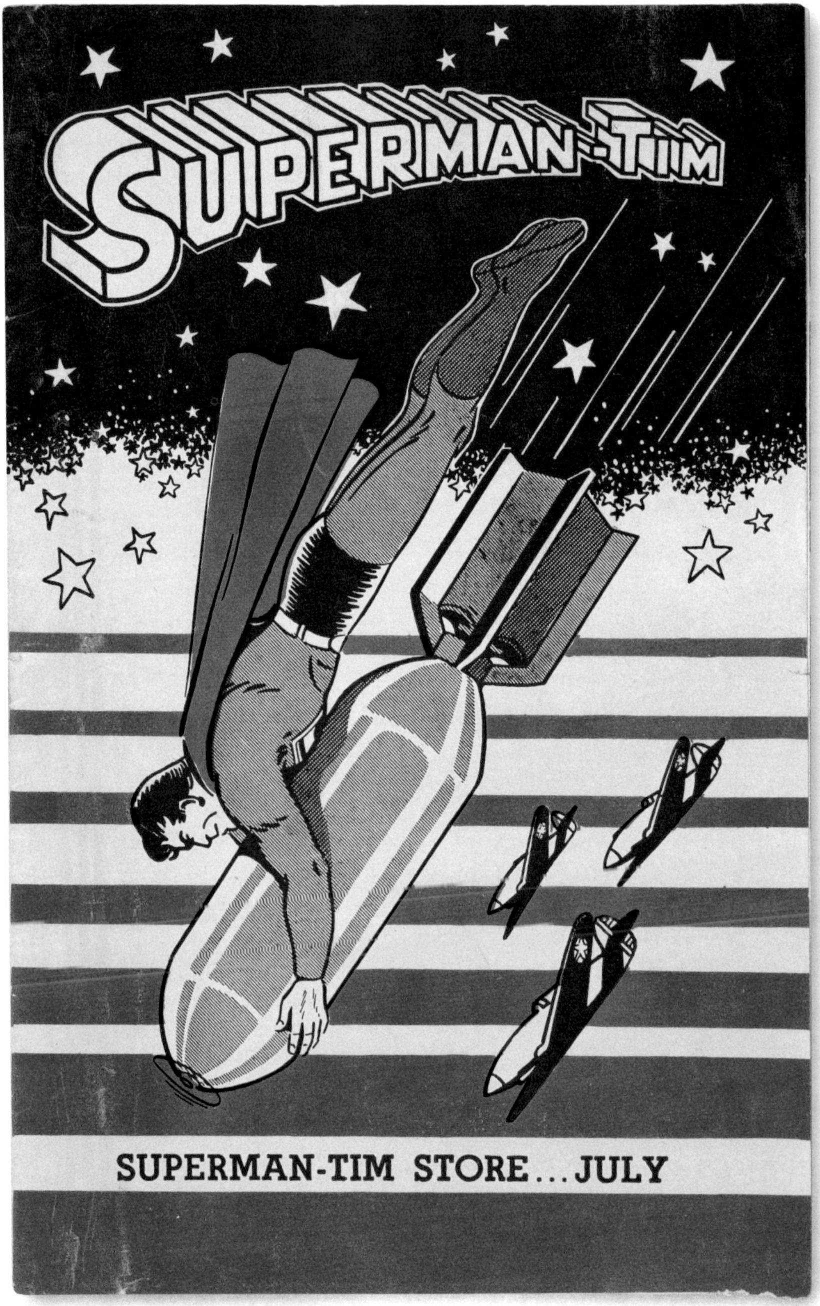
SUPERMAN-TIM
SUPERMAN-TIM STORE... JULY

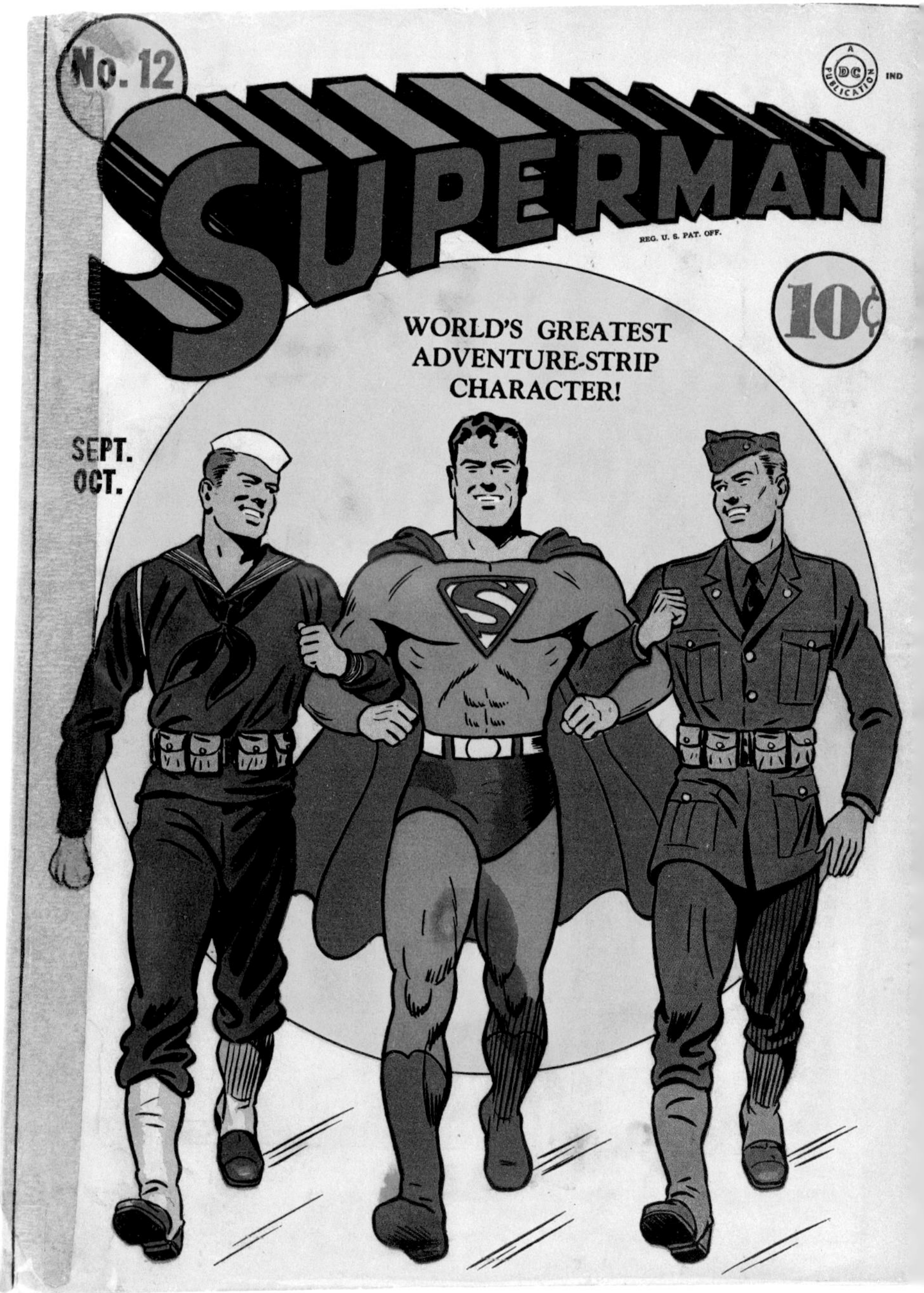
No. 12
A DC PUBLICATION
IND
SUPERMAN
REG. U. S. PAT. OFF.
10¢
WORLD'S GREATEST
ADVENTURE-STRIP
CHARACTER!
SEPT.
OCT.

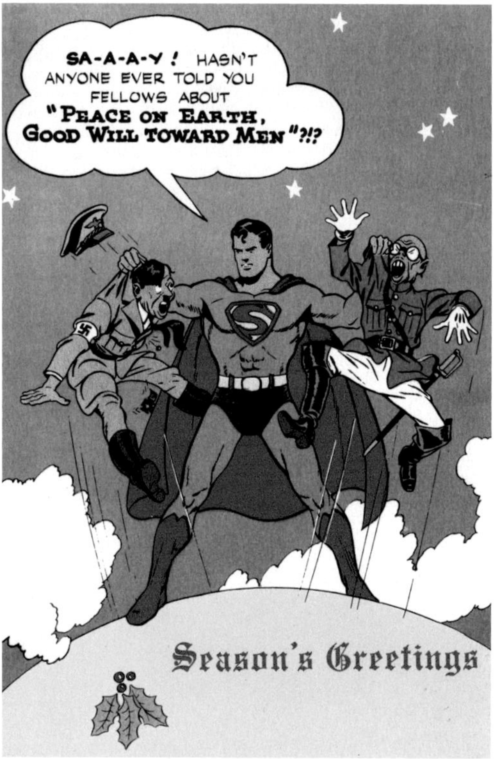
SA-A-A-Y ! HASN'T ANYONE EVER TOLD YOU FELLOWS ABOUT "PEACE ON EARTH, GOOD WILL TOWARD MEN"?!?
Season's Greetings

"[Comics] did more to unite and steel America for war than President Roosevelt's speeches."

—*THE TIMES LITERARY SUPPLEMENT*, MAY 29, 1953

SUPERMAN No. 12

Cover art, Fred Ray, September-October 1941. Many DC heroes waved the flag figuratively if not literally as the shadow of war fell over the United States. *All-American Comics'* Hop Harrigan was already a renowned civilian pilot and put his experience to good use as part of the U.S. Army Air Corps starting in 1942.

SUPERMAN HOLIDAY CARD

World War II–era card, 1940s.

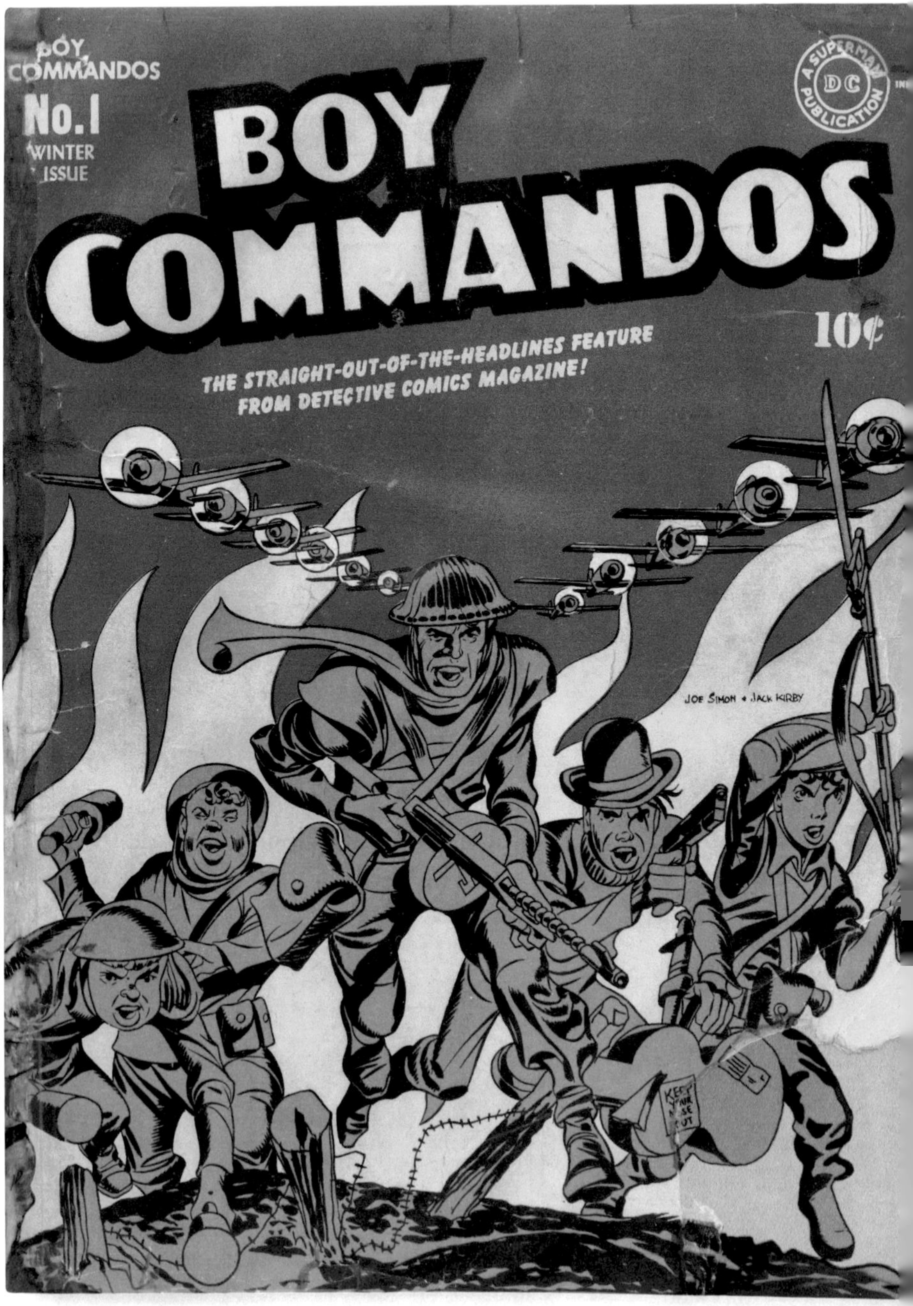
BOY COMMANDOS
No. 1
WINTER ISSUE
BOY COMMANDOS
A SUPERMAN DC PUBLICATION
10¢
THE STRAIGHT-OUT-OF-THE-HEADLINES FEATURE FROM DETECTIVE COMICS MAGAZINE!
JOE SIMON + JACK KIRBY

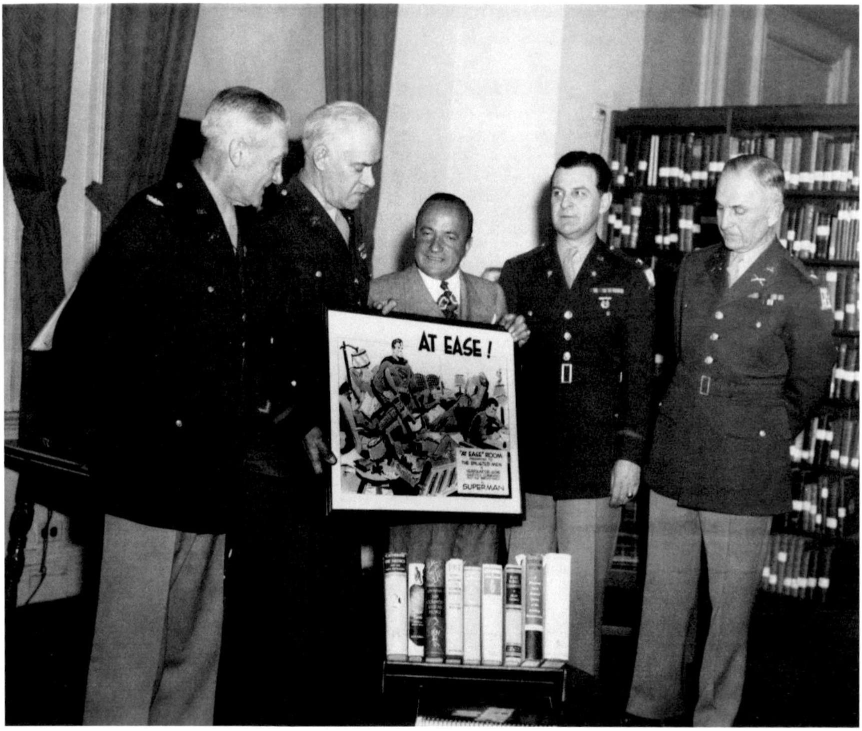
AT EASE !
"AT EASE" ROOM
SUPERMAN

BOY COMMANDOS No. 1

Cover art, Jack Kirby and Joe Simon, winter 1942–1943. With virtually every American supporting the war effort somehow, this series' far-fetched premise — a multinational kid gang physically battling Nazis — didn't prevent it from becoming a hit.

AT EASE

Photograph, Harry Donenfeld presents a wartime Superman poster to military personnel at Special Branch Headquarters Second Service Command, New York, ca. 1943. Harry Donenfeld capitalized on his connection to Superman during World War II, whether making public appearances at bond drives or preparing public service features. One story in *Superman* No. 25 was prepared on behalf of the Air Force's Technical Training Command and touted the skills of Yale University's cadets.

SENSATION COMICS No. 13

Cover art, H. G. Peter, January 1943.

ALL-STAR COMICS No. 21

Cover art, Joe Gallagher, summer 1944. A striking composition suggests the passage of time as members of The Justice Society travel back in time and change history on behalf of a remorseful dying man. The team made other trips forward and backward through time, but its most memorable exploit in that regard may have been *All-Star Comics* No. 35's "Day That Dropped out of Time," wherein the power-mad Degaton altered the present by changing the distant past.

HOW YOU CAN DEFEND YOUR HOME

Air raid defense manual written by M. C. Gaines, 1941. With the United States on the brink of war, the possibility of aerial attacks by enemy bombing planes was one of many fears to grip the American people. Indeed, London had been devastated during 1940 and 1941 by the Blitz, Nazi Germany's series of bombing raids for 76 consecutive nights. In short order, All-American publisher M. C. Gaines prepared a manual that citizens could refer to in the event of a similar crisis in the U. S. In 1942, Gaines and artist Sheldon Moldoff prepared a four-page comic pamphlet entitled "The Minute Man Answers the Call" to promote war bond sales.

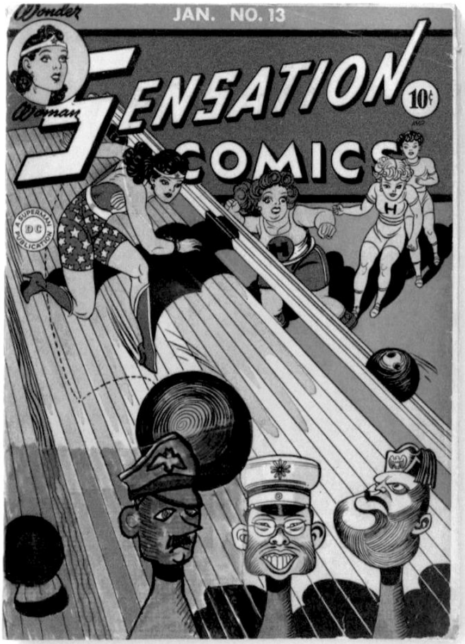
Wonder Woman
JAN. NO. 13
SENSATION COMICS
10¢
A SUPERMAN DC PUBLICATION

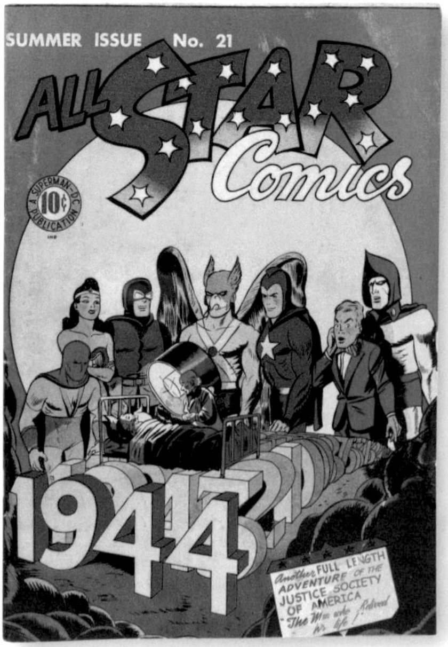
SUMMER ISSUE No. 21
ALL STAR Comics
10¢
A SUPERMAN-DC PUBLICATION
1944
FULL LENGTH ADVENTURE OF THE JUSTICE SOCIETY OF AMERICA

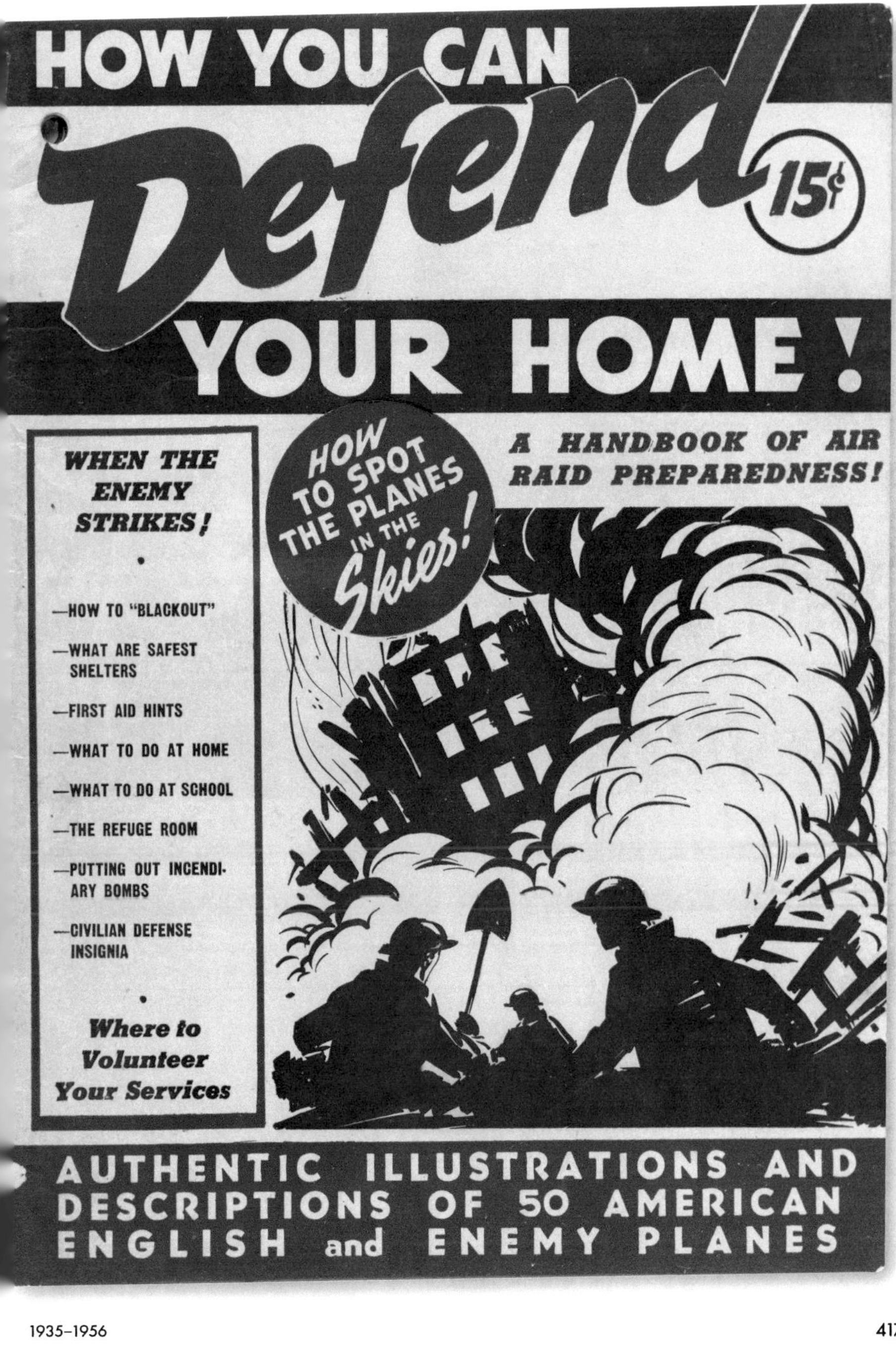
HOW YOU CAN
Defend
15¢
YOUR HOME!
HOW TO SPOT THE PLANES IN THE Skies!
A HANDBOOK OF AIR RAID PREPAREDNESS!
WHEN THE ENEMY STRIKES!
—HOW TO "BLACKOUT"
—WHAT ARE SAFEST SHELTERS
—FIRST AID HINTS
—WHAT TO DO AT HOME
—WHAT TO DO AT SCHOOL
—THE REFUGE ROOM
—PUTTING OUT INCENDIARY BOMBS
—CIVILIAN DEFENSE INSIGNIA
Where to Volunteer Your Services
AUTHENTIC ILLUSTRATIONS AND DESCRIPTIONS OF 50 AMERICAN ENGLISH and ENEMY PLANES

BATMAN
HERE'S A NEW GUN FROM THE FOLKS BACK HOME, SOLDIER!
YEP! THE FOLKS THAT'RE BACKING THE 7TH WAR LOAN

BATMAN
No.30
AUG...SEPT.
TEN CENTS
A SUPERMAN DC PUBLICATION
BATMAN
HERE'S A NEW GUN FROM THE FOLKS BACK HOME, SOLDIER!
YEP! THE FOLKS THAT'RE BACKING THE 7TH WAR LOAN!

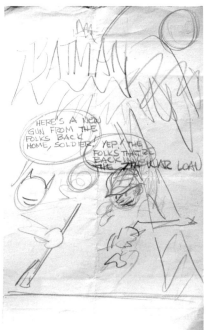

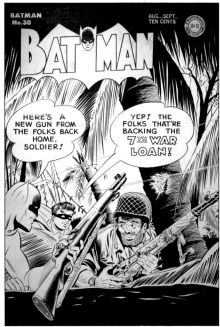

BATMAN No. 30

Concept notes, rough sketch, original art, and published cover art, Dick Sprang, August–September 1945. This issue's public-spirited cover referred to war bonds, certificates that citizens could purchase to provide funds to service the armed forces and create a sense of patriotism and involvement in the war overseas. There were eight campaigns to sell bonds, the seventh of which raised $26 billion. Seen here are editor Whitney Ellsworth's notes on the cover idea, Dick Sprang's rough sketch, and the finished product.

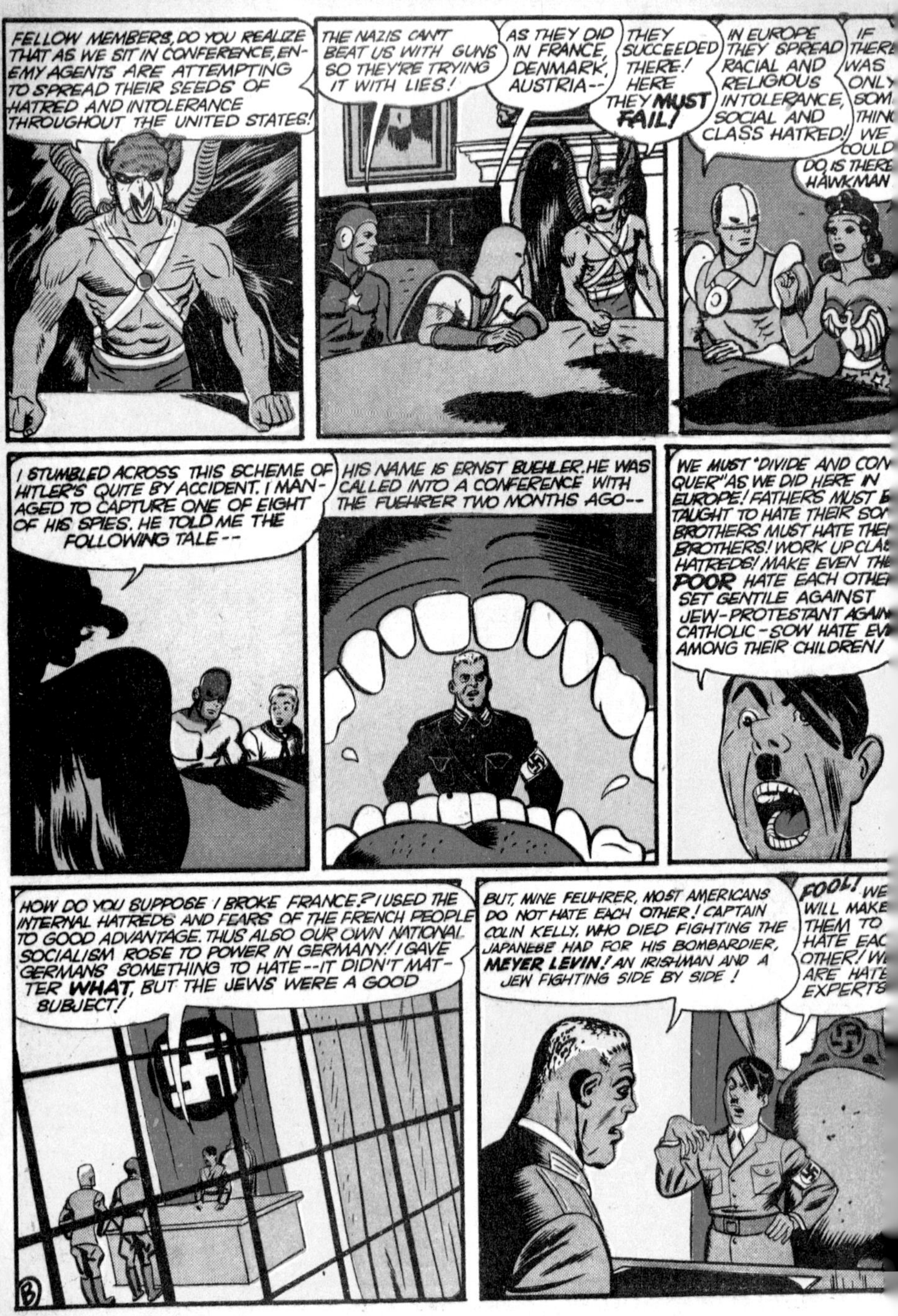
FELLOW MEMBERS, DO YOU REALIZE THAT AS WE SIT IN CONFERENCE, ENEMY AGENTS ARE ATTEMPTING TO SPREAD THEIR SEEDS OF HATRED AND INTOLERANCE THROUGHOUT THE UNITED STATES!
THE NAZIS CAN'T BEAT US WITH GUNS SO THEY'RE TRYING IT WITH LIES!
AS THEY DID IN FRANCE, DENMARK, AUSTRIA--
THEY SUCCEEDED THERE! HERE THEY **MUST FAIL!**
IN EUROPE THEY SPREAD RACIAL AND RELIGIOUS INTOLERANCE, SOCIAL AND CLASS HATRED!
IF THERE WAS ONLY SOM THING WE COULD DO, IS THERE HAWKMAN
I STUMBLED ACROSS THIS SCHEME OF HITLER'S QUITE BY ACCIDENT. I MANAGED TO CAPTURE ONE OF EIGHT OF HIS SPIES. HE TOLD ME THE FOLLOWING TALE--
HIS NAME IS ERNST BUEHLER. HE WAS CALLED INTO A CONFERENCE WITH THE FUEHRER TWO MONTHS AGO--
WE MUST "DIVIDE AND CON QUER" AS WE DID HERE IN EUROPE! FATHERS MUST B TAUGHT TO HATE THEIR SON BROTHERS MUST HATE THE BROTHERS! WORK UP CLA HATREDS! MAKE EVEN TH **POOR** HATE EACH OTHE SET GENTILE AGAINST JEW-PROTESTANT AGAI CATHOLIC-SOW HATE EV AMONG THEIR CHILDREN!
HOW DO YOU SUPPOSE I BROKE FRANCE? I USED THE INTERNAL HATREDS AND FEARS OF THE FRENCH PEOPLE TO GOOD ADVANTAGE. THUS ALSO OUR OWN NATIONAL SOCIALISM ROSE TO POWER IN GERMANY! I GAVE GERMANS SOMETHING TO HATE--IT DIDN'T MATTER **WHAT**, BUT THE **JEWS** WERE A GOOD SUBJECT!
BUT, MINE FEUHRER, MOST AMERICANS DO NOT HATE EACH **OTHER**! CAPTAIN COLIN KELLY, WHO DIED FIGHTING THE JAPANESE HAD FOR HIS BOMBARDIER, **MEYER LEVIN**! AN IRISHMAN AND A JEW FIGHTING SIDE BY SIDE!
FOOL! WE WILL MAKE THEM TO HATE EAC OTHER! W ARE HATE EXPERTS
8

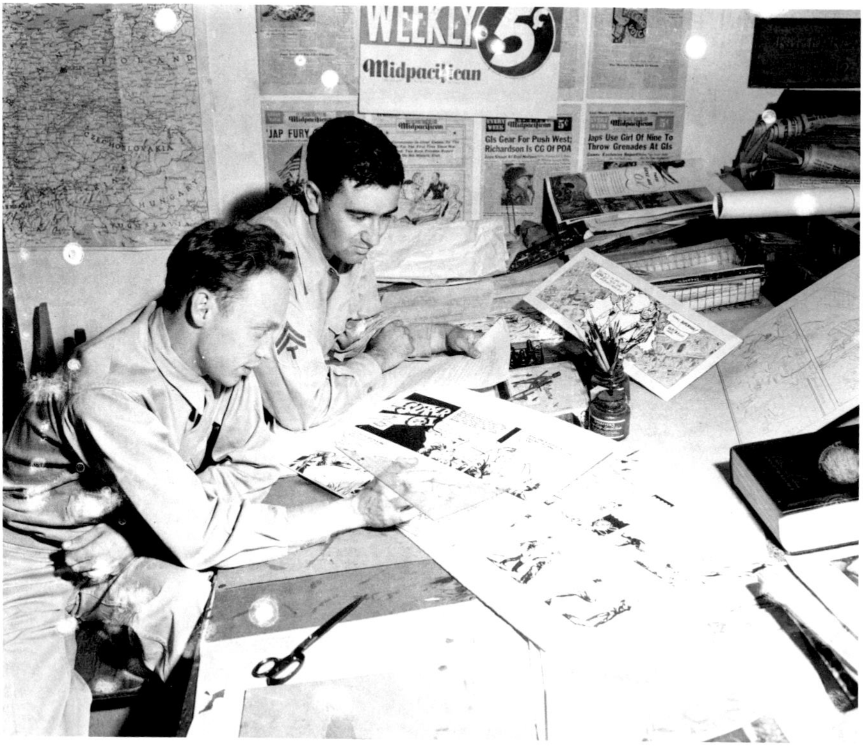
WEEKLY 5¢
JAP FURY
GIs Gear For Push West; Richardson Is CG Of POA
Japs Use Girl Of Nine To Throw Grenades At GIs

ALL-STAR COMICS No. 16

Interior, "The Justice Society Fights for a United America"; script, Gardner Fox; pencils and inks, Joe Gallagher. April–May 1943. The All-American line aggressively supported human rights during and after World War II, as in this early example from a Justice Society of America story. Nazi infiltrators make multiple attempts to divide United States communities along racial, religious, and class lines, but the heroes have none of it. The issue concludes with citizens of all creeds and colors standing with the JSA in an emphatic display of unity.

GERALD H. GREEN & JERRY SIEGEL

Photograph, Green and Siegel with their Super G.I. feature, December 1, 1944. Siegel's creativity continued undeterred in the Army, where he collaborated with "Doc" Green to create Joe Droop, aka Super G.I., for the armed forces newspaper *Midpacificman.*

ALL-STAR COMICS No. 46

Interior, "The Adventure of the Invisible Band"; script, John Broome; pencils, Irwin Hasen; inks, Bob Oksner. April–May 1949. Even with the war behind them, The Justice Society still viewed buying bonds as a good investment. Citizens who purchased United States Savings Bonds eventually received dividends on money that was put to use in the meantime to finance government expenses.

ALL-STAR COMICS No. 14

Cover art, Joe Gallagher, December 1942–January 1943. Hunger is rampant in areas of war-ravaged Europe, leading The Justice Society to provide a solution unavailable in the real world. Making their way to the hardest-hit areas of the continent, they distribute capsules that expand into full-course meals when treated with a special solution.

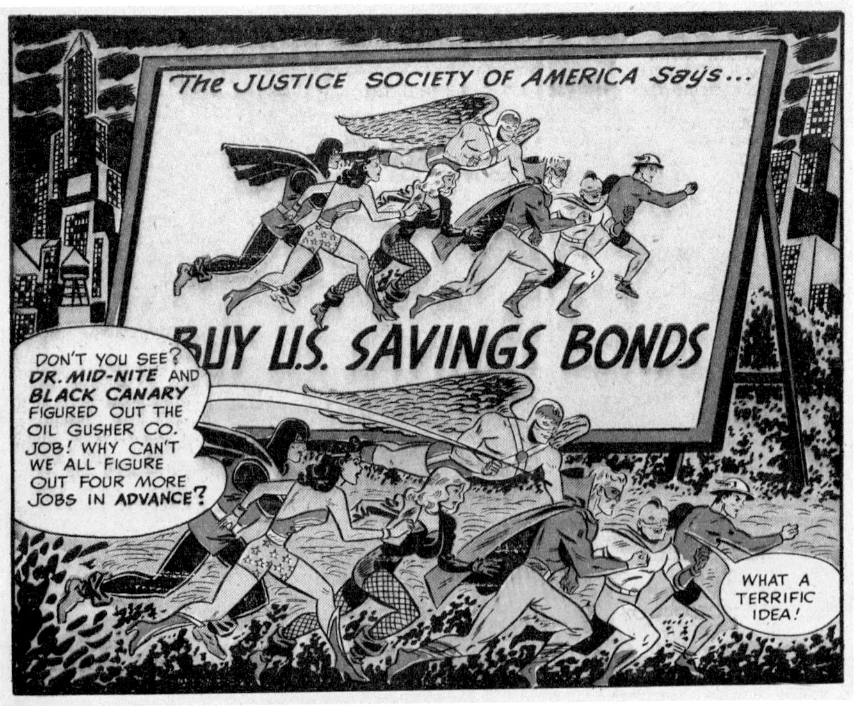
The JUSTICE SOCIETY OF AMERICA Says...
BUY U.S. SAVINGS BONDS
DON'T YOU SEE? DR. MID-NITE AND BLACK CANARY FIGURED OUT THE OIL GUSHER CO. JOB! WHY CAN'T WE ALL FIGURE OUT FOUR MORE JOBS IN ADVANCE?
WHAT A TERRIFIC IDEA!

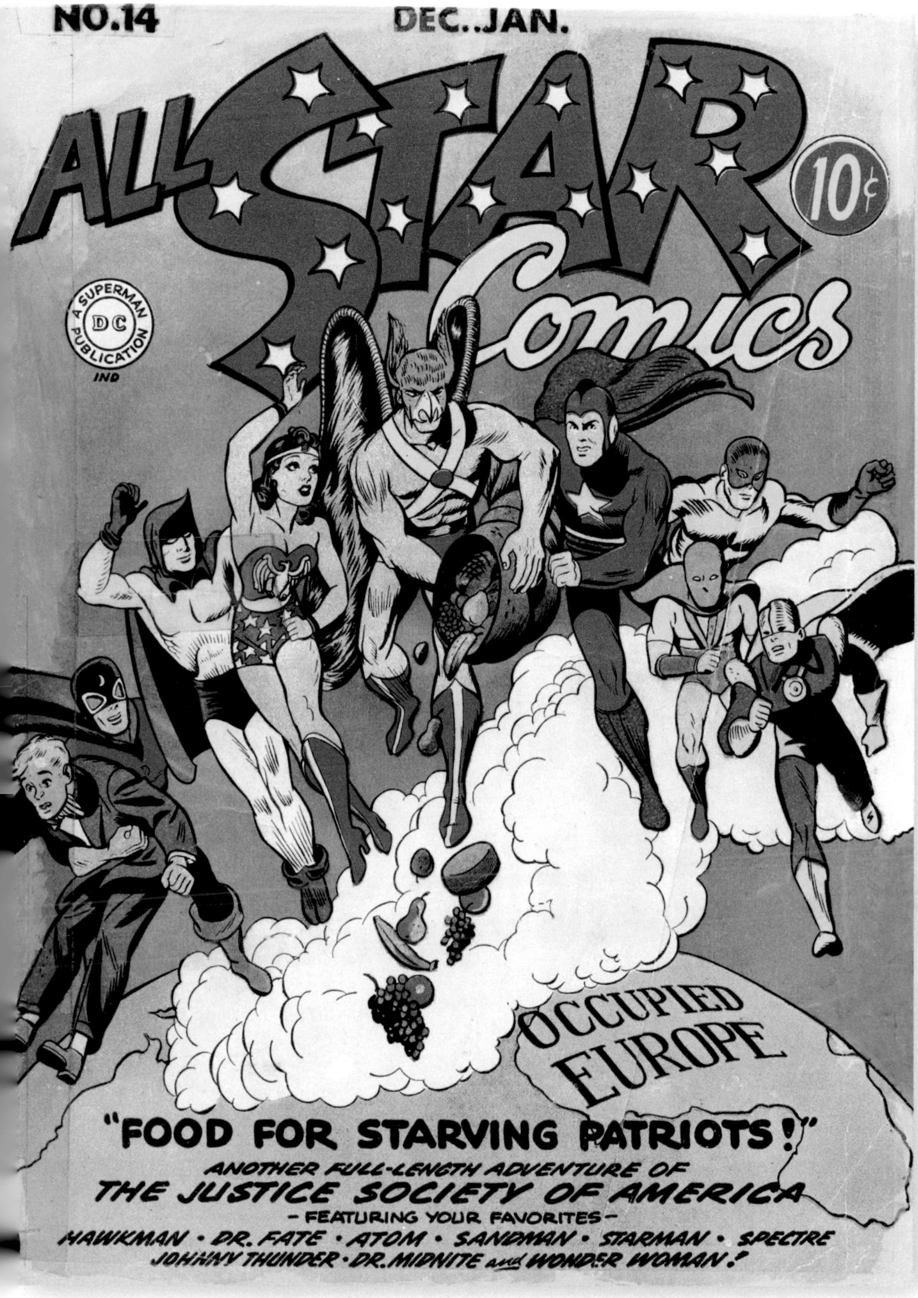
NO.14
DEC..JAN.
ALL STAR Comics
10¢
A SUPERMAN DC PUBLICATION
IND
OCCUPIED EUROPE
"FOOD FOR STARVING PATRIOTS!"
ANOTHER FULL-LENGTH ADVENTURE OF
THE JUSTICE SOCIETY OF AMERICA
-FEATURING YOUR FAVORITES-
HAWKMAN · DR. FATE · ATOM · SANDMAN · STARMAN · SPECTRE
JOHNNY THUNDER · DR. MIDNITE and WONDER WOMAN!

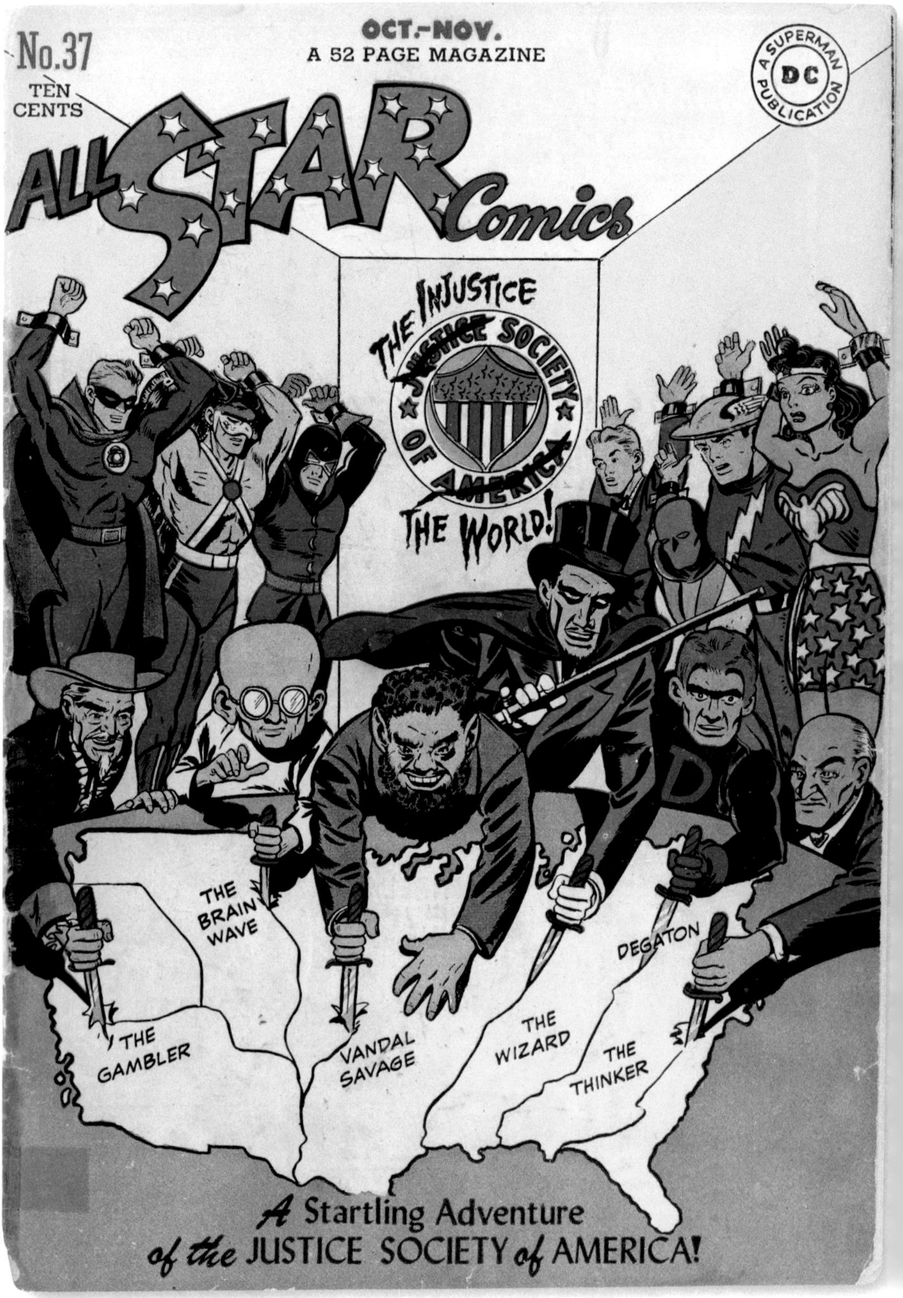
No.37
TEN CENTS
OCT.-NOV.
A 52 PAGE MAGAZINE
A SUPERMAN DC PUBLICATION
ALL STAR Comics
THE INJUSTICE ~~JUSTICE~~ SOCIETY OF ~~AMERICA~~ THE WORLD!
THE BRAIN WAVE
DEGATON
THE GAMBLER
VANDAL SAVAGE
THE WIZARD
THE THINKER
A Startling Adventure of the JUSTICE SOCIETY of AMERICA!

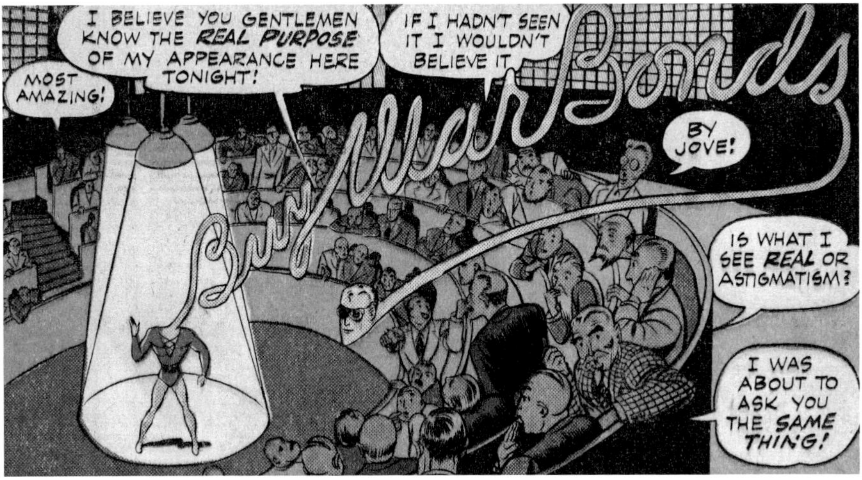
I BELIEVE YOU GENTLEMEN KNOW THE REAL PURPOSE OF MY APPEARANCE HERE TONIGHT!
MOST AMAZING!
IF I HADN'T SEEN IT I WOULDN'T BELIEVE IT
Buy War Bonds
BY JOVE!
IS WHAT I SEE REAL OR ASTIGMATISM?
I WAS ABOUT TO ASK YOU THE SAME THING!

ALL-STAR COMICS No. 37

Cover art, Irwin Hasen, October–November 1947.
The Injustice Society, composed of the captive heroes' individual and collective foes, was not the first team of costumed villains to pose a threat during the Golden Age, but it's certainly one of the most memorable.

POLICE COMICS No. 15

Interior, "Plastic Man"; script and art, Jack Cole. January 1943.
Plastic Man's advertisement of war bonds is a typically clever example of Jack Cole's use of the pliable hero's powers. It's also the only reference to the war in the story, a fairly typical instance in comic books of the period. Children were faced with an onslaught of reminders of the war in their daily life, not least of which was the absence of fathers and brothers. Mindful of that, many comic creators preferred to keep their product a relatively safe haven from the traumas of the real world.

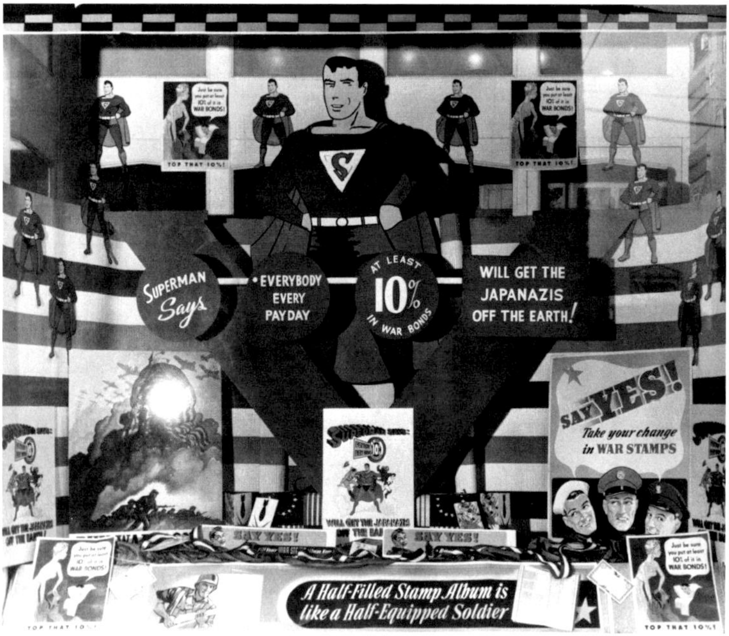
SUPERMAN Says
• EVERYBODY EVERY PAYDAY
AT LEAST 10% IN WAR BONDS
WILL GET THE JAPANAZIS OFF THE EARTH!
SAY YES!
Take your change in WAR STAMPS
A Half-Filled Stamp Album is like a Half-Equipped Soldier
TOP THAT 10%!

SUPERMAN WAR BOND DRIVE

Photograph, drug store window display, ca. 1942. Referring to the combined threats of two continents as "Japanazis," this display included a poster of Superman holding Hitler and Hirohito at bay that used the art from *Superman* No. 17's cover.

ACTION COMICS No. 58

Cover art, Jack Burnley, March 1943. "For the tough Marines, as for all U.S. Armed Forces, the Man of Steel is still super-favorite reading. But Superman is now in a really tough spot that even he can't get out of. His patriotism is above reproach. As the mightiest, fightingest American, he ought to join up. But he just can't.... To save Superman from this dilemma, plump, 27-year-old Superscriptman Jerry Siegel patched up a makeshift solution after Pearl Harbor. Superman, rejected for enlistment when his X-ray eyes inadvertently read the chart in the next room, set out to serve his country as No. 1 spy catcher. 'Of course,' says Ideaman Siegel, who admits that Superman frightens even him sometimes, 'if a sub comes to our shores and shells the U.S. we might have him take time out and administer the proper punishment.'" —*Time*, 1942

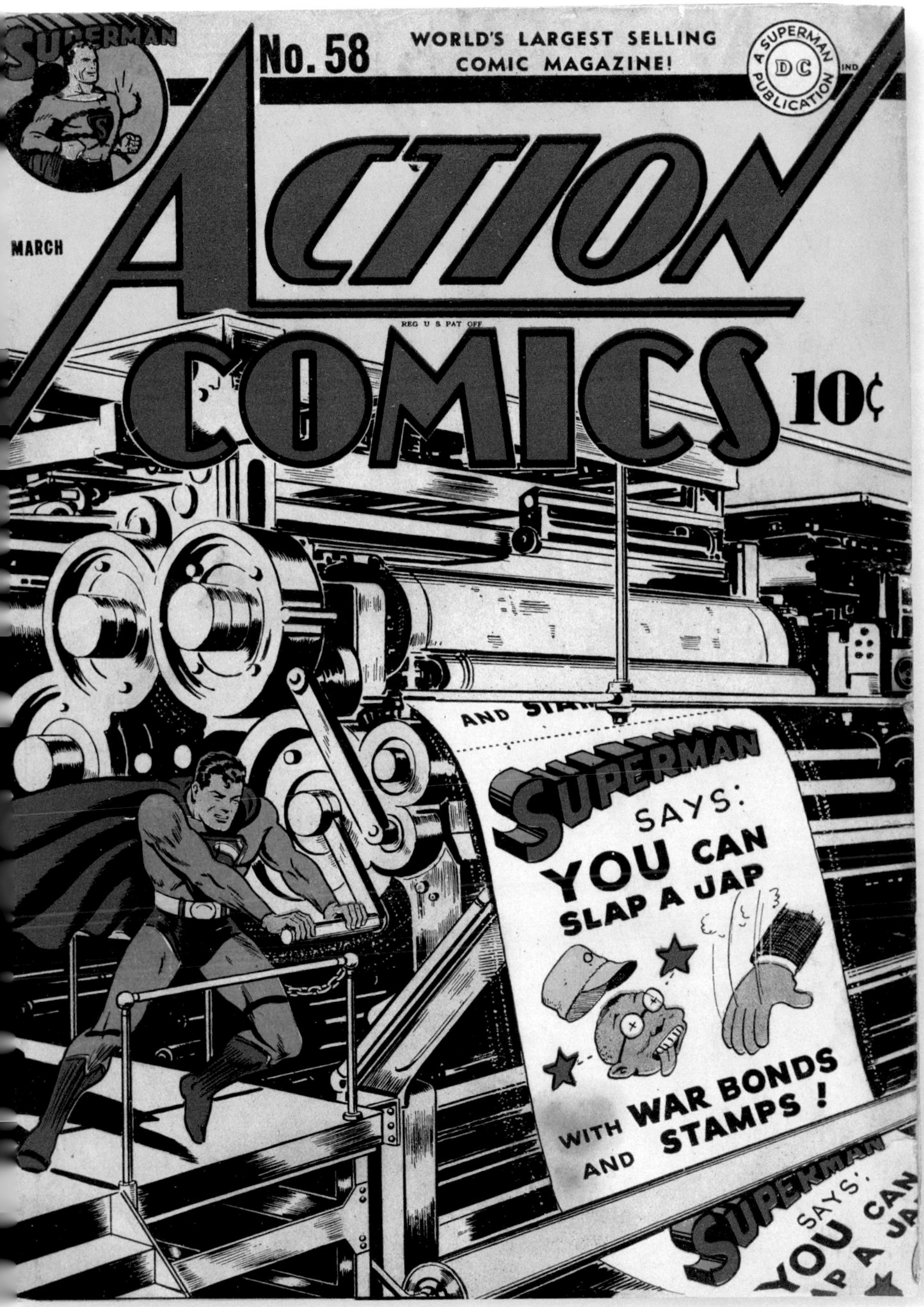
SUPERMAN
No. 58
WORLD'S LARGEST SELLING
COMIC MAGAZINE!
A SUPERMAN DC PUBLICATION INC
MARCH
ACTION
REG U S PAT OFF
COMICS
10¢
SUPERMAN
SAYS:
YOU CAN
SLAP A JAP
WITH WAR BONDS
AND STAMPS!

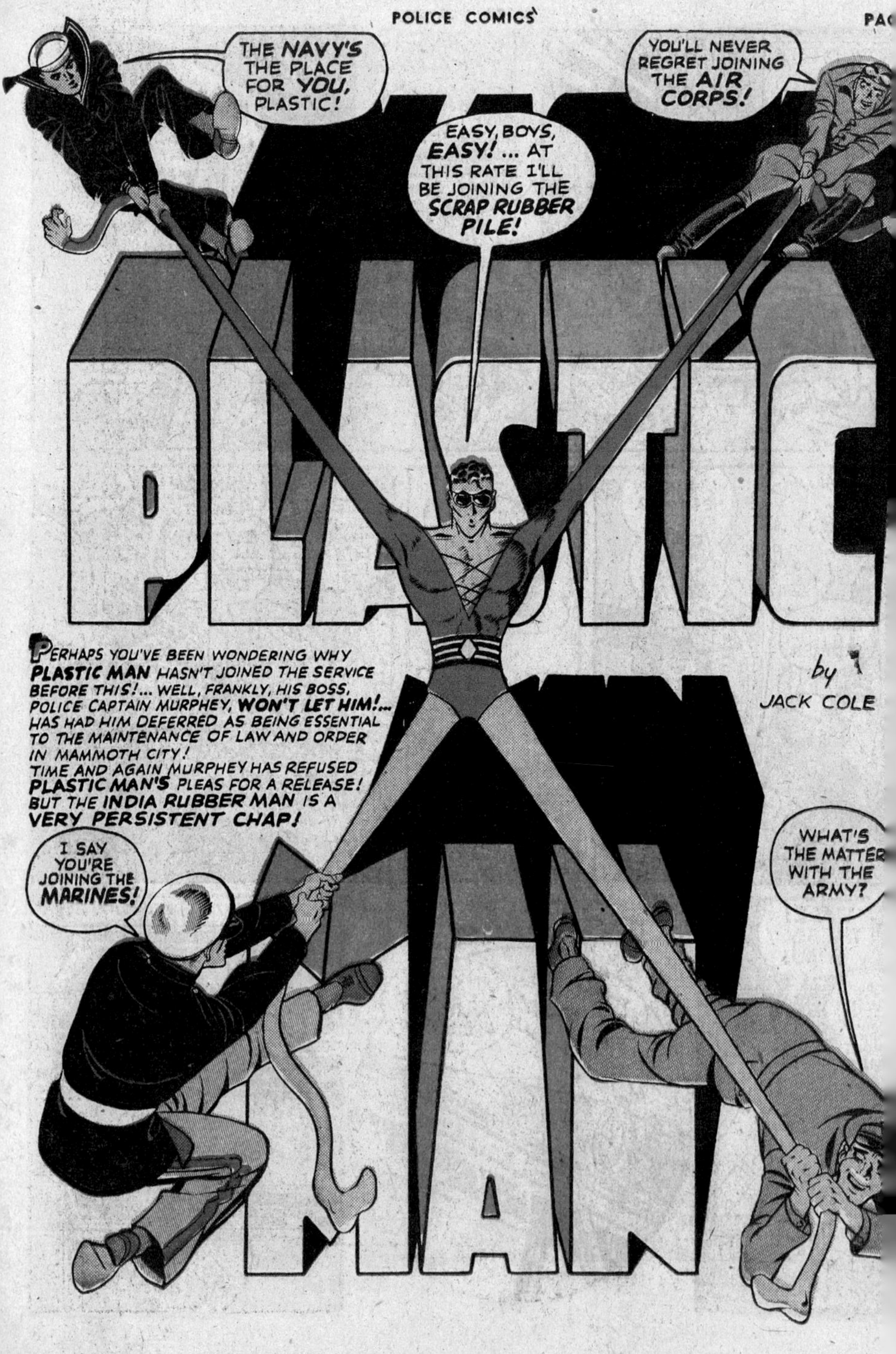
THE NAVY'S THE PLACE FOR YOU, PLASTIC!
YOU'LL NEVER REGRET JOINING THE AIR CORPS!
EASY, BOYS, EASY! ... AT THIS RATE I'LL BE JOINING THE SCRAP RUBBER PILE!
PLASTIC MAN
PERHAPS YOU'VE BEEN WONDERING WHY PLASTIC MAN HASN'T JOINED THE SERVICE BEFORE THIS!... WELL, FRANKLY, HIS BOSS, POLICE CAPTAIN MURPHEY, WON'T LET HIM!... HAS HAD HIM DEFERRED AS BEING ESSENTIAL TO THE MAINTENANCE OF LAW AND ORDER IN MAMMOTH CITY!
TIME AND AGAIN MURPHEY HAS REFUSED PLASTIC MAN'S PLEAS FOR A RELEASE! BUT THE INDIA RUBBER MAN IS A VERY PERSISTENT CHAP!
by JACK COLE
I SAY YOU'RE JOINING THE MARINES!
WHAT'S THE MATTER WITH THE ARMY?

POLICE COMICS No. 18

Interior, "Plastic Man"; script and art, Jack Cole. April 1943. The issue of which branch of the armed forces Plastic Man should join is settled by a letter from President Franklin Delano Roosevelt himself. He emphasizes that the hero would better serve his country by performing counterespionage work for the Federal Bureau of Investigation.

STAR SPANGLED COMICS No. 23

Interior, "Sweet Land of Liberty"; script, unknown; art, Hal Sherman. August 1943. The three leaders of the Axis powers—Germany's Adolf Hitler, Italy's Benito Mussolini, and Japan's Hideki Tojo—were among the most caricatured men of World War II. Though the real-life villains were often mocked in fantasy sequences, Hitler was also regularly shown having his plots against democracy thwarted by the likes of Wonder Woman or the Boy Commandos.

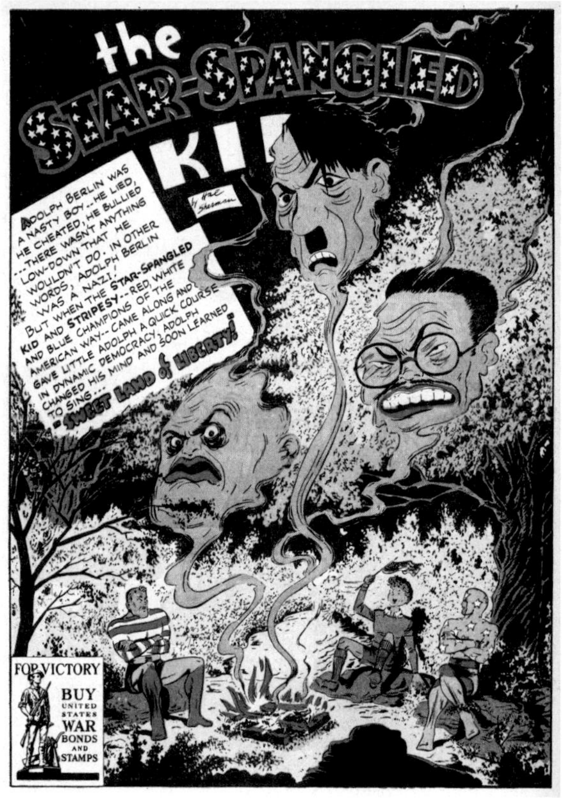
the STAR-SPANGLED KID
by Hal Sherman
ADOLPH BERLIN WAS A NASTY BOY...HE LIED, HE CHEATED, HE BULLIED ...THERE WASN'T ANYTHING LOW-DOWN THAT HE WOULDN'T DO. IN OTHER WORDS, ADOLPH BERLIN WAS A NAZI! BUT WHEN THE STAR-SPANGLED KID AND STRIPESY--RED, WHITE AND BLUE CHAMPIONS OF THE AMERICAN WAY--CAME ALONG AND GAVE LITTLE ADOLPH A QUICK COURSE IN DYNAMIC DEMOCRACY, ADOLPH CHANGED HIS MIND AND SOON LEARNED TO SING ... "SWEET LAND of LIBERTY!"
FOR VICTORY
BUY UNITED STATES WAR BONDS AND STAMPS

Be a Magician!
TURN WASTE PAPER INTO WAR WEAPONS!

HERE'S MY 100 LBS. SUPERMAN!

Special SUPERMAN SHOW Admission 100 lbs. OF WASTE PAPER

AND MINE!

OKAY, FOLKS! THE BIG ITEM ON THE SHOW TODAY IS A LITTLE MAGICAL STUNT THAT I'M GOING TO PERFORM.

SEE THIS 100 LB. PACKAGE OF WASTE PAPER? DOESN'T LOOK LIKE MUCH, DOES IT? BUT WATCH CLOSELY, FOLKS...

PRESTO!

PUFF!

CHANGO! NOW I HAVE 115 CARDBOARD BOXES, EACH OF WHICH HOLDS TEN MM. SHELLS. AMAZING WHAT YOU CAN TURN 100 LBS. OF WASTE PAPER INTO ISN'T IT? BUT IT'S LITERALLY TRUE!

AND THAT'S ONLY A SAMPLE! WASTE PAPER IS USED FOR MAKING MANY MILITARY ESSENTIALS, LIKE PARACHUTE FLARES, FUSE TANK LININGS, AIRPLANE SIGNALS, MAPS, ETC. AND WE **NEED** WASTE PAPER BADLY, BECAUSE WE HAVE A PAPER SHORTAGE!

YOU, TOO, CAN PERFORM MAGIC BY SALVAGING WASTE PAPER AND SELLING IT TO A DEALER, OR TURNING IT OVER TO YOUR LOCAL RED CROSS OR YOUR SCHOOL! THIS IS THE KIND OF MAGIC THAT WILL MAKE THE ENEMY DISAPPEAR!

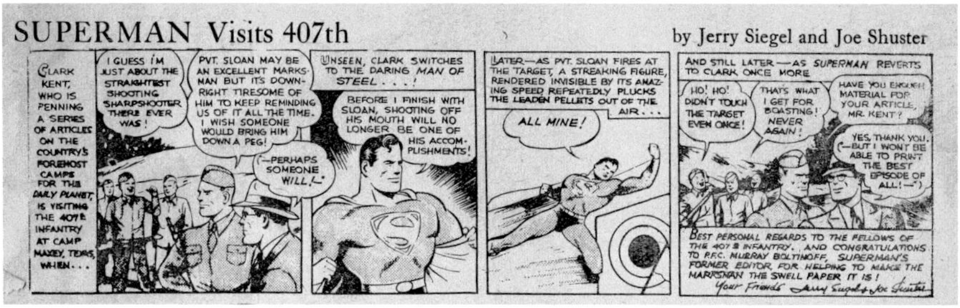
SUPERMAN Visits 407th
by Jerry Siegel and Joe Shuster
CLARK KENT, WHO IS PENNING A SERIES OF ARTICLES ON THE COUNTRY'S FOREMOST CAMPS FOR THE DAILY PLANET, IS VISITING THE 407th INFANTRY AT CAMP MAXEY, TEXAS, WHEN...
I GUESS I'M JUST ABOUT THE STRAIGHTEST SHOOTING SHARPSHOOTER THERE EVER WAS!
PVT. SLOAN MAY BE AN EXCELLENT MARKSMAN BUT IT'S DOWNRIGHT TIRESOME OF HIM TO KEEP REMINDING US OF IT ALL THE TIME. I WISH SOMEONE WOULD BRING HIM DOWN A PEG!
(—PERHAPS SOMEONE WILL!—)
UNSEEN, CLARK SWITCHES TO THE DARING MAN OF STEEL...!
BEFORE I FINISH WITH SLOAN, SHOOTING OFF HIS MOUTH WILL NO LONGER BE ONE OF HIS ACCOMPLISHMENTS!
LATER—AS PVT. SLOAN FIRES AT THE TARGET, A STREAKING FIGURE, RENDERED INVISIBLE BY ITS AMAZING SPEED REPEATEDLY PLUCKS THE LEADEN PELLETS OUT OF THE AIR...
ALL MINE!
AND STILL LATER—AS SUPERMAN REVERTS TO CLARK ONCE MORE
HO! HO! DIDN'T TOUCH THE TARGET EVEN ONCE!
THAT'S WHAT I GET FOR BOASTING! NEVER AGAIN!
HAVE YOU ENOUGH MATERIAL FOR YOUR ARTICLE, MR. KENT?
YES, THANK YOU. (—BUT I WON'T BE ABLE TO PRINT THE BEST EPISODE OF ALL!—)
BEST PERSONAL REGARDS TO THE FELLOWS OF THE 407th INFANTRY. AND CONGRATULATIONS TO P.F.C. MURRAY BOLTINOFF, SUPERMAN'S FORMER EDITOR, FOR HELPING TO MAKE THE MARKSMAN THE SWELL PAPER IT IS!
Your Friends Jerry Siegel & Joe Shuster

SUPERMAN No. 28

Interior, "Be a Magician! Turn Waste Paper into Weapons"; script, Jack Schiff; pencils and inks, George Roussos. May–June 1944. "Recognizing Superman as a wartime public relations expert, the War Department drafted him to spur drives to salvage fats, scrap iron, and wastepaper," editor Mort Weisinger once reported. "On one occasion Superman made an eloquent radio appeal, asking boys and girls to buy war stamps. Some 250,000 mailed in pledges." Ironically, the paper drives encouraged in this public service page resulted in the pulping of countless comic books and contributed to their scarcity today.

SUPERMAN VISITS 407TH

Specialty comic strip; script, Jerry Siegel; art, Joe Shuster Studio. March 31, 1943. While stationed at Camp Maxey, Texas, with the 407th regiment, former (and future) *Superman* editor Murray Boltinoff was recognized with this special comic strip.

BOY COMMANDOS No. 1

FOLLOWING SPREAD: *Interior, "Satan Wears a Swastika"; script and pencils, Jack Kirby; inks, Joe Simon. Winter 1942–1943.* "After a couple of verbal and physical initiation scraps with some of the more territorial newspaper boys, I was taken in as one of their own and I shilled my papers to passersby, whether they were on foot or slowing down for a traffic stoplight where I could hawk my papers at the driver's window.... My buddies —who I brought along with me the first time I tried to get a job hawking newspapers, and who also eventually dabbled in the trade—were for the most part jocks, geeks, scholars, and basically good guys all passing through the nation's worst Depression ever, looking to score a few coins to help our parents make ends meet." —Joe Simon

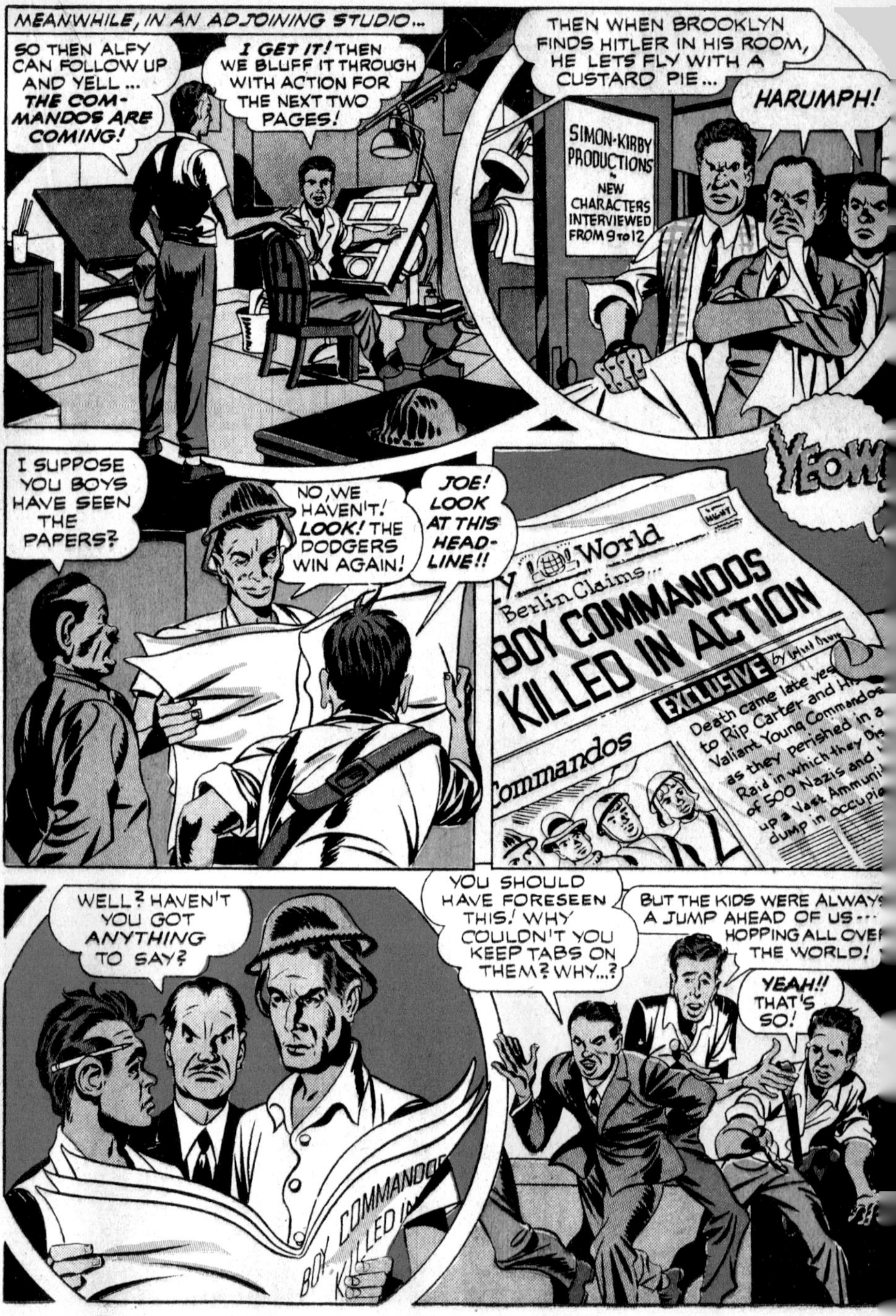
MEANWHILE, IN AN ADJOINING STUDIO...
SO THEN ALFY CAN FOLLOW UP AND YELL ... THE COMMANDOS ARE COMING!
I GET IT! THEN WE BLUFF IT THROUGH WITH ACTION FOR THE NEXT TWO PAGES!
THEN WHEN BROOKLYN FINDS HITLER IN HIS ROOM, HE LETS FLY WITH A CUSTARD PIE...
HARUMPH!
SIMON-KIRBY PRODUCTIONS
NEW CHARACTERS INTERVIEWED FROM 9 TO 12
I SUPPOSE YOU BOYS HAVE SEEN THE PAPERS?
NO, WE HAVEN'T! LOOK! THE DODGERS WIN AGAIN!
JOE! LOOK AT THIS HEADLINE!!
YEOW!
World
Berlin Claims...
BOY COMMANDOS KILLED IN ACTION
EXCLUSIVE
Death came late yes
to Rip Carter and
Valiant Young Commandos
as they perished in a
Raid in which they Dis
of 500 Nazis and
up a Vast Ammuni
dump in occupie
Commandos
Commandos
WELL? HAVEN'T YOU GOT ANYTHING TO SAY?
BOY COMMANDOS KILLED IN
YOU SHOULD HAVE FORESEEN THIS! WHY COULDN'T YOU KEEP TABS ON THEM? WHY...?
BUT THE KIDS WERE ALWAYS A JUMP AHEAD OF US--- HOPPING ALL OVER THE WORLD!
YEAH!! THAT'S SO!

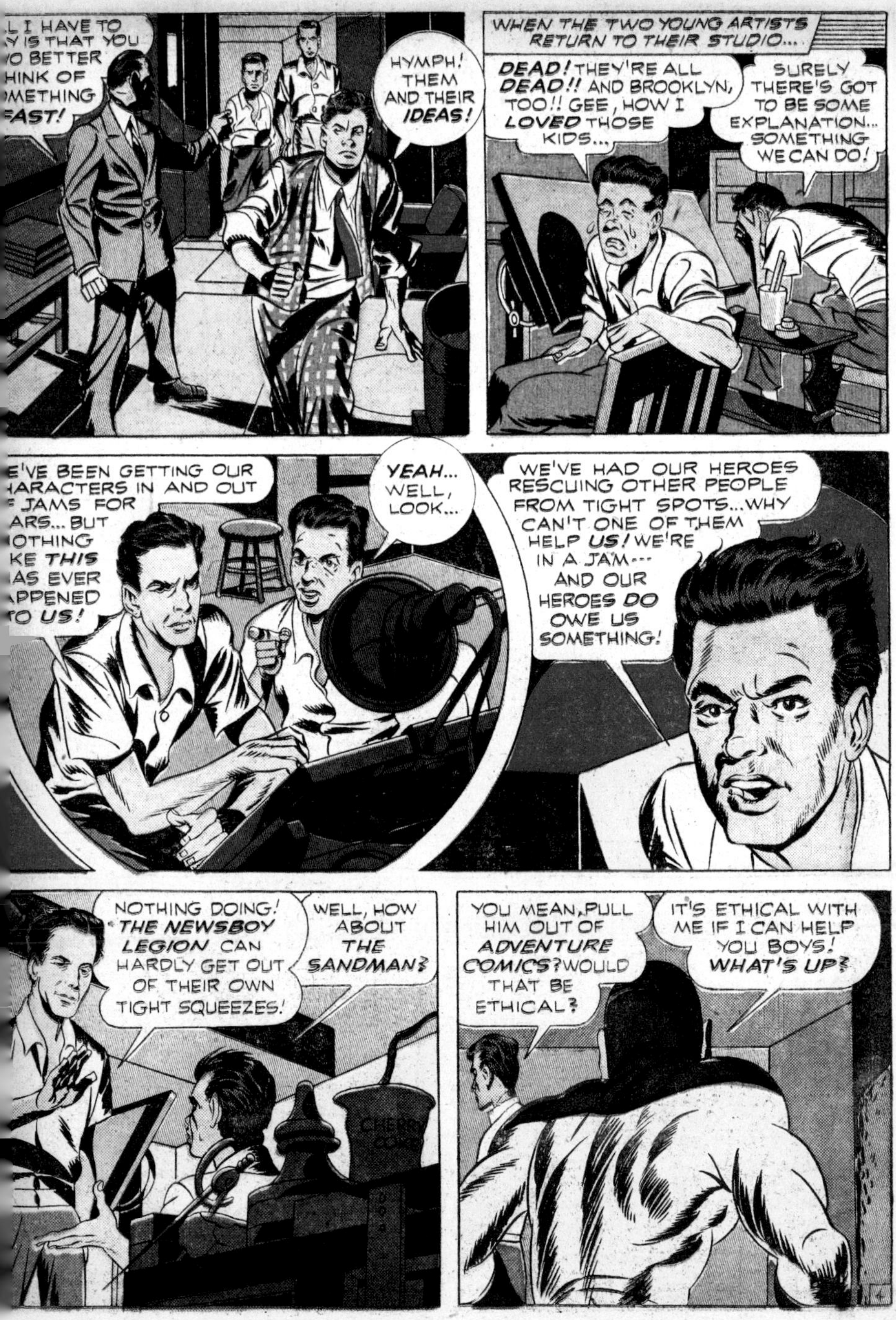
..L I HAVE TO ..Y IS THAT YOU ..O BETTER ..HINK OF ..OMETHING FAST!
HYMPH! THEM AND THEIR IDEAS!
WHEN THE TWO YOUNG ARTISTS RETURN TO THEIR STUDIO...
DEAD! THEY'RE ALL DEAD!! AND BROOKLYN, TOO!! GEE, HOW I LOVED THOSE KIDS...
SURELY THERE'S GOT TO BE SOME EXPLANATION... SOMETHING WE CAN DO!
..E'VE BEEN GETTING OUR ..HARACTERS IN AND OUT .. JAMS FOR ..ARS... BUT ..OTHING ..KE THIS ..AS EVER ..PPENED TO US!
YEAH... WELL, LOOK...
WE'VE HAD OUR HEROES RESCUING OTHER PEOPLE FROM TIGHT SPOTS...WHY CAN'T ONE OF THEM HELP US! WE'RE IN A JAM--- AND OUR HEROES DO OWE US SOMETHING!
NOTHING DOING! THE NEWSBOY LEGION CAN HARDLY GET OUT OF THEIR OWN TIGHT SQUEEZES!
WELL, HOW ABOUT THE SANDMAN?
YOU MEAN, PULL HIM OUT OF ADVENTURE COMICS? WOULD THAT BE ETHICAL?
IT'S ETHICAL WITH ME IF I CAN HELP YOU BOYS! WHAT'S UP?
4

WORLD'S FINEST COMICS No. 11

Cover art, Jack Burnley, autumn 1943. Another war initiative was the victory garden. As public food suppliers struggled to keep up with the additional demands necessary to feed soldiers, the general public was encouraged to grow their own vegetables in private gardens to reduce the strain. As with the sale of war bonds, the cultivation of victory gardens helped give citizens feelings of self-worth and patriotism. Superman, Batman, and Robin were happy to do their part.

WORLD'S FINEST COMICS No. 7

Cover art, Jack Burnley, autumn 1942. The image of the *World's Finest* heroes seated on the gun turrets of a battleship is one of DC's most striking covers during World War II. Inside the comic book, evidence of the war is primarily restricted to the Red, White and Blue feature (whose three heroes represented the Marines, Army, and Navy) and Stan Kaye's humor series *Drafty*.

No. 11
FALL ISSUE
15¢
WORLD'S FINEST
COMICS
A SUPERMAN DC PUBLICATION
R
VICTORY GARDEN
ONIONS
PEAS

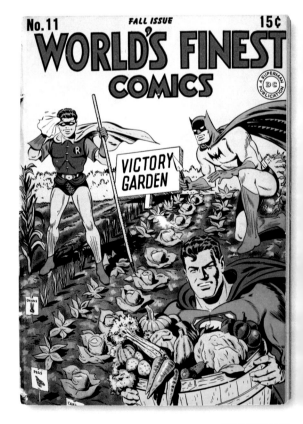

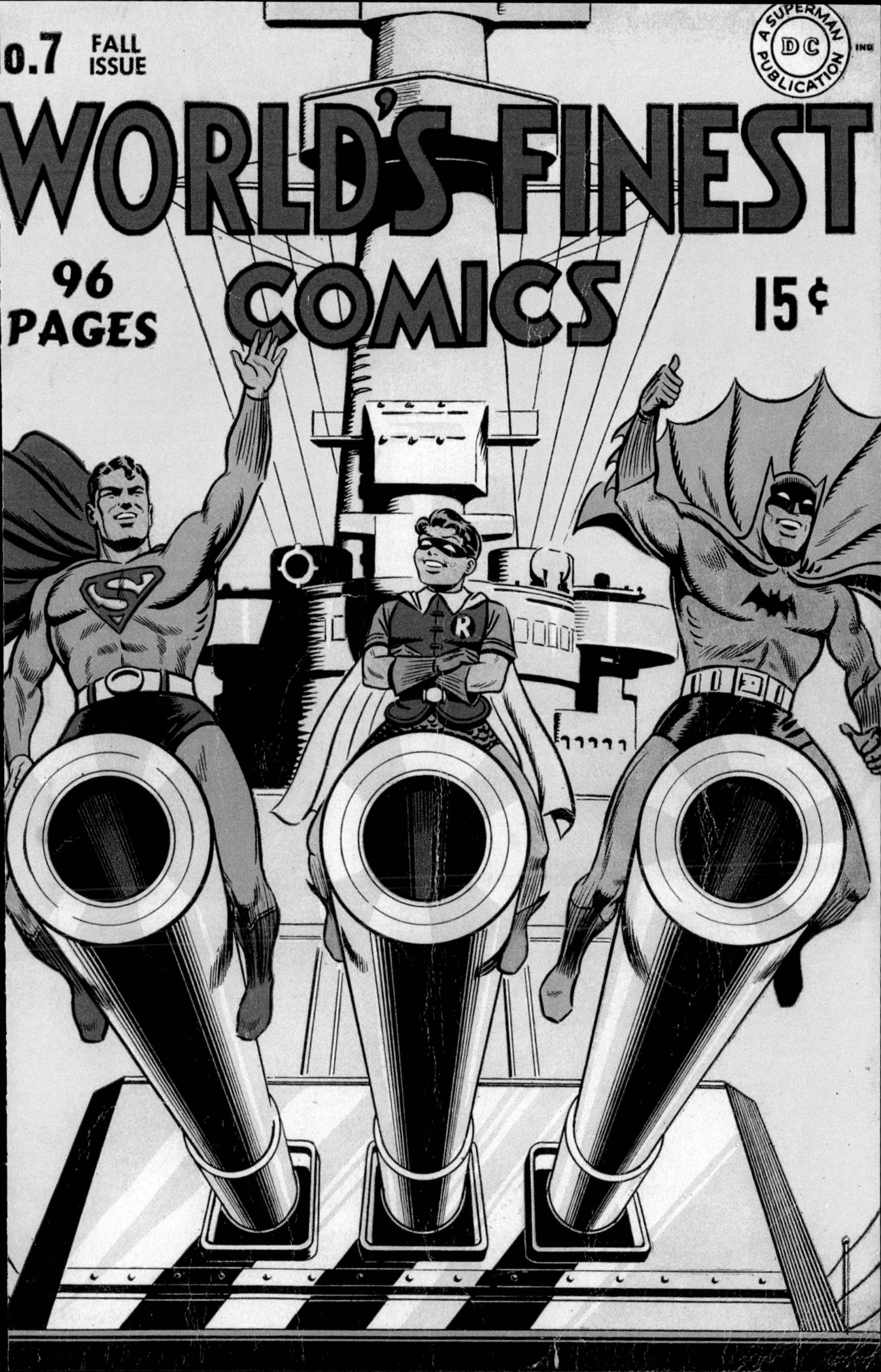

o.7
FALL ISSUE
A SUPERMAN DC PUBLICATION
IND
WORLD'S FINEST COMICS
96 PAGES
15¢

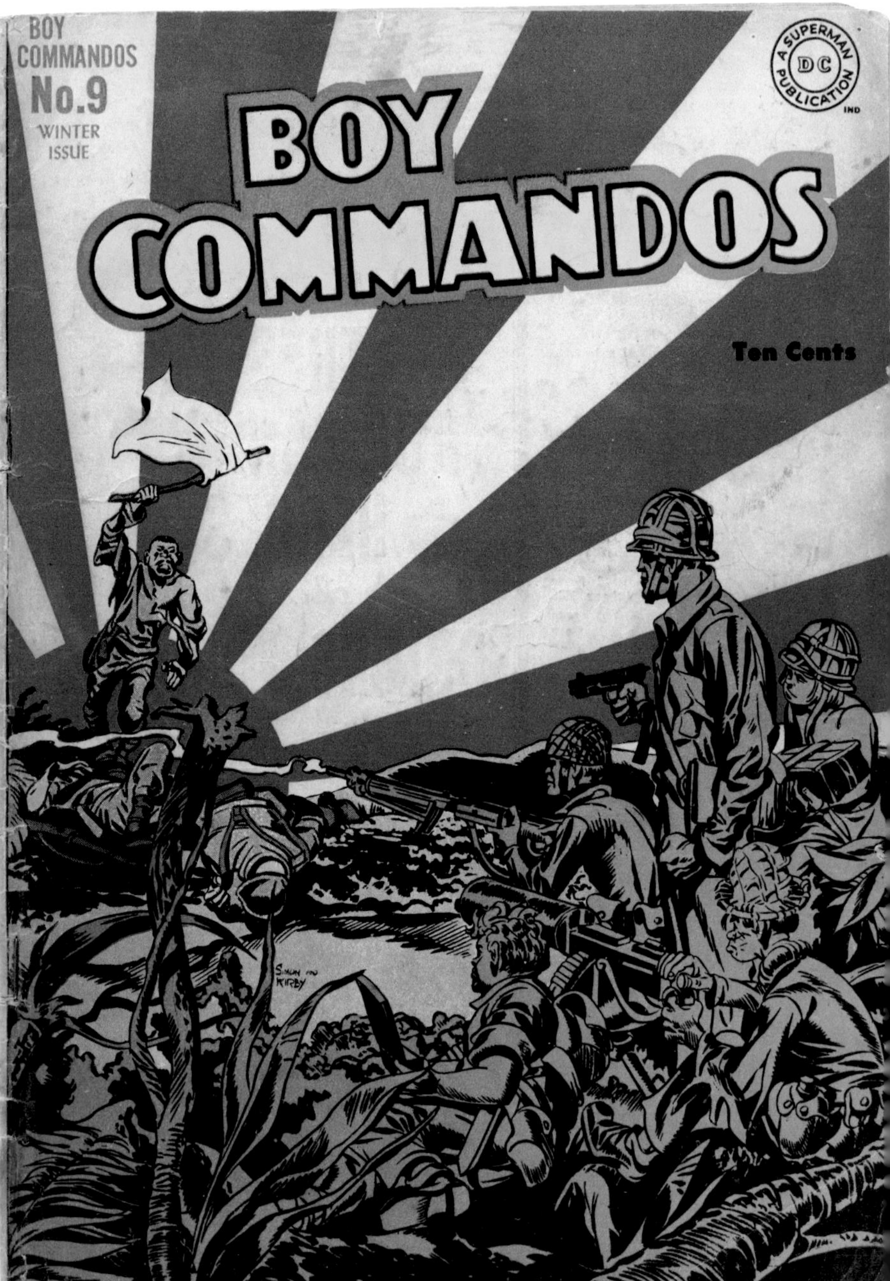
BOY COMMANDOS
No.9
WINTER ISSUE
A SUPERMAN DC PUBLICATION
IND
BOY COMMANDOS
Ten Cents

Joe Simon & Jack Kirby

"Before Simon and Kirby, the super hero was, in a sense, realistically oriented. Despite the characters' superhuman powers, they were not drawn in action in ways that suggested how extraordinary they were.... Nothing was the same after them."

—HARVEY KURTZMAN

BOY COMMANDOS No. 9

Cover art, Jack Kirby and Joe Simon, winter 1944–1945. Despite the fact that World War II was being fought on two fronts, the majority of DC's heroes seemed to focus their attention on the villainy of the Nazis, and the Boy Commandos were no exception. By 1944, the youthful quartet finally headed to Japan in an issue whose cover used the Japanese Imperial Army's rising sun flag as the backdrop for a surrendering soldier.

SIMON & KIRBY

Photograph, Joe Simon (left) and Jack Kirby (right) with writer Martin A. Bursten; Simon and Kirby studio, New York City. Ca. 1942.

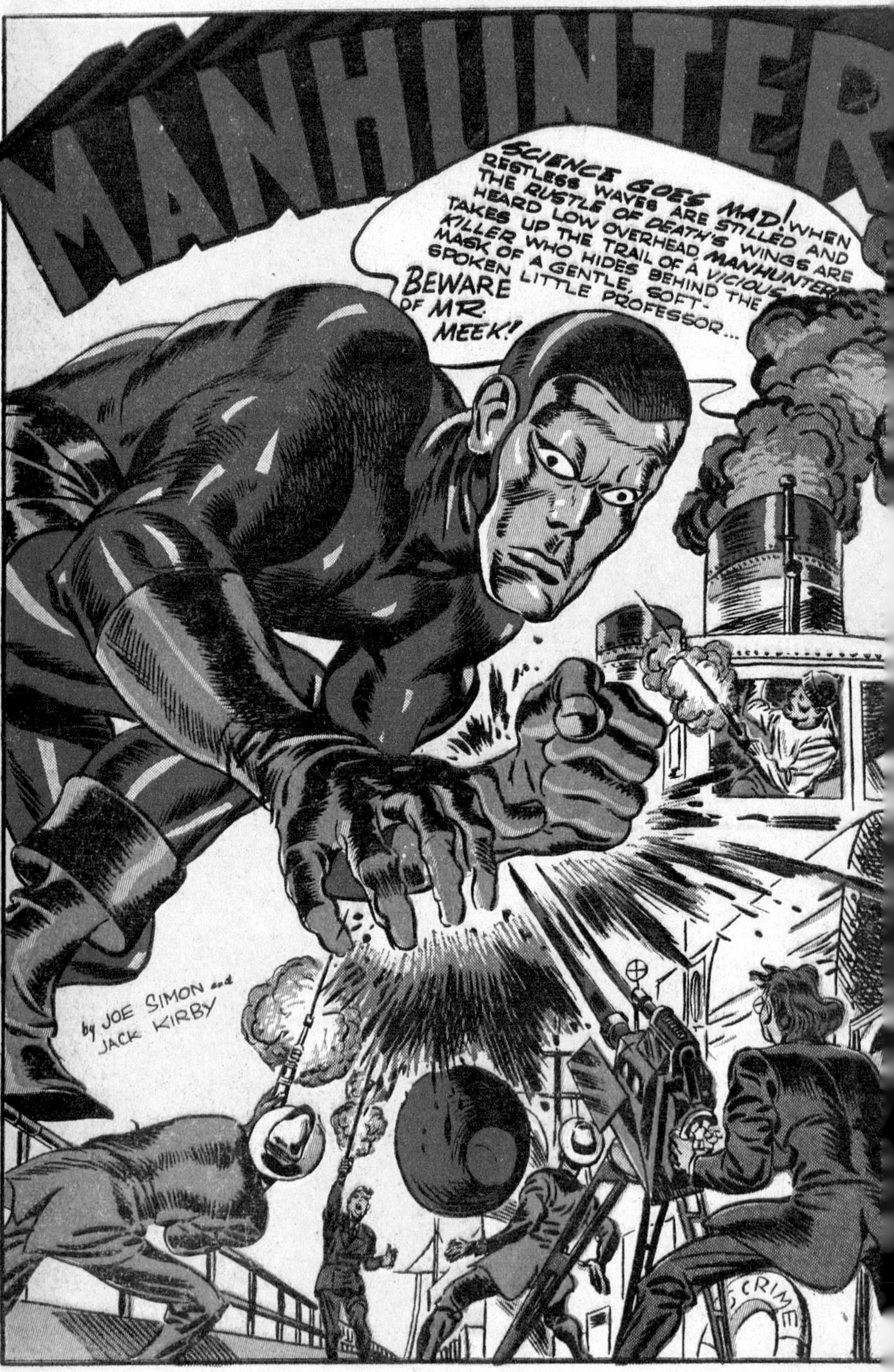
MANHUNTER
SCIENCE GOES MAD! WHEN RESTLESS WAVES ARE STILLED AND THE RUSTLE OF DEATH'S WINGS ARE HEARD LOW OVERHEAD MANHUNTER TAKES UP THE TRAIL OF A VICIOUS KILLER WHO HIDES BEHIND THE MASK OF A GENTLE, SOFT-SPOKEN LITTLE PROFESSOR... BEWARE OF MR. MEEK!
by JOE SIMON and JACK KIRBY

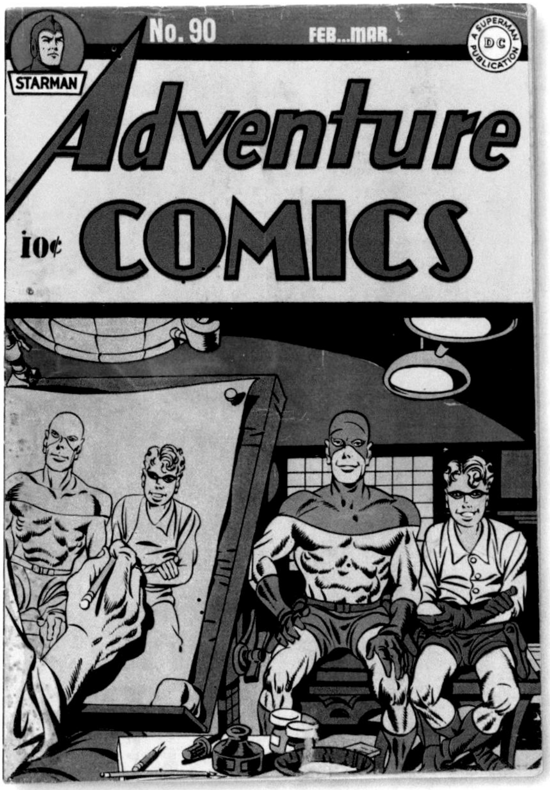
STARMAN
No. 90
FEB...MAR.
A SUPERMAN DC PUBLICATION
Adventure
10¢
COMICS

ADVENTURE COMICS No. 75

Interior, "Beware of Mr. Meek"; script and pencils, Jack Kirby; inks, attributed Joe Simon. June 1942. Like Jerry Siegel and Joe Shuster, the creative team of Joe Simon and Jack Kirby was a mark of quality and had a proven track record on hit comic books like Timely Comics' *Captain America*. Upon their arrival at DC, the duo revitalized the Sandman and developed new series starring the Boy Commandos, the Newsboy Legion, and Manhunter. Cloaked in the primary colors of red and blue, the latter character had the secret identity of Rick Nelson and replaced a detective feature called Paul Kirk, Manhunter. The Simon-Kirby Manhunter's civilian name was subsequently changed to Paul Kirk to create a link between the old series and the new one.

ADVENTURE COMICS No. 90

Cover art, Jack Kirby and unknown inker, February 1944.

ADVENTURE COMICS No. 84

Cover art, Jack Kirby and Joe Simon, March 1943. Simon and Kirby weren't above breaking the fourth wall, appearing in the same stories as their characters, the Boy Commandos and Sandman and Sandy.

ADVENTURE COMICS No. 73

Interior, "Bells of Madness"; script and pencils, Jack Kirby; inks, Joe Simon. April 1942. Originally an extension of pulp heroes, the Sandman acquired a colorful costume and kid sidekick shortly before Simon and Kirby were assigned the feature upon their arrival at DC. The duo kick-started the series with their dynamic layouts and added a specific hook to the series that found each story dealing with sleep or dreams.

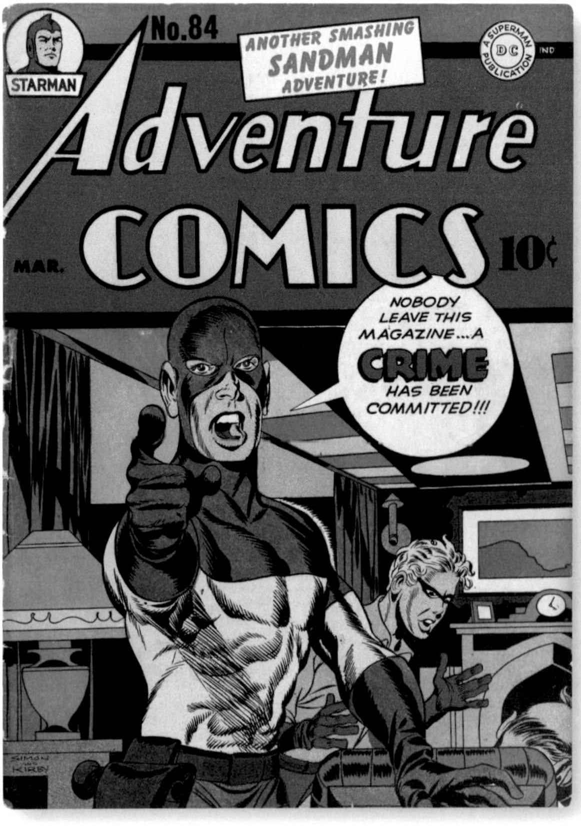
STARMAN
No.84
ANOTHER SMASHING SANDMAN ADVENTURE!
A SUPERMAN DC PUBLICATION
Adventure
MAR.
COMICS
10¢
NOBODY LEAVE THIS MAGAZINE...A CRIME HAS BEEN COMMITTED!!!
SIMON AND KIRBY

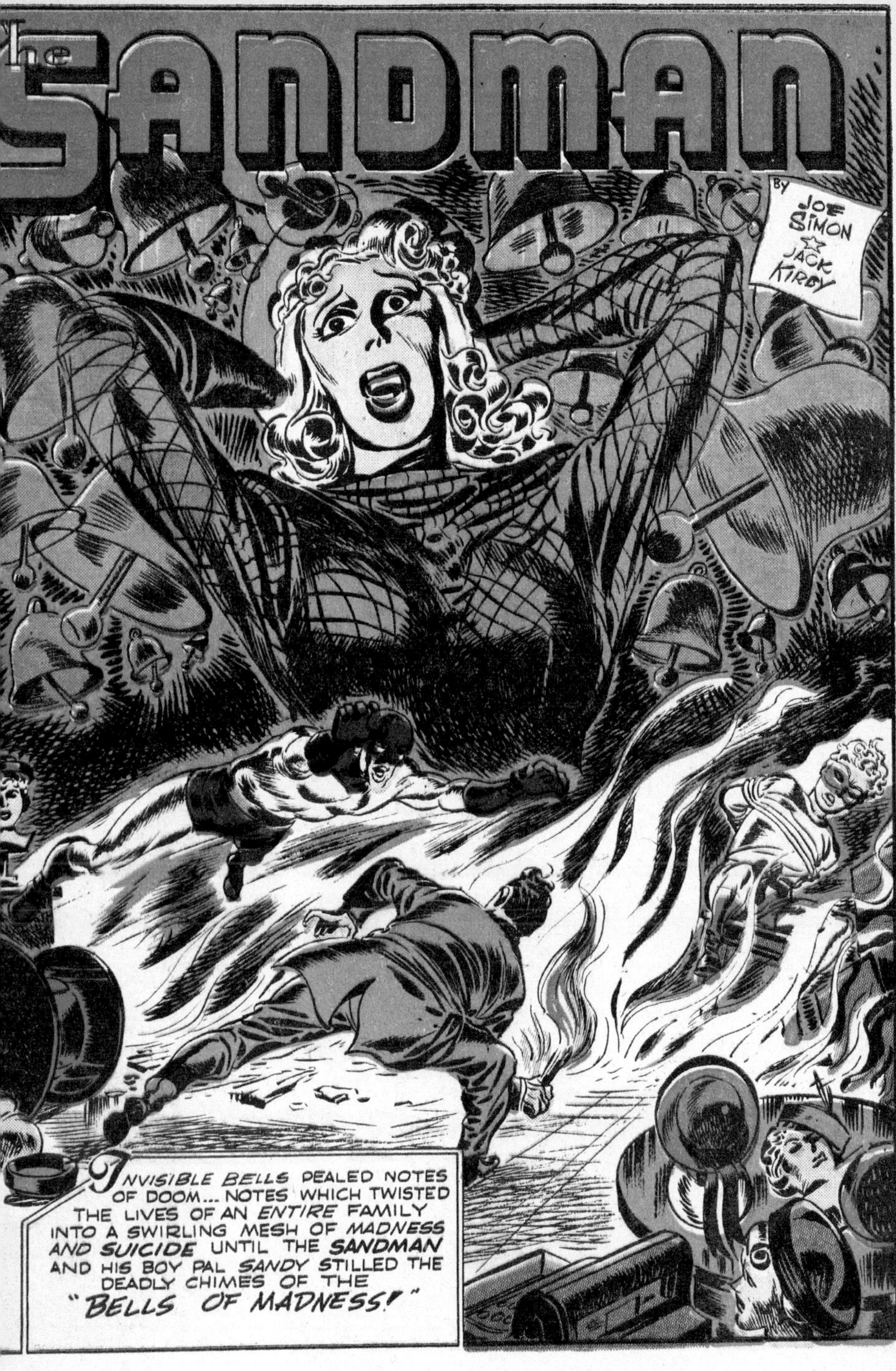

The SANDMAN
By JOE SIMON ☆ JACK KIRBY
INVISIBLE BELLS PEALED NOTES OF DOOM... NOTES WHICH TWISTED THE LIVES OF AN ENTIRE FAMILY INTO A SWIRLING MESH OF MADNESS AND SUICIDE UNTIL THE SANDMAN AND HIS BOY PAL SANDY STILLED THE DEADLY CHIMES OF THE "BELLS OF MADNESS!"

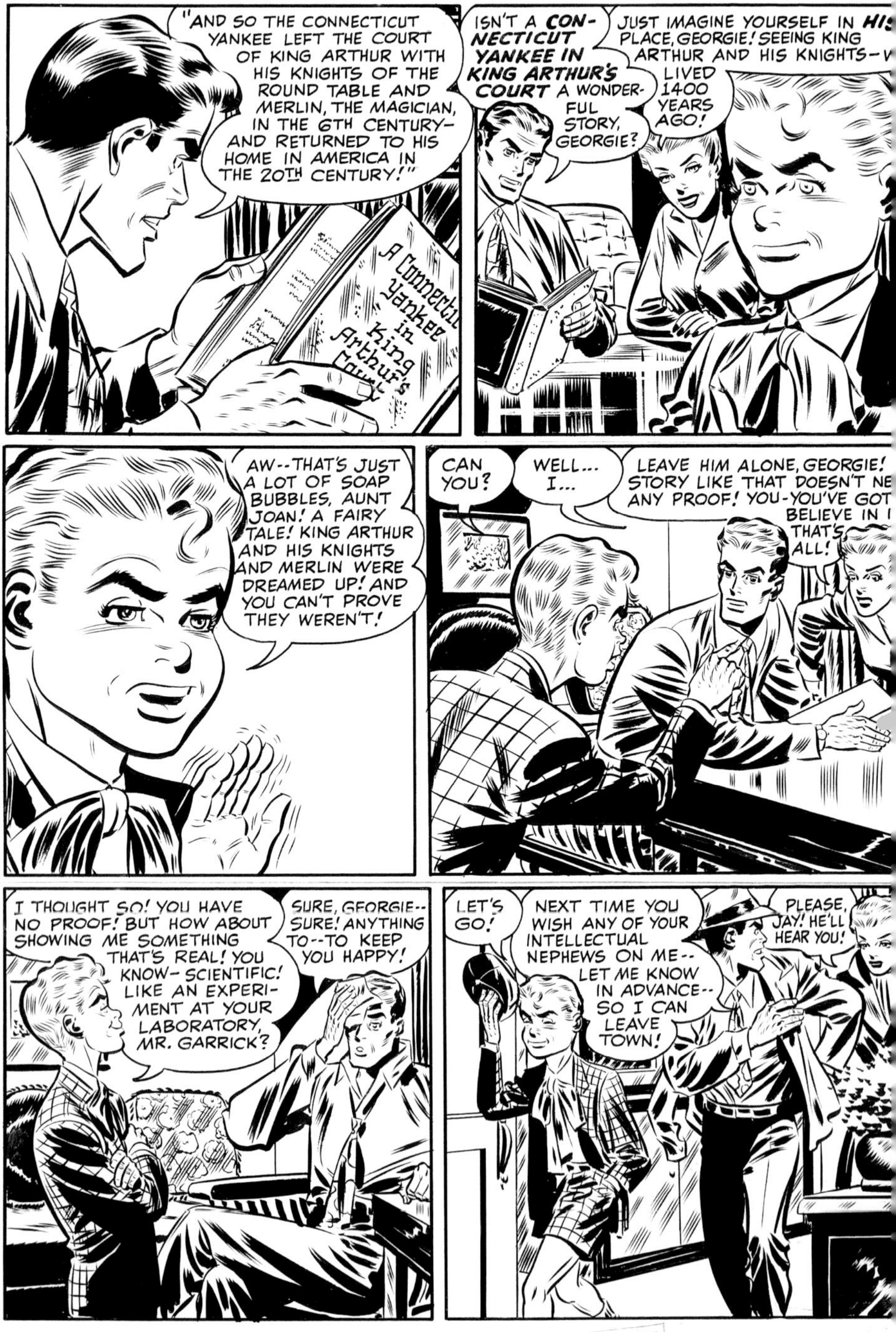
"AND SO THE CONNECTICUT YANKEE LEFT THE COURT OF KING ARTHUR WITH HIS KNIGHTS OF THE ROUND TABLE AND MERLIN, THE MAGICIAN, IN THE 6TH CENTURY-- AND RETURNED TO HIS HOME IN AMERICA IN THE 20TH CENTURY!"
A Connecticut Yankee in King Arthur's Court
ISN'T A CONNECTICUT YANKEE IN KING ARTHUR'S COURT A WONDERFUL STORY, GEORGIE?
JUST IMAGINE YOURSELF IN HIS PLACE, GEORGIE! SEEING KING ARTHUR AND HIS KNIGHTS--
LIVED 1400 YEARS AGO!
AW--THAT'S JUST A LOT OF SOAP BUBBLES, AUNT JOAN! A FAIRY TALE! KING ARTHUR AND HIS KNIGHTS AND MERLIN WERE DREAMED UP! AND YOU CAN'T PROVE THEY WEREN'T!
CAN YOU?
WELL... I...
LEAVE HIM ALONE, GEORGIE! STORY LIKE THAT DOESN'T NE ANY PROOF! YOU-YOU'VE GOT BELIEVE IN I THAT'S ALL!
I THOUGHT SO! YOU HAVE NO PROOF! BUT HOW ABOUT SHOWING ME SOMETHING THAT'S REAL! YOU KNOW- SCIENTIFIC! LIKE AN EXPERIMENT AT YOUR LABORATORY, MR. GARRICK?
SURE, GEORGIE-- SURE! ANYTHING TO--TO KEEP YOU HAPPY!
LET'S GO!
NEXT TIME YOU WISH ANY OF YOUR INTELLECTUAL NEPHEWS ON ME-- LET ME KNOW IN ADVANCE-- SO I CAN LEAVE TOWN!
PLEASE, JAY! HE'LL HEAR YOU!

FLASH COMICS No. 106

Sketches and art for Flash story left unpublished by Flash Comics'
cancellation; script, John Broome; pencils, Carmine Infantino; inks,
Bernard Sachs. 1948. Unpublished stories prepared for future
issues of *Flash Comics* remained in DC's inventory for two more
decades. When they were finally marked for destruction in the
1960s, quick-thinking young Marv Wolfman recognized their
historical significance and rescued fragments of many of the
stories from incineration, later recruiting other fans in his
mission. Some of the stories were later published by DC, while
others, like this page from a Flash adventure involving King
Arthur, remain incomplete and have appeared only in
historical publications.

STAR SPANGLED COMICS No. 13

Cover art, Jack Kirby and Joe Simon, October 1942. As a lesson in how to create visual excitement of a comic book page, legendary cartoonist Wally Wood drew examples of "22 panels that always work." One of them was the creative use of a newspaper page, a storytelling device also well recognized in film. It was particularly appropriate in the Newsboy Legion feature, whose stars actually sold newspapers.

STRANGE ADVENTURES No. 32

PAGE 446: *Interior, "The Atomic Invasion"; script, Sid Gerson; pencils and inks, Bernie Krigstein. May 1953.* In a world where the Korean War and escalating Cold War had heightened fears, a story entitled "The Atomic Invasion" couldn't help but send a chill down readers' spines. This particular plot had no connection to those real-world concerns, instead focusing on an alien invasion that was thwarted by an atom shifter created by two scientists. Similarly, the seeming missile hurtling toward a city on the cover of *Strange Adventures* No. 86 was really a somehow-less-threatening "space bomb." First and foremost, the goal of DC's science-fiction titles was to provide an escape from the real world's fears.

CAPTAIN MARVEL ADVENTURES No. 66

PAGE 447: *Interior, "Captain Marvel and the Atomic War"; script, Otto Binder; pencils and inks, C. C. Beck. October 1946.* Belying its reputation as a lighthearted super hero feature, this *Captain Marvel* story painted a surprisingly harrowing picture of the aftermath of a nuclear war. A mother and child die of radiation poisoning in the hero's arms before entire cities—and ultimately the world's entire population—are atomized in escalating retaliatory strikes. Only on the last page do readers learn that they've been watching a cautionary tale on television.

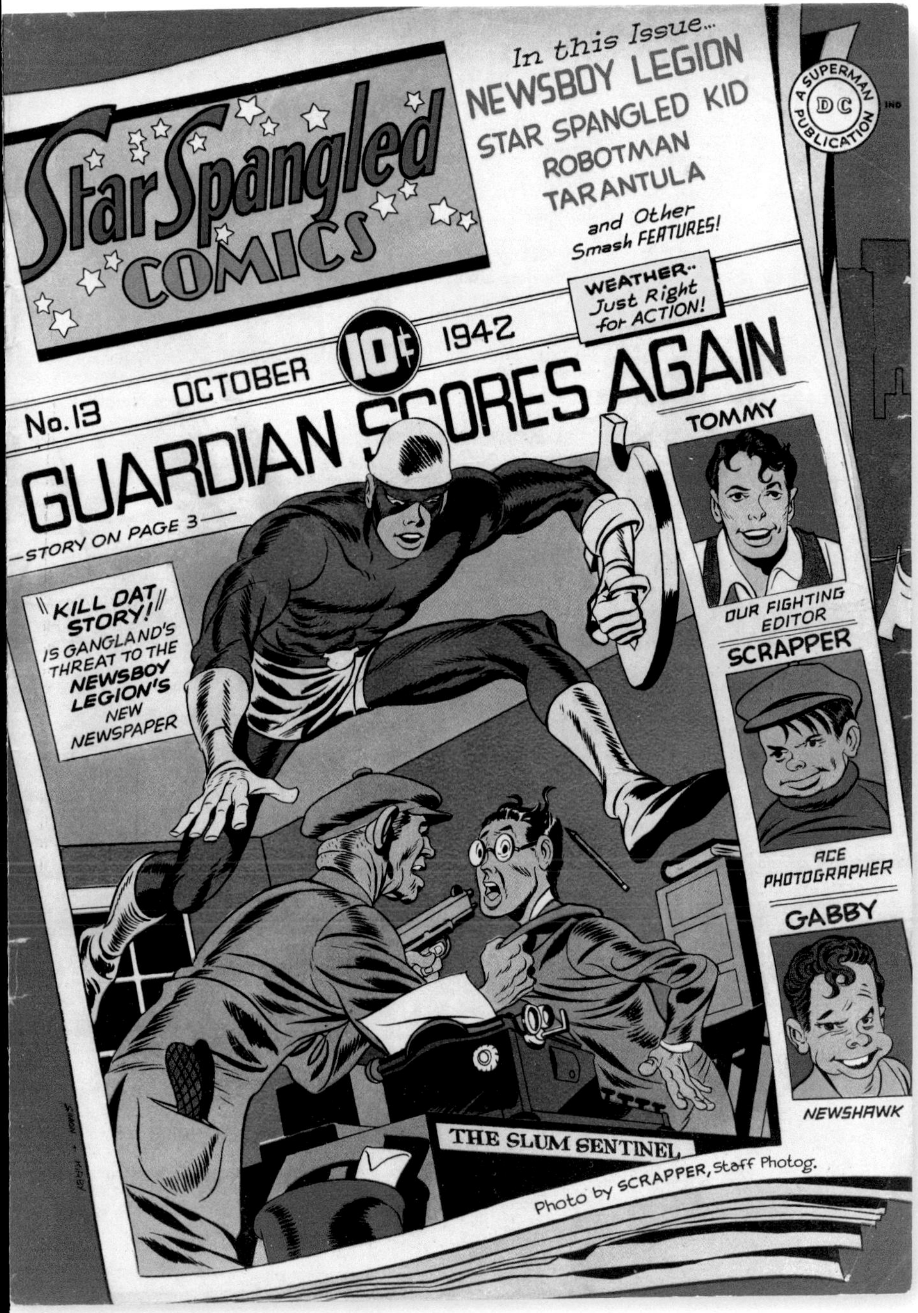

Star Spangled COMICS
In this Issue...
NEWSBOY LEGION
STAR SPANGLED KID
ROBOTMAN
TARANTULA
and Other Smash FEATURES!
A SUPERMAN DC PUBLICATION
WEATHER.. Just Right for ACTION!
No.13
OCTOBER
10¢
1942
GUARDIAN SCORES AGAIN
—STORY ON PAGE 3—
"KILL DAT STORY!" IS GANGLAND'S THREAT TO THE NEWSBOY LEGION'S NEW NEWSPAPER
TOMMY
OUR FIGHTING EDITOR
SCRAPPER
ACE PHOTOGRAPHER
GABBY
NEWSHAWK
THE SLUM SENTINEL
Photo by SCRAPPER, Staff Photog.

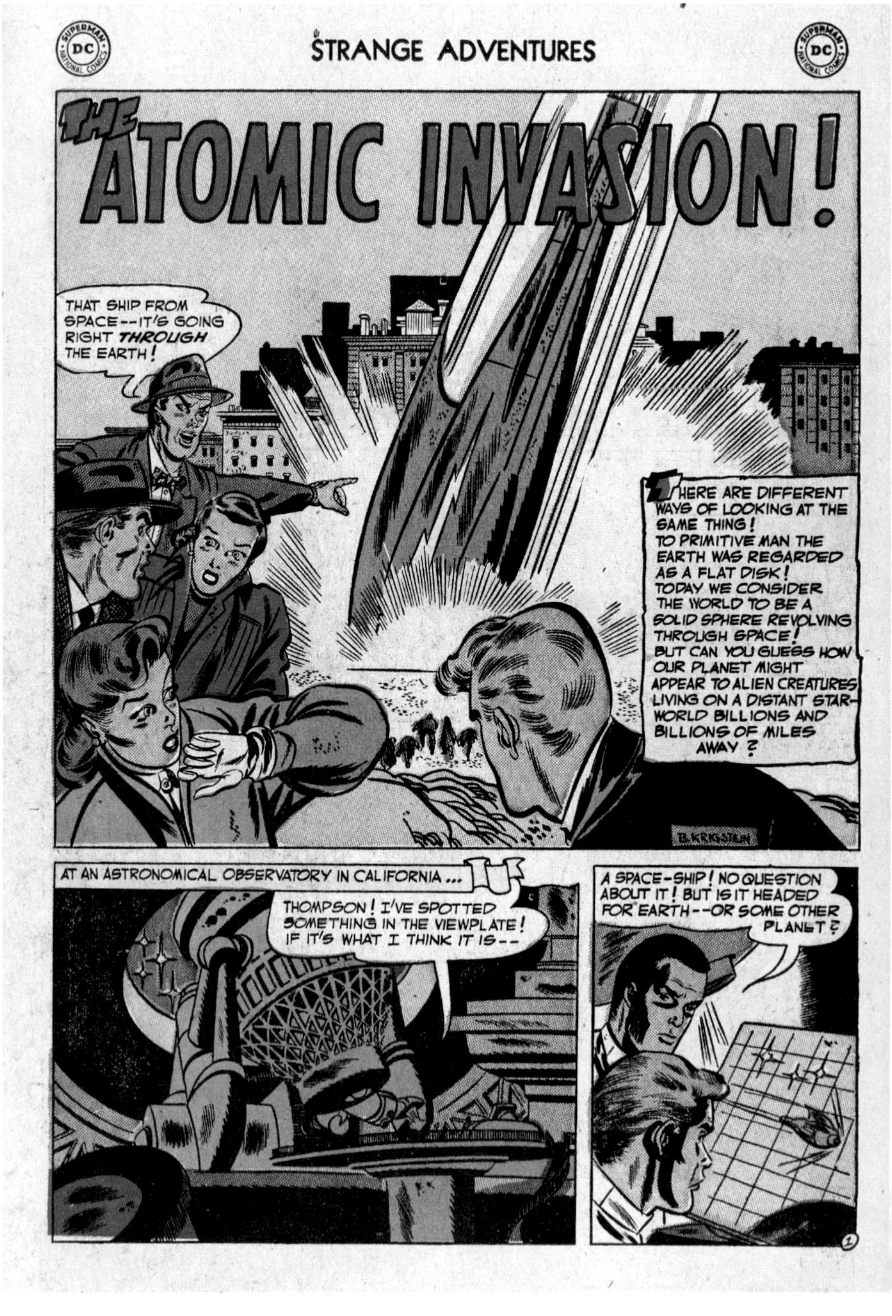
STRANGE ADVENTURES
THE ATOMIC INVASION!
THAT SHIP FROM SPACE--IT'S GOING RIGHT THROUGH THE EARTH!
THERE ARE DIFFERENT WAYS OF LOOKING AT THE SAME THING! TO PRIMITIVE MAN THE EARTH WAS REGARDED AS A FLAT DISK! TODAY WE CONSIDER THE WORLD TO BE A SOLID SPHERE REVOLVING THROUGH SPACE! BUT CAN YOU GUESS HOW OUR PLANET MIGHT APPEAR TO ALIEN CREATURES LIVING ON A DISTANT STAR-WORLD BILLIONS AND BILLIONS OF MILES AWAY?
B. KRIGSTEIN
AT AN ASTRONOMICAL OBSERVATORY IN CALIFORNIA...
THOMPSON! I'VE SPOTTED SOMETHING IN THE VIEWPLATE! IF IT'S WHAT I THINK IT IS--
A SPACE-SHIP! NO QUESTION ABOUT IT! BUT IS IT HEADED FOR EARTH--OR SOME OTHER PLANET?
1

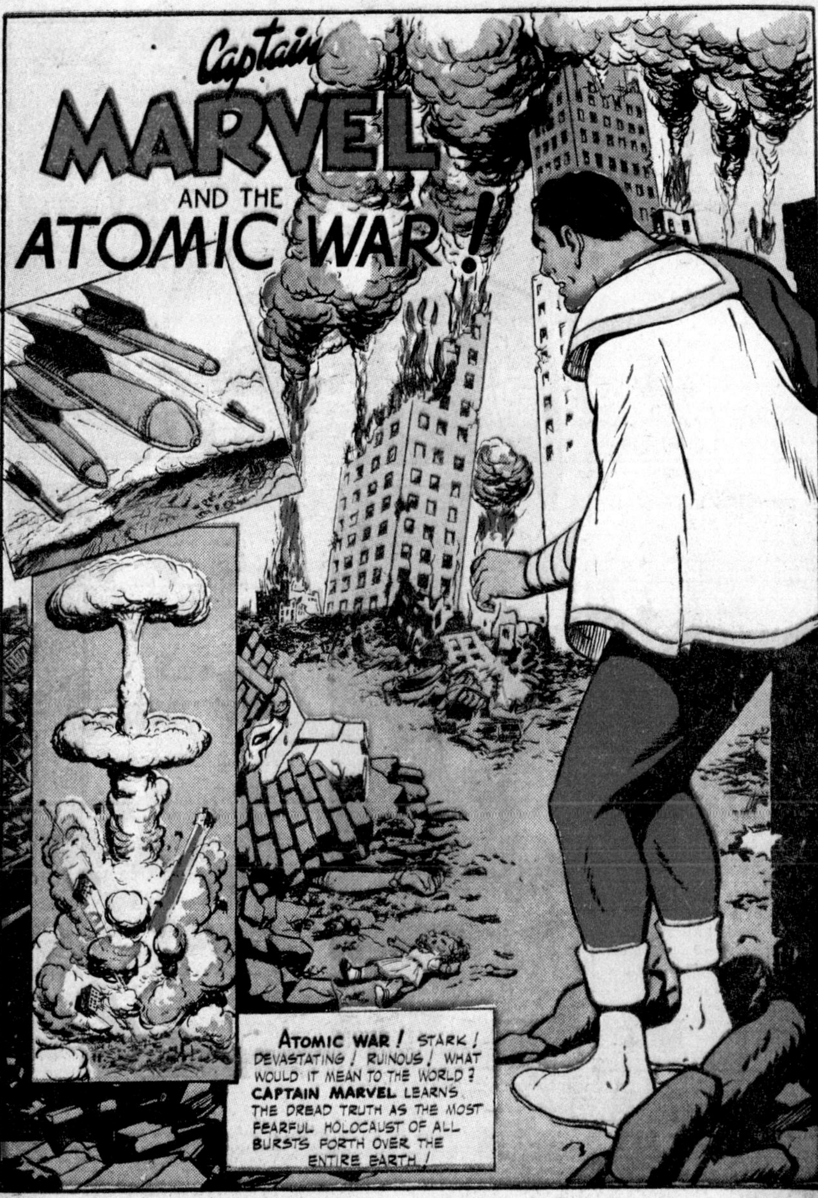
Captain
MARVEL
AND THE
ATOMIC WAR!
ATOMIC WAR! STARK! DEVASTATING! RUINOUS! WHAT WOULD IT MEAN TO THE WORLD? CAPTAIN MARVEL LEARNS THE DREAD TRUTH AS THE MOST FEARFUL HOLOCAUST OF ALL BURSTS FORTH OVER THE ENTIRE EARTH!

No.101
Ten Cents
OCT.
1946
ACTION
COMICS
IN THIS ISSUE!
SUPERMAN
COVERS ATOM
BOMB TEST!

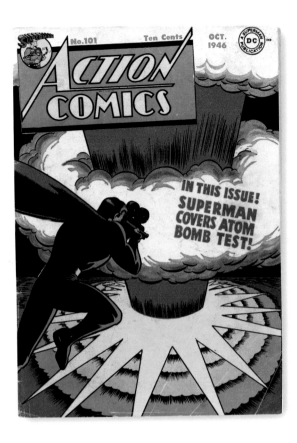

ACTION COMICS No. 101

Cover art, Win Mortimer, October 1946. Superman's postwar embrace of the Atomic Age was preceded by an innocent early-1945 story in his newspaper comic strip that caught the eye of the government. "The War Department stepped in to prevent Superman from pursuing his investigation of nuclear physics any further. 'Superman was denied,' wrote Louis N. Ridenour in *Fortune* (November 1945), 'a proposed bombardment of 3 million volt electrons from a cyclotron.'"
—John Lansdale Jr., *Harper's*, 1945

ACTION COMICS No. 138

Cover art, Al Plastino, November 1949. A teenage Al Plastino's blueprints of experimental model airplanes brought him to the attention of Grumman Aerospace during World War II, which led to a job drawing Army training manuals and, through connections there, a position drawing Superman for editor Mort Weisinger.

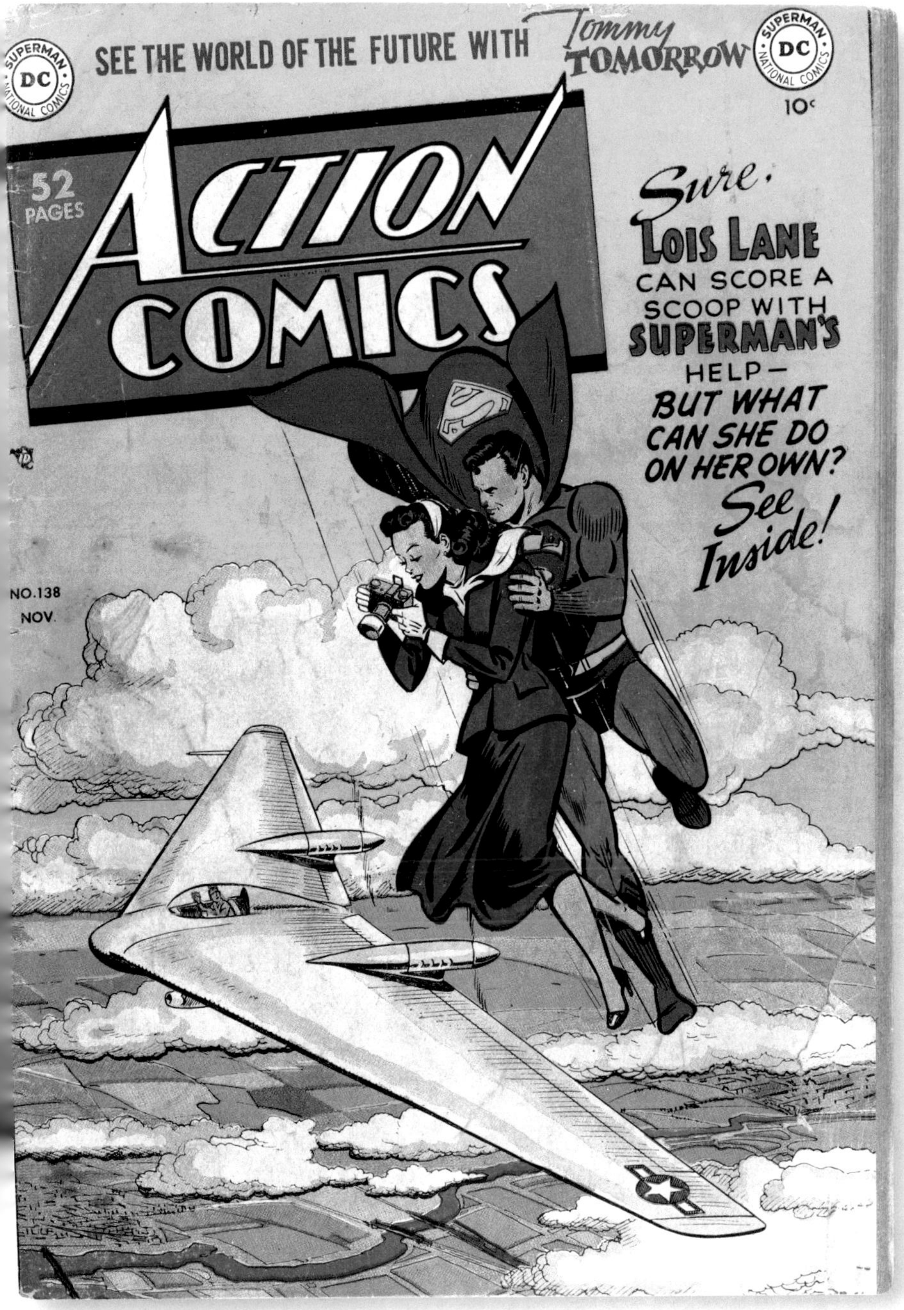
SEE THE WORLD OF THE FUTURE WITH Tommy TOMORROW
SUPERMAN DC NATIONAL COMICS
SUPERMAN DC NATIONAL COMICS
10¢
52 PAGES
ACTION COMICS
Sure, LOIS LANE CAN SCORE A SCOOP WITH SUPERMAN'S HELP— BUT WHAT CAN SHE DO ON HER OWN? See Inside!
NO.138
NOV.

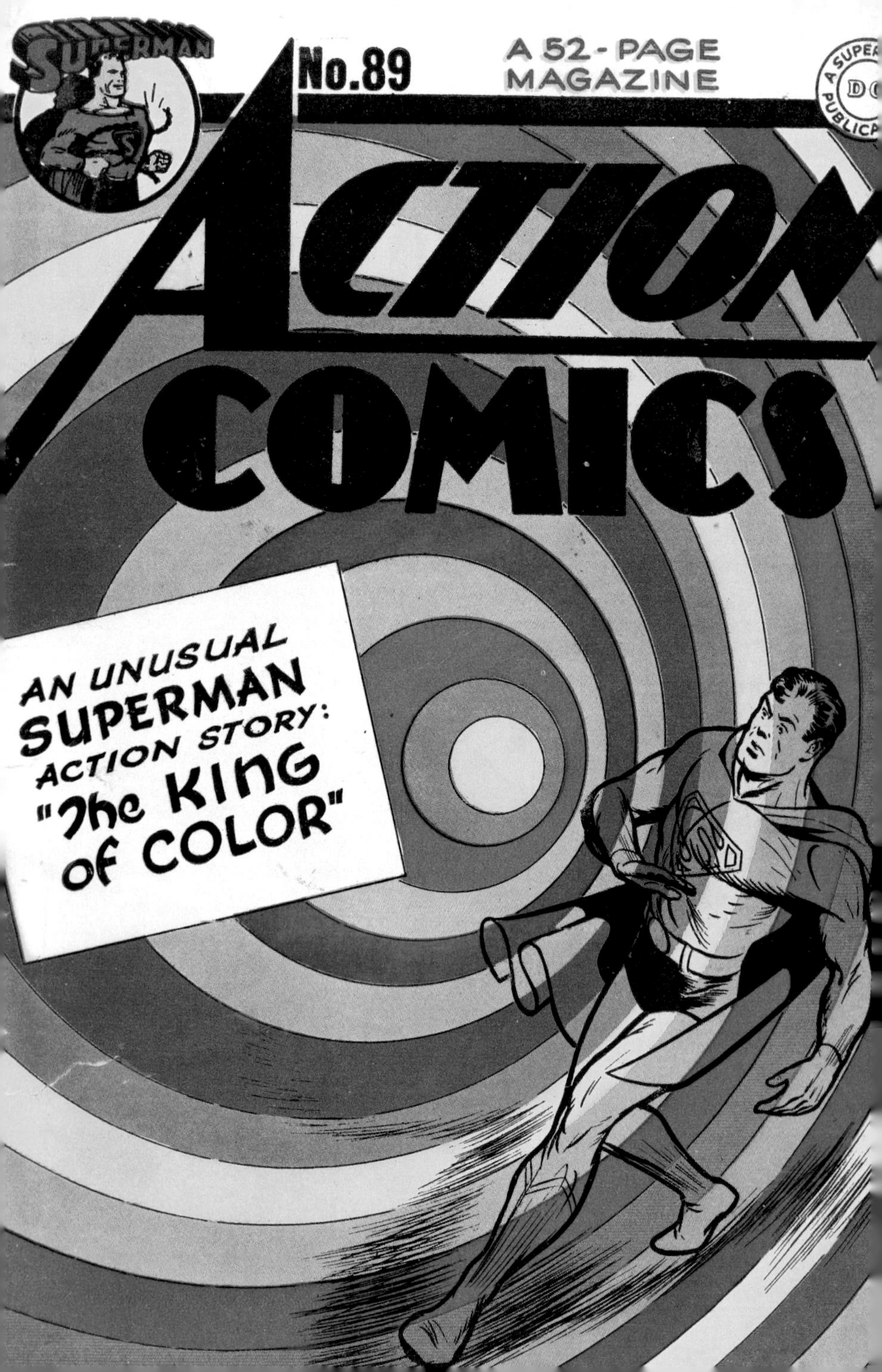
SUPERMAN
No.89
A 52-PAGE MAGAZINE
ACTION COMICS
AN UNUSUAL SUPERMAN ACTION STORY: "The KING of COLOR"

ACTION COMICS No. 89

Cover art, Wayne Boring and Stan Kaye, October 1945. Debates over which background colors would make covers more noticeable and sell better raged among editors and art directors throughout the nearly 50 years comics were distributed exclusively on newsstands. One truism that seems to have been universally accepted was that rainbow patterns were sure-fire attention-getters, as these covers attest. In this early Superman experiment, color is used to create a hypnotic effect to which even the Man of Steel seems vulnerable.

DETECTIVE COMICS No. 184

Cover art, Win Mortimer, June 1952. The Human Firefly, "the Man of a Thousand Lights," is the Batman antagonist brandishing the deadly rainbow ray. The character didn't exactly light up the sky for 1950s readers, so he appeared only once more, in 1959.

STAR SPANGLED COMICS No. 85

Cover art, Jim Mooney, October 1948. Here, a depiction of the aurora borealis provides an excuse to make this cover "pop" with a rainbow effect. The story it illustrates was not so colorful, however, being a solo adventure of Robin without Batman.

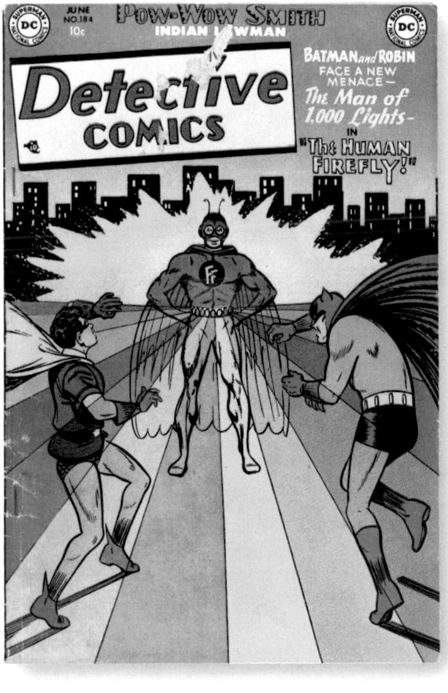
JUNE NO.184 10¢
POW-WOW SMITH
BATMAN and ROBIN FACE A NEW MENACE— The Man of 1,000 Lights— IN "The HUMAN FIREFLY!"
COMICS

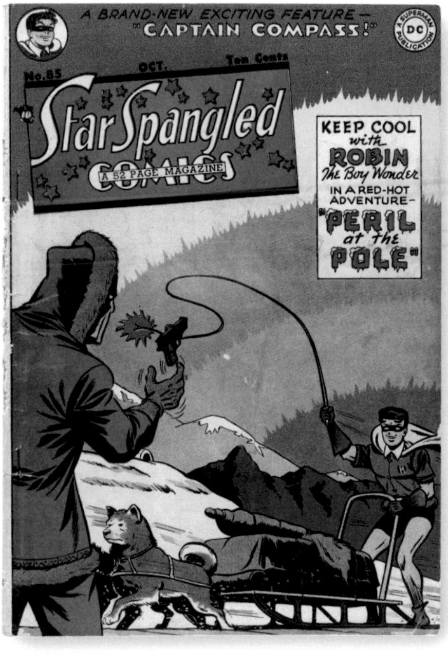
A BRAND-NEW EXCITING FEATURE— "CAPTAIN COMPASS!"
No.85
OCT.
Ten Cents
Star Spangled
A 52 PAGE MAGAZINE
KEEP COOL with ROBIN The Boy Wonder IN A RED-HOT ADVENTURE— "PERIL at the POLE"

"Besides being the greatest soliloquizer since Hamlet, Superman is also a humorist full of whimsy and light banter. No matter how rough the action or how grim the crisis, he is always ready to toss off some blithe gaiety."

— JOHN KOBLER, *THE SATURDAY EVENING POST*, JUNE 21, 1941

SUPERMAN No. 32
Cover art, Wayne Boring and Stan Kaye, January–February 1945.
Back when most covers did not illustrate a specific story, but were merely intended as eye-catching, provocative images, Superman's invulnerability was a popular theme.

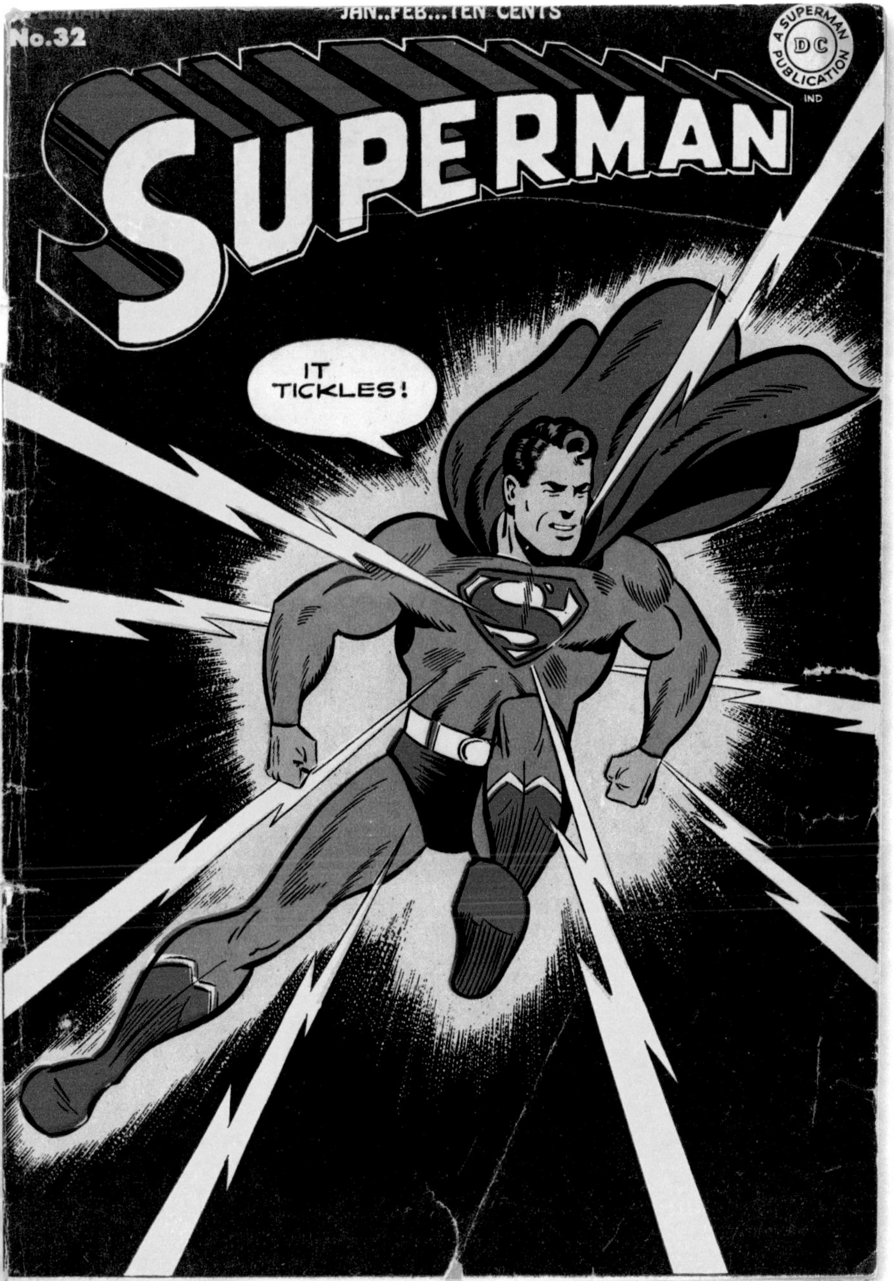
JAN..FEB...TEN CENTS
No.32
A SUPERMAN DC PUBLICATION
SUPERMAN
IT TICKLES!

No.21
JAN.- FEB.
Wonder Woman
A SUPERMAN DC PUBLICATION
TEN CENTS
H.G.PETER
Wonder Woman and the ADVENTURE of the ATOM UNIVERSE!

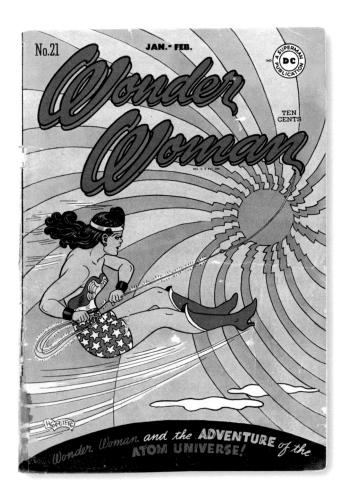

WONDER WOMAN No. 21

Cover art, H. G. Peter, January–February 1947. By the late 1940s, the increasingly competitive comic book environment motivated DC's editors to attempt hooking readers by dramatizing the interior's content on the cover, especially when that content comprised a book-length tale like this one. Some were less obvious than others, as is the case here, where the fact that the story in question takes place in a microminiature, subatomic universe is a bit difficult to discern from the stylized sunburst effect.

BATMAN No. 25

Cover art, Dick Sprang. October–November 1944.

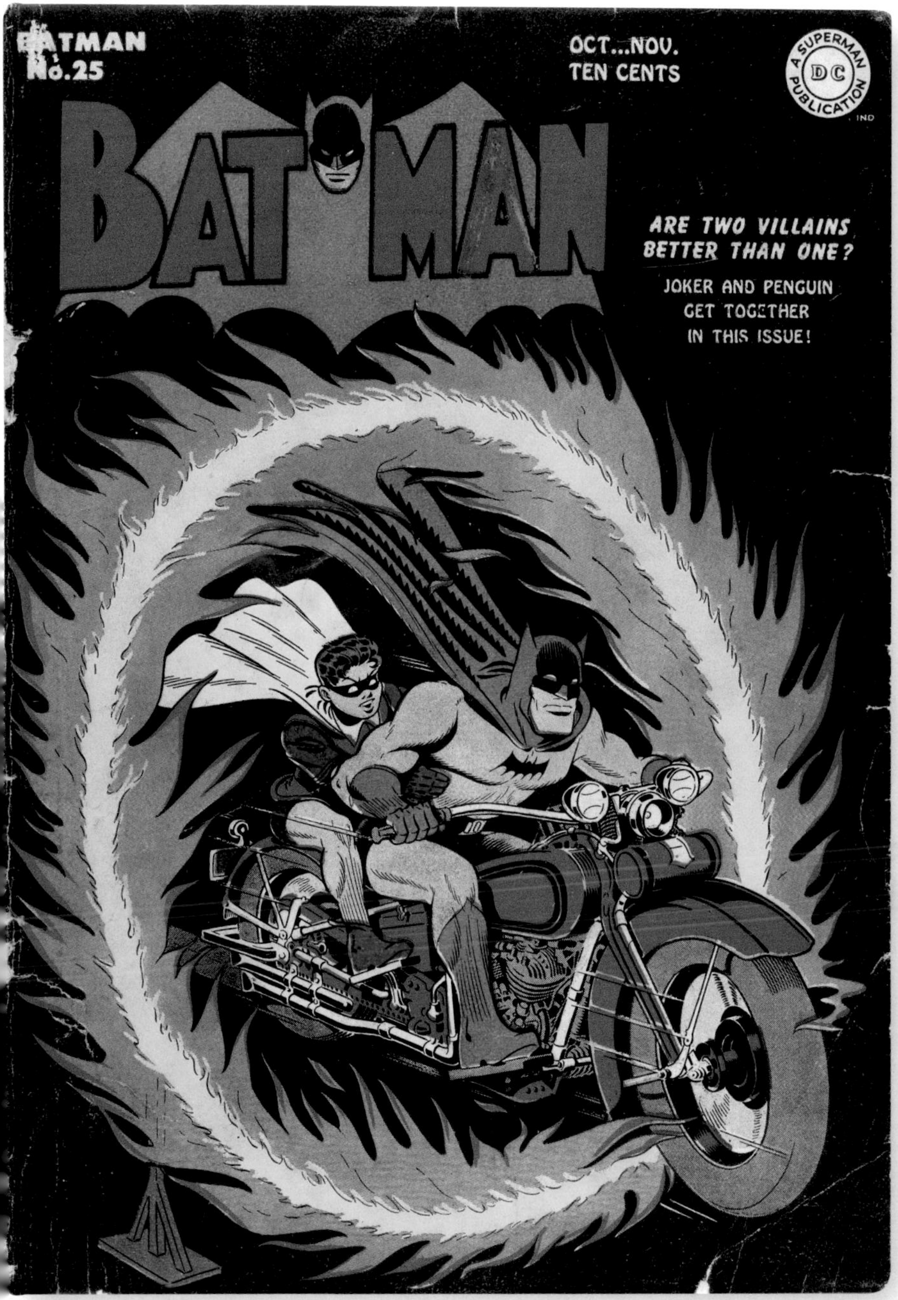
BATMAN
No.25
OCT...NOV.
TEN CENTS
A SUPERMAN
DC
PUBLICATION
IND
BATMAN
ARE TWO VILLAINS
BETTER THAN ONE?
JOKER AND PENGUIN
GET TOGETHER
IN THIS ISSUE!

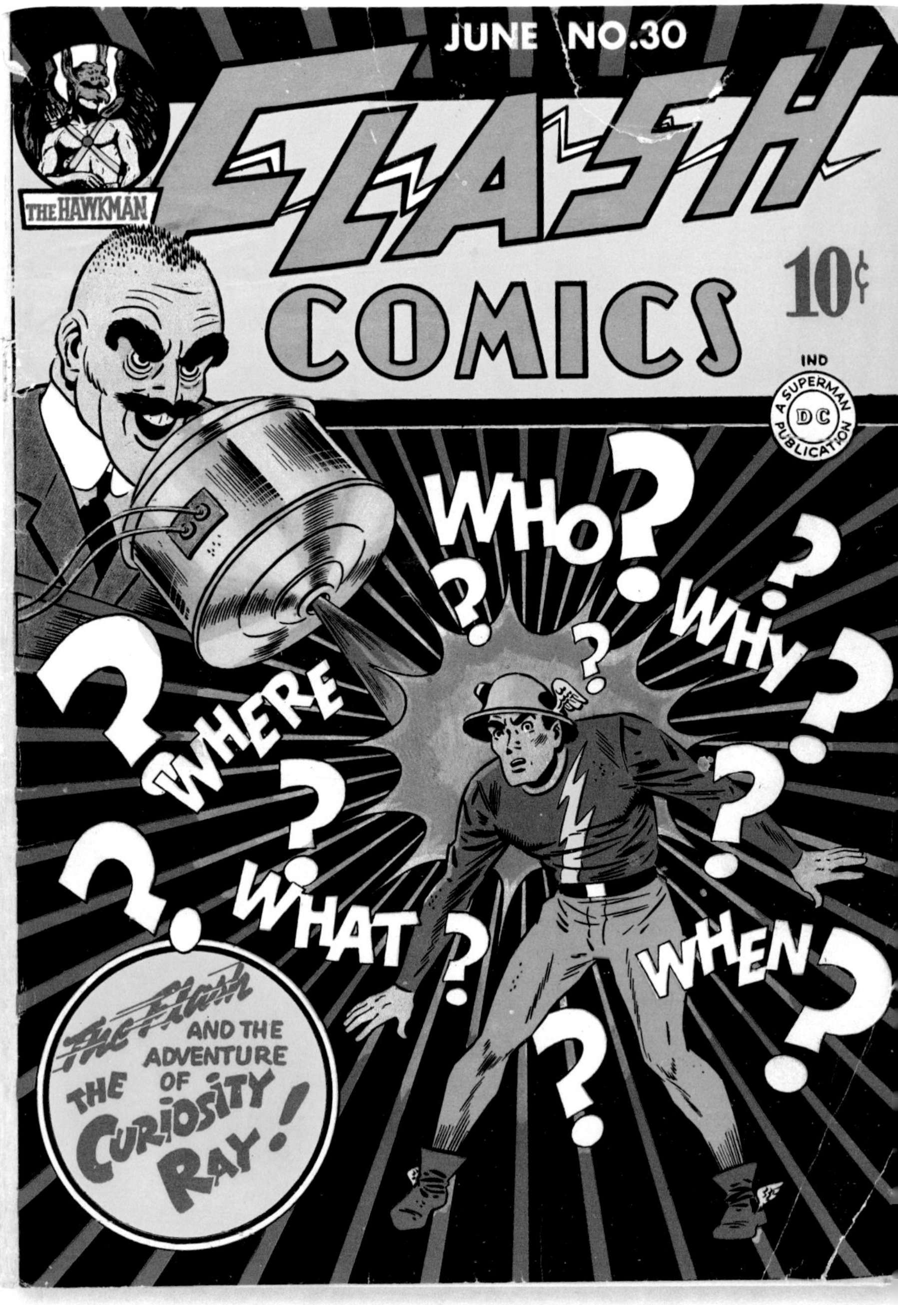
JUNE NO.30
THE HAWKMAN
FLASH COMICS
10¢
IND
A SUPERMAN DC PUBLICATION
WHO?
WHY?
WHERE?
WHAT?
WHEN?
The Flash AND THE ADVENTURE OF THE CURIOSITY RAY!

FLASH COMICS No. 30

Cover art, E. E. Hibbard, June 1942. Artist Everett Edward Hibbard brought a background in commercial art to the Flash as the series' primary artist from 1940 through 1946. His impeccable design sense and cartoony style endeared him to editor Sheldon Mayer, who also designated the illustrator to mimic the styles of several different artists when he gathered the members of The Justice Society in the landmark *All-Star Comics* No. 3.

ALL-AMERICAN COMICS No. 86

Cover art, Irwin Hasen, June 1947. "Since character development was the last thing to happen during the Golden Age, readers could count on their pick in heroes to act consistently toward the opposite sex.... The closest Alan Scott ever got to a woman was on the dance floor, and half the time, the lady was left stranded while Alan was putting in an appearance as Green Lantern." —Jerry Bails

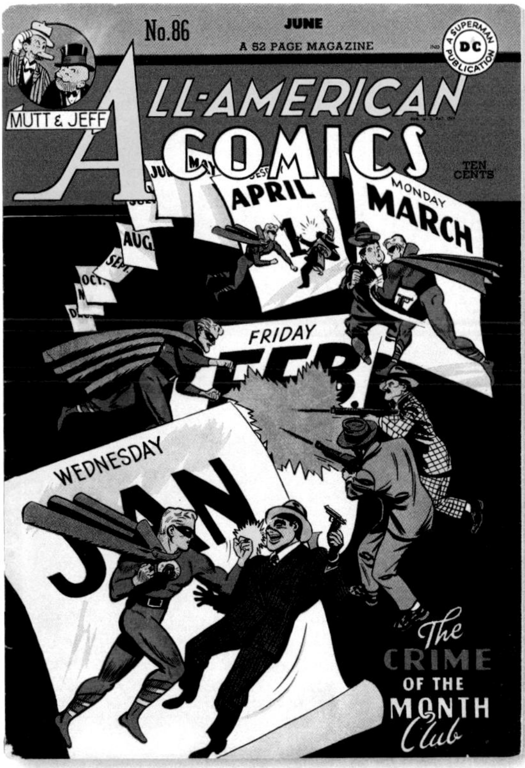
No.86
JUNE
A 52 PAGE MAGAZINE
A SUPERMAN DC PUBLICATION
MUTT & JEFF
ALL-AMERICAN
COMICS
TEN CENTS
APRIL
MONDAY
MARCH
AUG.
SEPT.
OCT.
FRIDAY
FEB.
WEDNESDAY
JAN
The
CRIME
OF THE
MONTH
Club

BATMAN No. 10

Cover art, Fred Ray and Jerry Robinson, April–May 1942.
"As a kid reader I hated kid sidekicks. How on earth could I, a slightly overweight, non-sports enthusiast comic book reader, identify with some super hero kid doing triple-flips on a high beam all the while spouting quick witticisms? I was the sidekick's age; I knew I could never be him. On the other hand, the adult hero was something I could, in my most insane fan delusion, aspire to become." —Marv Wolfman

WONDER WOMAN No. 45

Cover art, Irv Novick and Bernard Sachs, January–February 1951.
The eye-catching design of this cover likely also includes the influence of editor Robert Kanigher. A writer with a strong sense of what would make an effective visual display, as well as an occasional painter, he conceived similar images for the cover and splash page of the first Silver Age Flash story in 1956's *Showcase* No. 4 as well as the cover of *Wonder Woman* No. 103.

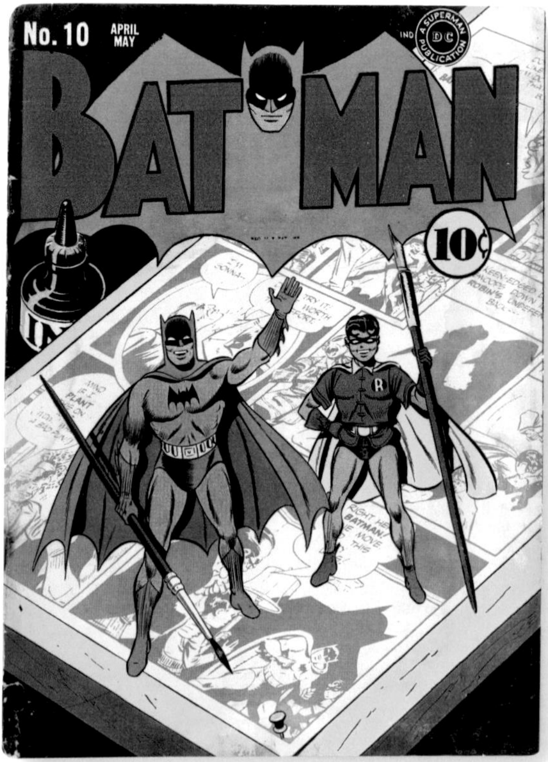
No. 10
APRIL
MAY
A SUPERMAN DC PUBLICATION
BATMAN
10¢

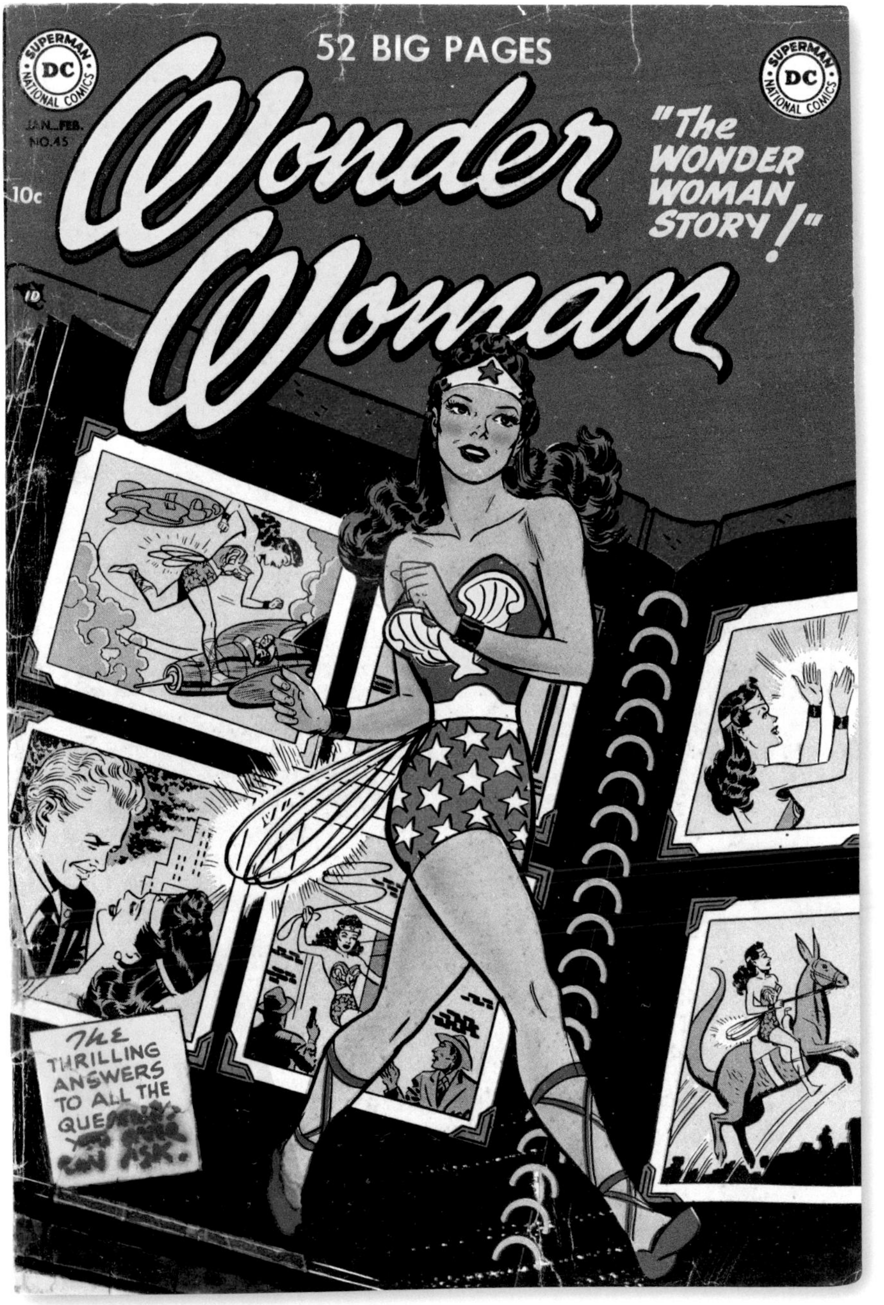
52 BIG PAGES
SUPERMAN DC NATIONAL COMICS
JAN.-FEB. NO.45
10c
Wonder Woman
"The WONDER WOMAN STORY!"
THE THRILLING ANSWERS TO ALL THE

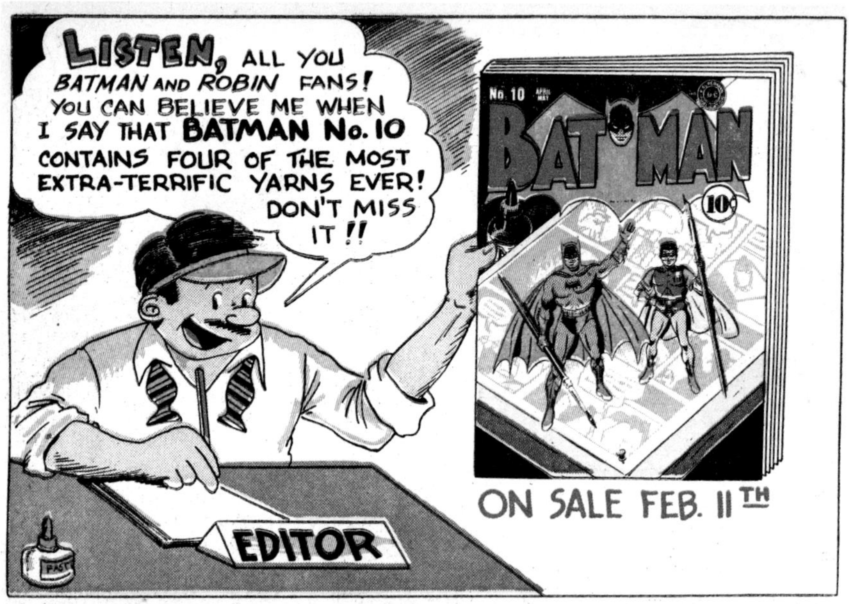
LISTEN, ALL YOU BATMAN AND ROBIN FANS! YOU CAN BELIEVE ME WHEN I SAY THAT BATMAN No. 10 CONTAINS FOUR OF THE MOST EXTRA-TERRIFIC YARNS EVER! DON'T MISS IT!!
No. 10
APRIL MAY
BATMAN
10¢
EDITOR
ON SALE FEB. 11TH

BATMAN No. 10 AD

Interior house ad from Detective Comics No. 61. Art, Vin Sullivan (editor), Fred Ray and, Jerry Robinson (Batman cover). March 1942. Editor Vin Sullivan's roots as a cartoonist were reflected in this early house ad.

WORLD'S BEST COMICS No. 1

Cover art, Fred Ray, spring 1941. The success of two previous issues of *New York World's Fair* demonstrated there was an audience for a 100-page comic book that cost 15 cents—particularly if Superman, Batman, and Robin were on the cover and inside. *World's Best* became *World's Finest Comics* with No. 2.

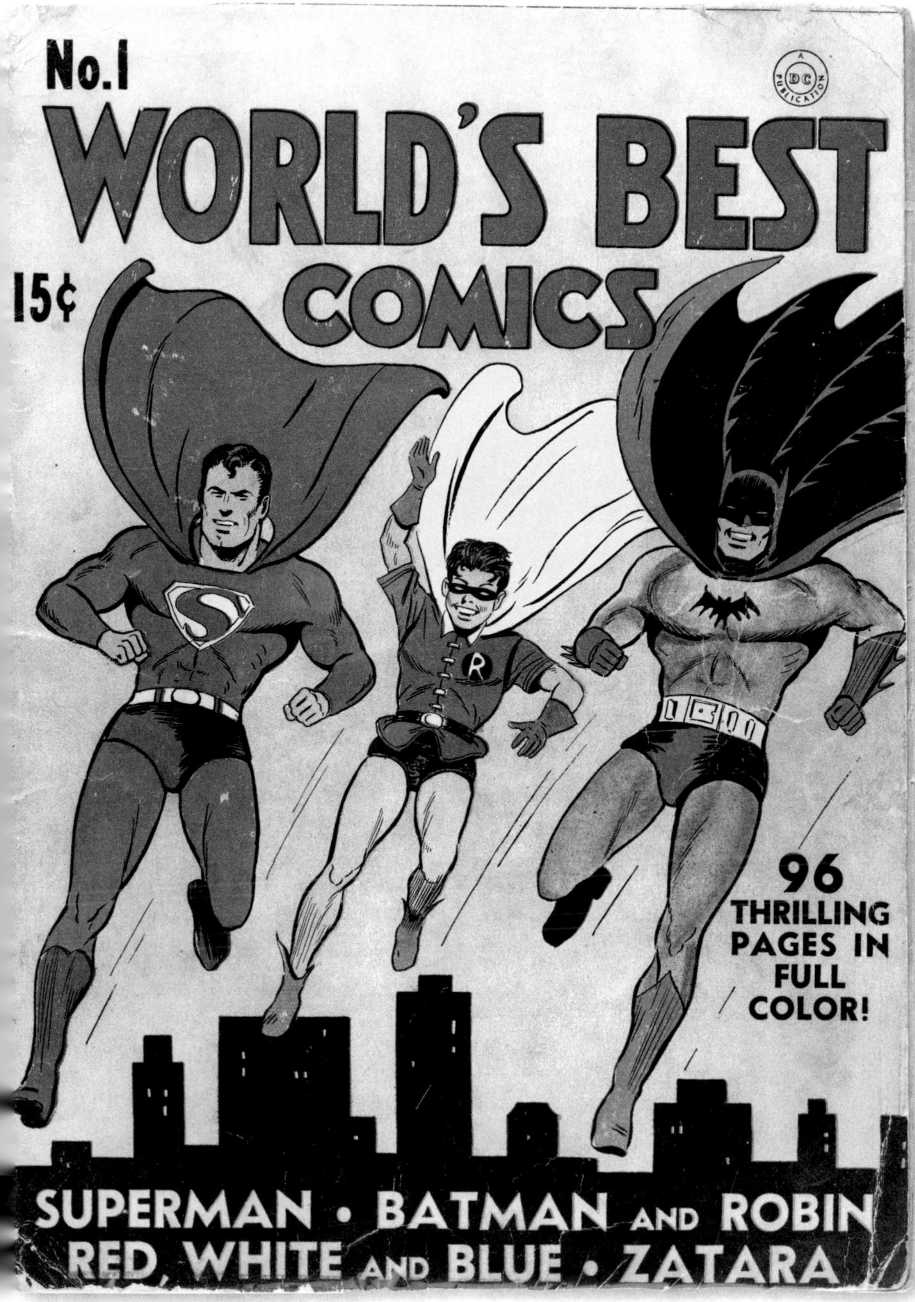
No. 1
WORLD'S BEST COMICS
15¢
A DC PUBLICATION
96 THRILLING PAGES IN FULL COLOR!
SUPERMAN • BATMAN AND ROBIN
RED, WHITE AND BLUE • ZATARA

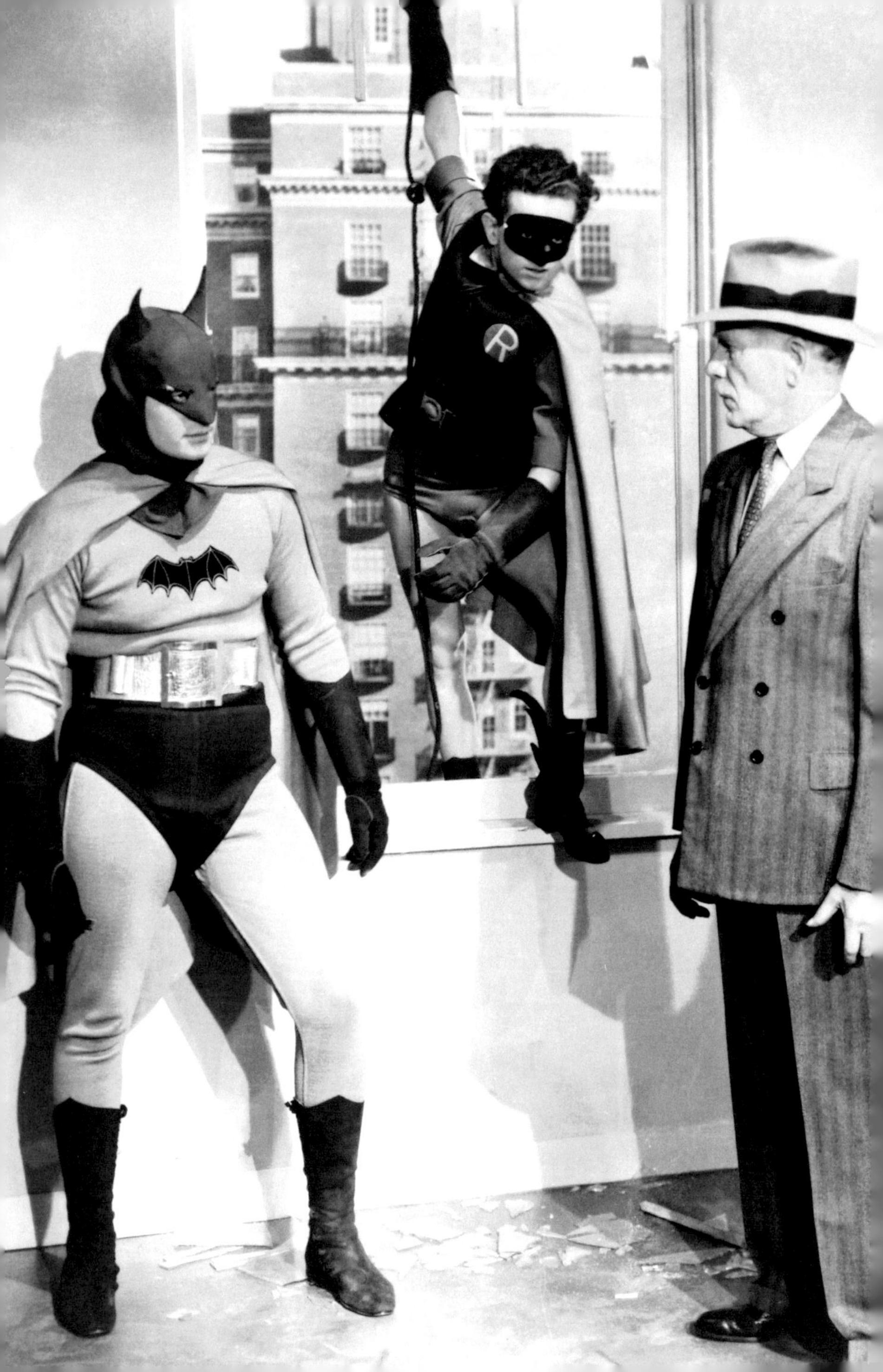

BATMAN AND COMEDY
PICTURES AT POPULAR PRICES
ROY ROGERS
TRIGGER
THRILLING CHAPTER
ROBIN
BATMAN

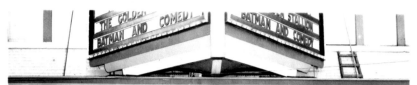

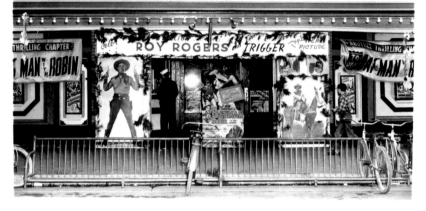

BATMAN MOVIE SERIAL

Film still; Lewis Wilson (Batman), Douglas Croft (Robin), and Gus Glassmire (Martin Warren), 1943. The ill-fitting costumes of Batman and Robin are only one indication of the incredibly low budget of the first movie serial featuring the characters. Released during the height of World War II, the story's villain is a stereotyped Japanese agent called Doctor Daka, played by J. Carrol Naish.

BATMAN MOVIE MARQUEE

Photograph, 1949. By the late 1940s, the popularity of movie serials was in decline, but they remained a major attraction for kids on a lazy Saturday. Super heroes like Batman and Robin had a comparatively small piece of the action in contrast to screen cowboys like Roy Rogers, soon to star in his own TV show.

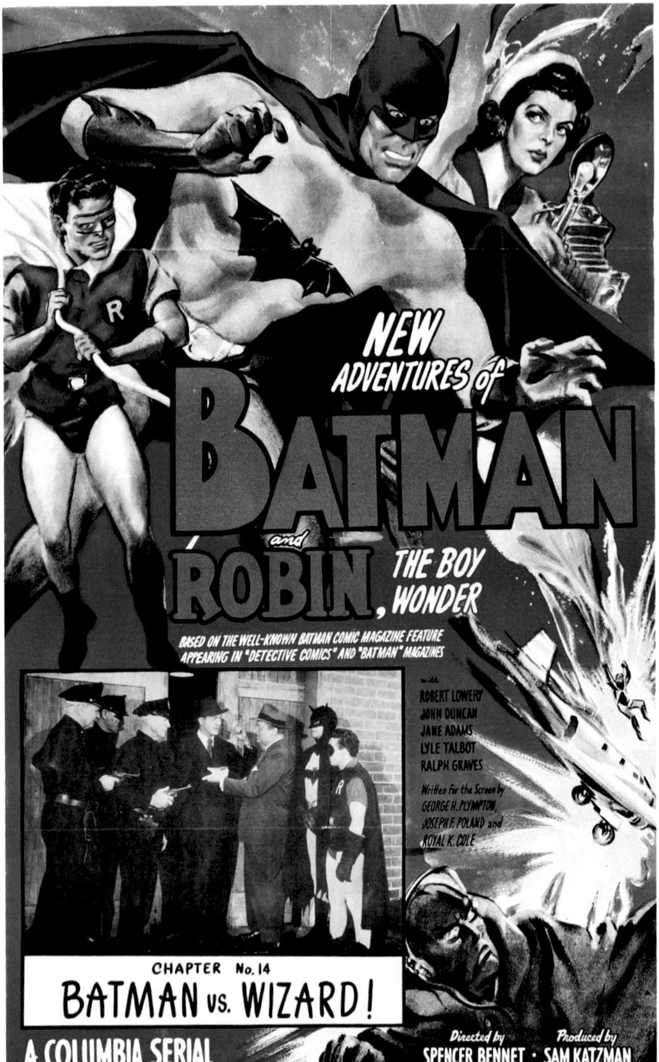
NEW
ADVENTURES of
BATMAN
and
ROBIN, THE BOY WONDER
BASED ON THE WELL-KNOWN BATMAN COMIC MAGAZINE FEATURE APPEARING IN "DETECTIVE COMICS" AND "BATMAN" MAGAZINES
with
ROBERT LOWERY
JOHN DUNCAN
JANE ADAMS
LYLE TALBOT
RALPH GRAVES
Written for the Screen by
GEORGE H. PLYMPTON,
JOSEPH F. POLAND and
ROYAL K. COLE
CHAPTER No. 14
BATMAN vs. WIZARD!
A COLUMBIA SERIAL
Directed by
SPENCER BENNET
Produced by
SAM KATZMAN

BATMAN MOVIE SERIAL

Movie poster, 1949.

BATMAN MOVIE POSTER

Movie poster, Belgium, 1949. The second Batman movie serial reached such countries as Argentina, Belgium, Greece, Portugal, and Serbia.

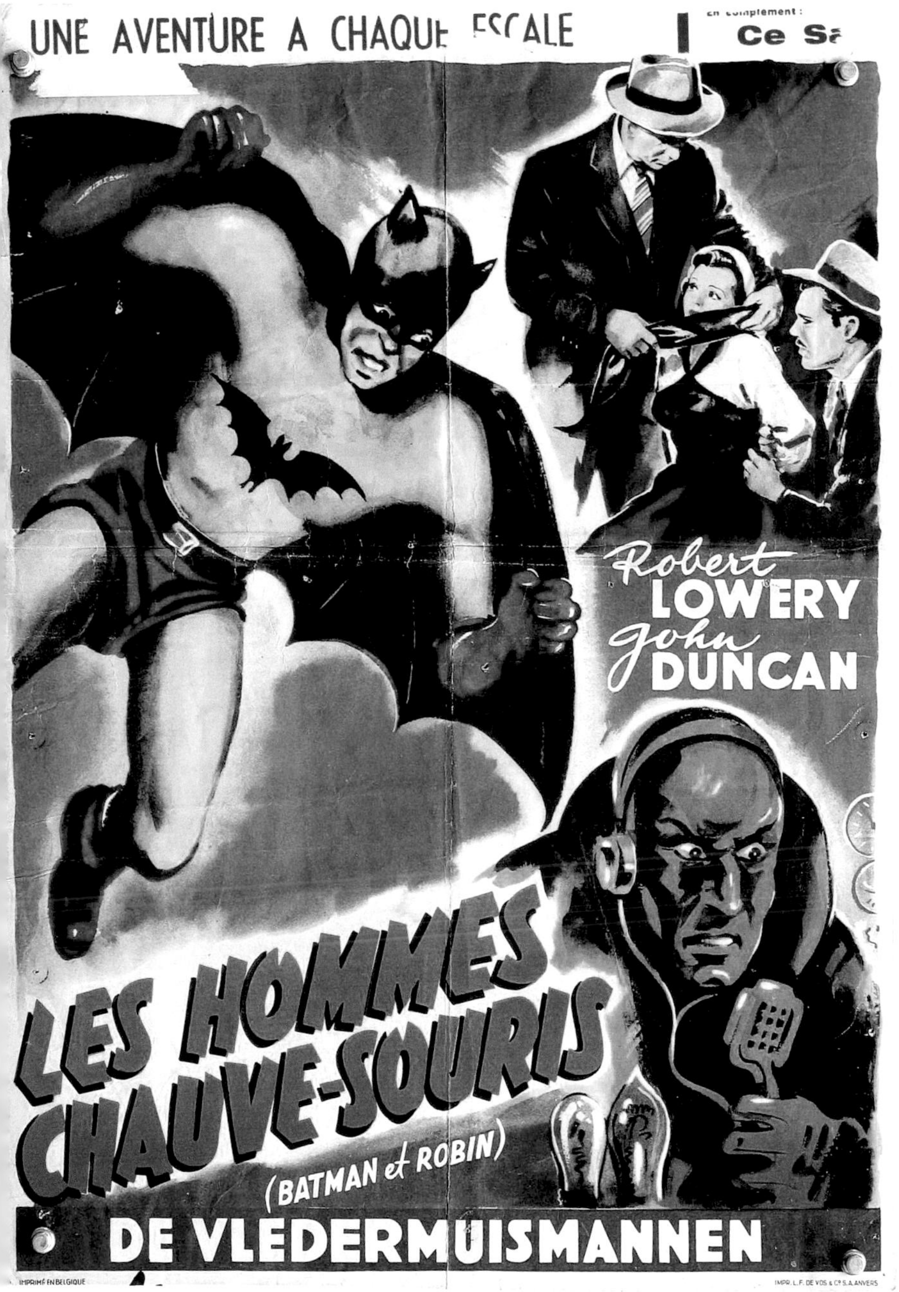
UNE AVENTURE A CHAQUE ESCALE
en complément :
Ce Sa
Robert
LOWERY
John
DUNCAN
LES HOMMES
CHAUVE-SOURIS
(BATMAN et ROBIN)
DE VLEDERMUISMANNEN
IMPRIMÉ EN BELGIQUE
IMPR. L.F. DE VOS & Cie S.A. ANVERS

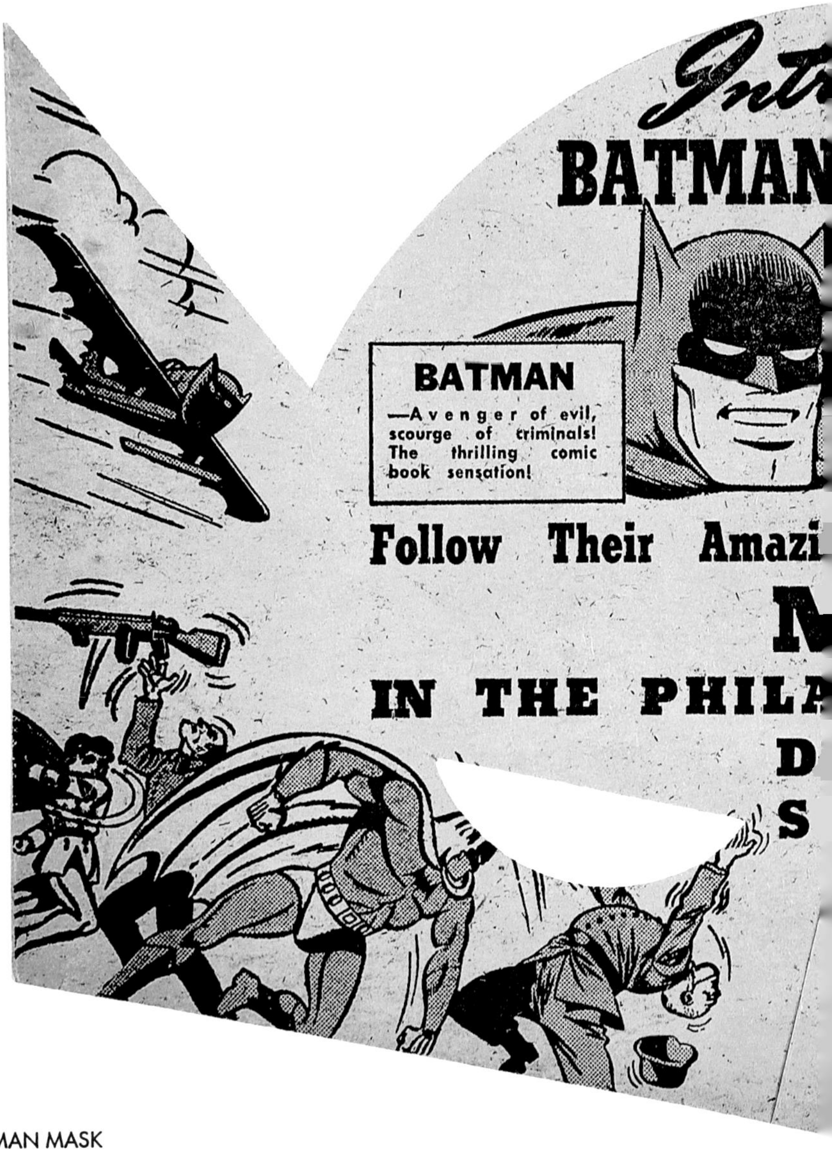
Intr
BATMAN
BATMAN
—Avenger of evil, scourge of criminals! The thrilling comic book sensation!
Follow Their Amazi
M
IN THE PHILA
D
S

BATMAN MASK

Promotional giveaway, 1943. In 1943, the *Philadelphia Record* newspaper printed 250,000 stylized masks to promote the debut of the "Batman" comic strip and used vendors and newspaper carriers to distribute them.

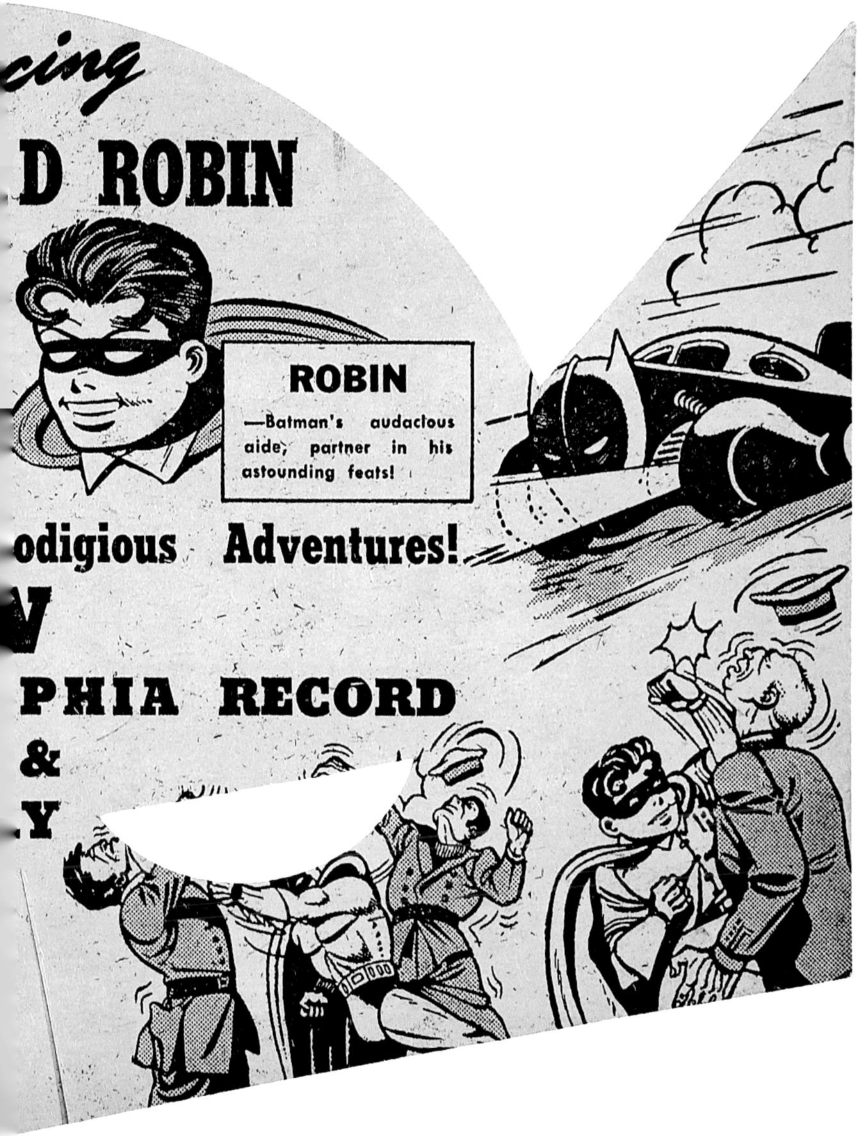
cing
D ROBIN
ROBIN
—Batman's audacious aide, partner in his astounding feats!
odigious Adventures!
V
PHIA RECORD
&
Y

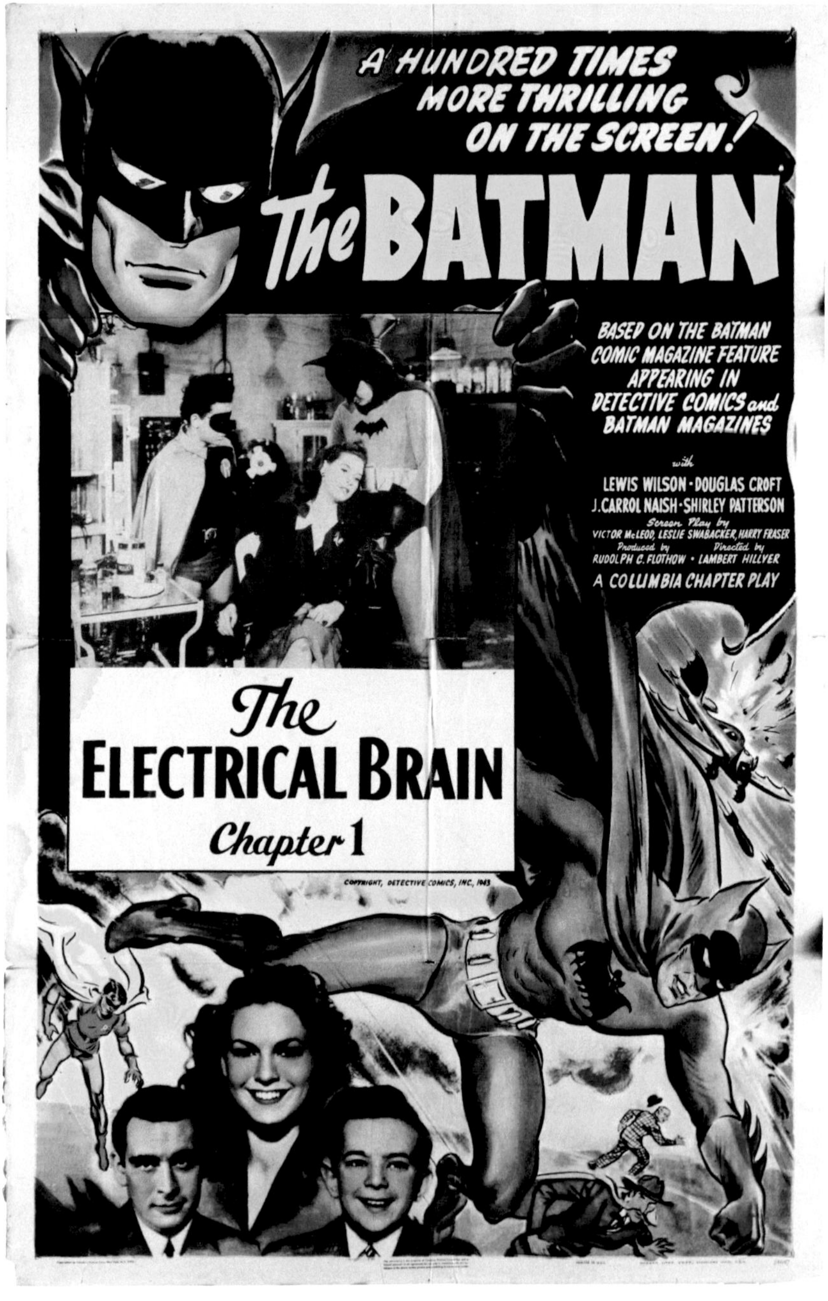
A HUNDRED TIMES
MORE THRILLING
ON THE SCREEN!
The BATMAN
BASED ON THE BATMAN
COMIC MAGAZINE FEATURE
APPEARING IN
DETECTIVE COMICS and
BATMAN MAGAZINES
with
LEWIS WILSON · DOUGLAS CROFT
J. CARROL NAISH · SHIRLEY PATTERSON
Screen Play by
VICTOR McLEOD, LESLIE SWABACKER, HARRY FRASER
Produced by
RUDOLPH C. FLOTHOW
Directed by
LAMBERT HILLYER
A COLUMBIA CHAPTER PLAY
The
ELECTRICAL BRAIN
Chapter 1
COPYRIGHT, DETECTIVE COMICS, INC., 1943

BATMAN MOVIE SERIAL

Poster, 1943. Although cheaply produced, the 1943 serial had a remarkable effect on Batman, referring to "the Bat's Cave" for the first time and depicting its entrance behind a grandfather clock as well as inspiring the slimmed-down Alfred in the comic book. The film's rerelease in 1965 — when its failings caused it to be viewed as a comedy — helped inspire the landmark TV series starring Adam West.

BATMAN ON ICE

Photograph, 1942. Republic Pictures' 1942 musical comedy *Ice Capades Revue* included a vividly costumed "bat-man."

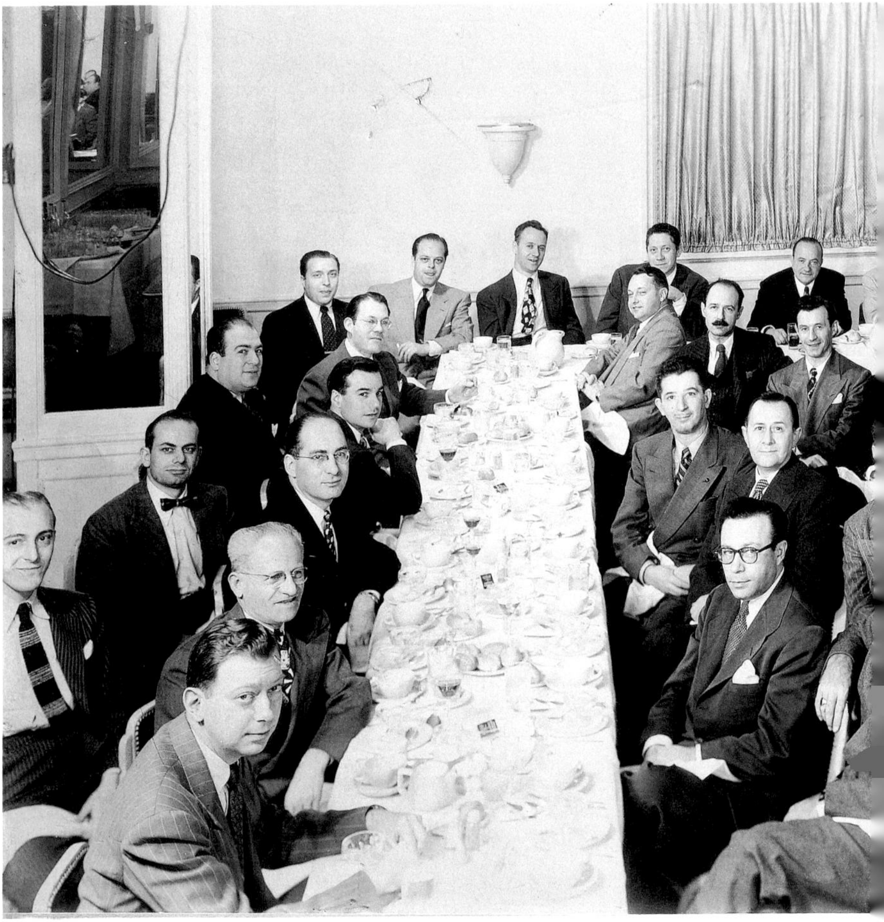

NATIONAL COMICS WHO'S WHO

Photograph, gathering of DC and AA's executives, editors, and related parties, ca. 1945. The circumstances behind this gathering are unknown but it represents a last glimpse at the collective braintrust that made up Detective Comics, Inc., and All-American Comics. Whitney Ellsworth, Harry and Irwin Donenfeld, Jack Liebowitz, and Paul Sampliner are in the center of the back row. Also in the crowd are Bill Finger, Julius Schwartz, Mort Weisinger, Robert Kanigher, Sol Harrison, Murray Boltinoff, Jack Schiff, M. C. Gaines, Robert Maxwell, and Sheldon Mayer. Soon after, M. C. Gaines sold the AA line to DC and the two companies officially merged as National Comics in 1946.

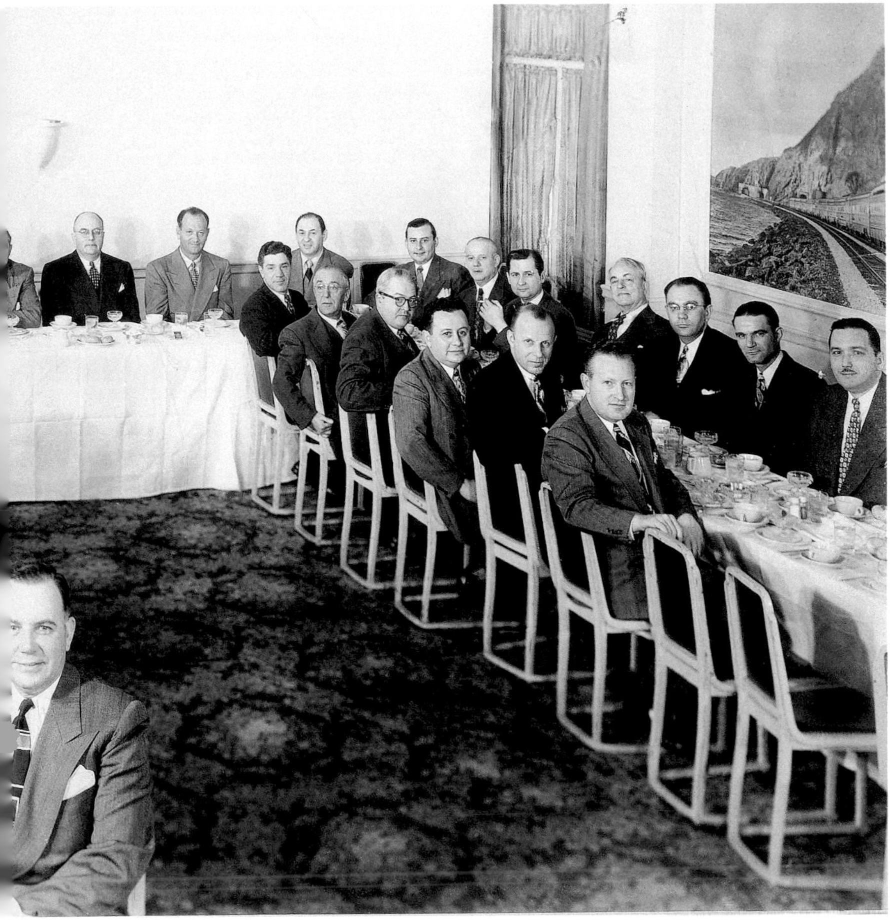

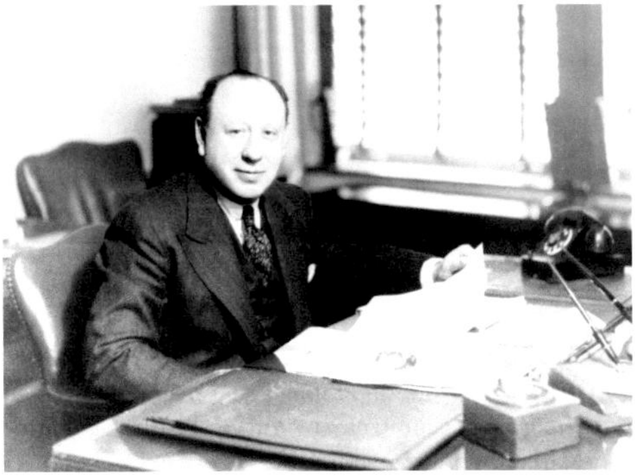

M. C. GAINES

Photograph, All-American publisher Max Gaines at his desk, ca. 1940.

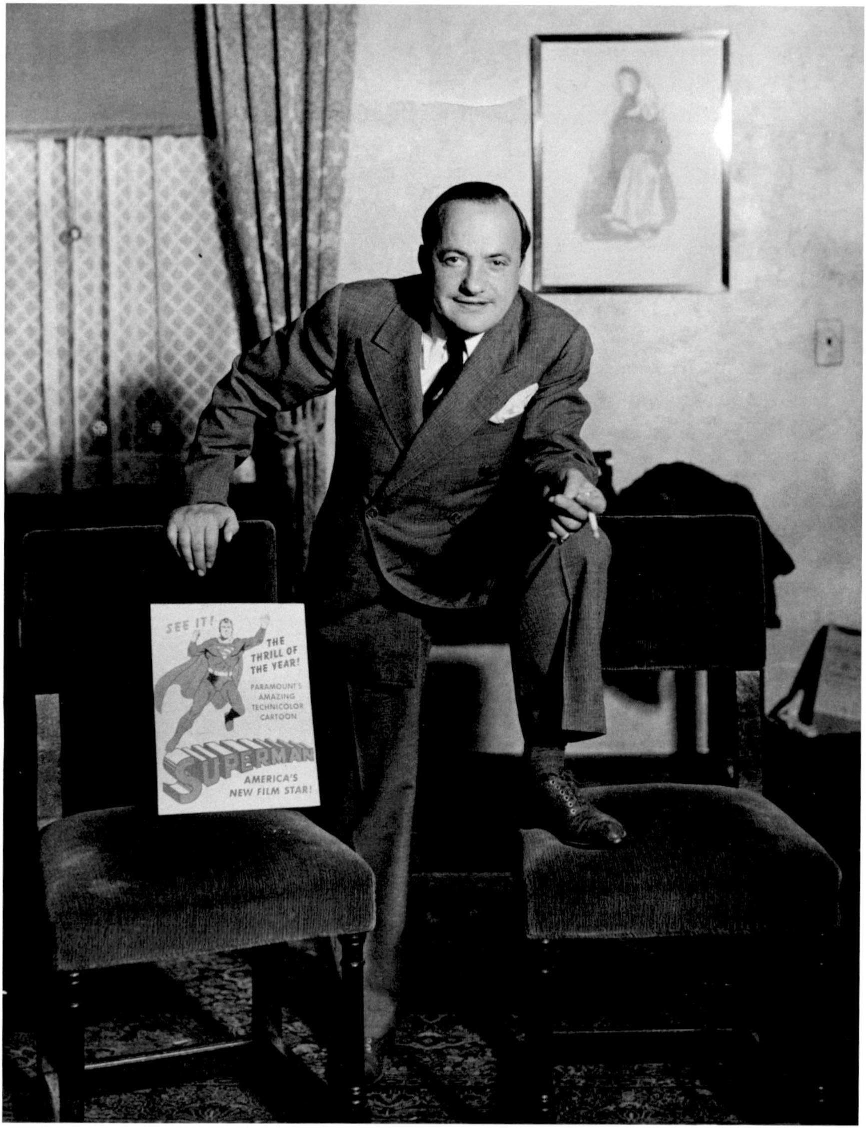
SEE IT!
THE THRILL OF THE YEAR!
PARAMOUNT'S AMAZING TECHNICOLOR CARTOON
SUPERMAN
AMERICA'S NEW FILM STAR!

HARRY DONENFELD

Photograph, 1940s. Harry Donenfeld took great pride in his connection to Superman, even wearing an "S" T-shirt beneath his suit that he'd expose on occasion.

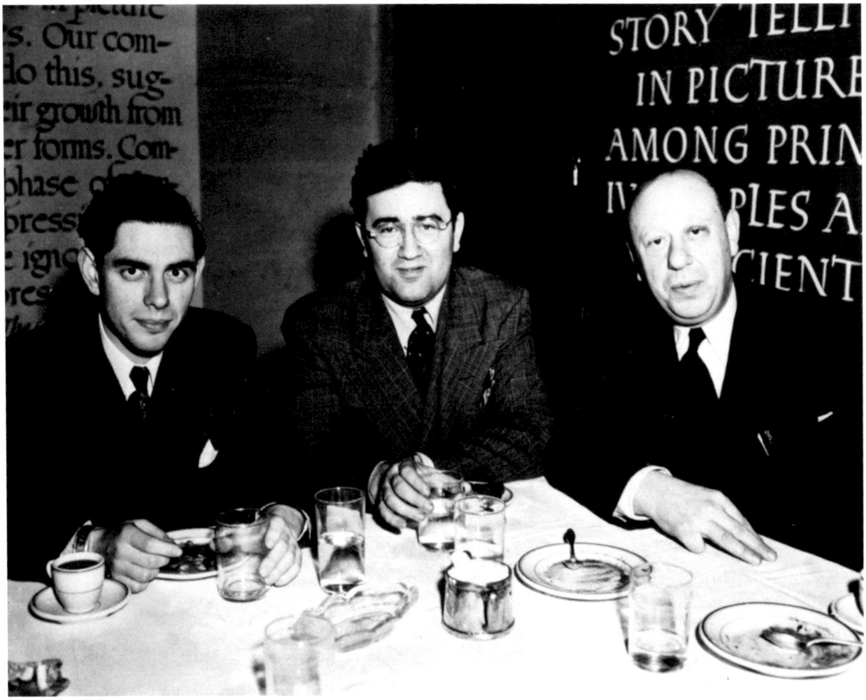
s. Our com-
do this, sug-
ir growth from
er forms. Com-
STORY
IN PICTURE
AMONG PRIN
PLES A
IENT

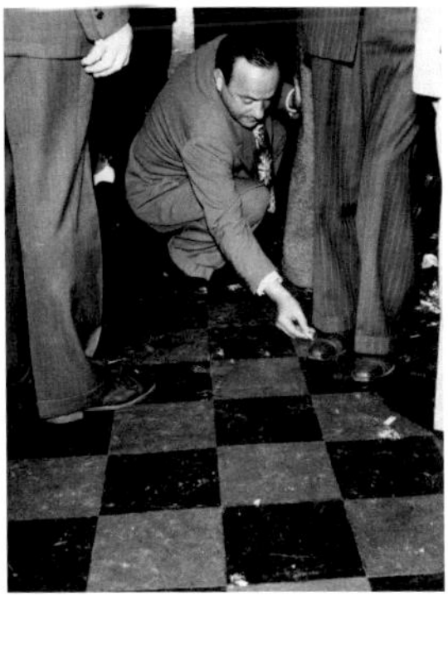

JOE SHUSTER, JERRY SIEGEL, AND M. C. GAINES
Photograph, 1940s. Publisher Max Gaines played a crucial role in Superman's published debut, recommending that Detective Comics Inc.'s new *Action Comics* include Siegel and Shuster's feature.

HARRY DONENFELD'S HOT FOOT
Photograph, ca. 1940s. Harry Donenfeld's penchant for pranks started early. Noting that a client had a stutter, the future publisher immediately introduced the man to his brother Irving, who also stuttered. The customer assumed Irving was making fun of him even as Harry's sibling fumed over what happened.

1950

FEB-MAR

52 BIG PAGES
ALL STAR COMICS
"INVADERS from the WORLD BELOW!"

450 66% 297
69% 310
(68)

APR-MAY

52 BIG PAGES
ALL STAR COMICS
"The Secret Conquest of the Earth!"

400 63% 252
63% 252
(68)

JUNE-JULY

52 BIG PAGES
ALL STAR COMICS
"The GUN THAT DROPPED THROUGH TIME!"

390 66% 257
68% 265
(68)

400
(73)

1951

FEB-MAR

ALL STAR COMICS
52 BIG PAGES
The MYSTERY of the VANISHING DETECTIVES!

400 63% 252
(70) 63% 252

APR-MAY

Strong Bow INDIAN WARRIOR!
ALL STAR WESTERN
"TWO-FISTED JUSTICE!"

390 64% 250
(66) 65% 254

JUN-JULY

DOUBLE ACTION DYNAMITE
ALL STAR WESTERN
"The TREASURE of the CLIFF DWELLERS!"

360 62% 223
(64) 63% 227

375
(71)

1952

FEB-MAR

32
ALL STAR WESTERN
Strong Bow DUELS THE MASTER OF INDIAN MAGIC IN DOOM of the LAKE DEMON!

400 63% 252
(66) 63% 252

APR-MAY

32
ALL STAR WESTERN
I NEVER THOUGHT I'D SEE THE TRIGGER TWINS WALKIN AROUND WITH EMPTY HOLSTERS!

400 59% 230
(60) 60% 234

JUN-JULY

32
ALL STAR WESTERN

375 56% 209
(61) 57% 213

375
(64)

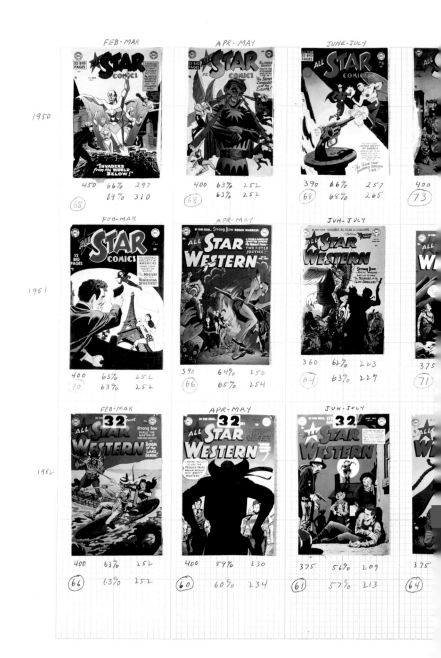

OCT-NOV

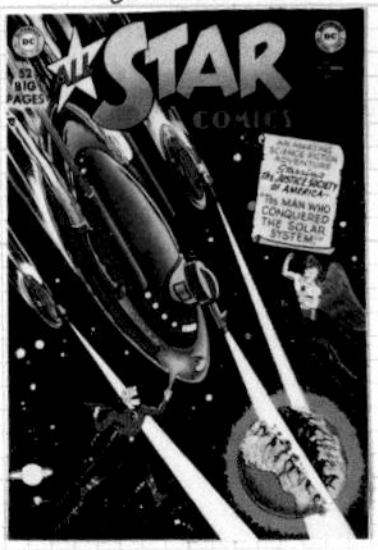
52 BIG PAGES
ALL STAR COMICS
The Justice Society of America
"The Man Who Conquered the Solar System"

390 71% 270

(75) 71% 270

DEC-JAN

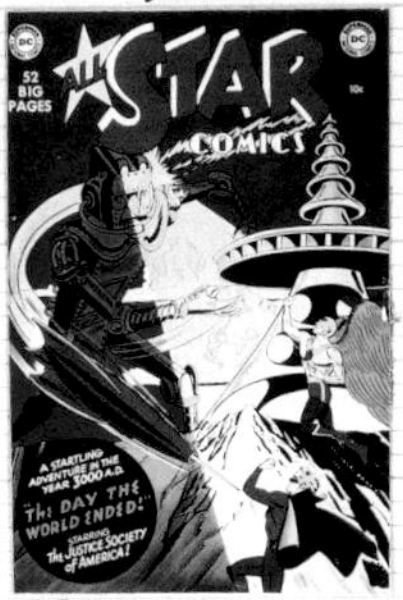
52 BIG PAGES
ALL STAR COMICS
A startling adventure in the year 3000 A.D.
"The Day the World Ended!"
Starring the Justice Society of America!

375 61% 229

(69) 60% 225

OCT-NOV

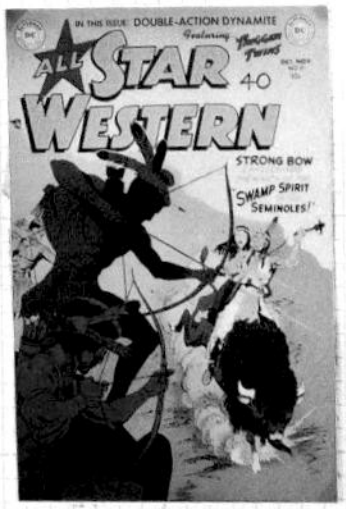
In this issue: Double-Action Dynamite
ALL STAR WESTERN
40
Strong Bow
Swamp Spirit Seminoles!

375 68% 255

(73) 68% 255

DEC-JAN

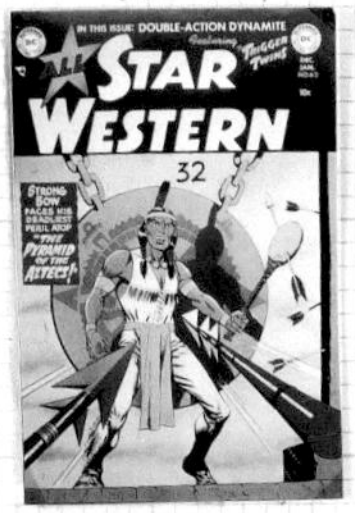
In this issue: Double-Action Dynamite
ALL STAR WESTERN
32
"The Pyramid of the Aztecs!"

375 60% 225

(64) 63% 236

OCT-NOV

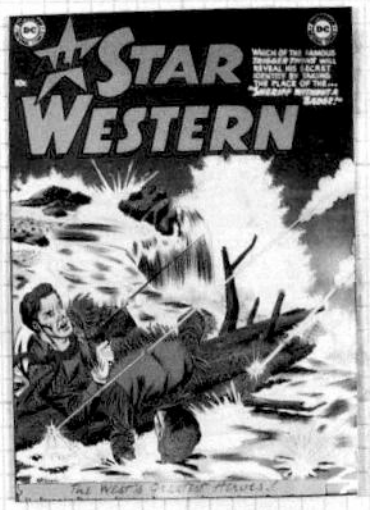
ALL STAR WESTERN

375 60% 225

(60) 60% 225

DEC-JAN

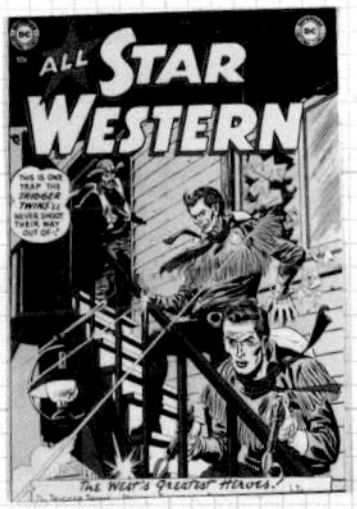
ALL STAR WESTERN
The West's Greatest Heroes!

350 59% 206

(57) 59% 206

ALL STAR

DONENFELD'S LOGS

THIS SPREAD AND FOLLOWING SPREAD: *Irwin Donenfeld's visual sales charts, 1950–1952 and 1953–1955.* To better gauge sales, Donenfeld created a chart that displayed the cover of each comic book and a variety of sales data. From this selection of information, he was able to determine that the super hero stories in *All-Star Comics* were in a downward cycle, prompting its transition to the more successful Western genre. Despite the overall lack of interest in super hero comics, Superman (along with Batman and, to a lesser degree, Wonder Woman) continued to thrive.

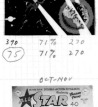

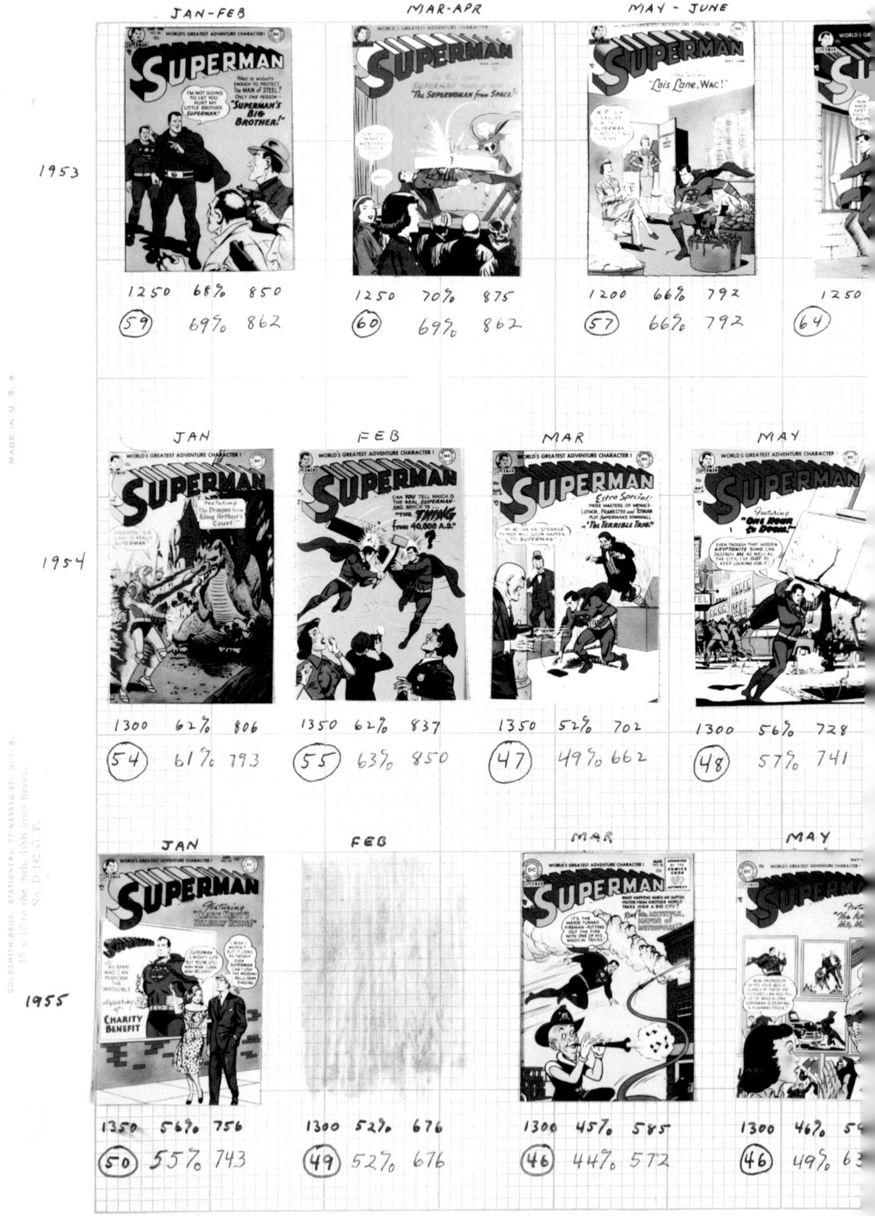
JAN-FEB
MAR-APR
MAY - JUNE
1953
SUPERMAN
"Superman's Big Brother!"
"The Superwoman from Space!"
"Lois Lane, Wac!"
1250 68% 850
59 69% 862
1250 70% 875
60 69% 862
1200 66% 792
57 66% 792
1250
64
JAN
FEB
MAR
MAY
1954
"The Dragon from King Arthur's Court!"
"The Thing from 40,000 A.D."
"The Terrible Trio!"
1300 62% 806
54 61% 793
1350 62% 837
55 63% 850
1350 52% 702
47 49% 662
1300 56% 728
48 57% 741
JAN
FEB
MAR
MAY
1955
CHARITY BENEFIT
1350 56% 756
50 55% 743
1300 52% 676
49 52% 676
1300 45% 585
46 44% 572
1300 46%
46 49%
MADE IN U. S. A.

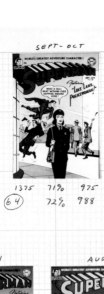

SEPT - OCT

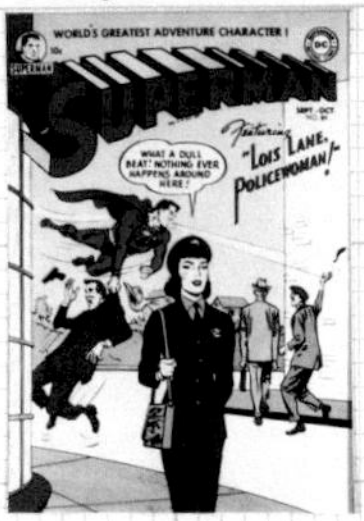
WORLD'S GREATEST ADVENTURE CHARACTER!
SUPERMAN
Featuring "LOIS LANE, POLICEWOMAN!"
WHAT A DULL BEAT! NOTHING EVER HAPPENS AROUND HERE!

1375 71% 975
(64) 72% 988

NOV - DEC

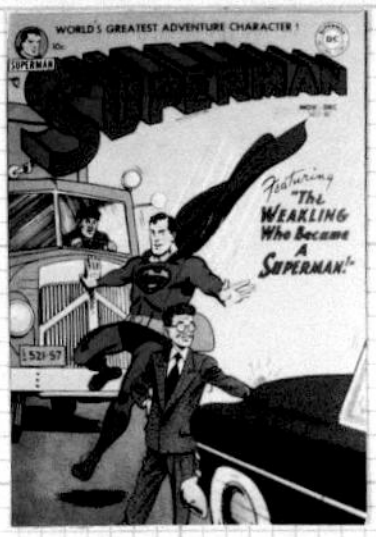
WORLD'S GREATEST ADVENTURE CHARACTER!
SUPERMAN
Featuring "The WEAKLING Who Became A SUPERMAN!"

1400 68% 952
(58) 70% 980

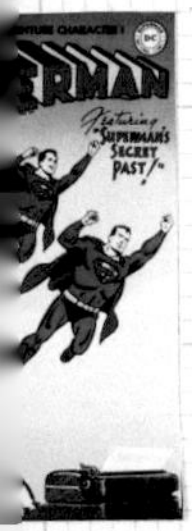
Featuring "SUPERMAN'S SECRET PAST!"

% 725
% 775

AUG

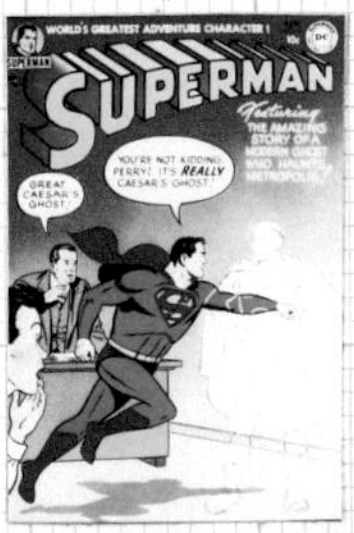
WORLD'S GREATEST ADVENTURE CHARACTER!
SUPERMAN
Featuring THE AMAZING STORY OF A MODERN GHOST WHO HAUNTED METROPOLIS!
GREAT CAESAR'S GHOST!
YOU'RE NOT KIDDING, PERRY! IT'S REALLY CAESAR'S GHOST!

1300 62% 806
(58) 63% 819

SEPT

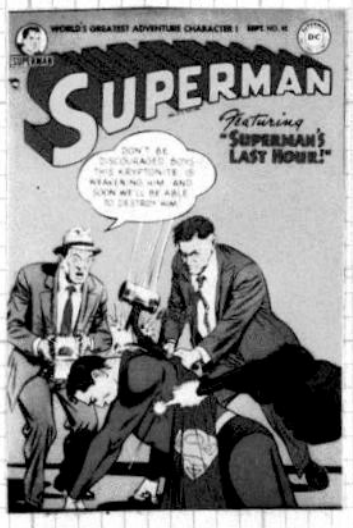
WORLD'S GREATEST ADVENTURE CHARACTER!
SUPERMAN
Featuring "SUPERMAN'S LAST HOUR!"
DON'T BE DISCOURAGED, BOYS! THIS KRYPTONITE IS WEAKENING HIM, AND SOON WE'LL BE ABLE TO DESTROY HIM!

1,300 62% 806
(61) 63% 819

NOV

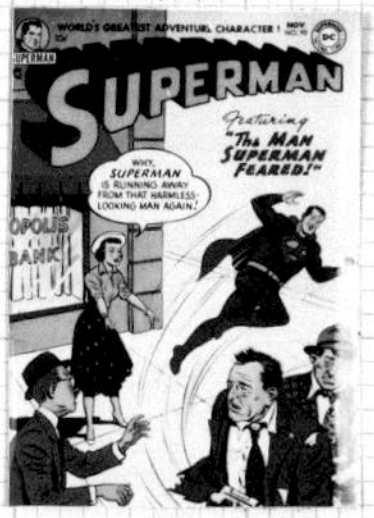
WORLD'S GREATEST ADVENTURE CHARACTER!
SUPERMAN
Featuring "The MAN SUPERMAN FEARED!"
WHY, SUPERMAN IS RUNNING AWAY FROM THAT HARMLESS-LOOKING MAN AGAIN!

1300 61% 793
(52) 60% 780

JULY

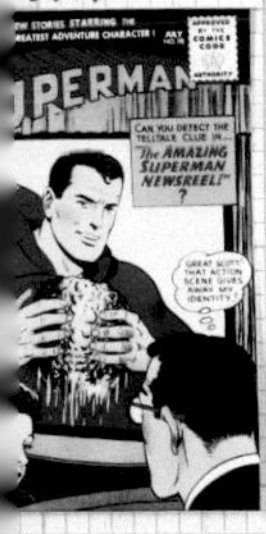
NEW STORIES STARRING THE WORLD'S GREATEST ADVENTURE CHARACTER!
SUPERMAN
CAN YOU DETECT THE TELLTALE CLUE IN... "The AMAZING SUPERMAN NEWSREEL!"?

49% 612
52% 649

AUG

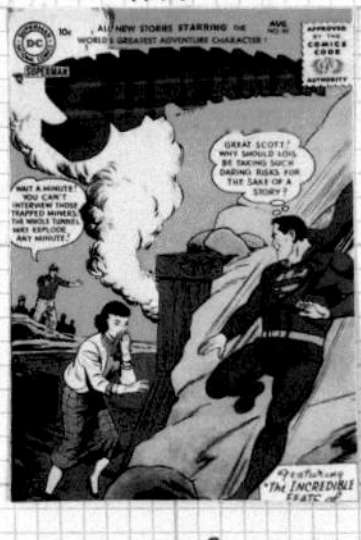
ALL NEW STORIES STARRING THE WORLD'S GREATEST ADVENTURE CHARACTER!
SUPERMAN
GREAT SCOTT! WHY SHOULD LOIS BE TAKING SUCH DARING RISKS FOR THE SAKE OF A STORY?
WAIT A MINUTE! YOU CAN'T INTERVIEW THOSE TRAPPED MINERS! THE WHOLE TUNNEL MAY EXPLODE ANY MINUTE!
Featuring "The INCREDIBLE FEATS of

1250 53% 662
(52) 53% 662

SEPT

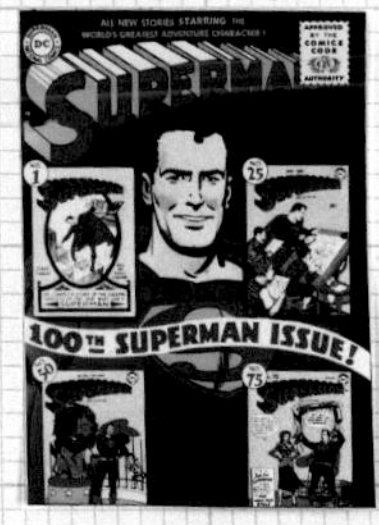
ALL NEW STORIES STARRING THE WORLD'S GREATEST ADVENTURE CHARACTER!
SUPERMAN
100TH SUPERMAN ISSUE!

1225 60% 735
(55) 62% 759

NOV

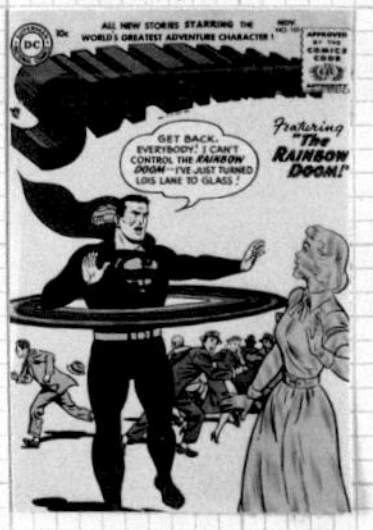
ALL NEW STORIES STARRING THE WORLD'S GREATEST ADVENTURE CHARACTER!
SUPERMAN
Featuring "The RAINBOW DOOM!"
GET BACK, EVERYBODY! I CAN'T CONTROL THE RAINBOW DOOM -- I'VE JUST TURNED LOIS LANE TO GLASS!

1100 63% 693
(49) 63% 693

SUPERMAN

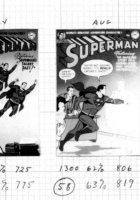

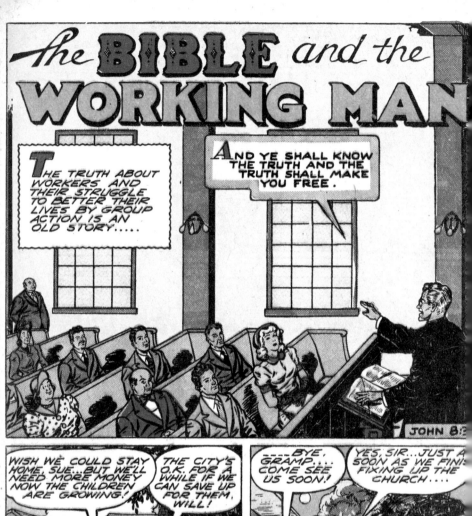

the BIBLE and the WORKING MAN

THE TRUTH ABOUT WORKERS AND THEIR STRUGGLE TO BETTER THEIR LIVES BY GROUP ACTION IS AN OLD STORY.....

AND YE SHALL KNOW THE TRUTH AND THE TRUTH SHALL MAKE YOU FREE.

JOHN 8:?

WISH WE COULD STAY HOME, SUE...BUT WE'LL NEED MORE MONEY NOW THE CHILDREN ARE GROWING!

THE CITY'S O.K. FOR A WHILE IF WE CAN SAVE UP FOR THEM, WILL!

---BYE, GRAMP.... COME SEE US SOON!

YES, SIR...JUST AS SOON AS WE FINISH FIXING UP THE CHURCH....

CLERGYMAN BROWN SEES HIS DAUGHTER'S FAMILY OFF....

1

THE BIBLE AND THE WORKING MAN

Cover, Dennis Neville, ca. 1944.

GAINES FILE COPIES

Identification card, Max C. Gaines, ca. 1944. Frank Jacobs wrote that All-American publisher Max Gaines was particularly proud of his *Picture Stories From the Bible* series "even though producing them brought no change to his blustering business methods. 'I don't care how long it took Moses to cross the desert,' he once screamed at an artist, 'I want it in three panels.'"

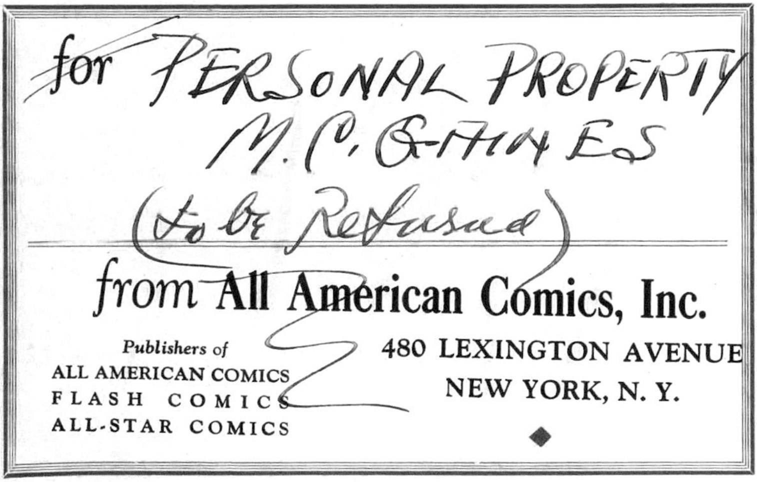

for PERSONAL PROPERTY
M. C. GAINES
from All American Comics, Inc.
Publishers of
ALL AMERICAN COMICS
FLASH COMICS
ALL-STAR COMICS
480 LEXINGTON AVENUE
NEW YORK, N. Y.

the KO PUNCH!
INTRODUCING THE STORY OF BIG DEAL AL JACKSON... HOW HE FOUGHT HIS WAY FROM THE BOTTOM TO THE TOP... AND HOW HIS WIFE, JEANIE, KEPT HIM FROM CRASHING DOWN AGAIN.

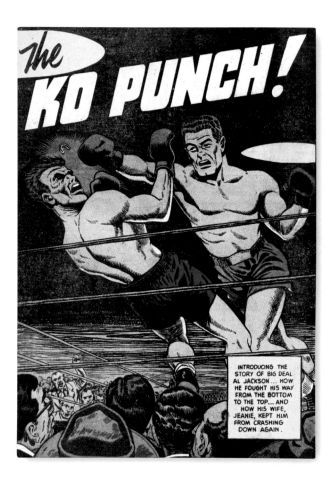

THE KO PUNCH!

Cover, Al Feldstein, 1954.

THE STORY OF RUBBER HEELS

Cover art, Bob Jenney, ca. 1945. M.C. Gaines was a strong advocate for using comic books to illuminate readers as well as entertain them. He'd published several public service pamphlets during World War II and created Educational Comics after selling most of his All-American line to DC in 1945. The market for creating specialty comics for businesses and schools was not as lucrative as Gaines imagined, however. After the publisher's death in 1947, his son Bill changed the company name to Entertaining Comics and began to produce radically different fare like *Tales from the Crypt* and *MAD*.

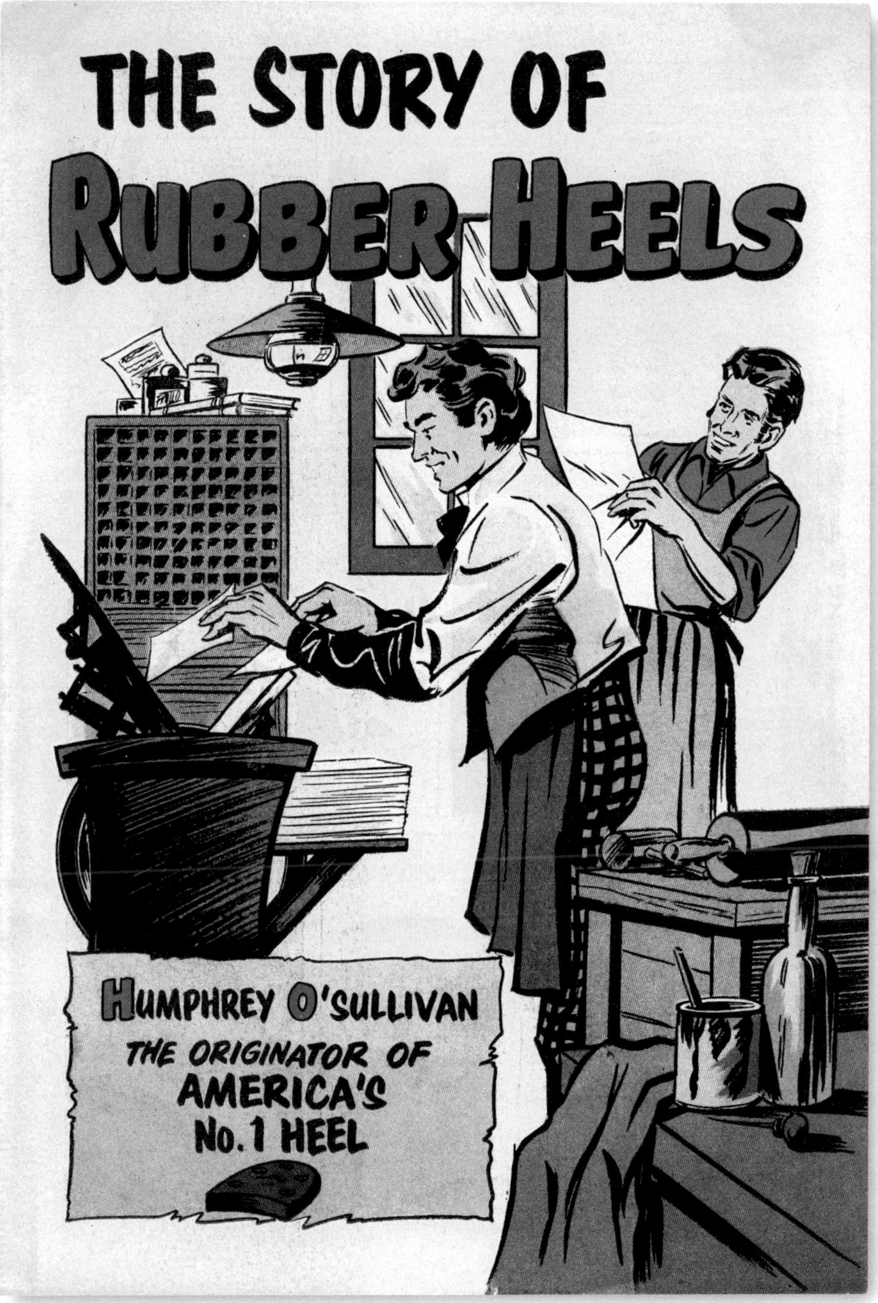
THE STORY OF
RUBBER HEELS
HUMPHREY O'SULLIVAN
THE ORIGINATOR OF
AMERICA'S
No. 1 HEEL

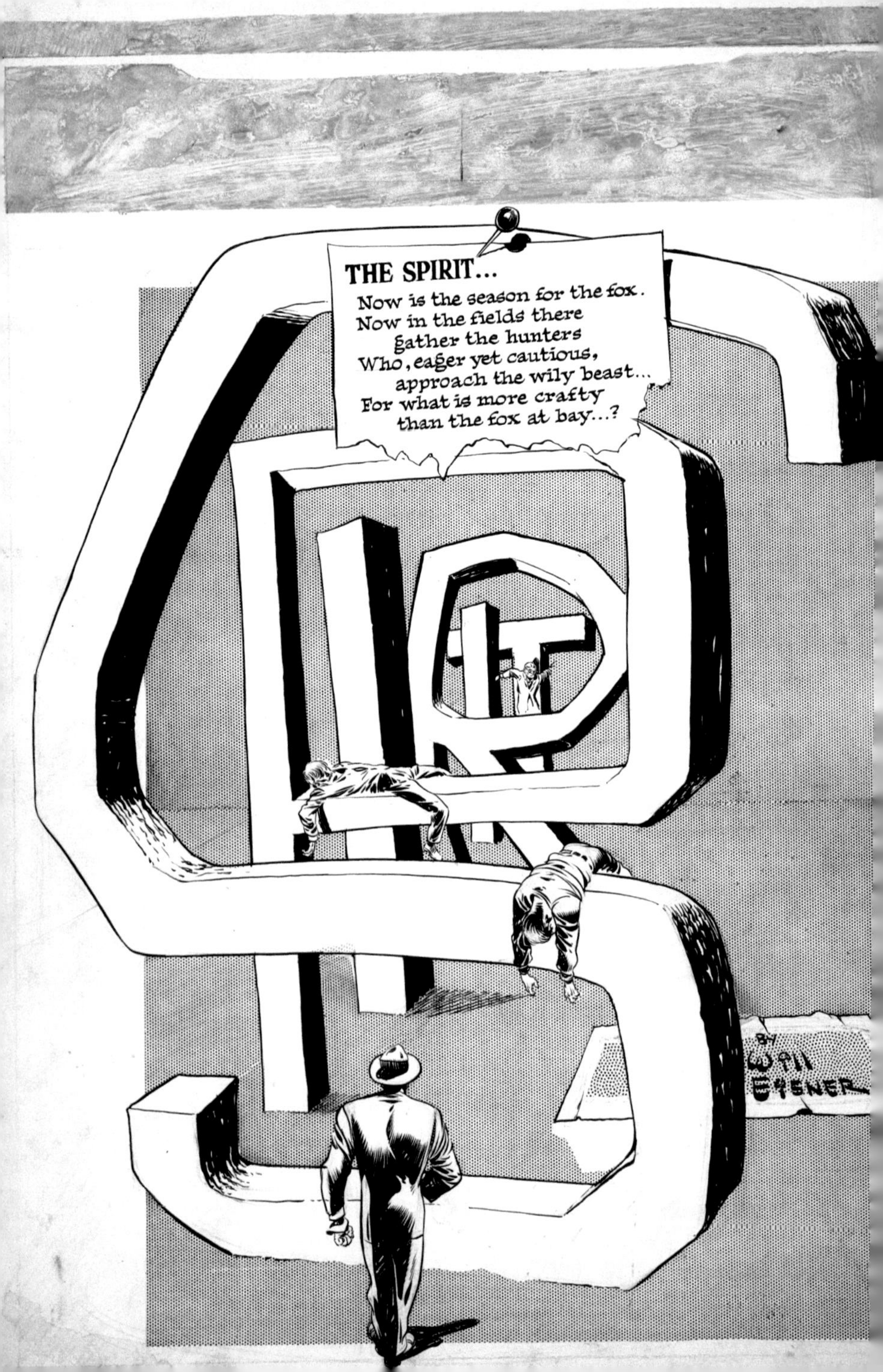
THE SPIRIT...
Now is the season for the fox.
Now in the fields there gather the hunters
Who, eager yet cautious, approach the wily beast...
For what is more crafty than the fox at bay...?
BY WILL EISNER

Will Eisner

"Eisner became a virtuoso cartoonist of a kind who had never been seen before in comic books — or, for that matter, in newspaper strips. He used all the elements of the comic-book page — dialogue, drawing, panel composition, color — with great daring, but never at the cost of narrative clarity."

— HARVEY KURTZMAN

THE SPIRIT No. 491
Original cover art, Will Eisner, October 23, 1949.

WILL EISNER STUDIO
Photograph, Will Eisner (left) with Nick Viscardi and Bob Powell, Tudor City studio, 1941. "Will Eisner is the single person most responsible for giving comics its brains." — Alan Moore

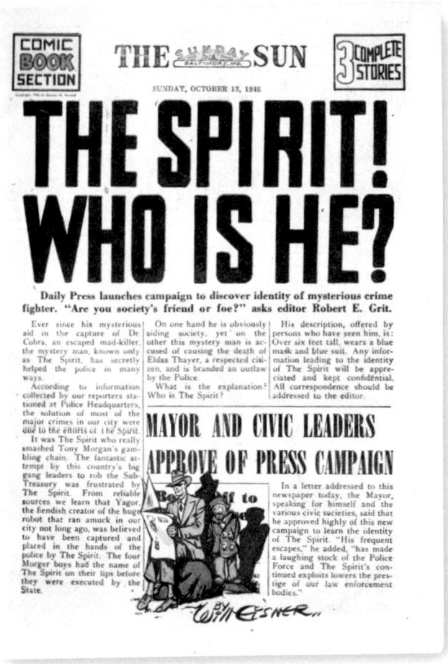
COMIC BOOK SECTION
THE SUNDAY SUN
3 COMPLETE STORIES
SUNDAY, OCTOBER 13, 1940
THE SPIRIT! WHO IS HE?
Daily Press launches campaign to discover identity of mysterious crime fighter. "Are you society's friend or foe?" asks editor Robert E. Grit.
Ever since his mysterious aid in the capture of Dr. Cobra, an escaped mad-killer, the mystery man, known only as The Spirit, has secretly helped the police in many ways.
According to information collected by our reporters stationed at Police Headquarters, the solution of most of the major crimes in our city were due to the efforts of The Spirit.
It was The Spirit who really smashed Tony Morgan's gambling chain. The fantastic attempt by this country's big gang leaders to rob the Sub-Treasury was frustrated by The Spirit. From reliable sources we learn that Yagor, the fiendish creator of the huge robot that ran amuck in our city not long ago, was believed to have been captured and placed in the hands of the police by The Spirit. The four Morger boys had the name of The Spirit on their lips before they were executed by the State.
On one hand he is obviously aiding society, yet on the other this mystery man is accused of causing the death of Eldas Thayer, a respected citizen, and is branded an outlaw by the Police.
What is the explanation? Who is The Spirit?
His description, offered by persons who have seen him, is: Over six feet tall, wears a blue mask and blue suit. Any information leading to the identity of The Spirit will be appreciated and kept confidential. All correspondence should be addressed to the editor.
MAYOR AND CIVIC LEADERS APPROVE OF PRESS CAMPAIGN
In a letter addressed to this newspaper today, the Mayor, speaking for himself and the various civic societies, said that he approved highly of this new campaign to learn the identity of The Spirit. "His frequent escapes," he added, "has made a laughing stock of the Police Force and The Spirit's continued exploits lowers the prestige of our law enforcement bodies."
BY WILL EISNER

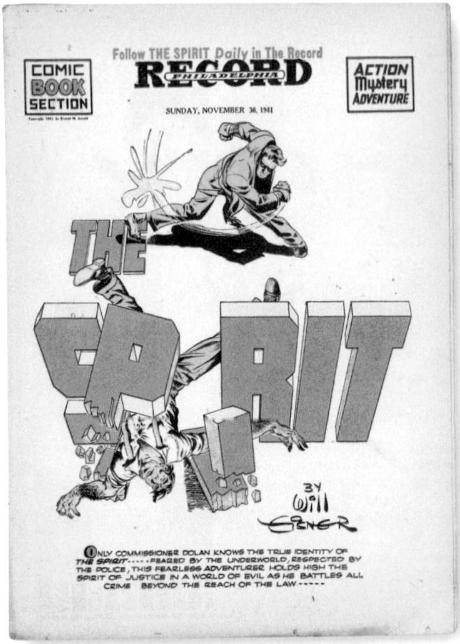
Follow THE SPIRIT Daily in The Record
RECORD PHILADELPHIA
COMIC BOOK SECTION
ACTION Mystery ADVENTURE
SUNDAY, NOVEMBER 30, 1941
THE SPIRIT
BY WILL EISNER
ONLY COMMISSIONER DOLAN KNOWS THE TRUE IDENTITY OF THE SPIRIT----FEARED BY THE UNDERWORLD, RESPECTED BY THE POLICE, THIS FEARLESS ADVENTURER HOLDS HIGH THE SPIRIT OF JUSTICE IN A WORLD OF EVIL AS HE BATTLES ALL CRIME BEYOND THE REACH OF THE LAW-----

THE SPIRIT No. 20

Cover art, Will Eisner, October 13, 1940. "By the time Denny Colt entered the field, all the good gimmicks had been taken. Superman had come from Krypton and was masquerading as Clark Kent. Batman was a wealthy ne'er-do-well who could afford to indulge his rather questionable taste for masquerading without a license. Denny Colt had to do it the hard way. No super powers, no vast source of wealth, no uniform gave him an edge over the dark forces of evil that beset society. He had to fight crime uninsulated. He always ran the risk of getting the stuffings kicked out of him." —Will Eisner

THE SPIRIT No. 79

Cover art, Will Eisner, November 30, 1941. Will Eisner used the superficial trappings of costumed heroes to draw in readers and challenged their expectations with unconventional stories like this tale told in verse.

THE SPIRIT No. 347

Interior, "The School for Girls"; script and art, Will Eisner, January 19, 1947. Discharged from the Army in 1945, Eisner was reunited with his creation at the end of the year, pushing the Spirit toward its artistic peak. Continuing to experiment with form and content, Eisner created pages like this one—a cutaway of a house where the events in each room moved the story to its payoff on the ground floor.

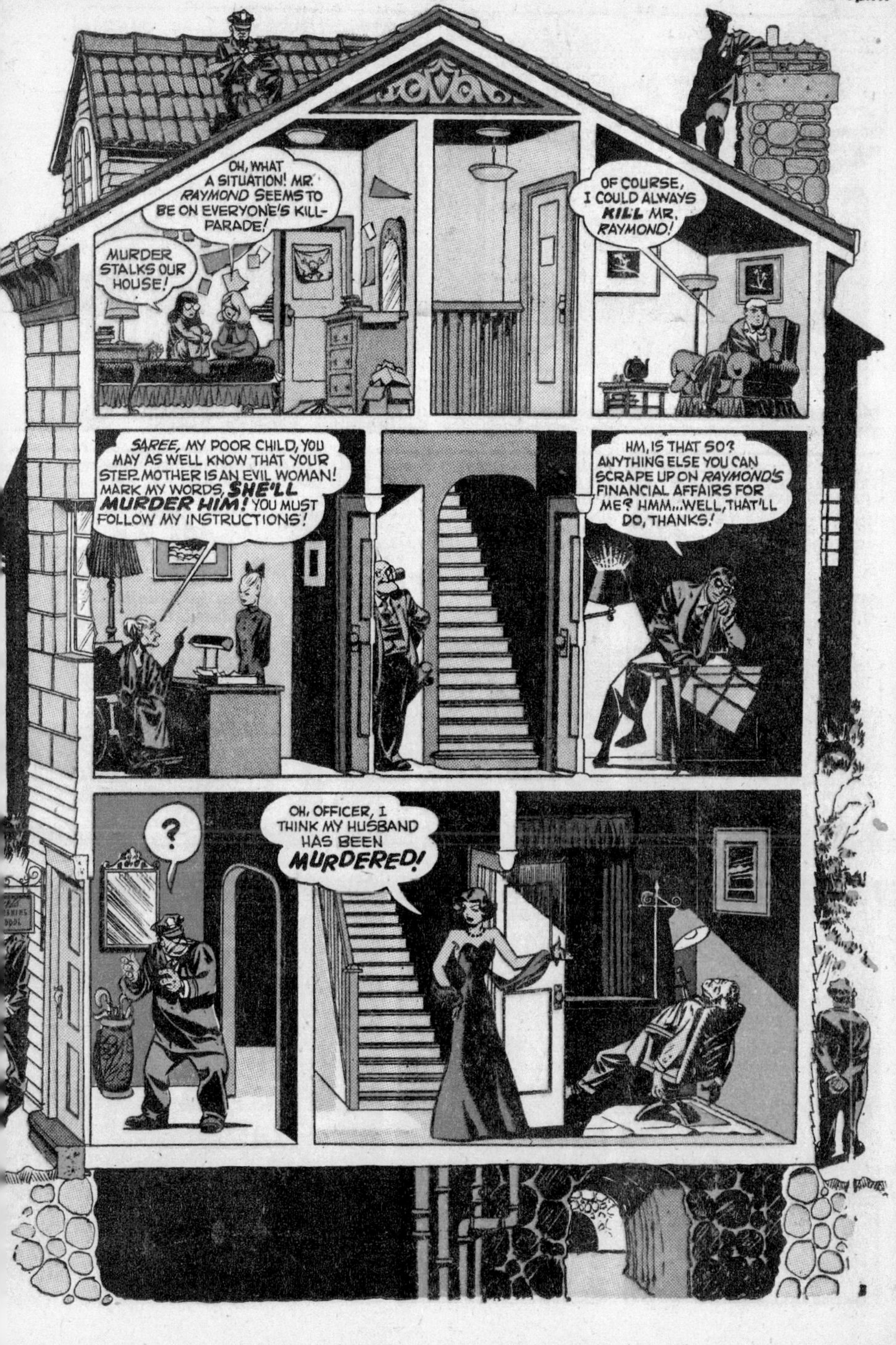

OH, WHAT A SITUATION! MR. RAYMOND SEEMS TO BE ON EVERYONE'S KILL-PARADE!
MURDER STALKS OUR HOUSE!
OF COURSE, I COULD ALWAYS KILL MR. RAYMOND!
SAREE, MY POOR CHILD, YOU MAY AS WELL KNOW THAT YOUR STEP-MOTHER IS AN EVIL WOMAN! MARK MY WORDS, SHE'LL MURDER HIM! YOU MUST FOLLOW MY INSTRUCTIONS!
HM, IS THAT SO? ANYTHING ELSE YOU CAN SCRAPE UP ON RAYMOND'S FINANCIAL AFFAIRS FOR ME? HMM...WELL, THAT'LL DO, THANKS!
?
OH, OFFICER, I THINK MY HUSBAND HAS BEEN MURDERED!

COMIC BOOK SECTION

Copyright, 1941, by Everett M. Arnold

RECORD *PHILADELPHIA*

SUNDAY, JUNE 22, 1941

ACTION Mystery ADVENTURE

THE Spirit

BY Will Eisner

or THE TALE OF THE DICTATOR'S REFORM

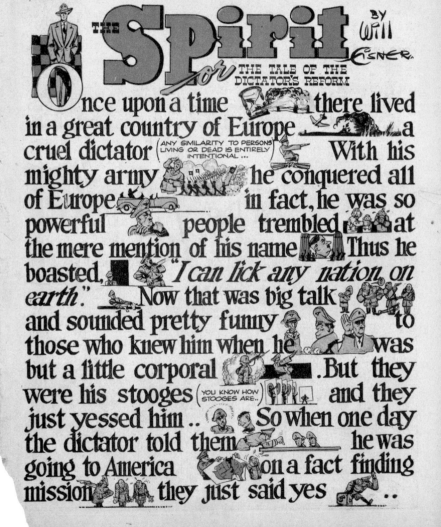

Once upon a time there lived in a great country of Europe a cruel dictator (ANY SIMILARITY TO PERSONS LIVING OR DEAD IS ENTIRELY INTENTIONAL ..) With his mighty army he conquered all of Europe in fact, he was so powerful people trembled at the mere mention of his name Thus he boasted, *"I can lick any nation on earth."* Now that was big talk and sounded pretty funny to those who knew him when he was but a little corporal. But they were his stooges (YOU KNOW HOW STOOGES ARE..) and they just yessed him .. So when one day the dictator told them he was going to America on a fact finding mission they just said yes ..

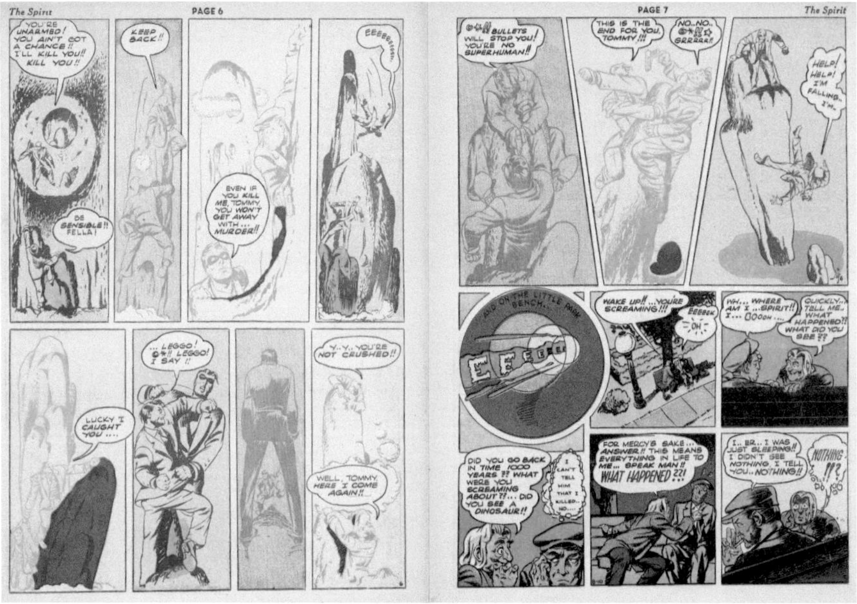
The Spirit
PAGE 6
YOU'RE UNARMED! YOU AIN'T GOT A CHANCE!! I'LL KILL YOU!! KILL YOU!!
BE SENSIBLE!! FELLA!
KEEP BACK!!
EVEN IF YOU KILL ME, TOMMY, YOU WON'T GET AWAY WITH... MURDER!!
LUCKY I CAUGHT YOU....
... LEGGO! LEGGO! I SAY!!
Y..Y.. YOU'RE NOT CRUSHED!!
WELL, TOMMY, HERE I COME AGAIN!!
PAGE 7
The Spirit
BULLETS WILL STOP YOU! YOU'RE NO SUPERHUMAN!!
THIS IS THE END FOR YOU, TOMMY!!!
NO..NO.. GRRRRR!!
HELP! HELP! I'M FALLING.. I'M..
AND ON THE LITTLE PARK BENCH..
WAKE UP!! ...YOU'RE SCREAMING!!!
EEEEEK
OH
WH... WHERE AM I ...SPIRIT!! I... OOOOH ....
QUICKLY.. TELL ME.. WHAT HAPPENED?? WHAT DID YOU SEE??
DID YOU GO BACK IN TIME 1000 YEARS?? WHAT WERE YOU SCREAMING ABOUT??... DID YOU SEE A DINOSAUR!!
I CAN'T TELL HIM THAT I KILLED.. NO....
FOR MERCY'S SAKE... ANSWER!! THIS MEANS EVERYTHING IN LIFE TO ME... SPEAK MAN!! WHAT HAPPENED??!
I.. ER.. I WAS JUST SLEEPING!! I DIDN'T SEE NOTHING, I TELL YOU.. NOTHING!!
NOTHING ??

THE SPIRIT No. 56

Cover art, Will Eisner, June 22, 1941. Like many cartoonists, Will Eisner addressed the threat of Hitler and Nazi Germany well before the United States joined the war. In this mid-1941 story, "the Dictator" secretly visits the U.S. and is successfully persuaded by the Spirit to abandon his mad ambitions. Upon his return, however, the reformed villain is immediately shot by his inner circle and replaced by a double.

THE SPIRIT No. 63

Interior, "The Element of Time"; script and art, Will Eisner, August 10, 1941. "Ultimately, Eisner began to tamper with the heroic detective-adventure formula itself, developing what comics critic Jules Feiffer called 'documentary fables — seemingly authentic when one reads them, but impossible after the fact.' One of Feiffer's favorite 'documentary fables' was 'The Oldest Man in the World,' a daring exercise in colouring as well as a cleverly complex story." — Catherine Yronwode

THE SPIRIT

THIS SPREAD AND FOLLOWING SPREAD: *Cover and interiors, "The Story of Gerhard Shnobble"; script and art, Will Eisner, September 5, 1948.* Eisner's *Spirit* stories were often short parables of humanity's foibles. Here, in the author's personal favorite, Eisner examines the wish that underlies the great super hero secret identity theme: that underneath our ordinary exteriors lies a dreamer who can fly. But unlike the celebrated heroes, Gerhard Shnobble's flight ends unnoticed and with his unmourned death, for Eisner always treasured humanity over the fantastic.

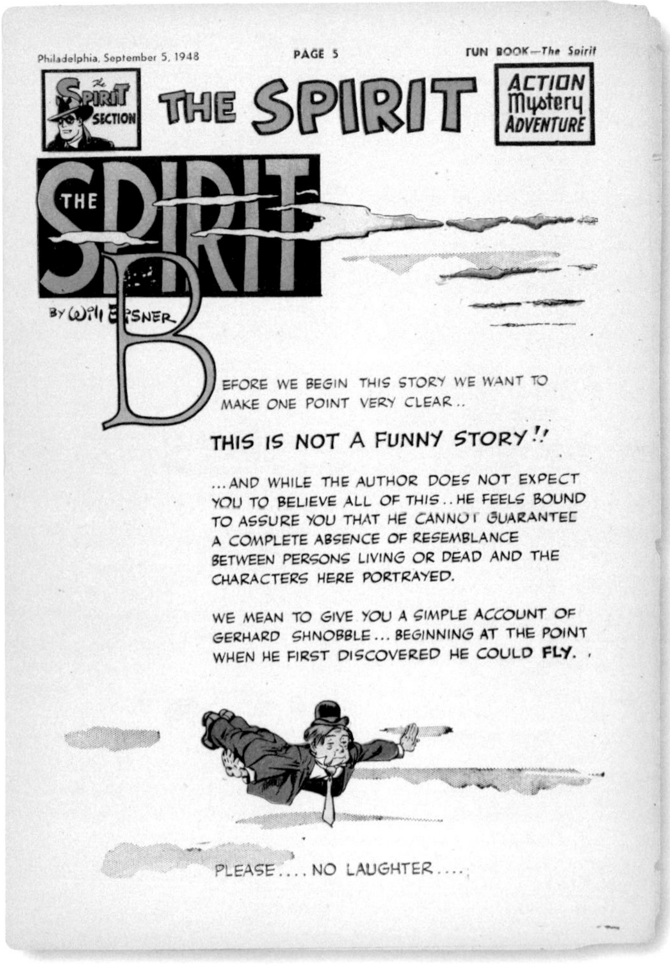
Philadelphia, September 5, 1948
PAGE 5
FUN BOOK—The Spirit
The SPIRIT SECTION
THE SPIRIT
ACTION Mystery ADVENTURE
THE SPIRIT
BY Will EISNER
BEFORE WE BEGIN THIS STORY WE WANT TO MAKE ONE POINT VERY CLEAR..
THIS IS NOT A FUNNY STORY!!
...AND WHILE THE AUTHOR DOES NOT EXPECT YOU TO BELIEVE ALL OF THIS..HE FEELS BOUND TO ASSURE YOU THAT HE CANNOT GUARANTEE A COMPLETE ABSENCE OF RESEMBLANCE BETWEEN PERSONS LIVING OR DEAD AND THE CHARACTERS HERE PORTRAYED.
WE MEAN TO GIVE YOU A SIMPLE ACCOUNT OF GERHARD SHNOBBLE... BEGINNING AT THE POINT WHEN HE FIRST DISCOVERED HE COULD FLY.
PLEASE.... NO LAUGHTER....

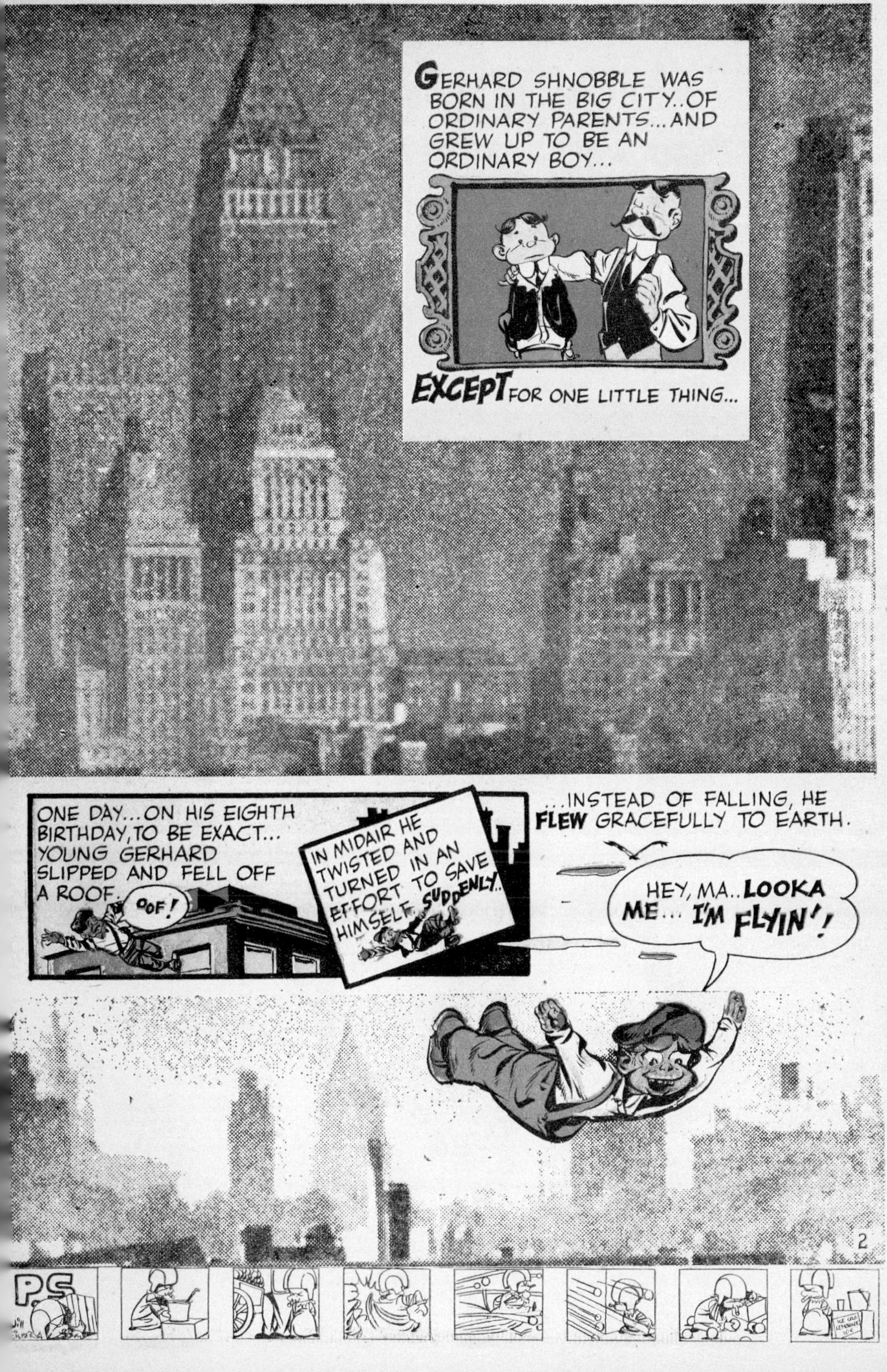
GERHARD SHNOBBLE WAS BORN IN THE BIG CITY..OF ORDINARY PARENTS...AND GREW UP TO BE AN ORDINARY BOY...
EXCEPT FOR ONE LITTLE THING...
ONE DAY...ON HIS EIGHTH BIRTHDAY, TO BE EXACT... YOUNG GERHARD SLIPPED AND FELL OFF A ROOF.
OOF!
IN MIDAIR HE TWISTED AND TURNED IN AN EFFORT TO SAVE HIMSELF. SUDDENLY..
...INSTEAD OF FALLING, HE FLEW GRACEFULLY TO EARTH.
HEY, MA..LOOKA ME... I'M FLYIN'!
2
PS

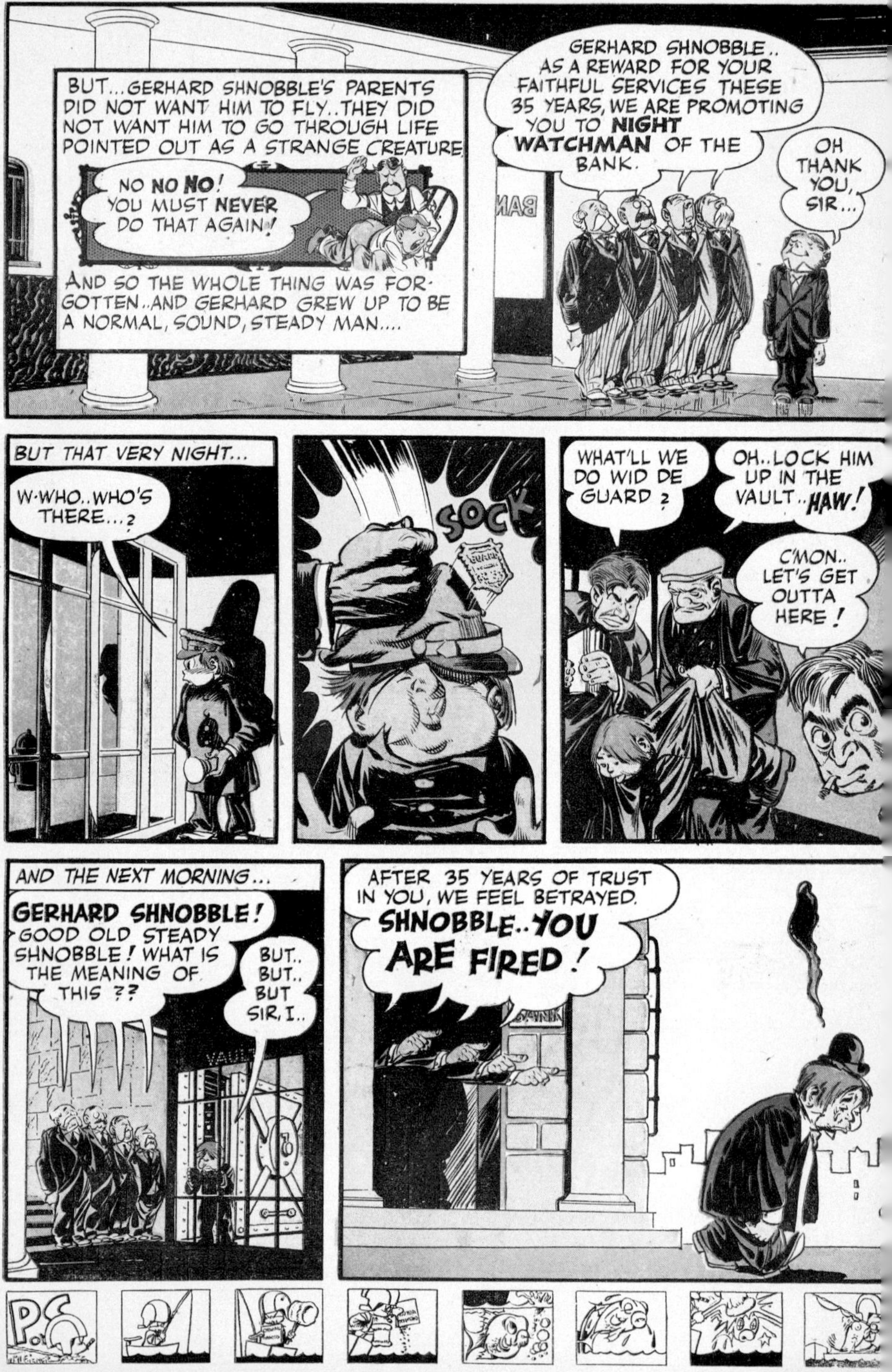
BUT... GERHARD SHNOBBLE'S PARENTS DID NOT WANT HIM TO FLY.. THEY DID NOT WANT HIM TO GO THROUGH LIFE POINTED OUT AS A STRANGE CREATURE
NO NO NO! YOU MUST NEVER DO THAT AGAIN!
AND SO THE WHOLE THING WAS FORGOTTEN.. AND GERHARD GREW UP TO BE A NORMAL, SOUND, STEADY MAN....
GERHARD SHNOBBLE.. AS A REWARD FOR YOUR FAITHFUL SERVICES THESE 35 YEARS, WE ARE PROMOTING YOU TO NIGHT WATCHMAN OF THE BANK.
OH THANK YOU, SIR...
BUT THAT VERY NIGHT...
W-WHO.. WHO'S THERE...?
SOCK
WHAT'LL WE DO WID DE GUARD ?
OH.. LOCK HIM UP IN THE VAULT.. HAW!
C'MON.. LET'S GET OUTTA HERE!
AND THE NEXT MORNING...
GERHARD SHNOBBLE! GOOD OLD STEADY SHNOBBLE! WHAT IS THE MEANING OF THIS ??
BUT.. BUT.. BUT SIR, I..
VAULT
AFTER 35 YEARS OF TRUST IN YOU, WE FEEL BETRAYED. SHNOBBLE.. YOU ARE FIRED!
BANK

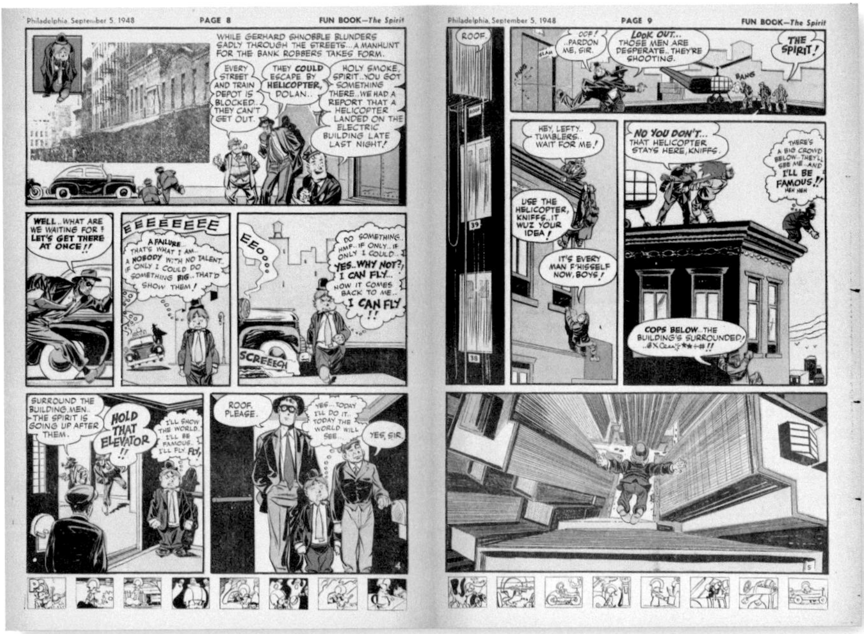
Philadelphia, September 5, 1948 PAGE 8 FUN BOOK—The Spirit
WHILE GERHARD SHNOBBLE BLUNDERS SADLY THROUGH THE STREETS... A MANHUNT FOR THE BANK ROBBERS TAKES FORM.
EVERY STREET AND TRAIN DEPOT IS BLOCKED. THEY CAN'T GET OUT.
THEY COULD ESCAPE BY HELICOPTER, DOLAN..
HOLY SMOKE, SPIRIT.. YOU GOT SOMETHING THERE.. WE HAD A REPORT THAT A HELICOPTER LANDED ON THE ELECTRIC BUILDING LATE LAST NIGHT!
WELL.. WHAT ARE WE WAITING FOR? LET'S GET THERE AT ONCE!!
EEEEEEEE
A FAILURE.. THAT'S WHAT I AM.. A NOBODY WITH NO TALENT.. IF ONLY I COULD DO SOMETHING BIG.. THAT'D SHOW THEM!
EEOooo
DO SOMETHING. HMF.. IF ONLY.. IF ONLY I COULD.. YES.. WHY NOT? I CAN FLY... NOW IT COMES BACK TO ME.. I CAN FLY!!
SCREEECH
SURROUND THE BUILDING, MEN.. THE SPIRIT IS GOING UP AFTER THEM.
HOLD THAT ELEVATOR!!
I'LL SHOW THE WORLD.. I'LL BE FAMOUS. I'LL FLY FLY
ROOF, PLEASE.
YES... TODAY I'LL DO IT.. TODAY THE WORLD WILL SEE...
YES, SIR.
Philadelphia, September 5, 1948 PAGE 9 FUN BOOK—The Spirit
ROOF.
OOF! ..PARDON ME, SIR.
LOOK OUT... THOSE MEN ARE DESPERATE.. THEY'RE SHOOTING.
THE SPIRIT!
BANG
HEY, LEFTY.. TUMBLERS.. WAIT FOR ME!
USE THE HELICOPTER, KNIFFS.. IT WUZ YOUR IDEA!
IT'S EVERY MAN F'HISSELF NOW, BOYS!
NO YOU DON'T... THAT HELICOPTER STAYS HERE, KNIFFS.
THERE'S A BIG CROWD BELOW.. THEY'LL SEE ME.. AND I'LL BE FAMOUS!! HEH HEH
COPS BELOW.. THE BUILDING'S SURROUNDED!

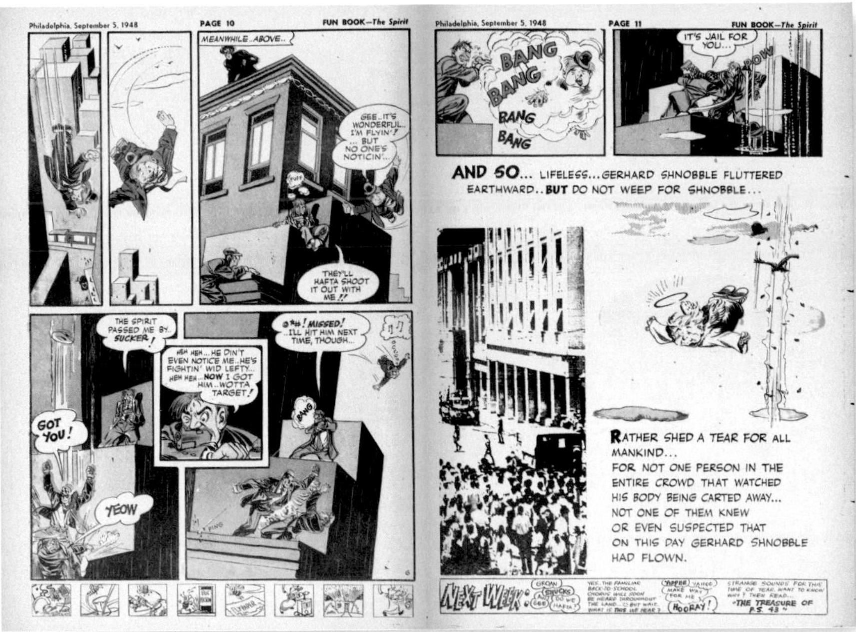
Philadelphia, September 5, 1948 PAGE 10 FUN BOOK—The Spirit
MEANWHILE.. ABOVE..
GEE.. IT'S WONDERFUL.. I'M FLYIN'! ... BUT NO ONE'S NOTICIN'..
THEY'LL HAFTA SHOOT IT OUT WITH ME!!
THE SPIRIT PASSED ME BY.. SUCKER!
HEH HEH... HE DIN'T EVEN NOTICE ME.. HE'S FIGHTIN' WID LEFTY.. HEH HEH... NOW I GOT HIM.. WOTTA TARGET!
MISSED! ..I'LL HIT HIM NEXT TIME, THOUGH...
GOT YOU!
BANG
YEOW
Philadelphia, September 5, 1948 PAGE 11 FUN BOOK—The Spirit
BANG BANG BANG BANG
IT'S JAIL FOR YOU...
POW
AND SO... LIFELESS... GERHARD SHNOBBLE FLUTTERED EARTHWARD.. BUT DO NOT WEEP FOR SHNOBBLE...
RATHER SHED A TEAR FOR ALL MANKIND... FOR NOT ONE PERSON IN THE ENTIRE CROWD THAT WATCHED HIS BODY BEING CARTED AWAY... NOT ONE OF THEM KNEW OR EVEN SUSPECTED THAT ON THIS DAY GERHARD SHNOBBLE HAD FLOWN.
NEXT WEEK:
HOORAY!
"THE TREASURE OF P.S. 43"

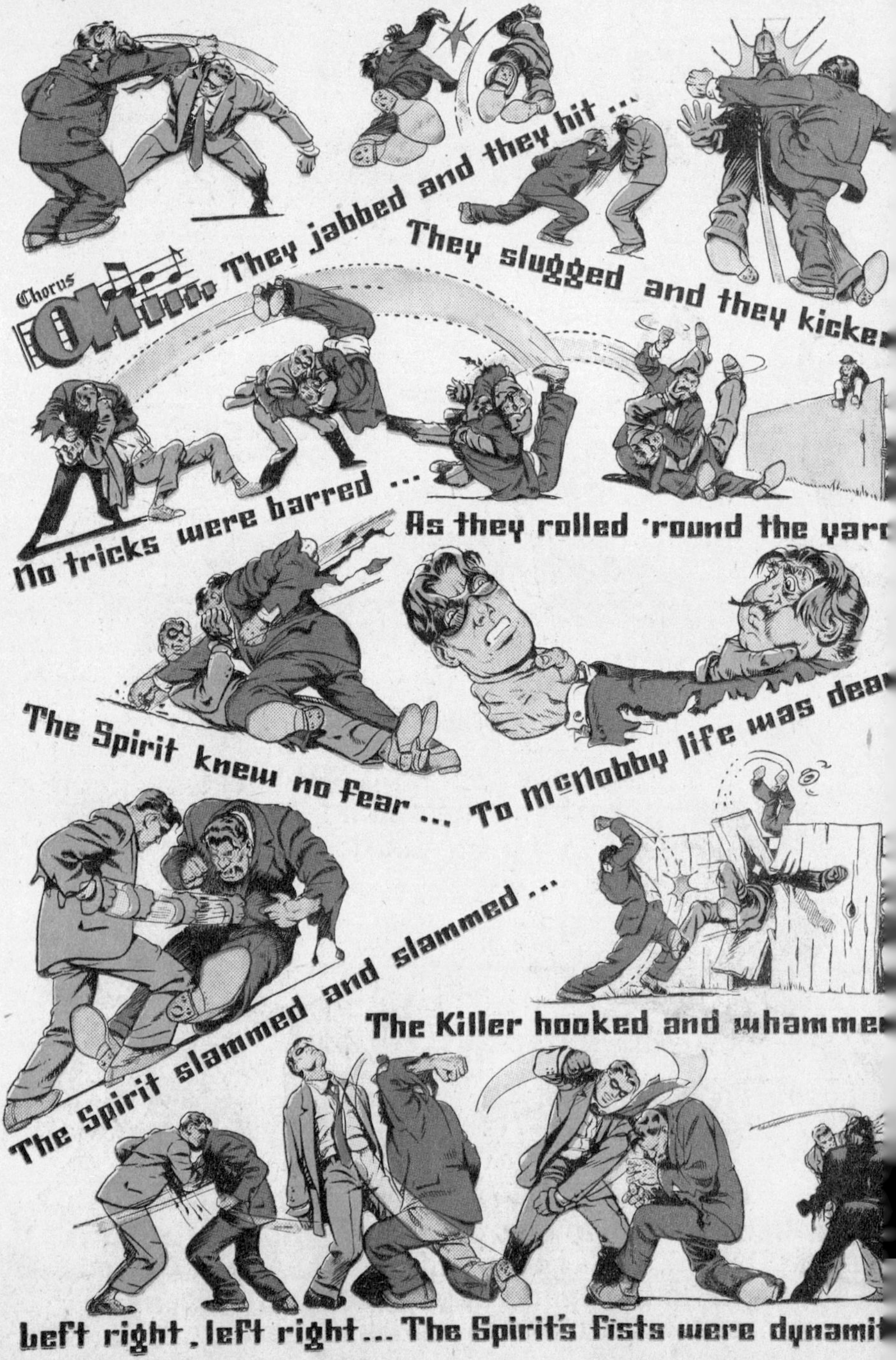
Chorus
Oh
They jabbed and they hit ...
They slugged and they kicked
No tricks were barred ...
As they rolled 'round the yard
The Spirit knew no fear ...
To McNobby life was dear
The Spirit slammed and slammed ...
The Killer hooked and whammed
Left right, left right ... The Spirit's fists were dynamite

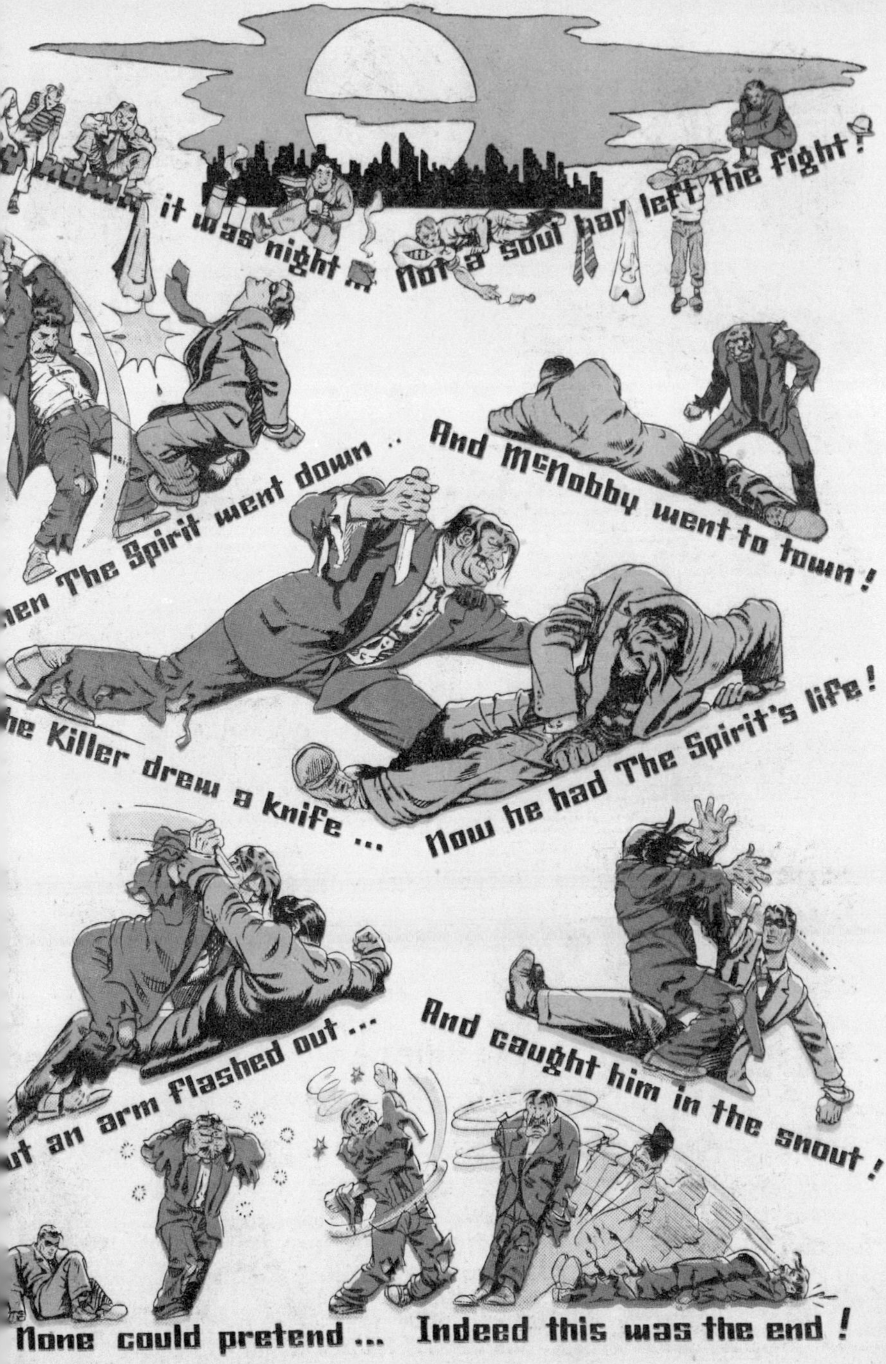
it was night ... Not a soul had left the fight!
hen The Spirit went down .. And McNobby went to town!
he Killer drew a knife ... Now he had The Spirit's life!
t an arm flashed out ... And caught him in the snout!
None could pretend ... Indeed this was the end!

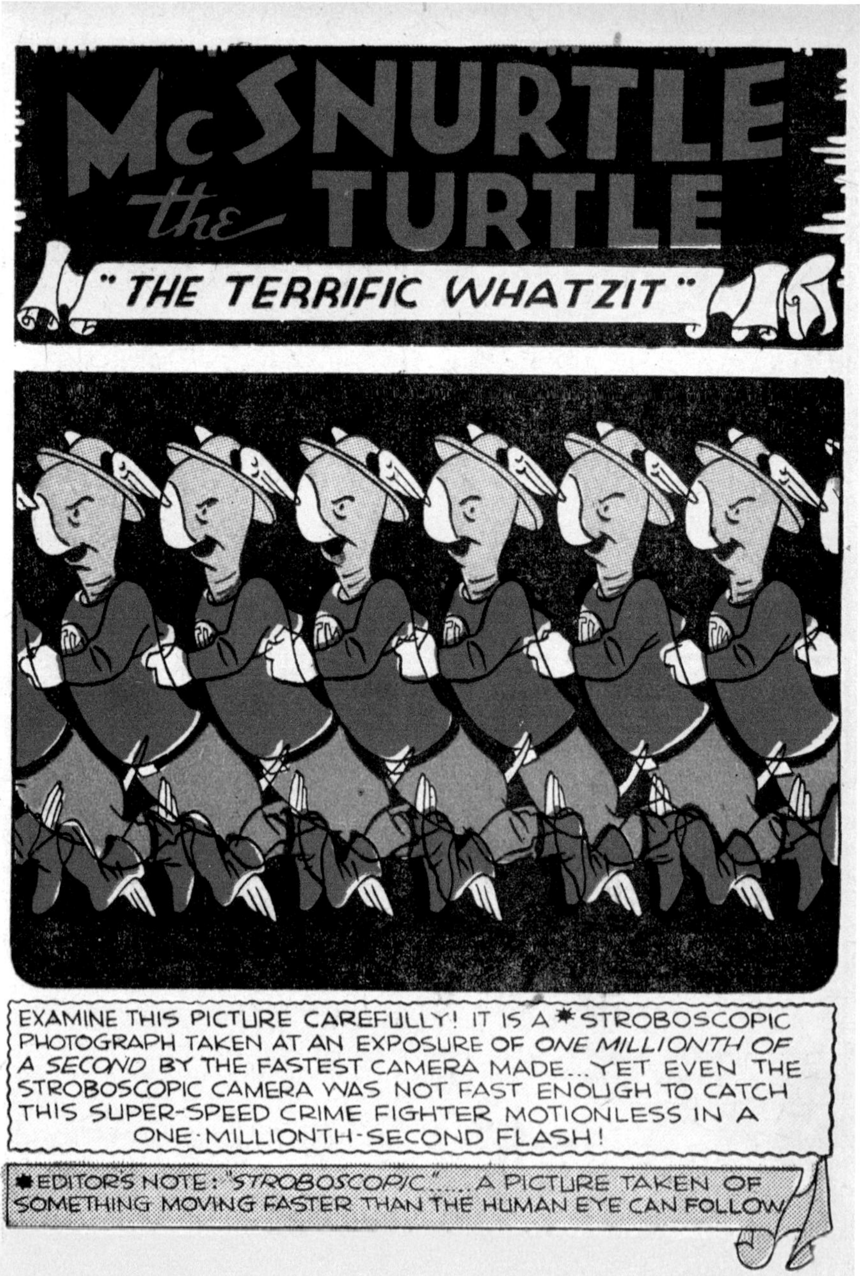
McSNURTLE the TURTLE
"THE TERRIFIC WHATZIT"
EXAMINE THIS PICTURE CAREFULLY! IT IS A ✱ STROBOSCOPIC PHOTOGRAPH TAKEN AT AN EXPOSURE OF ONE MILLIONTH OF A SECOND BY THE FASTEST CAMERA MADE... YET EVEN THE STROBOSCOPIC CAMERA WAS NOT FAST ENOUGH TO CATCH THIS SUPER-SPEED CRIME FIGHTER MOTIONLESS IN A ONE-MILLIONTH-SECOND FLASH!
✱ EDITORS NOTE: "STROBOSCOPIC"..... A PICTURE TAKEN OF SOMETHING MOVING FASTER THAN THE HUMAN EYE CAN FOLLOW

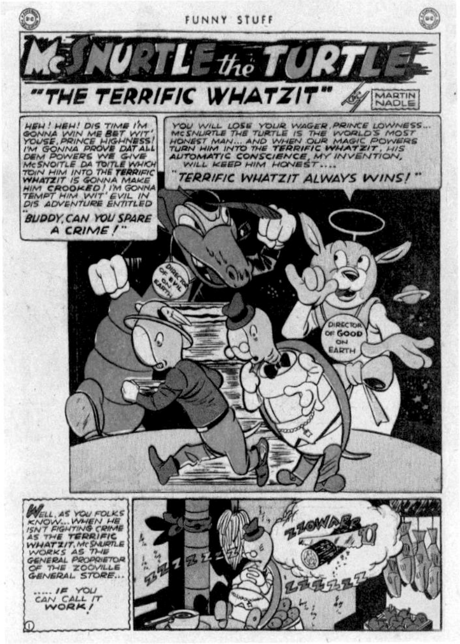
FUNNY STUFF
McSNURTLE the TURTLE
"THE TERRIFIC WHATZIT" by MARTIN NADLE
HEH! HEH! DIS TIME I'M GONNA WIN ME BET WIT' YOUSE, PRINCE HIGHNESS! I'M GONNA PROVE DAT ALL DEM POWERS WE GIVE McSNOITLE DA TOITLE WHICH TOIN HIM INTO THE TERRIFIC WHATZIT IS GONNA MAKE HIM CROOKED! I'M GONNA TEMPT HIM WIT' EVIL IN DIS ADVENTURE ENTITLED "BUDDY, CAN YOU SPARE A CRIME!"
YOU WILL LOSE YOUR WAGER, PRINCE LOWNESS... McSNURTLE THE TURTLE IS THE WORLD'S MOST HONEST MAN... AND WHEN OUR MAGIC POWERS TURN HIM INTO THE TERRIFIC WHATZIT, HIS AUTOMATIC CONSCIENCE, MY INVENTION, WILL KEEP HIM HONEST.... "TERRIFIC WHATZIT ALWAYS WINS!"
DIRECTOR OF EVIL ON EARTH
DIRECTOR OF GOOD ON EARTH
WELL, AS YOU FOLKS KNOW... WHEN HE ISN'T FIGHTING CRIME AS THE TERRIFIC WHATZIT, McSNURTLE WORKS AS THE GENERAL PROPRIETOR OF THE ZOOVILLE GENERAL STORE...
..... IF YOU CAN CALL IT WORK!
ZZOWARR
ZZZZZZZ

THE SPIRIT No. 53

PREVIOUS SPREAD: *Interiors, "Killer McKnobby"; script and art, Will Eisner. June 1, 1941.* Pronounced dead after being poisoned, Detective Denny Colt chose not to advertise his survival. Donning a small mask and calling himself the Spirit, he began fighting crimes beyond the reach of his friend and mentor, Police Commissioner Dolan.

FUNNY STUFF No. 1

Interior, "The Terrific Whatzit"; script, Sheldon Mayer; art, Martin Naydel. Summer 1944. The Terrific Whatzit faded away in 1946 as the super hero craze abated. Although McSnurtle the Turtle lost his series, he continued to appear throughout the 1950s as a supporting character in Sheldon Mayer features like Dizzy Dog and the Three Mouseketeers.

FUNNY STUFF No. 2

Interior, "McSnurtle the Turtle"; script, unknown; pencils and inks, Martin Naydel. Fall 1944. Edited by Sheldon Mayer, the Terrific Whatzit parodied a specific super hero, in this case All-American's Flash. The central gag was the fact the superfast hero's secret identity was the slow-moving McSnurtle the Turtle.

HOPPY THE MARVEL BUNNY No. 3

Interior, "Tugboat Millie"; script, unknown; art, Chad Grothkopf. July 1946. A funny animal variation of Fawcett Comics' Captain Marvel, Hoppy lost his super hero trappings in 1951 and was eventually sold to rival publisher Charlton.

COMIC CAVALCADE No. 44

Cover art, Rube Grossman, April–May 1951. Originally an animator for the Fleischer studios, Rube Grossman was a ubiquitous contributor to DC's funny animal line of the 1940s and 1950s.

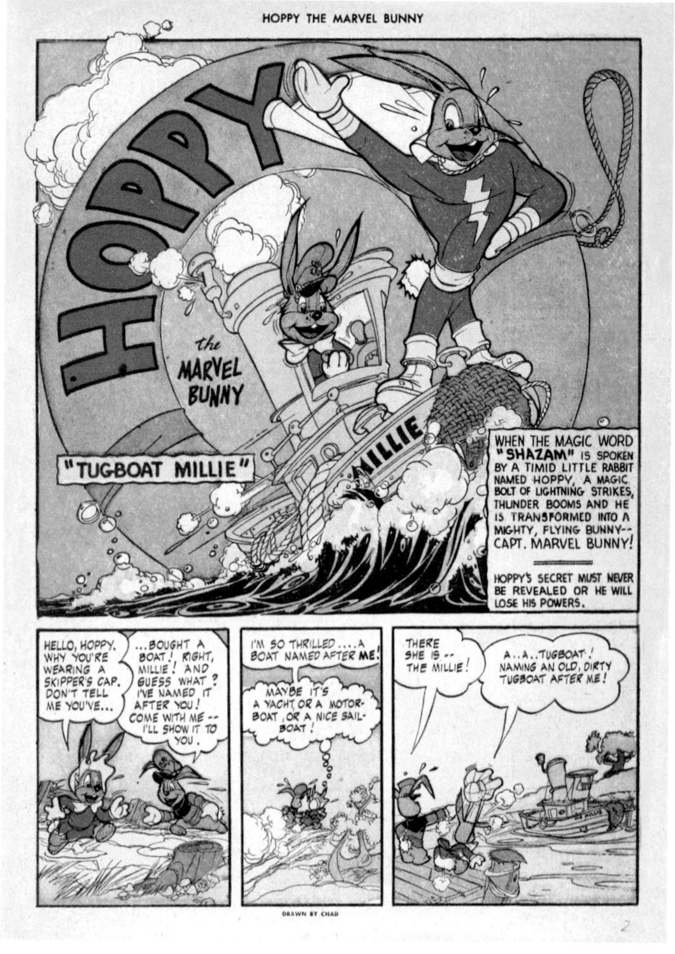
HOPPY THE MARVEL BUNNY
HOPPY
the MARVEL BUNNY
"TUGBOAT MILLIE"
MILLIE
WHEN THE MAGIC WORD "SHAZAM" IS SPOKEN BY A TIMID LITTLE RABBIT NAMED HOPPY, A MAGIC BOLT OF LIGHTNING STRIKES, THUNDER BOOMS AND HE IS TRANSFORMED INTO A MIGHTY, FLYING BUNNY-- CAPT. MARVEL BUNNY!
HOPPY'S SECRET MUST NEVER BE REVEALED OR HE WILL LOSE HIS POWERS.
HELLO, HOPPY. WHY YOU'RE WEARING A SKIPPER'S CAP. DON'T TELL ME YOU'VE...
...BOUGHT A BOAT! RIGHT, MILLIE! AND GUESS WHAT? I'VE NAMED IT AFTER YOU! COME WITH ME -- I'LL SHOW IT TO YOU.
I'M SO THRILLED....A BOAT NAMED AFTER ME!
MAYBE IT'S A YACHT, OR A MOTOR-BOAT, OR A NICE SAIL-BOAT!
THERE SHE IS -- THE MILLIE!
A..A..TUGBOAT! NAMING AN OLD, DIRTY TUGBOAT AFTER ME!
DRAWN BY CHAD

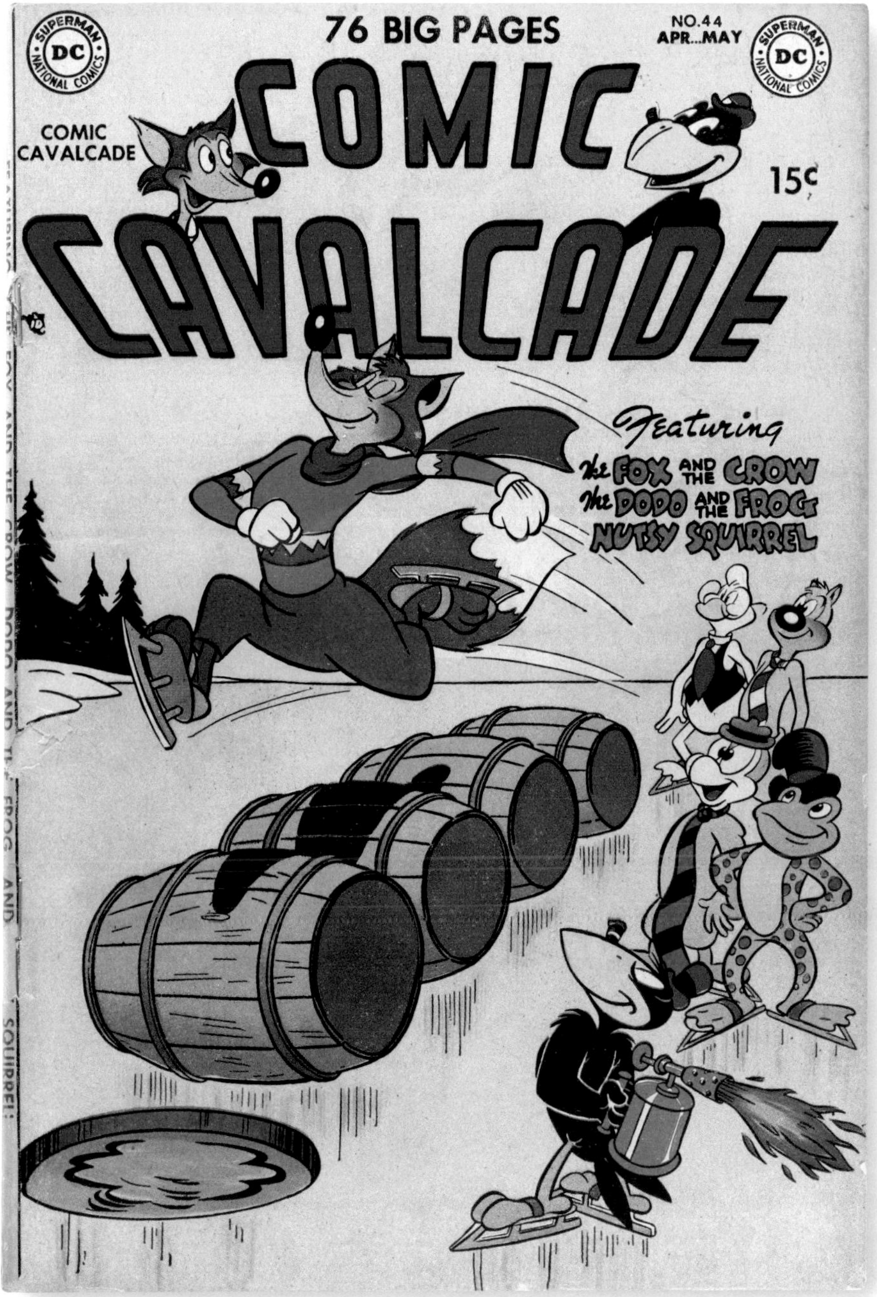

SUPERMAN DC NATIONAL COMICS
76 BIG PAGES
NO.44
APR...MAY
COMIC CAVALCADE
COMIC CAVALCADE
15¢
Featuring
The FOX AND THE CROW
The DODO AND THE FROG
NUTSY SQUIRREL

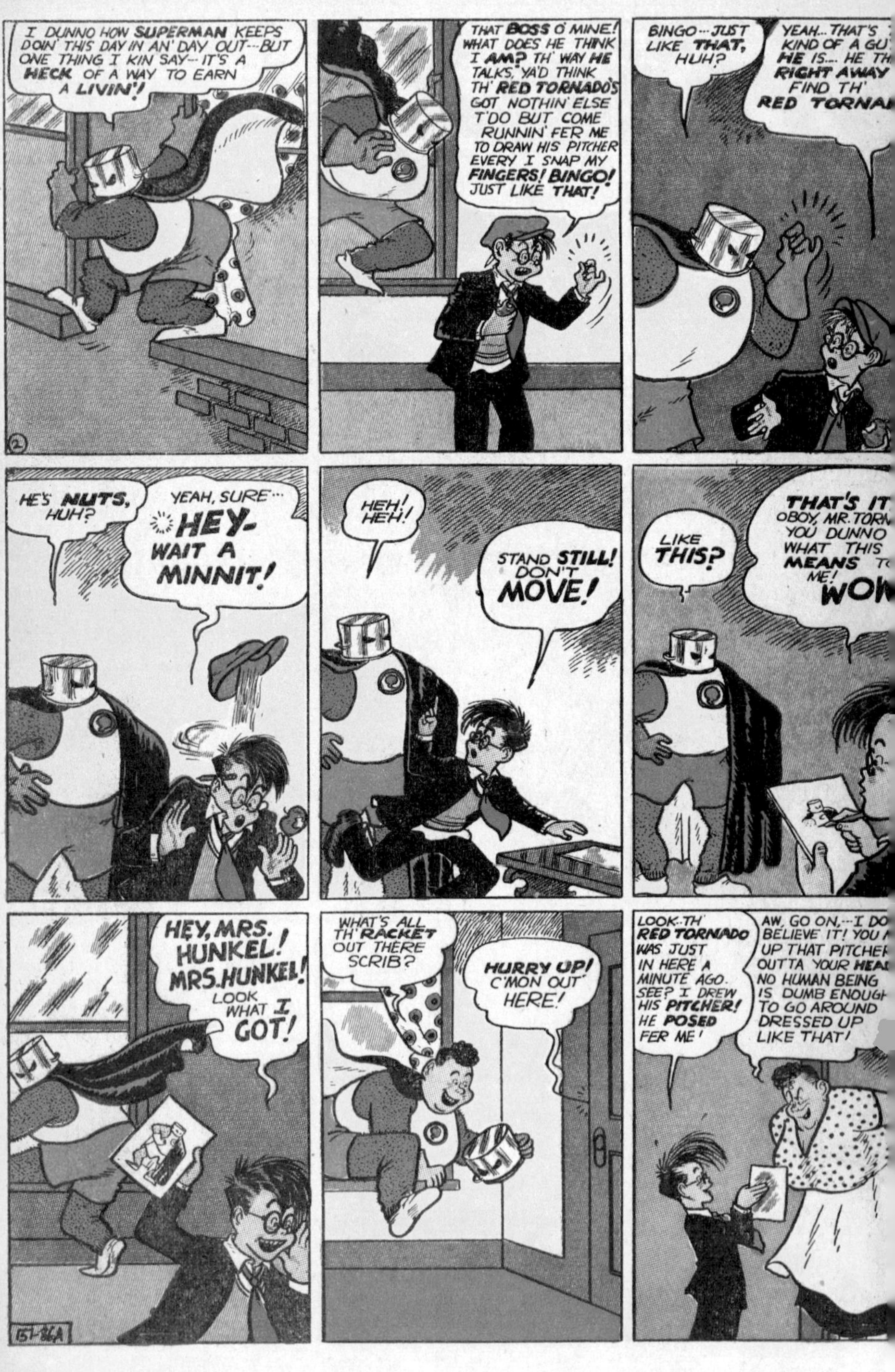

I DUNNO HOW SUPERMAN KEEPS DOIN' THIS DAY IN AN' DAY OUT--BUT ONE THING I KIN SAY-- IT'S A HECK OF A WAY TO EARN A LIVIN'!
2
THAT BOSS O' MINE! WHAT DOES HE THINK I AM? TH' WAY HE TALKS, YA'D THINK TH' RED TORNADO'S GOT NOTHIN' ELSE T'DO BUT COME RUNNIN' FER ME TO DRAW HIS PITCHER EVERY I SNAP MY FINGERS! BINGO! JUST LIKE THAT!
BINGO--- JUST LIKE THAT, HUH?
YEAH... THAT'S KIND OF A GU HE IS... HE TH RIGHT AWAY FIND TH' RED TORNA
HE'S NUTS, HUH?
YEAH, SURE... HEY- WAIT A MINNIT!
HEH! HEH!
STAND STILL! DON'T MOVE!
LIKE THIS?
THAT'S IT OBOY, MR. TORN YOU DUNNO WHAT THIS MEANS T ME! WOW
HEY, MRS. HUNKEL! MRS. HUNKEL! LOOK WHAT I GOT!
151-86A
WHAT'S ALL TH' RACKET OUT THERE SCRIB?
HURRY UP! C'MON OUT HERE!
LOOK-TH' RED TORNADO WAS JUST IN HERE A MINUTE AGO. SEE? I DREW HIS PITCHER! HE POSED FER ME!
AW, GO ON,--I DO BELIEVE IT! YOU A UP THAT PITCHER OUTTA YOUR HEAD NO HUMAN BEING IS DUMB ENOUGH TO GO AROUND DRESSED UP LIKE THAT!

Sheldon Mayer

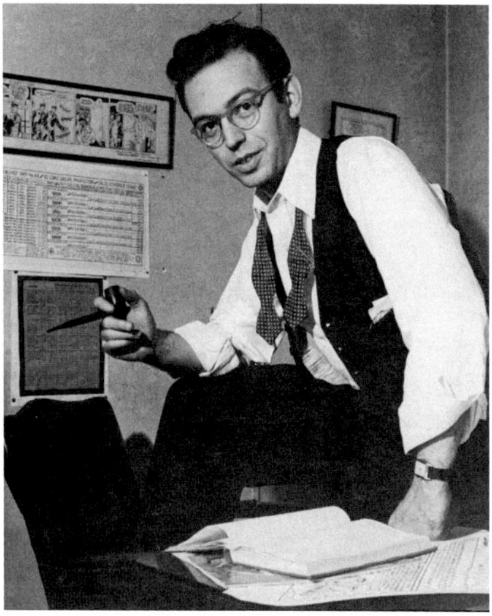

"Sheldon Mayer is a *rara avis*; one of the few creative men I've met in comics. He ran All-American like Charlie Chaplin opening the cabinet of Dr. Caligari. He mixed plots like D. W. Griffith and Mack the Knife sharing a Catskill Mountains kitchen. He was like one of the early barnstorming pilots who fearlessly flew across the unknown seas of imagination by the reckless seat of his pants."

—BOB KANIGHER

ALL-AMERICAN COMICS No. 22
Interior, "Scribbly"; script and art, Sheldon Mayer. January 1941.
With the super hero concept still in its infancy, Mayer was ready with his Red Tornado parody of the form in the Scribbly series. He also anticipated the sort of lampooning that the 1960s Marvel Comics characters would receive via references to his heroine as "the Red Tomato."

SHELDON MAYER
Publicity photo, the editor in his offices at All-American, 1945.
"I guess I was always a little jealous of my artists, because they were drawing pictures and I wasn't. The only time I was really happy was when I was drawing." —Sheldon Mayer, on his decision to leave editing and return to cartooning

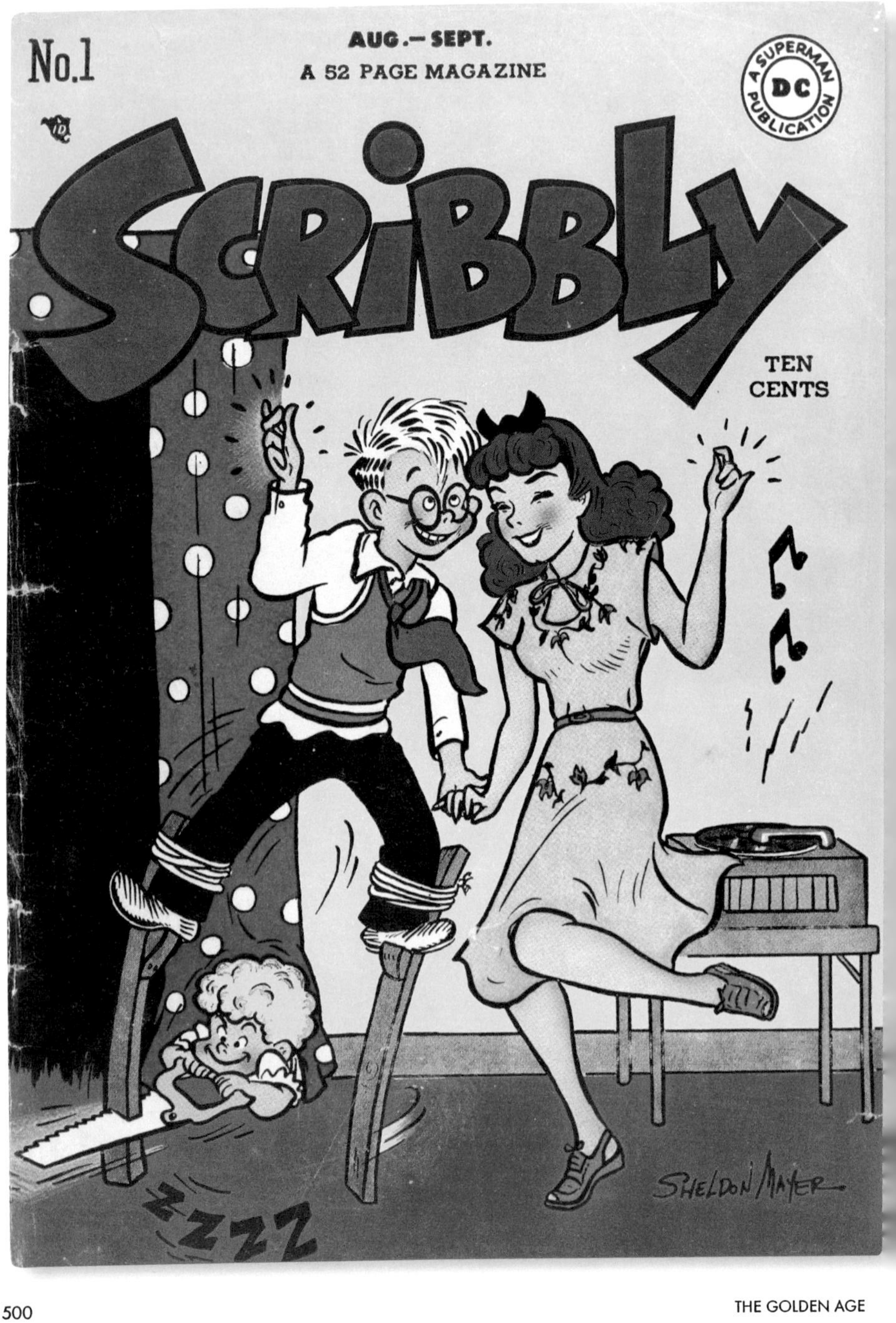
No.1
AUG.—SEPT.
A 52 PAGE MAGAZINE
A SUPERMAN DC PUBLICATION
SCRIBBLY
TEN CENTS
SHELDON MAYER
ZZZZ

COMIC CAVALCADE
No. 30
FIFTEEN CENTS
DEC-JAN.
A 76 PAGE MAGAZINE
BRAND NEW STORIES Featuring ALL YOUR OLD FAVORITES—
The FOX AND THE CROW
The DODO AND THE FROG
NUTSY SQUIRREL
AND OTHERS!

No. 1 SPRING ISSUE
TITO and his BURRITO
REAL SCREEN FUNNIES
TEN CENTS
featuring the FOX and the CROW
—AND OTHER FUNNY FAVORITES!

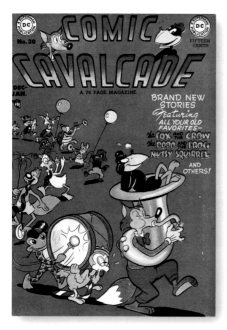

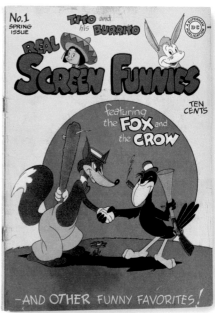

SCRIBBLY No. 1

Cover art, Sheldon Mayer, August–September 1948. Retiring as an editor, Mayer included a revival of his beloved Scribbly among his new cartooning projects. Though intended to tap the teen humor audience, Scribbly was still a kid cartoonist with a desire to draw Rational Comics' Terrificman.

COMIC CAVALCADE No. 30

Cover art, Rube Grossman, December 1948–January 1949. In a sign of the times, super heroes were evicted from *Comic Cavalcade* in favor of a funny animal lineup led by the Fox and the Crow, stars of several Screen Gems animated shorts.

REAL SCREEN FUNNIES No. 1

Cover art, Jim Davis, Spring 1945.

FUNNY STUFF No. 1

Cover art, Sheldon Mayer, summer 1944.

ANIMAL ANTICS No. 22

Cover art, Otto Feuer, September–October 1949. Most of DC's funny animal line consisted of original characters like the Raccoon Kids and the Three Mouseketeers. Much of the first wave was dropped in favor of later creations like Peter Porkchops and Dodo and the Frog. Like the Raccoon Kids, they each headlined their own comic book in the 1950s.

FUNNY STUFF No. 5

Interior, "J. Rufus Lion"; script and art, Sheldon Mayer. Summer 1945. "Mayer's raffish J. Rufus Lion story carries the lowlife scent of vaudeville that permeated many of the early humor comics. It manages to smash the fourth wall to smithereens years before Harvey Kurtzman's Hey Look! feature, and later *MAD*, atomized the smithereens, while painlessly introducing the notion of the unreliable narrator to young readers." —Art Spiegelman and Françoise Mouly

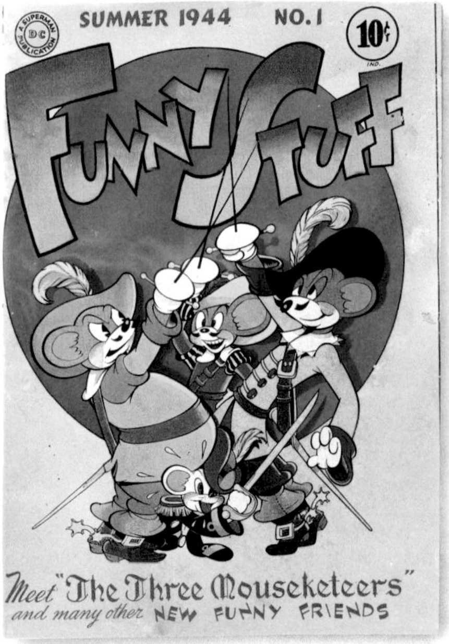
SUMMER 1944
NO. 1
10¢
FUNNY STUFF
Meet "The Three Mouseketeers"
and many other NEW FUNNY FRIENDS

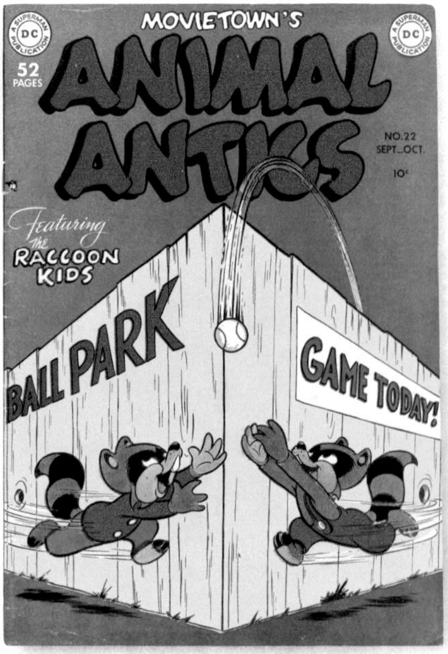
MOVIETOWN'S
52 PAGES
ANIMAL ANTICS
NO. 22
SEPT.-OCT.
10¢
Featuring the RACCOON KIDS
BALL PARK
GAME TODAY!

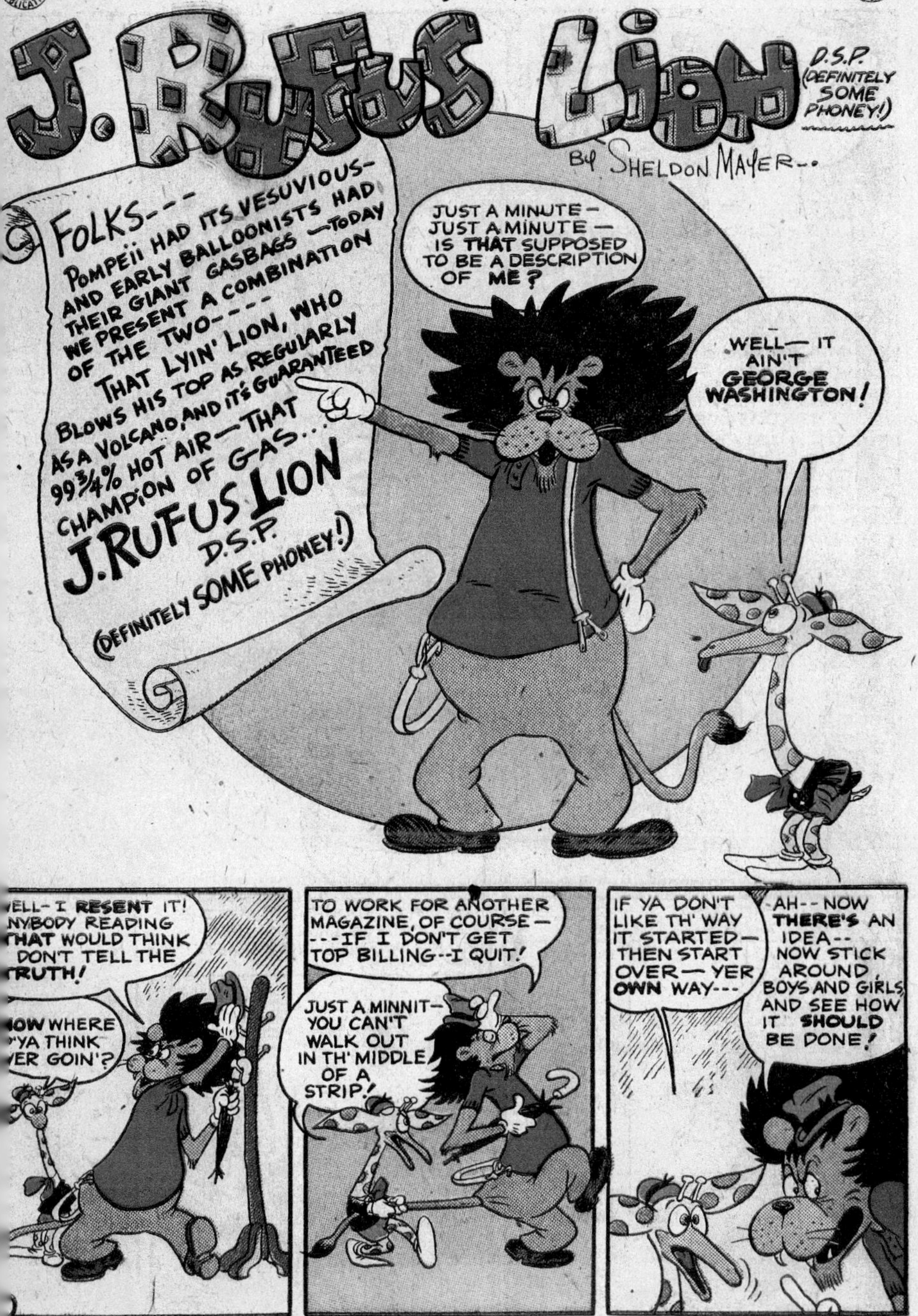
J. RUFUS LION
D.S.P. (DEFINITELY SOME PHONEY!)
BY SHELDON MAYER..
FOLKS--- POMPEII HAD ITS VESUVIOUS- AND EARLY BALLOONISTS HAD THEIR GIANT GASBAGS —TODAY WE PRESENT A COMBINATION OF THE TWO---- THAT LYIN' LION, WHO BLOWS HIS TOP AS REGULARLY AS A VOLCANO, AND IT'S GUARANTEED 99¾% HOT AIR— THAT CHAMPION OF GAS... J. RUFUS LION D.S.P. (DEFINITELY SOME PHONEY!)
JUST A MINUTE— JUST A MINUTE— IS THAT SUPPOSED TO BE A DESCRIPTION OF ME?
WELL— IT AIN'T GEORGE WASHINGTON!
VELL- I RESENT IT! NYBODY READING THAT WOULD THINK DON'T TELL THE RUTH!
OW WHERE 'YA THINK ER GOIN'?
TO WORK FOR ANOTHER MAGAZINE, OF COURSE— ---IF I DON'T GET TOP BILLING--I QUIT!
JUST A MINNIT— YOU CAN'T WALK OUT IN TH' MIDDLE OF A STRIP!
IF YA DON'T LIKE TH' WAY IT STARTED— THEN START OVER— YER OWN WAY---
AH-- NOW THERE'S AN IDEA-- NOW STICK AROUND, BOYS AND GIRLS, AND SEE HOW IT SHOULD BE DONE!

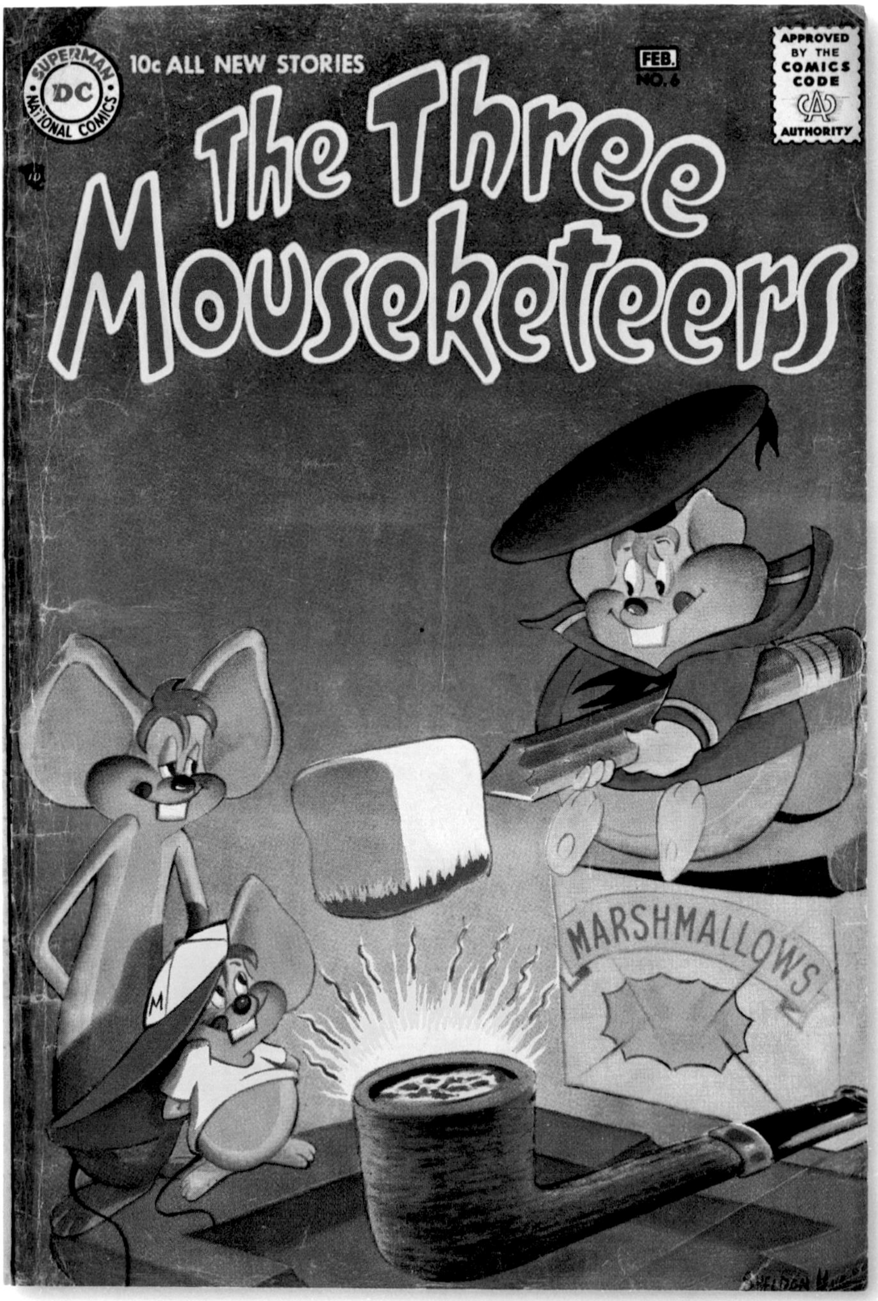
SUPERMAN DC NATIONAL COMICS
10c ALL NEW STORIES
FEB. NO. 6
APPROVED BY THE COMICS CODE AUTHORITY
The Three Mouseketeers
M
MARSHMALLOWS

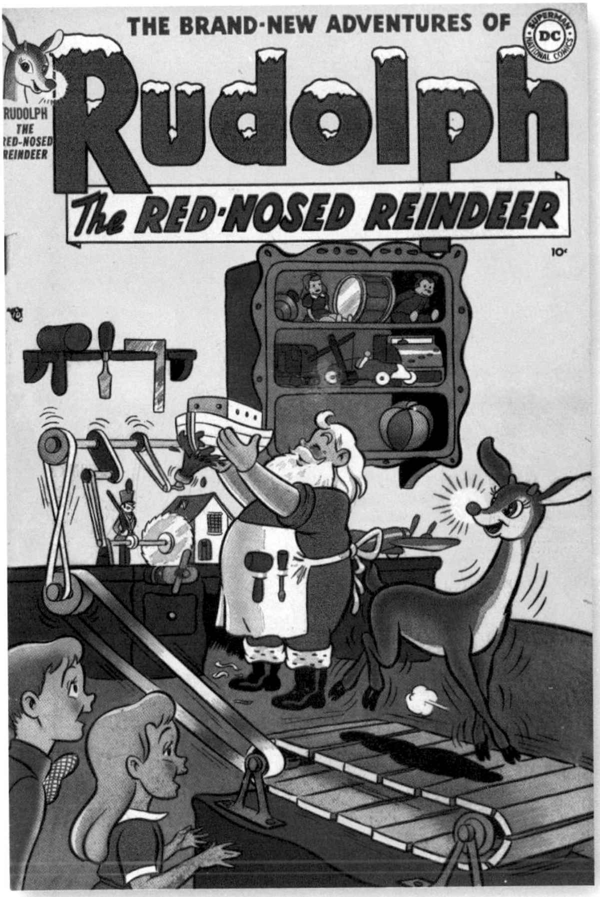
THE BRAND-NEW ADVENTURES OF
Rudolph
The RED-NOSED REINDEER
RUDOLPH THE RED-NOSED REINDEER
10¢

THE THREE MOUSEKETEERS No. 6

Cover art, Sheldon Mayer, January–February 1957. In 1955, DC put Sheldon Mayer to work on reviving its 1940s Three Mouseketeers feature. Unlike the early feature that was directly based on the Three Musketeers, the new version revolved around mouse kids Fatsy, Patsy, and Minus, who played in a tin can/clubhouse.

RUDOLPH THE RED-NOSED REINDEER No. 1

Cover art, Rube Grossman, 1950. First conceived by Robert L. May for a 1939 Montgomery Ward promotion, Rudolph was licensed by DC for an annual Christmas comic that ran for 12 years, and was later revived in the 1970s.

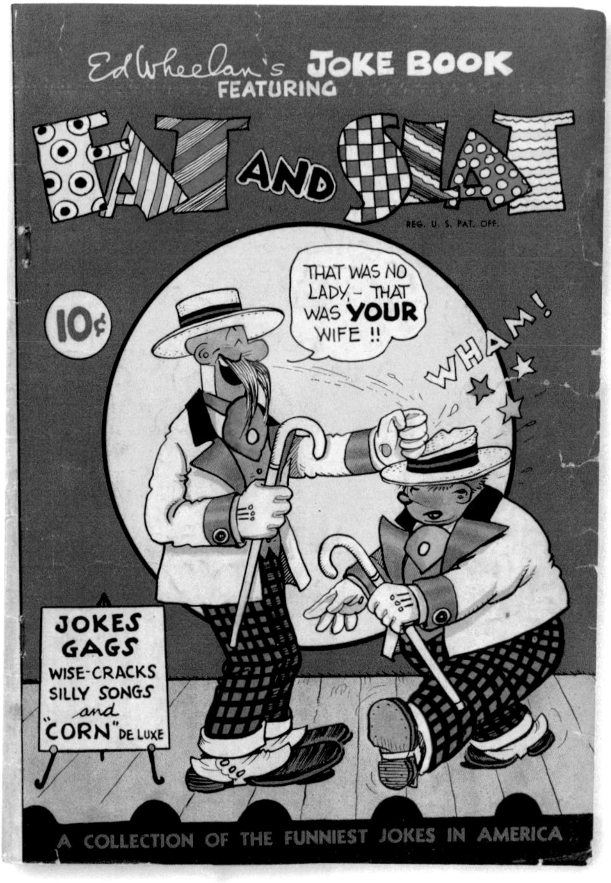
Ed Wheelan's JOKE BOOK
FEATURING
FAT AND SLAT
REG. U. S. PAT. OFF.
10¢
THAT WAS NO LADY, - THAT WAS YOUR WIFE !!
WHAM!
JOKES
GAGS
WISE-CRACKS
SILLY SONGS
and
"CORN" DE LUXE
A COLLECTION OF THE FUNNIEST JOKES IN AMERICA

ED WHEELAN'S JOKE BOOK No. 1

Cover art, Ed Wheelan, 1944. Longtime newspaper cartoonist Ed Wheelan brought his *Minute Movies* feature to the All-American line in the 1940s. This 1944 one-shot was filled with short vaudeville jokes delivered by Fat and Slat for the express purpose, the introduction explained, of delivering some levity into the grim wartime environment.

IT'S GAMETIME No. 3

Cover art, unknown, January–February 1956. Many 1950s DC titles were peppered with fillers featuring puzzles and word games. Given the low overhead in their production, DC published four issues of a title featuring nothing but those fillers before concluding there was no audience for them.

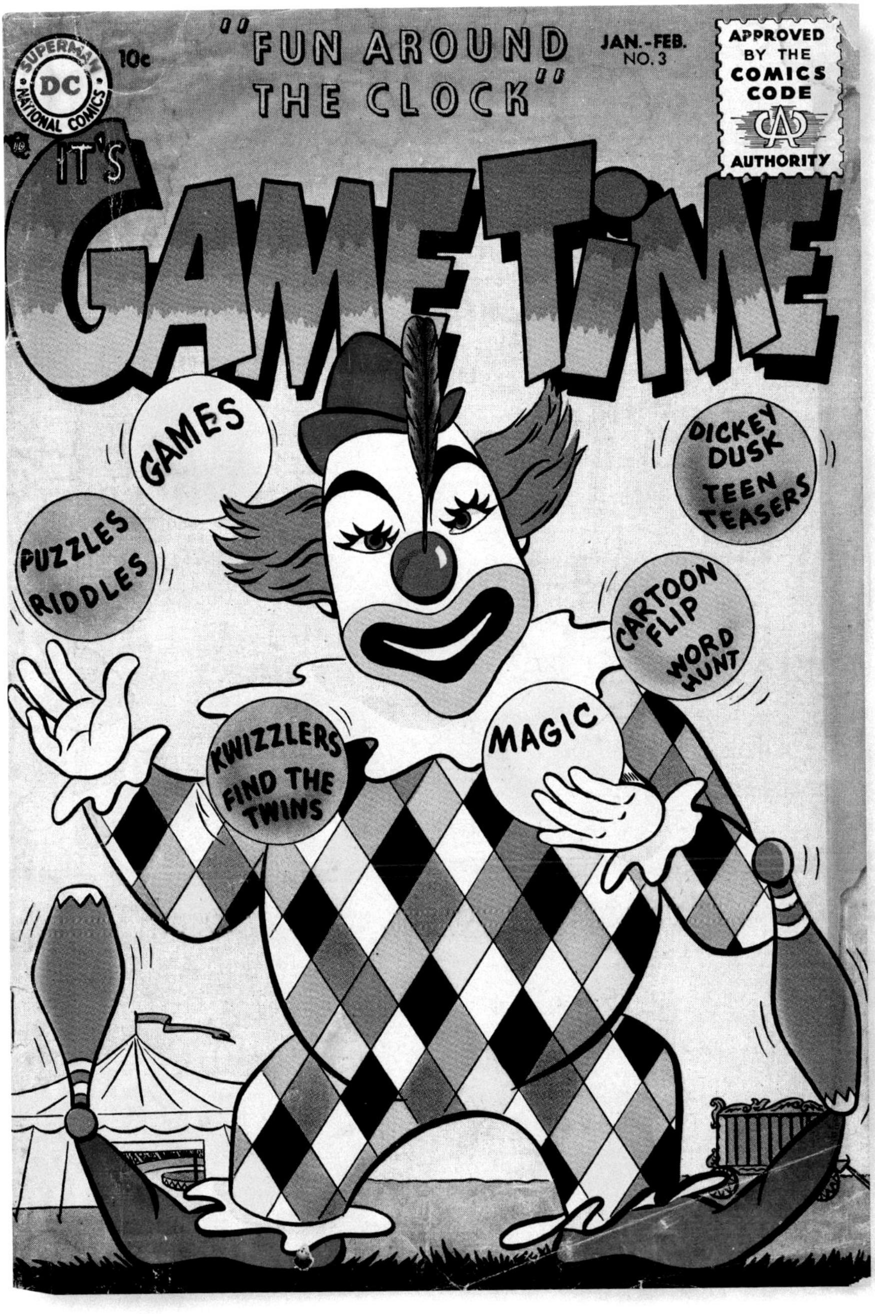
SUPERMAN DC NATIONAL COMICS
10c
"FUN AROUND THE CLOCK"
JAN.-FEB. NO. 3
APPROVED BY THE COMICS CODE AUTHORITY
IT'S
GAME TIME
GAMES
DICKEY DUSK
TEEN TEASERS
PUZZLES
RIDDLES
CARTOON FLIP
WORD HUNT
KWIZZLERS
FIND THE TWINS
MAGIC

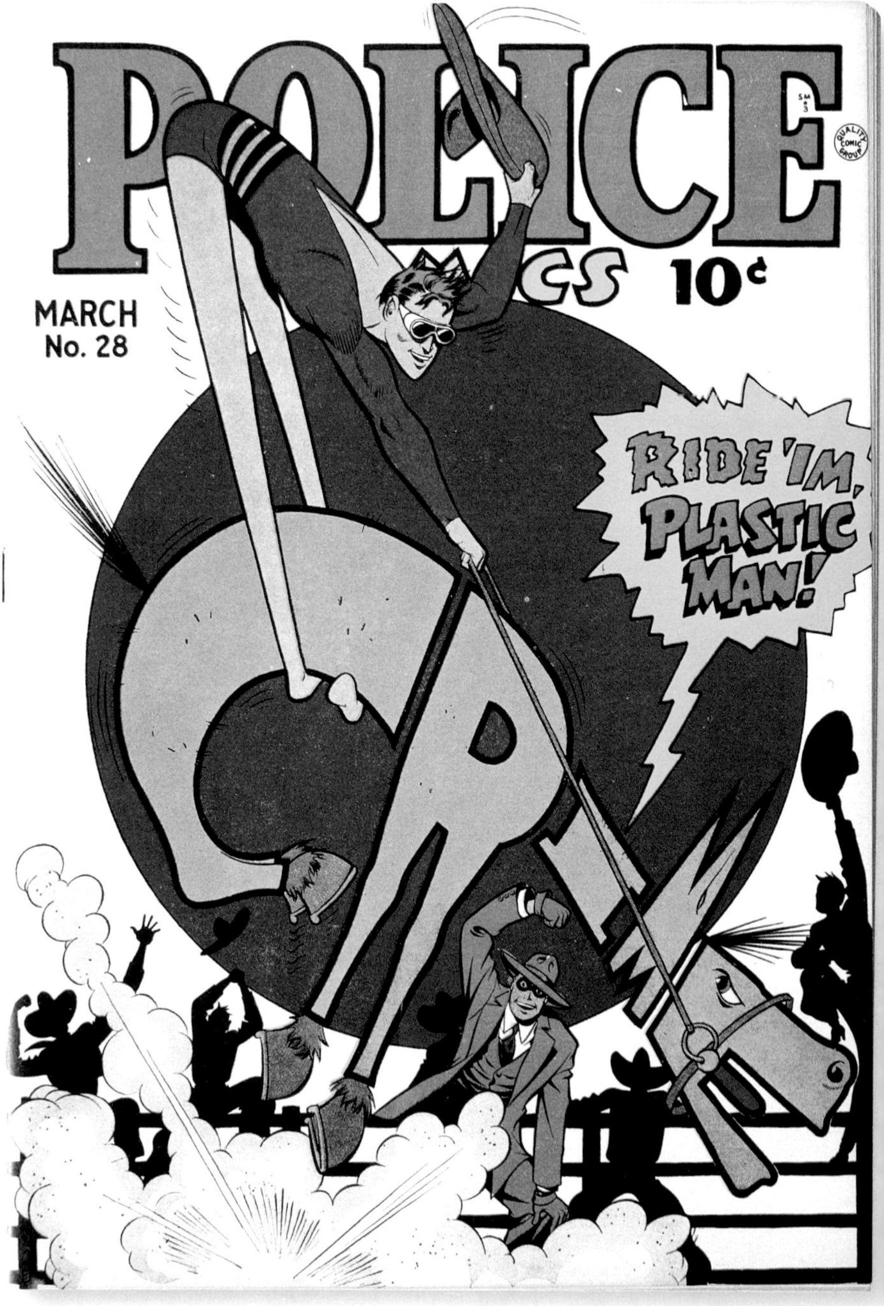
POLICE COMICS
10¢
MARCH
No. 28
QUALITY COMIC GROUP
RIDE 'IM, PLASTIC MAN!

Jack Cole

POLICE COMICS No. 28

Cover art, Jack Cole, March 1944. Two of the Golden Age's greatest cartoonists were both represented in *Police Comics*. Along with Cole's "Plastic Man," reprints of Will Eisner's syndicated feature "The Spirit" also appeared in the title. As a hedge against Eisner being drafted and "The Spirit" being discontinued, Quality Comics publisher Busy Arnold instructed Cole to create a visually similar character called Midnight, who appeared in *Smash Comics*.

JACK COLE

Photograph, Cole in his home studio, 1938. As part of the Harry "A" Chesler shop that produced material for earlier comic books, Cole's early work consisted primarily of humorous fillers.

"Jack Cole is one of the most innovative of the Golden Age comic book writer-illustrators.... Visually, Cole's humor is about as good as it gets.... Cole's extroverted zaniness in Plastic Man certainly forecasts the humor of *MAD* in the 1950s. There's no holding back with him; he literally comes at you from all angles."

—HARVEY PEKAR

PLASTIC MAN No. 1
Interior, "Plastic Man": script, pencils, and inks. Jack Cole. Summer 1943. Racial stereotyping was common throughout popular culture in this era, and Plastic Man was no exception. Before creating Plas, Jack Cole had produced a feature for *Smash Comics* starring Wun Cloo, the Defective Detective, a character who actually acquired stretchable powers in one story.

POLICE COMICS No. 38
Cover art, Jack Cole, January 1945.

THE GOLDEN AGE

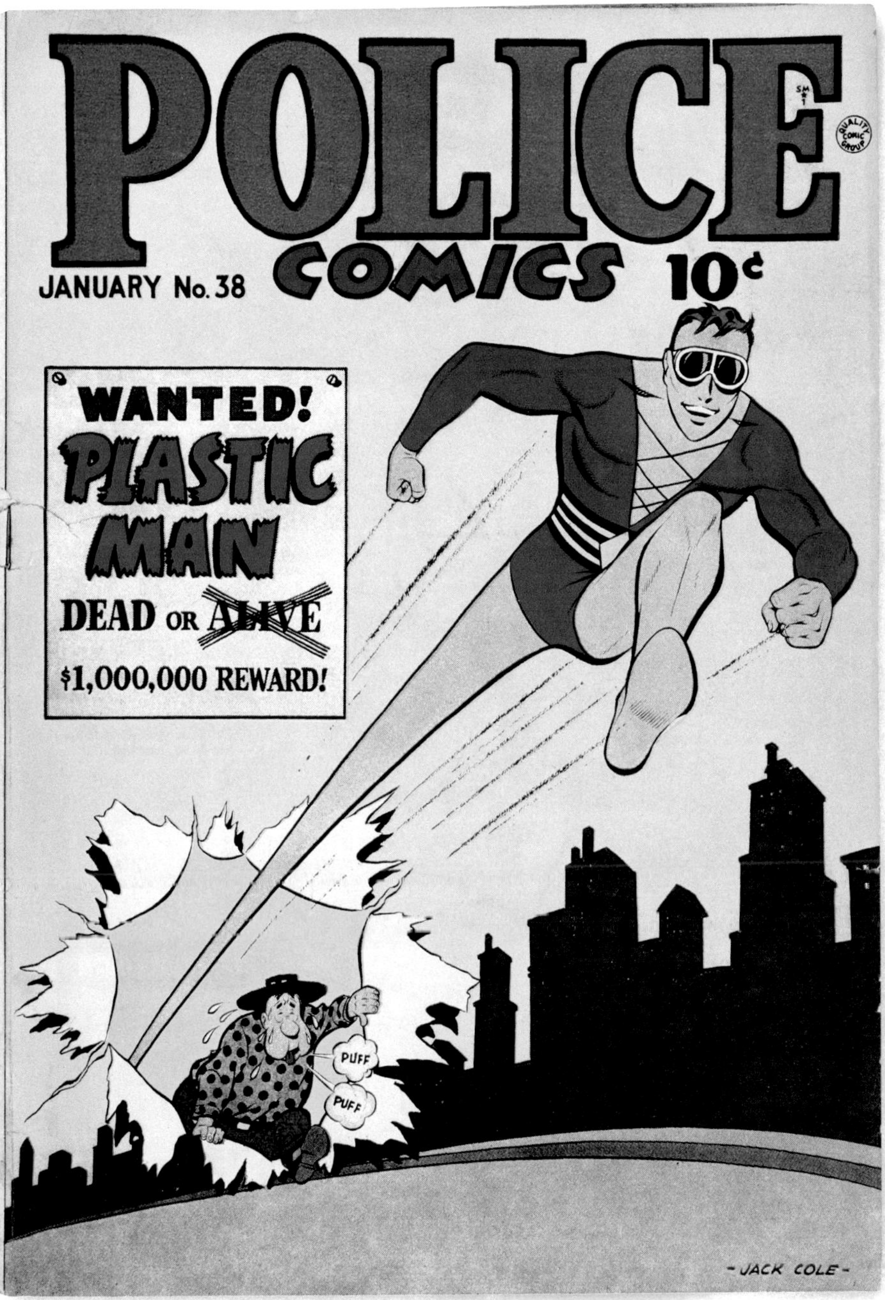
POLICE
COMICS
JANUARY No. 38
10¢
QUALITY COMIC GROUP
WANTED!
PLASTIC MAN
DEAD OR ~~ALIVE~~
$1,000,000 REWARD!
PUFF
PUFF
-JACK COLE-

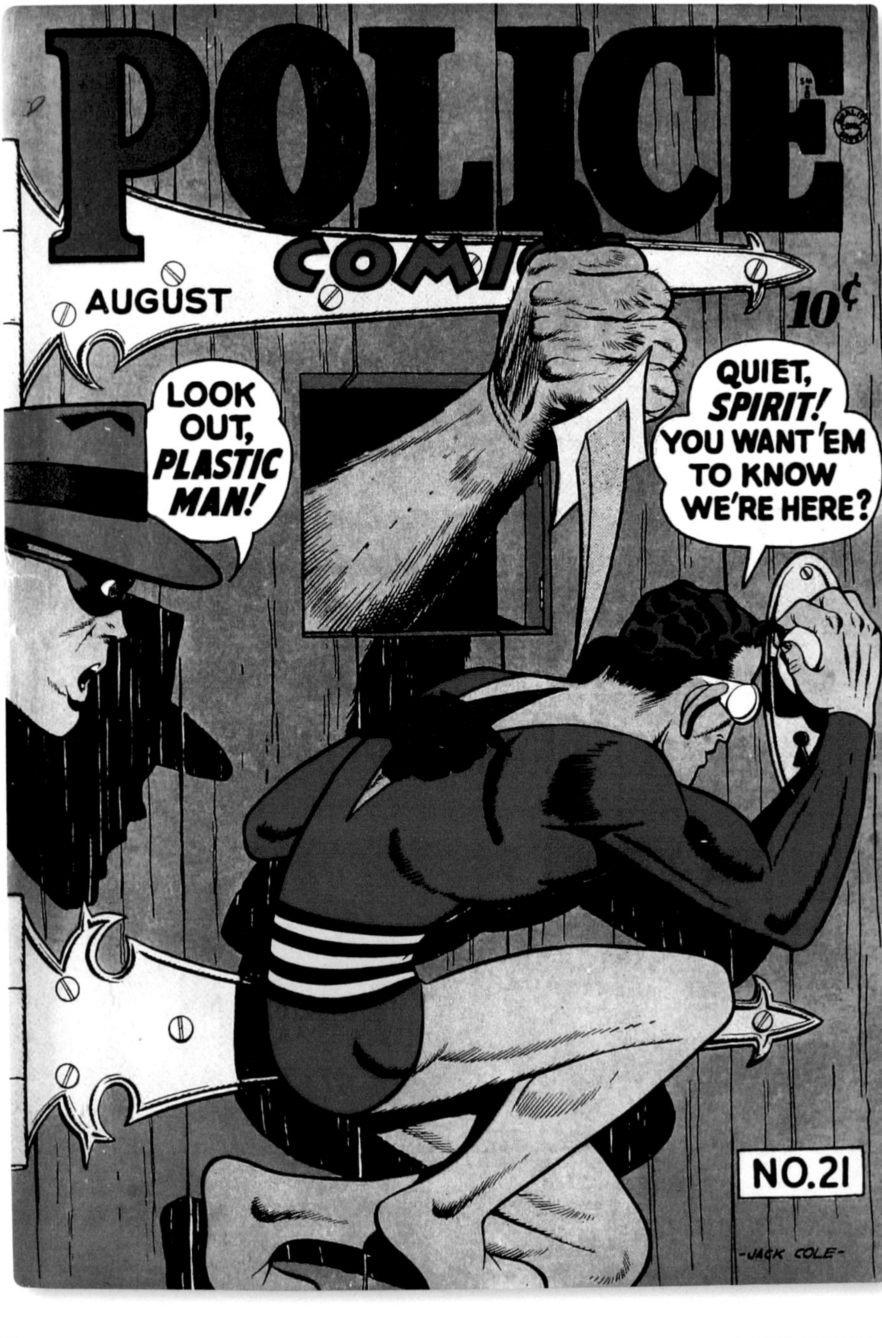
POLICE
COMICS
AUGUST
10¢
LOOK OUT, PLASTIC MAN!
QUIET, SPIRIT! YOU WANT 'EM TO KNOW WE'RE HERE?
NO.21
-JACK COLE-

POLICE COMICS No. 21

Cover art, Jack Cole, August 1943.

POLICE COMICS No. 9

Interior, "Satan's Son Sells Out to the Japs"; script and art, Jack Cole. May 1942. Despite reforming after he acquired his pliable body, Plastic Man maintained his gangster alter ego Eel O'Brian for more than a year. Now working for the FBI, Plas was finally found out, but his superior, Chief Branner, arranged for a full pardon.

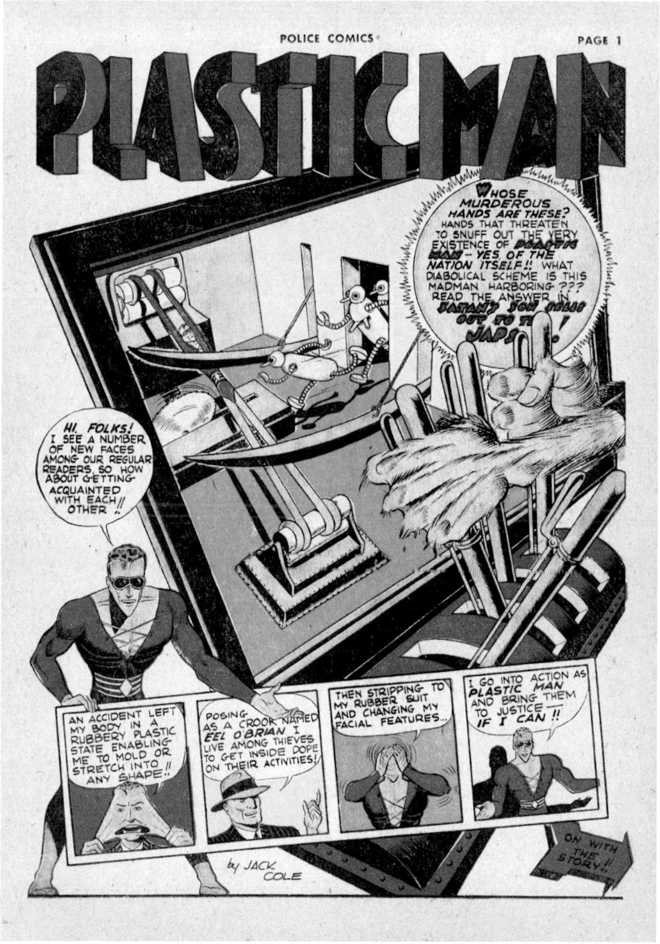

POLICE COMICS
PAGE 1
PLASTIC MAN
WHOSE MURDEROUS HANDS ARE THESE? HANDS THAT THREATEN TO SNUFF OUT THE VERY EXISTENCE OF
- YES, OF THE NATION ITSELF!! WHAT DIABOLICAL SCHEME IS THIS MADMAN HARBORING??? READ THE ANSWER IN
HI, FOLKS! I SEE A NUMBER OF NEW FACES AMONG OUR REGULAR READERS, SO HOW ABOUT GETTING ACQUAINTED WITH EACH OTHER !!
AN ACCIDENT LEFT MY BODY IN A RUBBERY PLASTIC STATE ENABLING ME TO MOLD OR STRETCH INTO ANY SHAPE!!
POSING AS A CROOK NAMED EEL O'BRIAN I LIVE AMONG THIEVES TO GET INSIDE DOPE ON THEIR ACTIVITIES!
THEN STRIPPING TO MY RUBBER SUIT AND CHANGING MY FACIAL FEATURES...
I GO INTO ACTION AS PLASTIC MAN AND BRING THEM TO JUSTICE — IF I CAN !!
by JACK COLE
ON WITH THE STORY!!

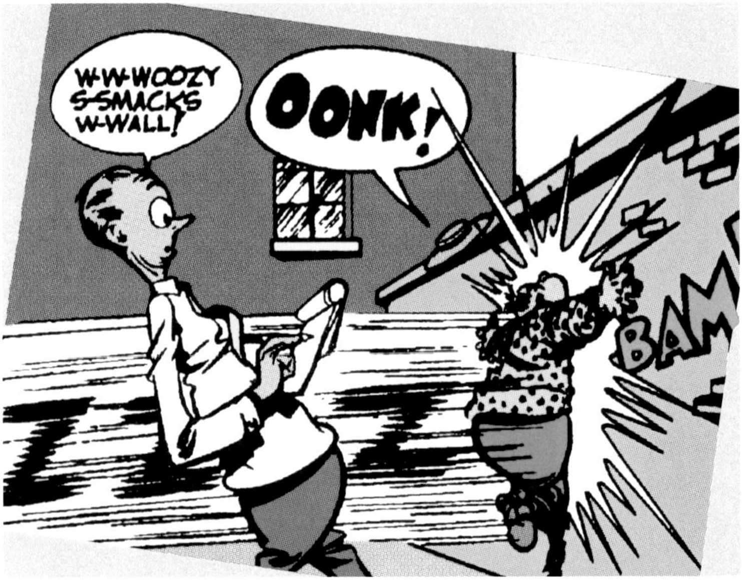
W-W-WOOZY S-SMACKS W-WALL!
OONK!
BAM

POLICE COMICS No. 20

Interior, "Woozy Winks Detective Agency"; script and art, Jack Cole. July 1943. Plastic Man creator Jack Cole periodically drew himself into his features, invariably portraying himself in an unflattering manner. In a Burp the Twerp episode in *Police* No. 2, Cole (as "Ralph Johns") killed a football team's lineup because he wanted to know how it "felt to make a dead-line!"

PLASTIC MAN No. 2

Interior, "Welcome to Coroner's Corners"; script and art, Jack Cole. August 1944. "As in animation, with its own laws of physics, where anything was possible, Cole extended those laws to his color pages—all in a fine sense of fun, mischief, discovery, achieving his goals in providing us more and more fast-moving kinetic action loops, panel to panel." —Alex Toth

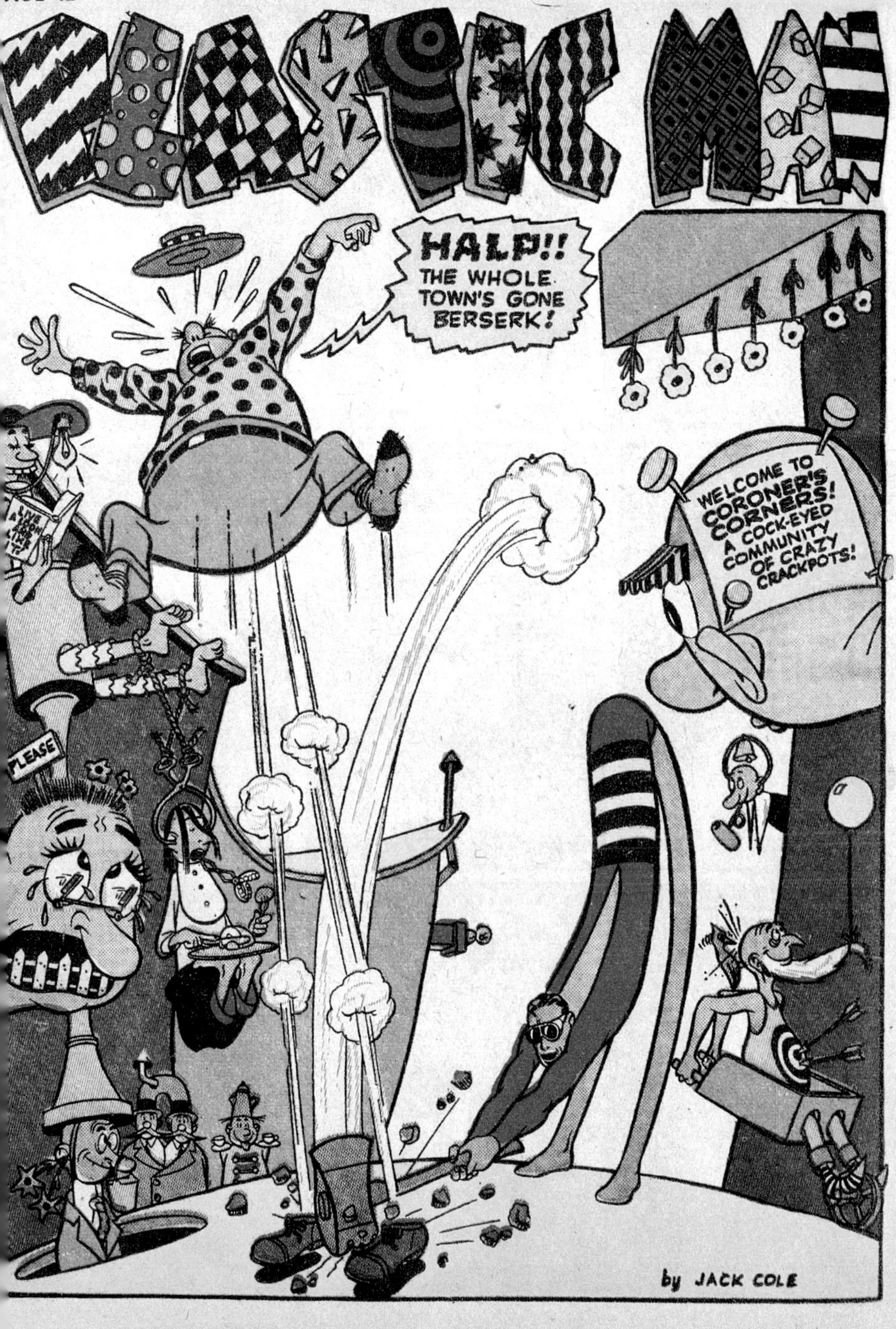
PLASTIC MAN
HALP!! THE WHOLE TOWN'S GONE BERSERK!
WELCOME TO CORONER'S CORNERS! A COCK-EYED COMMUNITY OF CRAZY CRACKPOTS!
PLEASE
by JACK COLE

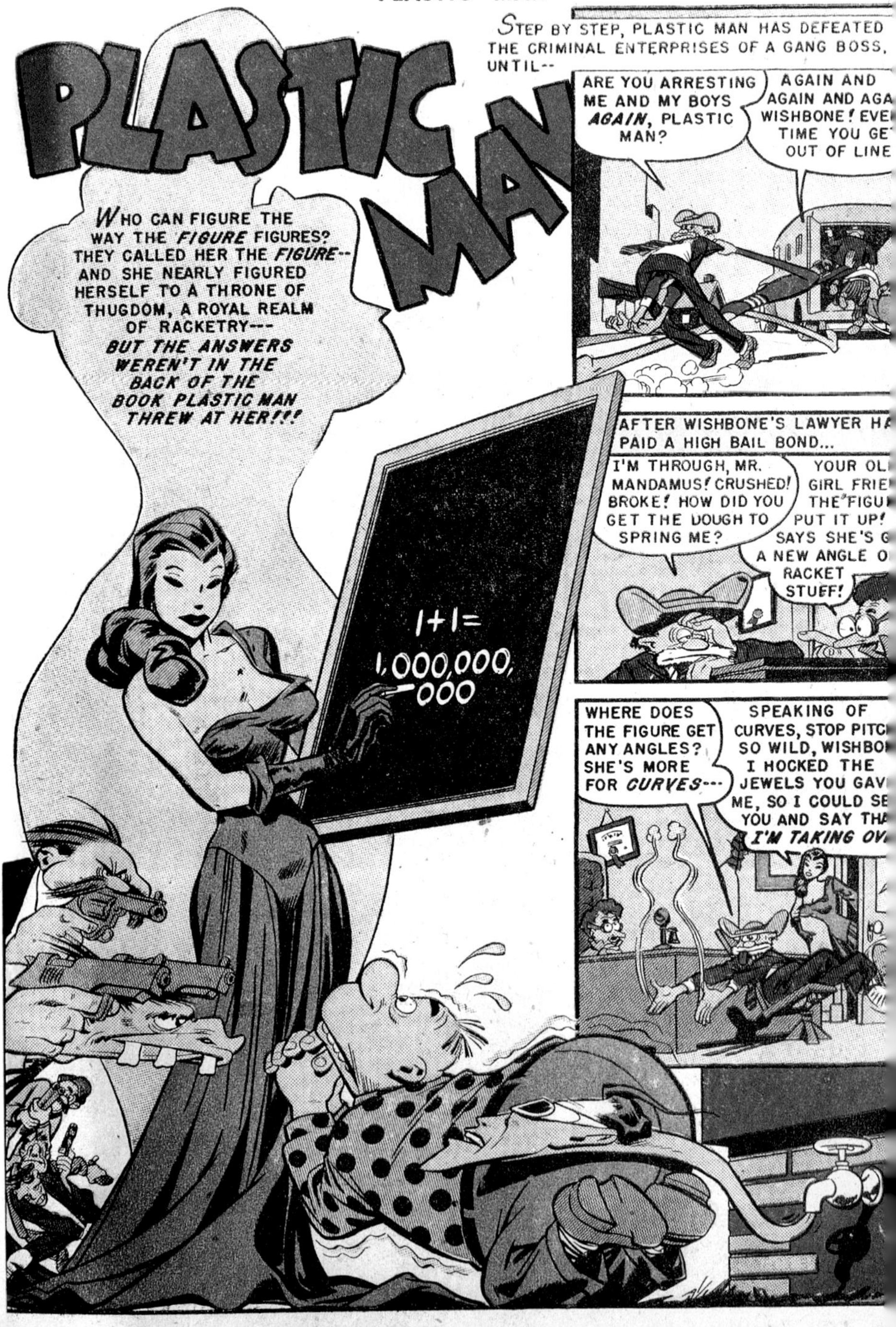
PLASTIC MAN
WHO CAN FIGURE THE WAY THE FIGURE FIGURES? THEY CALLED HER THE FIGURE-- AND SHE NEARLY FIGURED HERSELF TO A THRONE OF THUGDOM, A ROYAL REALM OF RACKETRY--- BUT THE ANSWERS WEREN'T IN THE BACK OF THE BOOK PLASTIC MAN THREW AT HER!!!
1+1= 1,000,000,000
STEP BY STEP, PLASTIC MAN HAS DEFEATED THE CRIMINAL ENTERPRISES OF A GANG BOSS, UNTIL--
ARE YOU ARRESTING ME AND MY BOYS AGAIN, PLASTIC MAN?
AGAIN AND AGAIN AND AGA WISHBONE! EVE TIME YOU GE OUT OF LINE
AFTER WISHBONE'S LAWYER HA PAID A HIGH BAIL BOND...
I'M THROUGH, MR. MANDAMUS! CRUSHED! BROKE! HOW DID YOU GET THE DOUGH TO SPRING ME?
YOUR OL GIRL FRIE THE FIGU PUT IT UP! SAYS SHE'S G A NEW ANGLE O RACKET STUFF!
WHERE DOES THE FIGURE GET ANY ANGLES? SHE'S MORE FOR CURVES---
SPEAKING OF CURVES, STOP PITC SO WILD, WISHBO I HOCKED THE JEWELS YOU GAV ME, SO I COULD SE YOU AND SAY THA I'M TAKING OV

"Although I'm slightly embarrassed to confess to being in love with a super hero comic, Jack Cole's Plastic Man belongs high on any adult's How to Avoid Prozac list, up there with the best of S. J. Perelman, Laurel and Hardy, Damon Runyon, Tex Avery, and the Marx Brothers."

—ART SPIEGELMAN

PLASTIC MAN No. 23

Interior. "The Figure"; script, unknown; pencils and inks, Jack Cole. August 1943. Beautiful women were as unattainable to Plastic Man as they were deadly. The Figure, Beauteous Bessie, and the Granite Lady were just a few of the femme fatales to cross his path. Cole, an unabashed fan of the woman's sensual form, went on to draw lush cartoons that were an artistic highlight of 1950s issues of Hugh Hefner's *Playboy* magazine.

POLICE COMICS No. 54

Cover art, Jack Cole, May 1946. "In Plastic Man's adventures, we see the dream images, fantasies, and strange dislocations of Dalí, de Chirico, and Magritte." —Peter L. Myer

POLICE COMICS No. 25

Interior, "The Rare Edition Murders"; script, pencils, and inks, Jack Cole. December 1943. The influence of Will Eisner's striking splash pages for *The Spirit* is evident in this nicely constructed piece that incorporates the Plastic Man logo into the design.

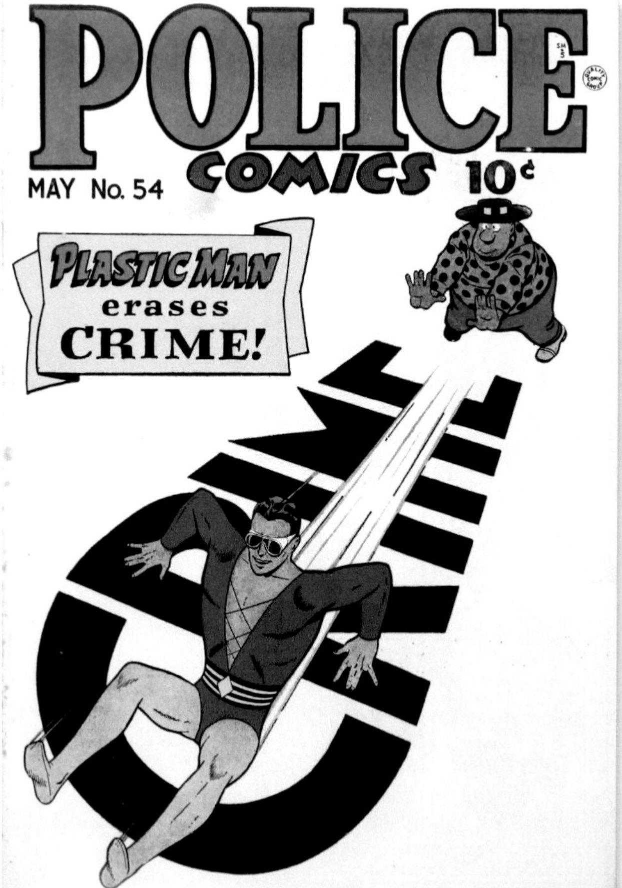
POLICE
COMICS
MAY No. 54
10¢
PLASTIC MAN
erases
CRIME!

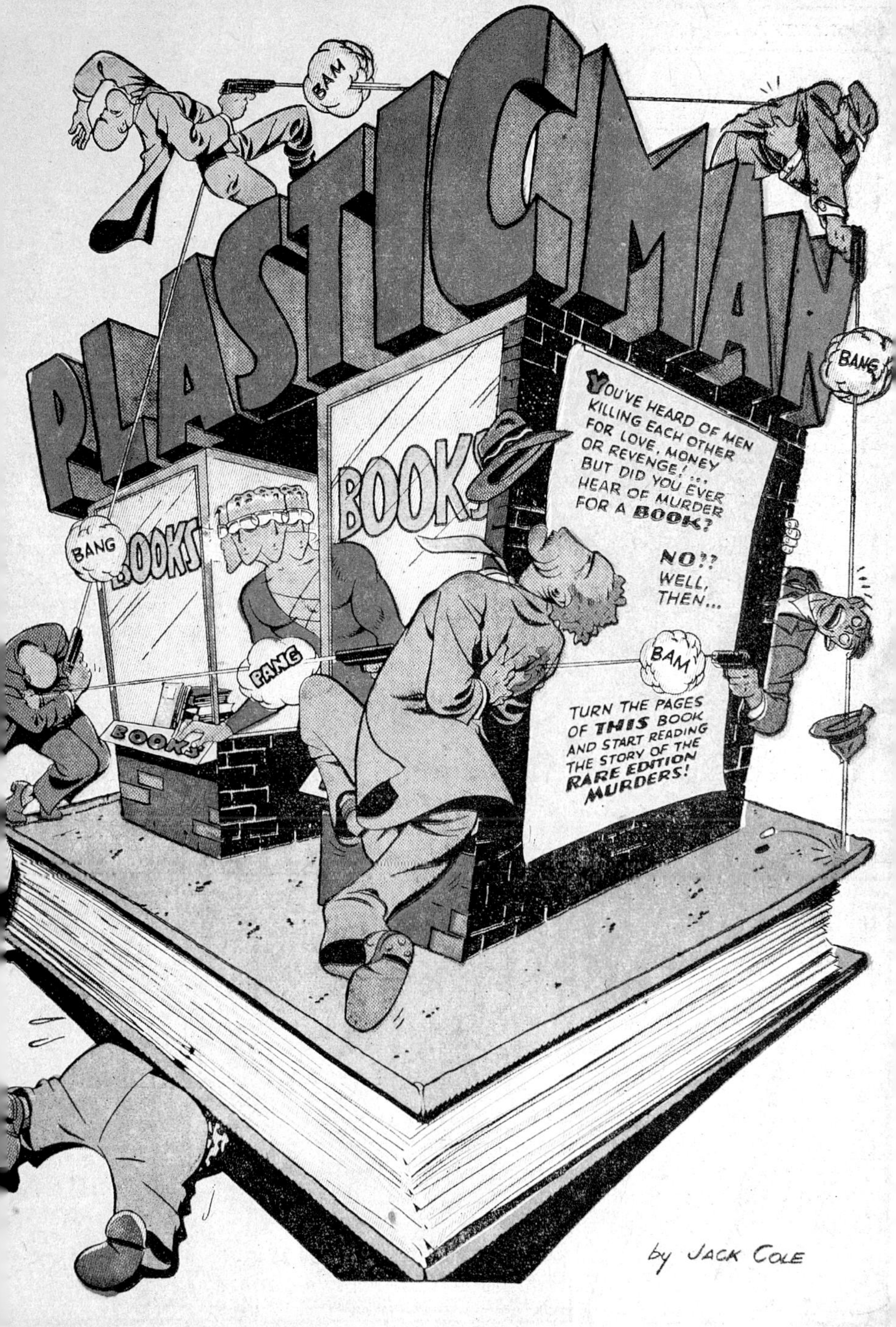
PLASTIC MAN
BAM
BANG
BOOKS
BOOKS
BANG
PANG
BOOKS
BAM
YOU'VE HEARD OF MEN KILLING EACH OTHER FOR LOVE, MONEY OR REVENGE! ... BUT DID YOU EVER HEAR OF MURDER FOR A BOOK?
NO?? WELL, THEN...
TURN THE PAGES OF THIS BOOK AND START READING THE STORY OF THE RARE EDITION MURDERS!
by JACK COLE

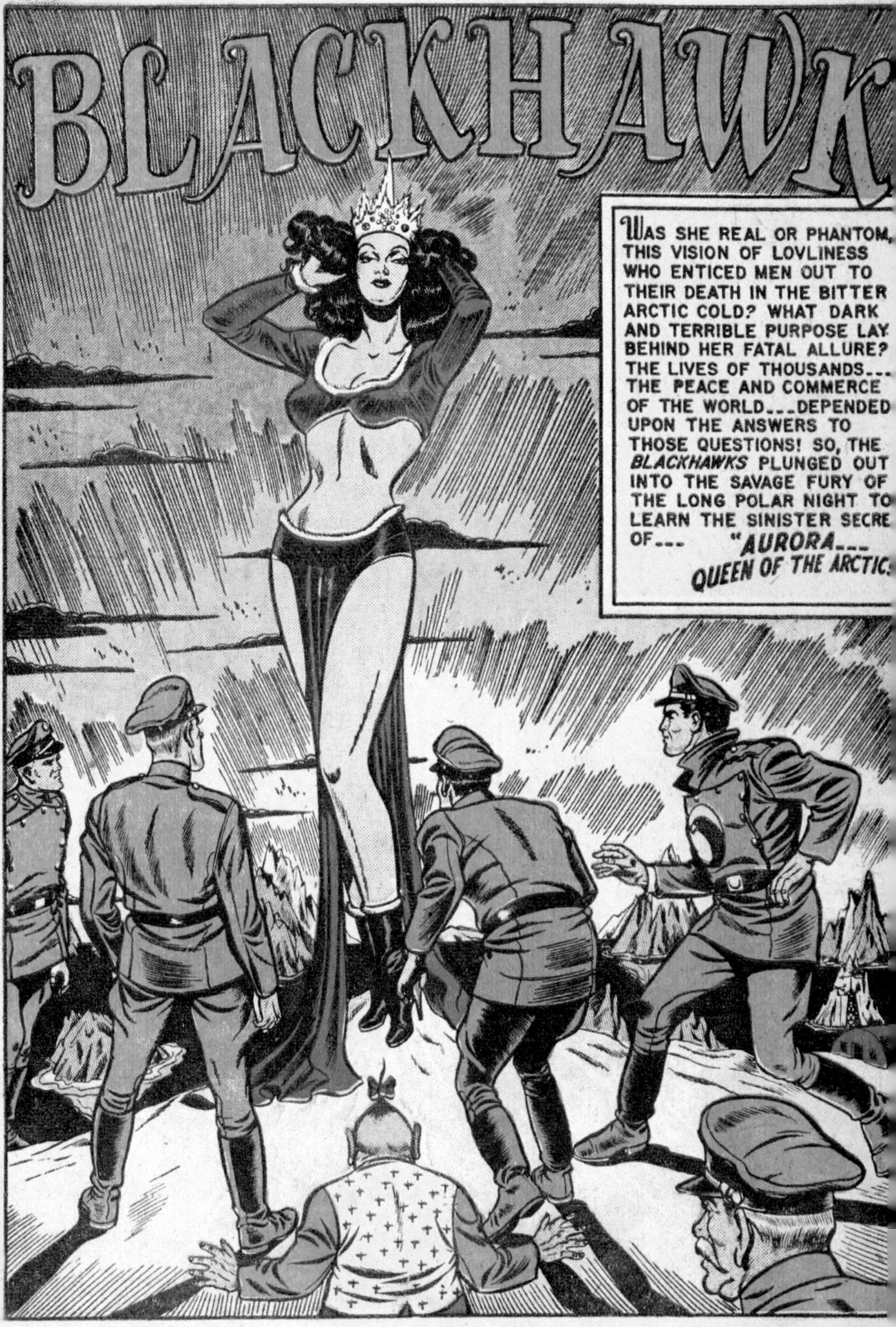
BLACKHAWK
WAS SHE REAL OR PHANTOM, THIS VISION OF LOVLINESS WHO ENTICED MEN OUT TO THEIR DEATH IN THE BITTER ARCTIC COLD? WHAT DARK AND TERRIBLE PURPOSE LAY BEHIND HER FATAL ALLURE? THE LIVES OF THOUSANDS... THE PEACE AND COMMERCE OF THE WORLD...DEPENDED UPON THE ANSWERS TO THOSE QUESTIONS! SO, THE BLACKHAWKS PLUNGED OUT INTO THE SAVAGE FURY OF THE LONG POLAR NIGHT TO LEARN THE SINISTER SECRE OF... "AURORA... QUEEN OF THE ARCTIC

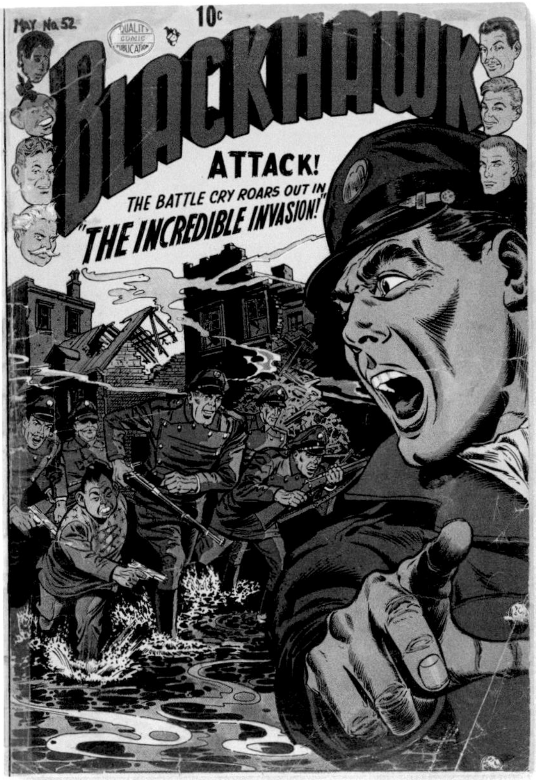
MAY No. 52
10¢
QUALITY COMIC PUBLICATION
BLACKHAWK
ATTACK!
THE BATTLE CRY ROARS OUT IN
"THE INCREDIBLE INVASION!"

BLACKHAWK No. 37

Interior, "Aurora... Queen of the Arctic"; script, unknown; pencils and inks, attributed Bill Quackenbush. February 1951. Much as Milton Caniff's "Terry and the Pirates" and Will Eisner's *The Spirit* often tempted its male heroes with the opposite sex, the Blackhawks regularly crossed paths with women who were as dangerous as they were beautiful. Most, like the ice queen Aurora, didn't survive for a rematch, but the exotic vigilante named Fear joined the aviators six times between 1946 and 1948.

BLACKHAWK No. 52

Cover art, Reed Crandall, May 1952. A hallmark of the *Blackhawk* series was the quality and precision of its artist, Reed Crandall. His initial period on the series was disrupted when he was drafted into the Army Air Force, but he returned following WWII to draw a celebrated run of stories through 1953, which brought about such classic menaces as Killer Shark and the War Wheel.

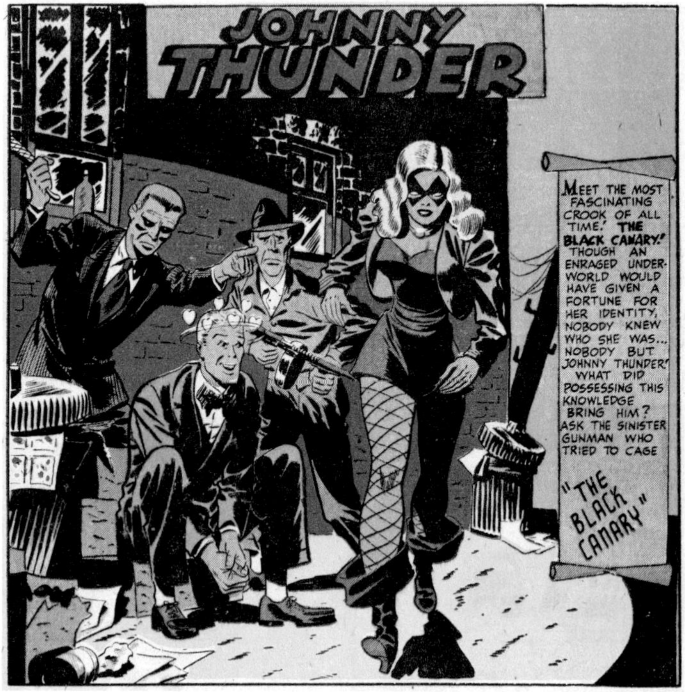
JOHNNY THUNDER
MEET THE MOST FASCINATING CROOK OF ALL TIME.' THE BLACK CANARY.' THOUGH AN ENRAGED UNDER-WORLD WOULD HAVE GIVEN A FORTUNE FOR HER IDENTITY, NOBODY KNEW WHO SHE WAS... NOBODY BUT JOHNNY THUNDER! WHAT DID POSSESSING THIS KNOWLEDGE BRING HIM? ASK THE SINISTER GUNMAN WHO TRIED TO CAGE
"THE BLACK CANARY"

FLASH COMICS No. 86

Interior, "The Black Canary"; script, Robert Kanigher; pencils, Carmine Infantino; inks, Joe Giella. August 1947. Introduced as a Robin Hood–style vigilante in the humorous Johnny Thunder series, Black Canary quickly established herself as a force for good, and actually replaced Johnny in *Flash Comics*. With a costume that included a blonde wig and fishnet stockings, the character was DC's last great heroine of the Golden Age and was awarded membership in The Justice Society of America.

TORCHY No. 1

Cover art, attributed Bill Ward, November 1949. The latter half of the 1940s saw a proliferation of what was later described as "good girl art," comic books featuring well-endowed women in revealing clothing. Cartoonist Bill Ward was one of the best-known practitioners of the form through his dim-witted comic heroine Torchy. Golden Age heroine Phantom Lady acquired an even skimpier costume and more-pronounced bosom in a 1947 revival by artist Matt Baker. The exaggerated emphasis on the female form soon became a point of contention with anticomics crusaders.

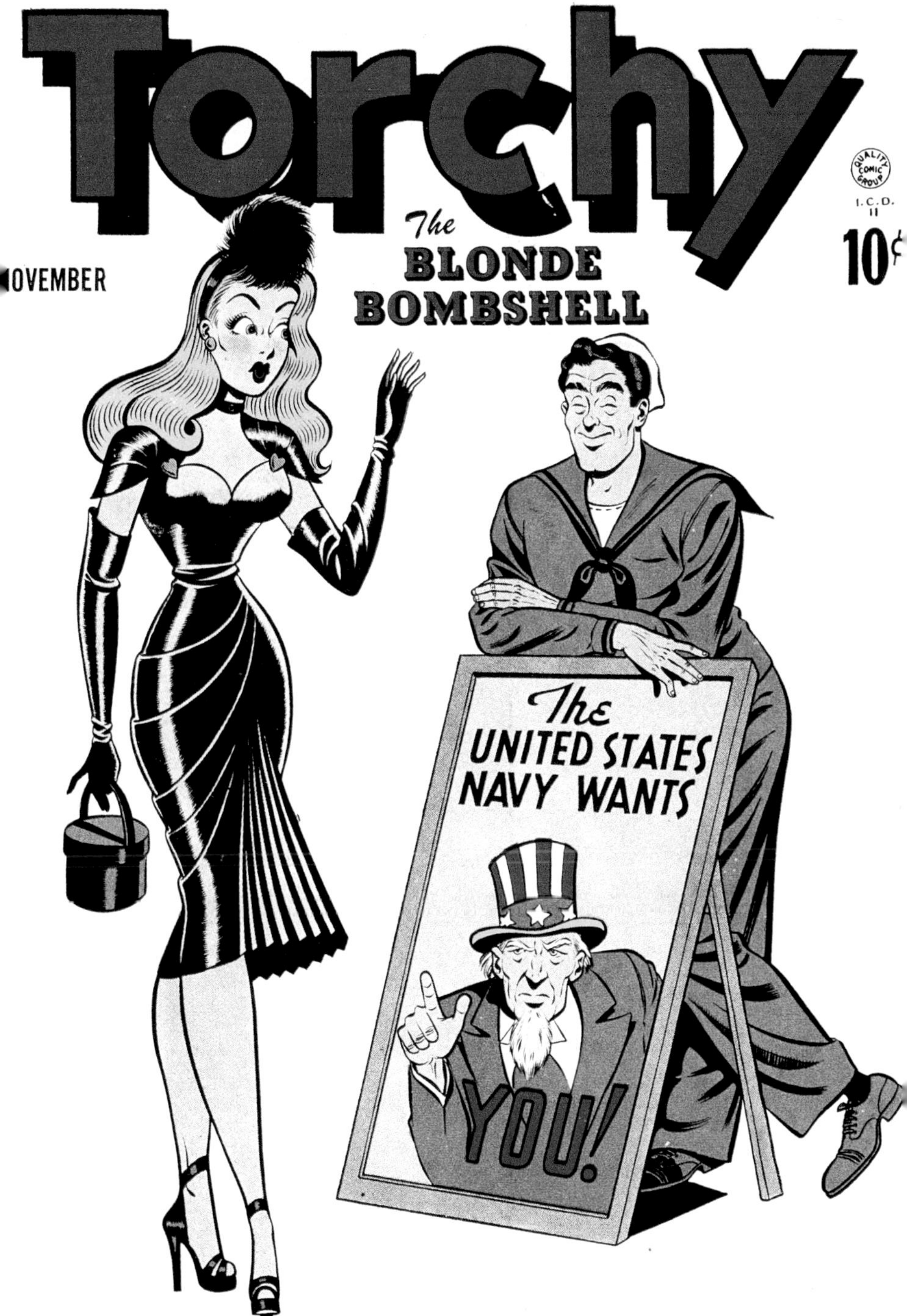
Torchy
The BLONDE BOMBSHELL
OVEMBER
QUALITY COMIC GROUP
I.C.D. 11
10¢
The UNITED STATES NAVY WANTS
YOU!

"Rarely by so much as a word or a glance is the tender passion suggested between Superman and Lois Lane. For one thing, Superman himself has shyly confessed that he would never embrace a girl, lest he inadvertently crack her ribs."

— JOHN KOBLER, *THE SATURDAY EVENING POST*, JUNE 21, 1941

SUPERMAN No. 63

Cover art, Al Plastino, March–April 1950. Beauty contests with women in bathing suits date back to 1921, but the competition in this story looked for females who also worked in dangerous professions. The finalists consisted of a cowgirl, a stuntwoman, a chemical engineer, and a trapeze artist.

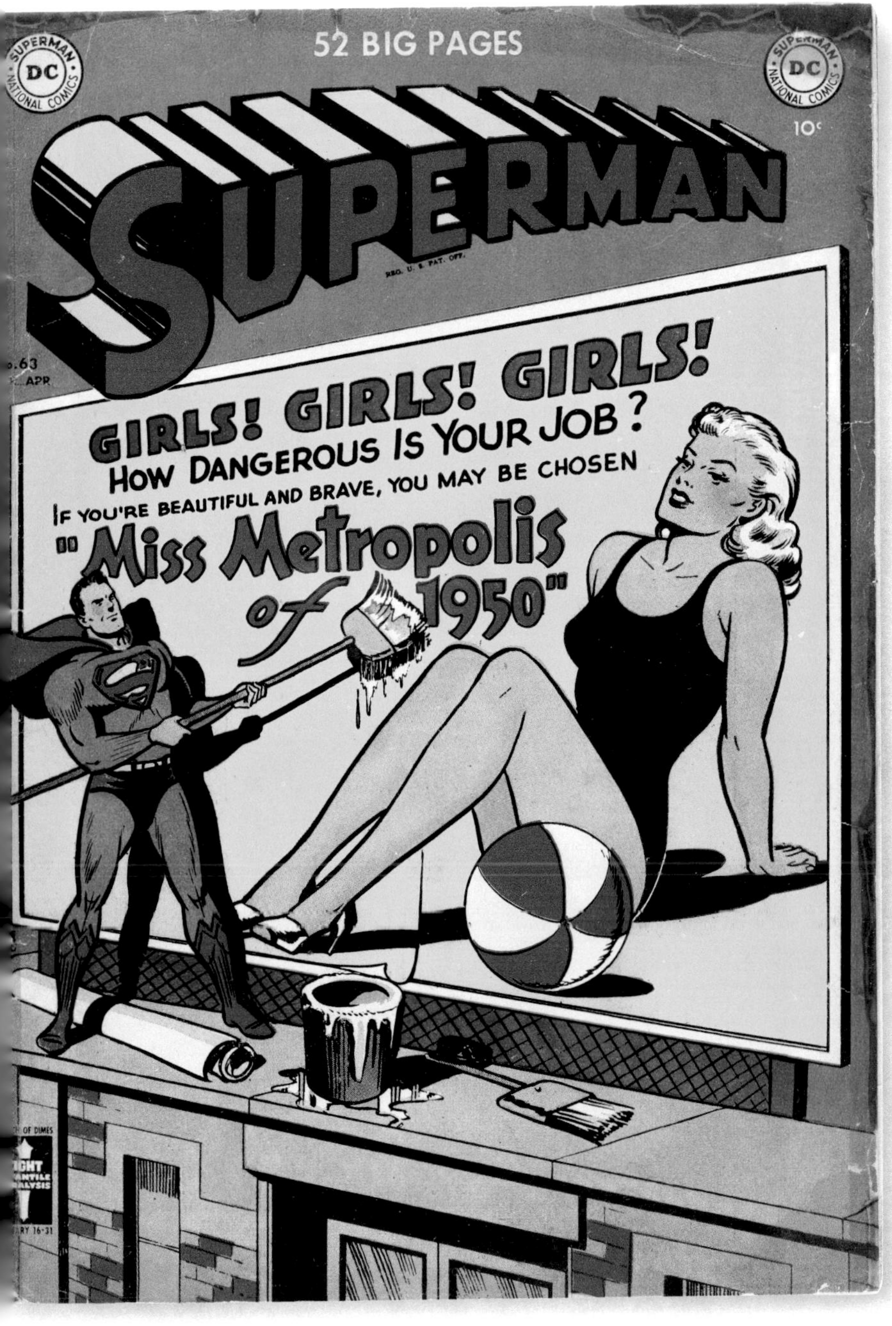
52 BIG PAGES
SUPERMAN
10¢
GIRLS! GIRLS! GIRLS!
HOW DANGEROUS IS YOUR JOB?
IF YOU'RE BEAUTIFUL AND BRAVE, YOU MAY BE CHOSEN
"Miss Metropolis of 1950"

SUPERMAN No. 67

Cover art, Al Plastino, November–December 1950. Lois doesn't think real-life singer Perry Como can hold a candle to Superman until she watches him perform. Realizing that he's disrupted the natural order of things, Como conspires to return the love-struck girl reporter's attention to the Man of Steel.

ACTION COMICS No. 154

Cover art, Win Mortimer, March 1951. What could be more romantic for a couple than being stranded together on a deserted island? In truth, the story behind the cover is more a battle of the sexes, with Clark Kent and Lois Lane engaging in a contest to determine which of them can better survive on the atoll.

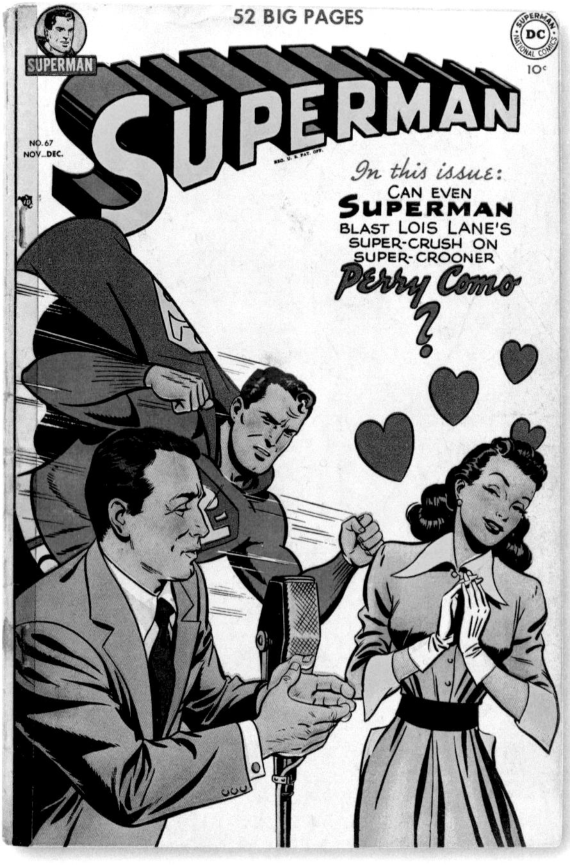
52 BIG PAGES
SUPERMAN
DC
10¢
SUPERMAN
NO. 67
NOV.–DEC.
In this issue:
CAN EVEN
SUPERMAN
BLAST LOIS LANE'S
SUPER-CRUSH ON
SUPER-CROONER
Perry Como
?

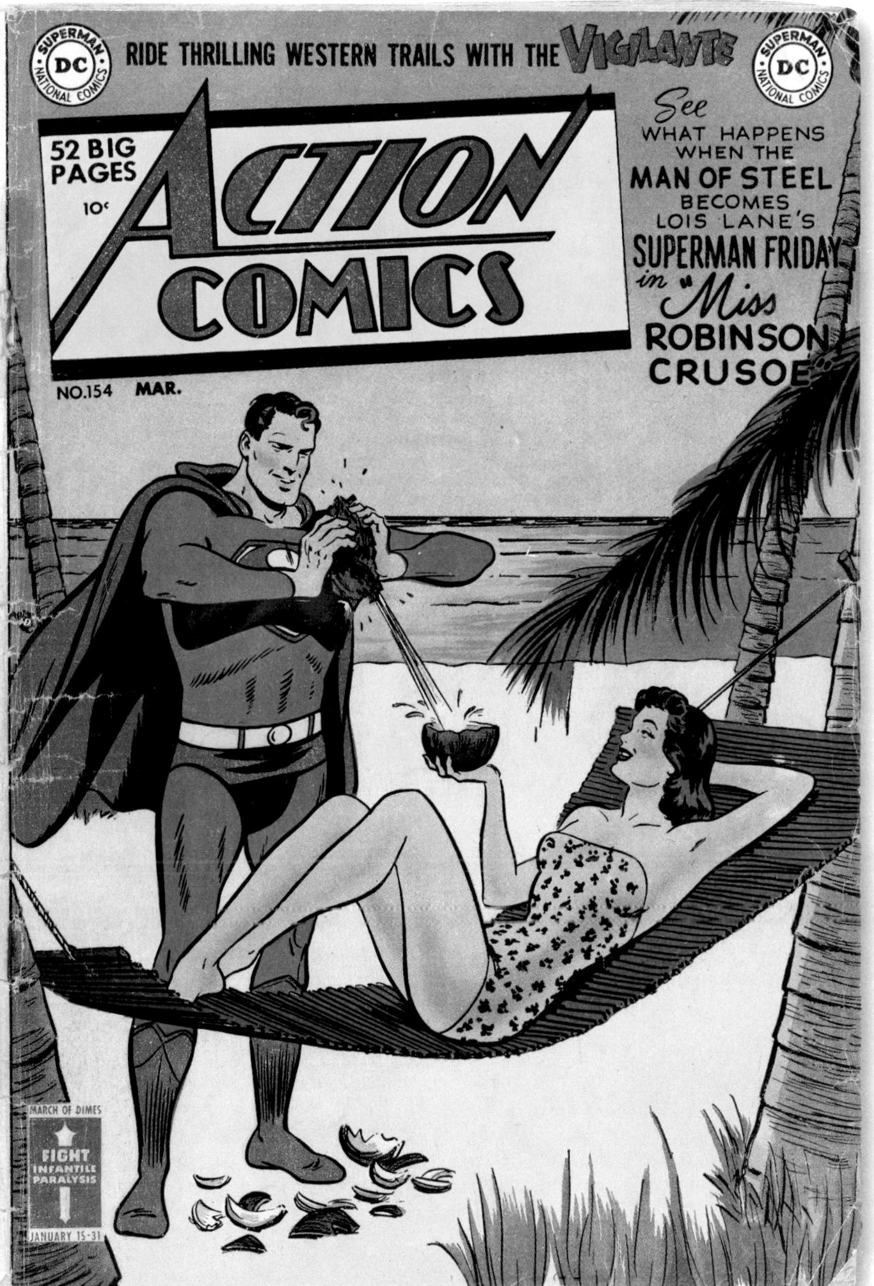
SUPERMAN DC NATIONAL COMICS
RIDE THRILLING WESTERN TRAILS WITH THE VIGILANTE
SUPERMAN DC NATIONAL COMICS
52 BIG PAGES
10¢
ACTION COMICS
NO.154 MAR.
See WHAT HAPPENS WHEN THE MAN OF STEEL BECOMES LOIS LANE'S SUPERMAN FRIDAY in "Miss ROBINSON CRUSOE"
MARCH OF DIMES
FIGHT INFANTILE PARALYSIS
JANUARY 15-31

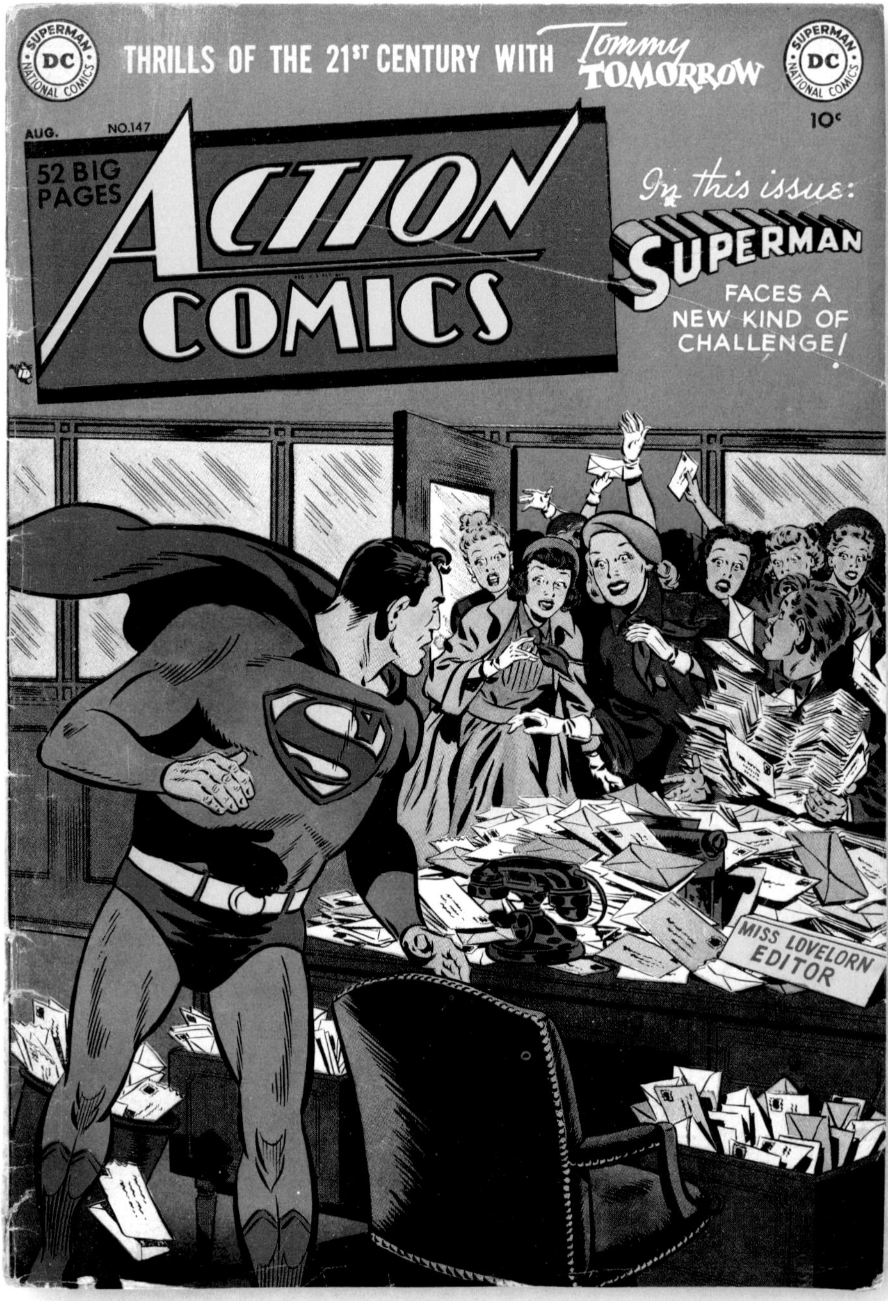
SUPERMAN DC NATIONAL COMICS
THRILLS OF THE 21ST CENTURY WITH Tommy TOMORROW
AUG.
NO.147
10¢
52 BIG PAGES
ACTION COMICS
In this issue:
SUPERMAN
FACES A NEW KIND OF CHALLENGE!
MISS LOVELORN EDITOR

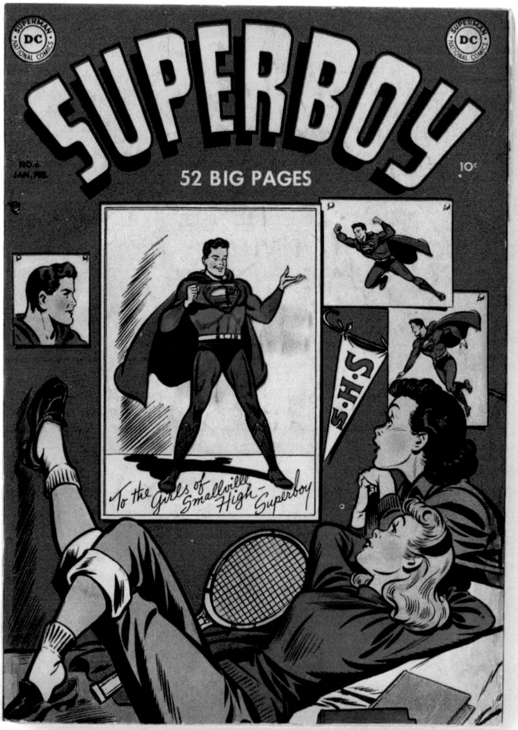
SUPERBOY
52 BIG PAGES
10¢
S·H·S
To the Girls of Smallville High - Superboy

ACTION COMICS No. 147

Cover art, Wayne Boring and Stan Kaye, August 1950. Lois Lane was far from alone in her yearning for Superman, although she didn't acquire any real competition until the 1950s, when newcomers like grade school and college sweethearts Lana Lang and Lori Lemaris were introduced. The women on this cover turn on Superman after he lets it slip that the writer of the *Daily Planet*'s lovelorn column is Clark Kent and not a sympathetic female as the newspaper implied.

SUPERBOY No. 6

Cover art, Al Plastino, January–February 1950. Even as super hero comic books were dying on the vine, *Superboy* was a surprise hit. It owed a share of its success to the fact that its teenage hero's interaction with bullies and girls had relevance to kids, but the fact that the feature was about the adventures of Superman as a boy surely didn't hurt.

SUPERBOY No. 12

FOLLOWING SPREAD: *Interior, Al Plastino, January 1951.*

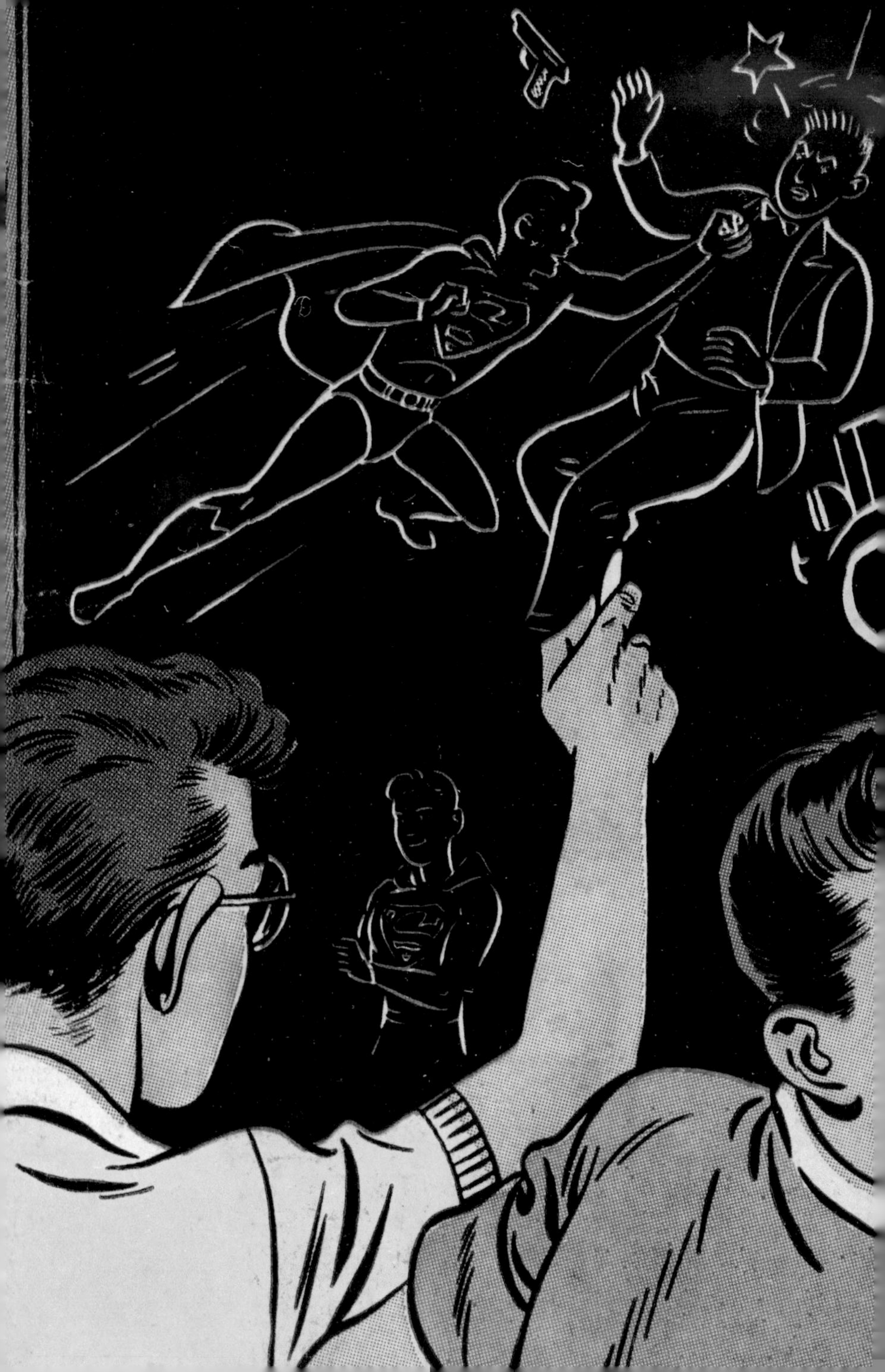

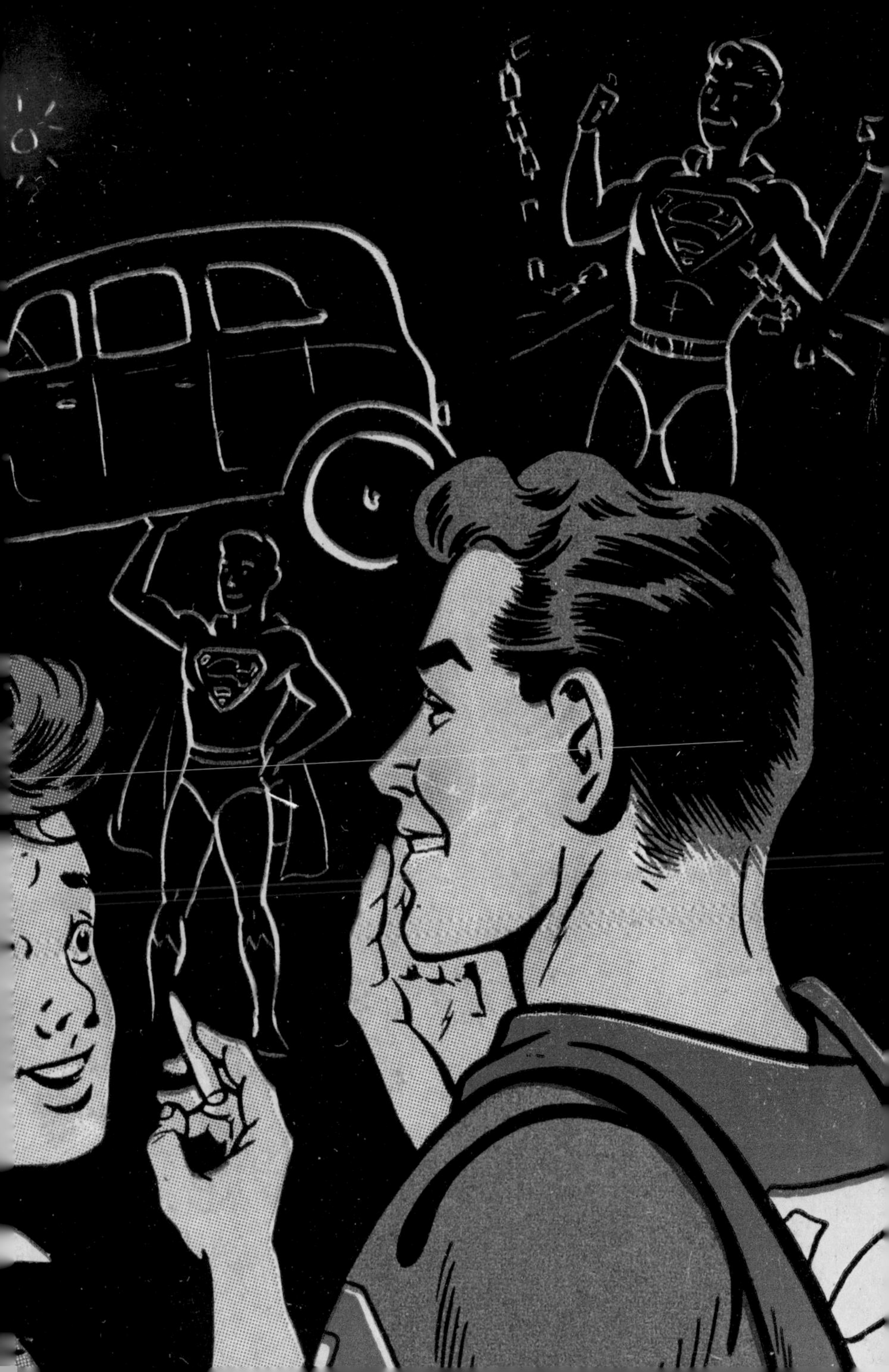

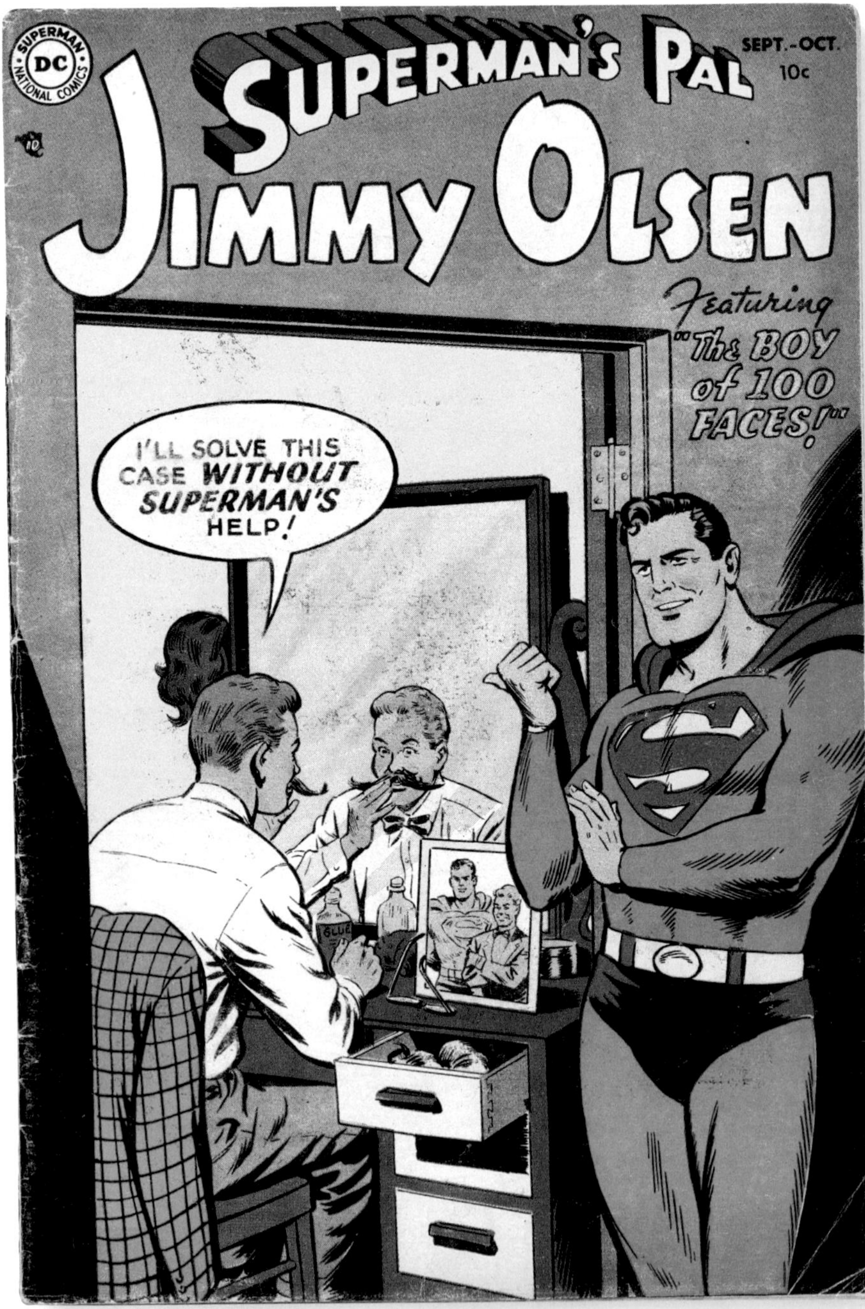
SUPERMAN DC NATIONAL COMICS
SUPERMAN'S PAL
SEPT.-OCT.
10c
JIMMY OLSEN
Featuring "The BOY of 100 FACES!"
I'LL SOLVE THIS CASE WITHOUT SUPERMAN'S HELP!
GLUE

SUPERMAN'S PAL, JIMMY OLSEN No. 1

Cover art, Curt Swan and Stan Kaye, September–October 1954. Much as Robin provided an identification for young Batman readers, Jimmy Olsen became a tremendous hit with fans through Jack Larson's portrayal of the character on the *Adventures of Superman* TV show. Although rarely featured in Superman comics prior to that point, the *Daily Planet* cub reporter was such a recognized character that DC had no qualms in giving him his own comic book.

LEAVE IT TO BINKY No. 11

Cover art, Bob Oksner, November–December 1949. With World War II over, high school students could worry less about being drafted into military service and more about cars and dating. The success of MLJ's Archie demonstrated that teenage humor comic books were an untapped market, and DC quickly followed suit, first with 1944's *Buzzy* and again with 1948's *Leave It to Binky*. Developed by Sheldon Mayer before he retired from editing, the series revolved around the antics of Binky Biggs, his girlfriend, Peggy, and their family and friends. Canceled after a decade, *Binky* was brought back in 1968 as a revival of teen humor comics began.

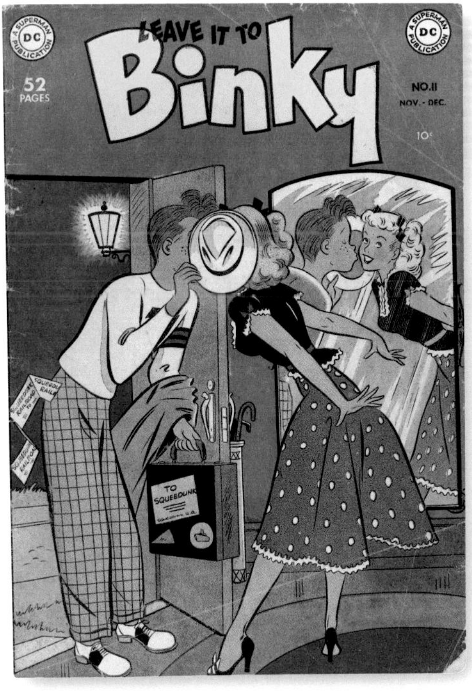
LEAVE IT TO
Binky
52 PAGES
NO. 11
NOV.-DEC.
10¢
TO SQUEEDUNK

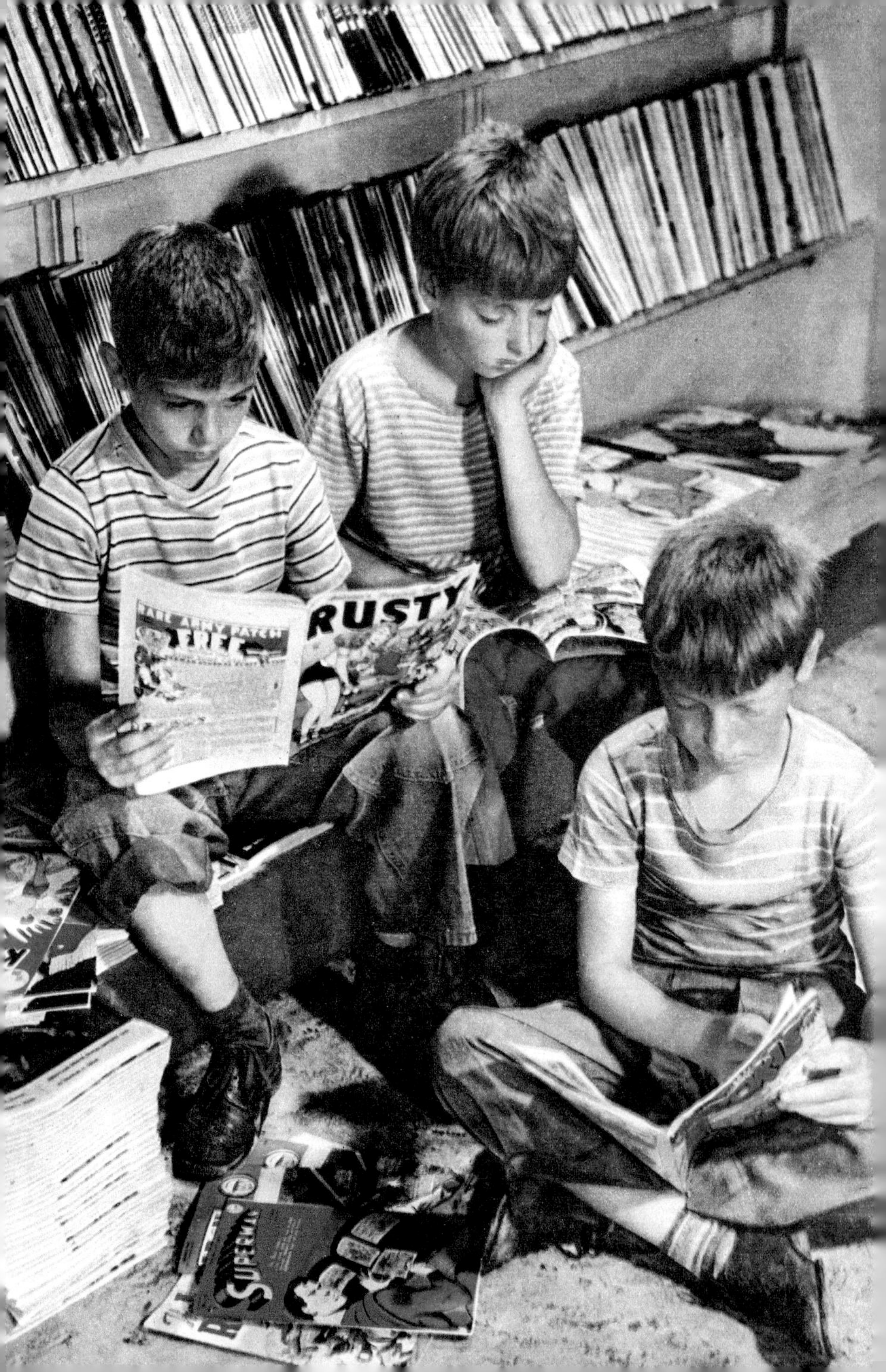
RUSTY
SUPERMAN

"If I were asked to express in a single sentence what has happened mentally to many American children I would say that they were conquered by Superman."

—FREDRIC WERTHAM

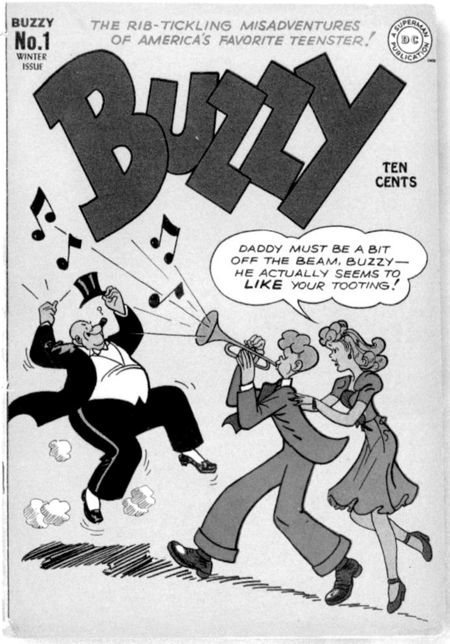

BUZZY
No.1
WINTER ISSUE
THE RIB-TICKLING MISADVENTURES OF AMERICA'S FAVORITE TEENSTER!
SUPERMAN DC PUBLICATION
BUZZY
TEN CENTS
DADDY MUST BE A BIT OFF THE BEAM, BUZZY— HE ACTUALLY SEEMS TO LIKE YOUR TOOTING!

NICKEL COMICS STAND

Photograph, ca. 1947. When comic book publishers spoke of their circulation, they often boosted the numbers by including pass-along readers—kids who read copies purchased by their friends. The pass-along effect was enhanced further through used book stores that sold old comic books for five cents, half the price of a new one.

BUZZY No. 1

Cover art, George Storm, winter 1944. DC's 1943 answer to *Archie*, which in 1941 put fledgling publisher MLJ on the map, was initially somewhat odd looking for teen humor, its art seeming curiously out of date. Original artist Storm seemed influenced by the "flapper" art of John Held Jr. After some editorial course correction, however, *Buzzy* enjoyed a run that lasted until 1958.

NO. 1
MAR...APR.
SUPERBOY
Ten Cents
SUPERMAN, WHAT WERE YOU LIKE WHEN YOU WERE A BOY?
IF THAT'S WHAT YOU'D LIKE TO KNOW, LOOK INSIDE!
GIVE

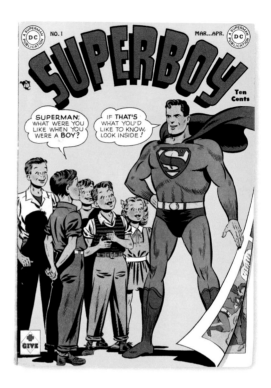

SUPERBOY No. 1

Cover art, Wayne Boring and Stan Kaye, March–April 1949. Originally conceived by Jerry Siegel to feature the comical antics of a preteen Superman who'd yet to adopt a costume, Superboy instead became a junior reflection of the Man of Steel with the same finely honed sense of morality and responsibility. Plans to publish a *Superboy* comic book during World War II were prevented by wartime paper shortages, and the character instead debuted without fanfare in 1944's *More Fun Comics* No. 101. After four years there and in *Adventure Comics*, the Boy of Steel finally won his own solo comic book.

STAR SPANGLED COMICS No. 14

Original interior original, "The Meanest Man on Earth"; script and art, Joe Simon and Jack Kirby. November 1942. If Superboy was a call-back to life in a small town, the Newsboy Legion was equally nostalgic for creators Jack Kirby and Joe Simon, who grew up in poor neighborhoods like their fictitious Suicide Slum. Life wasn't easy in the tenements, but it instilled the value of hard work and perseverance in both the Legionnaires and their creators.

FOUR MEMBERS OF THE NEWSBOY LEGION ARE SPENDING AN EVENING AT SOME NEAR SUICIDE SLUM... SHALL WE VISIT THEM? WHY NOT? LET'S DROP IN ON THEM...

WELL...THAT'S AN EDIFYING VIEW!

A BATH IS CERTAINLY REFRESHING AFTER A DAY'S WORK!

A BATH EVERY DAY! I NEVER HOID O' SUCH A DISGUSTIN' T'ING!!

COME ON, YOU GUYS! HUSTLE ALONG! WE'RE HAVIN' THAT COP, HARPER, OVER FOR SUPPER!

GADGETS! NOTHIN' BUT GADGETS!!! IT WAS EASIER IN THE OLD PLACE!

LATER, WHEN SUPPER IS SERVED... PATROLMAN JIM HARPER, GUARDIAN OF THE BOYS BY DECREE OF THE JUVENILE COURT, SITS DOWN TO A ROYAL REPAST!

YOU KIDS HAVE COME A LONG WAY FROM THE OLD DIGGINGS!

MAYBE! BUT THE COOKIN' AIN'T ANY BETTER!

WHAT'S WRONG WITH THESE PICTURES?

HOW COME OUR DIAMOND-IN-THE-ROUGH YOUNG FRIENDS, LAST SEEN LIVING IN A TUMBLEDOWN SHACK...ARE NOW RESIDING IN A MODERN UP-TO-DATE APARTMENT... PRACTICALLY THE LAP OF LUXURY FOR THESE SLUM KIDS..? WELL, IT'S QUITE A STORY...AND DESERVES TO BE TOLD FROM THE BEGINNING.... SIT IN....
YOU'LL LIKE IT!!

YOU SEE, MR. WILBUR WHILLING STARTED IT ALL WHEN HE FIRST GAZED AT THE ROTTEN SHAMBLES THAT WAS SUICIDE SLUM!

SOMETHING SHOULD BE DONE ABOUT THESE SLUMS... AND SOMETHING CAN BE DONE!

2

YOUNG LOVE No. 19

Cover art, Jack Kirby and Joe Simon, March 1951.

GIRLS' LOVE STORIES ASHCAN

Cover art, George Storm, 1949. Noting the proliferation of romance titles from other publishers, DC began locking down potential titles for their own love comics through ashcans produced to establish the trademark. The short-lived Western hybrid *Romance Trail* appeared first with *Girls' Love Stories* and *Secret Hearts* close behind.

FALLING IN LOVE No. 1

Cover art, Irv Novick, September–October 1955.

young Love
young Love
Big 52 pages! DON'T TAKE LESS!
10¢
MARCH No.19
the ORIGINAL YOUNG ROMANCE GROUP
JUMPING JUPITER! I DID NOTHING MORE THAN PAY THIS KID A FORMAL COMPLIMENT! AND SHE ACTS AS IF I JUST PROPOSED!
WHY DOESN'T NORA WAKE UP! SHE THINKS EVERY FELLOW IN TOWN IS HEAD OVER HEELS IN LOVE WITH HER! EVEN CLEOPATRA MUST HAVE BEEN PASSED UP BY A FEW MALES!
WHY, CHARLIE! I DIDN'T KNOW YOU FELT THIS WAY ABOUT ME! I THINK YOU'RE THE MOST WONDERFUL! GUY!

GIRLS' LOVE
STORIES
10 CENTS
COPR. 1949, NAT'L COMICS PUB., INC.
AUG. - SEPT.

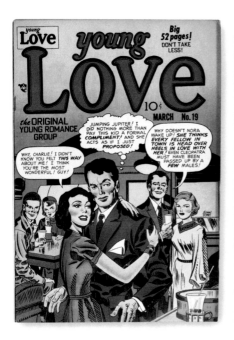

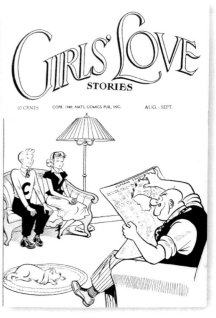

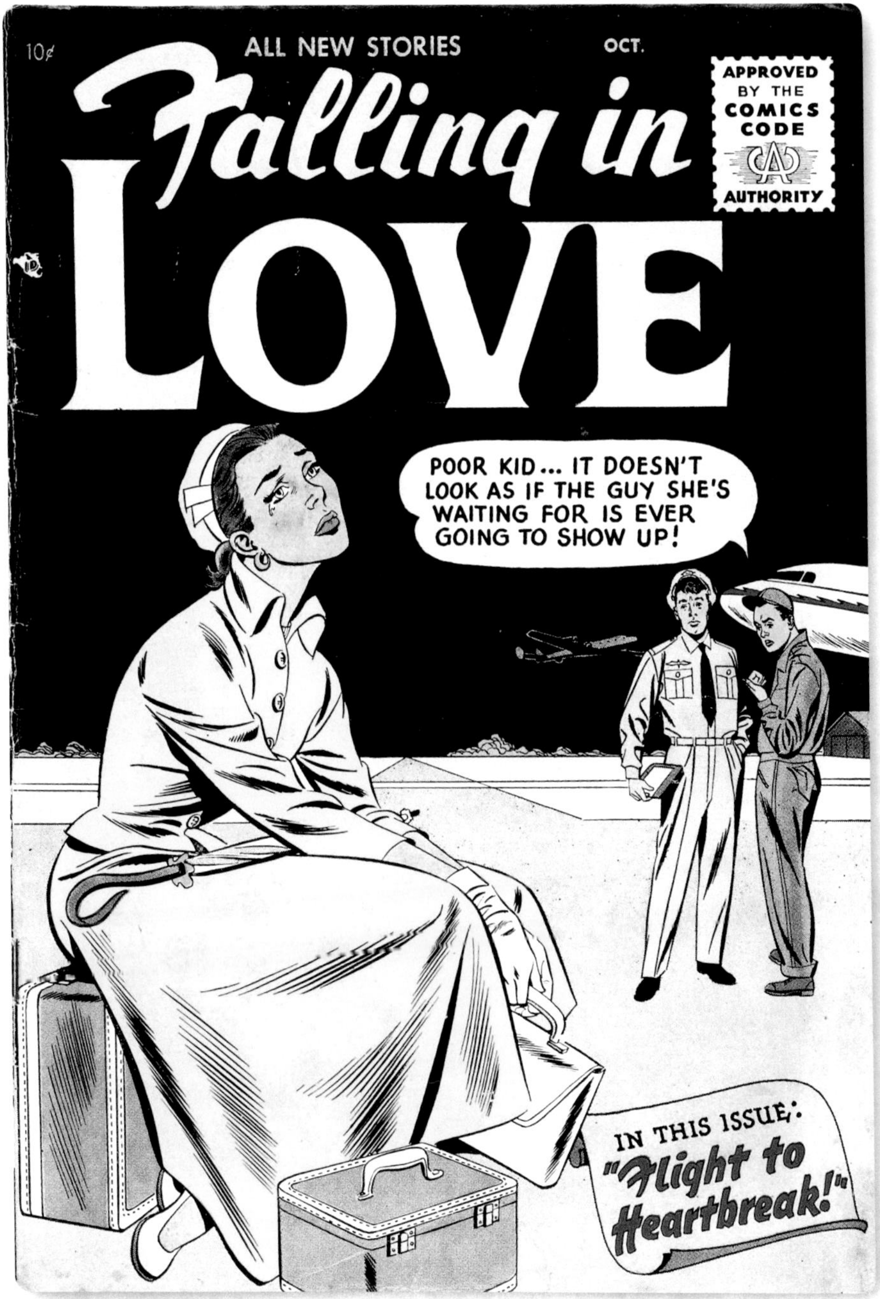

10¢
ALL NEW STORIES
OCT.
Falling in LOVE
APPROVED BY THE COMICS CODE AUTHORITY
POOR KID... IT DOESN'T LOOK AS IF THE GUY SHE'S WAITING FOR IS EVER GOING TO SHOW UP!
IN THIS ISSUE: "Flight to Heartbreak!"

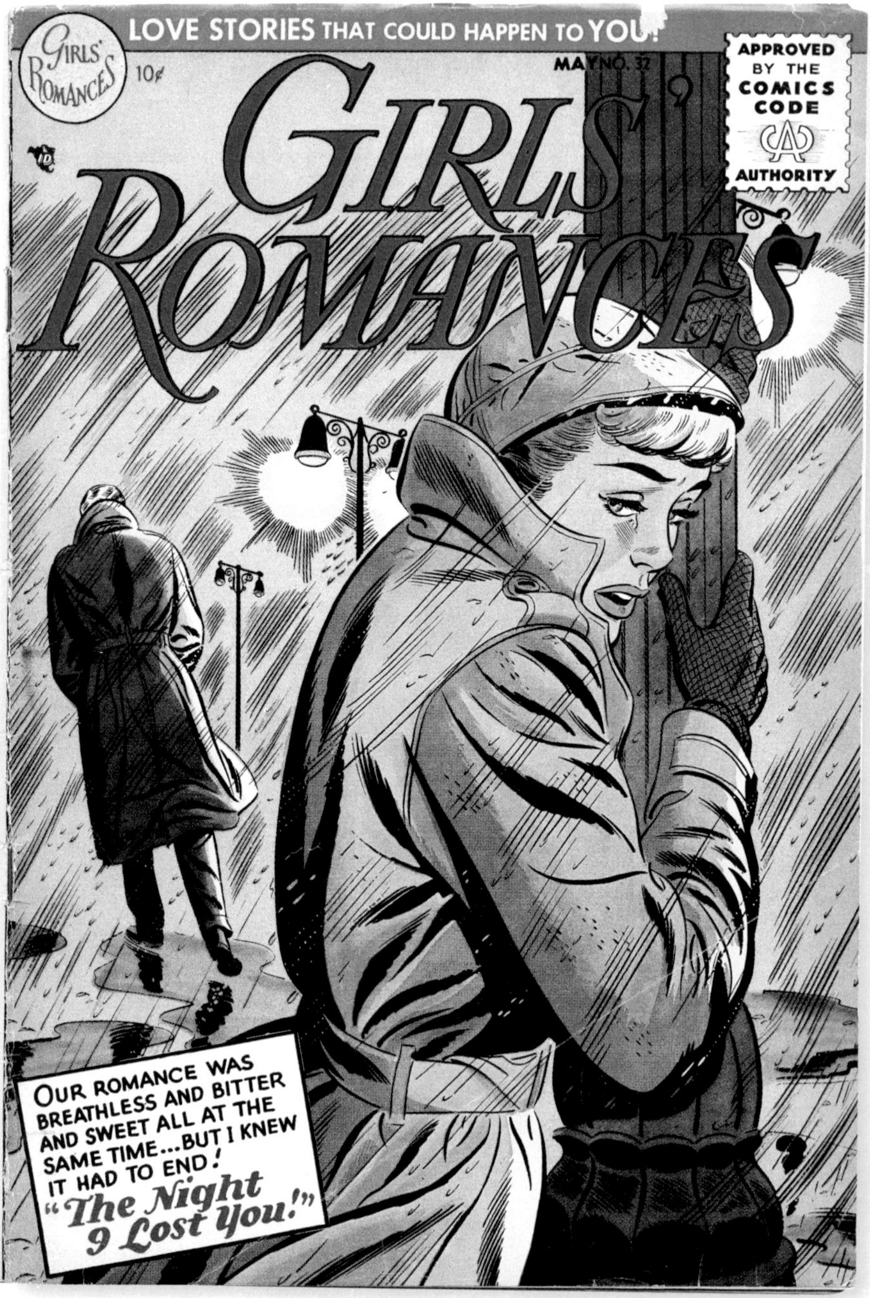

GIRLS' ROMANCES
LOVE STORIES THAT COULD HAPPEN TO YOU!
10¢
MAY NO. 32
APPROVED BY THE COMICS CODE AUTHORITY
GIRLS' ROMANCES
OUR ROMANCE WAS BREATHLESS AND BITTER AND SWEET ALL AT THE SAME TIME...BUT I KNEW IT HAD TO END!
"The Night I Lost You!"

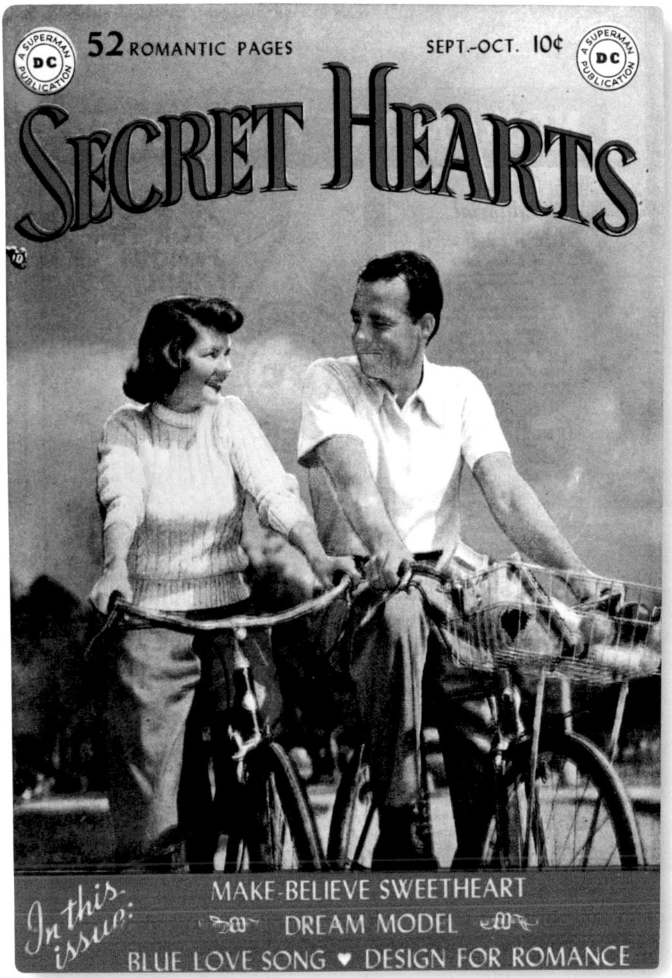
52 ROMANTIC PAGES
SEPT.-OCT. 10¢
SECRET HEARTS
MAKE-BELIEVE SWEETHEART
DREAM MODEL
In this issue:
BLUE LOVE SONG ♥ DESIGN FOR ROMANCE

GIRLS' ROMANCES No. 32

Cover art, Irv Novick and Mike Peppe, April–May 1955.
The DC logo — or any company icon — was conspicuously absent from their romance titles until well into the 1950s. The line was essentially a company within a company despite an overlap of talent with the official DC titles.

SECRET HEARTS No. 1

Cover photograph, Theda and Emerson Hall, September–October 1951.

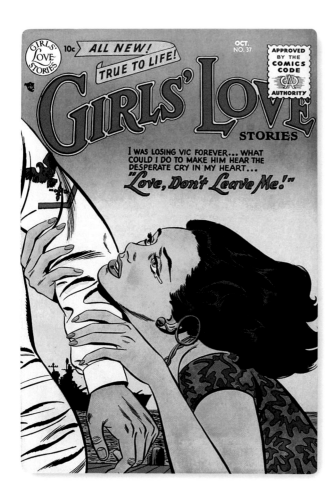

GIRLS' LOVE STORIES
10c
ALL NEW!
TRUE TO LIFE!
OCT.
NO. 37
APPROVED BY THE COMICS CODE AUTHORITY
GIRLS' LOVE
STORIES
I WAS LOSING VIC FOREVER... WHAT COULD I DO TO MAKE HIM HEAR THE DESPERATE CRY IN MY HEART...
"Love, Don't Leave Me!"

GIRLS' LOVE STORIES No. 37

Cover art, Tony Abruzzo and Bernard Sachs, September–October 1955. Tony Abruzzo possessed a distinctive angular style that stood out in the DC romance titles, where he worked exclusively from the mid-1950s to the late 1960s.

GIRLS' ROMANCES No. 12

Cover art, Irwin Hasen, December 1951–January 1952. For a time in the early 1950s, Irwin Hasen's art epitomized the style that DC was looking for in its romance line. During the same period, the artist was also assigned to draw the covers of *Wonder Woman*, making for a jarring contrast with the comparatively old-fashioned H.G. Peter art inside.

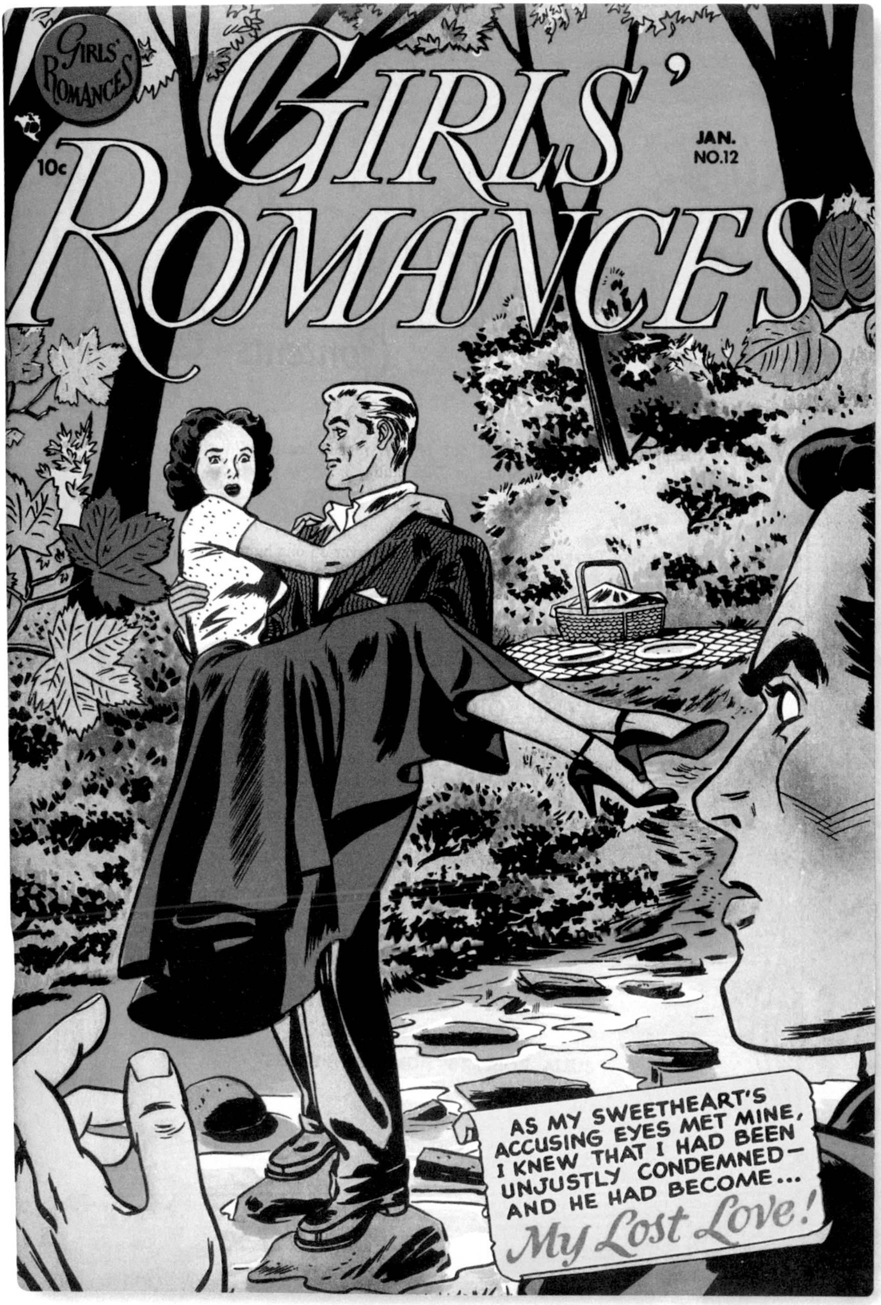
GIRLS' ROMANCES
10c
GIRLS' ROMANCES
JAN.
NO.12
AS MY SWEETHEART'S ACCUSING EYES MET MINE, I KNEW THAT I HAD BEEN UNJUSTLY CONDEMNED— AND HE HAD BECOME...
My Lost Love!

"Romance comics showed me that love is more important than career, that women should never chase men, and that only females cry. Even worse: They instilled in me a serious predilection for bright colors.... I adore people with bright blue eyes and bright orange hair."

—JEANNE MARTINET

GIRLS' ROMANCES No. 11
Cover art, Irwin Hasen, October–November 1951.

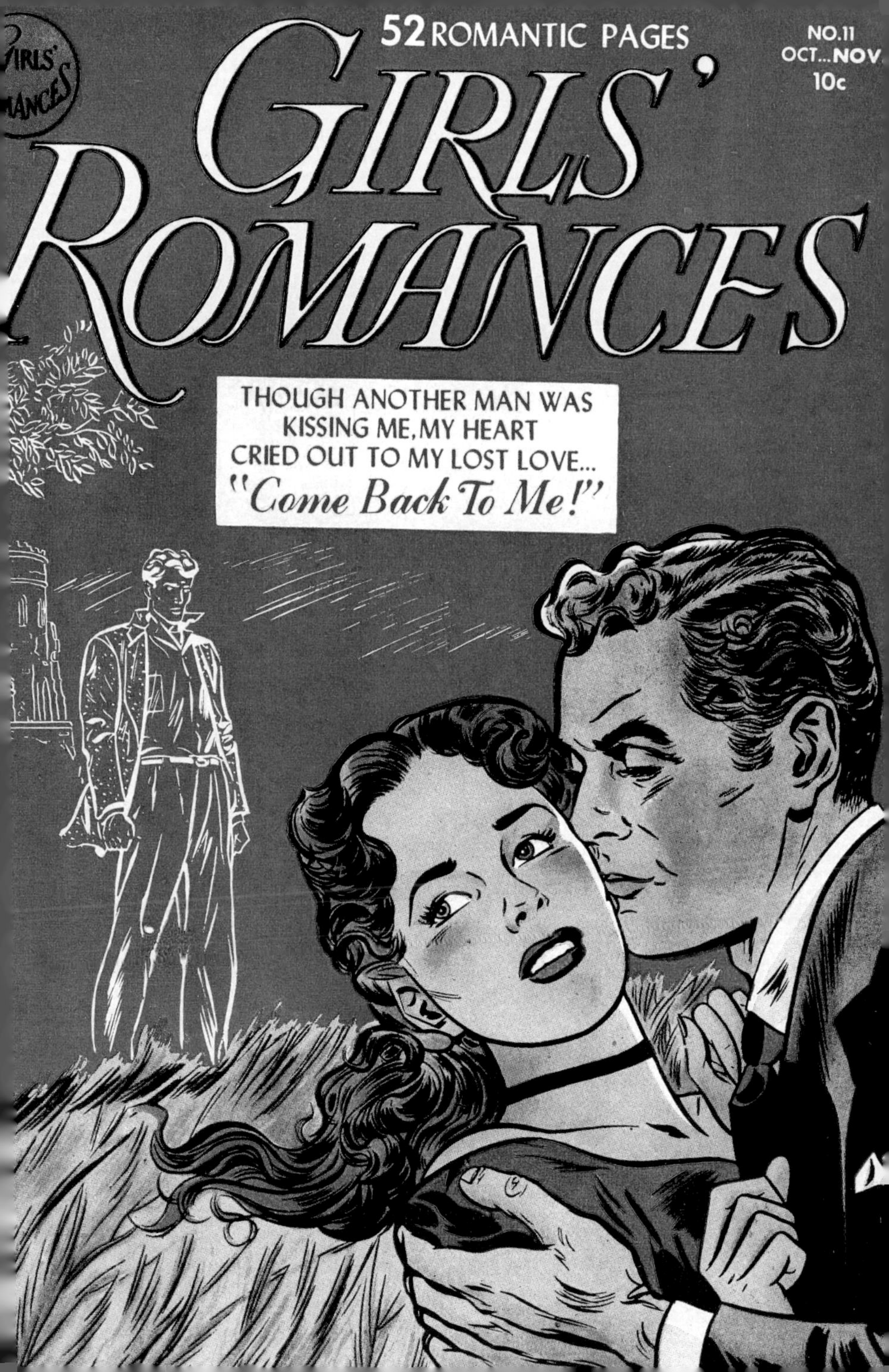

GIRLS' ROMANCES
52 ROMANTIC PAGES
NO. 11
OCT...NOV.
10c
GIRLS' ROMANCES
THOUGH ANOTHER MAN WAS KISSING ME, MY HEART CRIED OUT TO MY LOST LOVE... "Come Back To Me!"

GIRLS' LOVE STORIES No. 14
Cover art, Irwin Hasen, November–December 1951.

GIRLS' ROMANCES No. 7
Cover art, Frank Giacoia and Joe Giella, February–March 1951.

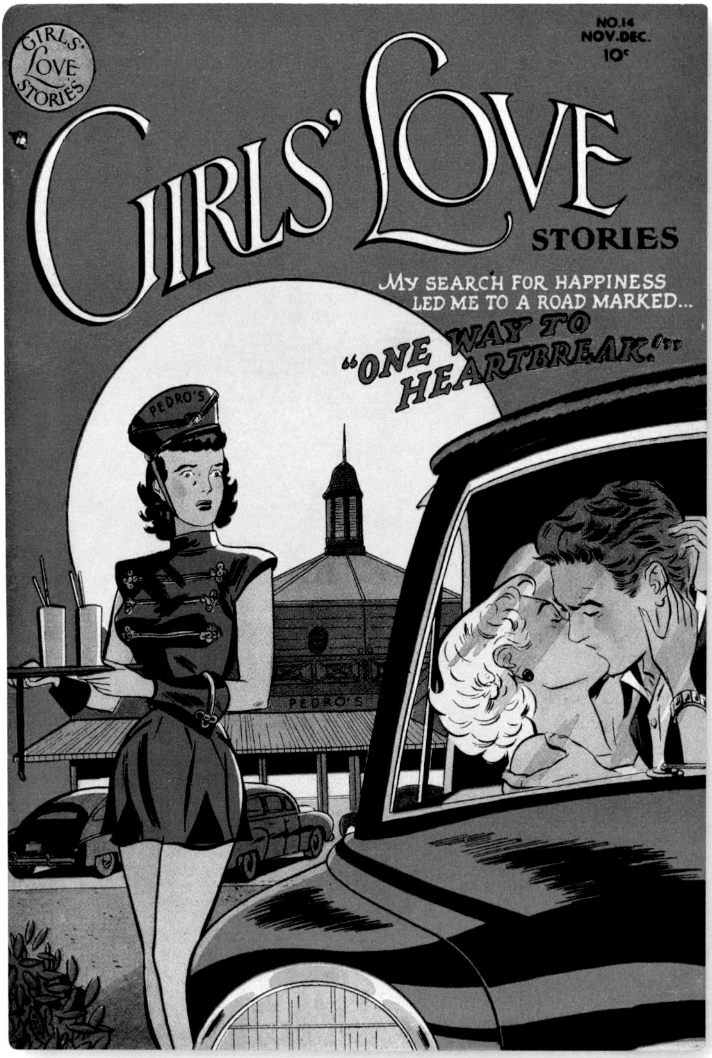

GIRLS' LOVE STORIES
NO.14
NOV.DEC.
10¢
GIRLS' LOVE
STORIES
MY SEARCH FOR HAPPINESS LED ME TO A ROAD MARKED...
"ONE WAY TO HEARTBREAK!"
PEDRO'S
PEDRO'S

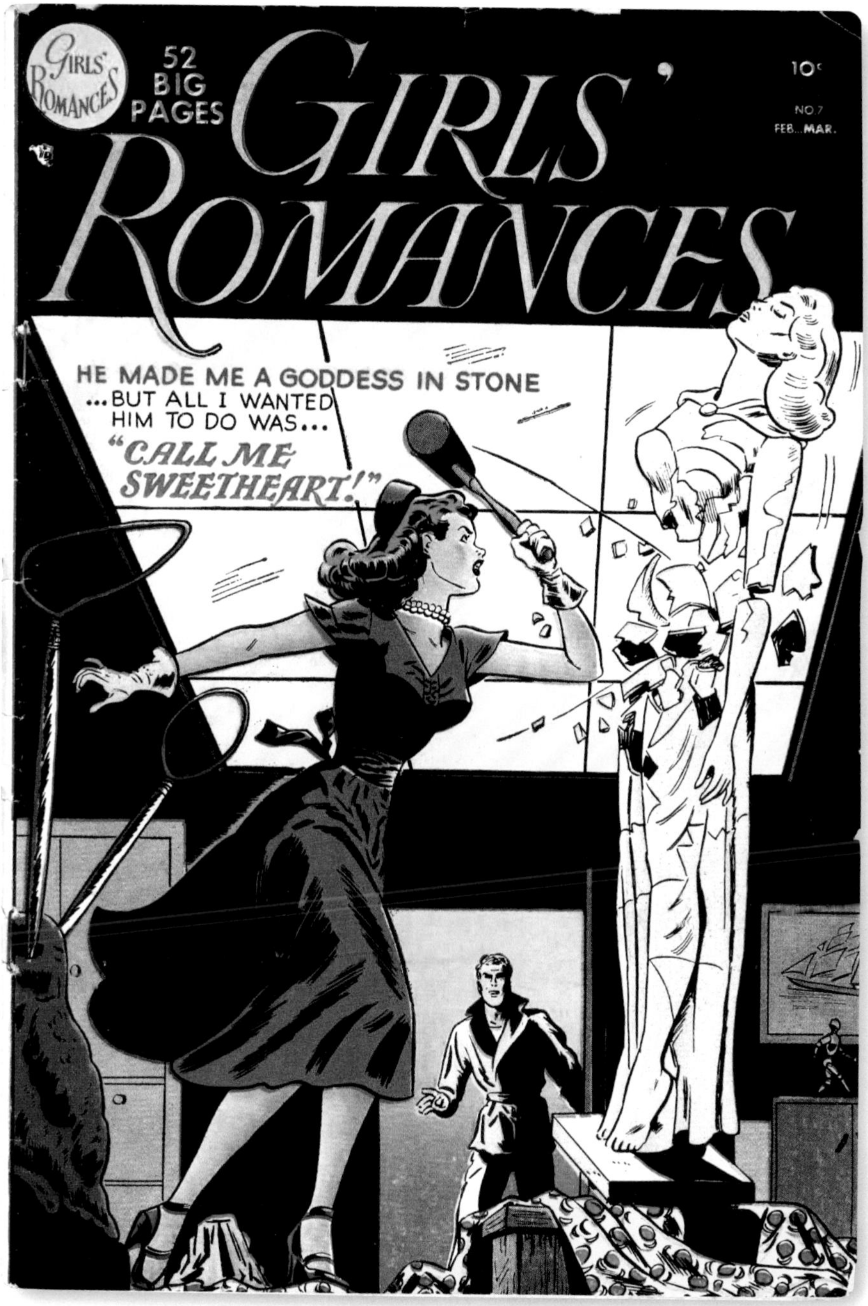

GIRLS' ROMANCES
52 BIG PAGES
GIRLS' ROMANCES
10¢
NO.7
FEB...MAR.
HE MADE ME A GODDESS IN STONE
...BUT ALL I WANTED HIM TO DO WAS...
"CALL ME SWEETHEART!"

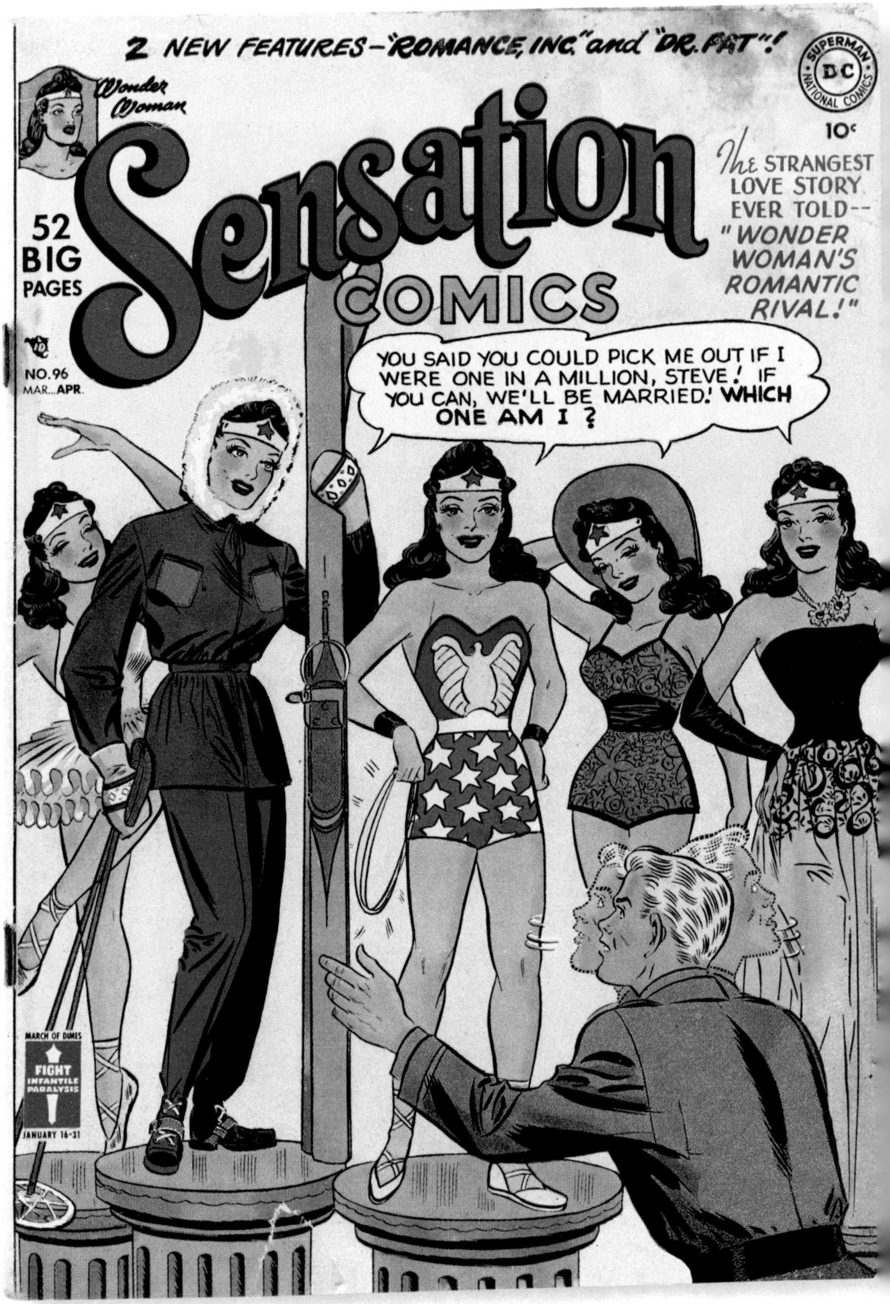
2 NEW FEATURES—"ROMANCE, INC." and "DR. PAT"!
Wonder Woman
SUPERMAN DC NATIONAL COMICS
10¢
Sensation COMICS
52 BIG PAGES
NO. 96
MAR...APR.
The STRANGEST LOVE STORY EVER TOLD-- "WONDER WOMAN'S ROMANTIC RIVAL!"
YOU SAID YOU COULD PICK ME OUT IF I WERE ONE IN A MILLION, STEVE! IF YOU CAN, WE'LL BE MARRIED! WHICH ONE AM I ?
MARCH OF DIMES
FIGHT INFANTILE PARALYSIS
JANUARY 16-31

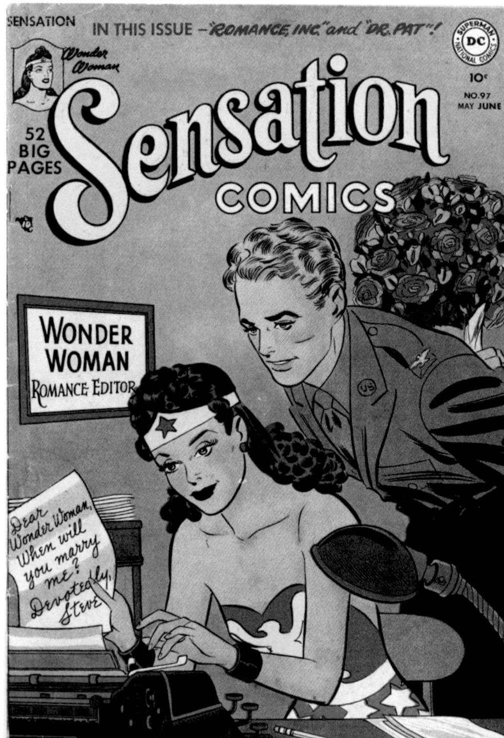
SENSATION
IN THIS ISSUE – "ROMANCE, INC." and "DR. PAT"!
Wonder Woman
52 BIG PAGES
Sensation
COMICS
10¢
NO. 97
MAY JUNE
DC
WONDER WOMAN
ROMANCE EDITOR
Dear Wonder Woman, When will you marry me? Devotedly, Steve

SENSATION COMICS No. 96

Cover art, Irwin Hasen, March–April 1950. Part of *Sensation Comics'* romance make-over was the implicit acknowledgment that the art style of Wonder Woman's original artist, H. G. Peter, was distinctly old-fashioned when compared with other comic books. While he continued to draw every story featuring the character until his death in 1958, Peter was replaced on the covers by artists like Irwin Hasen and Irv Novick, who drew prettier, more modern versions of the Amazing Amazon.

SENSATION COMICS No. 97

Cover art, Irwin Hasen, May–June 1950. When romance comics boomed for other publishers, *Sensation Comics* switched to that format in the hope of saving the title from cancellation. In addition to Wonder Woman's new job writing a newspaper advice column for young lovers, the comic book also featured series starring small-town female physician Dr. Pat and tales of Romance, Inc. with Ann Martin.

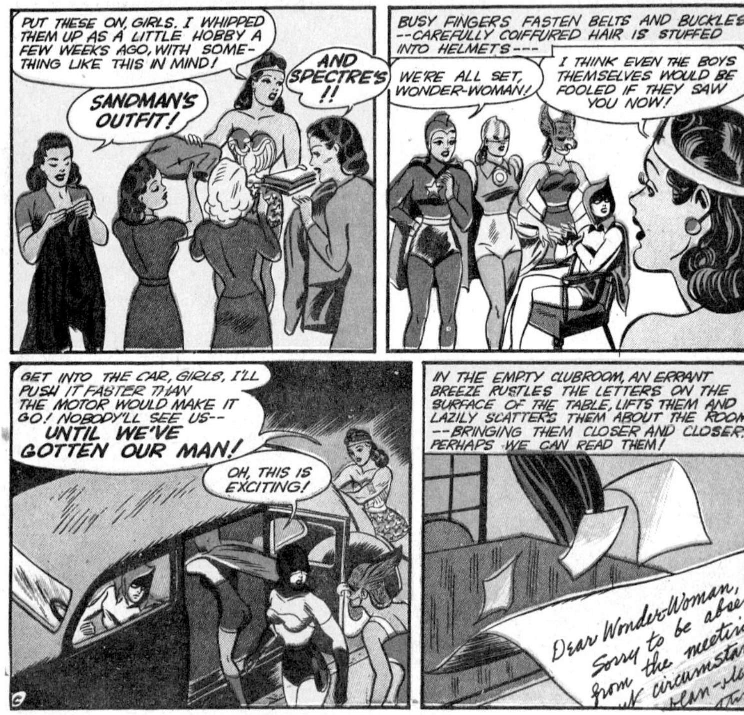
PUT THESE ON, GIRLS. I WHIPPED THEM UP AS A LITTLE HOBBY A FEW WEEKS AGO, WITH SOMETHING LIKE THIS IN MIND!
SANDMAN'S OUTFIT!
AND SPECTRE'S !!
BUSY FINGERS FASTEN BELTS AND BUCKLES --CAREFULLY COIFFURED HAIR IS STUFFED INTO HELMETS---
WE'RE ALL SET, WONDER-WOMAN!
I THINK EVEN THE BOYS THEMSELVES WOULD BE FOOLED IF THEY SAW YOU NOW!
GET INTO THE CAR, GIRLS, I'LL PUSH IT FASTER THAN THE MOTOR WOULD MAKE IT GO! NOBODY'LL SEE US-- UNTIL WE'VE GOTTEN OUR MAN!
OH, THIS IS EXCITING!
IN THE EMPTY CLUBROOM, AN ERRANT BREEZE RUSTLES THE LETTERS ON THE SURFACE OF THE TABLE, LIFTS THEM AND LAZILY SCATTERS THEM ABOUT THE ROOM --BRINGING THEM CLOSER AND CLOSER. PERHAPS WE CAN READ THEM!
Dear Wonder-Woman,
Sorry to be abs
from the meetin

ALL-STAR COMICS No. 15

Interior, "The Man Who Created Images"; script, Gardner Fox; pencils and inks, Joe Gallagher. February–March 1943. Despite being forced to sit out most of the early Justice Society adventures in the condescending role of recording secretary, Wonder Woman doesn't hesitate to rush to the rescue of the male members when they're captured by the Brain Wave. The heroes' girlfriends dress up in the costumes of their men to join the quest, although only Hawkgirl has experience in the role. This mirrored the experiences of American women who were filling in for their men, as embodied in the character of Rosie the Riveter…and like the real women's experience, many of those gains would be reversed quickly.

OUT OF THIS WORLD

"Superman" Sunday newspaper strip; script, unknown; artist, Wayne Boring. September 28, 1947. Character merchandising was already a massive part of DC's business, and perhaps the characters themselves understood that it was part of what ensured their continued survival as much as their superpowers.

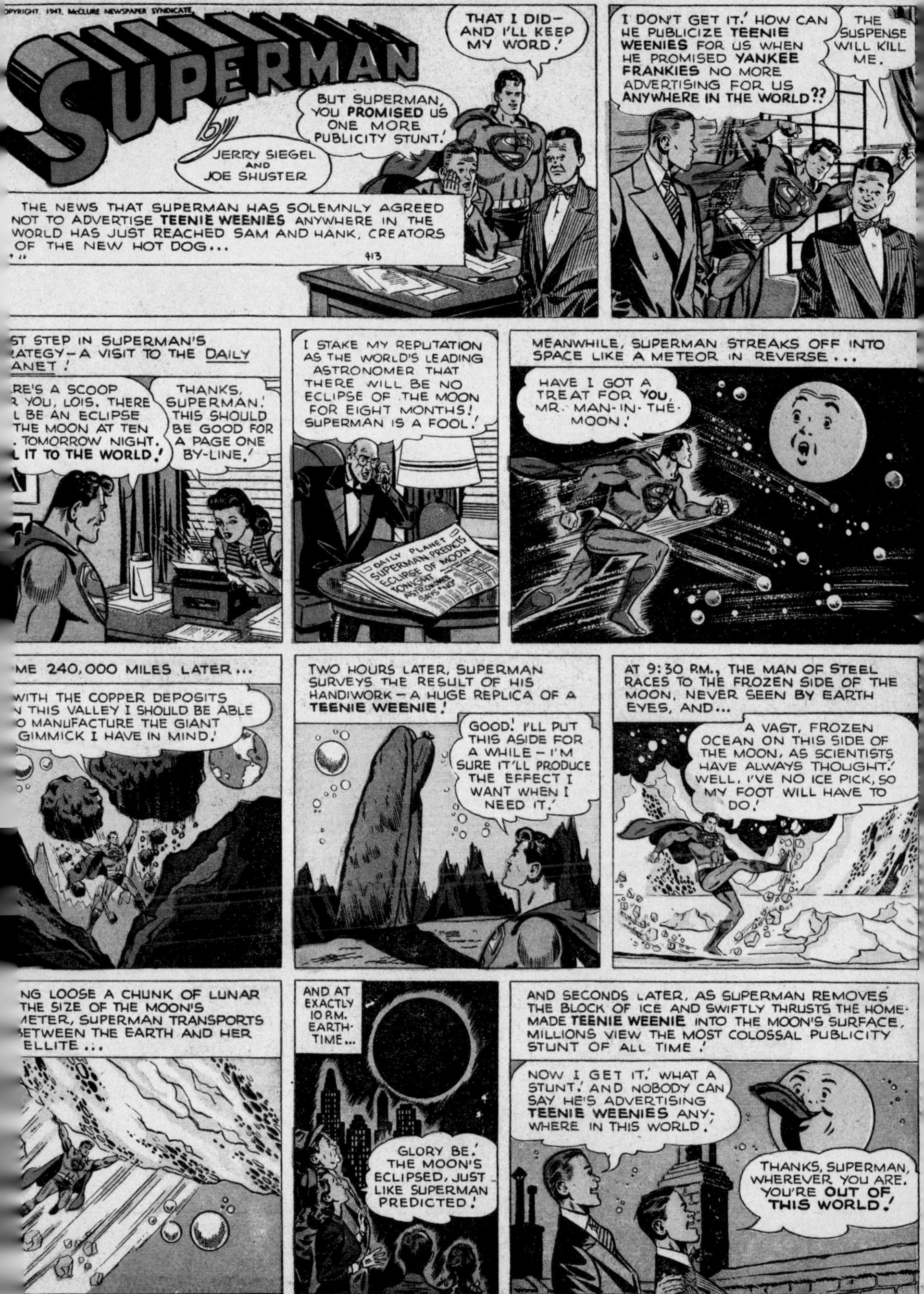
OPYRIGHT, 1947, McCLURE NEWSPAPER SYNDICATE
SUPERMAN
by JERRY SIEGEL AND JOE SHUSTER
THE NEWS THAT SUPERMAN HAS SOLEMNLY AGREED NOT TO ADVERTISE TEENIE WEENIES ANYWHERE IN THE WORLD HAS JUST REACHED SAM AND HANK, CREATORS OF THE NEW HOT DOG...
BUT SUPERMAN, YOU PROMISED US ONE MORE PUBLICITY STUNT!
THAT I DID— AND I'LL KEEP MY WORD!
413
I DON'T GET IT! HOW CAN HE PUBLICIZE TEENIE WEENIES FOR US WHEN HE PROMISED YANKEE FRANKIES NO MORE ADVERTISING FOR US ANYWHERE IN THE WORLD??
THE SUSPENSE WILL KILL ME.
ST STEP IN SUPERMAN'S RATEGY—A VISIT TO THE DAILY ANET!
RE'S A SCOOP R YOU, LOIS. THERE L BE AN ECLIPSE THE MOON AT TEN . TOMORROW NIGHT. L IT TO THE WORLD!
THANKS, SUPERMAN! THIS SHOULD BE GOOD FOR A PAGE ONE BY-LINE!
I STAKE MY REPUTATION AS THE WORLD'S LEADING ASTRONOMER THAT THERE WILL BE NO ECLIPSE OF THE MOON FOR EIGHT MONTHS! SUPERMAN IS A FOOL!
DAILY PLANET
SUPERMAN PREDICTS ECLIPSE OF MOON TONIGHT
ASTRONOMER SAYS "NO"
MEANWHILE, SUPERMAN STREAKS OFF INTO SPACE LIKE A METEOR IN REVERSE...
HAVE I GOT A TREAT FOR YOU, MR. MAN-IN-THE-MOON!
ME 240,000 MILES LATER...
WITH THE COPPER DEPOSITS N THIS VALLEY I SHOULD BE ABLE O MANUFACTURE THE GIANT GIMMICK I HAVE IN MIND!
TWO HOURS LATER, SUPERMAN SURVEYS THE RESULT OF HIS HANDIWORK—A HUGE REPLICA OF A TEENIE WEENIE!
GOOD! I'LL PUT THIS ASIDE FOR A WHILE—I'M SURE IT'LL PRODUCE THE EFFECT I WANT WHEN I NEED IT!
AT 9:30 P.M., THE MAN OF STEEL RACES TO THE FROZEN SIDE OF THE MOON, NEVER SEEN BY EARTH EYES, AND...
A VAST, FROZEN OCEAN ON THIS SIDE OF THE MOON, AS SCIENTISTS HAVE ALWAYS THOUGHT! WELL, I'VE NO ICE PICK, SO MY FOOT WILL HAVE TO DO!
NG LOOSE A CHUNK OF LUNAR THE SIZE OF THE MOON'S METER, SUPERMAN TRANSPORTS BETWEEN THE EARTH AND HER ELLITE...
AND AT EXACTLY 10 P.M. EARTH-TIME...
GLORY BE! THE MOON'S ECLIPSED, JUST LIKE SUPERMAN PREDICTED!
AND SECONDS LATER, AS SUPERMAN REMOVES THE BLOCK OF ICE AND SWIFTLY THRUSTS THE HOME-MADE TEENIE WEENIE INTO THE MOON'S SURFACE, MILLIONS VIEW THE MOST COLOSSAL PUBLICITY STUNT OF ALL TIME!
NOW I GET IT! WHAT A STUNT! AND NOBODY CAN SAY HE'S ADVERTISING TEENIE WEENIES ANY-WHERE IN THIS WORLD!
THANKS, SUPERMAN, WHEREVER YOU ARE. YOU'RE OUT OF THIS WORLD!

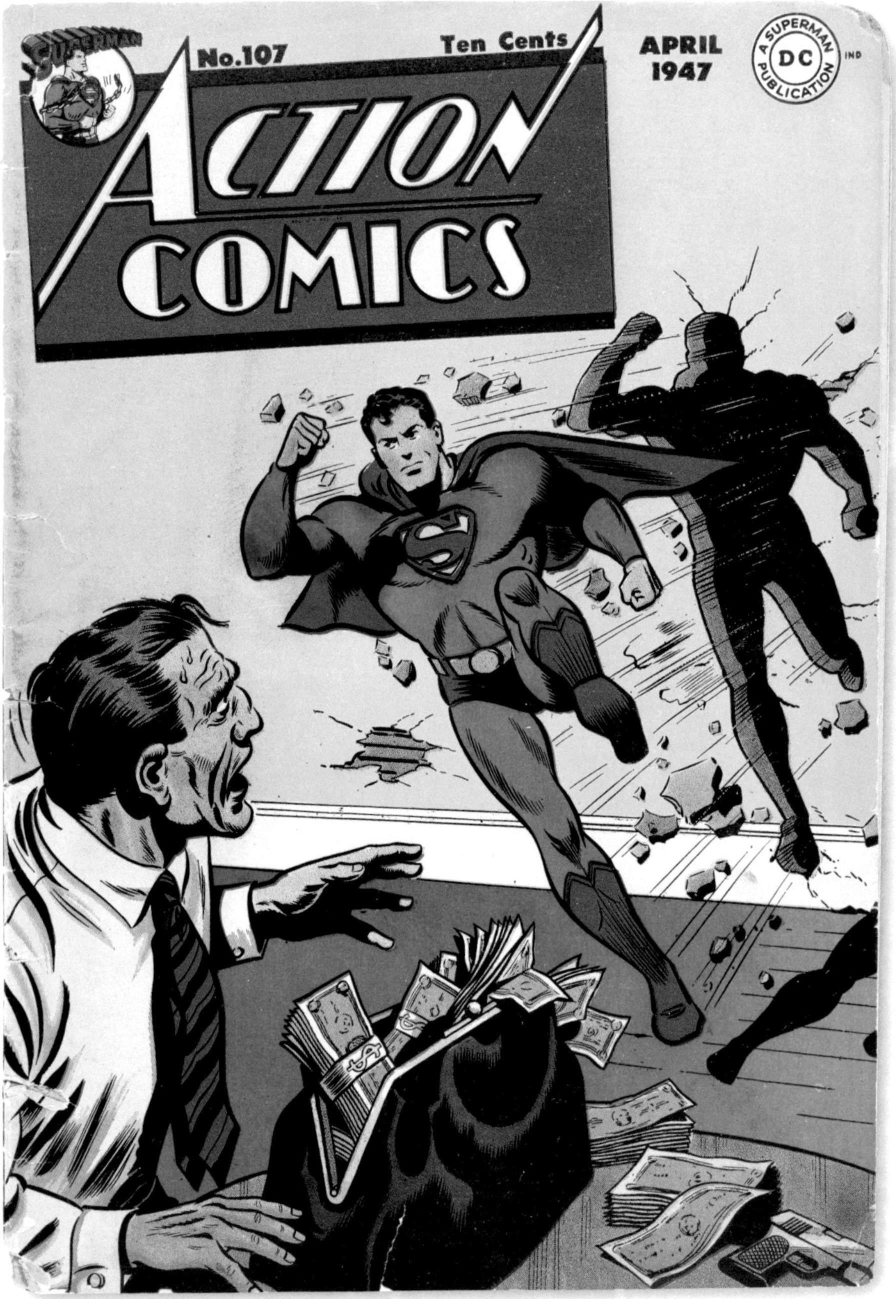
SUPERMAN
No.107
Ten Cents
APRIL
1947
A SUPERMAN
DC
PUBLICATION
IND
ACTION
COMICS

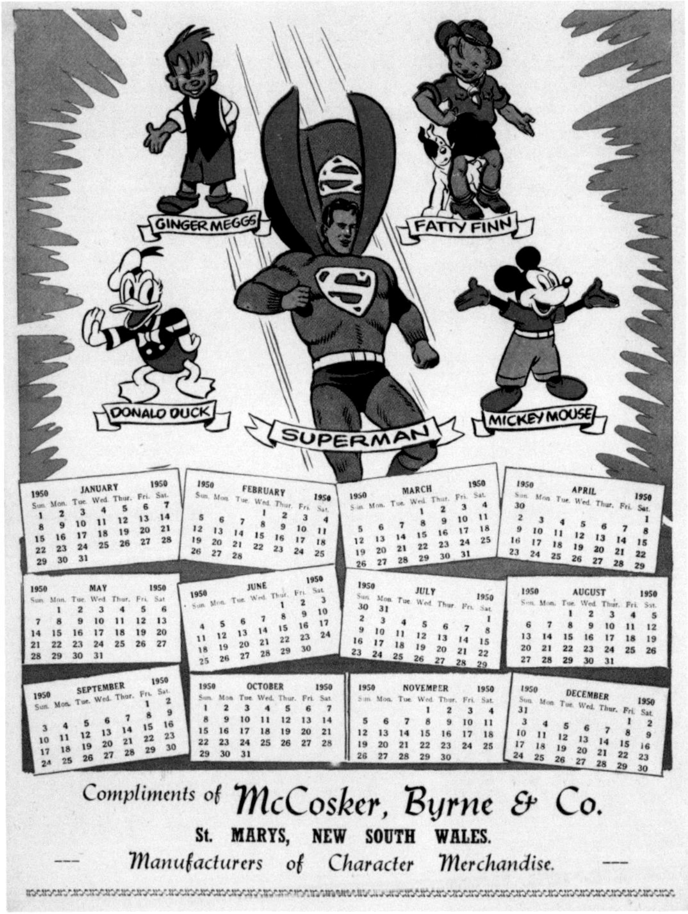
GINGER MEGGS
FATTY FINN
DONALD DUCK
SUPERMAN
MICKEY MOUSE
1950 JANUARY 1950
1950 FEBRUARY 1950
1950 MARCH 1950
1950 APRIL 1950
1950 MAY 1950
1950 JUNE 1950
1950 JULY 1950
1950 AUGUST 1950
1950 SEPTEMBER 1950
1950 OCTOBER 1950
1950 NOVEMBER 1950
1950 DECEMBER 1950
Compliments of McCosker, Byrne & Co.
St. MARYS, NEW SOUTH WALES.
Manufacturers of Character Merchandise.

ACTION COMICS No. 107

Cover art, Jack Burnley and Stan Kaye, April 1947. Charming scenes of Superman performing various feats of strength and skill were a staple of many comic book covers of the 1940s and rarely had any relation to the stories inside. It was a measure of the super hero's popularity that issues of his comic book could be sold purely on the basis of his name and superpowers rather than through teasers for the adventures inside.

COMICS CALENDAR

Calendar art, artist unknown, 1950.

ACTION COMICS No. 92

Cover art, Jack Burnley and Stan Kaye, January 1946. In contrast to the more cartoony versions of Superman by other artists, Jack Burnley's work stood out with its more realistic depictions of the human figure.

SUPERMAN No. 45

Cover art, Jack Burnley and George Roussos, March–April 1947. "Superman burrows faster and more silently than any excavating machine ever invented by man," declares *Superman* No. 11. It seems inevitable that the Man of Steel would eventually be used to illustrate the cliché of digging a hole to China, a gag also used in a few stories years later.

WORLD'S FINEST COMICS No. 76

Cover art, Win Mortimer, May–June 1955.

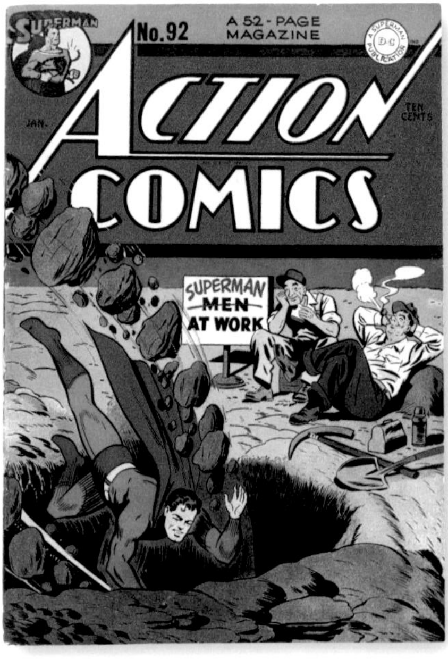

SUPERMAN
No.92
A 52-PAGE MAGAZINE
A SUPERMAN PUBLICATION DC
JAN.
ACTION COMICS
TEN CENTS
SUPERMAN MEN AT WORK

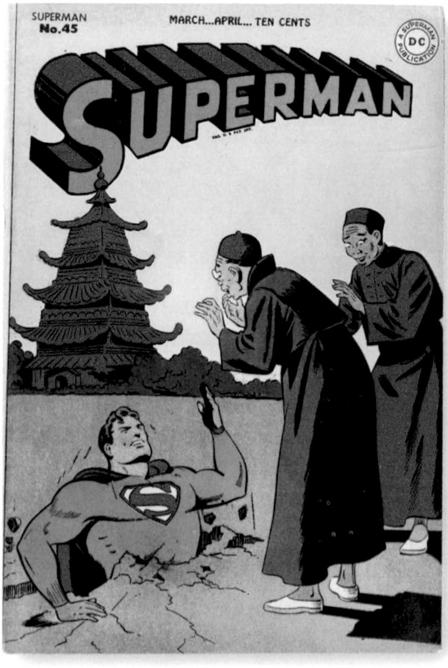

SUPERMAN No.45
MARCH...APRIL... TEN CENTS
A SUPERMAN PUBLICATION DC
SUPERMAN

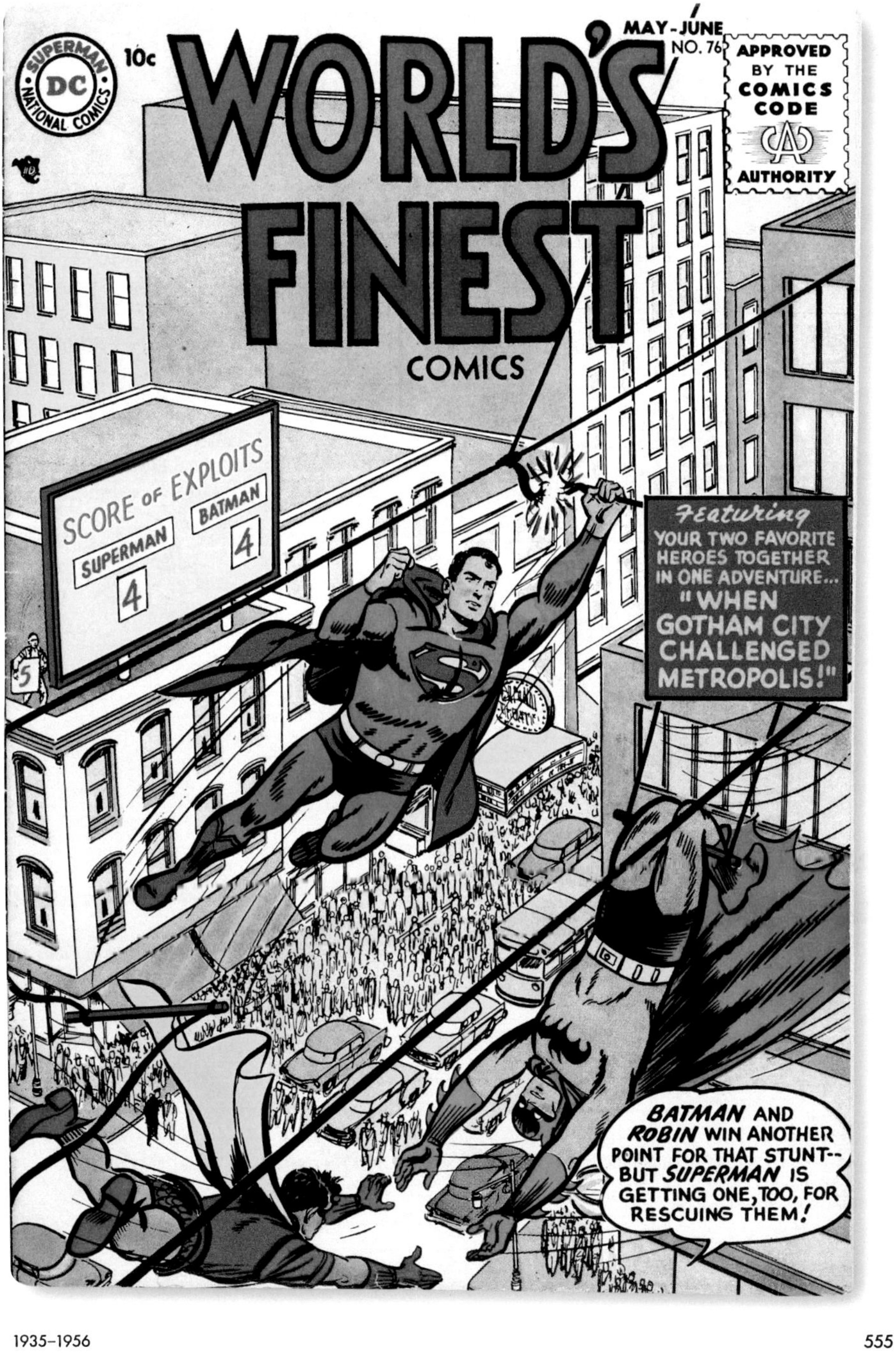
SUPERMAN
DC
NATIONAL COMICS
10c
WORLD'S FINEST COMICS
MAY-JUNE
NO. 76
APPROVED BY THE COMICS CODE AUTHORITY
SCORE OF EXPLOITS
SUPERMAN
4
BATMAN
4
5
Featuring YOUR TWO FAVORITE HEROES TOGETHER IN ONE ADVENTURE... "WHEN GOTHAM CITY CHALLENGED METROPOLIS!"
BATMAN AND ROBIN WIN ANOTHER POINT FOR THAT STUNT-- BUT SUPERMAN IS GETTING ONE, TOO, FOR RESCUING THEM!

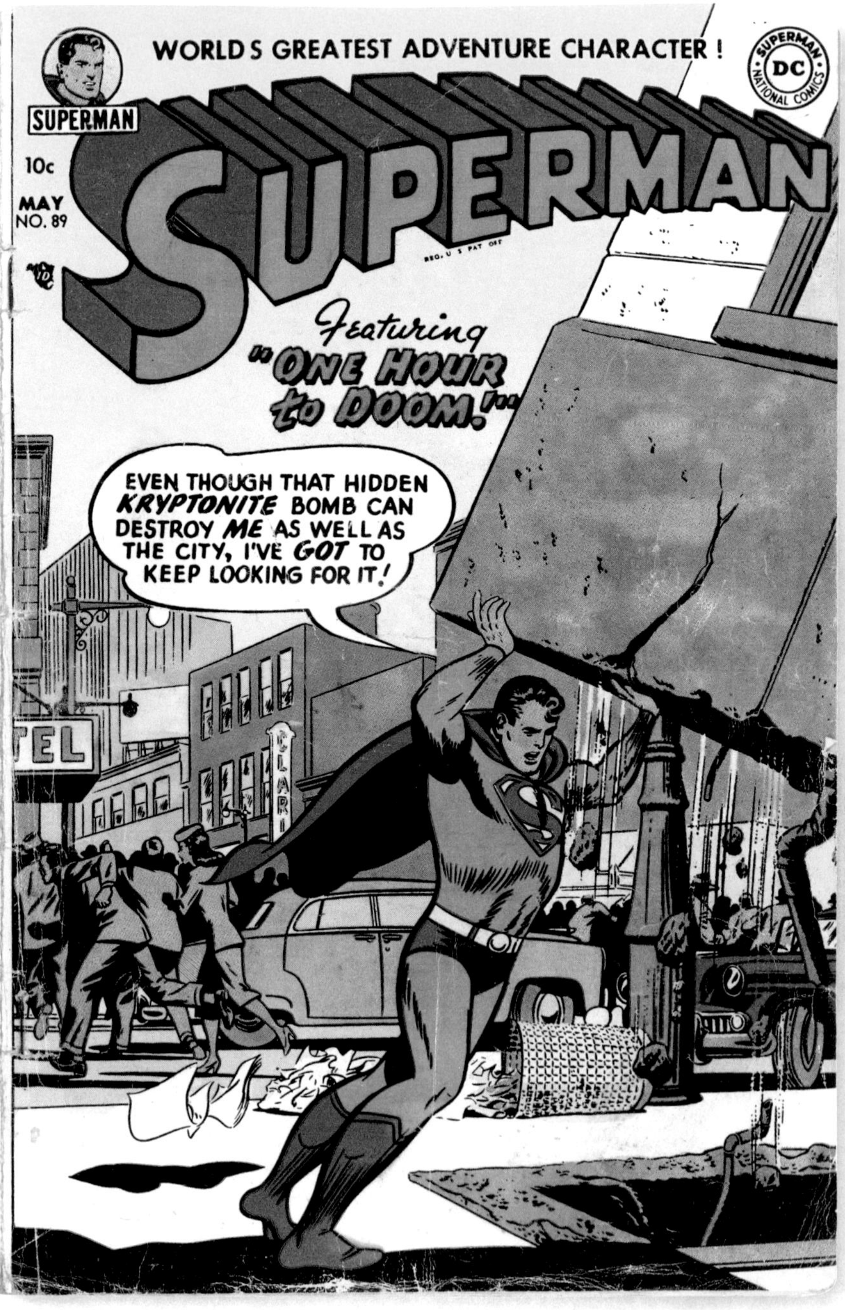

WORLD'S GREATEST ADVENTURE CHARACTER!
SUPERMAN
10c
MAY
NO. 89
SUPERMAN
Featuring "ONE HOUR to DOOM!"
EVEN THOUGH THAT HIDDEN KRYPTONITE BOMB CAN DESTROY ME AS WELL AS THE CITY, I'VE GOT TO KEEP LOOKING FOR IT!

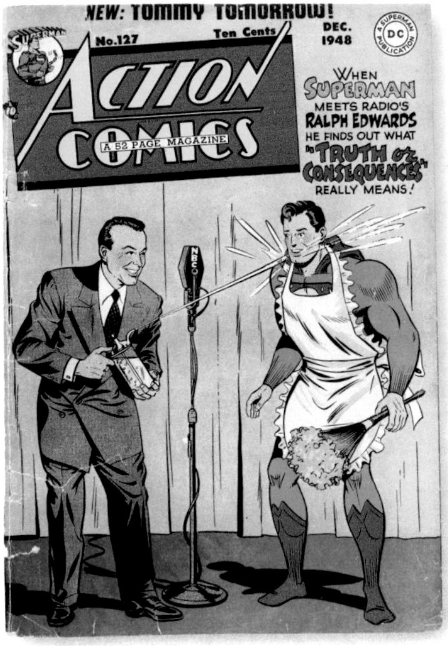
NEW: TOMMY TOMORROW!
No.127
Ten Cents
DEC. 1948
A SUPERMAN PUBLICATION
DC
ACTION COMICS
A 52 PAGE MAGAZINE
WHEN SUPERMAN MEETS RADIO'S RALPH EDWARDS HE FINDS OUT WHAT "TRUTH or CONSEQUENCES" REALLY MEANS!
NBC

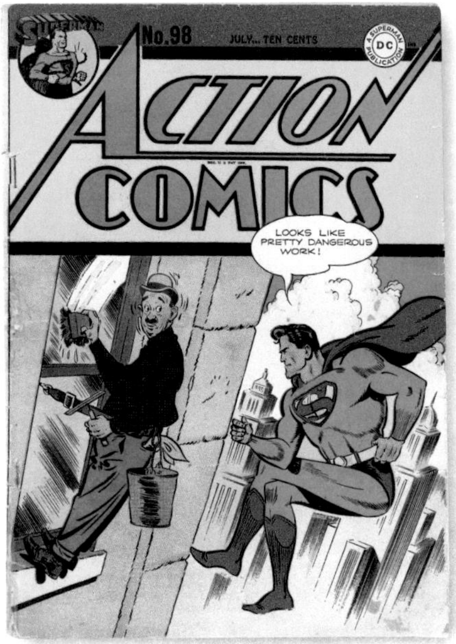
SUPERMAN
No.98
JULY... TEN CENTS
A SUPERMAN PUBLICATION
DC
ACTION COMICS
LOOKS LIKE PRETTY DANGEROUS WORK!

SUPERMAN No. 89

Cover art, Curt Swan and Stan Kaye, May 1954. Few artists were as closely linked to Superman as Curt Swan, whose realistic perspective on the Man of Steel and his world brought a comforting humanity and accessibility to the character. While a regular artist on offshoot features like Superboy and Jimmy Olsen, Swan drew only a handful of Superman stories during the 1950s. Instead, artists such as Wayne Boring and Al Plastino maintained the exaggerated visual style of the Man of Steel in his own comics while Swan projected a more contemporary image of the hero by drawing the covers.

ACTION COMICS No. 127

Cover art, Al Plastino, December 1948.

ACTION COMICS No. 98

Cover art, Wayne Boring and Ed Dobrotka, July 1946.

WHIT ELLSWORTH & JACK SCHIFF

Photograph, National offices, 1940s. Ellsworth played a crucial role in the development of the early Superman film projects, ultimately serving as producer on the *Adventures of Superman* TV show. As development began on the later *Batman* television series, Schiff was consulted for reference material and provided reprint giants filled with colorful costumed villains.

ACTION COMICS No. 130

Cover art, Al Plastino, March 1949. By the end of the 1940s, real-life celebrities had begun to show up in DC comics on occasion, but a guest appearance with Superman was a singular honor. Actress Ann Blyth's role in *Action Comics* No.130 promoted her part in the film *Mr. Peabody and the Mermaid.* Game show host and creator Ralph Edwards met the Man of Steel twice, once in 1948 when Superman appears on *Truth or Consequences* and again in 1959's *Superman's Girl Friend, Lois Lane* No.9, when the girl reporter is the subject of his later program *This Is Your Life.*

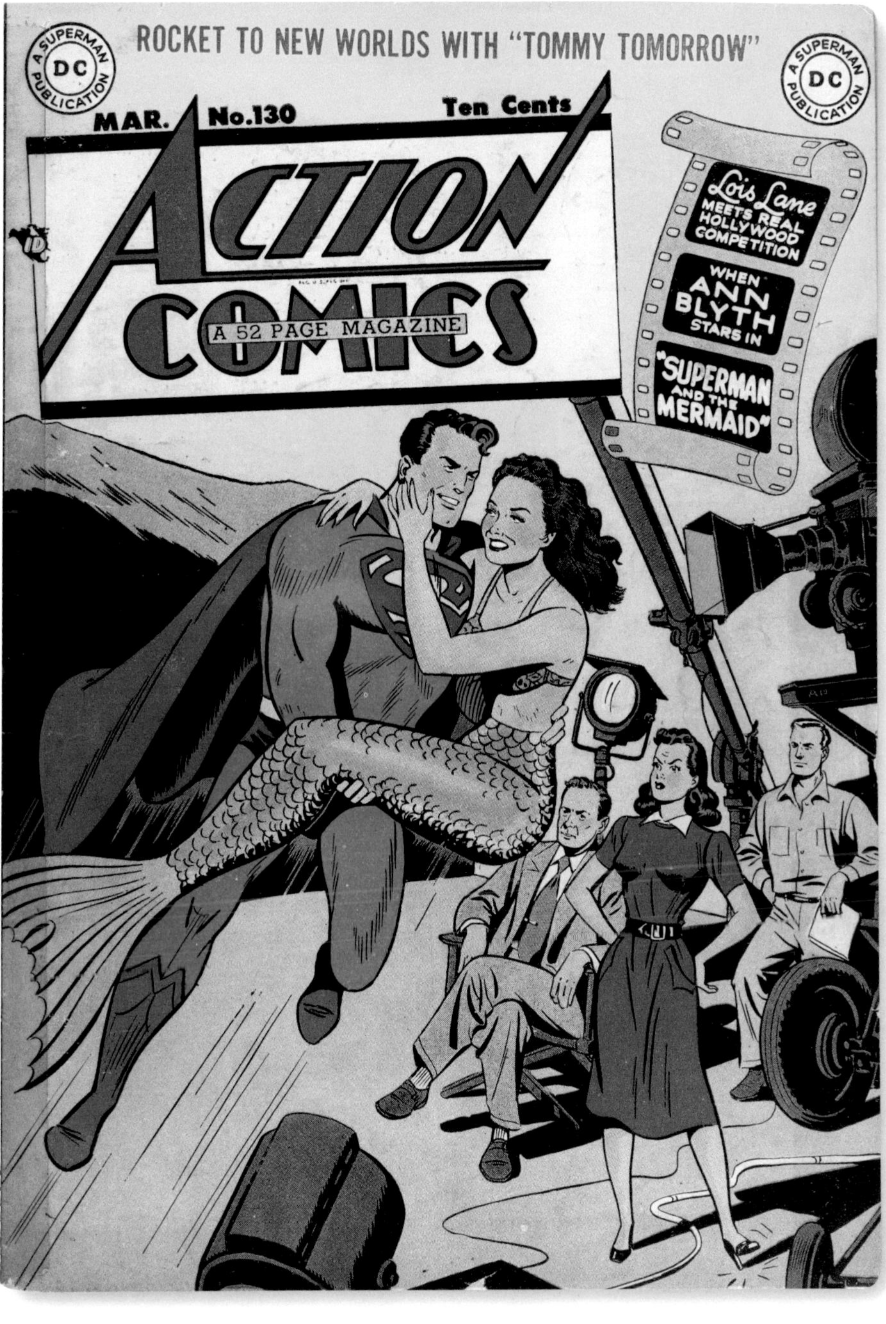

ROCKET TO NEW WORLDS WITH "TOMMY TOMORROW"
A SUPERMAN DC PUBLICATION
A SUPERMAN DC PUBLICATION
MAR.
No.130
Ten Cents
ACTION COMICS
A 52 PAGE MAGAZINE
Lois Lane MEETS REAL HOLLYWOOD COMPETITION
WHEN ANN BLYTH STARS IN
"SUPERMAN AND THE MERMAID"

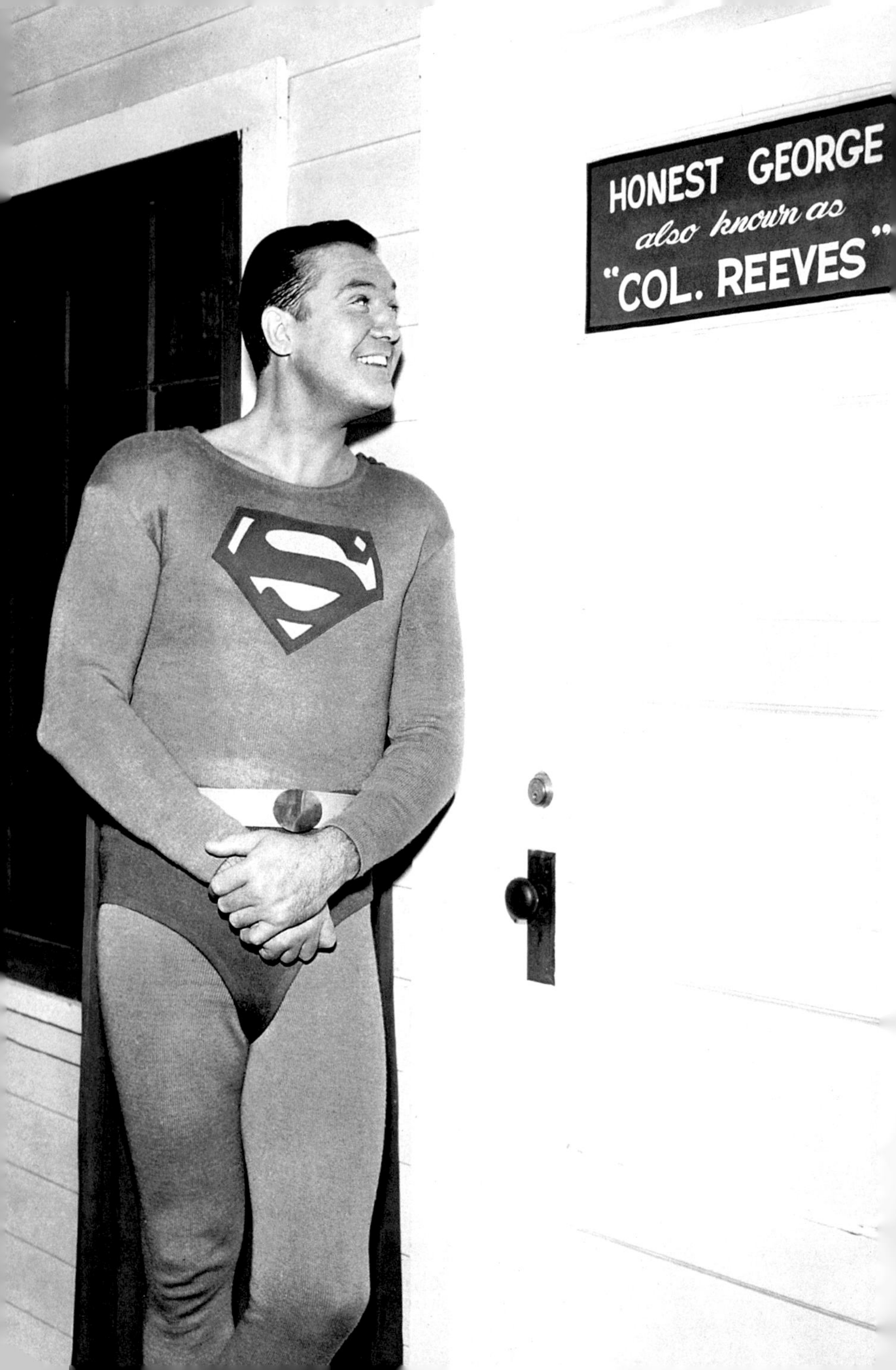
HONEST GEORGE
also known as
"COL. REEVES"

HONEST GEORGE
Photograph, George Reeves on Superman set, 1950s.

SUPERMAN MOVIE SERIAL
*Film still: Kirk Alyn (Superman) takes flight. Columbia Pictures,
1948.* Kirk Alyn was the first actor to portray Superman in a
live-action theatrical release, in movie serials in 1948 and 1950.
Efforts to portray the actor in flight were deemed a failure (the
wires attached to his body were too conspicuous). Instead, Alyn
was filmed leaping, and then he was replaced on screen by an
animated flying Superman.

1935–1956

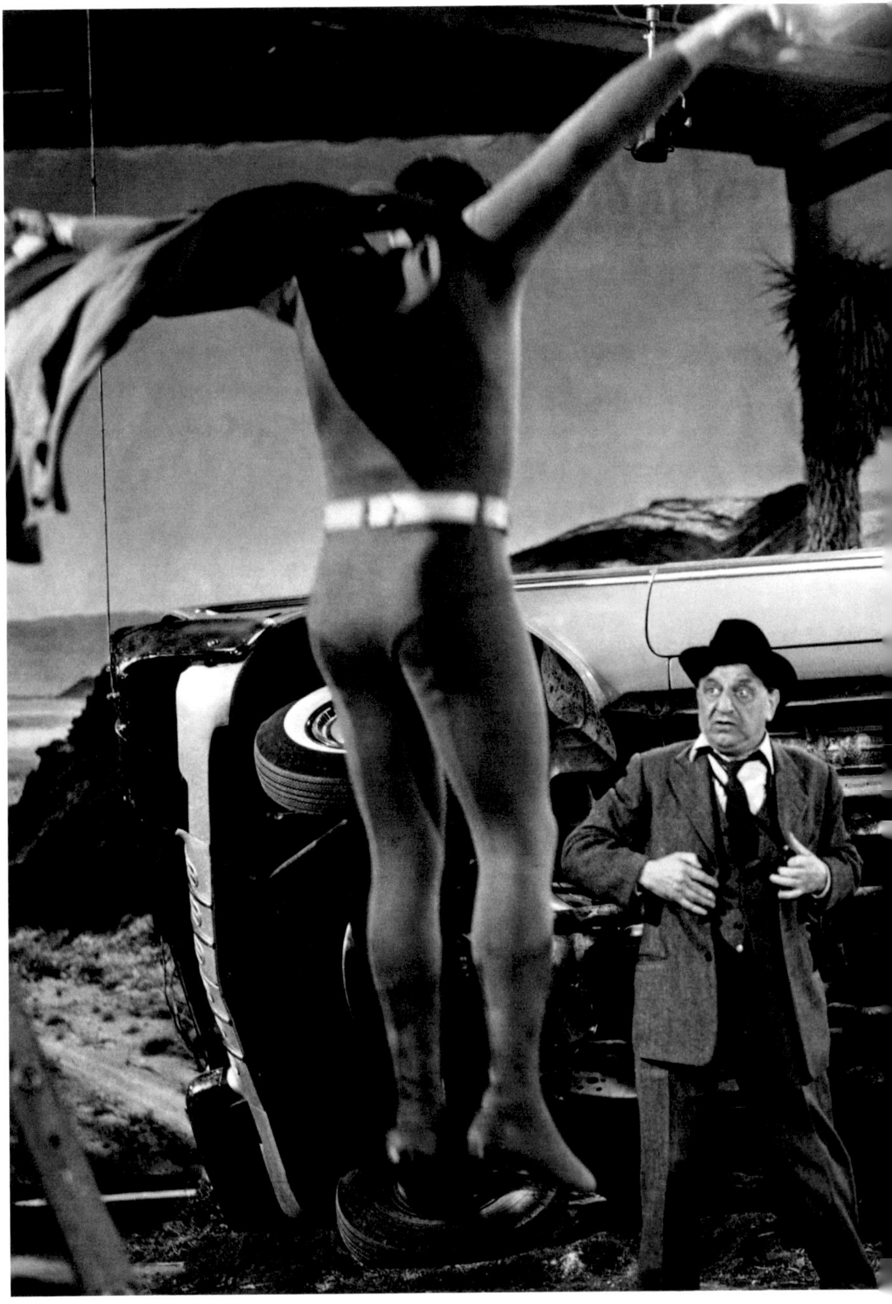

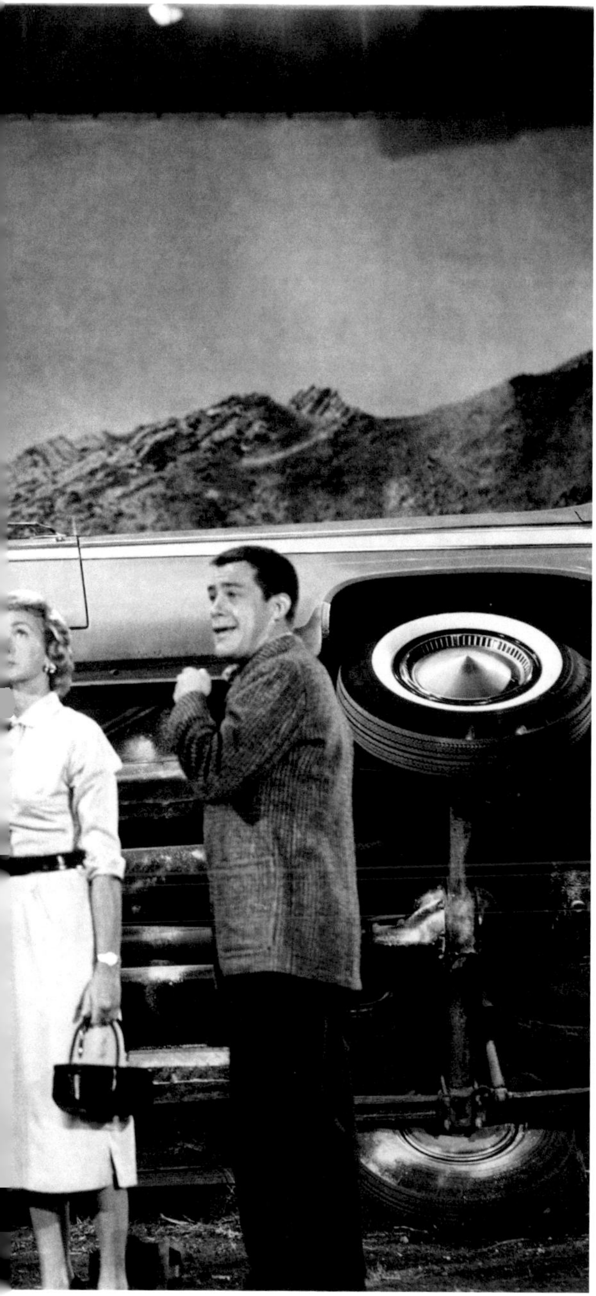

ADVENTURES
OF SUPERMAN

Film still, Superman drops from the sky, 1950s. Among the tricks used to create the illusion of flight was the use of wires to depict Superman in the air and a stunt that showed him dropping to the ground on his feet as if landing.

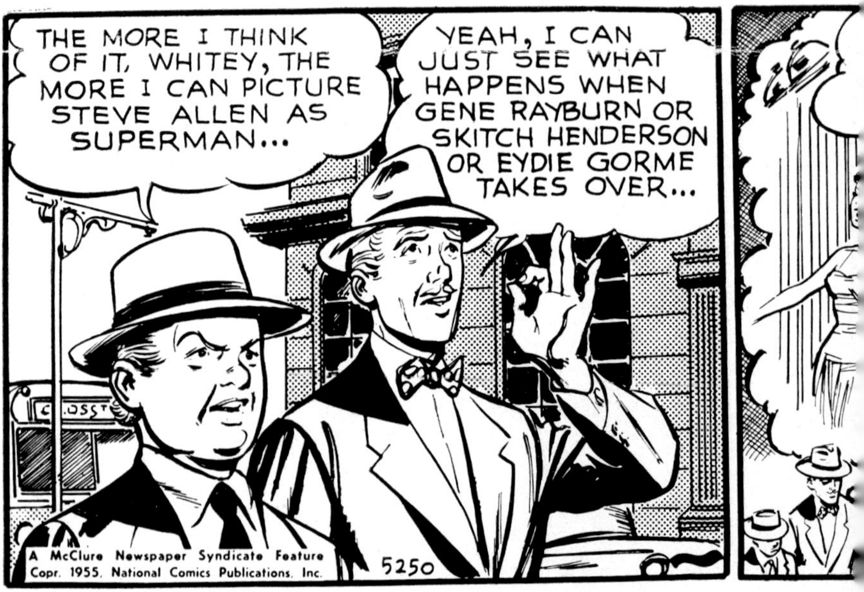
THE MORE I THINK OF IT, WHITEY, THE MORE I CAN PICTURE STEVE ALLEN AS SUPERMAN...
YEAH, I CAN JUST SEE WHAT HAPPENS WHEN GENE RAYBURN OR SKITCH HENDERSON OR EYDIE GORME TAKES OVER...
A McClure Newspaper Syndicate Feature
Copr. 1955, National Comics Publications, Inc.
5250

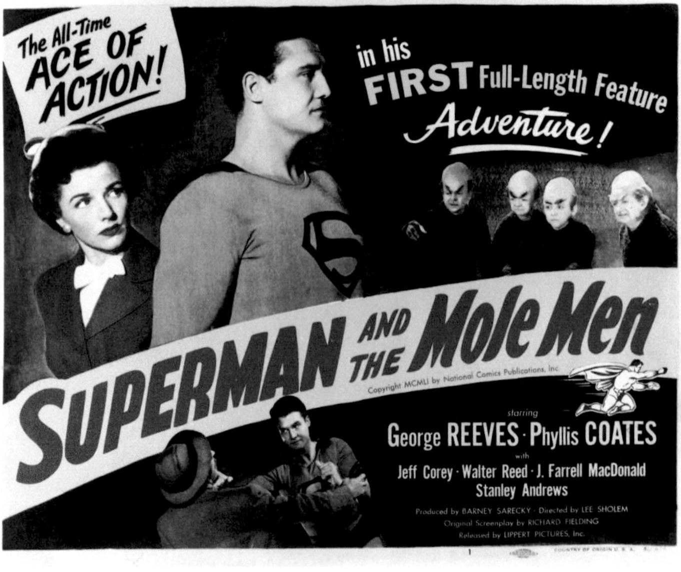
The All-Time ACE OF ACTION!
in his FIRST Full-Length Feature Adventure!
SUPERMAN AND THE Mole Men
Copyright MCMLI by National Comics Publications, Inc
starring
George REEVES · Phyllis COATES
with
Jeff Corey · Walter Reed · J. Farrell MacDonald
Stanley Andrews
Produced by BARNEY SARECKY · Directed by LEE SHOLEM
Original Screenplay by RICHARD FIELDING
Released by LIPPERT PICTURES, Inc.
COUNTRY OF ORIGIN U. S. A.

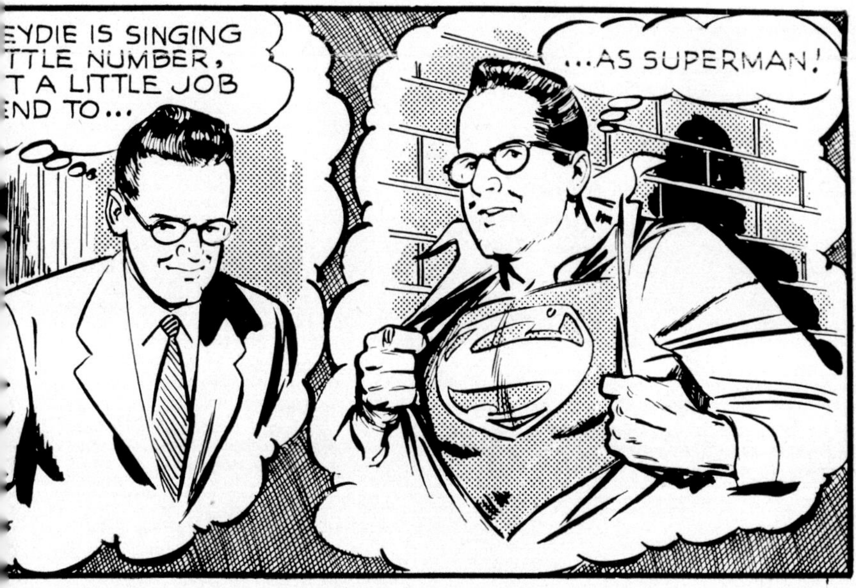
EYDIE IS SINGING
TTLE NUMBER,
T A LITTLE JOB
ND TO...
...AS SUPERMAN!

SUPERMAN COMIC STRIP

Newspaper comic strip, script, unknown; art, Win Mortimer. October 13, 1955. A year after becoming the first host of NBC's *Tonight Show*, Steve Allen was the subject of a story in the "Superman" newspaper strip that played on the bespectacled comedian's supposed remblance to Clark Kent.

SUPERMAN AND THE MOLE MEN

Lobby card, with George Reeves and Phyllis Coates, 1951.

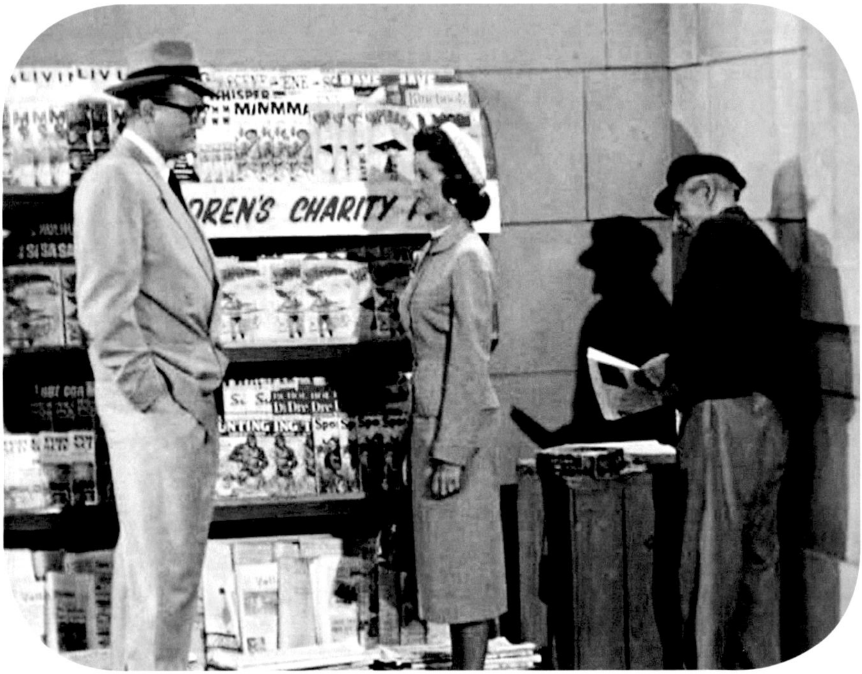
CHARITY

CLARK AND LOIS

Film still, George Reeves and Noel Neill, 1950s. Unlike George Reeves and Jack Larson (Jimmy Olsen), Noel Neill never appeared in a commercial for Kellogg's breakfast cereal broadcast during the *Adventures of Superman*. The sponsor feared that viewers would question why Clark Kent was having breakfast with Lois Lane.

ADVENTURES OF SUPERMAN

Photograph, Superman leaps into action, 1950s. George Reeves became Superman for an entire generation through his role on the 1950s TV series. Aware that viewers felt cheated by the movie serials' use of animation to make the Man of Steel fly, the show's producers developed an elaborate system to better simulate the appearance of flight. Ultimately, Reeves used a springboard to leap through a window onto an unseen mattress.

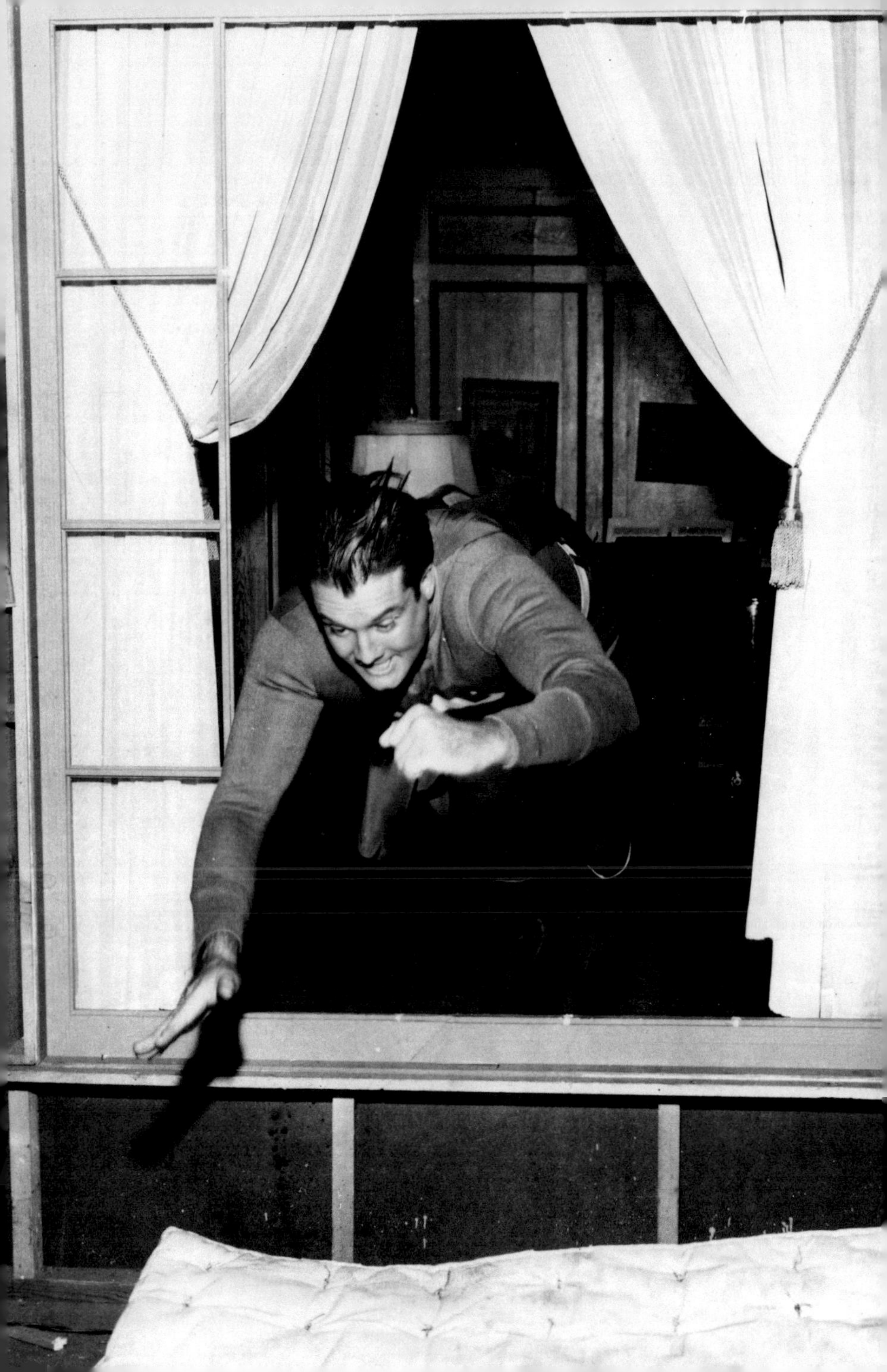

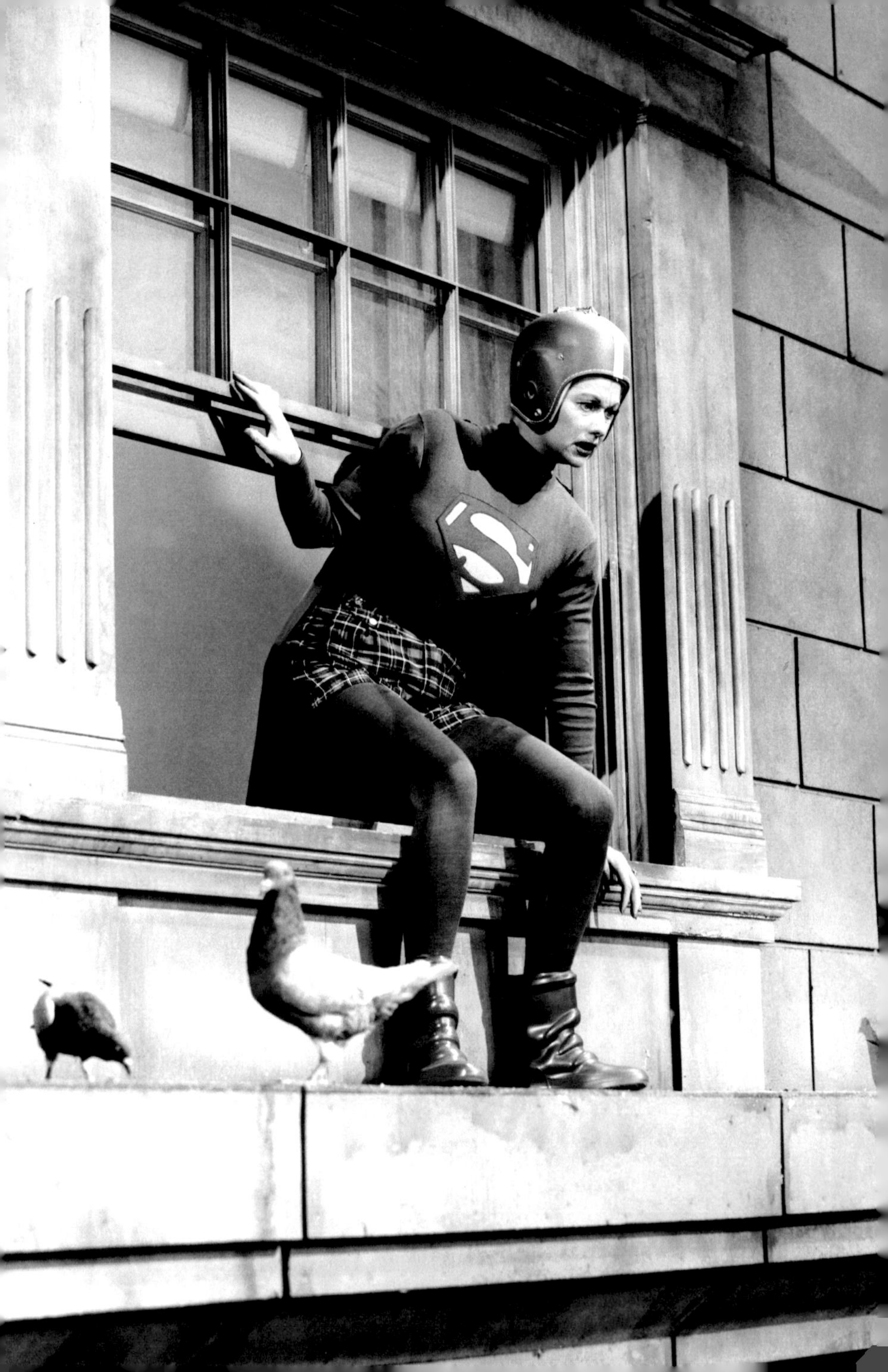

I LOVE LUCY

Film still, Lucille Ball impersonates Superman, "Lucy Meets Superman," 1957. I Love Lucy was the top-rated TV program in the United States when its writers decided on an unusual guest appearance by George Reeves as Superman. When Lucy Ricardo (Lucille Ball) is trapped on a window ledge while trying to appear at her son's birthday dressed as the TV hero, Reeves (in costume) helps rescue her. When he learns that her husband, Ricky, has been married to the zany redhead for 17 years, Reeves declares, "And they call *me* Superman!"

"HOW THEY MAKE SUPERMAN FLY"

Magazine article, TV Guide, *September 25, 1953.* The live-action *Adventures of Superman* TV show premiered on September 19, 1952. When the TV series was filmed in black and white, George Reeves wore a brown costume that was better suited to the flying special effects. Ironically, the correct blue that the actor switched to when the series began filming in color actually decreased the quality of the effects.

Can Sportscasters Spot A Curve?

TV GUIDE

VIEWING GUIDE TO WORLD SERIES

15¢

COMPLETE LOCAL PROGRAM LISTINGS
Week of Sept. 25 to Oct. 1

GEORGE REEVES——
MAN and SUPERMAN

HOW THEY MAKE
SUPERMAN FLY

It's a film trick, kiddies,
so don't try any take-offs

IT IS a mark of the deepest affection that the production crew which earns its daily bread by shooting the *Superman* TV film series refers to its star, George Reeves, as "Stuperman." In any other business, this would be insulting. In Hollywood, it is the accolade.

Reeves, a man who looks a good deal younger than he is, is as good-natured a hero as is extant in TV today. He carries the *Superman* role on his broad shoulders with a delicate sense of balance, kidding himself when among adults but taking it dead seriously when among the younger fry. To him, *Superman* is a cross between a job and a dedication. The same sense of dedication, inspired by Reeves' own genuine feeling on the subject, is evident in the attitude of the crew when one of them says, "Well, let's get Stuperman into his rig and get moving."

They're kidding on the square, ashamed to admit baldly that they go for this business of playing hero to the kids, yet at the same time sharing a secret satisfaction in knowing they

It's easy: Producer Whit Ellsworth tests the springboard, then *Superman* bounces when cue is given and, at top, he flies.

5

SUPER PUP

Film stills, Billy Curtis (as Superpup), 1958. Conceived by
Adventures of Superman producer Whitney Ellsworth, the
Adventures of Superpup reimagined the original show with
actors dressed as canines. Billy Curtis portrayed Superpup
and Bark Bent while *Daily Bugle* editor Terry Bite and reporter
Pamela Poodle were portrayed by Angelo Rossitto and Ruth
Delfino, respectively. The series never went beyond the pilot stage.

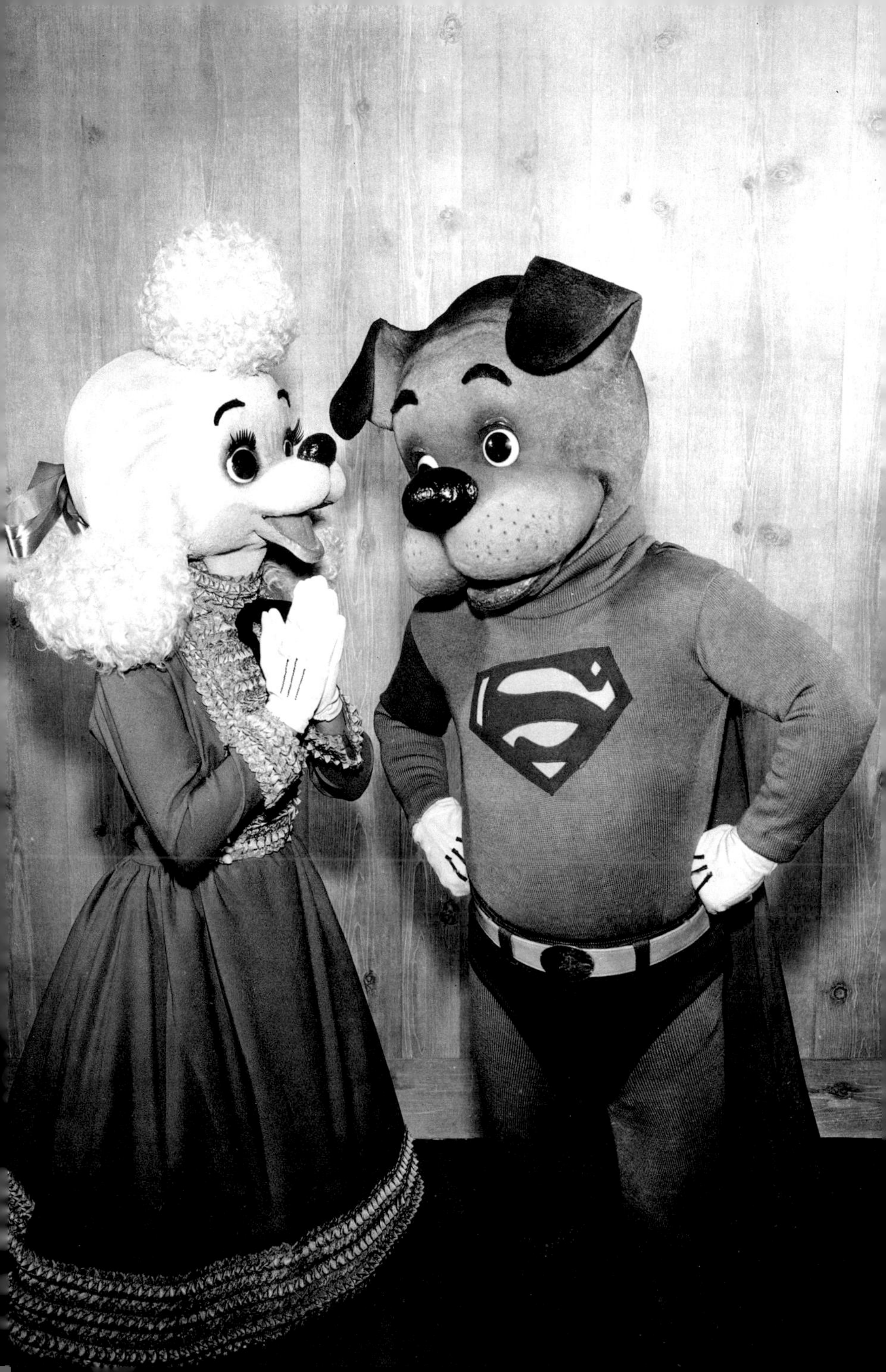

MISS BEVERLY HILLS OF HOLLYWOOD No. 1

Cover art, Bob Oksner, March–April 1949. Revolving around a budding actress, each issue of *Miss Beverly Hills* arranged for its star to run into Hollywood actors who'd agreed to license their image to comics for one story.

THE ADVENTURES OF ALAN LADD No. 4

Cover photograph, Theda and Emerson Hall, April–May, 1950. Although many silver screen cowboys licensed their images to comic books over the years, it was unusual to see an actor with a diverse dramatic résumé like Alan Ladd receive his own adventure comic book. A decade earlier, when *Green Lantern* was being developed, it was suggested that his civilian name be a variation on Aladdin but "Alan Ladd" was rejected as too improbable.

SUPERMAN DC PUBLICATION
Extra! BEVERLY meets ALAN LADD
SUPERMAN DC PUBLICATION
Miss BEVERLY HILLS of HOLLYWOOD
MAR. APR.
A 52 PAGE MAGAZINE
TEN CENTS
JAN 26
SCRIPT
Make-up Kit
"Road to Stardom" FEATURING WANDA HENDRIX

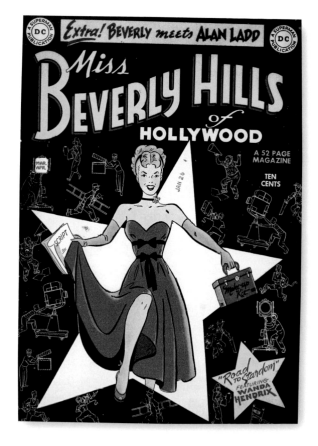

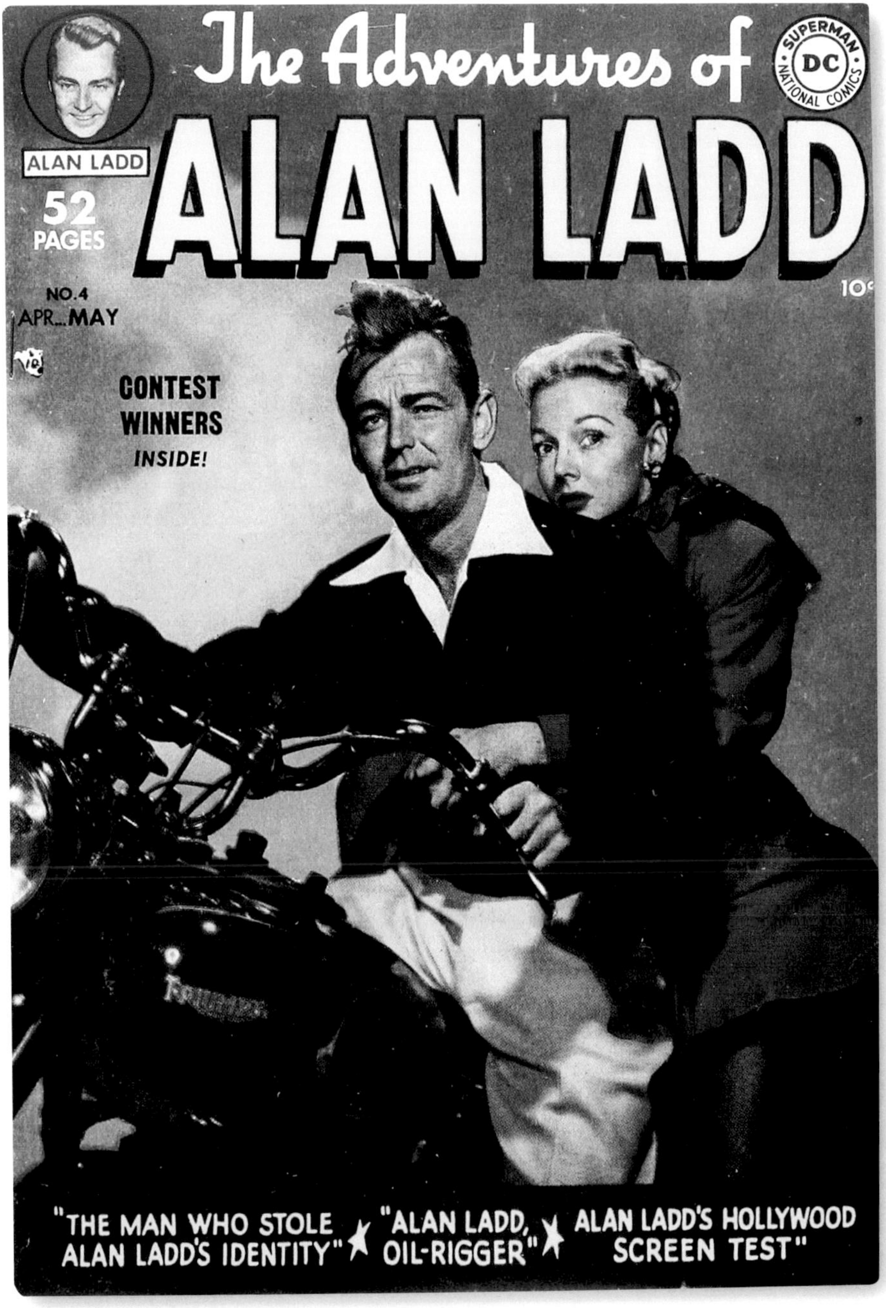
The Adventures of
ALAN LADD
ALAN LADD
52 PAGES
SUPERMAN DC NATIONAL COMICS
NO.4
APR...MAY
10¢
CONTEST WINNERS INSIDE!
"THE MAN WHO STOLE ALAN LADD'S IDENTITY"
"ALAN LADD, OIL-RIGGER"
ALAN LADD'S HOLLYWOOD SCREEN TEST"

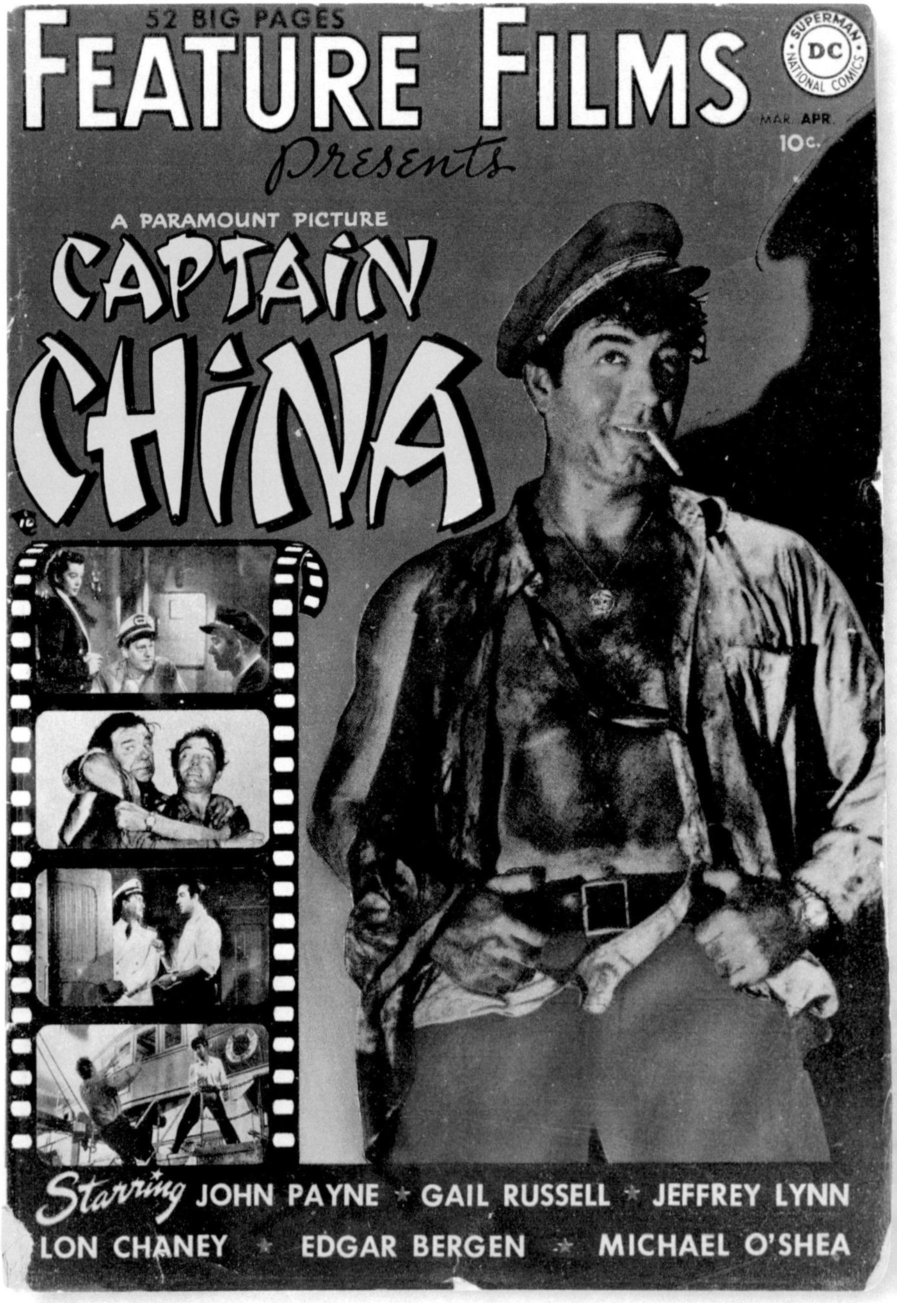
52 BIG PAGES
FEATURE FILMS
SUPERMAN DC NATIONAL COMICS
MAR. APR.
10c.
presents
A PARAMOUNT PICTURE
CAPTAIN CHINA
Starring JOHN PAYNE ★ GAIL RUSSELL ★ JEFFREY LYNN
LON CHANEY ★ EDGAR BERGEN ★ MICHAEL O'SHEA

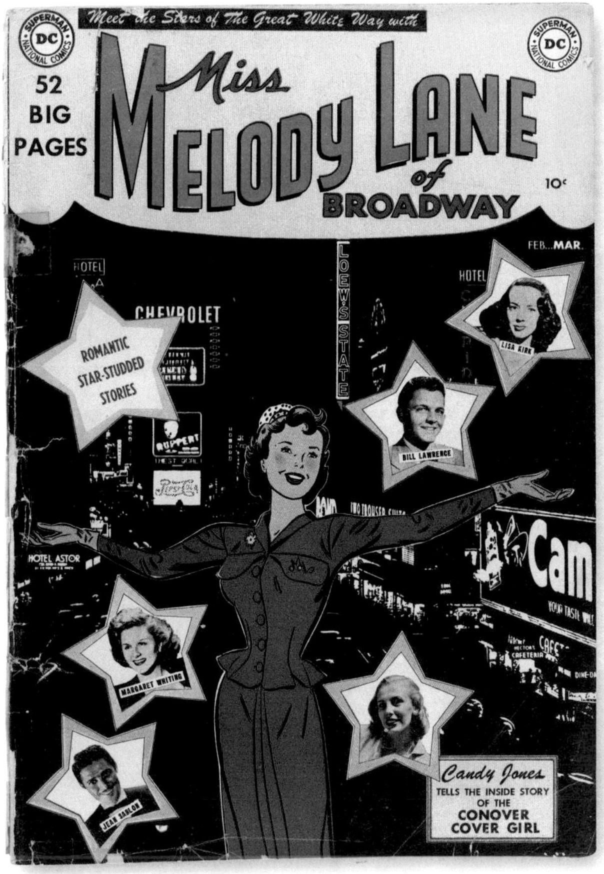
Meet the Stars of The Great White Way with
DC
52 BIG PAGES
Miss MELODY LANE of BROADWAY
10¢
FEB...MAR.
ROMANTIC STAR-STUDDED STORIES
LISA KIRK
BILL LAWRENCE
MARGARET WHITING
JEAN SABLON
Candy Jones TELLS THE INSIDE STORY OF THE CONOVER COVER GIRL
CHEVROLET
LOEW'S STATE
HOTEL ASTOR

FEATURE FILMS No. 1
Cover art, March–April 1950. While more polished than the art-photo hybrid of 1939's *Movie Comics, Feature Films'* adaptations of current theatrical releases survived a mere four issues.

MISS MELODY LANE OF BROADWAY No. 1
Cover art, Bob Oksner, February–March 1950. Before their TV shows made them household names in the 1950s, Sid Caesar and Ed Sullivan each guest starred with budding actress Miss Melody Lane. The comic book was an early attempt to capitalize on the infant television medium, and a skittish DC canceled it after three issues, replacing it on the schedule with *Strange Adventures.*

SERGEANT BILKO No. 1

Cover art, Bob Oksner, May–June 1957. Based on the TV series starring Phil Silvers, Sergeant Bilko proved popular enough to warrant the spin-off title *Sgt. Bilko's Pvt. Doberman* (based on a character played by Maurice Gosfield). Both comics ended shortly after the TV series' 1959 cancellation.

THE ADVENTURES OF BOB HOPE No. 13

Cover art, Owen Fitzgerald, February–March 1952. With firmly established screen personas, Bob Hope and the comedy team of Martin and Lewis made versatile leads in two of DC's longest-running humor titles. The exit of Dean Martin from the comedy team failed to affect their comic book in the least, which continued as *The Adventures of Jerry Lewis* until 1971. Hope's own title ended in late 1967, by which time he was better known to kids for his NBC-TV specials than his movies.

THE ADVENTURES OF DEAN MARTIN AND JERRY LEWIS No. 15

Cover art, Owen Fitzgerald, August 1954.

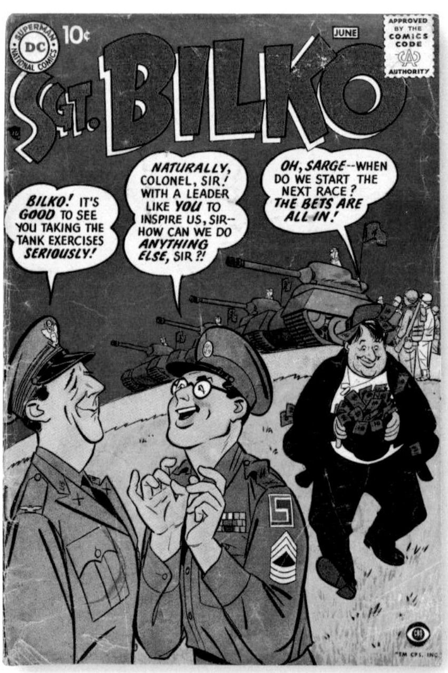
10¢
JUNE
APPROVED BY THE COMICS CODE AUTHORITY
SGT. BILKO
BILKO! IT'S GOOD TO SEE YOU TAKING THE TANK EXERCISES SERIOUSLY!
NATURALLY, COLONEL, SIR! WITH A LEADER LIKE YOU TO INSPIRE US, SIR--HOW CAN WE DO ANYTHING ELSE, SIR?!
OH, SARGE--WHEN DO WE START THE NEXT RACE? THE BETS ARE ALL IN!

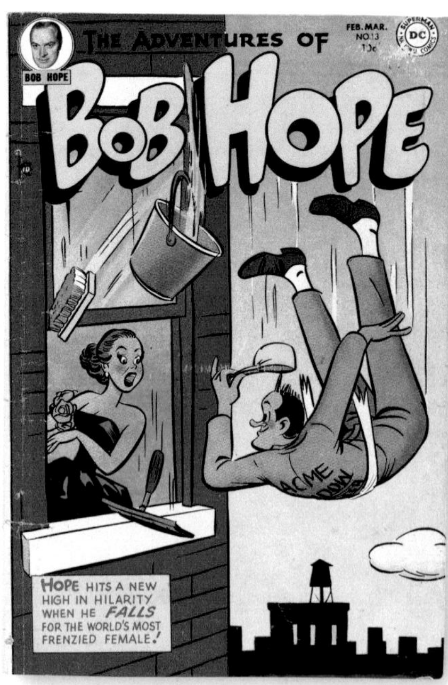
THE ADVENTURES OF
BOB HOPE
FEB.-MAR. NO. 13
BOB HOPE
ACME
HOPE HITS A NEW HIGH IN HILARITY WHEN HE FALLS FOR THE WORLD'S MOST FRENZIED FEMALE!

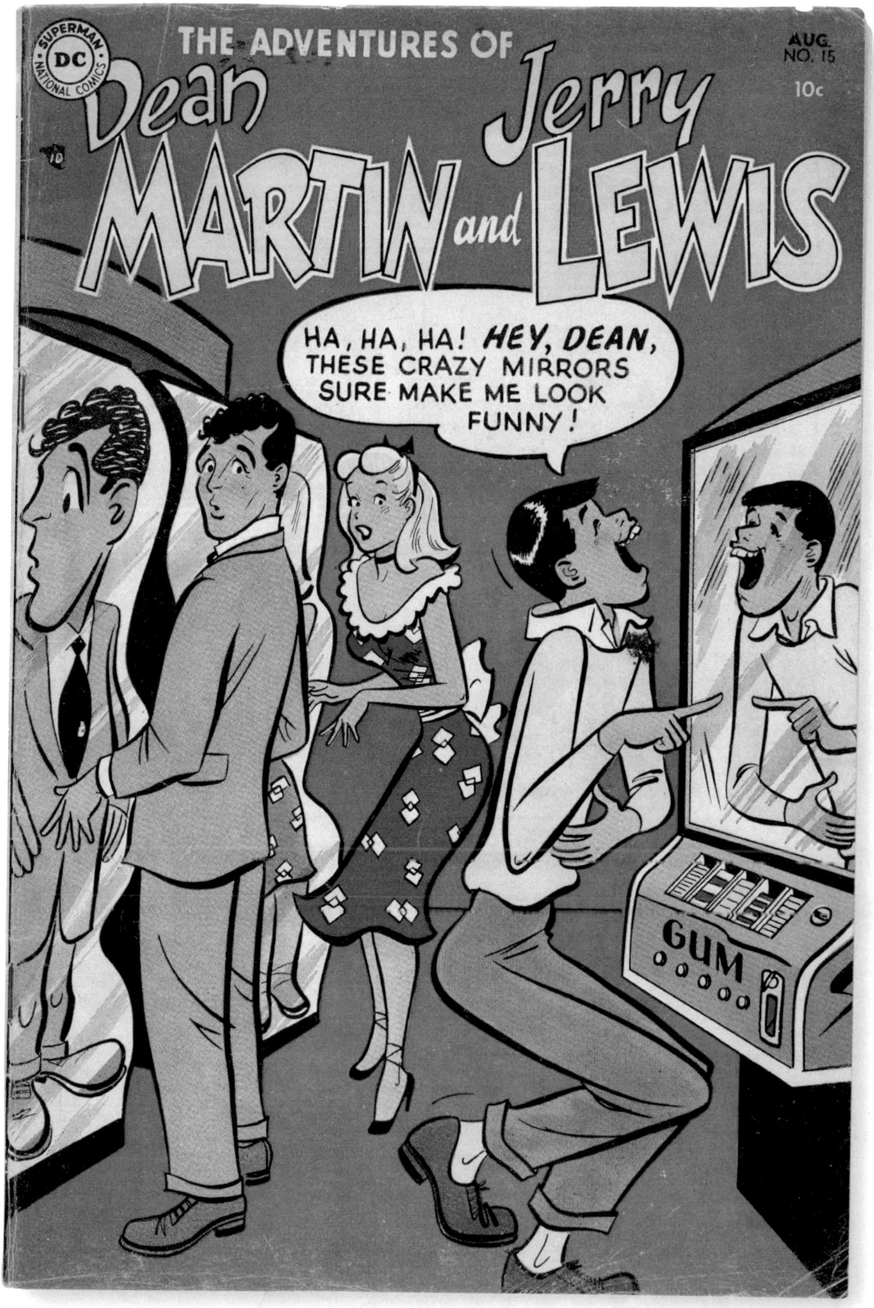
SUPERMAN DC NATIONAL COMICS
THE ADVENTURES OF
Dean Jerry
MARTIN and LEWIS
AUG. NO. 15
10c
HA, HA, HA! HEY, DEAN, THESE CRAZY MIRRORS SURE MAKE ME LOOK FUNNY!
GUM

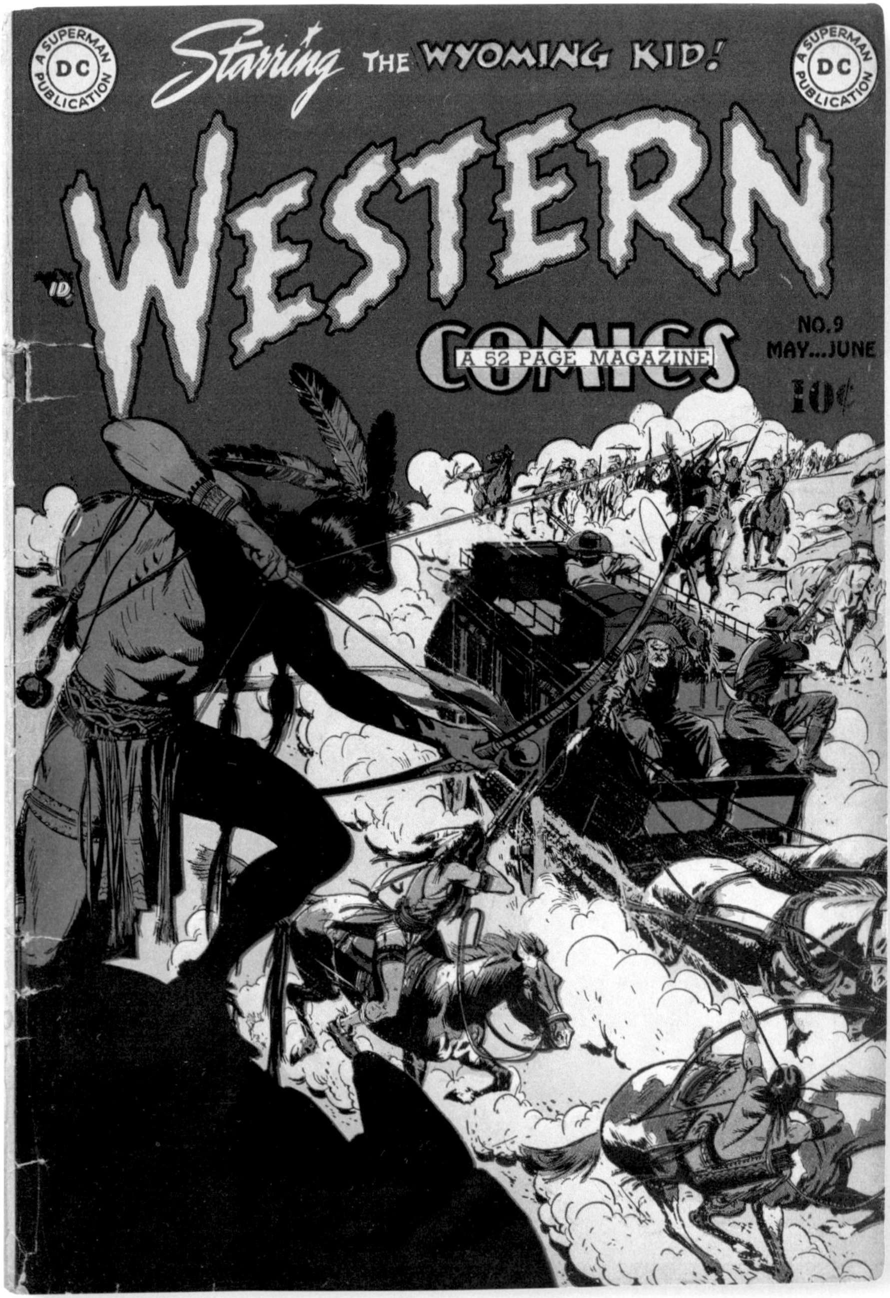
A SUPERMAN DC PUBLICATION
Starring THE WYOMING KID!
A SUPERMAN DC PUBLICATION
WESTERN
COMICS
A 52 PAGE MAGAZINE
NO.9
MAY...JUNE
10¢

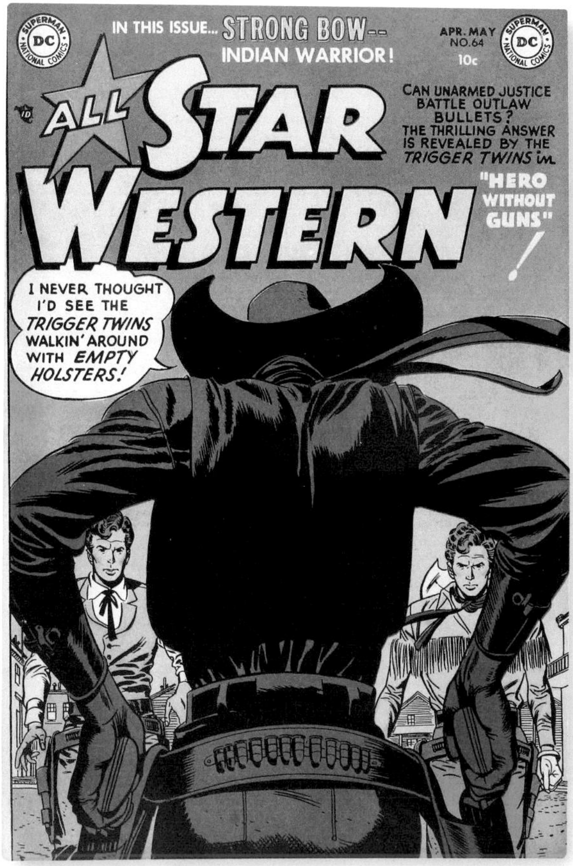
IN THIS ISSUE... STRONG BOW-- INDIAN WARRIOR!
APR.-MAY NO.64
10c
ALL STAR WESTERN
CAN UNARMED JUSTICE BATTLE OUTLAW BULLETS? THE THRILLING ANSWER IS REVEALED BY THE TRIGGER TWINS in
"HERO WITHOUT GUNS"!
I NEVER THOUGHT I'D SEE THE TRIGGER TWINS WALKIN' AROUND WITH EMPTY HOLSTERS!

WESTERN COMICS No. 9

Cover art, Leonard Starr, May–June 1949. Leonard Starr's lush, illustrative artwork came to symbolize the slick house look favored by DC editors. From 1957 to 1979, Starr produced the critically acclaimed "On Stage" newspaper strip. He moved on to a revival of the "Annie" comic strip, which he wrote and illustrated until his retirement in 2000.

ALL STAR WESTERN No. 64

Cover art, Carmine Infantino and Sy Barry, April–May 1952.

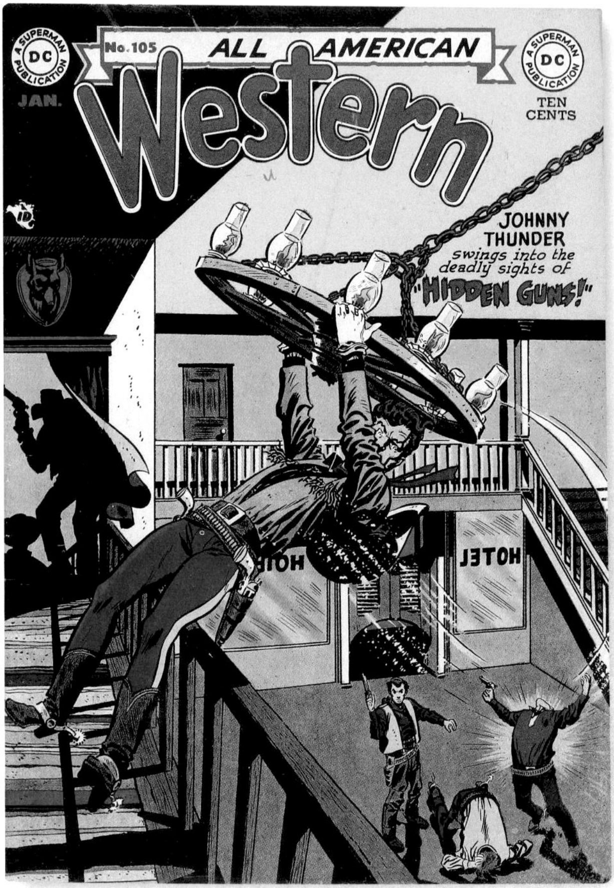
No. 105
ALL AMERICAN
Western
JAN.
TEN CENTS
JOHNNY THUNDER
swings into the deadly sights of
"HIDDEN GUNS!"
HOTEL
HOTEL

ALL-AMERICAN WESTERN No. 105

Cover art, Alex Toth and Sy Barry, January 1949.

ALL-AMERICAN WESTERN No. 103

Cover art, Alex Toth and Frank Giacoia, November 1948.
Determining that super heroes were on the way out, DC's Irwin Donenfeld evicted Green Lantern and company from *All-American Comics* and changed its title to *All-American Western*. The book's new star, Johnny Thunder, unrelated to the earlier comedic character, became a central part of DC's Western line during the decade, with a stronger start from the complex father-son relationship Robert Kanigher wove into the scripts and the striking compositions of artist Alex Toth.

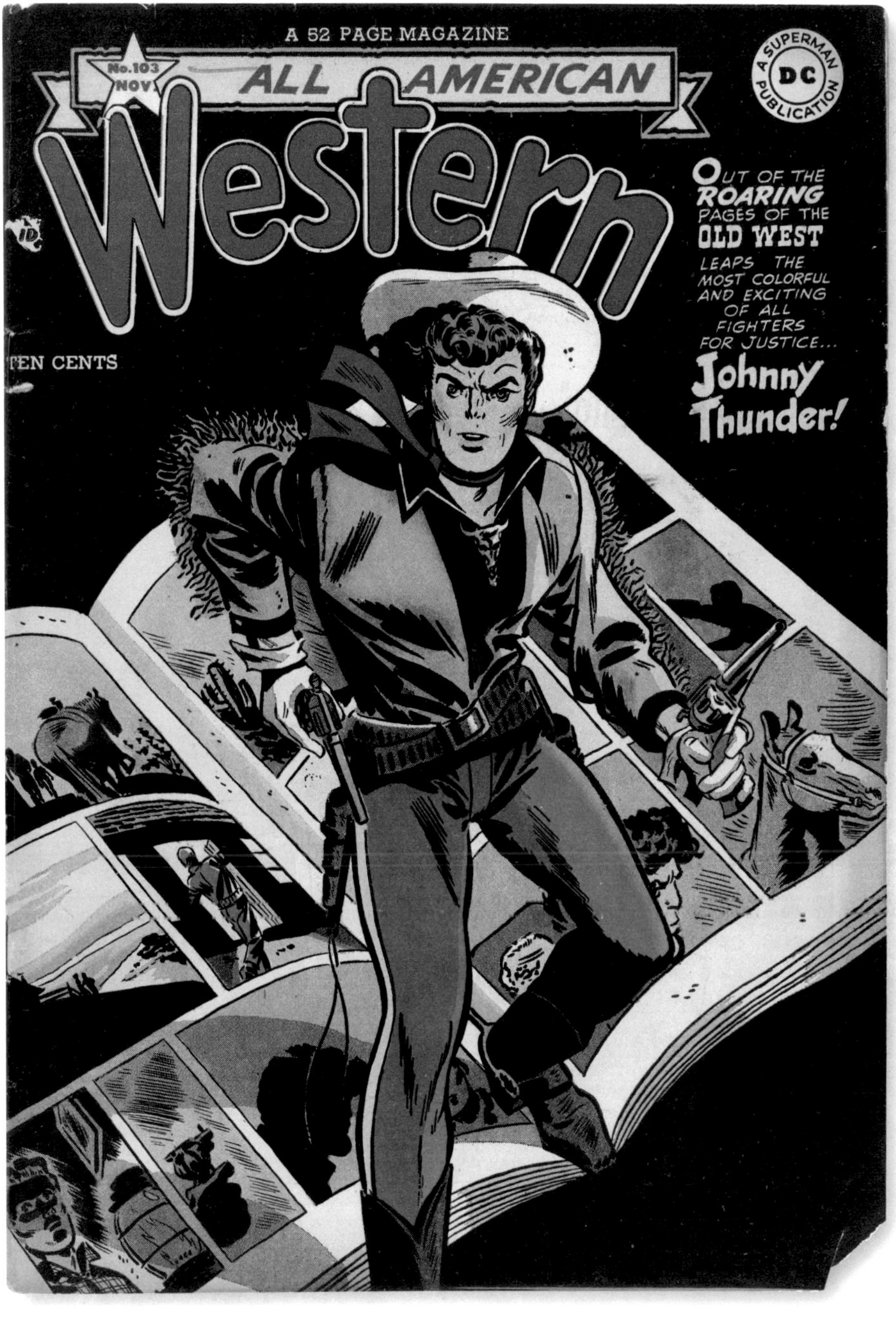
A 52 PAGE MAGAZINE
No.103 NOV.
ALL AMERICAN
Western
A SUPERMAN DC PUBLICATION
TEN CENTS
OUT OF THE ROARING PAGES OF THE OLD WEST LEAPS THE MOST COLORFUL AND EXCITING OF ALL FIGHTERS FOR JUSTICE...
Johnny Thunder!

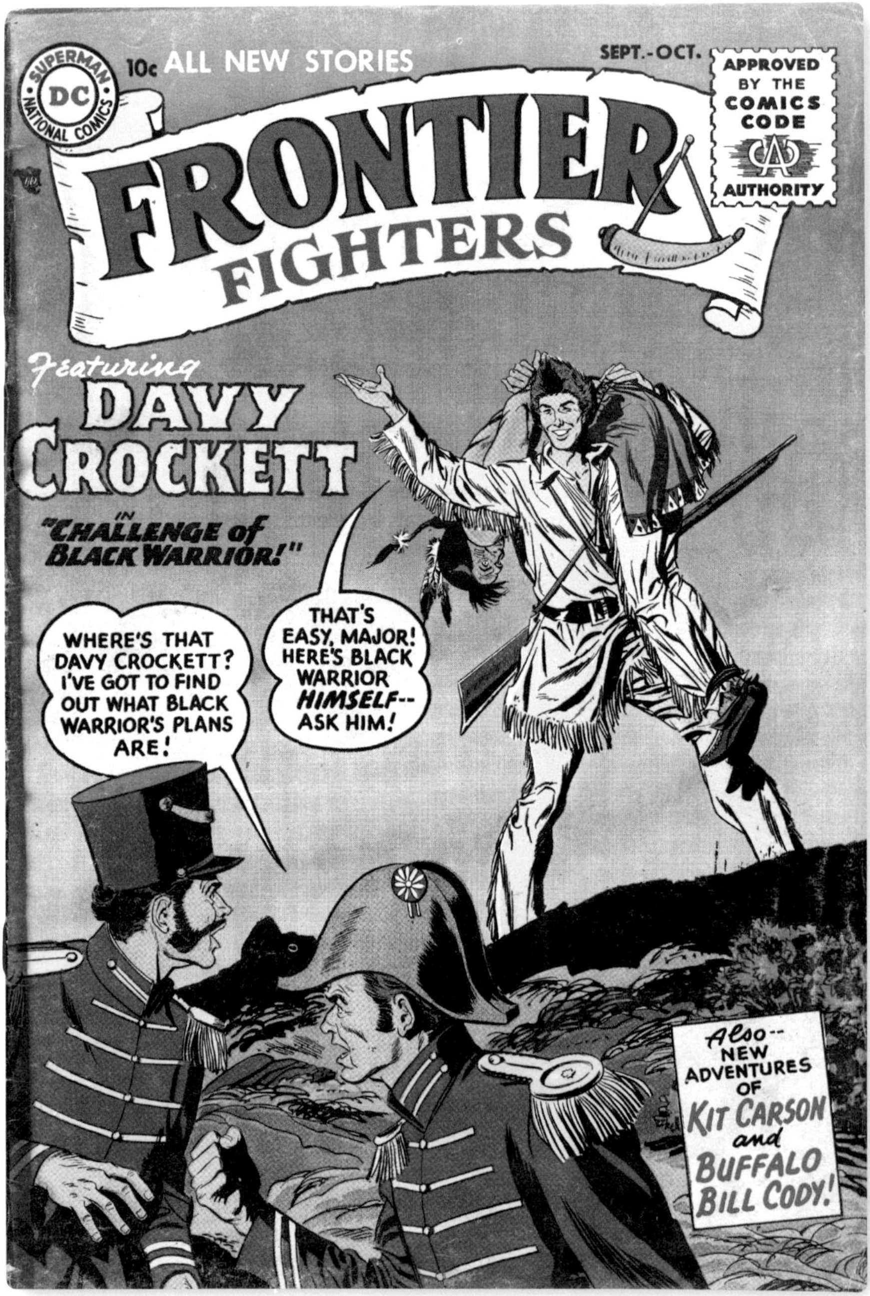
SUPERMAN DC NATIONAL COMICS
10c ALL NEW STORIES
SEPT.-OCT.
APPROVED BY THE COMICS CODE AUTHORITY
FRONTIER FIGHTERS
Featuring DAVY CROCKETT
IN "CHALLENGE of BLACK WARRIOR!"
WHERE'S THAT DAVY CROCKETT? I'VE GOT TO FIND OUT WHAT BLACK WARRIOR'S PLANS ARE!
THAT'S EASY, MAJOR! HERE'S BLACK WARRIOR HIMSELF-- ASK HIM!
Also-- NEW ADVENTURES OF KIT CARSON and BUFFALO BILL CODY!

FRONTIER FIGHTERS No. 1

Cover art, John Prentice, September–October 1955. Along with Davy Crockett, *Frontier Fighters* featured the adventures of other historical heroes like Buffalo Bill and Kit Carson.

ALL-AMERICAN WESTERN No. 111

Cover art, Alex Toth and Joe Giella, December 1949–January 1950.

A THRILLING "FOLEY OF THE FIGHTING FIFTH" ADVENTURE!
SUPERMAN DC NATIONAL COMICS
52 PAGES
NO.111
ALL AMERICAN
Western
10¢
DEC....JAN.
FATE CASTS FIGHTING
JOHNNY THUNDER
IN THE MOST AMAZING ROLE OF HIS CAREER, AS—
"The Gun-Shy Sheriff"

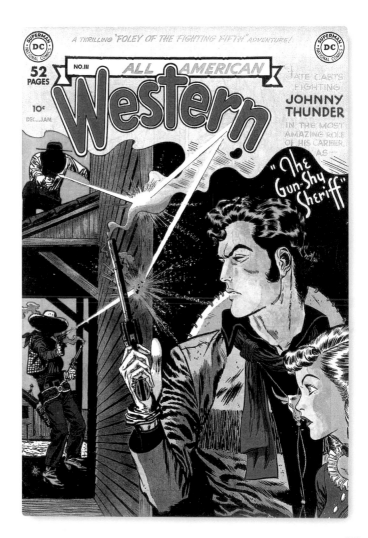

No. 4
Starring THE WYOMING KID!
A SUPERMAN PUBLICATION
DC
WESTERN
COMICS
A 52 PAGE MAGAZINE
JULY
AUG.
10¢

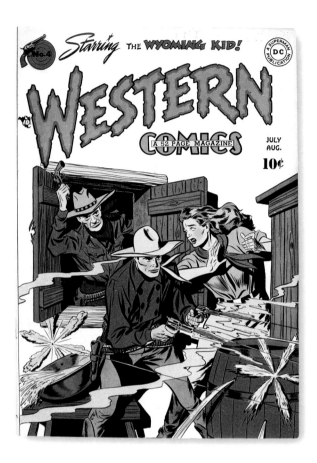

WESTERN COMICS No. 4

Cover art, Howard Sherman, July–August 1948. DC filled its first comic book devoted exclusively to Western heroes with several newcomers like the Cowboy Marshal, Rodeo Rick, and the Wyoming Kid. The Vigilante, the masked star of a longtime back-up strip in *Action Comics*, appeared in the first four issues before giving up his spot to another masked man—the Nighthawk.

STAR SPANGLED COMICS No. 116

Interior, "The Battle of Junction Fort"; script, unknown; art, Fred Ray. May 1951. Tomahawk's adventures in the Revolutionary War were a big enough draw that he bumped Robin the Boy Wonder as the cover star of Star-Spangled Comics in 1949.

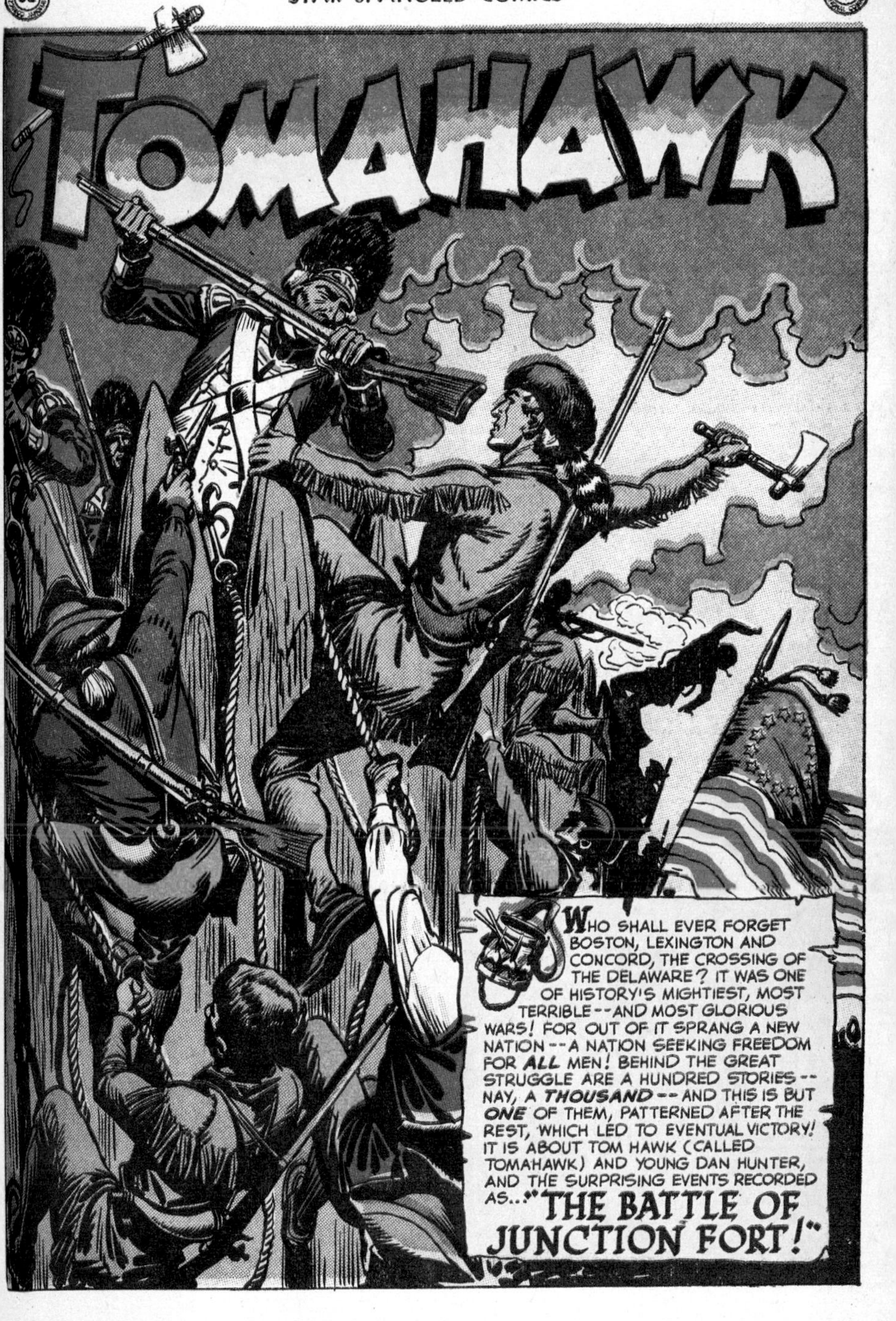
TOMAHAWK
WHO SHALL EVER FORGET BOSTON, LEXINGTON AND CONCORD, THE CROSSING OF THE DELAWARE? IT WAS ONE OF HISTORY'S MIGHTIEST, MOST TERRIBLE--AND MOST GLORIOUS WARS! FOR OUT OF IT SPRANG A NEW NATION--A NATION SEEKING FREEDOM FOR ALL MEN! BEHIND THE GREAT STRUGGLE ARE A HUNDRED STORIES--NAY, A THOUSAND--AND THIS IS BUT ONE OF THEM, PATTERNED AFTER THE REST, WHICH LED TO EVENTUAL VICTORY! IT IS ABOUT TOM HAWK (CALLED TOMAHAWK) AND YOUNG DAN HUNTER, AND THE SURPRISING EVENTS RECORDED AS..."THE BATTLE OF JUNCTION FORT!"

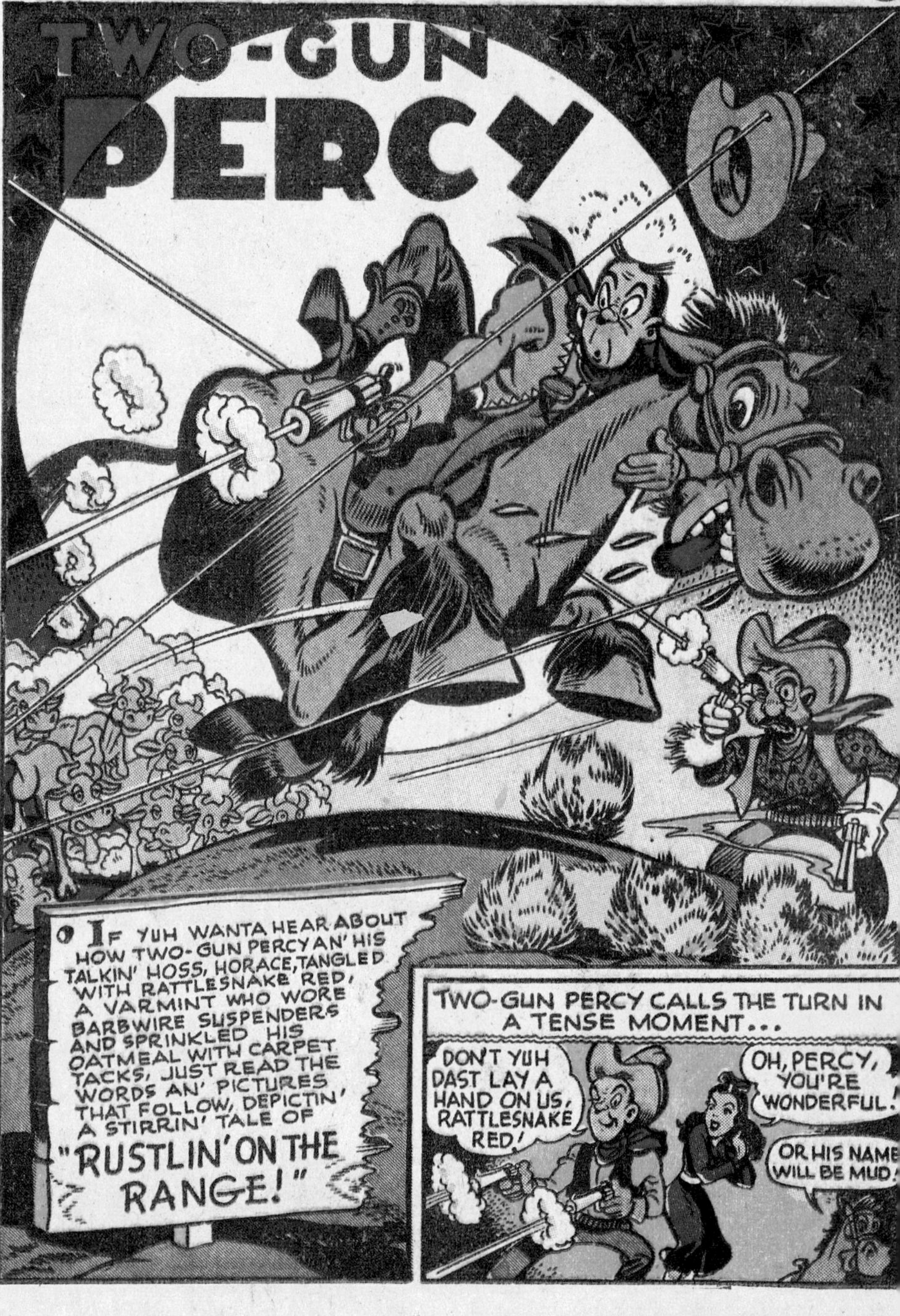

TWO-GUN PERCY
IF YUH WANTA HEAR ABOUT HOW TWO-GUN PERCY AN' HIS TALKIN' HOSS, HORACE, TANGLED WITH RATTLESNAKE RED, A VARMINT WHO WORE BARBWIRE SUSPENDERS AND SPRINKLED HIS OATMEAL WITH CARPET TACKS, JUST READ THE WORDS AN' PICTURES THAT FOLLOW, DEPICTIN' A STIRRIN' TALE OF "RUSTLIN' ON THE RANGE!"
TWO-GUN PERCY CALLS THE TURN IN A TENSE MOMENT...
DON'T YUH DAST LAY A HAND ON US, RATTLESNAKE RED!
OH, PERCY, YOU'RE WONDERFUL!
OR HIS NAME WILL BE MUD!

No.1
"QUEEN of the WESTERNS"
A SUPERMAN PUBLICATION DC
SEPT...OCT
TEN CENTS
DALE EVANS COMICS
PHOTO by LEE GREEN

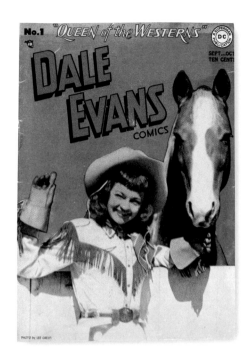

ALL FUNNY COMICS No. 13

Interior, "Rustlin' on the Range"; script, unknown; art, Jimmy Thompson. September–October 1946.

DALE EVANS COMICS No. 1

Cover photograph, Theda and Emerson Hall, September–October 1948. Dale Evans played a character by that name in her own comic book, but her sidekick there was the grizzled Uncle Six (who used a motorized wheelchair) rather than real-life husband Roy Rogers.

WONDER WOMAN No. 40

FOLLOWING SPREAD: *Interior, "Hollywood Goes to Paradise Island"; script, Robert Kanigher; pencils and inks, H. G. Peter and Win Mortimer (foreground celebrities only). March–April 1950.* In Hollywood to participate in a movie about her own adventures, Wonder Woman takes time to pose in a pinup featuring every screen performer then appearing in a DC comic book: Alan Ladd, Ozzie and Harriet Nelson, Bob Hope, Dale Evans, and Jimmy Wakely. A year before this story, Ladd crossed paths with Miss Beverly Hills of Hollywood in the first issue of her comic book, and Dale Evans co-starred with the Boy Commandos in No. 32 of their own title.

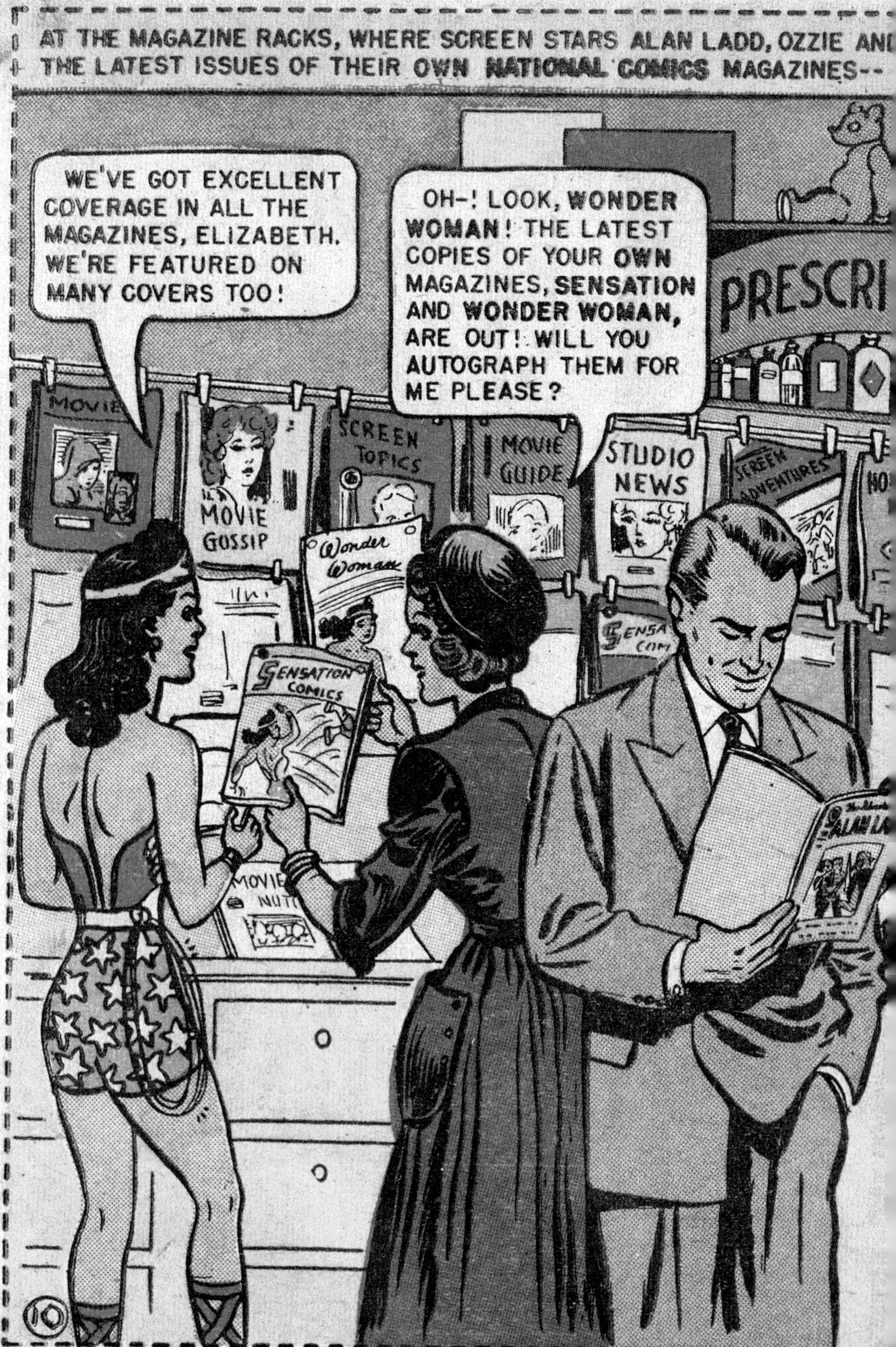
AT THE MAGAZINE RACKS, WHERE SCREEN STARS ALAN LADD, OZZIE AN
THE LATEST ISSUES OF THEIR OWN NATIONAL COMICS MAGAZINES--
WE'VE GOT EXCELLENT COVERAGE IN ALL THE MAGAZINES, ELIZABETH. WE'RE FEATURED ON MANY COVERS TOO!
OH-! LOOK, WONDER WOMAN! THE LATEST COPIES OF YOUR OWN MAGAZINES, SENSATION AND WONDER WOMAN, ARE OUT! WILL YOU AUTOGRAPH THEM FOR ME PLEASE?
PRESCRI
MOVIE
MOVIE GOSSIP
SCREEN TOPICS
MOVIE GUIDE
STUDIO NEWS
SCREEN ADVENTURES
Wonder Woman
SENSATION COMICS
MOVIE NUT
ALAN LA
10
CUT ALONG DOTTED LINE
CUT ALONG DOTT

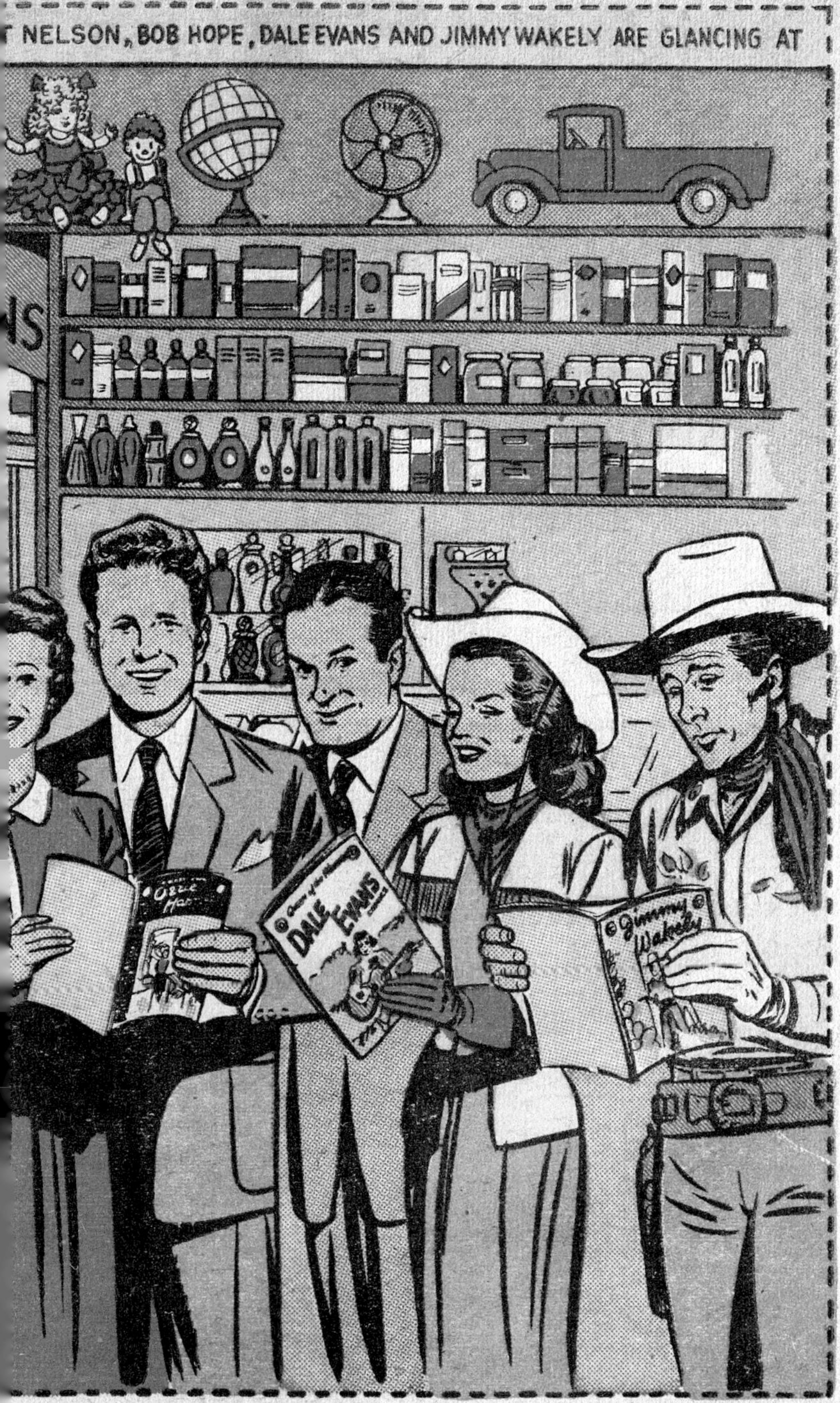
T NELSON, BOB HOPE, DALE EVANS AND JIMMY WAKELY ARE GLANCING AT
DALE EVANS
Jimmy Wakely

CUT ALONG DOTTED LINE

Wonder Woman

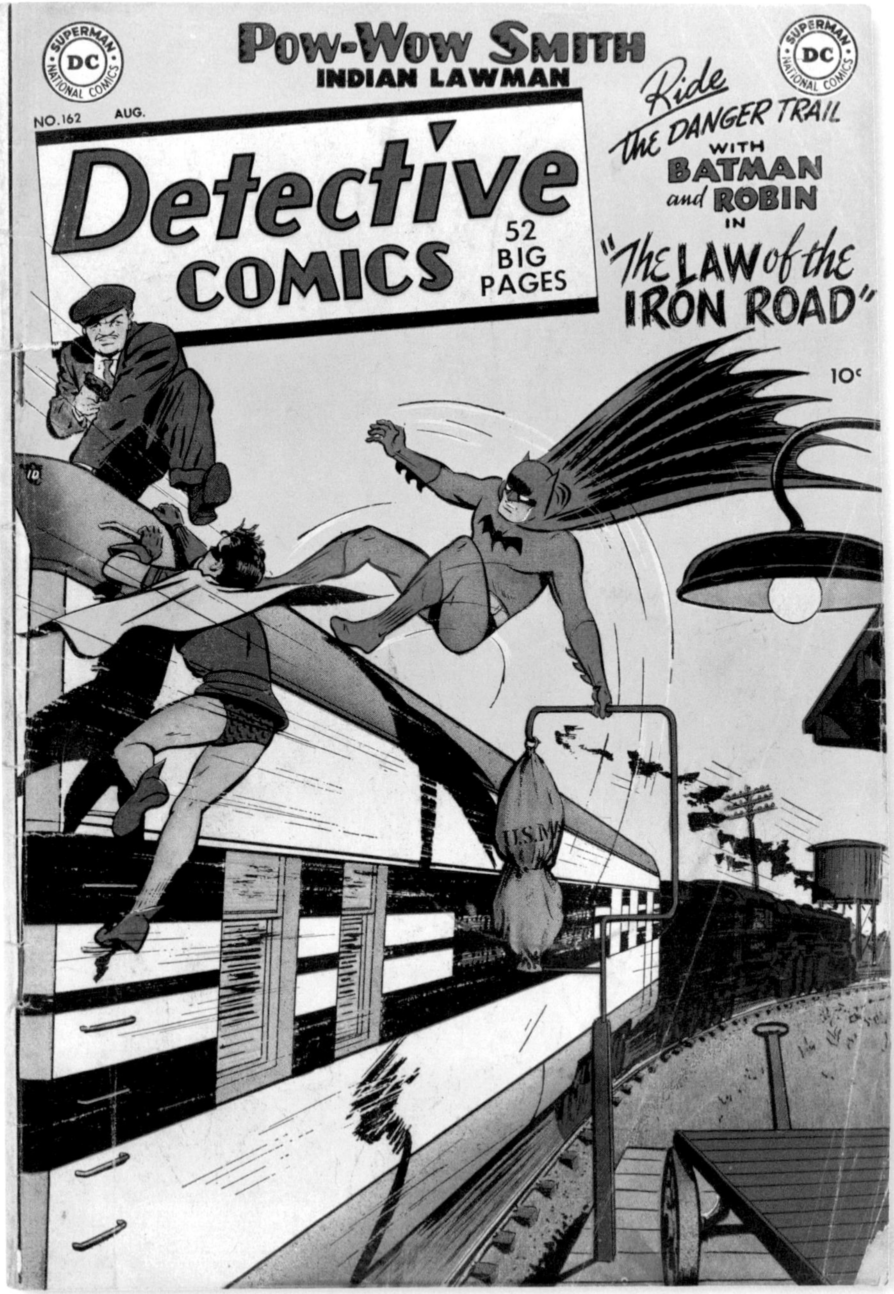
SUPERMAN DC NATIONAL COMICS
POW-WOW SMITH
INDIAN LAWMAN
SUPERMAN DC NATIONAL COMICS
NO.162
AUG.
Detective COMICS
52 BIG PAGES
Ride THE DANGER TRAIL WITH BATMAN and ROBIN IN
"The LAW of the IRON ROAD"
10¢
U.S.M.

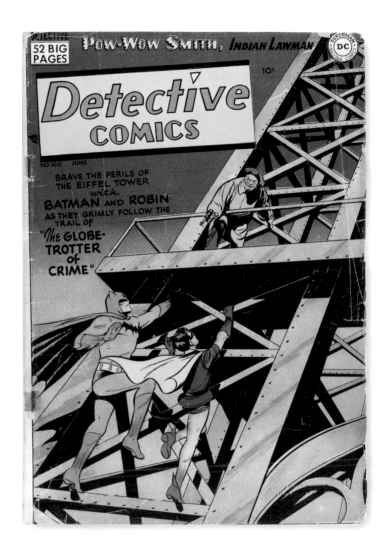

DETECTIVE
52 BIG PAGES
POW-WOW SMITH, INDIAN LAWMAN
SUPERMAN DC NATIONAL COMICS
10¢
Detective COMICS
NO. 160 JUNE
BRAVE THE PERILS OF THE EIFFEL TOWER with BATMAN AND ROBIN AS THEY GRIMLY FOLLOW THE TRAIL OF "The GLOBE-TROTTER of CRIME"

DECTECTIVE COMICS No. 162

Cover art, Win Mortimer, August 1950.

DECTECTIVE COMICS No. 160

Cover art, Win Mortimer, June 1950. Batman and Robin often left the confines of Gotham City in pursuit of lawbreakers, pushing past the throngs during Mardi Gras, scaling the Himalayas,or working with Scotland Yard or the Canadian Royal Police.

WONDER WOMAN No. 41

Cover art, Irwin Hasen and Bernard Sachs, May–June 1950. Although Diana Prince once established a detective agency in pursuit of a criminal, her alter ego of Wonder Woman gained a more long-lived occupation that same month in *Sensation Comics*: romance editor of the *Daily Globe*.

MR. DISTRICT ATTORNEY No. 1

Cover art, Sam Citron and Charles Paris, January–February 1948. Based on a popular radio drama that launched in 1939, *Mr. District Attorney* had an enduring 10-year run in comic books thanks to compact crime short stories. Once the D.A. began encountering Martians and men who walked through walls in 1958, the feature's glory days were behind it.

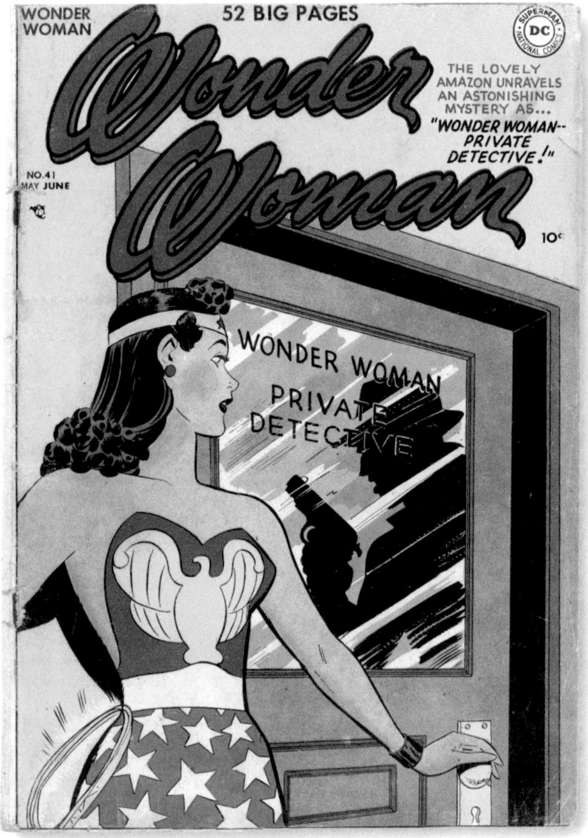
WONDER WOMAN
52 BIG PAGES
DC
Wonder Woman
THE LOVELY AMAZON UNRAVELS AN ASTONISHING MYSTERY AS...
"WONDER WOMAN-- PRIVATE DETECTIVE!"
NO.41 MAY JUNE
10¢
WONDER WOMAN PRIVATE DETECTIVE

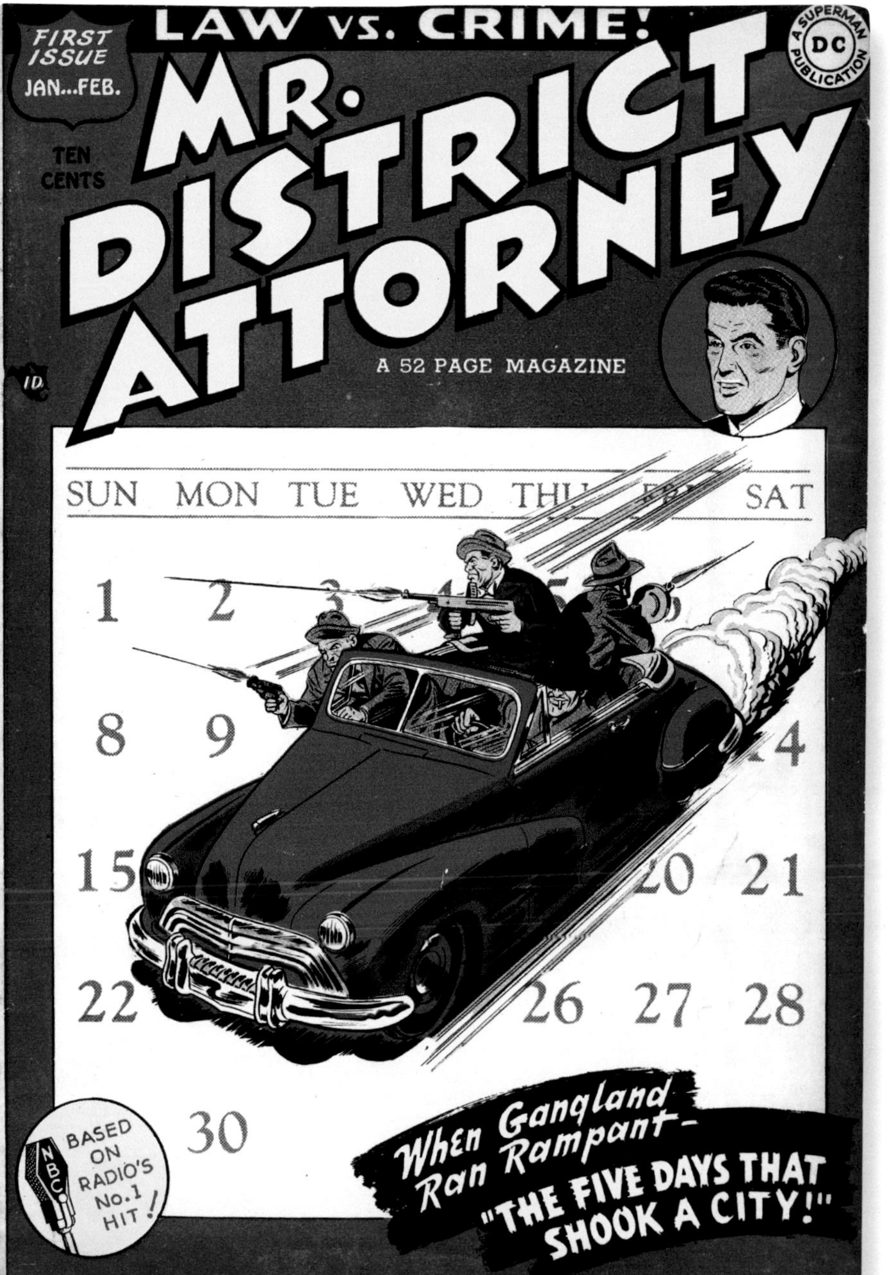
LAW vs. CRIME!
FIRST ISSUE
JAN...FEB.
TEN CENTS
MR. DISTRICT ATTORNEY
A SUPERMAN DC PUBLICATION
A 52 PAGE MAGAZINE
SUN MON TUE WED SAT
BASED ON RADIO'S No. 1 HIT!
NBC
When Gangland Ran Rampant—
"THE FIVE DAYS THAT SHOOK A CITY!"

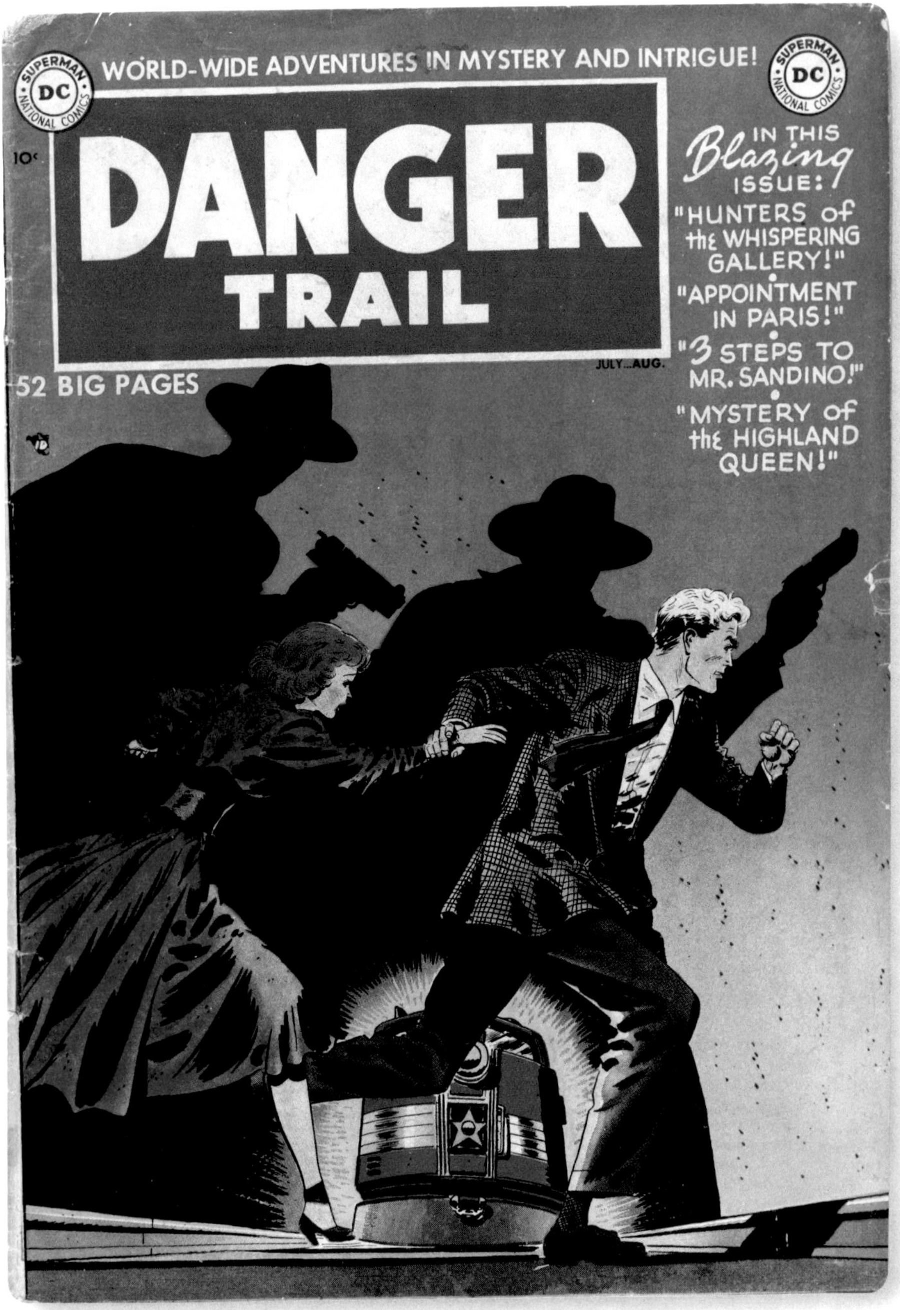
WORLD-WIDE ADVENTURES IN MYSTERY AND INTRIGUE!
SUPERMAN DC NATIONAL COMICS
SUPERMAN DC NATIONAL COMICS
10¢
DANGER TRAIL
IN THIS Blazing ISSUE:
"HUNTERS of the WHISPERING GALLERY!"
"APPOINTMENT IN PARIS!"
"3 STEPS TO MR. SANDINO!"
"MYSTERY of the HIGHLAND QUEEN!"
JULY...AUG.
52 BIG PAGES

NEW STORIES OF TV AND RADIO'S HIT SHOWS!
NOV. NO.11
10c
BIG TOWN
WILL ACE CRIME REPORTER STEVE WILSON'S BLAZING SCOOP TURN INTO HIS... "LAST HEADLINE"?

GANG BUSTERS
BRAND-NEW ADVENTURES OF RADIO'S COAST-TO-COAST FAVORITE
52 BIG PAGES
GANG BUSTERS
READ ABOUT NEW YORK'S MOST THRILLING MANHUNT IN "BROADWAY SQUAD!" THE INSIDE STORY OF THE MEN WHO PATROL THE GREAT WHITE WAY!
NO LEFT TURN
YOU CAN'T BEAT THE LAW!

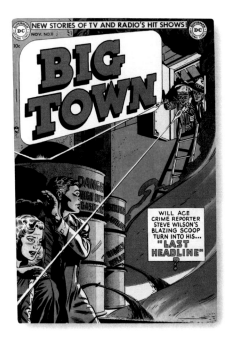

DANGER TRAIL No. 1

Cover art, Carmine Infantino and Joe Giella, July–August 1950. Touting global intrigue and adventure, *Danger Trail* never caught on with general readers, but it became a critical favorite with a later generation of fans. Although most stories in the series starred one-shot adventurers, each issue opened with the exploits of King Faraday, a secret agent created by Robert Kanigher and Carmine Infantino who'd be revived in the 1960s and again in the 1980s.

BIG TOWN No. 11

Cover art, Alex Toth, November 1951. Big Town continued in the vein of the radio and TV show it was licensed from with a succession of crime stories investigated by newspaper editor Steve Wilson and his team. The early issues were particularly handsome, sporting artwork by siblings Dan and Sy Barry.

GANG BUSTERS No. 19

Cover art, Dan Barry, December 1950–January 1951. Based on a popular radio series, *Gang Busters* was DC's way of gaining a foothold in the true crime genre. While lacking in the often lurid detail of series such as Lev Gleason's *Crime Does Not Pay, Gang Busters*' 11-year, 67-issue run brought a dignified credibility and realism to the form through contributions from artists including Curt Swan.

JIMMY WAKELY No. 18

Cover art, Gil Kane, July–August 1952. With most of the major movie cowboys already in deals with rival comic book companies, DC dug deep to license the image of Jimmy Wakely and capitalize on the rising popularity of Westerns. Flummoxed editor Julius Schwartz brought his trademark professionalism to bear on the series. Beyond top-flight artists Alex Toth and Carmine Infantino in each issue, the series also featured fillers by future superstars Frank Frazetta and Harvey Kurtzman. A secondary feature starred Kit Colby, Girl Sheriff, a rare Western heroine.

ALL STAR WESTERN No. 83

Cover art, Gil Kane and Joe Giella, June–July 1955.

DALE EVANS No. 2

Interior, "The Evil Eye of Eagle Eye"; script, unknown; pencils and inks, Jim McArdle. November–December 1948. One of the most famous women in Western movies, Dale Evans became the star of a DC comic book within months of her marriage to singing cowboy Roy Rogers. Just as many movie cowboys had funny sidekicks typified by Gabby Hayes, Dale's comic counterpart was assisted by her Uncle Six, an aged cowboy in a motorized wheelchair. Roy Rogers's own name and likeness were licensed to rival Dell Comics, which eventually published a Dale Evans comic book of its own after DC discontinued its series.

HOLLYWOOD'S SENSATIONAL COWBOY STAR!
JIMMY WAKELY 10¢
JULY-AUG. NO. 18
Jimmy Wakely
NOT EVEN BULLETS CAN STOP THE PHANTOM BRANDER!
AMERICA'S COWBOY CAVALIER DUELS A SPECTRAL FIGURE OF DOOM!

10¢ ALL NEW STORIES
JUNE-JULY NO. 83
APPROVED BY THE COMICS CODE AUTHORITY
ALL STAR WESTERN
TO SAVE A BOY'S LIFE, THE FIGHTING TRIGGER TWINS DELIBERATELY REVEAL THEIR SECRET IDENTITY! THRILL TO THE EXPLOSIVE CLIMAX OF THE... "SMOKESCREEN SHERIFF!"

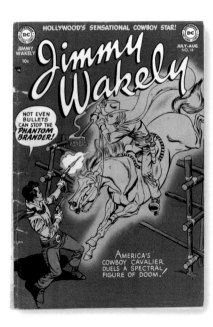

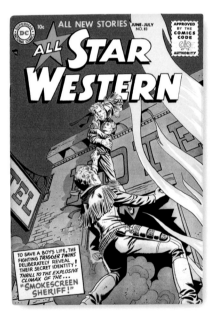

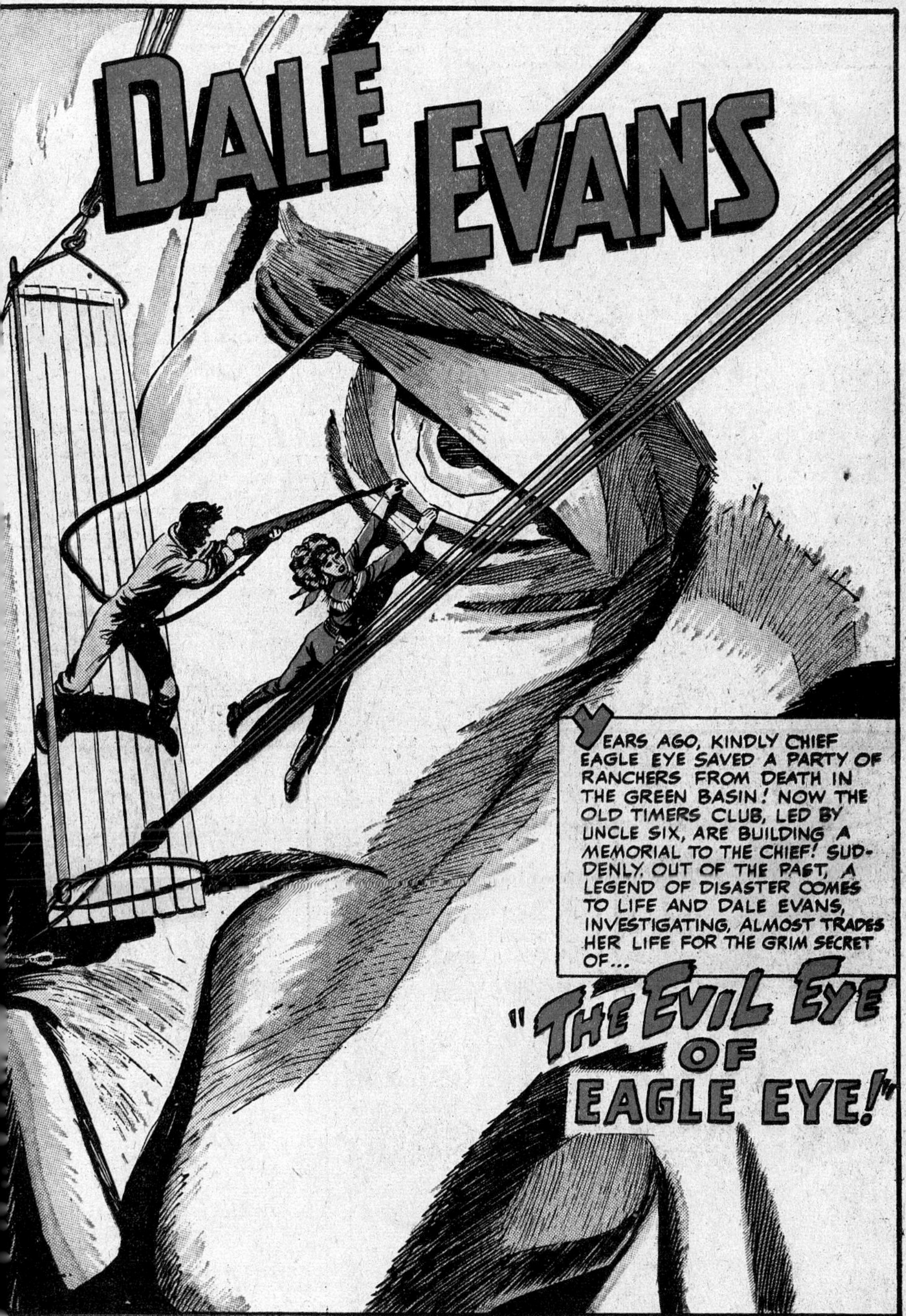
DALE EVANS
YEARS AGO, KINDLY CHIEF EAGLE EYE SAVED A PARTY OF RANCHERS FROM DEATH IN THE GREEN BASIN! NOW THE OLD TIMERS CLUB, LED BY UNCLE SIX, ARE BUILDING A MEMORIAL TO THE CHIEF! SUDDENLY, OUT OF THE PAST, A LEGEND OF DISASTER COMES TO LIFE AND DALE EVANS, INVESTIGATING, ALMOST TRADES HER LIFE FOR THE GRIM SECRET OF...
"THE EVIL EYE OF EAGLE EYE!"

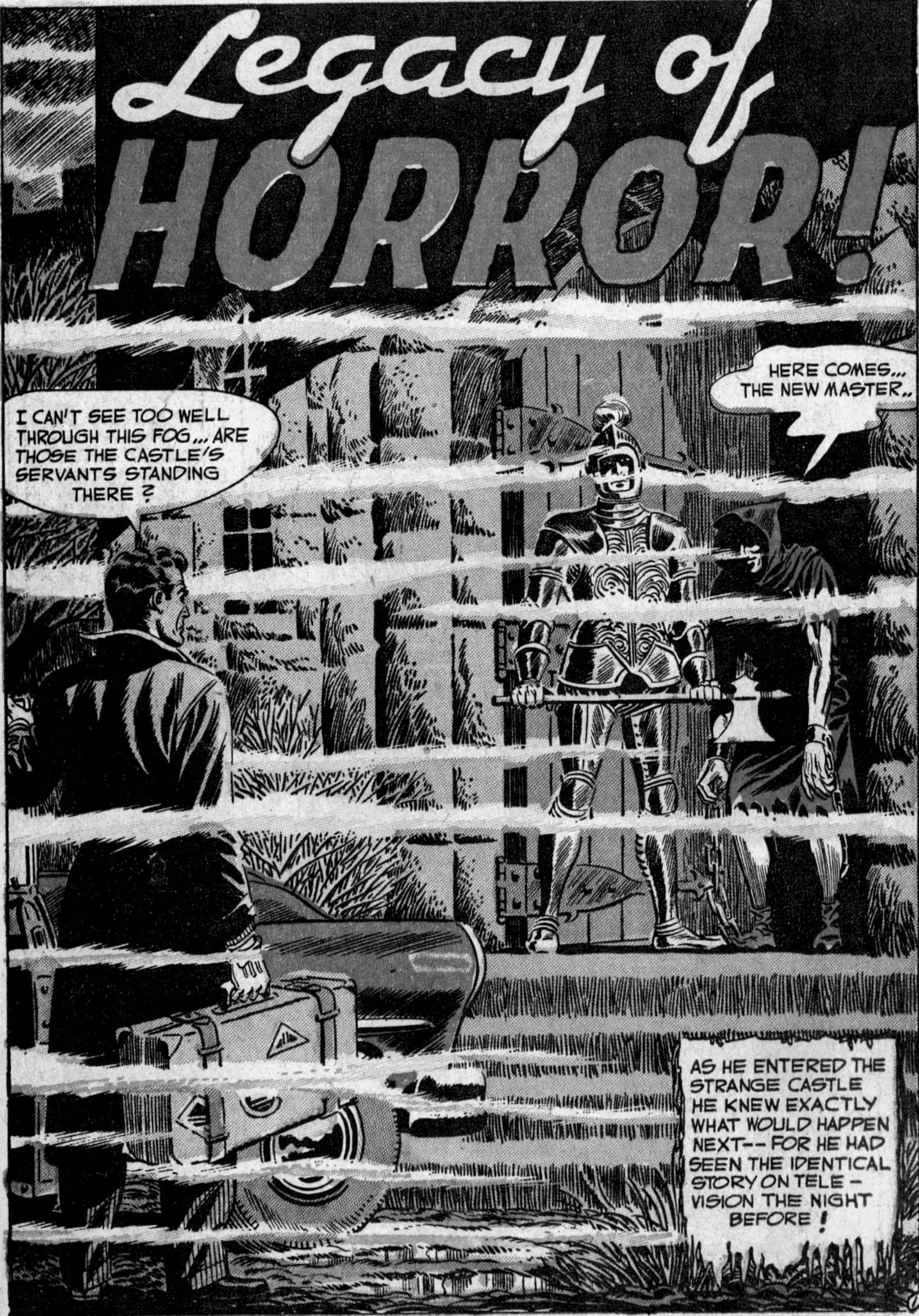
Legacy of HORROR!
HERE COMES... THE NEW MASTER..
I CAN'T SEE TOO WELL THROUGH THIS FOG... ARE THOSE THE CASTLE'S SERVANTS STANDING THERE ?
AS HE ENTERED THE STRANGE CASTLE HE KNEW EXACTLY WHAT WOULD HAPPEN NEXT-- FOR HE HAD SEEN THE IDENTICAL STORY ON TELE-VISION THE NIGHT BEFORE !

OCT.-NOV. NO. 2
IS HE MAN...OR GHOST?
THE PHANTOM STRANGER
10c
THE STRANGE STORY OF A CREEPING DOOM THAT STRUCK AT NIGHT...
"THE KILLER SHADOW!"

10c
HOUSE of MYSTERY
OCT. NO. 7
BLACK MAGIC HAS GIVEN ME EIGHT LIVES SO FAR-- AND NOW, THE NINTH FORCES ME TO KILL!
"The NINE LIVES of ROGER DENHAM"
"DEVIL MASK OF DEATH"
"RIDDLE OF THE SPLIT-SIAMESE TWINS"

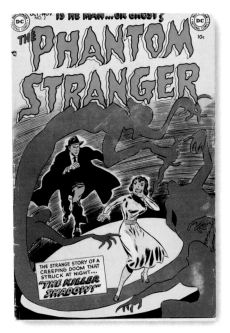

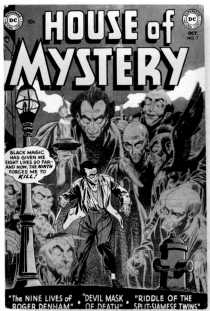

SENSATION MYSTERY No. 113

Interior, "Legacy of Horror"; script, unknown; pencils, Murphy Anderson; inks, Sy Barry. January–February 1953. As horror comic books surged in popularity, Wonder Woman was removed from *Sensation Comics* in favor of a suspense format and the new series title of *Sensation Mystery*. "Legacy of Horror" represented precisely the sort of visuals DC favored during the 1950s, with sturdy atmospheric pencils from mainstay Murphy Anderson and sleek inks by Sy Barry.

THE PHANTOM STRANGER No. 2

Cover art, Carmine Infantino and John Giunta, October–November 1952. The Phantom Stranger was inspired by Mark Twain's *The Mysterious Stranger* and was an effort to create a new suspense comic book centered on an actual leading man. As in DC's other mystery titles, there was no supernatural scenario that couldn't be rationally explained away, although the Stranger himself remained a mystery. Canceled after six issues, the series and its stories by John Broome and Carmine Infantino held a great mystique with fans.

HOUSE OF MYSTERY No. 7

Cover art, Ruben Moreira, October 1952. In contrast to the often-gruesome horror comics of its rivals, DC favored a more sedate approach. Suspenseful, well-drawn, and smartly designed covers drew readers in, but the strange situations invariably turned out to be hoaxes of some sort within the actual stories. Indeed, the very premise of the Dr. Thirteen feature — last seen in *House of Mystery* No. 7 — was that there was no such thing as ghosts.

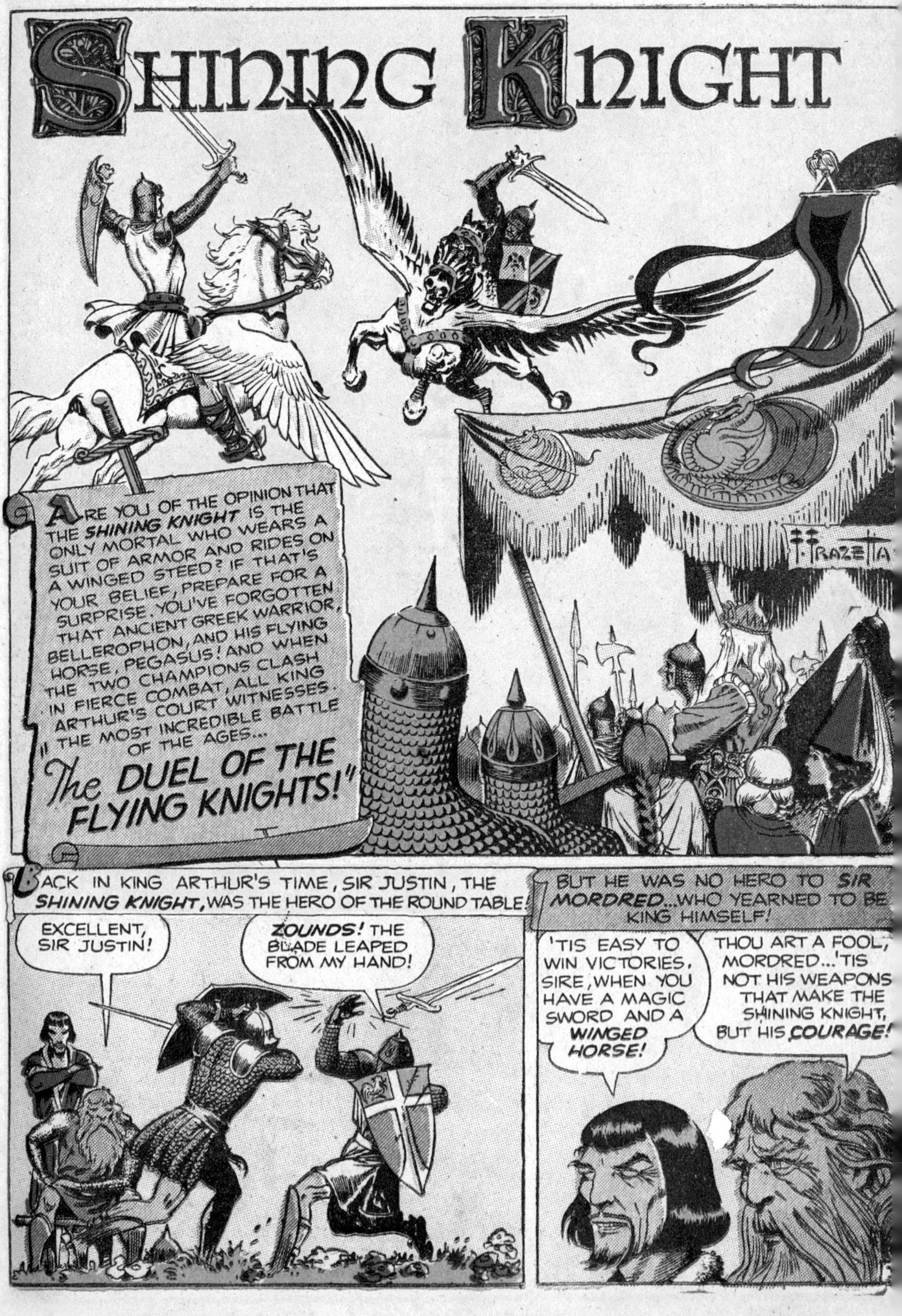
SHINING KNIGHT
F. FRAZETTA
ARE YOU OF THE OPINION THAT THE SHINING KNIGHT IS THE ONLY MORTAL WHO WEARS A SUIT OF ARMOR AND RIDES ON A WINGED STEED? IF THAT'S YOUR BELIEF, PREPARE FOR A SURPRISE. YOU'VE FORGOTTEN THAT ANCIENT GREEK WARRIOR, BELLEROPHON, AND HIS FLYING HORSE, PEGASUS! AND WHEN THE TWO CHAMPIONS CLASH IN FIERCE COMBAT, ALL KING ARTHUR'S COURT WITNESSES THE MOST INCREDIBLE BATTLE OF THE AGES...
"The DUEL OF THE FLYING KNIGHTS!"
BACK IN KING ARTHUR'S TIME, SIR JUSTIN, THE SHINING KNIGHT, WAS THE HERO OF THE ROUND TABLE!
EXCELLENT, SIR JUSTIN!
ZOUNDS! THE BLADE LEAPED FROM MY HAND!
BUT HE WAS NO HERO TO SIR MORDRED...WHO YEARNED TO BE KING HIMSELF!
'TIS EASY TO WIN VICTORIES, SIRE, WHEN YOU HAVE A MAGIC SWORD AND A WINGED HORSE!
THOU ART A FOOL, MORDRED...'TIS NOT HIS WEAPONS THAT MAKE THE SHINING KNIGHT, BUT HIS COURAGE!

ADVENTURE COMICS No. 153

Interiors, "The Duel of the Flying Knights"; script, Joe Samachson; art, Frank Frazetta. June 1950. Later to win accolades for his fantasy paintings, Frank Frazetta began his career as a comic book artist. At DC, small doses of his lush, detailed line work showed up primarily as filler stories, but he also drew eight celebrated installments of the decade-old Shining Knight feature between *Adventure Comics* Nos. 150 and 163. The episodes represented a sort of career peak for the displaced hero from King Arthur's court, and the series was discontinued three issues after Frazetta left.

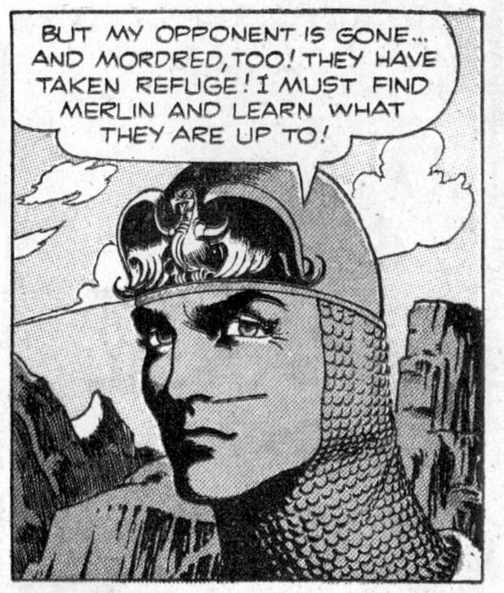

BUT MY OPPONENT IS GONE... AND MORDRED, TOO! THEY HAVE TAKEN REFUGE! I MUST FIND MERLIN AND LEARN WHAT THEY ARE UP TO!

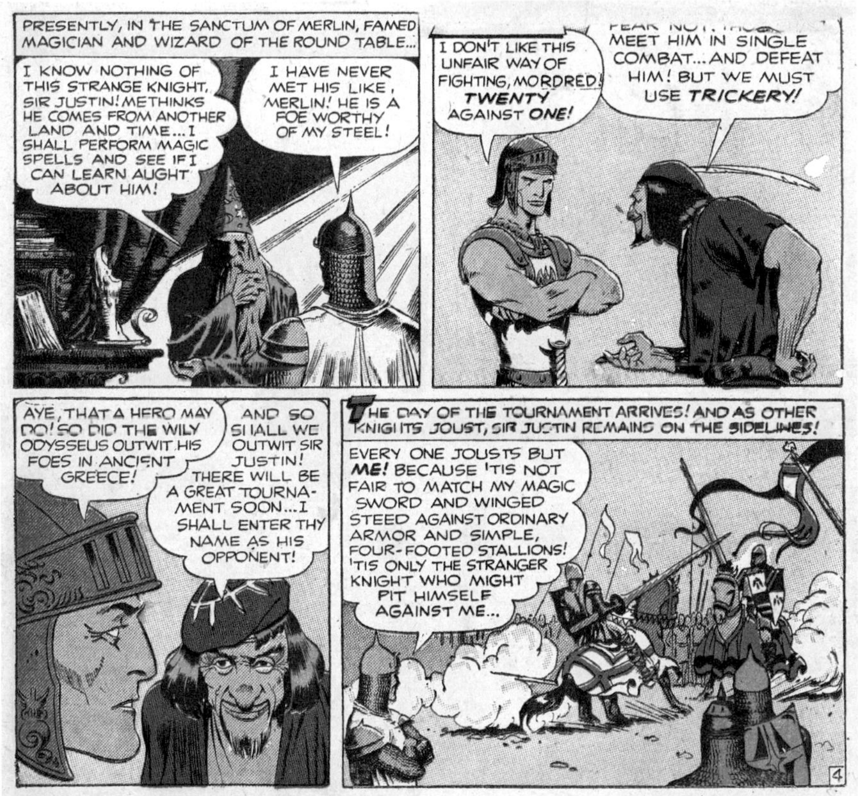

PRESENTLY, IN THE SANCTUM OF MERLIN, FAMED MAGICIAN AND WIZARD OF THE ROUND TABLE...
I KNOW NOTHING OF THIS STRANGE KNIGHT, SIR JUSTIN! METHINKS HE COMES FROM ANOTHER LAND AND TIME...I SHALL PERFORM MAGIC SPELLS AND SEE IF I CAN LEARN AUGHT ABOUT HIM!
I HAVE NEVER MET HIS LIKE, MERLIN! HE IS A FOE WORTHY OF MY STEEL!
I DON'T LIKE THIS UNFAIR WAY OF FIGHTING, MORDRED! TWENTY AGAINST ONE!
MEET HIM IN SINGLE COMBAT...AND DEFEAT HIM! BUT WE MUST USE TRICKERY!
AYE, THAT A HERO MAY DO! SO DID THE WILY ODYSSEUS OUTWIT HIS FOES IN ANCIENT GREECE!
AND SO SHALL WE OUTWIT SIR JUSTIN! THERE WILL BE A GREAT TOURNAMENT SOON...I SHALL ENTER THY NAME AS HIS OPPONENT!
THE DAY OF THE TOURNAMENT ARRIVES! AND AS OTHER KNIGHTS JOUST, SIR JUSTIN REMAINS ON THE SIDELINES!
EVERY ONE JOUSTS BUT ME! BECAUSE 'TIS NOT FAIR TO MATCH MY MAGIC SWORD AND WINGED STEED AGAINST ORDINARY ARMOR AND SIMPLE, FOUR-FOOTED STALLIONS! 'TIS ONLY THE STRANGER KNIGHT WHO MIGHT PIT HIMSELF AGAINST ME...
4

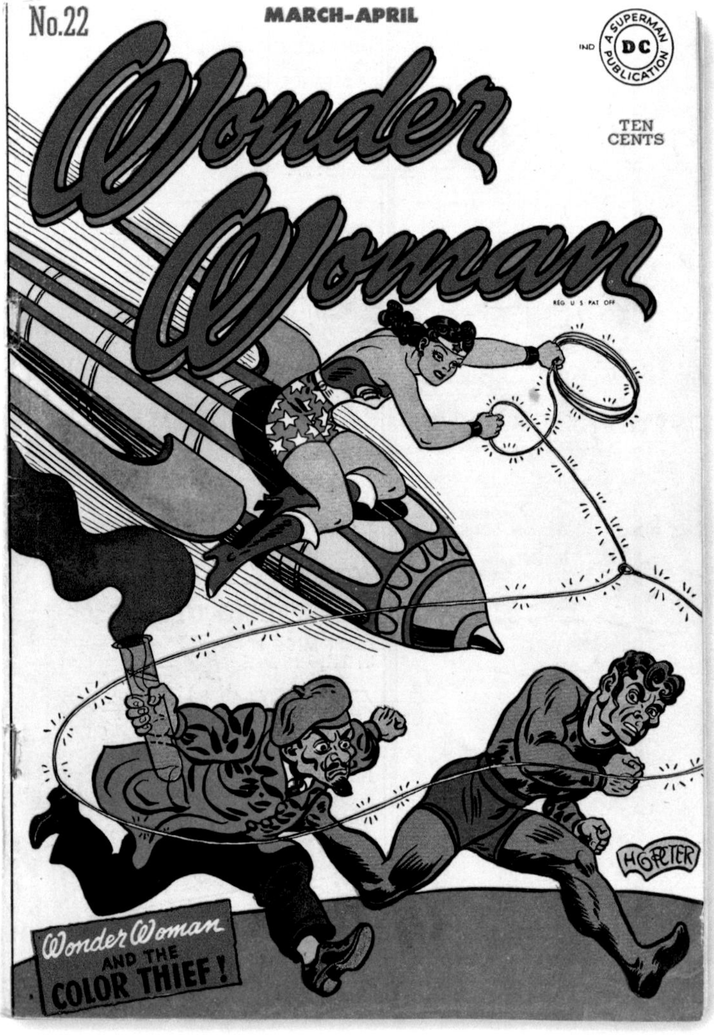
No.22
MARCH-APRIL
A SUPERMAN PUBLICATION
DC
IND
Wonder Woman
TEN CENTS
REG. U.S. PAT. OFF.
H.G. PETER
Wonder Woman AND THE COLOR THIEF!

WONDER WOMAN No. 22
Cover art, H. G. Peter, March–April 1947.

SENSATION COMICS No. 104
Cover art, Irwin Hasen and Bernard Sachs, July–August 1951. Wonder Woman seemed to have a particular problem with invaders from Mars, a planet that was home to her nemesis the Duke of Deception.

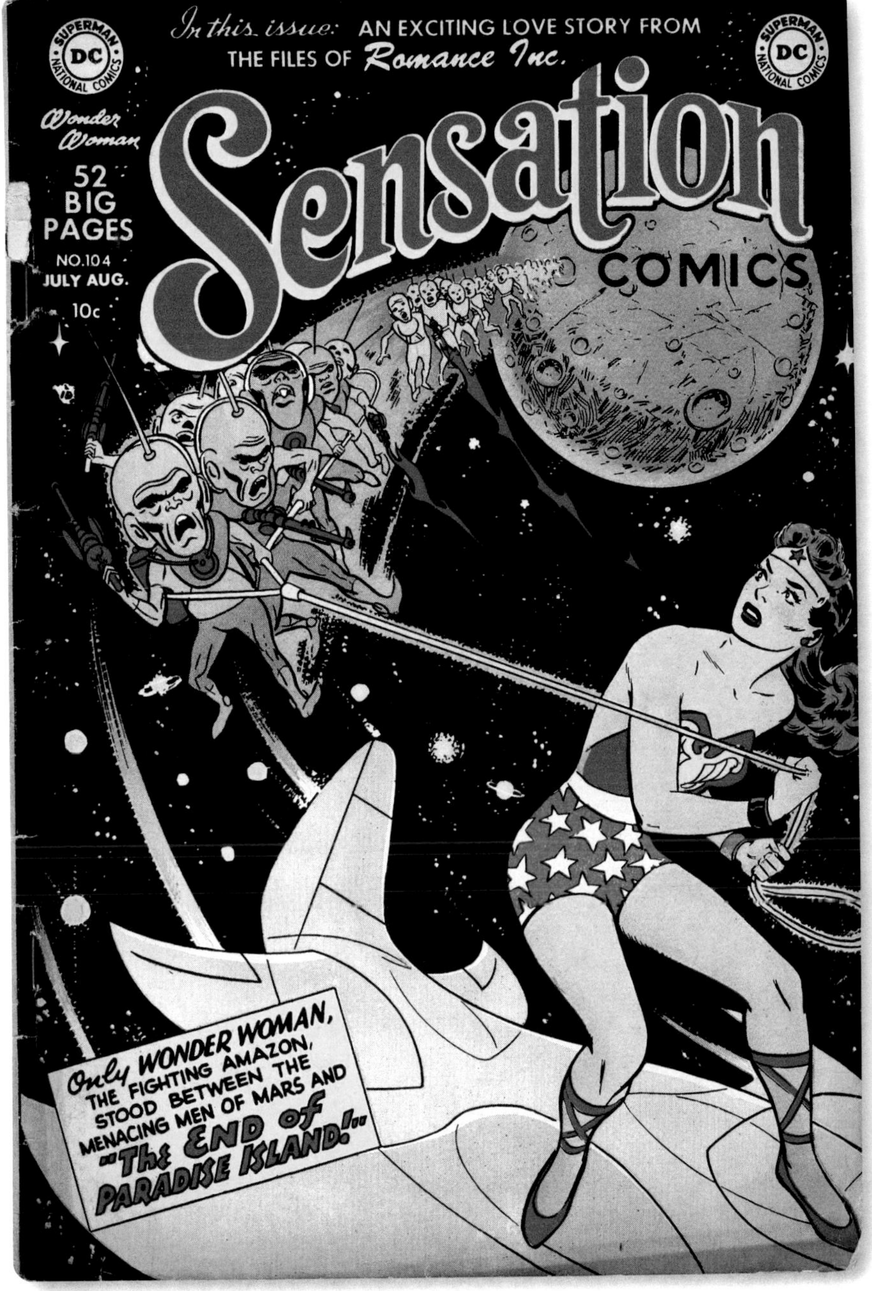
In this issue: AN EXCITING LOVE STORY FROM THE FILES OF Romance Inc.
SUPERMAN DC NATIONAL COMICS
SUPERMAN DC NATIONAL COMICS
Wonder Woman
52 BIG PAGES
NO.104 JULY AUG.
10c
Sensation
COMICS
Only WONDER WOMAN, THE FIGHTING AMAZON, STOOD BETWEEN THE MENACING MEN OF MARS AND "The END of PARADISE ISLAND!"

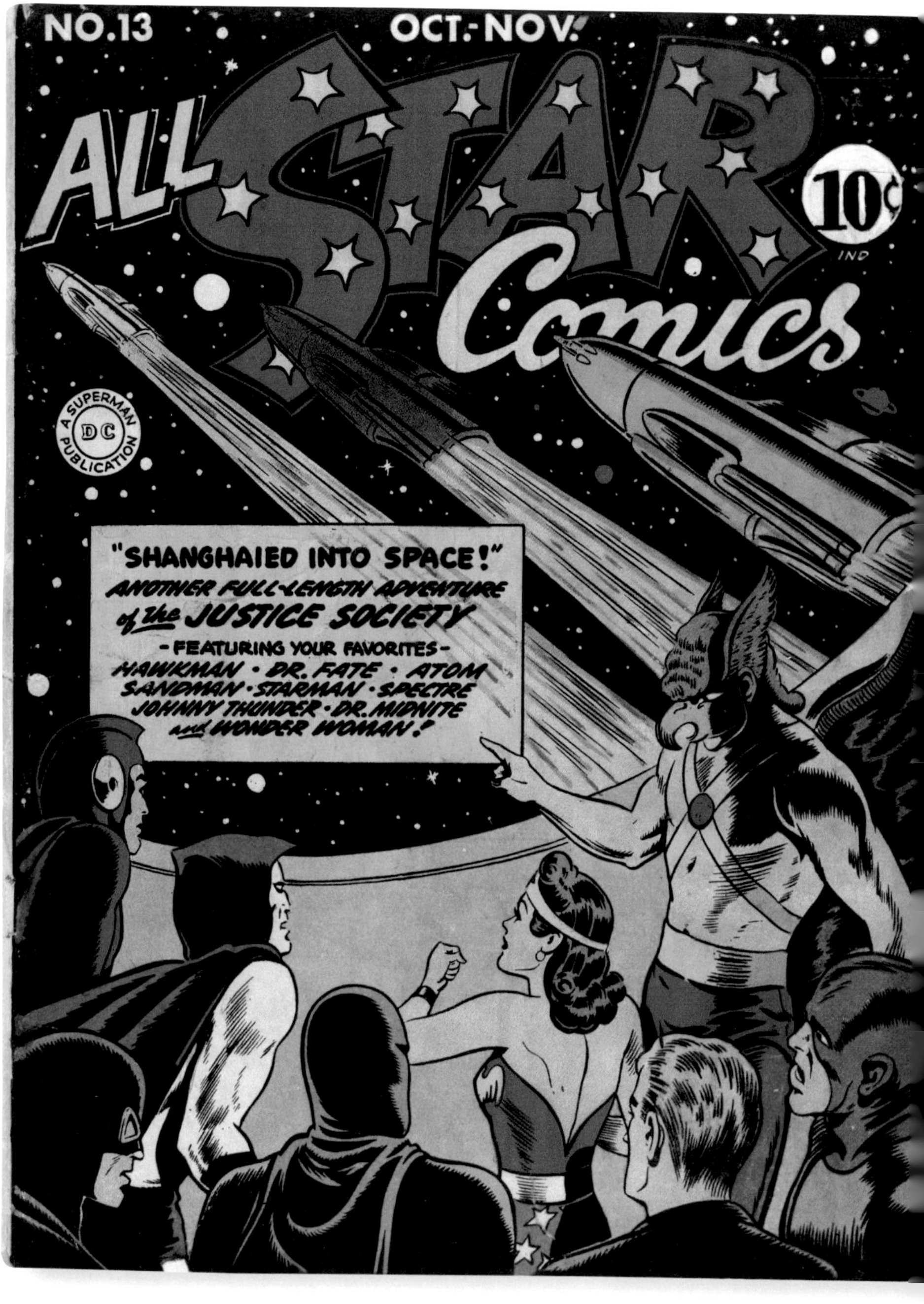
NO.13
OCT.-NOV.
ALL STAR Comics
10¢
IND
A SUPERMAN DC PUBLICATION
"SHANGHAIED INTO SPACE!"
ANOTHER FULL-LENGTH ADVENTURE of the JUSTICE SOCIETY
-FEATURING YOUR FAVORITES-
HAWKMAN · DR. FATE · ATOM
SANDMAN · STARMAN · SPECTRE
JOHNNY THUNDER · DR. MIDNITE
and WONDER WOMAN!

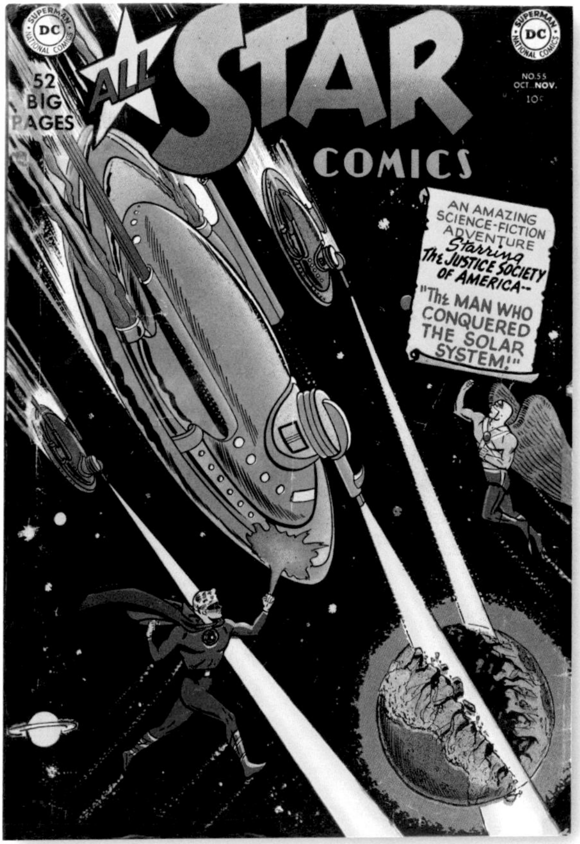
SUPERMAN DC NATIONAL COMICS
52 BIG PAGES
ALL STAR
COMICS
NO.55 OCT.-NOV.
10¢
AN AMAZING SCIENCE-FICTION ADVENTURE Starring The JUSTICE SOCIETY OF AMERICA--
"The MAN WHO CONQUERED THE SOLAR SYSTEM!"

ALL-STAR COMICS No. 13

Cover art, Jack Burnley, October–November 1942. Demonstrating a degree of technology that Nazi Germany could only dream of in the real world, Adolf Hitler attempted to get rid of the Justice Society by rocketing each member of the team to a different planet in the solar system.

ALL-STAR COMICS No. 55

Cover art, Arthur Peddy and Bernard Sachs, October–November 1950. After his comic book was canceled in 1949, Green Lantern continued to appear at the forefront of The Justice Society in *All-Star Comics* for another year and a half until it, too, was discontinued.

"The modern technological explosion profoundly affected American life. The Cold War spurred development in the science of rocket propulsion. The age-old dream of space exploration was not as fantastic as it once seemed."

—JERRY ROBINSON

ALL-AMERICAN COMICS No. 75

Cover art, Paul Reinman, July 1946. Along with Superman, Batman, the Flash, and Wonder Woman, Green Lantern was one of the elite five DC heroes of the 1940s to star in a comic book devoted exclusively to his adventures.

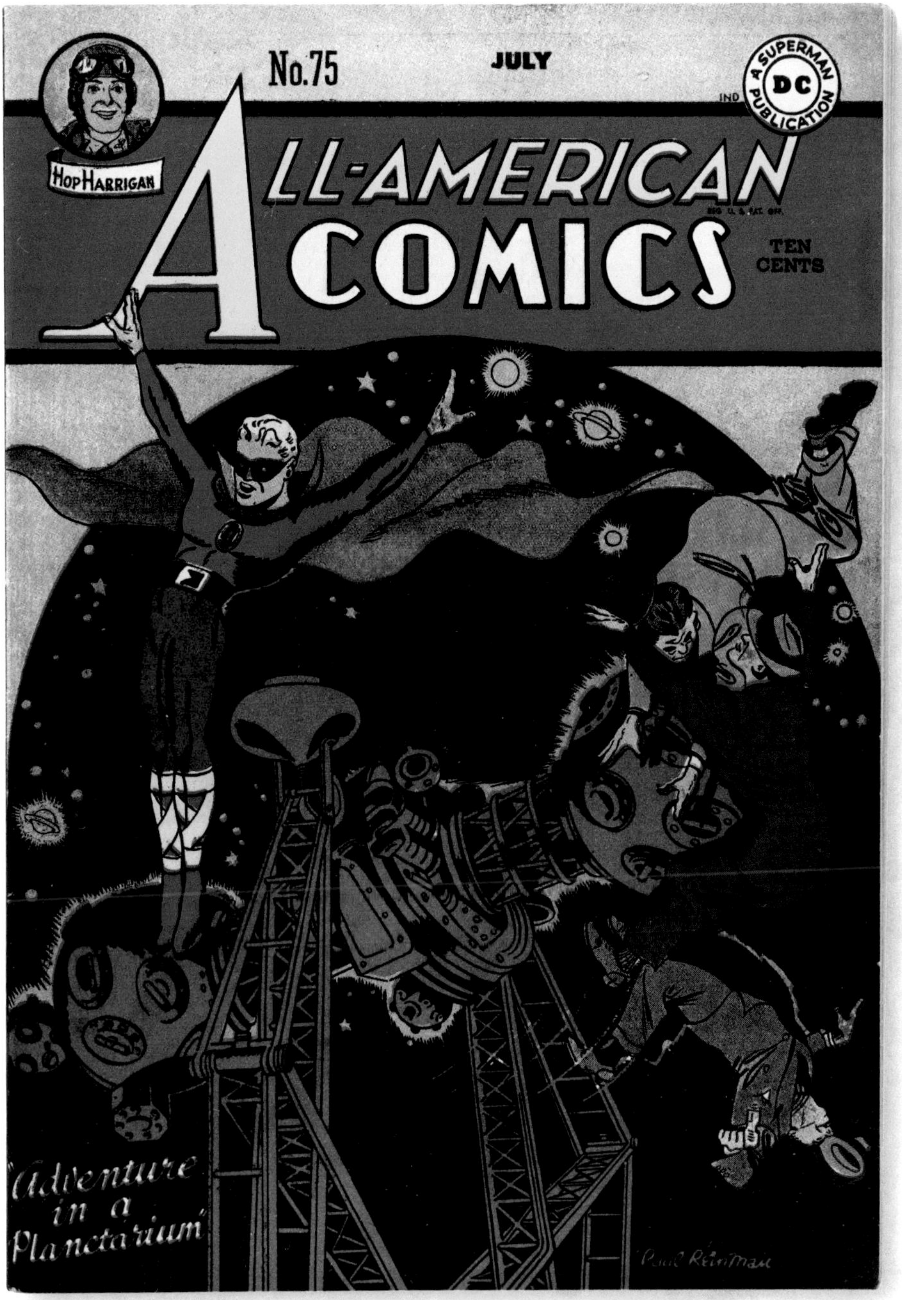
No.75
JULY
A SUPERMAN DC PUBLICATION
HOP HARRIGAN
ALL-AMERICAN COMICS
TEN CENTS
"Adventure in a Planetarium"
Paul Reinman

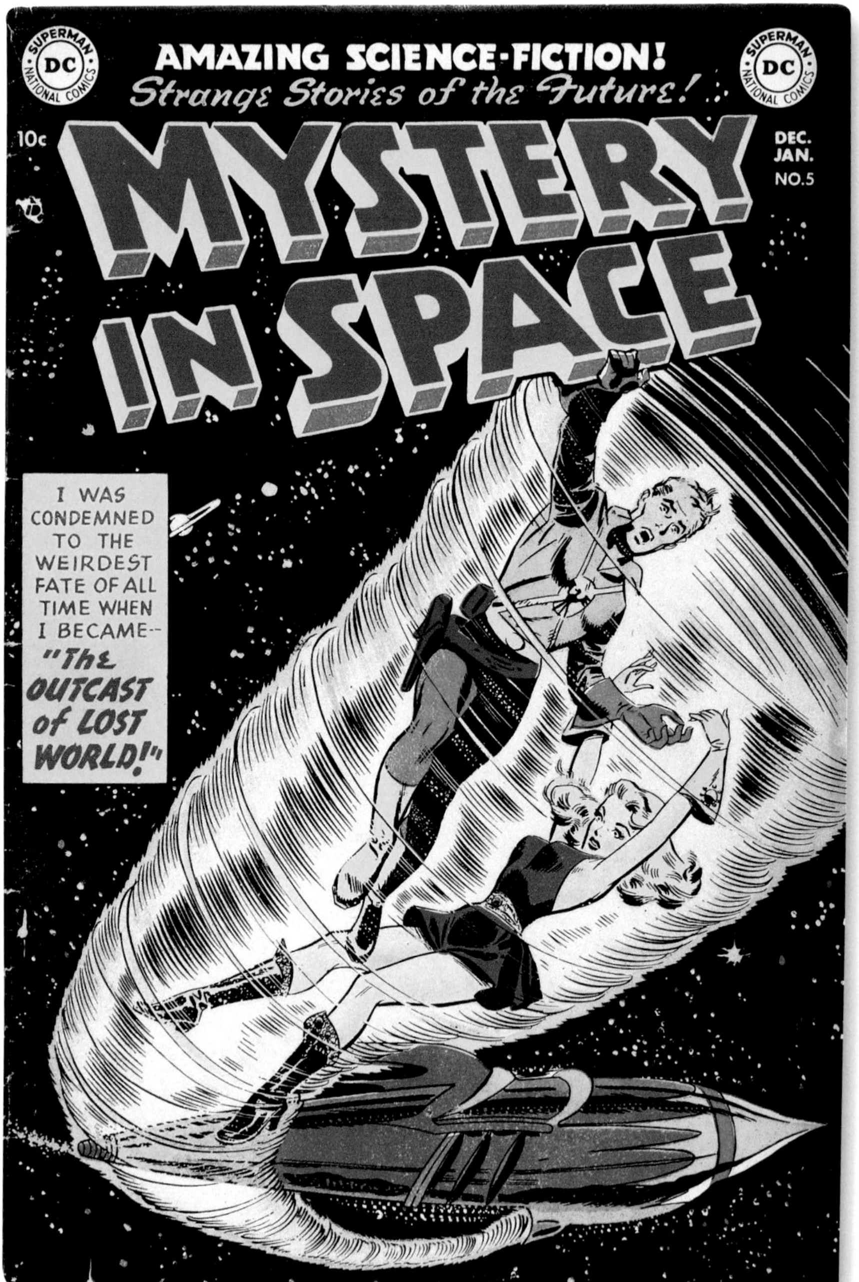
SUPERMAN DC NATIONAL COMICS
AMAZING SCIENCE-FICTION!
Strange Stories of the Future!
SUPERMAN DC NATIONAL COMICS
10c
MYSTERY IN SPACE
DEC. JAN.
NO.5
I WAS CONDEMNED TO THE WEIRDEST FATE OF ALL TIME WHEN I BECAME-- "The OUTCAST of LOST WORLD!"

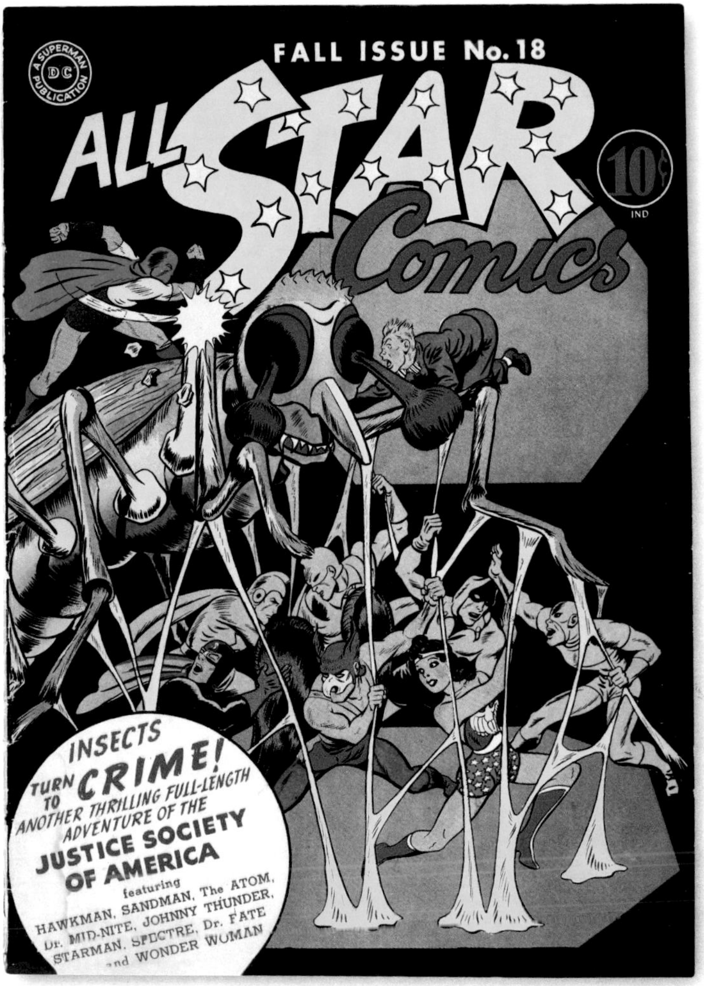
FALL ISSUE No. 18
A SUPERMAN DC PUBLICATION
ALL STAR Comics
10¢
IND
INSECTS
TURN TO CRIME!
ANOTHER THRILLING FULL-LENGTH ADVENTURE OF THE
JUSTICE SOCIETY OF AMERICA
featuring
HAWKMAN, SANDMAN, The ATOM,
Dr. MID-NITE, JOHNNY THUNDER,
STARMAN, SPECTRE, Dr. FATE
and WONDER WOMAN

MYSTERY IN SPACE No. 5

Cover art, Carmine Infantino, December 1951–January 1952. The futuristic Knights of the Galaxy defended the cosmos in the first eight issues of *Mystery in Space* before editor Julius Schwartz abandoned series characters in favor of episodic science fiction shorts.

ALL STAR COMICS No. 18

Cover art, Frank Harry, Fall 1943.

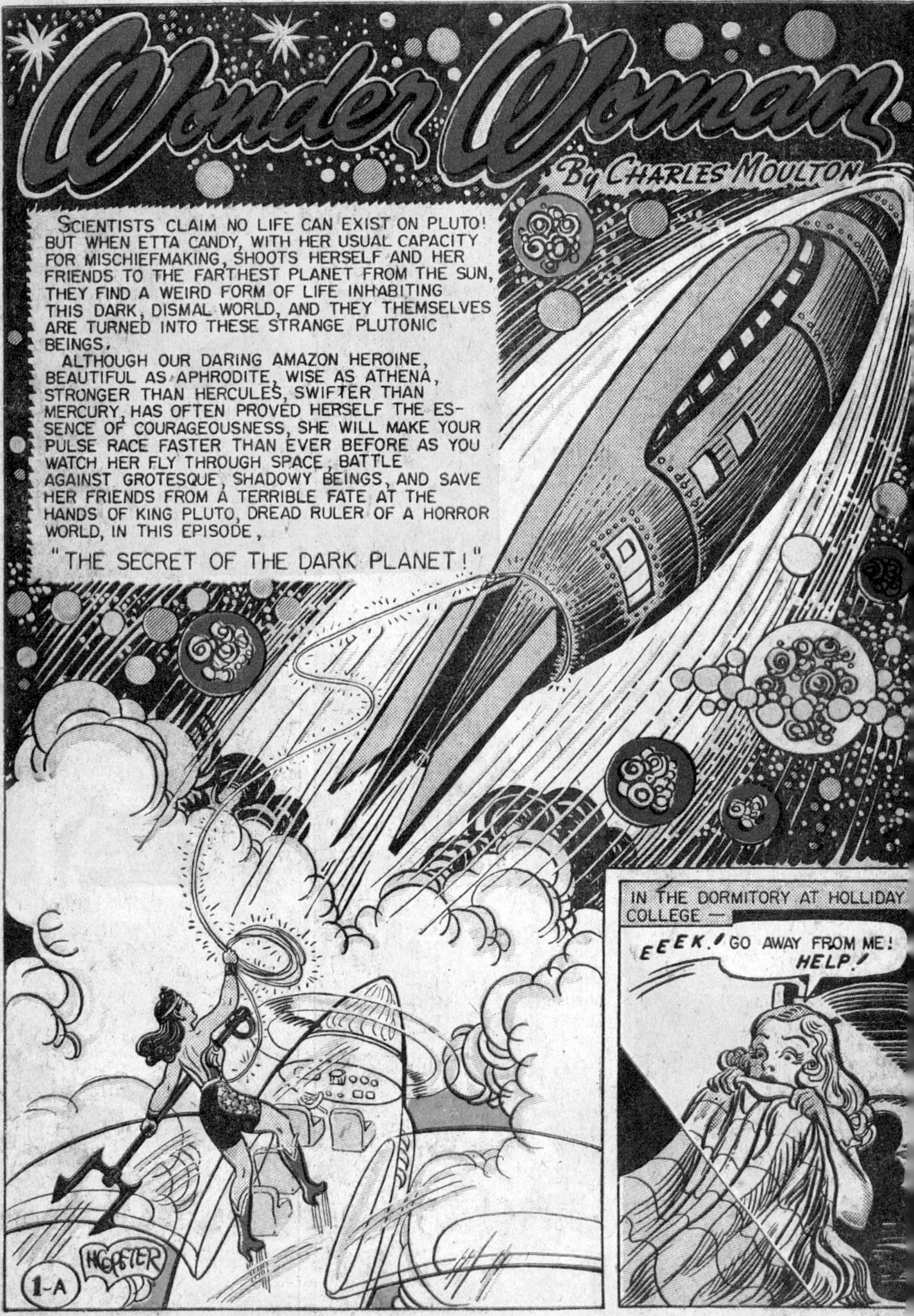
Wonder Woman
By CHARLES MOULTON
SCIENTISTS CLAIM NO LIFE CAN EXIST ON PLUTO! BUT WHEN ETTA CANDY, WITH HER USUAL CAPACITY FOR MISCHIEFMAKING, SHOOTS HERSELF AND HER FRIENDS TO THE FARTHEST PLANET FROM THE SUN, THEY FIND A WEIRD FORM OF LIFE INHABITING THIS DARK, DISMAL WORLD, AND THEY THEMSELVES ARE TURNED INTO THESE STRANGE PLUTONIC BEINGS.
ALTHOUGH OUR DARING AMAZON HEROINE, BEAUTIFUL AS APHRODITE, WISE AS ATHENA, STRONGER THAN HERCULES, SWIFTER THAN MERCURY, HAS OFTEN PROVED HERSELF THE ESSENCE OF COURAGEOUSNESS, SHE WILL MAKE YOUR PULSE RACE FASTER THAN EVER BEFORE AS YOU WATCH HER FLY THROUGH SPACE, BATTLE AGAINST GROTESQUE, SHADOWY BEINGS, AND SAVE HER FRIENDS FROM A TERRIBLE FATE AT THE HANDS OF KING PLUTO, DREAD RULER OF A HORROR WORLD, IN THIS EPISODE,
"THE SECRET OF THE DARK PLANET!"
HGPETER
1-A
IN THE DORMITORY AT HOLLIDAY COLLEGE —
EEEK! GO AWAY FROM ME! HELP!

WINTER ISSUE No. 7
Wonder Woman
10¢
FOR PRESIDENT
Wonder Woman for President
Wonder Woman 1000 YEARS in the Future!

WONDER WOMAN PREVIEWS THE STYLE FOR SECRETARIES 1000 YEARS HENCE

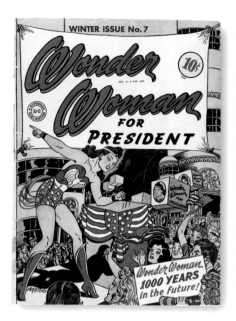

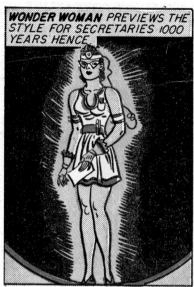

WONDER WOMAN No. 16

Interior, "The Secret of the Dark Planet"; script, Joye Murchison; pencils and inks, H. G. Peter. March–April 1946. Almost from the start, Wonder Woman brought her message of peace and equality to the people of other planets. She formed a close relationship with Queen Desira and the women of Venus, fought the war god Mars on the planet that bore his name, and even helped set diplomatic relations between Saturn and Earth. Sometimes those adventures came at the instigation of Wonder Woman's friend Etta Candy, who travels to the planet Pluto to rescue a classmate.

WONDER WOMAN No. 7

Cover art, H. G. Peter. Interior, "The Adventure of the Life Vitamin"; script, William Moulton Marston; pencils and inks, H. G. Peter. Winter 1943. William Moulton Marston's vision for the future was never more clear than in a full-length story depicting events in the 31st century and beyond. Beyond technological advances like a headband that transcribes thoughts into print, society becomes a utopia free of war and disease, and Diana (Wonder Woman) Prince becomes president of the United States — but only after apologetically resigning as secretary to the male General Darnell. "Men and women will be equal," the text asserts, "but women's influence will control most governments because women are more ready to serve others unselfishly."

GORILLA BOSS SKETCH

Pencil layout, Lew Sayre Schwartz, 1952. Schwartz would compose his entire Batman stories in notebooks, before transferring them to full-size pencils. Here, the Gorilla Boss of Gotham City prepares to strike.

CONGO BILL No. 1

Cover art, Nick Cardy, August–September 1954. After a long run as a back-up character in books like *Action Comics* and even a stint as the star of a movie serial, Congo Bill was briefly awarded his own comic book. Kid sidekick Janu was a new addition to the feature, having debuted in *Action* No. 191 just a few months earlier.

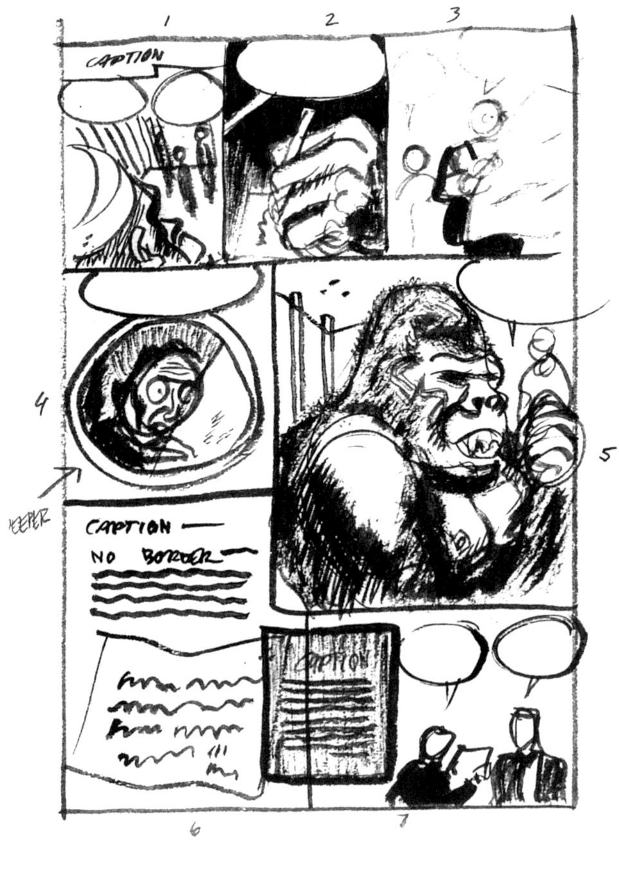

CAPTION
KEEPER
CAPTION —
NO BORDER —
CAPTION

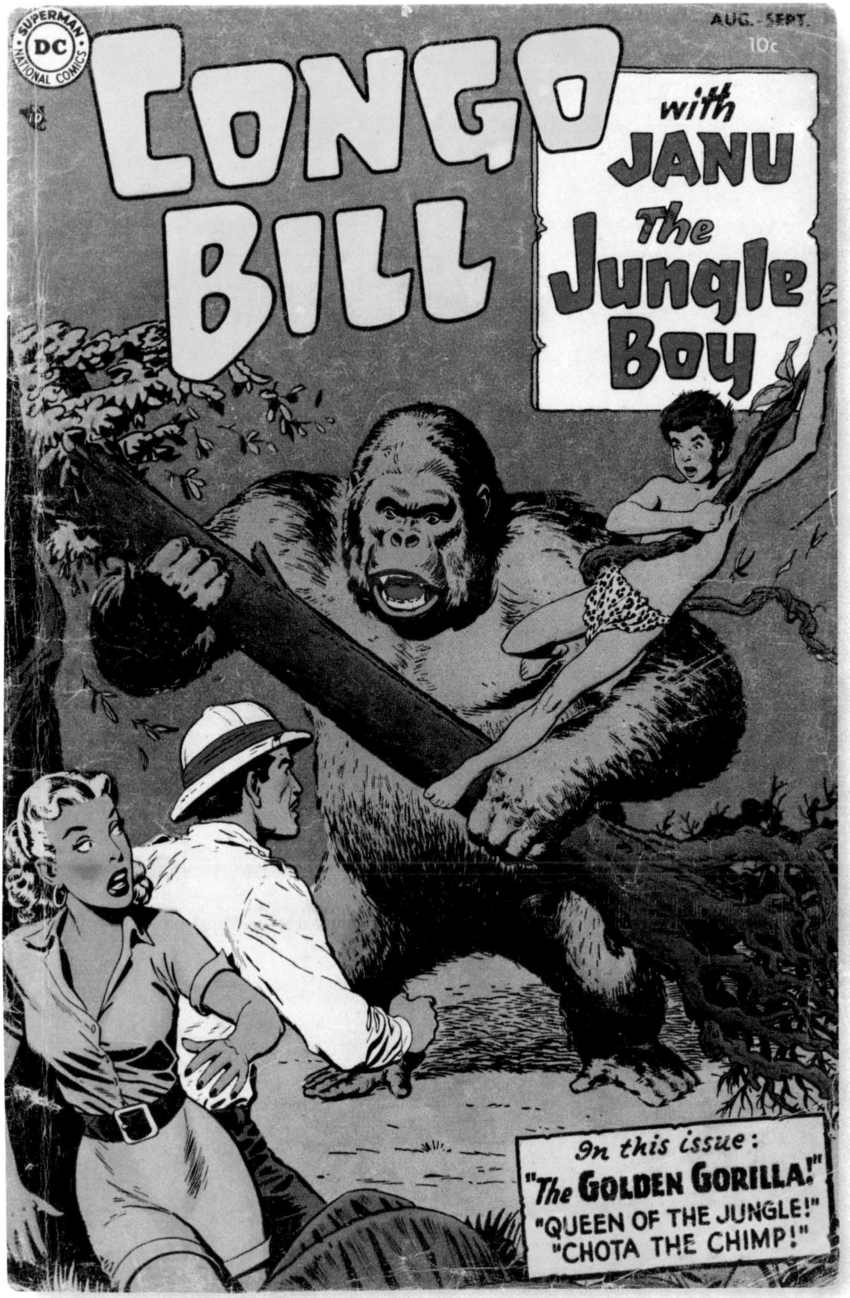
SUPERMAN DC NATIONAL COMICS
AUG.-SEPT.
10¢
CONGO BILL
with JANU The Jungle Boy
In this issue:
"The GOLDEN GORILLA!"
"QUEEN OF THE JUNGLE!"
"CHOTA THE CHIMP!"

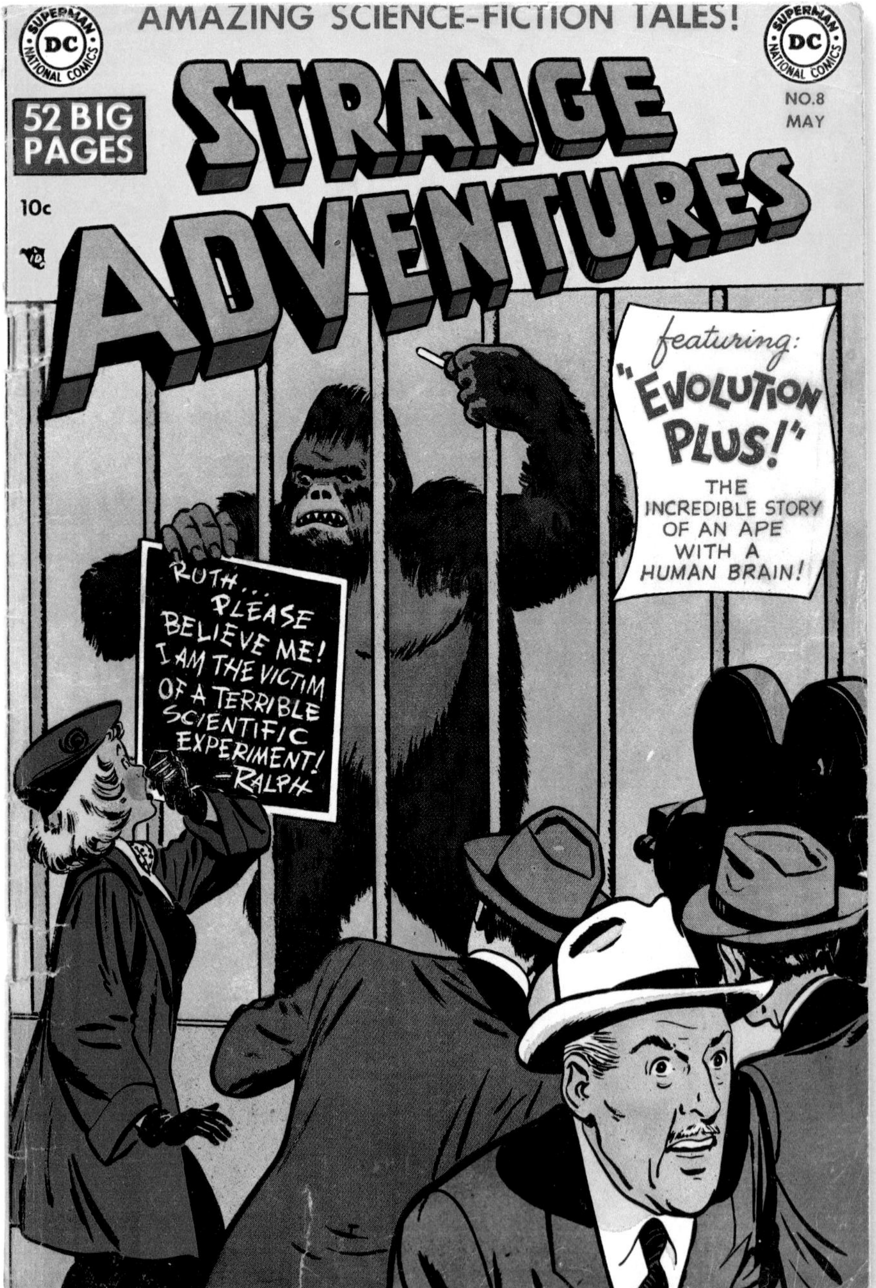
AMAZING SCIENCE-FICTION TALES!
SUPERMAN DC NATIONAL COMICS
52 BIG PAGES
10c
STRANGE ADVENTURES
NO.8
MAY
featuring: "EVOLUTION PLUS!"
THE INCREDIBLE STORY OF AN APE WITH A HUMAN BRAIN!
RUTH... PLEASE BELIEVE ME! I AM THE VICTIM OF A TERRIBLE SCIENTIFIC EXPERIMENT! —RALPH

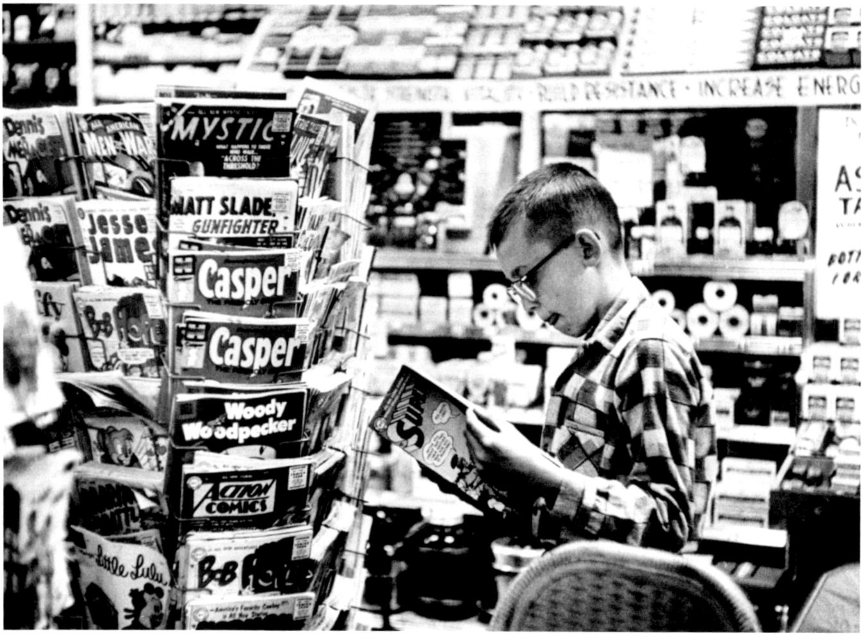
MYSTIC
"ACROSS THE THRESHOLD?"
MATT SLADE, GUNFIGHTER
Jesse James
Casper
Casper
Woody Woodpecker
ACTION COMICS
Little Lulu
BUILD RESISTANCE • INCREASE

STRANGE ADVENTURES No. 8

Cover art, Win Mortimer, May 1951. Canadian-born Win Mortimer was a quiet but versatile contributor to DC for almost five decades, and a major cover artist in the late Golden Age. Never closely associated with a particular character as its star artist, his fame never equaled his reliable presence on newsstands.

SPINNER RACK

Photograph, March 1956.

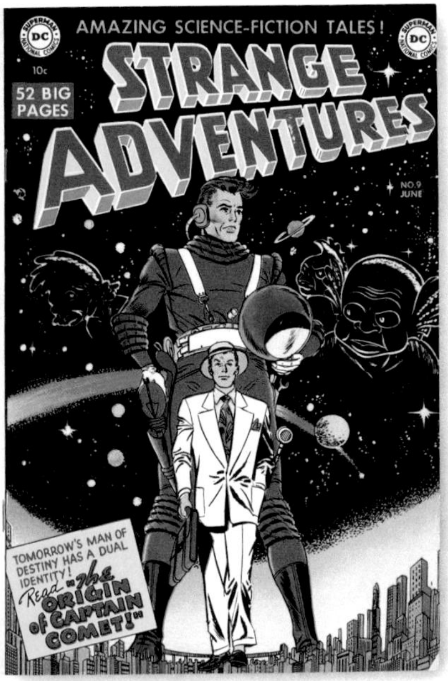
AMAZING SCIENCE-FICTION TALES!
STRANGE ADVENTURES
10c
52 BIG PAGES
NO. 9 JUNE
TOMORROW'S MAN OF DESTINY HAS A DUAL IDENTITY!
Read "The ORIGIN of CAPTAIN COMET!"

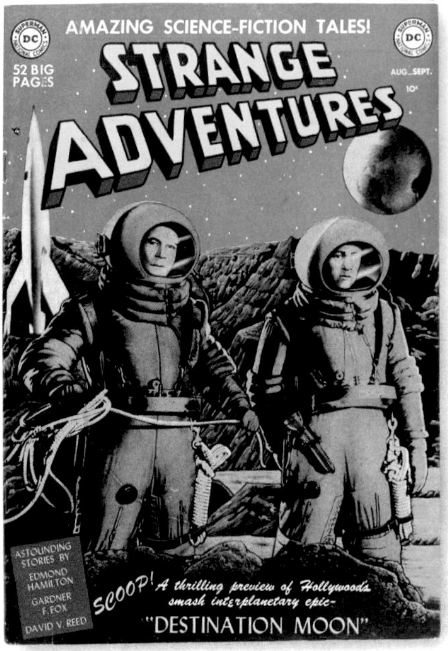
AMAZING SCIENCE-FICTION TALES!
STRANGE ADVENTURES
52 BIG PAGES
AUG.-SEPT.
10¢
ASTOUNDING STORIES BY EDMOND HAMILTON GARDNER F. FOX DAVID V. REED
SCOOP! A thrilling preview of Hollywood's smash interplanetary epic-
"DESTINATION MOON"

STRANGE ADVENTURES No. 9

Cover art, Carmine Infantino, June 1951.

STRANGE ADVENTURES No. 1

Cover art, unknown airbrush-photo artist, August–September 1950. The debut of a pure science-fiction book was a dream come true for editor Julius Schwartz; a lifelong fan of the genre, he'd been an agent for several authors before his comics career. The first issue included an adaptation of the movie *Destination Moon* and featured a photo cover, but the comic book found enduring success with stories and visually enticing concepts of its own creation.

STRANGE ADVENTURES No. 2

Cover art, Jim Mooney and Sy Barry, October–November 1950. Pulp science-fiction luminaries like artist Virgil Finlay and writer Edmond Hamilton were touted on early *Strange Adventures* covers, an extraordinary event in an era when most comics creators labored in anonymity.

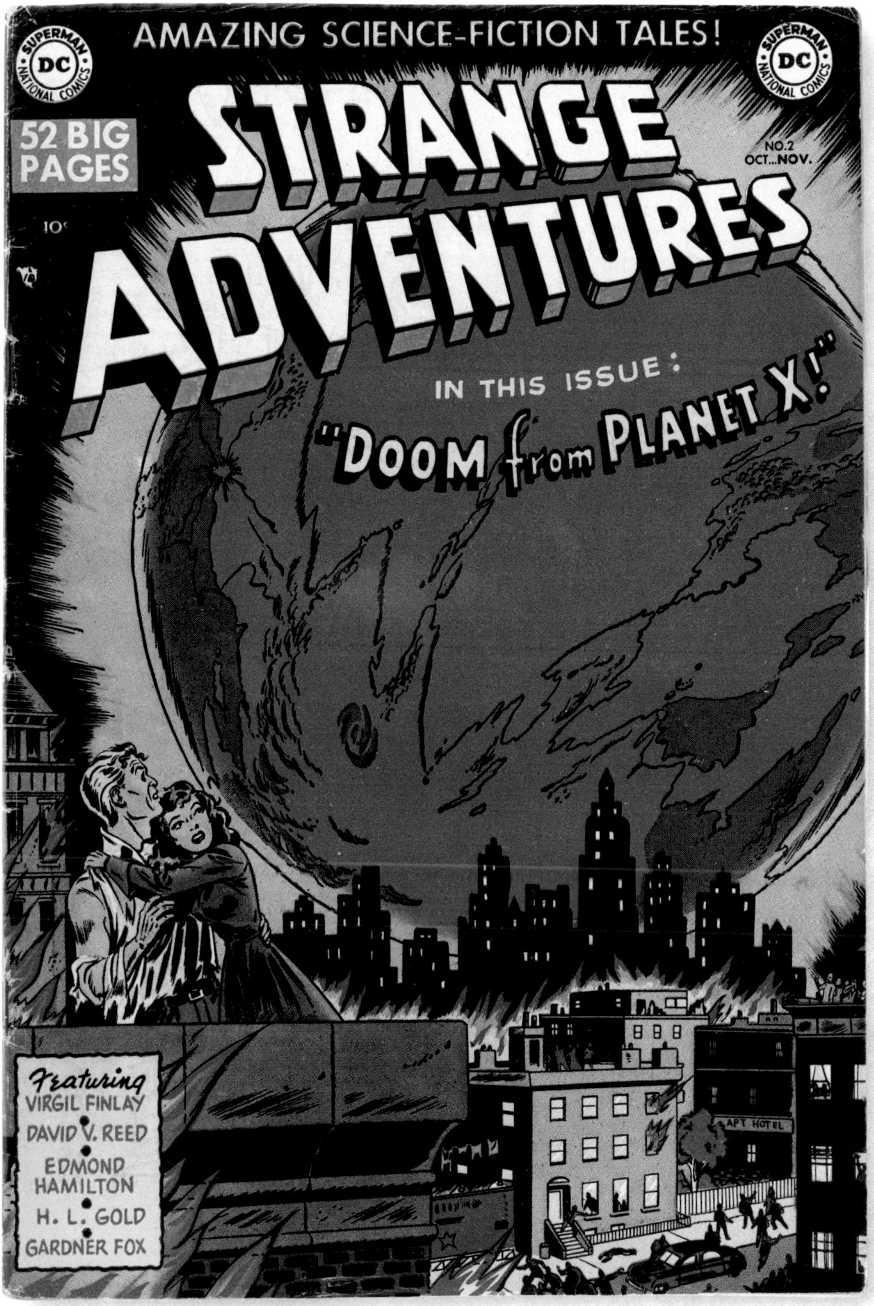
AMAZING SCIENCE-FICTION TALES!
SUPERMAN DC NATIONAL COMICS
52 BIG PAGES
10¢
STRANGE ADVENTURES
NO.2 OCT...NOV.
IN THIS ISSUE:
"DOOM from PLANET X!"
Featuring
VIRGIL FINLAY
DAVID V. REED
EDMOND HAMILTON
H. L. GOLD
GARDNER FOX
APT. HOTEL

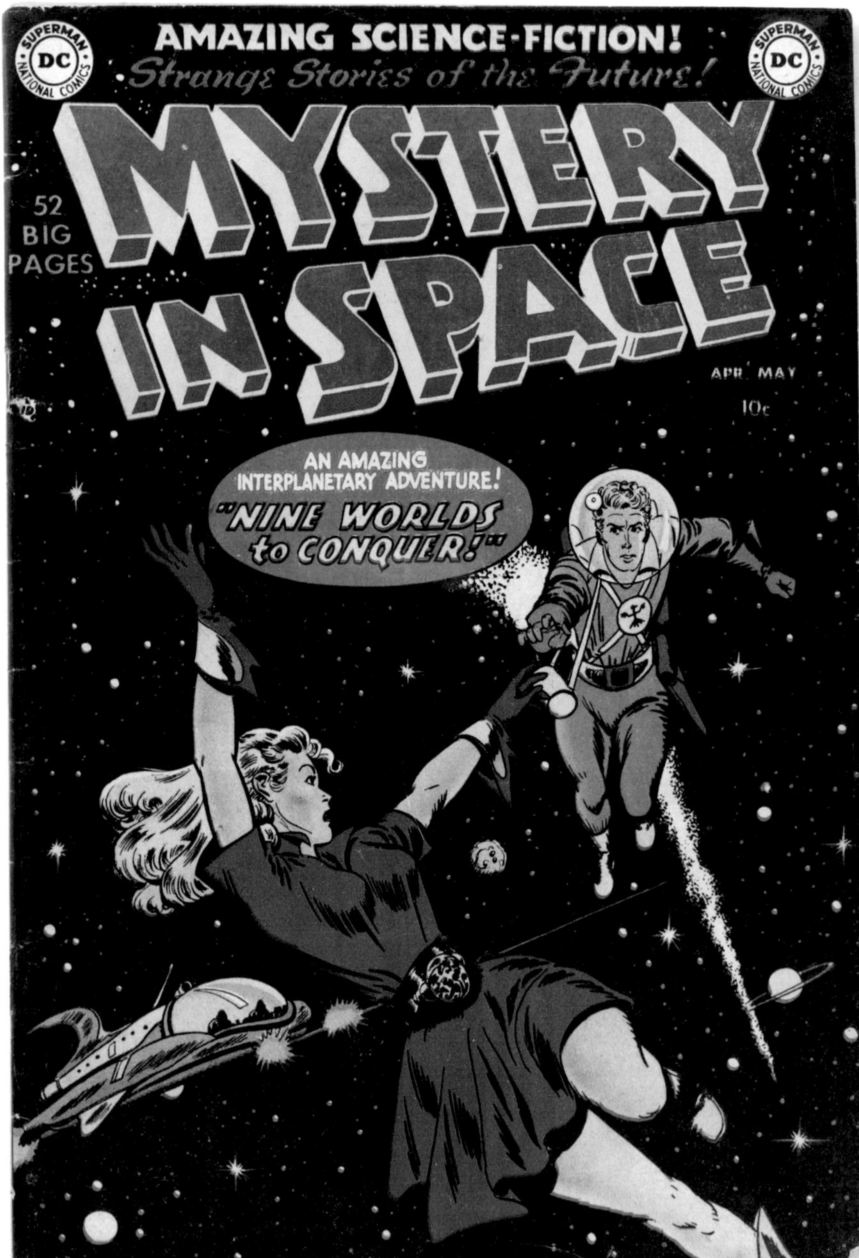
SUPERMAN DC NATIONAL COMICS
AMAZING SCIENCE-FICTION!
Strange Stories of the Future!
SUPERMAN DC NATIONAL COMICS
MYSTERY IN SPACE
52 BIG PAGES
APR. MAY
10c
AN AMAZING INTERPLANETARY ADVENTURE!
"NINE WORLDS to CONQUER!"

MYSTERY IN SPACE No. 1

Cover art, Carmine Infantino and Frank Giacoia, April–May 1951. The success of the *Strange Adventures* comic book inspired the *Mystery in Space* companion title. Its name came from editorial director Whitney Ellsworth, who explained to editor Julius Schwartz that he wanted to attract fans of both DC's science-fiction comic book and its suspense title, *House of Mystery*. The highlight of *Mystery in Space* No.1 was not the beginning of the short-lived Knights of the Galaxy series, but rather the story "Spores from Space," illustrated by Frank Frazetta, later to win accolades for his fantasy paintings.

MYSTERY IN SPACE No. 22

Cover art, Murphy Anderson, October–November 1954. Scenarios showing an altered planet Earth — whether changed into a cube or sliced in half — were another popular cover device.

MYSTERY IN SPACE No. 18

Cover art, Murphy Anderson and Joe Giella, February–March 1954. The imaginative situations on many of the science-fiction covers had a second life in the 1960s, when Julius Schwartz recycled them for *Justice League of America*. This particular layout was recycled on *JLA* No. 22 in 1963.

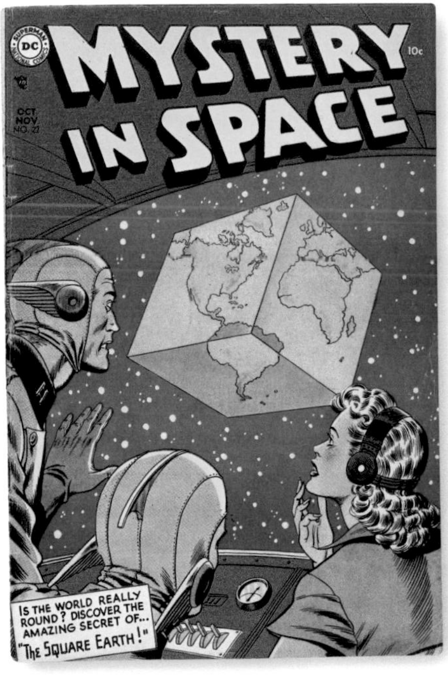
DC
MYSTERY IN SPACE
10c
OCT. NOV. NO. 22
IS THE WORLD REALLY ROUND? DISCOVER THE AMAZING SECRET OF...
"The SQUARE EARTH!"

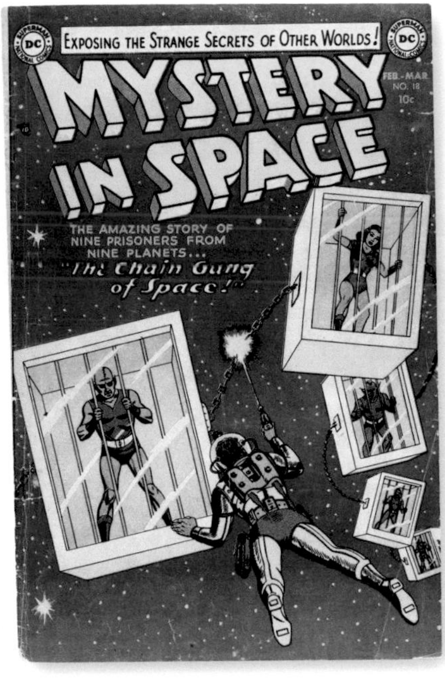
DC
EXPOSING THE STRANGE SECRETS OF OTHER WORLDS!
MYSTERY IN SPACE
FEB.-MAR. NO. 18
10c
THE AMAZING STORY OF NINE PRISONERS FROM NINE PLANETS...
"The Chain Gang of Space!"

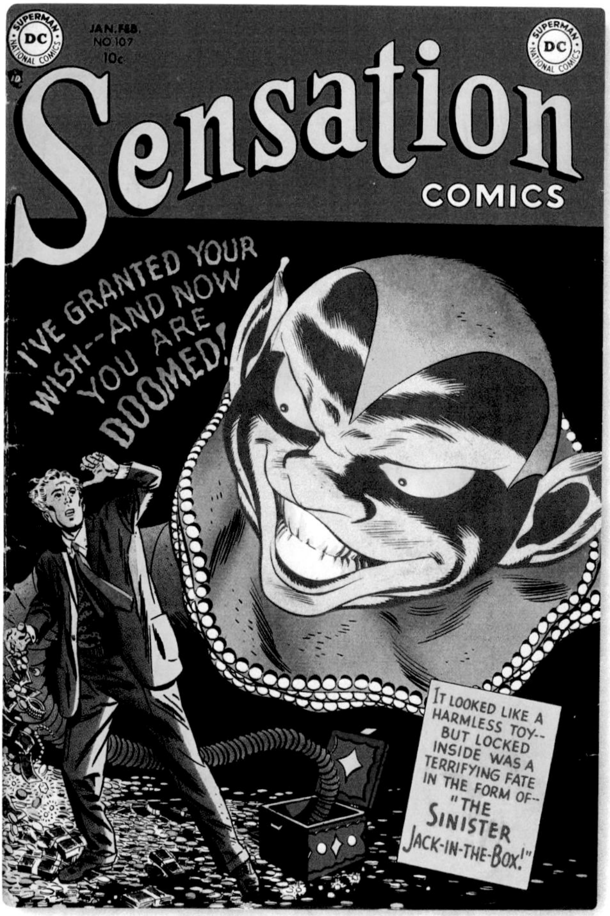
JAN.-FEB.
NO. 107
10c
Sensation
COMICS
I'VE GRANTED YOUR WISH--AND NOW YOU ARE DOOMED!
IT LOOKED LIKE A HARMLESS TOY-- BUT LOCKED INSIDE WAS A TERRIFYING FATE IN THE FORM OF-- "THE SINISTER JACK-IN-THE-BOX!"

SENSATION COMICS No. 107

Cover art, Alex Toth and Joe Giella, January–February 1952.

REAL FACT COMICS No. 6

Interior, "Columbus of Space"; script, Jack Schiff, George Kashdan, and Bernie Breslauer; pencils, Howard Sherman; inks, Virgil Finlay. January–February 1947. Intended as a generic representation of a future astronaut, Tommy Tomorrow took on a life of his own as the star of a long-running back-up feature in *Action Comics* and *World's Finest.*

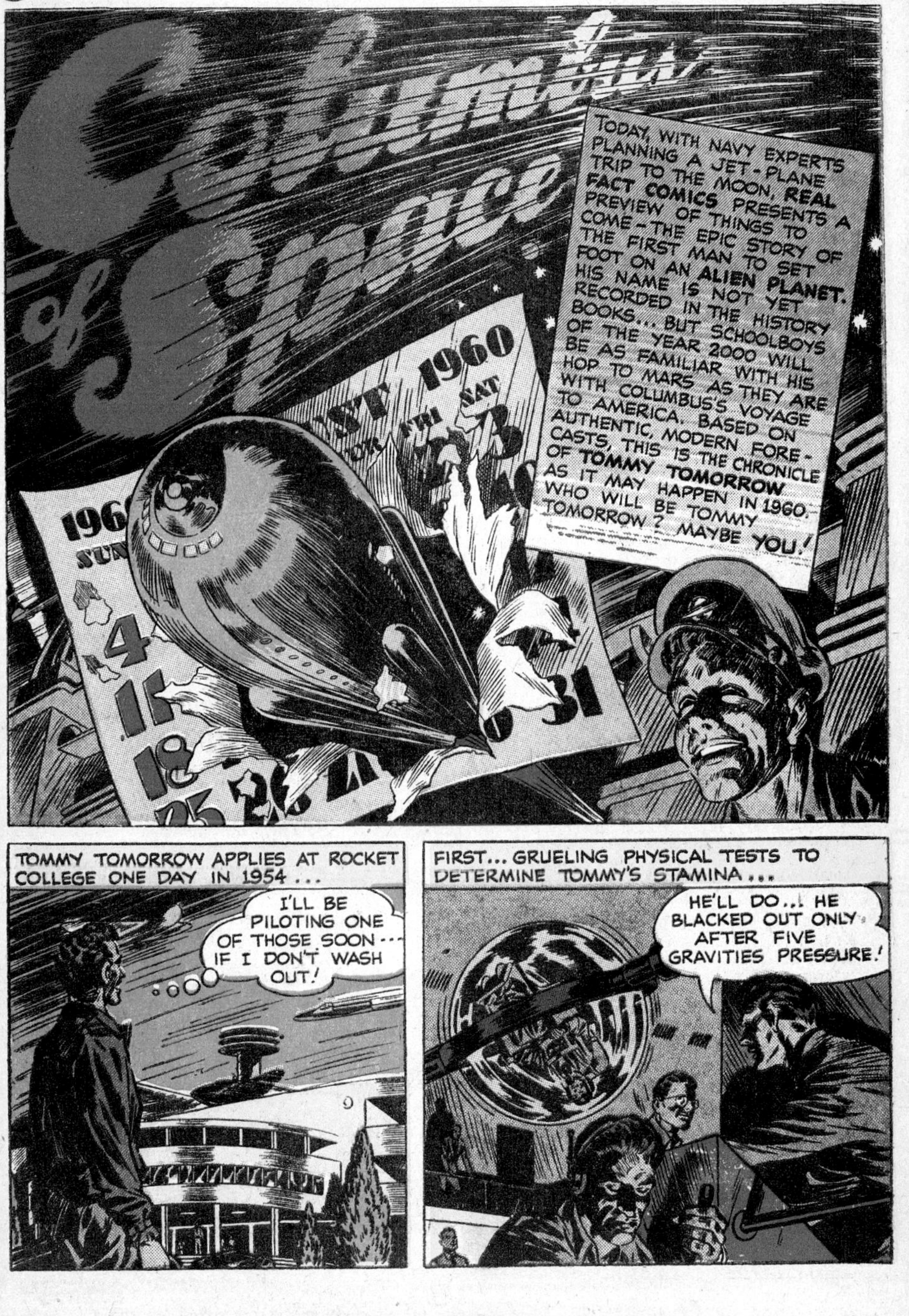
Columbus of Space
TODAY, WITH NAVY EXPERTS PLANNING A JET-PLANE TRIP TO THE MOON, REAL FACT COMICS PRESENTS A PREVIEW OF THINGS TO COME—THE EPIC STORY OF THE FIRST MAN TO SET FOOT ON AN ALIEN PLANET. HIS NAME IS NOT YET RECORDED IN THE HISTORY BOOKS... BUT SCHOOLBOYS OF THE YEAR 2000 WILL BE AS FAMILIAR WITH HIS HOP TO MARS AS THEY ARE WITH COLUMBUS'S VOYAGE TO AMERICA. BASED ON AUTHENTIC, MODERN FORE-CASTS, THIS IS THE CHRONICLE OF TOMMY TOMORROW AS IT MAY HAPPEN IN 1960. WHO WILL BE TOMMY TOMORROW? MAYBE YOU!
1960
TOMMY TOMORROW APPLIES AT ROCKET COLLEGE ONE DAY IN 1954...
I'LL BE PILOTING ONE OF THOSE SOON... IF I DON'T WASH OUT!
FIRST... GRUELING PHYSICAL TESTS TO DETERMINE TOMMY'S STAMINA...
HE'LL DO... HE BLACKED OUT ONLY AFTER FIVE GRAVITIES PRESSURE!

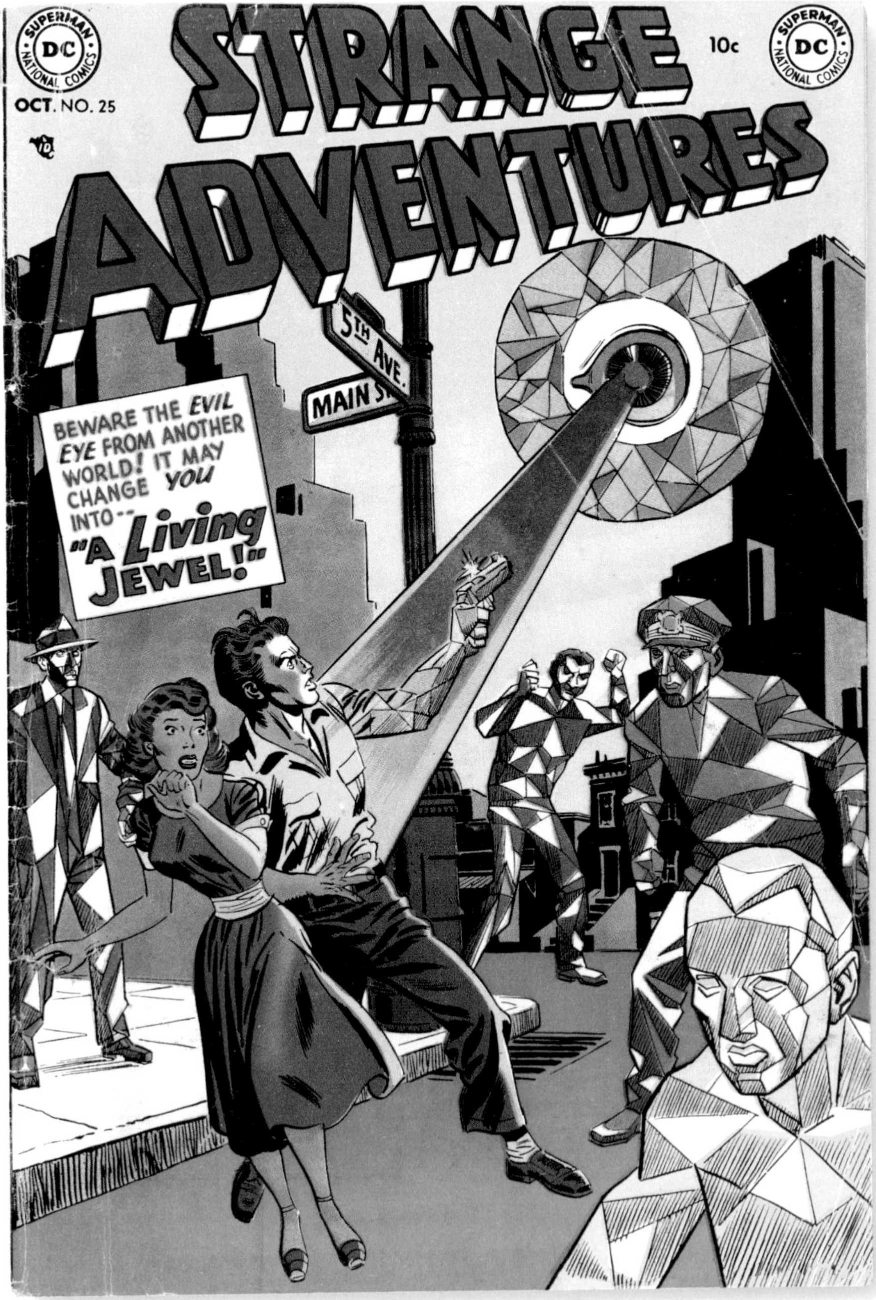
STRANGE ADVENTURES
SUPERMAN DC NATIONAL COMICS
10c
OCT. NO. 25
5TH AVE.
MAIN ST.
BEWARE THE EVIL EYE FROM ANOTHER WORLD! IT MAY CHANGE YOU INTO-- "A Living JEWEL!"

MAY–JUNE
NO.109
10¢
Sensation
COMICS
MY FINGERS --
ALIVE! AND
THREATENING
ME WITH --
DEATH!

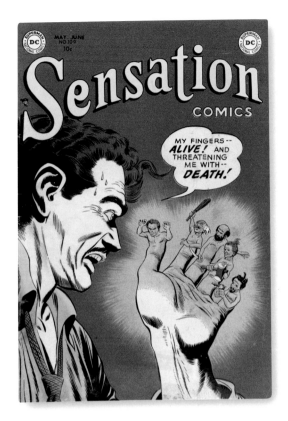

STRANGE ADVENTURES No. 25

Cover art, Gil Kane and Joe Giella, October 1952. Key to the success of Julius Schwartz's science-fiction comics was their strong covers. Bizarre, compelling situations such as a floating eye and its crystalline victims couldn't help but force youngsters to part company with their dimes to find out what happened next. Although Gil Kane pencilled occasional covers, Schwartz relied most heavily on artist Murphy Anderson, whose polished pencils and inks exemplified the slick style that DC held as its ideal.

SENSATION COMICS No. 109

Cover art, Murphy Anderson, May–June 1952. Following the eviction of Wonder Woman, *Sensation Comics* made a brief turn as a weird horror comic book, albeit one much milder than the more notorious examples being released by other publishers. This issue's bizarre concept was used as the basis for the cover of *Justice League of America* No.10 in 1962.

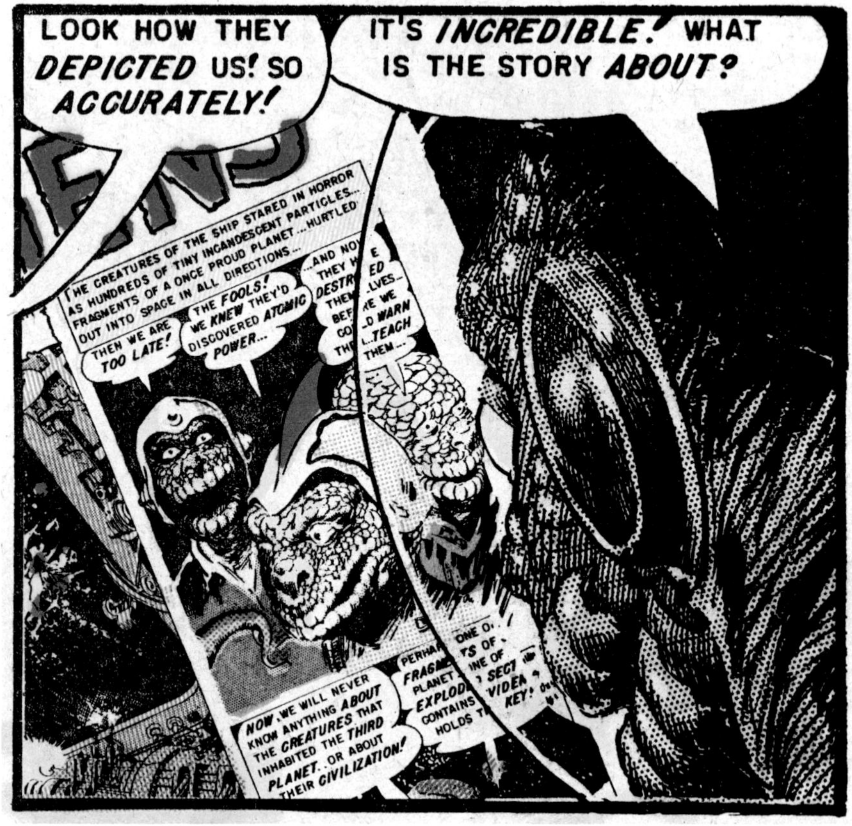
LOOK HOW THEY DEPICTED US! SO ACCURATELY!
IT'S INCREDIBLE! WHAT IS THE STORY ABOUT?
THE CREATURES OF THE SHIP STARED IN HORROR AS HUNDREDS OF TINY INCANDESCENT PARTICLES... FRAGMENTS OF A ONCE PROUD PLANET... HURTLED OUT INTO SPACE IN ALL DIRECTIONS...
THEN WE ARE TOO LATE!
THE FOOLS! WE KNEW THEY'D DISCOVERED ATOMIC POWER...
NOW WE WILL NEVER KNOW ANYTHING ABOUT THE CREATURES THAT INHABITED THE THIRD PLANET... OR ABOUT THEIR CIVILIZATION!

WEIRD FANTASY No. 17

Interior, "The Aliens"; script, Al Feldstein; pencils and inks, Al Williamson. January–February 1953. EC's science-fiction comic books had their humorous side, as in a tale where extraterrestrials rush to nuclear-war-ravaged Earth to discover an issue of *Weird Fantasy* depicting the aliens' expedition to the planet.

WONDER WOMAN No. 64

Cover art, Irwin Hasen, February 1954. In a typically bizarre plot, would-be invaders from Jupiter began transmitting creatures through 3-D filmstrips to determine if they could safely do the same. Wonder Woman stopped them by arranging for them to make their transfer on "a 3-D film of the most powerful hydrogen explosion we ever had," thus causing the Jovians to blow themselves up.

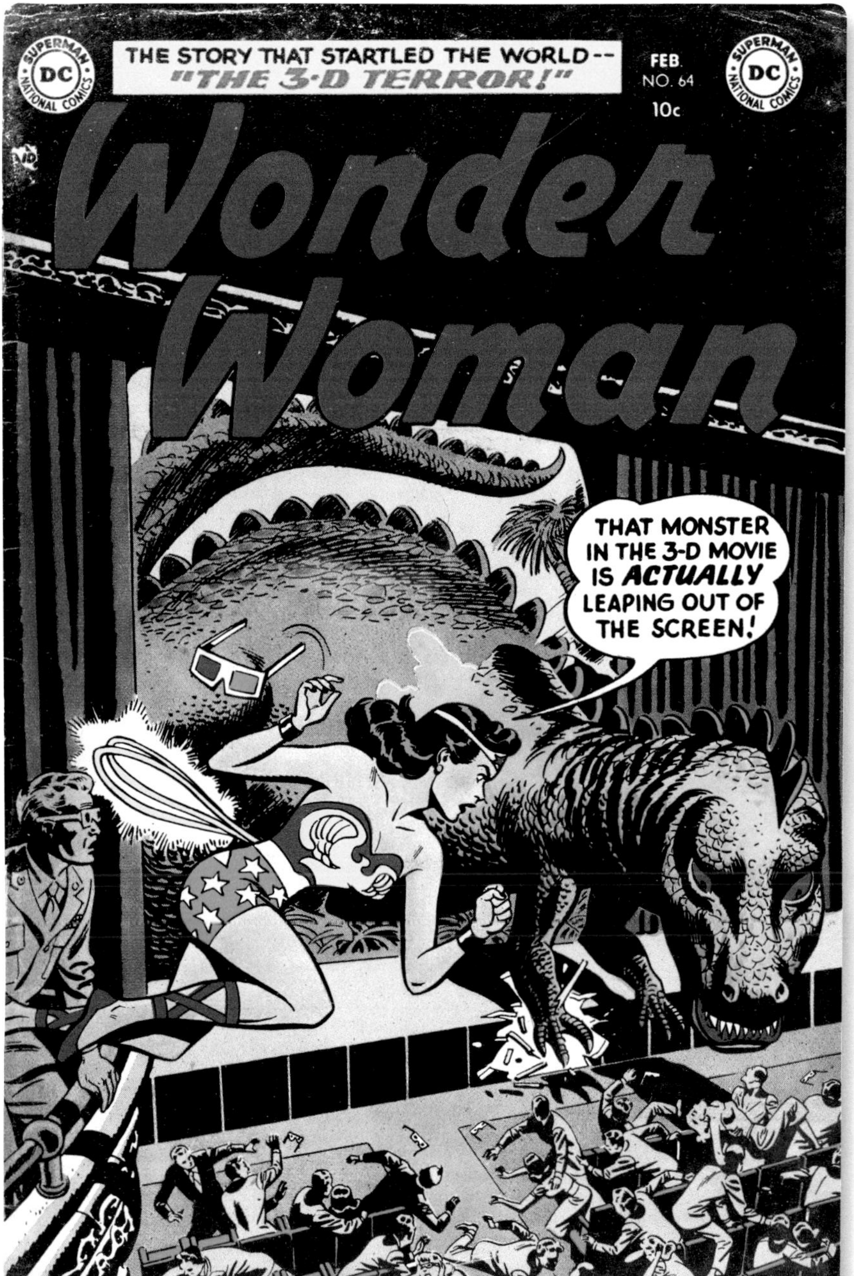
SUPERMAN DC NATIONAL COMICS
THE STORY THAT STARTLED THE WORLD--
"THE 3-D TERROR!"
FEB.
NO. 64
10c
Wonder Woman
THAT MONSTER IN THE 3-D MOVIE IS ACTUALLY LEAPING OUT OF THE SCREEN!

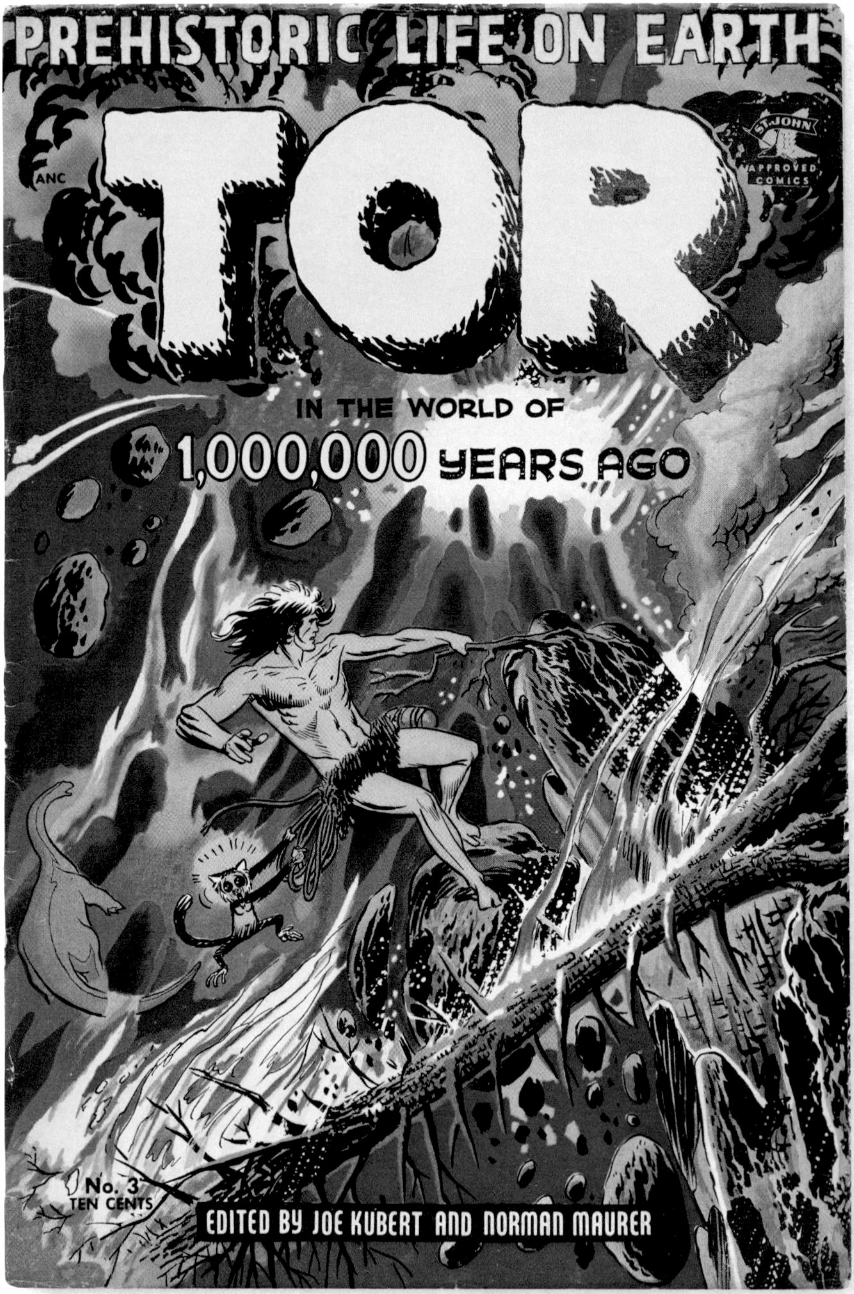
PREHISTORIC LIFE ON EARTH
TOR
ST. JOHN
APPROVED COMICS
ANC
IN THE WORLD OF
1,000,000 YEARS AGO
No. 3
TEN CENTS
EDITED BY JOE KUBERT AND NORMAN MAURER

TOR No. 3

Cover art, Joe Kubert, May 1954. Joe Kubert's Tor was one of the first comic books to exploit the 3-D craze. After two issues in the format, it returned to traditional 2-D. The entire *Tor* series has been reprinted many times in the years since, including a 1986 collection of the 3-D issues in that format.

THE MARVEL FAMILY No. 89

Cover art, Kurt Schaffenberger, January 1954. Agreeing to settle its lawsuit and stop publishing the adventures of Captain Marvel and company, Fawcett unintentionally ended the line with a cover full of irony. The last issue of *The Marvel Family* reduced its heroes to white silhouettes, with an accompanying title borrowed from mystery writer Agatha Christie: "And Then There Were None."

THREE-DIMENSION ADVENTURES SUPERMAN

Cover art, Curt Swan and Stan Kaye, 1953. The 3-D movie craze hit Superman and Batman with specialty comics devoted to each hero, the first DC titles to be published in traditional magazine size.

MORE PAGES OF YOUR FAVORITE COMIC CHARACTERS
JAN. NO. 89
THE MARVEL FAMILY
10¢
A FAWCETT PUBLICATION
HOLY MOLEY! WHAT HAPPENED TO THE MARVEL FAMILY?
Read AND THEN THERE WERE NONE!

THREE-DIMENSION ADVENTURES
SUPERMAN DC NATIONAL COMICS
SUPERMAN
25¢
in startling
3-D
LIFE-LIKE ACTION!
SUPER GLASSES INSIDE...

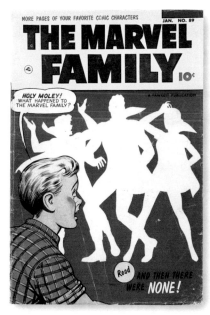

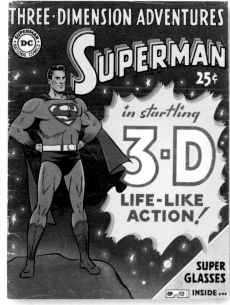

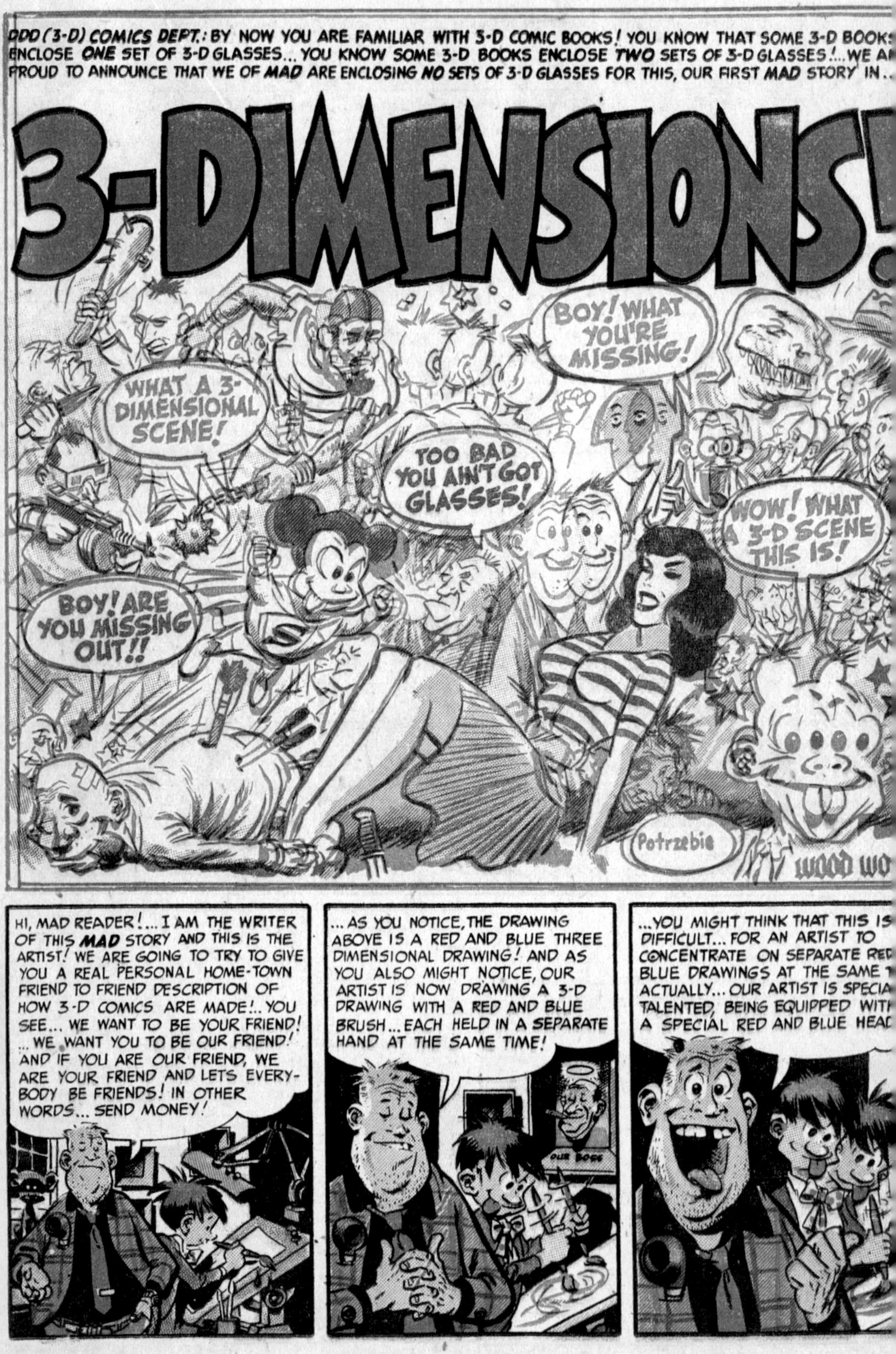
ODD (3-D) COMICS DEPT.: BY NOW YOU ARE FAMILIAR WITH 3-D COMIC BOOKS! YOU KNOW THAT SOME 3-D BOOKS ENCLOSE ONE SET OF 3-D GLASSES... YOU KNOW SOME 3-D BOOKS ENCLOSE TWO SETS OF 3-D GLASSES!...WE A
PROUD TO ANNOUNCE THAT WE OF MAD ARE ENCLOSING NO SETS OF 3-D GLASSES FOR THIS, OUR FIRST MAD STORY IN...
3-DIMENSIONS!
WHAT A 3-DIMENSIONAL SCENE!
BOY! WHAT YOU'RE MISSING!
TOO BAD YOU AIN'T GOT GLASSES!
WOW! WHAT A 3-D SCENE THIS IS!
BOY! ARE YOU MISSING OUT!!
Potrzebie
WOOD WO
HI, MAD READER!... I AM THE WRITER OF THIS MAD STORY AND THIS IS THE ARTIST! WE ARE GOING TO TRY TO GIVE YOU A REAL PERSONAL HOME-TOWN FRIEND TO FRIEND DESCRIPTION OF HOW 3-D COMICS ARE MADE!.. YOU SEE... WE WANT TO BE YOUR FRIEND! ...WE WANT YOU TO BE OUR FRIEND! AND IF YOU ARE OUR FRIEND, WE ARE YOUR FRIEND AND LETS EVERYBODY BE FRIENDS! IN OTHER WORDS... SEND MONEY!
...AS YOU NOTICE, THE DRAWING ABOVE IS A RED AND BLUE THREE DIMENSIONAL DRAWING! AND AS YOU ALSO MIGHT NOTICE, OUR ARTIST IS NOW DRAWING A 3-D DRAWING WITH A RED AND BLUE BRUSH... EACH HELD IN A SEPARATE HAND AT THE SAME TIME!
OUR BOSS
...YOU MIGHT THINK THAT THIS IS DIFFICULT... FOR AN ARTIST TO CONCENTRATE ON SEPARATE RED BLUE DRAWINGS AT THE SAME ACTUALLY... OUR ARTIST IS SPECIA TALENTED, BEING EQUIPPED WITH A SPECIAL RED AND BLUE HEAD

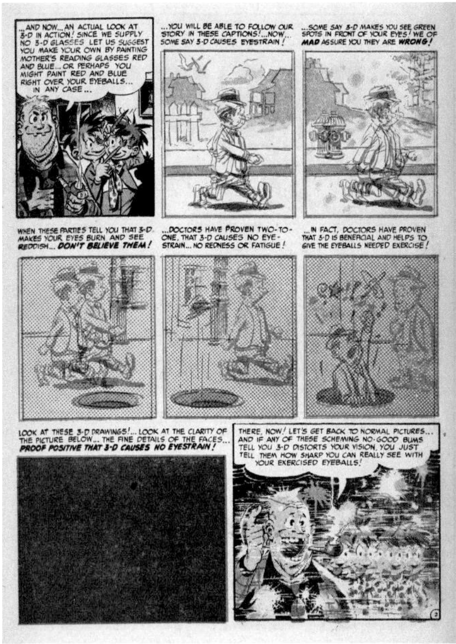
...AND NOW... AN ACTUAL LOOK AT 3-D IN ACTION! SINCE WE SUPPLY NO 3-D GLASSES LET US SUGGEST YOU MAKE YOUR OWN BY PAINTING MOTHER'S READING GLASSES RED AND BLUE... OR PERHAPS YOU MIGHT PAINT RED AND BLUE RIGHT OVER YOUR EYEBALLS... IN ANY CASE...
...YOU WILL BE ABLE TO FOLLOW OUR STORY IN THESE CAPTIONS!...NOW... SOME SAY 3-D CAUSES EYESTRAIN!
...SOME SAY 3-D MAKES YOU SEE GREEN SPOTS IN FRONT OF YOUR EYES! WE OF MAD ASSURE YOU THEY ARE WRONG!
WHEN THESE PARTIES TELL YOU THAT 3-D MAKES YOUR EYES BURN AND SEE REDDISH... DON'T BELIEVE THEM!
...DOCTORS HAVE PROVEN TWO-TO-ONE, THAT 3-D CAUSES NO EYE-STRAIN... NO REDNESS OR FATIGUE!
...IN FACT, DOCTORS HAVE PROVEN THAT 3-D IS BENEFICIAL AND HELPS TO GIVE THE EYEBALLS NEEDED EXERCISE!
LOOK AT THESE 3-D DRAWINGS!... LOOK AT THE CLARITY OF THE PICTURE BELOW... THE FINE DETAILS OF THE FACES... PROOF POSITIVE THAT 3-D CAUSES NO EYESTRAIN!
THERE, NOW! LET'S GET BACK TO NORMAL PICTURES... AND IF ANY OF THESE SCHEMING NO-GOOD BUMS TELL YOU 3-D DISTORTS YOUR VISION, YOU JUST TELL THEM HOW SHARP YOU CAN REALLY SEE WITH YOUR EXERCISED EYEBALLS!

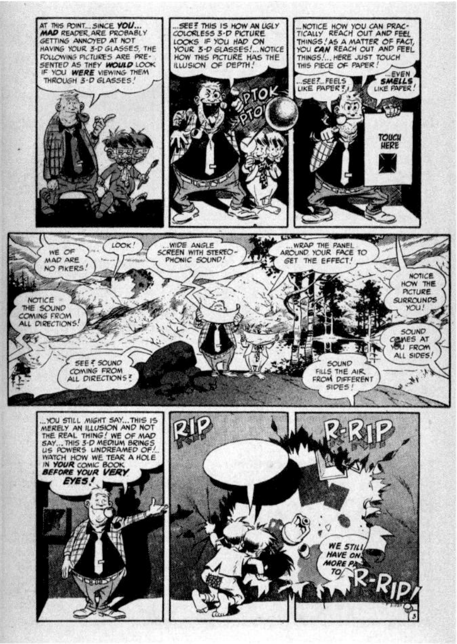
AT THIS POINT... SINCE YOU... MAD READER, ARE PROBABLY GETTING ANNOYED AT NOT HAVING YOUR 3-D GLASSES, THE FOLLOWING PICTURES ARE PRESENTED AS THEY WOULD LOOK IF YOU WERE VIEWING THEM THROUGH 3-D GLASSES!
...SEE? THIS IS HOW AN UGLY COLORLESS 3-D PICTURE LOOKS IF YOU HAD ON YOUR 3-D GLASSES!...NOTICE HOW THIS PICTURE HAS THE ILLUSION OF DEPTH!
PTOK
...NOTICE HOW YOU CAN PRACTICALLY REACH OUT AND FEEL THINGS! AS A MATTER OF FACT, YOU CAN REACH OUT AND FEEL THINGS!... HERE JUST TOUCH THIS PIECE OF PAPER!
...SEE?... FEELS LIKE PAPER?
...EVEN SMELLS LIKE PAPER!
TOUCH HERE
WE OF MAD ARE NO PIKERS!
LOOK!
...WIDE ANGLE SCREEN WITH STEREO-PHONIC SOUND!
...WRAP THE PANEL AROUND YOUR FACE TO GET THE EFFECT!
NOTICE HOW THE PICTURE SURROUNDS YOU!
NOTICE THE SOUND COMING FROM ALL DIRECTIONS!
SEE? SOUND COMING FROM ALL DIRECTIONS?
SOUND COMES AT YOU FROM ALL SIDES!
SOUND FILLS THE AIR FROM DIFFERENT SIDES!
...YOU STILL MIGHT SAY... THIS IS MERELY AN ILLUSION AND NOT THE REAL THING! WE OF MAD SAY... THIS 3-D MEDIUM BRINGS US POWERS UNDREAMED OF!... WATCH HOW WE TEAR A HOLE IN YOUR COMIC BOOK BEFORE YOUR VERY EYES!
RIP
R-RIP
R-RIP!

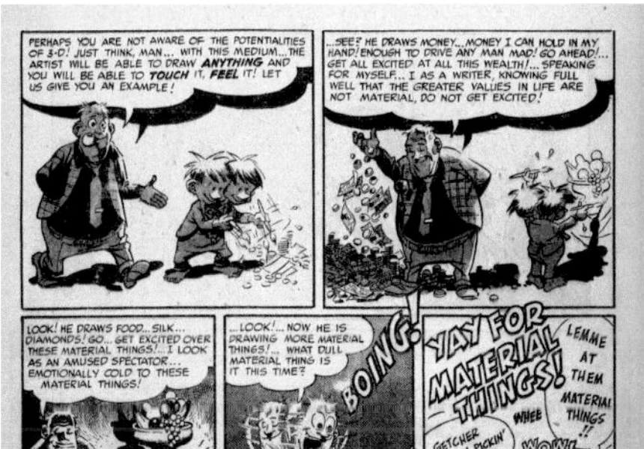
PERHAPS YOU ARE NOT AWARE OF THE POTENTIALITIES OF 3-D! JUST THINK, MAN... WITH THIS MEDIUM... THE ARTIST WILL BE ABLE TO DRAW ANYTHING AND YOU WILL BE ABLE TO TOUCH IT, FEEL IT! LET US GIVE YOU AN EXAMPLE!
...SEE? HE DRAWS MONEY... MONEY I CAN HOLD IN MY HAND! ENOUGH TO DRIVE ANY MAN MAD! GO AHEAD!... GET ALL EXCITED AT ALL THIS WEALTH!... SPEAKING FOR MYSELF... I AS A WRITER, KNOWING FULL WELL THAT THE GREATER VALUES IN LIFE ARE NOT MATERIAL, DO NOT GET EXCITED!
LOOK! HE DRAWS FOOD... SILK... DIAMONDS! GO... GET EXCITED OVER THESE MATERIAL THINGS!... I LOOK AS AN AMUSED SPECTATOR... EMOTIONALLY COLD TO THESE MATERIAL THINGS!
...LOOK!... NOW HE IS DRAWING MORE MATERIAL THINGS!... WHAT DULL MATERIAL THING IS IT THIS TIME?
BOING!
YAY FOR MATERIAL THINGS!
LEMME AT THEM MATERIAL THINGS!!
WHEE
WOW!
GETCHER COTTON PICKIN' HANDS OFFA ME!
Potrzebie?
Potrzebie!
HA, SEE? THE HOLE SHOWS THRO ON THIS SIDE, TOO!

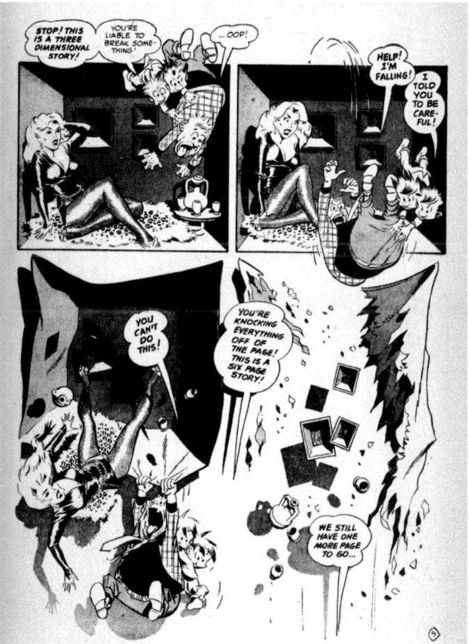
STOP! THIS IS A THREE DIMENSIONAL STORY!
YOU'RE LIABLE TO BREAK SOMETHING!
...OOP!
HELP! I'M FALLING!
I TOLD YOU TO BE CAREFUL!
YOU CAN'T DO THIS!
YOU'RE KNOCKING EVERYTHING OFF OF THE PAGE! THIS IS A SIX PAGE STORY!
WE STILL HAVE ONE MORE PAGE TO GO...

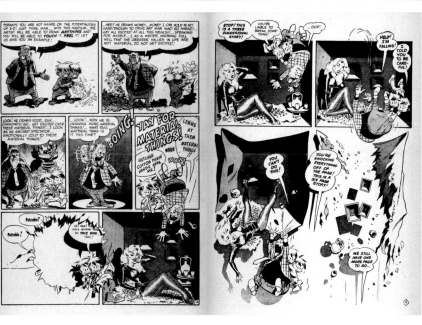

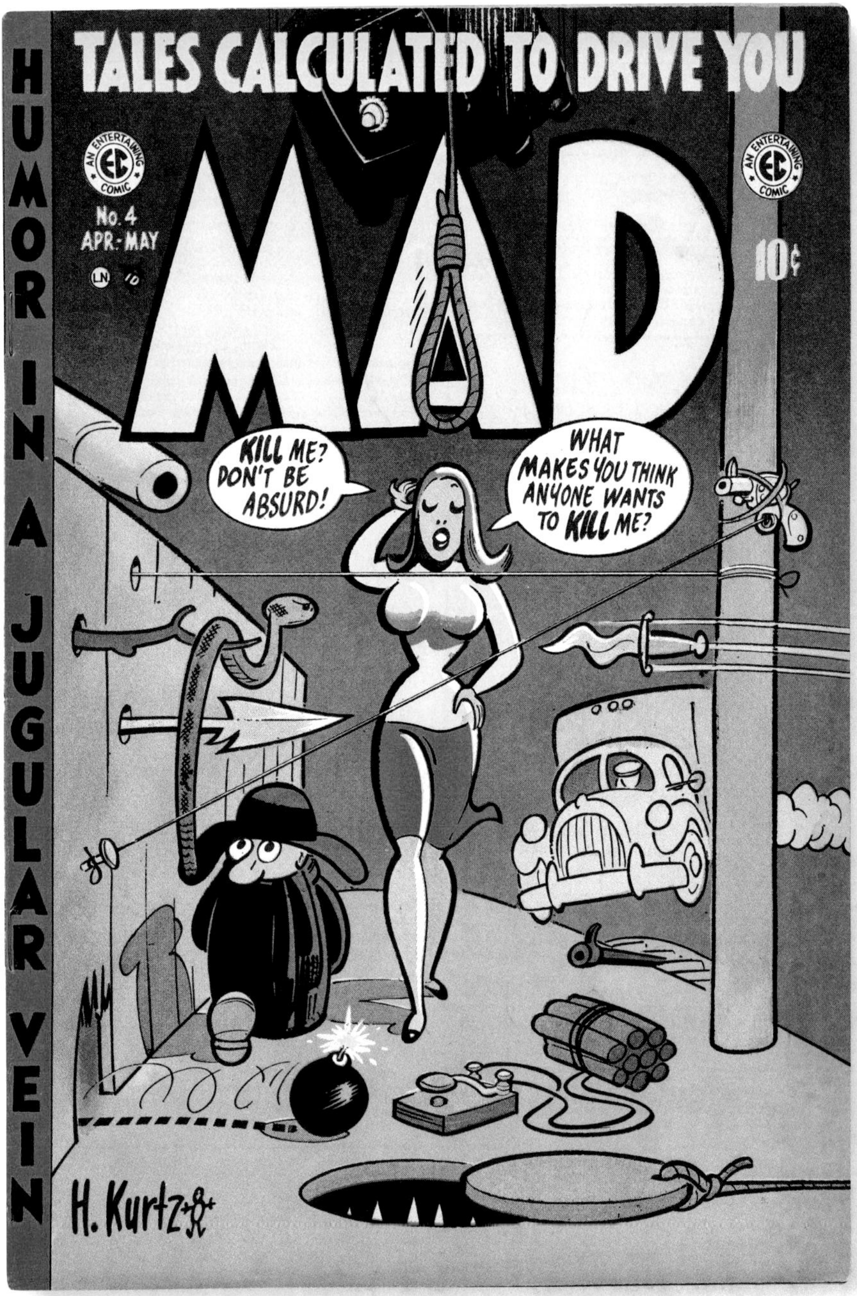
TALES CALCULATED TO DRIVE YOU
MAD
HUMOR IN A JUGULAR VEIN
AN ENTERTAINING EC COMIC
No. 4
APR.-MAY
10¢
KILL ME? DON'T BE ABSURD!
WHAT MAKES YOU THINK ANYONE WANTS TO KILL ME?
H. Kurtz

Harvey Kurtzman

"Kurtzman was eager to try anything that would make a reader pause and take notice, whether using innovative color effects, photos, or turning the magazine upside down so that the back cover was in reality the front cover."

—NICK MEGLIN

MAD No. 12

PREVIOUS SPREAD: *Interiors, "3-Dimensions"; writer, Harvey Kurtzman; artist, Wally Wood. June 1954.* Kurtzman and Wood's "3-Dimensions" made vivid use of color and the entire 3-D process. The visuals also made it unsuited for the black-and-white paperbacks that compiled the early *Mad* stories, and reprints of the episode in its proper form didn't appear for decades.

MAD No. 4

Cover art, Harvey Kurtzman, April–May 1953. Harvey Kurtzman's cover for this issue referenced his send-up of the Shadow, but the comic also skewered Robin Hood and led off with the famed "Superduperman," by Kurtzman and Wally Wood.

HARVEY KURTZMAN

Photograph, ca. 1960.

A FUNNY FUNNY BOOK
MAD
10
THAT THING! THAT SLITHERING BLOB COMING TOWARDS US!
WHAT IS IT?
IT'S MELVIN!

TALES CALCULATED TO DRIVE YOU
MAD
HUMOR IN A JUGULAR VEIN
No. 1 OCT.-NOV.
10¢
THAT THING! THAT SLITHERING BLOB COMING TOWARD US!
WHAT IS IT?
IT'S MELVIN!

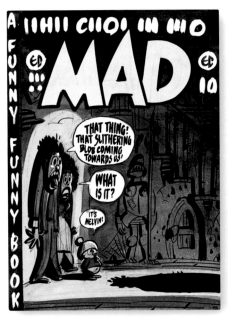

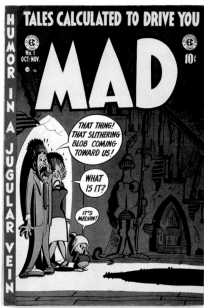

MAD No. 1

Color guide and final cover art, Harvey Kurtzman, April–May 1953. Like many truly revolutionary creations, *MAD* lost money in the beginning. In a society that preferred the safe and familiar, Harvey Kurtzman's "humor in a jugular vein" was more than a little unsettling. Kurtzman's role included not only writing and laying out most of the stories in the comic but also designing each cover. Marie Severin, one of the rare women working in the comics industry, was the colorist of the historic first issue's cover and interior stories.

MAD No. 4

OPPOSITE AND FOLLOWING SPREAD: *Interior original art and thumbnail layouts, "Superduperman"; script, Harvey Kurtzman; pencils and inks, Wally Wood. April–May 1953.* With incisive, hilarious commentary on topics like the Superman–Captain Marvel competition and Lois Lane's disdain for Clark Kent, "Superduperman" was the defining moment when *MAD* truly found its voice. Moving away from satires on genres like Westerns or horror, Harvey Kurtzman realized that it was more satisfying to target specific series that his audience knew well, whether it was comic books' Batman, comic strips' "Terry and the Pirates," or TV's *Howdy Doody*.

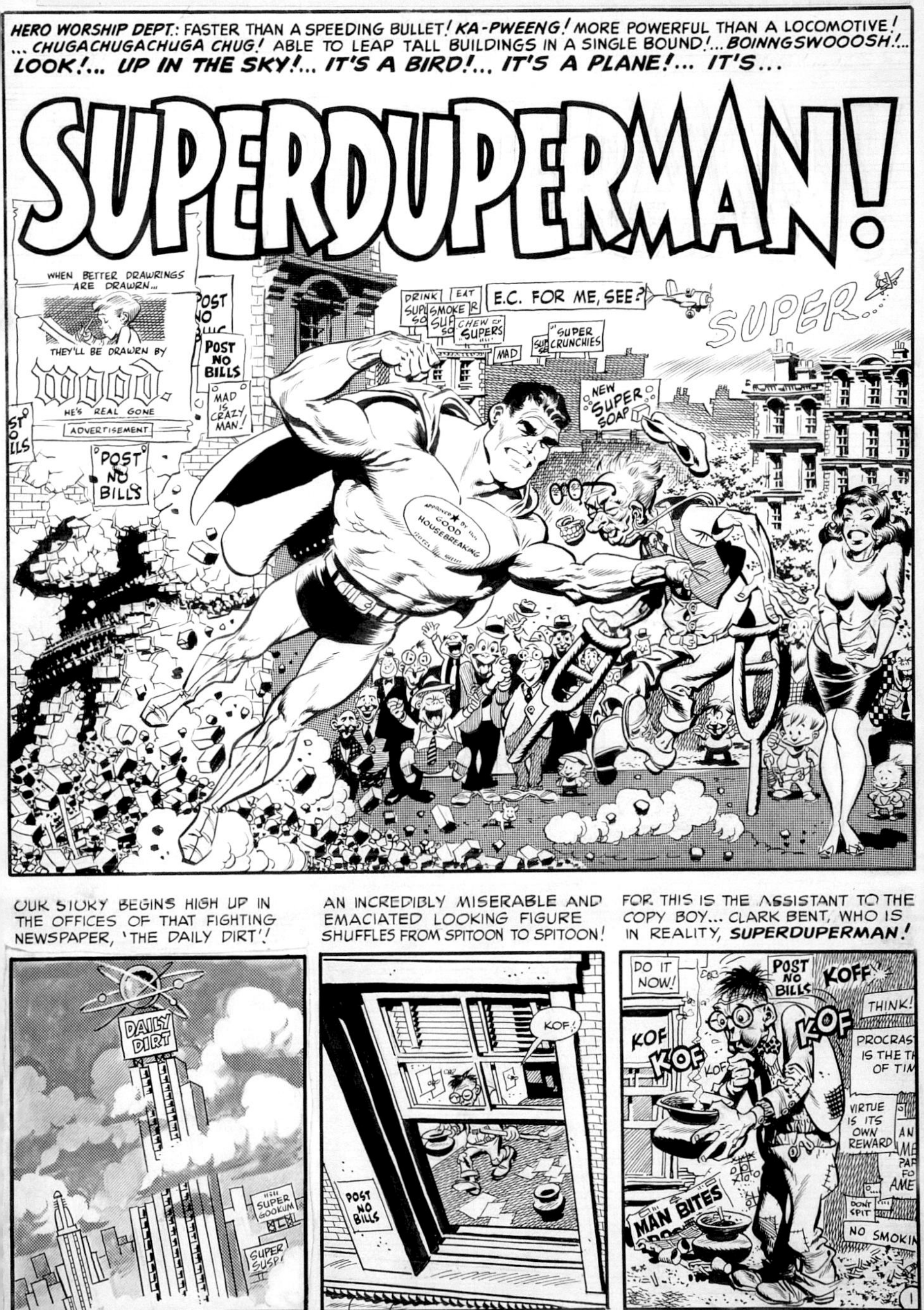
HERO WORSHIP DEPT.: FASTER THAN A SPEEDING BULLET! KA-PWEENG! MORE POWERFUL THAN A LOCOMOTIVE! ... CHUGACHUGACHUGA CHUG! ABLE TO LEAP TALL BUILDINGS IN A SINGLE BOUND!... BOINNGSWOOOSH!... LOOK!... UP IN THE SKY!... IT'S A BIRD!... IT'S A PLANE!... IT'S...
SUPERDUPERMAN!
WHEN BETTER DRAWRINGS ARE DRAWRN...
THEY'LL BE DRAWN BY
WOOD.
HE'S REAL GONE
ADVERTISEMENT
POST NO BILLS
MAD IS CRAZY MAN!
POST NO BILLS
E.C. FOR ME, SEE?
SUPER...
CHEW SUPERS
SUPER CRUNCHIES
MAD
NEW SUPER SOAP
GOOD HOUSEBREAKING
OUR STORY BEGINS HIGH UP IN THE OFFICES OF THAT FIGHTING NEWSPAPER, 'THE DAILY DIRT'!
DAILY DIRT
SUPER GOOKUM
AN INCREDIBLY MISERABLE AND EMACIATED LOOKING FIGURE SHUFFLES FROM SPITOON TO SPITOON!
KOF!
POST NO BILLS
FOR THIS IS THE ASSISTANT TO THE COPY BOY... CLARK BENT, WHO IS IN REALITY, SUPERDUPERMAN!
DO IT NOW!
POST NO BILLS
KOFF
THINK!
KOF
KOF
KOF
KOF
VIRTUE IS ITS OWN REWARD
MAN BITES
DON'T SPIT
NO SMOKIN
1

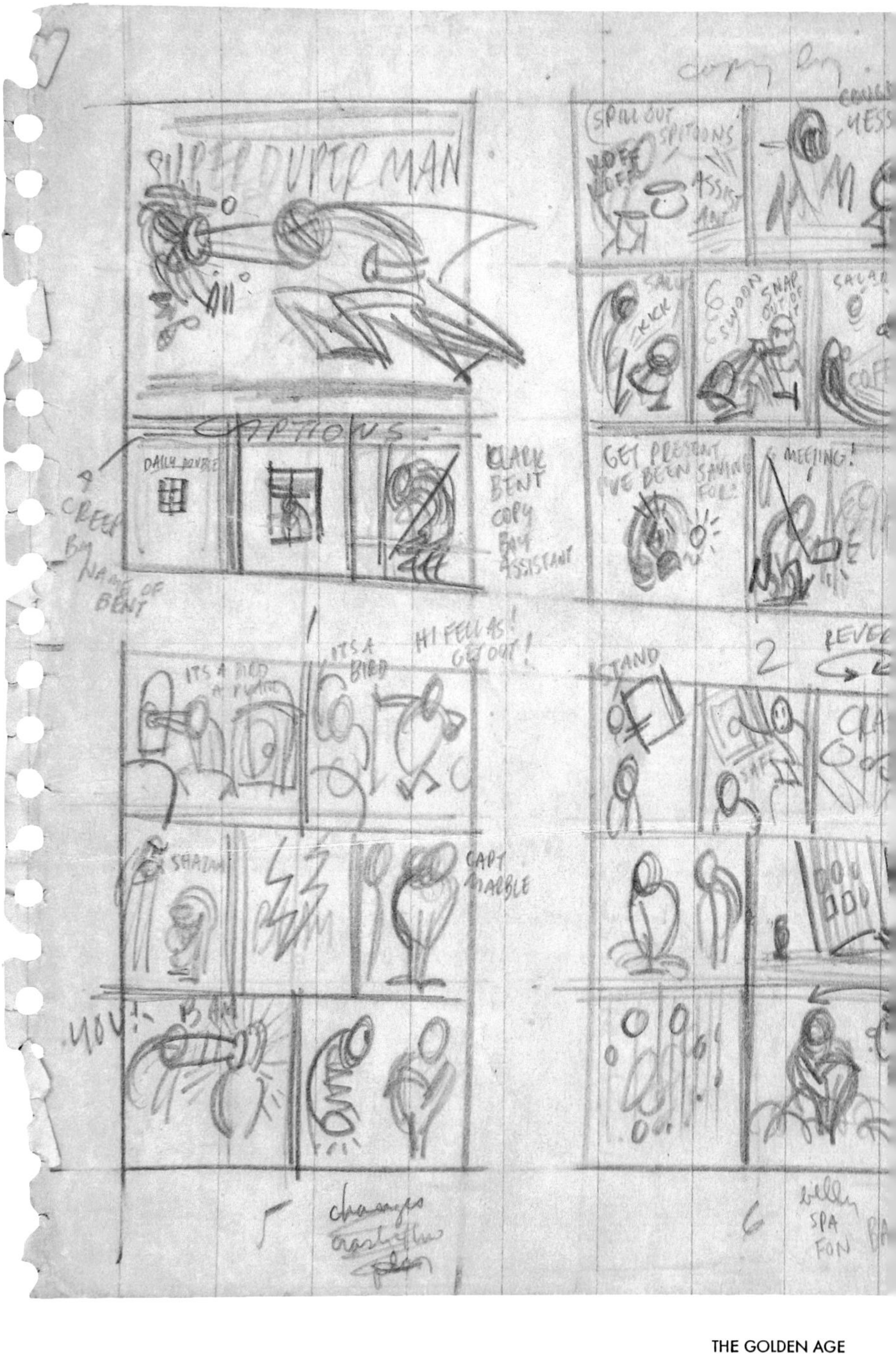
SUPER DUPER MAN
CAPTIONS
CLARK BENT COPY BOY ASSISTANT
A CREEP BY NAME OF BENT
1
ITS A BIRD
HI FELLAS! GET OUT!
SHAZAM
CAPT MARBLE
YOU!
BAM
5
changes
SPILL OUT SPITOONS
KICK
SWOON
SNAP OUT OF IT
GET PRESENT I'VE BEEN SAVING FOR
MEETING!
2
STAND
6
SPA FON

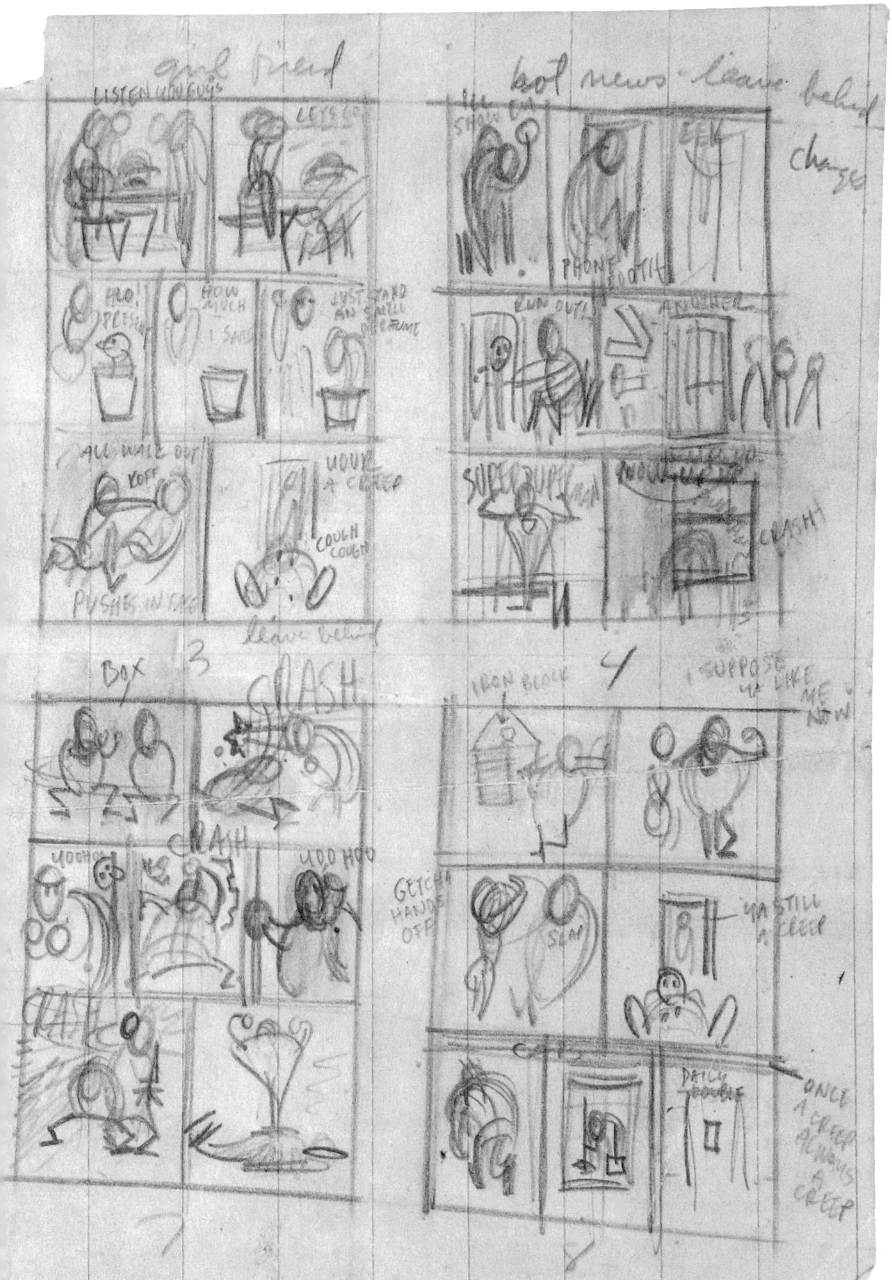

girl friend
LISTEN YOU GUYS
LETS GO
HOW MUCH
ALL WALK OUT
KOFF
YOUR A CREEP
COUGH COUGH
hot news
leave behind
change
PHONE BOOTH
CRASH
leave behind
BOX
3
CRASH
CRASH
YOO HOO
CRASH
4
IRON BLOCK
I SUPPOSE YA LIKE ME NOW
GETCHA HANDS OFF
SLAP
YA STILL A CREEP
DAILY DOUBLE
ONCE A CREEP ALWAYS A CREEP

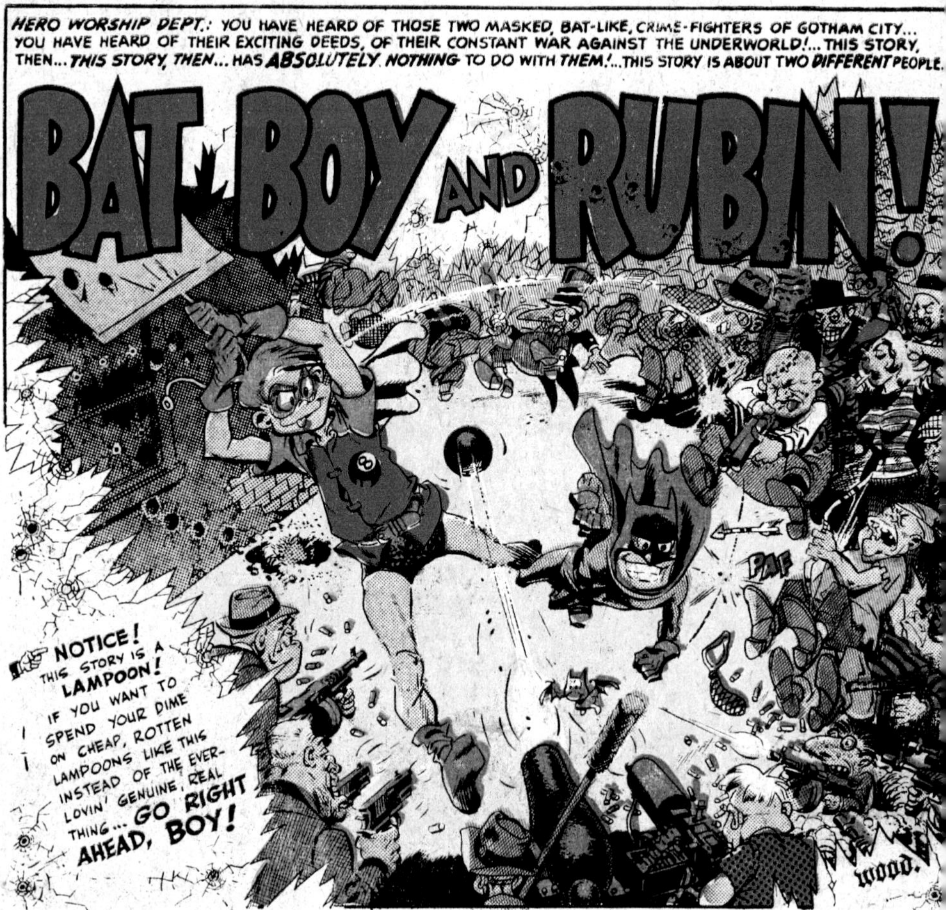
HERO WORSHIP DEPT.: YOU HAVE HEARD OF THOSE TWO MASKED, BAT-LIKE, CRIME-FIGHTERS OF GOTHAM CITY... YOU HAVE HEARD OF THEIR EXCITING DEEDS, OF THEIR CONSTANT WAR AGAINST THE UNDERWORLD!... THIS STORY, THEN... THIS STORY, THEN... HAS ABSOLUTELY NOTHING TO DO WITH THEM!...THIS STORY IS ABOUT TWO DIFFERENT PEOPLE.
BAT BOY AND RUBIN!
NOTICE! THIS STORY IS A LAMPOON! IF YOU WANT TO SPEND YOUR DIME ON CHEAP, ROTTEN LAMPOONS LIKE THIS INSTEAD OF THE EVER-LOVIN' GENUINE, REAL THING... GO RIGHT AHEAD, BOY!
PAF
WOOD.

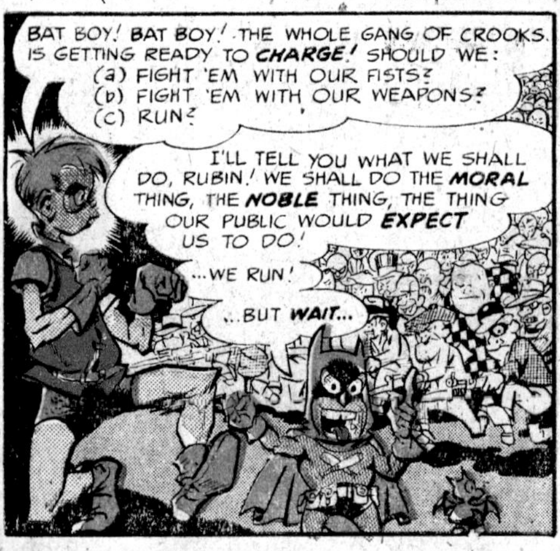
BAT BOY! BAT BOY! THE WHOLE GANG OF CROOKS IS GETTING READY TO CHARGE! SHOULD WE: (a) FIGHT 'EM WITH OUR FISTS? (b) FIGHT 'EM WITH OUR WEAPONS? (c) RUN?
I'LL TELL YOU WHAT WE SHALL DO, RUBIN! WE SHALL DO THE MORAL THING, THE NOBLE THING, THE THING OUR PUBLIC WOULD EXPECT US TO DO!
...WE RUN!
...BUT WAIT...

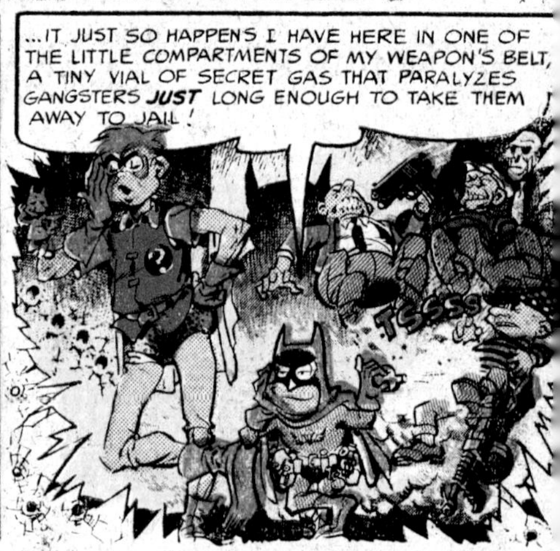
...IT JUST SO HAPPENS I HAVE HERE IN ONE OF THE LITTLE COMPARTMENTS OF MY WEAPON'S BELT, A TINY VIAL OF SECRET GAS THAT PARALYZES GANGSTERS JUST LONG ENOUGH TO TAKE THEM AWAY TO JAIL!
TSSSS

HERO WORSHIP DEPT.: 'SADDLESORE'... SIX FOOT LANKY TEXAN, 'SAURBRATTEN'... WALRUS-MUSTACHED DUTCHMAN, 'ROBESPIERRE'... SUAVE PARISIEN FROM LA BELLE FRANCE, 'BOSS HAWK', LEADER OF THE GANG, 'YOHNNY YOHNSON', FIGHTING SWEDE, AND 'CHOP CHOP CHOP'... CAMP FOLLOWER! ALL MEN OF PEP, VIM AND VIGOR, SNAP CRACKLE AND POP... ALL...
BLACK and BLUE HAWKS!
HAWKAAAAAAAAAAAAAAAAAAW!
woodhawk
YES, DEAR READER, THESE ARE THE BLACK AND BLUE HAWKS... FLYING, FLYING, DYING FOR THE FUN OF IT! OH, I'M TELLING YOU... WHAT FUN! COME, THEN! COME... TO A TINY ISLAND FAR OUT IN THE OCEAN! LATITUDE... ADVENTURE, LONGITUDE... DANGER! FOR THIS IS THE HOME OF... THE ROOST OF... THE COOP OF... THE BLACK AND BLUE HAWKS!
OVER LAND.. OVER SEA WE-EE FIGHT FOR DO-RE-MI...
HA CHA CHA
WE'RE BLACK AND BLUE HA
DAVY'S
HAW-KAW!
SING IT PRITTY, BOY!
AAAAA-HAW
HAWKA!

PLASTIC HERO WORSHIP DEPT.: WHERE ARE THE STRANGE CHARACTERS OF YESTERYEAR WHO USED TO HAUNT THE PAGES OF COMIC BOOKS? WHERE HAS THE 'FLASH' DASHED TO?... WHERE HAS 'SUB-MARINER' SWUM TO?... WHERE HAS 'CAPTAIN MARVEL' SHAZZAMED TO?... THIS STORY, THEN, IS DEDICATED TO THAT FAST-DYING RACE OF FREAKS... TO MEN LIKE...
PLASTIC SAM!
I AM PLASTIC SAM, THE MAN WITH THE 'SILLY-PUTTY' BODY! NOTICE HOW PEOPLE STARE FASCINATED AT ME STRETCHING MY BODY... THINKING THEY HAVE LOST THEIR SENSES!
I AM WHEEZY WUNKS, ASSISTANT TO PLASTIC SAM! NOTICE HOW PEOPLE STARE FASCINATED AT HIM STRETCHING HIS BODY THINKING HE HAS LOST HIS PANTS!
...AND, BY GEORGE, HE HAS! IT'S VERY DIFFICULT FINDING A MATERIAL FOR A SUIT THAT WILL STRETCH AND SHRINK WITH THE BODY!
HEATH
OUR STORY BEGINS IN COSMOPOLIS CITY IN THE HIDEOUT OF THIS HERE DIRTY BUNCH OF NO GOOD CROOKS PLANNING TO TAKE OVER THE U.S.A.! AS THE SCENE OPENS, WE HEAR...
...BOYS!... THERE'S ONLY ONE THING IN THE WAY OF US DIRTY BUNCH OF NO-GOOD CROOKS PLANNING TO TAKE OVER THE U.S.A.!!
OW! WATTAYA DOIN', BOSS?
WHY'D YA PULL MY NOSE?
...WHY'D YA BEND MY TOOTH?
WHY'D YA PINCH MY EYE-BALL?

MAD No. 8

Interior, "Bat Boy and Rubin"; script, Harvey Kurtzman; pencils and inks, Wally Wood. December 1953–January 1954.

MAD No. 5

Interior, "Black and Blue Hawks"; script, unknown; pencils and inks, Wally Wood. June–July 1953.

MAD No. 14

Interior, "Plastic Sam"; script, Harvey Kurtzman; pencils and inks, Russ Heath. August 1954. A huge fan of cartoonist Jack Cole and Plastic Man, Harvey Kurtzman later noted that it was difficult to parody a parody. Still, he found angles to mock, as in his observation that Sam's punches have no power since his body "has a consistency somewhere between window-putty and oatmeal."

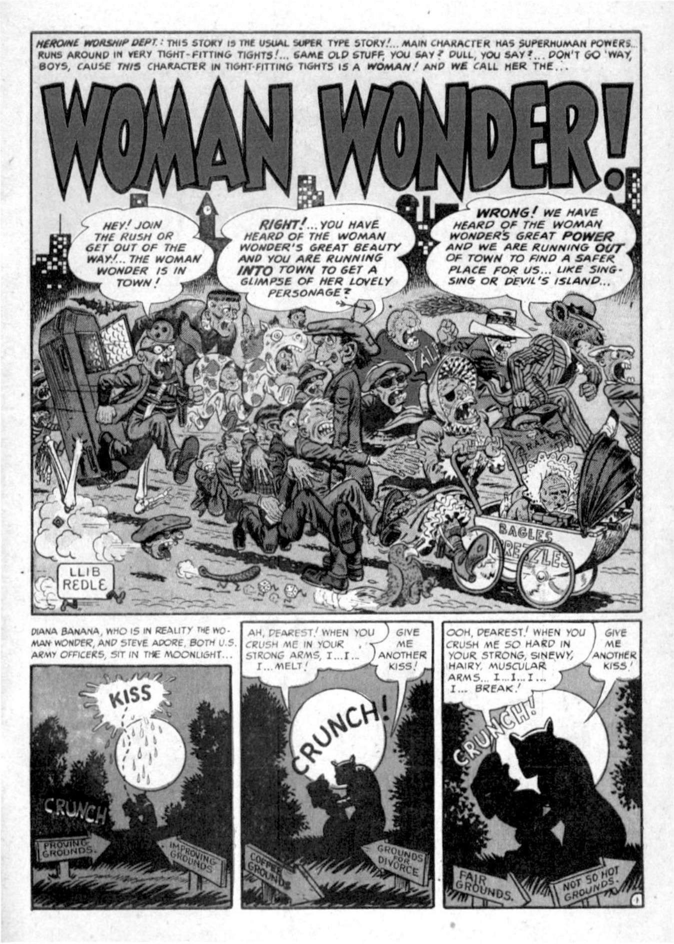
HEROINE WORSHIP DEPT.: THIS STORY IS THE USUAL SUPER TYPE STORY!... MAIN CHARACTER HAS SUPERHUMAN POWERS... RUNS AROUND IN VERY TIGHT-FITTING TIGHTS!... SAME OLD STUFF, YOU SAY? DULL, YOU SAY?... DON'T GO 'WAY, BOYS, CAUSE THIS CHARACTER IN TIGHT-FITTING TIGHTS IS A WOMAN! AND WE CALL HER THE...
WOMAN WONDER!
HEY! JOIN THE RUSH OR GET OUT OF THE WAY!... THE WOMAN WONDER IS IN TOWN!
RIGHT!... YOU HAVE HEARD OF THE WOMAN WONDER'S GREAT BEAUTY AND YOU ARE RUNNING INTO TOWN TO GET A GLIMPSE OF HER LOVELY PERSONAGE?
WRONG! WE HAVE HEARD OF THE WOMAN WONDER'S GREAT POWER AND WE ARE RUNNING OUT OF TOWN TO FIND A SAFER PLACE FOR US... LIKE SING-SING OR DEVIL'S ISLAND...
BAGLES
PREZLES
LLIB REDLE
DIANA BANANA, WHO IS IN REALITY THE WOMAN WONDER, AND STEVE ADORE, BOTH U.S. ARMY OFFICERS, SIT IN THE MOONLIGHT...
KISS
CRUNCH
PROVING GROUNDS.
IMPROVING GROUNDS
AH, DEAREST! WHEN YOU CRUSH ME IN YOUR STRONG ARMS, I...I... I...MELT!
GIVE ME ANOTHER KISS!
CRUNCH!
COFFEE GROUNDS
GROUNDS FOR DIVORCE
OOH, DEAREST! WHEN YOU CRUSH ME SO HARD IN YOUR STRONG, SINEWY, HAIRY, MUSCULAR ARMS... I...I...I... I... BREAK!
GIVE ME ANOTHER KISS!
CRUNCH!
FAIR GROUNDS.
NOT SO HOT GROUNDS.

MAD No. 10

Interiors, "Woman Wonder"; script, Harvey Kurtzman; pencils and inks, Bill Elder. April 1954. Kurtzman found ample material in the *Wonder Woman* series to mock, for example its 1940s fixation on bondage, the exhibitionism of the invisible plane, and Steve Trevor's unceasing lust. "Woman Wonder" concluded with the domestication of the character, forced to wait on her husband hand and foot. While still a potent symbol for young girls, the real Wonder Woman had been tamed to a degree herself since the death of her creator, William Moulton Marston.

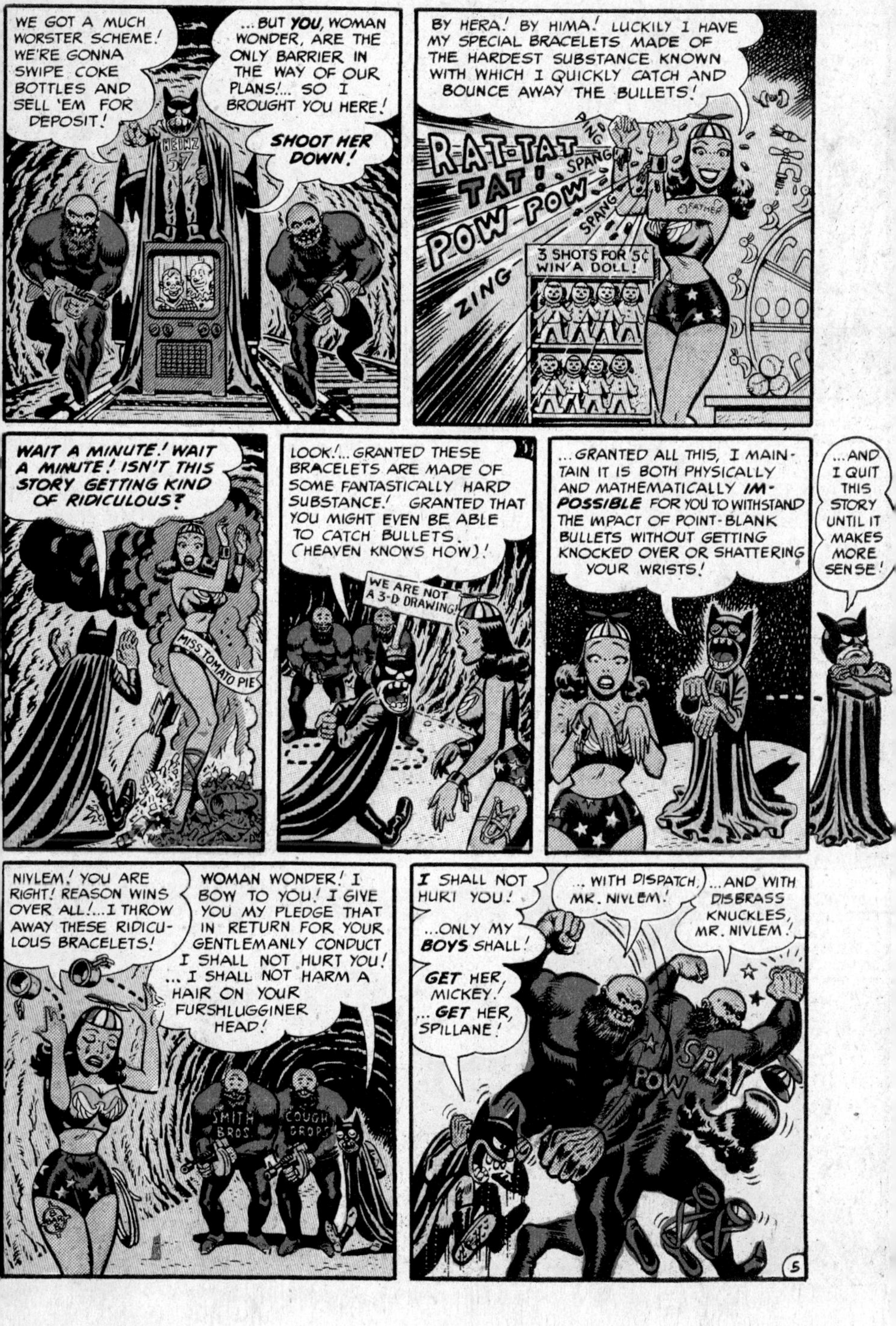
WE GOT A MUCH WORSTER SCHEME! WE'RE GONNA SWIPE COKE BOTTLES AND SELL 'EM FOR DEPOSIT!
...BUT YOU, WOMAN WONDER, ARE THE ONLY BARRIER IN THE WAY OF OUR PLANS!... SO I BROUGHT YOU HERE!
SHOOT HER DOWN!
HEINZ 57
BY HERA! BY HIMA! LUCKILY I HAVE MY SPECIAL BRACELETS MADE OF THE HARDEST SUBSTANCE KNOWN WITH WHICH I QUICKLY CATCH AND BOUNCE AWAY THE BULLETS!
RAT-TAT TAT!
POW-POW
PING
SPANG
SPANG
ZING
FATHER
3 SHOTS FOR 5¢ WIN A DOLL!
WAIT A MINUTE! WAIT A MINUTE! ISN'T THIS STORY GETTING KIND OF RIDICULOUS?
MISS TOMATO PIE
LOOK!... GRANTED THESE BRACELETS ARE MADE OF SOME FANTASTICALLY HARD SUBSTANCE! GRANTED THAT YOU MIGHT EVEN BE ABLE TO CATCH BULLETS. (HEAVEN KNOWS HOW)!
WE ARE NOT A 3-D DRAWING!
...GRANTED ALL THIS, I MAINTAIN IT IS BOTH PHYSICALLY AND MATHEMATICALLY IMPOSSIBLE FOR YOU TO WITHSTAND THE IMPACT OF POINT-BLANK BULLETS WITHOUT GETTING KNOCKED OVER OR SHATTERING YOUR WRISTS!
...AND I QUIT THIS STORY UNTIL IT MAKES MORE SENSE!
NIVLEM! YOU ARE RIGHT! REASON WINS OVER ALL!...I THROW AWAY THESE RIDICULOUS BRACELETS!
WOMAN WONDER! I BOW TO YOU! I GIVE YOU MY PLEDGE THAT IN RETURN FOR YOUR GENTLEMANLY CONDUCT I SHALL NOT HURT YOU! ...I SHALL NOT HARM A HAIR ON YOUR FURSHLUGGINER HEAD!
SMITH BROS.
COUGH DROPS
I SHALL NOT HURT YOU!
...ONLY MY BOYS SHALL!
GET HER, MICKEY! ...GET HER, SPILLANE!
...WITH DISPATCH, MR. NIVLEM!
...AND WITH DISBRASS KNUCKLES, MR. NIVLEM!
SPLAT
POW
5

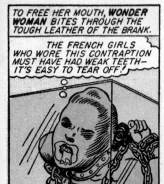

TO FREE HER MOUTH, **WONDER WOMAN** BITES THROUGH THE TOUGH LEATHER OF THE BRANK.

THE FRENCH GIRLS WHO WORE THIS CONTRAPTION MUST HAVE HAD WEAK TEETH—IT'S EASY TO TEAR OFF!

NEXT THE AMAZON GIRL REMOVES HER TIBETAN COLLAR BY TIGHTENING HER POWERFUL NECK MUSCLES.

WONDER WOMAN TRIES TO SEIZE THE MAGIC LASSO IN HER TEETH, BUT WITH HER EYES STILL BOUND, THE GOLDEN CORD ELUDES HER.

WHERE **IS** THAT LASSO LOOP? I CAN'T HOLD MY BREATH FOREVER!

THE AUDIENCE, MEANWHILE, BECOMES FRANTIC WITH FEAR FOR ITS IDOL.

WONDER WOMAN CAN'T BREAK LOOSE!

SHE'LL DROWN!

OPEN THAT TANK!

SMASH THAT GLASS! FREE **WONDER WOMAN!**

PRISCILLA RICH TRIES IN VAIN TO PREVENT SPECTATORS FROM INTERFERING.

OUT OF OUR WAY! RELEASE **WONDER WOMAN!**

PLEASE, EVERYBODY, KEEP BACK! YOU'LL SPOIL **WONDER WOMAN'S** ACT! SHE CAN BREAK **ANY** BONDS!

HA! EXCEPT THE MAGIC LASSO!

WONDER WOMAN, HER LUNGS BURSTING, TRIES AN ACROBATIC TRICK.

THAT'S BETTER—NOW I CAN SEE WHAT I'M DOING!

5A

GRIPPING THE MAGIC LASSO IN HER TEETH, **WONDER WOMAN** TEARS OFF THE GREEK FETTERS FROM HER ANKLES.

WONDER WOMAN, CAPTURED BY EVILESS ON PARADISE ISLAND, IS BOUND WITH THE MAGIC LASSO.

NOW, WE'LL TAKE YOU TO YOUR OWN AMAZON PRISON ON TRANSFORMATION ISLAND --HA HA!

THE CAPTIVE PRINCESS IS PLACED IN THE BOTTOM OF A BOAT.

I DON'T SEE CLEA, GIGANTA, ZARA, OR HYPNOTA--BUT THEY CAN FOLLOW IN ANOTHER BOAT. PULL AWAY, GIRLS!

WONDER WOMAN MAKES A NICE FOOT CUSHION!

NOW, MY PRISONER, YOU ARE SECURELY TIED. I COMMAND YOU TO MAKE NO ATTEMPT TO ESCAPE!

EVILESS WASN'T HOLDING THE LASSO WHEN SHE COMMANDED ME NOT TO ESCAPE SO I'M NOT COMPELLED TO OBEY HER! THEY BOUND ME VERY TIGHT BUT IF I CAN BEND MY LEGS A LITTLE--

SUDDENLY THE TIGHTLY BOUND AMAZON SPRINGS TO HER FEET.

AY-EE! HELP-- SEIZE THE

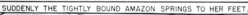

GREAT MEPHISTO--THAT AMAZON'S STRENGTH IS INCREDIBLE! BUT SHE'S STILL TIED TO THE BOAT--

WONDER WOMAN No. 6

PAGE 640: *Interior, "Wonder Woman and the Cheetah"; script, William Moulton Marston (as Charles Moulton); pencils and inks, H. G. Peter. Fall 1943.* "There was a certain symbolism that Marston engaged in, which was very simple and very broad. I suspect it probably sold more comic books than I realized, but every time I came across one of those tricks, I would try to clean it up. I probably made it worse." —Sheldon Mayer

SENSATION COMICS No. 9

PAGE 641: *Interior, "Wonder Woman"; script, William Moulton Marston; pencils and inks, H. G. Peter. September 1942. Seduction of the Innocent* author Fredric Wertham was far from alone in his concerns over the ever-present use of bondage in Wonder Woman stories. As early as 1943, All-American publisher M. C. Gaines had received enough criticism to futilely urge William Moulton Marston "to cut down the use of chains by at least 50 to 75%."

WONDER WOMAN No. 28

Interior original art, "Villainy, Inc."; script; William Moulton Marston; art, H. G. Peter. March–April 1948. In one of her last book-length adventures of the 1940s, Wonder Woman was attacked by a group of her greatest enemies.

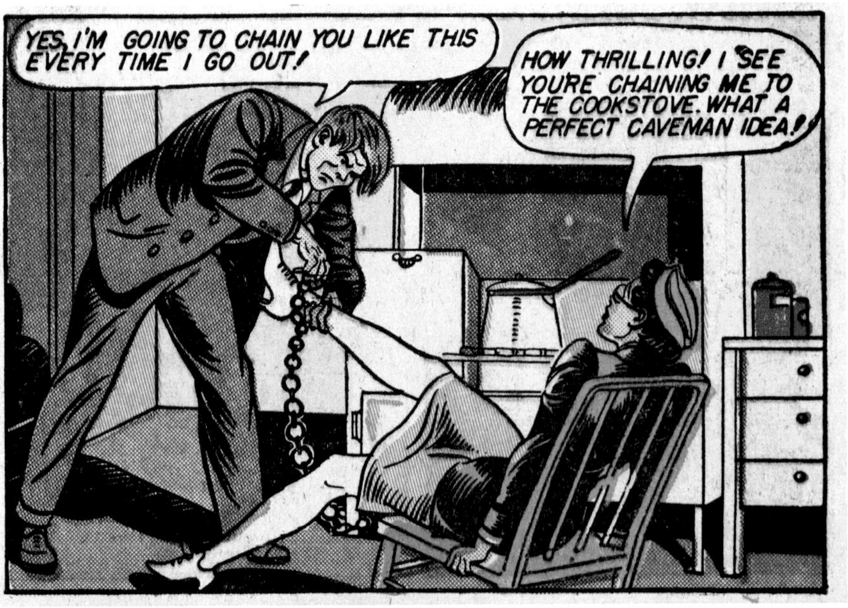
YES, I'M GOING TO CHAIN YOU LIKE THIS EVERY TIME I GO OUT!
HOW THRILLING! I SEE YOU'RE CHAINING ME TO THE COOKSTOVE. WHAT A PERFECT CAVEMAN IDEA!

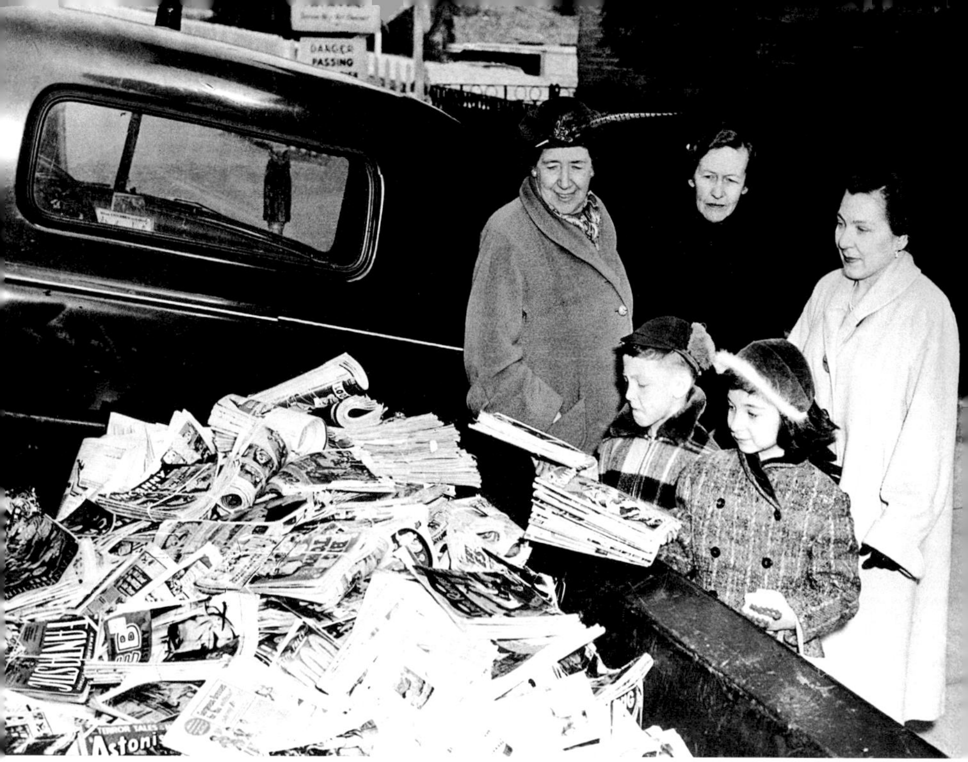
DANGER
PASSING

CONFISCATING COMICS

Photograph, members of the Women's Auxiliary of the American Legion collect comic books for incineration, Norwich, Connecticut, February 26, 1955. In 1953, Ray Bradbury's novel *Fahrenheit 451* projected a future where offensive books were routinely destroyed by groups called "firemen." For comic books, those forces included the Women's Auxiliary of the American Legion, which encouraged youngsters to trade in 10 comics for a "clean" book during a 1955 campaign. The American Book Publishing Council and American Civil Liberties Union were appropriately horrified at the prospect of the book burning that was scheduled to follow.

COMICS SEAL OF APPROVAL

FOLLOWING SPREAD: *Interiors, "What Do You Know About This Comics Seal of Approval?"; script, unknown; pencils and inks, Win Mortimer. 1955.* With its own code of conduct in place since the early 1940s and well respected for its monthly public service pages, DC was an appropriate choice to prepare a detailed comics pamphlet explaining the Comics Code's purpose and examination process. The account includes the ironic note that even violent material in recognized children's literature like Robert Louis Stevenson's *Treasure Island* would be censored.

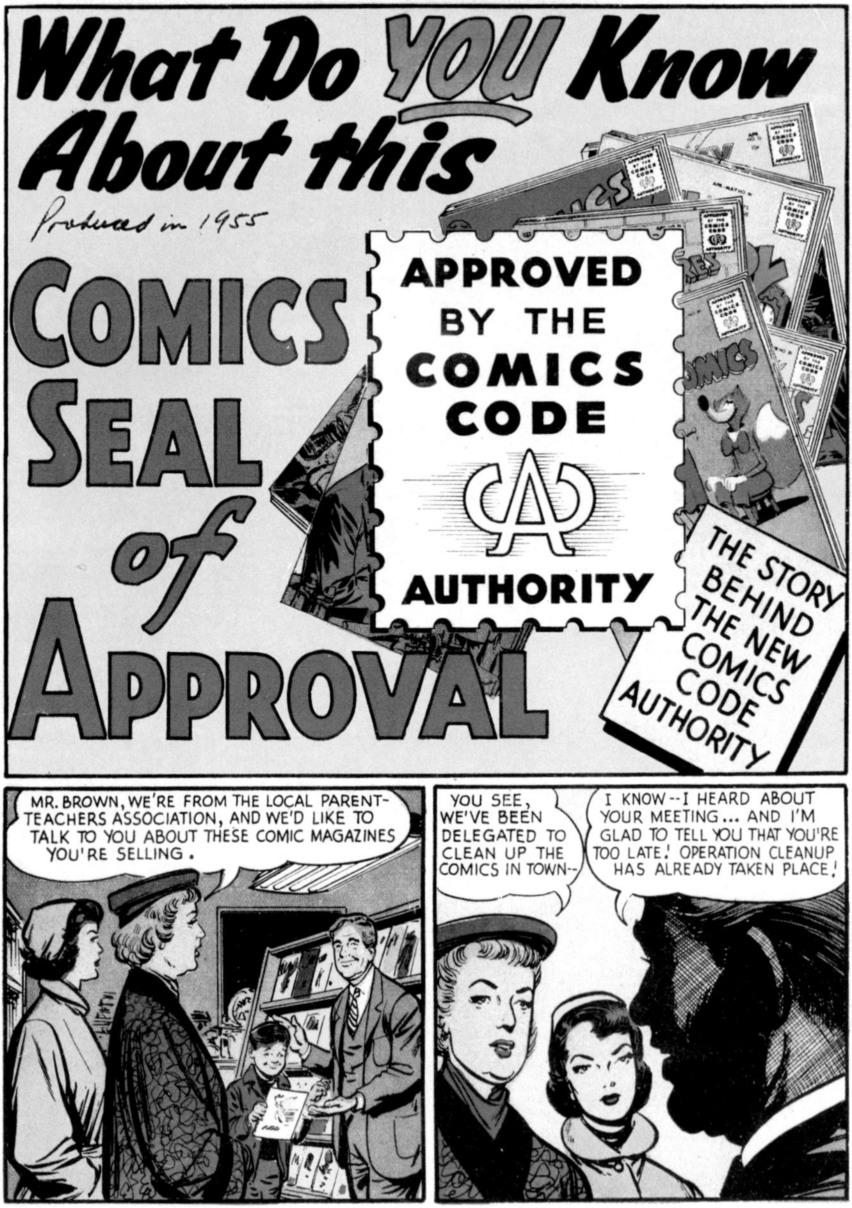
What Do YOU Know About this
Produced in 1955
COMICS SEAL of APPROVAL
APPROVED BY THE COMICS CODE AUTHORITY
THE STORY BEHIND THE NEW COMICS CODE AUTHORITY
MR. BROWN, WE'RE FROM THE LOCAL PARENT-TEACHERS ASSOCIATION, AND WE'D LIKE TO TALK TO YOU ABOUT THESE COMIC MAGAZINES YOU'RE SELLING.
YOU SEE, WE'VE BEEN DELEGATED TO CLEAN UP THE COMICS IN TOWN--
I KNOW--I HEARD ABOUT YOUR MEETING... AND I'M GLAD TO TELL YOU THAT YOU'RE TOO LATE! OPERATION CLEANUP HAS ALREADY TAKEN PLACE!

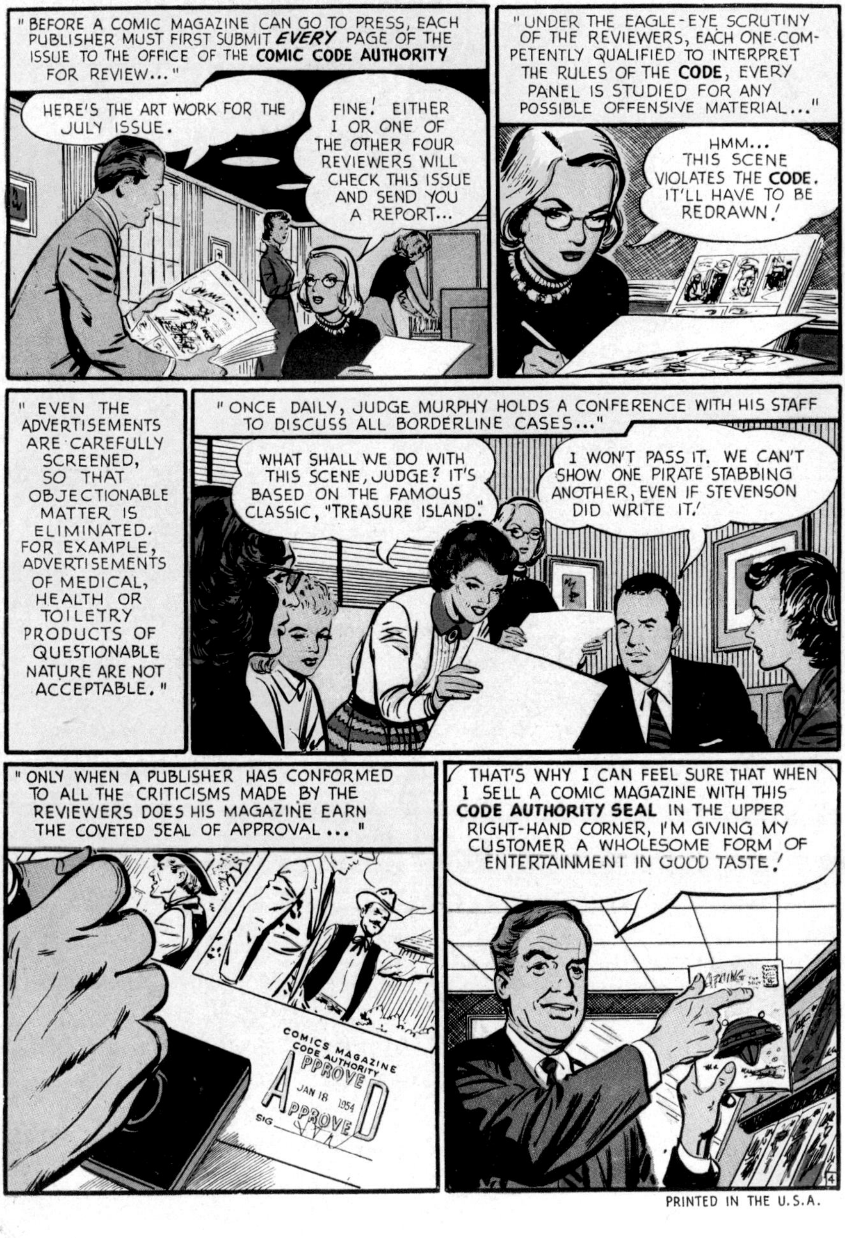

"BEFORE A COMIC MAGAZINE CAN GO TO PRESS, EACH PUBLISHER MUST FIRST SUBMIT *EVERY* PAGE OF THE ISSUE TO THE OFFICE OF THE **COMIC CODE AUTHORITY** FOR REVIEW..."
HERE'S THE ART WORK FOR THE JULY ISSUE.
FINE! EITHER I OR ONE OF THE OTHER FOUR REVIEWERS WILL CHECK THIS ISSUE AND SEND YOU A REPORT...
"UNDER THE EAGLE-EYE SCRUTINY OF THE REVIEWERS, EACH ONE COMPETENTLY QUALIFIED TO INTERPRET THE RULES OF THE **CODE**, EVERY PANEL IS STUDIED FOR ANY POSSIBLE OFFENSIVE MATERIAL..."
HMM... THIS SCENE VIOLATES THE **CODE**. IT'LL HAVE TO BE REDRAWN!
" EVEN THE ADVERTISEMENTS ARE CAREFULLY SCREENED, SO THAT OBJECTIONABLE MATTER IS ELIMINATED. FOR EXAMPLE, ADVERTISEMENTS OF MEDICAL, HEALTH OR TOILETRY PRODUCTS OF QUESTIONABLE NATURE ARE NOT ACCEPTABLE."
"ONCE DAILY, JUDGE MURPHY HOLDS A CONFERENCE WITH HIS STAFF TO DISCUSS ALL BORDERLINE CASES..."
WHAT SHALL WE DO WITH THIS SCENE, JUDGE? IT'S BASED ON THE FAMOUS CLASSIC, "TREASURE ISLAND."
I WON'T PASS IT. WE CAN'T SHOW ONE PIRATE STABBING ANOTHER, EVEN IF STEVENSON DID WRITE IT!
"ONLY WHEN A PUBLISHER HAS CONFORMED TO ALL THE CRITICISMS MADE BY THE REVIEWERS DOES HIS MAGAZINE EARN THE COVETED SEAL OF APPROVAL..."
COMICS MAGAZINE CODE AUTHORITY
APPROVED
JAN 18 1954
SIG
APPROVED
THAT'S WHY I CAN FEEL SURE THAT WHEN I SELL A COMIC MAGAZINE WITH THIS **CODE AUTHORITY SEAL** IN THE UPPER RIGHT-HAND CORNER, I'M GIVING MY CUSTOMER A WHOLESOME FORM OF ENTERTAINMENT IN GOOD TASTE!
4

PRINTED IN THE U.S.A.

AT EASE

Photograph, ca. 1951. American soldiers in Korea relax during
a break in the retreat. Reading comics was a common pastime
for troops stationed abroad, while public perception of the form
was beginning to shift at home. In the summer of 1952 *Life*
magazine reported that the "Pacific Fleet Command has
banned the sale of most war comic books in ships' stores on
the grounds that they are too gory for the American sailor."

STAR SPANGLED WAR STORIES No. 45

Cover art, Jerry Grandenetti, May 1956. A former assistant for
Will Eisner, Jerry Grandenetti was a prolific contributor to the
DC war titles, with the covers rendered in washtone by Jack
Adler still held in particularly high regard. The restless artist
continued to push his art style and periodically expressed his
gratitude that DC's editors allowed him to experiment with a
more exaggerated style that emerged in the 1970s.

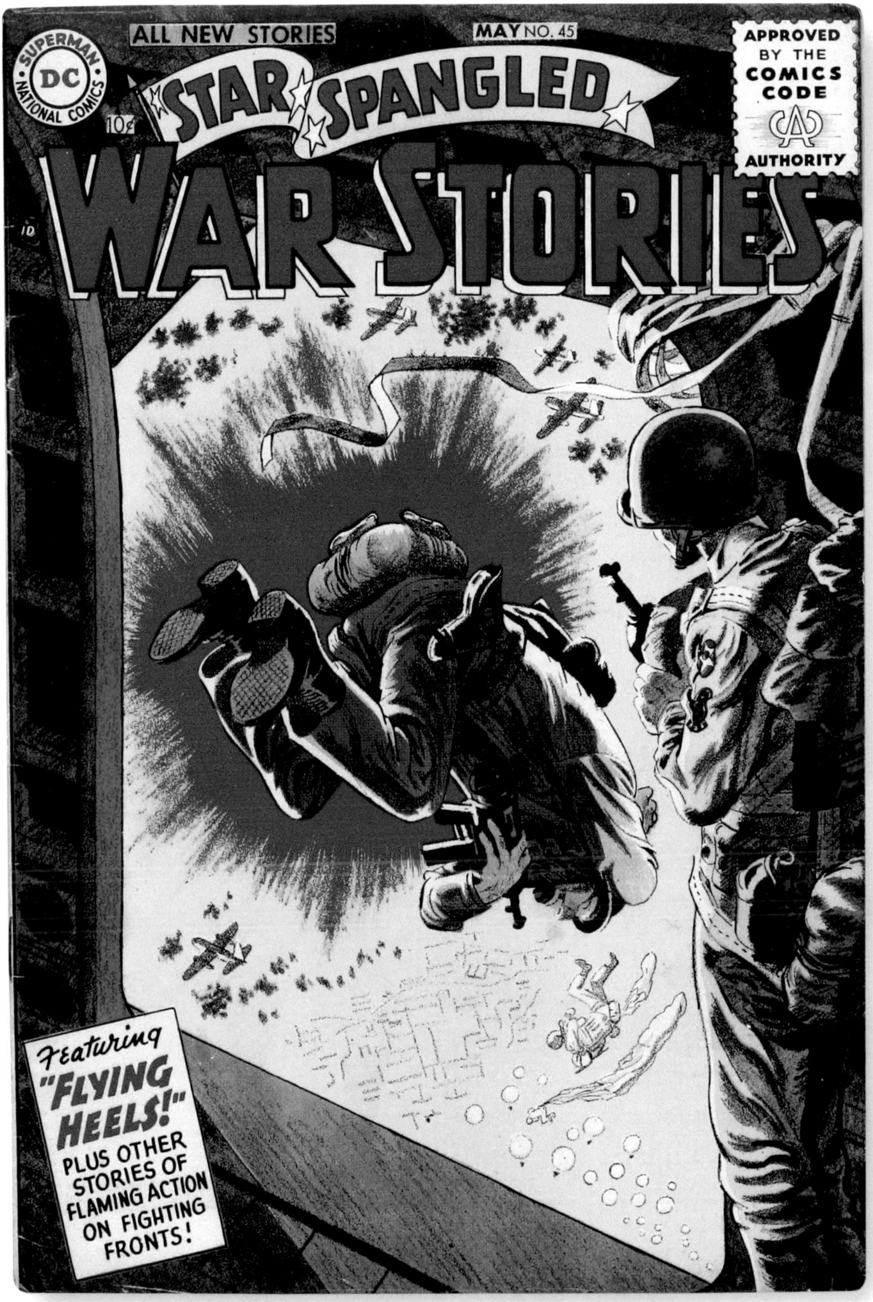
ALL NEW STORIES
MAY NO. 45
SUPERMAN
DC
NATIONAL COMICS
10¢
STAR SPANGLED
WAR STORIES
APPROVED
BY THE
COMICS
CODE
AUTHORITY
Featuring
"FLYING
HEELS!"
PLUS OTHER
STORIES OF
FLAMING ACTION
ON FIGHTING
FRONTS!

ALL AMERICAN MEN OF WAR ASHCAN

Cover art, Gil Kane and Frank Giacoia, August–September 1952.

OUR FIGHTING FORCES No. 1

Cover art, Jerry Grandenetti, October–November 1954. Our Fighting Forces was a comparatively late addition to the Robert Kanigher-edited war comics line. Like *Our Army at War, All-American Men of War,* and *Star Spangled War Stories,* the new title typically featured a quartet of short stories illustrated by a reliable pool of artists that included Jerry Grandenetti, Russ Heath, Irv Novick, and the Ross Andru–Mike Esposito team.

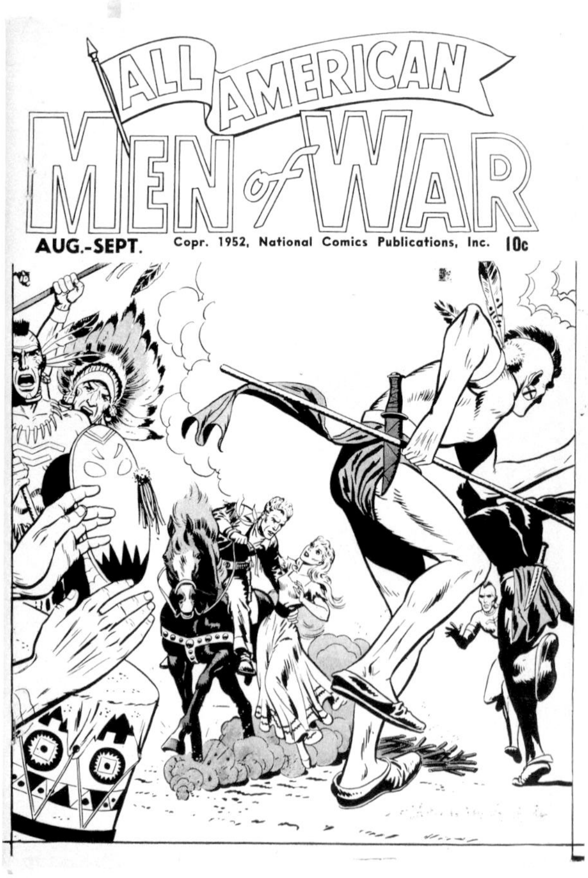
ALL AMERICAN
MEN of WAR
AUG.-SEPT.
Copr. 1952, National Comics Publications, Inc.
10c

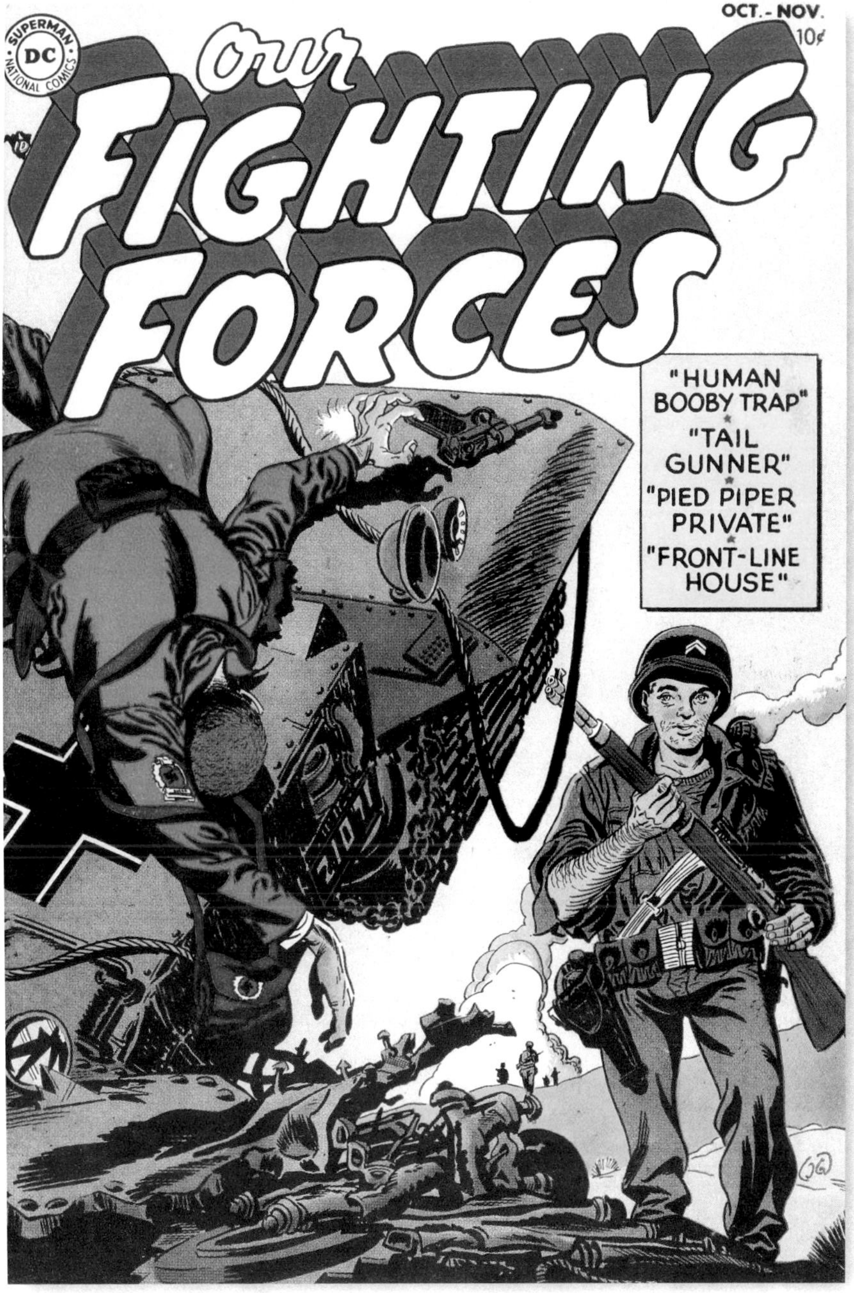
SUPERMAN DC NATIONAL COMICS
OCT.-NOV.
10¢
Our
FIGHTING
FORCES
"HUMAN BOOBY TRAP"
"TAIL GUNNER"
"PIED PIPER PRIVATE"
"FRONT-LINE HOUSE"

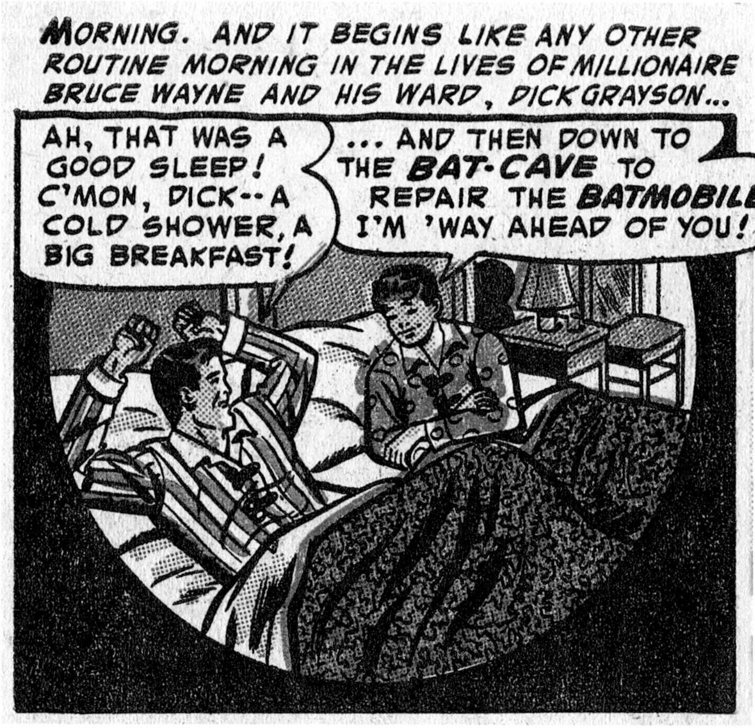
MORNING. AND IT BEGINS LIKE ANY OTHER ROUTINE MORNING IN THE LIVES OF MILLIONAIRE BRUCE WAYNE AND HIS WARD, DICK GRAYSON...
AH, THAT WAS A GOOD SLEEP! C'MON, DICK-- A COLD SHOWER, A BIG BREAKFAST!
... AND THEN DOWN TO THE BAT-CAVE TO REPAIR THE BATMOBILE! I'M 'WAY AHEAD OF YOU!

BATMAN No. 84

Interior, "Ten Nights of Fear"; script, David Vern Reed; pencils, Sheldon Moldoff; inks, Charles Paris. June 1954.

DETECTIVE COMICS No. 56

Interior original art, "Ride, Bat-Hombre, Ride": script, David Vern; pencils, Dick Sprang; inks, Charles Paris. December 1949–January 1950. A well-intentioned story found Batman traveling to a Latin American country at the behest of its dying President to train a "Bat-Hombre" who might root out villains like the cartoonish El Papagayo. Their best candidate was revealed as a scoundrel himself and perished in a fight with the real Batman.

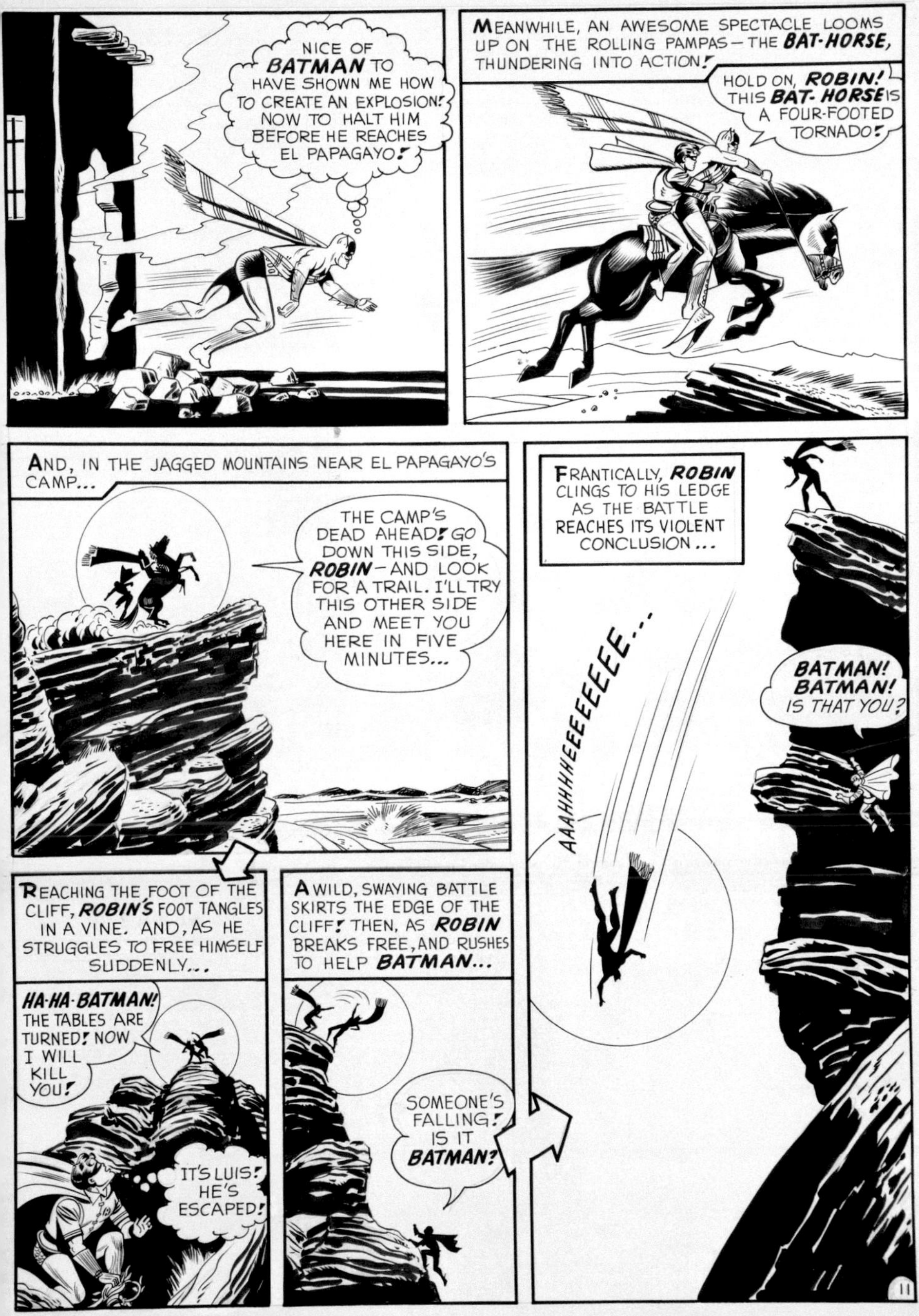
NICE OF BATMAN TO HAVE SHOWN ME HOW TO CREATE AN EXPLOSION! NOW TO HALT HIM BEFORE HE REACHES EL PAPAGAYO!
MEANWHILE, AN AWESOME SPECTACLE LOOMS UP ON THE ROLLING PAMPAS — THE BAT-HORSE, THUNDERING INTO ACTION!
HOLD ON, ROBIN! THIS BAT-HORSE IS A FOUR-FOOTED TORNADO!
AND, IN THE JAGGED MOUNTAINS NEAR EL PAPAGAYO'S CAMP...
THE CAMP'S DEAD AHEAD! GO DOWN THIS SIDE, ROBIN — AND LOOK FOR A TRAIL. I'LL TRY THIS OTHER SIDE AND MEET YOU HERE IN FIVE MINUTES...
REACHING THE FOOT OF THE CLIFF, ROBIN'S FOOT TANGLES IN A VINE. AND, AS HE STRUGGLES TO FREE HIMSELF SUDDENLY...
HA-HA-BATMAN! THE TABLES ARE TURNED! NOW I WILL KILL YOU!
IT'S LUIS! HE'S ESCAPED!
A WILD, SWAYING BATTLE SKIRTS THE EDGE OF THE CLIFF! THEN, AS ROBIN BREAKS FREE, AND RUSHES TO HELP BATMAN...
SOMEONE'S FALLING! IS IT BATMAN?
FRANTICALLY, ROBIN CLINGS TO HIS LEDGE AS THE BATTLE REACHES ITS VIOLENT CONCLUSION...
AAAHHHHEEEEEEEE...
BATMAN! BATMAN! IS THAT YOU?
11

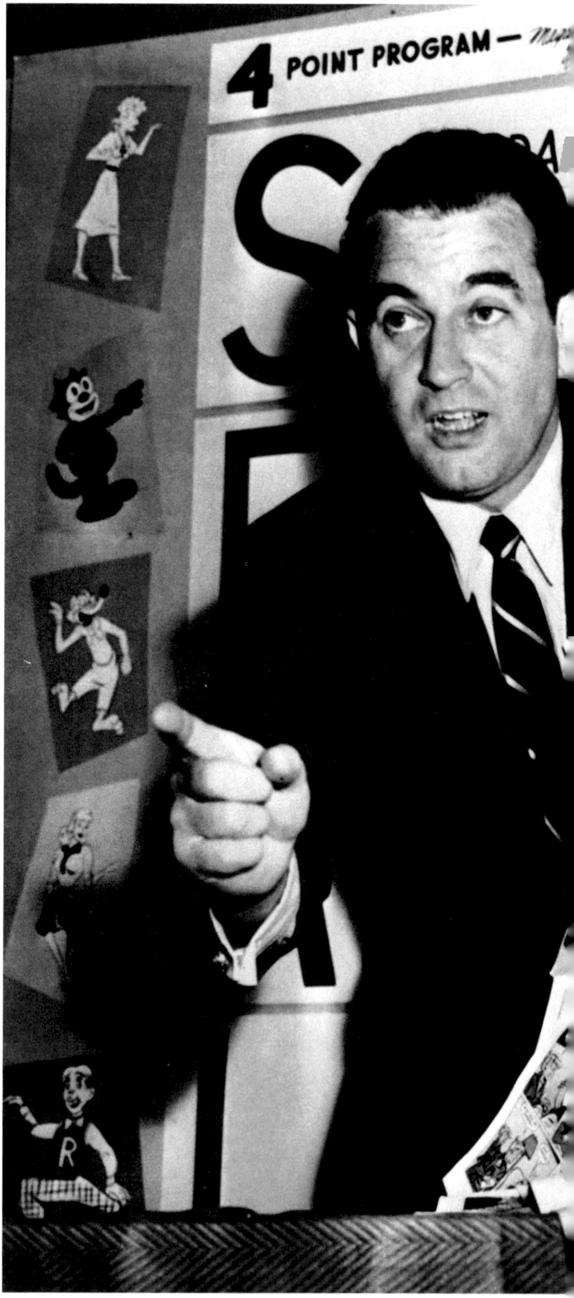
4 POINT PROGRAM —

VOICE OF AUTHORITY

Photograph, Charles F. Murphy, 1954. As administrator of the newly founded Comics Code Authority, Judge Murphy took great pains to demonstrate to the public how his reviewers would remove objectionable material from comic book pages before publication.

BATMAN No. 79

FOLLOWING SPREAD: *Interior, "Bride of Batman"; script, David Vern Reed; pencils, Dick Sprang; inks, Charles Paris. October–November 1953.* Batman's visible discomfort at the thought of marrying reporter Vicki Vale was rooted in the belief that the demands of married life would interfere with his fight against crime.

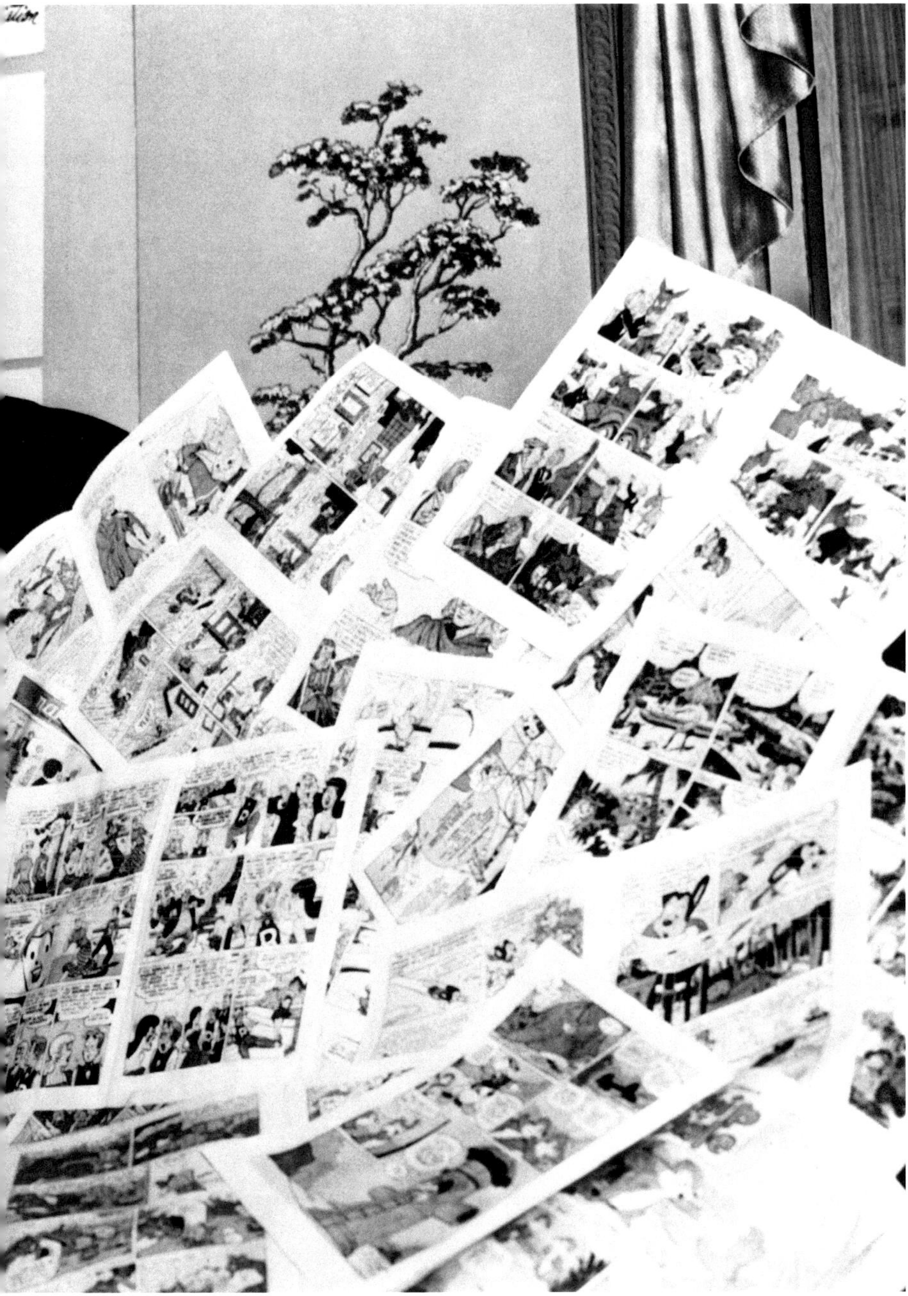

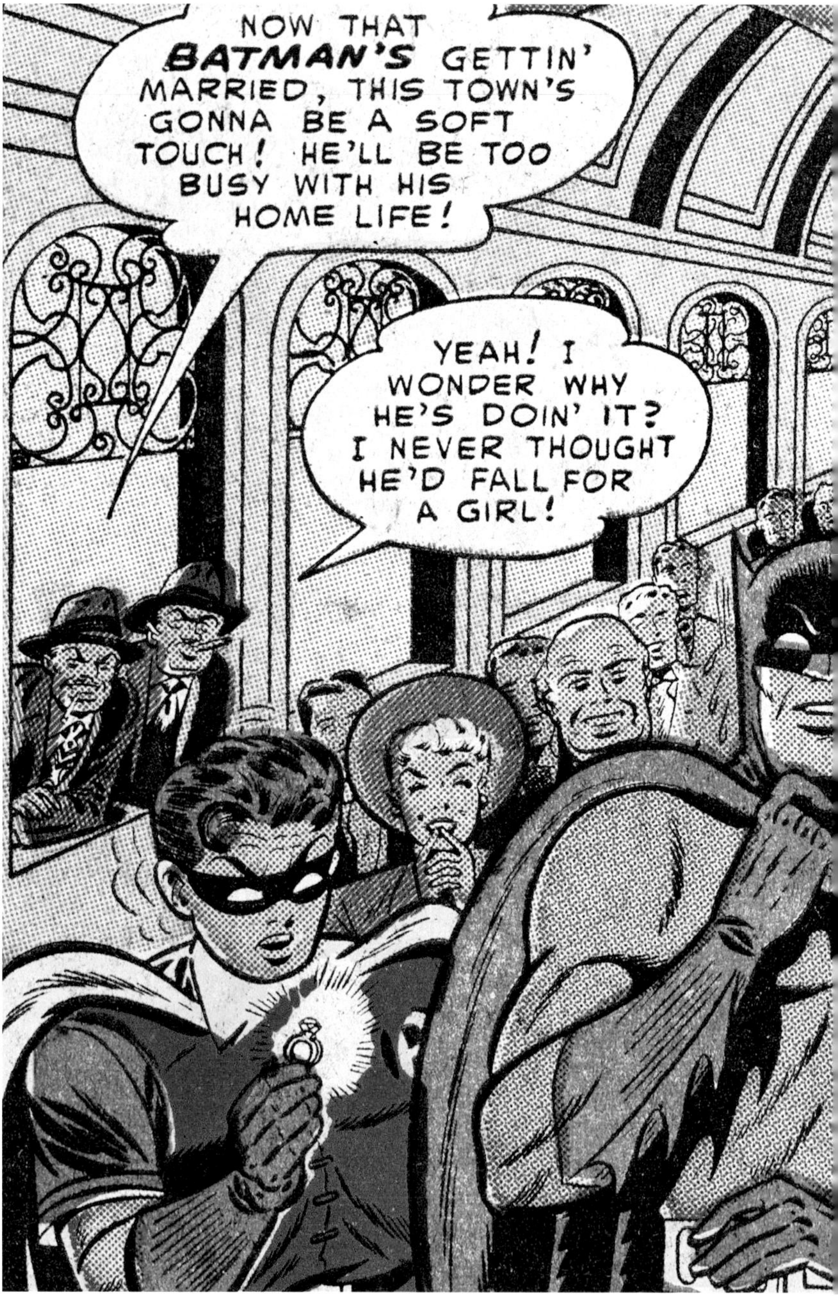
NOW THAT BATMAN'S GETTIN' MARRIED, THIS TOWN'S GONNA BE A SOFT TOUCH! HE'LL BE TOO BUSY WITH HIS HOME LIFE!
YEAH! I WONDER WHY HE'S DOIN' IT? I NEVER THOUGHT HE'D FALL FOR A GIRL!

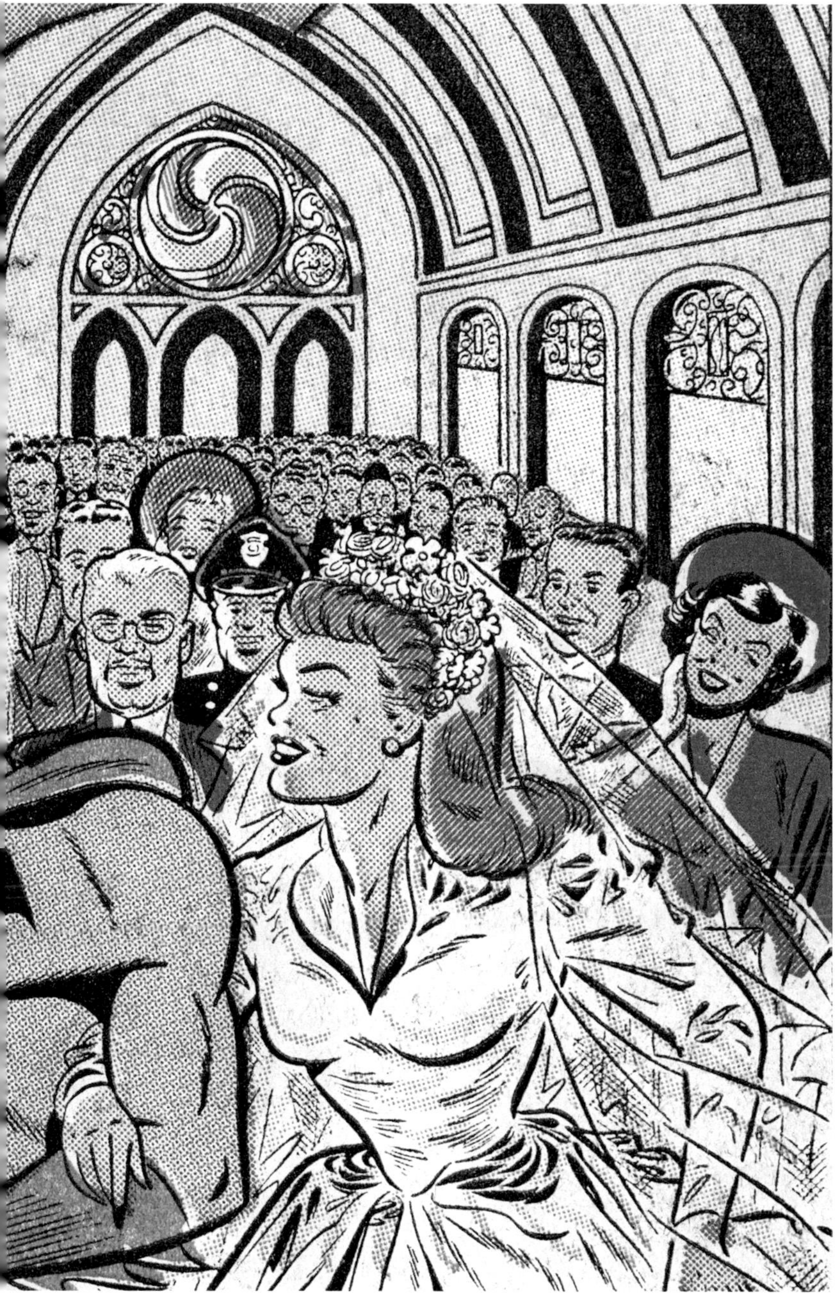

Bibliography

Daniels, Les. *Batman: The Complete History*. San Francisco: Chronicle Books, 1999.

Daniels, Les. *Comix*. New York: Outerbridge & Dienstfrey, 1971.

Daniels, Les. *DC Comics: Sixty Years of the World's Favorite Comic Book Heroes*. Boston: Bulfinch Press, 1995.

Daniels, Les. *Superman: The Complete History*. San Francisco: Chronicle Books, 1998.

Daniels, Les. *Wonder Woman: The Complete History*. San Francisco: Chronicle Books, 2000.

Feiffer, Jules. *The Great Comic Book Heroes*. New York: Dial Press, 1965.

Gabilliet, Jean-Paul. *Of Comics and Men: A Cultural History of American Comic Books*. Jackson, MS: University Press of Mississippi, 2010.

Grand Comics Database. *http://www.comics.org*.

Hadju, David. *The Ten-Cent Plague: The Great Comic-Book Scare and How It Changed America*. New York: Farrar, Straus and Giroux, 2008.

Jones, Gerard. *Men of Tomorrow: Geeks, Gangsters, and the Birth of the Comic Book*. New York: Basic Books, 2004.

Mike's Amazing World of DC Comics. *http://www. dcindexes.com*.

Overstreet, Robert. 1970–2010. *The Comic Book Price Guide*. 40 vols. Cleveland, TN: Overstreet Publications.

Pasko, Martin. *The DC Vault: A Museum-in-a-Book Featuring Rare Collectibles from the DC Universe*. Philadelphia: Running Press, 2008.

Spiegelman, Art, and Chip Kidd. *Jack Cole and Plastic Man*. San Francisco: Chronicle Books, 2001.

Steranko, Jim. 1970–1972. *History of Comics*. 2 vols. Reading, PA: Supergraphics.

Quotations are from 2010 interviews and:

Adams, Neal. *Comic Book Superheroes Unmasked*. History Channel, August 5, 2010.

Adler, Jack. "Scenemakers Behind the Scenes." By Carl Gafford. *Amazing World of DC Comics*, No. 10 (January 1976): 3–13.

Aleksander, Irina. "Diane von Furstenberg Channels Her Inner Wonder Woman, But Do Superheroes 'Work' in Fashion?" *New York Observer*, October 7, 2008.

Alter Ego, No. 1. Summer 1999.

Alter Ego, No. 25. June 2003.

Chabon, Michael. "The Amazing True Adventures of Michael Chabon." By Peter Quinones. *The Comics Journal*, No. 231 (March 2001): 89–97.

Arnold, Andrew D. "How Much for Those Comix?" *Time*. June 29, 2001.

Benton, Mike. *Superhero Comics of the Golden Age: The Illustrated History*. Dallas: Taylor Publishing, 1992.

Benton, Mike. *Superhero Comics of the Silver Age: The Illustrated History*. Dallas: Taylor Publishing, 1991.

Benton, Mike. *The Comic Book in America: An Illustrated History*. Dallas: Taylor Publishing, 1989.

Braun, Saul. "Shazam! Here Comes Captain Relevant." *The New York Times Magazine*. May 2, 1971.

Bridwell, E. Nelson. Introduction. In *Superman from the 30's to the 70's*. New York: Crown Publishers, 1972.

Bridwell, E. Nelson. Introduction. In *Shazam! from the 40's to the 70's*. New York: Crown Publishers, 1977.

Brown, Slayter. "The Coming of Superman." *The New Republic*. September 2, 1940.

Carter, Lynda. Interview by Les Daniels. Transcript. 1995.

Christensen, William and Mark Seifert. "Dark Legend." *Wizard*, No. 40. December 1994.

Coogan, Peter. *Superhero: The Secret Origin of a Genre*. Austin, TX: MonkeyBrain Books, 2006.

Eisner, Joel. *The Official Batman Book*. Chicago: Contemporary Books, 1986.

Eisner, Will. *Will Eisner's Spirit Casebook*. Princeton, WI: Kitchen Sink Press, 1990–1998.

Feiffer, Jules. "The Minsk Theory of Krypton." *The New York Times Magazine*. December 29, 1996.

Fifty Who Made DC Great: Suddenly, 50 Years Later. New York: DC Comics, 1985.

Finger, Fred. Interview by Dwight Jon Zimmerman. *Comics Interview*, No. 31 (1983): 3–11.

Flessel, Creig. "The Creig Flessel Interview." By Gary Groth. *The Comics Journal*, No. 245 (August 2002): 54–74.

Friedrich, Otto, Beth Austin, and Janice C. Simpson. "Up, Up and Awaaay!!!" *Time*. March 14, 1998.

Gaiman, Neil. Interview by Les Daniels. Transcript. 1995.

Gaiman, Neil. Official website. "Biography."

Gilmore, Mikal. "Comic Genius." *Rolling Stone*, No. 17 (March 1986): 56–58.

Haney, Bob. Interview by Les Daniels. Transcript. 1995.

Heller, Steven. "The Art of Rebellion." *The New York Times*. August 9, 2009, sec. BR12.

Jennings, Dana. "The Magic of Comics! While Batman Turns 64, a Fan Goes Back to 9." *The New York Times*, August 27, 2003.

Jensen, Jeff. "Heroic Effort: The Man of Steel first defended truth, justice, and the American way 63 years ago." *Entertainment Weekly*, June 6, 2001.

Johns, Geoff. "Geoff Johns brings the Legion to *Smallville*." By Jevon Phillips. *Los Angeles Times*, Hero Complex weblog, January 15, 2009.

Kane, Bob with Tom Adrae. *Batman and Me*. Forestville, CA: Eclipse Books, 1989.

Kobler, John. "Up, Up and Awa-a-y!" *The Saturday Evening Post*. June 21, 1941.

Kurtzman, Harvey. *From Aargh! to Zap!: Harvey Kurtzman's Visual History of the Comics*. New York: Prentice Hall, 1991.

Lansdale Jr., Lt.Col. John and the editors. "Superman and the Atom Bomb." *Harper's Magazine* (April 1948): 355.

Life 60, No.10. "The Whole Country Goes Super-mad." March 11, 1966.

Loeb, Jeph. Discussion at ICv2 Comics and Media Conference, San Diego, CA, July 22, 2009.

Los Angeles Times. "This Time, It Isn't Mr. Ali Who Gets in the Last Word." May 25, 1980, sec. C2.

Marston, William Moulton. Letter to Coulton Waugh, March 5, 1945. DC Comics Archive.

McKean, Dave. "A Decade in Comics: An Interview with Dave McKean." By Christopher Brayshaw. *The Comics Journal*, No.196 (June 1997): 58–89.

Moore, Alan. Introduction. In *Bill Sienkiewicz Sketchbook*. Seattle, WA: Fantagraphics Books, 1990.

Morrison, Grant. "Grant Morrison: The Comic Foundry Interview." By Laura Hudson. Comic Foundry, March 16, 2009.

Morrison, Grant. "Quotes." DC Comics Database.

Moldoff, Sheldon. "I Never Went a Day without Work." By Steve Ringgenberg. *The Comics Journal*, No.214 (July 1999): 90–107.

Musgrove, Michael. "Graphic Novels." *The Washington Post*. January 11, 1998.

National Periodical Publications Inc. President's Report, 1963.

Newsweek. "The Story of Pop." April 25, 1966.

Robinson, Jerry. *The Comics*. Newspaper Comics Council, 1974.

Ross, Alex. "The Alex Ross Interview." By Christopher Brayshaw. *The Comics Journal*, No.223 (May 2000): 38–74.

Sacks, Ethan. "Distinguished Company." *Wizard*, No.223 (April 2010).

Schelly, Bill. *Man of Rock: A Biography of Joe Kubert*. Seattle, WA: Fantagraphics Books, 2008.

Schwartz, Julius, with Brian M. Thomsen. *Man of Two Worlds: My Life in Science Fiction and Comics*. New York: HarperEntertainment, 2000.

Schwartz, Julius. "Strange Schwartz Stories." By Guy H. Lillian III. *Amazing World of DC Comics*, No.3 (November 1974): 2–11.

Siegel, Jerry and Joe Shuster. "Of Supermen and Kids with Dreams." By Rick Marshall. *Nemo* No.2 (August 1983): 6–19.

Publisher's Weekly. "DC's Vertigo Marks 10 Years." December 23, 2002.

Spiegelman, Art, and Françoise Mouly, eds. *The TOON Treasury of Classic Children's Comics*. New York: Abrams ComicArts, 2009.

Spurlock, J. David. *The Amazing World of Carmine Infantino*. Somerset, NJ: Vanguard Productions, 2001.

Starger, Steve and J. David Spurlock. *Wally's World: The Brilliant Life and Tragic Death of the World's 2nd Best Comic Book Artist*. Somerset, NJ: Vanguard Publications, 2006.

"Superman's Pal, Curt Swan." *Comics Values Monthly Special*, No.2 (1992).

Swan, Curt. "Drawing Superman." In *The Krypton Companion*, by Michael Eury. Raleigh, NC: TwoMorrows Publishing, 2006.

Time. The Press. "Superman's Dilemma." April 13, 1942.

Time. Show Business. "Onward and Upward with the New Superman." August 1, 1977.

Tollin, Anthony. "Origins of the Golden Age: Sheldon Mayer." *Amazing World of DC Comics*, No.5 (March–April 1975): 2–11.

Variety. "Action Comics Chief Liebowitz Spawned Superman in 1937." July 8, 1987.

Variety. "Superman Gets New 'Look,' Roots Return Under Byrne's Pen." July 8, 1987.

Wagner, Geoffrey. "Superman and His Sister." *The New Republic*. 1955.

Weisinger, Mort. "Here Comes Superman!" *Coronet*. July 1946.

Weist, Jerry. *100 Greatest Comic Books*. Atlanta: Whitman Publishing LLC, 2004.

Yronwode, catherine, with Denis Kitchen. *The Art of Will Eisner*. Princeton, WI: Kitchen Sink Press, 1982.

Credits

EDITORIAL NOTE

Early comics carried few credits or often credited creators of features rather than the actual talent producing the stories. We've endeavored to research credits for accuracy, and regret any errors. In order to provide the most accurate reproductions of the comics reading experience, we have dispatched photographers to work from the comics themselves…which, being artifacts that were often published on inexpensive paper and were read and collected, sometimes show their wear and tear. Collectors have graciously shared their treasures with us, and we have done our best to reverse the effect of time without altering the art. And treasures they are—despite the author's poor judgment in being unwilling to spend $130 for an *Action Comics* No.1 when the first Comic Book Price Guide came out in 1970, today that issue has sold for more than a million dollars and many other old DC issues have skyrocketed as well. The distances we went to in this quest are only hinted at by details like the odd UK tax stamps on a cover or two reproduced here. Other rare photos and original artwork have been treated with similar respect, but are subject to the same caveats that we have not always been able to identify the photographer or all the subjects.

It is our hope that you'll have been able to enjoy all these artifacts from the Golden Age (and earlier) as if you were actually holding them, or even more, since they're better reproduced and not crumbling.… This is our best approximation of inviting you into our personal library to sit down and share our delights.

The majority of the comics included in this series were photographed from The Ian Levine Collection.

Also featured are the collections of Art Baltazar, Ivan M. Briggs, Saul Ferris, Grant Geissman, Tom Gordon, Jim Hambrick, P.C. Hamerlinck, Philip Hecht, Bob Joy, Chip Kidd, Peter Maresca, Jim Nolt, Jerry Robinson, David Saunders, Anthony Tollin, Ellen Vartanoff, Jerome Wenker, Mark Zaid, and, notably, Mark Waid, Heritage Auctions, and Metropolis Comics.

Any omissions for copy or credit are unintentional and appropriate credit will be given in future editions if such copyright holders contact the publisher.

Acme Newspictures, Prints & Photographs Division, Library of Congress, LC-USZ62-59651: 393. Courtesy the Allan Asherman Collection: 400. American Heritage Center, University of Wyoming: 38, Mort Weisinger Photo File). AP Photo: 91 (bottom), 204, 643. AP Photo/ H. B. Littell: 216. © Bettmann/CORBIS: 90, 652-653. Courtesy www.betweenthecovers.com: 39 (bottom left), 76, 193 (top left). Courtesy Bob Ebert: 421. © Bob Kane Productions, Inc: 223. Courtesy Bob Underwood: 343. Copyright © 2009 Bonhams & Butterfields Auctioneers Corp. All Rights Reserved: 27. Photo by Carl Iwasaki/Time & Life Images/Getty Images: 615. Courtesy www.comiclink.com: 330-331. Courtesy Daniel Herman: 242, 257. Photo by David Saunders: 2. Courtesy Dick Cole: 509. Courtesy Denis Kitchen Art Agency Archives: 482, 483, 631, 632. Courtesy EC Comics, Inc: 88 (left). Photo by FPG/Hulton Archive/Getty Images: 321. Courtesy Gary Grossman, author *Superman: Serial to Cereal*: 568. © Harvey Kurtzman estate: 631, 634-635. Courtesy Heritage Auction Galleries: 13 (top), 15, 16, 19, 52 (top right), 67, 72, 88 (left), 89, 136, 160-161, 172, 193 (right), 231, 243 (top), 247, 308, 312 (left), 312 (right), 314 (top left and right), 318, 338, 340, 341, 342, 344, 356, 364, 387, 396, 403, 442, 464, 479, 497, 512, 518, 537, 538, 539, 540, 541, 542, 543, 545, 546, 547, 555, 573, 579, 580, 584, 592, 596 (right), 603, 608, 616 (left), 620, 633, 641, 647, 648, 649, 651. Courtesy Hershenson/Allen Archive: 50, 153, 378, 379, 401, 465. Courtesy the Ivan M. Briggs Collection: 96 (right), 183, 211 (top), 389, 463. Courtesy Jack Adler Estate: 9, 14. Courtesy Jim Bowers, creator CapedWonder.com, and John Field Collection: 562-563, 567. Courtesy/© Joe Kubert: 13 (top). Courtesy the Joe Rainone Collection: 49, 70, 170, 294. Photo by John Dominis/Time & Life Pictures/Getty Images, 646. Courtesy Mark Evanier: 437. Used with permission from Meredith Corporation. All rights reserved: 164, 346, 347, 534. Collection of Mike Glad: 380, 381. © New York City Municipal Archives: 134. Courtesy the P. C. Hamerlinck Collection: 58, 88 (right), 91 (top), 384, 385, 388, 392, 394, 397, 399, 447, 627 (left). © Copyright 2008 The Plain Dealer Publishing Co. All Rights Reserved: 44, 410. RKO/Album/AKG: 150. Courtesy Tom Gordon III: 61 (right), 466-467. Courtesy of *TV Guide* magazine, LLC © 1953: 569 (left and right). Ullstein bild/ Grange Collection: 270 (top). Photo by Walter Sanders/Time Life Pictures/Getty Images: 363. Courtesy the Wheeler-Nicholson Estate: 28. © Will Eisner Studios, Inc: 11, 482-493.

SUPERMAN PAINTING

PAGE 2: *Painting, H. J. Ward, oil on canvas, 45 x 60 in., 1940.*
Ward, who painted many covers for publisher Harry Donenfeld's pulps, created this promotional art for the Superman radio series' 1940 debut. It hung in Donenfeld's office and later was used as the cover of a 1974 reprint collection. DC archivists, however, believed it had been lost for more than 50 years. It was later discovered that the Donenfeld family had donated the painting to Lehman College in the Bronx, New York. Photo by David Saunders.

TOPS IN COMICS

PAGE 4: *House ad (Canadian), 1948.*

NEW COMICS NO. 7

PAGE 661: *Introductory page; script, Malcolm Wheeler-Nicholson; artist, Vin Sullivan. August 1936.* It was a simpler time, and this kid-friendly introduction betokened it. Comic strips also influenced National's practices in subtle ways: Like the strips, the early features were simply by "artists" — if there was a distinct writer, he was likely to be an uncredited ghost, working for a share of the $5-per-page rate that Wheeler-Nicholson typically paid.

THE END

PAGE 672: *Interior, "Detour,"* Comic Cavalcade *No. 18; script and art, Howard Purcell. December–January 1947.*

Acknowledgments

Thanks to Martin Pasko, Mark Waid, Daniel Wallace, and John Wells for research and writing assistance on captions, timelines and biographies; and to Joe Kubert for sharing his stories for this volume.

Special thanks to Ian Levine for allowing access to his amazing collection.

At DC Comics, thanks are due to Michael Acampora, Allan Asherman, Karen Berger, Roger Bonas, Georg Brewer, Richard Bruning, Mike Carlin, Christopher Cerasi, Mark Chiarello, Eddy Choi, Ivan Cohen, Dan DiDio, John Ficarra, Larry Ganem, Ben Harper, Bob Harras, Geoff Johns, Bob Joy, Hank Kanalz, Kevin Kiniry, Jay Kogan, Jim Lee, Evan Metcalf, Connor Michel, Lisa Mills, John Morgan, Diane Nelson, Scott Nybakken, Anthony Palumbo, Frank Pittarese, Barbara Rich, Cheryl Rubin, Andrea Shochet, Joe Siegel, Bob Wayne, Michael Wooten, and Dora Yoshimoto. At Warner Bros., my thanks to Josh Anderson and Leith Adams.

Many thanks to the numerous individuals who helped in the production of this book, including Jack Adler; Doug Adrianson; Teena Apeles; Dawn Arrington; Chris Bailey; Jerry Bails; Art Baltazar; John Barton; Jerry Beck; John Benson; Steve Bingen; Arnold Blumberg; Brian Bolland; Jim Bowers; Cindy Brenner; Ivan Briggs; Jonathan Browne; Scott Byers; Steve Carey; Pete Carlsson; Mildred Champlin; Dale Cendali; Ruth Clampett; Alice Cloos; Dick Cole; Wesley Coller; Gerry Conway; Margaret Croft; Les Daniels; Dave Davis; Jack Davis; Ken DellaPenta; Joe Desris; Lee Dillon; Michael Doret; Spencer Douglas; Paul Duncan; Mallory Farrugia; Saul Ferris; Stephen Fishler; Chaz Fitzhugh; Steve Fogelson; Danny Fuchs; Neil Gaiman; Craig B. Gaines; Grant Geissman; Dave Gibbons; Frank Goerhardt; Tom Gordon; Steven P. Gorman; Jared Green; Steven Grossfeld; James Halperin; Jim Hambrick; P. C. Hamerlinck; Yadira Harrison; Chuck Harter; Philip Hecht; Jim Heimann; Daniel Herman; Andy Hershberger; Jessica Hoffman; Martin Holz; Julia Howe; Adam Hyman; Lisa Janney; Klaus Janson; Jenette Kahn; Elizabeth Kane; Chip Kidd; Kirk Kimball; Denis and Stacy Kitchen; Stefan Klatte; Todd Klein; Florian Kobler; Charles Kochman; Christopher Kosek; Keith Krick; Joe Kubert; Danny Kuchuck; Amy Kule; Paul Kupperberg; Olive Lamotte; Caroline Lee; Hannah and Alfred Levitz; Jeanette, Nicole, Philip, and Garret Levitz; Steven Lomazow; Alice and Leonard Maltin; Tony Manzella; Peter Maresca; Byrne Marston; Pete Marston; Rachel Maximo; David Mazzucchelli; John Morrow; Mark McKenna; Ryann McQuilton; Eric Nash; Constantine Nasr; Meike Niessen; Scott Neitlich; Adam Newell; Maggie Nimkin; Jim Nolt; Jennifer Patrick; Kirstin Plate; Joe Orlando; Joe Rainone; Debbie Rexing; Dennis Robert; Jerry Robinson; Alex Ross; Barry Sandoval; Mike Sangiacomo; Jessica Sappenfield; David Saunders; Zina Saunders; Randy Scott; Susannah Scott; Jürgen Seidel; David Siegel; John Smedley; Ben Smith; Wayne Smith; Geoff Spear; Art Spiegelman; Bob Stein; Roy Thomas; Shane Thompson; Anthony Tollin; Ellen Vartanoff; Mark Voglesong; Mike Voiles; Phillip Wages; Chris Ware; William Wasson; Evan Weinerman; Jerry Weist; Sean Welch; Jerome Wenker; Josh White; Douglas Wheeler-Nicholson; Nicky Wheeler-Nicholson; Alex Winter; DebbySue Wolfcale; Marv Wolfman; Steve Younis; Mark Zaid; Thomas Zellers; Barry Ziehl; Marco Zivny; and Vincent Zurzolo.

And a special acknowledgment to Steve Korté, Josh Baker, and Nina Wiener, and the eagle eye of Benedikt Taschen, without whom this series of books would have been impossible.

— PAUL LEVITZ

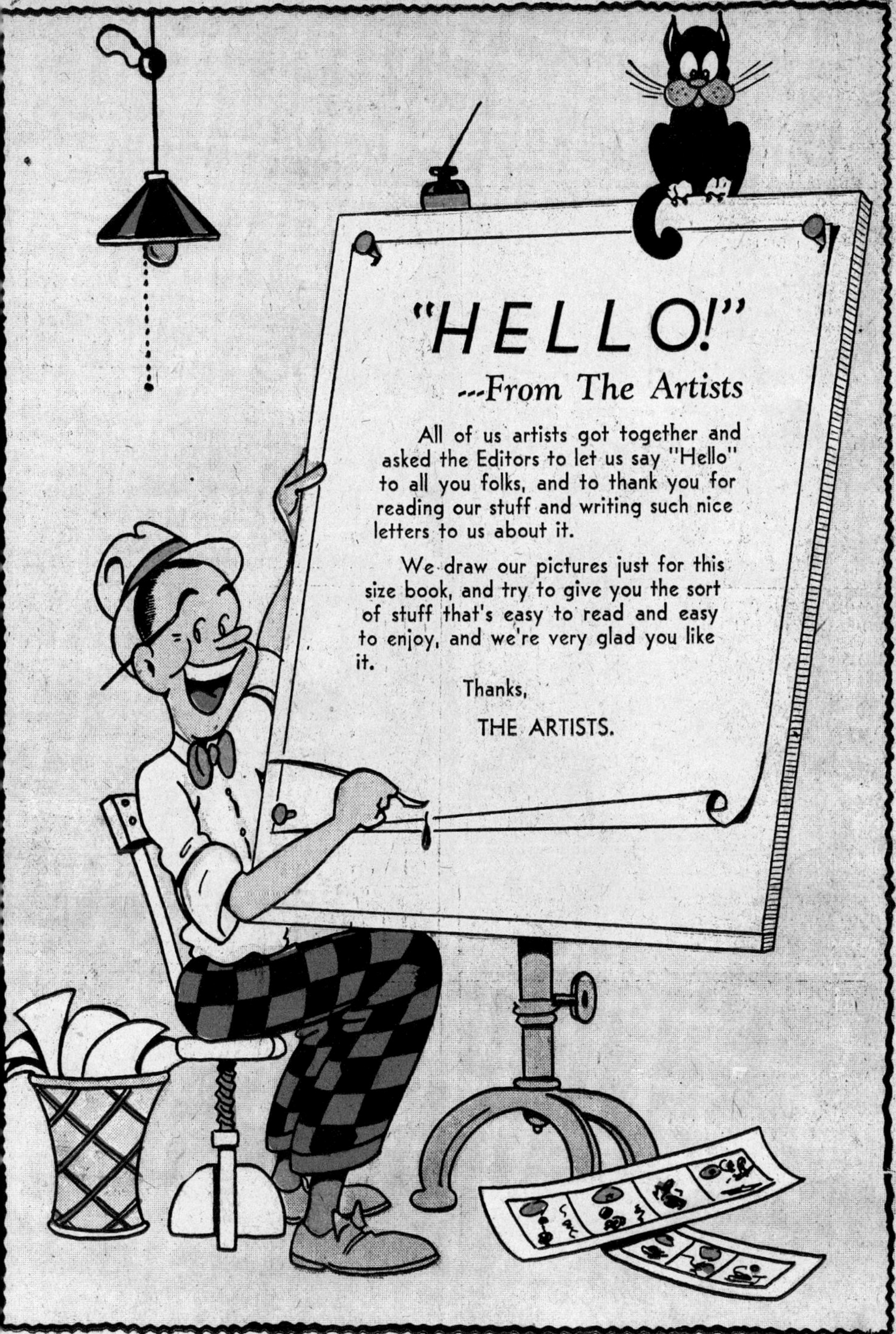
"HELLO!"
---From The Artists
All of us artists got together and asked the Editors to let us say "Hello" to all you folks, and to thank you for reading our stuff and writing such nice letters to us about it.
We draw our pictures just for this size book, and try to give you the sort of stuff that's easy to read and easy to enjoy, and we're very glad you like it.
Thanks,
THE ARTISTS.

100 Illustrators

Illustration Now!
Portraits

Illustration Now!
Fashion

100 Manga Artists

Logo Design

Fritz Kahn.
Infographics Pioneer

Bodoni. Manual of
Typography

The Package Design
Book

D&AD.
The Copy Book

Menu Design
in America

1000 Tattoos

Bookworm's delight:
never bore, always excite!

TASCHEN
Bibliotheca Universalis

The Circus.
1870s–1950s

Mid-Century Ads

1000 Pin-Up Girls

20th Century Fashion

20th Century Travel

20th Century
Classic Cars

1000 Record Covers

Funk & Soul Covers

Jazz Covers

Extraordinary
Records

Steinweiss

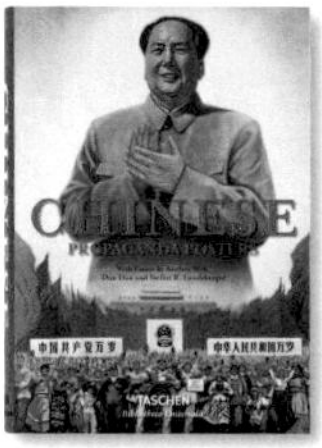
CHINESE
TASCHEN
Chinese Propaganda Posters

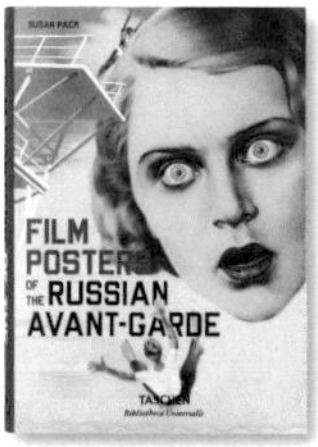
FILM POSTERS OF THE RUSSIAN AVANT-GARDE
TASCHEN
Film Posters of the Russian Avant-Garde

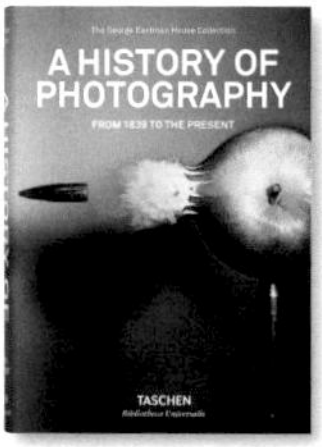
A HISTORY OF PHOTOGRAPHY
TASCHEN
A History of Photography

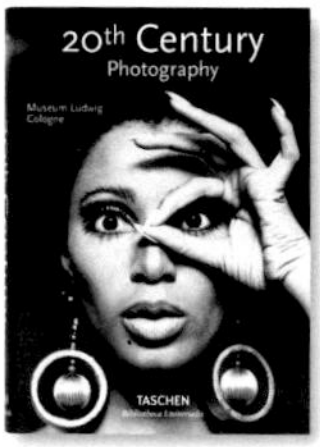
20th Century
Photography
TASCHEN
20th Century Photography

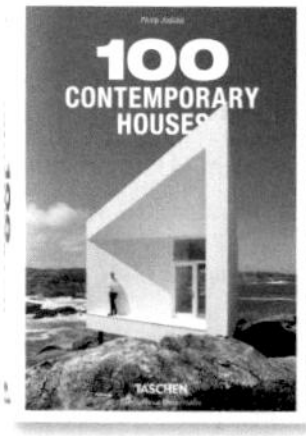
100
CONTEMPORARY HOUSES
TASCHEN
100 Contemporary Houses

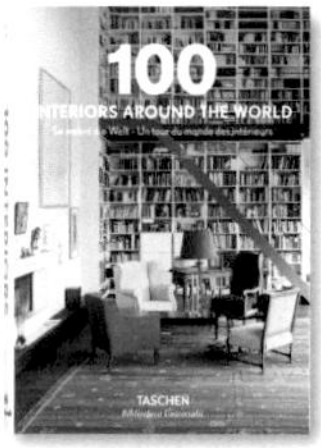
100
TASCHEN
100 Interiors Around the World

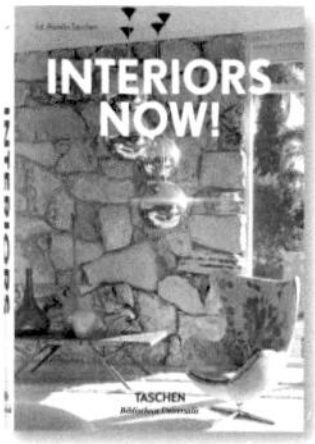
INTERIORS NOW!
TASCHEN
Interiors Now!

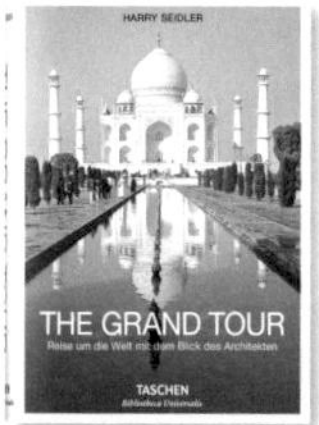
HARRY SEIDLER
THE GRAND TOUR
TASCHEN
The Grand Tour

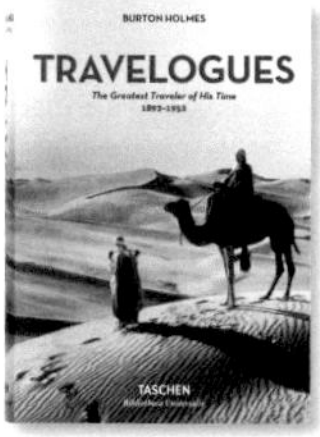
BURTON HOLMES
TRAVELOGUES
TASCHEN
Burton Holmes. Travelogues

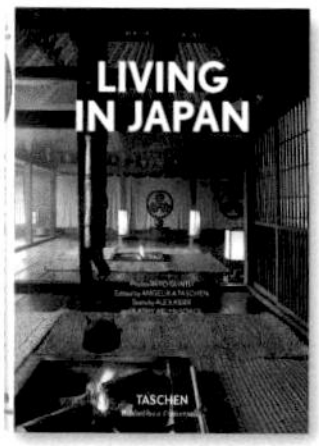
LIVING IN JAPAN
TASCHEN
Living in Japan

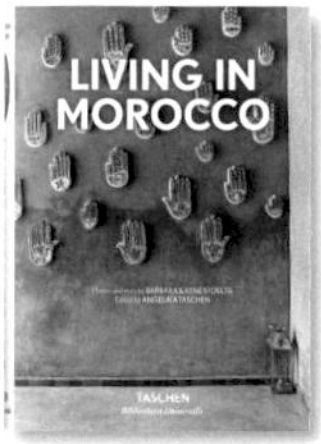
LIVING IN MOROCCO
TASCHEN
Living in Morocco

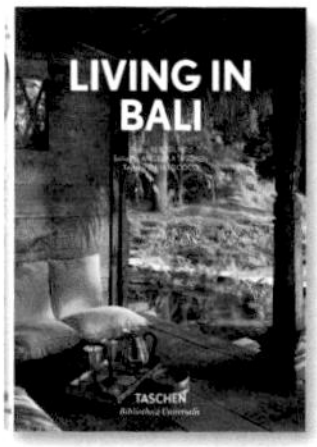
LIVING IN BALI
TASCHEN
Living in Bali

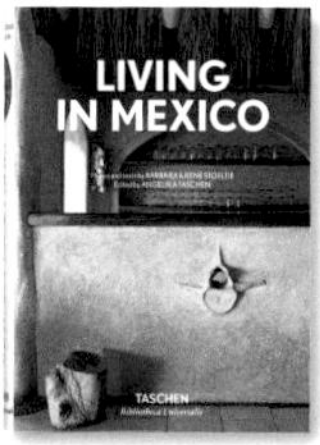
LIVING IN MEXICO
TASCHEN
Living in Mexico

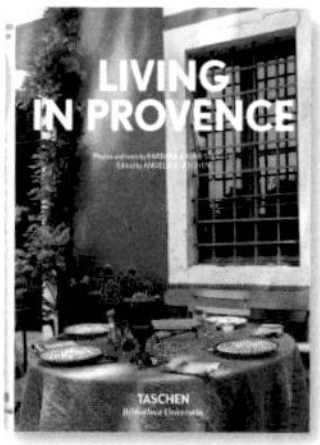
LIVING IN PROVENCE
TASCHEN
Living in Provence

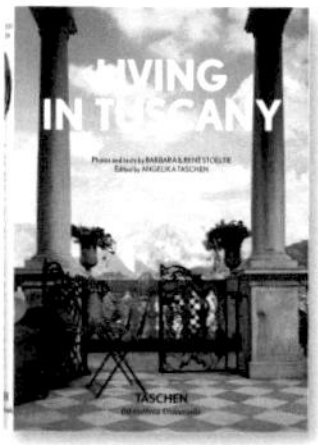
TASCHEN
Living in Tuscany

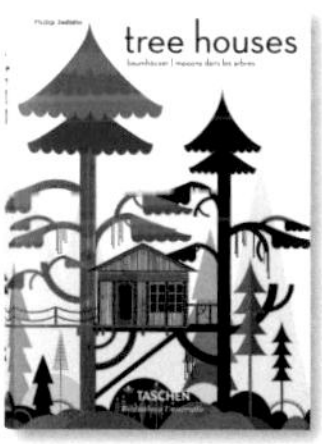
tree houses
TASCHEN
Tree Houses

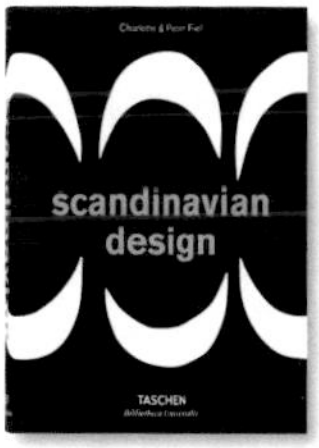
scandinavian design
TASCHEN
Scandinavian Design

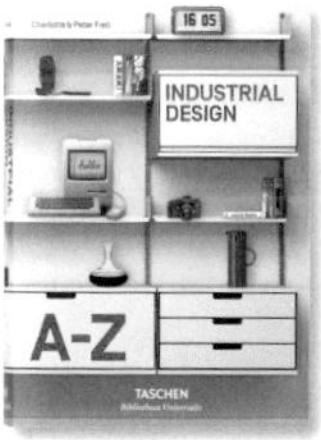
INDUSTRIAL DESIGN
A-Z
TASCHEN
Industrial Design A-Z

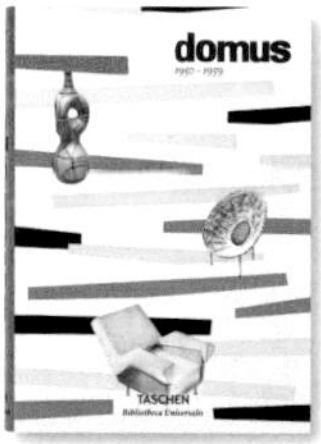
domus
TASCHEN
domus 1950s

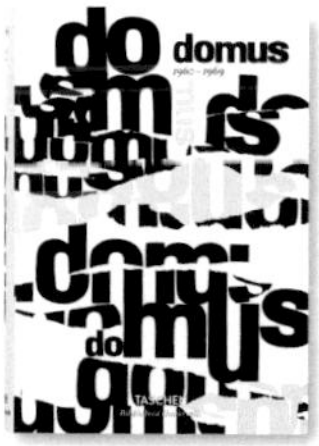
domus
TASCHEN
domus 1960s

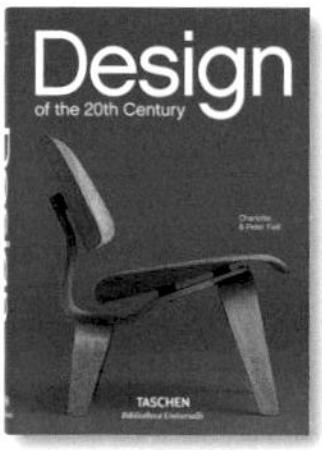
Design
of the 20th Century
TASCHEN
Design of the 20th Century

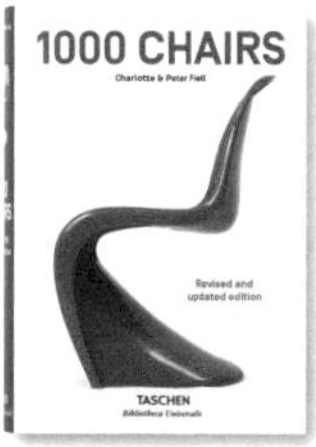
1000 CHAIRS
Charlotte & Peter Fiell
Revised and updated edition
TASCHEN
1000 Chairs

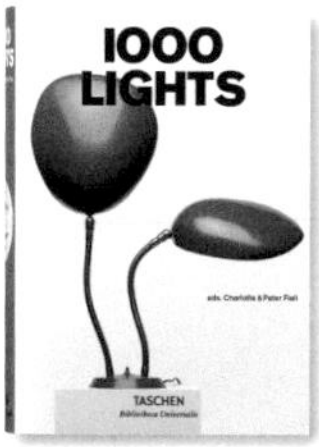
1000 LIGHTS
TASCHEN
1000 Lights

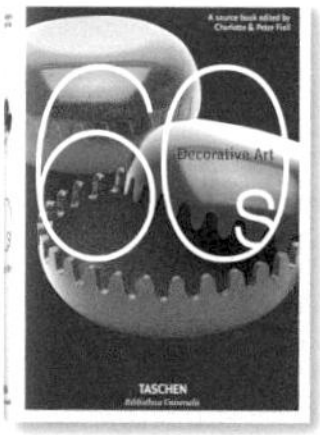
Decorative Art
TASCHEN
Decorative Art 60s

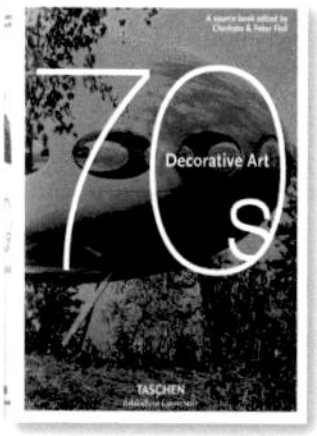
Decorative Art
TASCHEN
Decorative Art 70s

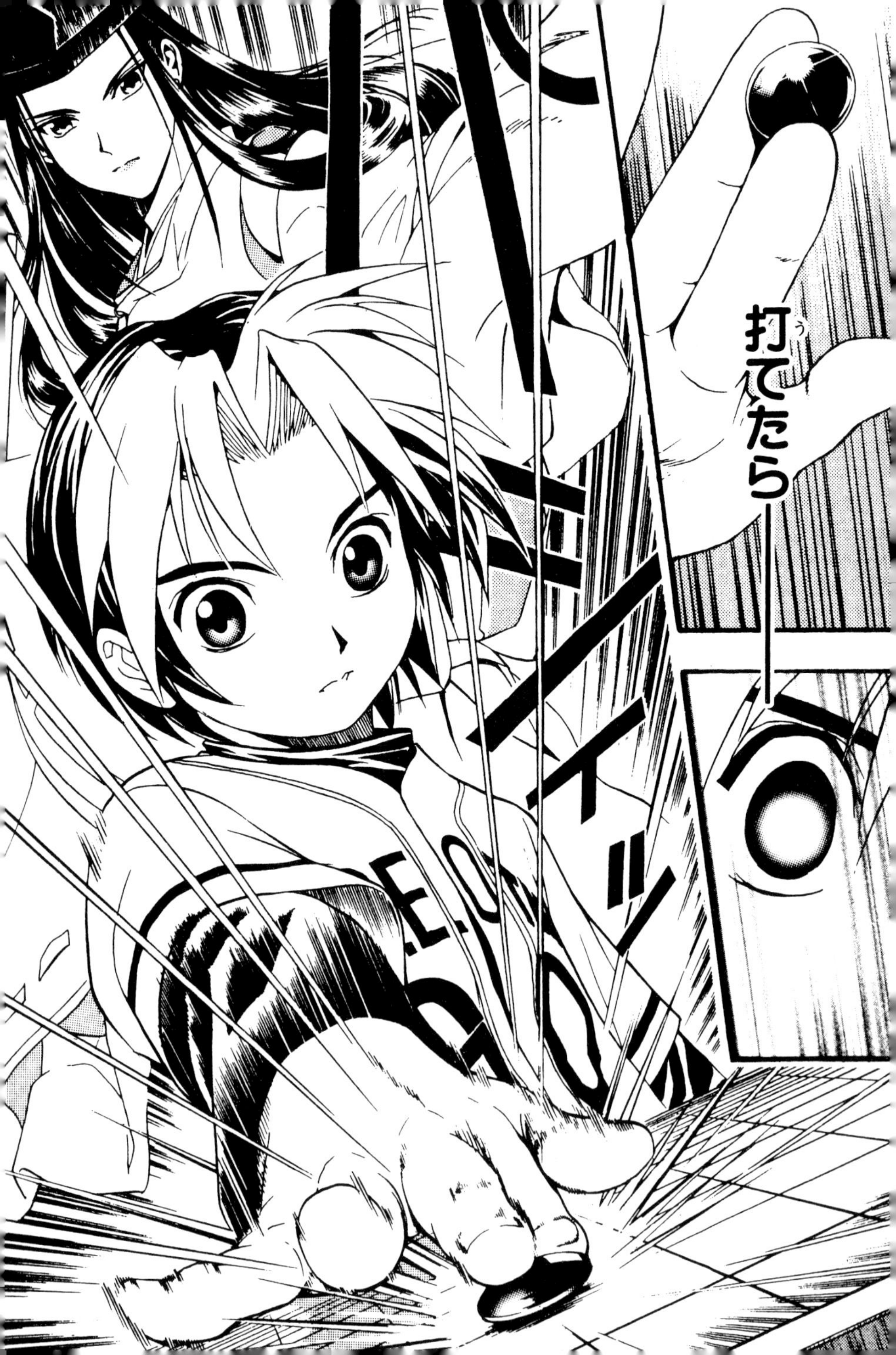
打てたら――

Manga-nificent

From Astro Boy to Akira, the superstars of the manga scene

Since the original TASCHEN edition of *Manga Design,* Japan's comic phenomenon has produced yet more captivating characters and a whole host of hot new talents. This revised and updated edition delivers the lowdown on the latest and the greatest makers and shapers of the manga scene. Through its A–Z directory we discover the superstars—both human and fictional—of what is now a vast global industry. From classic maestros—such as Osamu Tezuka (creator of Astro Boy) and Katsuhiro Otomo (creator of Akira)—to newcomers such as Hajime Isayama, each entry includes biographical and bibliographical information, descriptions of main characters, and of course plenty of examples of the artist's finest manga spreads and covers.

"This eye-popping survey of hundreds of Manga artists hurtles from *Sailor Moon* to stylish homoerotic porn, showing how Manga has influenced everything from advertising to movies like *Kill Bill.* Zap, wow, take that, Western literature!"

—*The Globe and Mail*, Toronto

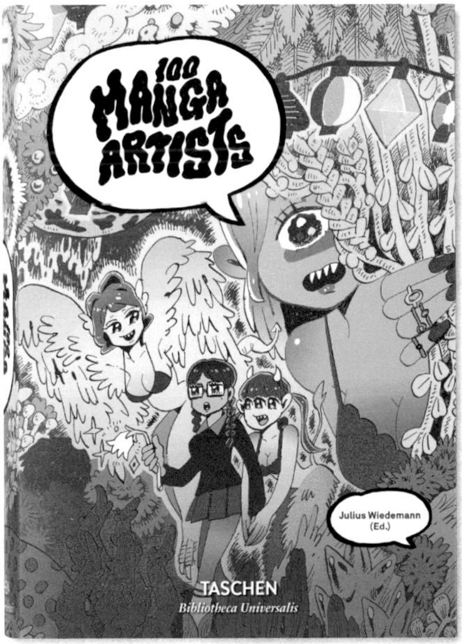
100 MANGA ARTISTS
Julius Wiedemann (Ed.)
TASCHEN
Bibliotheca Universalis

100 Manga Artists
Julius Wiedemann
672 pages
ENGLISH / GERMAN / FRENCH

2194

2195

2196

StickerNation.Net

2198

Swallow

2199

ZWERFVUIL
BLIKSEMSNEL IN DE BAK!

2200

2202

2203

2204

2206

2207

2208

Sure signs

Diverse logos from around the world

A good logo can glamorize just about anything. Now available in our popular *Bibliotheca Universalis* series, this sweeping compendium gathers diverse brand markers from around the world to explore the irrepressible power of graphic representation. Organized into chapters by theme, the catalog explores how text, image, and ideas distil into a logo across events, fashion, media, music, and retailers. Featuring work from both star names and lesser-known mavericks, this is an excellent reference for students and professionals in design and marketing, as well as for anyone interested in the visuals and philosophy behind brand identity.

"An excellent visual reference..."

—*Curve Magazine*, Sydney

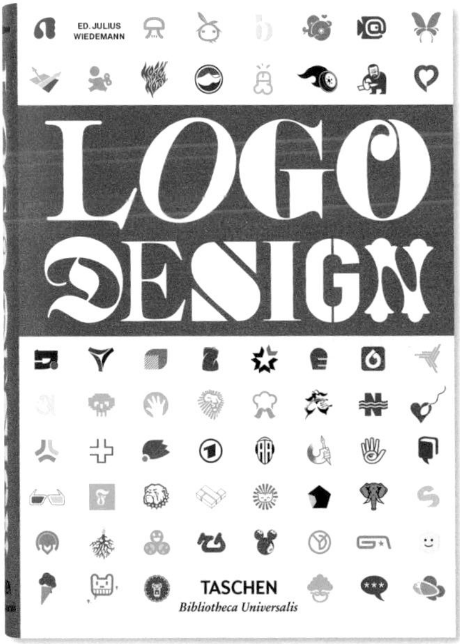
ED. JULIUS
WIEDEMANN
LOGO
DESIGN
TASCHEN
Bibliotheca Universalis

Logo Design
Julius Wiedemann
664 pages
ENGLISH / GERMAN / FRENCH

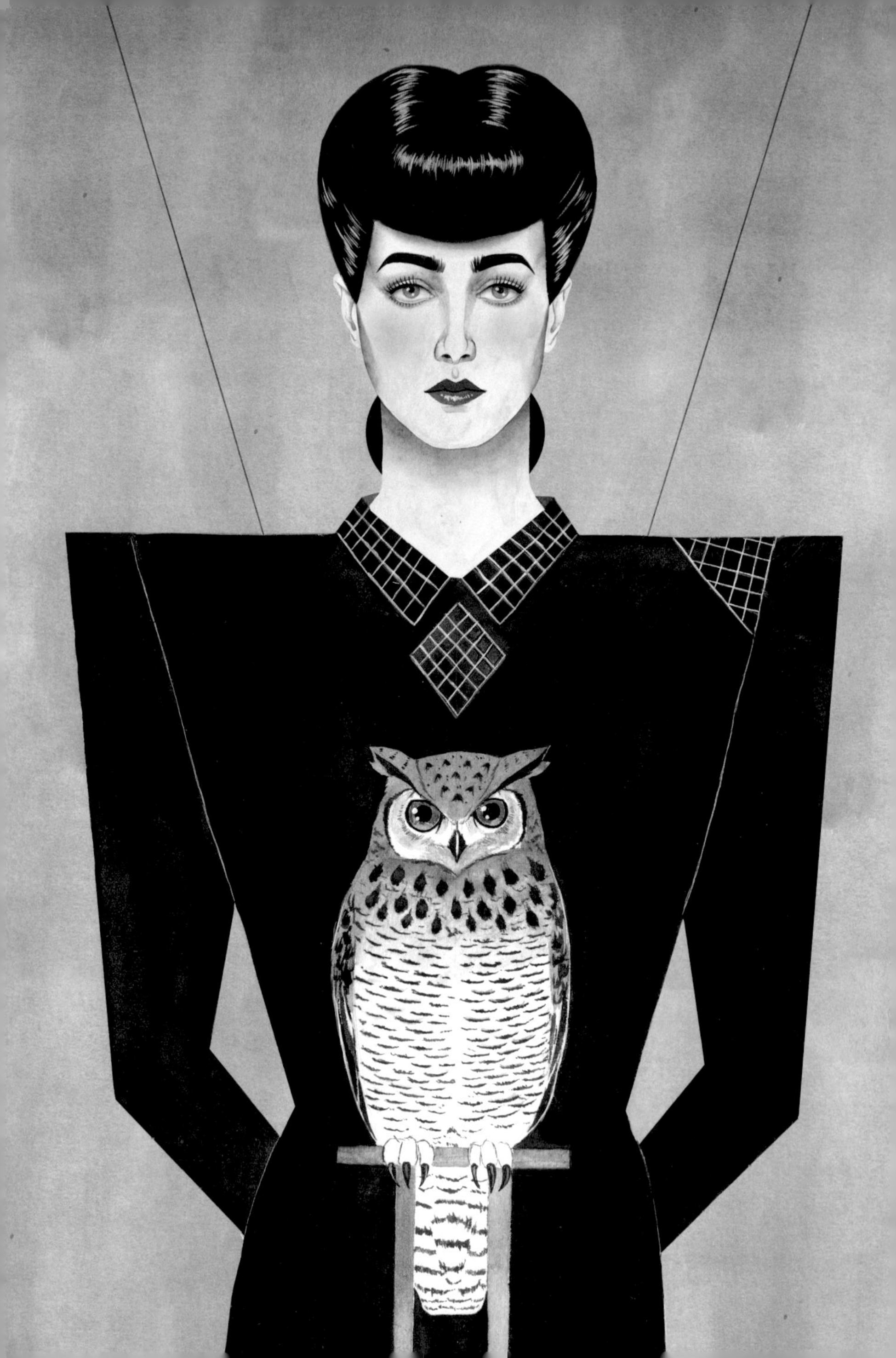

Perfect likeness

Portraiture today, from caricature to realism

The field of illustration has flourished over the last decade, with professionals working both on computers and by hand. In illustration, the single most challenging and captivating subject has been the portrait, frequently used in editorials, advertising, products, and most recently, being the subject of major exhibitions. With an introduction from Steven Heller, this collection gathers the portrait work of more than 80 illustrators including André Carrilho, Jody Hewgill, Anita Kunz, and Dugald Stermer.

"This is a multicultural selection, and hence a book of very beautiful, diverse signatures."

—*Design Week*, London

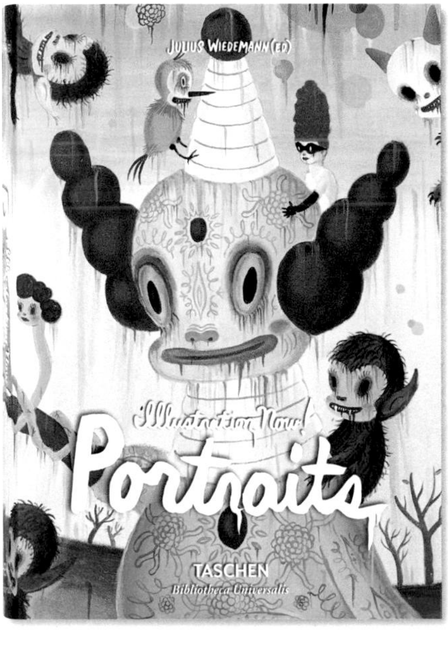
Julius Wiedemann (ed)
Illustration Now!
Portraits
TASCHEN
Bibliotheca Universalis

Illustration Now! Portraits
Julius Wiedeman, Steven Heller
576 pages
ENGLISH / GERMAN / FRENCH

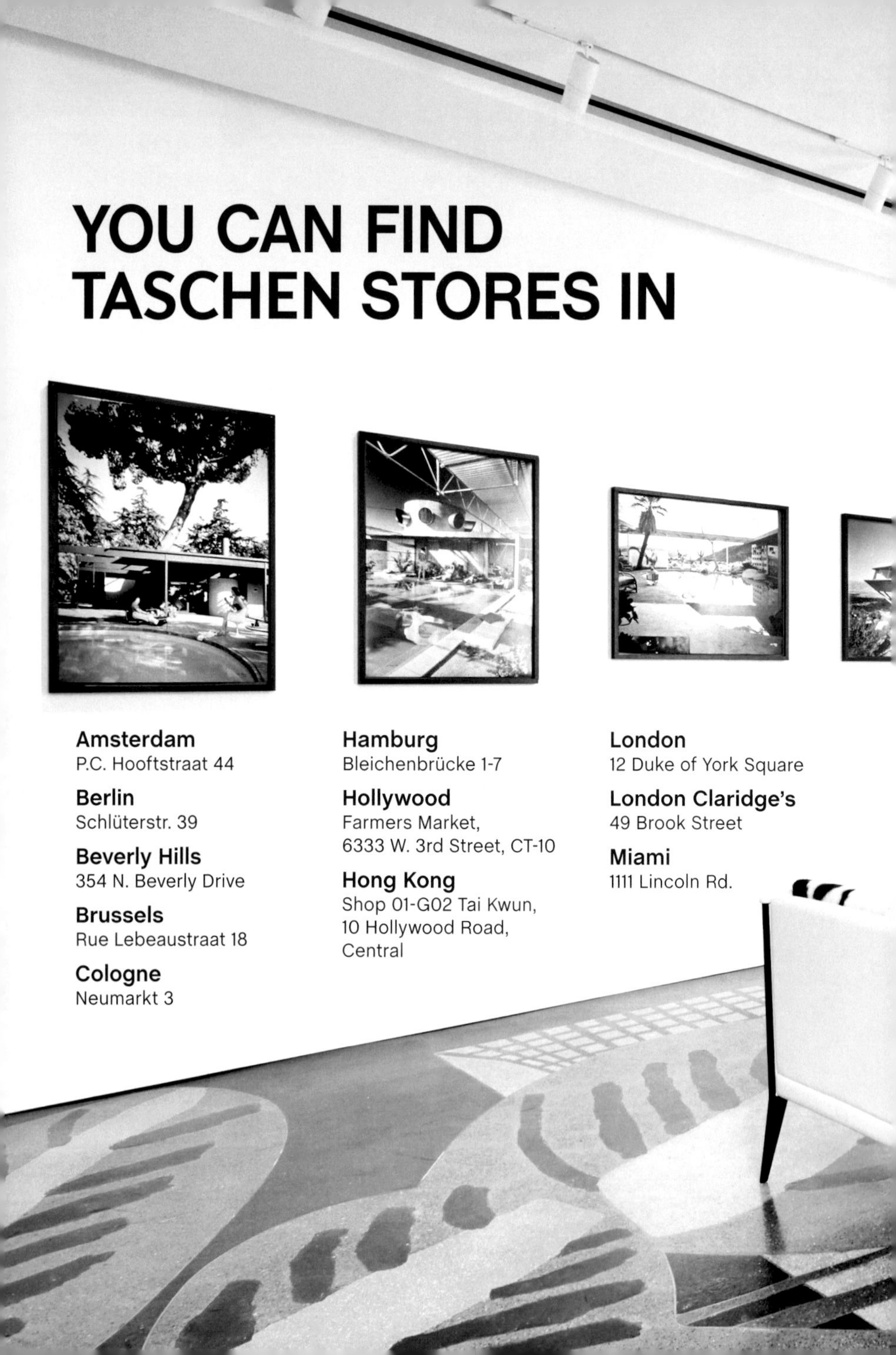

YOU CAN FIND TASCHEN STORES IN

Amsterdam
P.C. Hooftstraat 44

Berlin
Schlüterstr. 39

Beverly Hills
354 N. Beverly Drive

Brussels
Rue Lebeaustraat 18

Cologne
Neumarkt 3

Hamburg
Bleichenbrücke 1-7

Hollywood
Farmers Market,
6333 W. 3rd Street, CT-10

Hong Kong
Shop 01-G02 Tai Kwun,
10 Hollywood Road,
Central

London
12 Duke of York Square

London Claridge's
49 Brook Street

Miami
1111 Lincoln Rd.

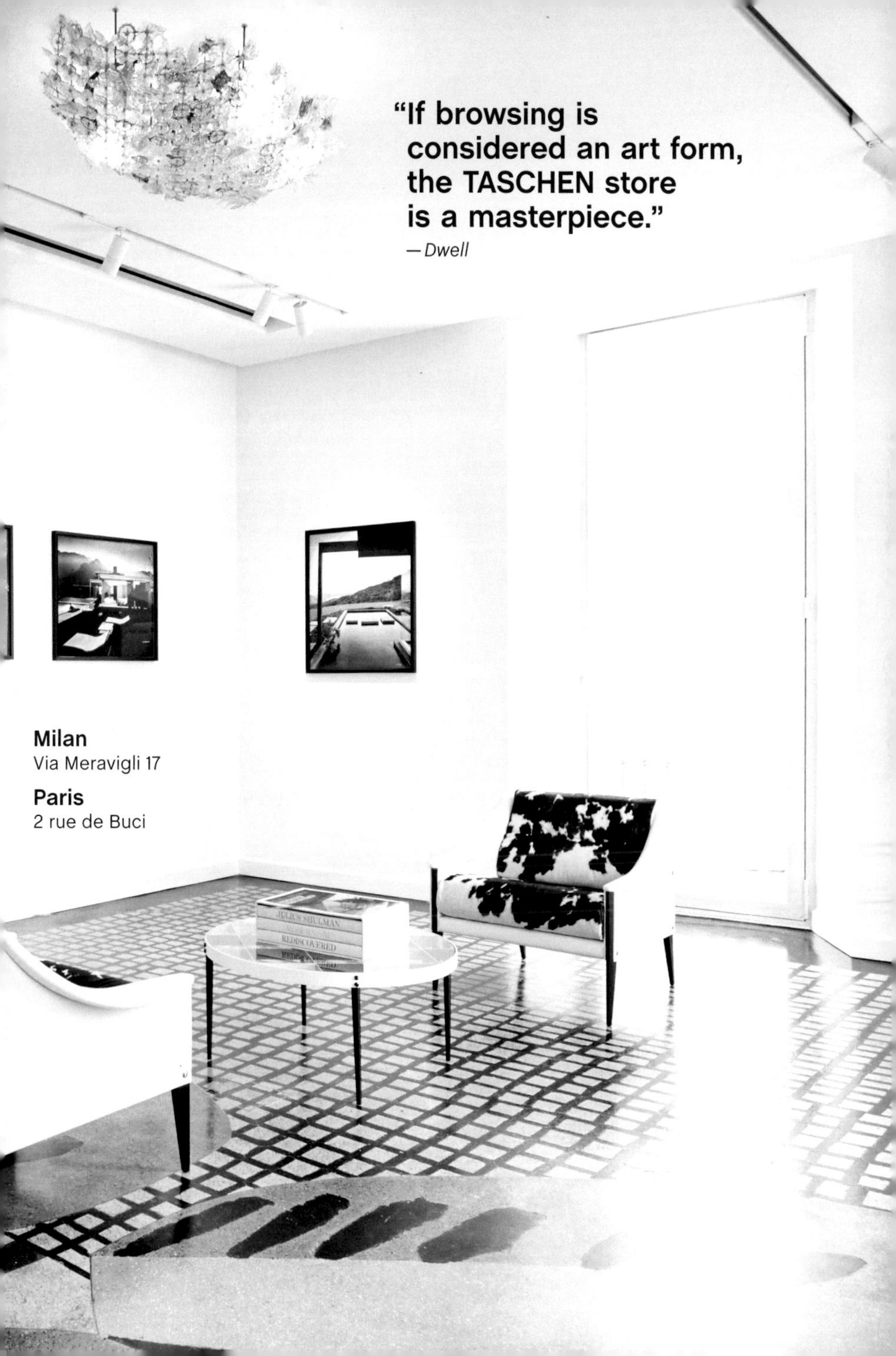
JULIUS SHULMAN
REDISCOVERED

“If browsing is considered an art form, the TASCHEN store is a masterpiece.”
— *Dwell*

Milan
Via Meravigli 17

Paris
2 rue de Buci

Imprint

EACH AND EVERY TASCHEN BOOK PLANTS A SEED!
TASCHEN is a carbon neutral publisher. Each year, we offset our annual carbon emissions with carbon credits at the Instituto Terra, a reforestation program in Minas Gerais, Brazil, founded by Lélia and Sebastião Salgado. To find out more about this ecological partnership, please check: www.taschen.com/zerocarbon
Inspiration: unlimited. Carbon footprint: zero.

To stay informed about TASCHEN and our upcoming titles, please subscribe to our free magazine at www.taschen.com/magazine, follow us on Twitter, Instagram, and Facebook, or e-mail your questions to contact@taschen.com.

TASCHEN GmbH
Hohenzollernring 53, D-50672 Köln
www.taschen.com

Art direction: Josh Baker, Los Angeles
Design: Birgit Eichwede, Cologne
Editors: Steve Korté, New York; Josh Baker and Nina Wiener, Los Angeles
Editorial consultants: Mark Waid, Martin Pasko, John Wells, and Daniel Wallace
Production: Stefan Klatte and Claire Deutsch, Cologne; Jennifer Patrick, Los Angeles
Layout: Nemuel DePaula, Los Angeles
Editorial coordination: Inka Lohrmann, Cologne

Printed in China
ISBN 978-3-8365-5656-9

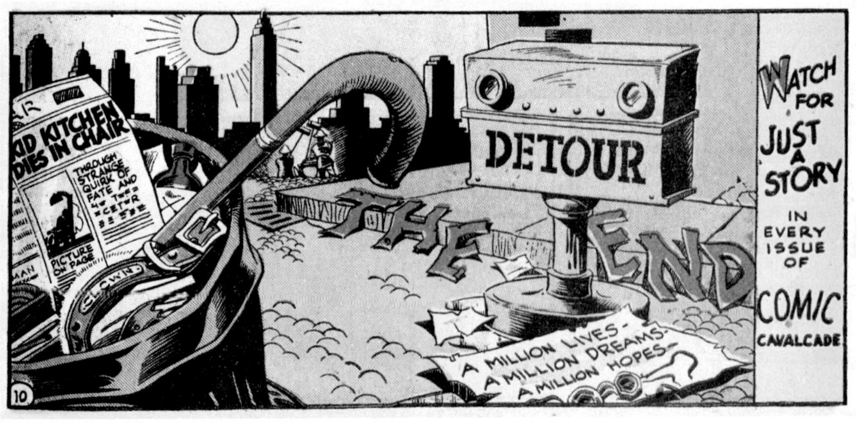
KID KITCHEN DIES IN CHAIR
THROUGH STRANGE QUIRK OF FATE AND
PICTURE ON PAGE
DETOUR
THE END
A MILLION LIVES - A MILLION DREAMS - A MILLION HOPES -
WATCH FOR JUST A STORY IN EVERY ISSUE OF COMIC CAVALCADE
10